CRIMINAL JUSTICE

Fourth Edition

CRIMINAL JUSTICE

Fourth Edition

James A. Inciardi
University of Delaware

Harcourt Brace Jovanovich College Publishers

Fort Worth   Philadelphia   San Diego   New York   Orlando   Austin   San Antonio
Toronto   Montreal   London   Sydney   Tokyo

Publisher	Ted Buchholz
Acquisitions Editor	Chris Klein
Senior Developmental Editor	Meera Dash
Senior Project Editor	Steve Welch
Senior Production Manager	Ken Dunaway
Senior Book Designer	John Ritland
Photo Editor	Mark G. Brelsford
Permissions Editor	Van Strength

On the Cover: Illustrated photograph by Norinne Betjemann. Norinne Betjemann is a Philadelphia-based artist who uses photography as her primary medium. Although the cover image, originally commissioned by the *Philadelphia Inquirer Magazine,* depicts Philadelphia's Eastern State Penitentiary, most of Betjemann's work melds together architectural elements from disparate sites in Europe, Central America, the Middle East, and India. Betjemann is a graduate of Moore College of Art and Design and is on the faculty of the University of the Arts. Her work has been in solo and group exhibitions throughout the United States as well as in Paris and London. Betjemann's mural-size pieces are in numerous corporate, museum, and private collections.

Address for Editorial Correspondence: Harcourt Brace Jovanovich College Publishers, 301 Commerce Street, Suite 3700, Forth Worth, TX 76102.

Address for Orders: Harcourt Brace Jovanovich, Inc., 6277 Sea Harbor Drive, Orlando, FL 32887. 1-800-782-4479, or 1-800-433-0001 (in Florida).

Acknowledgments and credits appear on pp. 749–751, which constitute a continuation of the copyright page.

Printed in the United States of America

Library of Congress Catalog Card Number: 91-78233

ISBN 0-15-500128-0

2 4 5 6 7 8 9 0 1   048   9 8 7 6 5 4 3 2 1

PREFACE

"Criminal justice" refers to the structure, function, and decision processes of agencies that deal with the management and control of crime and criminal offenders—police, courts, and correctional systems. It is often confused with the academic disciplines of criminology and police science. Criminology focuses on the role of crime in organized society, the nature and causes of crime and criminal behavior, and the relationships between crime and social behavior. Police science concentrates on the pragmatic aspects of law enforcement and peace-keeping operations—the prevention and detection of crime, the apprehension of criminal offenders, the location and preservation of evidence, the questioning of suspects, the application of police resources, and the development of police/community relations.

As an independent academic activity, the study of criminal justice is comparatively new in the United States. The first degree-granting program appeared half a century ago, and as recently as the 1950s fewer than five thousand college students were focusing on the study of crime and justice. During the past three decades, however, this situation has changed dramatically. During the middle and late 1960s interest in criminal justice education was spurred by the "war on crime" and the resulting massive federal funding for the upgrading of criminal justice personnel, agencies, technology, and programming. Currently criminal justice courses enroll well over 200,000 students annually, and the upward trend is expected to continue.

Although criminal justice is a relatively new course, the topics have been studied for centuries. It is indeed an interdisciplinary branch of knowledge. From the perspective of legal studies, it examines aspects of criminal law and procedure; from political science it takes elements of constitutional law and appellate court practice; from the viewpoint of sociology it examines the structures of certain social institutions and how they affect the administration of justice. Criminal justice also uses research from psychology, history, public administration, anthropology, economics, and many other disciplines.

NEW IN THIS EDITION

As criminal justice education has evolved and expanded, so too has research on the various processes of justice. This growth has resulted in a dramatic proliferation in the criminal justice literature as scholars, researchers, and administrators seek to disseminate their work. So great has been the demand for classroom materials that during the past decade publishers have responded with thousands of new textbooks, supplementary readings, manuals, anthologies, monographs, and reports. Several dozen new introductory criminal justice textbooks and revised editions appear every year.

It was in this context of rapid change that the first edition of *Criminal Justice* was published nearly a decade ago; and when a field changes rapidly, so must the classroom material—especially for introductory courses. For the Fourth Edition, new statistics, research findings, and significant court decisions were plentiful. Further, the major issues in criminal justice have changed as policies, procedures, and viewpoints have developed. The interests and concerns of instructors using the earlier editions also have developed. In response to the many favorable reviews and comments on the Third Edition from both instructors and students, the basic structure and organization of the book has remained unchanged.

Beyond the updating of facts, court decisions, issues, and research findings, there is one major change. As an outgrowth of the U.S. "war on drugs" during the 1980s and early 1990s, all phases of the criminal justice process have become "drug driven." In the legislative sector, new laws have been created to deter drug involvement and to increase penalties for drug-related crime. In the police sector, funding has served to expand street-level drug enforcement initiatives, which, in turn, have increased the number of drug-crime arrests. In the judicial sector, the increased flow of drug cases has resulted in overcrowded dockets and courtrooms, as well as the creation of new drug courts, special dispositional alternatives for drug offenders, and higher rates of conviction and incarceration. In the correctional sector, the results include the crowding of already overpopulated jails and penitentiaries, the establishment of liberal release policies, experimentation with new prison-based drug treatment programs, and the spread of AIDS among inmates — the result of the higher density of prison populations combined with the expanded presence in the penitentiary of intravenous drug users and others at risk for the disease. The Fourth Edition of *Criminal Justice* has attempted to address this shift.

FEATURES OF THE BOOK

Criminal Justice is designed to achieve a number of goals for introductory criminal justice courses. First, it offers basic information as to the nature of crime and the processes of justice. Second, in theme and perspective it provides an analysis of the administration of justice in its contemporary forms and historical roots. This approach reveals some of the myth, folklore, and stereotypical images that pervade thinking about crime and justice in the United States. Third, the textbook is conceived and written to interest a wide range of students. Intended for those at community colleges as well as four-year universities, the data and subject matter have been drawn from the professional and popular media and the fields of law, sociology, political science, history, popular culture, anthropology, and oral tradition. To explain certain phenomena more effectively, a portion of the more than two hundred photographs and cartoons — some comical, many serious, and all informative — emphasize the fads and foibles that have historically characterized the administration of justice in the United States. Fourth, and most important, this edition presents the many facets of justice administration in the context of the changing political, social, cultural, and economic events that have shaped the evolution and implementation of criminal justice in this century.

Each chapter ends with a Summary and a set of Key Terms, Questions for Discussion, and Suggested Readings. The text has an extensive end-of-book glossary of major and minor terms. Within the chapters, more than one hundred numbered Exhibits focus on important aspects of criminal justice processing, the history of criminal justice, and court cases mentioned in the text. All of the key terms, cases, and concepts are defined in the margins near their appearance in the text. In the Fourth Edition, graphs, tables, and quotations have been added to

the margin and tailored for use as an illustrative guide to the topics concerned.

ANCILLARIES

The Fourth Edition of *Criminal Justice* is accompanied by an expanded, integrated ancillary package. Each element is designed to facilitate both learning and teaching.

1. The Study Guide includes a summary, key terms, other important terms, objectives, practice test questions, supplementary readings, and removable exercises for each chapter of the textbook. The Study Guide also has a unique feature, "Understanding Supreme Court Opinions."
2. The Instructor's Resource Guide presents a summary, topic outline, review of the major objectives and key terms, and comments and answers for many of the discussion questions in each chapter. It also has extensive, useful lecture supplements, discussion topics, class projects, and transparency masters.
3. The Test Bank contains more than two thousand multiple-choice, true – false, and fill-in-the-blank questions with answers page-referenced to the text. The Test Bank is available in printed and computerized formats.
4. Computerized Test Bank and Gradebook Software are offered in IBM and Macintosh versions of the testing software, ExaMaster™. The testing software, new with the Fourth Edition, allows the instructor to create tests using few keystrokes and with all steps defined in easy-to-follow screen prompts. ExaMaster offers three easy-to-use options for test creation:
   a. EasyTest lets the instructor create an entire test from a single screen in a few easy steps. Instructors can select questions from the database or, using their own parameters, let EasyTest randomly select the questions.
   b. FullTest lets the instructor use the whole range of available options:
      - select questions as you preview them on the screen
      - edit existing questions or add your own questions
      - add or edit graphics in the MS-DOS version

- link related questions, instructions, and graphics
- randomly select questions from a wider range of criteria
- create specific criteria on two open keys
- block specific questions from random selection
- print up to ninety-nine different versions of the same test along with answer sheets

c. RequesTest is an option available to those who do not have access to a computer. When the instructor calls 1 (800) 447-9457, software specialists will compile the questions according to the instructor's criteria and either mail or fax the test within forty-eight hours.

Included with ExaMaster is Exam-Record, a gradebook program that allows instructors to record, curve, graph, and print out grades. ExamRecord takes raw scores and converts them into grades using the instructor's criteria. The distribution of grades can be set in a bar graph or a plotted curve.

If questions arise, the HBJ Software Support Hotline is available Monday through Friday 9 A.M. – 4 P.M. (Central Time) at 1 (800) 447-9457.

5. Overhead Transparency Acetates, new with the Fourth Edition, are available in addition to the transparency masters printed in the Instructor's Resource Guide. The set includes 35 color acetates reproduced from graphs and tables in the textbook.

ACKNOWLEDGMENTS

The number of debts one accumulates in writing a book is surprisingly large. Gratitude must first go to my wife, Carolyn J. Inciardi, for her continuous support and editorial assistance; to the team at Harcourt Brace Jovanovich — Chris Klein, Meera Dash, Steve Welch, John Ritland, Ken Dunaway, Mark Brelsford, and Van Strength — who were responsible for creating the Fourth Edition; to the many students and instructors who used the Third Edition and made recommendations for the Fourth; to Kenneth C. Haas, Valerie Hans, James Fyfe, Gennaro Vito, C. Ronald Huff, and James Marquart for their critical, yet needed, reviews of the material in the book; to Kenneth C. Haas, Patricia Loveless, and Duane C. McBride for their contributions to some of the exhibits; to Jeff Dunson and Tracy Tlumac for the many hours they spent in libraries retrieving updated material; and to Nova Lee McKernan and Mary-Ann Farrell for their assistance in the preparation of a clean manuscript. Finally, I wish to express my special debt to a wide selection of people who must remain anonymous, yet without whom portions of this book could not have been written.

James A. Inciardi

About the Author

James A. Inciardi is Director of the Center for Drug and Alcohol Studies and professor of sociology and criminal justice at the University of Delaware. He received his Ph.D. in sociology at New York University. He was director of the National Center for the Study of Acute Drug Reactions at the University of Miami School of Medicine, vice-president of the Washington, D.C.-based Resource Planning Corporation, and associate director of research for both the New York State Narcotic Addiction Control Commission and the Metropolitan Dade County (Florida) Comprehensive Drug Program.

Dr. Inciardi is the Principal Investigator of large federally funded drug treatment programs designed for criminal justice populations. He has done extensive consulting work nationally and internationally. He is the author of more than one hundred fifty articles, chapters, and books on criminal justice, substance abuse, history, folklore, criminology, medicine, law, public policy, and AIDS.

CONTENTS

PART ONE
The Foundations of Crime and Justice   37

PART TWO
The Police   161

PART THREE
The Courts   307

CHAPTER 9

Beyond the Limits of the Law: Police Crime, Corruption, and Brutality   *273*

CHAPTER 10

This is the House That Justice Built: The Structure of American Courts   *309*

PART FOUR
Corrections   493

PART FIVE
Juvenile Justice   677

CHAPTER 18

The Juvenile Justice System   679

EPILOGUE

The Changing Face of Criminal Justice in America 719

CHAPTER 1

The Rediscovery of Criminal Justice in America

There is one universal law. That law is justice. Justice forms the cornerstone of each nation's law.
—ALEXIS DE TOQUEVILLE

Justice is too good for some people and not good enough for the rest.
—NORMAN DOUGLAS

Only a socially just country has the right to exist.
—POPE JOHN PAUL II

Not even those who live by wickedness and crime can get on without some small element of justice.
—CICERO

ore than three decades ago, the noted scholar and columnist Max Lerner offered a rather curious description of criminal justice in America:

> The administration of American criminal justice has been often scored as inefficient, corrupt, and archaic, and all three charges are probably true, but again probably no truer than of past eras and other societies. The supervision of criminal justice is mainly in the hands of the local authorities; the Federal courts handle crimes under Federal jurisdiction but try to minimize the appeals from local and state jurisdictions. A lawbreaker is tracked down by local police, prosecuted by a local district attorney and defended by a local lawyer, tried in a local court house in a trial reported predominantly in the local press, convicted or cleared by a local jury, sentenced by a local judge, and shut up in a local or state prison. At every point there is a good deal of bungling, prejudice, poor judgement, or corruption. Yet on the whole there is a widespread feeling that the results are tolerably good and that the frailties of the whole process are a reflection of the frailties of the society in which it takes place.[1]

Lerner's comment, written in his widely acclaimed and sweeping reappraisal of American life, *America as a Civilization,* may appear to be somewhat cynical in its suggestion that the processes of justice are both lame and corrupt. Yet a glance over the twentieth century prior to his reflections offers considerable support. The literature on American law, crime, and justice clearly shows an overwhelming concern with inefficiency and corruption in the machinery of justice and crime control— problems emanating chiefly from the chaos that existed in urban areas throughout most of the nineteenth century. From the middle through late 1800s, criminal districts, street gangs, and political corruption were visible characteristics of major American cities. Initially, areas of vice and crime had appeared in which were concentrated houses of prostitution, dance halls, concert saloons, and gambling casinos. To these were added scores of organized street gangs, whose members stole and killed, as well as waged street battles against rival gangs. And finally, during the post– Civil War era, political corruption became commonplace, aiding and even helping shape the commercialization and organization of both vice and crime. The pleasure districts and urban guerrillas were able to operate openly because regular protection payments were made to corrupt police and political overlords.[2] The relentless muckraking of city presses and the resultant public outcry, however, started a reform movement at the turn of the century aimed at establishing political responsibility in public office.[3] But the reform movement was short-lived, and by 1910 the problem of crime in American cities was greater than ever before. The evils of the earlier decades seemed to have reemerged on an even larger scale, and the machinery available for social control was clearly ill-equipped to deal with the magnitude of the problem. As a consequence,

Nineteenth-Century Street Gangs

Street gangs were particularly prominent in U.S. cities during this era, using such colorful names as the Glee Club and Rising Stars in San Francisco; the Spiders and Yellow Henry's Mob in New Orleans; Bloody Maxwell's Boys and the Car Barn Bandits in Chicago; and the Bridge Twisters, Plug Uglies, Dead Rabbits, Dock Rats, Frog Hollows, and Hudson Dusters in New York. Especially notorious in New York's Lower Manhattan were the Whyos, who offered the following services:

punching	$ 2
both eyes blackened	4
nose and jaw broke	10
ear chewed off	15
leg or arm broke	19
shot in leg	25
stab	25
doing the big job	100 & up

SOURCES: Herbert Asbury, *The Gangs of New York* (New York: Knopf, 1928); James A. Inciardi, *Reflections on Crime* (New York: Holt Rinehart and Winston, 1978).

a series of crime surveys was made during the 1920s in various parts of the country, and for the first time in the national experience, the actual operations of the criminal justice process in urban America were closely and extensively examined.

THE 1920s: ATTEMPTS AT REFORM

The first of the crime surveys was made in Cleveland, Ohio, and began in 1920 on the assumption that criminal justice in what was then the country's fifth largest city was the least efficient function of government. The investigators set out to determine the system's defects and to trace them to their sources.[4] The effort in Cleveland was followed in 1925 by the *Missouri Crime Survey,* which examined state-level processes of law enforcement, judicial procedure, and correctional practice.[5] And finally, in 1926, the *Illinois Crime Survey* extensively investigated crime and justice in Cook County, Illinois, as well as completed a landmark study of organized crime in Chicago.[6] Collectively, the surveys resulted in a series of documents that clearly demonstrated the suspected faults with urban police and court systems and problems in local and state prison organization. Furthermore, combined with the unquestionable failure of the Prohibition Amendment and the rise of organized crime from the East to the Midwest, the findings resulted in a sweeping investigation by the National Commission on Law Observance and Enforcement. Known as the **Wickersham Commission** (its chairman was the former U.S. attorney general George W. Wickersham), it explored numerous aspects of crime and justice across America. Its conclusions were so damaging to the credibility of criminal justice administration that they resulted in public debate that would last for some time to come.[7]

CRIME AND JUSTICE: THE 1930s THROUGH THE 1950s

By the 1930s it was well established that justice in America was outmoded, inept, and marked by venality. The level of lawlessness in law enforcement, combined with the jaded quality of due process in the court system, was unprecedented. Yet few changes emerged from the decade of crime surveys, for the country suddenly had a host of new and more pressing concerns. In mid-October of 1929, America was a land of plenty, and average middle-class citizens saw a seemingly unlimited prosperity ahead. Newly inaugurated president Herbert Hoover announced that the conquest of poverty was no longer just a mirage, and economist Irving Fisher assured the people that the nation's economy was on a permanently high plateau. But by 1931, when the Wickersham Commission reports appeared in print, the national income had been cut in half. By 1932, unemployment had hit an all-time high, banks had begun to fail, and the shantytowns that sprang up on the outskirts of every city had become known as Hoovervilles.[8] This was the age of the Great Depression.

In the grimness of the national economic crisis, public interest was drawn to the great wave of crime that continued throughout the decade. The Depression years were the era of John Dillinger, Charles "Pretty

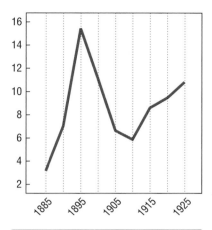

Homicide Rates (per 100,000 pop.) in the United States, 1885–1925

The Wickersham Commission: A federal inquiry into crime and the organization of justice in the United States.

During the Prohibition era, illegal saloons were commonplace. Called "speakeasies," the term likely came from the early 19th century English speak-softly-shop, an underworld designation for a smuggler's house where cheap liquor could be obtained.

Boy" Floyd, George "Baby Face" Nelson, and Bonnie Parker and Clyde Barrow.[9] Armed with machine guns and fast cars, the new breed of bandits recreated a frontier pattern of rapid assault followed by immediate and elusive retreat. Bank robbery was one of their usual crimes, and the masses of unemployed, absorbed in the exploits of this army of "public enemies" that was assaulting the very banking system they blamed for the loss of prosperity, had little reason to press for criminal justice reform. Later, as the thirties drew to a close and the nation began to pull out of the Depression, world events intervened, and again reform was pushed to the background. On December 7, 1941, the Japanese attacked the Pacific Fleet in Pearl Harbor, causing the deaths of more than three thousand American servicemen, and the greatest humiliation in American military history. The nation's energy was consumed by the urgency of World War II.

World War II

Shantytowns called "Hoovervilles" sprang up at the edges of U.S. cities during the Great Depression. This one sits grimly in New York's Central Park.

Running the Cat Roads *Among the most infamous of the 1930s "public enemies" was John Dillinger, who eluded the police and F.B.I. by "running the cat roads"—escaping through the many unmarked mid-west back-country roads. Dillinger's most notable bank robberies occurred during 1933–1934 in East Chicago (1), South Bend (2), Rockville (3), Greencastle (4), Indianapolis (5), Daleville (6), Muncie (7), Peru (8), Lima (9), Bluffton (10), Dayton (11), New Carlisle (12), and St. Mary's (13).*

The United States emerged from the war as the most powerful nation in the history of the world, not only in terms of its military capability, but in its technological and economic posture as well. The war ended the Great Depression and led to postwar prosperity. By 1947, the United States was producing 43 percent of the world's electricity, 57 percent of its steel, and 62 percent of its oil. Americans owned three-fourths of the automobiles in the world, and their average income was many times greater than that in other countries. By the close of the decade, unemployment had stabilized at about three million persons, roughly 5 percent of the labor force, and Americans, at least those in the white middle class, enjoyed an unprecedented state of economic privilege. In this opulent postwar society, which flowed with a superabundance of resources, the question of justice was of low priority, superseded by images of white houses with front lawns and all-electric kitchens.[10]

The "Fabulous Fifties"?

The prosperity of the late forties continued into what the nostalgia craze has called the "Fabulous Fifties." The 1950s has been romanticized as a golden age of simplicity and innocence, a thrilling time of bobby sox and soda fountains, Elvis Presley and James Dean, hot rods and "American Bandstand." There were no wars, no riots, and no protests. But the fifties was hardly a time of enthusiasm and contentment. To social critic Michael Harrington the period "was a moral disaster, an amusing waste of life," and author Norman Mailer pointedly described the fifties as "one of the worst decades in the history of man."[11] True, it *was* a time of leisure and cultural pursuit. In record numbers people traveled, listened to music, pulled weeds in their backyards, read *Reader's Digest* condensed books, and bought mink-trimmed clothespins and hula hoops. But it was also a time of fear and suspicion. The cold war with the Soviet Union, the perceived threat of communist infiltration, and the development of the hydrogen bomb were among the debilitating realities, crystallized by accusations, loyalty oaths, and the anticommunist witch hunts of Senator Joseph McCarthy. The fifties was also a time of conservatism. Life was bland, moral, and patriotic; people became suburbanized, domesticated, and buttoned-down. And the problems of poverty, sexual and racial discrimination, militarism, and ecology were ignored.[12]

In the area of crime and justice, American interest was focused on organized crime. From May 10, 1950, to May 1, 1951, the **Special Committee to Investigate Crime in Interstate Commerce** (the **Kefauver Committee**), chaired by Estes Kefauver, the U.S. senator from Tennessee, held hearings that were televised as a public service, but that rapidly became a media event. Although there were only 7,000 television sets in the country in 1946, the figure had increased to tens of millions by 1950, and many Americans were spending more hours watching their sets than they were spending at work. When the independent New York City station WPIX set up its cameras in Manhattan's Foley Square Courthouse where the Kefauver Committee was meeting, and began feeding the video to stations across the country, the potency of the hearings was felt almost immediately. Underworld figures like Frank Costello, Joe Adonis, Charlie Fischetti, and Ben Siegal became instant

The Kefauver Committee: A special Senate committee targeting organized crime in the United States. With exciting drama of the courtroom variety, its disclosures demonstrated the extent to which racketeers had established themselves in American society.

Senator Joseph McCarthy testifies during the McCarthy/Army hearings on the organization of the Communist Party in the United States, in June 1954.

I don't know anything about music. In my line, you don't have to.
—ELVIS PRESLEY, 1950s

Rock 'n' roll is part of a plot to undermine the morals of the youth of our nation. It is sexualistic, unmoralistic, and brings people of both races together.
—NORTH CAROLINA WHITE CITIZENS COUNCIL, 1950s

In the 1950s, the Russians launched Sputnik and we launched the Edsel.
—RICHARD FREEDMAN, *NEW YORK TIMES*, MARCH 5, 1978

The Apalachin Convention

visitors to American living rooms. An estimated 30 million people watched Costello's courtroom antics as network stations began carrying the full hearings, and the nation became totally absorbed:

> Merchants complained to the Committee that their businesses were paralyzed. Movie houses became ghost halls during the hours of the proceedings. . . . Housewives did their ironing and fed the baby in front of the set. In many big cities business and home life were noticeably affected. One Chicago department store manager took a look at the number of customers in his aisles and ran an ad: "Ten Percent Off During Kefauver Hours."[13]

Although most Americans were well aware that criminals existed at all levels of the social order, the impact of the Kefauver telecasts was staggering. People learned directly of the sordid intertwining of crime and politics and of the extent of dishonor in public life. Many questioned what could be done about these problems, but issues that were more pressing pushed such concerns about crime, once again, into the background.

The issues that claimed the country's attention this time included the "menace of domestic communists," as the late FBI director, J. Edgar Hoover, put it,[14] the cold war with the Soviet Union, and the growing hot war in Korea. There was also "the bomb" and nuclear war, for China had fallen to the communists and the Soviets possessed the plans for the atomic bomb. Then, on March 1, 1954, American scientists set off the first explosion of an H-bomb, and with that came a reshaping of the public mind. Overnight, private and public bomb shelters became necessities, and bombing and survival drills became common in schools and places of business.[15]

The specter of the bomb hovered over America throughout the fifties, but the early hysteria eventually waned. Also, the communist threat grew less impressive, and the Korean conflict came to an end. In addition, the fear of domestic espionage lessened, and Senator Joseph McCarthy fell from power.

This was the setting within which Max Lerner made his comments about criminal justice in *America as a Civilization*. It was within this context that he claimed that in spite of its bungling, prejudice, and corruption, people felt that the justice system was tolerably good. Perhaps Lerner's observations were not so cynical after all! The country was aware that there were difficulties with the justice system, but they had forgotten just how bad the problems actually were. Furthermore, during this same time, justice was swift and certain for those perceived as the most visible and wanton offenders. During the fifties, for example, more than 1,400 persons were legally executed for serious crimes. But the complacency that Lerner wrote about was to be short-lived, for the problems of organized crime, juvenile gangsterism, racism, and disenfranchised youth, combined with a nation guided by the hypocrisy of many of its political leaders, changed national priorities and ideologies for the coming decades.

In 1957, the year the Soviet Sputniks were placed into orbit, Jimmy Hoffa, already exposed as a labor racketeer by Arkansas Senator John L. McClellan, was named president of the Teamsters — the nation's largest union.[16] Many Americans then began questioning the democratic system's basic conceptions of justice and morality.[17] In November of that year, the country was again taken by surprise when scores of the nation's alleged crime leaders were inadvertently discovered at a meeting in the home of Joseph Barbara in Apalachin, New York. They had come from

● EXHIBIT 1.1 ●

Sidelights on Criminal Matters
The Apalachin Crime Conclave

On November 14, 1957, a group of 63 known crime syndicate bosses and other racketeers were discovered by police at the home of Joseph M. Barbara, president of the Canada Dry Bottling Company. Barbara's estate was in the hills near Apalachin, New York, a village in the western part of the state just a few miles north of the Pennsylvania line. Among the unprecedented assemblage of organized crime leaders and their sinister underlings were such notables as Vito Genovese, Carlo Gambino, Joseph Profaci, Joseph Bonanno, and Carmine Lombardozzi. Most of them had been arrested in the past on serious charges—murder, robbery, extortion, counterfeiting, blackmail, burglary, grand larceny, possession of firearms, gambling, and narcotics. They had come, they said, to ask after Mr. Barbara's health (and in fact he *was* ill, and died soon afterwards). Barbara remarked that he was surprised but pleased by the visit, and it was a fortunate coincidence that he happened to have 200 pounds of steak in his kitchen that day.

The "visit" to the Barbara estate on that November day raised numerous questions in the press, and in the minds of both the police and the courts. Many people who had rejected the notion of a nationwide criminal cartel felt that the presence of that many "retired" members of the underworld from all over the country had been more than a coincidence, and more than just a social gathering. Federal narcotics agents labeled the event a meeting of the grand council of the Mafia, although no credible evidence was ever advanced to support such a thesis. However, the Apalachin affair touched off numerous investigations into organized crime, and if subsequent syndicate "social gatherings" ever occurred in the years hence, they tended to be more discreet.

SOURCES: Virgil W. Peterson, *The Mob* (Ottawa, IL: Green Hill, 1983; Ralph Salerno and John S. Tompkins, *The Crime Confederation* (Garden City, NY: Doubleday, 1969).

all parts of the country: at least twenty-three from New York City or New Jersey, nineteen from upstate New York, eight from the Midwest, three from the West, two from the South, as well as two delegates from Cuba and one from Italy.[18] The reasons for the meeting were never uncovered, but its discovery strengthened the notion that organized crime was a nationwide and international alliance with monopolistic controls over numerous businesses, industries, and branches of government (see Exhibit 1.1). And in addition to the rediscovery of syndicate crime, there was a growing awareness of corruption in law enforcement, for the fifties were marked by a series of random exposures of police crime.[19] And to these issues were added the growing problems of juvenile delinquency and an apparent increase in street crime. But the most difficult problems —ones that had been festering since World War II—would not reach their fullest intensity until the decade of the sixties.

THE SIXTIES: A DECADE OF REBELLION

The fifties had been a decade of waste. In the belief that the good life had arrived, Americans rushed to the suburbs to escape urban congestion. Throughout the country, tract-built developments appeared, as landscapes were bulldozed flat. Between 1950 and 1960 the number of U.S. homeowners increased by 9 million to a total of almost 33 million.[20] This mass migration to the suburbs left the cities to deteriorate. In addition, Americans opted for the family automobile as never before, resulting in the construction of a 40,000-mile interstate highway system and an increase of more than 21 million in the number of cars registered. This reliance on the automobile, in turn, resulted in a breakdown in mass transportation, and in pollution, congestion, and a rapid depletion of fossil fuels. These problems were most deeply felt in the central cities, where the poor had been left behind.

The racism of the fifties also had consequences for the sixties. In that decade of growing prosperity, blacks continued to face the legacy of **Jim Crow.** Early in the fifties, for example, black war veteran Harvey Clark attempted to move his family into an apartment that he had leased in Cicero, Illinois. Police stopped Clark's van and the chief of police struck him, suggesting that he leave town or be shot. Upon Clark's second attempt to move into the apartment, the premises were besieged by a mob of 4,000 whites who, for four days, plundered the building and stole and destroyed Clark's belongings while the police stood idle. The mob was eventually dispersed and the case investigated, but those indicted were an NAACP attorney, the owner of the apartment building, her lawyer, and her rental agent. They were charged with conspiracy to injure property by causing "depreciation in the market selling price."[21]

In the South, blacks were repeatedly the victims of mob murders, lynchings, and all forms of disfranchisement. On August 28, 1955, Emmett Till, a 14-year-old black, was kidnapped from his Mississippi home after having allegedly whistled at a white woman. Four days later his body was recovered from the Tallahatchie River, and an all-white jury later acquitted the two white men accused of Till's murder. Racism was apparent, furthermore, not only for the poor or southern blacks, but for those in the northern middle class as well. In 1957, for example, William and Daisy Myers moved with their three children to Levittown, Pennsylvania, and immediately became the targets of stoning, burning crosses, and obscene phone calls. In addition, the house immediately behind theirs became the center for segregationist forces, who played "Old Man River" through loudspeakers around the clock.[22]

To add to these problems, the country's youth faced the enforcement of conformity, a transparency of sexual morals, and a set of cultural regulations and prohibitions that stressed achievement, prejudice, waste, compliance, and consensus, yet failed to explain or recognize the confusion and absurdity of it all. As a result of such contradictions, a teenage ethic emerged that made serious negative value judgments about the nature and meaning of life. As Kenneth Rexroth warned in an early issue of *Evergreen Review:*

> Listen you — do you *really* think your kids are like bobby soxers in those wholesome Coca-Cola ads? Don't you know that across the table from you at dinner sits somebody who looks on you as an enemy who is planning to kill him in the immediate future? Don't you know that if you were to say to your English class, "It is raining," they would take it for granted that you were a liar? Don't you know they never tell you nothing? that they can't? . . . they simply can't get through,

Jim Crow laws: Beginning in the 1880s, a number of oridinances were passed in southern states and municipalities legalizing segregation of blacks and whites. The term *Jim Crow* is believed to have derived from a character in a minstrel song. The Supreme Court ruling in *Plessey* v. *Ferguson* (1896) held that separate facilities for blacks and whites were constitutional. The decision in *Plessey* was ultimately overturned by *Brown* v. *Board of Education* in 1954.

The rebellion of youth

can't, and won't even try anymore to communicate. Don't you know this, really? If you don't, you're heading for a terrible awakening.[23]

The late social critic Paul Goodman tended to disagree with the conception that there had been a communication failure between youth and adult; he felt, on the contrary, that social messages had been communicated very clearly and that the young had found them totally unacceptable.[24] Whatever the reason, however, disaffection and rebellion were in the wings.

A recognition of the pressures on youth began to surface by the middle of the decade in the popular culture media. In 1954 Marlon Brando played in Columbia Pictures' *The Wild One* as a tough motorcycle leader whose gang rampages beyond his control and who is then unjustly attacked by adult mobs. The youth of the day recognized that adults distrusted their behavior somewhat, and they readily empathized with the brutality and perceived heroism of the young Brando character. The following year MGM's *Blackboard Jungle* examined another aspect of the youth problem, focusing on central city juvenile delinquency. Also appearing in 1955 was Warner Brothers' potent film *Rebel Without a Cause,* which targeted the disaffection of middle-class youth. In bringing delinquency from the slums to the suburbs, the film hinted that the social ills at the base of youthful rebellion were widespread.

In the sixties, the problems of enforced conformity, increasing rate of delinquency and youth rebellion, racism, crime and corruption, cultural values that canonized both consumption and waste, and other problems that had been growing through the late forties and fifties came to a head, together with the problems in the criminal justice system that had been ignored since the 1920s. These problems and contradictions resulted in perhaps the most violent era of the twentieth century.[25]

The turbulent events of the 1960s began in the South in early 1961, when civil rights workers sought to win enforcement of a 1958 Supreme Court ruling ordering the desegregation of bus line stations and waiting rooms. Led by James Farmer and the Congress of Racial Equality, two buses carrying thirteen Freedom Riders — six whites and seven blacks — left Washington, D.C., on May 4 for New Orleans. When they reached Alabama, one bus was firebombed and the demonstrators were beaten. The following year when James Meredith, a black student, attempted to enroll in the University of Mississippi at Oxford, the ensuing clash between thousands of southern whites and a small force of federal marshals lasted for more than fifteen hours and resulted in more than seventy casualties.* And while southern opposition to racial equality was generally expressed through violent mass protests, it also emerged through individual political murders. The list of civil rights workers, both black and white, who were martyred in the early 1960s is a lengthy one. It includes some well-known names: Medgar Evers, the NAACP field secretary; white civil rights volunteer Viola Liuzzo, a Detroit housewife and mother who was shot by nightriders while ferrying marchers between Selma and Montgomery, Alabama; and James Chaney, Andrew Goodman, and Michael Schwerner, three young civil rights workers murdered by members of the Ku Klux Klan in Mississippi, with the connivance of local law enforcement officers.

All three stars of Rebel Without a Cause *suffered premature violent deaths*—*James Dean at age 24, in a 1955 automobile crash; Natalie Wood at 43, in a 1981 drowning accident; and Sal Mineo at 37, in a 1976 street mugging.*

The Freedom Riders

America started the sixties thinking it could save the world and ended them wondering whether it could save face.
— James Reston, 1969

---

* An earlier attempt to desegregate an all-white southern college had been unsuccessful. In 1956, University of Alabama officials had expelled their first black student, Autherine Lucy, on the grounds that her presence was a threat to public order.

On August 28, 1963, in Washington, D.C., Martin Luther King, Jr., gave his historic speech in which he told all Americans, "I have a dream . . ."

George Lincoln Rockwell, leader of the American Nazi party, was murdered by one of his followers in 1967.

Also of national concern were the ghetto riots, brought on by racism, poverty, and the deterioration of central city slums. The first occurred in the early sixties in New York City's Brownsville, Bedford-Stuyvesant, and Harlem areas; they were followed in August 1965 by a riot in the Watts section of Los Angeles that began with an incident of alleged police brutality and ended with 34 persons killed and 1,032 injured, $40 million in property destroyed, 600 buildings damaged or demolished, and 4,000 persons arrested. By 1967 ghetto uprisings had erupted across the country. During the first nine months of that year there were some 164 disorders and 83 deaths, capped by major outbreaks in Newark, New Jersey, and Detroit, Michigan.

But the violence associated with the civil rights movement and oppression in the ghettos was only the beginning, for the decade was marked by considerable bloodshed of a highly political character. On November 22, 1963, John Fitzgerald Kennedy — the symbol of an era that, in hindsight, many believe to have been the beginning of an American Camelot — became the fourth U.S. president to be assassinated. His alleged assassin, Lee Harvey Oswald, was shot to death within thirty-six hours. Less than thirteen months later, Black Muslim leader Malcolm X was killed in a Harlem auditorium in New York City, thus becoming a cultural hero for a new and activist generation of black Americans. In 1967 George Lincoln Rockwell, leader of the American Nazi party — the extremist right-wing group dedicated to "saving" the United States from communists, blacks, and Jews — was murdered by one of his followers. And in 1968, civil rights leader Dr. Martin Luther King, Jr., and

Senator Robert F. Kennedy were assassinated. In addition, there were battles at Kent State, Ole Miss, Jackson State, and numerous other college campuses when students protesting the Vietnam War were fired upon by police and National Guardsmen.

Street crime also increased during the sixties. In 1960, for example, there were almost 300,000 known violent crimes. By the close of the decade the number of murders had increased by 76 percent, serious assaults by 117 percent, forcible rapes by 121 percent, and robbery by 224 percent. Furthermore, the number of burglaries had increased by 142 percent, larcenies by 245 percent, and the overall crime rate by 144 percent.[26]

But the final horror of the sixties came in August 1969, with antecedents in the **counterculture,** which had first become visible a few years earlier. The counterculture, as many have described it, was a whole complex of new behavior patterns and beliefs.[27] It was a revolution against the Protestant ethic and the bourgeois American concept of life that emphasized work, duty, morality, maturity, and success. Members of the counterculture rejected the traditionally accepted values of American culture; many lived in communes and used drugs; they wrote poetry, listened to acid rock music, embraced the teachings of mystical religions, and read *I Ching* or the *Tibetan Book of the Dead.* They were called "dropouts," "freaks," or, to use the term coined by a reporter from the *San Francisco Chronicle* during the summer of 1965, "hippies."

Then in 1967 came the "Summer of Love" and the "flower children." It all began on March 26 of that year when 10,000 youths congregated in New York City's Central Park to honor love. They joined hands in "love circles," flew kites, sang, and took drugs. On the West Coast that Easter Sunday, another 15,000 youths met in San Francisco and participated in a similar happening. The crossroads of the Summer of Love was the Haight-Ashbury section of San Francisco, where the

Counterculture: Associated with the "hippies" of the 1960s, it was a complex of ideas and behavior patterns that ran counter to those of traditional society.

The "Summer of Love"

Haight–Ashbury, home of the hippies of the 1960s and drug users of the 1970s, was invaded by the Yuppies (Young Urban Professionals) of the 1980s. Uncle Hock, a resident of the Haight since 1961, calls them "Yuffies," for Young Urban Failures.

We thought we could change a mammoth government by wearing flowers and holding hands.
—GRACE SLICK OF *JEFFERSON AIRPLANE,* FEBRUARY 23, 1976

natives were known as flower children. One participant described that historic summer scene:

> As we were traveling across, Scott McKenzie was singing on the radio, "If you're going to San Francisco, put flowers in your hair." Sure enough if we didn't arrive with flowers in our hair. We went into that town and I couldn't believe it. It was a carnival. That one big street, Haight Street . . . was just packed with every kind of freak you could imagine. Guys with Mohawk hair cuts, people walking around in commodore uniforms, you know, the hat with the fuzz all over it. Everything! You couldn't believe it. It was an incredible street scene.[28]

But as Ed Sanders described it in his book *The Family,* the Haight-Ashbury district of the flower children was "a valley of plump rabbits surrounded by wounded coyotes." [29] During the spring and summer of 1967, the word had gone out across the country to come to San Francisco for love and flowers. Yet other things also waited in "the Haight." There were vicious criminals who grew long hair, bikers who tried to take over the drug market with sadistic tactics, "speed freaks" going through aggressive paranoid delusions, and satanist-rapist death freaks. Among these last was a bearded little psychotic who haunted the Grateful Dead concerts at the Avalon Ballroon, curling into a fetal position on the dance floor. As William Manchester put it in *The Glory and the Dream,* "he would be well remembered in Hashbury." [30] And indeed he would — his name was Charles Manson.

The so-called Summer of Love ended on October 8, 1967, with the murder of Linda Rae Fitzpatrick in New York.[31] She had been raped four times, her face smashed, and her naked corpse found in the boiler room

From the world of darkness I loosed demons and devils to torment.
— CHARLES MANSON, 1976

A hippie "crash pad" of the 1960s

There are only three constants in the San Francisco hippie scene — music, grass, and LSD.
— A SAN FRANCISCO "FLOWER CHILD"

of a Lower East Side tenement. She had been a flower child, one of many who had met violent death. Later that week in San Francisco's Golden Gate Park other flower children burned a gray coffin marked "Summer of Love." That summer had been crippled by violence and came to an end, but the specter of the Haight's death freaks was soon to reemerge.

Charles Manson was not typical of the disaffected middle-class youth who made up the flower children. Born in Cincinnati, Ohio, in 1934, Manson was a wandering vagrant who was in trouble most of his life, spending much of his time in jails and reformatories throughout the country. At age 35, he was the organizer of a commune located on the edge of Death Valley that practiced free love and pseudoreligious ceremonies centering around his role as a Christ-like leader. On August 8, 1969, Manson directed five of his followers to the Los Angeles mansion of film director Roman Polansky. Spouting Manson's doctrines of "peace, love, and death," the group proceeded to brutally murder the five persons there. The victims were shot and stabbed to death, and various slogans were written on the walls of the house with the blood of those slain. Among the victims was Polansky's wife, actress Sharon Tate, and coffee heiress Abigail Folger. A few hours later, Manson's protégés —one man and three women—invaded the home of two additional victims, Leno and Rosemary LaBianca, leaving their bodies mutilated and arranged in grotesque positions.[32] (See Exhibit 1.2 for more on Manson and his "family.")

The decade of the sixties was marked by crime, violence, rebellion, and a discontentment with the processes of justice. Even before it ended, however, people began responding to the growing disorder and the criminal justice system's inability to manage it.

THE ISSUE OF LAW AND ORDER AND THE WAR ON CRIME

Emotionally charged appeals for **law and order** were heard well before the 1960s had reached their midpoint. The cries were, in part, a reflection of the temperament of grass-roots America, which was seeking a return to the morality of previous decades. But they came also from citizens who not only despised crime in general, but waste, anarchy, and government control over individual destinies as well. At the extreme right of this growing consciousness were organizations such as the John Birch Society and the Minutemen. The most visible was the John Birch Society, an ultraconservative, anticommunist organization founded in 1958 by manufacturer Robert Welch and named after Captain John Birch, a U.S. intelligence officer killed by communists in China in 1945. Although the original goal of the society was to fight subversive communism in the United States, it was also solidly opposed to integration and the New Left student movements.[33]

Also visible at this time was a trend toward the "nationalization" of the Bill of Rights. The writers of the Bill of Rights had intended that it apply on the national level—that is, the level of the federal government —and not the state level. Thus, defendants in state criminal trials were not accorded many of the constitutional protections that were routinely given to those tried in federal courts. But in the 1930s the U.S. Supreme Court began extending these rights to state defendants. It was not until the 1960s, however, that significant gains were made. By 1969, nearly all

Recalling the 1960s

At the close of the 1970s, two former members of the sixties generation surveyed 1,005 of their peers, attempting to learn exactly how involved they were in the culture of the era. Here are some of their findings.

In the 1960s, did you:

	yes
go to Haight-Ashbury during the Summer of Love	16%
wear love beads	50%
play in a rock band	16%
call cops "pigs"	73%
live in a commune	30%
consider yourself a "hippie"	62%
get busted	25%
own a waterbed	17%
believe in "flower power"	64%
stop using deodorant	37%
think last names were bullshit	25%
panhandle for "spare change"	23%
use LSD	58%
have a "bad trip" on LSD	33%

SOURCE: Adapted from Rex Weiner and Deanne Stillman, *Woodstock Census* (New York: Fawcett Columbine, 1979).

Law and order: A political ideology and slogan that sought a return to the morality and values of earlier times and rejected the growing permissiveness in government and social affairs.

The John Birch Society

Nationalization of the Bill of Rights

● **EXHIBIT** **1.2** ●

Whatever Happened to . . .

The Manson Family

At my will, I walk your streets and am right out there among you.
—Charles Manson, 1987

You're a mass murderin' dog, Charlie.
—Geraldo Rivera, 1988

Reports of the number of people who lived with Charles Manson at his commune on the edge of Death Valley varied—anywhere from twenty to forty at any given time. The bona fide members of Manson's "family," however, were relatively few, and included Susan Atkins, Patricia Krenwinkel, Leslie Van Houten, Charles Watson, Lynette Fromme, and Sandra Good.

It was Atkins, Krenwinkel, Van Houten, and Watson who actually carried out the Tate–Folger–LaBianca murders, under Manson's direction. All five were convicted in the slayings and were sentenced to death. In 1972, however, the death penalty was declared unconstitutional in California and their sentences were commuted to life. They became eligible for parole in 1978, but their releases were denied. Subsequent parole hearings had the same outcome.

Although behind bars, Manson has remained a visible personality, appearing in numerous magazine and television interviews over the years. In 1984 he was set afire by a fellow inmate at the California Medical Facility—a state prison for psychiatric cases—but recovered quickly.

Charles Manson, after some three decades in prison, remains a celebrity. Each month he receives dozens of letters from around the world and numerous requests for interviews.

As for his co-defendents in the murders, they maintain their innocence in the case, claiming that they had been seduced into committing the crimes and were under Manson's spell at the time. They describe their former leader as a charismatic sociopath for whom death was a blessing and murder a sacrament.

The other two members of Manson's group, Lynette Fromme and Sandra Good, also made their way into correctional institutions. On the morning of September 5, 1975, Fromme attempted to assassinate President Gerald R. Ford. Her purpose was to call attention to the fact that the world was being contaminated by pollutants. She felt that saving the world could be accomplished by killing those in high power who permitted such destruction. At her trial, against the advice of the court, she acted as her own attorney. For her efforts, she was convicted and sentenced to natural life.

Sandra Good, a close friend of Fromme and equally anxious to save the world from pollution, also found her way to prison in 1975. She had written such virulent letters to chemical industry executives and their wives and made so many verbal threats that she was convicted and sentenced to fifteen years. In 1985, after serving two-thirds of her term, she was eligible for release on the condition that she not associate with any members of the Manson family. At first she refused, stating, ". . . I want to be where my family is, and my family is in prison." By the close of the year, however, she exchanged her prison environment for supervised parole

the provisions of the Bill of Rights relating to criminal violations were binding on the states, including the prohibitions against compulsory self-incrimination, illegal search and seizure, and cruel and unusual punishment, as well as the rights to counsel, speedy trial, and confrontation of hostile witnesses.[34] Several of these decisions came early in the

Albert DeSalvo, the "Boston Strangler"

Angelo Buono, the "Hillside Strangler"

David Berkowitz, "Son of Sam"

Ted Bundy

John Wayne Gacy, the "Clown Killer"

in Vermont. At the close of the 1980s Good was still in Vermont —an environmental activist who went under the name of Blue Collins. Yet, while Manson ordered the Tate–Folger– LaBianca killings, he did not participate in them, and there are likely few people who even remember the names of the four actual killers—Susan Atkins, Patricia Krenwinkel, Leslie Van Houten, and Charles Watson. Furthermore, there have been homicides far more bizarre than those committed by the Manson family. For example, there was:

- Albert DeSalvo (the "Boston Strangler"), a rapist-killer of the early 1960s who left bows around the necks of his thirteen victims;

- Angelo Burno (the "Hillside Strangler"), who raped, tortured, and murdered at least nine California women in 1977–1978;

- David Berkowitz ("Son of Sam"), who stalked the lovers'

lanes of N.Y.C. in 1976–77 with his .44 magnum, killing six victims and wounding another seven;

- Ted Bundy, who admitted to brutally murdering twenty-eight women before he was executed in Florida's electric chair in 1989;

- John Wayne Gacy (the "Clown Killer") who likely committed more murders than any other person in the U.S.— at least thirty-three young men and boys from 1972–1977;

- Albert Fish, one of America's few known cannibals, who abducted twelve-year-old Grace Budd in 1928, butchered her alive, and ate her;

- Jeffrey Dahmer, the Milwaukee candy factory worker in whose apartment in 1991 police found rotting body parts stuffed in boxes and plastic bags, barrels filled with acid and bones, a refrigerator holding human skulls and genitals,

and photographs of nude, mutilated bodies.

By contrast, perhaps the continued fascination with Manson stems from media attention, since the gruesome killings involved a well-known actress. Perhaps it is because there was always something mystical about Manson—a long-haired Svengali described as a Christ-like leader who could mesmerize young women into submission with seductive rhetoric. Whatever the reasons, in the minds of many Americans, Charles Manson remains as the ultimate personification of evil.

sources: Clara Livsey, *The Manson Women: A "Family" Portrait* (New York: Richard Marek, 1980); *People,* September 13, 1982, p. 80; *New York Times,* June 14, 1981, p. 35; *USA Today,* September 26, 1984, p. 2A; *Time,* October 8, 1984, p. 74; *New York Times,* November 29, 1989, p. A22; *USA Today,* January 5, 1987, p. 2A; *Newsweek,* August 5, 1991, pp. 40–42.

1960s, and they were interpreted by many as Supreme Court attempts to "handcuff police" and "coddle criminals."

Law and order emerged as a political issue during the Johnson/ Goldwater presidential campaign of 1964. Barry Goldwater, the senior senator from Arizona and the choice of the Republican party, was an

The law-and-order issue in the Johnson/Goldwater campaign of 1964

extreme conservative. The GOP believed that throughout the nation there was a hidden conservative majority—a *silent majority*—that would swarm to the polls to elect a "real American," and Goldwater seemed to have the appropriate image. As William Manchester once described the candidate:

> Barry Goldwater was fifty-five years old, a man of absolute integrity, and one of the most charming politicians ever to run for the Presidency. Handsome, leonine, silver-haired, with the black horn-rimmed spectacles which were his trademark, he had become one of the most celebrated public men in the nation and certainly the best-known conservative. Goldwater represented a love for the best of the past and defiance toward the worst of the present. In his crisp, low, southwestern drawl he reminded the country of American maxims and ethical certitudes which had lost their validity but not their fascination. It was his special talent that he could make them seem both plausible and relevant.[35]

Goldwater's campaign issues included opposition to the absolute centralization of government, to the creation of a welfare state, and to accommodation to communism abroad. Also, he had voted against the 1964 Civil Rights Act, and he favored the replacement of U.S. Supreme Court justices whose decisions were allegedly handcuffing the police. As a mark of his general opposition to the growing permissiveness in the country, as well as to the government's failure to take a strong stand against communism, Goldwater billboards, pins, and bumper stickers read "In Your Heart You Know He's Right."[36]

Because of his attack on numerous sacred cows in the federal bureaucracy, many Americans came to believe in their hearts that Goldwater *was* right. But his comments were often rather bizarre. He offered to sell the Tennessee Valley Authority for $1, and he said that he wished it were possible to saw off the eastern seaboard and let it float out to sea.

This television commercial from the Democratic party was in response to Senator Barry Goldwater's suggestion that NATO be authorized to use nuclear weapons.

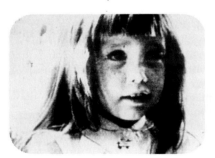

"Ten, nine, eight, seven . . .

six, five. four, three . . .

two, one . . .

These are the stakes. To make a world in which all of God's children can live . . .

or to go into the dark. We must either love each other or we must die. . . .

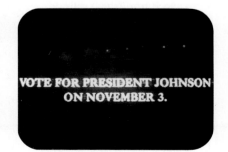

VOTE FOR PRESIDENT JOHNSON ON NOVEMBER 3.

The stakes are too high for you to stay home."

On these issues, Americans knew in their hearts that he was wrong, or "too far right." Then Goldwater brought the hydrogen bomb into the campaign, suggesting that NATO commanders be authorized to use tactical nuclear weapons; in one speech he suggested "lobbing one into the men's room in the Kremlin." In response, the Democrats came up with the slogan "In Your Heart You Know He Might!" Finally, Goldwater's law-and-order slogan got mixed up with civil rights. Because "law and order" was also the slogan of white segregationists, and because Goldwater had voted against civil rights, he became, like George Wallace, a segregationist hero. The end result was Goldwater's overwhelming defeat in the presidential election. He received only 38.5 percent of the national vote, and carried, in addition to his home state of Arizona, only the hardened segregationist states of Alabama, Georgia, Louisiana, Mississippi, and South Carolina.

Goldwater's defeat, however, did not mean the death of the law-and-order issue. Fear of crime in America was growing, as was discontent with the existing processes for crime control and prevention. "Law and order" became a shorthand term for the general fear not only of street crime but also of the violence and demonstrations surrounding the civil rights and antiwar movements. In response to the public's uneasiness, President Johnson launched his so-called war on crime only two months after his inauguration. In a message to the 89th Congress on March 8, 1965, Johnson commented that "crime had become a malignant enemy in America's midst." His strategy for the effort to combat crime involved federal intervention in the processes of criminal justice:

The war on crime

- increased federal law enforcement efforts
- assistance to local law enforcement efforts
- a comprehensive, penetrating analysis of the origins and nature of crime in modern America[37]

This growing fear of crime was further reflected in the May 1965 Gallup poll, which reported for the first time that crime was viewed by Americans as the most important problem facing the nation.[38] On July 25, 1965, the Johnson administration's "war on crime" was formally launched with the establishment of the **President's Commission on Law Enforcement and Administration of Justice.** And unknown to Americans, and even to Johnson himself, the President's Commission was to initiate a new era for criminal justice in the United States.

The President's Commission on Law Enforcement and Administration of Justice: A series of task forces appointed by President Johnson to study crime and justice in the United States and to make recommendations for change.

THE PRESIDENT'S CRIME COMMISSION

The President's Commission on Law Enforcement and Administration of Justice, more commonly referred to as the President's Crime Commission, appointed several task forces to study the crime problem and the structure of criminal justice administration, and to make recommendations for action. The commission, made up of nineteen commissioners, sixty-three staff members, 175 consultants, and hundreds of advisors, studied most aspects of the crime problem and the machinery of criminal justice. Even before its findings appeared, however, President Johnson announced to the nation that new approaches to old problems must be sought:

The problems of crime bring us together. Even as we join in common action, we know that there can be no instant victory. Ancient evils do not yield to easy conquest. We cannot limit our efforts to enemies we can see. We must, with equal resolve, seek out new knowledge, new techniques, and new understanding.[39]

After hundreds of meetings, tens of thousands of interviews, and numerous national surveys, the President's Crime Commission released a series of task force reports on the police, courts, corrections, juvenile delinquency, organized crime, science and technology, drunkenness, narcotics and drugs, and the assessment of crime, all of which were summarized in its general report, *The Challenge of Crime in a Free Society*.[40] This summary report targeted seven specific objectives, which in many ways would shape the direction of criminal justice for the years to come.

First, society must seek to prevent crime before it happens by assuring all Americans a stake in the benefits and responsibilities of American life, by strengthening law enforcement, and by reducing criminal opportunities.

Second, society's aim of reducing crime would be better served if the system of criminal justice developed a far broader range of techniques with which to deal with individual offenders.

Third, the system of criminal justice must eliminate existing injustices if it is to achieve its ideals and win the respect and cooperation of all citizens.

Fourth, the system of criminal justice must attract more people and better people — police, prosecutors, judges, defense attorneys, probation and parole officers, and corrections officials with more knowledge, expertise, initiative, and integrity.

Fifth, there must be much more operational and basic research into the problems of crime and criminal administration by those within and without the system of criminal justice.

Sixth, the police, courts, and correctional agencies must be given substantially greater amounts of money if they are to improve their ability to control crime.

Seventh, individual citizens, civic and business organizations, religious institutions, and all levels of government must take responsibility for planning and implementing the changes that must be made in the criminal justice system if crime is to be reduced.[41]

Besides these seven major objectives, the reports of the commission also made more than 200 specific recommendations.

The objectives and recommendations were, however, generally disappointing. The conclusions, for example, were very similar to those the Wickersham Commission had offered forty years earlier. In addition, the reasoning of the President's Crime Commission that by simply spending enough energy and money crime could be abolished was naive. But, although they were disappointing, the results were not, in retrospect, too surprising, since the commission's work was also part of the Johnson administration's Great Society effort — an ill-fated series of programs conceived in a utopian ethos for the purpose of upgrading the quality of American life. A Johnson biographer later described its agenda:

The Great Society would offer something to almost everyone: Medicare for the old, educational assistance for the young, tax rebates for business, a higher minimum wage for labor, subsidies for farmers, vocational training for the unskilled, food for the hungry, housing for the homeless, poverty grants for the poor, clean highways for commuters, legal protection for blacks, improved schooling for the

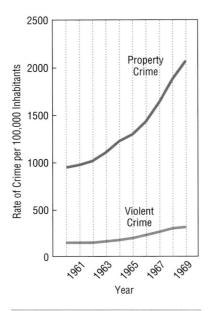

U.S. Crime Rates, 1960–1969

SOURCE: Uniform Crime Reports — 1969

The Great Society

Indians, rehabilitation for the lame, higher benefits for the unemployed, reduced quotas for the immigrants, auto safety for drivers, pensions for the retired, fair labeling for consumers, conservation for hikers and campers, and more and more and more.[42]

The commission, as well as the President himself, was naive to suggest, for example, that "warring on poverty, inadequate housing, and unemployment is warring on crime"; that "a civil rights law is a law against crime"; that "money for schools is money against crime." The relationship between crime and poverty had been studied at length for many generations, and the inescapable conclusion had been reached that the root causes of crime could not be found in any simplistic equation involving only the disadvantaged segments of society.

The war on poverty

Poverty and segregation may clearly serve to perpetuate crime, the noted criminologist Edwin H. Sutherland, among others, argued, but "poverty as such is not an important cause of crime."[43] Also, the peculiarity of the poverty–crime nexus was well targeted by Harvard University professor James Q. Wilson in his phrase "crime amidst plenty: the paradox of the sixties."[44] Wilson was referring to the fact that at the beginning of the 1960s, this country began the longest sustained period of prosperity since World War II. During this time the economy as a whole was strengthened, many of the financially disadvantaged improved their income positions, and the educational attainments of the young rose sharply. Yet, at the same time, crime increased at an alarming rate, along with youthful unemployment, drug abuse, and welfare. For the President's Commission to suggest, then, that the major weapon in the war on crime was to be simply money caused acute disappointment among those who had spent their lives studying the problem.

In contrast, the commission's analyses of the processes of criminal justice were to have a great impact. They awakened a consciousness of criminal justice as an integrated procedure, as a "system"—an orderly flow of managerial decision making that begins with the investigation of a criminal offense and ends with the offender's reintegration into the free community:

Criminal justice as a "system"

> The criminal justice system has three separately organized parts—the police, the courts, and corrections—and each has distinct tasks. However, these parts are by no means independent of each other. What each one does and how it does it has a direct effect on the work of the others. The courts must deal, and can only deal, with those whom the police arrest; the business of corrections is with those delivered to it by the courts. How successfully corrections reforms convicts determines whether they will once again become police business and influences the sentences the judges pass; police activities are subject to court scrutiny and are often determined by court decisions.[45]

According to the guidelines of the President's Crime Commission, **criminal justice** refers to the structure, functions, and decision processes of those agencies that deal with the management of crime—the police, the courts, and corrections. However, the concept of criminal justice, as described by the commission, is only an ideal. The notion of criminal justice operating as a system was at that time, and still is, somewhat of a myth. The unity of purpose and organized interrelationships among police, the courts, and corrections are beset with inefficiency, fallout, and failure. In most jurisdictions, the courts are a dumping ground for arrested offenders; correctional systems serve as holding pens for convicted offenders; and the free community—under the pro-

Criminal justice: The structure, functions, and decision processes of those agencies that deal with the management of crime—the police, the courts, and corrections.

The criminal justice "nonsystem"

tection and patrol of law enforcement — is the reentry point for those released from corrections. Rarely does each segment of the criminal justice system operate with a full awareness of the long-term cyclical implications of its activities. For this lack of coordination and failure of purpose, the American Bar Association has referred to criminal justice in America as a "nonsystem." [46]

The President's Crime Commission, however, was not altogether unaware of the shortcomings of what it called the "system" of criminal justice, and it called for extensive research and an upgrading of criminal justice personnel. In these areas, the commission had its most visible impact on criminal justice in America.

The Omnibus Crime Control and Safe Streets Act of 1968

Crime in the streets

The year 1968 occupies a unique summit in our ragged images of crime in America. It was a year of riots, protests, and assassinations. It was also a year of increasingly visible street crime. Among the 4.5 million known major crimes that occurred that year, there were almost 13,000 homicides, 31,000 rapes, 262,000 robberies, 283,000 serious assaults, 778,000 auto thefts, 1.3 million larcenies, and 1.8 million burglaries. Furthermore, at least 1 out of every 45 Americans was the victim of a serious crime. [47]

The drug revolution

In addition, 1968 marked the beginning of a new epoch in the drug revolution among American youth. Changes in drug technology that had begun almost two decades earlier were perfected, allowing a wide array of substances to be offered to an eager, drug-taking, disaffected youth. [48] Primary among these were newer varieties of amphetamine stimulants, sedatives, and hallucinogens, some of which could be produced in high school chemistry labs and fraternity house bathtubs. They were called "speed," "goofballs," "reds," "yellows," "blues," "black beauties," and other more colorful names. However, few drugs captured the attention and concern of the public as did marijuana and LSD.

Marijuana was not a new drug; it is a mild hallucinogenic substance derived from the crushed leaves and stems of the hemp plant and has been used for thousands of years. Before the late 1920s, few in the United States had heard of the drug, but by the close of the thirties it was being called the "weed of madness," "killer weed," a "sex-crazed drug menace," and "the burning weed of hell." Across the country, news stories detailed the insanity and violence resulting from marijuana use. The hysteria over the drug was provoked by a federal propaganda effort to outlaw its use, but the misinformation distributed about the drug served to type it as an "evil monster of destruction." [49] Even lawmakers of the day, who were creating legal controls on marijuana, were ignorant of its pharmacology and effects, as illustrated, for example, by the following comment from the January 29, 1929, issue of the *Montana Standard:*

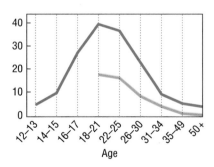

Marijuana Experience by Age   *Percent who have ever used marijuana (solid line) and of adults who use it now (dotted line)*

SOURCE: National Commission on Marijuana and Drug Abuse, 1972

> There was fun in the House Health Committee during the week when the Marihuana bill came up for consideration. Marihuana is Mexican opium, a plant used by Mexicans and cultivated for sale by Indians. "When some beet field peon takes a few rares of this stuff," explained Dr. Fred Fulsher of Mineral County, "he thinks he has just been elected president of Mexico so he starts out to execute all his political enemies. I understand that over in Butte where the Mexicans often go for the winter they stage imaginary bullfights . . . after a few whiffs of Marihuana. . . ." Everybody laughed and the bill was recommended for passage. [50]

An antimarijuana message in Omaha, Nebraska, in 1938 reflects misconceptions about the drug common until the 1960s.

Marijuana is not Mexican opium, and it does not have the properties of a narcotic drug. Furthermore, its use does not precipitate the execution of one's enemies — political or otherwise. Nevertheless, the concept of marijuana as a "weed of madness" that leads its user "along a path of destruction and death" persisted into the 1960s.

LSD (D-lysergic acid diethylamide), however, is another story. This drug was first isolated in 1938 by Dr. Albert Hoffman of Sandoz Research Laboratories, but its hallucinogenic properties were not discovered until years later. In the early 1960s, when it was still relatively unknown, two Harvard University psychologists, Timothy Leary and Richard Alpert, began experimenting with the drug on themselves and their colleagues, as well as on artists, writers, students, prison inmates, and others, to determine its effects. Although the two professors were eventually dismissed from Harvard, LSD had already gained a reputation. "Taking a trip" or "turning on" became a status symbol on college campuses. By the late sixties, LSD had become a household word, and chilling stories were told to scare potential users away from the drug (see Exhibit 1.3).[51] The 1967 Summer of Love, however, further escalated the popularity of hallucinogenic drugs, and not only LSD, but mescaline, peyote, and marijuana were sold openly. By 1968, marijuana and LSD use were believed to have reached epidemic proportions, and even the parents of young children became frightened when their sons and daughters returned home from their grade schools chanting, to the tune of "Frere Jacques":

Now they're calling taking drugs an "epidemic" — that's because white folks are doing it.
— RICHARD PRYOR, 1984

The psychedelic revolution

The term *psychedelic,* meaning "consciousness-expanding," is often used to describe such drugs as LSD, peyote, mescaline, DMT, and similar hallucinogenic drugs. From the Greek *psyche* (soul) and *delein* (to make manifest), the word was first proposed by LSD researcher Humphrey Osmond in 1956.

Mar – i – jua – na,   mar – i – jua – na   L – S – D,   L – S – D,

Coll-ege kids are mak-ing it, sch-ool kids are tak-ing it, Why can't we?   Why can't we?

• **EXHIBIT 1.3** •

Timothy Leary and LSD

Any idiot knows you don't take LSD above the ground floor.
— TIMOTHY LEARY, AUGUST 6, 1967

The drug scene of the 1960s had become the arena of "happening" America, and "turning on" to drugs for relaxation and to share friendship and love seemed to have become commonplace. And the prophet—the "high priest," as he called himself—of the new chemical age was a psychology instructor at Harvard University's Center for Research in Human Personality, Dr. Timothy Leary.

The saga of Timothy Leary had its roots, not at Harvard in the 1960s, but in Basel, Switzerland, just before the beginning of World War II. It was there, in 1938, that Dr. Albert Hoffman of Sandoz Research Laboratories first isolated a new chemical compound which he called D-lysergic acid diethylamide. More popularly known as *LSD,* it was cast aside in his laboratory where, for five years, it remained unappreciated, its properties awaiting discovery. On April 16, 1943, after absorbing some LSD through the skin of his fingers, Hoffman began to hallucinate. In his diary he explained the effect:

With closed eyes, multihued, metamorphizing, fantastic images overwhelmed me. . . . Sounds were transposed into visual sensations so that from each tone or noise a comparable colored picture was evoked, changing in form and color kaleidoscopically.[a]

Dr. Hoffman had experienced the first LSD "trip."

Dr. Humphrey Osmond of the New Jersey Neuropsychiatric Institute neologized a new name for LSD. "Psychedelic," he called it, meaning consciousness expanding. But outside of the scientific community, LSD was generally unknown—even at the start of the 1960s. This was quickly changed by Leary and his colleague at Harvard, Dr. Richard Alpert. They began experimenting with the drug—on themselves and with colleagues, students, artists, writers, clergymen, and volunteer prisoners. Although their adventures with LSD had earned them dismissals from Harvard by 1963, their message had been heard and LSD had achieved its reputation. Their revelations of the drug had been numerous and shocking to the political establishment and to hundreds of thousands of mothers and fathers across the nation.

In *The Realist,* a radical periodical of the 1960s, Leary commented:

I predict that psychedelic drugs will be used in all schools in the near future as educational devices—not only marijuana and LSD, but new and more powerful psychochemicals—to teach kids how to use their sense organs and other cellular equipment effectively . . . [b]

Elsewhere he wrote of the greatest fear that might be generated by psychedelic drug use, what he called "ontological addiction":

. . . the terror of finding a realm of experience, a new dimension of reality so pleasant that one will not want to return. This fear is based on the unconscious hunch . . . that normal consciousness is a form of sleepwalking and that somewhere there exists a form of awakeness, of reality from which one would not want to return.[c]

And then, perhaps most frightening of all to the older generation, were Leary's comments to some 15,000 cheering San Francisco youths on the afternoon of March 26, 1967. As a modern-day Pied Piper, Leary told his audience:

Turn on to the scene, *tune in* to what's happening; and *drop out*—of high school, college, grade school . . . follow me, the hard way.[d]

Leary's downfall came shortly thereafter, the result of conviction and imprisonment on drug trafficking charges, followed by a period of time as a fugitive in Algeria and Afghanistan after a prison escape. But Leary eventually rebounded. By 1976 he had straightened out his legal problems and become a free man. Since that time he has been "a cheerleader for scientific optimism," as he once put it. Throughout the 1980s, Leary was among the ranks of the most highly paid speakers on the college lecture circuit, often debating G. Gorden Liddy of Watergate fame. And quite curiously, Liddy was once his nemesis, having organized a raid in 1966 that led to one of Leary's early drug arrests.

The hysteria over Leary, LSD, and the other psychedelic substances had been threefold. *First,* the drug scene was especially frightening to mainstream society because it reflected a willful rejection of rationality, order, and predictability. *Second,* there was the stigmatized association of drug use with antiwar protests and antiestablishment, long haired, unwashed, radical "hippie" LSD users. And *third,* there were the drug's psychic effects, the reported "bad trips" that seemed to border on mental illness. Particularly with LSD, the rumors of how it could "blow one's mind" became legion. One story told of a youth high on the drug taking a swan dive in front of a truck moving at 70 mph. Another spoke of two "tripping" teenagers who stared directly into the sun until they were permanently blinded. A third described how LSD's effects on the chromosomes resulted in fetal abnormalities. The stories were never documented and were likely untrue. What *were* true, however, were the reports of LSD "flashbacks." Occurring with only a small percentage of users, individuals would reexperience the LSD-induced state days, weeks, and sometimes months after the original "trip," without having taken the drug again.

Despite the lurid reports, LSD was not in fact widely used on a regular basis beyond a few social groups that were fully dedicated to drug experiences. In fact, the psychedelic substances had quickly earned reputations as dangerous and unpredictable and were avoided by most. By the close of the 1960s all hallucinogenic drugs had been placed under strict legal control, and the number of users was minimal.[c]

Dr. Timothy Leary, the "high priest" of the psychedelic era

[a] Cited by William Manchester, *The Glory and Dream: A Narrative History of America, 1932–1972* (Boston: Little, Brown, 1974), p. 1362.

[b] *The Realist,* September 1966.

[c] Timothy Leary, "Introduction," in David Solomon (ed.), *LSD: The Consciousness-Expanding Drug* (New York: G. P. Putnam's, 1964), p. 17.

[d] Cited by William Manchester, op cit., p. 1366.

[e] National Commission on Marijuana and Drug Abuse, *Drug Abuse in America: Problem in Perspective* (Washington, D.C.: U.S. Government Printing Office, 1973), p. 81.

Heroin use had also reached significant proportions by 1968, having expanded from the ghettos to suburbia during the early part of the decade.[52] Usually associated with heroin use was street crime—burglaries, robberies, and muggings.

Fear of crime

It was in this setting of street crime, drug abuse, political protest, and violence that *fear of crime* emerged as an even more important concern than it had been when the President's Crime Commission was established. Noting this growing fear, the commission wrote that the purpose of its report was to reduce the fear of crime through its recommendations for a broad and comprehensive attack on the "root causes" of crime. Or as journalist Richard Harris described it:

> Like other crime studies, this one showed "that most crimes, wherever they are committed, are committed in cities." The facts were not particularly surprising, but to many readers the Commission's conclusions were. While it recommended immediate steps to upgrade the quality of the police and their methods, to revise outdated court systems, and to improve correctional techniques, it repeatedly stated that a lasting solution would require widespread recognition of basic matters that had long been overlooked or ignored and the development of a comprehensive program that would take as much money and understanding as the nation could muster.[53]

However, the recommendations of the commission did not and could not culminate in the type of war on crime that was envisioned. To launch a comprehensive attack on the "root causes" of crime was unrealistic, for the causes per se have never been fully known. The search for the causes of crime has been going on for generations with only minimal results. In fact, numerous researchers have concluded that a search for causes is a "lost cause" in criminology.[54]

The Omnibus Crime Control and Safe Streets Act: A piece of federal "law and order" legislation that was viewed by many as a political maneuver aimed at allaying fears of crime rather than bringing about criminal justice reform.

President Johnson's proposals for the war on crime resulted in the passage of the **Omnibus Crime Control and Safe Streets Act** of 1968, a piece of legislation that generated heated controversy in government, legal, and civil rights sectors across the nation. The act was not directly designed to bring about major reforms in the criminal justice system. Rather, it appeared to be more of a political maneuver aimed at allaying current fears about crime, and calming agitation over ghetto riots and anger over Supreme Court decisions that allegedly tied the hands of the police. One provision of the act (Title II) attempted to overturn numerous Supreme Court decisions by stating that all voluntary confessions and eyewitness identifications—regardless of whether a defendant had been informed of his or her rights of counsel—could be admitted in federal trials.[55] Title III of the act empowered state and local law enforcement agencies to tap telephones and engage in other forms of eavesdropping—for brief periods even without a court order. Primarily because of these two provisions, the Omnibus Crime Control and Safe Streets Act was looked upon as a bad law, one that constituted a significant move toward the establishment of an American police state. This concern was forcefully voiced by segments of liberal-minded America.

The Law Enforcement Assistance Administration

The Law Enforcement Assistance Administration (LEAA): A federal bureaucracy created to involve the national government in local crime control by supplying funds to the states for training and upgrading criminal justice agencies.

The primary provision of the Omnibus Crime Control and Safe Streets Act was Title I, which created the **Law Enforcement Assistance Administration.** More commonly known as LEAA, it was organized within the Department of Justice to develop new devices, techniques, and approaches in law enforcement; to award discretionary grants for special programs in the field of criminal justice; and to supply states and municipalities with funds to improve their criminal justice systems and for training and educating criminal justice personnel.[56]

During the early years of LEAA, the agency received considerable criticism for overemphasizing the funding of a "technological" war on crime and for providing grants for purposes beyond its original mission.[57] However, not all LEAA funds were misdirected or misused, nor were all funds channeled for the development of technological tools for a war on crime. A significant portion of LEAA expenditures were also targeted for social programming and research, court reform, and correctional programs. Furthermore, throughout the 1970s LEAA provided more than $40 million per year for the education of some 100,000 persons employed in or preparing for a career in criminal justice. Known as the Law Enforcement Education Program, the report of the Twentieth Century Fund Task Force, which examined the operation of LEAA, maintained that the education program was among the agency's most constructive and successful efforts. Nevertheless, and in spite of the many billions of dollars it spent, LEAA was deemed a failure. According to the Twentieth Century Fund:

> Since LEAA's establishment, crime rates—especially for violent crime—have continued to soar (except for a brief and unexplained respite in 1972). Last year alone, reported crimes went up 18 percent, the largest increase since the Federal Bureau of Investigation began collecting statistics almost 50 years ago. Meanwhile, all the manifest ills of the criminal justice system persist. State and local criminal justice systems remain as fragmented as ever. The courts are still overloaded; jails are still crowded; prosecutorial offices are generally underfunded; and sentencing and parole procedures and decisions remain arbitrary and uncoordinated. Nor do we know any more about the causes of crime than we did before LEAA came into being.[58]

THE NIXON–MITCHELL YEARS

The Johnson administration's war on crime continued into the early 1970s under President Richard M. Nixon and his attorney general, John Mitchell. It became muddled, however, by what is considered by many to be the major political scandal of the twentieth century.

The post–World War II era had witnessed the structuring of the Central Intelligence Agency (CIA) as an international secret police and as a mechanism of domestic social coercion that not only spied on Americans, but engaged in break-ins, burglaries, wiretapping, mail opening, and other forms of lawbreaking in an effort to control the government's political enemies—all in the name of national security.[59] During the same period, the Federal Bureau of Investigation (FBI) moved from pursuing "public enemies" into accumulating secret files on hundreds of thousands of Americans, including some high up in government. Under the directorship of J. Edgar Hoover, the FBI grew into a national police force, spying on selected groups in American society that did not agree with Hoover's own political philosophies.[60]

When the offices of the Democratic National Committee, located in the Watergate Hotel and office buildings in Washington, D.C., were broken into in June 1972, knowledge of the secret and illegal operations being pursued by the government slowly came to light. The actual Wa-

The rationale was to come up with a method of silencing you through killing you.

—Watergate conspirator G. Gorden Liddy in 1991 explaining to columnist Jack Anderson the plan to kill Anderson in 1972, following his muckraking reporting of the Watergate episode

The Watergate cover-up

I have many friends who live there and tell me it's very nice.
— RICHARD NIXON IN 1990 ON THE WATERGATE HOTEL/OFFICE COMPLEX

tergate burglary and wiretapping had been undertaken by a White House special investigations unit known as the "Plumbers," organized by White House assistant John Ehrlichman to plug White House "leaks." Their assignments included inquiries — accomplished through *any* necessary means — into the personal habits of President Nixon's political enemies. Watergate, and its subsequent "cover-up," were performed with the complicity of Nixon and Mitchell. These Watergate disclosures, combined with those concerning illegal CIA, FBI, and Internal Revenue Service (IRS) activities, not only helped discredit the Nixon administration, but deeply shook the public's confidence in American concepts of law and order as well.[61]

Also, the Nixon administration was prone to exaggerate about the crime problem in America. Law and order and the war on crime remained political issues, and by 1972 the fear of crime had climbed to new heights. According to a national Gallup poll of that year, almost half of those surveyed were afraid to walk in their neighborhoods at night, and drug addiction was cited among the major reasons for the high crime rate.[62] By January 1973, crime was ranked highest among the nation's urban problems, with drug use ranking third.[63] Nixon responded almost immediately, with a statement on March 14, 1973, reemphasizing the war on drugs:

> No single law enforcement problem has occupied more time, effort and money in the past four years than that of drug abuse and drug addiction. We have regarded drugs as "public enemy number one," destroying the most precious resource we have — our young people — and breeding lawlessness, violence and death.[64]

Richard Nixon and his staff in the White House

In one sense, Nixon was not exaggerating. Estimated federal expenditures for drug abuse prevention and law enforcement programs were indeed staggering—increasing from $150.2 million in 1971 to $654.8 million in 1973.[65] But his descriptions of the drug problem and its relation to crime often went beyond the parameters of reasonable estimate. He referred to the heroin problem as a plague that threatened every man, woman, and child in the nation with "the hell of addiction." Nixon based his statements on published data which noted that the number of addict-users had increased from 68,000 in 1969 to 550,000 in 1971. What he did not point out, however, was that these figures did not necessarily represent a real increase in the number of heroin users, but rather a change in the methods for counting them. The earlier estimate had been based solely on the number of users coming to the attention of federal authorities through arrest or placement in U.S. Public Health Service treatment facilities. By 1971, however, estimates were being made based on the results of systematic surveys of the population as a whole. Even more outrageous was the estimate the Nixon administration made of the amount of drug-related crime. White House officials indicated that addict crime—largely crime on the streets—cost the country roughly $18 billion. Yet, the $18 billion worth of crime the government claimed addicts were committing to buy their supply of heroin was actually over 25 times greater than the value of all property reported stolen and unrecovered throughout the United States in 1971.[66]

Investigative reporter Edward Jay Epstein has maintained that the Nixon administration, in making statements like these, was using the so-called war on heroin to increase the power of the White House bureaucracy:

> Under the aegis of a "war on heroin," a series of new offices were set up, by executive order, such as Office of Drug Abuse Law Enforcement and the Office of National Narcotics Intelligence, which, it was hoped, would provide the president with investigative agencies having the potential and the wherewithal and personnel to assume the functions of "the Plumbers" on a far grander scale. According to the White House scenario, these new investigative functions would be legitimized by the need to eradicate the evil of drug addiction.[67]

Whether the White House accomplished this goal, or whether it even *was* a goal of the Nixon administration, is not known and perhaps never will be. It is significant, however, that the momentum generated by the Johnson administration toward criminal justice reform, no matter how misconceived it may have been, was never supported through any direct action by the Nixon–Mitchell war on crime.[68]

The National Strategy to Reduce Crime

LEAA believed that change in the criminal justice process would be unlikely without specific standards and goals for police, courts, corrections, and crime prevention. Thus, on October 20, 1971, it appointed the National Advisory Commission on Criminal Justice Standards and Goals to formulate these specifics. After two years of study, this commission offered a national strategy to reduce crime, with the particular goal of reducing what it called "high fear" crime by 50 percent within ten years. It believed that by 1983 homicide could be cut by at least 25 percent, forcible rape by 15 percent, serious assault by 25 percent, robbery by 50 percent, and burglary by 50 percent.

Avoid all needle drugs. The only dope worth shooting is Richard Nixon.
—Abbie Hoffman, 1971

The so-called war on heroin

A Conservative is someone who believes in reform, but not now.
— MORT SAHL

A "conservative" is a liberal who was mugged last night.
— FRANK RIZZO, 1978

A "liberal" is a person who leaves the room when a fight begins.
— HAYWOOD BRAUN

I can remember way back when a liberal was one who was generous with his own money.
— WILL ROGERS

Unlike previous crime panels, however, no actual predictions were made. The commission felt that, by suggesting more than 400 standards and recommendations, it was offering not a solution, but a mechanism for a solution. Some attempts were made to implement the standards at the state and local levels, but on the whole they had little impact. By 1983, high-fear crime had not been cut in half. In fact, over the ten-year period from 1974 through 1983, the volume of serious crime in the United States had increased by almost 20 percent.[69]

THE REAGAN–MEESE YEARS

The 1980s witnessed a significant political shift to the conservative right. This was certainly clear in the election of Ronald Reagan to his first term as president of the United States. Voters left no doubt as to what they wanted. The 1980 election represented the strongest shift in three decades, hinting at a conservative domination that might conceivably last for the balance of the twentieth century. A telling factor, as well, was the shift back to "traditional" values by American youth, especially on college campuses. Each year, the University of California and the American Council on Education develop a national profile of college freshman characteristics and attitudes. Exhibit 1.4, which highlights selected areas of student response from this profile, clearly suggests that liberalism was not in vogue. Comparing the graduating classes of 1977 through 1995,

---

• EXHIBIT 1.4 •

Selected Attitudes of the Classes of 1977, 1984, 1987, 1992, and 1995

	Percent				
ATTITUDE	**CLASS OF 1977**	**CLASS OF 1984**	**CLASS OF 1987**	**CLASS OF 1992**	**CLASS OF 1995**
Political Views					
Far left	2.2	2.1	1.9	2.3	1.8
Liberal	32.6	19.6	19.2	22.0	22.6
Middle-of-the-road	50.7	60.0	60.3	53.9	54.7
Conservative	13.9	17.1	17.5	20.2	19.7
Far right	0.6	1.2	1.2	1.6	1.2
Proportions Who Agree That					
Courts are too concerned with the rights of criminals	50.1	65.9	68.8	69.1	66.3
The death penalty should be abolished	43.3	34.5	28.9	23.0	21.5
Marijuana should be legalized	48.2	39.3	25.7	19.3	18.6

SOURCE: The Chronicle of Higher Education, February 11, 1974, p. 8; February 9, 1981, p. 8; February 1, 1984, p. 14; January 11, 1989, p. 33; January 30, 1991, p. 30.

the number of liberals declined while conservatives and middle-of-the-roaders increased. Perhaps most significant was the trend toward more conservative views with respect to the rights of the accused, the death penalty, and the legalization of marijuana.

These data, combined with the conservatism among older Americans in the 1980s, suggest that the trend toward strict and rigid punishments for criminal offenders and the erosion of defendants' rights are the result of political views that stress societal protection over due process. And this, furthermore, was clearly the position of the Reagan administration.

The vehicle for President Reagan's criminal justice agenda was the federal courts. He was opposed to those judges who viewed courts as mechanisms for political action and social experimentation, while preferring those who exercised "judicial restraint."

At the helm of Reagan's reform movement was U.S. Attorney General Edwin Meese, an archconservative who had many liberal and moderate court observers worried. Meese's plan was to do more than just convict and incarcerate a greater number of serious criminal offenders. His aim was to fashion basic changes in the justice system that would tip the balance of advantage away from suspects and toward victims and the state. It was the position of both Meese and Reagan that during the 1960s and 1970s the judiciary became too lenient toward the accused and helped to accelerate a surge in crime.

The Reagan justice agenda, and particularly the role of Attorney General Meese, brought on controversy. On one occasion, for example, the attorney general stated that the "theory of incorporation," that is, the nationalization of the Bill of Rights, was on intellectually shaky ground and a questionable legal doctrine.[70] This drew rebuttal from Justices Brennan, Stevens, and Rehnquist, precipitating a debate that was unprecedented in recent history between the Supreme Court and the White House.[71] Meese's attempts at restructuring criminal justice in America fell short, however. Throughout the Reagan administration Meese's ethics had been questioned many times, thus hampering his goals. Furthermore, the hinting of his involvement in a major scandal led to his resignation as attorney general in mid-1988, thus ending his apparent crusade against liberalism.

The Reagan administration is the strongest and most supportive we have seen in as long as I can remember.
—JERALD VAUGHN, INTERNATIONAL ASSOCIATION OF CHIEFS OF POLICE, 1985

A Supreme Court decision does not establish a "supreme law of the land" that is binding on all persons and parts of government, henceforth and forevermore.

—EDWIN MEESE, 1986

GEORGE BUSH AND THE LEGACY OF THE GREAT DRUG WAR

During the closing years of the 1970s, just prior to the beginning of the Reagan presidency, a new epidemic of drug use was noticed in the United States. Rather than the heroin of the Nixon years, the problem this time was a derivative on the rather innocuous Peruvian shrub *Erythroxylum coca Lam.* — cocaine.[72]

Cocaine was nothing new to the United States, having first appeared a century earlier. However, by the late 1970s the drug was being smuggled into the United States from South America in record quantities. Moreover, the use of cocaine appeared to be escalating, particularly in the inner cities. And a concomitant of the increased presence of cocaine on the streets of America was a rising rate of crime — particularly violent crime.

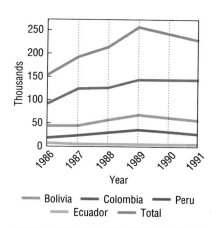

Coca Leaf Production in South America (in metric tons)

SOURCE: State Department

•   EXHIBIT   1.5   •

The Rediscovery of *Crack*-Cocaine

Crack is not a particularly new drug to the U.S., but goes back several decades, to a time when cocaine was still known as *charlie, corrine, bernice, schoolboy,* and the "rich man's drug." It was first reported in the literature during the early 1970s, but even then it had been known for a number of years. At that time, however, knowledge of crack, known then as "base" or "rock," seemed to be restricted to segments of cocaine's freebasing subculture. But since the drug contained many impurities, it was often referred to as "garbage freebase" by cocaine aficionados, and was quickly discarded.

The rediscovery of crack seemed to occur simultaneously on the East and West Coasts early in the 1980s. As a result of the Colombian government's attempts to reduce the amount of illicit cocaine production within its borders, it restricted the amount of ether available for transforming coca paste (an intermediate product in the processing procedure) into cocaine hydrochloride. The result was the diversion of coca paste from Colombia, through Central America and the Caribbean, into South Florida for conversion

into cocaine. Spillage from shipments through the Caribbean corridor reached local island populations, who developed the forerunner of *crack*-cocaine in 1980. Known as *baking-soda base, base-rock, gravel,* and *roxanne,* the prototype was a smokable product composed of coca paste, baking soda, water, and rum. Migrants from Jamaica, Haiti, Trinidad, and locations along the Leeward and Windward Islands chain introduced the crack prototype to Caribbean inner-city populations in Miami's immigrant undergrounds, where it was ultimately produced from *powder*-cocaine rather than paste. Apparently, at about the same time, a Los Angeles basement chemist rediscovered the rock variety of baking-soda cocaine, initially referred to as "cocaine rock."

It should be noted here that contrary to popular belief, crack is neither "freebase cocaine" nor "purified cocaine." Part of the confusion about crack comes from the different definitions of "freebase" in the drug community. "Freebase" (the noun) is a drug, a cocaine product converted to the base state from cocaine hydrochloride after adul-

terants have been chemically removed. Crack is converted to the base state *without* removing the adulterants. "Freebasing" (the act) means to inhale vapors of cocaine base, of which crack is but one form. Finally, crack is not purified cocaine, for during its processing, the baking soda remains as a salt, thus reducing its homogeneity somewhat. Informants in the Miami drug subculture indicate that the purity of crack ranges as high as 80 percent, but generally contains much of the filler and impurities found in the original cocaine hydrochloride, along with some of the baking soda (sodium bicarbonate) and *cuts* (expanders, for increasing bulk) from the processing. Interestingly, crack gets its name from the fact that the residue of sodium bicarbonate often causes a crackling sound when the substance is smoked.

SOURCES: James A. Inciardi, "Beyond Cocaine: Basuco, Crack, and Other Coca Products, *Contemporary Drug Problems,* 14 (Fall 1987), pp. 461–492; Anonymous, *The Gourmet Cokebook: A Complete Guide to Cocaine* (White Mountain Press, 1972); James N. Hall, "Hurricane Crack," *Street Pharmacologist,* 10 (September 1986), pp. 1–2.

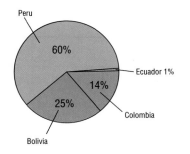

Major Producers of Coca 1991

The 1980s also witnessed the rediscovery of *crack*-cocaine (see Exhibit 1.5). The American crack experience is fairly well-known, having been reported (and perhaps over-reported) in the media since early in 1986. There are the "highs," binges, and "crashes" that induce addicts to sell their belongings and their bodies in pursuit of more crack; the high addiction liability of the drug that instigates users to commit any manner and variety of crimes to support their habits; the rivalries in crack distribution networks that turned some inner city communities into urban "dead zones," where homicide rates are so high that police have written them off as anarchic badlands; the involvement of many ghetto youths in the crack business, including the "peewees" and "wannabees" (want-to-be's), those street gang acolytes in grade school and junior high who patrol the streets with walkie-talkies in the vicinity of crack houses, serving in networks of look-outs, spotters, and steerers, and aspiring to be "rollers" (short for high-rollers) in the drug distribution business; the child abuse, child neglect, and child abandonment by crack-addicted mothers; and finally, the growing cohort of "crack babies" that appear troubled not only physically, but emotionally and behaviorally as well.[73]

As both drug use and crime escalated, the federal government, as well as legislators and criminal justice systems at all jurisdictional levels responded. From federal policy makers there were dramatic increases in the funding of a war on drugs, with much of the new monies earmarked for law enforcement activities. In addition, there were the RICO (Racketeer-Influenced and Corrupt Organizations) and CCE (Continuing Criminal Enterprise) statutes. As **asset forfeiture** provisions, RICO and CCE mandate forfeiture of the fruits of criminal activities. Their intent is to eliminate the rights of traffickers to their personal assets, whether these be cash, bank accounts, real estate, automobiles, jewelry and art, equity in businesses, directorships in companies, or any kind of goods or entitlement that are obtained in or used for a criminal enterprise.[74]

Another component in the federal drug war armamentarium was **"zero tolerance,"** a 1988 White House anti-drug policy that expanded the war on drugs from suppliers and dealers, to users as well — especially casual users — and meant that planes, vessels, and vehicles could be confiscated for carrying even the smallest amount of a controlled substance.[75] At state and local levels, zero tolerance gave birth to the many "user accountability" statutes. User accountability was based on the notion that if there were no drug users there would be no drug problems, and that casual users of drugs, like addicts, were responsible for creating the demand that made trafficking in drugs a lucrative criminal enterprise. As such, the new laws called for mandatory penalties for those found in possession of small quantities of drugs.[76] User accountability, however, played only a small part in the local initiatives against drugs. More significantly, drug enforcement measures in municipal and state police departments were expanded, new laws were enacted to create mandatory penalties for certain drug crimes, and special courts were established to process the increased number of drug cases.

When George Bush was sworn in as the forty-first president of the United States in 1989, the complexities involved in waging the drug war were well known to him. Not only had he served as vice president during Reagan's drug war, in the early part of the 1980s he had also directed the South Florida Task Force, a special federal anti-drug initiative designed to reduce the flow of cocaine through the Port of Miami.[77] As president, Bush expanded Reagan's anti-drug effort with increased funding. And finally, Bush's drug war policies were developed and coordinated through the newly established Office of National Drug Control Policy (ONDCP), a White House–level office that had been created by the National Narcotics Leadership Act of 1988, a piece of legislation drafted by Senator Joseph R. Biden of Delaware.

Amid a period of growing conservatism and rising crime rates, the escalating war on drugs has engendered a criminal justice process that appears to be "drug driven" in almost every respect. In the legislative sector, new laws have been created to deter drug involvement and to increase penalties for drug-related crime. In the police sector, funding has served to expand street-level drug enforcement initiatives which, in turn, have increased the number of drug-crime arrests. In the judicial

Asset forfeiture: The governmental seizure of personal assets obtained or used for a criminal enterprise.

Zero tolerance: A federal anti-drug measure that permits the confiscation of planes, vessels, or vehicles found to be carrying a controlled substance.

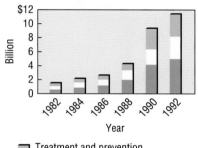

Treatment and prevention

International efforts and border control

Domestic enforcement

The Drug War's Growing Budget   *Obligated budget allocations for fiscal years through 1990, Congressionally enacted spending for 1991, and the Administration's budget request for 1992.*

SOURCE: Office of National Drug Control Policy

A legacy of the "war on drugs" has been a criminal justice process that appears to be *drug driven* in almost every respect.

In Bolivia's coca-growing regions, leaves of Erythroxylum coca Lam., the raw material from which cocaine is derived, are dried in the sun before processing.

sector, the increased flow of drug cases has resulted in overcrowded dockets and courtrooms, as well as the creation of new drug courts, special dispositional alternatives for drug offenders, and higher conviction and incarceration rates. In the correctional sector, the results include the further crowding of already overpopulated jails and penitentiaries, the establishment of liberal release policies, and experimentation with new prison-based drug treatment programs. The spread of AIDS among inmates is one result of the higher density of prison populations combined with the expanded presence of intravenous drug users and others at risk for the disease.

In the final analysis, the history of criminal justice in America is a series of episodes, each linked to social and political events and the attitudes and customs of society at large. Also, as demonstrated in chapters throughout this book, the course of criminal justice in the United States is in great part a reflection of changing police, court, and correctional priorities and decision-making practices.

SUMMARY

There were a variety of social, cultural, and political events that influenced the course of criminal justice in America during the twentieth century. The problems of crime and justice administration had been left untended during most of the first six decades of the century. Although there was dissatisfaction with the justice system of that era, other, more pressing concerns, such as the Great Depression and World War II, captured the nation's attention. With the onset of the 1960s a variety of events served to stimulate interest in criminal justice reform. For the first time in U.S. history, the federal government took an active role in the enhancement of state and local criminal processing.

During that decade and in the years that followed, however, neither the problems nor many of the inconsistencies in the administration of justice were solved. Nevertheless, the era did witness a rediscovery of the workings of the justice process in America, combined with a new interest in the quality of criminal justice policy and procedure.

KEY TERMS

asset forfeiture **(31)**
counterculture **(11)**
criminal justice **(19)**
Jim Crow laws **(8)**
law and order **(13)**
Law Enforcement Assistance
  Administration (LEAA) **(24)**

Omnibus Crime Control and
  Safe Streets Act **(24)**
President's Commission on Law
  Enforcement and
  Administration of
  Justice **(17)**

Special Committee to
  Investigate Crime in
  Interstate Commerce
  (Kefauver committee) **(5)**
Wickersham Commission **(3)**
zero tolerance **(31)**

QUESTIONS FOR DISCUSSION

1. Why can it be said that criminal justice was rediscovered during the late 1960s and early 1970s?

2. Why has the "war on crime" been considered a failure?

FOR FURTHER READING

Currie, Elliott. *Confronting Crime: An American Challenge.* New York: Panthean, 1985.

Gitlin, Todd. *The Sixties: Years of Hope, Years of Rage.* New York: Bantam Books, 1987.

Harris, Richard. *The Fear of Crime.* New York: Praeger, 1968.

Hofstadter, Richard. *The Age of Reform.* New York: Random House, 1955.

Inciardi, James A. *The War on Drugs II: The Continuing Epic of Heroin, Cocaine, Crack, Crime, AIDS, and Public Policy.* Mountain View, CA: Mayfield, 1992.

Viorst, Milton. *Fire in the Streets: America in the 1960s.* New York: Simon and Schuster, 1979.

Wilson, James Q. *Thinking About Crime.* New York: Vintage, 1983.

NOTES

1. Max Lerner, *America as a Civilization: Life and Thought in the United States Today* (New York: Simon and Schuster, 1957), p. 433.

2. For a discussion of and bibliography on this period, see James A. Inciardi, *Reflections on Crime* (New York: Holt, Rinehart and Winston, 1978), pp. 32–45.

3. See, for example, Richard Hofstadter, *The Age of Reform* (New York: Random House, 1955); Walter C. Reckless, *Vice in Chicago* (Chicago: University of Chicago Press, 1933).

4. The Cleveland Foundation Survey of the Administration of Justice in Cleveland, Ohio, *Criminal Justice in Cleveland* (Cleveland: Cleveland Foundation, 1922).

5. The Missouri Association for Criminal Justice, *The Missouri Crime Survey* (New York: Macmillan, 1926).

6. Illinois Association for Criminal Justice, *The Illinois Crime Survey* (Chicago: Illinois Association for Criminal Justice, 1929).

7. National Commission on Law Observance and Enforcement, *Wickersham Commission Reports.* 14 volumes (Washington, D.C.: U.S. Government Printing Office, 1931).

8. See Dixon Wecter, *The Age of the Great Depression* (New York: Macmillan, 1948).

9. See L. L. Edge, *Run the Cat Roads* (New York: December, 1981).

10. Godfrey Hodgson, *America in Our Time* (New York: Random House, 1976), pp. 19–20. See also Eric F. Goldman, *The Crucial Decade—And After: America, 1945–1960* (New York: Random House, 1960): Frederick Lewis Allen, *The Big Change: America Transforms Itself, 1900–1950* (New York: Harper & Brothers, 1952).

11. Cited by Douglas T. Miller and Marion Nowak, *The Fifties: The Way We Really Were* (Garden City, N.Y.: Doubleday, 1977), p. 6.

12. For commentaries on social and political life in the 1950s, see Miller and Nowak, *The Fifties;* David Caute, *The Great Fear: The Anti-Communist Purge under Truman and Eisenhower* (New York: Simon and Schuster, 1978); Daniel Bell, *The End of Ideology: On the Exhaustion of Political Ideas in the Fifties* (New York: Free Press, 1960).

13. Goldman, *The Crucial Decade,* p. 195. For a fuller discussion of the Kefauver hearings, see Estes Kefauver, *Crime in America* (New York: Greenwood Press, 1968).

14. J. Edgar Hoover, *Masters of Deceit: The Story of Communism in America and How to Fight It* (New York: Henry Holt, 1958), p. 4.

15. For a discussion of the political and social context within which the "bomb culture" emerged, see Theodore H. White, *In Search of History* (New York: Harper & Row, 1978), pp. 383–436.

16. See Walter Sheridan, *The Rise and Fall of Jimmy Hoffa* (New York: Saturday Review Press, 1972); John L. McClellan, *Crime Without Punishment* (New York: Duell, Sloan and Pearce, 1962).

17. See Frederic Sondern, *Brotherhood of Evil* (New York: Farrar, Straus, and Cudahy, 1959).

18. Donald R. Cressey, *Theft of the Nation: The Structure and Operations of Organized Crime in America* (New York: Harper & Row, 1969), p. 57.

19. Bell, *The End of Ideology,* pp. 162–163.

20. Miller and Nowak, *The Fifties,* pp. 7–8.

21. Fletcher Martin, "We Don't Want Your Kind," *Atlantic,* October 1958, p. 55, "Convictions in Cicero," *Newsweek,* June 16, 1952, pp. 34–35.

22. David B. Bittan, "Ordeal in Levittown," *Look,* August 19, 1958, pp. 84–85.

23. Kenneth Rexroth, "San Francisco Letter," *Evergreen Review,* Spring 1957, p. 11.

24. Paul Goodman, *Growing Up Absurd* (New York: Vintage, 1956).

25. For discussions of the social values and dissent of the 1960s, see Peter Joseph, *Good Times: An Oral History of America in the Nineteen Sixties* (New York: William Morrow, 1974); Roderick Aya and Norman Miller, eds., *The New American Revolution* (New York: Free Press, 1971); Hodgson, *America in Our Time.* Many of the violent episodes of the 1960s are described at length in H. D. Graham and T. R. Gurr, eds., *Violence in America: Historical and Contemporary Perspectives* (New York: Bantam, 1970); Richard Hofstadter and Michael Wallace, eds., *American Violence: A Documentary History* (New York: Random House, 1970).

26. J. Edgar Hoover, *Crime in the United States: Uniform Crime Reports — 1970* (Washington, D.C.: U.S. Government Printing Office, 1971), p. 65.

27. See, for example, Theodore Roszak, *The Making of a Counter Culture* (Garden City, N.Y.: Doubleday, 1969); also, Charles Perry, *The Haight-Ashbury: A History* (New York: Random House, 1984).

28. Joseph, *Good Times,* p. 133.

29. Ed Sanders, *The Family* (New York: Avon, 1972), pp. 39–40.

30. William Manchester, *The Glory and the Dream* (Boston: Little, Brown, 1974), p. 1368.

31. Manchester, *The Glory and the Dream,* pp. 1368–1370.

32. For an account of the Tate–LaBianca murders and the activities of the Manson clan, see Sanders, *The Family,* and Vincent Bugliosi and Curt Gentry, *Helter Skelter* (New York: W. W. Norton, 1974).

33. See J. Allen Broyles, *The John Birch Society: Anatomy of a Protest* (Boston: Beacon, 1964).

34. Henry J. Abraham, *Freedom and the Court: Civil Rights and Liberties in the United States* (New York: Oxford, 1977), pp. 33–105.

35. Manchester, *The Glory and the Dream,* p. 1257.

36. See Theodore H. White, *The Making of a President 1964* (New York: New American Library, 1965).

37. "Crime, Its Prevalence, and Measures of Prevention," Message from the President of the United States, House of Representatives, 89th Congress, March 8, 1965, Document No. 103.

38. James Q. Wilson, *Thinking About Crime* (New York: Basic Books, 1975), p. 65.

39. Lyndon B. Johnson, "Message to the Congress," March 9, 1966.

40. President's Commission on Law Enforcement and Administration of Justice, *The Challenge of Crime in a Free Society* (Washington, D.C.: U.S. Government Printing Office, 1967).

41. President's Commission, *The Challenge of Crime,* p. vi.

42. Doris Kearns, *Lyndon Johnson and the American Dream* (New York: Harper & Row, 1976), p. 216.

43. Edwin H. Sutherland and Donald R. Cressey, *Principles of Criminology* (Philadelphia: J. B. Lippincott, 1966), pp. 95, 241, 265.

44. Wilson, *Thinking About Crime,* p. 3.

45. President's Commission, *The Challenger of Crime,* p. 7.

46. American Bar Association, *New Perspectives on Urban Crime* (Washington, D.C.: ABA Special Committee on Crime Prevention and Control, 1972), p. 1.

47. J. Edgar Hoover, *Crime in the United States: Uniform Crime Reports — 1968* (Washington, D.C.: U.S. Government Printing Office, 1969).

48. James A. Inciardi, "Drugs, Drug-Taking and Drug-Seeking: Notations on the Dynamics of Myth, Change, and Reality," in *Drugs and the Criminal Justice System,* ed. James A. Inciardi and Carl D. Chambers (Beverly Hills: Sage, 1974), pp. 203–220.

49. For a discussion of marijuana use and the movement to criminalize it, see L. Sloman, *Reefer Madness: The History of Marijuana in America* (Indianapolis: Bobbs-Merrill, 1979).

50. Richard J. Bonnie and Charles H. Whitebread II, *The Marihuana Conviction: A History of Marihuana Prohibition in the United States* (Charlottesville: University of Virginia Press, 1974), p. 40.

51. The LSD phenomenon is described in David Solomon, ed., *LSD: The Consciousness-Expanding Drug* (New York: G. P. Putnam, 1964); Andrew I. Malcolm, *The Pursuit of Intoxication* (New York: Washington Square Press, 1972); Bernard Aaronson and Humphrey Osmond, eds., *Psychedelics: The Uses and Implications of Hallucinogenic Drugs* (Garden City, N.Y.: Doubleday, 1970).

52. See Leon Gibson Hunt and Carl D. Chambers, *The Heroin Epidemics* (New York: Spectrum Publications, 1976).

53. Richard Harris, *The Fear of Crime* (New York: Praeger, 1968), pp. 15–16.

54. Nigel D. Walker, "Lost Causes in Criminology," in *Crime, Criminology, and Public Policy,* ed. Roger Hood (New York: Free Press, 1974), pp. 47–62.

55. The Omnibus Crime Control and Safe Streets Act of 1968, Public Law 90-351, 90th Congress, June 1968, 18 U.S.C., Sec. 2518.

56. Twentieth Century Fund Task Force on the Law Enforcement Assistance Administration, *Law Enforcement: The Federal Role* (New York: McGraw-Hill, 1976), p. 4.

57. Jeff Gerth, "The Americanization of 1984," *Sundance Magazine* 1, April/May 1972, pp. 58–65.

58. Twentieth Century Fund Task Force, *Law Enforcement,* pp. 4–5.

59. See William R. Corson, *The Armies of Ignorance: The Rise of the American Intelligence Empire* (New York: Dial Press, 1977); Morton H. Halperin and Daniel Hoffman, *Freedom vs. National Security: Secrecy and Surveillance* (New York: Chelsea House, 1977).

60. See Pat Watters and Stephens Gillers, eds., *Investigating the FBI* (Garden City, N.Y.: Doubleday, 1973); David Wise, *The American Police State* (New York: Random House, 1977).

61. For intensive analyses of Watergate and its aftermath, see Carl Bernstein and Bob Woodward, *All the President's Men* (New York: Simon and Schuster, 1974); John Dean, *Blind Ambition: The White House Years* (New York: Simon and Schuster, 1976); Donald W. Harward, ed., *Crisis in Confidence: The Impact of Watergate* (Boston: Little, Brown, 1974).

62. *New York Times,* April 23, 1972, p. 23.

63. *Washington Post,* January 16, 1973, p. A3.

64. Cited by Carl D. Chambers and James A. Inciardi, "Forecasts for the Future: Where We Are and Where We Are Going," in *Drugs and the Criminal Justice System,* eds. Inciardi and Chambers, p. 221.

65. Chambers and Inciardi, "Forecasts for the Future," p. 222.

66. Edward Jay Epstein, *Agency of Fear* (New York: G. P. Putnam, 1977), pp. 174–179.

67. Epstein, *Agency of Fear,* p. 8.

68. For a discussion of the contrasts between the "mission of justice" under Johnson versus under Nixon, *see* Richard Harris, *Justice: The Crisis of Law, Order, and Freedom in America* (New York: E. P. Dutton, 1970).

69. Federal Bureau of Investigation, *Crime in the United States—1983* (Washington, D.C.: U.S. Government Printing Office, 1984), p. 43.

70. *New York Times,* October 17, 1985, p. B 10.

71. *New York Times,* October 26, 1985, p. 11.

72. See James A. Inciardi, *The War on Drugs II: The Continuing Epic of Heroin, Cocaine, Crack, Crime, AIDS, and Public Policy* (Mountain View, CA: Mayfield, 1992).

73. Ibid.

74. See John Dombrink and James W. Meeker, "Beyond 'Buy and Bust': Nontraditional Sanctions in Federal Drug Law Enforcement," *Contemporary Drug Problems,* 13 (Winter 1986), pp. 711–740; *New York Times,* 7 Jan. 1990, p. 13; *Drug Enforcement Report,* 23 April 1990, p. 8.

75. For a discussion of the philosophy of zero tolerance, see *Drug Abuse Report,* 19 April 1988, p. 6; U.S. Department of Transportation, Office of Public Affairs, *Transportation Facts,* "Zero Tolerance Policy on Illegal Drugs," 6 June 1988.

76. *Drug Abuse Report,* November 3, 1987, pp. 2–3; *Drug Enforcement Report,* November 9, 1987, p. 5; *Substance Abuse Report,* October 15, 1988, pp. 1–3; *Drug Enforcement Report,* September 23, 1988, pp. 1–2.

77. James A. Inciardi, "Revitalizing the War on Drugs," *The World & I,* February 1988, pp. 132–139.

PART

ONE

The Foundations of Crime and Justice

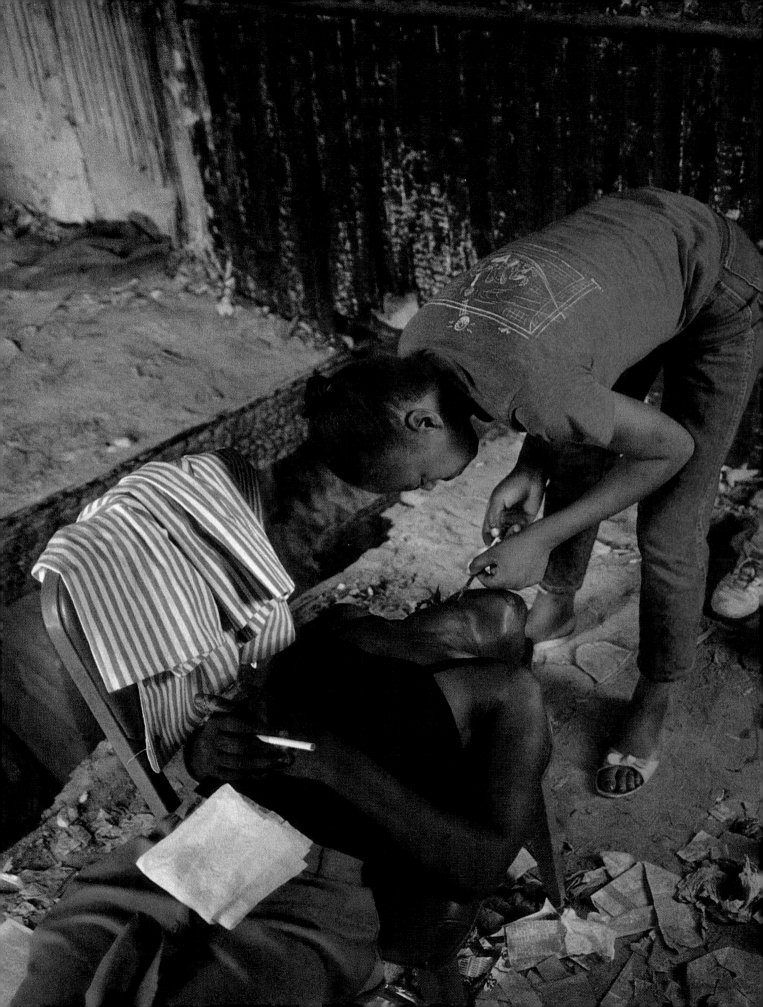

2

Crime and the Nature of Law

Morality cannot be legislated but behavior can be regulated.
—MARTIN LUTHER KING, JR.

Crime may be said to be injury inflicted in defiance of law.
—ARISTOTLE

Nobody ever commits a crime without doing something stupid.
—OSCAR WILDE

Too many criminals these days are giving crime a bad name.
—ANONYMOUS

Poor taste leads to crime.
—ARTHUR CONAN DOYLE

**Proportions of U.S. Population Reporting
Crime and *Poverty* as the Most Important
Problem Facing the Nation**

YEAR	CRIME	POVERTY
1970	4%	*
1971	7%	5%
1972	10%	10%
1973	17%	17%
1974	3%	3%
1975	5%	5%
1976	8%	8%
1977	6%	6%
1978	3%	*
1979	2%	*
1980	2%	*
1981	4%	*
1982	5%	*
1983	2%	*
1984	4%	3%
1985	4%	6%
1985	3%	6%
1986	3%	6%
1987	3%	6%
1988	*	7%
1989	6%	10%
1990	1%	6%
1991	*	12%

* denotes less than 1 percent
SOURCE: The Gallup Organization

The public's conception of crime

On January 21, 1958, Charles Raymond Starkweather set out on a murderous rampage across the American plains states, epitomizing the 1950s specter of teenage violence. His mass slaughter lasted only eight days, but it claimed the lives of ten people. Three of the victims were the parents and baby sister of Charlie's fourteen-year-old girlfriend, Caril Ann Fugate, who accompanied him on his trail of morbid violence. Yet curiously, while the nation was shocked by the murders, Charlie and Caril quickly became a macabre adornment of twentieth-century American folklore. People were fascinated with the seemingly matter-of-fact way in which much of the killing had been done. After shooting and stabbing three members of Caril's family, for example, the teenage couple ate sandwiches and watched television only a few yards from where their victims' bodies lay hidden.

But more importantly, Charlie Starkweather was a symbol. At age nineteen, he was a caricature of the then-popular James Dean image. Dean was the brilliant and eccentric star of *Rebel Without a Cause, Giant,* and *East of Eden* who, after his death in an automobile crash in 1955 at age twenty-four, became a symbol of the moral young outsider too sensitive to survive in a conformist adult society. For the many who had revered Dean in his films and who would continue to send him fan mail more than twenty years after his death, and to the rebellious youth of the decade for whom individuality and status meant confrontation by brute force, Charlie Starkweather was a hero. Like Robin Hood, Jesse James, and Billy the Kid, he had defied the established order, and had done so in a most visible and savage way. And like Dean, he too would become a martyr. When Starkweather was finally executed in the Nebraska State Penitentiary electric chair on June 24, 1959, his death was mourned by his followers — those across the country and those outside the prison walls who wanted to be with him to the very end.[1] In later years, Charlie Starkweather was the subject of Terrence Malick's 1973 movie *Badlands* and Bruce Springsteen's "Nebraska" album.

The episode of Charlie Starkweather is recalled here because it vividly illustrates the American fascination with crime. Stories of brutal violence and clever theft are continually offered to the public imagination, and the virtues and vices of such personages as Charles Manson, Al Capone, and Lee Harvey Oswald, to name only a few, have become well known. Murderers, rapists, and sinister sneak thieves are given prominent attention by the news media; violent crime is traditionally the major pursuit of the villains and scoundrels who appear in popular mystery and detective literature; and homicide, robbery, and assault are the common themes in both television and Hollywood portrayals of crime. In consequence, many Americans have developed rather distorted and one-sided conceptions of crime. Most of us feel that we have a reasonably good understanding of what crime is all about. We have learned, for example, to think of crime as something that is intrinsically evil, as something that threatens individual rights, civil liberties, and perhaps the very foundations of society. We are conscious of the presence of crime and respond to it by protecting ourselves — we lock our doors and windows to secure our property; we spend billions of dollars yearly to insure our valuables and precious possessions; we cautiously orient our activities away from dangerous places and situations to safeguard our lives. And we think of crime as something alien, something that exists outside of organized society. Our conceptions of crime lead directly to such common phrases as "organized crime," "crime in the streets," "gang delinquency," "the underworld," "crack houses," and "drug cartels."

However, even when we think about these common references to crime, we have only a minimal comprehension of what they really mean. "Organized crime" conjures up images of Eliot Ness and his "Untouchables," firing machine guns through the open windows of a speeding 1925 Packard; Al Capone and the St. Valentine's Day massacre; and such films as *The Godfather* and *Goodfellas*. Yet we have little idea of how organized crime actually affects our daily lives through its close associations with business, industry, and government.

Crime, in contrast, goes well beyond the undefined parameters of street crime and the limited catalog of violence and theft we find in the popular media. Furthermore, the volume and rates of crime vary considerably from what conventional knowledge might arbitrarily suggest.

Although violence and the most commonly discussed categories of theft may appear to be the most typical forms of lawbreaking, crime includes literally thousands of offenses. And the majority of these rarely come to our attention. White-collar crime, for example, is associated with the illegal activities of businesspeople that take place alongside the legitimate day-to-day activities of their business or profession. It involves billions of dollars annually in price fixing, embezzlement, restraint of trade, stock manipulation, misrepresentation, bribery, false advertising, and consumer fraud. The economic toll to the average citizen from white-collar crime well exceeds the dollar losses from all known robberies, burglaries, and other thefts — yet it is rarely considered. Also, the criminalization of conduct once deemed immoral — gambling, prostitution, alcohol and drug abuse — reflects an attitude that has resulted in the arrest and conviction of more persons than have the more serious offenses of larceny and assault. Violations in the areas of traffic control, building codes, fire ordinances, standards of quality, and safety precautions result in more deaths each year than criminal homicide. Corruption in public office and private business in the form of bribes, payoffs, fixes, and conflicts of interest occur in every branch of government and every kind of business, and at every level. And there is police crime, juvenile crime, and a range of property offenses that receive only minimal attention in the media.

At the same time, there are varieties of crime that the public associates only with the past, but that nevertheless continue to exist. When we think of pirates and buccaneers on the high seas, for example, we generally think of such colorful predators as Blackbeard, Henry Morgan, and Captain Kidd, who raised the Jolly Roger in the Caribbean and in the waters around India and Africa during the eighteenth century.[2] Yet piracy still lives and the Jolly Roger still flies — in the Caribbean, as part of the smuggling and trafficking of illegal drugs, and in the sea lanes of

Styles in crime seem boundless, including what amounts to free-lance demolition and theft. In Detroit, scavenger-crack addicts steal bricks from the foundations and walls of vacant buildings, which they sell to scrap dealers for $10 per hundred.

Man has excelled at everything, except crime.

— GOLDFINGER

When the President does it, that means it is not illegal.

— RICHARD M. NIXON

Southeast Asia, where fishing fleets and coastal freighters are hijacked.[3] Also common, but rarely presented by the media, are such crimes as animal poaching, cattle rustling, and even cactus filching.[4]

Finally, there are literally hundreds of activities that are considered crimes in some jurisdictions but not in others. There are events that were crimes at one time and are no longer considered as such. Additionally, there are behaviors people engage in daily that are viewed by many in society as normal and common but that, under the law, are defined as criminal.

Crime, then, is a term that is subject to both variable and uncritical usage, and conceptions of crime are often distorted and narrow, textured by misplaced emphasis on the more violent and lurid. The task of this discussion is to develop a fuller understanding of the meaning of crime, and to do so through an analysis of crime and its relation to law.

CRIME

Had I a hundred tongues, a hundred mouths, and a voice of iron, I could not sum up all the types of crime nor all their punishments.

— VIRGIL

Crime as drama

Crime as sin

Crime is an aspect of human experience that brings to mind images of evil and lawbreaking, and that has been subject to a variety of definitions and interpretations. For the classical and literary scholar, crime can be drama, a presentation of conflict between elements of the good and the profane as typified so eloquently in the Greek tragedies, Shakespeare's *Macbeth,* and Dostoyevsky's *Crime and Punishment.* To the moralist and reformer, crime is a manifestation of spiritual depravity; it is that festering evil and disease of the soul that must be eradicated both fully and immediately by the powers of restraint and virtue. Crime has also been equated with sin — with violations of a natural law, the Ten Commandments, or the proscriptions embodied in the Bible, the Talmud, and the Koran. For others, crime has different meanings: to the reporter it is news, to the detective it means work, to the thief it is business, and to the

Police officers examining the body of a victim of an apparent drive-by shooting

victim it suggests fear and loss. But to most individuals, crime is no more than the violation of a generally accepted set of rules that are backed by the power and authority of the state. Yet, while these and many other conceptions of crime may be important to a particular perspective, they are of little help in arriving at an explicit definition of crime. Nevertheless, the notion of crime as sin suggests a starting point, for the evolution of criminal definitions is intricately linked to historical images of right and wrong and the concepts of **natural law** (see Exhibit 2.1).

Natural law: generally refers to principles that determine what is right and wrong according to some higher power.

Crime as a Social Construction

A broad definition of crime in England is that it is any lower-class activity which is displeasing to the upper class.

— DAVID FROST, 1967

The ideas of natural law and natural crime assume the existence of universal standards as to what constitutes sin or immoral behavior, but a definition of crime framed in these terms lacks both clarity and precision. Furthermore, conceptions of crime as amoral behavior become even more confused when one considers that there is no moral code to which all persons, even in a single society or community, subscribe. A number of social scientists, therefore, have examined crime as a human construction. They suggest that the definition of behavior as "deviant" or "criminal" comes from individuals and social groups, and involves a complex social and political process that extends over a period of time. As such, they suggest, persons and social groups create crime by making rules whose infraction constitutes crime.

This more sociological view of deviance and crime rejects the notion that the rightness or wrongness of actions is of divine origin, and begins with an examination of how behaviors become deviant and criminal within societies. Known as the "sociology of deviance" or the "labeling perspective," this point of view focuses specifically on **deviance** — a concept considerably broader than that of crime. This position rests on the idea that rules that might be violated are not created spontaneously but, rather, come about only in response to behavior perceived to be harmful to a group. Thus, as sociologist Kai T. Erikson has suggested, "The term *deviance* refers to conduct which the people of a group consider so dangerous or embarrassing or irritating that they bring special sanctions to bear against the persons who exhibit it." [5] More specifically, and in contrast to the natural law concept,

> deviance is *not* a quality of an act the person commits, but rather a consequence of the application by others of rules and sanctions to an "offender." The deviant is one to whom that label has successfully been applied; deviant behavior is behavior that people so label.[6]

The mechanisms through which behavior becomes viewed as deviant were described by Howard S. Becker as a process of discovery undertaken by "crusading reformers," "rule creators," and "moral entrepreneurs." [7] The reformer or crusader views certain elements in society as truly, totally, and unconditionally evil, and feels that nothing can be right in the society until rules are made to correct and remove the wickedness he or she has perceived. The crusader's mission becomes a holy war, for the wrongs that have been observed are a breach in the stability of the social order, and only their eradication can ensure a better way of life for all. The crusader's role, then, involves bringing the evil to the attention of

Obviously, crime pays or there'd be no crime.

— G. GORDON LIDDY, 1986

When is conduct a crime? When somebody up there — a king, dictator, legislator, or pope so decrees!

— JESSICA MITFORD

It ain't no sin if you crack a few laws now and then, just so long as you don't break any.

— MAE WEST

Deviance: Conduct which the people of a group consider so dangerous, embarrassing, or irritating that they bring special sanctions to bear against the persons who exhibit it.

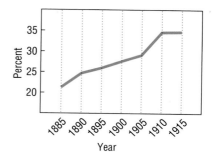

Alcoholic Beverage Consumption, Per Capita of Drinking Age (15+) Population (in gallons) in Years Prior to National Prohibition

SOURCE: Adapted from W. J. Rorabaugh, *The Alcoholic Republic* (New York: Oxford University Press, 1979), p. 233.

• EXHIBIT 2.1 •

Natural Law

Natural law, a concept that has run through human affairs for more than twenty centuries, focuses on perhaps the earliest understanding of crime. Natural law refers to a body of principles and rules, imposed upon individuals by some power higher than man-made law, that are considered to be uniquely fitting for and binding on any community of rational beings. As such, natural law is synonymous with "higher law" and is believed binding even in the absence of man-made law. As stated by Hugo Grotius, the Dutch jurist and statesman whose *De Jure Belli ac Pacis,* published in 1625, is regarded as the first work on international law:

The law of nature is a dictate of right reason which points out that an act, according as it is or is not in conformity with rational nature, has in it a quality of moral baseness or moral necessity; and that, in consequence, such an act is either forbidden or enjoined by the author of nature, God.[a]

Since natural law has generally referred to that which determines what is right and wrong and whose power is made valid by nature, it follows that its precepts should be eternal, universal, and unchangeable. But an examination of natural law from the time of the ancient Greeks to the present suggests that there is no single and unchanging view of the concept.[b] To Roman jurists, for example, *jus naturale,* or natural law, meant a body of ideal principles that people could understand rationally and that included the perfect standards of right conduct and justice. Throughout the Middle Ages the law of nature was identified with the Bible, with the laws and traditions of the Catholic church, and with the teachings of the church fathers.[c]

The cogency of natural law would suggest the existence of *natural crimes* — "thou shalt not kill" and "thou shalt not steal" —acts considered criminal by rational persons everywhere. However, research has failed to yield examples of activities that have been universally prohibited. Incest, for example, is believed by some to be a universal crime or taboo, for there are rules forbidding such behavior in one form or another in every known society.[d] However, there is considerable variation among societies and cultures as to what exactly constitutes incest. While it refers in virtually all settings to sexual relations between parents and children and between any sibling pair, it has been extended in others to include many categories of kin whose relationship may not be biological. Furthermore, in certain contexts—as in some royal marriages and sacred rituals—the incest taboo has been lifted.[e] As another example, even the act of murder is not universally viewed as criminal. In Comanche society, for example, for a husband to kill his wife —with or without good cause— was not murder. It was an absolute privilege and right that not even the family of the victim could challenge. In fact, the only crime in the Comanche legal system was excessive sorcery, for it was considered a threat to the tribe as a whole.[f]

Criminologist Hermann Mannheim has made a thorough and complex examination of the evolution of natural law throughout Western history,

the public at large, to the society's opinion makers, and ultimately to the designated rule creators and rule enforcers.

An illustration of this process was the antiliquor crusade that resulted in the ratification in 1919 of the Eighteenth Amendment to the United States Constitution, which prohibited the manufacture, sale, and distribution of intoxicating liquors. The prohibition "movement" asserted the rural Protestant ethic, which was in contrast to the urban culture that was emerging at the close of the nineteenth century. The earliest colonial settlers designated country and village life as good, and deemed only the farmer and his agrarian way of life to be pure and wholesome; life in the city was seen as wicked. The farmer was viewed as the solid man of the earth, the backbone of American democracy; living in communion with nature, he had an integrity that could never be attained by those surrounded with the evil and depravity of the city. This agrarian myth so permeated the ideals and thinking of the frontier people

concluding that even the concept of natural law has been subject to widely varying interpretations:

There is no single and unchanging concept of natural law. While its underlying idea is the longing of mankind for an absolute yardstick to measure the goodness or badness of human actions and the law of the State and to define their relations to religion and morality, the final lesson is that no such yardstick can be found.[g]

In sum, there has been a persistent conviction throughout history that there exist superior principles of right, some higher law, the violation of which constitutes crime. But the differing conceptions of natural law have served to discredit its importance in the understanding and definition of crime, which has led legal scholars and social scientists to other areas in their search for the meaning and parameters of crime.

Natural Law is significant, however, in both the evolution of criminal laws and modern conceptions of natural crimes. Elements of the natural law con-

cept were incorporated into the Code of Hammurabi, the first known written legal document, which dates back to about 1900 B.C. Natural law also played a key role in the formulation of Greco-Roman law, and it is a cornerstone of a portion of contemporary Anglo-American Law.

---

[a] Hugo Grotius, *De Jure ac Pacis,* cited by Cornelia Geer Le Boutillier, *American Democracy and Natural Law* (New York: Columbia University Press, 1950), p. 57.

[b] See Leo Strauss, *Natural Right and History* (Chicago: University of Chicago Press, 1953).

[c] See Charles Grover Haines, *The Revival of Natural Law Concepts* (Cambridge: Harvard University Press, 1930), pp. 6–11; Benjamin Fletcher Wright, *American Interpretations of Natural Law* (Cambridge: Harvard University Press, 1931), p. 6.

[d] Fernando Henriques, *Love in Action* (New York: Dutton, 1960), pp. 200–201.

[e] Margaret Mead, "Incest," in *International Encyclopedia of the Social Sciences,* ed. by David L. Sills (New York: Macmillan, 1968), vol. 7, pp. 115–122.

[f] E. Adamson Hoebel, *The Law of Primitive Man: A Study in Comparative Legal Dynamics* (Cambridge: Harvard University Press, 1954), pp. 127–142.

[g] Hermann Mannheim, *Comparative Criminology* (Boston: Houghton Mifflin, 1967), p. 47.

and their descendants that it tended to shape their perception of reality and overt behavior. Their anticity bias extended to drinking and the liquor trade, which they saw as symbols of urban morality — or immorality — and of urbanism in general. They viewed urbanism as diametrically opposed to the rural creeds of the Methodists, Baptists, Presbyterians, and Congregationalists, with their emphasis on individual human toil and a profound faith in the Bible. And to them, the commercialism of the cities was destroying the self-sufficiency of the farm and village, creating a situation of unwanted dependence. Urbanism, therefore, was the real sin in society, and the reform movement was simply an organization of rural interests striving against the wicked city and its impending dominance.

The crusading reformers included many members of the middle and upper classes who felt that prohibition would bring salvation to the cities and to the less privileged members of society. The best known of the

Rules are made for the obedience of fools and the guidance of wise men.
— SIR WINSTON CHURCHILL

reformers was Carry Nation, the uncrowned queen of the temperance movement, who often referred to liquor sellers as "booze-sodden, soul-killing, filth-smeared spawn of the Devil," or words to that effect.[8]

Note that although the deviance perspective can suggest how some deviance and crime can come into being, it fails to account for all definitions of crime. That is, some crimes may come into being by moral enterprise, and some behavior may become criminal when that label is applied to acts previously regarded as noncriminal; but this does not explain how or why many long-standing definitions regarding crimes against person and property came into being. Murder, for example, appears as a proscription in both the Old and New Testaments, and its designation as a capital offense appears in an early chapter of the Book of Genesis.

Furthermore, not all deviant behavior is criminal behavior, and conversely, not all criminal behavior is deviant behavior. Numerous kinds of activities receive social disapproval and may even be deemed as blatantly antisocial, but they are not necessarily crimes. While picking one's nose in public, espousing the doctrines of communism or nazism, or being an alcoholic are considered deviant by most Americans, the activities themselves are not criminal and they are not treated as such. Social disapproval might even be strong, with the deviants being subject to severe ostracism by their peers, but criminal sanctions would not be brought to bear against them.

By contrast, numerous other behaviors are indeed criminal, but the participants are not even called deviant. The Saturday night poker game for modest stakes may be a violation of the criminal law in some jurisdictions, yet to the society at large the occasional poker player is hardly a deviant. Similarly, many of the intimate sexual practices that occur be-

Is all crime deviant behavior, and is all deviant behavior crime?

The streets are safe in Philadelphia, it's only the people who make them unsafe.

— FRANK RIZZO

"My work environment was embezzlement-friendly."

tween adults in contemporary society may violate state and local criminal laws, but within the context of a consenting adult relationship the activities are considered normal.

And finally, although the labeling perspective fails to offer a basis for a working definition of crime, it does point out how some crime comes into being and, in that sense, how crime can be a social construction. More importantly, however, it provides a useful perspective for understanding how persons come to be labeled as deviant or criminal, how society may react to them, and how the process of labeling them as outsiders can affect their behavior. Society may react to disapproved behavior in a variety of ways — with disgust, anger, hate, gossip, isolation, physical punishment, incarceration, or even execution. Societal reaction is strong or weak depending upon the degree of antisocial behavior involved, how socially visible the behavior is, and the general norms and rules of the society regarding the particular behavior. The process of labeling individuals as deviants, delinquents, or criminals may result not only in rejection or punishment, but also in alteration of the intended behavior of both deviants and others. The anticipated effects of labeling, for example, may deter some persons from engaging in deviant or criminal acts. Furthermore, for those who already are considered deviants, delinquents, criminals, or outsiders, such labels may foster further unacceptable behavior. That is, the labels may lead them to view themselves as offenders who have only limited opportunities for socially approved pursuits.

Societal reaction to crime

Crime as a Legal Definition

I think crime pays. The hours are good and you travel a lot.
— WOODY ALLEN, 1969

If definitions of crime as violations of natural law or as antisocial behavior or deviance lack precision and are ambiguous, then we may need to look directly at law for a formal definition of crime. This need was best stated over half a century ago by Jerome Michael and Mortimer J. Adler during their attempt to unravel the nature of crime:

The law is sort of a hocus pocus science. It smiles in yer face while it picks yer pocket.
— CHARLES MACKLIN, 1797

> The most precise and least ambiguous definition of crime is that which defines it as behavior which is prohibited by the criminal code. The criminal law describes many kinds of behavior, gives them names such as murder and arson and rape and burglary, and proscribes them. If crime is defined in legal terms, the only source of confusion is such ambiguity as may inhere in the legal definitions of specific crimes. It is sometimes difficult to tell whether specific conduct falls within the legal definition, whether, for example, a specific homicide is murder or what degree of murder, as that offense is defined by law. But even so, the *legal rules are infinitely more precise than moral judgments or judgments with regard to the antisocial character of conduct* [emphasis added]. Moreover, there is no surer way of ascertaining what kinds of behavior are generally regarded as immoral or antisocial by the people of a community than by reference to their criminal code, for in theory, at least, the criminal code embodies social judgments with respect to behavior and, perhaps, more often than not, fact conforms to theory.[9]

The word *crime* has its roots in the Latin *crimen,* meaning judgment, accusation, and offense, and its origins are clearly legalistic. Numerous social scientists and legal scholars have offered definitions of crime within this legal perspective. The late Edwin H. Sutherland, perhaps the most renowned American criminologist of the mid-twentieth century,

It's strange that men should take up crime when there are so many legal ways to be dishonest.
— AL CAPONE

Crime: An intentional act or omission in violation of criminal law, committed without defense or justification, and sanctioned by the state as a felony or misdemeanor.

suggested that "the essential characteristic of crime is that it is behavior which is prohibited by the State and against which the State may react."[10] *Black's Law Dictionary* defines **crime** as "a positive or negative act in violation of the penal law; an offense against the state."[11] In the field of criminal justice it is defined simply as "a violation of the criminal law."[12] Yet these definitions, while correct in focusing on the law to delineate the limits of crime, fail to offer the kind of precision necessary for a full understanding of the term. We cannot simply call crime a violation of the law, for there are numerous circumstances under which identical behaviors would not be classified as criminal.

However, lawyer and sociologist Paul W. Tappan has offered a definition of crime that does mark its major boundaries:

> Crime is an intentional act or omission in violation of criminal law (statutory and case law), committed without defense or justification, and sanctioned by the state as a felony or misdemeanor.[13]

Tappan's definition will be accepted as the meaning of the term crime throughout this text. It is analyzed in detail in the following sections.

Crime Is an Intentional Act or Omission Central to the American system of law is the philosophy that a person cannot be punished for his or her thoughts. Thus, for there to be a crime, an act or the omission of an act that is legally required must be present. A person may wish to commit a crime, or think of committing a crime, but the crime does not occur until the action takes place. If one were to consider murdering a relative, there would be no crime until the killing, or its attempt, had actually occurred. Furthermore, one could conceivably *plan* for a long while to commit a crime, but again, the crime would not necessarily come into being until the action took place. In this respect, consider the case of Jack Gilbert Graham, who hoped to gain access to his mother's large estate by killing her. Graham went through some elaborate preparations to construct a bomb that he would place in her luggage, set to detonate ten minutes after her plane departed from Denver's Stapleton Airport bound for Seattle. In spite of his planning and his intent, had he dismantled the bomb and not placed it in his mother's suitcase, there would have been no crime. However, Graham did put his plan into action, and in the early evening of November 1, 1955, United Airlines flight 629 was blown apart over a beet farm near Longmont, Colorado, killing all 44 passengers and crew members aboard.[14]

Since crime is an intentional act or omission, persons cannot be punished for their thoughts.

Contrast the case of Jack Gilbert Graham, who acted alone, with the well-known Leopold and Loeb killing of 14-year-old Robert Franks. Nathan F. Leopold, Jr., was a graduate of the University of Chicago and the son of a multimillionaire shipping magnate; Richard A. Loeb was a University of Michigan graduate and the son of Sears, Roebuck and Company's vice president, Albert A. Loeb. Leopold and Loeb had structured what they felt would be the perfect crime — the kidnapping, ransoming, and killing of some innocent youth. Their planning extended over many weeks, and involved renting a car; opening a bank account for the ransom money; riding trains to the tentative ransom site; purchasing rope, a chisel, and hydrochloric acid with which they would garrote, stab, and mutilate their victim; gathering rags with which they would bind and gag the victim; selecting wading boots to be worn in the swamp where they would leave the victim's body; preparing a ransom note; and discussing potential victims. Unlike Graham, who had acted alone and who would have been innocent of any crime had he not planted the

bomb in his mother's belongings, Leopold and Loeb were already guilty of **conspiracy** to commit crime (see Exhibit 2.2). Their very agreement to murder, combined with their extensive preparations, constituted a crime. When Leopold and Loeb selected Robert Franks as their victim, and then abducted and murdered him, their crimes advanced from the conspiracy stage to include kidnapping and homicide.[15]

Failure to act in a particular case can also be a crime if there is some legal duty to do so. Consider, for example, the case of *People* v. *Beardsley,*[16] which involved a man who spent a weekend with his mistress. After a serious argument, the woman took an overdose of morphine tablets and the man made no attempt to obtain medical help to save her life. His failure to assist her did *not* constitute a crime. Although he may have had a moral obligation to help her, he had *no legal duty* to do so. There was no contractual relationship as might exist between parents and a day care center or between a patient and a hospital; there was no status relationship that imposed a legal duty such as that between husband and wife; and there was no legal statute imposing a legal duty on the man.

In contrast to *Beardsley,* in 1988 the California Supreme Court upheld manslaughter and felony child endangerment convictions of a woman who used prayer in lieu of medical attention in treating her 4-year-old's fatal attack of meningitis.[17] The defendant argued that the use of medicine violated her religious beliefs. The court countered that parents may not martyr their children to their own religious beliefs.

Less complex instances of failures to act that constitute crime can be found under the misprision of felony statutes. **Misprision of felony** refers to the offense of concealing a felony committed by another, even if the party to the concealment had not been part of the planning or execution of the felony.[18] Thus, if two individuals should overhear a group discussing their participation in a recent bank robbery, that couple would be guilty of misprision of felony if they failed to report the conversation to the authorities.

Criminal Intent   For an act or omission to be a crime, the law further requires criminal intent, or *mens rea* — from the Latin meaning "guilty mind." The concept of *mens rea* is based on the assumption that people have the capacity to control their behavior and to choose between alter-

Conspiracy: Concert in criminal purpose.

Legislatures have made conspiracy a separate offense because they perceive collective criminal activity to be a greater risk than individual actions.

Misprision of felony: The concealment of a felony committed by another.

Mens rea (criminal intent): A person's awareness of what is right and wrong under the law with an intention to violate the law.

● **EXHIBIT 2.2** ●

Conspiracy, "Smurfing," and the Bank Secrecy Act

Conspiracy means *concert in criminal purpose.* It refers to the combining of two or more persons to accomplish either an unlawful purpose or a lawful purpose by some unlawful means. Under federal statutes, four elements must be present for the crime of conspiracy to exist:

1. An act of agreement between two or more persons
2. An "object," or intention to do some unlawful act
3. A plan or scheme for accomplishing the object crime
4. An overt act implementing the agreement and intent

Thus, under federal law (18 U.S.C. 371),

if two or more persons conspire either to commit any offense against the United States, or any agency thereof in any manner or for any purpose, and one or more of such persons shall do any act to effect the object of the conspiracy, each shall be fined not more than $10,000 or imprisoned not more than five years, or both.

Many state conspiracy laws are similar to those at the federal level, but in some jurisdictions conspiracy becomes an offense as soon as the agreement to commit crime takes place. In most instances, however, some overt act that furthers the conspired crime must be apparent. This does not necessarily mean, though, that the intended crime must take place or even be attempted. And the overt act of implementation could be some minor *noncriminal* activity that sets the conspired plan into motion.

A case decided by the U.S. Court of Appeals in 1987 illustrates these many points (*U.S.* v. *Nersesian,* CA2, No. 86-1211, 6/29/87; 41 CrL 2311). The defendants in the case had been convicted of smuggling heroin into the United States from the Middle East. The conspiracy charges against them, however, involved the $117,000 in cash accrued from the distribution of the heroin and their efforts to convert it into money orders and travelers checks — a situation involving the federal Bank Secrecy Act.

The Bank Secrecy Act requires banks and other financial institutions (not individuals) to report cash transactions exceeding $10,000 in any single day to the Internal Revenue Service (IRS). The purpose of the act is to make the IRS aware of large cash transactions for the sake of levying and collecting any income taxes that might be due. To hide their $117,000 in illegal income from IRS, the defendants engaged in what has become known in the banking industry as "smurfing." They, and their couriers (*smurfs*) made numerous purchases of money orders and travelers checks in amounts of less than $10,000 — several times a day, on several different days, and at several different banks. At no time did any single transaction exceed $10,000.

These actions resulted in two separate charges of conspiracy. First, the defendants had conspired to prevent a financial institution from filing a currency transaction report that it was legally obligated to file. Second, the defendants had conspired to defraud the Internal Revenue Service by interfering with its collection of information about large currency transactions.

---

native courses of conduct. Thus, the notion of criminal intent suggests the actor's awareness of what is right and wrong under the law with an intention to violate the law, as contrasted with the retarded, the insane, or the young, who may not have their full use of reason.

Specific intent

Most legal commentaries divide *mens rea* into two basic types of intent: specific and general. *Specific intent* is present when one can gather from the circumstances of the crime that the offender must have consciously and subjectively desired the prohibited result. In the Leopold and Loeb case mentioned earlier, specific criminal intent was present. From the facts surrounding the case, it is clear that the murder of the victim was specifically intended. Similarly, the crime of burglary reflects the notion of specific intent. Burglary involves two broad elements: entry into the dwelling of another and the intention to commit a crime (usually a theft) therein. The burglar manifests specific intent because he or she consciously desires the prohibited result—theft.

By contrast, consider the case of a man outraged by his neighbor's barking dog. He expresses his disfavor by warning that if the dog is not quieted, he will shoot the animal. When the threat is ignored and the dog continues to bark, the angered man fires three shots through his neighbor's window intending to kill the dog. Instead, one of the bullets kills his neighbor. Although specific intent is not present in this case, general intent is. As such, *general intent* refers to a matter of conscious wrongdoing from which a prohibited result follows, without a subjective desire for the accomplishment of that result. Or more specifically, general criminal intent involves the conscious and intentional commission of a crime when the specific result of that crime was not necessarily intended.

General intent

Although criminal intent, whether specific or general, is necessary for an act to be a crime, there are some exceptions to this rule of law. Under the doctrine of **vicarious liability,** referred to in some jurisdictions as the doctrine of *respondeat superior,* liability can be imposed on an employer for certain illegal acts of his employees committed during the course and scope of their employment. This doctrine is generally directed at the protection of the public, as is indicated in the two following examples. In one case, the president of a pharmaceutical company was charged and convicted of a violation of the Pure Food and Drug Act of 1906. One provision of the act had required proper labeling of drugs, and unknown to him, his product had been mislabeled by his employees.[19] In another case, the defendant owned a tavern and his bartender had served minors in violation of the Pennsylvania Liquor Code. The tavern owner was neither aware that minors were served alcoholic beverages, nor was he present when the event occurred. Nevertheless, under the doctrine of *vicarious liability,* he was convicted. On appeal, the Pennsylvania Supreme Court upheld the conviction with the following statement:

Vicarious liability: The doctrine under which liability is imposed upon an employer for the acts of employees that are committed in the course and scope of their employment.

> While an employer in almost all cases is not criminally responsible for the unlawful acts of his employees, unless he consents to, approves, or participates in such acts, courts all over the nation have struggled for years in applying this rule within the framework of "controlling the sale of intoxicating liquor." We find that the intent of the legislature in enacting this Code was not only to eliminate the common law requirement of a *mens rea,* but also to place a very high degree of responsibility upon the holder of a liquor license to make certain that neither he nor anyone in his employ commit any of the prohibited acts upon the licensed premises. Such a burden of care is imposed upon the licensee in order to protect the public from the potentially noxious effects of an inherently dangerous business.[20]

As a final point here, when vicarious liability is imposed, only minor penalties are typically levied. In the Pennsylvania case noted above, the defendant was a second offender. As such, he faced a mandatory penalty of a $500 fine and three months in jail. However, only the fine was ordered, for as the court explained it, "A man's liberty cannot rest on so frail a reed as whether his employee will commit a mistake in judgment."

Violation of Criminal Law

For an act, or its omission to be a crime, not only must there be criminal intent, but the behavior must be in violation of the criminal law. **Criminal law,** as opposed to noncriminal law or civil law, is that branch of jurisprudence that deals with offenses committed against the safety and order of the state. As such, criminal law

Criminal law: The branch of jurisprudence that deals with offenses committed against the safety and order of the state.

Civil law: The body of principles that determines private rights and liabilities.

Statutory law: Law created by statute, handed down by legislatures.

Case law: Law that results from court interpretations of statutory law or from court decisions where rules have not been fully codified or have been found to be vague or in error.

Robinson v. California: In a new approach to the Eighth Amendment's ban on "cruel and unusual punishments," the United States Supreme Court declared in 1962 that sickness may not be made a crime, nor may sick people be punished for being sick. The Court viewed narcotic addiction to be a "sickness," and held that a state cannot make it a punishable offense any more than it could put a person in jail "for the 'crime' of having a common cold."

Common law: Customs, traditions, judicial decisions, and other materials that guide courts in decision making but have not been enacted by the legislatures into statutes or embodied in the Constitution.

relates to actions that are considered so dangerous, or potentially so, that they threaten the welfare of the society as a whole. And it is for this reason that in criminal cases the government brings the action against the accused. **Civil law,** by contrast, is the body of principles that determines private rights and liabilities. In these cases, one individual brings an action against another individual — a *plaintiff* versus a *defendant* — as opposed to the state versus an accused, as in criminal cases. More specifically, civil law is structured to regulate the rights between individuals or organizations; it involves such areas as divorce, child support, contracts, and property rights. Civil law also includes torts, civil wrongs for which the law gives redress.

Criminal law includes a variety of types: statutory law, case law, and common law. **Statutory law** is law passed from the legislatures, which create it by statute. Each state has a statutory criminal code, as does the federal government. The laws that define the boundaries of such commonly known offenses as homicide, rape, burglary, robbery, and larceny are generally of a statutory nature. By contrast, **case law** is law that results from court interpretations of statutory law or from court decisions where rules have not been fully codified or have been found to be vague or in error.

A classic example of case law is the Supreme Court decision involving *Robinson* **v.** *California,*[21] which resulted from Robinson's appeal of his conviction as a narcotic addict under a section of the California Health and Safety Code, which read:

> No person shall use, or be under the influence, or be addicted to the use of narcotics, excepting when administered by or under the direction of a person licensed by the State to prescribe and administer narcotics. It shall be the burden of the defense to show that it comes within the exception. Any person convicted of violating any provision of this section is guilty of a misdemeanor and shall be sentenced to serve a term of not less than 90 days nor more than one year in the county jail.

Robinson had been convicted after a jury trial in the Municipal Court of Los Angeles. In terms of evidence, the arresting officer testified that he had observed scar tissue, discoloration, and what appeared to be needle marks on the inside of the defendant's left arm, and that the defendant had admitted to the occasional use of narcotics. Under the California law, the use of narcotics was considered a status or condition — not an act; it was a continuing offense that could subject the offender to arrest at any time before he or she "reformed." Robinson was convicted of the offense charged. He then took his case to the Appellate Department of the Los Angeles County Superior Court, where the original judgment of conviction was affirmed. Upon appeal to the United States Supreme Court, the decision was reversed on the grounds that status offenses such as "being addicted to the use of narcotics" were unconstitutional, and that imprisonment for such an offense was cruel and unusual punishment in violation of the Eighth Amendment to the Constitution. Thus, the *Robinson* v. *California* case, after the lower court's decisions were reversed, represented case law in that it defined narcotic addiction as a status that was no longer punishable under the law.

Common law refers to those customs, traditions, judicial decisions, and other materials that guide courts in decision making but that have not been enacted by the legislatures into statutes or embodied in the Constitution. Among the better-known aspects of common law are the rights set forth in the Declaration of Independence, and other doctrines protecting life, liberty, and property.

Defense or Justification   For an act (or the omission thereof) to be a crime, it must not only be intentional and in violation of the criminal law, but it must also be committed without defense or justification. **Defense** is a broad term that can refer to any number of causes and rights of action that would serve to mitigate or excuse an individual's guilt in a criminal offense. Defenses most commonly raised include insanity, mistake of fact, mistake of law, duress and consent, consent of the victim, entrapment, and justification.

Insanity is any unsoundness of mind, madness, mental alienation, or want of reason, memory, and intelligence that prevents an individual from comprehending the nature and consequences of his or her acts or from distinguishing between right and wrong conduct. Insanity is a legal concept rather than a medical one. Furthermore, it is a complex legal issue. A few jurisdictions recognize that some defendants can be partially insane in respect to the circumstances surrounding the commission of a crime, but sane as to other matters. The cornerstone of the insanity defense emerged from the case of Daniel M'Naghten in 1843. M'Naghten killed the secretary to England's Sir Robert Peel. At his trial he claimed that at the time he committed the act he had not been of a sound state of mind. From this came the **M'Naghten Rule** — the "right-or-wrong" test of criminal responsibility — which states:

> If the accused was possessed of sufficient understanding when he committed the criminal act to know what he was doing and to know that it was wrong, he is responsible therefore, but if he did not know the nature and quality of the act or did know what he was doing but did not know that it was wrong, he is not responsible.[22]

The M'Naghten test has been severely criticized on the grounds that it is arbitrary and applies to only a small percentage of people who are actually mentally ill. In 1954 the U.S. court of appeals for the District of Columbia broadened the M'Naghten test in favor of what has become known as the **Durham Rule** in *Durham* v. *United States.*[23] It was held that an accused is not criminally responsible if he or she suffers from a diseased or defective mental condition at the time the unlawful act is committed. This rule has also been criticized, but on opposite grounds from M'Naghten. Critics claim that it is far too broad and places too much power in the hands of psychiatrists and juries for determining the legal issue of insanity.

In retrospect, the defense of "not guilty by reason of insanity" has been debated for generations. Critics of the defense argue that defendants acquitted on insanity pleas spend less time in mental institutions than do those sent to prison for similar crimes. Supporters of the insanity defense claim that it would be morally unjust to convict and punish an individual who acted under the condition of an unsound mind. Or as Harvard University law professor Alan M. Dershowitz once put it, "Would anyone seriously think of convicting someone for murder who thought he was shooting a robot or squeezing a melon?"[24]

John W. Hinckley, Jr. was tried in the shooting of President Ronald Reagan in 1981. His acquittal on insanity grounds the following year fully rekindled the controversy over the insanity defense. Confidence was lost in the criminal justice system because in this case it was unable to punish a man who admitted trying to assassinate the President of the United States. There were calls for reform, even abolition of the insanity defense entirely.[25]

In the aftermath of the Hinckley verdict, Montana and Idaho barred the insanity defense except in extreme cases. Several other states adopted a procedure that permits juries to find defendants "guilty but mentally

---

Defense: Any number of causes and rights of action that serve to excuse or mitigate guilt in a criminal offense.

Insanity

M'Naghten Rule: The "right-or-wrong" test of criminal responsibility.

Durham Rule: An accused is not criminally responsible if he or she suffers from a diseased or defective mental condition at the time the unlawful act is committed.

It's a rich man's defense — if you can afford enough psychiatrists and psychologist, you're probably going to get off.
— Utah Senator Orrin Hatch in 1982 on the insanity plea

The insanity plea should not be abolished. It's been with us since biblical times. It reflects a very important moral notion about criminal responsibility.
— Alan Dershowitz, 1982

Following the Hinckley trial in 1982, a telephone survey of 434 adults yielded the following opinions on the insanity plea and the verdict of *not guilty by reason of insanity* (NGRI).

Fairness of Hinckley verdict:	
Unfair	53.7%
Somewhat or slightly fair	37.8%
Very fair	8.5%
Respondent's verdict:	
Guilty	73.3%
NGRI	14.7%
Don't know	12.0%
Is Hinckley insane?	
No	65.7%
Yes	24.4%
Don't know	10.0%
Is the insanity defense a loophole?	
Yes	87.1%
No	6.8%
Don't know	6.1%
What should happen to Hinckley?	
Punishment	26.4%
Treatment	14.1%
Punishment and treatment	59.5%

SOURCE: Valerie P. Hans and Dan Slater, "John Hinckley, Jr. and the Insanity Defense: The Public's Verdict," *Public Opinion Quarterly*, 47 (1983), p. 206.

Mistake of fact

Mistake of law is no release from prosecution.

ill." The aim of such a finding is to guarantee psychiatric treatment to an offender while insuring that he or she will serve as much prison time as another convicted person.[26] Moreover, the 1983 United States Supreme Court's decision in *Jones* v. *U.S.*[27] held that persons found not guilty of crimes by reason of insanity may be confined to mental hospitals for a longer time than they would have spent in prison if convicted—a ruling that applied to John W. Hinckley, Jr.

Yet despite the new state statutes and the ruling in *Jones,* the insanity defense has actually been expanded in the post-Hinckley era. A number of Vietnam veterans suffering from the disorientation and flashbacks associated with P-TSD (post traumatic stress disorder) have successfully argued that the intense reliving of their war experiences destroyed their ability to distinguish between right and wrong. The P-TSD insanity defense has been used to acquit veterans accused of homicide, armed robberies, and drug law violations.

The problem with the insanity defense is that insanity is a legal, not a medical term. Furthermore, there is little agreement on the actual meaning of the word. On the other hand, and in contrast to conventional wisdom, few serious offenders use the insanity plea to avoid incarceration. Studies demonstrate that the plea is used in less than one percent of serious criminal cases, is rarely successful, and when it is, defendants generally spend more time in mental institutions than they would have spent in prison had they been convicted.

Mistake of fact is any erroneous conviction of fact or circumstance resulting in some act that would not otherwise have been undertaken. Mistake of fact becomes a defense when an individual commits a prohibited act in good faith and with a reasonable belief that certain facts are correct, which, if they were indeed accurate, would have made the act innocent. Further, the mistake must be an honest one and not the result of negligence or poor deliberation.

For example, if Smith walks away with Jones's suitcase thinking that it is his own, Smith's defense would be that he was operating under a mistake of fact since both parties had identical luggage. Such a mistake precludes Smith from having criminal intent and, as a result, he has a defense against a conviction for larceny. Mistake of fact has been used as a defense in cases of statutory rape. Statutory rape refers to sexual intercourse with a female under a certain age (usually sixteen or eighteen) despite her consent. Although a defendant may claim that his underage female partner looked older than her actual age, or even misrepresented her age, the courts are decidedly mixed in their acceptance of the defense. In 1984, for example, the Utah Supreme Court accepted the defense of reasonable mistake of age on the grounds that "a person cannot be found guilty of a criminal offense unless he harbors a requisite criminal state of mind."[28] During the same year, however, the Michigan Supreme Court refused to recognize the defense, holding that the statutory-rape laws impose criminal liability without requiring proof of specific criminal intent.[29]

Mistake of law is any want of knowledge or acquaintance with the laws of the land insofar as they apply to the act, relation, duty, or matter under consideration. There is a well-worn cliché that "ignorance of the law is no excuse," which suggests that the notion of mistake of law offers no release from prosecution of such a crime. Indeed, simple ignorance of forbidden behavior is not usually an acceptable defense against crime; all persons are assumed to have knowledge of the law. This is true for both citizens and aliens alike. If an Englishman, for example, were to take a

---

EXHIBIT 2.3

Ignorance of the Law

Lambert v. California, 355 U.S. 225 (1957)

Despite the rule that "ignorance of the law is no excuse," *Lambert* v. *California*, decided by the United States Supreme Court in 1957, highlights a major exception.

Section 52.38(a) of the Los Angeles Municipal Code defined a "convicted person" as follows:

Any person who, subsequent to January 1, 1921, has been or hereafter is convicted of an offense punishable as a felony in the State of California, or who has been or who is hereafter convicted of any offense in any place other than the State of California, which offense, if committed in the State of California, would have been punishable as a felony.

The Los Angeles code also made it unlawful for any "convicted persons" to remain in the city for more than five days without registering with the police; or if they lived outside of the city, to enter the city on five or more occasions during a thirty-day period without registering.

In *Lambert*, the petitioner was found guilty of failing to register, fined $250, and placed on probation for three years. On appeal to the United States Supreme Court, the conviction was reversed. The Court recognized the importance of the rule that ignorance of the law is not an excuse. However, as Justice William O. Douglas commented:

Due process places some limits on its exercise. Engrained in our concept of due process is the requirement of notice. Notice is sometimes essential so that the citizen has the chance to defend charges. . . . Notice is required in a myriad of situations where a penalty or forfeiture might be suffered for mere failure to act.

That is, where a person did not know of the duty to register and where there was no proof of the probability of such knowledge, he or she may not be convicted with due process. Were it otherwise, the evil would be as great as when the law is written in print too fine to read or in a language foreign to the community.

---

motor tour of the United States and unknowingly drive on the left side of the road as is the law in his native land, his ignorance would be no defense against a U.S. traffic violation. Similarly, in many jurisdictions it is a crime to fail to come to the aid of a police officer when so ordered and if the request is not hazardous to the citizen. This law is not well known to most citizens. Nevertheless, should an individual fail to comply with such an order on the basis of ignorance, his or her lack of knowledge of the law would not be an adequate defense against the crime. In contrast, however, as the Supreme Court ruled in *Lambert* v. *California*,[30] ignorance of the law may be a defense against crime if the law has not been made reasonably well known (see Exhibit 2.3).

Duress and consent is any unlawful constraints exercised upon an individual forcing him or her to do some act that would not have been done otherwise. Duress implies that one is not acting of his or her own free will, and the American system of law emphasizes both criminal intent and responsibility. A typical example of duress and consent has

Lambert v. *California:* The Supreme Court held that due process requires that ignorance of a duty must be allowed as a defense when circumstances that inform a person as to the required duty are completely lacking.

Duress and consent

been seen often in television and movie themes. The local bank official is forced to aid the thieves in a bank robbery while his wife and children are held captive by a second group of bandits. If the banker fails to cooperate, his family will be harmed. In this case duress and consent is a legal defense against crime, since there is no criminal intent and since the rule includes injuries, threats, and restraints exercised not only against the individual, but on his or her parent, child, or spouse as well. However, such threats or restraints must be against the person (as opposed to property), and they must be immediate (not future). Had the bank official been threatened with the slaying of his family at some future date, there would be no immediate and imposing threat. Similarly, if the threat was to destroy his house, again the notion of duress would be a poor defense.

Consent of the victim

Consent of the victim is any voluntary yielding of the will of the victim, accompanied by his or her deliberation, agreeing to the act of the offending party. The victim's consent to a crime can be a defense recognized by the law, but there are several elements to a defense of consent. First, the victim must be capable of giving consent, and this rule excludes any consent offered by the insane, the retarded, or those below the age of reason. Second, the offense must be a "consentable" crime. Murder is considered to be a nonconsentable crime, as is statutory rape. Furthermore, there are offenses such as disorderly conduct for which no consent can generally be given. Third, the consent cannot be obtained by fraud. For example, should an auto mechanic suggest to a customer that her transmission must be fully replaced when indeed only a small bolt requires tightening, the victim's consent to have it replaced is not a legal defense. Fourth, the person giving consent must have the authority to do so. Although one party may have the right to give consent to have his or her property taken, such authority cannot be given to the property of another party.

Entrapment: The inducement of an individual to commit a crime not contemplated by him or her.

Entrapment is the inducement of an individual to commit a crime not contemplated by him or her, undertaken for the sole purpose of instituting a criminal prosecution against the offender. Cases of entrapment occur when law enforcement officers, or civilians acting at their behest, induce a person to commit a crime that he or she would not have otherwise undertaken. *Inducement* is the key word in the entrapment defense and refers to the fact that the accused had no intention of committing the crime until persuaded to do so by the law officer. Should police officer Jones approach Smith and convince him to rob Brown, and then place Smith under arrest after the crime is committed, the defense of police entrapment would be available. Similarly, in some jurisdictions, if a vice squad officer in plain clothes approaches a prostitute and offers her a sum of money for sexual favors, and then arrests her after their encounter, entrapment might be an available defense. Even though the accused is by profession a prostitute, the case could nevertheless be one of entrapment since the particular offense for which she was arrested had occurred only because of police inducement.

I didn't make him buy the damn drugs, I just offered them for sale.
— A SAN FRANCISCO POLICE OFFICER
ACCUSED OF ENTRAPMENT, 1991

In recent years, the strength of the entrapment defense has been weakened by court decisions that have considered the offender's "predisposition" to committing a crime. In the 1976 case of *Hampton* v. *United States,*[31] the Supreme Court ruled that it was not entrapment for an undercover agent to supply illicit drugs to a suspected dealer and then for another agent to act as a buyer, when there was reason to believe that the suspect was inclined, or "predisposed," to commit the crime anyway.

What makes this case different from that of the prostitute is the legality of the primary behavior in question. Sexual intercourse, whether the female partner is or is not a prostitute, is generally legal behavior. What constituted the crime was her acceptance of money for the sexual act, and what constituted entrapment was the plain-clothes officer's inducement of money. In contrast, Hampton's dealing in illicit drugs was illegal behavior, and it was not the undercover agent's inducement that made the primary act illegal. Furthermore, as opposed to the case of Officer Jones convincing Smith to rob Brown, Hampton was reputedly a drug dealer while Smith was not by trade a robber.

Justification is any just cause or excuse for the commission of an act that would otherwise be a crime. The notion of justification as a defense against crime typically involves the use of force or violence in the protection of one's person or property, the lives and property of others, the prevention of crime, and the apprehension of offenders. *Justifiable homicide* includes those instances of death that result from legal demands — the execution of a duly condemned prisoner, the killing of a fleeing inmate by a prison guard, or the shooting of an armed robber by a police officer. *Excusable homicide* includes death from accidents or misfortunes that may occur during some lawful act. Self-defense or the defense of some other individual can be viewed as either a justifiable or excusable act depending on the circumstances surrounding the particular case.

Beyond these general areas, some jurisdictions have particular statutes that may extend the boundaries of justifiable cause or excuse. Until 1974, for example, a Texas law defined as justifiable homicide a husband's shooting and killing his wife's lover if he found them in the very midst of the act of adultery. The law specified, however, that the actual shooting had to occur before the couple separated and that the husband must not have been a party to, or approved of, the adulterous connection. (Interestingly, this Texas statute did not extend to women who found their husbands engaging in adultery.)

Finally, there are many issues raised as defenses against crime that in most instances are not allowed by the courts. Although the First Amendment to the Constitution guarantees religious freedom, *religious practice* that violates criminal law can generally not be used to justify or excuse criminal conduct. Similarly, if it is *custom* that a given law is typically not enforced, such a tradition does not justify the violation of that law. Finally, many have attempted to use *intoxication* as a defense against crime, claiming that while under the influence of alcohol or drugs they were not in control of their behavior and therefore not criminally responsible. However, most jurisdictions make a distinction between voluntary and involuntary intoxication. Voluntary intoxication is not a defense under most circumstances. In cases of involuntary intoxication, however, where liquor or drugs are forced upon an individual, a reasonable defense can be mounted depending on the defendant's "degree of intoxication" at the time of the criminal act.

On the other hand, there have been a number of unusual defenses that the courts have periodically accepted. In 1984, a New Jersey appeals court ruled that medical *necessity* was a legitimate defense for a man charged with possession of marijuana. The decision involved a quadriplegic who argued that he smoked marijuana to relieve his chronic pain, and that the marijuana had fewer side effects than prescription drugs.[32] Similarly, in *People* v. *Lovercamp*[33] in 1975 and *Jorgensen* v. *State*[34] in 1984, courts have accepted the necessity defense for inmates charged

---

Justification

Justifiable homicide includes instances of death that result from legal demands, whereas *excusable homicide* includes deaths from misfortunes that occur during some lawful act.

Police Entrapment

If a cop comes up to a prostitute and engages in vague generalities or responses to her leads, this is not entrapment.

The scenario might go something like this:

HE: Hi.
SHE: Hi, wanna party?
HE: Sure. What's the tariff, and what do you do?
SHE: Fifty dollars for a blow job.

This is a perfectly legitimate vignette for a legal arrest. The twist on this exchange would be:

HE: Hi.
SHE: Hi.
HE: I'm willing to give you $50 for a blow job, how about it?
SHE: Sure.

Because the officer initiated the action . . . the arrest, if made, would be illegal.

—FORMER MINNEAPOLIS POLICE CHIEF
ANTHONY V. BOUZA, 1990

The necessity defense

• EXHIBIT 2.4 •

Sidelights on Criminal Matters
"Zero Tolerance" and the Innocent-Owner Defense

One of the more debated aspects of the late 1980s war on drugs was "zero-tolerance." Mentioned briefly in the closing section of Chapter 1, it was a 1988 White House anti-drug policy that was never fully articulated in the national media. It would appear that zero tolerance was based on a number of premises: 1) that if there were no drug abusers there would be no drug problem; 2) that the market for drugs is created not only by availability, but also by demand; 3) that drug abuse starts with a willful act; 4) that the perception that drug users are powerless to act against the influences of drug availability and peer pressure is an erroneous one; 5) that most illegal drug users can choose to stop their drug-taking behaviors and must be held accountable if they do not; 6) that individual freedom does not include the right to self and societal destruction; and, 7) that public tolerance for drug abuse must be reduced to *zero*.ª As such, the

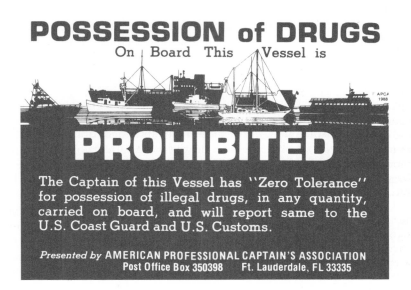

POSSESSION of DRUGS
On Board This Vessel is
PROHIBITED

The Captain of this Vessel has "Zero Tolerance" for possession of illegal drugs, in any quantity, carried on board, and will report same to the U.S. Coast Guard and U.S. Customs.

Presented by AMERICAN PROFESSIONAL CAPTAIN'S ASSOCIATION
Post Office Box 350398   Ft. Lauderdale, FL 33335

zero-tolerance policy expanded the war on drugs from suppliers and dealers, to users as well — especially casual users — and meant that planes, vessels, and vehicles could be confiscated for carrying even the smallest amount of a controlled substance.

Not surprisingly, the policy quickly became unpopular, particularly with non-drug-using owners of confiscated boats. As a case in point, during May 1988 the Coast Guard seized the *Ark Royal,* a $2.5 million, 133-ft. yacht that was in international waters between Mexico

---

She was saying, "You son of a bitch; you fucking can't do this to me; I'm a doctor. I hope you get shot and come into my hospital so I can refuse to treat you, or if any other troopers get shot, I will also refuse to treat them."
— A VIRGINIA STATE TROOPER IN 1991 DESCRIBING THE ARREST OF AN ORTHOPEDIC SURGEON, WHO CONVINCED A JUDGE THAT HER ERRATIC BEHAVIOR HAD BEEN CAUSED BY PREMENSTRUAL SYNDROME, NOT DRUNKENNESS

with escaping prison custody. In both cases, the prisoners were faced with threats of forcible sexual attack or death (see chapter 16). For more than a century the courts have accepted the *PMS defense* (premenstrual syndrome) in a wide variety of cases.[35] Going further, in 1987 there was the *seat-belt defense,* in which a Michigan jury acquitted a driver of negligent homicide because his auto-accident victims had failed to obey the state's seat-belt law.[36] In 1989 there was the *toxin defense* — the successful claim in an Arizona murder case in which a public defender argued that his client was brain damaged (and hence, temporarily insane) as the result of radiation from uranium near his home.[37] And finally, there is the *innocent owner defense,* a legacy of the federal "zero tolerance initiative" (see Exhibit 2.4).

and Cuba. The on-board drug stash was one-tenth of an ounce of marijuana, and because only the captain and crew were on board at the time of the raid, it was not even apparent that the drug had been used by the vessel's owner.[b] Also seized was the luxury yacht *Monkey Business*—the rental party boat that had gained notoriety in 1987 for carrying presidential hopeful Gary Hart and model Donna Rice to Bimini.[c]

U.S. Customs Service activity during the first six months of zero tolerance resulted in the arrest of 3,540 people; and the seizure of 4,282 private automobiles, pickup trucks and vans valued at some $20 million; the seizure of 145 commercial trucks valued at almost $5 million; the seizure of six aircraft valued at $386,000; and the seizure of 107 boats valued at over $60 million.[d] So many of these vehicles and vessels were confiscated that complaints lead to an easing of the zero-tolerance policy. An "innocent owner's" defense was established to protect against forfeiture when someone else's "personal use" drugs were found.[e] And to emphasize the notion of an "innocent owner," fishing and charter boat captains began displaying plaques on their vessels which stated that **POSSESSION OF DRUGS ON BOARD THIS VESSEL IS PROHIBITED.**

[a] U.S. Department of Transportation, Office of Public Affairs, *Transportation Facts*, "Zero-Tolerance Policy on Illegal Drugs," June 6, 1988; Department of the Treasury, U.S. Customs Service, "Zero Tolerance Made Plain," *Southern Boating*, October 1988, pp. 86–88; *New York Times*, April 12, 1988, pp. A1, A10.

[b] *Time*, 23 May 1988, p. 55; *Boat/U.S. Reports*, XXIV (May 1989), pp. 1, 7.

[c] *Miami Herald*, May 20, 1988, pp. 1A, 24A.

[d] *USA Today*, October 19, 1988, p. 4A.

[e] *National Law Journal*, November 7, 1988, pp. 3, 9; *In Command*, Fall 1989, p. 5; *Drug Enforcement Report*, April 24, 1989, p. 4; *Drug Enforcement Report*, November 8, 1989, p. 4; *Boat/U.S. Reports*, XXIII (Nov./Dec. 1988), pp. 1–2.

Law Sanctioned by the State Under the American system of law the maxim *nullum crimen sine poena* (no crime without punishment) dictates that a law must be written, that persons cannot be tried for acts that are not crimes in law, and that persons cannot be punished for acts for which the state provides no penalty. In the absence of such doctrines a social order would quickly fall into a state of *anomie*. If a legal system had no written law, *any* act could potentially be construed as a crime at the pleasure of the court or state, resulting in a situation of ironbound tyranny. Furthermore, if certain types of behavior were defined as crimes but no penalties were embodied in the law for their commission, then again a hopeless level of confusion and disregard for law would likely ensue. In contrast, American law consists of written codes describing the

Anomie is a condition within a society or group in which there exists a weakened respect or lack of adherence to some or most of the norms.

*Prostitution—*mala in se, *or a consequence of the legislation of morality?*

various prohibited forms of behavior and the range of punishments that would occur for their commission.

The law must be specific, however, for there are many acts that, depending upon the attendant circumstances, may or may not be crimes. The physical act of sexual intercourse, for example, describes any number of situations, including adultery, fornication, forcible and statutory rape, seduction, and incest. And, in addition to these six different crimes, it is also a normal, lawful act between mates. However, as a lawful act even between married couples, the act might be called obscenity, pornography, indecent exposure, or disorderly conduct, depending on the place it occurs. Further, at one time the ethnicity of each partner might have been considered, and it could have been called *miscegenation* (marriage involving people of different races), which was a crime. Thus, the law must be specific as to what sex acts are prohibited and among whom and where and under what circumstances they may and may not occur.

Also significant in American criminal law is the doctrine that only the offender can be punished. This posture has its roots in the Old Testament, that "every man shall be put to death for his own sin," and has endured in current legal doctrine. However, there are a variety of situations in which this may not necessarily be the case. Recall, for example, the doctrine of vicarious liability, which says an employer can be held responsible for certain crimes of his employees.

Felonies and Misdemeanors Crimes have been classified in many ways, among which are *mala in se* and *mala prohibita* offenses. Acts are considered to be *mala in se* when they are inherently and essentially evil — immoral in their nature and injurious in their consequences — such as murder, rape, and theft. *Mala prohibita* crimes are those that may not necessarily be wrong in themselves, but that are wrong simply be-

Mala in se

Mala prohibita

cause they have been prohibited by statute. Moral turpitude, that is, depravity or baseness of conduct, is the basis of distinction between these two types of crime, but since attitudes regarding moral turpitude tend to vary from one jurisdiction to the next, the distinction that is almost universally used instead is that between felonies and misdemeanors.

Historically, under common law felonies were crimes punishable by death or forfeiture of property, and included such offenses as murder, rape, theft, arson, and robbery. Misdemeanors were considered lesser offenses that lacked the moral reprehensibility of felonies. The current distinction between the two is similar. In most jurisdictions, **felonies** are serious crimes punishable by death or by imprisonment (usually for one year or longer) in a federal or state penitentiary. **Misdemeanors** are minor offenses generally punishable by no more than a $1,000 fine and/or one year of imprisonment, typically in a local institution. The felony–misdemeanor classification goes beyond the *mala se – mala prohibita* distinction, since a number of felonies fail to reflect moral turpitude. For example, the crimes of prison escape, wiretapping, carrying a concealed deadly weapon, or possession of forgery instruments are felonies in some jurisdictions in spite of the perpetrator's lack of moral turpitude.

In the legal codes of most jurisdictions, felonies and misdemeanors encompass the boundaries of what is defined as crime. In a few states, however, there is a third generic category. This category has resulted from the redefinition of certain offenses as less serious than misdemeanors; such offenses are generally referred to as *violations*. In the New York Penal Law, for example:

> "Violation" means an offense for which a sentence to a term of imprisonment in excess of fifteen days cannot be imposed.[38]

Included in this category of violations are such minor offenses as disorderly conduct, loitering, public intoxication, and patronizing a prostitute.

Felony: A crime punishable by death or by imprisonment in a federal or state penitentiary.

Misdemeanor: A crime punishable by no more than a $1,000 fine and/or one year of imprisonment, typically in a local institution.

CRIMINAL LAW

Law is experience developed by reason and applied continually to further experience.

— Roscoe Pound

Law is a statement of the circumstances in which the public force will be brought to bear upon man through the courts.

— Justice Oliver Wendell Holmes, Jr.

Legal scholars Sir Frederick Pollock and F. W. Maitland have commented that "law may be taken for every purpose, save that of strictly philosophical inquiry, to be the sum of the rules administered by the courts of justice."[39] To legal scholar Sir James Fitzjames Stephen, law is "a system of commands addressed by the sovereign of the state to his subjects, imposing duties and enforced by punishments."[40] There have been numerous attempts to frame more philosophical definitions of law, but few have been widely accepted. Even more numerous have been definitions that are more pragmatic. These have all generally signified

The good of the people shall be the highest law.

— Cicero

Law is the crystallized prejudices of the community.

— GOLDFINGER

A misdemeanor is an infraction of the law having less dignity than a felony and constituting no claim to admittance into the best criminal society.

— AMBROSE BIERCE, THE DEVIL'S DICTIONARY, 1911

Common law originated in the customs of the people.

Selected Capital Offenses from the *Original Criminal Code of 1676*

If any person within this Government shall deny the true God and His attributes, he shall be put to death.

If any person shall commit any wilful and premeditated murder he shall be put to death.

If any person slayeth another with a sword or dagger who hath no weapon to defend himself, he shall be put to death.

If any man bear false witness maliciously and on purpose to take away a man's life, he shall be put to death.

If any child or children, above sixteen years of age, and of sufficient understanding, shall smite their natural father or mother, unless thereunto provoked and forced for their self-protection from death or maiming, at the complaint of said father and mother, and not otherwise, there being sufficient witness thereof, that child or those children so offending shall be put to death.

that law is a body of rules of human conduct that the courts recognize and enforce.

The origins of law are buried in antiquity, for they likely date before the beginning of recorded history. It would be safe to assume, however, that even the crudest forms of primitive social organization needed some regulation, and law quickly evolved to fill that need.

Since the beginnings of civilization a number of distinct legal systems have emerged, including the Egyptian, Mesopotamian, Chinese, Hindu, Hebrew, Greek, Roman, Celtic, Germanic, Catholic church (canon), Japanese, Islamic, Slavic, Romanesque, and Anglican.[41] The earliest of these was the Egyptian, dating to perhaps 4000 B.C., followed by the Mesopotamian in 3500 B.C., and the Chinese in 3000 B.C. United States law is comparatively recent; it draws from Greek, Roman, and Catholic church law, but has its major roots in the Anglican or English common law. Other sources of U.S. law include the state and federal constitutions, statutory law, and the regulations of administrative agencies.

Common Law

The history of common law can be traced to eleventh-century England, when the existing collection of rules, customs, and traditions were declared the law of the land by King Edward the Confessor. Much of it was unwritten, "preserved mainly in the breasts and closets of the clergy, who, as a rule, were the only persons educated in the law; in the knowledge and recollection of the thanes [barons] and the land owners whose lands and whose persons were governed by it; and in the traditions handed down from fathers to sons." [42] During the years after the Norman Conquest in 1066 when William the Conqueror seized the English throne, he found a system of law that was not based on statute, but on the customs of the people as reflected in the decisions of judges:

> Common law was judge-made law — molded, refined, examined, and changed in the crucible of actual decision, and handed down from generation to generation in the form of reported cases. In theory, the judges drew their decisions from existing principles of law; ultimately these principles reflected the living values, attitudes, and ethical ideas of the English people. In practice, the judges relied on their own past actions, which they modified under the pressure of changing times and changing patterns of litigation.[43]

As time passed, a process emerged whereby this largely unwritten customary law of the land was translated into specific rules. As judges reached their decisions in judicial proceedings, a body of maxims and principles developed that was derived, in theory, from customs. The result was a set of legal rules in the form of judicial decisions, rather than legislative statutes, that provided precedents for the resolution of future disputes. It is this body of decisions that became what is referred to as common law. Thus, common law was case law as opposed to law created by statute. Much of common law, furthermore, reflected natural law ideas of right and wrong, as well as direct statements from the Holy Scriptures.

The early criminal laws of the American colonies developed within the tradition and structure of English common law and the English charters for the founding of settlements in the New World. As the colonies became more mature, they developed their own legal systems, but in substance these varied little from English common law. The *Original Criminal Code of 1676,* for example, handed down by the Duke of York and applied to the residents of the Pennsylvania colony, was among the early bodies of law in the New World. Much of it was based on common law, combined with a series of rules structured for maintaining British dominance over colonial interests. The influence of biblical proscriptions was also apparent in this code, with many capitol offenses drawn virtually from the Ten Commandments.[44]

Other Sources of Criminal Law: Constitutional Law, Statutory Law, and Administrative Law

Although English common law rests at the foundation of American criminal law, contemporary criminal codes also reflect the content of constitutional law, administrative law, and federal and state statutory laws. At the apex of American legal system is **constitutional law,** or law set forth in the Constitution of the United States and in the constitutions of the various states. Constitutional law is the supreme law of the land. As such, it presents the legal rules and principles that define the nature and limits of governmental power as well as the rights and duties of individuals in relation to the state and its governing organs, and that are interpreted and extended by courts exercising the power of judicial review.

Constitutional law: The legal rules and principles that define the nature and limits of governmental power, and the duties and rights of individuals in relation to the state.

The U.S. Constitution, which embodies the fundamental principles upon which the affairs of the United States are conducted, was drawn up at the Federal Constitutional Convention in Philadelphia in 1787. The Constitution was signed on September 17, 1787, was ratified by nine states by June 21, 1788, and superseded the Articles of Confederation — the original charter of the United States — which had been in force since 1781. It is brief and concise, and includes a preamble, seven articles, and twenty-six amendments. Although not all of the Constitution relates to criminal law, Supreme Court and lower court interpretations of its articles and amendments have had a direct impact on criminal law and criminal procedure, as will be seen throughout this text.

Next in order of authority to constitutional law are the federal statutes, enacted by Congress, and state statutes, ordained by state legislatures. Federal statutes must conform to the prescriptions and proscriptions of the Constitution, and state statutes must conform to the Constitution as well as to that of the jurisdiction in which they are enacted.

Federal statutes

With fifty separate state legislatures creating laws, and an even greater number of separate court systems interpreting them, the application of statutory laws becomes exceedingly complex. Furthermore, statutory laws are far from uniform. For this reason criminal laws established by statute tend to vary from one jurisdiction to another, and what may be a violation of the criminal law in one state may not necessarily be so in another.

Finally, criminal law can descend from **administrative law,** a branch of public law that deals with the powers and duties of government agencies. More specifically, administrative law refers to the rules and regulations of administrative agencies; the thousands of decisions made by them; their orders, directives, and awards; and the court opinions dealing with appeals from the decisions and with petitions by the agencies to the courts for the enforcement of their orders and directives.

Administrative law: A branch of public law that deals with the powers and duties of government agencies.

Much of the content of administrative law is not concerned directly with criminal behavior. Nevertheless, the rules of certain agencies bear directly on violations of behavior that would be dealt with by the criminal courts. The scheduling of drugs by the Drug Enforcement Administration, for example, is an administrative regulation that has been translated into criminal statutes in the federal as well as many state jurisdictions.

SUMMARY

The concept of crime is only minimally understood by most people. It goes well beyond the rather imprecise boundaries of "street crime" or the limited issues of violence and theft that are focused upon by mass-media news and entertainment. Drawing upon standards of what constitutes "sin" or immoral behavior, people have often defined crime as violations of natural law. Many social scientists have focused on the processes through which crime comes into being and have suggested that crime is a social construction. The only precise definition of crime, however, comes from a more legalistic posture. As such, crime is an intentional act or omission in violation of criminal law (statutory and case law), committed without defense or justification, and sanctioned by the state as a felony or misdemeanor.

KEY TERMS

administrative law **(63)**
case law **(52)**
civil law **(52)**
common law **(52)**
conspiracy **(49)**
constitutional law **(63)**
crime **(48)**
criminal law **(51)**

defense **(53)**
deviance **(43)**
Durham Rule **(53)**
entrapment **(56)**
felony **(61)**
Lambert v. *California* **(55)**
mens rea **(49)**
misdemeanor **(61)**

misprision of felony **(49)**
M'Naghten Rule **(53)**
natural law **(43)**
Robinson v. *California* **(52)**
statutory law **(52)**
vicarious liability **(51)**

QUESTIONS FOR DISCUSSION

1. How do natural law conceptions of "sin," sociological considerations of deviance, and legalistic definitions of crime differ?
2. In the Leopold and Loeb case, when did the conspiracy actually begin? What elements were present?
3. Under what kinds of circumstances would the consent of the victim be an acceptable defense against crime? What are some examples?
4. What should be done about the insanity plea? Why?

FOR FURTHER READING

Allen, William, *Starkweather: The Story of a Mass Murderer.* Boston: Houghton Mifflin, 1976.
Erikson, Kai T. *Wayward Puritans: A Study in the Sociology of Deviance.* New York: Wiley, 1966.
Friedman, Lawrence M. *A History of American Law.* New York: Simon and Schuster, 1973.
Morris, Norval. *Madness and the Criminal Law.* Chicago: University of Chicago Press, 1982.

NOTES

1. See James M. Reinhardt, *The Murderous Trail of Charles Starkweather* (Springfield, Ill.: Charles C. Thomas, 1960); William Allen, *Starkweather: The Story of a Mass Murderer* (Boston: Houghton Mifflin, 1976).

2. See Hugh F. Rankin, *The Golden Age of Piracy* (New York: Holt, Rinehart and Winston, 1969).

3. See G. O. W. Mueller and Freda Adler, *Outlaws of the Ocean* (New York: Hearst Marine Books, 1985).

4. *Time,* September 7, 1987, p. 62; *USA Today,* April 23, 1985, p. 3A; *Christian Science Monitor,* September 8, 1986, p. 3; *New York Times,* July 26, 1987, pp. 1, 16; *Newsweek,* October 6, 1980, p. 16.

5. Kai T. Erikson, *Wayward Puritans: A Study in the Sociology of Deviance* (New York: Wiley, 1966), p. 6.

6. Howard S. Becker, *Outsiders: Studies in the Sociology of Deviance* (New York: Free Press, 1963), p. 9.

7. Becker, *Outsiders,* pp. 147–163.

8. See J. C. Furnas, *The Life and Times of the Late Demon Rum* (New York: Capricorn, 1973).

9. Jerome Michael and Mortimer J. Adler, *Crime, Law and Social Science* (New York: Harcourt, Brace, 1933), p. 2.

10. Edwin H. Sutherland, *White Collar Crime* (New York: Dryden, 1949), p. 31.

11. Henry Campbell Black, *Black's Law Dictionary,* 4th ed. (St. Paul, Minn.: West, 1968), p. 444.

12. George B. Rush, *Dictionary of Criminal Justice* (Boston: Holbrook, 1977), p. 92.

13. Paul W. Tappan, *Crime, Justice, and Correction* (New York: McGraw-Hill, 1960), p. 10.

14. "Case of 44 Mid-Air Murders," *Life,* November 28, 1955.

15. For the story of the Leopold and Loeb case, see Nathan F. Leopold, *Life Plus Ninety-Nine Years* (New York: Doubleday, 1958).

16. *People* v. *Beardsley,* 113 N. W. 1128 (1907).

17. *Walker* v. *Superior Court* (1988) 44 CrL 2193.

18. *United States* v. *Perlstein,* C.C.A.N.J., 126 F. 2d 789, 798.

19. *United States* v. *Dotterweich,* 320 U.S. 277 (1943).

20. *Commonwealth* v. *Koczwara,* 155 A. 2d 825 (1959, Penna.).

21. *Robinson* v. *California,* 370 U.S. 660 (1962).

22. Black, *Black's Law Dictionary,* p. 1101.

23. *Durham* v. *United States,* C.A.D.C., 214 F. 2d 862 (1954).

24. *National Law Journal,* May 3, 1982, pp. 1, 11–13.

25. Valerie P. Hans and Dan Slater. "John Hinckley, Jr., and the Insanity Defense: The Public's Verdict," *Public Opinion Quarterly* 47 (1983), pp. 202–212.

26. Lincoln Caplan, *The Insanity Defense and the Trial of John W. Hinckley, Jr.* (Boston: David R. Godine, 1984).

27. *Jones* v. *U.S.,* 33 Cr.L. 3233 (1983).

28. *State* v. *Elton,* Utah SupCt (35 CrL 2071).

29. *People* v. *Cash,* Mich SupCt (35 CrL 2345).

30. *Lambert* v. *California,* 355 U.S. 225 (1957).

31. *Hampton* v. *United States,* 425 U.S. 484 (1976).

32. *New York Times,* December 9, 1984, p. 78.

33. *People* v. *Lovercamp,* 118 Cal Rptr 110 (1975).

34. *Jorgensen* v. *State,* Nev SupCt (1984) 36 CrL 2093.

35. Allen D. Spiegel, "Temporary Insanity and Premenstrual Syndrome: Medical Testimony in an 1865 Murder Trial," *New York State Journal of Medicine,* 88 (September 1988), pp. 482–492.

36. *National Law Journal,* February 16, 1987, pp. 3, 32.

37. *National Law Journal,* May 1, 1989, p. 9.

38. State of New York, *Penal Law,* 10.00 (3).

39. Sir Frederick Pollack and F. W. Maitland, *The History of English Law Before the Time of Edward I* (Cambridge: University Press, 1911), p. xxv.

40. Sir James Fitzjames Stephen, *History of the Criminal Law of England,* vol. 2 (New York: Macmillan, 1883), p. 75.

41. John H. Wigmore, *A Panorama of the World's Legal Systems* (Washington, D.C.: Washington Law Book Co., 1936), p. 4.

42. F. A. Inderwick, *The King's Peace* (London: Swan Sonnenschein, 1895), p. 3.

43. Lawrence M. Friedman, *A History of American Law* (New York: Simon and Schuster, 1973), p. 17.

44. Harry Elmer Barnes, *The Repression of Crime: Studies in Historical Penology* (New York: George H. Doran, 1926), pp. 44–45.

CHAPTER

3

Legal and Behavioral Aspects of Crime

Crime, like virtue, has its degrees.
—Jean Racine

A kleptomaniac is a person who helps himself because he can't help himself.
—Anonymous

Crime in every possible form, like business, has progressed to the stage where the little unorganized participant hasn't much chance of success.
—Emanuel H. Lavine

A thief believes that everybody steals.
—E. W. Howe

A burglar who respects his art always takes his time before taking anything else.
—O. Henry

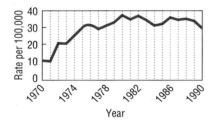

Pickpocketing in the U.S.   1970–1990
SOURCE: UCR

When Thomas Bartholomew Moran died in 1971 at the Miami Rescue Mission, he was a vagrant, a derelict, and his pockets were empty—a rather ironic ending to a life spent emptying the pockets of others. Yet, in spite of the dismal circumstances of his death, Moran had been a celebrated criminal whom many considered to be the dean of American pickpockets. His career in crime had been a lengthy one. It began in 1906 when, as a youth of only fourteen years, he would pass through the crowded streets and stores of downtown Kansas City, opening women's purses and removing small change. The practice was called "moll-buzzing," and was looked down upon by the more accomplished thieves of his day since women were considered easy "marks" (victims) and the targets of only rank amateurs. By age seventeen, Moran had graduated to the more complex problems of stealing from men. Under the tutelage of Mary Kelly, a well-known pickpocket in both the United States and Great Britain during the latter part of the nineteenth century, he polished his approaches to the point where he could remove a diamond pin from a garment, a watch from a vest, and a wallet from a suit coat or pants pocket, all without his victim's knowing that a theft was taking place.[1] Moran quickly achieved the rank of "class cannon," a designation that typified him as a thief with the skill and daring to devote a lifetime to stealing from the pockets of live victims. Moran was also an accomplished shoplifter and forger, although picking pockets was always his prime vocation. He worked the streets and stores of almost every major city in the United States; he followed the circuses and carnivals that traveled across America, lured by the thousands of "rubes" (farmers and hicks) who crowded the midways in search of thrills and excitement; and he visited the resort towns, preying on the wealthy who were careless as they leisured in the sun and at the race tracks. And early in his career, Moran had even been aboard the *Titanic* when it left on its ill-fated maiden voyage. Traveling in steerage under an assumed name, his purpose was to benefit handsomely from the more than 300 first-class passengers whose collective wealth exceeded $250 million. His immediate ambitions were dimmed, however, when the *Titanic* brushed an iceberg in the north Atlantic at 11:40 P.M. on April 15, 1912, sinking only two hours and forty minutes later. But Moran was among the 705 survivors who managed to find space in one of the ship's twenty lifeboats, and his career in crime continued to flourish for the better part of the fifty-nine remaining years of his life.[2]

Contrast Moran with John Janus Powell, also a pickpocket, shoplifter, and forger. As opposed to Moran, who distinguished himself in the professional underworld, Powell was a product of the American ghetto and a self-styled street hustler. He was born in 1948 in the Brownsville section of Brooklyn and by age sixteen he was stealing regularly to support his daily heroin habit. His exploits were less colorful than those of Moran, for they were limited to the forgery of stolen welfare checks, picking pockets in supermarkets, and shoplifting in department stores and specialty shops — all in his local neighborhood. Powell had few skills, for the pressures of drug addiction never afforded him the luxuries of time and patience to develop his techniques as a thief. And unlike Moran, Powell's career was a short one, ending in a heroin overdose on a Brooklyn side street in late 1967.[3]

These brief episodes from the lives of Moran and Powell have been mentioned here not because they are interesting anecdotes from the annals of crime, but because they illustrate some of the complex issues surrounding the nature and meaning of crime. Although crime may be conduct that is prohibited by criminal law, its dynamics go well beyond the sterile descriptions of classifications, provisions, and subsections that appear in state and federal criminal codes. Crime includes patterns and systems of behavior that occur at one or several points in time. It can involve varying sets of circumstances and victim–offender relationships. And too, crime can be an isolated event that occurs at only one point in the offender's lifetime; it can reflect the best-developed aspects of a well-established career in illicit enterprise; or it can be the product of an organization structured for the pursuit of illegal behavior. In any study of crime it is important to understand not only the content of criminal codes, but the behavior systems that surround the prohibited acts as well — for all of these factors influence the images of crime, the societal reactions to crime, and the criminal justice management of crime. Moran and Powell were both pickpockets, shoplifters, and forgers; both committed the same crimes for economic gain. But beyond this, the two were quite dissimilar. Moran was what a select corner of the underworld would call a "professional thief"; he was a member of a small and exclusive fraternity of criminals. Crime was Moran's chosen career, and he approached it as a full-time profession. There was a certain mystique about his predatory behavior; he was romanticized by many and admired by most. Although Moran was arrested often, he was liked even by many of the police officers who pursued him. Furthermore, he was rarely convicted for his crimes. In contrast, Powell's criminal acts were haphazard and unplanned, although frequent. He was an inept street hustler for whom crime was the only available means to a specific and immediate end. He was liked by few; even his family, from whom he often stole, avoided him. To the agents of the criminal justice system Powell was just another junkie who was responsible for raising central-city crime rates and keeping court calendars crowded. During his limited criminal career of only five years, Powell spent most of his time in jails, reformatories, and prisons.

Studies of behavior systems in crime are generally the subject matter of courses in criminology, and are only rarely discussed in basic texts on criminal justice. Yet such designations as "professional theft," "organized crime," and "white-collar crime" reflect criminal acts that are undertaken within the context of specific behavior systems. As such, this chapter first discusses the legal aspects of various crimes as they are described in criminal codes, and then briefly analyzes the behavior systems within which they most often occur.

Thomas B. Moran was a world-class pickpocket. He is shown here in the Dade County (Miami), Florida, stockade after his sixty-ninth arrest for picking pockets.

LEGAL ASPECTS OF CRIME CATEGORIES

As noted in Chapter 2, there are literally thousands of acts that are prohibited by law and that are designated as felonies, misdemeanors, and infractions in federal, state, and local criminal codes. There is also the area of administrative law, which sets forth an alternative list of criminal violations. All these laws result in a potential catalog of behaviors defined as crime that is so long that even their numbers would be difficult to count. Of course, due to space limitations only a few categories of crime can be discussed here, and those chosen for study are the ones that appear most often in our local criminal courts and the ones that receive the most attention from state-level criminal justice agencies. The crime categories to be covered here include the following:

- Criminal homicide
- Assault (except sexual assault)
- Robbery
- Arson
- Burglary
- Other property offenses
- Sex offenses
- Drug law violations
- Crimes against public order and safety

This list, although brief, encompasses more than 90 percent of the criminal law violations handled by state and local criminal justice agencies. This is not to say that other crimes are not serious or important, of course. Treason, for example, the only crime specifically mentioned in the Constitution of the United States, is clearly an act that can threaten the society as a whole. Yet treason is relatively infrequent, and only rarely does it come to the attention of a local criminal justice system. Kidnapping is another offense that is well feared by the community, yet it too occurs infrequently.

Treason is the only crime specifically mentioned in the Constitution of the United States.

Criminal Homicide

Homicide: The killing of one human being by another.

Homicide is the killing of one human being by another. If it is not excusable or justifiable (see Chapter 2), it is called criminal homicide. Criminal homicide is usually divided by statute into murder and manslaughter, each of which is typically subdivided into many degrees.

Murder: The felonious killing of another human being with malice aforethought.

Murder Under common law, **murder** was defined as the felonious killing of another human being with malice aforethought. That last phrase implies a definite malicious intent to kill. Common law did not differentiate between murder in the first or second degree, however, and difficulties in proving cases often emerged due to varying interpretations of *malice, aforethought,* and the two terms taken together as a phrase. In modern criminal codes the law is more specific, and the concepts of malice aforethought, deliberation, and premeditation are all crucially different.

Also, today, murder is generally divided into two degrees: first and second. In most jurisdictions, *first-degree murder* includes the notions of malice aforethought, deliberation, and premeditation. **Malice aforethought** refers to the intent to cause death or serious harm, or to commit

Malice aforethought: The intent to cause death or serious harm, or to commit any felony whatsoever.

any felony whatsoever. **Deliberation** refers to a full and conscious knowledge of the purpose to kill, suggesting that the offender has considered the motives for the act and its consequences. **Premeditation** refers to a design or plan to do something before it is actually done; it is a conscious predecision to commit the offense even though such a decision may occur only moments before the final act.

There are many instances of murder in the first degree every year, but a good illustration involving malice aforethought, deliberation, and premeditation was the infamous "trick-or-treat" murder of 1974 in Pasadena, Texas. The victim was 8-year-old Tim O'Bryan, one of four children who had been given tubes of candy on Halloween night that had been laced with enough potassium cyanide to kill a dozen adults. Tim was the only youngster to eat the candy, and shortly after returning to his home he fell into convulsions, lapsed into a coma, and died. Upon investigation, it was proven that the murderer was the boy's father, Ronald O'Bryan. The senior O'Bryan was somewhat of an incompetent who had lost twenty-one jobs in ten years and was deeply in debt. Without his wife's knowledge, he carried $31,000 insurance policies on each of his young children, both of whom he had intended to kill. His planning was elaborate, although not particularly clever. He had made inquiries in his local area as to the shops that carried cyanide, and he had even questioned a neighbor as to how much of the chemical would be needed to kill a person. On the evening of the murder, O'Bryan gave the poisoned Halloween candy not only to his two children, but to others as well in order to divert suspicion. His intent to kill his children for the insurance money resulted in a conviction of murder in the first degree and three counts of attempted murder.[4] (See Exhibit 3.7 for more on O'Bryan.)

In a number of jurisdictions, statutes also designate murder to be in the first degree depending on the specific circumstances involved. In twenty-two states, for example, murder by poisoning automatically carries a first-degree charge, and in some areas the "murder-one" charge is also mandatory if the homicide involved torture, ambush, the use of destructive devices, the killing of a law enforcement officer, or a murder for hire.[5]

Deliberation: The full and conscious knowledge of the purpose to kill.

Premeditation: A design or conscious decision to do something before it is actually done.

All creatures kill — there seems to be no exception. But of the whole list man is the only one that kills for fun; he is the only one that kills in malice; the only one that kills for revenge.
— MARK TWAIN

Homicide *is the slaying of one human being by another. There are four kinds of homicide: felonious, excusable, justifiable, and praiseworthy, but it makes no great difference to the person slain whether he fell by one kind or another — the classification is for the advantage of the lawyers.*
— AMBROSE BIERCE, *THE DEVIL'S DICTIONARY,* 1911

Murder in the second degree

Murder in the second degree refers to instances of criminal homicide committed with malice aforethought but without deliberation and premeditation. Murders of this type are often the impulse killings that occur among members of a family, or lovers, often as the outgrowth of an argument or difference of opinion. It is that spur-of-the-moment episode that occurs without planning or full consideration.

Currently, thirty-three states and the District of Columbia divide murder into at least two degrees. Three states, however — Florida, Minnesota, and Wisconsin — have more than two degrees of murder, the aim being to limit the use of the death penalty without reducing the seriousness of the crime. In many convictions for murder in the third degree, the case involved the felony-murder doctrine, discussed next.

Felony-murder doctrine: if a death occurs during the commission of a felony, the person comitting the primary offense can also be charged with murder in the first degree.

The Felony-Murder Doctrine The common law conception of the felony-murder doctrine maintained that any death resulting from the commission of, or attempt to commit, the crimes of arson, burglary, larceny, rape, or robbery was murder. In many contemporary legal statutes, the **felony-murder doctrine** provides that if a death occurs during the commission of a felony, the person committing the primary offense can also be charged with murder in the first degree.[6] Thus, should an individual commit the felonious crime of arson by setting fire to his place of business, and should one of his employees be killed in that fire, the arsonist would be charged with first-degree murder.

Murder in the first degree includes murder which is willful, deliberate or premeditated, or which is committed in the perpetration, or attempt to perpetrate robbery.
— ARIZONA REVISED STATUTES

A great deal of confusion surrounds this doctrine. First, the statute is unusual in that although under the law first-degree murder requires malice aforethought, deliberation, and premeditation, with the felony-murder rule these three essential elements are treated as being implied. The offender is seen to act in a deliberate manner and is thus responsible for any natural and probable consequences. A second difficult issue in the doctrine is whether the felon must be the agent of the killing. Thus, if a case of arson results in the death of a fireman who is fighting the fire, can the arsonist be charged with first-degree murder under the felony-murder doctrine? Exhibit 3.1 summarizes two cases in which the felony-murder doctrine was accepted by the courts.

Manslaughter: The unlawful killing of another, without malice.

Manslaughter Manslaughter is an alternative category of criminal homicide, typically charged when a killing occurs under circumstances not severe enough to constitute murder but nevertheless beyond the defenses of justifiable or excusable homicide. **Manslaughter** is distinguished from murder in that the latter implies malice while manslaughter does not. Furthermore, some jurisdictions divide manslaughter into as many as four degrees, although most differentiate only between voluntary and involuntary manslaughter.

Voluntary manslaughter refers to intentional killings in the absence of malice and premeditated design, whereas *involuntary* manslaughter exists when a death results unintentionally as the consequence of some unlawful act or through negligence.

Voluntary manslaughter refers to intentional killings committed in the absence of malice and premeditated design. Its essential elements include a legally adequate provocation resulting in a killing done during the heat of passion. Thus, if two persons become involved in a quarrel and one kills the other, the offender can be charged with voluntary manslaughter. In contrast, *involuntary manslaughter* exists when a death results unintentionally as the consequence of some unlawful act or through negligence. For example, if a motorist is driving while seriously under the influence of alcohol and loses control of the vehicle, killing a pedestrian, involuntary manslaughter could be charged. In this case, the killing would be unintentional, yet the motorist's intoxicated condition while driving is a violation of the law. (In some jurisdictions, the charge might be vehicular homicide or driving while intoxicated.)

EXHIBIT 3.1

Applying the Felony-Murder Doctrine

On the basis of recent trial and appellate court interpretations of the felony-murder doctrine, it appears that the blanket rule has wide acceptance.

In the California case of *Carlos* v. *Superior Court,* for example, the defendant and Manuel Perez, both armed, robbed a Safeway supermarket. As they left the store they were confronted by an off-duty deputy sheriff who had been walking to the market with his three-year-old daughter. Carlos immediately fled, but a gun battle then occurred between the deputy and Perez. Caught in the crossfire, the child suffered fatal head wounds. Although Carlos had left the scene before the shooting started, he was nevertheless convicted of murder. In the Florida case of *State* v. *Amaro,* three participants in an illegal drug transaction were arrested and taken into custody. Moments later, a fourth participant entered upon the scene and fired upon the arresting officer, killing him. All four participants were convicted under the felony-murder doctrine.

Felony-murder has been accepted by the courts on the grounds that a killing is a foreseeable, predictable result of the commission of a felony. This was the rationale in both *Carlos* and *Amaro.* The courts have had difficulty and mixed opinions, however, in the application of the death sentence to defendants convicted under felony-murder statutes.

SOURCES: *Carlos* v. *Superior Court,* Calif SupCt (34 CrL 2289); *State* v. *Amaro,* Fla CtApp (34 CrL 2016).

It has long been a well-stated principle that the commission of unlawful sexual intercourse with a female relative is an act obviously calculated to arouse ungovernable passion, and that the killing of the seducer or adulterer under the influence or in the heat of that passion constitutes voluntary manslaughter, and not murder.

—FROM THE OPINION IN *State* v. *Thornton,* Tennessee Supreme Court, 41 CrL 2162 (1987), in which the defendant appealed his first-degree murder conviction in the slaying of his wife's lover after discovering them *inflagrante delicto* (engaged in sexual intercourse).

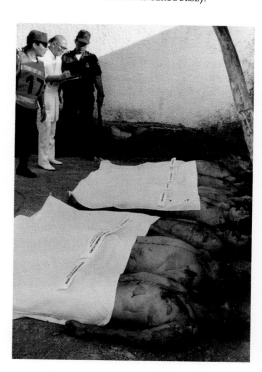

The bodies of several members of the Medellin cartel killed by the Colombian military

---

A 1985 case in Conroe, Texas, demonstrates how broadly the involuntary manslaughter statutes can be interpreted. A nineteen-year-old customer in a local saloon lapsed into a coma and later died after consuming beer and two 15-ounce "kamikaze" drinks made with 190-proof liquor. His blood alcohol content was 0.485 percent — more than four times the legal definition of intoxication. The two bartenders who prepared and served the drinks were charged with negligent homicide.[7] Similarly, in 1989 a DeKalb County, Georgia man was convicted of involuntary manslaughter and sentenced to five years in prison after three of his pit bull terriers killed a four-year-old boy.[8] His prosecution was based on the *doctrine of implied malice,* in which a person can be convicted of criminal homicide if "wanton disregard for human life" can be proved. In Florida, furthermore, manslaughter statutes include a *vessel homicide* law aimed at unsafe boat operators — a legislative reaction to the state's more than 100 boating fatalities each year.[9]

As a final note, since voluntary manslaughter can refer to deaths resulting from unlawful acts, it must be differentiated from the felony-murder doctrine. In jurisdictions where all homicides occurring during the commission of a felony are classified as murder, then involuntary manslaughter can apply only to misdemeanor cases. Also, in many cases the differences that separate second-degree murder from voluntary man-

Implied malice

Vessel homicide

slaughter are not always immediately clear. Both offenses, for example, can relate to crimes of passion, and what differentiates one from another is often a reflection of the degree of passion involved, the court's interpretation of the circumstances of the killing, and the particular legal codes that define the boundaries of the two offenses in a given jurisdiction.

Assault

Assault: An intentional attempt or threat to physically injure another.

Assault and battery: An assault carried into effect by doing some violence to the victim.

Contrary to popular notions, **assault** does not refer to the infliction of an injury on another person. Rather, in legal terms, it is simply an intentional attempt or threat to physically injure another. *Battery* is the nonlethal culmination of an assault. Thus, **assault and battery** is an assault carried into effect by doing some violence to the victim. Aggravated assault refers to an assault made with the intent to commit murder, rape, robbery, or to inflict serious bodily harm; simple assault is one in which the intended harm fails or where no serious harm was ever intended.

Although aggravated assaults are usually felonies and simple assaults are misdemeanors, many jurisdictions separate the two according to degree of assault rather than name. Furthermore, some states have defined specific kinds of assault as distinct offenses. For example, while assault in the third degree can generally be construed as simple assault and a misdemeanor, other categories of nonfelonious assault might include *menacing* (touching a person with an instrument or part of the body causing offense or alarm to that person).[10] Similarly, although *mayhem* can be considered as a serious and aggravated assault, in some states, such as California, it is classified as a separate felony:

Menacing

Mayhem

> Every person who unlawfully and maliciously deprives a human being of a member of his body, or disables, disfigures, or renders it useless, or cuts or disables the tongue, or puts out an eye, or slits the nose, ear, or lip, is guilty of mayhem.[11]

Jostling

Perhaps the most peculiar of the categories of assault are to be found in the jostling statutes. *Jostling* refers to the pushing or crowding of an individual, and it is generally believed that pickpockets jostle their victims (bump into and throw them off balance) while stealing their money. In New York the jostling statute enables police officers to arrest pickpockets even though they are not caught stealing.[12] In fact, this statute is so widely used in some areas that many career pickpockets have numerous arrests for jostling and few for actually stealing. It might be added, however, that expert pickpockets rarely jostle their victims. As one "class cannon" commented on the subject:

> No, you never throw them the jostle. . . . All that does is wake up the mark and tell him that something's happening. . . . If a cop knows you and thinks you're going to score, he'll grab you and call it jostling, even though you did nothing.[13]

Robbery

Robbery: The felonious taking of the money or goods of another, from his person or in his presence and against his will, through the use or threat of force and violence.

Robbery is the felonious taking of the money or goods of another, from his person or in his presence and against his will, through the use or threat of force and violence. As such, robbery is an offense involving aspects of both theft and assault, and since the use or threat of violence is present, it is generally classified as a crime against the person. The specific elements necessary for a robbery to take place are clear in its definition: (1) the felonious taking (with the intent to steal) (2) of the money or goods of another (3) from his person or in his presence (or in his custody, care, or control) (4) against his will (5) through the use or threat of force and violence. If one or more of these elements were missing there would be no robbery, but rather, some other crime or no crime at all. If the use or threat of force were absent, for example, the crime would be one of theft.

The two elements of robbery that have received the most discussion in the courts have centered around the issues of "felonious taking" and "from his person or in his presence." The notion of felonious taking suggests an intent to steal. But what of instances in which a person might use or threaten force to recover what he believes to be his or her own property? Would there be the crime of robbery? In one California case, the defendant had used force to recover money that he had lost in an illegal gambling game. The court ruled that intent to steal was lacking in the case, and offered the following comment:

> It is the law in this state that certain games of chance . . . are illegal; that the winner gains no title to the property at stake nor any right to possession thereof; and that the participants have no standing in a court of law or equity. In jurisdictions where such is the state of the law the weight of authority appears to favor the view that the recaption by force or fear of money lost at illegal games is not robbery although the act may be punishable as an unlawful assault or trespass.
>
> The courts recognize that in such a case, whatever other element of crime may be present, there cannot exist an intent to steal or take feloniously the property of another, which is an essential element of the crime of robbery.[14]

On the second issue, "from his person" means the victim's body or clothing that he or she is wearing, and "in his presence" refers to within the sight or hearing of the victim. The courts have agreed, however, that the meaning of the term "presence" can vary from one case to the next, suggesting that the victim's presence need be only proximate rather than immediate. In another California case, two men asked a hotel clerk to show them a room. After entering the room, the men seized the clerk, gagged and bound him to one of the bedposts, and returned to the hotel desk, where they removed the contents of the cash register. The men were later apprehended and convicted of robbery, but they appealed the case on the grounds that the money had been taken neither from the clerk's person nor even in his presence, since he was in another part of the building when the property was taken. The appellate court affirmed the trial court's decision, however, suggesting that proximity and consciousness may create a presence, and furthermore:

> At least as early as the time when the clerk was induced to leave the hotel office for the purpose of "showing" the room to defendant and his companion the crime of robbery was commenced; it was an overt act connected with the commission of the offense, at which time the clerk was "immediately" present. The trick or device by which the physical presence of the clerk was detached from the property under his protection and control should not avail defendant in his claim that the property was not taken from the "immediate presence" of the victim.[15]

Finally, some jurisdictions divide robbery into degrees. Robbery in the first degree is charged when the offender is armed with a deadly weapon or dangerous instrument. Others have specific statutes that recognize unarmed robbery, armed robbery, train robbery, and safe and vault robbery.

"At least it doesn't appear to be a case of senseless violence."

Robbery involves both theft and assault and is a crime against the person.

Robbery by Reptile

It was no dream. Antonio Zavala, abruptly awakened in his Chicago apartment, was really seeing the head of a boa constrictor pointed menacingly toward his face. The rest of the snake, all 6 ft. of it, was being held by a teen-age acquaintance of Zavala's who hissed, "Give me your money." Zavala prudently handed over $6. The intruder, wreathed in the coils of his accomplice, fled.

The police were intrigued by the thief's modus operandi. Said Sergeant Arthur Nielsen: "This is only the second armed animal robbery case I've seen in 21 years. We once caught a guy who was using a big German shepherd to scare money out of his victims." The snake, which police found sleeping under a nearby porch, was turned over to the Lincoln Park Zoo. The snake was thus freed, after a fashion; only its master must still face the scales of justice.

—Time, August 11, 1980, p. 23.

Arson

Arson: The willful or malicious burning or attempt to burn, with or without intent to defraud, any dwelling, other building, vehicle, or personal property.

Common law conceptions of **arson** referred to the malicious burning of the dwelling of another, but modern statutes have extended the parameters of arson in a variety of ways. First, while arson originally carried the ideas of fire and burning, most jurisdictions now include the use of explosives. Second, contemporary statutes include not only dwellings, but also other types of buildings, as well as the property of the arsonist if there is an attempt to defraud an insurer or if the building is occupied. Thus, a person is guilty of arson when he or she intentionally damages a building by starting a fire or causing an explosion.[16]

Arson is a felony in all jurisdictions, and most often is divided into at least two degrees and sometimes three. In general, if the premises set afire are occupied, the charge will be first-degree arson. If they are unoccupied, the case will be one of second-degree arson. A person is guilty of arson in the third degree if the premises burned are his or her own, if they are unoccupied, and if the purpose is to defraud the insurer.

The professional arsonist builds vacant lots for money.
— Jimmy Breslin

From a legalistic perspective, the major problem in arson cases is the element of criminal agency, or *intent*. A conviction depends on the state's proving that an accused had both the intent and opportunity to commit arson, which is difficult in many cases. Studies have shown that the reasons for arson are both numerous and obscure, and sometimes hard to detect. There are "revenge firesetters," for example, whose crimes result from anger, hatred, or jealousy in personal relationships; there are "excitement firesetters," who simply enjoy watching fires and the operations of fire equipment; there are "insurance-claim firesetters," who incinerate business property for its insurance value; there are "vandalism firesetters," who set buildings ablaze as part of adolescent peer-group activities; there are "criminal vindication firesetters," who use arson for hiding the evidence of other crimes.[17] To these might be added the "professional torches," who incinerate buildings for a fee, the "firebombers" of activist and political liberation organizations, the large number of skid row vagrants who seem to be overrepresented among those arrested for arson, and the many other types for whom intent and motivation are not altogether clear.

Burglary

Burglary

At one time, burglary was viewed as a crime against the habitation — that is, an invasion of the home — and referred only to the breaking and entering of a dwelling, at night, with the intent to commit a felony therein. The term comes directly from English common law and has its roots in the Saxon words *burgh* (a house) and *laron* (theft). The offense has been materially broadened in current statutes: it includes structures other than a dwelling; it is applicable whether the illegal entry occurs during the night or day; and it can involve an intended felony or misdemeanor.

Breaking and entering: The forcible entry into a building or structure, with the intent to commit a crime therein.

The term **breaking and entering** is often used synonymously with *burglary,* but this can be misleading since both breaking and entry need not be formally present for a burglary to occur. "Breaking" suggests forcible entry, but the mere opening of a closed door is sufficient to constitute a breaking. Furthermore, simply remaining in a building until after it has closed, for some criminal purpose, can also constitute a burglary, even though there is no actual breaking aspect. *Entry* is the more essential element; it can be limited to the insertion of any part of the body or any instrument or weapon, and still be sufficient to constitute a burglary.

Burglary is one of those offenses that appears in any number of degrees and varieties. A person is typically guilty of burglary in the third degree when he or she knowingly enters or remains unlawfully in a building with the intent to commit a crime therein. The burglary becomes an offense in the second degree if the building happens to be a dwelling, or if the offender is armed, or if there is physical injury to any person who is not a participant in the crime. Burglary in the first degree involves unlawful entry or remaining in a dwelling at night, combined with the offender being armed or causing physical injury.[18]

Since there is a criminal intent aspect to burglary, that is, unlawful entry for some criminal purpose, two additional points must be stressed. First, even if the purpose of the entry involves only a minor crime, such as petty theft or some other misdemeanor, the burglary has been consummated and a felony has been committed. Further, the offender can be charged not only with burglary, but with the other offense as well. Second, the criminal intent aspect has resulted in a number of jurisdictions structuring their laws so that attempted burglary is included in the definition of burglary.

Closely related to burglary are a number of other crimes that are generally defined in separate statutes. For example, in many jurisdictions the very possession of burglar's tools can be prosecuted as a felony:

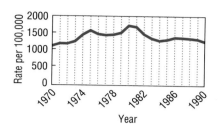

Burglary in the U.S.   1970–1990
SOURCE: UCR

"I said no to drugs, but I couldn't say no to drug money."

Possession of burglar's tools

A person is guilty of possession of burglar's tools when he possesses any tool, instrument, or other thing adapted, designed, or commonly used for committing or facilitating offenses involving unlawful entry into premises, or offenses involving forcible breaking of safes or other containers or depositories of property, under circumstances evincing an intent to use or knowledge that some other person intends to use the same in the commission of an offense of such character.[19]

Under the law, then, burglar's tools can include any number and type of devices, ranging from sophisticated lock picks and explosives to simple everyday tools such as screwdrivers and chisels.

Criminal trespass

Also related to burglary are the crimes described as *criminal trespass*. These are generally misdemeanors or violations and are differentiated from burglary when breaking with criminal intent is absent, or when the trespass involves property that has been fenced in a manner designed to exclude intruders.

Property Offenses

Attempting to approach the full range of property offenses in some systematic way is difficult, for most jurisdictions use alternative ways of defining and categorizing them. In Louisiana, for example, the technical dimensions of the theft statute are quite broad:

Theft is the misappropriation or taking of anything of value which belongs to another, either without the consent of the other to the misappropriation or taking, or by means of fraudulent conduct, practices, or representations. An intent to deprive the other permanently of whatever may be the subject of the misappropriation or taking is essential.[20]

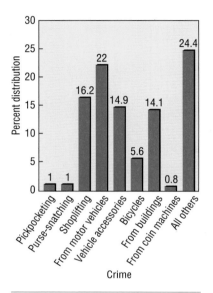

U.S. Larceny Theft in 1990
SOURCE: UCR

Thus, the Louisiana definition covers a multitude of property crimes, including what other states may separately define as larceny, embezzlement, and fraud. Further, while many states may have a broad *larceny* statute, which refers to the taking and carrying away of the personal property of another with the intent to deprive permanently, other states, such as Delaware, define shoplifting—a clear instance of larceny—as a separate offense.[21] In Ohio and several other jurisdictions, theft statutes include the unlawful use of a person's service.[22] In general, however, **theft** seems to be the broadest of terms relating to property offenses, and can be loosely defined as the unlawful taking, possession, or use of another's property, without the use or threat of force, and with the intent to deprive permanently. Within the boundaries of this definition, theft would include the following:

Theft: The unlawful taking, possession, or use of another's property, without the use or threat of force, and with the intent to deprive permanently.

Larceny   The taking and carrying away of the personal property of another with the intent to deprive permanently.

Shoplifting   The theft of goods, wares, or merchandise from a store or shop.

Pickpocketing   The theft of money or articles directly from the garments of the victim.

Embezzlement   The fraudulent appropriation or conversion of money or property by an employee, trustee, or other agent to whom the possession of such money or property was entrusted.

Fraud   Theft by false pretenses; the appropriation of money or property by trick or misrepresentation, or by creating or reinforcing a false impression as to some present or past fact that would adversely affect the victim's judgment of a transaction.

The times keep changing on what's the hot items. I suppose it's like the fashion world.

—Holyoke, Mass. Police Capt. Richard Page on how some street thieves were selling stolen Tylenol, Pampers, and baby formula (1990)

Forgery   The making or altering of any document or instrument with the intent to defraud.

Counterfeiting   The making of imitation money and obligations of the government or corporate body.

Confidence games   The obtaining of money or property by means of deception through the confidence a victim places in the offender.

Blackmail   The taking of money or property through threats of accusation or exposure.

Plagiarism   The copying or adopting of the literary, musical, or artistic work of another and publishing or producing it as one's own original work.

Removal of landmarks   The relocation of monuments or other markings that designate property lines or boundaries for the purpose of fraudulently reducing the owner's interest or holdings in lands and estates.

Criminal bankruptcy   The fraudulent declaration of a person's excessive indebtedness or insolvency in an effort to avoid partial or full payment of one's debts.

Usury   The taking of or contracting to take interest on a loan at a rate that exceeds the level established by law.

Ransom   The demanding of money for the redemption of captured persons or property.

Buying, receiving, or possessing stolen goods   The purchase, receipt, or possession of any property or goods known to be stolen.

This list may be longer or shorter depending on how an offense is interpreted in a particular jurisdiction. *Extortion,* for example, is included in the theft statutes of some states, and can be defined to include not only the taking of money or property under threat of physical injury if the property is not delivered (which may also be construed as a form of robbery), but also what has been defined as blackmail. *Theft of services* also appears as a separate offense in some areas. This refers, for example, to a situation in which a homeowner illegally taps into another's electric meter or alters the mechanism in his own meter, thus avoiding his or her due payment for electric service. Furthermore, the list is by no means

He who holds the ladder is as bad as the thief.

—German proverb

Plunder: To take the property of another without observing the decent and customary reticences of theft.

—Ambrose Bierce, *The Devil's Dictionary,* 1911

Extortion

Theft of services

Larceny: The taking and carrying away of the personal property of another, with the intent to deprive permanently.

Carrier's Case: A person in possession of another's packaged goods, who opens the package and misappropriates its contents, is guilty of larceny.

Pear's Case: A person who has legal control of another's property, and converts that property so as to deprive the owner of his possessory rights, is guilty of larceny.

Thieves respect property; they merely wish the property to become their property that they may more perfectly respect it.

—G. K. Chesterton

mutually exclusive. What has been defined as counterfeiting may appear under forgery statutes; confidence games are clearly special varieties of fraud; and shoplifting and pickpocketing are forms of larceny. The most attention is devoted here to **larceny,** since this classification includes many types of theft, and because, at least in terms of official criminal statistics, larceny is the most common of all major crimes.

Given the legal definition provided in the previous list, the crime of larceny includes five essential elements: (1) the taking (2) and carrying away (3) of the personal property (4) of another (5) with the intent to deprive permanently. The element of *taking* suggests that the offender has no legal right to possession of the property in question. In this sense, taking involves a trespass in that the possession of property has been wrongfully obtained. And this point highlights the difficult distinctions among *possession, custody,* and *control* as they relate to the parameters of larceny. The renowned *Carrier's Case* of 1473 provided an initial interpretation of this distinction when a mover, entrusted with the task of transporting bales of wool dye and thus having legal custody of them, broke into several bales and took part of the contents. From this case came the time-honored doctrine of "breaking bulk," which maintained that although the mover or carrier had legal custody of the property, his breaking into the bales was a trespass against the possessory interests of the owner, and as such was larceny.[23] In 1779, the famous *Pear's Case* approached an alternative situation in which the accused hired a horse from a livery stable, gave the owner a false address, and then took the animal to a local market and sold it as his own. The legal issue was that the stableman had willingly delivered the animal and that Pear had not used force or stealth to obtain its custody. The court ruled that it was larceny "by trick." The horse had been hired for a purpose that the accused never intended to execute, and as such, his taking of the horse with the intention of selling it was a trespass against the stableman's right of possession.[24] The point, then, is that a taking can occur even when a person has authorized custody or control of an object if his or her conversion of that object ultimately deprives someone else of their possessory rights.

The *carrying away* aspect of larceny, also known as "asportation," involves the removal of the property from the place it formerly occupied. The distance of movement, however, need not be significant. The removal of a wallet from a pocket, for example, represents complete asportation.

Personal property, as the third element of larceny, refers to anything that is capable of ownership except land or things permanently affixed to it. The property must also be that of *another,* since larceny is a crime against possession and therefore cannot occur with what one already possesses.

The final element of larceny involves *intent* — intent to permanently deprive. If the intent is to deprive only temporarily, then there is no larceny, although many states have structured their criminal codes to cover these latter situations with such lesser offenses as unauthorized use of a vehicle and misappropriation of property. Whether the intent is to deprive permanently or only temporarily, however, is a question of fact on which the court must rule, and the distinction between permanent and temporary can be a matter of interpretation. In *United States* v. *Sheffield,* the defendant had taken an automobile without consent and by stealth. After driving through several states he reversed his course to the general direction from which he started, but was arrested while in a state other than the one from which he had taken the vehicle. Sheffield was convicted of auto theft in a Maryland court. He appealed on the defense that he intended to return the auto to the vicinity from which it had been removed. The conviction was upheld, however, supported by the following opinion of the court:

> When an automobile is taken without right of colorable authority and by stealth and to be used by the taker for his own use and benefit for an indefinite period of time, I think there is properly a presumption, or at least sufficient evidence, for an inference of fact that it is being taken to deprive the owner of the rights and benefits of his property; and the mere statement of a defendant who has so feloniously taken a motor car that he intended to abandon it somewhere in the same city . . . is not sufficient to destroy the inference unless well supported by collateral facts.[25]

The distinction between larceny as a felony or misdemeanor, or "grand larceny" versus "petty larceny," is of a statutory nature. As indicated in Exhibit 3.2, the dividing point ranges from as little as $50 in Oklahoma, to as much as $2,500 in Arkansas. At a value below these amounts the larceny is a misdemeanor, while anything valued at or above the statutory figure is a felony.

EXHIBIT 3.2

Dollar Amounts at Which Larcenies Shift from Petty to Grand

State	Amount	State	Amount	State	Amount
Alabama	$ 100	Kentucky	$100	North Dakota	$ 500
Alaska	500	Louisiana	100	Ohio	300
Arizona	100	Maine	500	Oklahoma	50
Arkansas	2,500	Maryland	300	Oregon	200
California	400	Massachusetts	100	Pennsylvania	2,000
Colorado	300	Michigan	100	Rhode Island	500
Connecticut	1,000	Minnesota	250	South Carolina	100
Delaware	500	Mississippi	100	South Dakota	200
District of Columbia	250	Missouri	150	Tennessee	200
Florida	300	Montana	300	Texas	750
Georgia	500	Nebraska	300	Utah	250
Hawaii	200	Nevada	100	Vermont	100
Idaho	150	New Hampshire	500	Virginia	200
Illinois	300	New Jersey	500	Washington	250
Indiana	250	New Mexico	100	West Virginia	200
Iowa	500	New York	250	Wisconsin	500
Kansas	150	North Carolina	400	Wyoming	2,000

NOTE: In some jurisdictions, the dollar amounts at which larcenies shift from petty to grand depend on the type of property stolen.

SOURCE: Wayne Logan, Lindsay S. Stellwagen, and Patrick A. Langan, *Felony Laws of the 50 States and the District of Columbia* (Washington, D.C.: Bureau of Justice Statistics, 1987).

In 1981, the California statutory rape law was challenged before the U.S. Supreme Court on the ground that it discriminated on the basis of gender — men alone were criminally liable under the statute. The Court upheld the power of the states to enact such statutes since they were intended to prevent teenage pregnancies. (Michael M. *v.* Superior Court of Sonoma County, 458 U.S. 747 [1981])

Adultery is the application of democracy to love.

—H. L. MENCKEN

Bigamy is a mistake in taste for which the wisdom of the future will adjudge a punishment called trigamy.

—AMBROSE BIERCE, THE DEVIL'S DICTIONARY, 1911

Sex Offenses

The scope of illegal sexual activity is quite broad in American society. This is due in part to the legacy of the early Puritan codes and the Holy Scriptures; to attempts to maintain standards of public decency through the legislation of morality; to requirements of community consensus as to an individual's right to sexual self-determination; and to an effort to protect those who are too young or otherwise unable to make decisions as to their own sexual conduct. Although in recent years the codes regulating many sexual activities, such as contraception and miscegenation, have been eliminated or severely limited, the list is still long and includes the following:

Forcible rape   Having sexual intercourse with a female against her will and through the use of threat of force or fear.

Statutory rape   Having sexual intercourse with a female under a stated age (usually sixteen or eighteen, but sometimes fourteen), with or without her consent.

Seduction   The act of enticing or luring a woman of chaste character to engage in sexual intercourse by fraudulently promising to marry her or by some other false promise.

Fornication   Sexual intercourse between unmarried persons.

Adultery   Sexual intercourse between a man and woman, at least one of whom is married to someone else.

Incest   Sexual intercourse between parent and child, any sibling pair, or between close blood relatives.

Sodomy   Certain acts of sexual relationship including *fellatio* (oral intercourse with the male sex organ), *cunnilingus* (oral intercourse with the female sex organ), *buggery* (penetration of the anus), *homosexuality* (sexual relations between members of the same sex), *bestiality* (sexual intercourse with an animal), *pederasty* (unnatural intercourse between a man and a boy), and *necrophilia* (sexual intercourse with a corpse).

Indecent exposure (exhibitionism)   Exposure of the sexual organs in a public place.

Lewdness   Degenerate conduct in sexual behavior that is so well known that it may result in the corruption of public decency.

Obscenity   That which is offensive to morality or chastity and is calculated to corrupt the mind and morals of those exposed to it.

Pornography   Literature, art, film, pictures, or other articles of a sexual nature that are considered obscene by a community's moral standards.

Bigamy   The act of marrying while a former marriage is still legally in force.

Polygamy   The practice of having several spouses.

Prostitution   The offering of sexual relations for monetary or other gain.

Child molesting   The handling, fondling, or other contact of a sexual nature with a child.

Sexual assault   Any sexual contact with another person (other than a spouse) that occurs without the consent of the victim or is offensive to the victim.

Voyeurism (peeping)   The surreptitious observance of an exposed body or sexual act.

Although the offenses of forcible rape, incest, and child molesting appear in all jurisdictions throughout the United States in one form or another, not all of the sexual behaviors listed are universally prohibited. Fornication, seduction, and pornography are disappearing from the penal codes of many state and local areas; indecent exposure, in the form of topless dancing and live sex shows, have been decriminalized in several jurisdictions; and prostitution is legal in one jurisdiction — in Las Vegas County, Nevada, outside the city limits of Las Vegas. However, American sodomy statutes, although neither uniform nor universal, and in most instances unenforced, continue to persist in modern criminal codes. The great majority of sodomy arrests that occur in the United States involve male homosexuals caught in the act of fellatio in public restrooms, parks, and other public places. Other sodomous acts, however, can be and are prosecuted. Even acts of fellatio and cunnilingus between husband and wife have resulted in criminal processing (see Exhibit 3.3). Furthermore, violation of the sodomy statutes is a felony in a number of jurisdictions, and in 1986 the U.S. Supreme Court ruled that homosexuals do *not* have a constitutional right to engage in sodomy, even when the act is consensual and occurs in private.[26] Similarly, adultery statutes remain in force in most states. Furthermore, in Alabama, Wisconsin, Michigan, and Oklahoma, adultery continues to be a felony.[27]

Attitudes About Rape in the U.S

Would you classify the following as rape or not?

		YES
A man has sex with a woman who has passed	FEMALE	88%
out after drinking too much	MALE	77%
A married man has sex with his wife even though she	FEMALE	61%
does not want him to	MALE	56%
A man argues with a woman who does not want to have sex until she agrees	FEMALE	42%
to have sex	MALE	33%
A man uses emotional pressure, but not physical force, to get a woman to	FEMALE	39%
have sex	MALE	33%

Do you believe a woman who is raped is partly to blame if:

	AGE	YES
She is under the influence	18–34	31%
of drugs or alcohol	35–49	35%
	50+	57%
She initially says yes to	18–34	34%
having sex and then	35–49	43%
changes her mind	50+	43%
She dresses provocatively	18–34	28%
	35–49	31%
	50+	53%
She agrees to go to the	18–34	20%
man's room or home	35–49	29%
	50+	53%

Adapted from a telephone poll of 500 American adults taken for *Time*/CNN on May 8, 1991, by Yankelovich Clancy Shulman. Sampling error is plus or minus 4.5 percent.

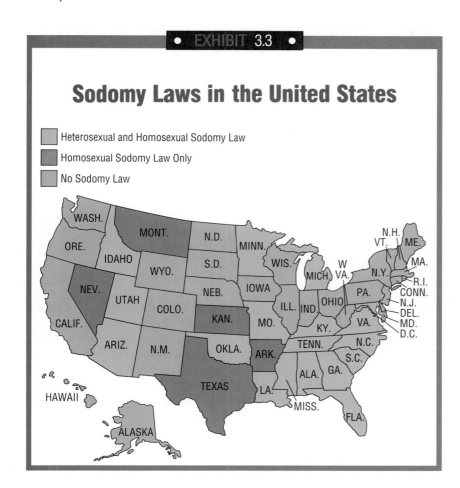

● EXHIBIT 3.3 ●

Sodomy Laws in the United States

- Heterosexual and Homosexual Sodomy Law
- Homosexual Sodomy Law Only
- No Sodomy Law

It'll be a sad day for sexual liberation when the pornography addict has to settle for the real thing.
— BRENDAN FRANCIS

The worst that can be said about pornography is that it leads not to "anti-social" acts but to the reading of more pornography.
— GORE VIDAL

Pornography is the undiluted essence of anti-female propaganda.
— SUSAN BROWNMILLER

Bigamy is having one spouse too many. Monogamy has been called the same thing.
— ANONYMOUS

Obscenity can be found in every book except the telephone directory.
— GEORGE BERNARD SHAW

Rape: The unlawful carnal knowledge of a female without her consent and against her will.

Carnal knowledge is the act of having sexual bodily connection. Under many statutes, there is carnal knowledge if there is the slightest penetration of the sexual organ of the female by the sexual organ of the male; it is not necessary that the vaginal canal be entered. Sexual contact without any penetration is generally referred to as carnal abuse.

Prostitution

Procuring

I don't know of many people who think that two people living together ought to be a crime.

— MASSACHUSETTS GOV. MICHAEL DUKAKIS, SIGNING A MEASURE IN 1987 REPEALING A 200-YEAR-OLD STATE LAW BANNING COHABITATION

Cocaine isn't habit-forming. I should know, I've been using it for years.

— TALLULAH BANKHEAD

Without doubt, forcible rape is the one sex offense about which there is the most concern, and it is a crime whose statutes are often quite peculiar. In most jurisdictions, **rape** is defined as the unlawful carnal knowledge of a female without her consent and against her will. This suggests that the law of rape defines men as the only possible offenders and women as the only possible victims.* However, one cannot discount the many instances of homosexual assault that occur in American prisons and jails,[28] or the cases of forced oral-genital and other body contacts attempting to simulate heterosexual intercourse that have been manifest in women's institutions.[29] Furthermore, this raises the question as to whether a man can be raped by a woman. Authors Neil C. Chamelin and Kenneth R. Evans have suggested that a female *cannot* acutally rape a male.[30] But, although it is unlikely that any man raped by a woman would bring the crime to the attention of the authorities for fear of ridicule, this does not mean it cannot happen. Numerous such cases have been documented, and studies by sex therapists Philip M. Sarrel and William H. Masters have indicated that male victims of sexual assault by women suffer aftereffects similar to those seen in women who have been raped.[31]

Rape is considered the most serious of the sex offenses, but prostitution seems to the most visibly common. Prostitution is sex for hire, implying some gain, typically money. It includes not only sexual intercourse, but also any other form of sexual conduct with another person for a fee. Where prostitution is illegal, it is typically a misdemeanor or some lesser offense.

Related to prostitution is *procuring,* also referred to as pandering or "pimping." Procuring involves promoting prostitution through the operation of a house of prostitution or managing the activities and contacts of one or more prostitutes for a percentage of their earnings. Procuring is most often a felony at the state level, and in some circumstances can be prosecuted under federal law. For example, the White Slave Traffic Act of 1910, more commonly known as the *Mann Act,* prescribes a heavy fine and imprisonment for the transportation of a woman in foreign or interstate commerce for immoral purposes. The act was intended to intervene in the practice of white slavery, which was allegedly common at the turn of the twentieth century, and which involved the large-scale transportation of women and young girls and their detention in vice resorts for the purpose of forced prostitution. The statute was also aimed at controlling the importation of alien women for immoral purposes. More currently, the law remains as part of Congress's regulatory power over interstate commerce.

Drug Law Violations

The federal and state statutes that regulate the nonmedical use of drugs as well as control the manufacture, sale, and distribution of "dangerous" drugs are relatively recent, having evolved only during the current century. Although a few local ordinances focused on certain types of drug use and sale during the late 1800s, the Pure Food and Drug Act of 1906 was the first piece of federal legislation that targeted the distribution of what were considered dangerous drugs. The purpose of the law was to limit the uncontrolled manufacture of patent medicines and

---

* Maine is one of the few states in which rape is considered a "gender-neutral" offense. See *National Law Journal,* July 14, 1986, p. 10.

This series of photos shows a drug sale in Detroit where the buyer indicates how much he wants, places his money in a cup attached to a twenty-foot piece of twine, which is raised by the drug dealer, who then throws the crack to the buyer below.

The Harrison Act

over-the-counter drugs containing cocaine, opium, and other narcotics. The *Harrison Act of 1914,* initially a revenue measure designed to make narcotics transferals a matter of record, evolved into a sweeping law that defined as criminal any manufacture, prescription, transfer, or possession of narcotics by persons who were not authorized to pay a tax on them.[32] In 1937, the *Marijuana Tax Act,* modeled after the Harrison Act, resulted in a total prohibition of marijuana, and during the 1950s a series of federal statutes were passed to increase the penalties associated with the sale and use of narcotics, marijuana, and cocaine.[33]

The *Comprehensive Drug Abuse and Control Act of 1970,* in effect since May 1, 1971, brought together under one law most of the drug controls that had been created since the Harrison Act in 1914. Title II of the new law, known separately as the **Controlled Substances Act,** categorized certain substances into five "schedules" and defined the offenses and penalties associated with the illegal manufacture, distribution, and dispensing of any drug in each schedule (see Exhibit 3.4).

Prior to the enactment of the Controlled Substances Act in 1970, federal and state drug laws often varied greatly from one another, and the penalties for many drug violations varied considerably from one jurisdiction to another. Many state marijuana laws, for example, specified that the penalties for marijuana should be the same as those for heroin, and in at least nineteen jurisdictions there was no distinction in the law between the penalties for the mere possession of one marijuana cigarette or "reefer" and those for the sale of large quantities of heroin. By 1972, however, the majority of the states adopted the provisions of the Controlled Substances Act, thus helping standardize drug laws in most parts of the nation.

In contrast, the laws in jurisdictions that have not adopted the full text of the federal model vary considerably. While the federal penalties for the possession of even small quantities of marijuana call for a sen-

The Controlled Substances Act

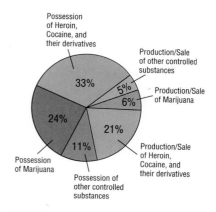

Possession of Heroin, Cocaine, and their derivatives **33%**

Production/Sale of other controlled substances **5%**

Production/Sale of Marijuana **6%**

Production/Sale of Heroin, Cocaine, and their derivatives **21%**

Possession of other controlled substances **11%**

Possession of Marijuana **24%**

Drug Law Arrests, 1990
SOURCE: UCR

> • EXHIBIT 3.4 •

Drug Schedules Under the Controlled Substances Act

Schedule I includes drugs with a high potential for abuse, which have no currently accepted medical use in the United States, and drugs where there is a lack of accepted safety for use under medical supervision. Schedule I lists a variety of opiates and their derivatives, and numerous hallucinogenic substances, including *heroin, LSD, marijuana,* mescaline, peyote,* and *psilocybin.*

Schedule II includes drugs where there is a high potential for abuse, which are currently used for medical treatment in the United States, and which if abused could lead to physical or psychological dependence. Examples of Schedule II drugs in-

clude *opium, morphine, cocaine,* and *methadone.*

Schedule III includes drugs that have a potential for abuse less than those in Schedules I and II, which are currently accepted for medical use in the United States, and which may lead to moderate or low physical dependence or high psychological dependence. Examples of Schedule III drugs includes *amphetamines* (such as Benzedrine and Dexedrine), *methamphetamine, phenmetrazine* (Preludin), *barbiturates* (such as Tuinal, Seconal, and Nembutal), *codeine,* and *phencyclidine* (PCP).

Schedule IV includes drugs that have a low potential for abuse and are currently accepted for

use in the United States which, if abused, could lead to limited physical or psychological dependence. Examples of Schedule IV drugs include the *long-acting barbiturates* such as phenobarbital, *minor tranquilizers* such as Librium, Valium, and Miltown, and *chloral hydrate.*

Schedule V includes drugs that have a potential for abuse and dependence lower than those listed in Schedule IV. Examples of Schedule V drugs are those that contain limited quantities of narcotics, such as *codeine cough syrup.*

* The rescheduling of marijuana from I to II is currently under consideration.

tence of up to one year imprisonment and/or fines up to $5,000, or probation, penalties in some jurisdictions range from as little as a citation without arrest (Oregon), to imprisonment up to 10 years in Georgia, Texas, and Louisiana.[34]

In addition to laws that control the manufacture, transfer, distribution, sale, and possession of drugs, some jurisdictions have legislation against and penalties for the possession of narcotics paraphernalia — typically hypodermic syringes and needles. Furthermore, some states require that controlled substances, such as prescription drugs, be kept in the containers in which they were originally dispensed.

Crimes Against Public Order and Safety

Public order crimes are generally misdemeanor crimes against public order and safety.

They shoulda called me Little Cocaine, *I was sniffing so much of the stuff! My nose got big enough to back a diesel truck in, unload it, and drive it out again.*
— LITTLE RICHARD

The final category, crimes against public order and safety, or public order crimes, tends to be a rather sweeping collection of offenses, mostly misdemeanors, that nevertheless account for a considerable portion of criminal justice activity. The criminal codes that have been structured for the maintenance of public order and safety tend to vary considerably from place to place, but the following crimes all seem to appear in one form or another in most jurisdictions:

Disorderly conduct Any act that tends to disturb the public peace, scandalize the community, or shock the public sense of morality.

Disturbing the peace   Any interruption of the peace, quiet, and good order of a neighborhood or community.

Breach of the peace   The breaking of the public peace by any riotous, forcible, or unlawful proceeding.

Harassment   Any act that serves to annoy or alarm another person.

Drunkenness   The condition of being under the influence of alcohol to the extent that it renders one helpless.

Public intoxication   The condition of being severely under the influence of alcohol or drugs in a public place to the degree that one may endanger persons or property.

Loitering   Idling or lounging upon a street or other public way in a manner that serves to interfere with or annoy passersby.

Criminal nuisance   Any conduct that is unreasonable and that endangers the health and safety of others.

Vagrancy   The condition of being idle and having no visible means of support.

Desecration   The defacing, damaging, or mistreatment of a public structure, monument, or place of worship or burial.

Driving while intoxicated (DWI) or Driving Under the Influence (DUI)   The operation of a motor vehicle while under the influence of alcohol or illegal drugs.

Gambling   The playing or operation of any game of chance that involves money or property of any value that is prohibited by the criminal code.

Violation of privacy   Any unlawful trespass, interception, observation, eavesdropping, or other surveillance that serves to infringe on the private rights of another.*

The only reason that cocaine is such a rage today is that people are too drunk and lazy to get themselves together to roll a joint.

—JACK NICHOLSON

---

* Some violations of privacy may be classified as sex offenses, such as voyeurism or exhibitionism.

Disorderly conduct

Many of these offenses tend to overlap with one another, and, depending on the jurisdiction, one or more of these crimes against public order and safety may fall under the proscriptions of a single criminal code. In Colorado, for example, the existing *disorderly conduct* statute includes what has been separately defined in the preceding list as disorderly conduct, disturbing the peace, breach of the peace, harassment, and criminal nuisance. In addition, this same Colorado law extends to the public display of a deadly weapon. Thus, in Colorado,

a person commits disorderly conduct if he intentionally, knowingly, or recklessly:

(a) Makes a coarse and obviously offensive utterance, gesture, or display in a public place; or

(b) Abuses or threatens a person in a public place in an obviously offensive manner; or

(c) Makes unreasonable noise in a public place or near a private residence that he has no right to occupy; or

(d) Fights with another in a public place except in an amateur or professional contest of athletic skill; or

(e) Not being a peace officer, discharges a firearm in a public place except when engaged in lawful target practice or hunting; or

(f) Not being a peace officer, displays a deadly weapon in a public place in a manner calculated to alarm.[35]

In recent years, the constitutionality of many criminal codes designed for the preservation of public order and safety has been challenged. Numerous cases of disorderly conduct, breach of the peace, and vagrancy have come before the Supreme Court on the grounds that they violate First Amendment protections of free speech and assembly or because they are too vague. Furthermore, the use of such statutes as mechanisms for penalizing those who are viewed in some communities as political and social undesirables has been questioned as a violation of rights of due process. Nevertheless, these statutes remain in force in the criminal codes of most American jurisdictions, and arrests for vagrancy and disorderly conduct alone approach one million annually.

BEHAVIOR SYSTEMS IN CRIME

The preceding discussion provides a basis for understanding the legal definitions and boundaries of the major categories of crime. However, in their descriptions of prohibited acts and their delineations of penalties, what the criminal codes cannot do is offer some insight and explanation of the social and behavioral contexts in which certain crimes tend to occur, the lifestyles associated with particular offenses, and the relationship of certain criminal acts to the wider social order. Further, the criminal law tells us nothing of the differences in styles and patterns of crime, of the various types of offenders, of victim–offender relationships, of varying techniques for committing crimes, and of how all of these affect the criminal justice management of crime. In short, each variety of crime has two important aspects — its legal description as stated in the law, and the behavior system that brings it into being. Consider, for example, the crime of shoplifting, which penal codes define as the theft of money, goods, or other merchandise from a store or shop. As such, the law is quite clear as to what may constitute shoplifting. But the law cannot help us understand the numerous behavior patterns associated with shoplifting. For example, there are many pensioners, students, and others for whom an instance of shoplifting may be a first or only offense, committed perhaps out of desperation or for the sake of excitement. There are also numerous department store employees who pilfer merchandise in an attempt to supplement their legal incomes in a potentially safe manner. There are street hustlers in the central cities for whom shoplifting is but one of many petty crimes undertaken on a sporadic basis for the sake of economic gain. And finally, there are professional *boosters,* a small fraternity of skilled thieves who have elevated their techniques to an art form and carry them out regularly as a full-time business and vocation. The skills and techniques of the four types vary considerably, as do the frequency of their thefts and their methods for the disposal of the stolen goods. Furthermore, the first two varieties of shoplifters rarely view themselves as criminals, while the others are often proud of the labels of "hustler" and "professional thief."

Within this context, then, we can examine six behavior systems in crime: (1) violent personal crime, (2) occasional property crime, (3) organized robbery and gang theft, (4) white-collar and corporate crime, (5) organized crime, and (6) professional theft. Before proceeding with this analysis, however, two points must be emphasized. First, while this list of six behavior systems includes a wide variety of criminal activities and offense categories, it clearly does not include all prohibited acts. Any attempt to construct a schema that includes all types of behavior designated by the law as criminal would be pointless, primarily because the resulting classification would be so long and complex that it would be of minimal value for the purposes intended here. However, what is included reflects the vast majority of serious criminal activities. Second, a given criminal offense can fall within one or more behavior systems. For example, shoplifting can be carried out in different ways, under different circumstances, with different levels of skill, and with different relationships to the offender's social, economic, and criminal careers.

Six behavior systems in crime

Violent Personal Crime

Violent personal crime consists of criminal acts resulting from conflicts in personal relations in which death or physical injury is inflicted. Thus, violent personal crime is a reflection of individual and personal violence, and includes specific forms of criminal homicide, assault, forcible rape, and child abuse.

The boundaries of violent personal crime are somewhat limited. First, studies of murder, assault, rape, and child abuse have suggested that in many cases (particularly in crimes of passion), the offenders had limited, if any, prior involvement in crime. Second, murderers, assaulters, and rapists generally do not view themselves as criminals, and their crimes are not always a predominant part of their life organization. Finally, most instances of personal violence are not a reflection of some group activity — rather, the violence is directed by the offender against a specific victim.[36]

A further aspect of personal violence is the victim-offender relationship, a factor which suggests that a large portion of such behavior is well beyond the control of law enforcement. In the case of murder, for example, the majority of offenses occur among persons who know one another. In 1990, for example, of the 20,045 murders reported during that

Violent personal crime: Criminal acts resulting from conflicts in personal relations in which death or physical injury is inflicted.

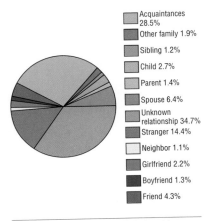

Acquaintances 28.5%

Other family 1.9%

Sibling 1.2%

Child 2.7%

Parent 1.4%

Spouse 6.4%

Unknown relationship 34.7%

Stranger 14.4%

Neighbor 1.1%

Girlfriend 2.2%

Boyfriend 1.3%

Friend 4.3%

Murder Circumstances by Relationship

SOURCE: UCR

year, 5.4 percent of the victims were spouses, 7.2 percent involved other family members, and 37.4 percent included neighbors or other close acquaintances. In the remaining cases, the homicide was of the "stranger-to-stranger" type, or the relationship could not be established. Interestingly, the majority of these killings involved circumstances of "romantic triangles," quarrels over money or property, or other arguments.

Although official statistics on assaults are not as complete as those on criminal homicide, similar patterns of personal violence are apparent. Street muggings do indeed occur, but it is also relatively clear that nearly two-thirds of all known aggravated assaults result from domestic quarrels, altercations, jealousies, and arguments over money and property. Further, victim–offender relationships are typically intimate, close, and frequent, primarily involving family members and close acquaintances.[37]

Child abuse, which is a particular variety of homicide or assault directed against children, is a form of personal violence that has received attention only during recent years. Known in medical terminology as the "battered child syndrome," it is but one of the many forms of family violence. Studies suggest that the offenders are typically parents or guardians; that they do not view themselves as criminals; and that although the abuse of their children may be an enduring pattern of behavior, they rarely have generalized criminal careers. Rather, they are individuals who are provoked by the forms of aggravation that can be typical of children — persistent crying, failure to use the toilet, aggression toward siblings, breaking toys or household items, or disobedience — and who respond by anger that strikes out in full force.

Not all forms of personal violence are clear-cut instances of differences of opinion in personal relations as are most homicides and assaults. Rape, for example, is not generally a crime that evolves from an intimate personal relationship, although in many cases the victim and offender are known to one another, and in some instances forced intercourse results from an anticipated sexual encounter. Recent studies have documented an increased number of stranger-to-stranger rapes, and available data suggest that forcible rape is but one of many crimes in the offenders' criminal careers.[38] Similarly, child molestation does not follow the general pattern of personal violence. In fact, much of what is called child molesting is not violence in the strict sense of the word. It may include instances of forcible rape, but its most frequent manifestations involve parent–child incest, the sexual fondling of a child, or the persuasion or coercion to engage in or submit to oral-genital contacts or to masturbate the adult.[39] Few cases have been reported where direct physical assault was associated with such "carnal abuse" of children. Nevertheless, child molesting is generally viewed as a variety of personal violence since it involves a sexual attack on persons who are not fully capable of making decisions as to their own sexual conduct. And for similar reasons, the use of cocaine during pregnancy is increasingly being defined by the courts as a variety of personal violence (see Exhibit 3.5).

However, most homicides, assaults, rapes, and incidents of child abuse and molesting can be grouped into a single behavior system in crime because they are all invasions of the rights of the victim's person. Whether the crime be direct assault or indecent liberties, the violence is of a personal nature. Furthermore, it is "individual violence," with the aggression directed typically by a single offender.

Occasional Property Crime

Occasional property crime refers to those types and instances of burglary, larceny, forgery, and other thefts undertaken infrequently or irregularly, and often quite crudely. Offenders who engage in this level of property crime do not pursue it as a career. They include amateur thieves for whom crime is incidental to their way of life, as well as the rank and file of urban street criminals or youthful groups who partake in sprees of burglaries, auto thefts, shoplifting, and vandalism as part of peer-group activities or for economic gain.

Offenders of this type generally have a petty or noncriminal orientation. They are often first or infrequent offenders who do not view themselves as criminals. They are unacquainted with criminal subcultures; their techniques for committing crimes are unskilled and undeveloped; they have little or no access to structured mechanisms for the disposal of stolen property. Rather, they generally steal for their own immediate purposes and little planning is apparent. Young vandals and burglars see themselves more often as "pranksters" than as thieves. Nonprofessional forgers, shoplifters, and pilferers are typically victims of temporary or desperate financial situations, or they engage in an occasional theft for the sake of adventure and excitement.

Edwin M. Lemert's study of "naive check forgers," undertaken many decades ago, clearly illustrates the factors associated with one common form of occasional property crime as a behavior system. Lemert found that many arrested forgers included professional, clerical, skilled, and craft workers who were, for the most part, respectable members of their communities. Many had no prior criminal records, and those who did had been involved in only minor offenses on an infrequent basis. The situations that led them into forgery included such contingencies as business failure, unemployment, gambling losses, alcoholic sprees, family or marital conflict, and separation or divorce. Elaborate planning of the forgery was quite untypical of this group of offenders, and the forgeries were extremely simple — the forgers wrote fictitious checks, passed falsified checks, and issued personal checks without sufficient funds. And finally, Lemert's "naive" check forgers were easily identified and apprehended, and readily admitted their guilt.[40]

Shoplifting has persisted as the most common form of occasional property crime throughout the twentieth century. Patterns of shoplifting have been studied at length, and although professional *boosters* appear in every location, most thieves are of the occasional type and include amateur pilferers and store employees who steal for their own use. These offenders are generally law-abiding types who slip a few articles into their pockets, purses, and shopping bags, generally restricting their thefts to expensive pieces of clothing, electronic gadgets, jewelry, leather goods, and small appliances — all for personal consumption.[41]

Finally, not all instances of occasional property crime are totally nonviolent. In many robberies and armed holdups the predators are amateur, first-offender types, and the patterns and contingencies are the same as those apparent among naive check forgers and shoplifters. Consider, for example, the case of a nineteen-year-old Wilmington, Delaware, youth who had an urgent need for cash to cover the impending cost of extensive car repairs. His crime was the armed robbery of a local liquor retailer. The event was his first criminal offense and his lack of aptitude was apparent from the very beginning. With little planning, the youth

Occasional property crime: Burglary, forgery, larceny, and other thefts undertaken infrequently or irregularly, and often quite crudely.

I'm convinced that every boy, in his heart, would rather steal second base than an automobile.
— SUPREME COURT JUSTICE TOM CLARK

The "naive check forger"

Shoplifting

• EXHIBIT 3.5 •

Cocaine, Fetal Rights, and the Prosecution of Pregnant Addicts

- In 1988, Brenda Vaughan of Washington, D.C. spent nearly four months in jail—an unusually long time for a first offender convicted of check forgery. However, the presiding judge felt he had to protect her fetus from cocaine.

- Pamela Stewart of San Diego, after defying her physician's advice to stop using street drugs during pregnancy, was arrested and incarcerated on a charge of failing to provide for her baby. Her child was subsequently born brain damaged and died after only six weeks.

- Bianca Green of Rockford, Illinois, was born in February 1989 suffering from severe oxygen deprivation and died two days later. After cocaine was found in the baby's urine, as well as in the bloodstream of her mother Melanie, the mother was arrested and charged with child abuse, supplying drugs to a minor, and involuntary manslaughter.

With almost 400,000 drug-exposed infants being born each year in the United States, state and county attorneys across the nation have become more inclined to prosecute mothers-to-be who abuse their fetuses by taking illegal drugs. Charges have included child abuse, child neglect, assault, manslaughter, and drug delivery.

At issue is whether pregnant women who use drugs should be considered a public health problem, or one for the criminal justice system. Without question, cocaine babies are at risk. Crack and cocaine abusing women are more likely to miscarry, give birth prematurely, and have low-weight babies. In addition, infants born to cocaine users tend to have abnormally small heads and brains, suffer deformities of the genital organs and urinary tract, and experience higher rates of sudden infant death syndrome, or SIDS (crib death). They can also suffer subtle neurological damage leading to extraordinary irritability during infancy and learning disorders in later years. A number of these problems may be exacerbated during the early months of life, since intoxicating levels of cocaine can be ingested through breastfeeding.

Prosecutors argue that the threat of criminal charges will help deter pregnant women from using drugs, saving babies from the wide spectrum of ill effects that prenatal drug use can cause. At the same time, "fetal rights" and pro-life advocates insist that the state must intervene to ensure proper medical care for both mother and child. There is also the not-so-hidden pro-life agenda to chip away at the 1972 decision in *Roe* v. *Wade* (410 U.S. 13), which granted women the right to an abortion, and hence, gave no rights to fetuses.

By contrast, public health officials and women's advocates claim that the threat of prosecution will instead scare women away from the medical help they need. Along with many drug abuse clinicians and researchers, they further argue drug use during pregnancy is a community health problem that is more properly addressed through the expansion of drug treatment services designed specifically for mothers-to-be.

How this controversy will ultimately be settled is difficult to predict. On the one hand, the growing number of cocaine-babies (or "tox babies" as they are often called, for the toxico-

parked his car directly in front of the establishment he had targeted for the crime. In the presence of at least five witnesses, he emerged from his vehicle with his gun already drawn and entered the store. By the time he had completed the robbery, his license plate had been recorded and the police had been contacted. And if this identification had not been sufficient, the youth left his jacket, containing his wallet, driver's license, name, address, and phone number, behind at the scene of the crime.

Perhaps the most spectacular and well-known of the occasional offender types was D. B. Cooper, the man who boarded a Northwest Orient Airlines jet on November 24, 1971, and then hijacked it. After

D. B. Cooper

logical examinations they undergo) has become a major public health problem in some locales. (In New York City, for example, the rate of known cases of drug use during pregnancy increased by some 270 percent during the 1980s, largely attributable to the more widespread use of cocaine.) On the other, court decisions that would grant legal rights to fetuses could unleash a torrent of fetal protection cases that would have mothers-to-be (drug-using or not) seeing more of their lawyers than their physicians. Perhaps the compromise position is mandatory drug treatment in lieu of prosecution for *all* drug-dependent individuals, pregnant or not, who come to the attention of the criminal justice system for drug-related crimes. (Compulsory treatment is examined in considerable detail in Chapter 17.)

SOURCES: Rorie Sherman, "Keeping Baby Safe From Mom," *National Law Journal,* October 2, 1988, pp. 1, 24–25; Ira J. Chasnoff, Douglas E. Lewis, and Liza Squires, "Cocaine Intoxication in a Breast-Fed Infant," *Pediatrics,* 80 (December 1987), pp. 836–838; *U.S. News & World Report,* February 6, 1989, p. 50; *New York Times,* April 20, 1991, p. 6; *Newsweek,* April 29, 1991, pp. 52–53.

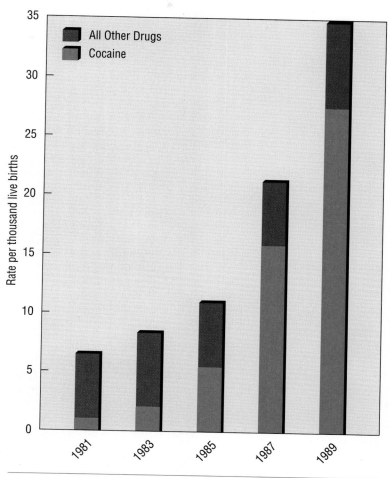

Drug Use During Pregnancy per 1,000 Live Births*

* As reported on New York City birth certificates 1980–1988, showing the rise in cocaine use.
SOURCE: New York City Department of Health.

receiving the $200,000 ransom and parachute he had demanded from airline officials, Cooper jumped from the jetliner over a rural area of Washington State. Cooper was not a known criminal, and all indications suggested that his ransom of the jetliner had been undertaken with little planning and expertise.[42] (For more about Cooper, see Exhibit 3.7.)

Organized Robbery and Gang Theft

Organized robbery and gang theft, often called professional "heavy" crime, involves highly skilled criminal activities using or threatening to

Organized robbery and gang theft:
Highly skilled criminal activities using or threatening to use force, violence, coercion, and property damage, and accompanied by planning, surprise, and speed to diminish the risks of apprehension.

use force, violence, coercion, and property damage, and accomplished by planning, surprise, and speed in order to diminish the risks of apprehension.

"Heavy" criminals of this type pursue crime as a career for financial gain; they generally work in teams and are heavily armed; their planning is careful and their timing precise; and their pursuits include armed robbery, hijacking, kidnapping, and large-scale industrial theft. Although there is some variation from group to group, most organized robberies and gang thefts follow a planned pattern: (1) there is a definite target, ensuring a profitable outcome; (2) the target is fully studied (*cased*) in advance; (3) mock or practice trials are made; (4) timetables are established and escape routes are charted; (5) there is a getaway vehicle with a special driver; (6) there is a lookout person and a gunman with an accomplice for inside operations; and (7) there is a planned time, place, and method for the division of the plunder.

With organized armed robberies and hijacks, although they are generally planned in advance, the skill levels can vary. For example, as Werner J. Einstadter has pointed out, robbery tactics can emerge at any of three basic levels:

1. *The ambush*   Little planning; participants attack an establishment in guerrilla fashion; random selection of the victim; high incidence of violence
2. *The selective raid*   Some planning; limited analysis of site conditions; tentative plan of approach and escape
3. *The planned operation*   Well planned and well structured in every aspect; risks held to a minimum[43]

Three levels of skill in robbery tactics

Individuals who engage in organized robbery and gang theft are usually long-term criminals who move from petty offenses to auto theft, burglary, and robbery. Their repeated experiences as young adults with police, courts, and reformatories add to their sophistication in criminality and to criminal self-conceptions. They live on the fringes of organized society, and they view the "heavy" rackets as a way to "get rich quick," to become socially mobile, or to start anew, rather than as a vocation or occupational career.

Perhaps the best known of the "heavy" offenders was Willie Sutton, America's most famous bank burglar. During his half-century career, Sutton plundered almost one hundred banks using a variety of ruses, disguises, pioneering safecracking techniques, and the timing of an athlete. (See Exhibit 3.7.) As for his general preparations for stealing from a bank, Sutton once commented:

Willie Sutton, the best known "heavy" offender

I studied the habits of the employees and the guards and the cops on the beat. I learned the complete layout of the bank, and drew a plan. . . . I learned the location of every burglar alarm and safeguard. . . . I rehearsed my men thoroughly in their parts.[44]

The most recent forms of organized robbery and gang theft to come to the attention of law enforcement agencies occur within the industrial sector, with losses accumulating to billions of dollars annually. Armed robbers, thieves, hijackers, and river pirates now focus on farm and construction equipment, loaded gasoline trucks, and energy pipelines. Raids occur at railroad yards, construction sites, and plants and wholesaling locales where goods are stored or shipped.

It is a rather pleasant experience to be alone in a bank at night.
— WILLIE SUTTON

White-collar and Corporate Crime

White-collar crime and corporate crime refer to those offenses committed by persons acting in their legitimate occupational roles. The offenders include businesspeople, members of the professions and government, and other varieties of workers who, in the course of their everyday occupational activities, violate the basic trust placed in them or act in unethical ways. Crime is neither the way of life nor the chosen career of white-collar or corporate offenders, but rather something that occurs in conjunction with their more legitimate work activities. For example:

- In the business sector—financial manipulations, unfair labor practices, rebates, misrepresentation of goods and consumer deception by false labeling, fencing of stolen goods, shortchanging, overcharging, black-marketeering

White-collar crime: Offenses committed by persons acting in their legitimate occupational roles.

A "dishonest crime" is when somebody else creates the situation for which you are convicted.
— FORMER U.S. SENATOR HARRISON WILLIAMS, ON HIS PRISON SENTENCE IN 1987 FOR ACCEPTING ILLEGAL FUNDS

- In the labor sector—misuse of union funds, failing to enforce laws affecting unions, entering into collusion with employers to the disadvantage of union members, illegal mechanisms for controlling members
- In the corporate sector—restraint of trade, infringement of patents, monopolistic practices, environmental contamination, misuse of trademarks, manufacture of unsafe goods, false advertising, disposal of toxic wastes
- In the financial sector—embezzlement, violation of currency control measures, stock manipulation
- In the medical sector—illegal prescription practices, fee-splitting, illegal abortions, fraudulent reports to insurance companies
- In the legal sector—misappropriation of funds in trusts and receiverships, securing prejudiced testimony, bribery, instituting fraudulent damage claims
- In the criminal justice sector—accepting bribes, illegal arrest and detention practices, illegal correctional practices
- In the civil sector—illegal commissions, issuance of fraudulent licenses and certificates, illegal tax evaluations, misuse of campaign funds, illegal campaign practices

At all levels of white-collar criminality, the offenders have no criminal self-concept. Rather, they rationalize their behavior as sharp business practice, taking advantage of an "easy rip-off," or maintaining that certain laws are unfair or that whatever they gained "was coming to them."

Currently, losses through white-collar and corporate crime are estimated to be as high as $200 billion annually.[45] Such an estimate might be quite conservative, however, since crimes of this type pervade all levels of the economic spectrum. Many white-collar thefts are small, but even these can accumulate to extensive capital losses. Consider for example, the proprietor of a small grocery store in Brooklyn, New York, known to the author some years ago. This shopkeeper kept a small $2.98 broom at the end of his checkout counter, which he would routinely ring up as part of the purchases of transient customers. The broom would never be packed with the customers' goods, and if a buyer later returned to complain about the questionable $2.98 charge on the register receipt, the grocer would simply say "Sir," or "Madam, you forgot your broom!" That same broom, or some similarly priced item, was sold at least ten times each day, and over one year's time the fraud would accumulate to thousands of dollars. Alternatively, there was Raymond A. Galati, former fire chief of New Britain, Connecticut, who pleaded guilty to white-collar crimes including bribery and extortion. Galati was involved in selling jobs and promotions, with firm price tags on every forthcoming civil service examination in his department—$1,000 for the answers to the lieutenant exam and $3,000 for the assistant chief exam.[46]

At the other end of the spectrum, E. F. Hutton, Wall Street's fifth largest brokerage firm, was found guilty in 1985 of more than 2,000 separate charges of mail and wire fraud. Hutton executives had engaged in a sophisticated form of *check kiting* to avoid high interest rates. They deposited funds in local banks and then wrote checks for sums greater than the amounts in the accounts. Those checks were then covered a few days later by checks from other Hutton branches. The practice provided E. F. Hutton with interest-free loans of as much as $250 million a day.[47] Another case involved Texaco and Pennzoil. For much of the 1980s they

Any company executive who overcharges the government $5 million will be fined $50 or have to go to traffic school three nights a week.
—Art Buchwald

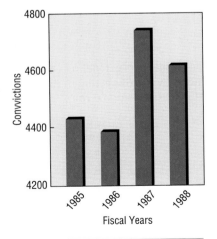

4800

Convictions

4600

4400

4200

1985 1986 1987 1988

Fiscal Years

White-Collar Crime Program
SOURCE: Federal Bureau of Investigation, 1991

"Kickbacks, embezzlement, price fixing, bribery . . . this is an extremely high-crime area."

represented corporate America's equivalent of Iran and Iraq, fielding armies of lawyers and paralegals to pound each other with hundreds of briefs and appeals. At issue was whether Texaco had illegally acquired Getty Oil, thus shutting Pennzoil out of the deal. In 1985 a jury decided in favor of Pennzoil, assessing Texaco with a $10.5 billion penalty.[48]

For years it has been argued that white-collar criminals are rarely punished, and that if and when penalties are imposed, corporate officers generally escape criminal sanctions. This certainly has been the case in the past, but there are indications that the trend may be reversing. In 1985, for example, Paul Thayer, the chairman of LTV Corporation and former President Reagan's deputy secretary of defense for a time was given a $5,000 fine and a four-year prison term for stock manipulation.[49] In another case, a Chicago judge decided that under certain conditions an industrial death could be defined as murder. The case involved the cyanide poisoning death of a worker in an Illinois silver recovery plant. On the basis of their total disregard for safety regulations, the three officers in charge of the plant were found guilty of murder and sentenced to twenty-five-year prison terms.[50]

How many criminals can claim 56,000 victims?

— Banker Marvin Warner in 1987 as Judge Richard Niehaus sentenced Warner to 3½ years in prison and a $22 million fine for his role in the collapse of a Cincinnati savings bank

Organized Crime

Organized crime designates business activities directed toward economic gain through unlawful means. Organized crime provides illegal goods and services through activities that include gambling, loan-sharking, commercialized vice, bootlegging, trafficking in narcotics and other drugs, disposing of stolen merchandise, and infiltrating legitimate businesses.

Organized crime: Business activities directed toward economic gain through unlawful means.

• EXHIBIT 3.6 •

Sidelights on Criminal Matters
The Cali Cartel

Travel guides say little about Cali, Colombia—only that it is a city of 1.33 million located 180 miles southwest of Bogota; that it is the sugar capital of the country; and that apart from its *salsa* music and a few nice churches and museums, it doesn't have much to offer. They don't mention that Cali is the headquarters of what has become known as the "Cali cartel" —reckoned to be the largest and wealthiest criminal organization on Earth.

The Cali cartel is a loosely integrated criminal enterprise involving some fifteen lesser organizations that deal in drugs, murder, arms, politics, and money. Principally, it stands at a pivotal place in the international network of cocaine trafficking. Operating out of Cali and the nearby homesteads of Colombia's Cauca Valley, the cartel purchases *coca paste* (an intermediate product in the transformation of coca leaves into street cocaine) in Bolivia and Peru, transforms it into almost pure cocaine in jungle laboratories, and transports it to the United States, Europe, Africa, and Japan by air and sea. It is estimated that the Cali cartel produces 70 percent of the cocaine reaching the United States, and 90 percent of what is sold elsewhere in the world.

The cartel's rise to prominence began at the end of the 1980s with the Colombian government's war against the larger and better known Medellin (*Med-ah-een*) cartel, notorious for its systematic brutalization and assassination of journalists, judges, political leaders and candidates, police officers, citizens, and others who openly opposed its drug trafficking activities. In 1990 and 1991, Colombian security forces killed or jailed most of the Medellin organization's top leaders. During the same period, the Cali group expanded its operations by stealth and accommodation, rather than by violence.

The creativity of Cali combine is best seen in its imaginative smuggling techniques. Whereas the Medellin group brazenly shipped cocaine across borders in fast boats or light

---

I know what the Mafia can do to a man who has crossed them. One day you wake up with your head in one room and your legs in another.
— Vincent "Big Vinnie" Teresa

At the heart of what is often meant by organized crime are the types of enterprises just noted that sell illegal goods and services to customers. Such activities, however, are not always highly organized. Instead, they range on a continuum from freelance prostitutes and neighborhood bookies, on the one hand, to regionally organized gambling or drug syndicates, on the other.

Organized crime, as a behavior system, is typically pursued as an occupational career. In its most organized aspects, there is a hierarchical structure that includes leaders (or "godfathers," as mass media and

planes, the Calenos use the slower, yet far safer merchant marine. The cartel devised endless ways to hide its cocaine in commercial cargo. Moreover, with United States Customs agents checking no more than 3 percent of the some 9 million shipping containers entering U.S. ports annually, the odds are quite favorable for Cali.

The leaders of the Cali group take a percentage on shipments by the numerous smaller organizations with which they are aligned. In return, they provide such services as transportation, distribution channels in the consumer nations, as well as muscle and firepower when needed. Generally maintaining its low profile, Cali has been dubbed the "quiet cartel."

SOURCES: *New York Times,* July 14, 1991, pp. 1, 6; *Time,* July 1, 1991, pp. 29–34; Attorney General of the United States, *Drug Trafficking: A Report to the President of the United States* (Washington, DC: U.S. Department of Justice, 1989), pp. 17–22; *Miami Herald,* June 21, 1991, pp. 1A, 10A.

New Routes for the Drug Trade

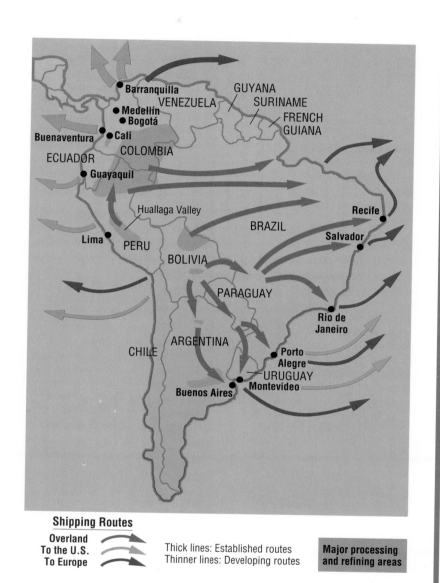

Shipping Routes

Overland
To the U.S.
To Europe

Thick lines: Established routes
Thinner lines: Developing routes

Major processing and refining areas

---

popular culture would insist) at the uppermost levels, followed by a middle echelon of gangsters and "lieutenants" who carry out the orders of their "bosses." And at the bottom of the structure are people only marginally associated with the "organization" — prostitutes, "enforcers," drug sellers, bookies — who may sometimes operate independently of the power structure and who typically deal directly with the public.

People who pursue organized crime as an occupational career most often focus on this type of criminality as a mechanism of upward mobility and are recruited on the basis of kinship, friendship, or contacts

Organized crime takes in over $40 billion a year and spends very little on office supplies.

—WOODY ALLEN

● EXHIBIT 3.7 ●

Whatever Happened to . . .

Candy Man Ronald O'Bryan

It did not take Pasadena, Texas, police long to solve the 1974 "trick-or-treat" murder. O'Bryan had made inquiries about how much cyanide it would take to kill a person, and he had been seen purchasing the poison not long before his eight-year-old son died from the lethal dose he had given him. Moreover, he had been seen giving cyanide-laced candy to his son and several other children.

On June 3, 1975, after a two-week trial in which O'Bryan claimed his innocence, it took the jury only 45 minutes of deliberation to convict him. The following day he was sentenced to die in the electric chair. Then the appeals process began, and continued for eight years, nine months, and five days. In the meantime, Texas changed its method of execution from electrocution to lethal injection.

O'Bryan never received a new trial, and on March 30, 1984,

any further stays of execution were denied. At 12:04 A.M. the following day, O'Bryan was strapped to the hospital gurney in the execution room at the Texas State Penitentiary in Huntsville. At 12:27, a needle was inserted into his arm and saline solution began flowing into his vein. At 12:40, the lethal injection began. Thirty seconds later he was dead.

Skyjacker D. B. Cooper

After receiving the $200,000 ransom he had demanded from Northwest Orient Airlines officials on January 24, 1971, Cooper parachuted from the plane over Ariel, Washington. The FBI launched a massive manhunt, but Cooper was never found. However, almost immediately he became a modern-day folk hero — a twentieth-century Robin Hood. Popular mythology holds that he got away, that he beat the system. Every year

A police sketch of the missing skyjacker D. B. Cooper

on the Saturday after Thanksgiving in Ariel, the festivities of D. B. Cooper Day are held. Hundreds of people, some from as far away as England, clog the little town's only street to pay tribute to the perpetrator of America's only unsolved skyjack-

Do you know what the Mafia is?
What?
The Mafia? M-a-f-i-a?
I'm sorry, I don't know what you're talking about.
— AN EXCHANGE BETWEEN A GOVERNMENT LAWYER AND RACKETEER SALVATORE MORETTI DURING THE KEFAUVER COMMITTEE HEARINGS IN 1950

within lower-class environments, where such activities are sought out as means for economic respectability. Whether individual criminals are within a highly structured "syndicate" or are low-level independent prostitutes or bookies, their commitment to the career is long-term and their whole social organization and lifestyle revolve around crime.[51]

Historically, discussions of organized crime have focused almost exclusively on such activities as prostitution and gambling, such groups as the Mafia and Cosa Nostra, and such individuals as Al Capone, Meyer Lansky, and others of similar images. More recent analyses, however, have extended their interest to other criminal groups, such as those involved in the international trafficking of cocaine (see Exhibit 3.6).

Professional Theft

Professional theft refers to nonviolent forms of criminal occupation pursued with a high degree of skill to maximize financial gain and minimize the risks of apprehension. The more typical forms of professional

ing. It is an article of faith among them that somehow, somewhere, Cooper is managing to live a discreetly decadent life on his marked money. But what the cultists do not understand, or refuse to believe, is that when Cooper jumped from the plane at an altitude of 10,000 feet into 200 mile-per-hour air and freezing rain, dressed only in a light business suit and raincoat, it is likely that his body was thrown into immediate shock and that he did not stay conscious long enough to even open his parachute.

Bank Robber Willie Sutton

Willie Sutton's career in crime was a long one, providing him with an estimated $2 million over a period of 35 years. Moreover, his techniques earned him many names. For his use of ingenious disguises he became known as Willie "the Actor." Because he went over the wall of New York's Sing Sing Prison on more than one occasion, he was called Willie "the Escape Artist." And because he dug under the wall of Pennsylvania's "escape-proof" Holmesburg Prison, he was dubbed Willie "the Mole." Sutton died of a stroke on November 2, 1980, at the age of 79. In an epitaph, columnist Pete Axthelm suggested that Sutton should more properly be called Willie "the Loser." Sutton had spent almost half his life in jails and penitentiaries, and died without a nickel of the $2 million he claimed to have heisted.

The Medellin Cartel

When the Medellin cartel ruled the cocaine business in the 1980s, its top leaders were Carlos Lehder, Jose Gonzalo Gacha, Jorge Ochoa, and Pablo Escobar.

In 1987, Lehder was arrested by Colombian authorities, extra-dited to the U.S., convicted on numerous counts of cocaine trafficking, and sentenced to a term of life plus 135 years. In August 1989, after Colombia's leading presidential candidate was assassinated and the Medellin cartel was accused of the murder, Colombian President Virgilio Barco Vargas initiated a vigorous war against the cartel and its leadership. In December of 1989, Jose Gacha was slain in a shootout with police near Cartagena, Colombia. In 1991, fearing capture and extradition to the U.S., both Jorge Ochoa and Pablo Escobar negotiated their surrender to Colombian authorities — after guarantees of light sentences in Colombian prisons. Escobar, the leader of the cartel, approved in advance the jail facilities where he would be held.

With its leadership dismantled, the Medellin cartel endured, but with less visibility and a considerably smaller market share of the world's cocaine trade.

theft include pickpocketing, shoplifting, safe and house burglary, forgery, counterfeiting, sneak-thieving, and confidence swindling.

What separates professional thieves from other criminals who engage in the same types of offense behavior are the social organization and occupational structure that circumscribe their criminal activities. Professional thieves make a regular business of stealing; it is their occupation and means of livelihood, and they devote their entire working time and energy to stealing. Professional thieves also operate with proficiency. Like members of legitimate professions, they have an organized body of knowledge and skills that they utilize in the planning and excecution of their activities, and they are graduates of a developmental process that includes the acquisition of specialized attitudes, knowledge, skills, and experience. Moreover, in identifying themselves with the world of crime, they are members of an exclusive fraternity that extends friendship, understanding, sympathy, congeniality, security, recognition, and respect. As residents of this remote corner of the underworld, they also have access to specialized patterns of communication, a complex system of

Professional theft: Nonviolent forms of criminal occupation pursued with a high degree of skill to maximize financial gain and minimize the risks of apprehension.

Mob boss John Gotti raises his fist in victory as he leaves the New York State Supreme Court in Manhattan in February 1990. The jury found him not guilty of assault and conspiracy in the shooting of carpenters' union leader John O'Connor. After a subsequent trial in 1992, however, Gotti was convicted on thirteen counts of murder and racketeering.

argot, and a network of contacts within the legal profession and criminal justice system that enable them to steal for long periods of time without going to prison.

The first intensive examination of professional theft as a behavior system appeared more than four decades ago in Edwin H. Sutherland's *The Professional Thief.*[52] The work of Sutherland and later researchers documented the fact that professional theft was an outgrowth of the disintegration of the feudal order in Europe during the years 1350–1550, and that it remained relatively unchanged for centuries. The types of crime, techniques, skills, attitudes, patterns of recruitment and training, interactional setting, style of life, and to some extent the argot of twentieth-century professional thieves were characteristically like those of previous periods. This system of criminal behavior seemed to persist in its unchanged and unmolested state in spite of social and technological changes and the repressive efforts of the criminal justice system, due to a highly functional structure of low visibility built around its subculture.

Professional thieves, for example, maintained a low profile in the nexus of victim–offender relationships due to the nature of the crimes and victims that were targeted. Confidence games and extortion presented little risk since the victims themselves were violators of the law and were acting in collusion with the thieves. Shoplifting offered only a limited danger since businesspeople were reluctant to accuse those persons of theft who often appeared to be legitimate customers. In other instances, such as pickpocketing, the thief's manipulative abilities often allowed him to arrange payments of restitution in lieu of complaint and prosecution. Immunity was furthered by the thief's many contacts, who could fix many of the criminal cases that did come to the attention of the criminal justice system.

Although this criminal behavior system sustained itself for many centuries, historical study indicates that it began to decline shortly after World War I and all but perished by the 1970s. The development of

Professional theft declined after World War I and by the 1970s was nearly extinct.

private police systems and police technology and communications, the bureaucratization of the criminal justice system, the enactment of federal laws aimed at interstate flight, and the shrinkage of vice areas all served to erode the foundations of the professional criminal underworld. Over time, thieves were more often identified, apprehended, prosecuted, convicted, and sentenced. The result of these efforts was to make the enterprise unprofitable, severely curtailing the number of new recruits to the profession.[53]

Nevertheless, professional theft in this classic form continues to persist at some levels. Specifically, recent research has documented that the social organization and occupational structure of professional pickpockets or "class cannons" endures in the style of nineteenth- and early twentieth-century professional thieves.[54] There is evidence that highly skilled thieves of the professional caliber continue to operate in overly lucrative enterprises. In March 1980, for example, Miami's Trendline Jewelry, a large wholesaler of precious metals, was the victim of still unknown and highly sophisticated groups. The thieves thwarted complex alarm systems that used sonar equipment and electric eyes, and then proceeded to carry off thousands of 14-karat bracelets and ring mountings plus over 800 pounds of gold and 3,000 pounds of silver.[55] And too, there are continual reports of confidence games conducted in the same manner as the professional thieves of years past.[56]

As a final note, it must be emphasized again that these six behavior types—violent personal crime, occasional property crime, organized robbery and gang theft, white-collar and corporate crime, organized crime, and professional theft—do not represent the full spectrum of criminal behavior systems. There remains, for example, *political crime,* which includes treason, sedition, espionage, sabotage, war collaboration, radicalism, and protest, in which offenders violate the law when they feel that such illegal activity is essential and appropriate in achieving necessary changes in society. There is also public order or "victimless" crime, which reflects a major segment of police arrest activity and includes many public safety and minor sex offenses, drug violations, and nuisance offenses. In such crimes, no real injury to another person is involved, nor is the theft of goods and services involved. Rather, the morals, safety, and tranquility of the community is placed at risk, and typically the offenders are not viewed by others or even themselves as criminals per se, but rather as drunks, hookers, perverts, and junkies.

According to the terms of Medellin cartel leader Pablo Escobar's surrender, he was to be held at Envigdo Rehab Center, a drug treatment facility reportedly built with his own contributions. Located in the hills overlooking Escobar's home town and converted to a jail according to his specifications, it included a large recreation room and soccer field.

Political crime

SUMMARY

There are thousands of acts that are prohibited by law and designated as felonies or misdemeanors in federal, state, and local criminal codes across the United States. Such crime categories as homicide, assault, robbery, arson, burglary, sex offenses, drug law violations, and offenses against the public order and safety are by no means all that appear in criminal statutes and codes, but they account for some 90 percent of the criminal law violations that are processed by U.S. courts. However, although crime may be conduct prohibited by criminal law, its dynamics include certain patterns and systems of behavior. It is important for any student of crime and criminal justice to understand not only the content of criminal codes, but the behavior systems that surround the prohibited acts as well.

KEY TERMS

arson (**76**)
assault (**74**)
assault and battery (**74**)
breaking and entering (**76**)
Carrier's Case (**80**)
Controlled Substances
    Act (**85**)
deliberation (**71**)
felony-murder doctrine (**72**)

homicide (**70**)
larceny (**80**)
malice aforethought (**70**)
manslaughter (**72**)
murder (**70**)
occasional property crime (**91**)
organized crime (**97**)
organized robbery and gang
    theft (**93**)

Pear's Case (**80**)
premeditation (**71**)
professional theft (**100**)
rape (**84**)
robbery (**74**)
theft (**78**)
violent personal crime (**89**)
white-collar crime (**95**)

QUESTIONS FOR DISCUSSION

1. In cases where the felony-murder doctrine has been invoked, the intent to commit murder has often been absent. In such circumstances, is conviction of murder in the first degree a just disposition? Why or why not?
2. Which sex offenses, if any, should be abolished from contemporary criminal codes? Why?
3. Are there any types of property offenses other than those listed in this chapter?
4. Should penalties for white-collar crimes be equal to those for street crimes when victims' losses are similar? Why or why not?
5. Should pregnant addicts be prosecuted for child abuse?

FOR FURTHER READING

Batey, Robert and Sandra Anderson Garcia, "Prosecution of the Pregnant Addict: Does the Cruel and Unusual Punishment Clause Apply?" *Criminal Law Bulletin,* 27 (March–April, 1991), pp. 99–113.

Girgliotta, Guy and Jeff Leen. *Kings of Cocaine,* New York: Simon and Schuster, 1989.

Meier, Robert F., ed. *Major Forms of Crime.* Beverly Hills: Sage, 1984.

Reis, Gilbert "From Deuteronomy to Deniability: A Historical Perlustration on White-Collar Crime," *Justice Quarterly,* 5 (March, 1988), pp. 7–32.

NOTES

1. James A. Inciardi, "In Search of the Class Cannon: A Field Study of Professional Pickpockets," in *Street Ethnography: Selected Studies of Crime and Drug Use in Natural Settings,* ed. Robert S. Weppner (Beverly Hills: Sage, 1977), pp. 55–77.
2. This incident in the life of Thomas Bartholomew Moran was reported to the author by Hester Marc, an old-line professional pickpocket who had worked on and off with Moran for more than thirty years. Corroborating evidence of the presence of career thieves on the *Titanic* and other Atlantic liners during the early part of this century appears in the unpublished working papers of the late Edwin H. Sutherland. For a discussion of the era of the luxury liners and the sinking of the *Titanic,* see Walter Lord, *A Night to Remember* (New York: Holt, Rinehart and Winston, 1955).
3. John Janus Powell was an alias used by a heroin addict personally known to the author.
4. John Godwin, *Murder U.S.A.: The Ways We Kill Each Other* (New York: Ballantine, 1978), pp. 29–31.
5. Paul B. Weston and Kenneth M. Wells, *Criminal Law* (Santa Monica: Goodyear, 1978), pp. 184–185.
6. Jerome Hall, "Analytic Philosophy and Jurisprudence," *Ethics* 77 (October 1966): 14–28.
7. *USA Today,* January 25, 1985, p. 3A.
8. *USA Today,* December 6, 1989, p. 3A.
9. *Miami Herald,* March 23, 1988, p. 3B.
10. *Delaware Code,* Title 11, Section 601.
11. *Penal Code of California,* Section 203.
12. David M. Maurer, *Whiz Mob* (New Haven: College and University Press, 1964), p. 68.
13. This comment was made to the author by a Miami Beach pickpocket in early 1976. Additional comments on this topic can be found in James A. Inciardi, "The Pickpocket and His Victim," *Victimology: An International Journal* 1 (Fall 1976): 446–453.
14. *People* v. *Rosen,* 11 Cal. 2d 147 (1938).
15. *People* v. *Lavender,* 31 P.2d 439 (1934).
16. John F. Boudreau, Quon Y. Kwan, William E. Faragher, and Genevieve C. Denault, *Arson and Arson Investigation: Survey*

and Assessment (Washington, D.C.: U.S. Government Printing Office, 1977), p. 1.

17. James A. Inciardi, "The Adult Firesetter: A Typology," *Criminology: An Interdisciplinary Journal* 8 (August 1970): 145–155; James A. Inciardi, *Reflections on Crime* (New York: Holt, Rinehart and Winston, 1978), pp. 127–128.

18. See, for example, *Delaware Code,* Title 11, Sections 824, 825, 826.

19. 58 *Delaware Laws,* c. 497, Section 1.

20. *Louisiana Criminal Code,* Section 67.

21. *Delaware Code,* Title 11, Section 840.

22. *Ohio Code,* 2913.02.

23. Carrier's Case, Yearbook, 13 Edward IV, 9, pl. 5 (1473).

24. Pear's Case, 1 Leach 212, 168 Eng. Rep. 208 (1779).

25. *United States* v. *Sheffield,* 161 F. Supp. 387 (1958, Md.).

26. *Bowers* v. *Hardwick,* 30CrL3261 (1986).

27. *National Law Journal,* April 20, 1987, p. 14: *New York Times,* May 9, 1990, p. A26.

28. See, for example, David M. Petersen and Marcello Truzzi, eds., *Criminal Life; Views from the Inside* (Englewood Cliffs, N.J.: Prentice-Hall, 1972), p. 165; Haywood Patterson and Earl Conrad, *Scottsboro Boy* (Garden City, N.Y.: Doubleday, 1950).

29. David A. Ward and Gene G. Kassebaum, *Women's Prison: Sex and Social Structure* (Chicago: Aldine, 1965); Rose Giallombardo, *Society of Women: A Study of a Women's Prison* (New York: Wiley, 1966); Dorothy West, "I Was Afraid to Shut My Eyes," *The Saturday Evening Post* (July 13, 1968), p. 23.

30. Neil C. Chamelin and Kenneth R. Evans, *Criminal Law for Policemen* (Englewood Cliffs, N.J.: Prentice-Hall, 1976), p. 109.

31. *Miami Herald,* September 17, 1982, p. 1B; *Psychology Today,* September 1983, pp. 74–75.

32. See David F. Musto, *The American Disease: Origins of Narcotic Control* (New Haven: Yale University Press, 1973).

33. For a brief history of drug use in the United States, see James A. Inciardi, *The War on Drugs II* (Mountain View, CA: Mayfield, 1991), Chapters 1 & 2.

34. *A Guide to State-Controlled Substances Acts* (Washington, DC: Bureau of Justice Assistance, and the National Criminal Justice Association, 1988).

35. *Colorado Penal Code,* 18-9-106.

36. See Marvin Wolfgang, *Patterns in Criminal Homicide* (Philadelphia: University of Pennsylvania Press, 1958); David J. Pittman and William Handy, "Patterns in Criminal Aggravated Assault," *Journal of Criminal Law, Criminology and Police Science* 55 (December 1964): 462–470; Marshall B. Clinard and Richard Quinney, *Criminal Behavior Systems: A Typology* (New York: Holt, Rinehart and Winston, 1967), pp. 20–33.

37. President's Commission on Law Enforcement and Administration of Justice, *The Challenge of Crime in a Free Society* (Washington, D.C.: U.S. Government Printing Office, 1967), p. 18.

38. See Duncan Chappell, Robley Geis, and Gilbert Geis, eds., *Forcible Rape: The Crime, the Victim, and the Offender* (New York: Columbia University Press, 1977); D. J. West, C. Roy, and F. L. Nichols, *Understanding Sexual Attacks* (London: Heinemann, 1978).

39. Charles H. McCaghy, "Child Molesters: A Study of Their Careers as Deviants," in *Criminal Behavior Systems,* ed. Clinard and Quinney, pp. 75–88; Vincent De Frances, "Protecting the Child Victim of Sex Crimes Committed by Adults," *Federal Probation* 35 (September 1971): 15–20; Robert L. Geiser, *Hidden Victims: The Sexual Abuse of Children* (Boston: Beacon Press, 1979).

40. Edwin M. Lemert, "An Isolation and Closure Theory of Naive Check Forgery," *Journal of Criminal Law, Criminology, and Police Science* 44(1953): 296–307.

41. Mary Owen Cameron, *The Booster and the Snitch* (New York: Free Press of Glencoe, 1964); Loren E. Edwards, *Shoplifting and Shrinkage Protection for Stores* (Springfield, Ill.: Charles C. Thomas, 1958).

42. Robert J. Trotter, "Psyching the Skyjacker," *Science News* 101 (February 12, 1972): 108–110; Sam A. Angeloff, "The FBI Agent Who Has Tracked D. B. Cooper for Nine Years Retires, but the Frustrating Search Goes On," People, March 3, 1980, pp. 45–46; *New York Times,* November 25, 1979, p. 45.

43. Werner J. Einstadter, "The Social Organization of Armed Robbery." *Social Problems* 17 (Summer 1969): 64–83.

44. Quentin Reynolds, *I, Willie Sutton* (New York: Farrar, Straus & Young, 1953), p. 19; see also Willie Sutton with Edward Linn, *Where the Money Was* (New York: Viking Press, 1976).

45. *U.S. News & World Report,* May 20, 1985, p. 83.

46. *New York Times,* March 30, 1980, p. E5.

47. *Time,* May 13, 1985, p. 51.

48. *Time,* December 28, 1987, p. 63.

49. *Newsweek,* May 20, 1985, p. 54.

50. *Newsweek,* July 8, 1985, p. 58.

51. For a discussion of organized crime, see Joseph L. Albini, *The American Mafia: Genesis of a Legend* (New York: Appleton-Century-Crofts, 1971); Daniel Bell, *The End of Ideology: On The Exhaustion of Political Ideas in the Fifties* (New York: Free Press, 1962), pp. 127–150; Norval Morris and Gordon Hawkins, *The Honest Politician's Guide to Crime Control* (Chicago: University of Chicago Press, 1970), pp. 202–235; James A. Inciardi, *Careers in Crime* (Chicago: Rand McNally, 1975), pp. 109–121.

52. Edwin H. Sutherland, *The Professional Thief* (Chicago: University of Chicago Press, 1937).

53. Inciardi, *Careers in Crime,* pp. 5–82.

54. Inciardi, "In Search of the Class Cannon," pp. 55–77.

55. *Time,* March 24, 1980, p. 28.

56. See *New York Times,* August 21, 1988, p. 33.

4

Criminal Statistics and the Extent of Crime

In the war on crime the bad guys are ahead.

—THOMAS PLATE, 1975

Arresting a single drunk or a single vagrant who has harmed no identifiable person seems unjust, and in a sense it is. But failing to do anything about a score of drunks or a hundred vagrants may destroy an entire community.

—JAMES Q. WILSON

In the war on drugs the bad guys are ahead.

—STATE DEPARTMENT OFFICIAL, 1991

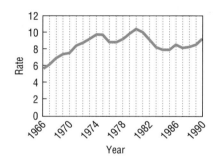

Murder Rates in the U.S.   *1965 – 1990*
SOURCE: *UCR*

Occupational Homicides Among U.S. Women

According to the Centers for Disease Control, homicide is the leading cause of job-related death among women. Of an estimated 7,000 fatal work-related injuries each year, some 13 percent result from homicide. Among women, who represent 47 percent of the work force, homicide accounts for 42 percent of the deaths — the most common case is a robbery-related shooting. Although the majority of on-the-job deaths involve men, who dominate the more dangerous occupations, homicides represent only 12 percent of the deaths.

SOURCE: *Morbidity and Mortality Weekly Report*, August 17, 1990, pp. 544 – 545.

During the latter years of the nineteenth century, French sociologist Emile Durkheim commented that the relative amount of crime experienced by a community remained fairly stable over time.[1] Durkheim's point was that this relative stability was a function of a community's ability to recognize crime; that the number of crimes known to a society or community was limited by the kinds of equipment employed to detect and count it, and by the size and complexity of the available means to control it.

With Durkheim's thoughts in mind, consider the following comments by New York City journalist Lincoln Steffens:

> Every now and then there occurs the phenomenon called a crime wave. New York has such things periodically; other cities have them; and they sweep over the public and nearly drown the lawyers, judges, preachers, and other leading citizens who feel that they must explain these extraordinary outbreaks of lawlessness. Their diagnosis and their remedies are always the same: the disease is lawlessness; the cure is more law, more arrests, swifter trials, and harsher penalties.[2]

These curious and rather cynical comments, written by Steffens over half a century ago, are resurrected here because they relate to a series of events that remain pertinent to discussion of and reflections on the extent and measurement of crime. In 1891, Steffens inaugurated the era of journalistic "muckraking" — so-called by Theodore Roosevelt — by publishing a series of exposés of corruption in business and city government. Throughout most of the 1880s Steffens was a police reporter for the New York *Evening Post;* much of his leisure time was spent in the basement of police headquarters trading stories of the underworld with detectives, prisoners, and other reporters. It was on one of these occasions that he, with the help of rival reporter Jacob Riis, actually started what appeared to be a crime wave in New York City.

One evening at police headquarters, Steffens was told the story of how an old professional thief, with the aid and protection of the police, had burglarized the Madison Avenue home of a popular Wall Street broker. Steffens put together the facts of the crime and reported them in the *Post* the following day. Jacob Riis, who was the police reporter for the New York *Evening Sun* at that time, was immediately called down by his city editor and criticized for not having the story of such a sensational crime. That afternoon Riis "scooped" a new burglary, reported it in his column, and the competition had begun in earnest. What followed over the succeeding weeks was a growing series of crime stories in the *Post,* the *Sun,* and the other New York dailies, written in a manner that suggested that there was indeed a crime wave on the streets of the city. As Steffens himself described it:

I called on my assistant, Robert, and told him we must get some crimes. We spent the day buttonholing detectives; I sat an hour asleep in the basement in vain. Nothing but old stories. Robert saved the day. He learned, and I wrote, of the robbery of a Fifth Avenue club. That was a beat, but Riis had two robberies that were beats on me. By that time the other evening papers were having some thefts of their own. The poker club reporters were loafers only by choice. They could get the news when they had to, and being awakened by the scrap between Riis and me, they broke up their game and went to work, a combine, and they were soon beating me, as Riis was. I was sorry I had started it. Robert or I had to sleep in turns in the basement, and we picked up some crimes, but Riis had two or three a day, and the combine had at least one a day. The morning newspapers not only rewrote ours; they had crimes of their own, which they grouped to show that there was a crime wave.[3]

Because of the sudden and persistent "outbreak of crime," explanations were demanded from the police for the increased lawlessness and their inability to deal with New York's criminal element. Ultimately, Theodore Roosevelt, who was then president of New York City's Board of Police Commissioners, ordered Steffens and Riis to discontinue their lurid reporting of robberies and thefts, and the period of sudden lawlessness quickly abated.

In retrospect, Lincoln Steffens and Jacob Riis had generated what appeared to be a crime wave by taking reports of robberies and run-of-the-mill burglaries and thefts from police blotters and featuring them in black headlines. Yet there had not been a crime wave in New York during that period, but rather a "crime-reporting wave," spirited by overzealous police reporters and competition among the daily presses. This pattern, initiated by Steffens and Riis, continues in many communities. Radio, television, and newspaper accounts of lawbreaking and scandal, combined with word-of-mouth reports by victims and their families, are the main sources of the public's knowledge and images of crime. Crime stories do have some impact on newspaper circulation and local television news ratings. Furthermore, even when crime is not overplayed in the media, the very mechanisms through which information on crime is collected and compiled are beset with so many difficulties that even honest attempts to report on the magnitude and rates of crime are distorted. In short, although there are likely more data on crime than on any other social phenomenon, there are also so many problems associated with using crime statistics that we must be aware of their limitations if we are to understand them and use them properly.

This chapter describes the major sources of information on the magnitude and trends of crime. It explains how the information is compiled, what it includes, how it might be best interpreted, and how it has been misused. The shortcomings and the usefulness of official crime statistics are also discussed. The final section looks at alternate and supplementary sources of crime data.

Women as Victims of Violence

- Every hour 16 women are confronted by rapists, and one woman is raped on the average of every 6 minutes.

- Millions of women are battered each year, and a woman is beaten on the average of every 18 seconds.

- 3 out of 4 women will be the victims of at least one violent crime during their lifetime.

- The United States has a rape rate nearly 4 times higher than Germany's, 13 times higher than Britain's, and more than 20 times higher than Japan's.

SOURCE: Senate Judiciary Committee, 1990

THE *UNIFORM CRIME REPORTS*

The uniform collection of crime statistics on a national basis in this country began only about half a century ago. At the 1927 annual meeting of the International Association of Chiefs of Police, the Committee

The **Uniform Crime Reports:** The annual publication of the FBI presenting official statistics on the rates and trends in crime in the United States.

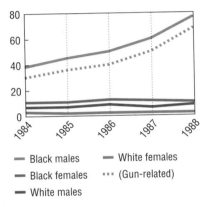

Homicide Rates *Per 100,000 in category, age 15–19*

SOURCE: Centers for Disease Control

Legend:
- Black males
- Black females
- White males
- White females
- (Gun-related)

A teen shoplifter

The crime clock

on Uniform Crime Reports was appointed to respond to a demand for national crime data. It was commissioned to prepare a manual on standardized crime reporting for use by local police agencies. Based on the efforts of this committee, Congress, on June 11, 1930, authorized the Federal Bureau of Investigation (FBI) to collect and compile nationwide data on crime.[4] Pursuant to the congressional order, the FBI assumed responsibility for directing the voluntary recording of data by police departments on standardized forms provided by the FBI and for compiling and publishing the data received. Known as the **Uniform Crime Reports (UCR),** they were issued monthly at first, quarterly until 1941, semiannually through 1957, and annually since 1958.

As early as 1932, FBI director J. Edgar Hoover was boasting in his congressional testimony about the value and usefulness of the *UCR.* The purpose, Hoover maintained, was "to determine whether there is or is not a crime wave and whether crime is on the increase or decrease."[5] From that time on, crime often reflected a statistical increase, and the FBI charted the degree and nature of that increase, any geographical variations, and other trends that were deemed significant.

The main publication of the *UCR* is an annual booklet, *Crime in the United States,* which has helped to establish the FBI's image as the nation's leading authority on crime trends. This annual periodical is the only source of information on the magnitude and trends of crime in the United States. It is relied upon heavily by administrators, politicians, policy and opinion makers, the press, criminal justice agencies, and the public at large. Yet the FBI reports have their problems. They are incomplete and structurally biased, resulting in the creation and persistence of many myths about crime in the United States. Furthermore, they have been misused and misinterpreted. In consequence, inaccurate and distorted representations of crime are continually being offered to both professional and lay audiences, and public pronouncements about "the crime problem" often have only limited basis in fact. The following commentary includes an explanation of official criminal statistics, an examination of their reliability, and a discussion of how these and other sources of information can be used to understand the nature and extent of crime in America.

Structure and Content

The FBI's *Uniform Crime Reports* presents us with a nationwide view of crime based on statistics submitted by city, county, and state law enforcement agencies throughout the country. As of 1990, more than 16,000 law enforcement agencies were contributing crime data to this reporting program, representing coverage for more than 98 percent of the national population.[6]

The *UCR* begins with a rather alarming *crime clock.* The one in Exhibit 4.1 suggests that in 1990 there was one murder every twenty two minutes, one forcible rape every five minutes, one robbery every forty-nine seconds, a property crime every two seconds, as well as other crimes in similarly frequent intervals. The reader is quickly cautioned in the FBI report that the crime clock display should not be interpreted to imply some regularity in the commission of crimes; it simply represents the annual ratio of crime to fixed time intervals. Unfortunately this cautionary comment is easily overlooked, and invariably, mass-media commentary on crime in the United States makes frequent reference to the literal meaning of the crime clock.

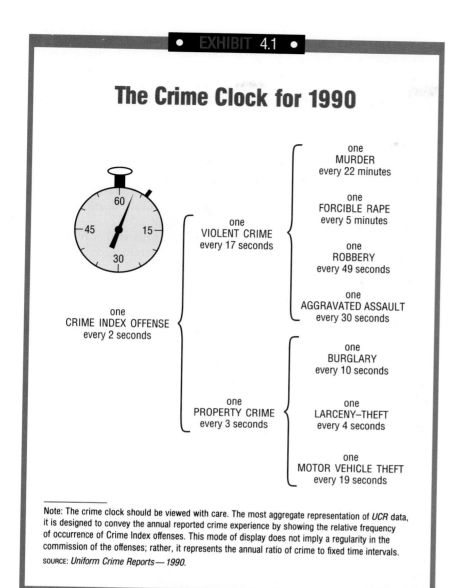

EXHIBIT 4.1

The Crime Clock for 1990

one
CRIME INDEX OFFENSE
every 2 seconds

one
VIOLENT CRIME
every 17 seconds

one
MURDER
every 22 minutes

one
FORCIBLE RAPE
every 5 minutes

one
ROBBERY
every 49 seconds

one
AGGRAVATED ASSAULT
every 30 seconds

one
PROPERTY CRIME
every 3 seconds

one
BURGLARY
every 10 seconds

one
LARCENY–THEFT
every 4 seconds

one
MOTOR VEHICLE THEFT
every 19 seconds

Note: The crime clock should be viewed with care. The most aggregate representation of *UCR* data, it is designed to convey the annual reported crime experience by showing the relative frequency of occurrence of Crime Index offenses. This mode of display does not imply a regularity in the commission of the offenses; rather, it represents the annual ratio of crime to fixed time intervals.
SOURCE: *Uniform Crime Reports — 1990.*

Percent Increase in Murders, 1985 – 1990

- In America's *Historic* Murder Capitals

Washington, D.C.	+195%
Atlanta	+ 70%
New York	+ 37%
Los Angeles	+ 13%
Miami	no change

- In America's *Newest* Murder Capitals

Milwaukee	+126%
New Orleans	+101%
Jacksonville	+ 84%
Memphis	+ 71%
Charlotte	+ 60%

SOURCE: *Uniform Crime Reports.*

Aggregate crime rates, such as those depicted in the *UCR* "crime clocks," should not be used to assess one's personal risk of crime victimization. One's individual risk varies enormously by age, gender, lifestyle, geographic location, and a whole range of other variables.

The *UCR* places its compilations into two categories: *"crimes known to the police"* and *arrests.* "Crimes known to the police" include all events either reported to or observed by the police in those categories of crime that the FBI designates as **Part I offenses:**

1. **Criminal homicide**   a. Murder and nonnegligent manslaughter: the willful [nonnegligent] killing of one human being by another. Deaths caused by negligence, attempts to kill, assaults to kill, suicides, accidental deaths, and justifiable homicides are excluded. Justifiable homicides are limited to: (1) the killing of a felon by a law enforcement officer in the line of duty; and (2) the killing of a felon by a private citizen. b. Manslaughter by negligence: the killing of another person through gross negligence. Excludes traffic fatalities. While manslaughter by negligence is a Part I crime, it is not included in the Crime Index.

"Crimes known to the police" and arrests are the two categories of crimes compiled in the *UCR.*

Part I offenses: Crimes designated by the FBI as the *most serious* and compiled in terms of the number of reports made to law enforcement agencies and the number of arrests made.

2. **Forcible rape**   The carnal knowledge of a female forcibly and against her will. Included are rapes by force and attempts or assaults to rape. Statutory offenses (no force used — victim under age of consent) are excluded.

3. **Robbery**   The taking or attempting to take anything of value from the care, custody, or control of a person or persons by force or threat of force or violence and/or by putting the victim in fear.

4. **Aggravated assault**   An unlawful attack by one person upon another for the purpose of inflicting severe or aggravated bodily injury. This type of assault usually is accompanied by the use of a weapon or by means likely to produce death or great bodily harm. Simple assaults are excluded.

5. **Burglary – breaking or entering**   The unlawful entry of a structure to commit a felony or a theft. Attempted forcible entry is included.

6. **Larceny-theft (except motor vehicle theft)**   The unlawful taking, carrying, leading, or riding away of property from the possession or constructive possession of another. Examples are thefts of bicycles or automobile accessories, shoplifting, pocket-picking, or the stealing of any property or article which is not taken by force and violence or by fraud. Attempted larcenies are included. Embezzlement, "con" games, forgery, worthless checks, etc., are excluded.

7. **Motor vehicle theft**   The theft or attempted theft of a motor vehicle. A motor vehicle is self-propelled and runs on the surface and not on rails. Specifically excluded from this category are motorboats, construction equipment, airplanes, and farming equipment.

8. **Arson**   Any willful or malicious burning or attempt to burn, with or without intent to defraud, a dwelling house, public building, motor vehicle or aircraft, personal property of another, etc.

Arrests include compilations of arrest reports for all the Part I offenses *combined with* those of twenty-one additional categories, which the FBI designates as **Part II offenses:**

9. **Other assaults (simple)**   Assaults and attempted assaults where no weapon was used and which did not result in serious or aggravated injury to the victim.

10. **Forgery and counterfeiting**   Making, altering, uttering, or possessing, with intent to defraud, anything false which is made to appear true. Attempts are included.

11. **Fraud**   Fraudulent conversion and obtaining money or property by false pretenses. Included are confidence games and bad checks, except forgeries and counterfeiting.

12. **Embezzlement**   Misappropriation or misapplication of money or property entrusted to one's care, custody, or control.

13. **Stolen property; buying, receiving, possessing**   Buying, receiving, and possessing stolen property, including attempts.

14. **Vandalism**   Willful or malicious destruction, injury, disfigurement, or defacement of any public or private property, real or personal, without consent of the owner or person having custody or control.

15. **Weapons; carrying, possessing, etc.**   All violations of regulations or statutes controlling the carrying, using, possessing, furnishing, and manufacturing of deadly weapons or silencers. Included are attempts.

16. **Prostitution and commercialized vice**   Sex offenses of a commercialized nature, such as prostitution, keeping a bawdy house, procuring, or transporting women for immoral purposes. Attempts are included.

17. **Sex offenses (except forcible rape, prostitution, and commercialized vice)**   Statutory rape and offenses against chastity, common decency, morals, and the like. Attempts are included.

18. **Drug abuse violations**   State and local offenses relating to narcotic drugs, such as unlawful possession, sale, use, growing, and manufacturing of narcotic drugs.

19. **Gambling**   Promoting, permitting, or engaging in illegal gambling.

20. **Offenses against the family and children**   Nonsupport, neglect, desertion, or abuse of family and children.

21. **Driving under the influence**   Driving or operating any vehicle or common carrier while drunk or under the influence of liquor or narcotics.

22. **Liquor laws**   State or local liquor law violations, except "drunkenness" (offense 23) and "driving under the influence" (offense 21). Federal violations are excluded.

23. **Drunkenness**   Drunkenness or intoxication. Excluded is "driving under the influence" (offense 21).

24. **Disorderly conduct**   Breach of the peace.

25. **Vagrancy**   Vagabondage, begging, loitering, etc.

26. **All other offenses**   All violations of state or local laws, except offenses 1–25 and traffic offenses.

27. **Suspicion**   No specific offense; suspect released without formal charges being placed.

28. **Curfew and loitering laws**   Offenses relating to violation of local curfew or loitering ordinances where such laws exist.

• EXHIBIT 4.2 •

Index of Crime for the United States, 1981–1990

	Total U.S. Population	Total Crime Index*	Violent Crime	Property Crime	Murder
1981	229,146,000	13,423,800	1,361,820	12,061,900	22,520
Rate per 100,000 inhabitants	—	5,858.2	594.3	5,263.9	9.8
1990	248,709,873	14,475,600	1,820,130	12,655,500	23,440
Rate per 100,000 inhabitants	—	5,820.3	731.8	5,088.5	9.4
Percent change, 1981–1990					
by crimes	—	+7.8%	+33.7%	+4.9%	+4.1%
by rate	—	−0.6%	+23.1%	−3.3%	+4.1%

* Arson is not included due to incomplete reporting.

SOURCE: *Uniform Crime Reports — 1990.*

29. Runaways Limited to juveniles taken into protective custody under provisions of local statutes.

Note that these definitions of offense categories vary somewhat from the strict legal definitions discussed in Chapter 3. These more simplified and less technical definitions are given in a uniform crime reporting handbook provided by the FBI to law enforcement agencies as a guide for the compiling and reporting of local data.

Information on Part I offenses, which are the most widely quoted and often misinterpreted, are grouped by city, metropolitan area, state, region, and the nation as a whole to reflect an "Index of Crime" for the given year, and it is these **Crime Index** data that are relied upon for estimating the magnitude and rates of crime. A sample of the *UCR* data appears in Exhibit 4.2, which contains ten classifications of crime, their absolute numbers, rates, and percent changes between 1981 and 1990. Some of the terms and variables in the table are important for reading and interpreting any crime statistics:

> *Total Crime Index* The sum of all Part I offenses reported to or observed by the police (that is, "crimes known to the police") during a given period of time in a particular place (in this example, during 1990 for the total United States).
>
> *Violent Crime* The sum of all Part I violent offenses (homicide, forcible rape, robbery, and aggravated assault).
>
> *Property Crime* The sum of all Part I property offenses (burglary, larceny-theft, motor vehicle theft, and arson).

The Crime Index: The sum of Part I offenses reported in a given place for a given period of time.

Forcible Rape	Robbery	Aggravated Assault	Burglary	Larceny, Theft	Motor Vehicle Theft
82,500	592,910	663,900	3,779,700	7,194,400	1,087,800
36.0	258.7	289.7	1,649.5	3,139.7	474.7
102,560	639,270	1,054,860	3,073,900	7,945,700	1,635,900
41.2	257.0	424.1	1,235.9	3,194.8	657.8
+24.3%	+7.8%	+58.9%	−18.7%	+10.4%	+50.4%
+14.4%	−0.7%	+46.4%	−25.1%	+1.8%	+38.6%

Rate per 100,000 inhabitants The **crime rate,** or the number of offenses that occurred in a given area for every 100,000 persons living in that area, calculated as follows:

$$\frac{\text{Total Crime Index}}{\text{Population}} \times 100,000 = \text{Rate}$$

Crime rate: The number of Part I offenses that occur in a given area per 100,000 inhabitants living in that area.

In Exhibit 4.2, the crime rate in the United States for 1990 was 5,820 per 100,000 inhabitants. That is, 5,820 Part I offenses were "known to the police" for every 100,000 persons in the nation. As such:

$$\frac{\text{1990 Total Crime Index}}{\text{1990 Population}} \times 100,000 = \text{Rate}$$

$$\frac{14,475,613}{248,709,873} \times 100,000 = 5,820$$

Percent change The percentage of increase or decrease (+ or −) in the crime index or crime rate over some prior year, calculated as follows:

$$\frac{\text{Current Total Crime Index} - \text{Previous Total Crime Index}}{\text{Previous Total Crime Index}} = \text{Percent change}$$

The Total Crime Index was 14,251,000 in 1989. The Total Crime Index increased by 1.61 percent from 1989 to 1990. This percentage is calculated according to the following equation.

Murder City

What city was the murder capital of the world during the 1980s? Miami? New York? Washington? Bogota? Hong Kong? Medellin? Rome? Moscow? What? (See below for details.)

In the 1980s, murders increased dramatically in several American cities, particularly Washington, D.C. But *murder city* was not Washington, or New York, or even Miami as folklore suggests. It was Medellin, Colombia, where homicides increased in tandem with expansions in cocaine trafficking. Medellin's murder rate began to rise in the late 1970s, and to skyrocket in 1986. It peaked in 1988 with an average of ten homicides a day, which was more than New York, Los Angeles, Detroit, and Washington, D.C., combined that year. For those who said Miami, the murder rate actually declined there by about 40 percent during the decade of the '80s.

$$\frac{1990 \text{ Total Crime Index} - 1989 \text{ Total Crime Index}}{1989 \text{ Total Crime Index}} = \text{Percentage change}$$

$$\frac{14,475,600 - 14,251,400}{14,251,400} = \text{Percent change}$$

$$\frac{224,200}{14,251,400} = 0.016 = 1.6 \text{ Percent}$$

While most *UCR* data present Part I offense information for thousands of cities and towns throughout the nation (some 200 pages of tables in 1990), other material also appears. For example arrest data are broken down for each offense by the age, sex, and race of those arrested, and by population area, for both Part I and Part II offenses. In addition, the *UCR* provides totals of the number of law enforcement personnel in the communities that contribute to the reporting system, as well as extensive information on the number of law enforcement officers assaulted or killed during the given year.

The Extent of Crime

The data presented in Exhibit 4.2 provide some preliminary indicators of the extent of crime in the United States, at least in terms of those Index crimes that become known to the police. There were about 14.5 million Part I crimes reported during 1990, including 23,440 murders, 102,560 rapes, 639,270 robberies, 1,054,860 serious assaults, 3,073,900 burglaries, 7,945,700 larcenies, and 1,635,900 motor vehicle thefts.

It was noted earlier that Part II offenses are reported in the *UCR* only in terms of arrests. Therefore, there is no measure of even the relative incidence and prevalence of these crimes throughout the nation. As indicated in Exhibit 4.3, however, there were approximately 14,195,100 arrests during 1990, of which over eleven million involved Part II – type crimes.

Reliability of Estimates

It must be emphasized at the outset that with the exception of the data on homicide, *UCR* estimates of the volume and rates of crime are considerably lower than the actual frequency of such occurrences. Homicide figures tend to be nearly complete, since most deaths and missing persons are investigated in one way or another. Furthermore, comparisons of homicide rates compiled by the FBI and by the Office of Vital Statistics reflect similar figures.[7] But in all other crime categories *UCR* estimates are severely deficient.

Crime, by its very nature, is not easily measurable. It is subject to both concealment and nonreporting — concealment by victims and offenders, and nonreporting by authorities — with the result that official crime statistics fall significantly short of the full volume and range of offenses. There are, for example, wide areas of criminal behavior that rarely find their way into official compilations. When sex, family, and other human relationships are involved, criminal codes are often in sharp conflict with emotions and social norms, resulting in the concealment of homosexual relations, statutory rape, adultery, sodomy, illegal abortion, desertion, and nonsupport. In the legal and health professions there are unreported white-collar crimes by both practitioners and clients, primarily in the areas of illegal child adoption practices, fee-splitting, illegal

● EXHIBIT 4.3 ●

Total Estimated Arrests for the United States in 1990

Crime	Number of Arrests	Crime	Number of Arrests
Total	14,195,100	Embezzlement	15,300
Murder and nonnegligent manslaughter	22,900	Stolen property; buying, receiving, possessing	165,200
Forcible rape	39,160	Vandalism	326,000
Robbery	167,990	Weapons; carrying, possessing, etc.	221,200
Aggravated assault	475,330	Prostitution and commercialized vice	111,400
Burglary	432,600	Sex offenses (except forcible rape and prostitution)	107,600
Larceny-theft	1,554,800		
Motor vehicle theft	211,300	Drug abuse violations	1,089,500
Arson	19,100	Gambling	19,300
Violent crime[a]	705,500	Offenses against family and children	85,800
Property crime[b]	2,217,800	Driving under the influence	1,810,800
Crime Index Total[c]	2,923,300	Liquor laws	714,700
		Drunkenness	910,100
Other assaults	1,014,100	Disorderly conduct	733,000
Forgery and counterfeiting	94,800	Vagrancy	38,500
Fraud	291,600	All other offenses (except traffic)	3,267,800
		Suspicion (not included in totals)	22,200
		Curfew and loitering law violations	80,800
		Runaways	174,200

Note: Arrest totals are based on all reporting agencies and estimates for unreported areas. Because of rounding, items may not add to totals.
[a] Violent crimes are offenses of murder, forcible rape, robbery, and aggravated assault.
[b] Property crimes are offenses of burglary, larceny-theft, motor vehicle theft, and arson.
[c] Includes arson.

SOURCE: *Uniform Crime Reports—1990.*

prescription and drug dispensing practices, falsification of claims, perjury, bribery, and conflicts of interest. Within the business sector there are instances of consumer fraud, purchase and sale of stolen merchandise, shortchanging, price-fixing, and concealment of income. As noted in Chapter 3, employees are responsible for countless cases of embezzlement and pilferage, while customers engage in shoplifting, tag-switching, and petty check forgery. Within the public sector there is untold bribery and corruption, and to these offenses can be added "victimless crimes" and syndicate rackets involving prostitution, procuring, commercialized vice, drugs, gambling, and liquor violations, which involve another group of nonreporting clientele. Finally, to these might be added the perhaps millions of victims of Part I and Part II offenses who fail to report crimes to the police out of fear of publicity and reprisal, a lack of confidence in law enforcement or other criminal justice authorities, or a desire not to want to get involved with crime reporting and control.[8]

A classic case of people not wishing "to get involved" with the reporting of crime occurred during the killing of Kitty Genovese — although in this instance the nonreporting was by witnesses rather than victims. On March 14, 1964, at 3:20 A.M., 28-year-old Kitty Genovese returned home from work and parked her car only 150 feet from her apartment at 82-70 Austin Street in Queens County, New York, a residential borough of New York City. Ms. Genovese had walked only a few feet when a man came out of the shadows, stabbed her, and began to sexually assault her. She began to scream and lights blinked on in the apartment houses along Austin Street. For the next twenty-five minutes the attacker stalked, assaulted, and stabbed Ms. Genovese until she eventually died just before 3:50 A.M. Although thirty-seven witnesses heard the woman's cries for help and watched the assault, the first call to the police did not occur until some minutes after her death — almost half an hour after the attack began. Days later, while the nation was still shocked over the witnesses' behavior during the crime, the *New York Times* published the following editorial comment:

The killing of Kitty Genovese

> Seldom has the *Times* published a more horrifying story than its account of how thirty-seven respectable, law-abiding middle-class Queens citizens watched a killer stalk his young woman victim in a parking lot in Kew Gardens over a half-hour period, without one of them making a call to the police department that would have saved her life. They would not have been exposed to any danger themselves: a simple telephone call in the privacy of their own homes was all that was needed. How incredible it is that such motives as "I didn't want to get involved" deterred them from this act of simple humanity. Does residence in a great city destroy all sense of personal responsibility for one's neighbors? Who can explain such shocking indifference on the part of a cross section of our fellow New Yorkers?[9]

The story of Kitty Genovese is not unique. It is repeated in big cities everywhere. On July 16, 1989, for example, a Jacksonville, Florida man was beaten to death on a city bus, while other riders sat out the confrontation and watched.

SOURCE: *Miami Herald*, July 17, 1989, p. 3A

There are many specific reasons for not wishing to become involved with the police, including one that came from a liquor shop owner in New York City whose place of business was held up at gunpoint on three separate occasions. His combined losses were more than $10,000 in money and goods, which could have been reimbursed by his insurance coverage had he reported the robberies to the authorities. He did not, however, for he was hoping to sell his business and felt that if word got out that his establishment was a "target," its potential market value would have diminished significantly.

At the same time, crime statistics are also subject to concealment, nonreporting, overreporting, and other manipulations by criminal justice authorities, either for political and public relations purposes or for reasons of personnel shortage. Law enforcement agencies wishing to secure more equipment and staff, for example, typically report (on some occasions overreport) all officially known complaints. However, if such equipment or personnel has already been obtained, the agencies may report fewer crimes, in order to suggest an efficient use of prior funding.[10]

Also, methods of recording crimes at the local level can have an impact on the reliability of statistics. Studies by the National Opinion Research Center (NORC) at the University of Chicago suggest that police may report only three-fourths of the complaints received for certain crimes.[11] Other studies have documented that as many as 20 percent

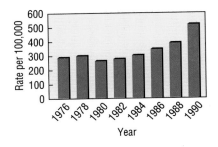

Drug-Related Arrests *1975–1990*

SOURCE: *UCR*

● EXHIBIT 4.4 ●

Sidelights on Criminal Matters
The Strange Career of "Detective Can"

Throughout the 1960s, in one of the most active police precincts in New York City, it was observed by the author that on busy nights less than half of the "in person" complaints to the desk officer were either acted upon or recorded. If the victim was intoxicated, an adolescent, or black and the crime was a purse snatching, simple assault, or burglary, the complainant was told to go home and return some other time. If the victims insisted on making a complaint, many were harassed and threatened with arrest for interfering with police officers in the performance of their duties. Those who did manage to have their case put on paper were unaware that as soon as they left the squad room the matter was thrown in the wastebasket.

This practice was not at all new in New York City. A decade earlier, substantial increases had suddenly become apparent in all of the Part I offense categories listed in the *Uniform Crime Reports*. In its investigation into these drastic changes, the New York City Institute of Public Administration found that the problem stemmed from the new police commissioner's demand that more honest and complete records be maintained. In other words, as in the "crime wave" started by Lincoln Steffens and Jacob Riis during the 1890s, New York was simply experiencing a "crime-reporting wave." The final report on the matter pointed out that

in most cases arising prior to October 1950, the information furnished by a complaint quickly found its way to a wastebasket. This practice was referred to cynically as "canning" a complaint or referring the matter to "Detective Can."

During the 1980s, "Detective Can" reappeared in Chicago, but this time as a police captain. Television station WBBM charged that for decades police officers in that city had been burying many of their cases in order to keep crime statistics down. City officials ultimately admitted that the exposé was correct, that detectives had been routinely transferring victims' files to "Captain Can," chief of the "circular precinct." Procedures were changed, and during the months that followed, crime statistics jumped by 25 percent, a clear example of a "paper crime wave."

SOURCE: Intitute of Public Administration, *Crime Records in Police Management* (New York: Institute of Public Administration, 1952); *Newsweek,* May 16, 1983, p. 63.

of citizen complaints may not be recorded in police figures, depending on the presence or absence of a suspect; the victim–offender relationship; and the victim's age, ethnicity, and methods of interacting with law officers (see Exhibit 4.4).[12]

Clearly, procedures such as these can have serious effects on the compilation of crime statistics. In 1984, for example, in a study sponsored by the Justice Department it was found that the FBI was not informed of about one in every five crimes reported by the public.[13]

In addition to these problems of concealment and nonreporting, which occur at the victim and agency levels, there are other contaminations of the statistics that result from the *UCR* process itself.

As noted earlier, the FBI's *Uniform Crime Reporting Handbook* provides specific definitions of the twenty-nine crime categories in the *UCR;* the FBI also provides standardized reporting forms to police agencies across the country for compiling their data. However, not all law enforcement bureaucracies follow directions and instructions to the letter, resulting in many contaminated categories. In 1985, for example, the FBI estimated that some 7,000 inaccurate reports were being received daily in the area of stolen vehicles alone.[14]

One reason many people do not want to become involved in reporting a crime, or even in coming to the aid of the victim, may be the number of other people around. The more crowded the city street, as in this scene, the fewer may be willing to help.

The *UCR* in Retrospect

How useful, then, are the *Uniform Crime Reports*? Are they reliable enough to provide the researcher, administrator, and observer with baseline data on the phenomenon of crime? As has been pointed out, the *UCR* data do have limitations, including incompleteness and bias, and they fall considerably short in reporting the full extent of crime in the United States.

By examining *UCR* figures within the perspective of rates and proportions, as opposed to absolute numbers, a degree of bias is eliminated. Such analyses can help determine the overall growth, decline, or persistence of particular offense behavior; they can be a mechanism for determining the extent to which the phenomenon is or is not being brought under control; they can suggest the parameters of the population cohort or cohorts most responsible for a particular form of criminality; and they can indicate the changing social and economic severity of a given offense.

Second, the most effective use of rate and proportion analysis occurs at the local level. Combining existing *UCR* data with statistical compilations available from local, county, and state criminal justice agencies provides planners, administrators, and observers with the specific information necessary for isolating community crime trends.

Incident-based reporting

In 1987, the Department of Justice began a redesign of the *UCR* program, with the testing and implementation of a new *Incident-Based Reporting* (IBR) system. When the new IBR system is fully set in motion,

in each of twenty-four crime categories data will be collected and reported with regard to the:

- *incident* — date and time;
- *offense* — whether offense(s) were completed or attempted, type(s) of criminal activity, weapons or force involved, premises involved and method of entry (if applicable), location of offense, whether computer equipment was used in the offense, and whether the offender used alcohol/drugs during or before the crime;
- *property* — type of property loss, value, recovery date, type/quantity of drugs involved (if appropriate);
- *victim* — type (person or business), victim characteristics (age, sex, race, ethnicity), circumstances if homicides/assaults (such as lovers' quarrel, killed in line of duty, etc.), victim/offender relationship;
- *offender* — offender characteristics (age, sex, race), date of arrest, and arrest offense.[15]

Since conversion to the Incident-Based Reporting system will require computerization, training, technical assistance, and support at each reporting, full implementation on a nationwide basis is not expected before the year 2000.

DRUG USE AMONG VIOLENT OFFENDERS

Robbers are the most likely to have used drugs daily, and rapists and other sex offenders the least likely. Of violent offenders, 23 percent incarcerated for robbery had used drugs daily, compared to 9 percent of those incarcerated for rape and 6 percent of those incarcerated for other sex offenses.

SOURCE: Bureau of Justice Statistics, 1991

VICTIM SURVEY RESEARCH

In 1965, in an effort to determine the parameters of crime that did not appear in official criminal statistics, the President's Commission on Law Enforcement and Administration of Justice initiated the first national survey of crime victimization ever conducted. During that year, the National Opinion Research Center (NORC) surveyed 10,000 house-

Victimization surveys: Surveys of the victims of crime based on interviews with representative samples of the household population.

Crime Rate Comparisons Between the First NORC Survey and the *UCR*

CRIME	NORC	*UCR*
Homicide	3.0	5.1
Forcible rape	42.5	11.6
Robbery	94.0	61.4
Aggravated assault	218.3	106.6
Burglary	949.1	605.3
Larceny	606.5	393.3
Motor vehicle theft	206.2	251.0
Total violent crimes	357.8	184.7
Total property crimes	1,761.8	1249.6

SOURCE: President's Commission on Law Enforcement and Administration of Justice, 1967

Is this violence, or are they just clowning around? It may be difficult for a bystander to tell.

Reasons for nonreporting of crimes

holds, asking whether the person questioned, or any member of his or her household, had been a victim of crime during the preceding year, whether the crime had been reported to the police, and if not, the reasons for not reporting.[16] The households were selected so that they would be representative of the nation as a whole, and as is the case with political polling and election forecasting, the results were considered to be accurate within a small degree of error. More detailed surveys were undertaken in medium- and high-crime areas in Washington, D.C., Boston, and Chicago by the Bureau of Social Science Research, located in Washington, and the Survey Research Center of the University of Michigan.

These **victimization surveys** quickly demonstrated that the actual amount of crime in the United States at that time was likely to be several times that reported in the *UCR*. The NORC survey suggested that during 1965, forcible rapes were almost four times the reported rate, larcenies were almost double, and burglaries and robberies were 50 percent greater than the reported rate. Vehicle theft was lower, but by a smaller amount than the differences between other categories of crime, and the homicide figure from the NORC survey was considered too small for an accurate statistical projection. As high as the NORC rates were for violent and property crimes, they were still considered to have understated the actual amounts of crime to some degree, since the victimization rates for every member of the surveyed household were based on the responses of only one family member interviewed.

The National Crime Survey

The interest and knowledge generated by the initial victim survey research stimulated the Law Enforcement Assistance Administration (LEAA) to continue the effort with surveys of its own. Its first survey, conducted by the U.S. Bureau of Census in 1972, further documented the disparities between unreported crime and "crimes known to the police." In some cities the ratio of the two was greater than 5 to 1.[17]

Since this 1972 effort, victimization research has continued under the title of the National Crime Survey (NCS). NCS data reflect the nature and extent of criminal victimization, the characteristics of the victim, victim–offender relationships, the times and places of the crimes, the degree of weapon use, extent of personal injury, extent of victim self-protection, amount of economic and worktime loss due to victimization, the degree to which crimes are reported to police, and the reasons for nonreporting.[18] For example, 1990 survey findings were based on interviews with 95,000 occupants in 47,000 housing units and projected to the population of the nation as a whole. Although NCS and *UCR* data are not fully comparable (this is discussed in the next section), Exhibit 4.5 suggests that the 2,458,000 violent cimes projected by the NCS go well beyond what appeared in *UCR* data for the same year.

The major reason for these large discrepancies is that significant numbers of these crimes were not reported to the police by victims. The NCS chart in Exhibit 4.6 suggests that the reporting rate for violent crimes was about half; for larcenies, less than a third. The major reason for this high level of nonreporting was the victims' beliefs that there was nothing the police could do about the crimes or their beliefs that the victimizations were simply not important enough to report. Less frequently mentioned were such reasons as fear of reprisal, reporting was too inconvenient or time-consuming, the police would not want to be bothered, or the crime was a private and personal matter.

• EXHIBIT 4.5 •

Crimes of Violence: National Crime Survey and *Uniform Crime Reports*, 1990

CRIME	National Crime Survey		Uniform Crime Reports	
	NUMBER	RATE	NUMBER	RATE
Total	2,458,000	1,420	1,820,130	731.8
Forcible rape	130,000	60	102,560	41.2
Robbery	1,150,000	570	639,270	257.0
Aggravated assault	1,601,000	790	1,054,860	424.1

Note: The National Crime Survey rate per 100,000 persons is based on a survey population of all persons ages 12 years and over. The *Uniform Crime Reports* rate per 100,000 is based on the total U.S. population.

SOURCES: *Criminal Victimization* 1990, Bureau of Justice Statistics Bulletin, October 1991; *Uniform Crime Reports — 1990.*

Although *UCR* and NCS data have been often compared, the two are still not fully comparable. First, the *UCR* bases its crime rates on the total U.S. population, while the NCS victimization data relate only to those persons who are ages twelve years and older. Second, the NCS measures crime by the *victimization* rather than by the incident, and for crimes against persons the number of victimizations is normally greater than the number of incidents, since more than one person can be involved in any given incident. Third, NCS and *UCR* crime classifications are not always uniform. While purse snatching is included with robbery according to *UCR* definitions, it appears as theft in NCS data. Fourth, NCS data on homicide are considered to be unreliable because violence of that type is relatively rare, and the few unreported instances that do emerge during a survey of a population cross-section are too small in numbers to project accurately for the nation as a whole.

Comparisons between NCS and *UCR* crime figures and rates must be viewed with caution. Neither reporting mechanism alone can offer a fully accurate picture of the extent of specific crimes. Nevertheless, comparisons do indicate some general weaknesses of the *Uniform Crime Reports* and suggest the relative amounts of crime that go unreported to the police.

Victimization Survey Applications and Limitations

The rediscovery of the victim as a more complete source of information on instances of criminal activity has been the chief contribution of victim survey research. The material derived from crime victim surveys helps

The uses of victimization surveys

determine to a great degree the extent and distribution of crime in a community. In addition, the surveys target not only victimizations but also public conceptions of the fear of crime, characteristics of the victim and offender, conceptions of police effectiveness, as well as other data. Therefore victim-focused studies such as these can also be used to do the following:

1. Describe the characteristics of victims and high crime areas
2. Evaluate the effectiveness of specific police programs
3. Develop better insights into certain violent crimes through the analysis of victim–offender relationships
4. Structure programs for increased victim reporting of crimes to the police
5. Sensitize the criminal justice system to the needs of the victim
6. Develop training programs that stress police–victim and police–community relations
7. Structure and implement meaningful public information and crime prevention programs

The limitations of victimization data

Nevertheless, victimization studies do have limitations. A number of weaknesses affect their accuracy. The researchers who conduct these surveys find that those interviewed tend to incorrectly remember exactly when a crime occurred; in property offenses, they forget how much the losses were. Furthermore, the same respondents are used from one year to the next. As a result, respondents may be prone to "panel bias," the tendency of some of those who are continually selected to become less willing to cooperate in the long and complex interviewing process.[19] But by far the major problem associated with the victimization survey technique is its cost. The greatest advantages come from surveys at the local level that focus on what can be done to upgrade neighborhood crime prevention and police effectiveness programs. One such community-based study occurred during 1974 in Pueblo, Colorado, a small city of some 100,000 persons at that time.[20] The cost of the Pueblo study exceeded $50,000. The cost of conducting similar studies on an annual basis in most communities would be staggering, and most communities would simply not be able to afford them.[21]

SELF-REPORTED CRIMINAL BEHAVIOR

Since the 1930s, when the FBI began publishing the *Uniform Crime Reports,* criminological research has produced studies confirming the limitations of official crime statistics. Among the earliest of these research efforts was a rudimentary victimization survey in 1933, which found that of some 5,314 instances of shoplifting that occurred in three Philadelphia department stores, less than 5 percent were ever reported to the police.[22]

Self-reported crime: Crime statistics compiled on the basis of self-reports by offenders.

Another primary mechanism for determining the nature and extent of this "dark figure," or *unknown crime,* has been the study of self-reported offense behavior, or **self-reported crime.** The first major study of self-reported crime came in 1947, when two researchers obtained completed questionnaires from 1,020 men and 678 women of diverse ages and with a wide range of conventional occupations regarding their involvement in forty-nine different offenses. Ninety-nine percent of the respondents admitted committing one or more of the offenses listed.

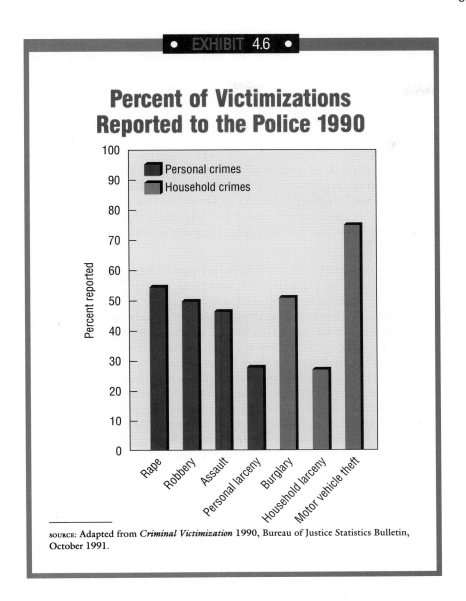

● EXHIBIT 4.6 ●

Percent of Victimizations Reported to the Police 1990

- Personal crimes
- Household crimes

Percent reported

Rape · Robbery · Assault · Personal larceny · Burglary · Household larceny · Motor vehicle theft

SOURCE: Adapted from *Criminal Victimization* 1990, Bureau of Justice Statistics Bulletin, October 1991.

The percentages of both men and women who had engaged in many types of crime were significant:[23]

CRIME	Percentage Engaging in Crime	
	MEN	WOMEN
Petty theft	89	83
Disorderly conduct	85	76
Malicious mischief	84	81
Assault	49	5
Tax evasion	57	40
Robbery	11	1
Fraud	46	34
Criminal libel	36	29
Concealed weapons	35	3
Auto theft	26	8
Other grand theft	13	11
Burglary	17	4

The uses and advantages of self-report studies

This pioneer effort demonstrated that criminal activity was considerably more widespread than police files even began to suggest. Since then, studies of self-reported criminal involvement have become more common. In addition to their use as a check on the limitations of standard crime-reporting mechanisms, they can also be used to determine

1. the extent of crime commission within the "normal" (typically noncriminal) population
2. what kinds of crime typically remain unknown
3. how the official system of crime control selects its cases
4. whether certain categories of offenders are over- and under-selected by official control mechanisms
5. whether explanations and theories of crime developed for officially known offenders apply to nonregistered offenders as well.[24]

The limitations of self-reports

Validity

Reliability

Studies of self-reported crime have provided numerous insights into these issues, but such research has not been without limitations and problems. First, there are methodological questions of validity and reliability. *Validity* refers to how good an answer the study yields. When the respondents admit to criminal behavior, are their answers true? Do they underreport or exaggerate their offense behavior? Are the respondents' estimates of the frequency of their crimes accurate? *Reliability* refers to the precision or accuracy of the instruments used to record and measure self-reported behavior. In other words, does the interview measure what it is intended to measure? Does the respondent interpet the meaning of words such as *burglary, robbery,* or some other offense the same way the researcher does? Besides these potential methodological problems there are other possible sources of error, such as the following:

- Those who agree to answer questions may be markedly different from those who refuse, which leaves in doubt the representativeness of any sample of persons interviewed.

- Those who respond to such inquiries may be truthful in their answers but may elect to conceal large segments of their criminal backgrounds.

- Most studies have focused on groups of students and other juveniles, stressing the incidence of unrecorded *delinquency,* while few efforts have targeted populations of adult offenders.

One of the more recent studies that did examine the extent of unknown crime within an adult population involved the collection of extensive self-reported data on drug use and criminality in Miami, Florida, between 1988 and 1991. The sample included 699 crack and cocaine users, the majority of whom were actively using drugs and committing crimes in the community at the time of the interview. All subjects were interviewed at length about the number of their crimes and arrests during the previous ninety days. According to the study's findings, the incidence of crime was strikingly high while the rate of arrest was almost insignificant (see Exhibit 4.7). There were a total of 1,766,630 offenses; *less than 1 percent resulted in arrest.* Although most of these offenses were the "victimless" crimes of procuring, drug sales, prostitution, and gambling, the number of Index crimes was significant — almost 5,000 robberies and assaults and more than 20,000 larcenies of one type or another.

In general, despite sample biases and other methodological limitations, the studies of self-reported crime that have been made over the past four decades are important to criminological research. First, there are the

Criminal Activity of 699 Cocaine Users During Their Last 90 Days on the Street in Miami, Florida

Crime	Number of Offenses	Percentage of Total Offenses	Percentage of Sample Involved	Percentage of Offenses Resulting in Arrest
Robbery	3,223	0.2	9.7	0.7 ($n = 23$)
Assault	1,499	0.1	11.6	0.3 ($n = 5$)
Weapons (show/use)	23,714	1.3	23.7	<0.1 ($n = 8$)
Burglary	2,128	0.1	16.9	1.8 ($n = 38$)
Motor vehicle theft	1,110	0.1	8.6	1.9 ($n = 21$)
Shoplifting	7,970	0.5	41.8	0.3 ($n = 23$)
Theft from vehicle	4,257	0.2	26.0	0.1 ($n = 6$)
Pickpocketing	32	<0.1	1.1	0.0 ($n = 0$)
Prostitute's theft	873	<0.1	8.2	0.0 ($n = 0$)
Drug theft	1,730	0.1	7.7	0.0 ($n = 0$)
Sneak theft	3,203	0.2	12.6	<0.1 ($n = 2$)
Con games	12,425	0.7	16.0	0.0 ($n = 0$)
Bad checks, credit cards, etc.	3,534	0.2	34.3	0.2 ($n = 6$)
Sell/trade stolen goods	15,746	0.9	37.1	0.1 ($n = 14$)
Wholesale drug business	16,670	0.9	9.3	<0.1 ($n = 1$)
Make/smuggle drugs	2,379	0.1	6.4	<0.1 ($n = 1$)
Retail drug business	1,639,428	92.8	72.4	<0.1 ($n = 22$)
Prostitution	15,803	0.9	17.7	<0.1 ($n = 4$)
Procuring	10,600	0.6	14.9	0.0 ($n = 0$)
Professional gambling	306	<0.1	0.3	0.0 ($n = 0$)
Totals	1,766,630	100.0	91.6	<0.1 ($n = 174$)

SOURCE: "Crack Abuse Patterns and Crime Linkages" (National Institute on Drug Abuse Grant #DAO4862), James A. Inciardi, Principal Investigator.

advantages mentioned earlier. Second, studies that focus on particular populations (such as drug users) can tell us more about the patterns and styles of criminal careers than any other form of data.

OTHER SOURCES OF DATA ON CRIME AND JUSTICE

Throughout the history of crime statistics in the United States, writers in this field have recognized the gaps and abuses in crime data and have stressed the need for a comprehensive statistics program that would give an accurate picture of crime in the United States. One of the earliest suggestions for achieving this appeared in Louis Newton Robinson's *History and Organization of Criminal Statistics in the United States* in 1911. Robinson proposed to use a model designed by the Bureau of the Census for collecting mortality statistics, with the responsibility for compilation resting with individual states and cities.[25] In 1931, the National Commission on Law Observance and Enforcement (the Wickersham Commission) recommended the development of a comprehensive plan for a complete body of statistics covering crime, criminals, criminal justice, and correctional treatment of federal, state, and local levels, with the responsibility of the program entrusted to a single federal agency.[26] More than thirty years later, in 1967, the President's Commission on Law Enforcement and Administration of Justice again called for a national crime statistics program.[27] In 1973, the same plea was made by the National Advisory Commission on Criminal Justice Standards and Goals.[28] As recently as 1984, the Justice Department made a similar recommendation.[29]

To date, the long-awaited national statistics program has yet to emerge. The *Uniform Crime Reports* still continues as the primary data source on crime, supplemented to some extent by victimization surveys, and to a lesser degree by a smattering of self-report studies. However, these are not the only sources of data on crime, criminals, and criminal justice processing. Many state and federal agencies compile data on their own particular areas of interest, which are available to students and researchers in crime and justice. These appear in the *Sourcebook of Criminal Justice Statistics,* published annually by the U.S. Department of Justice.

Given the extent to which the use of illegal drugs has impacted crime rates and criminal justice processing, more than two dozen new databases have been developed on drug use patterns, trends, and correlates. Although most are used regularly by researchers and policy makers, perhaps most significant to the criminal justice field are:

- the *National Household Survey of Drug Abuse,* sponsored by the National Institute on Drug Abuse (NIDA) and conducted on a regular basis.[30] This survey projects estimates of the use of the major drugs of abuse by persons in the general household population of the United States. As such, the estimates tend to be incomplete, since they do not include people living in jails, prisons, and other institutions, on military bases, the homeless, and others living "on the streets."

- the *High School Senior Survey,* also sponsored by NIDA, and conducted annually with a representative sample of high school seniors.[31] The high school survey explores trends in drug use, attitudes and values about drug and alcohol use, and lifestyle orientations of American youth. However, since it excludes high school dropouts from its sampling frame, significant numbers of drug-using adolescents are likely missing from its estimates.

- the **Drug Use Forecasting** (DUF) program, sponsored by the National Institute of Justice and the Bureau of Justice Assistance, offers data on recent drug use by arrestees in selected jurisdictions across the nation.[32] As indicated in Exhibit 4.8, DUF urine test results suggest that the majority of arrestees in most large cities in the United States were under the influence of illegal drugs at the time of arrest.

Drug Use Forecasting (DUF): A Dept. of Justice program that compiles data on drug use by arrestees in selected cities.

• EXHIBIT 4.8 •

The Drug Use Forecasting (DUF) Program

In operation since 1987, the DUF program collects data in booking facilities throughout the United States. For approximately fourteen consecutive evenings each quarter, voluntary and anonymous urine specimens and interviews are collected from samples of booked arrestees. As indicated below, based on samples collected during the second quarter of 1990, significant numbers of arrestees tested positive for drug use in every city, with cocaine emerging as the major drug in most locales.

In addition to providing data on recent drug use by arrestees who may not be contacted through other drug use surveys, the DUF program also provides each participating city with information for:

• detecting drug epidemics early;
• planning and allocation of law enforcement resources; and
• determining local drug abuse treatment and prevention needs.

The major limitation of the DUF data is the lack of a probability sampling plan permitting generalization of results to the total arrestee population in each city represented.

SOURCES: *Federal Drug Data for National Policy* (Washington, D.C.: U.S. Dept. of Justice, Office of Justice Programs, April 1990); *Drug Use Forecasting* (Washington, D.C.: National Institute of Justice, April 1991).

Drug Use by Arrestees

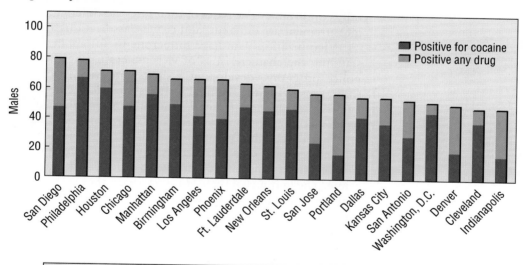

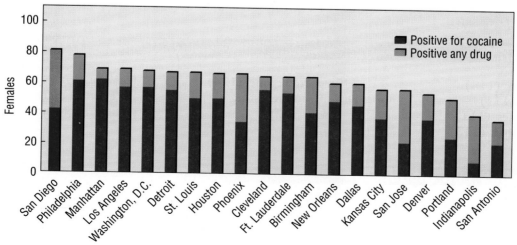

SUMMARY

Most of the data on the nature, extent, and trends of crime in the United States comes from official crime statistics. Official statistics are collected and compiled by the FBI and published annually as the *Uniform Crime Reports (UCR)*. The *UCR* includes "crimes known to the police" and arrests. Data are broken down into Part I and Part II offenses, and arrests are subdivided by age, race, and sex. The *UCR* also includes rates of crime, percent changes from year to year, and breakdowns by region, state, and metropolitan area.

Although official statistics are the primary source of crime data, they have numerous shortcomings. Most criminal acts are not reported to the police, and statistical data are subject to concealment, overreporting, nonreporting, and other manipulations. On the other hand, despite these difficulties, *UCR* data are useful for gaining insight into the relative amount of crime and for analyzing crime and arrest trends.

In an effort to determine the parameters of crime that did not appear in official statistics, in 1965 the President's Commission initiated the first national survey of crime victimization ever conducted. Similar surveys have been undertaken since then. These surveys demonstrate that the actual amount of crime is probably several times greater than that estimated in the *UCR*. Victimization and *UCR* data, however, are not fully comparable. The bases of their rates are different, the yardsticks of measurement are different, and crime classifications are not uniform.

Victimization data have numerous useful applications for understanding the characteristics of victims, evaluating the effectiveness of police programs, developing insights into victim–offender relationships, sensitizing the criminal justice system to the needs of the victim, and structuring more focused crime prevention programs. On the other hand, victimization surveys have their shortcomings. They are expensive and they raise a number of basic methodological issues.

Self-reported data on offenses represent a third source of information on crime. This data reflects the so-called "dark figure" or unknown crime. The findings of these studies suggest the extent of crime in "normal" populations, what kinds of crimes are committed that typically remain unknown, and how the offical system of crime control may select its cases. Self-report studies, however, have problems of validity and reliability.

KEY TERMS

Crime Index **(114)**
crime rate **(114)**
Part I offenses **(111)**
Part II offenses **(113)**

self-reported crime **(124)**
Drug Use Forecasting (DUF) **(128)**

Uniform Crime Reports (UCR) **(110)**
victimization surveys **(122)**

QUESTIONS FOR DISCUSSION

1. What issues of validity and reliability are most apparent with regard to official criminal statistics?
2. Can the *UCR* be improved? How?

3. How might official statistics, victimization data, and self-reported crime data be collected and combined to provide a more accurate picture of crime in the United States?

FOR FURTHER READING

Black, D. I., "Production of Crime Rates," *American Sociological Review* 35 (1970): 735–739.

Jencks, Christopher, "Is Violent Crime Increasing?," *The American Prospect,* Winter 1991, pp. 98–109.

O'Brian, Robert M., *Crime and Victimization Data.* Beverly Hills: Sage, 1985.

NOTES

1. Emile Durkheim, *The Rules of Sociological Method,* trans. S. A. Solovay and J. H. Meuller (Glencoe, IL: Free Press, 1958).

2. Lincoln Steffens, *The Autobiography of Lincoln Steffens* (New York: Harcourt, Brace, 1931), p. 285.

3. Steffens, *Autobiography,* pp. 287–288.

4. Albert Morris, *What Are the Sources of Knowledge About Crime in the U.S.A.?* United Prison Association of Massachusetts, Bulletin No. 15, November 1965.

5. Sanford J. Ungar, *FBI* (Boston: Little, Brown, 1976), p. 387.

6. Federal Bureau of Investigation, *Crime in the United States— 1990* (Washington, D.C.: U.S. Government Printing Office, 1991). Throughout this text, these FBI crime reports will be referenced simply as *Uniform Crime Reports.*

7. Daniel Glaser, "National Goals and Indicators for the Reduction of Crime and Delinquency," *The Annals* 371 (May 1967): 104–126.

8. See Harry Manuel Shulman, "The Measurement of Crime in the United States," *Journal of Criminal Law, Criminology and Police Science* 57(1966): 483–492; Donald R. Cressey, "The State of Criminal Statistics in the United States— 1960," *Journal of Criminal Law, Criminology and Police Science* 51(1960): 49–65.

9. Cited by Jonathan Craig and Richard Posner, *The New York Crime Book* (New York: Pyramid, 1972), p. 176.

10. See D. Seidman and M. Couzens, "Getting the Crime Rate Down: Political Pressure and Crime Reporting," *Law and Society Review* 8(1974): 457–493; C. C. Van Vechten, "Differential Case Mortality in Select Jurisdictions," *American Sociological Review* 7(1942): 833–839.

11. President's Commission on Law Enforcement and Administration of Justice, *Crime and Its Impact: An Assessment* (Washington, D.C.: U.S. Government Printing Office, 1967).

12. D. I. Black, "Production of Crime Rates," *American Sociological Review* 35 (1970): 735–739.

13. *New York Times,* November 19, 1984, p. B11.

14. *Christian Science Monitor,* August 28, 1985, p. 15.

15. *Structure and Implementation Plan for the Enhanced UCR Program* (Washington, D.C.: Federal Bureau of Investigation, 1989).

16. President's Commission on Law Enforcement and Administration of Justice, *Crime And Its Impact—An Assessment* (Washington, D.C.: U.S. Government Printing Office, 1967), p. 17.

17. Law Enforcement Assistance Administration, *Criminal Victimization in the United States— 1977* (Washington, D.C.: U.S. Government Printing Office, 1979).

18. LEAA, *Criminal Victimization— 1977.*

19. See James Garofolo, *An Introduction to the National Crime Survey* (Washington, D.C.: U.S. Government Printing Office, 1977), p. 5.

20. E. L. Willoughby and James A. Inciardi, "Estimating the Incidence of Crime: A Survey of Crime Victimization in Pueblo, Colorado," *Police Chief* (August 1975): 69–70.

21. For a more detailed discussion of the victim survey research technique, see Richard F. Sparks, Hazel G. Genn, and David J. Dodd, *Surveying Victims: A Study of the Measurement of Criminal Victimization* (New York: Wiley, 1977).

22. Thorsten Sellin, *Research Memorandum on Crime in the Depression* (New York: Social Science Research Council, 1937).

23. James S. Wallerstein and Clement J. Wyle, "Our Law-Abiding Law-Breakers," *Probation* 35 (April 1947): 107–118.

24. J. Andenaes, N. Christie, and S. Skirbekk, "A Study in Self-reported Crime," in *Scandinavian Studies in Criminology,* Scandinavian Research Council on Criminology (Oslo: Universitelsforloget, 1965), pp. 87–88.

25. Louis Newton Robinson, *History and Organization of Criminal Statistics in the United States* (New York: Hart, Schaffner & Marx, 1911).

26. U.S. National Commission of Law Observance and Enforcement, *Report on Criminal Statistics* (Washington, D.C.: U.S. Government Printing Office, 1931).

27. President's Commission on Law Enforcement and Administration of Justice, *The Challenge of Crime in a Free Society* (Washington, D.C.: U.S. Government Printing Office, 1967), pp. 123–137.

28. National Advisory Commission on Criminal Justice Standards and Goals, *A National Strategy to Reduce Crime* (Washington, D.C.: U.S. Government Printing Office, 1973).

29. *New York Times,* November 19, 1984, p. B11.

5

The Process of Justice: An Overview

The Constitution . . . shall be the Supreme law of the land.
— U.S. CONSTITUTION, 1787

The general law of the land is in favour of the wager of battle, and it is our duty to pronounce the law as it is, and not as we may wish it to be. Whatever prejudices therefore may justly exist against this mode of trial, still as it is the law of the land, we must pronounce judgment for it.
— THE LORD CHIEF JUSTICE EDWARD LAW, EARL OF ELLENBOROUGH, 1818

The Constitution of the United States speaks of liberty and prohibits the deprivation of liberty without due process of law.
— CHIEF JUSTICE CHARLES EVANS HUGHES, SUPREME COURT OF THE UNITED STATES, 1935

Our Constitution is in active operation, everything appears to promise that it will last, but in this world nothing is certain but death and taxes.
— BENJAMIN FRANKLIN, 1789

The inquisitorial system of justice: A system in which the accused was considered guilty until he could prove himself innocent.

The inquiry system of justice: A system in which all participants in a proceeding are obliged to cooperate with the court in its inquiry into the crime.

hrough the ages, processes of justice have emerged in numerous and varied forms. During the early centuries of Christianity, for example, when a thief was detected in the act of stealing, no trial was considered necessary. If he was a poor man who could not pay even the smallest of fines, he was simply put to death with little formality. But in the more doubtful cases, some degree of innocence or guilt had to be determined. Typical in such instances was the *ordeal by water,* adopted by the Catholic church and carried out by a priest.

Before the *trial by ordeal* actually began, a cauldron of boiling water was placed in the center of the church. Spectators, who were required to be fasting and "abstinent from their wives during the previous night," assembled into two rows on either side of the church and were blessed by the priest. While they prayed that God would "make clear the whole truth," the priest bandaged the arm of the accused. Into the bottom of the vat of boiling water the priest dropped a small stone.

If the accused were to undergo only the single ordeal, he had simply to place his hand into the water up to his wrist; but if the more serious triple ordeal had been prescribed, he then had to plunge his entire forearm to the bottom of the cauldron and pluck out the stone. After three days, the bandages were removed, and evidence of scalding was deemed proof of guilt.[1]

This ordeal by water, not formally abolished in England until 1219, could be replaced by similar tests. The accused could be ordered to walk barefoot over red-hot ploughshares, to place his hand into a glove of near-molten metal, or to walk three paces carrying in his bare hands an iron bar reddened with heat. In these cases as well, it was believed that God would make known the truth, and the accused, if innocent, would not be burned. In other circumstances, for those who were not friendless, guilt or innocence could be determined by *compurgation.* Here, although perjury was considered common, the accused would assemble a number of his peers who would make an oath with him that he was innocent.

Trials by ordeal, or perhaps by battle, were the cornerstone of the **inquisitorial system** of justice. The assumption of guilt was the guiding factor, and the accused was considered guilty until he could prove himself innocent. Inquisitorial justice became manifest when some form of divine intervention spared the accused from pain, suffering, and death, or when the accused would readily admit his or her guilt, usually elicited through torture or other forms of corporal punishment. This system — which now might more properly be called the **inquiry system** so as to remove from it the aura of terror associated with the word *inquisition* — still exists in a modified form in most countries of the world that did not evolve from English or American colonial rule. In the modern inquiry court, all persons — judge, prosecutor, defense attorney, defendant, and witnesses—are obliged to cooperate with the court in its inquiry into the crime. Out of this inquiry (an inquisition, in a value-free sense of the term) it is believed that the truth will emerge.

By contrast, American judicial process reflects the **adversary system,** in which the innocence of the accused is presumed, and the burden of proof is placed on the court. In the adversary court, the judge is an impartial arbiter or referee between battling adversaries—the prosecution and defense. Within strict rules of procedure, the opposing sides fight to win, and it is believed that the side with truth will be victorious. Adversary proceedings are grounded in the right of the defendant to refrain from hurting himself or herself (as opposed to the lack of such a right in an inquiry court), and in the notion of **due process of law,** a concept that asserts fundamental principles of justice and implies the administration of laws that do not violate the sacredness of private rights.

The following discussion examines the concept of due process of law and how it emerged in American law. In addition, the various stages of the criminal justice process are introduced. A more complete analysis of the process is presented in later chapters.

The adversary system of justice: A system in which the innocence of the accused is presumed and the burden of proof is placed on the court.

Due process of law: A concept that asserts fundamental principles of justice and implies the administration of laws which do not violate the sacredness of private rights.

CRIMINAL DUE PROCESS

No person shall be . . . deprived of life, liberty, or property, without due process of law.

—FROM THE FIFTH AMENDMENT

. . . Nor shall any State deprive any person of life, liberty, or property, without due process of law.

—FROM THE FOURTEENTH AMENDMENT

To this day, no one knows precisely what the words "due process of law" meant to the draftsmen of the fifth amendment, and no one knows what these words meant to the draftsmen of the fourteenth amendment.

—ARTHUR SUTHERLAND, 1965

During the age of chivalry, when the championing of the weak was emphasized as the ideal and when valor, courtesy, generosity, and dexterity in arms were the summit of any man's attainment, inquisitorial justice was dominant. In the Middle Ages "due process" meant nothing more than adhering to the *law of the land,* and torture was the common method of ascertaining guilt. Periods of active torture were usually preceded by imprisonment in some foul dungeon or small cell. Defendants were ill-fed and left in an uncomfortable and half-starved condition to contemplate the infinitely worse treatment that awaited them.

Eventually, the defendant was brought to a torture room to face his or her accusers and those in charge of the gruesome ceremonies. Common to the torture room was the "strappado"—considered to cause only minor pain, a mechanism used only in the early phases of torture. The hands of the accused were tied behind the back and then drawn up by a rope and pulley, thus wrenching the shoulders from their sockets without leaving outward marks. Later phases of torture included the application of thumbscrews or "Spanish boots," through which pieces of wood were pressed down on thumbs or shins in such a way as to crush

The law of the land

Medieval torture and "due process"

Flaying alive (at left) and the rack were sixteenth-century conceptions of "due process of law."

Ashford v. *Thornton*

A constitution should be short and obscure.

— Napoleon Bonaparte

both flesh and bone. Also common was the German "schnüre," in which a piece of rope was sawed back and forth across the limbs of the accused until the flesh was rubbed away, exposing the bone. If confessions could not be forced by these and numerous other exercises in horror, the final stage of torture, which typically led to death, was initiated. Devices used here included spiked barrels and cradles in which the accused was rocked back and forth, or the infamous iron maiden. The latter was a hollow statue constructed of wood or iron and braced with metal strips. Long spikes were attached to the inside, and when the accused was placed inside and the vessel closed, the spikes entered the eyes and body, producing certain death. This, during the Middle Ages, was viewed as "due process," since the use of torture for eliciting confessions was sanctioned by existing law.

The case of *Ashford* v. *Thornton* illustrates a less gruesome, although equally curious, reflection of early conceptions of due process.[2] Ashford appeared before the king's justices charging Thornton with murder. He swore that Thornton had raped and drowned Mary Ashford, the accuser's young sister. The sheriff found Thornton, brought him to court, and the justices ordered him to make his plea. "Not guilty," he maintained, "and I am ready to defend the same with my body." Thornton then drew off his glove and threw it to the floor of the court, a signal that he was demanding trial by battle. It would be his life against Ashford's, and if Thornton won, he would be judged innocent. Ashford argued that the circumstances were so exceptional that Thornton should be denied the right to defend himself in battle, but the justices were not persuaded. They ruled that the established procedure for cases of this kind must be followed—that is, trial by battle. Ashford refused to fight and due process followed its course: the judgment was that Thornton should go free.

Distinguished attorney and legal writer Charles Rembar points out that the case of *Ashford* v. *Thornton* did not occur during the age of the Norman or the Plantagenet kings, but rather, less than two centuries ago.[3] The year was 1818, almost thirty years after both the United States Constitution and its Bill of Rights, which were the basis of the emerging system of modern rational jurisprudence, had been written.

But even in the United States at that time, the concept of due process was vague at best. The framers of the Constitution had stated in the Fifth Amendment that persons shall not be deprived of life, liberty, or property "without due process of law." The due process guarantee was repeated when the Fourteenth Amendment was added to the Constitution in 1868. But what was intended by these words?

The Bill of Rights

During the First Congress, in June 1789, two years after the signing of the Constitution, James Madison of Virginia, who was later to become the fourth president of the United States, proposed a dozen constitutional amendments. Congress approved ten of the amendments in September 1791, and they took effect on December 15 of that year, after ratification by the requisite number of states. These first ten amendments to the Constitution have become known as the **Bill of Rights** (see Exhibit 5.1).*

The significance of the Bill of Rights is that it restricts government rather than individuals and private groups. It was added to the Constitution at the insistence of those who feared a strong central government. U.S. Supreme Court Chief Justice Earl Warren commented on this more than a century and a half later:

> The men of our First Congress . . . knew . . . that whatever form it may assume, government is potentially as dangerous a thing as it is a necessary one. They knew that power must be lodged somewhere to prevent anarchy within and conquest from without, but that this power could be abused to the detriment of their liberties.[4]

Within the Bill of Rights, the *First Amendment* prohibits laws and practices that have the effect of establishing an official religion, and protects the freedoms of speech, the press, religion, assembly, and the right to petition the government for redress of grievances; the *Second* ensures the right to keep and bear arms as part of a well-regulated militia; the *Third* forbids the government to quarter soldiers in people's homes; and the *Fourth* protects a person's right to be secure in his or her person, house, papers, and effects against unreasonable searches and seizures. The *Fifth Amendment* requires indictments for proceedings in serious

---

* Most authorities refer to the first ten amendments as the Bill of Rights; others include only the first eight or nine.

The Bill of Rights: The first ten amendments of the Constitution of the United States, which restrict government actions.

Identifying the Bill of Rights

To coincide with the 200th anniversary of the ratification of the Bill of Rights in 1991, the American Bar Association commissioned a nationwide poll to determine what proportion of adults could identify the content and purpose of this historic document. Multiple choice questions were provided, and the answers were as follows:

1. What is the Bill of Rights?
   a) the Preamble to the U.S. Constitution 28%
   b) the Constitution's first 10 amendments 33%
   c) Any rights bill passed by Congress 22%
   d) A message of rebellion from the Founding Fathers to the British monarchy 7%
   e) Don't know 10%
2. What was the Bill's original purpose?
   a) To limit abuses by the Federal government 9%
   b) To limit abuses by states 1%
   c) To insure equality for all citizens . 33%
   d) All of the above 55%
   e) Don't know 2%

The proportions of correct answers (b and a) suggests that most Americans don't know much about their Constitution.

● EXHIBIT 5.1 ●

The Bill of Rights

I

Congress shall make no law respecting an establishment of religion, or prohibiting the free exercise thereof; or abridging the freedom of speech or of the press; or the right of the people peaceably to assemble, and to petition the government for a redress of grievances.

II

A well-regulated militia being necessary to the security of a free state, the right of the people to keep and bear arms shall not be infringed.

III

No soldier shall, in time of peace, be quartered in any house without the consent of the owner, nor in time of war, but in a manner to be prescribed by law.

IV

The right of the people to be secure in their persons, houses, papers, and effects, against unreasonable searches and seizures, shall not be violated, and no warrants shall issue but upon probable cause, supported by oath or affirmation, and partic-

ularly describing the place to be searched, and the persons or things to be seized.

V

No person shall be held to answer for a capital or otherwise infamous crime, unless on a presentment or indictment of a grand jury, except in cases arising in the land or naval forces or in the militia when in actual service in time of war or public danger; nor shall any person be subject for the same offence to be twice put in jeopardy of life or limb; nor shall be compelled in any criminal case to be a witness against himself, nor be deprived of life, liberty, or property, without due process of law; nor shall private property be taken for public use without just compensation.

VI

In all criminal prosecutions the accused shall enjoy the right to a speedy and public trial, by an impartial jury of the State and district wherein the crime shall have been committed, which district shall have been previously ascertained by law, and to be informed of the nature and cause of the accusation; to be confronted with the witnesses against him; to have compulsory

process for obtaining witnesses in his favor, and to have the assistance of counsel for his defense.

VII

In suits at common law, where the value in controversy shall exceed twenty dollars, the right of trial by jury shall be preserved, and no fact tried by a jury shall be otherwise re-examined in any court of the United States, than according to the rules of the common law.

VIII

Excessive bail shall not be required, nor excessive fines imposed, nor cruel and unusual punishments inflicted.

IX

The enumeration in the Constitution of certain rights, shall not be construed to deny or disparage others retained by the people.

X

The powers not delegated to the United States by the Constitution, nor prohibited by it to the States, are reserved to the States respectively, or to the people.

A bill of rights is what the people are entitled to against every government on earth.

—Thomas Jefferson, 1787

criminal offenses: it forbids compelling an individual to incriminate himself or herself or trying a person twice for the same offense ("double jeopardy"); it also contains the initial constitutional statement on "due process of law." The *Sixth Amendment* sets out certain requirements for criminal trials, including the defendant's right to counsel, notification of the charges, a speedy and public trial before an impartial jury in the jurisdiction in which the crime was allegedly committed, and the related rights to confront hostile witnesses and to have compulsory processes for obtaining defense witnesses. The *Seventh* preserves the right to a jury trial in common-law civil suits in which twenty dollars or more are at stake; and the *Eighth* forbids excessive bail, excessive fines, and cruel and unusual punishment. The *Ninth Amendment* has never been cited as the sole basis of a U.S. Supreme Court decision and there has long been a debate over what the Founding Fathers of the Constitution intended to do.[5] On its face, it states that the enumeration of specific rights elsewhere in the Constitution should not be taken to deny or disparage unenumerated rights retained by the people. The *Tenth Amendment* clearly was designed to protect states' rights and guard against the accumulation of excessive federal power, but it, too, is subject to a variety of interpretations by judges and legal scholars.

Since no rights are absolute, and since they are subject to reasonable regulation through law, *the original intent of due process was not self-evident.* Madison, the father of these amendments, expected the federal courts to play the major role in implementing their guarantees, and clearly emphasized this point to his fellow members of Congress:

> Independent tribunals of justice will consider themselves in a peculiar manner the guardians of those rights; they will be an impenetrable bulwark against every assumption of power in the Legislative or Executive; they will naturally be led to resist every encroachment upon rights expressly stipulated for in the Constitution by the declaration of rights.[6]

During the decades immediately following the ratification of the Bill of Rights, the Supreme Court had little occasion to apply the promises of due process. Slavery, for example, was viewed as a matter of property rights, not human rights; and the constitutional guarantees of civil liberties and due process placed restrictions on government only at the federal level. The passage of the Alien and Sedition Acts in 1798, however, created the potential for constitutional challenge. These four acts, passed by a Federalist-controlled Congress, were designed to combat pro-French Jeffersonian Republicans. The laws extended the residency requirement for naturalization from five to fourteen years, provided for deportation of aliens by the president and for the arrest of editors, writers, and speakers charged with attacking the government. Under the terms of these stringent acts, scores of Jeffersonian leaders and supporters were arrested, convicted, and imprisoned — in direct violation of the First Amendment guarantee of free speech — yet the arrests were never challenged before the High Court.

The Nationalization of the Bill of Rights

In 1833, the Supreme Court made it quite clear that the Bill of Rights provided no protection against state or local action, but only against that of federal authority. In **Barron v. Baltimore,**[7] the owner of a wharf challenged a local action that seriously impaired the value of his wharf by creating shoals and shallows around it. Barron maintained that this represented a "taking" of his property without just compensation, in violation of the Fifth Amendment. Chief Justice John Marshall ruled, however, that the Bill of Rights had been adopted to secure individual rights only against the encroachments of the federal government.

Barron v. *Baltimore* seemingly had closed the judicial door on the argument that the provisions of the Bill of Rights should provide protection against abuses of individual rights by state and local governments.

The Second Amendment and Gun Control

The controversy over gun control is rooted in the Second Amendment, which provides, "A well-regulated Militia, being necessary to the security of a free State, the right of the people to keep and bear Arms, shall not be infringed."

What does all of this really mean? Is there a constitutional right to bear arms, or isn't there? Opinions differ. Pro-gun advocates interpret the amendment phrase-by-phrase, and quite literally too, concluding that the right to bear arms is self evident. Gun control advocates argue the reverse, that the amendment is distorted when split into phrases; that taken as a whole, it restricts the right to activities that the state determines necessary to maintain a militia.

Although the gun lobby and some legal scholars are convinced that U.S. citizens have a constitutional right to carry a gun, state and federal courts have not supported this interpretation. Where do you stand?

Average Number of Annual Handgun Crimes

Murder	9,200
Rape	12,100
Robbery	210,000
Assault	407,600
Total	638,900

SOURCES: Bureau of Justice Statistics, *Handgun Crime Victims*, July 1990; Ellen Alderman and Caroline Kennedy, *In Our Defense: The Bill of Rights in Action* (New York: William Morrow, 1991).

The Alien and Sedition Acts

Barron v. Baltimore: The Supreme Court ruling that the Bill of Rights was added to the Constitution to protect citizens only against the action of the federal, not the state or local, government.

The Fourteenth Amendment

However, with the ratification of the **Fourteenth Amendment** to the Constitution in 1868, it once again became possible to argue that the Bill of Rights should be understood to restrict the powers of the state and local governments as well as the federal government. This is because of the following language in Section 1 of the Amendment:

> No State shall make or enforce any law which shall abridge the privileges or immunities of citizens of the United States; nor shall any State deprive any person of life, liberty, or property, without due process of law; nor deny to any person within its jurisdiction the equal protection of the laws.

Legal historians disagree on the question of whether Congress intended these words to make all of the provisions of the Bill of Rights binding on the states.[8] In its first decisions after the ratification of the Fourteenth Amendment, the Supreme Court rejected the notion that the due process clause of the Fourteenth Amendment ("nor shall any State deprive any person of life, liberty, or property, without due process of law") had "incorporated" the Bill of Rights, thus making each of the provisions of the Bill of Rights applicable to state and local governments. For example in *Hurtado* v. *California* (1884),[9] the High Court declared that the states were under no obligation to follow the Fifth Amendment's requirement that those prosecuted for a capital or "otherwise infamous crime" must first be indicted by a grand jury. The practical result of *Hurtado* was that California was permitted to use the practice of "information" (a process in which the prosecutor merely submits his charges in an affidavit of evidence, supported by sworn statements) as a substitute for the more time-consuming and difficult requirement of obtaining an indictment from a grand jury. But the most important aspect of the *Hurtado* decision was the Court's holding that the Fourteenth Amendment's due process clause did not obligate the states or localities to adhere to the specific provisions of the Bill of Rights.*

"Incorporating" the Bill of Rights

Hurtado v. *California*

Constitutions should consist only of general provisions; the reason is that they must necessarily be permanent and they cannot calculate for the possible change of things.
    —ALEXANDER HAMILTON, 1788

Only one Supreme Court Justice dissented from the Court's anti-incorporation position in *Hurtado* v. *California.* Justice John Marshall Harlan, often referred to as "the great dissenter," insisted that all of the rights in the Bill of Rights were "fundamental" and that there was ample evidence that Congress had intended the Fourteenth Amendment to make each and every provision of the Bill of Rights binding upon the states. In his dissents in *Hurtado* and several other notable cases,[10] Justice Harlan unsuccessfully endeavored to convince a majority of his colleagues that "no judicial tribunal has authority to say that [the Bill of Rights] may be abridged by the States."[11]

Gitlow v. New York Justice Harlan died in 1911, not knowing that his stand in favor of incorporation would be largely vindicated by future Supreme Court decisions. The first step toward incorporating most of the provisions of the Bill of Rights came in 1925 in the famous case of **Gitlow v. New York.**[12] Benjamin Gitlow, a member of the Socialist Party, had been convicted of violating a New York sedition law because he had printed and distributed some 16,000 copies of the "Left Wing Manifesto." This tract called for the overthrow of the United States government by "class action of the proletariat in any form . . ." and urged the proletariat to "organize its own state for the coercion and suppression of the bourgeoisie."

Gitlow v. New York: The Supreme Court ruling that the First Amendment prohibition against government abridgement of the freedom of speech applies to state and local governments as well as to the federal government.

---

* The facts of the *Hurtado* case are presented in Chapter 12.

Gitlow appealed his conviction to the Supreme Court, his primary contention being that the New York statute unconstitutionally deprived him of his First Amendment right to freedom of speech. The High Court ultimately sustained Gitlow's conviction, holding that free speech was not an absolute right and the Gitlow's manifesto fell within the category of speech that could properly be prohibited by law. Over the dissenting votes of Justices Louis Brandeis and Oliver Wendell Holmes, both of whom argued that political speech should be proscribed only when it created a "clear and present danger" to the security of the nation, the majority of the Justices reasoned that Gitlow's tract could properly be suppressed even if it merely contained language that tended to have the effect of inciting violent attempts to overthrow the government (the so-called bad tendency test).

Although Benjamin Gitlow lost his effort to overturn his conviction, he won one of his other arguments — a victory that would come to have enormous influence on the evolution of the American criminal justice. To convince the Justices to hear his appeal, Gitlow had asserted that the First Amendment rights of free speech and free press were enforceable against the states. If the High Court did not accept this proposition, it would lack any legal basis for accepting the case for review and considering the merits of Gitlow's First Amendment arguments. But in a seemingly casual passage in his majority opinion, Justice Edward T. Sanford made judicial history by formally accepting the principle of incorporation of the free speech and free press provisions of the Bill of Rights:

> For present purposes we may and do assume that freedom of speech and of the press — which are protected by the First Amendment from abridgement by Congress — are among the fundamental personal rights and "liberties" protected by the due process clause of the Fourteenth Amendment from impairment by the States.

Benjamin Gitlow

It soon became apparent that *Gitlow's* incorporation decision was no aberration, but the first step in a case-by-case process that would significantly expand the Supreme Court's authority to protect individual rights against the unconstitutional acts of state and local government officials. In 1927, a unanimous Supreme Court confirmed the incorporation of freedom of speech in the case of *Fiske* v. *Kansas.*[13] Four years later, in *Near* v. *Minnesota,*[14] the Court again declared that freedom of press was enforceable against state infringement when it struck down the so-called Minnesota Gag Law as an infringement of the liberty of the press that is guaranteed by the Fourteenth Amendment.

Fiske v. *Kansas*

Near v. *Minnesota*

In 1932, the Court overturned the convictions of seven indigent, illiterate black youths who had been convicted of the rapes of two white women in a one-day trial in a raucous Alabama courtroom without the opportunity to consult with a defense attorney. The case was *Powell* v. *Alabama,*[15] the first of the notorious Scottsboro Boys cases, and the Court's seven-to-two holding made it obligatory for the states to provide defense counsel in capital cases in which indigent defendants faced such disadvantages as illiteracy, ignorance, and extreme community hostility. Although the *Powell* ruling affected only certain types of capital trials, it represented at least the partial incorporation of the Sixth Amendment's right to counsel clause. (See Chapter 11 for a more detailed examination of the Scottsboro case and the evolution of the right to counsel in American criminal justice.)

Powell v. *Alabama*

The Scottsboro Boys with their attorney Sam Leibowitz

Whatever is forbidden by the Fifth Amendment is forbidden by the Fourteenth also.
——from Frank Palko's appeal to the United States Supreme Court in 1937

What do you want? Blood?
——Supreme Court Justice Pierce Butler during oral argument in *Palko*, to the state attorney representing Connecticut

Our recent cases have thoroughly rejected the Palko *notion that basic constitutional rights can be denied by the states. . . .*
——Justice Thurgood Marshall in *Benton* v. *Maryland*, thirty-two years after Frank Palko was executed

Palko* v. *Connecticut   The next provisions of the Bill of Rights to be nationalized were the First Amendment's guarantees of freedom of religion,[16] freedom of assembly, and freedom to petition the government for a redress of grievances.[17] By 1937, the process of incorporation was well underway. But many questions remained unanswered. Should all of the commands of the Bill of Rights be made binding upon the states, as Justice Harlan had argued in 1884? Were only certain provisions worthy of nationalization? If so, what guiding principles should the Court apply in deciding which provisions to incorporate? What was needed was an opportunity to elaborate more fully the legal and philosophical issues involved in nationalizing the Bill of Rights.

That opportunity came in the historic 1937 case of *Palko* v. *Connecticut*.[18] The State of Connecticut had charged Frank Palko with first degree murder for the shooting deaths of two policemen. However, the jury chose to convict Palko of second degree murder—a decision that resulted in a sentence of life imprisonment, but spared Palko from the death penalty that surely would have followed a conviction for murder in the first degree. Undaunted, the prosecutor, citing a Connecticut statute that permitted prosecutorial appeals based upon an "error of law to the prejudice of the state," sought and won a retrial on the original first degree charges. At the second trial, the unfortunate Palko was promptly convicted and sentenced to die in Connecticut's electric chair. After losing all of his appeals in the courts of the state, he and his attorneys

An Overview of the Criminal Justice Process

EXHIBIT 5.2

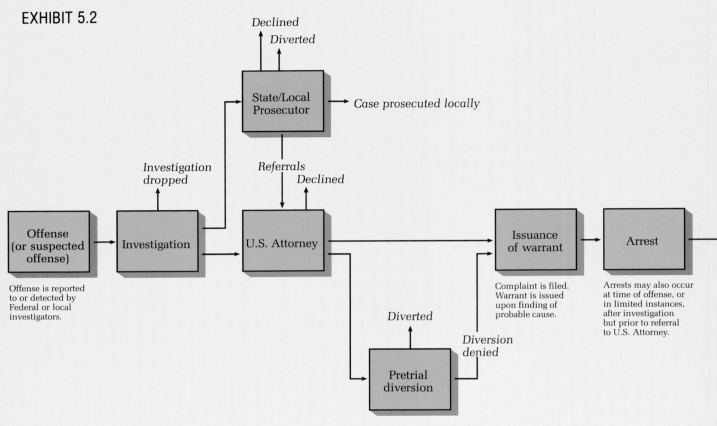

Declined
Diverted

State/Local Prosecutor → Case prosecuted locally

Investigation dropped

Referrals
Declined

Offense (or suspected offense) → **Investigation** → **U.S. Attorney** → **Issuance of warrant** → **Arrest** →

Offense is reported to or detected by Federal or local investigators.

Diverted

Diversion denied

Pretrial diversion

Complaint is filed. Warrant is issued upon finding of probable cause.

Arrests may also occur at time of offense, or in limited instances, after investigation but prior to referral to U.S. Attorney.

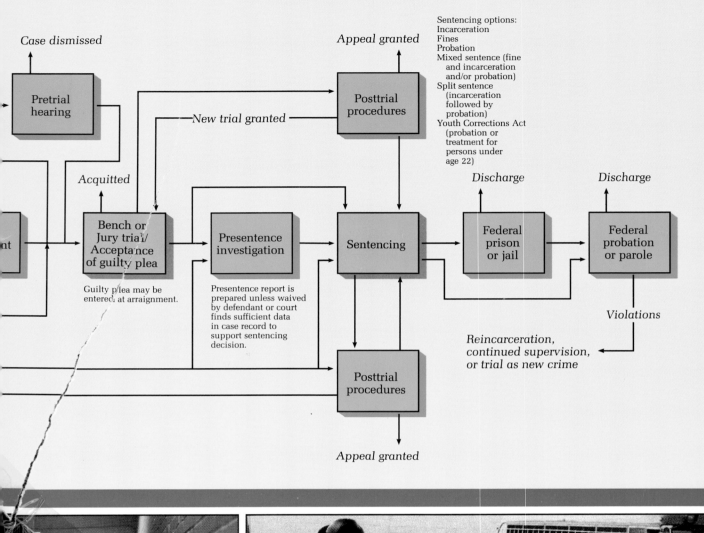

Case dismissed

Pretrial hearing

Acquitted

New trial granted

Posttrial procedures

Appeal granted

Sentencing options:
Incarceration
Fines
Probation
Mixed sentence (fine
   and incarceration
   and/or probation)
Split sentence
   (incarceration
   followed by
   probation)
Youth Corrections Act
   (probation or
   treatment for
   persons under
   age 22)

Discharge

Discharge

Bench or Jury trial/ Acceptance of guilty plea

Presentence investigation

Sentencing

Federal prison or jail

Federal probation or parole

Guilty plea may be entered at arraignment.

Presentence report is prepared unless waived by defendant or court finds sufficient data in case record to support sentencing decision.

Posttrial procedures

Violations

Reincarceration, continued supervision, or trial as new crime

Appeal granted

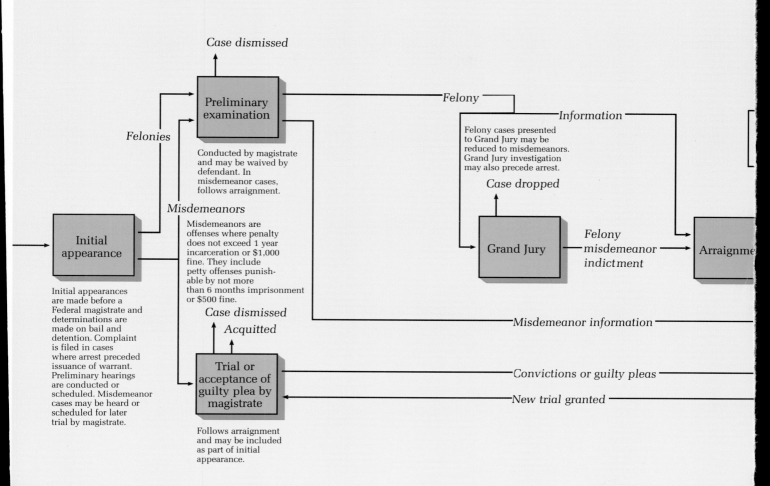

Case dismissed

Preliminary examination

Conducted by magistrate and may be waived by defendant. In misdemeanor cases, follows arraignment.

Felonies

Misdemeanors

Misdemeanors are offenses where penalty does not exceed 1 year incarceration or $1,000 fine. They include petty offenses punishable by not more than 6 months imprisonment or $500 fine.

Felony

Information

Felony cases presented to Grand Jury may be reduced to misdemeanors. Grand Jury investigation may also precede arrest.

Case dropped

Grand Jury

Felony misdemeanor indictment

Arraignme

Initial appearance

Initial appearances are made before a Federal magistrate and determinations are made on bail and detention. Complaint is filed in cases where arrest preceded issuance of warrant. Preliminary hearings are conducted or scheduled. Misdemeanor cases may be heard or scheduled for later trial by magistrate.

Case dismissed

Acquitted

Trial or acceptance of guilty plea by magistrate

Follows arraignment and may be included as part of initial appearance.

Misdemeanor information

Convictions or guilty pleas

New trial granted

appealed to the U.S. Supreme Court on the grounds that his second trial constituted a violation of the Fifth Amendment protection against double jeopardy and that the Fifth Amendment was binding upon the states as a result of the Fourteenth Amendment's due process clause. (See Chapter 12 for more discussion of double jeopardy.)

There was—and is—no question that Frank Palko's retrial and conviction had violated the double jeopardy clause. In a majority opinion authored by Justice Benjamin Cardozo, however, the Supreme Court ruled against his claims and Palko was subsequently electrocuted. But, ironically, it would be reasonable to say that Frank Palko did not die in vain. For Justice Cardozo's majority opinion laid the foundation—a series of guidelines and principles—that would eventually lead to the incorporation of not only the double jeopardy clause, but nearly all of the other key provisions of the Bill of Rights.

At the heart of Justice Cardozo's *Palko* opinion was his rejection of the notion of total incorporation and an effort to establish what has been called the "Honor Roll of Superior Rights." Cardozo wrote eloquently of "those fundamental principles of liberty and justice which lie at the base of all our civil and political institutions." He cited freedom of speech as the cardinal example of a "fundamental right," stressing that the right to speak freely "is the matrix, the indispensable condition, of nearly every other form of freedom." Justice Cardozo also cited freedom of the press and the Fifth Amendment's prohibition against governmental takings of private property without just compensation (the so-called eminent domain clause) as examples of fundamental rights in a democratic society.

On the other end of the continuum of rights, however, were "formal" rights that were admirable and worthy of respect, but without which "justice would not perish." As examples, Cardozo cited the Sixth Amendment right to trial by jury and the Fifth Amendment right to be indicted by a grand jury when charged with "a capital or otherwise infamous crime." Such rights, he explained,

are not of the essence of a scheme of ordered liberty. To abolish them is not to violate a principle of justice so rooted in the traditions and conscience of our people as to be ranked as fundamental.

Justice Cardozo next turned to the Fifth Amendment protection against compulsory self-incrimination. This too was not a "fundamental" right, he asserted, because "justice would not perish if the accused were subject to a duty to respond to orderly inquiry." Having articulated the standards to be applied, Cardozo finally posed the question that would determine the fate of Frank Palko: Did Connecticut's denial of Palko's Fifth Amendment protection against double jeopardy violate those "fundamental principles of liberty and justice which lie at the base of all our civil and political institutions"?

The answer "surely must be 'no'," wrote Justice Cardozo. The State of Connecticut wasn't trying to harass and wear down Mr. Palko by repeatedly charging him with the same crime; the Connecticut authorities merely were asking that "the case against him . . . go on until there shall be a trial free from the corrosion of substantial legal error." This, asserted Cardozo, was no great affront to fundamental principles of justice. Indeed, "the edifice of justice stands, in its symmetry, to many, greater than before." And thus the double jeopardy clause failed to make "the Honor Roll of Superior Rights," thereby leaving the states free to pass laws in violation of the Fifth Amendment's command that no

The Fifth Amendment double jeopardy protection safeguards an accused from being tried more than once for the same offense.

Supreme Court Justice Benjamin Nathan Cardozo. Cardozo was born in New York City in 1870. His parents were descendants of Sephardic Jews who settled in New York earlier in the century; one of his ancestors authored the words at the base of the Statue of Liberty. At age fifteen, Benjamin Cardozo was admitted to Columbia University, graduating with honors in 1889, and completing his master's degree and entering law school the following year. In 1891 he was admitted to the New York bar without a law degree. After twenty-three years as a private lawyer, he was elected to the New York Supreme Court. In 1932 President Herbert Hoover appointed Cardozo to the U.S. Supreme Court, where he served until his death six years later.

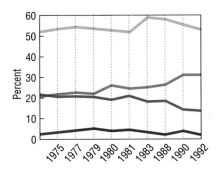

Percent

— Legal under certain circumstances
— Legal in all cases
— Illegal in all cases
— No opinion

Opinions on Abortion, 1975–1990 Do you
think abortions should be legal in all cases,
under certain circumstances, or not at all?

SOURCE: Gallup Poll, April 1990

person shall "be subject for the same offense to be twice put in jeopardy of life or limb."

Justice Cardozo's distinctions between "fundamental" rights, on the one hand, and "formal" rights, on the other hand, are still in effect. The criteria articulated in *Palko* are firmly in place and unlikely ever to be modified or transformed by the Supreme Court. And, in fact, Justice Cardozo's "Honor Roll" itself changed only twice between 1937 and 1961. In 1947, the Court added the First Amendment's requirement of "separation of church and state" to the list of rights that applied to the states as an element of the Fourteenth Amendment's due process clause.[19] One year later, the Sixth Amendment's guarantee of the right to a "public trial" was incorporated, thus prohibiting the states from conducting trials and sentencings in secret.[20]

The Criminal Law "Revolution" By the early 1960s, the composition of the Supreme Court had changed and so, arguably, had the beliefs and values of the American people. Under Chief Justice Earl Warren, who had been appointed by President Eisenhower in 1953, the Supreme Court had made it clear that constitutional rights were not static concepts, frozen in eighteenth century notions of justice and fairness. The protections of the Bill of Rights, in Chief Justice Warren's memorable phrase from *Trop* v. *Dulles,*[21] "must draw [their] meaning from evolving standards of decency that mark the progress of a maturing society."

The year 1961 marks the beginning of what many legal scholars call "the criminal law revolution." Throughout the 1960s, the Supreme Court, applying the very same guiding principles articulated by Justice Cardozo in *Palko,* expanded the "Honor Roll of Superior Rights" considerably. By 1969, almost all of the criminal law–related provisions of the Bill of Rights had been made binding upon the states as elements of Fourteenth Amendment due process.

Mapp v. *Ohio*

In the historic 1961 case of *Mapp* v. *Ohio,*[22] the High Court declared that both the Fourth Amendment's proscription of "unreasonable searches and seizures" and the exclusionary rule (prohibiting the use of illegally seized evidence in a criminal trial) were applicable to the states (see Chapter 8). The Eighth Amendment's ban on cruel and unusual punishments was incorporated in 1962.[23] and the Sixth Amendment's right to counsel was imposed on the states one year later in the famous case of *Gideon* v. *Wainwright* (see Chapter 11).[24] In 1964, the Fifth Amendment's protection against self-incrimination was incorporated,[25] and in 1965, the Sixth Amendment right to confront hostile witnesses was given the same status.[26] The year 1967 saw two Sixth Amendment protections added to the Honor Roll: the guarantee of a speedy trial[27] and the right to compulsory processes for obtaining defense witnesses.[28]

Gideon v. *Wainwright*

The process of nationalizing the Bill of Rights reached its climax in two decisions announced shortly before the end of the Warren Court era. In 1968, the Court declared that the Sixth Amendment's guarantee of trial by jury applies to state criminal trials involving serious offenses.[29] And in the 1969 case of *Benton* v. *Maryland,*[30] the Justices finally ruled that the time had come to make the Fifth Amendment ban on double jeopardy binding upon the states. The *Benton* Court's determination that the provision against double jeopardy was indeed a "fundamental right that was implicit in the concept of ordered liberty" overruled *Palko* v. *Connecticut* (thirty-two years too late for Frank Palko) and completed — for now — the process of nationalizing the Bill of Rights.

Benton v. *Maryland*

Since *Benton,* the Supreme Court has not incorporated any more of the specific provisions of the Bill of Rights. However, it is worth mentioning that in 1965, the Court in *Griswold v. Connecticut*[31] incorporated the right to "privacy"—a right not specifically cited in the Bill of Rights (or anywhere else in the U.S. Constitution). The Court overturned a Connecticut law that made it a crime for any person, married or single, to use any kind of contraceptive. Speaking through a majority opinion written by Justice William Douglas, the Court reasoned that a right to privacy was implicit in the Constitution as a result of "zones of privacy" created by the "liberty" safeguards in the due process clauses of the Fifth and Fourteenth Amendments and by the "penumbras" surrounding the First, Third, Fourth, Fifth, and Ninth Amendments.

Griswold v. Connecticut: The Supreme Court ruling that a right of personal privacy is implicit in the Constitution.

The question of whether it was proper for the Court to find a right to privacy in the Constitution remains controversial today. Certainly, the most famous application of this newly discovered right to privacy came in January 1973 with the announcement of the Court's decision in *Roe* v. *Wade.*[32] In *Roe,* the Court held that the right of privacy rendered unconstitutional all state laws that made it a crime or otherwise restricted a woman's right to obtain an abortion in the first three months of pregnancy. On the other hand, in 1986, in *Bowers* v. *Hardwick*[33] (touched on briefly in Chapter 3), a five-to-four majority of the Court held that this same right to privacy could not be used to invalidate state laws making it a crime for consenting adults to engage in homosexual sodomy in the privacy of their own homes. Thus, at this point, it seems safe to say that a right to privacy has been found to be implicit in the Constitution and enforceable against the states, but the precise scope of this right will have to be decided by the Court on a case-by-case basis.

Roe v. *Wade*

Bowers v. *Hardwick*

The Law of the Land

Currently, nearly all of the specific provisions of the Bill of Rights and the *Griswold*-created right of privacy are binding upon the states as elements of the Fourteenth Amendment due process clause. The easiest way to remember what is and is not incorporated is to list the rights that have not been made obligatory upon the states. Of the first eight amendments (the amendments that refer to the specific rights of individuals), these are the only provisions that have not been incorporated:

1. The Second Amendment right to bear arms as part of a well-regulated militia
2. The Third Amendment protection against the involuntary quartering of soldiers in our houses
3. The Fifth Amendment protection against being prosecuted for "a capital or otherwise infamous crime"
4. The Seventh Amendment right to a jury trial in cases involving more than $20
5. The Eighth Amendment protection against excessive bail
6. The Eighth Amendment protection against excessive fines

This textbook traces the case-by-case process by which incorporation has occurred in greater detail in such areas as self incrimination and search and seizure (Chapter 8), the right to counsel (Chapter 11), and protection against cruel and unusual punishments (Chapter 13). For now, it is important to understand that although the Supreme Court has not fulfilled Justice Harlan's hope for total incorporation of the Bill of

Selective incorporation

Rights, it has achieved what legal scholars call *selective incorporation*. This means simply that most, but not all, of the provisions of the Bill of Rights are binding upon the states. This accomplishment — the nationalization of the Bill of Rights — has radically altered the American system of criminal justice as practiced by state and local governments. None of the major Court-imposed changes in criminal procedure to be discussed in this text (such as the exclusionary rule, the Miranda rule, and changes in death penalty laws) could have occurred in the absence of selective incorporation.

Due process in American law

The process of selective incorporation also added greater specificity to the meaning of words "due process of law." But the concept of due process is anything but precise. Whether a particular police practice or court rule is held to violate due process will always depend upon the totality of facts and circumstances in a particular case and upon a court's effort to apply those facts and circumstances in the context of one or more principles of law. Thus, due process should be understood as asserting a fundamental principle of justice rather than a specific rule of law. It implies and comprehends the administration of laws that do not violate the very foundations of civil liberties; it requires in each case an evaluation based on a disinterested inquiry, on a balanced order of facts exactly and fairly stated, on the detached consideration of conflicting claims, and on a judgment mindful of reconciling the needs of continuity and change in complex society. Or as statesman Daniel Webster maintained, due process suggested "the law which hears before it condemns; which proceeds upon inquiry, and renders judgement only after trial." [34] Yet even these comments fail to explain fully the due process clause. A better understanding might be achieved by considering due process in its two aspects: *substantive* and *procedural*.

We justices read the Constitution the only way we can: as 20th century Americans. The genius of the Constitution rests not in any static meaning it might have had in a world that is dead and gone, but in the adaptability of its great principles to cope with current problems.

— FORMER SUPREME COURT JUSTICE
WILLIAM BRENNAN

Substantive Due Process

Substantive due process: Due process protection against unreasonable, arbitrary, or capricious laws or acts.

Substantive due process refers to the content or subject matter of a law. It protects persons against unreasonable, arbitrary, or capricious laws or acts by all branches of government. In the criminal justice process, one illustration of substantive due process in the **void-for-vagueness doctrine.** Under its precepts, due process requires that a criminal law must

necessarily guess at its meaning and differ as to its application." [35] The Supreme Court has struck down criminal statutes and local ordinances that, for example, made it unlawful to wander the streets late at night "without lawful business," [36] to "treat contemptuously the American flag," [37] and to willfully "obstruct public passages." [38] In all of these cases, the issue of substantive due process and the void-for-vagueness doctrine came into play because the statutes were neither definite nor certain as to the category of persons they referred to or the conduct that was forbidden.

A landmark case involving substantive due process occurred in **Buck v. Bell** in 1927.[39] Carrie Buck was an 18-year-old feebleminded white woman, who was committed in 1924 to the Virginia State Colony for Epileptics and the Feeble Minded. Carrie was also the daughter of a feebleminded mother, and the mother of a feebleminded, illegitimate baby. A Virginia statute at that time provided that the health of the patient and the welfare of society may be promoted in certain cases by the sterilization of mental defectives, and that the superintendent of the state colony where Carrie resided could recommend to its board of directors that the sterilization occur. The sterilization was ordered, and although Carrie may have been feebleminded, she understood what was about to happen to her and initiated the appeals procedure.

The county circuit court as well as the Virginia Supreme Court of Appeals both affirmed the sterilization decree, agreeing that such a sterilization law was a "blessing" for feebleminded persons like Carrie. Her lawyers then appealed to the United States Supreme Court on the grounds that the *substance* of the Virginia law represented a denial of due process, that the law was arbitrary, capricious, and unreasonable, and that it was a violation of the Fourteenth Amendment guarantee of equal protection. Chief Justice Oliver Wendell Holmes, Jr., upheld the Virginia statute, and offered the following comment:

The void-for-vagueness doctrine: The rule that criminal laws that are unclear or uncertain as to *what* or to *whom* they apply violate due process.

***Buck* v. *Bell*:** The Supreme Court ruling that Virginia did not violate the Fourteenth Amendment's due process guarantee when it sterilized, without her consent, a mentally defective mother.

Law and justice are not always the same. When they aren't, destroying the law may be the first step toward changing it.

—GLORIA STEINEM

Drawing by P. Steiner © 1982 *The New Yorker Magazine, Inc.*

"Remember, gentlemen, we aren't here just to draft a constitution. We're here to draft the best damned constitution in the world."

It is better for all the world, if instead of waiting to execute degenerate offspring for crime, or to let them starve for their imbecility, society can prevent those who are manifestly unfit from continuing their kind. . . . Three generations of imbeciles are enough.[40]

Carrie Buck was ultimately sterilized, and the philosophy of *Buck* v. *Bell* has been the object of heavy criticism. Nevertheless, it illustrates the concept of substantive due process and its inherent problems. In *Skinner* v. *Oklahoma*,[41] however, which was a test of the constitutionality of Oklahoma's Habitual Criminal Sterilization Act in 1942, the High Court ruled in favor of Arthur Skinner, a third-felony offender duly sentenced to a term of imprisonment for larceny. The sterilization law was struck down for its denials of both equal protection, since it applied only to certain types of felony offenses while not considering such crimes as embezzlement, political offenses, and violations of revenue acts, and of substantive due process.

Skinner v. *Oklahoma*

Procedural Due Process

Neither *Buck* v. *Bell* nor *Skinner* v. *Oklahoma* had any argument with the procedures through which the decision to sterilize had been made. Rather, they were attacking the *substance* of the laws that demanded sterilization. By contrast, **procedural due process** is concerned with the notice, hearing, and other procedures that are required before the life, liberty, or property of a person may be taken by the government. In general, procedural due process requires the following:

Procedural due process: The procedures that are required before the life, liberty, or property of a person may be taken by the government.

1. Notice of the proceedings
2. A hearing
3. Opportunity to present a defense
4. An impartial tribunal
5. An atmosphere of fairness

U.S. v. *Valdovinos-Valdovinos* in 1984,[42] a case in which the United States District Court for the Northern District of California considered the government's conduct so outrageous that the charges had to be dismissed, focused on the issue of procedural due process. In *Valdovinos-Valdovinos,* the Immigration and Naturalization Service (INS) was attempting to stem the flow of illegal aliens from Mexico. The major investigator tool was what is known as a ''cold line,'' an undercover telephone operation in which agents posing as U.S. employers offered to reimburse aliens for their smuggling expenses and to give them jobs. The INS disseminated the cold-line telephone number in Mexico and used the operation to advise Mexican nationals still within Mexico that it was appropriate to violate United States law. The district court ruled that the procedure was a violation of due process; the operation was not for the purpose of infiltrating crime, but ''the generation by police of new crimes merely for the sake of pressing criminal charges.'' As such, the INS cold-line procedure was no more than entrapment.

Since the criminal law revolution of the 1960s, when questions concerning the procedural rights of criminal defendants came under closer and more frequent scrutiny by the United States Supreme Court, the due process clause of the Fifth and Fourteenth Amendments has been clarified and extended. The decisions handed down by the High Court have had a significant impact on the processing of defendants and offenders through all phases of the criminal justice process — from arrest

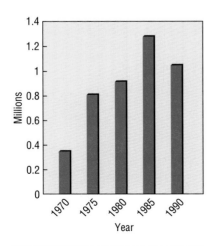

Illegal Immigrants Entering the U.S.

to trial and from sentencing through corrections. In the remainder of this chapter, these phases of the criminal justice process are outlined and described. The influence of the Supreme Court's decisions involving questions of due process and other constitutional rights in arrest, trial, and sentencing practices are examined in later sections.

THE CRIMINAL JUSTICE PROCESS

Criminal justice in the United States exists for the control and prevention of crime, and as a "process"—the **criminal justice process**—it involves those agencies and procedures set up to manage both crime and the persons accused of violating the criminal law. As an organizational complex, criminal justice includes the agencies of law enforcement charged with the prevention of crime and the apprehension of criminal offenders; it includes the court bureaucracies charged with determining the innocence or guilt of accused offenders and with the sentencing of convicted criminals; and it includes the network of corrections charged with the control, custody, supervision, and treatment for those convicted of crime.

There are many steps in the criminal justice process. The three-part fold-out Exhibit 5.2 broadly outlines the phases of case processing at the federal level. The federal system is the general model followed by most state and local courts.

The criminal justice process: The agencies and procedures set up to manage both crime and the persons accused of violating the criminal law.

Prearrest Investigation

Although the first phase of the criminal justice process would seem logically to be arrest, this is usually the case only when a crime is directly observed by a law enforcement officer. In other situations, the process begins with some level of investigation. Prearrest investigation can be initiated when police receive either a complaint from a victim or witness, knowledge from informers, or through surveillance. Typically, investigative activities include an examination of the scene of a crime, a search for physical evidence, interviews with victims and witnesses, and the quest for the perpetrator. Data from informers or general surveillance can suggest that some "suspicious" activity is occurring—perhaps gambling, drug sales, prostitution, or disorderly behavior—at which point an officer's or a detective's "go-out-and-look" investigations take place.

Prearrest investigations can also occur in another manner, sometimes even before a crime has actually been committed. Law enforcement agencies at the local, state, and federal levels become involved in long-term investigations when crime is not necessarily known, but is strongly suspected or believed about to occur. This type of investigation is most typical of federal enforcement agencies, such as the Federal Bureau of Investigation, the Internal Revenue Service, the Customs Service, and the Postal Inspection Service. Such investigations, which include the use of informers, undercover agents, surveillance, and perhaps wiretapping and other electronic eavesdropping devices, have been common in recent years in investigations of international money laundering operations (see Exhibit 5.3).

It should be noted that in all types of prearrest investigation, it is possible for the investigation activities to continue beyond the point at which the evidence necessary for an arrest has been gathered.

● EXHIBIT 5.3 ●

Sidelights on Criminal Matters
"Laundering" Cocaine Cash

"Money laundries" have been used for decades by organized crime figures and others wanting to keep large amounts of money from being taxed. Currently, the widest use of these laundering operations occurs among high-level drug dealers and traffickers who accumulate millions of dollars each week. Because of the amount of funds involved, the dollars cannot be spent or invested without attracting government attention. Thus, the "dirty" money must be "cleaned." Hence, the need for "laundering" or "rinsing."

Federal investigations have found that a common form of money laundering occurs through banks in Miami, the Bahamas, the Grand Cayman Islands, Switzerland, Hong Kong, and elsewhere. The pattern involves the depositing of, say, $10 million in cash in a U.S. bank. Although the Bank Secrecy Act (discussed earlier in Exhibit 2.2) requires that deposits of $10,000 or more must be reported by banks to the Internal Revenue Service (IRS), for a 2 percent fee some banks "forget" to file the proper notice

with the IRS. The American bank then wires the money to an account in the Cayman Islands, a country with strict banking laws that protect the privacy and identity of depositors. The account to which the money is wired belongs to a bogus Cayman Islands corporation owned by the drug trafficker. The corporation, by way of the Cayman Islands bank, returns the money to the drug dealer in the form of a "loan." In this way the dealer gets his money back, "clean," in an ostensibly lawful manner. Since the money is in the form of a loan, it is not subject to taxation.

Investigators and analysts from the Drug Enforcement Administration, the Internal Revenue Service, and the Central Intelligence Agency report that more complex money laundering operations follow the same basic scheme, divided into three intricate stages — placement, layering, and integration.

Placement involves positioning literally tons of cash into financial institutions so that it can be turned into a paperless deposit. Launderers can fly or

smuggle the money to foreign banks with lax reporting rules, or use businesses in the U.S. as fronts to explain the cash deposits.

Layering involves electronic transfers of money from the U.S. or foreign banks to countries with strict bank secrecy rules. They might use "shell" corporations in several nations to hold the deposits. Those corporations are owned by other corporations in other countries. The whole idea is to create so many layers in so many secrecy havens that the money is impossible to trace.

Integration involves sending the money back to the dealer or trafficker disguised as a "loan," or as salary or profits from a foreign business or investment. The money can be used to purchase real estate, gold, and businesses. Moreover, the money is now integrated into the legitimate economy, and the trafficker's affluent lifestyle becomes plausible because he appears to be a successful businessman.

SOURCES: *New York Magazine,* October 31, 1983, pp. 30–36; *Miami Herald,* February 11, 1990, pp. 1A, 24A–25A; *Insight,* August 21, 1989, pp. 8–17.

Arrest

Arrest: The action of taking a person into custody for the purpose of charging with a crime.

When an investigation suggests that a crime has been committed, or when a crime has been directly observed by a law enforcement officer, an **arrest** is made. Although the legal definition of the arrest tends to vary from one jurisdiction to another, it is simply the action of taking a person into custody for the purpose of charging him or her with a crime. In most jurisdictions, an arrest *warrant* is necessary in misdemeanor cases, unless the crime has been observed by a police officer. The warrant is a written order giving authorization to arrest and is issued by a magistrate or someone of equal authority. Felony arrests can be made without a warrant if the officer has reasonable certainty that the person being arrested is indeed the offender. *Reasonable certainty* (or probable cause) refers to the arresting officer's "rational grounds of suspicion, supported by circumstances sufficiently strong in themselves to warrant a cautious man in believing the accused to be guilty."[43]

Arrests can be made not only by law enforcement officers, but by private citizens as well. The following is an excerpt from the Idaho Code of Criminal Procedure:

A private person may arrest another:

1. For a public offense committed or attempted in his presence.
2. When the person arrested has committed a felony, although not in his presence.
3. When a felony has been in fact committed, and he has reasonable cause for believing the person arrested to have committed it.[44]

The statutes of most jurisdictions governing arrest are quite specific. Criminal codes designate who can make arrests, the circumstances under which arrests can be made, and the conditions under which an arrest warrant is and is not mandatory. There are exceptions, however, which can place law enforcement agencies, private citizens, and other individuals in criminal justice proceedings in a tenuous position with regard to the constitutionality of how they make an arrest. Chapter 62 of the *West Virginia Code,* for example, which designates the laws of criminal procedure for that state, makes no mention of who may make an arrest, when an arrest can be made, and under what circumstances an arrest warrant is not necessary.[45] (Chapter 8 discusses arrests in detail.)

Booking

In some lesser offenses—as in New York state, for example, where prostitution is a minor offense punishable in some circumstances by no

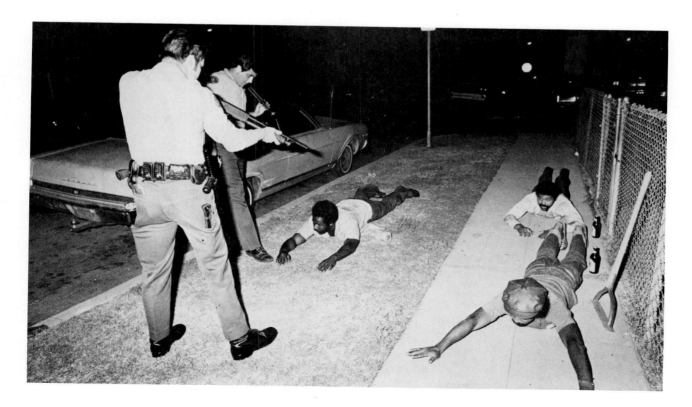

Booking: the police administrative procedures for officially recording an arrest.

more than a fine[46]—the police may be permitted to issue a *citation,* which is an order to appear before a judge at some future date. In all other circumstances, however, a physical arrest occurs when the suspect is present, and the process continues to the booking phase.

Booking refers to the administrative steps and procedures carried out by the police in order to record an arrest properly and officially. At the time of booking the accused's name and address, the time and place of arrest, and the arrest charge are entered into the police log. Booking can also include fingerprinting and photographing of the suspect.

The booking phase is the first point at which the accused can drop out of the criminal justice process with no further criminal proceedings. Charges may be dropped if the suspect has been arrested for a minor misdemeanor, or if there was a procedural error by the police, such as a lack of probable cause for arrest or illegal search and seizure. In the case of a procedural error, the decision to drop the charges can be made by an assistant prosecutor or by someone of high rank in the police system. Booking is also the first point at which some defendants can be released on bail.

Bail, taken from the French term *baillier* meaning "to deliver or give," is the most common form of temporary release. It involves the posting of financial security by the accused (or by someone in his or her behalf), guaranteeing an appearance at trial. (Bail is discussed in detail in Chapter 12.)

"Oh, yeah—I'm just as supreme as you are!"

Initial Appearance

Due process requirements mandate that within a reasonable (not extreme or arbitrary) time after arrest, the accused must be brought before a magistrate and given formal notice of the charge. Such notice occurs at the initial appearance. At this same time, the accused is also notified of his or her legal rights, and bail is determined for those who did not receive such temporary release during the booking phase. Release on recognizance (ROR), a substitute for bail, can also occur, typically at the recommendation of the magistrate when there seems to be no substantial risk that the accused will fail to appear for trial. The accused is released on his or her own personal *recognizance,* or obligation. (Chapter 12 discusses release on recognizance more fully.)

For some kinds of minor offenses, such as being drunk and disorderly, or in other cases where a simple citation has been issued, summary trials and sentencing are conducted at this initial appearance, with no further court processing. In other situations, the magistrate presiding at the initial appearance may determine that the evidence available is not sufficient to warrant further criminal processing and consequently may dismiss the case.

Preliminary Hearing

Due to the complexity of criminal processing and the delays generated by overloaded court calendars, in many jurisdictions, defendants have the option to bypass the initial appearance and instead proceed directly to the preliminary hearing.

The major purpose of the preliminary hearing is to protect defendants from unwarranted prosecutions. Thus, the presiding magistrate seeks to:

The preliminary hearing helps protect defendants from unwarranted prosecution.

- determine whether a crime has been committed
- determine whether the evidence establishes probable cause to believe that the defendant committed it
- determine the existence of the probable cause for which a warrant was issued for the defendant's arrest
- inquire into the reasonableness of the arrest and search and the compliance of the executing officer with the requirements of the warrant
- fix the appropriate bail or temporary release, if this was not already done

Preliminary hearings, like the initial appearance, are not always held. In some jurisdictions, the defense may waive this hearing in order to keep damaging testimony temporarily out of the official records in the hope that by the time the trial does occur witnesses may have forgotten some things, become confused, or disappeared.[47] However, other defense attorneys insist on this hearing as a tactic for gaining insight into the strengths and weaknesses of the state's case.

Determination of Formal Charges

Whether the initial court processing does or does not include an initial appearance or preliminary hearing, the next step in the criminal justice

Indictment

True bill

No bill

Information

The defendant makes one of the four primary pleas at arraignment.

process is the formalization of charges. One mechanism is the indictment by a grand jury. The *indictment* is a formal charging document based on the grand jury's determination that there is sufficient cause for a trial. The decision must be a majority decision, and when it is reached, a *true bill* is signed, containing the following information:

- the type and nature of the offense
- the specific statute alleged to have been violated
- the nature and elements of the offense charged
- the time and place of the occurrence of the crime
- the name and address of the accused or, if not known, a description sufficient to identify the accused with reasonable certainty
- the signature of the foreman of the grand jury to verify that it has been returned as a true bill
- the names of all codefendants in the offense charged, as well as the number of criminal charges against them

Since the grand jury does not weigh the evidence presented, its finding is by no means equivalent to a conviction; it simply binds the accused over for trial. If this tribunal returns a *no bill* — that is, if it fails to achieve the required majority vote and thus refuses the indictment — the accused is released.

Grand juries are available in about half of the states and in the federal system, but in only a limited number of jurisdictions are they the exclusive mechanism for sending a defendant to trial. The most common method for bringing formal charges is the *information,* a charging document drafted by a prosecutor and tested before a magistrate. Typically, this testing occurs at the preliminary hearing. The prosecutor presents some, or all, of the evidence in open court — usually just enough to convince the judge that the defendant should be bound over for trial. As indicated earlier, however, the preliminary hearing is sometimes waived, and in those circumstances the information document is not tested before a magistrate.

Arraignment

After the formal determination of charges through the indictment or information, the actual trial process begins. The first phase in this segment of the criminal justice process is the arraignment, at which the accused is taken before a judge, the formal charges are read, and the defendant is asked to enter a plea. There are four primary pleas in most jurisdictions:

1. *Not guilty* If the not-guilty plea is entered, the defendant is notified of his or her rights, a determination is made of competence to stand trial, counsel is appointed if indigency is apparent, and in some jurisdictions the defendant can elect to have a trial by judge or a trial by jury.
2. *Guilty* If a plea of guilty is entered, the judge must determine if the plea was made voluntarily and if the defendant has an understanding of the full consequences of such a plea. If the judge is satisfied, the defendant is scheduled for sentencing; if not, the judge can refuse the guilty plea and enter "not guilty" into the record.

3. *Nolo contendere*   This plea, not available in all jurisdictions, means "no contest" or "I will not contest it." It has the same implication as the guilty plea but is of considerably different legal significance in that an admission of guilt is not present and cannot be introduced in later trials.

4. *Standing mute*   Remaining mute results in the entry of a not-guilty plea. Its advantage is that the accused does not waive his or her right to protest any irregularities that may have occurred in earlier phases of the criminal justice proceedings.

The Trial Process

The complete trial process can be long and complex (see Chapter 12). It may begin with a hearing on pretrial motions entered by the defense to *suppress* evidence, *relocate* the place of the trial, *discover* the nature of the state's evidence, or *postpone* the trial itself. After the *pretrial motions* (if there are any) the jury is selected and the trial proceeds as follows:

Pretrial motions

1. *Opening statements by prosecution*   The prosecutor outlines the state's case, and how the state will introduce witnesses and physical evidence to prove the guilt of the accused.

2. *Opening statements by the defense*   The defense, if it elects to do so, explains how it plans to introduce witnesses and evidence in its own behalf.

3. *Presentation of the state's case*   The state calls its witnesses to establish the elements of the crime and to introduce physical evidence; the prosecutor accomplishes this through direct examination of the witnesses followed by their cross-examination by the defense.

4. *Presentation of the defense's case*   The defense may open with a motion for dismissal on the grounds that the state failed to prove the defendant guilty "beyond a reasonable doubt." If the judge concurs, the case is dismissed and the accused is released; if the judge rejects the motion, the defense's case proceeds in the same manner as the state's presentation.

5. *Prosecutor's rebuttal*   The prosecutor may elect to present new witnesses and evidence, following the format of the state's original presentation.

6. *Defense's surrebuttal*   The defense may again make a motion for dismissal; if denied, it too can introduce new evidence and witnesses.

7. *Closing statements*   The defense attorney, followed by the prosecutor, make closing arguments, which sum up their cases and the deductions that can be made from the evidence and testimony.

8. *Charging the jury*   In jury trials, the judge instructs the jury as to possible verdicts and charges them to retire to the jury room to consider the facts of the case, to deliberate on the testimony, and to return a just verdict.

9. *Return of the verdict*   Once the jury has reached a decision, they return to the courtroom with a verdict, which is read aloud by a member of the court. The jury may be *polled,* at the request of either the defense or the prosecution; that is, each member is asked individually whether the verdict announced is his or her individual verdict.

Posttrial motions

In the case of a trial by judge, the steps involving the jury are eliminated and the judge makes the determination of innocence or guilt.

Posttrial motions can also occur if the defendant is found guilty, and the defense is given the opportunity to seek a new trial or have the verdict of the jury *set aside* (revoked).

Sentencing

After conviction or the entry of a guilty plea, the defendant is brought before the judge for the imposition of the sentence. The sentencing process may begin with a presentence investigation, which summarizes the offender's family, social, employment, and criminal history, and serves as a guide for the presiding judge in determining the type of sentence to be imposed. Depending on the nature of the offense and the sentencing guidelines established by statute, a simple fine or adjudication to probation in the community might be imposed. Sentences can also include other forms of community-based corrections, imprisonment, and even death.

Appeals and Release

Subsequent to conviction and sentencing, defendants found guilty may appeal their case to a higher court. Appeals are based on claims that due process was not followed, that new evidence has become available, or that the sentence imposed was "cruel and unusual," in violation of constitutional rights.

Parole

Release from imprisonment occurs after the time specified in the sentence has been served, or if the offender is released on *parole* — a conditional release that occurs after only a portion of the sentence has been served. Release from prison, or any type of sentence, can also occur

Pardon

through *pardon* — a "forgiveness" for the crime committed that bars any

Reprieve

further criminal justice processing. Other factors that can affect a sentence are the *reprieve,* which delays the execution of a sentence, and the

Commutation

commutation, which reduces a sentence to a less severe one.

CRIMINAL JUSTICE AS A "SYSTEM"

Criminal justice as a "system"

The preceding summary of the various stages in the criminal justice process might suggest that the administration of justice is a *criminal justice "system"* — some orderly flow of managerial decision making that begins with the investigation of a criminal offense and ends with a correctional placement. And this indeed was the ideal fostered by the President's Commission on Law Enforcement and Administration of Justice some years ago in its commentary on criminal justice in America.

> The criminal justice system has three separately organized parts—the police, the courts, and corrections—and each has distinct tasks. However, these parts are by no means independent of each other. What each one does and how it does it has a direct effect on the work of the others. The courts must deal, and can only deal, with those whom the police arrest; the business of corrections is with those delivered to it by the courts. How successfully corrections reforms convicts determines whether they will once again become police business and influences the sentences the judges pass; police activities are subject to court scrutiny and are often determined by court decisions. And so reforming or reorganizing any part or

procedure of the system changes other parts or procedures. Furthermore, the criminal process, the method by which the system deals with individual cases, is not a hodgepodge of random actions. It is rather a continuum — an orderly progression of events — some of which, like arrest and trial, are highly visible and some of which, though of great importance, occur out of public view. A study of the system must begin by examining it as a whole.[48]

However, the notion of criminal justice operating as an orderly system was and remains a myth. The justice process is composed of a series of bureaucracies operating along alternative and often conflicting paths; also, one segment of the system often serves as a dumping ground for each of the others. In addition, questions of definition and interpretation can confound the complexities of criminal procedure even further:

The criminal justice "nonsystem"

Law enforcement agents interpret the definition of a situation to determine if a law has been indeed violated. Prosecutors and defense attorneys interpret the law and the social situation of the alleged offense to determine which laws were violated and to assess the culpability of the accused. Juries interpret the information provided by the police and courts to determine the innocence or the extent of guilt of the defendant. Judges interpret the evidence presented and the character of the offender to determine the nature and type of sentence and to insure that "due process" has been achieved. And finally, correctional personnel interpret their knowledge of the law, social science, correctional administration, and human behavior to determine the appropriate custodial, correctional, rehabilitative, and punitive treatment for each convicted criminal.[49]

A simplified guide to the criminal justice system

Not only is there a lack of unity of purpose and organized interrelationships among police, courts, and corrections, but also, individual interpretations of crime, law, evidence, and culpability at every phase of the process create further inefficiency. Criminal justice in the United States, therefore, is hardly a "system." However, this is to be expected from a process of justice in a democratic society where checks and balances have been built in at every level so that the fairness of due process can be achieved.

SUMMARY

Interpretations of the meaning of "due process" have varied throughout history. Currently, due process of law, as guaranteed by both the Bill of Rights and the Fourteenth Amendment, implies and comprehends the administration of laws that do not violate the very foundations of civil liberties. It requires in each case an evaluation based on disinterested inquiry, a balanced order of facts exactly and fairly stated, the detached consideration of conflicting claims, and a judgment mindful of reconciling the needs of continuity and change in a complex society. The criminal justice process, from investigation and arrest through trial and sentencing, is structured to guarantee due process of law at each of its many stages. Moreover, it is designed to be a system, an orderly flow of managerial decision making that begins with the investigation of a criminal offense and ends with a correctional placement. It can be argued, however, that the criminal justice process is anything but a system, that it lacks a unity of purpose and organized interrelationships among its various components.

KEY TERMS

adversary system (**135**)
arrest (**150**)
Barron v. *Baltimore* (**139**)
Bill of Rights (**137**)
booking (**152**)
Buck v. *Bell* (**147**)

criminal justice process (**149**)
due process of law (**135**)
Fourteenth Amendment (**140**)
Gitlow v. *New York* (**140**)
Griswold v. *Connecticut* (**145**)
inquiry system (**134**)

inquisitorial system (**134**)
procedural due process (**148**)
substantive due process (**146**)
void-for-vagueness
   doctrine (**147**)

QUESTIONS FOR DISCUSSION

1. What do you think the framers of the Constitution meant by due process of law?
2. How does due process of law differ from the law of the land?

3. What other rights and liberties do you think should have been incorporated into the Bill of Rights?
4. How do *you* interpret the Second Amendment?

FOR FURTHER READING

Cox, Archibald. *The Court and the Constitution.* Boston: Houghton Mifflin, 1987.
Alderman, Ellen, and Caroline Kennedy. *In Our Defense: The Bill of Rights in Action.* New York: William Morrow, 1991.

Rembar, Charles. *The Law of the Land: The Evolution of Our Legal System.* New York: Simon and Schuster, 1980.

NOTES

1. Luke Owen Pike, *A History of Crime in England,* vol. 1 (London: Smith, Elder, 1873–1876), pp. 52–55; Christopher Hibbert, *The Roots of Evil* (Boston: Little, Brown, 1963), pp. 5–8.

2. Cited by Charles Rembar, *The Law of the Land: The Evolution of Our Legal System* (New York: Simon and Schuster, 1980), pp. 18–23.

3. Rembar, *Law of the Land,* p. 19.

4. Henry M. Christman, ed., *The Public Papers of Chief Justice Earl Warren* (New York: Simon and Schuster, 1959), p. 70.

5. See Randy E. Barnett (ed.), *The Rights Retained by the People: The History and Meaning of the Ninth Amendment* (Fairfax, VA: George Mason University Press, 1989).

6. Irving Brant, *The Bill of Rights* (Indianapolis: Bobbs-Merrill, 1965), pp. 49–50.

7. Barron v. Baltimore, 7 Pet. 243 (1833).

8. See, Richard C. Cortner, *The Supreme Court and the Second Bill of Rights* (Madison: University of Wisconsin Press, 1981), pp. 3–11; Henry J. Abraham, *Freedom and the Court: Civil Rights and Liberties in the United States,* 4th edition (New York: Oxford University Press, 1982), pp. 30–48.

9. *Hurtado* v. *California,* 110 U.S. 516(1884).

10. See, *Maxwell* v. *Dow,* 176 U.S. 581 (1900); *Twining* v. *New Jersey,* 211 U.S. 78 (1908).

11. *Maxwell* v. *Dow,* 176 U.S. 581, 616 (1900).

12. *Gitlow* v. *New York,* 268 U.S. 652 (1825).

13. *Fiske* v. *Kansas,* 274 U.S. 380 (1927).

14. *Near* v. *Minnesota,* 283 U.S. 697 (1931).

15. *Powell* v. *Alabama,* 287 U.S. 45 (1932).

16. *Hamilton* v. *Regents of the University of California,* 293 U.S. 245 (1934). Some legal scholars argue that the Court did not make it entirely clear that it intended to incorporate the freedom of religion clause until *Cantwell* v. *Connecticut,* 310 U.S. 296 (1940).

17. Both of these First Amendment rights were incorporated in *DeJonge* v. *Oregon,* 299 U.S. 353 (1937).

18. *Palko* v. *Connecticut,* 302 U.S. 319 (1937).

19. *Everson* v. *Board of Education,* 330 U.S. 1 (1947).

20. In re Oliver, 333 U.S. 257 (1948).

21. *Trop* v. *Dulles,* 356 U.S. 86 (1958).

22. *Mapp* v. *Ohio,* 367 U.S. 643 (1961).

23. *Robinson* v. *California,* 370 U.S. 660 (1962).

24. *Gideon* v. *Wainwright,* 392 U.S. 335 (1963).

25. *Malloy* v. *Hogan,* 378 U.S. 1 (1964).

26. *Pointer* v. *Texas,* 380 U.S. 400 (1965).

27. *Klopfer* v. *North Carolina,* 386 U.S. 213 (1967).

28. *Washington* v. *Texas,* 388 U.S. 14 (1967).

29. *Duncan* v. *Louisiana,* 391 U.S. 145 (1968).

30. *Benton* v. *Maryland,* 395 U.S. 784 (1969).

31. *Griswold* v. *Connecticut,* 381 U.S. 479 (1965).

32. *Roe* v. *Wade,* 410 U.S. 113 (1973).

33. *Bowers* v. *Hardwick,* 106. S. Ct. 2841 (1986).

34. *Dartmouth College* v. *Woodward,* 4 Wheat 519 (1819).

35. Peter W. Lewis and Kenneth D. Peoples, *The Supreme Court and the Criminal Process—Cases and Comments* (Philadelphia: W.B. Saunders, 1978), p. 92.

36. *Coates* v. *City of Cincinnati,* 402 U.S. 611 (1971).

37. *Smith* v. *Goguen,* 415 U.S. 566 (1974).

38. *Cox* v. *Louisiana,* 379 U.S. 536 (1965).

39. *Buck* v. *Bell,* 274 U.S. 200 (1927).

40. Cited by Abraham, *Freedom and the Court,* pp. 111–114.

41. *Skinner* v. *Oklahoma,* 316 U.S. 535 (1942).

42. *U.S.* v. *Valdovinos-Valdovinos,* USDC N Calif (1984) 35 CrL 2216.

43. *Brinegar* v. *United States,* 338 U.S. 161 (1949).

44. *Idaho Code,* 19–604.

45. *West Virginia Code,* 62:1–14.

46. State of New York, *Penal Code,* 40, 80.05.

47. Herbert Jacob, *Justice in America: Courts, Lawyers, and the Judicial Process* (Boston: Little, Brown, 1978), p. 173.

48. President's Commission on Law Enforcement and Administration of Justice. *The Challenge of Crime in a Free Society* (Washington, D.C.: U.S. Government Printing Office, 1967), p. 7.

49. James A. Inciardi, *Reflections on Crime* (New York: Holt, Rinehart and Winston, 1978), p. 160.

PART

TWO

The Police

6

Law Enforcement in the United States: History and Structure

Every policeman knows that, though governments may change, the police remain.
—LEON TROTSKY, 1932

Far more university graduates are becoming criminals than are becoming policemen.
—PHILIP GOODHART, 1960

Very few people ever consider the police as human beings with some of the virtues, failures, and talents common to all.
—SIR ROBERT MARK, 1983

Cops and taxis have one thing in common. . . . they're never around when you need them most.
—A NEW YORK SHOPKEEPER, 1979

Cocaine trafficking through Miami and snowstorms in Alaska have at least one thing in common; you can't stop either.
—A U.S. CUSTOMS OFFICER

The police are the largest and most visible segment of the criminal justice process. As organized agents of law enforcement, police officers are charged with the prevention and detection of crime, the apprehension of criminal offenders, the defense of constitutional guarantees, the resolution of community conflicts, the protection of society, and the promotion and preservation of civil order. They have often been referred to as that "thin blue line" between order and anarchy.

The starting points for an analysis of police in the United States are its history and structure, both of which reflect a number of curiosities. Moreover, policing is a relatively modern phenomenon, having emerged as a formally organized institution just over a century and a half ago. At the same time, however, the origins of policing go back many hundreds of years, and to numerous European cultures. Structurally, policing in the United States has the characteristic of decentralization. That is, there is no national police force per se. Rather, there are literally thousands of independent police agencies throughout the country that developed separately and operate under a policy of local autonomy. In spite of this diversity, though, the organization of these enforcement units is remarkably similar.

THE EMERGENCE OF MODERN POLICE

Mutual pledge: Alfred the Great's system of internal policing that organized the people into tithings, hundreds, and shires.

The constable

The sheriff

The night watch

Policing can be traced to the latter part of the ninth century when England's Alfred the Great was structuring the defenses of his kingdom against an impending Danish invasion. Part of Alfred's strategy depended on internal stability. To gain this, he instituted a system of **mutual pledge,** which organized the country at several levels. At the lowest level were *tithings,* ten families grouped together who each assumed responsibility for the acts of their members. At the next level, ten tithings, or 100 families, were grouped together into a *hundred;* the hundred was under the charge of a *constable.* Hundreds within a specific geographic area were combined to form *shires* — administrative units (now called counties) under royal authority that were governed by a *shire-reeve,* or *sheriff.*[1] In thirteenth-century England, the *night watch* appeared in urban areas to protect late-night city streets; the watch represented the most rudimentary form of metropolitan policing.[2] Modern police forces did not emerge, however, until centuries later, due to the efforts of Henry and John Fielding, Patrick Colquhoun, and Sir Robert Peel.

Magistrates, Constables, Beadles, and Thief-takers

At least metaphorically, every citizen in seventeenth-century England was a policeman, and every policeman was a citizen. That is, law enforcement was the duty of all the people. In practice, however, this system was ineffectual, even including the few officials whose duties included enforcing the law and keeping the peace. There were *magistrates,* for example, who not only presided in courts, but ordered arrests, called witnesses, and examined prisoners. There were *parish constables,* carryovers from the days of Alfred the Great, who had limited powers of arrest and whose authority was confined to relatively small districts. And there were *beadles,* constables' assistants, who were paid £20 a year and who did little more than clear vagrants from the city streets. But the impact of magistrates and constables was minimal, for most were corrupt and justice rarely prevailed.

To these could be added the **thief-takers** — private detectives of a sort who were paid by the Crown on a piecework basis.[3] They had no official status as police and no more authority than the private citizen, and anyone could be a thief-taker. Like the bounty hunters of the American West, thief-takers received a reward in return for the apprehension of a criminal.

Thief-takers: Citizens who received a reward for the apprehension of a criminal.

Thief-takers emerged in England in response to the troublesome nature of highway robbery, which had been flourishing since the early years of such legendary outlaws as Robin Hood and Little John. By the seventeenth century, although romanticized in literature, highway robbery in the grand manner of Jack Sheppard, Dick Turpin, Claude Duval, and Captain Lightfoot made traveling through the English countryside so perilous that no coach or traveler was safe. As a result, in 1693 an Act of Parliament established a reward of £40 for the capture of any highwayman or road agent.[4] The reward was payable upon conviction, and to the thief-taker also went the highwayman's horse, arms, money, and property, unless these were proven to have been stolen.

This system was extended during the reigns of Anne and George I to cover offenses other than highway robbery, and soon a sliding scale of parliamentary rewards came into existence. Burglars, housebreakers, and footpads (street robbers), for example, were worth the same as the highwayman, but the sheep stealer brought only £10, and the army deserter only £1. In some communities, homeowners joined together and offered supplementary rewards, typically £20, for the apprehension of any highwayman or footpad within their district. When there were especially serious crime waves, Parliament provided special rewards of £100 for particular felons.

As the system expanded, a class of professional thief-takers sprang up. Not unexpectedly, many thief-takers were themselves criminals, since the offer of a pardon was an additional incentive. But thief-taking also had its drawbacks. Arresting desperate criminals was dangerous, rewards were not paid if the criminal was acquitted, and thief-takers always had to fear the private revenge of their victims' friends and associates.

The result was that thief-takers often became *thief-makers.* Many would seduce youngsters into committing crimes, then have another thief-taker arrest the youth in the midst of the offense. Others framed innocent parties by planting stolen goods on their persons or in their homes. Although some real criminals were apprehended by the professional thief-takers, the system generally created more crime than it suppressed.[5]

Thief-makers

Henry Fielding, the "Blind Beak," and the Bow Street Runners

Henry Fielding: The eighteenth-century British novelist and magistrate who laid the foundation for the first modern police force.

Although probably best known as the eighteenth-century novelist who wrote *Tom Jones,* **Henry Fielding** might also be credited with laying the foundation for the first modern police force. In 1748, during the age of English highwaymen, Fielding was appointed magistrate in Westminster, a city adjacent to central London. He located himself in a house on Bow Street that became both his home and his office, and it was there that the first English police force began to form.

It was a time when burglaries, street and highway robberies, and other thefts had reached new heights, and it was Fielding's aim to reduce the profitability of such criminal activities. First he established relationships with local pawnbrokers, provided them with lists and descriptions of recently stolen property, and urged them to notify him should the contraband come to their attention. He then inserted the following notice into the London and Westminster newspapers:

> All persons who shall for the future suffer by robbers, burglars, etc., are desired immediately to bring or send the best description they can of such robbers, etc., with the time and place and circumstances of the fact, to Henry Fielding Esq., at his house in Bow Street.[6]

What Fielding suggested was original for his time, for few people had ever before reported thefts to the authorities. Although Fielding could accomplish little singlehandedly, within a year he had obtained the cooperation of Saunders Welch, the High Constable of Holborn, and several other public-spirited constables. Together they formed a small but unofficial investigative division that was the first organized force ever used in England against criminals. Fielding's constables — the **Bow Street Runners** — were not paid as police officers, but they were nevertheless entitled to the standard thief-takers' rewards.

The Bow Street Runners: Henry Fielding's unofficial band of constables who were paid as thief-takers.

In time, Henry Fielding's efforts were noticed by the government, and some £200 was periodically provided to support the activities of his Bow Street Runners. Only four years after his appointment as magistrate, however, Fielding's health began to deteriorate, forcing him into a wheelchair. He then persuaded the authorities to appoint his half-brother, John Fielding, to share his magistracy. John soon took over the operations of the unofficial Bow Street Police, and was quickly dubbed the "Blind Beak." This name derived from the facts that John was blind, and that in English cant — the slang of the London underworld — "beak" was a term referring to any judge or magistrate.[7]

The Bow Street Runners endured, but only on a small scale. Then in 1763, Fielding was allotted £600 to set up a civilian Horse Patrol of eight men for the direct curtailment of robbers and footpads on the London streets. The patrol seemed to be a success, but after only nine months it was disbanded due to a lack of support by the English government. During the next decade, however, a permanent Foot Patrol was established, and in 1804, some twenty-two years after John Fielding's retirement, a new Horse Patrol was set up. It included two inspectors and fifty two men, outfitted in red vests and blue jackets and trousers. This was England's first uniformed police.[8]

The Horse Patrol, England's first uniformed police

Patrick Colquhoun and Sir Robert Peel

The Bow Street Runners had been born and nurtured to some extent in secrecy, for had it been known that even an unofficial band of police were being supported with public funds, it would have been denounced as an instrument of oppression and tyranny. Even John Fielding's Horse Patrol, as effective as it had been, was disbanded for this very reason. The English people were emphatic that they did not want a professional police force because of their love of freedom, their faith in private enterprise, their respect for tradition, and their dislike for spending public money. In spite of these feelings, which were deeply rooted in English culture, when Glasgow businessman Patrick Colquhoun was appointed as a London magistrate he soon crystallized the idea of a "new science of preventive police."[9] His suggestions for a large, organized police force for greater London were quickly rejected, but in 1789 he did form a special river police patterned after Fielding's Bow Street model. Although successful, Colquhoun's efforts met with little support, for throughout that century and decades thereafter the English continued to harbor mistrust for enforcement authority.

Although popular belief has credited Sir Robert Peel with the establishment of a professional police force of the modern variety,[10] it is clear that others came before him. Nevertheless, Peel was a significant figure in this evolutionary process, for it was he who, basing his thoughts on the ideas of Colquhoun, in 1828 drew up the first police bill that was ultimately passed by Parliament. London's new Metropolitan Police, established in 1829, was a centralized agency with the responsibilities of both the prevention of crime and the apprehension of offenders, and thus, modern policing finally came into being.

LONDON POLICE.—MOUNTED FORCE,

Early nineteenth-century London "bobbies"

LAW AND ORDER IN EARLY AMERICA

From the time the first were founded, the villages and towns in the New World were constantly threatened — on land by Indians and from the sea by pirates and foreign enemies. These problems of defense were dealt with by the military. The towns had no protection, however, against their own disorderly, lawbreaking inhabitants. Then in the seventeenth century, village authorities began selecting men to serve as guardians of the peace. The titles and functions of these first police officers were similar to those of the English constable, and the range of their duties can be seen from a typical Massachusetts law of 1646, reprinted here in the style of its colonial authors:

> Evry cunstable . . . hath, by virtue of his office, full powr to make, signe, & put forth pursuits, or hues & cries, after murthrers, manslayrs, peace breakrs, theeves, robers, burglarers, where no ma[gis]trate is at hand; also to apphend without warrant such as are our taken with drinke, swearing, breaking ye Saboth, lying, vagrant psons, night walkers, or any other yt shall break o[u]r laws; . . . also to make search for all such psons . . . in all houses licensed to sell either beare or wine, or in any othr suspected or disordered places, & those to apphend, & keepe in safe custody.[11]

Colonial constables and watches

Constables, or *schouts* in the Dutch settlements, appeared in all the colonies as soon as local governments were organized. They were paid for their services through fines. Nighttime security was provided by "military watches," "rattle watches" composed of paid volunteers, "bellmen," and other forms of the night watch. By the eighteenth century, the daytime peacekeeping of the constables and the nighttime protection of the watches was common everywhere. Unlike England, where the notion of a paid police force was despised, most colonial peacekeeping activities were supported by municipal authority.

Jailer, San Angelo (Texas) County Jail, 1915

The duties of sheriffs in the trans-Mississippi West

The posse comitatus: The able-bodied men of a county who were at the disposal of a sheriff when called for service.

As the colonial towns grew, the number of street riots, drunken brawls, and other types of violent behavior increased considerably. Those charged with keeping the peace were not only incapable of enforcing all of the laws, but often they were lax in their duties, as was noted in Massachusetts's *Bristol Journal* on March 16, 1760:

> *The watch burn Tobacco while Houses are burning,*
> *And the Glass, not the Watch, goes its rounds,*
> *A burning shame this and sad subject of mourning,*
> *That our Guard's such a mute Pack of Hounds.*[12]

Despite these difficulties, however, the constable and the watch were maintained throughout the 1700s and into the early part of the next century as the only sources of urban law enforcement. Some cities did expand the numbers of these paid officers, but to little avail. And growing levels of lawlessness combined with corruption within the ranks of the watch ultimately led to the organization of formal police forces by mid-century.

The Trans-Mississippi West

As settlers moved west, they reached the frontier well before peace officers and courts of law. Violence and crime were inevitable in these sparsely populated regions. Frontiersmen, who used firearms for hunting and self-defense, turned easily to fists, knives, and pistols to settle disputes. Indian tribes, often with cultures that glorified war and acts of revenge, naturally resisted white encroachment. Whites themselves, with European traditions of feuding and revenge, applied these practices to both their neighbors and the Indians. In the absence of any formal mechanisms of frontier justice, the West also served as a sanctuary for a lawless minority of outlaw and criminal migrants.

The *sheriff,* the first of the formal law enforcement agents to appear in the vast territories beyond the Mississippi River, was closely modeled after the British counterpart. But while the powers of the English sheriff had diminished over time, those of the American sheriff expanded to include not only the apprehension of criminals, but also the conducting of elections, the collection of taxes, and the custody of public funds. Furthermore, the sheriffs of the new republic were eventually chosen by popular election.

As the West became more populated, and more lawless, the sheriff evolved into an active agent of law enforcement. Duties as fiscal administrator and executive arm of the courts were quickly subordinated to the more colorful activities of rounding up cattle thieves, highwaymen, and other bandits, and engaging in gun play with serious outlaws. Typically, the local sheriff's office did not include a paid staff of trained deputies that could, for example, be called upon to track fleeing outlaws. Thus, use of the posse became crucial in frontier law enforcement. (For weaknesses of the sheriff system, see page 180.)

During the time of Alfred the Great, when mutual pledges bound together the members of a tithing, one of the peacekeeping instruments was the **posse comitatus,** Latin for "the power of the county," which consisted of all the able-bodied men in a county. This group was at the absolute disposal of a sheriff, and members were required to respond when called to do so. The institution of posse comitatus was transferred intact to American soil.[13] Here, it became an important component of criminal justice machinery as the frontier moved westward, for it could place the entire power of a community under the leadership of the sheriff (see Exhibit 6.1).

Also among the lawmen of the West were territorial police agencies. The **Texas Rangers,** known well in both history and legend, was the first of these. Equipped by Stephen Austin in 1823 to help protect settlers against the Indians, the Rangers were organized as a corps of irregular fighters at the outbreak of the Texas revolution against Mexico in 1835. After 1870, the Rangers evolved into an effective law enforcement agency.[14] Following the lead of the Texas Rangers, the Arizona Rangers was established in 1901 and the New Mexico Mounted Police in 1905, but these were primarily border patrol forces and were abandoned within a few years after their inception.[15]

Federal marshals were also a part of law enforcement in the American West. When the United States came into being with the ratification of the Constitution, the dual sovereignty of state and republic required the designation of special officers to represent the authority of the federal courts. In 1789, Congress established appointive positions of federal marshals, but they did not come into particular prominence until after the Civil War. The popular image of federal marshals and their deputies maintaining law and order along the trail and in the violent mining communities, however, has little foundation in fact. Most of their working time was spent on routine functions related to civil and criminal court activity. Criminal investigation and the apprehension of outlaws did occur on occasion, but these constituted only a fraction of the duties performed.[16]

The Texas Rangers: Founded by Stephen Austin in 1823, the first territorial police agency in the United States.

Company D of the Texas Rangers, 1893

Posse Comitatus Act: An act of Congress that prohibited the military from enforcing federal, state, and local civilian law.

• EXHIBIT 6.1 •

Posse Comitatus, "Fat Albert," and the War on Drugs

Traditionally in the Old West, a posse consisted of the entire population of a county above age fifteen that could be summoned to assist the local sheriff. During the post–Civil War years, U.S. marshals in occupied southern states often called upon federal troops to form a posse for purposes of enforcing local laws. Once southern states regained representation in Congress, it became a unanimous goal of southern congressmen to prevent such practices in the future. The result was the **Posse Comitatus Act,** passed by the 45th Congress on June 18, 1878. The law prohibited the army, and eventually other branches of the military, from enforcing federal, state, and local civilian law, and from supplementing the efforts of civilian law enforcement agencies.

But the Posse Comitatus Act was never a constitutionally mandated statute. In fact, its very wording permitted the assistance of the military if specifically authorized by an act of Congress. Over the years, Congress has approved the use of military forces for the control of civil disorder, and it was for this reason that Chicago's Mayor

Richard Daley was able to call in the Illinois National Guard and regular army troops at the Democratic National Convention in 1968. Moreover, the act did not prevent the United States Coast Guard from intercepting and seizing vessels at sea that were transporting contraband to American ports.

When President Ronald Reagan signed the Department of Defense Authorization Act of 1982 into law, it included several amendments to the century-old Posse Comitatus Act. Although military personnel were still prohibited from physically intercepting suspected drug vessels and aircraft, conducting searches and seizures, and making arrests, the entire war chest of the U.S. military became available to law enforcement for training, intelligence gathering, and detection. Moreover, members of the Army, Navy, Air Force, and Marines could operate military equipment for civilian agencies charged with the enforcement of drug laws.

Beginning in 1982, the "war on drugs" had a new look. Put into force was the Bell 209 assault helicopter, more popularly known as the Cobra. No heli-

Finally, it should be noted that not all marshals were federal marshals. There were also city and town marshals appointed by a mayor or city council. These were community lawmen who served purely as local police. "Wild Bill" Hickok, for example, was a local marshal in the towns of Hays City and Abilene, Kansas, as was Wyatt Earp in Dodge City, Kansas.

Policing the Great Metropolis

In 1845, New York City established the first organized metropolitan police force in the United States. But this occurred only because the fear

copter in the military arsenal was faster, and in its gunship mode it could destroy a tank. There was the Navy's EC-2, an aircraft equipped with a radar disc capable of detecting other aircraft from as far as 300 miles away. There was "Fat Albert" and his pals—surveillance balloons 175 feet in length equipped with sophisticated radar and listening devices. Albert could not only pick up communications from Cuba and Soviet satellites, but could also detect traffic in "Smugglers' Alley," a wide band of Caribbean sky that is virtually invisible to land-based radar systems. And there were NASA satellites to spy on drug operations as far apart as California and Colombia, airborne infrared sensing and imaging equipment that could detect human body heat in the thickest underbrush of Florida's Everglades, plus a host of other high technology devices.

Although the infusion of military resources has had some success in the war on drugs, civil libertarians were opposed to this militarization from the very beginning. They feared that the use of the military in civilian law enforcement would lead to an erosion of private rights and a

"Fat Albert" surveillance balloon ready for duty in the Florida Keys

broadening of military power in civilian life. To date, civil liberties have not been compromised by the military, and Fat Albert continues to roam Smugglers' Alley.

SOURCES: James A. Inciardi, *The War on Drugs II: The Continuing Epic of Heroin, Cocaine, Crack, Crime, AIDS, and Public Policy* (Mountain View, CA: Mayfield, 1992); National Drug Policy Board, *National and International Drug Law Enforcement Strategy* (Washington, DC: Dept. of Transportation, 1987).

of crime and ensuing social disintegration were stronger than cultural opposition to a standing army.

At the beginning of the nineteenth century, New York was no longer the homogeneous community with a common culture and a shared system of values and moral standards that it had been in colonial times. During the five and a half decades before the establishment of the new police force, the population of the city had increased by more than 1,000 percent—from 331,131 in 1790 to 371,223 by 1845.[17] With a significant proportion of the new immigrants being of foreign birth, the city had become a mosaic of subcommunities, separated from one another by

Arrests in New York City, 1845–1850

Arson	87
Assault with intent to kill	490
Assault and battery	13,896
Assault/interfering w. police	733
Attempt at rape	82
Attempt to steal	545
Attempt at burglary	157
Aiding/assisting to escape	212
Abandonment	336
Burglary	751
Bigamy	66
Bastardy	187
Constructive larceny	171
Disorderly conduct	20,252
Deserters	316
Driving without licence	184
Embezzlement	75
Escaped convicts	303
Forgery	89
Felony	159
Fraud	101
Fighting in the street	1,987
Gambling	435
Grand larceny	2,055
Insanity	1,484
Intoxication	36,675
Intox. & disorderly conduct	29,190
Indecent exposure	351
Insulting females in street	138
Keeping disorderly houses	228
Misc. felonies/misdemeanors	4,039
Murder	64
Obtain. goods by false pretenses	240
Petit larceny	14,454
Pickpockets	215
Passing counterfeit money	425
Perjury	29
Rape	68
Robbery in 1st degree	169
Receiving stolen goods	183
Runaway apprentices	175
Selling liquor without license	39
Threatening life	189
Vagrancy	11,347
Violation of corp. ordinances	1,093
Total	144,364

SOURCE: A. E. Costello, *Our Police Protectors* (New York: Author's Edition, 1885), p. 116

barriers of class, culture, language, attitudes, and behavior derived from vastly different traditions.

The increased population combined with growing levels of poverty served to increase the crime rate. The rise in the population brought with it greater conflicts associated with class and cultural differences. A highly visible and mobile wealth attracted criminal predators, both foreign and domestic, resulting in sharp increases in crime and vice. In 1840, New York's *Commercial Advisor* commented on how the city's streets had become pathways of danger:

> Destructive rascality stalks at large in our streets and public places, at all times of day and night, with none to make it afraid; mobs assemble deliberately . . . in a word, lawless violence and fury have full dominion over us. . . .[18]

And in 1842, a special citizens' committee made melodramatic reference to the constant increase in crime and the inability of the police to deal with it:

> The property of the citizen is pilfered, almost before his eyes. Dwellings and warehouses are entered with an ease and apparent coolness and carelessness of detection which shows that none are safe. Thronged as our city is, men are robbed in the street. Thousands that are arrested go unpunished, and the defenseless and the beautiful are ravished and murdered in the daytime, and no trace of the criminals is found.[19]

During this period the city was patrolled by a few hundred marshals, constables, and watchmen who were unsalaried, but received fees for their services. As with the British experience, this system resulted in numerous instances of graft, corruption, laxity, and misdirected effort. Officers concentrated on duties that would earn them money rather than on bringing criminals to justice. Since the recovery of stolen property brought a greater fee than the apprehension of an offender, for example, few thieves were deliberately sought out. This situation also led to arrangements between police and criminals before some robberies and burglaries actually took place — an officer would know of a crime in advance, would recover the stolen property, and would forward a share of the reward to the thief.[20]

From 1841 to 1844, several plans for the organization of a London-style police force were introduced in the city, but none could command enough support for adoption. In 1844, however, the New York state legislature authorized communities to organize police forces and appropriate special funds to be given to cities to provide 24-hour police protection. When the Democrats won the city's mayoral election of 1845, Mayor William F. Havermeyer called for the adoption of the new state statute. The bill was signed into law on May 23, 1845, and a police force akin to London's was finally created. By the outbreak of the Civil War, Chicago, New Orleans, Cincinnati, Baltimore, Newark, and a number of the other large cities had followed New York's lead. The foundation of today's municipal police departments had thus been established.

N.Y.P.D. Salary Schedule in 1845	
Superintendent	$1,250
Captains	700
Assistant Captains	600
Sergeants	550
Policemen	500

SOURCE: A. E. Costello, *Our Police Protectors* (New York: Author's Edition, 1885), p. 103

POLICE SYSTEMS IN THE UNITED STATES

With a population of some two hundred fifty million people, all of whom are under the authority of competing political jurisdictions at federal, state, county, and local levels, law enforcement in the United States today reflects a structure more complex than in any other country. There are 20,000–25,000 professional police agencies in the public sector alone — each representing the enforcement arm of a specific judicial body. To these can be added numerous others in the private sphere. The duties and authority of each are generally quite clear, but in many respects they can also be rather vague and overlapping. Although enforcing the law and keeping the peace may be the responsibilities of a *municipal* police agency within a small suburban village, for example, also active in that same community may be the officers from a county sheriff's department, a state police bureaucracy, and numerous federal enforcement bodies. This level of complexity can be further complicated by possible jurisdictional disputes, agency rivalries, lack of coordination and communication, and failure to share intelligence and other resources.

Consider, for instance, the jurisdictional and administrative complexities that exist in Dade County, Florida. Located at the southeastern tip of the state of Florida, Dade County has a population of more than 1.9 million, and occupies some 2,109 square miles — a land area larger than the entire state of Delaware or Rhode Island. In addition to the city of Miami Beach, the county includes 26 other incorporated municipalities. Each of these is an independent political jurisdiction with its own municipal police force. Also included in this essentially urban-suburban county is the Dade County Public Safety Department —

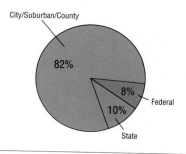

Distribution of Sworn Police Officers in the United States

Jurisdictional complexities in modern policing

● EXHIBIT 6.2 ●

The Federal Law Enforcement Agencies

Department of Justice

Federal Bureau of Investigation (FBI)

The chief investigative body of the Justice Department, with legal jurisdiction extending to all federal crimes that are not the specific responsibility of some other federal enforcement agency. The more significant crimes that fall into FBI jurisdiction are kidnapping, crimes against banks, aircraft piracy, violations of the Civil Rights Act, interstate gambling, organized crime, and interstate flight to avoid prosecution, custody, or confinement.

Drug Enforcement Administration (DEA)

The DEA was formed in 1973 as a consolidation of other drug enforcement agencies. Its major responsibility is control of the use and distribution of narcotics and other dangerous drugs. During the latter part of 1981, the DEA merged with the FBI, becoming a semiautonomous subsidiary of the FBI.

Immigration and Naturalization Service (INS)

Created in 1891, it is responsible for administering the laws that regulate the admission, exclusion, naturalization, and deportation of aliens. Its *Border Patrol* is charged with preventing the illegal entry of aliens and the smuggling of illegal goods.

U.S. Marshals Service

Under the direct authority of the U.S. Attorney General's Office, it has the power to enforce all federal laws that are not the specific responsibility of some other federal agency, although its major activities involve administering proceedings at the federal courts. U.S. marshals also protect relocated witnesses.

Organized Crime and Racketeering Section (OCR)

It was created in 1954 to coordinate investigations of organized crime with responsibilities in the areas of intelligence gathering, investigation, and prosecution.

SOURCE: Donald A. Torres, *Handbook of Federal Police and Investigative Agencies* (Westport, CT: Greenwood Press, 1985).

whose jurisdiction is countywide — as well as the Florida State Police and the Florida Marine Patrol. At the federal level, the following agencies also have jurisdiction: the Federal Bureau of Investigation, the Immigration and Naturalization Service, the Drug Enforcement Administration, the Internal Revenue Service, the Customs Service, the United States Coast Guard, and a number of others. Within the private sphere, detective agencies control all security operations at the Miami International Airport and other locations; the railroad industry has its own police force; and hundreds of other businesses and industries use private police agencies.

New York City reflects another complex situation. In addition to the New York City Police Department, whose jurisdiction covers the five boroughs that make up the city as a whole, both the transit system and

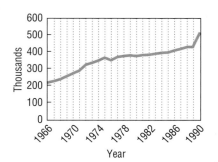

U.S. Police Empoyees 1966–1990

Treasury Department

Internal Revenue Service (IRS)

As the federal agency responsible for the administration and enforcement of the federal tax laws, its major enforcement activities in the criminal area fall within the Intelligence Division, which investigates possible criminal violations of the tax law.

Secret Service

Known primarily for its role in protecting the president of the United States, his family, and other government officials, its investigative units focus on the forgery and counterfeiting of U.S. currency, checks, bonds, and federal food stamps.

Bureau of Alcohol, Tobacco and Firearms (ATF)

Originally organized to enforce Prohibition, ATF has responsibility for enforcing the tax laws that relate to the manufacture of alcohol and tobacco, and for enforcement of the Gun Control Act of 1972. As of early 1986, the future of this agency was uncertain. Late in 1981 its dissolu-

tion was recommended by President Reagan, with many of its functions to be transferred to the Justice Department.

Customs Service

The Customs Service has both inspectors and investigators, whose responsibilities include the administration of laws related to the importation of foreign goods; the collection of duties, penalties, and other fees; and the prevention of smuggling.

United States Postal Service

Postal Inspection Service

As the law enforcement and audit arm of the Postal Service, it has jurisdiction in all criminal matters infringing on the integrity and security of the mail, and the safety of all postal valuables, property, and personnel.

Department of Transportation

Coast Guard

A special naval force with responsibilities for suppressing contraband trade and aiding vessels in distress. It was formed in

1915 when an act of Congress combined the Revenue Cutter Service (established in 1790 to prevent smuggling) and the Life Saving Service.

Department of the Interior

National Park Service

Established in 1916, the purpose of the National Park Service is to control and manage national parks and monuments. The more typical activities of park rangers include search and rescue missions, emergency medical services, and management of park recreation and services. Ranger law enforcement activities focus on violations of park regulations and crimes committed within park boundaries.

Inspectors General

Every cabinet department has an Office of Inspector General (except Justice, which refers to it as the office of Professional Responsibility). Each investigates criminal and administrative wrongdoing related to its particular agency business.

the public housing authority have their own public police forces, each of which is larger than some state police agencies. There are also the state police, private police, federal enforcement bodies, and an interstate agency — the New York/New Jersey Port Authority Police, whose jurisdiction and authority cross both state and county lines.

Because of such complexities, jurisdictional issues in law enforcement are often ignored in studies of police. The rest of this chapter attempts to differentiate among these various levels of authority.

Federal Law Enforcement Agencies

Federal law enforcement agencies have two features that make them unique within the spectrum of police activity. First, since they were structured to enforce specific statutes—those contained in the U.S. Criminal Code—their units are highly specialized, often with specialized resources and training. Second, since they are the enforcement arms of the federal courts, their jurisdictional boundaries, at least in theory, have been limited by congressional authority. The major agencies include the **Federal Bureau of Investigation** (FBI); the Drug Enforcement Administration (DEA); the Immigration and Naturalization Service (INS); the U.S. Marshals Service; the Organized Crime and Racketeering Section (OCR) of the U.S. Department of Justice; the Intelligence Division of the Internal Revenue Service (IRS); the Secret Service; the Bureau of Alcohol, Tobacco, and Firearms (ATF); the Customs Service; the Postal Inspection Service; the U.S. Coast Guard; and the National Parks Service (see Exhibits 6.2 and 6.3).

In addition to these, there are a variety of other federal agencies with enforcement functions. For example, the Departments of Labor, Agriculture, Defense, Interior, and others have developed enforcement or quasi-enforcement units to deal with operations of a criminal or regulatory nature. Independent regulatory bodies such as the Interstate Commerce Commission (ICC), the Securities and Exchange Commission (SEC), and the Federal Trade Commission (FTC) require enforcement powers to ensure compliance. During peacetime, the Department of Transportation has administrative authority over the Coast Guard, whose enforcement powers overlap with those of the Customs Service, FBI, DEA, and INS. Special investigative and enforcement bodies appear

Federal Bureau of Investigation: The chief investigative body of the Justice Department, with jurisdiction extending to all federal crimes that are not the specific responsibility of some other federal enforcement agency.

A border patrolman escorts illegal aliens captured near San Diego, California

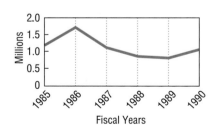

Alien Apprehensions in Millions

SOURCE: Border Patrol

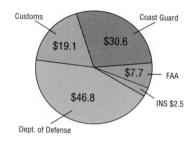

Federal Spending on the Drug War *Drug Interception Programs*

Federal Spending on the Drug War *in the Criminal Justice Sector*

from time to time, descending directly from the executive, judicial, or legislative branches of government. As a case in point, on October 14, 1982, President Ronald Reagan announced the formation of the **Organized Crime Drug Enforcement Task Force (OCDETF)** program.[21] Composed of thirteen task forces covering all fifty states, Puerto Rico, and the U.S. Virgin Islands, membership includes the FBI, DEA, U.S. Attorneys Office, Marshals Service, Customs Service, ATF, IRS, Coast Guard, and state and local law enforcement agencies. Coordinated by the U.S. Attorneys Office in each region, more than federal 1,200 agents are charged with "targeting, investigating, and prosecuting individuals who organize, direct, finance, or are otherwise engaged in *high-level* illegal drug trafficking enterprises."[22] Although the OCDETF program has received little attention in the media, it appears to be a successful enforcement initiative. From its inception in 1982 through mid-1991, it initiated 3,486 investigations of major drug trafficking organizations, convicting 16,658 persons with an average prison term of 7.5 years. Moreover, during fiscal years 1983 through 1990, the program seized $1.92 billion in cash and real estate.[23]

Organized Crime Drug Enforcement Task Force Program: A joint federal, state, and local law enforcement initiative against high-level drug trafficking organizations.

• EXHIBIT 6.3 •

The FBI: In Search of Public Enemies

Although almost all police work is undertaken by county and municipal law enforcement agencies, the Federal Bureau of Investigation also does its share. Somewhat controversial at times, the FBI is considered to be the nation's elite law enforcement body, and it is among the most famous police agencies in the world.

The beginnings of the FBI can be traced to President Theodore Roosevelt's "trust-busting" and his war with the "malefactors of great wealth" and their kept men in Congress. Roosevelt was handicapped in these efforts against industrial combines and graft because, when the need to gather evidence arose, the Department of Justice's lack of an investigative arm forced the president to borrow detectives from other federal agencies. As a result of this problem, Roosevelt's attorney general, Charles J. Bonaparte (who was also the grandnephew of Emperor Napoleon I), appealed to Congress in 1907 and 1908 to create a permanent detective force in Justice. Bonaparte's requests were denied. The major reason was the Congress's expressed fear that a "secret police" would be created—a force so powerful that it might escape all control and turn its investigative energies against even Congress itself.

Congressional response to Bonaparte's appeal went even beyond denial, however. On May 30, 1908, Congress passed a law that specifically forbade the Justice Department from borrowing any investigative agents from other federal organizations. Nevertheless, on July 1, 1908, some 30 days after Congress had adjourned, Bona-

parte went ahead and quietly established in the Justice Department the very investigative force that the Congress had refused to authorize. He called it the Bureau of Investigation.

During its earliest years, the Bureau occupied itself with small investigations—antitrust prosecutions, bankruptcy and fraud cases, crimes committed on government reservations, and interstate commerce violations. But with the passage of the Mann Act in 1910, sponsored by Congressman James Robert Mann, the Bureau of Investigation stepped into a more national posture.

It was a time when prostitution and commercialized vice had become big business, and there was growing worry over the number of women and young girls who were being imported into the United States "for immoral purposes." Proponents of Victorian morality led an outcry for stern law enforcement action. Under the Mann Act, officially known as the White Slave Traffic Act, it was forbidden to transport women for immoral purposes in interstate or foreign commerce, to assist in procuring transportation for immoral purposes, or to persuade or induce any female to cross state lines for such purposes.

Stanley W. Finch, appointed the first director of the Bureau by Charles J. Bonaparte, saw the Mann Act as an opportunity to secure funds for the expansion of his agency. He portrayed white slavery as a national menace, suggesting that only his Bureau could save the American people from such a festering horror. He offered grim descriptions of white slave traffic:

Unless a girl was actually confined in a room and guarded, there was no girl, regardless of her station in life who was altogether safe. . . . There was need that everyone be on his guard, because no one could tell when his daughter or his wife or his mother would be selected as a victim.

Not unexpectedly, with the virtue of every wife, mother, and daughter in the nation at stake, the Bureau got its funding and the full support of Congress. Bureau agents proceeded with zeal, and by 1916 some 2,414 cases had been prosecuted.

During the years that followed, the Bureau began investigating a new "menace" to American society—the radical alien. Among the more onerous statutes passed by Congress during World War I was the Alien Act of 1918, a law designed to exclude and expel from the United States any aliens who were considered to be anarchists. In 1919, as the result of numerous postwar bombings attributed to subversive organizations, William J. Flynn, former head of the Secret Service, was named the new Bureau director and given the mission of a holy war against radicals and dissidents. The General Intelligence Division was organized to concentrate on the alleged alien menace, and the first assistant in charge of the new GID was a twenty-four-year-old up-and-coming Justice Department lawyer named John Edgar Hoover.

In 1922, congressional investigations into rumors of graft and corruption within the Harding administration left the image of the Bureau somewhat tarnished. The secretary of the interior was found to have accepted a bribe and leased naval oil reserves at Teapot Dome, Wyoming, to a private oil company; the attorney general was found to have taken money in lieu of prosecuting Prohibition law violators; and the head of the Veterans' Bureau was convicted of fraud, bribery, and conspiracy. Where, asked congressional critics, had been the watchdog of Justice while the naval oil reserves were being looted? Had it been sleeping, or had it simply closed its eyes?

In the aftermath of the implied involvement of the Bureau in the Teapot Dome scandal, President Calvin Coolidge appointed Harlen Fiske Stone as his new attorney general. Stone was ordered to find a new director of the Bureau of Investigation. On May 10, 1924, the position was offered to young J. Edgar Hoover. Hoover set out to clean house and build a new image for his national police force. He established new qualifications for his agents, preferring those with legal or accounting backgrounds; he improved existing training standards; and he created a career service in which the salaries and retirement benefits would be better than in any comparable agency in the federal government or elsewhere. And Hoover did more.

By 1935, when the name of his agency had been changed to the Federal Bureau of Investigation, he had established a vast fingerprint file, a crime laboratory, the Uniform Crime Reporting system, and a training academy. During the same decade, he mounted a campaign to offset the glamorous publicity that was given John Dillinger, Alvin Karpis, Bonnie Parker and Clyde Barrow, and other criminals. For a time his "G-men" were included among the top heroes of American culture. The Bureau's list of "ten most wanted criminals" and "public enemies" provided a continuing scoreboard of Hoover's successes against bank robbers, kidnappers, gangsters, and other lawbreakers, and the entire agency reveled in its image of fearless law enforcement — an image that endured for many decades.

By 1960, Hoover's FBI was considered to be the finest law enforcement agency in the world. It had the respect of the American people. Its 6,000 agents were deployed in a manner that would enable the Bureau to place one of them at the scene of a federal crime anywhere in the nation within an average of one hour or less.

With the revolution in values that occurred in the United States during the 1960s, however, FBI activities became better known, and the image of both Hoover and his empire began to pale. The Bureau had grown into an enormous bureaucracy, with far-reaching power over the life of the nation. It led an autonomous existence and its director had lasted through eight presidencies. Information began to leak out as to the number of files the Bureau had developed on tens of thousands of noncriminals, including presidents and members of the Senate and House.

Disclosures revealed the FBI to have engaged in illegal wiretapping, a mail-opening program aimed at American citizens, the discrediting of its political enemies by attempting to destroy their jobs and credit ratings, accepting kickbacks and bribes, systematically stealing government property, and inciting radicals to commit illegal acts.

Amidst the turmoil surrounding his years as director, J. Edgar Hoover died on March 2, 1972, at the age of seventy-seven. In the years hence, there has been a succession of directors, and the agency has taken on a new image. Agents are chasing fewer bank robbers and car thieves, and are focusing more on organized and white-collar crime, public corruption, espionage, terrorism, and drug trafficking. But the *new* FBI has not managed to sidestep all controversy. During the latter part of the 1980s, for example, it became known that the FBI had conducted surveillance of American citizens and groups opposed to the Reagan Administration's policies in Latin America. Furthermore, scandal once again rocked the agency during the late 1980s and early 1990s when it was charged with widespread harassment of its black and Hispanic agents.

SOURCES: Fred J. Cook, *The FBI Nobody Knows* (New York: Macmillan, 1964); Don Whitehead, *The FBI Story* (New York: Random House, 1956); Sanford J. Unger, *FBI* (Boston: Little, Brown, 1976); Nelson Blackstock, *COINTELPRO: The FBI's Secret War on Political Freedom* (New York: Vintage, 1976); John Dean, *Blind Ambition* (New York: Simon and Schuster, 1976); *Time*, May 1, 1978, p. 18; *National Law Journal*, June 6, 1983, pp. 1, 8, 25; *New York Times*, January 28, 1988, pp. A1, A18; *New York Times*, April 6, 1991, p. 1.

Interpol: An international police organization of 120 member countries that serves as a depository of intelligence information on wanted criminals.

Interpol and the U.S. intelligence community also play a role in the federal law enforcement bureaucracy. **Interpol,** the International Criminal Police Organization, headquartered in St. Cloud, France, is an international organization of 120 member countries that serves as a clearinghouse and depository of intelligence information on wanted criminals. For example, it keeps data on criminal identification and circulates wanted notices. It is neither an investigative nor an enforcement agency. The Treasury Department is the United States's representative to this international group, and its American liaison office is staffed by federal law enforcement personnel.[24]

State Police Agencies

The Texas Rangers, as noted earlier, was the earliest form of a state police body to appear on American soil. It was established during the earliest days of the Texas Republic, largely for military service along the Mexican border, and even today it retains some of its original frontier flavor. In other locales, state police forces emerged through a slow process of evolution. In 1865, for example, the governor of Massachusetts appointed a small force of "state constables," primarily for the suppression of commercialized vice. In 1879, the group was reorganized into the Massachusetts District Police and was granted more general police powers.[25] In 1920 it was absorbed into a new department of public safety and designated as the Massachusetts State Police.

During this period other states began experimenting with similar forces, all because of the basic deficiencies in existing rural police administration and practices. In the decades that followed the Civil War and Reconstruction, population growth and demographic shifts, changing economic conditions, and the numerous complexities characteristic of any pluralistic society resulted in numerous increases in crime. The office of the sheriff, the only form of law enforcement that existed in many communities, manifested a variety of weaknesses that limited its effectiveness in the prevention and control of crime. Most sheriffs were elected by popular vote for terms of only two years, a practice that inhibited freedom from political and local influence and limited the possibility of securing sheriffs with professional qualifications and experience. Statutes in many states prohibited incumbents of the office from succeeding themselves, and in many instances deputies could not even succeed their sheriffs. Furthermore, sheriffs were responsible for the execution of civil processes, for the administration of the county jail, and in some cases for the collection of taxes as well. Also, the fee system under which they received compensation made civil duties more attractive, resulting in an unwillingness to exercise their law enforcement powers. These difficulties also existed in communities where civil and police duties were in the hands of local constables.[26]

Weaknesses of the sheriff system

If the unwillingness and inability of sheriffs and constables to combat rural crime were not enough, there was an additional problem that affected both rural and urban areas. Crime had become more global in nature and was less often localized in a particular community. Improvements in transportation and communication had opened new vistas for criminals, providing them with convenient access to numerous geographical areas and ready means of escape to others. Yet there was no effective communication or cooperation between the police of one municipality and those of other cities and towns. The emergence of state police agencies was in direct response to these issues. The agencies were a mechanism of law enforcement that was geographically unconfined, with organization, administration, resources, training, and means of communication adaptable to an entire state.

The beginning of modern state police administration dates to 1905, with the creation of the Pennsylvania State Constabulary. It was the first professional statewide force whose superintendent had extensive administrative powers and was responsible only to the governor. From the beginning it operated as uniformed force, used a system of troop headquarters and widely distributed substations as bases of operations, and patrolled the entire state, including the most remote rural areas.[27] In the years that followed, other states established state police departments based on the Pennsylvania model, and by 1925, formal state police departments existed throughout most of the nation.

Currently, each state has its own police apparatus, and although the structures and functions of these fifty state organizations vary somewhat, they all generally fulfill some of the regulatory and investigative roles of the federal enforcement groups as well as some of the uniformed patrol duties of local police. In general, they are organized into one of two models. Some, like the Michigan State Police and the state forces in New York, Pennsylvania, Delaware, Vermont, and Arkansas, have general police powers and enforce state laws. In addition to performing routine patrol and traffic regulation, they have a full range of support services including specialized units that investigate major crimes, intelligence units that investigate organized criminal activities, and drug trafficking, juvenile units, crime laboratories, and statewide computer facilities for identification and intelligence information. Other state police agencies direct most of their attention to enforcing the laws that govern the operation of motor vehicles on public roads and highways. These state highway patrols, as in California, Ohio, Georgia, Florida, and the Carolinas, are not limited to the enforcement of traffic laws, however. In some cases they also have the responsibility to investigate crimes that occur in specific locations or under particular circumstances — such as on state highways or state property, or crimes that involve the use of public carriers. State police operations can also include investigative functions relating to alcoholic beverage control, racetrack operations, and environmental pollution.

County and Municipal Policing

Despite the existence of the large federal enforcement bureaucracies and the state police agencies, most law enforcement and peacekeeping in rural, urban, and unincorporated areas is provided by county and municipal authorities.

The office of sheriff has been established by either a state constitution or statutory law in all states but Alaska, Hawaii, and New Jersey. The sheriff serves as the chief law enforcement officer in his or her county and has countywide jurisdiction. In most counties the sheriff is elected. In years past, this practice brought into question the qualifications of sheriffs as professional police agents as well as the effectiveness of county police organizations in enforcing the law, and it continues to do so today.

Currently, the sheriff's office has three primary responsibilities in most jurisdictions. First, it provides law enforcement services to the county. Second, it maintains the county jail and receives prisoners who

Modern state police administration began in 1905.

The Florida marine patrol cruising the waters of Miami's Biscayne Bay

The modern sheriff's office and its duties

are in various stages of the criminal justice process or who are awaiting transportation to a state institution. Third, as an officer of the county courts, the sheriff provides personnel to serve as court bailiffs, to transport defendants and prisoners to and from the courts or to various institutions; and to act in civil matters such as in delivering divorce papers or subpoenas and enforcing court-ordered liens, eviction notices, forfeitures of property, and the administration and sale of foreclosed property.*

With the establishment of city, town, and other municipal police agencies during the twentieth century, a number of jurisdictional disputes emerged between county and municipal police. Currently, many states have given cities and towns statutory authority to provide for their own police protection, thus limiting the sovereignty and jurisdiction of the county police or sheriff's office to rural and unincorporated areas. In other instances, agreements have been reached between county and town police departments whereby sheriffs will not enforce the criminal laws in particular municipalities, except in instances of civil strife, police corruption, or when called upon to do so.

Police in the Private Sector

With the rising concern over street crime during the past few decades, combined with the dramatic increases during the 1970s and 1980s in industrial thefts, shoplifting, and employee pilferage, there has been a growing awareness of and interest in the structure and roles of private policing. Police in the private sector are not new, either to the United States or civilization as whole. In fact, before formal public police agencies were organized in Europe and America during the nineteenth century, *all* policing, with the exception of the military, was private. The constables, shire-reeves, and members of the tithings and hundreds in Alfred the Great's ninth-century England were essentially a form of private police. Along with those who functioned in the night watches, they were private citizens performing either at the pleasure or request of royal authority, or on a fee-for-service basis. The thief-takers of London, as well as Henry and John Fielding's Bow Street Runners, were also private agents of law enforcement, pursuing the cause of law and order for the bounties, rewards, and other fees offered for the apprehension and conviction of highwaymen and other offenders.

The rudimentary forms of law enforcement that emerged and persisted during the period of American colonial expansion were modeled after the British. But during the last 100 or so years, private policing in the United States has taken on both new and varied forms, functioning in areas of law enforcement where conventional police are unable, unwilling, ill-equipped, or otherwise prohibited to operate.

In history, folklore, and popular culture, both the significance and impact of private police in the United States are profound. One of the most famous private policing agencies in the world is the Pinkerton National Detective Agency, founded in 1850 in a small Chicago office by Scottish immigrant *Allan Pinkerton*. "The Pinkertons," as they were called, initially gained notoriety just before the Civil War through their thwarting of the alleged "Baltimore Plot" to assassinate president-elect

Allan Pinkerton

---

* It should be pointed out here that while many sheriff's offices do all of these things, some do not. A number are not full service police agencies and only serve subpoenas, transport prisoners, and supervise certain civil processes.

Abraham Lincoln. During the decades that followed, Pinkerton agents played major roles in numerous industrial clashes between workers and management. The best know of these were the one involving the Molly Maguires in 1874–1875 and the Homestead strike in Pittsburgh in 1892. Hired to protect the railroads during the era of America's outlaw West, they were responsible for the arrests of John and Simeon Reno, who were credited with having organized the nation's first band of professional bank robbers. They were persistent adversaries of Jesse James, Cole Younger, and other members of the James–Younger gang. In Texas, they were retained by railroad executives to hunt down the legendary Sam Bass, and have been credited with the deaths of Jim and Rube Burrows — well known in the 1880s as proficient robbers of both trains and express offices. And they appear in the annals of Western Americana as the group who rid Montana and Wyoming of Robert Leroy Parker (Butch Cassidy), Harry Longbaugh (the Sundance Kid), Blackjack Ketchum, Etta Place, and other members of the now romanticized Wild Bunch from Robbers Roost. Allan Pinkerton himself, with his insistence on detailed descriptions of known criminals — including physical characteristics, background, companions, and hideouts — was the first in America to devise what is today's "rogues' gallery." [28] And curiously, the Pinkerton National Detective Agency is responsible for the term *private eye* in the American language. The firm's trademark is an open eye, underlined with the slogan, "We never sleep" (see Exhibit 6.4).

Pinkerton's was not the only private law enforcement agency in the American West. In competition with the Pinkerton agency during the latter part of the eighteenth century was the Rocky Mountain Detective Association, begun by a former major general of the Colorado Militia, David J. Cook. With agents in all the principal cities in the United States, Cook's army of private operatives focused on the pursuit and apprehension of the bank and train robbers, cattle thieves, murderers, and road agents who plundered the towns, highways, and mining communities throughout the territory north of Mexico between the Missouri River and the Pacific. [29]

There was also a corps of detectives hired by the railroads. These detectives instituted a variety of measures to increase the risks and diminish the profits of the ever-rising levels of train robbery: baggage cars were equipped with ramps and stalls containing fast horses for the immediate pursuit of bandits; detectives and guards rode unobtrusively in coaches to spot potential trouble; and single locomotives were kept ready on sidings to speed alarms and transport agents. [30] The best-known agency of this type was *Wells, Fargo & Co.*, begun in 1852 by Henry Wells and William G. Fargo as a joint stock association to capitalize on express, banking, and other business opportunities in California. Wells, Fargo was actually a banking institution, an express and mail-carrying service, and a stage line that operated out of more than a hundred offices in the western mining districts. But since the company carried millions of dollars in gold dust in an area beset with bandits, and since it had advertised that there would never be a loss to any customer, it was forced to structure its own elaborate security system. Treasure boxes and express coaches were protected by armed guards, and outlaws who held up Wells, Fargo banks and carriers were relentlessly hunted down by specially trained and equipped couriers and agents. [31]

Private policing today includes a variety of nonpublic organizations and individuals who provide guard, patrol, detection, protection, and

Wells, Fargo

• EXHIBIT 6.4 •

Sidelights on Criminal Matters
The Pinkerton Rogues' Gallery

The Pinkerton rogues' gallery was the forerunner of today's police "mug books." Allan Pinkerton insisted on having detailed descriptions of known criminals, including their physical characteristics, backgrounds, companions, and hideouts. His organization never closed a rogues' gallery case until the individual was officially declared dead.

Here are four typical criminals from the Pinkerton rogues' gallery:

• Maximilian Shinburn, 1839–1919. Known as the "King of Bank Burglars."

• Charles Bullard. Accomplished burglar and pianist. Distinguishing features: speaks fluent French.

• Sophie Lyons, 1850–1924. Occupation: criminal tendencies since early childhood. Criminal occupations: pickpocket, shoplifter, blackmailer, stall for bank sneaks.

• Frederick J. Wittrock, 1858–1921. Occupation: store proprietor. Criminal occupation: express robbery. Distinguishing features: reads dime novels voraciously.

*MAX SHINBURN alias "Max Shinborn"
Bank burglar*

I can see the day when an entrepreneur will come along and say, "I can police the Bronx for $50 million less and do a better job."
— MINNEAPOLIS POLICE CHIEF
ANTHONY V. BOUZA, 1984

We are like a private FBI.
— WAYNE BLACK, DIRECTOR OF
WACKENHUT'S SPECIAL INVESTIGATIONS
SERVICE

What it comes down to is Wackenhut is an army for hire.
— AFL-CIO REPRESENTATIVE, COMMENTING IN 1990 ABOUT MANAGEMENT'S USE OF WACKENHUT ARMED GUARDS TO PROTECT STRIKEBREAKERS AND REPLACEMENT WORKERS

alarm services, as well as armored car transportation, crowd control, insurance investigation, and retail and industrial security. Pinkerton's continues to operate in these areas, and Wells, Fargo & Co. has also endured, principally as a worldwide banking firm and armored car service. Currently most notable, however, is the Wackenhut Corp., a South Florida–based former mom-and-pop private-eye shop that has grown into what some call a free-market army. In early 1991, Wackenhut had some 40,000 employees, and annual revenues in excess of $500 million. In addition to the more routine private policing chores, Wackenhut guards and monitors public and privately owned nuclear facilities, Department of Energy sites, the Alaska pipeline, and the Strategic Petroleum Reserve to name but a few major posts. And then there is Wackenhut Corrections, a subsidiary which designs, builds, staffs, and operates jails and prisons for local and state governments.[32]

In general, the efforts of private police agencies are clearly separate from those of city, county, state, and federal law enforcement. Public police have the primary responsibility for maintaining order, enforcing the law, preventing and investigating crimes, and apprehending criminals. They are also responsible for policing public property. In contrast, policing *private* property is to some extent the responsibility of its owners or managers, and private security and police are often used for this job. In addition, there are areas of criminal and noncriminal activity that conventional law enforcement is either ill-equipped or otherwise pro-

CHARLES BULLARD alias "Piano Charley"
Burglar

SOPHIE LYONS alias "Sophie Levy,"
"Jane Smith," "Mme de Verney"
Pickpocket

FRED WITTROCK alias "Terrible Fred"
Highwayman

hibited from handling. In cases of suspected insurance fraud, for example, most public police agencies have neither the personnel nor the financial resources to undertake intensive investigations. The search for runaway children is also far too large a problem for public agencies, and the surveillance of unfaithful spouses is beyond the authority and jurisdiction of any public service agency.

But there are problems with policing in the private sector. Nationally, private police — or "rent-a-cops," as they have come to be called — currently total more than one million persons, far more than the total number of federal, state, and local police. These private agents sometimes exceed the bounds of their authority. There have been occasions, for example, when uniformed and armed private police have shot shoplifters and disorderly persons and have fired upon people out of anger and frustration. The problem stems from the fact that there are only limited controls over private agencies and from the lack of training available to security personnel. In a study done by the Rand Corporation, a California consulting firm, it was found that fewer than half of the private security guards were high school graduates, their average age was fifty-two years, fewer than 50 percent knew that their arrest powers were no greater than those of the average citizen, and most were untrained and poorly paid.[33]

By the mid-1980s, new standards for private policing were implemented and more stringent legislation governing their activities was

A quick look around reveals a ragtag army of uniformed security personnel minding property, affording serenity to high-rise dwellers, protecting private functions, body-guarding dignitaries, and generally affording tranquility, in an uncertain age, to those rich enough to buy their own police forces.

—FORMER MINNEAPOLIS POLICE CHIEF
ANTHONY V. BOUZA, 1990

Vigilante justice: Extralegal criminal justice activities by individuals or groups who take the law into their own hands for the sake of establishing "law and order."

George Witherell was lynched on December 4, 1888, for an alleged multiple murder.

passed. But how these changes have affected police in the private sector is difficult to measure. What is clear is that the dramatic growth in the private police industry has had an impact on the quality of public policing. As many budget-conscious communities trim the size of their police forces, the number of private police agents continues to expand.[34] And in conjunction with this, there has been the growing tendency to use private police for the provision of services typically done by public agencies (see Exhibit 6.5).

Volunteer Police and the American Vigilante Tradition

The vigilante tradition, in its most classic sense, refers to the organized and extralegal movements of individuals who take the law into their own hands. From the 1760s through the beginning of the twentieth century, vigilante activity was an almost constant factor in American life. It appeared in numerous forms, ranging from unorganized mobs to quasi-military groups that banded together to establish "law and order" and administer **vigilante justice** in areas where courts and law officers were nonexistent, corrupt, unwilling, or incapable of dealing with the problems at hand. Unlike the frontier lynch mobs, the better-known vigilante groups, such as the South Carolina Moderators (1767), the East Texas Regulators (1840–1844), and the California Vigilance Committees (1850–1856), were highly structured and served in all phases of their own criminal justice proceedings. University of Oregon history professor Richard Maxwell Brown describes their vigilante operations in this way:

> The characteristic vigilante movement was organized in command or military fashion and usually had a constitution, articles, or a manifesto to which the members would subscribe. Outlaws or other malefactors taken up by vigilantes were given formal (albeit illegal) trials, in which the accused had counsel or an opportunity to defend himself. An example of a vigilante trial is found in the northern Illinois regulator movement of 1841. Two accused horse thieves and murderers were tried by 120 regulators in the presence of a crowd of 500 or more. A leading regulator served as judge. The defendants were given a chance to challenge objectionable men among the regulators, and, as a result, the number of regulators taking part in the trial was cut by nine men. Two lawyers were provided—one to represent the accused and one to represent the "people." Witnesses were sworn, an arraignment was made, and the trial proceeded. In summation, the prosecuting attorney urged immediate execution of the prisoners. The crowd voted unanimously for the fatal sentence, and, after an hour allotted to the two men for prayer, they were put to death. The accused were almost never acquitted, but the vigilantes' attention to the spirit of law and order caused them to provide, by their lights, a fair but speedy trial.[35]

Not all vigilante and regulator groups were this well organized, and not all followed rules of criminal procedure. Like the posse comitatus, in taking the law into their own hands they often seized innocent persons, and they were guilty of depriving all persons—innocent and guilty—of justice and constitutional rights.

There was a noticeable decline in the incidence of vigilantism by the close of the nineteenth century, but it never fully disappeared. During periods of stress, fear, and intergroup tension, it periodically reemerged in rural areas. In the turbulent and crime-ridden years since the early 1960s, a number of quasi-vigilante groups have emerged. Some have

• EXHIBIT 6.5 •

Private Police in the Public Sector

In recent years, an expanding number of municipalities have been turning to private organizations for the provision of services typically supplied by local government. Trash collection and emergency medical services are among the more common examples of relatively low-cost yet high-quality services being transferred to the private sector. Moreover, a move has occurred in some jurisdictions toward the "privitization of corrections" (see Chapter 16). A similar trend is emerging with regard to police support services.

Although the private sector has long since been performing duties for police and sheriff's departments on a fee basis in the areas of data processing, management planning, accounting and auditing, and equipment repair, contracts for police support services are relatively new. *Police support services* include those kinds of activities that support the broader law enforcement and peace-keeping roles of state and municipal police agencies. Typical examples include towing of illegally parked vehicles, traffic control, guarding public buildings and sports arenas, fingerprinting prisoners, and conducting background checks on job applicants—all of which are duties commonly associated with police officers. The Wackenhut Corp., for example, in addition to these activities, transports prisoners and suspects, traces stolen money, and conducts kidnap negotiations.

The reasons for the transfer of police services to the private sector are several. The first is cost. Since police support services can be effectively accom-

plished by persons with less skill and experience than police officers, labor costs are lower in private security firms. In addition, private sector fringe benefit packages tend to be less costly than those in civil service, and since the more dangerous

aspects of law enforcement and peace keeping are not undertaken, liability insurance premiums are lower than those paid by government agencies.

Related to cost is the practice of some police agencies of increasing services without raising personnel budgets. In counties

and municipalities experiencing fiscal limitations and taxpayer revolts, contracting for additional services tends to be more politically feasible than adding staff to payrolls.

Using private police also increases a department's flexibility and responsiveness. In times of crisis or for special events when there is a need for increased "blue visibility" on the streets, private police services can be contracted on a temporary "on demand" basis for the more routine tasks of policing. This allows municipalities the opportunity to shift personnel to where it is needed without having to hire, train, or maintain new staff.

Despite the trend toward the privitization of police support services, it appears unlikely that the entirety of policing will be transferred to the private sector. Policing involves such varied activities and skills that it would not be profitable for private firms to train and maintain the necessary staff. Moreover, both the government and the taxpayers view law enforcement and peace keeping as public service tasks that should not be performed by private enterprise.

SOURCES: Marcia Chaiken and Jan Chaiken, *Public Policing—Privately Provided* (Washington, DC: National Institute of Justice, 1987); William C. Cunningham and Todd H. Taylor, *The Hallcrest Report: Private Security and Police in America* (Portland: Chancellor Press, 1985); *Business Week,* September 26, 1988, pp. 86–87; Deanna Hodgin, "Private Crime Fighting for a Profit," *Insight,* January 21, 1991, pp. 44–45.

• EXHIBIT 6.6 •

Urban Vigilantism

Crime and the fear of crime in urban areas have combined in recent decades to add a new chapter to the history of American vigilantism. Groups have organized to protect city neighborhoods where police patrols appear inefficient or ill-equipped to deal with the growing levels of lawlessness. Similarly, as reflections of the avenging vigilante portrayed by actor Charles Bronson in his well known *Death Wish* films, there are those who have carried out their own versions of "street justice." The most notable of these groups and individuals include the Guardian Angels, Bernhard Goetz of New York City, and the "Mad Dads" of Omaha.

Vigilante "Paul Kersey" (played by Charles Bronson) takes aim at murderous street punks in Death Wish 3.

The Guardian Angels

In T-shirts and red berets, they stand where civilization ends and the jungle begins.
— NEW YORK DAILY NEWS, 1982

The Guardian Angels were founded by Brooklyn-born Curtis Sliwa, whose job had him riding New York City's No. 4 subway, known as the "mugger's express." To protect the riders on the No. 4, arch-Angel Sliwa organized a group of his friends as "The Magnificent Thirteen," and on February 13, 1979, they went on their first subway patrol. They quickly expanded into the Guardian Angels, a group of unarmed but streetwise youths, self-appointed peacekeepers who patrol the city's buses, subways, and streets. Dressed in white T-shirts and red berets, the 700-person force has had a reassuring effect on many New Yorkers. Because they have broken up numerous fights and made hun-

dreds of civilian arrests, New York City police authorities consider their presence to be significant in the prevention of crime.

The popularity of the Guardian Angels enabled the group to expand to dozens of cities by 1991, but they have also been controversial. Some city officials consider them to be untrained and unregulated meddlers out to make police look bad. A Chicago police administrator branded them a "goon squad"; to others, they are no more than urban vigilantes who take the law into their own hands for the sake of some perverted ego fulfillment.

Their less-than-cordial acceptance in some locales has been based on several beliefs: that the roles of enforcing the law and keeping the peace should be filled only by well-trained police officers, that the Angel's presence in some situations might provoke trouble, and that they themselves run the risk of serious harm. Yet despite the mixed reactions, the Guardian Angels have endured and

continue to expand, not only in cities but in suburban areas as well.[a]

Bernhard Goetz, the "Subway Vigilante"

Everyone was talking about Goetz, and board games like Trivial Pursuit were popular. And it all sort of fell together.
— MIKE MARINE, CREATOR OF THE SUBWAY VIGILANTE BOARD GAME, IN WHICH PLAYERS START WITH A "GUN" AND SIX "BULLETS" AND MUST GET FROM "BROOKLYN" TO "THE BRONX" ALIVE, 1987

On December 22, 1984, urban vigilantism took on an altogether new look when Bernhard Hugo Goetz, a thirty-seven-year-old-self-employed electrical engineer, gunned down four youths who demanded $5 from him on a New York City subway car. The youths had criminal records, and for urban dwellers who were fed up with crime in the streets, Goetz was an immediate hero. Subsequent evidence suggested that Goetz's actions

A patrol of Guardian Angels in a confrontation with two men on a New York City street

may have been unprovoked, but when one of his victims was arrested six months later on rape and robbery charges, New York's "subway vigilante" received new support. In a national poll conducted by the Roper organization during September 1985, Goetz ranked sixth (following Lee Iacocca, Dan Rather, Peter Jennings, Mike Wallace, and Tom Brokaw) among the most admired personalities in the nation.[b]

Goetz was ultimately charged with attempted murder, assault, and illegal possession of a firearm, but his only conviction was on the gun charge. He was sentenced to six months in jail and ordered to pay a $5,000 fine.

The "Mad Dads" of Omaha, Nebraska

I'm a mad dad.
— MAD DAD FOUNDER JOHN FOSTER,
AFTER HIS SON WAS ASSAULTED BY A
BAND OF STREET YOUTHS

Mad Dads (an acronym for Men Against Destruction/Defending Against Drugs and Social Dis-

order), was established at the close of the 1980s to provide role models for black youths in Omaha and to provide a positive presence on the city's violence and crack–ravaged streets. A 600-member biracial group of fathers, their primary purpose is to offer alternatives to crime and gang violence. Much of their volunteer work involves cleaning up neighborhoods, painting over graffiti, and keeping drug gangs away from public housing projects. Although Omaha police were at first fearful that Mad Dads was just another publicity-seeking vigilante group, the "quality behavior" of its members quickly won police trust. In 1990, the group began opening chapters in other cities across the nation.[c]

SOURCES:
[a] *New York Daily News,* January 17, 1982, pp. 5, 61; *Newsweek,* July 1, 1985, p. 45; *New York Times,* June 15, 1988, p. B4; *New York Times,* July 13, 1988, pp. B1, B4.
[b] *Newsweek,* January 7, 1985, pp. 10–11; *National Law Journal,* June 29, 1987, pp. 24–27.
[c] *New York Times,* June 10, 1990, p. 25.

The process of law is a little slow. So this is the road you'll have to go. Murderers and thieves Beware! PEOPLE'S VERDICT.

— A JINGLE FOUND IN 1902 PINNED TO THE BODY OF A MAN HANGED BY THE VIGILANTES OF CASPER, WYOMING

Many thanks, sir for trying to do something to help the problems in this country.

— MARION, INDIANA JUDGE ROY JONES IN 1990, TO A DEFENDANT WHO SHOT AN ALLEGED PURSE SNATCHER

Police reserves

quickly come and gone, while others persist. Characteristically, they cooperate to some extent with the police, and their main activity is patrolling in radio-equipped vehicles for the purposes of spotting, reporting, and discouraging criminal acts against the residents of their communities. On the other hand, newer types of urban vigilantes have emerged in recent years that have generated great concern among both law enforcement groups and political officials (see Exhibit 6.6).

In contrast to vigilantes, auxiliary police groups consist of volunteer civilians working *with* local police. They come under the direct supervision of police, are trained and uniformed, and serve as the "eyes and ears" of law enforcement. Auxiliary police reserves, however, do not have formal enforcement powers, and they are not armed. In addition, they have no more authority than ordinary citizens, and they typically do not take direct action against suspects.

Auxiliary police currently exist in most major cities. In New York, for example, each police precinct has a volunteer auxiliary police unit. Members do not receive compensation, but they are supplied with uniforms and some equipment. Volunteers may not issue summonses and are not allowed to carry firearms, but they do have the power of arrest and may use physical force when necessary. Applicants must meet certain minimum requirements and, once accepted, are required to attend a ten-week lecture course. Each member of this auxiliary reserve usually patrols three nights a week and must put in at least eight hours per month to remain active. At last count, the New York Auxiliary Police had about 3,200 volunteers, with an additional 1,100 in training.[36]

In contrast are volunteer *police reserves* — armed and uniformed groups with powers similar to those of full-time officers. The reserve units emerged during the early 1940s when many police officers were drafted for the war effort. Today they are popular in many large cities — including Los Angeles, Washington, D.C., Dallas, and Miami — that do not have the fiscal means to hire additional full-time officers. The Los Angeles County Sheriff's Department currently has the largest and perhaps the most structured national police reserve corps. There are some 1,200 reserve police, the majority of whom are uniformed officers with 24-hour-a-day police authority. But to qualify they must pass a physical and psychological screening and take 600 hours of classroom and field training over a six-month period, a course with a nearly 50 percent dropout rate. They have to work at least two eight-hour tours a month to stay accredited. The program has been deemed a success and shoulders almost 10 percent of the sheriff's department workload.[37]

SUMMARY

The police represent the largest and most visible segment of the criminal justice system and are charged with enforcing the law and keeping the peace.

Modern policing has its roots in the latter part of the ninth century and the mutual pledge system of England's Alfred the Great. By the seventeenth century, thief-takers were being used by the Crown as private detectives paid on a piecework basis. The foundations for the first modern police were put into place by Henry Fielding in 1748. His Bow Street Runners were an organ zed investigative division that earned the

standard thief-takers' rewards. The later efforts of Patrick Colquhoun and Sir Robert Peel led to the establishment of the first modern police force.

In the United States, constable and night watch systems were common in most colonial communities. As settlers moved west, sheriffs emerged as active agents of law enforcement. They were assisted by the posse comitatus, which consisted of all the able-bodied men in a county. Nineteenth-century America also saw the establishment of state police agencies of federal marshals. In addition, cities set up metropolitan police forces after the London model.

Today there are more than 40,000 public police agencies across the United States at the federal, state, and local levels. Federal law enforcement agencies enforce specific statutes as contained in the U.S. Criminal Code, and their units are highly specialized. State police agencies generally fulfill a number of the regulatory and investigative roles of the federal enforcement groups as well as a portion of the uniformed patrol duties of local police. The majority of modern policing, however, is provided by county and municipal authority.

Police in the private sector became well known in this country during the last century with the efforts of the Pinkerton National Detective Agency. Private police today include a variety of organizations and individuals who provide guard, patrol, detection, and alarm services, armored-car transportation, crowd control, insurance investigation, and retail and industrial security. Nonpublic police also include civilian police auxiliaries and neighborhood watch groups.

Members of New York City's Veterans Civilian Observation Patrol help make their neighborhoods safe at night. Operating under the auspices of the local police, many of these volunteers are Vietnam veterans, and have become reassuring sights on lonely streets and subway cars.

KEY TERMS

Bow Street Runners **(166)**
Federal Bureau of
  Investigation **(176)**
Henry Fielding **(166)**
Interpol **(180)**

mutual pledge **(164)**
Organized Crime Drug
  Enforcement Task
  Force **(177)**
posse comitatus **(168)**

Posse Comitatus Act **(170)**
Texas Rangers **(169)**
thief-takers **(165)**
vigilante justice **(186)**

QUESTIONS FOR DISCUSSION

1. What has been the role of the sheriff down through the ages?
2. To what extent do the functions of federal, state, and local police vary and overlap?
3. Do private police agencies create more problems than their protection is worth? Why or why not?
4. Should quasi-vigilante groups be permitted to patrol the streets?

FOR FURTHER READING

Inciardi, James A. and Juliet L. Dee "From the Keystone Cops to *Miami Vice:* Images of Policing in American Popular Culture," *Journal of Popular Culture,* Fall 1987, pp. 84–102.
Klockars, Carl B. *The Idea of Police.* Beverly Hills: Sage, 1985

Miller, Wilbur R. "Cops and Bobbies, 1830–1870," *Journal of Social History,* Winter 1975, pp. 81–101.
Reppetto, Thomas A. *The Blue Parade.* New York: Free Press, 1978.

NOTES

1. Luke Owen Pike, *A History of Crime in England,* vol. 2 (London: Smith, Elder, 1873–76), pp. 457–462.
2. Pike, *Crime in England,* vol. 1, p. 218.
3. See Patrick Pringle, *Hue and Cry: The Story of Henry and John Fielding and Their Bow Street Runners* (New York: William Morrow, 1965), pp. 29–58.
4. Arthur L. Hayward, *Lives of the Most Remarkable Criminals* (New York: Dodd, Mead, 1927), p. 234.
5. See Patrick Pringle, *The Thief-Takers* (London: Museum Press, 1958).
6. Pringle, *Hue and Cry,* p. 81.
7. For the derivation of the term "beak" and a discussion of underworld cant, see James A. Inciardi, *Careers in Crime* (Chicago: Rand McNally, 1975), pp. 136–139.
8. The complete story of the Bow Street Runners can be found in the works of Patrick Pringle, *Hue and Cry,* as well as in his *Highwaymen* (New York: Roy, 1963).
9. Patrick Colquhoun, *A Treatise on the Police of the Metropolis* (London: J. Mawman, 1806).
10. Thomas A. Reppetto, *The Blue Parade* (New York: Free Press, 1978), p. 14.
11. Cited by Carl Bridenbaugh, *Cities in the Wilderness: Urban Life in America, 1625–1742* (New York: Capricorn, 1964), pp. 63–64.
12. Cited by Carl Bridenbaugh, *Cities in the Revolt: Urban Life in America, 1743–1776* (New York: Knopf, 1965), p. 107.
13. Bruce Smith, *Rural Crime Control* (New York: Columbia University Institute of Public Administration, 1933), pp. 61–63.
14. Walter Prescott Webb, *The Texas Rangers: A Century of Frontier Defense* (Boston: Houghton Mifflin, 1935).
15. Bruce Smith, *Police Systems in the United States* (New York: Harper & Brothers, 1949), p. 168.
16. Frank R. Prassel, *The Western Peace Officer: A Legacy of Law and Order* (Norman: University of Oklahoma Press, 1972).
17. Ira Rosenwaike, *Population History of New York City* (Syracuse, N.Y.: Syracuse University Press, 1972), pp. 18–36.
18. *Commercial Advisor,* August 20, 1840, cited by James F. Richardson, *The New York Police: Colonial Times to 1901* (New York: Oxford University Press, 1970), p. 26.
19. Cited by Richardson, *New York Police.*
20. Richardson, *New York Police,* p. 31.
21. *Organized Crime Drug Enforcement Task Forces* (Washington, DC: U.S. General Accounting Office, December 9, 1983).
22. "Organized Crime Drug Enforcement Task Forces: Goals and Objectives," *Drug Enforcement,* 11 (Summer 1984), pp. 3–15.
23. *Drug Enforcement Report,* June 24, 1991, p. 6.
24. R. H. Whitten, *Public Administration in Massachusetts* (New York: Columbia University Studies, 1898).
25. Bruce Smith, *The State Police: Organization and Administration* (New York: Columbia University Institute of Public Administration, 1925), pp. 1–40.
26. Katherine Mayo, *Justice To All: The Story of the Pennsylvania State Police* (New York: Putnam, 1917).
27. See Advisory Commission on Intergovernmental Relations, *State–Local Relations in the Criminal Justice System* (Washington, D.C.: U.S. Government Printing Office, 1971).

28. James D. Horan and Howard Swiggett, *The Pinkerton Story* (New York: G. P. Putnam's Sons, 1951); James D. Horan, *The Pinkertons: The Detective Dynasty That Made History* (New York: Crown, 1967).

29. D. J. Cook, *Hands Up* (Denver: Republican, 1882).

30. Eugene B. Block, *Great Train Robberies of the West* (New York: Avon, 1959); Stuart H. Holbrook, *The Story of American Railroads* (New York: Bonanza, 1962); Freeman H. Hubbard, *Railroad Avenue* (New York: McGraw-Hill, 1945).

31. See Edward Hungerford, *Wells Fargo: Advancing the American Frontier* (New York: Bonanza, 1949); Carolyn Lake, *Undercover for Wells Fargo* (Boston: Houghton Mifflin, 1969).

32. Deanna Hodgin, "Private Crime Fighting for a Profit," *Insight,* January 21, 1991, pp. 44–45.

33. James S. Kakalik and Sorrel Wildhorn, *The Private Police: Security and Danger* (New York: Crane, Russak, 1977).

34. For the most recent comprehensive examination of private policing in the United States, see Clifford D. Shearing and Philip C. Stenning [eds.], *Private Policing* (Newbury Park, CA: Sage, 1987).

35. Richard Maxwell Brown, "The American Vigilante Tradition," in *Violence in America: Historical and Comparative Perspectives,* ed. Hugh Davis Graham and Ted Robert Gurr (Beverly Hills: Sage, 1979), p. 162.

36. National Advisory Commission on Criminal Justice Standards and Goals, *Community Crime Prevention* (Washington, D.C.: U.S. Government Printing Office, 1973), p. 318; *New York Times,* August 20, 1988, pp. 29–30.

37. *Wall Street Journal,* December 21, 1983, pp. 1, 12.

7

Enforcing the Law and Keeping the Peace: The Nature and Scope of Police Work

There is a sleeping cop in all of us. He must be killed.

—FRENCH GRAFFITI, 1968

The policeman is the little boy who grew up to be what he said he was going to be.

—RAYMOND BURR, 1968

You can't measure what a patrolman standing on a corner has prevented. There is no product at the end of a policman's day.

—CHARLES E. McCARTHY, 1968

I have never seen a situation so dismal that a policeman couldn't make it worse.

—IRISH PLAYWRIGHT
BRENDAN BEHAN, 1962

Whether they emerge from the antiestablishment graffiti of a European student movement, the script of a primetime television series, a police inspector's comments in a newspaper interview, or the discontented grumblings of a noted playwright, attitudes about police and policing in modern society reflect a broad range of opinion. Michael Harrington, a leading exponent of democratic socialist philosophy in the United States, commented in his well-known book *The Other America* that "for the middle class, police recover stolen property, give directions, and help old ladies," but "for the urban poor, police are those who arrest you." For others, police are "pigs" and "fascists" or simply just "cops" and the "men in blue."

Such a range of opinion is likely to endure for as long as the police establishment continues as the visible machinery of law and order. Also, the more emotional and compelling opinions about police will remain negative. This kind of criticism and hostility is, to some extent, a function of the role police officers must play in maintaining social order; but to suggest that antipolice sentiment is justified is another matter entirely.

Police abuse of authority has been well documented, and, as is discussed in Chapter 9, incidents of corruption, brutality, and the unwarranted use of force and power, particularly against minority groups, are not uncommon. Furthermore, it is these abuses that we are likely to remember when we think about police. In general, however, people's ambivalence toward the police and their negative opinions of police work and behavior come mainly from a lack of understanding of the nature of police work and of the social, organizational, and legalistic constraints that shape its course. This ambivalence is further fueled by scandals and individual events of great importance. Karl Menninger, perhaps the most admired and widely acclaimed American psychiatrist of this century, summed it up quite accurately when he commented:

> There is no question that the police are misunderstood, looked down upon, unfairly treated, ridiculed, criticized, underestimated, and generally given a bad go of it in America.[1]

This chapter examines the character and structure of police work and offers some perspectives on the complexities and frustrations of attempting to enforce the law and maintain order in a democratic society. The following analysis seeks to answer such questions as these: What do police do? What do citizens ask them to do? What do they decide to do upon their own initiative? And what influences their decisions to do what they do?

THE FUNCTIONS OF POLICE

I guess what our job really boils down to is not letting the assholes take over the city. Now I'm not talking about your regular crooks . . . they're bound to wind up in the joint anyway. What I'm talking about are those shitheads out to prove that they can push everybody around. Those are the assholes we gotta deal with and take care of on patrol. They're the ones that make it tough on the decent people out there. You take the majority of what we do and it's nothing more than asshole control.

—A VETERAN POLICE OFFICER[2]

Police work suggests dramatic confrontations between police and law-breakers, with victory going to those with the greater strength, power, and resources. It suggests initiation of the process of justice, an enterprise bounded by the dusting for fingerprints and the search for elusive clues, the investigation and chase, and the ultimate apprehension and arrest of the suspected offender. It might also suggest that the functions of law enforcement are only the control of crime and the protection of society. But police work goes well beyond these tasks.

I'm not against the police, I'm just afraid of them.

—ALFRED HITCHCOCK

The Police Role

Although police work does entail the dangerous and competitive enterprise of apprehending criminals, officers assigned to patrol duties, even in large cities, are typically confronted with few, if any, serious crimes during the course of a single assignment. In smaller cities and towns such

Peacekeeping can involve many things—including bicycles and bermuda shorts as part of a Los Angeles beach patrol.

Police work is 70 percent common sense. That's what makes a policeman, common sense and the ability to make a quick decision.

— JOSEPH WAMBAUGH

Police patrol

The peacekeeping operations of the police are primarily of a nature not involving criminal activities.

Police arrest activity

crimes occur with even less frequency, and in some rural jurisdictions they may be extremely rare. Most police work is a *peacekeeping* operation. In this capacity it can include intervening in situations that may represent only potential threats to the public order — sidewalk agitators exercising their rights of free speech amidst hostile crowds, street-corner gatherings whose intentions seem questionable, belligerent drinkers who annoy or intimidate passersby. It can include the enforcement of civil ordinances whose violation can in no way be construed as criminal activity, but that is illegal nevertheless — for example, issuing citations for parking and minor traffic offenses, vending merchandise without a license, obstructing sidewalks, failing to post certain certificates of authority to conduct business, or perhaps even littering. Peacekeeping can also include more general areas of public service that are in no way related to the violation of law: directing traffic, settling disputes, locating missing children, returning lost pets, offering counsel to runaways, providing directions to confused pedestrians, and delivering babies.

Police work encompasses preventive and protective roles as well, for peacekeeping also includes *patrol,* which lessens opportunities to commit crimes. In addition, prevention and protection can involve initiating programs to reduce racial tensions, promote safe driving, reduce opportunities for crime victimization, and educate the public about home security measures.

Finally, police work involves many tasks that occur well beyond public notice and that are often time-consuming, overly routine, and excessively burdensome. Such activities include maintaining extended surveillances, transporting suspects, protecting witnesses, writing arrest and other reports, and testifying in court.[3] In short, peacekeeping operations generally do not involve criminal activities, and often are not even in the area of law enforcement.[4]

Even in the law enforcement aspects of police work, a significant proportion of activity does not involve "dangerous crime." One perspective on this issue emerges through an examination of police *arrest activity.* Exhibit 7.1 gives arrest statistics for the nation as a whole during 1990 as compiled by the FBI. Of the 14,195,100 arrests, only 20.6 percent involved the more serious Index crimes of homicide, forcible rape, robbery, aggravated assault, burglary, larceny, vehicle theft, and

• EXHIBIT 7.1 •

Number and Percent Distribution of Arrests in the United States for 1990

Crime	Number of Arrests		Percent	
Murder and nonnegligent manslaughter		22,900		0.2
Forcible rape		39,160		0.3
Robbery		167,990		1.2
Aggravated assault		475,330		3.3
Burglary		432,600		3.0
Larceny-theft		1,554,800		11.0
Motor vehicle theft		211,300		1.5
Arson		19,100		.1
Violent crime	705,500		5.0	
Property crime	2,217,800		15.6	
Crime Index total	2,923,300		20.6	
Other assaults		1,014,100		7.1
Forgery and counterfeiting		94,800		0.7
Fraud		291,600		2.1
Embezzlement		15,300		0.1
Stolen property; buying, receiving, possessing		165,200		1.2
Vandalism		326,000		2.3
Weapons; carrying, possessing, etc.		221,200		1.6
Prostitution and commercialized vice		111,400		0.8
Sex offenses (except forcible rape and prostitution)		107,600		0.8
Drug abuse violations		1,089,500		7.7
Gambling		19,300		0.1
Offenses against family and children		85,800		0.6
Driving under the influence		1,810,800		12.8
Liquor laws		714,700		5.0
Drunkenness		910,100		6.4
Disorderly conduct		733,000		5.2
Vagrancy		38,500		0.3
All other offenses (except traffic)		3,267,800		23.0
Suspicion (not included in total)		22,200		—
Curfew and loitering law violations		80,800		0.6
Runaways		174,200		1.2
Total*		14,195,100		100.0

Note: Arrest totals based on all reporting agencies and estimates for unreported areas.
* Because of rounding, items do not add to totals.
SOURCE: *Uniform Crime Reports*—1990.

arson. In contrast, almost one-third of the arrests were for such lesser crimes as gambling, driving while intoxicated, liquor law violations, disorderly conduct, prostitution, vagrancy, and drunkenness.

These data should not be interpreted as suggesting that arrest activity in areas other than Index crime is either unimportant or not dangerous. On the contrary, of the tens of thousands of assaults on police officers that occur in the United States each year, one-third result from the follow-up of "disturbance" calls. Less than a fourth result from responding to robbery and burglary calls and attempting other arrests.

The data from these and other studies of the police testify to the fact that police work involves keeping the peace more so than enforcing the law. And the value of police peacekeeping activities should not be underestimated. A large proportion of the annual homicide and assault rates is an outgrowth of various kinds of disputes, and responding to such disputes takes up a considerable amount of police time. If police no longer intervened in these disputes, we could expect a considerable increase in assaults.

The Right to Use Force

Peacekeeping role: The legitimate right of police to use force in situations in which urgency requires it.

The **peacekeeping role** is what mainly separates the functions of police from those of private citizens. This role involves the legitimate right to use force in situations whose urgency requires it. One police observer described it this way:

> I share a property line with my neighbor. About one foot to my side of the property line there stands my horticultural pride and joy: a 25-foot apple tree. (Needless to say, a small portion of this gorgeous tree graces my neighbor's yard.) Though the tree is mine and I am willing to share its bounty with my neighbor, he does not like apples. He likes still less the fact that my apples fall off, rot, and litter his yard. One day he gets fed up with my stinking apples and yells to me that he is going to cut down my tree unless I do. "No way," I say. He revs up his chain saw.
>
> Modern democratic society offers me two options in such a situation. First, I can drive to court and file a civil suit against my neighbor and, years hence, recover damages from him. The problem with this remedy is that I love my apple tree and don't want it cut down even if at some time in the future I am rewarded handsomely for its loss. Hence, modern democratic society offers me another option: call the cops and get them to stop my chain saw–wielding neighbor before his chain bites the bark. What police have that suits them to this task is a right to use coercive force. That is they can tell my neighbor to stop and if he doesn't, they can use whatever force is necessary to stop him.
>
> This is not true of me, of course. I do not have a general right to use coercive force. Modern democratic society would look very dimly on me if I appeared on the scene with a gun and threatened to blast my neighbor and his revving chain saw into the great orchard in the sky.[5]

Police are social agents that stand ready to employ force upon the citizenry on the basis of situationally defined exigencies.
—PETER K. MANNING

The police can't use clubs or gas or dogs. I suppose they will have to use poison ivy.
—WILLIAM F. BUCKLEY, JR.

The point is simply that modern democratic society severely restricts the right of private citizens to use force and urges them to use legal channels to work out their disputes. This restriction extends to virtually all cases except self-defense; and even there one must show that all reasonable means of retreat were exhausted. The law does recognize, however, that there are occasions in which something has to be done immediately—occasions in which resort to the courts or other mechanisms of dispute settlement would simply take too long and the damage would already be done. It is for handling such occasions that there are

police—an idea based on the notion that it is better to have a small group of people (police) with a monopoly on the legitimate right to use force than to allow anyone with a club, gun, knife, or chain saw to use force in such immediately demanding situations. That right to use force in situations that demand it is held by the police in modern democratic society and justifies their role in crime control, peacekeeping, traffic, and everything else they do. In short, this is the essence of the peacekeeping role of the police.

THE POLICE BUREAUCRACY

Policemen are soldiers who act alone; soldiers are policemen who act in unison.
— HERBERT SPENCER, 1851

The analogy between police and soldiers given by English philosopher Herbert Spencer more than a century ago remains appropriate today, for virtually every police organization throughout the Western world is structured around a military model. Furthermore, combined with their paramilitary character and with modifications related to size, police departments are bureaucratically structured. Thus, there are clearly defined roles and responsibilities. Activities are guided by rules and regulations, and there is both a chain of command, and an administrative staff charged with maintaining and increasing organizational efficiency. Both the military and bureaucratic characteristics of police organizations are best illustrated by a description of the organizations' division of labor, its chain and units of command, and its rules, regulations, and discipline.

The military model of police organization

Division of Labor

All large police organizations and many smaller ones have a relatively fixed and clearly defined division of labor. As indicated in Exhibit 7.2, a diagram of the organization of the Los Angeles Police Department, each separate responsibility falls within a specific unit, and the designated tasks of one division are precluded from being carried out in others.

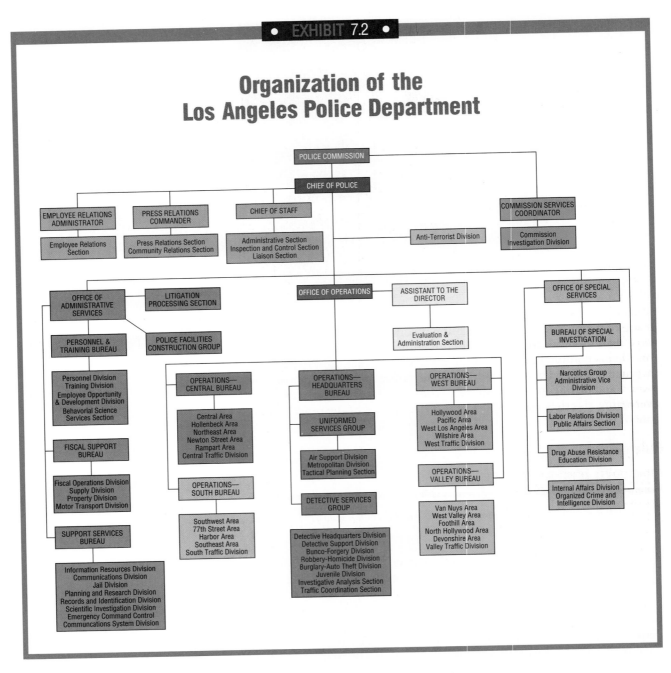

● EXHIBIT 7.2 ●

Organization of the Los Angeles Police Department

Narcotics, labor relations, air support, detective services, and personnel and training clearly fall within the authority of separate divisions and sections, and only under extraordinary circumstances would the personnel assigned to one division work in the area of another. Furthermore, within the detective services group, there are numerous separate divisions. The organizational arrangements of smaller police agencies are similar, although scaled down in proportion to their size and workload.

Chain and Units of Command

In theory at least, individual orders, requests, or any other types of information should flow up or down through each level of the organizational hierarchy, and no level of supervision or command should be

Let me explain something to you. When the police PR (public relations) man says that "an arrest is imminent" in some highly visible case, he's usually full of shit. What that line really means is that the police have no leads, no clues, no suspects, no idea of who did it, no nothin'.
—A MASSACHUSETTS POLICE OFFICIAL

bypassed. Referring again to Exhibit 7.2, for example, should a detective in the juvenile division have a request that must be acted upon by the chief of police, the communication would go up through the chain of command—from the detective to the head of the juvenile division, to the commander in charge of the detective services group, to operations headquarters, to the office of operations, and finally, to the chief of police.

Within this structure, each employee of a police agency has but one immediate superior to whom he or she must answer. In addition, the bureaucratic principle of delegation of responsibility is quite refined. Supervisors in the chain of command have complete and full authority over their subordinates, and the subordinates, in turn, are fully responsible to their immediate superiors.

Although no uniform terminology has been adopted in American police service for ranks, grades of authority, functional units, territorial units, and time units, those most commonly used are military-style designations. Ranks and titles include *officers, commanders, sergeants, lieutenants, captains, majors, chiefs,* and sometimes even *colonels.* Functional units include *bureaus,* which are composed of *divisions,* and these, in turn, can include *sections, forces,* or *squads.* Territorial units may be called *posts* (fixed locations to which officers are assigned for duty), *routes* or *beats* (small areas assigned for patrol purposes), *sectors* (areas containing two or more posts, routes, or beats), and *districts* and *areas* (large geographic subdivisions). Finally, time units include *watches* and *shifts,* and those assigned to a particular watch or shift are members of a *platoon* or *company.*[6]

Police and Public Service

When a sample of Lansing, Michigan, residents were asked to choose the most important public service-oriented activities that police should engage in, the following were indicated by the majority of respondents:

assisting stranded motorists	85%
checking/welfare of senior citizens	79%
investigation of vehicle accidents	77%
teaching rape prevention programs	52%
home security checks for vacationers	56%
teach pedestrian safety to children	54%

SOURCE: National Neighborhood Foot Patrol Center, Michigan State University

Rules, Regulations, and Discipline

Most police organizations have a complex system of rules and regulations designed to control and guide the actions of officers. Operations manuals and handbooks are generally lengthy, containing regulations and procedures to guide conduct in most situations (although, unlike the military, there are no rule books suggesting "proper" conduct for officers' spouses). In New York City, the current rule book is almost one foot thick.[7] Officers are instructed as to when they can legitimately fire weapons (clear and present danger of injury to an officer or citizen, no warning shots, and never from a moving car). If any shots are indeed fired, there are detailed rules and procedures for "sweeping the street" (locating spent bullets and determining if any injury or property damage occurred at the base of the trajectory of a bullet that missed its target). Reports of such matters must follow certain guidelines and their preparation must be done in a specific manner (in black ink with no erasures). Elaborate regulations also exist dealing with such varied phases of a police agency's internal operations as the receipt of complaints from citizens, the keeping of records, the transportation of nonpolice personnel in official vehicles, and the care and replacement of uniforms, ammunition, and other equipment. And there are policies and rules to guide the manner in which an officer makes an arrest, deals with medical emergencies, inspects the residence of a vacationing citizen, or takes a stray dog into custody. There are even rules governing procedures for mundane activities:

> *Even going to the toilet* . . . the rules dictate the formula by which . . . [an officer] . . . must request permission from a superior officer to leave post for "personal necessity."[8]

Gentlemen, there is a rule for everything.

—Police Academy instructor, New Jersey State Police, 1988

If you aren't in complete control of a situation, anything you do will make it worse.

—Howard Leary, former commissioner, New York City Police Department

While the existence of so many rules may seem absurd at first glance, most were established with good reason. In organizations with such crucial responsibilities, particularly one that can use deadly force, rules must be carefully spelled out. Even the procedure for taking care of "personal necessity" is not without importance, for it involves an officer leaving his or her assigned post. Over time, as circumstances change or become more complex, the number of rules tends to grow.

Most observers of police activity agree, however, that many police rules and regulations are essentially useless and for the most part unenforceable. The police process demands compliance with departmental regulations as well as vigorously productive law enforcement. These demands sometimes conflict, and when they do, proper conduct must often take a back seat to the desirability of "good 'collars' [arrests]." Furthermore, although in theory some procedures seem explicit and comprehensive, in practice they are no more than vague sermonizing as to what should be done. For example, in the area of police intervention in domestic disputes, no single rule can cover the possible number of contingencies. Officers are told to deal politely, impartially, and uniformly with citizens, but in a domestic quarrel one or more persons may express aggression, fear, or anger. One might be ill, the other might be drunk and abusive, and there could be children or other parties involved. What the officer must do depends more often on the nuances of the situation than on any regulation or published procedure.

There are other areas as well—because of the very nature of police work—where rules can be unenforceable. Since most officers are assigned to some type of patrol work on the street or in cars, they are unsupervised and their superiors have no way of determining what they actually are or are not doing.[9] Patrick V. Murphy, former police chief in the cities of New York, Detroit, and Washington, D.C., recalled a situation regarding the regulations that existed in his day as a rookie cop during World War II:

> Take the police signal box system. Its official purpose was to maintain a management check on the movement of officers out on patrol. Each precinct had a large number of call boxes that were laid out in the pattern of an electronic grid, more or less in a logical schematic pattern across the territory of the precinct. However, there was a hitch in the scheme's logic which required all officers to phone the precinct switchboard once an hour, the line on which the call was received identifying the caller's location.
>
> The hitch was that there might be two to four boxes on the same line. One learned this beat-the-system fact on the first day. "Kid," one veteran explained, "you can call in on any one of these three boxes, and for all they know at the switchboard, you could be at any one of the three locations. They're all on the same line. You can call up and say, 'This is Murphy on Box Four,' and since Four is connected to Six and Eight, be at either place." What the experienced hand was saying was that Murphy could be playing poker in a "coop"* near Box Four, but could call in and give the impression that he was blocks away. An hour later, to give the impression that he was on the move, he could call back from the same box and give a different location entirely. Yet the system was designed, and publicized, as a management control measure to insure constant movement; this was the great police omnipresence.[10]

Because many rules are unenforceable, police management must practice strategic leniency. Administrators routinely ignore the minor violations of departmental regulations in exchange for adherence to a

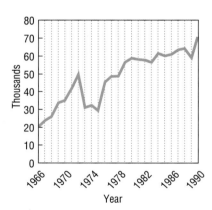

Police Officers Assaulted 1965–1990

SOURCE: UCR

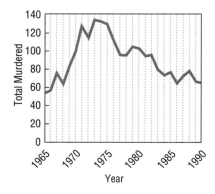

Police Officers Slain on Duty 1965–1990

SOURCE: UCR

---

* A sleeping or loafing location kept by officers.

few important rules and a modicum of organizational loyalty. Urban ethnographer Jonathan Rubinstein offers the following illustration:

> Although nobody questions a supervisor's right to punish his men . . . he will exhaust every available alternative before exercising his formal authority. For example, the operations room occasionally fills up with men who come in to drop off their reports and hang around to drink a cup of coffee . . . The supervisors, even when they are annoyed, rarely tell the men in a direct fashion to get back on the street . . . One day a captain from outside the district was about to enter the operations room when he noticed how many policemen were standing inside. He quickly turned away and walked over to the drinking fountain, where he took a long drink. Their sergeant, who had been urging the men to move . . . said only, "I think he wants to come in here, but he does not want to embarrass anyone so he is waiting for you to leave."[11]

As a final point, it should be emphasized here that it is not the titles and uniforms *per se* that make the police quasi-military. If police officers were suddenly put in jeans and crew neck sweaters and their titles were changed to workers, supervisors, and enforcers, police departments would remain quasi-military organizations. What makes them quasi-military is their *punitive* administrative approach: the specification of numerous rules and regulations and punishing deviations from them as a way of gaining compliance.

THE ORGANIZATION OF POLICING

As bureaucratic organizations, most police agencies are broken down into a variety of administrative components — all of which focus either directly or indirectly on the basic police mission. *Line services* include such activities as patrol, criminal investigation, and traffic control. Depending on the size of the agency, line services might also have specific divisions or units that focus on vice, organized crime, intelligence, and juvenile crime. There are also a variety of *administrative services,* which are structured to back up the efforts of the line staff and include such activities as training, personnel issues, planning and research, legal matters, community relations, and internal investigation. *Auxiliary services* assist the line staff in carrying out the basic police function, with specialized units assigned to communications, record keeping, data processing, temporary detention, laboratory studies, and supply and maintenance.

Line services

Administrative services

Auxiliary services

A number of the staff and auxiliary services, such as internal investigations, are discussed elsewhere in this book. However, we examine the basic activities of the line services in greater detail in the following sections since they reflect the primary and most visible aspects of policing.

Line services are the primary aspect of policing.

Patrol

For generations, the "cop on the beat" has been considered the mainstay of policing. In fact, to most people, the omnipresent force of officers dispersed throughout a community, in uniform, armed, and on call twenty-four hours a day, *is* policing. Whether officers are on foot or in cars, **patrol** remains basic to police work in both concept and technique.

Policing city streets entails a variety of tasks. Some of these are mundane, others are somewhat routine and boring, and a few can be

Patrol: A means of deploying police officers that gives them responsibility for policing activity in a defined area and that usually requires them to make regular circuits of that area.

dangerous. Patrol work includes such a wide spectrum of activities that it defies any specific description. It could involve dog-catching, administering first aid, breaking up family fights, pursuing a fleeing felon, directing traffic, investigating a crime scene, calming a lost child, or writing a parking ticket. Whatever the tasks might include, the patrol force is the foundation of the police department and its largest operating unit. In both cities and towns, along highways and in rural areas, uniformed patrol personnel directly perform all the major functions of modern law enforcement.

The functions of police patrol

More specifically, police patrols have five distinct functions: to protect public safety, to enforce the law, to control traffic, to conduct criminal investigations, and to interpret the law.[12] In their role as *protectors,* patrols promote and preserve the public order, resolve conflicts, and respond to requests for defensive service. Patrol enforcement duties include both the preservation of constitutional guarantees and the enforcement of legal statutes. The *traffic* control functions of patrol involve enforcing the motor vehicle and traffic laws, and handling accidents and disasters. As *investigators,* police officers on patrol conduct preliminary examinations of complaints of criminal acts, gather physical evidence and interview witnesses. During such investigations they may also uncover evidence, identify and apprehend suspects, and recover stolen property. Finally, patrol officers have *quasi-judicial functions:* they make the first interpretation of whether a law has been violated, it is here that the discretionary aspects of policing begin to surface. In such circumstances police may choose to take no action or to arrest, or they may only advise, instruct, or warn.

Traditionally, the prevention and suppression of crime was regarded as the mission of police patrols. For decades, if not a century or more, this interpretation of duties was accepted by the police, public officials,

Police work is often routine and boring.

and the general public. As an historical outgrowth of the early watch system, the first formal police patrols were on foot, and the cop on the beat became the symbol and very essence of policing in America. But even as early as the 1930s, well before the automobile had fully become part of the American way of life, foot patrols were beginning to vanish.[13] By the 1960s, their efficiency was being more seriously called into question. Foot patrols were deemed geographically restrictive and wasteful of personnel. Close supervision of officers had proven difficult, and without immediate transportation, foot patrols could not be deployed quickly to locations where their services might be needed.[14] Furthermore, the International Association of Chiefs of Police took the matter one step further, strongly advocating the idea of a conspicuous patrol that conveyed a sense of police omnipresence. The association felt that this could be best achieved using a highly mobile force of one-person cars:

> The more men and more cars that are visible on the streets, the greater is the potential for preventing a crime. A heavy blanket of conspicuous patrol at all times and in all parts of the city tends to suppress violations of the law. *The most economical manner of providing this heavy blanket of patrol is by using one-man cars when and where they are feasible.*[15]

With the start of the 1970s, police officers on foot patrol were seen less often, and one-person motor patrols became more common. However, because of the general lack of police–citizen contact that has resulted from motorized patrols, there are indications that current trends are turning once again in favor of putting the cop back on the beat. By the mid-1980s, foot patrols had reappeared in Oakland, Los Angeles, Newark, Detroit, New York, Houston, Boston, Minneapolis, Cincinnati, and other locales, and the trend continues to spread[16] (see Exhibit 7.3).

Whether police are deployed singularly or in teams, in vehicles or on foot, however, the essential value of police patrol in the prevention and suppression of crime has been called into question. In a study conducted by the Police Foundation during the 1970s, three different levels of preventive patrol in Kansas City were closely compared. The setting was fifteen police beats, which were divided into five groups of similarly matched beats. One beat in each of the five groups was randomly selected for each of the three levels of patrol: normal, proactive, and reactive. *Normal* patrol involved a single car cruising the streets when not responding to calls; the *proactive* patrol strategy involved increasing the level of preventive patrol and police visibility by doubling or tripling the number of cruising cars; *reactive* patrol was characterized by the virtual elimination of cruising cars, with police entering the designated areas only in response to specific requests. At the conclusion of the study, no significant differences were found in any of the areas — regardless of the level of patrol — in the amount of crime officially reported to the police or according to victim surveys, observed criminal activity, citizen fear of crime, or the degree of citizen satisfaction with police.[17] In effect, the Kansas City experiment suggested that police patrol was not deterring crime.

Detective Work

Although patrol units conduct preliminary investigations of criminal acts, most sustained investigations are assigned to a police department's detective force, which specializes in the apprehension of offenders. Detective-level policing, specifically *detective work;* includes a variety of

I'd love to be a policeman here, but I'm not brave enough.
— BRITISH CONSTABLE, TRAINING IN NEW YORK CITY

Motorized patrols

The reappearance of foot patrols in major cities

The Kansas City Experiment
Kansas City is a large, rambling city in which police presence per square mile is very low. Would the study have shown the same effects had it been conducted in a place in which police beats were small and police presence per square mile were higher? I'm not sure, but I suspect that people notice more when cops are taken off half-square mile radio car beats than when they are taken off twenty-square mile beats.

— JAMES J. FYFE

It makes about as much sense to have police patrol routinely in cars to fight crime as it does to have firemen patrol routinely to fight fire.
— CARL B. KLOCKARS

• EXHIBIT 7.3 •

Recent Research on Police Foot Patrols
by George L. Kelling

During the late 1970s, experiments were initiated in Newark, New Jersey, and Flint, Michigan. The findings in the two studies were remarkably consistent:

- When foot patrol is added in neighborhoods, levels of fear decrease significantly.

- When foot patrol is withdrawn from neighborhoods, levels of fear increase significantly.

- Citizen satisfaction with police increases when foot patrol is added in neighborhoods.

- Police who patrol on foot have greater appreciation for the values of neighborhood residents than police who patrol the same areas in automobiles.

- Police who patrol on foot have a greater job satisfaction, less fear, and higher morale than officers who patrol in automobiles.

The Flint experiment yielded two additional important findings. First, in areas where there was aggressive foot patrol, calls for service via telephone were reduced by more than 40 percent. Second, there was a modest reduction in crime. (There were no changes in crime levels in Newark as a result of use of foot patrols.)

In sum, foot patrol has been shown to reduce citizen fear, increase citizen satisfaction, improve the attitudes of police officers, and improve the job satisfaction among police officers. In addition, foot patrol shows some potential for reducing calls for service via telephone and, although the findings are not strong, it has some crime reduction potential. The questions to be asked then are the following: What are the public policy implications of the political popularity of foot patrol and the empirical findings about its impact? Do these findings indicate that all cities should immediately return to the wholesale use of foot patrol?

Before these questions can be answered directly, the findings regarding fear reduction need to be discussed briefly.

Criminologists and persons concerned with public policy about crime were perplexed during the 1970s by the relationship between crime and fear of crime. There were many neighborhoods in which the levels of crime were modest but the level of citizen fear of crime was high; there were many other neighborhoods in which crime was high but fear levels low.

During the early 1980s, it was discovered that fear of crime was not primarily associated with crime, although that certainly was an important contributor to fear levels. Instead, fear was found to relate to disorder: gangs, disorderly persons, drunks, panhandlers, street prostitution, and other forms of behavior that were threatening but not necessarily criminal. These findings did not surprise citizens or police officials who had worked closely with citizen anti-crime groups. The anticrime groups had been emphasizing problems of community disorder and trying to convince the police to do something about them for some time.

These insights helped analysts interpret the findings regarding the fear reduction impact of foot patrol. It was likely that fear was reduced both as a result of the felt presence of police and of their activities in maintaining order during patrol. Thus, to the extent that police defined disorder and citizen fear as signifi-

---

The duties and responsibilities of detectives

responsibilities, all of which fall into the area of criminal investigation: (1) the identification, location, and apprehension of criminal offenders; (2) the collection and preservation of physical evidence; (3) the location and interviewing of witnesses; and (4) the recovery and return of stolen property. In addition, detective duties may involve some of the law enforcement functions of patrol units, such as responding to the dispatch of a "burglary in progress," but these would generally be exceptions rather than general practice.

In small police departments, detective functions are often carried out by members of the patrol force, or there may be a single detective generalist who handles all or most of the criminal investigations. In the

cant problems, foot patrol is an important police tactic. Moreover, according to the analysts, foot patrol also might have some anticrime potential. It may keep minor disorders from escalating into more serious events; it may encourage citizens to take action on their own behalf; and it certainly positions patrol officers to receive and interpret information necessary to solve crimes.

What then is the significance of foot patrol? Should police departments in every city immediately abandon automobile patrol and install foot patrol as the primary tactic? Probably not. The public yearning for foot patrol and the empirical findings regarding its significance suggest that foot patrol is one more important police tactic. In a city like Boston, for example, where population density is very high, foot patrol could be used on a widespread basis. Many areas of New York and Philadelphia have a population density that makes them amenable to the use of foot patrol. In Chicago, Milwaukee, and many other cities, foot patrol would be valuable in some areas. Yet in a rambling city like Houston, relatively few

areas lend themselves to foot patrol. Similarly, foot patrol may be more or less valuable during particular times of the day. Foot patrol may be very important in neighborhood shopping centers where merchants need help controlling students who pass through the area after school.

It has become apparent over the past few years that citizens desire a more intimate and pervasive police presence in their communities. Citizens, as individuals and in groups, want police to help them keep order and prevent crime as well as to have police take action on their own. This wisdom — that peaceful communities emerge as the result of the social obligation of all citizens to each other, and that the police's role is to support that expression of social obligation — is perhaps the most important conclusion to be gained from police research, not just research into foot patrol, but almost all of the research conducted by police over the last twenty years.

SOURCE: Adapted from George L. Kelling, *Foot Patrol* (Washington, DC: National Institute of Justice, 1991).

larger departments, however, there are not only detective squads, but special investigative units that focus only on homicides, robberies, burglaries, or rape. Typically, a detective unit will handle the investigation of all crimes that occur in its geographically assigned area; not all homicides or robberies or burglaries would necessarily be assigned to detectives from one of the specialized units. However, should the nature and method of the offense suggest a link to similar crimes in other areas, or if it is determined that the crime might have political repercussions, then the specialized unit would become involved in the case.

In cities and metropolitan areas where crime rates are high, there may be numerous and sometimes exotic sounding detective units whose

concerns are narrowly focused. The Los Angeles Police Department has its "Bunco-Forgery" squad; Detroit has its "Squad Six," which handles only drug-related homicides; and New York has its Safe, Loft & Truck Squad. So large, in fact, is the detective bureau of the N.Y.P.D., that it has literally dozens of divisions, units, sections, and squads. Special detective sections and teams may also be organized for specific instances of crime or investigation.

Media portrayals of detectives suggest that they spend much of their time in the pursuit of criminal offenders and that their efforts at detection are quite successful. But in reality this is simply not the case. Former police administrator Herman Goldstein has pointed this out in his *Policing a Free Society:*

> Part of the mystique of detective operations is the impression that a detective has difficult-to-come-by qualifications and skills; that investigating crime is a real science; that a detective does much more important work than other police officers; that all detective work is exciting; that a good detective can solve any crime. It borders on heresy to point out that, in fact, much of what detectives do consists of very routine and rather elementary chores, including much paper processing; that a good deal of their work is not only not exciting, it is downright boring; that the situations they confront are often less challenging and less demanding than those handled by patrolling police officers; that it is arguable whether special skills and knowledge are required for detective work; that a considerable amount of detective work is actually undertaken on a hit-or-miss basis; and that the capacity of detectives to solve crimes is greatly exaggerated.[18]

In fact, detectives are responsible for proportionately few arrests. They generally receive their cases in the form of reports of criminal incidents written by patrol officers. Although practically all serious offenses are investigated by detectives in one way or another, such crimes are extremely difficult (and often impossible) to solve. In most robberies, burglaries, and thefts — which account for the majority of the FBI Index offenses — physical evidence that can be subjected to any kind of serious analysis is rarely found. Furthermore, if witnesses to a crime are available, many are unwilling to cooperate or their descriptions of the offender are so vague that they are of little value to an investigator. Even victims themselves are typically uncertain about the facts of the case.

All but about 5 percent of serious crimes that are solved by detectives are solved because a witness tells the detective whodunit, or by thoroughly routine clerical procedures.
—CARL B. KLOCKARS

EXHIBIT 7.4

"Cops" and "Coppers" Some Etymological Considerations

American slang has a long and curious history, and much of it is traceable to the underworlds of vice and crime of past centuries. Such currently popular slang terms as "beef" (to complain), "fence" (a receiver of stolen goods), "hick" (a farmer), "hump" and "screw" (sexual intercourse), "lush" (a drunk), "snitch" (to inform on someone), and "tail" (a woman's buttocks or sexual intercourse) have their origins in the cant, or slang, of the sixteenth-century Elizabethan professional thief. Other slang usages date back to seventeenth-century England.

"Cop" and "copper," both meaning a policeman, also have their origins in the underworld.

Etymological investigation suggests that *cop* is associated with the root of the Latin *capere* (to seize or snatch) or the Gypsy *kap* and *cop* (to take). In the nineteenth-century cant of both English and American thieves, "to cop" came to mean to snatch, grab, or arrest; hence, the "cop" or "copper" was the policeman who grabbed a thief or made an arrest. And from the same root came such slang terms as "copped" (arrested), "cop a plea" (accept a plea of guilty to

a lesser crime), "cop a feel" (to surreptitiously touch or grab a woman's breasts), and "cop out" (to offer a plea or excuse). Some obsolete terms of this genre include "copper house" (a police station), and "copperhearted" (at heart a policeman).

The following excerpt, taken from George W. Matsell's *The Rogue's Lexicon,* published in 1859, illustrates some of these usages in nineteenth-century American underworld slang:

The knuck was copped to rights, a skin full of honey was found in his kick's poke by the copper when he frisked him.

That is, the pickpocket was arrested, and a purse full of money was found in his pants pocket by the policeman when he searched him.

sources: Godfrey Irwin, ed., *American Tramp and Underworld Slang* (New York: Sears, 1931); George W. Matsell, *Vocabulum; or, The Rogue's Lexicon* (New York: Matsell & Co., 1859); J. S. Farmer and W. E. Henley, *Slang and Its Analogues*(1890–1904, 7 vols.; reprint ed., New York: Arno Press, 1970); Eric Partridge, *Dictionary of Slang and Unconventional English* (New York: Bonanza Books, 1961); James A. Inciardi, *Careers in Crime* (Chicago: Rand McNally, 1975).

Only in those few instances where positive information can be found at the scene of a crime, or when victims or witnesses can provide substantial information to an investigating detective, are crimes likely to be solved. As a result, detectives engage in a selecting-out process when making decisions as to which crimes to investigate.[19] Detectives are evaluated on a variety of criteria, including their success with major cases, their ability to keep up with paper work, their skill at handling special types of cases, their capacity to reflect a positive and professional image, and importantly, the number of felony arrests they make during the course of a year and the "clearance rate" for specific crimes. A crime is "cleared" when the offender has been taken into custody, and the **clearance rate** refers to

Clearance rate: The proportion of crimes that result in arrest.

the proportion of crimes that result in arrest. Thus, detectives generally choose to investigate seriously and intensively only those crimes that are most likely to be cleared. It is for this reason that clearance rates for homicide, aggravated assault, and forcible rape are relatively high. A large proportion of these offenses occur as the result of differences of opinion in personal relations, and the victims and offenders are often at least minimally acquainted. Thus, in many cases victims or members of their families can provide detectives with the identity of the offender or with leads and clues that can result in a possible identification. In contrast, clearance rates for robbery and burglary are quite low.

Since detective bureaus are under organizational, administrative, and political pressure to solve crimes, they also use a variety of mechanisms, sometimes illegitimate, to increase local clearance rates. Through the *multiple-clearance method,* one single arrest may ultimately clear numerous unsolved crimes. In the Son of Sam case (noted earlier in Chapter 1, Exhibit 1.2), for example, the arrest of David Berkowitz resulted in the clearing of six homicides and numerous felony assaults.[20] Similarly, if an individual is arrested for purse-snatching, detectives may contact recent purse-snatch victims to see if they can identify the suspect in an effort to clear previous, unsolved cases. But the multiple-clearance method can also be abused. One Miami Beach detective told the author this story several years ago:

The multiple-clearance method

> It was a damn good *collar* [arrest]. The officer catches him climbing ass first out of a kitchen window with a TV set under his arm. . . . He *bags* [arrests] him, and finds a *piece* [gun] in his back pocket, burglar's tools in his raincoat, and three bags of heroin in his sock. . . . Now we know that this junkie burglar has been doing his thing up and down the coast all year, so we offer him a deal: "You help us and we'll help you." . . . In the end, he *cops* [admits] to twenty-odd burglaries so we can get them off the books, and we drop the gun charge and tell the prosecutor that he's just some poor junkie stiff that cooperated and just needs a little help with his drug problem.

Unfounding and reclassification are also reliable, although sometimes illegitimate, methods of increasing clearance rates and getting the crime rate down.[21] *Unfounding* is a formal declaration that certain crimes previously thought to have occurred never actually happened. *Reclassification* is the reduction of certain crimes from felonies to misdemeanors. There are also "exceptional clearances," when some element beyond police control precludes taking the offender into custody, such as the death of a known but unapprehended criminal, a deathbed confession, or the refusal of a victim to prosecute after the perpetrator is identified.

All of this should not suggest that clearance rates are always or regularly manipulated. However, it is clear that different police agencies have different policies and practices in claiming and calculating clearance rates, so much so, in fact, that clearance rates are very poor indicators of the effectiveness of a detective bureau. It is also important to note that detectives, who constitute less than 15 percent of the sworn officers in most well-managed departments, "clear" far fewer cases than the considerably larger number of officers assigned to patrol. Yet one should not become cynical about the actual value of detective work. The perseverance of many detectives can be impressive. And routine follow-up investigations often produce new information that can lead to the identity of a perpetrator. In addition, the public relations value of detective work is immeasurable. Victims treated sympathetically offer greater assistance to the police in the future, and detective advice to victims plays an important role in crime prevention.

Crimes Cleared by Arrest, 1990

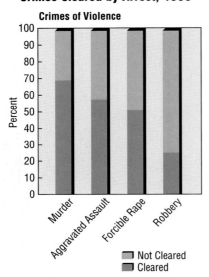

Crimes of Violence

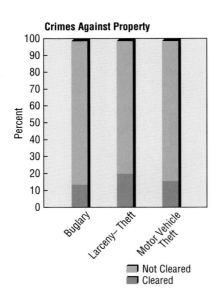

Crimes Against Property

Specialized Police Units

In addition to the patrol and investigative aspects of police work, there are numerous specialized approaches to crime control that occur within the context of highly focused bureaus and squads. For example, many large urban police departments have juvenile or *youth bureaus,* which employ proactive strategies to prevent and deter delinquent behavior. These large departments also have specialized units for enforcing vice laws or gathering intelligence concerning organized crime.

Youth bureaus

Of a less conventional nature is the use of police decoys and "blending"—essentially, two related types of undercover work. In *decoy* operations, nonuniformed officers pose as potential high-risk victims —drunks, tourists, young women, the elderly, and the disabled—in high-crime areas in order to attract and apprehend street criminals. *Blending* involves the use of police officers posing as ordinary citizens, who are strategically placed in high-risk locations to observe and intervene should a crime occur. Among the more effective decoy and blending operations was New York City's Taxi-Truck Surveillance Unit, launched to combat the growing number of night assaults on truck and cab drivers. For a period of five years, specially equipped officers from both patrol and detective bureaus were selected to play the roles of cabbies and truckers; this undercover approach ultimately reduced the assaults and robberies by almost 50 percent.[22]

Police decoys

Blending

The most controversial of the special approaches to crime control are the elite police teams that use aggressive military procedures in exceptionally dangerous or potentially explosive situations. The forerunner of these groups was perhaps New York City's Tactical Patrol Force TPF, a fast-moving battalion of shock troops trained in mob control and culled from the very best of police academy recruits. During the 1960s and early 1970s, the TPFs, as they are still known, viewed their 1,000-member force as the elite of incorruptible law enforcement. In addition to mob and riot control, the TPFs swept into high-crime areas to hunt down muggers and robbers, often using a variety of decoy units that readily blended into the life on the street.[23] Even more visible and controversial are the newer commando-style police units known under such names as SWAT (Special Weapons and Tactics), ERT (Emergency Response Team), and TNT (Tactical Neutralization Team). SWAT teams, which are carefully chosen and trained in the use of weapons and strategic invasion tactics and are typically used in situations involving hostages, airplane hijackings, and prison riots. The first of these police "guerrilla" units was the Philadelphia Police Department's 100-man Special Weapons and Tactics squad, which was organized in 1964 in response to the growing number of bank robberies throughout the city.[24] SWAT teams were also created in other cities during the 1960s, generally in response to riots and similar disturbances, that erupted. By the mid-'70s, SWAT teams had become popular among police agencies throughout the nation, with squads ranging in size from small two-person teams in suburban and rural areas to large 160-member teams in densely populated metropolitan regions.[25]

Sting operations have also become a part of urban law enforcement in recent years. The typical sting involves using various undercover methods to control large-scale theft. Police officers pose as purchasers of stolen goods ("fences"), setting up contact points and storefronts wired for sound and videotape. And finally, almost every urban locale has one or more specialized drug enforcement units, organized to disrupt street-level drug dealing and/or cooperate with state and federal drug enforce-

Sting operations

• EXHIBIT 7.5 •

Sidelights on Criminal Matters
Drug Enforcement in Urban Areas

Just as yellow fever was successfully attacked by draining the swamps and morasses where it bread, so the attack on crime is, at least, a matter of eliminating its breeding spaces. Every city has its vicious spots—its points of contagion. . . . The various rendezvous where narcotics are illegally obtained are breeding grounds of crime to which the conscientious police executive will give careful attention.

—RAYMOND B. FOSDICK, *AMERICAN POLICE SYSTEMS*, 1920

Although warring on drugs is a relatively recent phenomenon, drug enforcement has been recognized as an important aspect of American policing for more than a hundred years. As early as 1886, for example, Inspector Thomas Byrnes of the New York City Police Department addressed the need for targeting those urban locales where narcotics were sold and used, and by the first decade of the twentieth century drug squads had become active in a number of urban police organizations.

Since the 1970s, drug enforcement has become a conspicuous part of policing in both large and small departments. In many municipal jurisdictions, for example, there are one or more of the following:

• *drug enforcement task forces*—cooperative efforts with state and federal law enforcement agencies structured to develop lengthy investigations of upper echelon drug law violators and individuals participating in drug trafficking networks;

• *tactical narcotics teams*—structured to disrupt street-level trafficking and collect intelligence to support major case investigations;

• *precinct-based street drug enforcement units*—uniformed officers on proactive and reactive patrol to address local street drug offenses;

• *street crime units*—tactical forces of plainclothes and decoy officers that can be quickly deployed to specific areas to address local community concerns without depleting existing precinct staff.

Recognized as an "exceptional scheme" of drug law enforcement by the U.S. Attorney General is the Tampa, Florida, "Q.U.A.D. Squad" program. The Q.U.A.D. (Quick Uniform Attack on Drugs) program was established in 1989 to suppress

ment groups in the investigation and apprehension of upper-level trafficking organizations (see Exhibit 7.5).

Police Discretion and Selective Law Enforcement

The policeman on post is in all truth the court of first instance; he is a de facto judge just as truly as any ermined magistrate, and a wise patrolman can be guide, philosopher and friend as he carries on his daily, hourly court.

—ARTHUR WOODS, FORMER COMMISSIONER, NEW YORK CITY POLICE DEPARTMENT

Among the major roles of police peacekeeping operations is the enforcement of laws that protect people and property. In carrying out this directive, police have the power to make arrests—official accusations of law violation. Thus, police officers stand on the front lines of the criminal justice process and must serve as chief interpreters of the law. Based on their knowledge of criminal codes, they must make immediate judgments as to whether a law has been violated, whether to invoke the powers of arrest, and whether to exercise the use of force when invoking that power. This situation tends to be exceedingly complex, especially since laws are not and cannot be written to take into account the specific circumstances surrounding every police confrontation. Moreover, all laws cannot be fully enforced, and most police officers, having only minimal if any legal training, are not equipped to deal with the intrica-

street-level drug sales in open-air markets. By responding to all citizen complaints about drug dealing, openly confronting suspected dealers and buyers, purchasing drugs and making arrests, conducting sting operations, attending meetings of local community groups, and working with the media in a public awareness campaign, the program successfully eliminated 95 percent of Tampa's 154 open-air drug markets in just two years.

Yet in spite of the mounting number of drug arrests throughout the nation, there are those who maintain that drug enforcement does *not* work very well. Or as the highly regarded former Minneapolis Police Chief Anthony V. Bouza noted in 1990:

Nothing works. New York freezes areas and saturates them with a blue carpet of cops. It doesn't work. Los Angeles does roundups and sweeps. They don't work. Minneapolis works with the feds, in task forces, and targets the bigger dealers. . . . And it doesn't work.

The overriding and strongest lesson is that nothing is working in this war. We lack a unified vision, a single, coherent national strategy.

SOURCES: Anthony V. Bouza, *The Police Mystique: An Insider's Look at Cops, Crime, and the Criminal Justice System* (New York: Plenum, 1990); Thomas Byrnes, *Professional Criminals of America* (New York: G. W. Dillingham, 1886); Donald C. Dilworth (ed.), *The Blue and the Brass: American Policing, 1890–1910* (Gaithersburg, MD: International Association of Chiefs of Police, 1976); Raymond B. Fosdick, *American Police Systems* (New York: Century, 1920); *Drug Enforcement Report*, June 24, 1991, p. 4.

cies of law. Therefore, police must exercise a great deal of discretion in deciding what constitutes a violation of the law, which laws to enforce, and how and when to enforce them.

To define **police discretion** in a single phrase or sentence would be difficult, for the term has come to mean different things to different people. In the broadest sense, discretion exists whenever a police officer or agency is free to choose among various alternatives — to enforce the law and to do so selectively, to use force, to deal with some citizens differently than with others, to provide or not provide certain services, to train recruits in certain ways, to discipline officers differently, and to organize and deploy resources in a variety of forms and levels. Most discussions of police discretion seem to focus on a narrower area, examining decisions regarding only when and how to enforce the law, and hence, invoke the criminal justice process.

By and large, police discretion is paradoxical since it appears to flout legal demands. In most jurisdictions the police officer is charged with the enforcement of laws — *all* laws! Yet discretion in terms of selective enforcement is necessary because of limited police resources, the ambiguity and breadth of criminal statutes, the informal expectations of legislatures, and the often conflicting demands of the public. The potential for discretion exists whenever an officer is free to choose from two or more

Police discretion: The freeedom to choose among a variety of alternatives in conducting police operations.

task-relevant, alternative interpretations of the events reported, inferred, or otherwise observed in any police–civilian encounter.

Studies of actual police practices demonstrate that discretion is not only widespread, but also that it occurs in many different kinds of situations. Based on extensive field observations of police practices, sociologist Wayne R. LaFave identified many of the reasons for this exercise of discretion.

A. Circumstances in which the conduct in question is clearly unlawful, but where police believe that the legislature may not have intended full enforcement. This would involve decisions not to arrest when:
(1) the law is ambiguous (e.g., complaints regarding obscene materials);
(2) the statutes are vague and may appear to have been designed as devices to deal with nuisance behavior rather than to call for full criminal processing (e.g., vagrancy and loitering);
(3) the statutes were written ever so broadly for the purpose of simply foreclosing any "loophole" opportunities for criminal entrepreneurs (e.g., laws which not only prohibit large-scale organized gambling, but friendly poker games as well);
(4) the intent of the law was seemingly to express a moral standard without an expectation of its full enforcement (e.g., the sodomy statutes which prohibit certain sexual acts among consenting adults);
(5) the legislation is apparently out of date (e.g., the age-old "blue laws" which regulate the sale and/or consumption of alcoholic beverages).

B. Circumstances in which police action would place constraints on a law enforcement agency's time, personnel, and financial resources. This would include decisions not to arrest when:
(1) the offenses are trivial (e.g., smoking in an elevator);
(2) the conduct is considered common, even accepted, among a particular group even though generally prohibited by statute (e.g., barroom fights or family assaults within certain ethnic, national, or socioeconomic groups);
(3) the victim refuses to bring a complaint or testify at a trial (e.g., rape victims who do not wish the additional humiliation associated with trial proceedings);
(4) the victim is a party to the offense (e.g., the client of a massage parlor who complains of being "rolled" by a prostitute).

C. Circumstances in which an arrest would have been technically correct and where legislative intent or limited resources are not at issue. This would include decisions not to arrest when:
(1) arrests would be inappropriate or ineffective (e.g., arrests of skid row drunks);
(2) arrests would cause loss of public support (e.g., sudden crackdowns on gambling);
(3) arrests that would endanger long-range enforcement goals (e.g., arrests of police informants or states' witnesses);

Patrol car theft foiled — by the cop inside

New York Times Service

NEW YORK — The annals of crime in New York City plumbed a bizarre new dimension Friday with a report that a Bronx man tried to steal a well-marked transit police car — with a uniformed officer seated in it.

"I gotta go! I gotta go!" the intruder shouted as he jumped in beside Officer Daniel Daly.

After a fierce, cramped struggle, the strange encounter Thursday was over quickly.

Sgt. Peter Sweeney could recall nothing comparable in his 25 years with the Police Department.

The suspect, 26-year-old Aundray Burns, was charged with attempted robbery, assault and resisting arrest.

"We think he was overcome by the sight of this magnificent white-and-blue patrol car," said Al O'Leary, a police spokesman.

SOURCE: *Miami Herald*, March 30, 1991, p. 1A.

(4) arrests that would cause undue harm to the offender (e.g., young first offenders or persons with good reputations whose offenses were only minor).[26]

The issue of police discretionary power is a problematic one, for the need for selective law enforcement is inescapable. **Full enforcement** of the law would involve an investigation of every disturbing event and every complaint, and the tenacious enforcement of each and every statute on the books—from homicide, robbery, and assault, to spitting on the sidewalk or littering the street. Full enforcement would mean arresting the little old lady down the street for gambling at an illegal bingo game, arresting your neighbor for not having his dog licensed, or perhaps even arresting your spouse for initiating oral sexual contacts on your wedding night.

Full enforcement, of course, is impossible and undesirable. It establishes mandates that exceed the capabilities and resources of police agencies and the criminal justice system as a whole. It places demands on police officers that exceed their conceptions of justice and fairness. And it transcends the public's conception of the judicious use of police power. Thus, police departments and officers are forced to select the options of underenforcement of some laws and nonenforcement of others, according to the dictates of any given situation. However, there are few clear-cut policies available to police describing when to invoke powers of arrest, and therein lies the problem. The very nature of police discretion creates situations in which good judgment suggests that enforcement should be initiated, *but it is not,* and others in which police power ought not be invoked, *but it is.*

Studies of police discretionary power have demonstrated that the most significant factor in the decision to arrest is the seriousness of the offense committed. This is supplemented by other information such as the offender's current mental state, past criminal record (when known to the arresting officer), whether weapons were involved, the availability of the complainant, and the relative danger to the officer involved.[27] In addition to these seemingly objective criteria, other factors come into play as well. What many police view as "safe" arrests often involve individuals without the power, resources, or social position to "cause trouble" for the officer. The social position of the complainant is also a matter of concern. In addition, a variety of studies have documented that police use their discretionary power of arrest more often when "disrespect" is shown them. Irving Piliavin and Scott Briar's well-known study, "Police Encounters with Juveniles," gives a particularly useful perspective on these aspects of discretion and differential law enforcement.[28] Their research demonstrated that, with the exception of offenders who had committed serious crimes or who were already wanted by the authorities, the disposition of juvenile cases depended largely on how a youth's character was evaluated by an officer. Such evaluations and decisions were typically limited to the information gathered by police during their actual encounters with juveniles. Piliavin and Briar found that this had serious implications for both the accused and the system of justice as a whole. When police officers believed that a youth's demeanor, race, or style of dress were good indicators of future behavior or criminality, arrests became totally discriminatory—the youths who were arrested were those who typically did not fit the officer's idea of normalcy.

Full enforcement: The tenacious enforcement of every statute in the criminal codes.

Selective law enforcement is inescapable, for full enforcement of the law is both impossible and impractical.

They came through the door like renegades from some warrior cop hell. Mad Max, Robo Cop, and the Terminator all flashed before my eyes.
—A RESEARCHER/BYSTANDER IN A MIAMI CRACK HOUSE COMMENTING ON A RAID BY DEA AGENTS

This is unfair. You have a boat.
—A BURGLARY SUSPECT TO A MASSACHUSETTS POLICE OFFICER, WHO ARRESTED HIM AS HE TRIED TO SWIM AWAY IN THE ATLANTIC OCEAN

The more problematic aspects of police discretion have become manifest in numerous other ways. Consider, for example, the following conversations on May 27, 1991, between unidentified callers and members of the Milwaukee Police Department, the Fire Department, and the 911 emergency service:

911 OPERATOR: Operator 71.

CALLER: Hi, I'm on 25th and State, and there is this young man. He's butt naked. He has been beaten up. He is very bruised up. He can't stand up. He has no clothes on. He is really hurt. I got no coat on. I just seen him. He needs some help.

OPERATOR: Where, where is he at?

CALLER: 25th and State. At the corner of 25th and State.

OPERATOR: He's just on the corner of the street?

CALLER: Yeah, he's in the middle of the street. He fell out. We're trying to help him. Some people are trying to help him.

OPERATOR: O.K. And he's unconscious right now?

CALLER: They're getting him. He's bruised up. Somebody must have jumped on him and stripped him or whatever.

OPERATOR: O.K. Let me put the Fire Department on the line. They'll send an ambulance. Just stay on the phone, O.K.?

CALLER: O.K.

The phone rings and a man answers " Fire Department."

CALLER: Can you send an ambulance to the corner of 25th and State?

FIRE OPERATOR: What's the problem?

CALLER: This butt naked young boy, or man, or whatever. He's butt naked. He's been beaten up real bad and he's fell out and people are trying to help him stand up. He can't stand up. He's butt naked. He has no clothes on. He is very hurt.

FIRE OPERATOR: Is he awake?

CALLER: He ain't awake. They're trying to get him to walk. But he can't walk straight. He can't even see straight. Every time he stands up, he falls out.

FIRE OPERATOR: 25th and State?

CALLER: Yeah, a one way.

FIRE OPERATOR: O.K.

CALLER: O.K. Bye.

The police were then dispatched.

OFFICER: The intoxicated Asian naked male was returned to his sober boyfriend.

In the background, there was some laughter, although it is unclear whether the laughter occurred in the police car or at the police dispatcher.

CALLER: A moment ago, 10 minutes, my daughter and my niece flagged down a policeman when they walked upon a young child being molested by a male guy. And no information or anything was being taken but they were taken downtown. I was wondering. . . . I mean I'm sure further information must be needed. The boy was naked and bleeding.

OFFICER: O.K.

The caller was transferred by the dispatcher to another police officer, where the woman caller went through her story again.

CALLER:	I wondered if this situation was being handled. This was a male child being raped and molested by an adult.
POLICE:	Where did this happen?

She was transferred to another officer.

POLICE:	Hello, this is the Milwaukee police.
CALLER:	Yes, there was a Squad Car No. 68 that was flagged down earlier this evening, about fifteen minutes ago.
OFFICER:	That was me.
CALLER:	Yeah, uh, what happened? I mean my daughter and niece witnessed what was going on. Was there anything done about the situation? Do you need their names, or information or anything from them?
OFFICER:	No, not at all.
CALLER:	You don't?
OFFICER:	It was a young intoxicated boyfriend of another boyfriend.
CALLER:	Well how old was this child?
OFFICER:	He was more than a child. He was an adult.
CALLER:	Are you sure?
OFFICER:	Yup.[29]

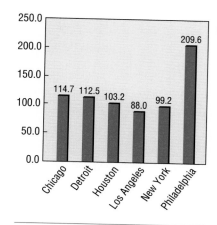

Calls For Police Service Per 100 Residents in 6 Selected Cities In Philadelphia, where residents are encouraged to call the police for a wide variety of services, police received in 1986 nearly 210 calls per 100 residents—more than two a person. In other cities residents call the police considerably less often.

SOURCE: Anthony Pate and Edwin E. Hamilton, *The Big Six: Policing America's Largest Cities* (Washington, DC: Police Foundation, 1991).

The subject of these conversations was Konerak Sinthasomphone, a fourteen-year-old Laotian boy who had apparently escaped from the home of Jeffrey L. Dahmer. The police considered the incident a domestic dispute between homosexuals and returned the boy to Dahmer. Two months later, Dahmer was arrested and charged with multiple murders. He admitted to dismembering numerous bodies and boiling several skulls to remove the flesh. Konerak Sinthasomphone's body was among the many found.

A different level of police discretion involves decisions made by police command staff regarding departmental objectives, enforcement policies, the deployment of personnel and resources, budget expenditures, and the organizational structure of police units. Known as *command discretion,* it is implicit in the very structure and organization of a police force. It tends to be less problematic than other types of discretion since it provides at least some uniform guidelines for street-level decision making.[30] Examples of command discretion might involve orders to "clear the streets of all prostitutes," or conversely, "look the other way" when observing the smoking of marijuana at rock concerts. A curious example of this level of discretion occurred when the police chief of a small town in New Jersey made it departmental policy that there would be a moratorium on the issuance of citations for parking and minor traffic violations. The police department had run low on its stock of summonses, and new supplies would not be readily forthcoming.[31]

Command discretion

Exactly how police discretion can be effectively controlled poses a complex dilemma, for it must be done in a manner that does not destroy the polar objectives of law enforcement—effective crime control and the protection of the rights of citizens. On this point, Professor Herman Goldstein commented:

As a minimum it would seem desirable that discretion be narrowed to the point that all officers in the same agency are operating on the same wavelength. The limits on discretion should embody and convey the objectives, priorities, and operating philosophy of the agency. They should be sufficiently specific to enable an officer to make judgments in a wide variety of unpredictable circumstances in a manner that will win the approval of top administrators, that will be free of personal prejudices and biases, and that will achieve a reasonable degree of uniformity in handling similar incidents in the community.[32]

THE POLICE SUBCULTURE

A *subculture* is the normative system of a particular group that is smaller than and essentially different from the dominant culture. It includes learned behavior common to the group and characterizes ways of acting and thinking that, together, constitute a relatively cohesive cultural system. The police are members of a subculture. Their system of shared norms, values, goals, career patterns, style of life, and occupational structure, and thus their social organization, is essentially different from those of the wider society within which they function and are charged to protect. Entry into the **police subculture** begins with a process of socialization whereby police recruits learn the values and behavior patterns characteristic of experienced officers. Ultimately, many develop an occupational or working personality, as a response to the danger of their work and their obligation to exercise authority.

Police subculture: The values and behavior patterns characteristic of experienced police officers.

The Police Personality

For generations, the notion that policing attracts persons predisposed toward authoritarianism and cynicism has been shared by many. There is even a body of research that supports this point of view.[33] Yet, the overwhelming majority of studies over the past two decades have consistently indicated that policing does *not* attract a distinctive personality type, but rather, that the nature of police socialization practices create a working personality among many patrol officers.[34]

Perhaps the most definitive statement on the development of the police personality comes from Jerome H. Skolnick, who summarized the process as follows:

> The policeman's role contains two principal variables, danger and authority, which should be interpreted in the light of a "constant" pressure to appear efficient. The element of danger seems to make the policeman especially attentive to signs indicating a potential for violence and lawbreaking. As a result, the policeman is generally a "suspicious" person. Furthermore, the character of the policeman's work makes him less desirable as a friend, since norms of friendship implicate others in his work. Accordingly, the element of danger isolates the policeman socially from that segment of the citizenry which he regards as symbolically dangerous and also from the conventional citizenry with whom he identifies.[35]

Criminals are not "criminals," they're perpetrators, *and they're not "arrested," they're* apprehended.
— New Castle County, Delaware Sheriff's Deputy, on police language, 1991

Skolnick further suggests that the element of authority reinforces the element of danger in isolating the policeman. That is, police are required to enforce laws that are unpopular, some of which are more morally conservative and others which are more morally liberal than the values of the communities in which they work. Police are also charged with enforcing the traffic laws and other codes that regulate the flow of public activity. In these situations, where police direct the citizenry and enforce unpopular laws that come from some idealized middle-class morality, they become viewed as adversaries. The public denies any recognition of police authority, while stressing the police obligation to respond to danger.

Riot police carry away a protestor during an antinuclear rally.

Skolnick and others have elaborated on other elements that contribute to the development and crystallization of the police **working personality.** All officers, for example, enter the police profession through the same mechanism: academy training followed by the constabulary role of the "cop on the beat." Because of this, officers share early experiences in a paramilitary organization that places a high value on similarity, routine, and predictability. Furthermore, as functionaries charged with enforcing the law and keeping the peace, police are required to respond to all assaults against persons and property. Thus, in an occupation characterized by an ever-present potential for violence, many police develop a perceptual shorthand to identify certain kinds of people as "symbolic assailants." [36] As a consequence, police develop conceptions that are shaped by persistent suspicion. In fact, police are specifically *trained* to be suspicious.

In sum, the police personality emerges as a result of the very nature of police work and of the kindred socialization processes in which most police officers seem to partake. To combat the social isolation that descends from the authoritarian role of the police, they develop resources within their own world — other police officers — to combat social rejection. In the end, most police become part of a closely knit subculture that is protective and supportive of its members, and that shares similar attitudes, values, understandings, and views of the world. This sense of isolation and the solidarity that grows out of it is typified by the following comment made to the author by a Delaware state trooper:

Working personality: A personality characterized by authoritarianism, cynicism, and suspicion developed in response to danger and the obligation to exercise authority.

Police solidarity

After only three months on the job I sensed that things were changing. I heard less and less from my high school buddies, old friends didn't call me over to play some poker or have a beer, even my own brother got a little distant. . . . My wife and I didn't get invited to parties any more — maybe they thought I'd arrest them if they pulled out a joint. . . . Enough was enough. We started sticking with the people from Troop 6 . . . and it was better, they were police people.

Police cynicism: The notion that all people are motivated by evil and selfishness.

Finally, an integral part of the police personality is **cynicism** — the notion that all people are motivated by evil and selfishness. Police cynicism develops among many officers through their contact with the police subculture and by the very nature of police work. Police officers are set apart from the rest of society because they have the power to regulate the lives of others, a role symbolized by their distinctive uniform and weapons. Moreover, their constant dealing with crime and the more troublesome aspects of social life serve to diminish their faith in humanity. (See Exhibit 7.6.) As the late Arthur Niederhoffer put it:

> Cynicism is an emotional plank deeply entrenched in the ethos of the police world, and it serves equally well for attack or defense. For many reasons police are particularly vulnerable to cynicism. When they succumb, they lose faith in people, society, and eventually in themselves. In their Hobbesian view, the world becomes a jungle in which crime, corruption, and brutality are normal features of the terrain.[37]

Police Operational Styles

O.K., maybe I am too suspicious. But you have to admit that with the kind of work I do, suspicion breeds like bacteria in pus.
— N.Y.P.D. UNDERCOVER NARCOTICS DETECTIVE, 1988

Without question, not all police officers manifest the level of cynicism expressed here, and there are others who possess little, if any, cynicism at all. Furthermore, the degree to which police officers develop the outstanding characteristics of the working personality also varies widely. In addition, approaches to police work reflect considerable variation. Research on police behavior suggests that most police adopt an operational style, a general role to which they tend to conform that embodies an abstract perception of law enforcement and their responsibilities to the community they are pledged to serve. The primary roles played by individual police officers are those of the enforcer, the idealist, the realist, and the optimist. No officer conforms solely to one of these roles in his or her behavior to the exclusion of the others — they are not specific personality types or pure categories of policing — but rather manifests the general attitude associated with one of these ideal types.[38]

Enforcers   Enforcers include police officers who place high merit on maintaining order and "keeping society safe," and a relatively low value on individual rights and constitutional due process. Since removing dangerous criminals from the streets is their main preoccupation, enforcers are generally critical of the Supreme Court and its decisions, which serve to "handcuff the police," and of police administrators, politicians, and others "who think that they know more about the law than the policeman does."

In general, enforcers express considerable dissatisfaction with their jobs. Even though they may arrest murderers and thieves, they see the same criminals being released and begin to wonder if their time has been well spent. They adapt by becoming resentful, cynical, and distrustful, and tend to stereotype people in various ways. Furthermore, as guardians of the public safety they see less serious crimes as being of little importance. They view intervening in domestic disputes or enforcing the traf-

● EXHIBIT 7.6 ●

Police Cynicism

"I look back over almost thirty-five years in the police service, thirty-five years of dealing with the worst that humanity has to offer. I meet the failures of humanity daily, and I meet them in the worst possible context. It is hard to keep an objective viewpoint." [a]

"The policeman's world is spawned of degradation, corruption, and insecurity. He sees men as ill-willed, exploitative, mean and dirty; himself a victim of injustice, misunderstood and defiled." [b]

"The whole damn area is made up of junkies and thieves —every last one of them. There's only one way to clean it up. Round them all up and put them on an island in the Pacific. Then give each of them $100, a bag of heroin, and a knife. They'll end up killing each other off." [c]

"What the hell do you expect from an animal like that. In fact they're *all* animals!" [d]

"I am convinced that we are turning into a nation of thieves.

I have sadly concluded that nine out of ten persons are dishonest." [e]

"It's the ass-hole of the city. All you have to do is rub your fingers on any wall and ten thieves jump out." [f]

"I hate citizens." [g]

SOURCES:
[a] *The Police: An Interview by Donald McDonald with William H. Parker, Chief of Police of Los Angeles* (Santa Barbara: Center for the Study of Democratic Institutions, 1962), p. 25.
[b] William A. Westley, "The Police: A Sociological Study of Law, Custom, and Morality." (Ph.D. dissertation, University of Chicago, 1951), p. ii.
[c] Personal communication from a New York City detective, February 7, 1981.
[d] Personal communication from a New York City Transit Authority police officer, June 18, 1980.
[e] Dorothy Crowe, "Thieves I Have Known," *Saturday Evening Post,* February 4, 1961, p. 78.
[f] Statement by a police officer patrolling New York's Times Square, cited in James A. Inciardi, *Careers in Crime* (Chicago: Rand McNally, 1975), p. 52.
[g] Elaine Cumming, Ian Cumming, and Laura Edell, "Policeman as Philosopher, Guide, and Friend," *Social Problems* 12 (Winter 1965):285.

fic laws as a poor use of their time. On the other hand, although they are unhappy with police work, enforcers are committed to upholding "the law." They wish to return to "the good old days" when there was respect for the law and the cop on the beat.

Idealists Idealists share many of the characteristics of enforcers, but in other ways they are very different. While placing a high value on maintaining order and protecting society, they also take seriously such notions as individual rights and due process of law. At the same time, while emphasizing the need to deal with dangerous criminals, idealists accept the notion that police officers should be involved in a wide variety of activities, even those not necessarily related to law enforcement.

The dissatisfactions and occupational frustrations known among enforcers are also manifest among idealists. Although concerned with rights and due process, they do see inequities within the courts. Furthermore, they view their jobs as difficult and feel rejection when under-

Dallas police prepared for riot control.

standing and respect for their contributions is not forthcoming. Although more flexible than enforcers, idealists also tend to become cynical.

Realists Realists share many of the same resentments and dissatisfactions with the court system and other social institutions as do other types of officers, but they are less frustrated with their roles in life. Since they place relatively low emphasis on both maintaining order and individual rights, they more easily find ways to cope with their jobs.

Realists see due process of law as an obstacle to effective enforcement and simply conclude that keeping society safe is impossible. What remains for these officers, then, is the "police group" — the group loyalty, mutual support, and the special ethos of being a police officer. Realists do not try to change the world, offenders, or even the police department, and cynicism becomes a very real part of their thinking. They internalize the idea that if you can't succeed because of the courts, or because of the politicians and public who do not understand the difficulties of police work, "then the hell with it — just don't let it get to you."

Optimists Optimists are the most people-oriented members of the police force. They place a high value on individual rights and are less likely to define their jobs as keeping society safe. Optimists see law enforcement as providing opportunities to help people in trouble. Since

There is no such thing as perfect justice.
— BIRMINGHAM POLICE OFFICER, 1990

much of police work involves activities other than crime fighting, optimists find much of their job rewarding. Although they are indeed full-fledged members of the police subculture, they tend to manifest little frustration, dissatisfaction, or cynicism.

There are many police officers wo could be readily described as enforcers, idealists, realists, or optimists. However, there are numerous others who manifest characteristics of several of these types, and still more who reflect totally different operational styles. James Q. Wilson has identified an alternative type, for example—the *watchman*—who reflects a number of the attitudes of both the enforcer and the idealist. The watchman style of policing involves keeping a low profile, and intervening only when there is a clear indication of public danger and disorder. These types of officers realize the importance of enforcing the law, but they tend to do so only when the public safety appears threatened.[39]

SUMMARY

Police have many functions. In a democratic society like the United States they serve as enforcers, protectors, investigators, and traffic controllers, and they act in many other roles as well. Yet, contrary to popular notions, their chief function is not enforcing the law but keeping the peace. This peacekeeping role is the key factor that separates the police from private citizens. Peacekeeping involves the mobilization of the legitimate right to use force in situations where urgency requires it.

Police departments are bureaucratically structured on a military model. All large police organizations and many smaller ones have a fixed division of labor, chains and units of command, and rules, regulations, and discipline.

Patrol is the most basic concept and technique of police work. It is by means of patrol that police protect public safety, enforce the law, control traffic, conduct criminal investigations, and interpret the law. In years past, foot patrols were considered the mainstay of policing. They have been replaced almost universally by motor patrols, but currently there is a trend favoring "putting the cop back on the beat" to increase contact between police and citizens.

A police department's detective force specializes in the apprehension of offenders. Detective work includes the identification and arrest of criminal offenders, the collection and preservation of physical evidence, the locating and interviewing of witnesses, and the recovery and return of stolen property. In spite of this concentrated activity, however, for their numbers detectives make proportionately few arrests.

Police officers, whether detectives or those in uniform, are called on to judge immediately whether a law has been violated, whether to invoke the powers of arrest, and whether to use force in invoking that power. Considerable discretion must be used in making these judgments. An outgrowth of this discretionary power is selective law enforcement.

Finally, there is a police subculture—a system of shared norms, values, goals, and style of life that is essentially different from that of the wider society within which officers function and which they are charged to protect. Within this subculture there are numerous styles of policing, including those of enforcer, idealist, realist, optimist, and watchman.

Up With the Cops

Most Americans believe that cops are doing their best to fight the drug war, though a full third disagree. Sixty-one percent of those polled would pay extra taxes to support larger police staffs.

Do you think the police in your community are working as hard as they can to combat drugs?

55% Yes   36% No

If more money is spent to fight crime, what should it go for?

44%   More drug treatment
         programs and social services
28%   More police
17%   More prisons
4%   More judges

Would you be willing to pay extra taxes for a larger police force in your community or not?

61% Yes   35% No

For this NEWSWEEK Poll, The Gallup Organization interviewed a national sample of 602 adults by phone May 17–18. The margin of error is plus or minus 4 percentage points. "Don't know" and other answers omitted. The NEWSWEEK Poll © 1989 by NEWSWEEK, Inc.

KEY TERMS

clearance rate **(211)**

cynicism **(222)**

full enforcement **(217)**

patrol **(205)**

peacekeeping role **(200)**

police discretion **(215)**

police subculture **(220)**

working personality **(221)**

QUESTIONS FOR DISCUSSION

1. What is the relative importance of patrol units, detective forces, and specialized squads to big-city policing?

2. In what ways are police agencies similar to military organizations? If you could imagine a police department *not* organized along military lines, what would it be like?

3. Do the advantages of police discretion outweigh the disadvantages?

4. What might be the most effective combination of foot patrols, motor patrols, and one-person patrols versus team patrols?

5. If there were more police on foot patrol, would there be more order and less crime?

FOR FURTHER READING

Bouza, Anthony V. *The Police Mystique: An Insider Looks at Cops, Crime, and the Criminal Justice System.* New York: Planum, 1990.

Bristow, Allen P. *Rural Law Enforcement.* Boston: Allyn and Bacon, 1982.

Goldstein, Herman. *Problem-Oriented Policing.* New York: McGraw Hill, 1990.

Rubinstein, Jonathan. *City Police.* New York: Farrar, Straus and Giroux, 1973.

NOTES

1. Karl Menninger, *A Psychiatrist's World: Selected Papers* (New York: Viking Press, 1959).

2. Quoted in John Van Maanen, "The Asshole," in Peter K. Manning and John Van Maanen, *Policing: A View From the Street* (Santa Monica: Goodyear, 1978), p. 221.

3. For a more detailed discussion of police tasks, see Egon Bittner, *The Functions of Police in Modern Society* (New York: Jason Aronson, 1975); Jonathan Rubinstein, *City Police* (New York: Farrar, Straus and Giroux, 1973); Herman Goldstein, *Policing a Free Society* (Cambridge, Mass.: Ballinger, 1977).

4. James Q. Wilson, *Varieties of Police Behavior: The Management of Law and Order in Eight Communities* (Cambridge, Mass.: Harvard University Press, 1968); Albert J. Reiss, Jr., *The Police and the Public* (New Haven, Conn.: Yale University Press, 1971); Richard J. Lundman, "Police Patrol Work: A Comparative Perspective," *Police Behavior: A Sociological Perspective,* ed. Richard J. Lundman (New York: Oxford University Press, 1980), pp. 52–65.

5. Carl B. Klockars, *The Idea of Police* (Beverly Hills: Sage, 1985), pp. 15–16.

6. O. W. Wilson and Ray C. McLaren, *Police Organization* (New York: McGraw-Hill, 1977), pp. 70–73.

7. Lawrence W. Sherman, *Scandal and Reform: Controlling Police Corruption* (Berkeley: University of California Press, 1978), p. 128.

8. Arthur Niederhoffer, *Behind the Shield* (Garden City, N.Y.: Doubleday, 1967), pp. 41–42.

9. Richard J. Lundman, *Police and Policing* (New York: Holt, Rinehart and Winston, 1980), p. 53; Bittner, *Functions of Police in Modern Society,* p. 56; President's Commission on Law Enforcement and Adminstration of Justice, *Task Force Report: The Police* (Washington, D.C.: U.S. Government Printing Office, 1967), p. 17.

10. Patrick V. Murphy and Thomas Plate, *Commissioner: A View from the Top of American Law Enforcement* (New York: Simon and Schuster, 1977), pp. 32–33.

11. Rubinstein, *City Police,* pp. 41–42.

12. National Advisory Commission on Criminal Justice Standards and Goals, *Police* (Washington, D.C.: U.S. Government Printing Office, 1973), p. 192.

13. Bruce Smith, *Police Systems in the United States* (New York: Harper & Brothers, 1949), p. 14.

14. President's Commission on Crime in the District of Columbia, *A Report on the President's Commission on Crime in the District of Columbia* (Washington, D.C.: U.S. Government Printing Office, 1966), p. 53; Police Department of Kansas City, *1966 Survey of Municipal Police Departments* (Kansas City, Mo.: Police Department, 1966), p. 53.

15. International Association of Chiefs of Police, *A Survey of the Police Department of Youngstown, Ohio* (Washington, D.C.: International Association of Chiefs of Police, 1964), p. 89.

16. Robert C. Trojanowicz and Dennis W. Banas, *Perceptions of Safety: A Comparison of Foot Patrol Versus Motor Patrol Officers* (East Lansing: National Neighborhood Foot Patrol Center, School of Criminal Justice, Michigan State University, 1985).

17. George L. Kelling, *The Kansas City Preventive Patrol Experiment: A Summary Report* (Washington, D.C.: Police Foundation, 1974).

18. Goldstein, *Policing a Free Society,* pp. 55–56.

19. See, for example, Donald J. Black, "The Social Organization of Arrest," *Stanford Law Review* 23 (June 1971): 1087–1111; Jan Chaiken, Peter Greenwood, and Joan Petersilia, "The Criminal Investigation Process: A Summary Report," *Policy Analysis,* 3 (1977), pp. 187–217.

20. See Lawrence D. Klausner, *Son of Sam* (New York: McGraw-Hill, 1981).

21. Lundman, "Police Patrol Work," pp. 64–65.

22. Patrick J. McGovern and Charles P. Connolly, "Decoys, Disguises, Danger—New York City's Nonuniform Street Patrol," *Law Enforcement Bulletin* (October 1976): 16–26; Carl B. Klockars, "The Modern Sting," in Carl B. Klockars [ed.], *Thinking About Police: Contemporary Readings* (New York: McGraw-Hill, 1983), pp. 217–226.

23. Charles Whited, *The Decoy Man* (New York: Playboy Press, 1973), p. 12.

24. Philadelphia *Bulletin,* March 28, 1976, section 3, p. 1.

25. See William L. Tafoya, "Special Weapons and Tactics," *Police Chief* (July 1975): 70–74; "The SWAT Squads," *Newsweek,* June 23, 1975, p. 95; Jenkins, C. Gordon, "Countdown to Teamwork," *Security Management,* (March 1989): 46–49; *Washington Post,* April 1, 1991, p. A8.

26. Wayne R. LaFave, *Arrest: The Decision to Take a Person into Custody* (Boston: Little, Brown, 1965).

27. Larry J. Siegel, Dennis Sullivan, and Jack R. Greene, "Decision Games Applied to Police Decision Making," *Journal of Criminal Justice* (Summer 1974): 131–142; Kenneth Culp Davis, *Police Discretion* (St. Paul, Minn.: West, 1975).

28. Irving Piliavin and Scott Briar, "Police Encounters with Juveniles," *American Journal of Sociology* 70 (September 1964): 206–214.

29. *New York Times,* August 2, 1991, p. A10.

30. Paul M. Whisenand and R. Fred Ferguson, *The Managing of Police Organizations* (Englewood Cliffs, N.J.: Prentice-Hall, 1973), pp. 199–201.

31. WCAU-TV News, Philadelphia, February 16, 1981.

32. Goldstein, *Policing a Free Society,* p. 112.

33. For example, see Richard Bennett and Theodore Greenstein, "The Police Personality: A Test of the Predispositional Model," *Journal of Police Science and Adminstration* 3 (1975): 439–445.

34. The most significant studies of this viewpoint include Niederhoffer, *Behind the Shield;* Jerome H. Skolnick, *Justice Without Trial: Law Enforcement in Democratic Society* (New York: Wiley, 1966).

35. Skolnick, *Justice Without Trial,* p.44.

36. Skolnick, *Justice Without Trial,* p.45–46.

37. Niederhoffer, *Behind the Shield,* p. 9.

38. This discussion is based on the typology found in John J. Broderick, *Police in a Time of Change* (Morristown, N.J.: General Learning Press, 1977). See also, W. K. Muir, *Police: Streetcorner Politicians* (Chicago: University of Chicago Press, 1977).

39. Wilson, *Varieties of Police Behavior,* pp. 140–141.

8

The Law of Arrest, Search, and Seizure: Police and the Constitution

The Constitution of the United States was made not merely for the generation that then existed, but for posterity.
—HENRY CLAY (1777–1852)

Policing constantly places its practitioners in situations in which good ends can be achieved by dirty means.
—CARL B. KLOCKARS, 1980

I'd like to tell the Supreme Court where it can put its search and seizure rules.

—A FORMER KEY WEST
POLICE OFFICIAL, 1985

The constitutional debate tends to center on the question of the power and efficiency of the state versus the freedom of the individual. Characteristically, cries of "handcuffing the police" and "coddling of criminals" attend decisions that restrict and define police powers more closely. Cries of "fascist" and "oppressor" usually accompany decisions described as conservative, which favor the power of the police over the rights of the individual.
—FORMER MINNEAPOLIS POLICE CHIEF
ANTHONY V. BOUZA, 1990

olice powers are numerous, and can be broadly divided into two general areas: investigative powers and arrest powers.[1] Police *investigative powers* include, but are not necessarily limited to:

- the power to stop
- the power to frisk
- the power to order someone out of a car
- the power to question
- the power to detain

Police *arrest powers* include:

- the power to use force
- the power to search
- the power to exercise seizure and restraint

Because the Constitution of the United States was designed to protect each citizen's rights, it placed certain restrictions on the exercise of these powers. This chapter discusses the legal constraints on police powers and traces their evolution through Supreme Court decisions, focusing on the Court's impact on law enforcement practice.

SEARCH WARRANTS

The right of the people to be secure in their persons, houses, papers, and effects, against unreasonable searches and seizures, shall not be violated, and no warrants shall issue, but upon probable cause, supported by oath or affirmation, and particularly describing the place to be searched, and the persons or things to be seized.

— FOURTH AMENDMENT, CONSTITUTION OF THE UNITED STATES

The law enforcement functions of the police are accomplished through the investigation of crimes and the apprehension of offenders. Each of these functions becomes manifest by means of a complex and interrelated series of specific activities. The first objective of investigation is to determine if a crime has been committed (although not all crimes require investigation) and, if so, what type of crime it was. Police generally analyze the available information to learn if the elements are present that constitute violation of criminal codes. The next objective is to identify the offender through further gathering of intelligence. When the investigation has been fruitful, an arrest is made; that is, a suspect is taken into custody. Beyond the investigation and apprehension aspects of law en-

I recall once in South America that I complained to the police that a camera had been stolen and they ended up arresting me. I hadn't registered or something. In other words, once you get them on the scene they really start nosing around. Once the law starts asking questions there's no stopping them.

— BEATNIK AUTHOR WILLIAM BURROUGHS

Call it a ticket, call it a summons, call it a citation, or even call it a mistake. Whatever. But by any name, consider it an affirmation that this is an ordered society that you are visiting.

— A MIAMI POLICE OFFICER TO A BRAZILIAN TOURIST IN 1991, WHEN CITING HER FOR PARKING HER RENTAL CAR ON THE SIDEWALK IN FRONT OF THE SHOP SHE WAS VISITING

forcement, police also have responsibility for gathering additional evidence if necessary, and for perserving it so that the prosecution phase of the criminal justice process can be effective. Yet each and every action in police investigation and apprehension is circumscribed by procedural issues that are governed by law and constitutional rights, and it is when these procedures and issues are called into question that law enforcement practice becomes a matter for judicial review.

At the onset, evidence gathering typically depends on *search* — the examination or inspection of premises or person with a view to discovering stolen or illicit property or evidence of guilt to be used in the prosecution of a criminal action. Associated with search is *seizure* — the taking of a person or property into the custody of the law in consequence of a violation of public law. **Search and seizure,** then, involves means for the detection and accusation of crime: the search for and taking of persons and property as evidence of crime.

The very language of the *Fourth Amendment,* however, prohibits "unreasonable searches and seizures." Unreasonableness, in the constitutional sense, is an elastic term with an ambiguous definition that may vary depending on the particular considerations and circumstances of a given situation. In general, however, it refers to that which is extreme, arbitrary, and capricious, and which is not justified by the apparent facts and circumstances.

Search warrants obviate much of the problematic nature of search and seizure, for they reflect the formal authority of the law in their sanctioning of the use of police search powers. A **search warrant** is a written order, issued by a magistrate and directed to a law enforcement officer, commanding search of a specified premises for stolen or unlawful goods, or for suspects or fugitives, and the bringing of these, if found, before the magistrate.

Search and seizure: The search for and taking of persons and property as evidence of crime.

Search warrant: A written order, issued by a magistrate and directed to a law enforcement officer, commanding a search of a specified premises.

PROBABLE CAUSE

Warrants authorizing a search must pass the constitutional test of reasonableness. In the language of the Fourth Amendment, "no warrants shall issue, but upon probable cause." **Probable cause,** in the constitutional sense, refers to facts or apparent facts that are reliable and generate a reasonable belief that a crime has been committed. In the absence of such "facts," the probable cause element has not been met, and the validity of the warrant can be questioned. And while probable cause "means less than evidence which would justify condemnation," [2] it does require "belief that the law was being violated on the premises to be searched; and the facts are such that a reasonably discreet and prudent man would be led to believe that there was a commission of the offense charged." [3]

Establishing probable cause for the issuance of a search warrant is a matter that the Supreme Court has addressed at length in recent years. As a result of *Aguilar* v. *Texas* in 1964 and *Spinelli* v. *United States* in 1969, [4] the general rule for many years was that probable cause for search could not be based solely on hearsay information received by the police. Rather, a valid warrant had to contain a statement that there was a reasonable cause to believe that property of a certain kind might be found "in or upon a designated or described in place, vehicle, or person," combined with "allegations of fact" supporting such a statement.

Probable cause: Facts or apparent facts that are reliable and generate a reasonable belief that a crime has been committed.

Aguilar v. *Texas*
Spinelli v. *United States*

• EXHIBIT 8.1 •

Illinois v. *Gates:* From the Supreme Court's Opinion

On May 3, 1978, the police department of Bloomingdale, Illinois, received an anonymous letter which included statements that Mr. and Mrs. Gates were engaged in selling drugs; that the wife would drive their car to Florida on May 3 to be loaded with drugs, and the husband would fly down in a few days to drive the car back; that the car's trunk would be loaded with drugs; and that Mr. and Mrs. Gates presently had over $100,000 worth of drugs in their basement. Acting on the tip, a police officer determined the Gates's address and learned that the husband had made a reservation on a May 5 flight to Florida. Arrangements for surveillance of the flight were made with an agent of the Drug Enforcement Administration (DEA). The surveillance disclosed that Mr. Gates took the flight, stayed overnight in a motel room registered in his wife's name, and left the following morning with a woman in

a car bearing an Illinois license plate issued to Mr. Gates, heading north on an interstate highway used by travelers to the Bloomingdale area. A search warrant for the defendants' residence and automobile was then obtained from an Illinois state court judge, based on the Bloomingdale police officer's affidavit setting forth the foregoing facts and a copy of the anonymous letter. When Mr. and Mrs. Gates arrived at their home, the police were waiting and discovered marijuana and other contraband in the defendants' car trunk and home. Prior to their trial on charges of violating state drug laws, the court ordered suppression of all the items seized, and the Illinois Appellate Court affirmed. The Illinois Supreme Court also affirmed, holding that the letter and affidavit were inadequate to sustain a determination of probable cause for issuance of the search warrant under *Aguilar* v. *Texas,* and *Spinelli* v. *United*

States, because they failed to satisfy the "two-pronged test" of (1) revealing the informant's "basis of knowledge" and (2) providing sufficient facts to establish either the informant's "veracity" or the "reliability" of the informant's report. The Court held the following:

1. The question—which this Court requested the parties to address—whether the rule requiring the exclusion at a criminal trial of evidence obtained in violation of the Fourth Amendment should be modified so as, for example, not to require exclusion of evidence obtained in the reasonable belief that the search and seizure at issue was consistent with the Fourth Amendment will not be decided in this case, since it was not presented to or decided by the Illinois courts. . . . Nor does the State's repeated opposition to respondents' substantive

---

Illinois* v. *Gates: The Supreme Court ruling that in establishing probable cause for the issuance of a search warrant, magistrates may make a common sense decision, given all the circumstances set forth in the affidavit, whether there is a fair probability that contraband can be found in a particular place.

The High Court's ruling in *Illinois* v. *Gates* in 1983,[5] however, eliminated the *Aguilar-Spinelli* test, replacing it with a "totality of circumstances analysis." *Gates* required magistrates to simply make a practical, commonsense decision whether, given all the circumstances set forth in the affidavit, there was a fair probability that contraband would be found in a particular place (see Exhibit 8.1).

WARRANTLESS SEARCH

A civilized system of law is as much concerned with the means employed to bring people to justice as it is with the ends themselves. A first principle of jurisprudence is that the ends do not justify the means.
—JUSTICE WILLIAM O. DOUGLAS, 1956

Fourth Amendment claims suffice to have raised the separate question whether the exclusionary rule should be modified. The extent of the continued vitality of the rule is an issue of unusual significance, and adhering scrupulously to the customary limitations on this Court's discretion promotes respect for its adjudicatory process and the stability of its decisions. . . .

2. The rigid "two-pronged test" under *Aguilar* and *Spinelli* for determining whether an informant's tip established probable cause for issuance of a warrant is abandoned, and the "totality of the circumstances" approach that traditionally has informed probable-cause determinations is substituted in its place. The elements under the "two-pronged test" concerning the informant's "veracity," "reliability," and "basis of knowledge" should

be understood simply as closely intertwined issues that may usefully illuminate the common-sense, practical question whether there is "probable cause" to believe that contraband or evidence is located in a particular place. The task of the issuing magistrate is simply to make a practical, common-sense decision whether, given all the circumstances set forth in the affidavit before him, there is a fair probability that contraband or evidence of a crime will be found in a particular place. And the duty of a reviewing court is simply to ensure that the magistrate had a substantial basis for concluding that probable cause existed. This flexible, easily applied standard will better achieve the accommodation of public and private interests that the Fourth Amendment requires than does the approach that has developed from *Aguilar* and *Spinelli*.

3. The judge issuing the warrant had a substantial basis for concluding that probable cause to search respondents' home and car existed. Under the "totality of the circumstances" analysis, corroboration of details of an informant's tip by independent police work is of significant value. Here, even standing alone, the facts obtained through the independent investigation of the Bloomingdale police officer and the DEA at least suggested that respondents were involved in drug trafficking. In addition, the judge could rely on the anonymous letter, which had been corroborated in major part by the police officer's efforts.

SOURCE: *Illinois* v. *Gates,* 462 U.S. 213 (1983).

Although the general rule regarding the application of the Fourth Amendment is that any search or seizure undertaken without a valid search warrant is unlawful, there are exceptions, provided that the arrest, search, and seizure are not unreasonable. The major exceptions include:

- a search incident to a lawful arrest
- stop and frisk procedures
- proabable cause and inventory searches of automobiles
- fresh pursuit
- consent searches

Search Incident to Arrest

Traditionally, a search without a warrant is allowable if it is made incident to a lawful arrest. The Supreme Court explained why in 1973:

It is the fact of the lawful arrest which establishes the authority to search, and we hold that in the case of a lawful custodial arrest a full search of the person is not only an exception to the warrant requirement of the Fourth Amendment, but is also a "reasonable" search under that Amendment.[6]

But given the language expressed by the Court, what would constitute a lawful arrest?

Until recently, it was generally assumed that the Fourth Amendment did not require the issuance of a warrant for an arrest to be lawful. Moreover, in 1976, the Supreme Court ruled that a police officer could make an arrest in a public place without a warrant even if he had enough time to obtain one.[7] However, in 1980 the Court ruled that in the absence of exigent circumstances the home of an accused could not be entered to make an arrest without a warrant.[8]

The foregoing at least suggests that arrests made *with* warrants are lawful, assuming, of course, that the arrest warrants themselves are procedurally correct. Furthermore, as indicated in the language of *Gates,* the provisions that determine the validity and legality of search warrants also apply to arrest warrants.

In the absence of a warrant, the legality of an arrest can be somewhat more problematic. As a general rule of common law, an arrest could not be made without a warrant, but if the felony or breach of the peace that was threatened or committed occurred within the view of an officer who was authorized to make an arrest, it was that officer's duty to arrest without warrant. If a felony had been committed and there was probable cause to believe that the particular person was the offender, then he or she could be arrested without a warrant. This common law rule of arrest, which is not at odds with constitutional guarantees, tends nevertheless to be vague, leaving much to the interpretation of the individual police officer. Even in the more definitive statements of this rule as they appear in the criminal procedure codes of most jurisdictions, it is the officer's

responsibility to fully determine the probable cause for, and hence the potential legality of, an arrest. For example, Section 1b-10-3 of the code of criminal procedure of the state of Alabama states:

An officer may arrest any person without a warrant, on any day and at any time, for:

1. Any public offense committed or a breach of the peace threatened in his presence;
2. When a felony has been committed, though not in his presence, by the person arrested;
3. When a felony has been committed and he has reasonable cause to believe that the person arrested committed it;
4. When he has reasonable cause to believe that the person arrested has committed a felony, although it may afterwards appear that a felony had not in fact been committed; or
5. On a charge made, upon reasonable cause, that the person arrested has committed a felony.

In most warrantless arrest situations, when one of these conditions prevails, the arrest is lawful and the search incident to the arrest is also lawful.

Although a warrantless search incident to a lawful arrest is permissible, the Supreme Court has placed limitations on the *scope* of such a search. The key case in this regard was *Chimel* v. *California*,[9] decided in 1969.

By way of introduction to this important case, it can be safely suggested that Ted Steven Chimel was not a particularly astute thief. Prior to the burglary of the coin store for which he was arrested and convicted, Chimel had engaged in a variety of incriminating blunders. He approached the owner of the store, told him that he was planning a big robbery, and questioned him about his alarm system, insurance cover-

Chimel v. *California:* The Supreme Court ruling that a search incident to a lawful arrest in a home must be limited to the area into which an arrestee might reach in order to grab a weapon or other evidentiary items.

age, and the location of the most valuable coins. Chimel also carefully cased the store. Following the burglary, he called the owner of the shop and accused him of robbing himself. When the victim suggested to Chimel that the crime had been sloppy, Chimel argued that it had been "real professional." And on the night of the burglary itself, Chimel declined an invitation for a bicycle ride, commenting that he "was going to knock over a place" and that "a coin shop was all set."

According to the facts in *Chimel,* on the afternoon of September 13, 1965, three police officers arrived at Ted Chimel's Santa Ana home with a warrant authorizing his arrest for the burglary of the coin shop. The officers knocked at the door, identified themselves to Chimel's wife, who admitted them inside, where they waited until Chimel returned from work. Upon his arrival, the officers handed him the arrest warrant and asked permission to "look around." He objected, but was advised that although no search warrant had been issued a search could nevertheless be conducted on the basis of the lawful arrest.

Accompanied by Chimel's wife, the police officers searched the entire three-bedroom house, during which time they requested that she open drawers in the master bedroom and sewing room and physically move contents of the drawers from side to side so that they might view any items that would have come from the burglary. When the full search was completed, the officers seized a variety of items, including a number of coins.

At Chimel's trial on two counts of burglary, the coins were admitted into evidence against him in spite of his objections that they had been illegally seized. Chimel was convicted, and the judgment was later affirmed by the California Supreme Court.

On appeal to the U.S. Supreme Court, however, Chimel's conviction was reversed, and the majority opinion of the Court analyzed the constitutional principle underlying search incident to arrest:

> When an arrest is made, it is reasonable for the arresting officer to search the person arrested in order to remove any weapons that the latter might seek to use in order to resist arrest or effect his escape. Otherwise, the officer's safety might well be endangered, and the arrest itself frustrated. In addition, it is entirely reasonable for the arresting officer to search for and seize any evidence on the arrestee's person in order to prevent its concealment or destruction. And the area into which an arrestee might reach in order to grap a weapon or evidentiary items must, of course, be governed by a like rule. A gun on a table or in the drawer in front of one who is arrested can be dangerous to the arresting officer as one concealed in the clothing of the person arrested. There is ample justification, therefore, for a search of the arrestee's person and the area "within his immediate control"—construing that phrase to mean the area from within which he might gain possession of a weapon or destructible evidence. There is no comparable justification, however, for routinely searching rooms other than that in which an arrest occurs—or, for that matter, for searching through all the desk drawers or other closed or concealed areas in that room itself. Such searches, in the absence of well-recognized exceptions, may be made only under the authority of a search warrant. The "adherence to judicial processes" mandated by the Fourth Amendment requires no less.

The consequences of "unlawful" arrest

There can be several consequences of "unlawful" or "false" arrest. First, evidence seized as an outgrowth of an unlawful arrest is inadmissible. Similarly, any conviction resulting from an illegal arrest may be overturned. Typically, however, if it is clear in the early stages of the criminal justice process that the arrest in question was indeed unlawful, it is likely that the charges against the suspect will be dropped before adversary proceedings follow their full course. Second, in most jurisdictions a citizen wrongly taken into custody can institute a civil suit against the officer and the police department that initiated or authorized the arrest (although these suits are seldom won).

However, a number of other issues associated with wrongful arrest vary greatly from state to state. Under Tennessee law, for example, as early as 1860 and as recently as the 1970s, numerous court decisions have declared that if "the officer acts at his peril, if he has no right to make an arrest without a warrant, or if his warrant is not valid, he is a trespasser." [10] Under such circumstances, the police officer is liable for money damages. However, where the arrest "would have been proper without a warrant, it is immaterial whether or not the warrant was good or bad." [11]

In Tennessee, Alabama, and numerous other jurisdictions, case law has dictated that every person has a right to resist an unlawful arrest, and "in preventing such illegal restraint of his liberty he may use such force as may be necessary." [12] In Idaho, by contrast, the suspect has no such right. [13] Further, in those jurisdictions where resistance to wrongful arrest is lawful, the means or amount of resistance cannot be disproportionate to the effort of the police officer to execute the arrest.

Finally, virtually all states place no liability for wrongful arrest on police officers if the arrest was made on the basis of a valid warrant or on probable cause, but a verdict of not guilty was returned. Thus, an acquittal is not tantamount to a finding of no reasonable grounds for arrest. [14] However, in 1986 the Supreme Court ruled in *Malley* v. *Briggs* [15] that a police officer could be held liable for damages if an arrest was made *without* probable cause —*even if he or she had obtained an arrest warrant.*

Stop and Frisk

Field interrogation or *stop and frisk* procedures can be a useful mechanism for police officers in areas where crime rates are high or where the potential risk for crime seems visibly present. In fact, it is not uncommon for police to stop on the street persons whose behavior seems suspicious, to detain them briefly by questioning for identification purposes, and to

Excessive Force and Resisting Arrest

In the absence of excessive or unnecessary force by an arresting officer, a person may not use force to resist an arrest by one who he knows or he has good reason to believe is an authorized police officer, engaged in the performance of his duties, regardless of whether the arrest was unlawful in the circumstances. But if an officer uses excessive or unnecessary force to subdue the arrestee, then regardless of whether the arrest is lawful or unlawful, the arrestee may defend himself by employing such force as reasonably appears to be necessary.
—From the opinion in Commonwealth v. Moreira, Massachusetts Supreme Judicial Court, 33 CrL 2078 (1983)

Malley v. *Briggs*

Stop and frisk is not uncommon where crime rates or the potential for crime is high.

Crack confiscated during a Los Angeles drug raid

• EXHIBIT 8.2 •

Terry v. Ohio

At 2:30 P.M. on October 31, 1963, the attention of Cleveland police detective Martin McFadden was drawn to the activities of two men, Richard Chilton and John Terry, who were conversing at the intersection of two downtown thoroughfares. Periodically, one of the men would separate from the other, walk southwest along one of the streets, pause for a moment to peer into a particular store window, walk on a short distance, and then turn around and head back to the corner, pausing once again to look into the same window. The two men would then confer briefly before the second man would repeat the identical process of strolling down the street and looking into the very same store window. Detective McFadden observed Chilton and Terry repeat this reconnaissance ritual roughly a dozen times until a third man appeared, spoke with them briefly, and departed down one of the streets. Chilton and Terry resumed their pacing, peering, and conferring for another ten minutes, after which they departed together, following the path taken earlier by the third man.

At this point, the police detective was thoroughly convinced that Chilton and Terry were "casing a job, a stick-up." He followed them, and when they stopped to converse with the third man who had met them earlier on the street corner, he decided to intervene. Detective McFadden approached the three men, identified himself as a police officer, and asked for their names. When the men "mumbled something" in response to his inquiries, McFadden spun Terry around so he was facing the other two men, patted down the outside of his clothing, and felt what he believed to be a pistol. A more thorough search found that it was a .38-caliber revolver, and a frisk of the other two men revealed a revolver in Chilton's overcoat pocket. All three of the suspects were taken to the police station, where Chilton and Terry were formally charged with carrying concealed weapons.

Terry became an interesting case in law, for the prosecution argued that the guns had been "seized" in a "search" incident to a lawful arrest. The defense, however, maintained that Detec-

tive McFadden had no probable cause for arrest and the guns ought to be suppressed as evidence obtained through illegal search and seizure.

Not surprisingly, the court recognized that McFadden's search was *not* incident to a lawful arrest, for no arrest had been made prior to the search; rather, it was clearly a case of stop and frisk. In fact, it was the court's opinion that it "would be stretching the facts beyond reasonable comprehension" to find that the officer had probable cause to arrest the three men of attempted robbery *before* he patted them down for weapons. Nonetheless, the Ohio trial court did rule that Detective McFadden's method of obtaining the evidence had been lawful: he had a duty to investigate the observed suspicious activity and had an absolute right to protect himself by frisking for weapons.

Chilton and Terry were both convicted of the weapons charge, and Terry was sentenced to a term of one to three years in the state penitentiary. Two appellate courts in Ohio upheld Terry's conviction, and the U.S.

Terry v. Ohio: The Supreme Court ruling that when a police officer observes unusual conduct and suspects a crime is about to be committed, he may "frisk" a suspect's outer clothing for dangerous weapons.

frisk (conduct a limited search by running the hands over the outer clothing) those whose answers or conduct suggest criminal involvement or threaten police safety.

Before the Supreme Court finally clarified the legal status of stop and frisk procedures in *Terry* **v. Ohio** (see Exhibit 8.2),[16] the authority for stop and frisk came from individual department directives, state judicial policy, police discretionary practices, and legislative statutes. In *Terry,* decided in 1968, the Supreme Court held that a police officer is not entitled to seize and search every person he sees on the streets and of whom he makes inquiries. Before placing a hand on the person of a citizen in search of anything, the officer must have constitutionally adequate, reasonable grounds for doing so.

Supreme Court granted *certiorari* (review) in 1967 in order to consider a number of questions concerning the constitutional validity of the stop and frisk practice. Showing rare solidarity, the High Court decided by an 8-to-1 margin to uphold a police officer's right to frisk and seize weapons under such circumstances. The Court ruled that Detective McFadden had reasonable grounds to believe that the "suspects" were armed and dangerous, that swift measures were necessary for the protection of himself and others, and that his frisk was appropriately limited to a patting down of the outer clothing until he felt weapons.

But central to the decision in *Terry* was the Court's general concern over police–citizen street encounters. Delivering the opinion of the Court on this issue, Chief Justice Earl Warren stated the following:

Our first task is to establish at what point in this encounter the Fourth Amendment becomes relevant. That is, we must decide whether and when Officer McFadden "seized" Terry and whether and when he conducted a

"search." There is some suggestion in the use of such terms as "stop" and "frisk" that such police conduct is outside the purview of the Fourth Amendment because neither action rises to the level of a "search" or "seizure" within the meaning of the Constitution. We emphatically reject this notion. It is quite plain that the Fourth Amendment governs "seizures" of the person which do not eventuate in a trip to the station house and prosecution for crime— "arrests" in traditional terminology. It must be recognized that whenever a police officer accosts an individual and restrains his freedom to walk away, he has "seized" that person. And it is nothing less than sheer torture of the English language to suggest that a careful exploration of the outer surfaces of a person's clothing all over his or her body in an attempt to find weapons is not a "search." Moreover, it is simply fantastic to urge that such a procedure performed in public by a policeman while the citizen stands helpless, perhaps facing a wall with his hands raised, is a "petty indignity." It is a serious intrusion upon the sanctity of the person, which may inflict great indignity and arouse strong resentment, and it is not to be undertaken lightly.

The *Terry* decision also provided standards for stop and frisk encounters, indicating that there had to be specific facts that could justify the police intrusion. In the words of Chief Jus-

tice Warren, there were five conditions that justified a stop and frisk action:

1. Where a police officer observes unusual conduct which leads him reasonably to conclude in light of his experience that criminal activity may be afoot;
2. and that the person with whom he is dealing may be armed and dangerous;
3. where in the course of investigating this behavior he identifies himself as a policeman;
4. and makes reasonable inquiry;
5. and where nothing in the initial stages of the encounter serves to dispel his reasonable fear for his own or others' safety . . .

Chief Justice Warren also emphasized, however, that the frisk was to be a limited search of the outer clothing in an attempt to discover weapons, and that the scope of any frisk or search associated with stop and frisk procedures was limited by the circumstances of the particular encounter.

SOURCE: *Terry* v. *Ohio*, 392 U.S. 1 (1968).

Any evidence found during the course of a frisk that is contrary to the *Terry* decision falls under the long-standing **fruit of the poisonous tree** doctrine. Under this rule, evidence seized illegally is considered "tainted" and cannot be used against a suspect. Furthermore, subsequent evidence derived from the initially tainted evidence must also be suppressed.

Related to both *Terry* and the poisonous tree doctrine is *California* v. *Hodari D.,*[17] decided by the Supreme Court in 1991 — a case precipitated to a great extent by the nation's "war on drugs." It seems that two officers on a routine drug patrol in a high-crime Oakland neighborhood spotted a group of youths who fled upon seeing the police approaching. The officers had *not* seen anything illegal happen, yet they knew that drug

Fruit of the poisonous tree: The doctrine that evidence seized illegally is considered "tainted" and cannot be used against a suspect.

In *California* v. *Hodari D.,* the Supreme Court ruled that a chase by police officers does not amount to a seizure, and therefore, evidence dropped by a fleeing suspect can be used even if police did not have any lawful reason for initiating the chase.

sales were common in the area. Given this, one of the officers chased Hodari D., a sixteen-year-old, and saw him toss away a small rock that the officer believed to be crack-cocaine. At that point, the officer tackled and restrained Hodari, and retrieved the "rock" (which was indeed crack-cocaine). The California Court of Appeal ruled that Hodari had been "seized" when he saw the officer running toward him, and that such a seizure was unreasonable under the Fourth Amendment. As such, the crack was the *fruit* of an illegal seizure. The U.S. Supreme Court reversed this decision, however, arguing that the police chase was not a "seizure," but a "show of force" that is not limited by the Constitution. The seizure did not occur until the officer tackled Hodari, but by that time, the officer's observance of the discarded rock represented the necessary probable cause.

Automobile Searches

As early as 1925, the Supreme Court established that due to the extreme mobility of motor vehicles, there were situations under which their warrantless search could be justified. In *Carroll* v. *United States,*[18] petitioner George Carroll was convicted of transporting liquor for sale in violation of the federal prohibition law and the Eighteenth Amendment. The contraband liquor used as evidence against him had been taken from his car by government agents acting without a search warrant. But the Supreme Court sustained Carroll's conviction against his contention that the seizure violated his Fourth Amendment rights. The Court determined that there had been probable cause for search. Chief Justice William Howard Taft explained the decision:

> The guaranty of freedom from unreasonable searches and seizures by the Fourth Amendment has been construed practically since the beginning of the government, as recognizing a necessary difference between a search of a store, dwelling house, or other structure in respect of which a proper official warrant readily may be obtained and a search of a ship, motor boat, wagon, or automobile for contraband goods, where it is not practicable to secure a warrant, because the vehicle can be quickly moved out of the locality or jurisdiction in which the warrant must be sought.

The Carroll Doctrine: The ruling, from the Supreme Court's decision in *Carroll* v. *United States,* that warrantless searches of vehicles were permissible where reasonable suspicion of illegal actions existed.

Known as the **Carroll Doctrine,** the High Court's decision maintained that an automobile or other vehicle may, upon probable cause, be searched without a warrant even though in a given situation there might be time to obtain one. Subsequent rulings made clear the breadth of the Carroll Doctrine. In 1931, the Court upheld the search of a parked car as reasonable, since the police could not know when the suspect might move it.[19] The Carroll Doctrine was reaffirmed in 1970 when the Supreme Court held that a warrantless search of an automobile that resulted in the seizure of weapons and other evidence, but conducted at a police station many hours after the arrests of the suspects, was lawful.[20]

United States v. *Ross*

A related issue here involves how *extensive* the search of an automobile may be in the absence of a warrant. In *United States* v. *Ross,*[21] decided in 1982, the Supreme Court held that where police have probable cause to search an entire vehicle, they may do so, including containers and packages which may conceal the items being sought. Moreover, *New York* v. *Belton*[22] a year earlier examined the scope of a vehicle search incident to arrest. In *Belton,* two principles were established. First, following a custodial arrest, police officers may search the entire passenger

In *New York* v. *Belton,* the Supreme Court imposed no limits on the scope of a search of a vehicle's passenger compartment when such a search was incident to an arrest.

compartment of the vehicle as an incident of that arrest. Second, if during the course of the search any containers are found, they may be opened and searched. Effectively, the decision in *Belton* seemed to impose no limits on the scope of a search of a vehicle's passenger compartment. And going one step further, in *California* v. *Acevedo,*[23] decided in 1991, the High Court permitted police to open and search a closed container found in an automobile, without a warrant, if they had probable cause to believe that the container contained contraband or evidence of a crime.

Related to automobile searches are the random stopping of cars, and the searches and arrests that may follow. Known as *spot checks,* the random stopping of automobiles for the purpose of checking drivers' licenses and vehicle registrations has often been used as a form of proactive police patrol. One New York City patrolman reflected on this practice:

> You try to stop the cars and drivers that look suspicious, but other times you go the pot luck route to break the monotony and start with every 20th car. Some nights we'll stop just blue cars, and other times it'll be big cars or old cars or whatever. Other times we'll pull over just blacks, or white guys with beards.[24]

Spot checks can aid in the apprehension of criminals, as this Miami Beach police officer found:

> Depending on the time of night and where you are, maybe you'll pick up something. A few weeks back I see this guy stop at a light and I just don't like the looks of him . . . so I pull him over. . . . It ends up that the car is stolen and he's wanted in two other states on forgery charges.[25]

The reflections of these police officers point to the dangers of spot checks, for although they can result in the apprehension of some offenders, they also lend themselves to discriminatory enforcement procedures.

The Supreme Court has taken a strong stand against random spot checks, as was indicated in *Delaware* v. *Prouse.*[26] On November 30, 1976, at about 7:30 P.M., a New Castle County, Delaware, police officer stopped the automobile in which William J. Prouse was riding. The car belonged to Prouse, but he was not the driver. As the patrolman approached the vehicle, he smelled marijuana smoke, and when he came abreast of the window he observed marijuana on the floor of the automobile. Prouse was arrested and later indicted for illegal possession of the drug.

At a hearing on Prouse's motion to suppress the marijuana seized as a result of the stop, the New Castle County police officer characterized the stopping of the car as "routine," explaining that "I saw the car in the area and was not answering any complaints so I decided to pull them off." He further indicated that before stopping the vehicle he had not observed any traffic or equipment violations, nor was he acting in accordance with directives relating to spot checks of automobiles.

After the suppression hearing, the trial court ruled that the stop and detention had been wholly capricious and therefore violative of Prouse's Fourth Amendment rights. When the prosecution appealed, the Delaware Supreme Court ruled in favor of Prouse, and the case went on to the United States Supreme Court. The High Court granted *certiorari* in an effort to resolve the conflict between the Delaware Supreme Court decision and similar decisions in five other jurisdictions, and the opposite

In *California* v. *Acevedo,* the Supreme Court held that a closed container inside a car may be searched without a warrant if there is probable cause to believe that it contains contraband or evidence of a crime.

Whereas a *Belton* container search springs from a search incident to arrest, an *Acevedo* container search stems from a probable cause belief that the container contains contraband.

Police spot checks

Delaware v. Prouse: The Supreme Court ruling that police may not randomly stop motorists, without any probable cause to suspect crime or illegal activity, to check their drivers' license and auto registration.

"Caught in the act" in Miami, this sixteen-year-old youth became stuck in the iron bars of the house he was trying to enter. He was able to call the emergency number for the police to rescue him and was charged with burglary and booked.

decision, which had been rendered in six jurisdictions, that the Fourth Amendment does *not* prohibit the kind of automobile stop that occurred.

Ultimately, the Supreme Court ruled that random spot checks were a violation of constitutional rights. In so doing, however, the Court did not preclude states from devising methods for making spot checks of driver's credentials that do not involve the unconstrained exercise of police discretion, such as roadlock inspections in which *all* motorists are stopped. Since *Prouse,* a number of states have established roadblock-type stops, primarily for combatting drunk driving. Although several state supreme courts (including Oregon and Louisiana) have held that these sobriety checkpoints violate their state constitutions' prohibition of unreasonable search and seizure, the Supreme Court ruling in *Michigan Department of State Police* v. *Stiz*[27] in 1990 upheld the procedure.

Fresh Pursuit

Warrantless arrest and search is permissible in the circumstance of *fresh,* or "hot," *pursuit,* which involves chasing an escaping criminal or suspect into a house — and consequently searching that house — or into an adjoining jurisdiction. In common law, fresh pursuit referred to the immediate pursuit of a person for the purpose of arrest — pursuit that continued without substantial delay from the time of the commission or the discovery of an offense. Thus, fresh pursuit is the following of a fleeing suspect who is endeavoring to avoid immediate capture.

In contemporary statutes the notion of fresh pursuit has been broadened considerably. In Tennessee, for example, which reflects the comparative legislation in most state jurisdictions, the law reads as follows:

> The term "fresh pursuit" shall include fresh pursuit as defined by the common law, and also the pursuit of a person who has committed a felony or who is reasonably suspected of having committed a felony. It shall also include the pursuit of a person suspected of having committed a supposed felony, though no felony has actually been committed, if there is reasonable ground for believing that a felony has been committed. Fresh pursuit as used herein shall not necessarily imply instant pursuit, but pursuit without unreasonable delay.[28]

Although there is statutory authority for hot pursuit, the practice of high-speed automobile chases has raised considerable controversy in recent years. The National Highway Safety Administration has estimated that more than 250 people are killed and another 20,000 injured each year because of high-speed police pursuits.[29] Many of these deaths and injuries involve bystanders. Police departments have responded with new regulations and training initiatives. Similarly, the courts are also examining the matter.[30] Ultimately, the issue is a matter of police discretion, with individual officers having to balance the demands of law enforcement duty with the risks to public safety.

At any time the hazards of the pursuit outweigh the necessity of apprehension, the pursuit will be discontinued.

— FLORIDA HIGHWAY PATROL
POLICY MANUAL

Consent Searches

Warrantless searches may be undertaken by law enforcement officers when the person in control of the area or object consents to the search. But consent searches can often precipitate complex and problematic legal issues, since a consent to search waives a person's right to the Fourth Amendment protection against unreasonable search and seizure.

Thus, in a consent search, neither probable cause nor a search warrant is required, but when using evidence obtained through such a search the burden of proving consent becomes the responsibility of the prosecution. The issues involved are (1) *who* can give consent to search what, (2) *what* constitutes free and voluntary consent, and (3) is there a principle of *limited* consent?

Ordinarily, courts are unwilling to accept blindly the simple waiver of a defendants' Fourth Amendment right and require the state to prove that the consent was voluntarily given. In *Wren* v. *United States*,[31] the United States Court of Appeals ruled that a consent was indeed "voluntary" when the search was expressly agreed upon or invented by the person whose right was involved. *United States* v. *Matlock* expanded the range of voluntary consent to third parties who possessed common authority with the defendant over the property or premises to be searched.[32] In *Bumper* v. *North Carolina*,[33] the issue of coercion by law enforcement officers was addressed. In *Bumper,* the police had obtained the consent of the defendant's grandmother to search her house in connection with a crime he was suspected of committing. But the police had incorrectly informed the woman that they had a lawful search warrant, and it was on that premise that she had consented to the search. The Court ruled that it was *not* a constitutionally valid consent. Finally, in *Schneckloth* v. *Bustamonte*,[34] the Supreme Court ruled that police officers are not required to advise the persons whose consent they are seeking that they are not obliged to give consent.

Although *Wren, Matlock,* and *Schneckloth* offer police wide latitude and discretion in the area of consent searches, the Supreme Court has also ruled that voluntary consents are also, to some degree, limited consents. The Court has ruled that a search based on voluntary consent must be limited to those items connected to the crime that triggered the desire to search and to other items clearly connected to that crime.[35] Yet by contrast, in 1991 the Supreme Court ruled in two cases that expanded the scope of consent. In *Florida* v. *Jimeno*,[36] for example, the Court held that a consent to search an automobile automatically includes a consent to search any closed containers found therein. In **Florida** v. **Bostick**,[37] the Court cleared away the all constitutional doubts about the drug interdiction technique known as "working the buses" (see Exhibit 8.3).

Other Warrantless Searches

In addition to lawful arrest, stop and frisk, automobile searches, fresh pursuit, and consent, there are numerous other instances in which the search warrant requirement has been waived. Some examples are private searches, border searches, inventory searches, electronic eavesdropping, and searches of abandoned property and open fields.

Private Searches As early as 1921, the Supreme Court ruled in *Burdeau* v. *McDowell* that the Fourth Amendment protects individuals only against searches and seizures by government agents, not against such actions undertaken by private individuals not acting in concert with law enforcement authorities.[38]

Border Searches Although a series of rulings in the mid-1970s made it clear that warrantless searches of persons entering the United States at its borders violated the Fourth Amendment guarantee, *United States* v.

Florida v. *Bostick:* The Supreme Court ruling that police officers' conduct in boarding stopped passenger buses and approaching seated passengers to ask them questions and to request consent to search their luggage does not constitute a Fourth Amendment "seizure" in every instance, but instead must be evaluated in each case.

This Court is not empowered to forbid law enforcement practices simply because it considers them distasteful.

— FROM THE MAJORITY OPINION IN
FLORIDA v. *BOSTICK,* 1991

● EXHIBIT 8.3 ●

Sidelights on Criminal Matters
The Court, Bostick, *and the War on Drugs*

Drug interdiction efforts have led to the wider use of police surveillance at airports, train stations, and bus depots. Officers approach individuals, either randomly or because they suspect illegal activity, and ask them potentially incriminating questions. The Broward County, Florida, Sheriff's Department uses such a technique, in which officers board buses at scheduled stops and ask passengers for permission to search their luggage.

When officers boarded a Miami to Atlanta bus during a stopover in Fort Lauderdale during 1985, without any particular suspicion they conversed with passenger Terrance Bostick. After telling him that he could refuse, they requested his consent to search his luggage. He agreed, and the officers found cocaine in his bag. Bostick was arrested and charged with drug trafficking, but he argued that the seizure of the cocaine was in violation of the Fourth Amendment.

After the case moved through the Florida courts, the Supreme Court ultimately ruled against Bostick, holding that "bus sweeps" for drugs do not inevitably result in "seizures" requiring reasonable suspicion. The Court explained that it was only applying the same constitutional rules it had developed for police encounters on the street and in other public places to sweeps on buses, trains, and commercial aircraft. The ruling "follows logically," the Court argued, from prior decisions permitting police to approach individuals for questioning even when the officers have no "reasonable suspicion" that crime was afoot. The Court did emphasize, however, that in such cases: 1) consent prior to search is required; 2) officers may not convey a message that passenger compliance with their request is required; and, 3) police may not use intimidating gestures or actions to coerce a consent to a search.

SOURCE: *Florida* v. *Bostick,* 49 CrL 2270 (1991).

Martinez-Fuerte in 1976 established that border patrol officers need not have probable cause or a warrant before they stopped cars for brief questioning at fixed checkpoints.[39]

Inventory Searches In 1976 the Supreme Court established an inventory search exception to the warrant rule when it held that police with custody of a lawfully impounded automobile do not need a warrant or the owner's consent before routinely inventorying items left in plain view or the glove compartment.[40]

Electronic Eavesdropping Subsequent to *Katz* v. *United States* in 1967,[41] in which the Supreme Court ruled that conversations intercepted through warrantless electronic eavesdropping were in violation of the Fourth Amendment, Congress authorized the passage of the Omnibus Crime Control and Safe Streets Act of 1968, which included a provision involving electronic surveillance. The new act represented statutory authorization for the federal use of wiretaps and other eavesdropping devices through the issuance of warrants that could be approved only by the attorney general of the United States or his designated assistant.

Abandoned Property In the 1960 case of *Abel* v. *United States,*[42] the Supreme Court spelled out an "abandoned property exception" to the warrant rule. In *Abel,* a hotel manager had given consent to an FBI agent to search a room that had been previously occupied by the petitioner. During the search, incriminating evidence was found in a wastepaper basket. The Court held that once Abel vacated the room the hotel had exclusive right to its possession and could freely give a consent to search.

Although decided on an expectation of privacy rather than an abandoned property doctrine, *California* v. *Greenwood*[43] is an important case of related interest. In 1984, after learning from an informant that Billy Greenwood of Laguna Beach might be dealing in drugs, and after observing a parade of cars making brief nocturnal stops at his home, a police asked the local refuse collector to turn over the brown plastic trash bags in front of Greenwood's house. Clawing through the garbage uncovered a rich nest of drug paraphernalia, including razor blades, straws containing cocaine residue, the phone bills listing calls to people with drug records. Based on this evidence, the police obtained a warrant to search the house, found hashish and cocaine inside, and arrested Greenwood. Two California courts ruled that the searches of Greenwood's garbage were in violation of the Fourth Amendment ban against unreasonable search and seizure. The High Court ruled against Greenwood, however, thus giving the police broad power to search trash. Writing for the majority, Justice Byron White commented:

> It is common knowledge that garbage bags left on or at the side of a public street are readily accessible to animals, children, scavengers, snoops, and other members of the public. Requiring police to seek warrants before searching such refuse would therefore be inappropriate.

Open Fields

As early as 1924, in *Hester* v. *United States,*[44] the Supreme Court established the "open fields exception," declaring that police officers may enter and search a field without a warrant. In *Oliver* v. *United States* (and the companion case of *Maine* v. *Thornton*),[45] decided in 1984, the Court went further by holding that fences and "No Trespassing" signs provide no reasonable expectation of privacy to owners of properties large enough to include areas that extend beyond the curtilage of houses or other buildings. As such, the decision in *Oliver* assured police that even if they enter such property by going over fences and ignoring "No Trespassing" signs in criminal violation of state law, any evidence they discover on the property is nevertheless admissible at trial.

The "Plain View" Doctrine

Pertinent to this discussion of warrantless search and seizure is the highly controversial **"plain view" doctrine**, examined by the Supreme Court in *Harris* v. *United States* in 1968.[46] In *Harris,* the Court ruled that

In *California* v. *Greenwood*, the Supreme Court approved the warrantless search and seizure of garbage left for collection outside the *curtilage* (yard or other ground inside a fence) of a house, since there is no expectation of privacy in trash that is disposed of in that manner.

The worst peril of garbage searching is dirty diapers.
—ANONYMOUS FBI AGENT, 1988

Looking through garbage really calls for care. Let's face it, nobody wants to be poked by an AIDS-infected needle.
—ANONYMOUS DEA AGENT, 1991

Oliver v. *United States* is an important, yet often overlooked case, since it holds, in effect, that police conduct may be reasonable even though it is illegal.

"Plain view" doctrine: The rule, from the Supreme Court decision in *Harris* v. *United States,* that anything a police officer sees in plain view when he has a right to be where he is, is not the product of a search and is therefore admissible as evidence.

Crack has been a real boon to both buyer and seller. It's cheap, real cheap. Anybody can come up with $5 or $10 for a trip to the stars. But most important, it's easy to get rid of in a pinch. Drop it on the ground and it's almost impossible to find; step on it and the damn thing is history. All of a sudden your evidence ceases to exist.
—A MIAMI NARCOTICS DETECTIVE, 1986

Why is it that so many drug users seem to suffer from an allergy which causes them to drop things in the presence of a police officer?
—STEVEN M. GREENBERG, 1974

The protective sweep doctrine: The rule that when police officers execute an arrest on or outside private premises, they may conduct a warrantless examination of the entire premises for other persons whose presence would pose a threat, either to their safety or to evidence capable of being removed or destroyed.

anything a police officer sees in plain view when he has a right to be where he is, is not the product of a search and is therefore admissible as evidence. In the *Harris* case, James E. Harris's automobile had been observed leaving the scene of a robbery in Washington, D.C. The vehicle was traced, and Harris was later arrested near his home as he was getting into his car. The arresting officer made a quick inspection of the car and then took his suspect to the police station.

After some discussion, a decision was made to impound the car as evidence. Harris's vehicle was towed to the station house about ninety minutes after the arrest, arriving there with its doors unlocked and its windows open. Then it began to rain.

According to police procedures in the District of Columbia, the arresting officer in instances such as these is required to thoroughly search the impounded vehicle, remove any valuables, prepare a written inventory, and submit a report detailing the impounding. The officer undertook his search, and tied a property tag to the steering wheel. After this was done, he began to close up and lock the auto. When he opened the front door on the passenger side for the purpose of rolling up the window the officer for the first time observed a registration card, which lay face up on the metal stripping over which the door closes. The card, which was in "plain view," belonged to the victim of the robbery.

Harris moved to suppress the registration card on the grounds that its seizure was not contemporaneous with his arrest. In the Supreme Court's opinion, however, the observation of the card was not the outcome of a search, but rather, came about from a measure to protect the vehicle while in police custody. As such, the seizure was lawful.

Although the Court made the nature of "plain view" relatively clear in this case, a few police officers have apparently perjured themselves in using the doctrine as a mechanism for justifying illegal searches. If one were to sit in a courtroom in a large urban area where drug trafficking is high, he or she would very quickly get the impression than many drug users suffer from "dropsy." Miami attorney Steven M. Greenberg explained the phenomenon:

> Dropsy is claimed by the police in situations where they have searched a suspect without probable cause or consent and found contraband. To insure the admission of the illegally seized evidence the police will "improvise" a story similar to the following: As I drove past ——— School, I noticed two or three suspicious-looking suspects standing in the schoolyard, who glanced apprehensively at me as I passed. I drove on down the street, parked my vehicle, and walked toward them. As I approached, one of the suspects reached into his pocket and dropped a clear plastic bag at his feet. I bent down to pick it up and noticed that it contained a substance which resembled marijuana.[47]

Greenberg goes on to suggest that this is extraordinary clumsiness, since both the officer and the suspect know that a search will not be lawful under these circumstances. But given the fact that the alleged marijuana suddenly comes into plain view, the seizure can be explained.

Under the **protective sweep doctine,** examined in numerous court cases during recent years, the scope of plain view has been considerably expanded. The protective sweep doctrine, as it is currently understood, suggests that when law enforcement officers execute an arrest on or outside private premises, they may, despite the absence of a search warrant, examine the entire premises for other persons whose presence would pose a threat, either to their safety or to evidence capable of being removed or destroyed. Furthermore, these protective sweep procedures may be initiated even if there is only a suspicion that other such persons are present on the premises, and any evidence falling in plain view during the search, or sweep, may be lawfully seized.[48]

THE EXCLUSIONARY RULE

In 1914, the U.S. Supreme Court announced its well-known and highly controversial **exclusionary rule,** which prohibited the use in federal courts of evidence seized by federal agents in violation of the Fourth Amendment prohibition against unreasonable search and seizure. The rule was an outgrowth of *Weeks* v. *United States,*[49] and during the eight decades since *Weeks,* it has been hotly debated whether the decision has been an effective remedy or an expensive constitutional right.

Exclusionary rule: The constitutional guarantee that prohibits, in court, the use of illegally obtained evidence.

Weeks v. United States

In common law proceedings, the admissibility of evidence in criminal cases was unrelated to any illegal actions the police may have engaged in when securing such evidence. An attorney might argue that a certain piece of evidence was immaterial, inappropriate, irrelevant, or even incompetent, but if it passed these tests it was clearly admissible. The courts, even at the appellate and supreme levels, had no concern with the legality of the methods used to obtain it. If the evidence had been stolen, common law provided for the prosecution of the thief, or a civil action for trespass and return of the property, but the illegally obtained evidence was nevertheless allowable in court proceedings.

Yet it had long been argued that any evidence illegally obtained should not be admissible, and that such a refusal would provide the only

Weeks v. *United States:* The Supreme Court ruling that a person whose Fourth Amendment rights of security against unreasonable search and seizure are violated by federal agents has the right to require that evidence obtained in the search be excluded from use against him or her in federal courts.

"Struck down anything interesting lately?"

effective deterrent to illegal search and seizure. Even the Supreme Court adhered to the common law principle, as in *Adams* v. *New York*[50] in 1904 when it ruled that the admissibility of evidence was not affected by the illegality of the means by which it was obtained.

In *Weeks,* the defendant was arrested at his place of business. The police officer then searched Weeks's house and turned over the articles and papers found there to a United States marshal. Thereupon, the marshal, accompanied by police officers, repeated the search of Weeks's room and confiscated other documents and letters. No warrants had been obtained for the arrest or the search. Before his trial, Weeks petitioned the federal district court for the confiscated articles and papers, but the court refused, and allowed the materials to be used against him at trial, resulting in his conviction.

On appeal, the Supreme Court ruled in Weeks's favor, thus initiating the exclusionary rule. Speaking for the Court, Justice William R. Day explained:

> If letters and private documents can thus be seized and held and used in evidence against a citizen accused of an offense, the protection of the Fourth Amendment, declaring his right to be secure against such searches and seizures, is of no value, and, so far as those thus placed are concerned, might as well be stricken from the Constitution. The efforts of the courts and their officials to bring the guilty to punishment, praiseworthy as they are, are not to be aided by the sacrifice of these great principles established by years of endeavor and suffering which have resulted in their embodiment in the fundamental law of the land.

The decision in *Weeks* quickly became the subject of much legal controversy. By denying prosecutors the use of certain evidence, the rule sometimes caused the collapse of the government's case and the freeing of a defendant against whom there was strong evidence of guilt. In 1931, George W. Wickersham, Chairman of the National Commission on Law Observance and Enforcement, commented that the "guarantees as to searches and seizures are often in the way of effective detection."[51] Justice Benjamin Cardozo wrote before he came to the Supreme Court bench, "The criminal is to go free because the constable has blundered."[52]

Weeks was only a parial victory for the Fourth Amendment.

"Silver platter" doctrine

But *Weeks* was only a partial victory of the Fourth Amendment. *The exclusionary rule applied only to material obtained in an unconstitutional search and seizure by a federal agent in a federal case, and did not pertain to state actions.* In addition, *Weeks* made possible the *"silver platter" doctrine,* which permitted federal prosecutors to use evidence obtained by state agents through unreasonable search and seizure — provided that the evidence was obtained without federal participation and was turned over to federal officials.[53]

Wolf v. Colorado

In 1949, the Supreme Court made a somewhat vague move toward applying *Weeks* to state court actions. The case was *Wolf* v. *Colorado,*[54] in which a deputy sheriff seized a physician's appointment book without a warrant, interrogated patients whose names appeared in the book, and thereby obtained evidence to charge Wolf with performing illegal abortions. Wolf was convicted.

On appeal to the Supreme Court, Wolf challenged the use of the evidence, arguing that it had been illegally seized. But the Court sustained (upheld) Wolf's conviction. At the same time, the Court held that

the Fourth Amendment guarantee protected individuals against state as well as federal action. What the Court did not do, however, was extend the exclusionary rule to the states. In essence, then, the Supreme Court had put forth a rather astonishing legal dichotomy. In effect, it had announced the incorporation of the Fourth Amendment's pertinent guarantees, but immediately neutralized or negated them by continuing to sanction the admissibility of evidence illegally obtained by the states. As explained by legal scholar Henry J. Abraham, *Wolf* prohibited unreasonable searches and seizures by the states, but if the evidence was trustworthy (that is, if it was "material, relevant, and competent" as required by common law), it was admissible regardless of how it was acquired.[55]

In spite of the Supreme Court's refusal in *Wolf* to apply the exclusionary rule to illegally seized evidence at the state level, it subsequently ruled in **Rochin v. California** that evidence acquired in a manner that "shocks the conscience" would be invalid (see Exhibit 8.4).[56]

In the decade that followed *Rochin,* two loopholes in the exclusionary rule as it applied to the federal system were closed. In *Rea* v. *United States,*[57] federal law enforcement officials were prohibited from turning over evidence unconstitutionally seized by them to state prosecutors for use in state courts. And in 1960, the "silver platter" doctrine was put to rest by *Elkins* v. *United States,*[58] which made inadmissible in federal courts any evidence seized in an unconstitutional fashion by state officials and handed over to a federal prosecutor.

Rochin v. *California:* The Supreme Court ruling that evidence acquired in a manner that "shocks the conscience" is in violation of the Fourth Amendment.

Mapp v. Ohio

It was not until almost a half century after the Supreme Court first announced the exclusionary rule in *Weeks* that it fully extended the principle to the states. The precipitating case was **Mapp v. Ohio,**[59] decided in 1961.

The *Mapp* case began on May 23, 1957, when three Cleveland police officers arrived at the residence of Mrs. Dollree ("Dolly") Mapp. The visit was pursuant to information that a suspect, wanted for questioning in a recent bombing, was hiding out in her home, and also that a large amount of gambling paraphernalia was being concealed at the residence.

Mapp v. *Ohio:* The Supreme Court ruling that evidence obtained in violation of the Fourth Amendment must be excluded from use in state as well as federal trials.

• EXHIBIT 8.4 •

Rochin v. California

On the morning of July 1, 1949, three Los Angeles County deputy sheriffs entered Rochin's home without the benefit of a warrant, on the basis of "some information" that he was selling narcotics. Upon locating Rochin in his bedroom, the officers observed "two capsules" on his bedside table and inquired about them. Rochin "seized the capsules and put them in his mouth," and after he swallowed them, the officers forcibly took him to a hospital where they had his stomach pumped.

The Supreme Court ruled Rochin's conviction invalid, and in delivering the opinion of the Court, Justice Felix Frankfurter stated it this way:

We are compelled to conclude that the proceedings by which this conviction was obtained do more than offend some fastidious squeamishness or private sentimentalism about combatting crime too energetically. This is conduct that shocks the conscience. Illegally breaking into the privacy of Rochin, the struggle to open his mouth and remove what was there, the forcible extraction of his stomach's contents — this course of proceedings by agents of government to obtain evidence is bound to offend even hardened sensibilities. They are methods too close to the rack and screw to permit of constitutional differentiation.

The *Rochin* reversal was not based on the police's warrantless search on less than probable grounds, but on the finding that the seizure was a blatant violation of the concept of due process of law as found in the Fifth and Fourteenth Amendments.

SOURCE: *Rochin* v. *California*, 342 U.S. 165 (1952).

Mrs. Mapp, and her daughter by a former marriage, lived on the top floor of the two-family dwelling. Upon arriving, the police knocked at the door and demanded entry. Mapp, after telephoning her attorney, refused to admit them without a search warrant. The officers then advised their headquarters of the situation and undertook a surveillance of the house.

The police again sought entrance some three hours later when at least four additional officers arrived on the scene. When Mapp did not come to the door immediately, the police forced their way into the dwelling. Meanwhile, Mapp's attorney arrived, but the police prohibited him from either seeing his client or entering the house. From the testimony, Mapp was apparently about halfway down the stairs from the second floor when the police broke into the lower hall. She demanded to see the search warrant. Thereupon one of the officers held up a paper, which he claimed to be a warrant.

Mapp grabbed the alleged warrant and stuffed it into her bra. A struggle ensued during which the officers removed the paper and at the same time handcuffed her because she had reportedly been "belligerent" in resisting their official rescue of the warrant paper from her person. Running roughshod over Mrs. Mapp, the officers then took her forcibly, in handcuffs, to her bedroom where the officers searched a dresser, a chest of drawers, a closet, and some suitcases. They also looked through a photo album and some of Mapp's personal papers.

The search then spread to the remainder of the second floor, including the child's bedroom, the living room, the kitchen, and the dining area. The basement of the building and a trunk found there were also searched. Neither the bombing suspect nor the gambling paraphernalia were found, but the search did turn up an unspecified amount of pornographic literature.

Following the search, Mapp was arrested on a charge of possessing "lewd and lascivious books, pictures, and photographs," and was subsequently convicted in an Ohio court on possession of obscene materials. At the trial, no search warrant was produced by the prosecution, nor was the failure to produce one ever explained or accounted for.

The issue in *Mapp,* of course, was the legality of the arrest, search, and seizure. There was no search warrant and no consent to search, but one could argue, as the prosecution heatedly did, that at the time the police applied force and searched her apartment, Dolly Mapp was indeed under arrest—hence, it was a search incident to arrest. Yet, as the defense pointed out, and the facts of the case substantiated, there was no "probable cause" for arrest. The only background data the police had was "information that a fugitive was hiding in her home."

It was on the basis of these facts, or rather the lack of them, that the Supreme Court reversed the decision of the Ohio court and extended the exclusionary rule to all fifty states. The Supreme Court indicated that the Fourth Amendment is incorporated, by inference, in the due process clause of the Fourteenth, and from the day of its decision, June 19, 1961, any evidence that was illegally obtained by the police would be inadmissible in any and every courtroom in the country! In the Court's opinion, as Justice Clark eloquently stated:

> The ignoble shortcut to conviction left open to the State tends to destroy the entire system of constitutional restraints on which the liberties of the people rest. Having once recognized that the right to privacy embodied in the Fourth Amendment is enforceable against the States, and that the right to be secure against rude invasions of privacy by state officers is, therefore, constitutional in origin, we can no longer permit that right to remain an empty promise. Because it is enforceable in the same manner and to like effect as other basic rights secured by the Due Process Clause, we can no longer permit it to be revocable at the whim of any police officer who, in the name of law enforcement itself, chooses to suspend its environment. Our decision, founded on reason and truth, gives to the individual no more than that which the Constitution guarantees him, to the police officer no less than that to which honest law enforcement is entitled, and, to the courts, that judicial integrity so necessary in the true administration of justice.

Reactions to Mapp

The *Mapp* case was a controversial decision, both within and outside the Supreme Court. It had been reached by a 5-to-3 majority (with Justice Potter Stewart abstaining). Among those concurring with the Court's opinion was Justice William O. Douglas, who asserted that "once evidence, inadmissible in a federal court, is admissible in a state court a 'double standard' exists which leads to 'working arrangements' that undercut federal policy and reduce some aspects of law enforcement to a shabby business." Justice Black, however, although also concurring with the opinion, commented that he was "still not persuaded that the Fourth Amendment, standing alone, would be enough to bar the introduction into evidence against an accused of papers and effects seized from him in violation of its commands." Among the dissenters, Justice Harlan was of the view that "the *Wolf* rule represents sounder constitutional doctrine than the new rule which now replaces it." And Justice Potter Stewart refused to deal with the constitutional issue that was the basis of the *Mapp* reversal. In a separate memorandum to the Court, Stewart commented that the Ohio obscenity law under which Mrs. Mapp was convicted in the first place was itself unconstitutional.*

Beyond the chambers of the Supreme Court there were also strong and opposing opinions regarding the *Mapp* decision. The very next day, the *New York Times* referred to *Mapp* as "an historic step," and Harvard Law School dean Ervin Griswold — soon to be solicitor-general of the United States — saw the case as requiring "a complete change in the outlook and practices of state and local police."[60] In contrast, *Mapp* produced a frantic torrent of complaints from outraged police across the nation, who felt they were being deprived of their legal right to search for and obtain evidence.[61] In response to police complaints, University of Michigan law professor Yale Kamisar argued:

> What law-enforcement officers were really bristling about was tighter enforcement of long-standing restrictions. Not *Mapp,* but state and federal constitutional provisions that had been on the books for decades, banned arbitrary arrests and unreasonable searches. The police never had the authority to proceed without "probable cause," only the incentive. And the principal contribution of *Mapp* was to reduce that incentive.[62]

The Impact of *Mapp*

In 1965, the Court held in *Linkletter* v. *Walker* that the *Mapp* decision would not be retroactively applied to overturn state criminal convictions that occurred prior to the expansion on the exclusionary rule in 1961.[63] The Court stated that the purpose of *Mapp* was to deter future unlawful police conduct and thereby carry out the guarantee of the Fourth Amendment against unreasonable searches and seizures. The purpose was to deter, not to redress the injury to the privacy of a former search victim, and no deterrent function could be served by making the rule retroactive. But despite *Linkletter,* to the twenty-six state jurisdictions that had rejected the exclusionary rule in toto prior to *Mapp,* the *Mapp* decision was an explosive one. Not only were police search and seizure procedures required to change suddenly, but the rule also immediately applied to all cases that were currently under court review.

The Retreat from *Mapp*

Throughout the 1960s and into the following decade, dissatisfaction with the *Mapp* suppression rule continued. Considerable agitation for the rule's abridgment, if not outright abolition, was manifest not only in Congress, but on the bench of the Supreme Court and among the public at large, who were fearful of the increased levels of street crime.

The justices who wished to modify *Mapp* — including John Marshall Harlan, Byron Raymond White, Henry Andrew Blackmun, and Warren Earl Burger, who was the new Chief Justice of the United States as confirmed by the Senate on June 9, 1964, by a 74-to-3 vote — thought it had developed into a series of confusing and complicated requirements

---

* The Supreme Court subsequently invalidated all state laws prohibiting the private possession of pornography in the home. See *Stanley* v. *Georgia,* 394 U.S. 557 (1969).

that puzzled the police more than it restrained them. The Fourth Amendment prohibited "unreasonable" searches, but *unreasonable* was a term that had never been fully defined by either the Constitution or the Court. Furthermore, the Fourth Amendment also required that police obtain a warrant, and that it be issued only when "probable cause" was shown. Yet the Court, over the years, had allowed numerous exceptions to this warrant requirement.

Chief Justice Burger, even prior to his appointment to the Supreme Court, had been an articulate advocate of a change in the exclusionary rule. He argued, both on and off the bench, that society had paid a monstrous price for the rule, that evidence should be suppressed only when there was genuine police misconduct, that it was absurd to free a thief or murderer because a police officer had made a minor error in an application for a search warrant, that the rule had little deterrent effect on police misconduct, and that in place of the rule there should be a remedy such as disciplinary action against police officers who abused constitutional rights.

While Harlan, White, Blackmun, and Burger opposed *Mapp,* Justices Thurgood Marshall, William Joseph Brennan, and William O. Douglas were its strong supporters. Justice Potter Stewart, although undecided, had views similar to those of Harlan, and Justice Hugo Black—a judge since 1910 and a member of the Supreme Court bench since 1937—was also in doubt. Black's position was that rather than overrule *Mapp,* a clear checklist should be created of what was and was not a reasonable search, and when evidence could and could not be excluded.

The retreat from *Mapp* began in 1974 with the Supreme Court's ruling in *United States* v. *Calandra*.

The "good faith" exception to the exclusionary rule

United States v. *Leon:* The Supreme Court ruling that the Fourth Amendment exclusionary rule does not bar the use of evidence obtained by police officers acting in objectively reasonable reliance on a search warrant issued by a magistrate but ultimately found to be unsupported by probable cause.

This was the situation on *Mapp* as it existed among the members of the Court bench in the spring of 1971.[64] Fearing the "death of *Mapp*," and possibly of *Weeks* as well, Justices Brennan and Marshall instructed their clerks not to accept cases involving the Fourth Amendment until the positions of Black and Stewart were fully clear. The message was communicated: no free shots at the Fourth Amendment would be given; *certiorari* would be granted only in the cases involving flagrant police violations, not in those intended to "right little wrongs." But the case awaiting decision at this point was *Coolidge* v. *New Hampshire,*[65] a case that involved numerous Fourth Amendment issues — arrest, probable cause seizure, plain-view seizure, arrest–search, and consent–search. The facts in *Coolidge* were so hopelessly convoluted, however, that it was decided that it would not be the case on which the future of *Mapp* would be decided.

The retreat from *Mapp* began instead less than three years later, with *United States* v. *Calandra,*[66] decided on January 8, 1974. In *Calandra,* the Court ruled that the exclusionary rule was not applicable to the presentation of illegally obtained evidence at grand jury proceedings.

In 1976, the Court's decision in *Stone* v. *Powell* practically closed the federal courtroom doors to state prisoners convicted by means of illegal searches and seizures.[67] Under the common law principle of *habeas corpus,* state prisoners who had allegedly been convicted and incarcerated through illegally secured evidence could appeal to the federal courts. In *Powell,* the Court ruled that federal courts were under no constitutional obligation to use the writ of *habeas corpus** to order release of persons who argued that their convictions in state courts had been obtained with illegally seized evidence. So long as the state provided an opportunity for a full and fair hearing of the defendant's challenge to the evidence, the Court held, there was no obligation at the federal level to use the *habeas corpus* to enforce the exclusionary rule.

A further setback for the exclusionary rule came in 1984 with the Supreme Court's long anticipated enunciation of the *"good faith"* exception. The announcement came in **United States v. Leon** and **Massachusetts v. Sheppard,**[68] two cases involving defective search warrants. In *Leon,* the leading case, probable cause to support the warrant was lacking, yet this defect had not been ascertained by the prosecutors who reviewed the application, the magistrate who approved the warrant, or the officers who executed the search in accordance with its authorization (see Exhibit 8.5). In *Sheppard,* an inappropriate warrant form had been used. Moreover, it had been improperly filled out. Trial courts had held that these defects required the suppression of evidence seized under the Fourth Amendment's exclusionary rule. Disagreeing with this result, the Supreme Court adopted a good faith exception to the rule in *Leon* and then applied the exception in *Sheppard,* thus allowing the evidence as a result of the warrants to be admissible.

As a footnote to this discussion, two years after *Leon* the Supreme Court added a second good faith exception to the exclusionary rule. In *Illinois* v. *Krull,*[69] the Court justified the admissibility of evidence obtained by police officers who carry out a search under a state law subsequently found to be unconstitutional. In *Murray* v. *United States,*[70] decided in 1988, the Court also added an "independent source" exception to the exclusionary rule. In *Murray,* it was held that evidence dis-

---

* *Habeas corpus* is explored at length in Chapter 16.

covered by police during an initial, warrantless entry into a warehouse is admissible if the same evidence is discovered in a second search, pursuant to a search warrant that is based on information obtained independently of the initial, illegal search.

CUSTODIAL INTERROGATION

No person . . . shall be compelled in any criminal case to be a witness against himself.

—FROM THE FIFTH AMENDMENT

In all criminal prosecutions the accused shall enjoy the right . . . to have the assistance of counsel for his defense.

—FROM THE SIXTH AMENDMENT

Confessions, the Supreme Court stated more than a century ago in *Hopt* v. *Utah,*[71] are "among the most effectual proofs of the law," but by constitutional implication they are admissible as evidence only when given voluntarily. This has long since been the rule in the federal courts where the *Fifth Amendment* clearly applies. A confession, whether written or oral (but now usually recorded), is simply a statement by a person admitting to the violation of a law. In *Hopt,* the Court stressed that for a confession to be valid it had to be *voluntary,* defining as involuntary or coerced any confession that "appears to have been made, either in consequence of inducements of a temporal nature . . . or because of a threat or promise . . . which, operating upon the fears or hopes of the accused . . . deprive him of that freedom of will or self-control essential to make his confession voluntary within the meaning of the law." In 1896, the Court restated this position, ruling that the circumstances surrounding the confession had to be considered in order to determine if it had been voluntarily made.[72]

The Fifth Amendment

In *Hopt* v. *Utah,* decided in 1884, the Supreme Court ruled that for a confession to be admissible as evidence in federal cases, it had to be given voluntarily.

Twining v. New Jersey

The inadmissibility of involuntary confessions, however, did not apply to the states. The 1908 decision in *Twining* v. *New Jersey* specifically emphasized this.[73] In the *Twining* case, defendants Albert C. Twining and David C. Cornell, executives of the Monmouth Safe and Trust Company, were indicted by a New Jersey grand jury for having knowingly displayed a false paper to a bank examiner "with full intent to deceive him" as to the actual condition of their firm. At trial, Twining and Cornell refused to take the stand, and presiding judge Webber A. Heisley commented both extensively and adversely on this point. To the jury Heisley stated:

> Because a man does not go upon the stand you are not necessarily justified in drawing an inference of guilt. But you have a right to consider the fact that he does not go upon the stand where a direct accusation is made against him.[74]

The jury returned a verdict of guilty, at which point Twining and Cornell appealed to the U.S. Supreme Court. They contended that the exemption from self-incrimination was one of the privileges and immunities which the Fourteenth Amendment forbade the states to abridge, and that the alleged compulsory self-incrimination constituted

●   EXHIBIT 8.5   ●

United States v. Leon

In *United States* v. *Leon,* a California district court judge issued a search warrant based on information from a confidential source and a lengthy police investigation. The warrant authorized the search of three houses and several automobiles. The subsequent search produced large quantities of cocaine and methaqualone. Defendants filed a pretrial motion to suppress the evidence seized in the search on the grounds that the affidavit was insufficient to establish probable cause. The district court granted part of the motion and the U.S. Court of Appeals for the Ninth Circuit affirmed. The government's petition for *certiorari* presented only the question of whether a "good faith" exception to the exclusionary rule should be adopted.

Justice White, writing for the majority, reversed the decision of the court of appeals and finally announced the long-awaited good faith exception to the exclusionary rule. The majority based its decision on two independent grounds. First, it said that the Fourth Amendment does not contain any expressed provisions precluding the use of evidence obtained in violation of its commands. Once the illegal search is completed, the wrong prohibited by the Fourth Amendment is "fully accomplished" and "the exclusionary rule is neither intended nor able to cure the invasion of the defendant's rights which he has already suffered." The judicially created rule acts only to safeguard Fourth Amendment rights through its deterrent effect.

Second, the majority said that the question of whether a party's Fourth Amendment rights were violated is a separate issue from the question of whether the exclusionary rule should be imposed. In *Leon,* only the latter question had to be resolved. The Court reasoned that it would be resolved by "weighing the costs and benefits of preventing the use . . . of inherently trustworthy tangible evidence." The Court noted that the costs exacted by the exclusionary rule were "substantial." Excluding relevant, probative evidence impedes the "truthfinding" function of judge and jury, which further results in the objectionable consequence that "some guilty defendants may go free. . . ." Such a benefit to guilty defendants is particularly offensive to the criminal justice system when the illegal acts of law enforcement are minor and were done in good faith. Therefore, the indiscriminate application of the exclusionary rule under such circumstances might result in "disrespect for the law and the administration of justice." Thus, after applying a cost–benefit analysis test, the Court concluded that the exclusionary rule should be modified to allow introduction of unconstitutionally obtained evidence where officers acted in "reasonable good faith belief that such a search or seizure was in accord with the Fourth Amendment."

The majority further supported this new exception in those areas where the deterrent effect of the exclusionary rule would not be achieved. In those

---

In *Twining* v. *New Jersey,* decided in 1908, the Supreme Court inferred that *state* defendants did not enjoy the Fifth Amendment privilege against compelled self-incrimination.

a denial of due process. In an 8-to-1 decision, the Court ruled against Twining and Cornell, stating that the privilege against self-incrimination was "not fundamental in due process of law, not an essential part of it."

Twining was not a case of forced confession in the strictest sense of the term, for no confession had actually occurred. But as an issue in self-incrimination, the notion of a potentially involuntary confession was inferred, and the resulting decision in 1908 was that *state* defendants did not enjoy the Fifth Amendment privilege against compelled self-incrimination.

Brown v. Mississippi

Although more than half a century would pass before the Supreme Court would specifically apply the Fifth Amendment privilege against state action, the Court, through its unanimous decision in *Brown* v. *Missis-*

situations, the benefits of the rule "would not outweigh its costs." "In short . . . the Court has applied, in deciding whether exclusion is appropriate in a particular case, attempts to mark the point at which the detrimental consequences of illegal police action became so attenuated that the deterrent effect of the exclusionary rule no longer justifies its cost." This balancing approach provides strong support for adopting a good-faith modification.

The Court concluded that even if the rule effectively "deters *some* police misconduct . . . it can not be expected and should not be applied, to deter objectively reasonable law enforcement activity." Excluding evidence will not in any appreciable way further the ends of the exclusionary rule where the officer's conduct is objectively reasonable. "This is particularly true when an officer acting with good faith has obtained a search warrant from a . . . magistrate and acted within its scope."

Under this rule, suppression of evidence would be an appropriate remedy when the issuing magistrate was misled by information that the affiant knew was false. This exception would also not apply when the issuing magistrate disregards his role in such a manner that "no reasonable well-trained officer should rely on the warrant." Nor would the police be acting in objective good faith if the affidavit was "so lacking of probable cause as to render official belief in its existence unreasonable."

The majority concluded that this good-faith exception was not intended to signal an unwillingness to enforce Fourth Amendment requirements. Nor would it preclude judicial review concerning the constitutionality of searches and seizures.

SOURCE: J. Michael Hunter, "Is the Exclusionary Rule a Relic of the Past? *Leon, Sheppard,* and 'Beyond,'" *Ohio Northern Law Review* 12 (November 1985). Reprinted by permission of the author.

Dick Wright, Scripps-Howard Newspapers

sippi,[75] forbid states in 1936 to use coerced confessions to convict persons of crimes.

In *Brown,* three black men were arrested for the murder of a white man. At trial, they were convicted solely on the basis of their confessions, and sentenced to death. But the confessions had been coerced. The defendants had been tied to a tree, whipped, twice hanged by a rope from a tree, and told that the process would continue until they confessed. And although the use of torture to elicit the confessions was undisputed, the convictions were affirmed by the Mississippi Supreme Court.

On appeal to the U.S. Supreme Court, Mississippi defended its use of the confessions extracted through beatings and torture by citing the earlier *Twining* decision — that state defendants did not enjoy the Fifth Amendment privilege. The Court agreed with *Twining,* but rejected the Mississippi defense maintaining that the state's right to withdraw the privilege of self-incrimination was not the issue. In speaking for the Court, Chief Justice Charles Evans Hughes saw a distinction between

In *Brown* v. *Mississippi,* decided in 1936, the Supreme Court held that physically coerced confessions could not serve as the basis for a conviction in a state prosecution. Just as these confessions could not be introduced in federal criminal trials under the *Fifth* Amendment they could not be allowed in state courts under the *Fourteenth* Amendment's due process clause.

"No state shall make or enforce any law which shall abridge the privileges or immunities of citizens of the United States; nor shall any state deprive any person of life, liberty, or property, without due process of law; nor deny to any person within its jurisdiction the equal protection of the laws. . . ."

— FROM THE FOURTEENTH AMENDMENT

"compulsion" as forbidden by the Fifth Amendment, and "compulsion" as forbidden by the Fourteenth Amendment's due process clause:

> The compulsion to which the Fifth Amendment refers is that of the processes of justice by which the accused may be called as a witness and required to testify. Compulsion by torture to extort a confession is a different matter. . . .
>
> Because a state may dispense with a jury trial, it does not follow that it may substitute trial by ordeal. The rack and torture chamber may not be substituted for the witness stand. . . . It would be difficult to conceive of methods more revolting to the sense of justice than those taken to procure the confessions of these petitioners, and the use of the confessions thus obtained as the basis for conviction and sentence was a clear denial of due process.

In the years that followed, the Supreme Court reversed numerous decisions in which confessions had been compelled, examining in every instance the totality of circumstances surrounding the arrest and the interrogation procedures. The Court's philosophy made it clear that coercion could be psychological as well as physical. As summarized by Justice Felix Frankfurter in 1961:

> Our decisions . . . have made clear that convictions following the admission into evidence of confessions which are involuntary . . . cannot stand. This is so not because such confessions are unlikely to be true but because the methods used to extract them offend an underlying principle in the enforcement of our criminal law: that ours is an accusatorial and not an inquisitorial system—a system in which the State must establish guilt by evidence independently and freely secured and may not by coercion prove its own charge against an accused out of his own mouth.[76]

The Prompt Arraignment Rule

Just before the turn of the twentieth century, the Supreme Court had implied that delay in charging a suspect with a crime might be one of the factors in determining whether a confession had been voluntary or not.[77] A number of federal statutes served to clarify the Court's intent. Their purpose was to prevent federal law enforcement agents from using post-arrest detention as a way of exacting confessions through interrogation, and from justifying illegal arrests through confessions subsequently obtained by means of prolonged questioning.

McNabb v. *United States*

But the rules had no compelling force until 1943, when the Supreme Court ruled in *McNabb* v. *United States* that confessions obtained after "unreasonable delay" in a suspect's arraignment could not be used as evidence *in a federal court.*[78] In *McNabb*, five Tennessee mountaineers were arrested when federal agents closed in on their moonshining operations, and during the course of the raid one of the agents was killed. Two of the defendants were convicted of second-degree murder on the strength of their confessions and were sentenced to forty-five years' imprisonment. Their incriminating statements had come after *three days* of questioning in the absence of any counsel and before they were charged with any crime. The Court overturned the *McNabb* convictions, not on the basis of the Fifth Amendment, but on the existing *prompt arraignment* statutes as well as on the High Court's general power to supervise the functioning of the federal judicial system. Speaking for the Court, Justice Frankfurter addressed the purpose of the ban on unnecessary delay between arrest and arraignment:

Prompt arraignment

This procedural requirement checks resort to those reprehensible practices known as the "third degree" which though universally rejected as indefensible, still find their way into use. It aims to avoid all the evil implications of street interrogation of persons accused of crime. It reflects not a sentimental but a sturdy view of law enforcement. It outlaws easy but self-defeating ways in which brutality is substituted for brains as an instrument of crime detection.

The Federal Rules of Criminal Procedure subsequently incorporated this rule. In *Mallory* v. *United States*,[79] almost fifteen years after *McNabb*, the High Court reaffirmed its prompt arraignment mandate by nullifying the death sentence imposed on a convicted rapist who "confessed" to the crime during a delay of more than eighteen hours between his arrest and arraignment. The defendant, Andrew Mallory, had been arrested in the District of Columbia, and during his long period of interrogation no attempt was made to bring official charges against him—even though arraigning magistrates were available in the same building throughout the period of questioning.

Mallory v. *United States*

In both *McNabb* and *Mallory,* the Supreme Court did not rule on whether or not the confessions had been obtained voluntarily. Rather, the cases were decided on the basis of the Court's authority to police the federal judicial system. But the Court's decision in *Mallory* received fierce criticism. By reversing the conviction on the basis of the prompt arraignment rule, the Court was saying that any evidence gathered during the delay had been acquired unlawfully, and hence was inadmissible —even if it included a confession that was indeed voluntary.

The *McNabb–Mallory* prompt arraignment rule, however, would not stand the test of time. At the state level, the example set by the federal courts was never fully followed. And even the decisions in *McNabb* and *Mallory* were ultimately diluted. Less than a month after *Mallory* had been handed down, a subcommittee of the House Judiciary Committee began hearings to reverse the Supreme Court decision. Although no "corrective" legislation came out of the House, in 1968 Congress incorporated a section into the Omnibus Crime Control and Safe Streets Act that related directly to *Mallory.* The act modified the *Mallory* decision to provide that a confession made by a person in the custody of law officers was not to be inadmissible as evidence *solely* because of delay in arraigning the defendant if the confession were found to be voluntary, if the weight to be given the confession were left to jury determination, and if the confession were given within six hours immediately following arrest. The measure also provided that confessions obtained after this six-hour limit could be admissible if the presiding trial judge found the further delay to be not unreasonable.[80]

Confessions and Counsel

Prior to the 1960s, the Fifth Amendment privilege against self-incrimination and the *Sixth Amendment* right to counsel were not effectively linked. The *Brown* v. *Mississippi* decision in 1936 had ruled on the inadmissibility of confessions obtained by physical compulsion. In delivering the Court's opinion in that case, Chief Justice Hughes also highlighted the constitutional issue that "the state may not deny to the accused the aid of counsel." But in 1958, the Court's decision in *Crooker* v. *California* held that confessions could be both voluntary and admissible even when obtained from a suspect who was denied the opportunity to consult with legal counsel during interrogation by the police.[81]

The Sixth Amendment

• EXHIBIT 8.6 •

Escobedo v. Illinois

On the night of January 19, 1960, Manuel Valtierra, the brother-in-law of twenty-two-year-old Danny Escobedo, was fatally shot in the back. Several hours later Escobedo was arrested without a warrant and was interrogated for some fifteen hours. During that period he made no statements to the police, and was released after his attorney had obtained a writ of *habeas corpus*. Eleven days after the shooting of Valtierra, Escobedo was arrested for a second time and again taken to a police station for questioning. Shortly after Escobedo was brought to the Chicago police station, his attorney also arrived but the police would not permit him to see his client. Both the attorney and Escobedo repeatedly requested to see each other, but both were continually denied the privilege. Escobedo was told that he could not see his attorney until the police had finished their questioning. It was during this second period of interrogation that Escobedo made certain incriminating statements that would be construed as his voluntary confession to the crime.

Danny Escobedo was convicted of murder and sentenced to a twenty-two-year prison term. On appeal to the state supreme court of Illinois, Escobedo maintained that he was told that "he would be permitted to go home if he gave the statement and would be granted an immunity from prosecution." The statement in question referred to the complicity of his four codefendants, who had all been arrested on the murder charge. The Illinois Supreme Court reversed Escobedo's conviction, but the state petitioned for, and the court granted, a rehearing of the case. The decision was again reversed, sustaining the trial court's original conviction, and Escobedo still faced the twenty-two-year prison term. Escobedo's counsel appealed further, and the U.S. Supreme Court granted *certiorari*.

On June 22, 1964, the Court ruled in favor of Danny Escobedo by a 5-to-4 decision. In delivering the opinion of the

Through *Brown* and *Crooker,* the Court was taking a firm stand on coerced confessions but nevertheless was limiting the right to counsel.

With the criminal law revolution of the 1960s, under the stewardship of Chief Justice Earl Warren, a series of Supreme Court decisions ensued that served to unite more fully the provisions of the Fifth and Sixth Amendments and at the same time strengthen defendants' rights. In 1964, the Court reversed its position in *Crooker,* declaring in *Massiah* v. *United States* that an indicted person could not be properly questioned or otherwise persuaded to make incriminating statements in the absence of his or her attorney.[82] Shortly thereafter, the Court's decision in *Malloy* v. *Hogan* finally extended the privilege against self-incrimination to state defendants.[83] At the same time, it laid the groundwork for its most important decision of the 1964 term, *Escobedo* v. *Illinois* (see Exhibit 8.6).[84]

Court, Justice Arthur Goldberg noted that it was based on five pivotal facts in the interrogation. We hold, therefore, that where . . .

[1] the investigation is no longer a general inquiry into an unsolved crime but has begun to focus on a particular suspect,

[2] the suspect has been taken into police custody,

[3] the police carry out a process of interrogations that lends itself to eliciting incriminating statements,

[4] the suspect has requested and been denied an opportunity to consult with his lawyer, and

[5] the police have not effectively warned him of his absolute constitutional right to remain silent,

the accused has been denied "the assistance of counsel" in violation of the Sixth Amendment of the Constitution as "made obligatory upon the states by the Fourteenth Amendment" . . . and that no statement elicited by the police during the interrogation may be used against him in a criminal trial.

SOURCE: *Escobedo* v. *Illinois*, 378 U.S. 478 (1964).

Danny Escobedo

The *Escobedo* decision required that an accused be permitted to have an attorney present during police interrogation. The majority view held that the adversary system of justice had traditionally been restricted to the trial stage, and that the system was long overdue to be hauled back into the earlier stages of criminal proceedings. It was also contended, however, that the *Escobedo* decision need not affect the powers of the police to investigate unsolved crimes. But when "the process shifts from investigatory to accusatory," the Court stated, "when its focus is on the accused and its purpose is to elicit a confession, our adversary system begins to operate, and, under the circumstances here, the accused must be permitted to consult with his lawyer."

The four dissenting justices were not convinced, and the overall tenor of their opinions was that the decision would hamper criminal law enforcement. Across the country police and prosecutors alike echoed the

Escobedo v. *Illinois:* The Supreme Court ruling that when the process shifts from the investigatory to the accusatory and its purpose is to elicit a confession, the accused may be permitted to consult with his attorney.

feelings of the dissenting justices. To interrogate a suspect behind closed doors in order to secure a confession was an aspect of policing based on centuries-old custom and usage and a deeply entrenched police practice. No longer would the well-developed "third degree" and sometimes melodramatic "good guy – bad guy" interrogation routines be as readily possible.

Miranda v. Arizona

In the final analysis, *Escobedo* seemed to raise more questions than it answered regarding police conduct during arrest and interrogation. In the Court's discussion of the conditions that existed in Danny Escobedo's interrogation and that led to a reversal of his conviction, was it being suggested that *all* of these conditions had to be met in order for a confession to be admissible? Were police required to warn suspects of their right to remain silent? If a suspect requested counsel but none was at hand, could a police interrogation continue? If a suspect did not wish counsel, what then? And most importantly, how were the police to determine when an investigation began to "focus," to use the Court's term, on a particular suspect?

Given these unsettled issues, by January 1966, two separate United States courts of appeals had interpreted *Escobedo* in diametrically opposed ways. As referee of the conflict, the U.S. Supreme Court sifted through some 170 confession-related appeals, granting *certiorari* to four cases: **Miranda v. Arizona,** *Vignera* v. *New York, Westover* v. *United States,* and *California* v. *Stewart.*[85] Known by its leading case, *Miranda* (see Exhibit 8.7), the package consolidated the appeals of four persons, all convicted on the basis of confessions made after extended questioning by police officers in which the defendant's right to remain silent had not been made known to them. In all four cases, the crimes for which the defendants had been convicted involved major felonies — Miranda had been convicted of kidnapping and rape, Vignera had been convicted of robbery in the first degree, Westover had been convicted of bank robbery, and Stewart had been convicted of robbery and first-degree murder. The convictions were reversed by the Supreme Court, and from this decision came the well-known *Miranda* warning rules, which every police officer must state to a suspect prior to any questioning:

1. "You have a right to remain silent."
2. "Anything you say can and will be held against you in a court of law."
3. "You have a right to consult with a lawyer and to have the lawyer present during any questioning."
4. "If you cannot afford a lawyer, one will be obtained for you if you so desire."

The reactions to *Miranda,* even from within the Supreme Court, were immediate. Four justices prepared a dissenting opinion, and it has been reported as well that Justice Harlan, his face flushed and his voice occasionally faltering with emotion, denounced the decision orally from the bench, terming it "dangerous experimentation" at a time of a "high crime rate that is a matter of growing concern" and a "new doctrine" without substantial precedent, reflecting "a balance in favor of the accused."[86]

Beyond the chambers of the Supreme Court, the *Miranda* decision was bitterly attacked for what was considered a handcuffing of the police

Miranda v. *Arizona:* The Supreme Court ruling that the guarantee of due process requires that suspects in police custody be informed that they have the right to remain silent, that anything they say may be used against them, and that they have the right to counsel — before any questioning can permissibly take place.

The idea that the police cannot ask questions of the person that knows most about the crime is an infamous decision.

— Attorney General Edwin Meese on *Miranda,* September 1, 1985

• EXHIBIT 8.7 •

Miranda v. Arizona

Ernesto Miranda, a twenty-three-year-old Mexican with less than a ninth-grade education, was arrested at his home in Phoenix on March 13, 1963, and taken to a local police station for questioning. He was suspected of having kidnapped and raped an eighteen-year-old woman. At the Phoenix police station, Miranda was placed in a lineup and identified by the victim, after which he was interrogated for two hours. At the close of the interrogation, the questioning officers emerged with a written confession signed by Miranda. The confession was admitted at trial, over Miranda's objections, and he was convicted of kidnapping and rape and received a twenty-to-thirty year sentence on each count. On appeal to the Arizona Supreme Court the conviction was affirmed.

The U.S. Supreme Court's decision reversed Miranda's conviction, based on its view of the relationships between custodial interrogation and genuinely voluntary confessions, combined with the constitutional rights of suspects as promulgated by the Fourth, Fifth, Sixth, and Fourteenth Amendments. In the Court's opinion, custodial interrogation was inherently coercive, and the procedures for advising suspects of their rights — if present — were rarely sufficiently clear.

In a 5-to-4 majority decision, Chief Justice Earl Warren offered the following statement:

Our holding will be spelled out with some specificity in the pages which follow but briefly stated it is this: the prosecution may not use statements, whether exculpatory or inculpatory, stemming from custodial interrogation of the defendant unless it demonstrates the use of procedural safeguards effective to secure the privilege against self-incrimination. By custodial interrogation, we mean questioning initiated by law enforcement officers after a person has been taken into custody or otherwise deprived of his freedom of action in any significant way. As for the procedural safeguards to be employed, unless other fully effective means are devised to inform accused persons of their right of silence and to assure a continuous opportunity to exercise it, the following measures are required. Prior to any questioning, the person must be warned that he has a right to remain silent, that any statement he does make may be used as evidence against him, and that he has a right to the presence of an attorney, either retained or appointed. The defendant may waive effectuation of these rights, provided the waiver is made voluntarily, knowingly and intelligently. If, however, he indicates that he wishes to consult with an attorney before speaking there can be no questioning. Likewise, if the individual is alone and indicates in any manner that he does not wish to be interrogated, the police may not question him. The mere fact that he may have answered some questions or volunteered some statements on his own does not deprive him of the right to refrain from answering any further inquiries until he has consulted with an attorney and thereafter consents to be questioned.

SOURCE: *Miranda* v. *Arizona,* 384 U.S. 436 (1966).

in their efforts to protect society against criminals. It was asserted that more than three-fourths of the convictions in major crimes depended on confessions; and police officers and prosecutors across the country, together with some courts, echoed the belief of New York City's police commissioner, Patrick V. Murphy, that "if suspects are told of their rights they will not confess."[87]

At least one study, however, has suggested that *Miranda* had little or no effect on law enforcement. In New Haven, Connecticut, for example, some police simply did not comply with the decision in many cases.[88] Detectives gave the *Miranda* warnings only about 20 percent of the time, and few suspects were ever informed of their right to counsel. In instances when the warnings *were* given, the detectives had a number of ways to nullify their effect. Some altered the wording slightly: "Whatever you say may be used *for* or against you in a court of law." Others inserted some qualifying remarks: "You don't have to say a word, but you ought to get everything cleared up," or "You don't have to say anything, of course, but you can explain how . . ."

The Erosion of *Miranda*

During his presidential campaign in 1968, Richard M. Nixon promised to appoint men to the Supreme Court who would be less receptive to the arguments of criminal defendants and more responsive to the needs and reasoning of law enforcement officers. The first of the Nixon appointees, Warren Burger, came in early 1969. Burger was a conservative appeals court judge, and he replaced the retiring Earl Warren as the Court's chief justice. Burger clearly espoused "law and order" concepts, which made him attractive to the Senate Judiciary Committee, and he was known in Washington circles as Nixon's "hatchet man." As the new chief justice, he announced from time to time to the other justices exactly which previous decisions the Court now had to overrule—*Miranda, Mapp, Chimel,* and others—and he eyed closely the votes that might be marshalled to achieve that result.[89] In 1970, Burger was joined on the bench by another Nixon appointee, Harry A. Blackmun, and in 1971 by Lewis F. Powell and William H. Rehnquist—the four comprising what quickly became known as the "Nixon Court." *Miranda* itself was not overturned, but in the 1970s the Court clearly began a retreat from *Miranda.* For example, in *Harris v. New York,*[90] by a 5-to-4 vote, the Court held that although statements made by a defendant during interrogation and before he was advised of his rights could not be used as evidence against him, those statements could be used to impeach his credibility as a witness if he took the stand in his own defense and made statements conflicting with those made before trial. In *Michigan v. Tucker,*[91] the Court upheld the prosecution's use of a witness whose identity was revealed during an interrogation contaminated by *Miranda* violations. Police had arrested Tucker for rape but failed to advise him of his right to free counsel. While being questioned, Tucker provided the name of a witness who could document his activities at the time of the crime. When contacted, the "alibi's" statements seriously incriminated Tucker. In *Michigan v. Mosley,*[92] the Court ruled that although a suspect's assertion of his right to silence must terminate police questioning about one crime, it does not foreclose subsequent police efforts, after an interval and a second reading of his rights, to question him about another crime.

The Supreme court faced only one serious challenge to *Miranda* during the 1970s, in *Brewer v. Williams* (see Exhibit 8.8).[93] At the close of the decade, *Miranda* had yet to be overthrown, but during the 1980s further erosion became apparent. In *New York v. Quarles,*[94] a "public safety" exception to *Miranda* was established. Benjamin Quarles was taken into custody shortly after a woman had approached the arresting officer and told him that she had been raped by an armed assailant. After frisking and handcuffing Quarles, the officer asked him where the gun was. Upon being told, he retrieved Quarles's pistol, but no *Miranda* warnings had been given prior to this questioning. The Court held that the officer's failure to read the *Miranda* warnings before seeking to locate the firearm was justified in the interests of public safety.

In *Nix v. Williams,*[95] a later chapter in the case of *Brewer v. Williams* created an "inevitable discovery" exception to the *Miranda* rule (see Exhibit 8.9). In *Moran v. Burbine,*[96] the Supreme Court declared that a police department's failure to inform a suspect undergoing custodial interrogation of his attorney's attempts to reach him does *not* constitute a violation of the *Miranda* rule. The High Court reasoned that events occurring that are unknown to a defendant have no bearing on his capacity to knowingly waive his rights.

Brewer v. Williams: The Supreme Court ruling that the use of subterfuge or trickery to elicit incriminating information from a suspect constitutes "custodial interrogation" and is bound by the holding in *Miranda.*

Brewer v. Williams

On Christmas Eve, 1968, in Des Moines, Iowa, ten-year-old Pamela Powers was abducted, raped, and strangled to death. Two days later Robert Williams, who had recently escaped from a mental institution and who resided at the Des Moines YMCA where the child had been abducted, surrendered to police in Davenport, Iowa, some 160 miles away. Williams had surrendered at the advice of his lawyer, Henry McKnight, and when it was learned that a detective would be transporting Williams back to Des Moines, McKnight insisted that no interrogation take place during the trip. The police agreed.

Knowing that Williams was a religious man, the detective addressed him as "Reverend" during the trip; he did not interrogate Williams, but presented him with a series of statements referred to in the record as the "Christian burial speech":

I want to give you something to think about while we're traveling down the road. . . . Number one, I want you to observe the weather conditions, it's raining, it's sleeting, it's freezing, driving is very treacherous, visibility is poor, it's going to be dark early this evening. They are predicting several inches of snow for tonight, and I feel that you yourself are the only person that knows where this little girl's body is, that you yourself have only been there once, and if you get a snow on top of it you yourself may be unable to find it. And, since we will be going right past the area on the way into Des Moines, I feel that we could stop and locate the body, that the parents of this little girl should be entitled to a Christian burial for the little girl who was snatched away from them on Christmas Eve and murdered. And I feel we should stop and locate it on the way in rather than waiting until morning and trying to come back out after a snowstorm and possibly not being able to find it at all.

Shortly after the detective's "Christian burial speech," Williams directed the officer to Pamela Powers's dead and frozen body.

Williams was convicted of murder, in spite of his counsel's objections to the admission of the evidence resulting from the incriminating statements Williams made during the trip. The Iowa Supreme Court affirmed the conviction, and on appeal to the U.S. Supreme Court, Iowa's attorney general, along with the National District Attorneys Association and Americans for Effective Law Enforcement, requested that the court overrule *Miranda*.

By a 5-to-4 decision, the Supreme Court ruled that Williams had not waived his right to counsel during his ride from Davenport to Des Moines, and that the detective's "Christian burial speech" constituted "custodial interrogation." Chief Justice Warren Burger castigated his more liberal colleagues in open court, stating in his strongly worded opinion that "the result by the Court in this case ought to be intolerable in any society which purports to call itself organized society."

SOURCE: *Brewer* v. *Williams*, 430 U.S. 387 (1977).

At the close of the 1980s and the beginning of the 1990s, the case-by-case dismantling of *Miranda* continued. *Duckworth* v. *Eagan*[97] in 1989, for example, permitted a police *Miranda* warning to state "We have no way of giving you a lawyer, but one will be appointed for you, if you wish, if and when you go to court." Writing for the Court in this 5-to-4 decision, Chief Justice Rehnquist stressed that the Court never insisted that the *Miranda* warning be given in the exact form described in Chief Justice Warren's *Miranda* majority opinion delivered in 1966. In *Illinois* v. *Perkins*,[98] decided in 1990, the Court held that the use of "jailhouse plants" to elicit incriminating statements from incarcerated suspects does *not* constitute custodial interrogation within the meaning of *Miranda*.

The only recent exception to the case-by-case erosion of *Miranda* was *Mississippi* v. *Minnick*,[99] decided in 1991. In this case, the Court held that once a criminal suspect asserts his or her right to an attorney, police may not question the suspect without an attorney present unless the suspect initiates the questioning.

Miranda *warnings are not required when the suspect is unaware that he is speaking to a law enforcement officer and gives a voluntary statement.*
— FROM THE MAJORITY OPINION IN
ILLINOIS V. *PERKINS*

● EXHIBIT 8.9 ●

Whatever Happened to . . .

Dollree Mapp

When the *Mapp* v. *Ohio* decision in 1961 extended the exclusionary rule to the states, Dollree

In 1970, nine years after her conviction was overturned by the Supreme Court on the grounds of illegal search and seizure, Dollree Mapp was arrested when police, armed with a search warrant this time, found heroin and stolen property in her home.

Mapp's conviction for the illegal possession of obscene materials was overturned on the grounds of illegal search and seizure. Many years later, Mapp again came into contact with the law. On November 2, 1970, some two years after relocating from Cleveland to New York City, she was arrested by detectives of the Narcotics Division and the Safe, Loft, and Truck Squad of the New York Police Department. Mapp was suspected of dealing in stolen property, and the detectives, pursuant to a search warrant, raided her home and found 50,000 envelopes of heroin and stolen property valued at over $100,000. On April 23, 1971, she was convicted of the felonious possession of dangerous drugs and sentenced to a term of twenty years to life.

Throughout her trial, Mapp argued against the legality of the search warrant, but three lower courts as well as the federal court of appeals sustained her conviction. However, on December 31, 1980, New York Governor Hugh Carey commuted her minimum sentence, making her eligible for parole the following day.

Danny Escobedo

The Supreme Court's *Escobedo* v. *Illinois* decision in 1964 overturned Danny Escobedo's murder conviction on the grounds that his constitutional rights had been violated when police refused him access to an attorney before he confessed to the slaying of his brother-in-law.

Within two years of the High Court's decision, however, Escobedo was making regular appearances before Chicago magistrates. During 1966 and 1967, he was arrested on various charges of disorderly conduct, burglary, weapons violations, and drug sales. On the burglary and drug charges, Escobedo was convicted and received concurrent sentences of twenty-two and twenty years. He was ultimately paroled in 1975.

Escobedo made the headlines on several occasions during the 1980s. In 1984 he was sentenced to twelve years in prison on conviction of taking indecent liberties with a thirteen-year-old girl. While free on bond pending an appeal of that conviction, in 1985 he was arrested in Chicago on a charge of attempted mur-

Show-ups, Line-ups, and Exemplars

A final aspect of this discussion of police and the Constitution involves a variety of investigating techniques law enforcement officers employ to detect and identify criminal offenders. Among these are show-ups, line-ups, photographs, and other forms of "nontestimonial" material that the Supreme Court has allowed, given certain conditions, as admissible evidence.

The *show-up* is a procedure that generally takes place shortly after a crime has been committed when a victim or witness is taken to a police station and confronted with a suspect. In the show-up, the victim or witness is not offered an array of individuals from which a suspect is to be

der. In 1987 he pleaded guilty, and received a sentence of eleven years.

Ernesto Miranda

The *Miranda* v. *Arizona* decision in 1966, which laid out the well-known "Miranda warning rules," did not end Ernesto Miranda's legal entanglements. In February 1967, he was tried again on the kidnapping and rape charges, for when the Supreme Court overturned his original conviction it had not quashed the indictment, and Miranda was granted a new trial. During his second trial, Miranda's common-law wife, Twila Hoffman, testified that he had admitted kidnapping and raping the victim. Miranda was convicted and sentenced to a twenty- to thirty-year term in state prison. He was paroled in 1972. Two years later, he was arrested on a gun charge and for possession of drugs, but the cases were dismissed due to Fourth Amendment violations. In 1975, Miranda was returned for a brief period to Arizona State Prison for parole violation,

but he was released later that year. In early 1976, at age thirty-four, Ernesto Miranda was slain in a Phoenix skid row bar during a quarrel over a card game. When the police arrested the suspect in the killing, they appropriately recited the *Miranda* warning rules.

Robert Williams

After the High Court's 1977 ruling in *Brewer* v. *Williams* (see Exhibit 8.8), Robert Williams was returned to the Iowa courts for a second trial for the 1968 murder of ten-year-old Pamela Powers. At this new trial, evidence about Powers's body was admitted, but not Williams's involvement in its discovery. Williams was convicted of first-degree murder, and the Iowa Supreme Court affirmed. In subsequent *habeas corpus* proceedings, the federal district court, denying relief, agreed with the Iowa trial and appeals courts, that the victim's body would inevitably have been found. However, the U.S. Court of Appeals for the Eighth Circuit reversed, holding that—even assuming that there

is an "inevitable discovery" exception to the exclusionary rule—the state had not met the exception's requirement that it be proved that the police did not act in bad faith. At that point, the state of Iowa appealed the court of appeals decision to the United States Supreme Court. The case was *Nix* v. *Williams*, and the High Court's ruling came in 1984.

By a vote of 7-to-2, the Supreme Court endorsed the "inevitable discovery" exception. Chief Justice Warren Burger noted that some 200 volunteers had been searching for Pamela Powers's body at the very time that Williams led police to it, and that it would have been "inevitably discovered" by lawful means without his help. That being so, wrote Burger in the Court's opinion, it "would reject logic, experience and common sense" to apply the exclusionary rule and bar the evidence. Sixteen years after the Christmas Eve slaying of Pamela Powers, Robert Williams's life sentence for the crime was fully endorsed.

possibly chosen, as in a line-up. Rather, it is often a one-on-one confrontation, presented in such a context as "Is he the one?" *Show-up* is a term that is not consistently used by either the police or the courts; *line-up* is more popular. However, *show-up* does seem to be used more often in the context of one-on-one identifications. Here is an example of a show-up, described in the 1972 case of *Kirby* v. *Illinois*.[100]

> After Kirby and his alleged accomplice Ralph Bean were arrested, police officers brought Willie Shard, the robbery victim, to a room in a police station where Kirby and Bean were seated at a table with two other police officers. Shard testified at trial that the officers who brought him to the room asked him if Kirby and Bean were the robbers and he indicated they were.

In the *line-up,* the suspect is placed together with several other persons and the victim or witness is then asked to pick out the suspect.

The constitutional issues in the use of line-ups and show-ups have generally focused on the fairness of these procedures, and on the suspects' and defendants' rights to counsel during identification. In *Foster* v. *California,*[101] for example, there was only one witness to a robbery. The suspect, who was six-feet-tall, was first placed in a line-up with two other men who were several inches shorter. Also, he was wearing a leather jacket similar to the one the witness had seen one of the robbers wearing. The witness thought the suspect was indeed the robber, but was not absolutely sure. Several days later another line-up was held, and the suspect was the only one in the second line-up who had been in the earlier one. At this point the witness positively identified the suspect as the robber. The Supreme Court did not allow this type of identification procedure to stand, stating that "in effect, the police repeatedly said to the witness, *'This is the man.'* "

United States v. *Wade:* The Supreme Court ruling that a police line-up identification of a suspect, made without the suspect's attorney present, is inadmissible as evidence at trial.

United States v. **Wade** addressed the issue of a defendant's right to counsel during a line-up.[102] In *Wade,* the defendant had been shown to witnesses before trial at a postindictment line-up, without notice of the line-up to the accused or his attorney, and without his attorney present. The Court recognized in this case that the chances of an unfair identification were so great, either through inadvertence or design, that it ruled that a person who is subjected to a pretrial line-up or show-up is entitled to be represented by counsel at that time. Importantly, however, the *Wade* case referred only to postindictment line-ups, and not to those occurring in earlier phases of the criminal justice process.

Nontestimonial exemplars include: Voice, blood, handwriting, and other specimens used as evidence.

With respect to nontestimonial exemplars, the Supreme Court has maintained a firm position:

- In *Schmerber* v. *California,*[103] the Court ruled that the forced extraction of a blood sample from a defendant who was accused of driving while intoxicated was admissible at trial.
- In *United States* v. *Dionisio,*[104] the Court held that a suspect could be forced to provide voice exemplars.
- In *United States* v. *Mara,*[105] the Court held that a suspect could be compelled to provide a handwriting exemplar.
- In *United States* v. *Ash,*[106] the Court held that the Sixth Amendment does not grant the right to counsel at photographic displays conducted for the purpose of allowing a witness to attempt an identification of an offender.

The position of the Court in these cases has been that the Fifth Amendment privilege protects an accused only from being compelled to testify against himself — that is, from evidence of a communicative nature. On the other hand, in *Winston* v. *Lee* the Court held that a suspect cannot be forced to undergo surgery to remove a bullet from his chest, even though probable cause exists that the surgery would produce evidence of a crime.[107]

SUMMARY

The police have both investigative and arrest powers. Investigative powers include the power to stop and frisk, to order someone out of a vehicle, to question, and to detain. Arrest powers include the power to use force, to search, and to exercise seizure and restraint. The Constitution places restrictions on the exercise of these powers, but determining the specific intent of the Constitution in this behalf has been left to the courts.

Search and seizure refers to the search for and taking of persons and/or property as evidence of crime. The Fourth Amendment prohibits "unreasonable" searches and seizures. The Supreme Court has ruled on guidelines for the issuance of search warrants, searches incident to arrest, and the circumstances involving stop and frisk, fresh pursuit, random automobile checks, consent search, and "plain view" seizure.

The Supreme Court's exclusionary rule prohibits in court the use of any evidence seized in violation of the Fourth Amendment ban against unreasonable search and seizure. In *Weeks* v. *United States* in 1914, the Court established the exclusionary rule for federal prosecutions; *Mapp* v. *Ohio* extended this rule to the states in 1961. Since *Mapp,* however, there has been dissatisfaction with the exclusionary rule. As a result, there has been a retreat from *Mapp.*

In criminal prosecutions, the Constitution prohibits forced confessions and guarantees the assistance of counsel. However, these restrictions were applied to the states only recently. *Brown* v. *Mississippi* in 1936 began a movement that culminated with *Escobedo* and *Miranda* during the 1960s. As with *Mapp,* there was dissatisfaction with the *Miranda* rule, and over the years its original strength has been diluted.

KEY TERMS

Brewer v. *Williams* **(264)**
Carroll Doctrine **(240)**
Chimel v. *California* **(235)**
Delaware v. *Prouse* **(241)**
Escobedo v. *Illinois* **(261)**
exclusionary rule **(247)**
Florida v. *Bostick* **(243)**

fruit of the poisonous tree **(239)**
Illinois v. *Gates* **(232)**
Mapp v. *Ohio* **(249)**
Miranda v. *Arizona* **(262)**
"plain view" doctrine **(246)**
probable cause **(231)**
protective sweep doctrine **(246)**

Rochin v. *California* **(249)**
search and seizure **(231)**
search warrant **(231)**
Terry v. *Ohio* **(238)**
United States v. *Leon* **(254)**
United States v. *Wade* **(268)**
Weeks v. *United States* **(247)**

QUESTIONS FOR DISCUSSION

1. Given the facts in *Chimel* v. *California,* could the prosecution have applied the doctrines of "plain view" and protective sweep?
2. What are the various rights of the accused during the pretrail phases of the criminal justice process?
3. Applying the concept of probable cause, what

specifically was considered "unreasonable" about the searches and seizures in *Aguilar* v. *Texas* and *Mapp* v. *Ohio*?
4. What are your opinions of the reasonableness of the Supreme Court decisions in *Escobedo* v. *Illinois, Miranda* v. *Arizona,* and *Brewer* v. *Williams*?

FOR FURTHER READING

Abraham, Henry J. *Freedon and the Court: Civil Rights and Liberties in the United States.* New York: Oxford University Press, 1977.
Ginger, Ann Fagan. *The Law, the Supreme Court, and People's Rights.* Woodbury, N.Y.: Barron's, 1973.
Kelder, Gary, and Alan J. Statman. "The Protective Sweep Doctrine: Recurrent Questions Regarding the Propriety of Searches Conducted Contemporaneously with an Arrest on or near Private Premises." *Syracuse Law Review* 30 (1979): 973–1092.
Lippman, Matthew. "Stop and Frisk: The Triumph of Law Enforcement Over Private Rights." *Criminal Law Bulletin* 24 (Jan–Feb 1988): 24–47.

NOTES

1. J. Shane Creamer, *The Law of Arrest, Search, and Seizure* (New York: Holt, Rinehart and Winston, 1980); p. 3.
2. *Locke* v. *United States*, 7 Cr. 339 (1813).
3. *Dumbra* v. *United States*, 268 U.S. 435 (1925).
4. *Aguilar* v. *Texas*, 378 U.S. 108 (1964); *Spinelli* v. *United States*, 393 U.S. 410 (1969).
5. *Illinois* v. *Gates*, 462 U.S. 213 (1983).
6. *United States* v. *Robinson*, 414 U.S. 218 (1973).
7. *United States* v. *Watson*, 423 U.S. 455 (1976).
8. *Payton* v. *New York*, 455 U.S. 573 (1980).
9. *Chimel* v. *California*, 395 U.S. 752 (1969).
10. *McQueen* v. *Heck*, 41 Tenn. 212 (1860); *Shelton* v. *State*, 3 Tenn. Cr. App. 310, 460 S.W. (2d) 869 (1970).
11. *Harris* v. *State*, 206 Tenn. 276 (1960).
12. *Lowery* v. *State*, 39 Ala. 659, 107 So. 2d 366 (1958).
13. *State* v. *Autheman*, 47 Idaho 328, 274 P. 305, 62 A.L.R. 195 (1929); *Appleton* v. *State*, 61 Ark. 590, 33 S.W. 1066 (1896).
14. For example, *Neal* v. *Joyner*, 89 N.C. 287 (1883).
15. *Malley* v. *Briggs*, 38 CrL 3169 (1986).
16. *Terry* v. *Ohio*, 392 U.S. 1 (1968).
17. *California* v. *Hodari D.*, 49 CrL 2050 (1991).
18. *Carroll* v. *United States*, 267 U.S. 132 (1925).
19. *Husty* v. *United States*, 282 U.S. 694 (1931).
20. *Chambers* v. *Maroney*, 399 U.S. 42 (1970).
21. *United States* v. *Ross*, 456 U.S. 798 (1982).
22. *New York* v. *Belton*, 453 U.S. 454 (1981).
23. *California* v. *Acevedo*, 49 CrL 2210 (1991).
24. Personal communication, October 31, 1970.
25. Personal communication, June 19, 1975.
26. *Delaware* v. *Prouse*, 24 CrL 3079 (1979).
27. *Michigan Department of State Police* v. *Stiz*, 47 CrL 2155 (1990).
28. *Tennessee Code*, Title 40, Section 811.
29. Louis P. Mitchell, "High Speed Pursuits," *C.J., The Americas*, 2 (January 1990), p. 18.
30. Geoffrey P. Alpert, "Analyzing Police Pursuit," *Criminal Law Bulletin*, 27 (July–August 1991), pp. 358–367.
31. *Wren* v. *United States*, 352 F 2d 617 (1965).
32. *United States* v. *Matlock*, 415 U.S. 164 (1974).
33. *Bumper* v. *North Carolina*, 391 U.S. 543 (1968).
34. *Schneckloth* v. *Bustamonte*, 412 U.S. 218 (1973).
35. *United States* v. *Dichiarinte*, 445 F 2d 126 (1921).
36. *Florida* v. *Jimeno*, 49 CrL 2175 (1991).
37. *Florida* v. *Bostick*, 49 CrL 2270 (1991).
38. *Burdeau* v. *McDowell*, 256 U.S. 465 (1921).
39. *United States* v. *Martinez-Fuerte*, 428 U.S. 543 (1976).
40. *South Dakota* v. *Opperman*, 428 U.S. 364 (1976).
41. *Katz* v. *United States*, 389 U.S. 347 (1967).
42. *Abel* v. *United States*, 362 U.S. 217 (1960).
43. *California* v. *Greenwood*, 43 CrL 3029 (1988).
44. *Hester* v. *United States*, 265 U.S. 57 (1924).
45. *Oliver* v. *United States*, US SupCt (1984) 35 CrL 3011; *Maine* v. *Thornton*, US SupCt (1984) 35 CrL 3011.
46. *Harris* v. *United States*, 390 U.S. 234 (1968).
47. Steven M. Greenberg, "Compounding a Felony: Drug Abuse and the American Legal System," in *Drugs and the Criminal Justice System*, ed. James A. Inciardi and Carl D. Chambers (Beverly Hills, Calif.: Sage, 1974), p. 200.
48. Gary Kelder and Alan J. Statman, "The Protective Sweep Doctrine: Recurrent Questions Regarding the Propriety of Searches Conducted Contemporaneously with an Arrest on or near Private Premises," *Syracuse Law Review* 30 (1979): 973–1092.
49. *Weeks* v. *United States*, 232 U.S. 383 (1914).
50. *Adams* v. *New York*, 192 U.S. 585 (1904).
51. National Commission on Law Observance and Enforcement, *Report on Prosecution* (Washington, D.C.: U.S. Government Printing Office, 1931), p. 24.
52. *People* v. *Defore*, 242 N.Y. 13 at 21 (1926).
53. Elder Witt, ed., *Guide to the U.S. Supreme Court* (Washington, D.C.: Congressional Quarterly, 1979), p. 549.
54. *Wolf* v. *Colorado*, 338 U.S. 25 (1949).
55. Henry J. Abraham, *Freedom and the Court: Civil Rights and Liberties in the United States* (New York: Oxford University Press, 1977), pp. 71–72.
56. *Rochin* v. *California*, 342 U.S. 165 (1952).
57. *Rea* v. *United States*, 350 U.S. 214 (1956).
58. *Elkins* v. *United States*, 364 U.S. 206 (1960).
59. *Mapp* v. *Ohio*, 367 U.S. 643 (1961).
60. *New York Times*, June 20, 1961, p. 1.
61. Arthur Niederhoffer, *Behind the Shield* (Garden City, N.Y.: Doubleday, 1967), p. 159.
62. Yale Kamisar, "Criminals, Cops, and the Constitution," *The Nation* 199 (November 9, 1964): 323.
63. *Linkletter* v. *Walker*, 381 U.S. 618 (1965).
64. See Bob Woodward and Scott Armstrong, *The Brethren: Inside the Supreme Court* (New York: Simon and Schuster, 1979), pp. 112–119.
65. *Coolidge* v. *New Hampshire*, 403 U.S. 443 (1971).
66. *United States* v. *Calandra*, 414 U.S. 338 (1974).
67. *Stone* v. *Powell*, 428 U.S. 465 (1976).
68. *United States* v. *Leon*, US SupCt (1984) 35 CrL 3273; *Massachusetts* v. *Sheppard*, US SupCt (1984) 35 CrL 3296
69. *Illinois* v. *Krull*, 40 CrL 3327 (1987).
70. *Murray* v. *United States*, 43 CrL 3168 (1988).
71. *Hopt* v. *Utah*, 110 U.S. 574 (1884).
72. *Wilson* v. *United States*, 162 U.S. 613 (1896).
73. *Twining* v. *New Jersey*, 211 U.S. 78 (1908).
74. Cited by Abraham, *Freedom and the Court*, p. 59.
75. *Brown* v. *Mississippi*, 297 U.S. 278 (1936).
76. *Rogers* v. *Richmond*, 365 U.S. 534 (1961).
77. *Bram* v. *United States*, 168 U.S. 532 (1897).
78. *McNabb* v. *United States*, 318 U.S. 332 (1943).
79. *Mallory* v. *United States*, 354 U.S. 449 (1957).
80. Elder Witt, *Guide to the U.S. Supreme Court*, p. 679. See also Richard Harris, *The Fear of Crime* (New York: Praeger, 1969).
81. *Crooker* v. *California*, 357 U.S. 433 (1958).
82. *Massiah* v. *United States*, 377 U.S. 201 (1964).
83. *Mallory* v. *Hogan*, 378 U.S. 1 (1964).
84. *Escobedo* v. *Illinois*, 378 U.S. 478 (1964).
85. *Miranda* v. *Arizona, Vignera* v. *New York, Westover* v. *United States, California* v. *Stewart*—all 384 U.S. 436 (1966).
86. *New York Times*, June 14, 1966, p. 1.
87. Robert F. Cushman, *Cases in Constitutional Law* (Englewood Cliffs, N.J.: Prentice-Hall, 1979), p. 400.
88. Richard Ayres, "Confessions and the Court," in *The Ambivalent Force: Perspectives on the Police*, ed. Arthur Neiderhoffer and Abraham S. Blumberg (Hinsdale, Ill.: Dryden, 1976), pp. 286–290.

89. William O. Douglas, *The Court Years: 1939–1975* (New York: Random House, 1980), p. 231.
90. *Harris* v. *New York,* 401 U.S. 222 (1971).
91. *Michigan* v. *Tucker,* 417 U.S. 433 (1974).
92. *Michigan* v. *Mosley,* 423 U.S. 96 (1975).
93. *Brewer* v. *Williams,* 430 U.S. 387 (1977).
94. *New York* v. *Quarles,* US SupCt (1984) 35 CrL 3135.
95. *Nix* v. *Williams,* US SupCt (1984) 35 CrL 3119.
96. *Moran* v. *Burbine,* 106 S. Ct. 1135 (1986).
97. *Duckworth* v. *Eagan,* 45 CrL 3172 (1989).
98. *Illinois* v. *Perkins,* 47 CrL 2131 (1990).
99. *Mississippi* v. *Minnick,* 48 CrL 2053 (1991).
100. *Kirby* v. *Illinois,* 406 U.S. 682 (1972).
101. *Foster* v. *California,* 394 U.S. 440 (1969).
102. *United States* v. *Wade,* 388 U.S. 218 (1967).
103. *Schmerber* v. *California,* 384 U.S. 757 (1966).
104. *United States* v. *Dionisio,* 410 U.S. 1 (1973).
105. *United States* v. *Mara,* 410 U.S. 19 (1973).
106. *United States* v. *Ash,* 413 U.S. 300 (1973).
107. *Winston* v. *Lee,* US SupCt (1985) 53 U.S.L.W. 4367.

CHAPTER 9

Beyond the Limits of the Law: Police Crime, Corruption, and Brutality

There is more law in the end of a policeman's nightstick than in any decision of the Supreme Court.
—ALEXANDER "CLUBBER" WILLIAMS, 1881

The .38 service revolver is a police officer's final authority.
—FROM *COPS*, BY MARK BAKER, 1985

The word is that the precinct is . . . going up in smoke. I heard that you and several other people are going down. They have you on video doing something. That's what I heard the word is. And also that you're a rat. So stay away from me.
—FROM *BUDDY BOYS*, BY MIKE MCALARY, 1987

A cop who fingers a colleague guilty of armed robbery, drug dealing, or even murder will still be ostracized by many of his fellow officers.
—FROM *COP HUNTER*, BY VINCENT MURANO, 1990

Being a cop today is a stop-and-go nightmare.
—*U.S. NEWS AND WORLD REPORT*, DECEMBER 3, 1990

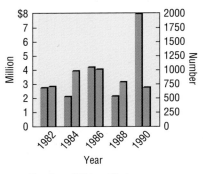

Claims of Police Misconduct in Los Angeles, 1981–1990

SOURCE: City of Los Angeles. Dollar amounts exclude legal fees.

When a group of white officers from the Los Angeles Police Department clubbed Rodney King fifty-six times in the early morning hours of March 3, 1991, little did they know that the L.A.P.D. would never be the same. Their beating of King, an unemployed black construction worker, had been taped by a bystander. Within days, television stations across the nation were replaying the grisly images, provoking protests and discussions of police brutality throughout the country.

The case of Rodney King and the L.A.P.D. became a notorious case, but only because it had been videotaped and given a national audience. But the problems of brutality, as well as those of police crime and corruption, are likely as old as policing itself. And a retrospective glance suggests that brutality and corruption were apparent from the first days of organized policing in the United States.

Among the more publicized figures in nineteenth-century police history was Alexander S. Williams, a Canadian immigrant whose career with the New York City Police spanned almost three decades. Born in Nova Scotia in 1839, Williams moved to New York at midcentury in search of work as a ship's carpenter, and quickly established himself in the world of shipbuilding.[1] During the Civil War, Williams became the first Westerner to construct a ship in Japan, undertook salvage work for the United States government, and ultimately became a partner in a growing shipbuilding firm. Labor problems in that industry, however, quickly put an end to his business aspirations, and as an alternative he joined the New York City police force in 1866.

After only two years as a patrolman, Williams made the first of a series of moves that would ultimately make him well known among his fellow officers, within the underworld, and to the citizens of New York as well. In 1868, he was assigned to the Broadway Squad in lower Manhattan, where many police officers before him had been either seriously assaulted or murdered by the numerous gang members, street brawlers, and other violent criminals who ranged through the area. On his second day at the new post, Patrolman Williams positioned himself in front of the Florence Saloon — a notorious resort of local thieves, muggers, and other types of criminals located at the intersection of Broadway and Houston Street — where he selected two of the neighborhood's toughest characters, picked fights with them, knocked them unconscious with his nightstick, and hurled their bodies through the plate glass window of their hangout. According to local folklore, ten of their comrades came to the rescue, but Williams, a large and powerful man, stood his ground and mowed them down one after another with his hardwood club. Thereafter, he averaged a fight a day for almost four years.[2] His skill with the nightstick was said to be so extraordinary and the force of his blows so powerful that he was hailed as "Clubber" Williams—a title he retained throughout his life.

Following his assignment to the Broadway Squad, Williams' career moved quickly. In July 1871, he was promoted to the rank of sergeant. Only two months later he became a captain, and from there he moved on to become a police inspector. His fame grew so rapidly in New York that he once commented, "I am so well known here in New York that car horses nod to me every morning."[3] He was the star feature of police parades and received constant attention from the daily press. He even refereed a major prizefight—in full uniform—at Madison Square Garden.

But there was another side to Alexander Williams, for he also epitomized the kinds of brutality and corruption that were characteristic of the New York police during the latter part of the nineteenth century. His use of the nightstick was not limited to warding off thugs and street brawlers, but was applied to strikers and sleeping drunks as well. And Williams was also known for clubbing spectators at parades as a means of crowd control.[4] His technique with the nightstick reflected both sadism and brutality. Williams often spoke of how his stick could be used for knocking a man unconscious, for killing him, or for just battering him to pieces. In terms of "art for art's sake," he discussed on many occasions how a tap with the stick on the head, hands, or feet could send a current through the spine to make a prisoner stand up or lie down.

As for graft and corruption within the ranks of policing, Williams was an entrepreneur. It was "Clubber" Williams who reportedly coined the term "tenderloin" as the designation for areas of vice and nightlife. When he was transferred from the not-too-lucrative downtown Broadway precinct to the area bounded by Manhattan's Fourteenth to Forty-second Streets and Fifth and Seventh Avenues, Williams was quite pleased. His new sector was so wide open as a vice resort that New Yorkers called it Satan's Circus. But Williams gave it the new nickname. As he took over his post, he commented, "I've had nothing but chuck steaks for a long time, and now I'm going to get me a little of the tenderloin."[5]

Williams, of course, was speaking of opportunities for graft, and bountiful it was for him, for by imposing tribute on every kind of illegal activity he quickly became a wealthy man. Houses of prostitution paid him initiation fees plus monthly charges for protection; saloons paid to stay open after hours; gambling halls paid monthly contributions; and pickpockets, burglars, and other thieves paid him a percentage of the stealings.

The adventures of Alexander "Clubber" Williams were typical, although on a larger scale, of the graft and corruption within the ranks of policing made possible by the politics of city bossism that existed during that period of American history. Although police corruption in this grand and open manner has all but disappeared, William's exploits are nevertheless colorful illustrations of the problems that continue to exist. In contrast with the days of "Clubber" Williams, however, police corruption and brutality are no longer openly tolerated.

The balance of this chapter focuses on two areas of police misconduct: corruption and violence. Police corruption involves illegal activities for economic gain, including payment for services that police are sworn to carry out as part of their peacekeeping role. Police violence, in the forms of brutality and the misapplication of deadly force, involves the wrongful use of police power.

Clubs, Clubbers, and the Clubbed

It's the funniest sight in the world to see the effect of a proper lick with a stick on a man's two feet. You don't get the chance to try it often. In my day we old cops used to practice it, very easy, on one another, and when you could do it you'd go out and find your bum. I remember the first time I got one just right. He was asleep on his back on a park bench, his two feet stuck out clear and even. Gosh, I was glad, and careful, I sneaked up on him from behind, knelt down, spit on my hand, and aimed. I was so nervous that I dropped my raised arm twice before I felt steady and ready. Then—say, but then I let her go, I whacked level and straight, hitting the bottoms of both boots at the same instant, and, well, it happened—what they always said would happen. That bum rose, still like a stick, he didn't bend a knee or move an arm. I think he didn't wake up. He just rose up, running—I mean that he was running by the time he came erect, and with never a holler or a look behind, he was running hell-bent across that park and—I watched him; I walked over in the direction he disappeared and—he's running yet. Yep! I bet that when he woke up, he was surprised to find himself running; it was so unusual for him to run that it woke him, but he couldn't stop of course.

—A NEW YORK PATROLMAN, AS TOLD TO JOURNALIST LINCOLN STEFFENS IN THE EARLY 1890s

CORRUPTION

Police corruption reflects illegal activities for economic gain; police violence involves the wrongful use of police power.

Police corruption begins with the notion that policemen by some divine right are entitled to free meals, free movies, and cut-rate prices on virtually everything they buy.

— DAVID BURNHAM, 1970

Research in the area of white-collar crime, combined with government inquiries targeting the internal operations of organized crime, labor unions, and various business enterprises, have demonstrated that work-related law-breaking can be found within every profession and occupation. In the health field, for example, fee splitting, diversion of drugs and medical supplies, fraudulent reports to insurance companies, and unlawful prescription practices are undertaken by physicians, pharmacists, nurses, and hospital personnel. In the business sector, such unlawful activities as employee pilferage, financial manipulations, labor racketeering, consumer fraud and deception, misrepresentation of goods, sales of stolen goods, black marketeering, shortchanging, and overcharging occur among both executives and workers. Moreover, a wide spectrum of criminal activities has been found within the legal profession, civil service, banking and finance, labor, education, and professional sports.

Similarly, illegal job-related activities involving graft, corruption, theft, and other practices are comparably evident within the ranks of the police. Yet crime and corruption may be considerably more widespread than in most other occupations. Virtually every urban police department in the United States has experienced both organized corruption and some form of scandal, and similar problems have been uncovered in small towns and rural sheriff's departments.[6] During the 1970s, for example, the Police Foundation arranged to receive newspaper clippings detailing incidents of police corruption across the United States. In a period of only sixty days, the foundation received articles from as many as thirty states. The articles reported on allegations of graft and corruption in major urban centers, small cities, sheriffs' offices, state police forces, and suburban departments. They reflected practices ranging from accepting bribes from traffic offenders to accepting payment to

No police department can remain free of corruption in a community where bribery flourishes in public office and private enterprise; a corrupt police department in an otherwise corruption-free society is a contradiction in terms.

— ORLANDO W. WILSON, FORMER SUPERINTENDANT OF POLICE, CHICAGO

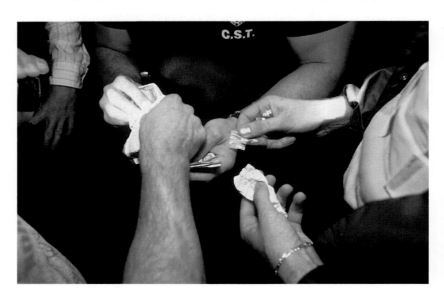

alter testimony at trials.[7] During approximately the same period, an analysis of police practices in Philadelphia noted that officers saw themselves operating in a world where "notes" (payoffs) were constantly floating about, "and only the stupid, the naive, and the faint-hearted are unwilling to allow some of them to stick to their fingers."[8] In New York, the findings of the Knapp Commission asserted that more than half of the city's 29,600 police officers had taken part in corrupt practices,[9] and throughout the 1980s and early 1990s the media has continually reported incidents of drug-related corruption in police agencies in all parts of the nation.

The problem lies in the fact that policing is rich in opportunities for corruption—more so than in most, if not all other occupations. The police officer stands at the front lines of the criminal justice system in a nation where crime rates are high and where the demands for illegal goods and services are widespread. These conditions, combined with a range of numerous other variables, create a situation in which police officers are confronted daily with opportunities for accepting funds in lieu of fully discharging their duties.

Police corruption is best defined as misconduct by police officers in the forms of illegal activities for economic gain and accepting gratuities, favors, or payment for services that police are sworn to carry out as part of their peacekeeping role. It occurs in many forms, and observers and researchers of police behavior tend to agree that it is most manifest in nine specific areas:[10]

1. meals and services
2. kickbacks
3. opportunistic theft
4. planned theft and robbery
5. shakedowns
6. protection
7. case fixing
8. private security
9. patronage

Police corruption: Misconduct by police officers in the forms of illegal activities for economic gain and accepting gratuities, favors, or payment for services that police are sworn to carry out as part of their peacekeeping role.

Meals and Services

Free or discount meals are available to police officers in almost every American city.[11] A number of restaurant chains have a policy of providing meals to officers on a regular basis, and these are tabulated daily, with records kept so they can demonstrate their goodwill to both the department and the city. Numerous diners, coffee shops, and other small restaurants have a similar policy, but in these the policy is maintained for the sake of **"police presence"** in the establishment. Many owners of diners and restaurants feel that if they can attract officers, it will extend a measure of security to their place of business. Unquestionably, it does; holdups are much less likely to occur at locations regularly visited by police, and if a crime or altercation happens nevertheless, police response is typically more rapid. Such deterrent presence is also "purchased" by other types of establishments—hardware stores, dry cleaners, small food shops, clothing outlets, liquor stores, and the like—generally by offering members of the police force goods and services at discount prices.

"Police presence": The almost continuous presence of police officers in a place of business for the crime deterrent effects if affords.

However, in some places the providing of meals, goods, and services at reduced rates or even at no cost is forced through implicit or direct coercion. In such instances, shopkeepers are reluctant to donate food or "gifts" of any sort to officers, yet they understand that it is expected of them. They comply out of fear—fear that the patrolman will "look the other way" when trouble occurs, and fear that the local precinct will search harder for violations of some kind on the business premises. For

Drugs corrupt both cops and robbers.
— FORMER MINNEAPOLIS POLICE CHIEF ANTHONY V. BOUZA

example, a Brooklyn, New York, liquor store owner reported the following incident to the author:

> Less than two weeks after I opened this place, two cops walk in and tell me they're from this sector. Then they start fingering some bottles of Scotch so I ask them if they need any help. They ask me if I give special discounts and I say no, everything is already marked down. With that they just give me a funny look and walk out of the store. I guess it made them mad, 'cause from then on I never got any cooperation from the police.
>
> Then comes Christmas time and I guess they figured they'd give me a second chance. One of the same two cops walks in and announces "I've come to say Merry Christmas." So I say Merry Christmas to him, and give him a calendar. Well that must have really ticked him, 'cause three days later they set me up for a bust. This kid walks in asking for a fifth of Canadian, and he looked like he was about twenty-two or so, so I don't ask him for his ID. And wouldn't ya know it! . . . as soon as I take the money and give him the bottle, the same two cops walk in and tell me the kid is under age. It turns out that he's only sixteen. I get stuck with a summons, a trip to court, a fine, a hearing before the state liquor authority, another fine, and the threat of a suspended license if it happens again. . . .
>
> So now they get their Christmas gifts, and Easter gifts, and Columbus Day gifts . . . and gifts and gifts and gifts.

Kickbacks

Police officers have numerous opportunities to direct individuals in stressful situations to persons who — for a profit — can assist them. And police can receive a fee for referring arrested suspects to bailbonds agents and defense attorneys, for placing accident victims in contact with physicians and lawyers who specialize in filing personal injury claims, for sending tow trucks and ambulances to accident scenes, and for arranging for the delivery of bodies to specific funeral homes.

Given the very nature of routine police patrol work, opportunities such as these are not uncommon, and the potential for small kickbacks on a regular basis is always present. However, some officers look upon kickbacks as a business enterprise and actively seek out new and more lucrative areas of endeavor. In Tampa, Florida, for example, one police officer made highly profitable use of his access to departmental files. The names of burglary victims were turned over to a dealer in home security systems, who would then apply high-pressure salesmanship to demonstrate the advantages of residential burglar alarms. The names of victims who lived in apartments were given to other sources in order to generate sales of locks and renter's insurance. Information about robbery, assault, and rape victims was directed to dealers who could provide weapons and instruction in self-defense. All combined, the kickbacks from these contacts, which were paid on a commission basis, amounted to many thousands of dollars each year.[12]

Items From a Detroit Police Blotter

—January: an officer is arrested for loitering in a suspected crack den with $2,615 in her pocket.

—March: an officer is accused of murder after allegedly strangling a suspect.

—April: two officers are charged with stealing $700 from an elderly street vendor outside a rock concert.

—June: a rookie cop, already suspended for cashing his partner's paycheck, kills his wife, her lover, and himself.

—July: four officers are charged with breaking into a suspected drug den looking for drugs, possibly for themselves.

SOURCE: *Newsweek*, September 5, 1988, p. 37.

Opportunistic Theft

Police are presented with numerous opportunities as well to appropriate unlawfully various items of value. Such "opportunistic theft" typically involves jewelry and other goods taken from the scene of a burglary or from a suspect; narcotics confiscated from drug users and dealers; merchandise found at the scene of a fire; funds taken during a gambling raid; money and personal property removed from the bodies of drunks, crime victims, and deceased persons; and confiscated weapons. For example:

- During the course of a search incident to an arrest for purse-snatching, the police officer found seventy-two diamond pinky rings in the pockets of the suspect — the proceeds of an earlier theft from a local diamond exchange. Only seventy rings were turned in as evidence.

- When detectives were dusting an apartment for fingerprints following a burglary, one of the investigators removed a man's gold watch that had been left behind. Placing it in his pocket, he commented: "They've got theft insurance."

- The "store" of a local receiver of stolen goods was raided by police, and the alleged contraband was confiscated. Prior to any full accounting of the "hot" property, three color television sets, a dozen transistor radios, and several musical instruments were removed and placed in an officer's private automobile. The stolen property was later distributed among the officers involved.

- In response to a call that a "suspicious and sickening stench" was emanating from a locked room in a skid row rooming house, two police officers discovered the bloated and decomposing body of a well-known neighborhood eccentric. He had apparently died a few days earlier from strangulation during an epileptic seizure. During a search of the deceased's room in an effort to locate personal papers that might identify his next of kin, the officers found some $18,000 in small bills. The two officers divided the money equally between themselves.[13]

Some examples of opportunistic theft

Planned Theft

Planned theft and robbery as a variety of police corruption refers to the direct involvement of police in predatory criminal activities. During the last two decades, either through complicity with criminals or as undertaken directly by police, it has occurred in Denver, Des Moines, Chicago, Nashville, New York, Philadelphia, Buffalo, Birmingham, Cleveland, New Orleans, Miami, and numerous other cities. A typical case involved a Greenville, South Carolina, police officer who was routinely stealing from establishments he was assigned to protect. The officer was found to be burglarizing homes and businesses along his patrol route regularly.[14] Similar examples appear throughout police literature.

One of the recent and more celebrated episodes of planned theft and robbery by police involved a group known as the "Miami River Cops" — a textbook case of police officers trading on the influence of their badges, uniforms, and patrol cars to stage bold drug rip-offs and intimidate drug dealers. In one incident (portrayed in a larger than life manner in a 1988 episode of television's "Miami Vice,") the officers had learned that a lobster boat tied to a pier in the Miami River contained a considerable amount of cocaine. They raided the boat and removed 323 pounds of the drug. Then they called their more law-abiding police colleagues who seized the boat and another 850 pounds of cocaine that was left aboard. The "River Cops" staged other raids as well, but were eventually arrested on various charges of robbery, theft, and conspiracy.[15]

Characteristically, however, planned theft and robbery by police officers, unlike some other forms or corruption is rarely tolerated by police departments. Although there might be passive support for such activity, as soon as knowledge of this type of enterprise becomes known to the public, even corrupt departments generally react in a forceful manner.[16]

Shakedowns

The "shakedown" racket

Shakedowns are forms of extortion in which police officers accept money from citizens in lieu of enforcing the law. The term *shakedown* has its roots in the nineteenth century British underworld. A "shakedown" was a temporary substitute for a bed, as was common in many an English prostitute's room. Hence, her quarters also became known as a shakedown. Commonplace in the underworld of the time was the practice of an extortion scheme that had several variations, usually involving the collective efforts of sneak thieves, prostitutes, and other types of criminals. In a typical situation, an attractively dressed female approached a country gentleman, explaining that she was a victim of circumstances and was thus forced for the first time in her life to accost a man. After naming a modest sum for her charms, he would accompany her to her room, bolting the door. While he engaged in sexual relations with the young woman, a wall panel would slide open from which a thief would enter, replace the money in the victim's pocket with paper, and silently exit. After the theft had taken place, a sound would be heard that the woman would claim to be her husband. The gentleman would quickly dress and hastily leave through a rear door, unaware that he had been robbed. It was from rackets such as this that most forms of extortion became known as shakedowns — appropriately named after the place where they occurred: the "shakedown," the prostitute's room.[17]

Police have been known to shake down tavern owners by threatening to enforce obscure liquor laws, and restaurant owners and shopkeepers by threatening to enforce health regulations and zoning violations. Perhaps most common, however, are shakedowns involving traffic violations. For example, the victim of one police shakedown reported the following story to the author:

> It was on the New Jersey turnpike on a Monday night, and it was dark and raining and I just couldn't see a damn thing — so I decide to drive off the highway and rest until things let up. All of a sudden I see the red lights of a squad car behind me. It seems that I was going the wrong way on an exit ramp. . . .
>
> Well, the trooper gives me this long story as to how dangerous my driving was and all that could have happened, but then tells me that a twenty could square things.

Protection

The protection of illegal activities by police has been known in this country for well over a century. Such protection usually involves illegal goods and services such as prostitution, gambling, narcotics, and pornography, and the resulting corruption is typically well organized. In Mayor Richard Daley's Chicago, such corruption was apparent throughout the police hierarchy, according to journalist Mike Royko.

> Some taverns paid him to stay open beyond the 2 A.M. closing hour. He was less expensive than a 4 A.M. license. Others paid him to assure that if a bartender

worked a customer over, the customer would be charged with assault. He didn't keep it all: the detectives on his shift got some, and the lieutenant in a little office in the back got more. And his collection was small change compared to what the captain's bag man picked up during the day.

The captain's bag man made the rounds of the bookies, the homosexual bars, the hotels and lounges that were headquarters for prostitution rings. That's where the real money was, but the captain didn't keep it all. He got some, but most of it went to the ward committeeman. That's why the captain was running the station: the ward committeeman had put him there because he trusted him to collect the payoffs and give an honest accounting and a fair split. If he didn't, the ward committeeman would call downtown to headquarters and have the captain transferred to a paper-shuffling job somewhere. Not that this was likely to happen: the captain knew what he was supposed to do, or the ward boss wouldn't have had him promoted through the ranks all the way to captain.[18]

Police corruption in the form of protection of illegal activities was apparently most widespread during the years prior to the investigation by the Knapp Commission of the early 1970s, in New York City. The Commission found that more than half of New York's almost 30,000 officers took part in corrupt practices during 1971, much of which involved protection rackets.[19] More recently, there have been numerous incidents of protection and other crimes associated with cocaine trafficking (see Exhibit 9.1).

Drug abuse by police officers is the New York City Police Department's No. 1 corruption hazard
— REPORT TO N.Y.P.D. COMMISSIONER BENJAMIN WARD, 1984

Case Fixing

As a form of corruption, case fixing has appeared at all levels of the criminal justice process and has involved not only police, but bailiffs, court personnel, members of juries, prosecutors, and judges. Fixing a case with a police officer, however, is the most direct, and often the least complicated and least expensive method. The most common form involves a bribe to an officer in exchange for not being arrested—a practice most typically initiated by pickpockets, prostitutes, gamblers, drug users, the parents of juvenile offenders, members of organized crime, and sometimes burglars. Case fixing can also take the form of an officer perjuring himself or herself on the witness stand, reducing the seriousness of a charge against an offender, or agreeing to drop an investigation prematurely by not pursuing leads that might produce evidence supporting a criminal charge.[20]

Traffic-ticket fixing is likely the most common form of case fixing, and often it does not involve any monetary payment.[21] In some jurisdictions, simply "knowing" someone on the police force is all that is needed to have a summons discharged, and in other instances a call to a police chief can be effective. There may also be long-standing complex arrangements. In Brooklyn, New York, a "protected" gambling establishment had no facilities for customer parking, forcing bettors to park illegally. After numerous complaints to the local police captain, an arrangement was structured:

Here in Bogotá, you can buy your way out of an arrest with a carton of Marlboro.
— AMERICAN DIPLOMAT, 1982

You see, there's always been pressure on the cops to enforce the traffic laws down here, so there's no way I could get them to stop "writing." Now, for a $25 ticket for double parking, the customer gives me $5. At the end of the day the money and a list of the ticket numbers goes over to the desk sergeant. As I understand things, 50 percent goes to the captain, 20 percent to the sergeant, and the rest goes to someone downtown . . . We're talking sometimes to about as many as eighty to ninety tickets a week.[22]

● EXHIBIT 9.1 ●

Sidelights on Criminal Matters
Cocaine Trafficking and Police Corruption

The corrupting power of drug money is one of the obvious reasons why this number one crime problem must be conquered.

— FORMER FBI DIRECTOR WILLIAM H. WEBSTER

Drug abuse is generally understood in terms of a limited number of issues. First, it is a public health problem. Illicit drugs, whether narcotics, stimulants, depressants, or hallucinogens, have been found to cause a range of physical and psychosocial complications. Drug abuse can place at risk the productivity of a potentially large segment of the population. Second, there is the link between drug abuse and the crime rate. The connection between drug use and street crime has been well documented, for the drug-taking and drug-seeking activities of narcotics addicts and other types of drug users indeed affect the rates of burglaries, larcenies, and robberies. Further, the drug trafficking and distribution marketplace has increased the profits and power of criminal syndicates,

and violent crime has come to be closely associated with the competition that seems to exist at all levels of the drug distribution network.

Yet drug use and trafficking have a larger effect on the social, economic, and political organization and functioning of a nation or community. In South America, for example, cocaine trafficking has exacerbated the effects of inflation, altered economic planning, affected property values and inflated wages, and swung government power toward wealthy drug dealers. In *all* nations where drug use and trafficking are commonplace, the corruption of individuals is widespread, particularly of those charged with enforcement of the drug laws.

For as long as drug enforcement has been a part of American policing, there has been drug-related corruption. Some police officers have accepted bribes in lieu of enforcing the drug laws; others have directly participated in the actual trafficking of illegal substances. Yet

the problem was rarely widespread and never endemic to any given police force. All of this seemed to change, however, with the arrival of the cocaine era of the 1980s.

The high price of cocaine, and the billions of dollars accumulated by cocaine traffickers, have brought about the wholesale corruption of law enforcement in some communities. In New York City and other urban areas, the number of police officers charged with selling drugs or involved with drug-related graft and extortion markedly increased during the 1980s. In Miami and other parts of South Florida, cocaine-related corruption became so commonplace that by the mid-1980s reports of new scandals no longer received extensive media coverage. In Key West, the involvement of police officers and administrators in cocaine trafficking became so enduring and pervasive that in 1985 federal prosecutors accused that city's entire police department of being a "continuing criminal enterprise." Even the

And more recently, a Dade County, Florida, pawn shop owner reported a very similar arrangement:

> You see, we has no place to put the cars of the folks who do business here. So when the police ticket them, I take the tickets and get to the officers later and make an arrangement.[23]

Private Security

Corruption in the form of private security involves providing more police protection or presence than is required by standard operating

FBI became tarnished by the cocaine trade when one of its agents accepted almost $1 million in bribes and skimmed forty-two kilos from a load of cocaine he helped to seize.

Most recently, an alliance between drug enforcement officers in the Los Angeles Police Department and the Los Angeles County Sheriff's Department made national headlines in 1991 for the special activities that were organized to target local cocaine dealers. It would appear that the officers were beating suspects, falsifying search warrants, "flaking" suspects (planting cocaine on alleged dealers), stealing cash and valuables from homes during drug raids, filing false police reports, and maintaining a coordinated "conspiracy of silence."

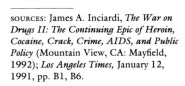

SOURCES: James A. Inciardi, *The War on Drugs II: The Continuing Epic of Heroin, Cocaine, Crack, Crime, AIDS, and Public Policy* (Mountain View, CA: Mayfield, 1992); *Los Angeles Times,* January 12, 1991, pp. B1, B6.

Confiscated cash, cocaine, and weapons in a corruption case

procedures.[24] Examples might include checking the security of private premises more frequently and intensively than is usual, escorting businesspeople to make bank deposits, or providing more visible police presence in stores or establishments in order to keep out undesirables. In such instances, payoffs are less likely to be made in cash but more typically in goods, services, and favors.

Some officers hire themselves out as bodyguards. A Miami Beach officer who weighed more than 250 pounds and who was proficient with weapons, in the martial arts, and in stunt driving often placed himself at the disposal of cocaine dealers who were carrying large amounts of cash and drugs. He commented to a professional informant:

•   EXHIBIT 9.2   •

Private Employment of Public Police

For much of their history, police officers worked long tours without additional pay, and supplementary employment was prohibited. With the growth of police brotherhoods and unions, the length of tours was reduced to the conventional three shifts of eight hours each, the work week was reduced to five tours, and extra pay was added for any additional hours (overtime). Shorter tours and a reduced workweek created the possibility for supplementary earnings from secondary employment. Many departments refused to permit it, however, largely on the grounds that an officer was obliged at all times to enforce the law and to be available for duty when summoned.

Despite prohibitions against secondary employment, a sizable minority of police officers began in the 1930s to take a second job —a practice commonly known as "moonlighting." Many police departments tolerated moonlighting if there was no conflict of interest for the officer or the police department. Specifically, this meant that secondary employment was tacitly permitted if it involved manual or other forms of work altogether unrelated to protective services or to public morals. Suspension and possible discharge awaited the moonlighter caught violating these informal conventions.

Gradually, police officials recognized that they had no

means to control secondary employment other than to sanction violators. Sanctioning violators was difficult not only because it was hard to detect who was moonlighting, but also because there was growing resistance to sanctioning violators. Consequently, departments moved to

control rather than prohibit outside employment by requiring a work permit. In permitting employment, police officials were able to specify what kinds of outside employment were acceptable to the department and to approve work on a specific job for a specific employee.

An off-duty St. Petersburg, Florida, police officer stops traffic for a private yacht being transported by truck. Officers on private duty are allowed to use their uniforms, badges, guns, and sometimes even their patrol cars.

I'm as big as any fullback on the Dolphins, and they know I hit like one. Besides, they know I'm a cop . . . so they know it's best to stand clear.[25]

This should not suggest, however, that all policing in the private sector by public police is corrupt. On the contrary, "extra-duty policing," as it has come to be known, is common in many parts of the nation (see Exhibit 9.2).

The work permit was originally based on the idea that a police officer could hold a second job provided it was a regular part-time civilian job with the same employer who was responsible for supervising and paying the employee. The police department simply controlled the kind of employment to ensure there was no conflict of interest for the officer holding that position. There was a clear presumption that the officer would not be called on to enforce the law in his work.

At the same time, demand arose for police service and security. This demand was met by the growth of private security businesses. But private security agencies lacked the essential police powers to carry out the duties demanded by private interests, such as controlling crowds. Other public authorities found it in their best interest to secure police service from the public police rather than to employ their own police or private security agents. Among the public and quasi-public authorities demanding police service were public housing authorities, civic and sports centers, and public utilities. Both public and private corporations and agencies sought such service. Although many police departments regularly provided this service, over time they were less able to meet this demand by assignment from their regular police force because the growth of police personnel lagged behind the growth in demand for regular police services. The large untapped reserve workforce available for meeting this sporadic and variable demand was the off-duty police employee with sworn authority. Supply and demand merged when public police departments permitted officers to work on permit as off-duty police officers with full police authority.

The demand for extra-duty uniformed police officers varies widely from city to city — as does their supply. In most larger municipal police departments, there are several conditions that warrant demand for uniformed officers.

- **Traffic control and pedestrian safety** — Road construction and repair, access to utility lines under public thoroughfares, and construction sites all pose problems of control of traffic and pedestrian movement. In some states, one or more officers must be stationed at such sites. Traffic control also may be required for funerals, business openings or promotions, and other private events.

- **Crowd control** — Major private events that attract large paid audiences or public ones sponsored by nonprofit organizations pose problems of crowd control. Some, such as rock concerts and jazz festivals, may require large numbers of officers to prevent disorder as well as to ensure the orderly behavior of the crowd. Others, such as local religious or neighborhood festivals, ordinarily require far fewer officers. County and municipal sports arenas, concert halls, and public and private school events likewise demand these services.

- **Private security and protection of life and property** — Many private businesses as well as public authorities demand uniformed officers as a visible preventive or deterrent to violations of law. They may perform duties that are commonly performed by private security officers but with the additional expectation that they will enforce the law by arrest, if necessary.

- **Routine law enforcement for public authorities** — in large cities, the scale of public authorities such as housing, airport, and parks usually leads to their employing a separate enforcement staff with full police powers. But in smaller municipalities such police service may be obtained on a contract basis with the city police department for extra-duty employees.

SOURCE: Albert J. Reiss, Jr., *Private Employment of Public Police* (Washington, D.C.: National Institute of Justice, 1988).

Patronage

Patronage can occur in a variety of ways, all of which involve the use of one's official position to influence decision making. Historically, patronage has meant making governmental appointments so as to increase one's political strength, and it has always been a part of political life in one form or another. Political patronage has been comically illustrated by journalist and author William Safire with a note allegedly written by New York political boss William Marcy Tweed to Pennsylvania politician Matthew Quay during the 1870s:

> Dear Tit:
>   The bearer understands addition, division, and silence.
> Appoint him!
>
> > Your friend,
> > Bill[26]

Although there may be ethical issues surrounding the practice of political patronage, it is not necessarily illegal in all of its forms. However, patronage clearly becomes corruption when payments are made for political favors. Within the ranks of policing, corruption by patronage can occur through the granting of promotions and transfers for a fee. Arranging access to confidential department records of agreeing to alter such records may also be construed as patronage. In addition, influencing department recommendations regarding the granting of licenses is patronage.

Patronage can emerge in other ways as well. Within a police department itself, for example, inside people have been payed to falsify attendance records, influence the choice of vacations and days off, report officers as on duty when they are not, and provide passing grades in training programs and promotion exams.

EXPLANATIONS OF POLICE CORRUPTION

A number of hypotheses as to why police corruption occurs have been offered. The three most common interpretations are that police corruption is caused by society at large, by influences within police departments, or by a disposition towards corruption in individuals who become police.[27]

The Society-at-Large Explanation

The society-at-large explanation comes from the late O. W. Wilson, based on his observations and experiences as Chicago's Superintendent of Police. As Wilson put it:

> This force was corrupted by the citizens of Chicago. . . . It has been customary to give doormen, chauffeurs, maids, cooks and delivery men little gifts and gratuities. . . . It is felt that the level of service depends on these gratuities.[28]

Such practices, in turn, lead to small bribes, such as accepting money in lieu of enforcing traffic laws on minor city ordinances. Accepting small payoffs from drivers and business operators then extended to more serious crimes. Wilson called this progression the *slippery slope hypotheses* — that corruption begins with apparently harmless and well-intentioned practices and leads, eventually — in individual police officers or in departments as a whole — to all manner of crimes for profit.

The Structural Explanation

In his well-known *Behind the Shield,* the late Arthur Niederhoffer made the following comment:

Actual policemen seem to accept graft for other reasons than avarice. Often the first transgression is inadvertent. Or, they may be gradually indoctrinated by older policemen. Step by step they progress from a small peccadillo [trifling sin] to outright shakedown and felony.[29]

Going further, this step by step progress results from the contradictory sets of norms that police officers see both in the world at large and in their own departments. Officers, particularly those in large cities, are exposed to a steady diet of wrongdoing. They discover, furthermore, that dishonesty and corruption are not limited to those the community views as "criminals," but also to individuals of "good reputation"— including fellow officers with whom they must establish some mutual trust and reliance. In time, they develop a cynical attitude in which they view corruption as a game in which every person is out to get a share.[30]

The Rotten-Apple Explanation

The "bad" or rotten-apple view is perhaps the most popular explanation of police corruption. It suggests that there are a few bad officers in an otherwise honest department, who are operating on their own. Corruption is the result of the moral failure of just a few officers, but spreads, for after all, as the old proverb suggests, "one rotten apple spoils the rest of the barrel."

In retrospect, there is likely no *single* explanation that accounts for all police corruption. The three discussed here are the principle views, and likely work in conjunction with one another. The "rotten-apple" explanation, although the most popular, is also the most criticized, for it fails to explain why individual officers become corrupt. Or more specifically:

If corruption is to be explained in terms of a few "bad" people, then some departments attracted a disproportionately high number of rotten apples over long periods of time.[31]

Ten or twenty years ago, when you talked about a bribe, it was a $20 bill in a matchbook. Today, you have people in the drug culture saying, "There's ten grand in the bag, and it's yours if you let me go."
—SHELDON GREENBERG, POLICE EXECUTIVE RESEARCH FORUM, 1990

POLICE VIOLENCE

Officer, would you be terribly upset if your suspect here should accidentally get himself a broken jaw?
—A NEW YORK DETECTIVE, 1964

He called me a racist pig! So I hit him.
—A MIAMI POLICE OFFICER, 1976

Always carry a throwaway. *
—AN OAKLAND PLAINCLOTHES OFFICER, 1981

Police violence in the form of brutality, unwarranted deadly force, and other mistreatment of citizens is not uncommon in American history. Commentaries documenting the growth and development of both the urban metropolis and the rural frontier testify amply to the unwarranted

Police violence in U.S. history

Every situation I go through I assume right away I'm going to be outgunned.
—A CLEVELAND POLICE OFFICER, 1990

---

* A *throwaway* is generally an unregistered, untraceable pistol (or sometimes a knife) carried by some police officers. In the event of an accidental or unwarranted shooting of a citizen by an officer, the throwaway is placed on or in the vicinity of the body of the victim. The police officer then claims that the shooting was in self-defense.

use of force throughout the ranks of policing. Law enforcement records in the trans-Mississippi West provide numerous examples of the "shoot first and ask questions later" philosophy of many American lawmen. Moreover, the brutal and sadistic applications of the policeman's nightstick to demonstrate that "might makes right" appears often in the histories of urban police systems.

In 1903, New York City magistrate and former police commissioner Frank Moss commented:

> For three years, there has been through the courts and the streets a dreary procession of citizens with broken hands and bruised bodies against few of whom was violence needed to effect an arrest. Many of them had done nothing to deserve an arrest. In a majority of such cases, no complaint was made. If the victim complains, his charge is generally dismissed. The police are practically above the law.[32]

Moss was expressing his frustrations as both a member of the bench and a police reformer about a problem that was widespread during his time, but which received little attention. And the ambivalence over police violence has continued throughout the better part of the twentieth century.

It was not until the 1960s that the issue of police misconduct in the forms of brutality and deadly force assumed any public and political urgency, and this can be attributed to two phenomena. The first was the "criminal law revolution" carried on by the Supreme Court under the leadership of Chief Justice Earl Warren. The second was the findings of the Kerner Commission — the National Advisory Commission on Civil Disorders.

Brown v. *Mississippi*

Brown v. *Mississippi* in 1936 established the Court's position on brutality, at least as far as coerced confessions were concerned.[33] It was the first time a state conviction was overturned because it had been obtained by using a confession extracted by torture. But the importance of *Brown* remained unnoticed for twenty-five years, until the High Court finally developed some hard and fast rules concerning the methods of interrogation of suspects while in police custody. *Rogers* v. *Richmond* in

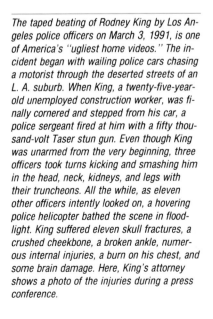

The taped beating of Rodney King by Los Angeles police officers on March 3, 1991, is one of America's "ugliest home videos." The incident began with wailing police cars chasing a motorist through the deserted streets of an L. A. suburb. When King, a twenty-five-year-old unemployed construction worker, was finally cornered and stepped from his car, a police sergeant fired at him with a fifty thousand-volt Taser stun gun. Even though King was unarmed from the very beginning, three officers took turns kicking and smashing him in the head, neck, kidneys, and legs with their truncheons. All the while, as eleven other officers intently looked on, a hovering police helicopter bathed the scene in floodlight. King suffered eleven skull fractures, a crushed cheekbone, a broken ankle, numerous internal injuries, a burn on his chest, and some brain damage. Here, King's attorney shows a photo of the injuries during a press conference.

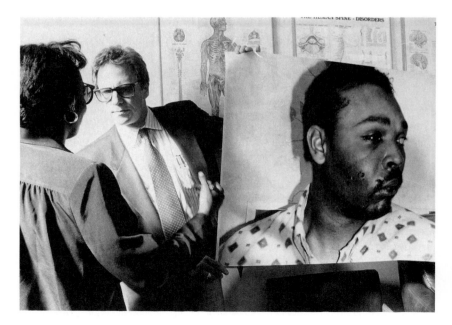

1961, *Greenwald* v. *Wisconsin*, *Georgia* v. *Sims* and *Florida* v. *Brooks* in 1968 asserted that the Fourteenth Amendment bars confessions when "the methods used to extract them offend the underlying principle in the enforcement of our criminal law," especially those which reflect "shocking displays of barbarism."[34]

While the Supreme Court examined police violence within the context of the brutality of squad room interrogations, the Kerner Commission targeted the wider issue of street justice in all of its varied and callous forms. Known more formally as the National Advisory Commission on Civil Disorders, its purpose was to investigate the causes of the rioting and destruction that occurred in Detroit, Los Angeles, Newark, New York, and twenty other urban areas during the summer of 1967. The commission concluded that there were numerous causes but ranked as the primary stimuli police practices in patrolling urban ghettos. Aggressive preventive patrol, combined with police misconduct in the forms of brutality, unwarranted use of deadly force, harassment, verbal abuse, and discourtesy were sources of aggravation among blacks, and complaints of such practices were found in all of the locations studied.[35]

> The Kerner Commission investigated the causes of urban violence that took place in the summer of 1967.

Brutality

Although the Supreme Court and the Kerner Commission were significant in giving greater attention and public visibility to police violence during the 1960s, the subject had long since been the focus of rigorous study.

In 1949, for example, sociologist William A. Westley surveyed police officers in Gary Indiana, asking the question: "When do you think a policeman is justified in roughing a man up?"[36] Seventy-four officers responded, and the major reasons given covered a variety of areas.*

> *If his honor asks how come the suspect has his jaw wired and a few broken teeth, tell him the asshole tripped and fell in a sewer.*
> — BOSTON POLICE OFFICER, 1985

- Disrespect for police   27%
- When it is impossible to avoid   17%
- To obtain information   14%
- To make an arrest   6%
- For the hardened criminal   5%
- When you know the person is guilty   2%
- For sex criminals   2%

Systematic observations in Boston, Chicago, and Washington, D.C., during 1966 reflected similar patterns.[37] National attention has focused more recently on allegations of police brutality in numerous cities across the nation.[38] Among the more conspicuous of these have been Houston and San Antonio, where there were isolated incidents of torturing prisoners, and New York, where it was alleged in 1985 that officers in one precinct had systematically assaulted, beaten, and burned a number of suspects.[39] Then in 1991 there was the videotaped assault of Rodney King by L.A.P.D. officers, noted at the beginning of this chapter.[40]

In the past, **police brutality** was considered to be a practice limited only to those few sadistic officers who were seen as "bad apples." However, more recent commentaries suggest that police violence is the result

> **Police brutality:** The unlawful use of physical force by officers in the performance of their duties.

---

* These percentages must be viewed with some caution. Most of the officers responded "never" to the question asked, and of the balance, many gave multiple answers. Thus, although the percentages total to seventy-three, considerably fewer officers felt that roughing someone up was justified.

The "watchman's style" of policing may contribute to police brutality.

There's a great potential for an officer abusing steroids to physically mistreat people.
— RICHARD WITT, POLICE CHIEF, HOLLYWOOD, FLORIDA

of norms shared throughout a police department, and that it is best understood as an unfortunate consequence of the police role. Police are given the unrestricted right to use force in situations where their evaluation of the circumstances demands it. Yet this mandate has never been precisely defined or limited. Moreover, some officers show characteristics of the police "working personality": the feeling of constant pressure to perform, along with elements of authoritarianism, suspicion, racism, hostility, insecurity, and cynicism. Police norms that emphasize solidarity and secrecy allow a structure in which incidents of brutality and other misconduct will not draw the condemnation of fellow officers.

Also contributing to the existence of police brutality is the type of policing described by political scientist James Q. Wilson as the "watchman's style."[41] Watch-style departments tend to be located in the older American cities, where there are high concentrations of poor and minority citizens combined with machine politics. In such cities, police officers act primarily as reluctant maintainers of order. They ignore many minor problems — those involving the poor, gambling, traffic violations, misdemeanors, juvenile rowdiness, and domestic disputes. Officers act tough in serious situations, but in most others they often follow the path of least resistance, which is generally to render curbstone justice. Furthermore, many officers tend to be poorly trained, and the departments rarely meet even the most minimum standards for planning, research, and community relations. The consequence of this watch style is undefined boundaries and expectations of police behavior that become manifested in the form of organized corruption discriminatory arrests, and unnecessary police violence.

Going beyond the "working personality" and the "watchman's style" as factors contributing to unnecessary police violence, sociologist Richard J. Lundman has focused on three additional issues related to violence that apply to most police organizations:

1. police perceptions that citizen acceptance of police authority is fundamental to effective policing
2. police judgments of the "social value" of certain citizens
3. the conservative nature of police decision making[42]

Police Authority Because authority is both central and essential to the police roles of enforcing the law and keeping the peace, persons who question or resist that authority represent a challenge to officers, detectives, and the organizations they represent. Challenges are not taken lightly; they are seen as barriers to effective policing. Often police use intense verbal coercion to establish their authority quickly. Should that fail, some use physical force to elicit compliance from citizens. A Baltimore, Maryland, patrol officer recalled the following incident:

> I pulled this kid over one Sunday night for a defective tail light and I asked him for his license and registration. When he started making excuses I told him very clearly: "Look kid, it's late, you're a hazard to other motorists, and I don't want any of your shit!" When he continued to whine about getting a ticket I grabbed him by the jaw and told him that he'd either quit stalling or get his ass kicked from here to kingdom come.[43]

Judgments of Social Value In the view of many law enforcement officers, certain citizens—drunks, juvenile gang members, homosexuals, sex offenders, drug users, hardened criminals—have little to contribute to society. Many officers do not consider such people worth protecting, or they protect them using different norms than those that guide their policing of other citizens. Some police even single these people out for physical abuse. A Delaware state police officer put it this way: "So what if we knocked him around a little; he was nothing but a dirty junkie."[44]

Police Decision Making Since police work requires officers to make quick decisions, often on the basis of only fragmentary information, both officers and their superiors tend to defend the use of violence as a means of rapid problem resolution. As Richard J. Lundman has pointed out, many members of the criminal justice system and the public at large also hold this view.[45] He cites the example of *Chicago Daily News* journalist John O. Linstead, who was assaulted by police officers during the 1968 Chicago Democratic convention. Linstead observed police beating three bystanders and intervened in the situation by shouting obscenities at the officers. They turned on him. The officers were charged with the assault, and the evidence against them was overpowering. But the jury returned a verdict of not guilty, and the judge congratulated them with the following comments:

> The language that Mr. Linstead used . . . was vile and degrading to the officers. He charged some of the officers with committing incest with their mothers in the lowest gutter language, which I suggest would be provoking in such a manner that any red-blooded American would flare up.[46]

Deadly Force

In common law, police were authorized to use deadly force as a last resort to apprehend a fleeing felon. This common law rule dates back to the Middle Ages, when all felonies were punishable by death, and thus the killing of the felon resulted in no greater consequence than that authorized for the punishment of the offense. This "shoot to kill" doctrine based on common law principles persists in one form or another in many jurisdictions throughout the United States, for there are few operational guidelines in the use of deadly force by police. The *Code of Alabama* illustrates this point: "An officer may use reasonable force to

Writing on the Wall

Two years before the videotaped beating of Rodney King, television viewers were shocked by footage of a white patrolman in Long Beach, Calif., apparently ramming a black man's head through a plate-glass window. The victim was Don Carlos Jackson, who has devoted himself to exposing police racism since he himself retired from the police force of Hawthorne, Calif., in 1989.

Jackson has assembled a collection of bigoted materials he has found in police departments. Among them: an "Official Running Nigger Target," depicting a grossly caricatured nude black male, posted in a station house in Glendale, Calif.; and a memorandum he found in Los Angeles reading, "Effective immediately, Negroes are no longer to be called 'niggers' or 'jigs'—but seagulls. they cruise all night, squawk all day, s____ on everybody. And are protected by the Federal Government."

Jackson argues that for many officers, "the definition of a criminal suspect is almost synonymous with a black male face." Most departments have rules forbidding the display of racist materials. All too often those regulations are ignored.

SOURCE: *Time*, April 1, 1991.

When police officers fire their guns, the immediate consequences of their decisions are realized at the rate of 750 feet per second.
—James J. Fyfe, 1988

Tennessee v. Garner: Deadly force against a fleeing felon is proper only when it is necessary to prevent the escape *and* when there is probably cause to believe that the suspect poses a significant threat to the officers or others.

Police work on inner-city streets is a domestic Vietnam, a dangerous no-win struggle fought by confused, misdirected and unappreciated troops.
— U.S. News and World Report, December 3, 1990

At 1:59 on the morning of December 17, 1979, a lone black man was said to have crashed his motorcycle while dodging Miami police at speeds up to one hundred miles per hour. He supposedly battled with police officers, who subdued him with nightsticks. He died four days later of head injuries. The victim was Arthur McDuffie, a thirty-three-year-old ex-Marine and insurance salesman. Upon investigation of the incident, it was learned that McDuffie was driving with a suspended license and had tried to elude police. The officers decided to "teach him a lesson." Four white officers were indicted for manslaughter, but when they were acquitted by an all-white jury, angry blacks took to the streets. After three days of racial fury, fifteen people were dead and Miami's financial toll exceeded some $200 million. As shown here, National Guardsmen were brought in during the "McDuffie riot" to restore order. In the aftermath of the riot, bumper stickers read: "VISIT MIAMI. IT'S A RIOT."

arrest, but is without privilege to use more force than is necessary to accomplish the arrest."[47]

The lack of specificity in such codes, and in similar case and statutory laws, demonstrates that the decision to use deadly force for making an arrest largely remains a matter of discretion. All jurisdictions permit officers to use lethal force in defense of themselves, and most allow firing on a fleeing felon. Yet prior to *Tennessee v. Garner*[48] in 1985, the conditions under which such force could be applied to a fleeing felon were variable. Some jurisdictions required the suspect to be a "known" felon; others required that the officer be a witness to the felony; and still others permitted deadly force when the officer had a "reasonable belief" that the fleeing individual committed the felony in question. In *Garner,* the Supreme Court held that deadly force against a fleeing felon was proper *only* when it was necessary to prevent the escape *and* if there was probable cause to believe that the suspect posed a significant threat of death or serious physical injury to the officer or others.

When it comes to explaining the use of force, both lethal and non-lethal, James J. Fyfe points out that many discussions of the topic fail to distinguish between police violence that is clearly extralegal and abusive, and violence that is the unnecessary result of police incompetence.[49] He argues that such a distinction is important because the causes and motivations for the two vary greatly. Extralegal violence involves the willful and wrongful use of force by officers who knowingly exceed the bounds of their office. Unnecessary violence, by contrast, and including *deadly force,* occurs when well-meaning officers prove incapable of dealing with the situations they encounter without needless or too hasty resort to force. An example of this is what Fyfe refers to as the "split-second syndrome" (see Exhibit 9.3).

Although the number of people killed each year by "police intervention" is relatively small, there is a widespread perception that blacks are singled out as victims. More importantly, however, a number of studies have demonstrated that minority group members are statistically over-represented among the victims in police killings.[50] But an explanation of the phenomenon is less clear. Radical sociologist Paul Takagi states that "police have one trigger finger for whites and another for blacks," suggesting that police are engaged in a form of genocide against minority

groups.[51] This, however, seems to be a naive oversimplification of a very complex issue, for many factors are operating simultaneously. Another explanation is that communities get the number of killings by police that they deserve.[52] Researchers Richard Kania and Wade Mackey found that police killings are statistically associated with violent crimes in a community, and they argue that "the police officer is reacting to the community as he perceives it." A third view is the "bad apple" theory, which puts the blame on a few uncontrollable police officers.[53]

In all likelihood, however, the reasons for the disproportionate number of minority group members killed by police involve all of these explanations. In addition, the most recent analysis of the police use of deadly force suggests that its frequency is heavily influenced by individual departmental policies on the use of force, combined with the fact that blacks and other minorities tend to be overrepresented in the most violent and criminogenic neighborhoods.[54]

CONTROLLING POLICE MISCONDUCT

Without question, policing is rich in opportunities for corruption, brutality, the abuse of discretionary powers, the violation of citizens' rights, and other forms of misconduct. Furthermore, "policing the police" is difficult, for a variety of reasons. Corruption generally occurs in the most covert of circumstances and involves a willingness and cooperation on the part of many citizens. In addition, the victims of the misconduct —of the brutality, abuse of discretionary powers, and violations of due-process rights — are often reluctant, prevented, or otherwise indisposed to making the misconduct fully public. Further, police operations are in many ways invisible to disciplinary mechanisms, since officers operate alone or in small teams — beyond the observation of departmental supervisors. Finally, the "legitimation" at the administrative levels of the internal policing of certain abusive practices, combined with the elements of secrecy and solidarity that are characteristic of all police organizations, inhibit many police agencies from making instances or misconduct a matter of public record.

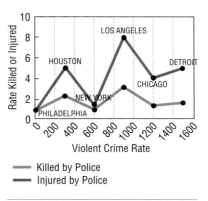

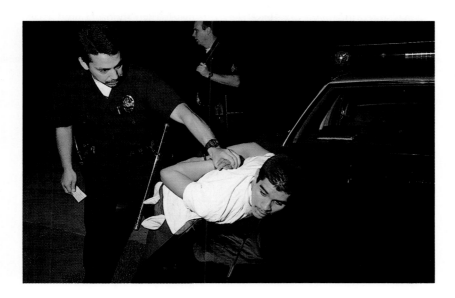

Violent Crime and Police Use of Force
SOURCE: Police Foundation

● EXHIBIT 9.3 ●

The Split-Second Syndrome
by James J. Fyfe

It is difficult to define the factors that led well-meaning officials to make the bad decisions just reviewed, but it appears that they are reflections of what might be called a "split-second syndrome" that affects police decision-making in crises. This syndrome serves both to inhibit the development of greater police diagnostic expertise and to provide after-the-fact justification for unnecessary police violence. It also serves as a guide to many of the equally unfortunate low-visibility decisions made by individual police officers every day.

The split-second syndrome is based on several assumptions. First, it assumes that, since no two police problems are precisely alike, there are no principles that may be applied to the diagnosis of specific situations. Thus, no more can be asked of officers than that they respond as quickly as possible to problems, devising the best solutions they can on the spur of the moment. This, of course, places an extraordinary burden upon officers, who must make life-or-death decisions under the most stressful and time-constrained conditions.

Second, because of these stresses and time constraints, a high percentage of inappropriate decisions should be expected, but any subsequent criticism of officers' decisions — especially by those outside the police, who can have no real appreciation of the burdens upon officers — is an unwarranted attempt to be wise after the event. Thus, if we are to maintain a police service whose members are decisive in the crises to which we summon them, we had best learn to live with the consequences of the decisions we ask them to make. If we do not, we risk damaging police morale and generating a police service whose members are reluctant to intervene on our behalf.

Finally, the split-second syndrome holds that assessments of the justifiability of police conduct are most appropriately made on the exclusive basis of the perceived exigencies of the moment when a decision had to be taken. So long as a citizen has, intentionally or otherwise, provoked the police at that instant, he, rather than the police, should be viewed as the cause of any resulting injuries or damage, no matter how excessive the police reaction and no matter how directly police decisions molded the situation that caused those injuries or damages.

Thus, should police receive a report of an armed robbery in a crowded supermarket, they should be granted great leeway in their manner of response, because no two armed-robbery calls are precisely alike. If, in the course of responding, they decide that, to prevent the robber from escaping, the best course of action is to confront him immediately in the midst of a crowd of shoppers, they should not be told they should have acted otherwise. When they do challenge the alleged robber and he suddenly reacts to their calls from behind by turning on them with a shiny object in his hand, the only issue to be decided by those who subsequently review police actions is whether, at that instant, the suspect's actions were sufficiently provocative to justify their shooting him. That is so regardless of how the prior

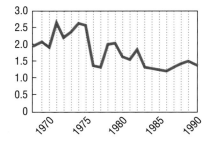

People Killed by Police Officers in the U.S., Per Million People

SOURCES: F.B.I. Uniform Crime Reports

This is not to say, however, that police abuses cannot be brought under greater control. There are many mechanisms that can affect police behavior for the better, including the legislature, the community, and the police system itself.

Legislative Control

Although the Civil Rights Act of 1964, was a decision of Congress, it is actually implemented by the courts; as such it is not a direct legislative control over police behavior. However, state and local legislative bodies can have a specific impact on the conduct of law enforcement through a reevaluation of certain laws that create the potential for police violations and corruption.

actions of the police may have contributed to their peril; regardless of how predictable it was that the suspect would be alarmed and would turn toward the police when they shouted to him; regardless of how many innocent bystanders were hit by bullets; and regardless of whether the reported armed robber was in fact an unhappy customer who, with pen in hand to complete a check for his purchase, had been engaged in a loud argument with a clerk during which he had said that the store's prices were "robbery."

The underpinning of the split-second syndrome, in short, is the assumption that the sole basis on which any use of force by the police needs to be justified is the officers' perceptions of the circumstances prevailing at the instant when they decide to apply force. The officers involved in the incident described above did, of course, possess much information that would lead them to believe that the subject of their call was a robber. When he turned on them, they were entitled, in the heat of the moment, to believe that their

lives were in imminent danger. When they made the split-second decision to pull the trigger, they were also entitled to believe that no less drastic action would adequately protect their lives, so they were fully justified in shooting. Under the split-second syndrome, this shooting was a legitimate use of force under provocation.

But such an analysis lends approval to unnecessary violence, and to failure of the police to meet their highest obligation: the protection of life. Split-second analysis of police action focuses attention on diagnoses and decisions made by the police during one frame of an incident that began when the police became aware that they were likely to confront a violent person or situation. It ignores what went before. As the successful application of hostage techniques illustrates, it also ignores the fact that there are general principles that may be applied by officers to a variety of highly predictable, potentially violent situations.

It requires no great diagnostic ability to determine that the

officers involved made a significant contribution to the bloody finale of the incident described above. Officers who respond to reports of robberies by charging through the front door and confronting suspects from exposed positions are almost certain to find themselves in great danger, real or perceived, and to face split-second decisions involving their lives, the lives of suspects and the lives of bystanders. Thus, instead of asking whether an officer ultimately had to shoot or fight his way out of perilous circumstances, we are better advised to ask whether it was not possible for him to have approached the situation in a way that reduced the risk of bloodshed and increased the chances of a successful and non-violent conclusion.

Reprinted from James J. Fyfe, "The Split-Second Syndrome and Other Determinants of Police Violence," in Anne Campbell and John Gibbs (eds.), *Violent Transactions* (New York: Basil Blackwell), 1986.

Throughout the history of the United States, criminal justice has been faced with the problem of overcriminalization due to the legislation of morality and the overregulation of civilian conduct. The laws that impose restrictions on alcohol consumption, drug use, prostitution, gambling, and other "victimless" crimes, combined with the numerous public health and other regulations over certain business enterprises, are typically the areas in which police corruption occurs. Thus, if legislatures are to control police conduct, one could argue that they might begin by decriminalizing these victimless crimes. That anything will be done in this area seems unlikely, however. The continued existence of many of the victimless crimes that generate the potential for corruption is the result of legislative unwillingness to repeal them for fear of committing political suicide. Nevertheless, a few changes have

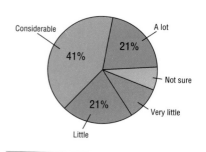

Nationwide, How Much Police Brutality Do You Think Exists Against Minorities?
SOURCE: *Newsweek* Poll of 3/14–16/91

The Public Views the Police

TOTAL		WHITES	BLACKS
	CONFIDENCE		
55%	Say they have a great deal or quite a lot of confidence in the local police	59%	30%
44	Say they have very little or just some confidence	39	70
	BRUTALITY		
	Say when they hear charges of police brutality they are . . .		
67	. . . likely to think charges are justified	65	82
24	. . . not likely to think they are justified	27	11
27	Say they think the police in their own neighborhood rough up people unnecessarily when arresting them or afterwards	25	42
63	Say the police in their own neighborhood don't rough people up unnecessarily	66	47
	EQUAL TREATMENT OF RACES		
	Say the police in big cities . . .		
51	. . . are tougher on blacks than on whites	48	67
34	. . . treat blacks and whites the same	36	15
	Say the police in their own community . . .		
19	. . . are tougher on blacks than on whites	16	42
66	. . . treat blacks and whites the same	69	45

New York Times/CBS News Poll of April 1–3, 1991.

occurred. Gambling laws have been relaxed through the establishment of state-run lotteries and off-track betting; prostitution has been legalized in one jurisdiction and reduced to a minor violation in others; and a number of the unreasonable restriction placed on business owners, landlords, and the building construction industry have been eliminated. However, a major portion of police corruption is an outgrowth of the laws controlling the possession of cocaine, crack, heroin, and numerous other drugs, and it is unlikely these will be legalized in any great hurry, if ever.[54]

By contrast, Section 1983 of the Civil Rights Act of 1871 authorizes suits for damages for violations of one's constitutional rights. By invoking Section 1983, an individual can hold a law enforcement agency or municipality liable for an incident of police misconduct. (For a closer look at such suits, see Exhibit 9.4.)

Civilian Review Boards

The influence of citizens on police behavior is most evident in small communities. There is closer contact between the police and members of the community, officers are typically longtime residents of the locations they patrol, police officials are often dependent on public support for their departmental finances and tenure, and police behavior in general has a higher grass-roots visibility. Further, the opportunities for police abuse are less widespread in small cities, towns, and rural areas. The reverse seems to be true in large urban centers, where community control over policing is almost totally absent. There have been a number of suggestions made over the years concerning how to counter this problem, including "putting the cop back on the beat," sensitivity training for police recruits, and the establishment of civilian review boards to enforce police discipline. Some two decades ago, author Arthur I. Waskow offered the following three-part formula for placing control of the police system in the hands of the citizenry.

> *First,* police forces should be restructured along neighborhood lines with control over each force residing in elected officials from the neighborhood; *second,* organizations should be developed to protect those who are policed; and *third,* community control should be established informally by changing the police "profession" so that police are not isolated from the rest of the community.[55]

Waskow's suggestions are likely correct, at least from a technical point of view. But they are based on an idealized concept of police–community relations and are probably unworkable. The paramilitary character of police organizations, the conservative nature of police decision making, and the elements of the police culture that stress secrecy and solidarity, all combine to create a situation where police would be highly resistant to outside control. The experience with civilian review boards illustrates this point.

Prior to 1958, all the power to discipline law enforcement personnel was in the hands of police departments, generally in the form of some internal review committee composed of one or more police officials. But during the late 1950s and early 1960s, concern about this system surfaced when the United States Commission on Civil Rights found that many blacks felt powerless to do anything about police malpractice. These revelations were later confirmed by a number of studies conducted by the American Civil Liberties Union (ACLU), the National Association for the Advancement of Colored People (NAACP), and the University of California, which pointed to a range of dissatisfactions with internal police review boards: (1) They could not be impartial in judging fellow officers; (2) the procedures for filing complaints were so cumbersome that they discouraged citizen reporting; (3) they made no effort to solicit complaints; (4) they insulated police officers and departments from public accountability; and (5) they rarely disciplined officers, thus giving the impression that they were simply whitewash efforts.[56] The ACLU also found that in an effort to protect the reputation of their departments, the internal affairs units and other special police squads that were structured for "policing the police" employed a host of reprehensible tactics to discourage citizens from filing complaints against officers. In New York City, they threatened complainants with criminal libel; in Cleveland, they forced them to take lie detector tests; and in Philadelphia, Washington, D.C., and Los Angeles, they took them into custody on charges of resisting arrest, disorderly conduct, or some other minor offense. Other departments intimated witnesses, deprived complainants of access to departmental files, or otherwise acted as though the citizens were on trial.[57]

Led by the ACLU, the NAACP, and other citizen groups, public opinion urged police authorities to shift the responsibility for handling complaints to citizen-controlled outside review boards. The boards envisioned were to serve several purposes:

1. They would restrain those officers who engaged in brutality, harassment, and other abusive and even illegal practices.
2. By insuring a thorough and impartial investigation of all complaints, they would protect other officers against malicious, misguided and otherwise unfounded accusations.

After four police officers were acquitted in the beating of Rodney King, there was a spasm of rage, incendiary violence, and looting in Los Angeles. The chaos quickly spread to a few other cities. In this scene, three men smashed the window of a downtown Seattle liquor store. They were with a group of about fifty people who went through the downtown area breaking windows. Police followed just 50 yards behind.

• **EXHIBIT** 9.4 •

Police Malpractice Suits

Physicians are not the only defendants in malpractice suits. In recent years, more citizens have been suing police departments for brutality, for the misuse of deadly force, and for ineptitude and carelessness that result in the injury and death of innocent bystanders.

The greater tendency for courts to compensate victims or their families for injuries and "wrongful deaths" at the hands of the police is an outgrowth of several historical factors. First was the steady erosion of the doctrine of **sovereign immunity,** the principle that the state cannot be sued in its own courts or in any other court without its consent and permission. This erosion began during the 1960s when Section 1983 of the Civil Rights Act of 1871 was recognized to be an appropriate way of bringing suit against state officers in prisoners' rights cases (see Chapter 16). A second factor was the U.S. Supreme Court's ruling in *Monell* v. *New York City Department of Social Services* in 1978.[a] Although *Monell* focused on a maternity leave policy rather than a criminal justice issue, the conclusion of the Court was that cities and other local governments could be sued directly under Section 1983 for damages if the action alleged to be unconstitutional

implemented or executed a policy statement, ordinance, regulation, or decision officially adopted and promulgated by that body's officers. In employing Section 1983 and *Monell,* the suits alleging police malpractice have involved such issues as deadly force, brutality, innocent bystanders, and failure to protect citizens.

Cases evolving from police misuse of deadly force have been numerous. *Tennessee* v. *Garner* was the first such case to reach the Supreme Court. A more notorious case, however, was *Prior* v. *Woods* in 1981,[b] which resulted in a $5.7 million award — one of the largest in police malpractice history. On the morning of July 31, 1979, twenty-four-year-old David Prior was parked in front of his home in a Detroit suburb. Two police officers had been briefed earlier that David would be staying in his van in an effort to catch a thief who had twice stolen stereo equipment from the vehicle. Mistaken for a burglar, however, Prior was shot and killed by two police officers.

Beyond the issue of the misuse of deadly force, there have been other types of police malpractice cases. *Biscoe* v. *Arlington* in 1984 and *Grandstaff* v. *Borger* in 1985 both dealt with loss of life or serious injury to innocent

bystanders.[c] In *Biscoe,* $5 million was awarded to Alvin B. Biscoe and his wife stemming from an incident that occurred in 1979. While waiting to cross a street in downtown Washington, D.C., Mr. Biscoe lost both his legs after he was hit by a car involved in a high-speed police chase. In *Grandstaff,* an award of $1.4 million went to the family of a man who had been mistaken for a fugitive and was killed in a barrage of gunfire. In both cases, the awards were grounded in the logic of *Monell,* that the constitutional injury was an outgrowth of an "official policy." The official policy in the *Biscoe* case was clear, for high-speed chases were sanctioned by the offending police department without regard to potential risk of harm to bystanders. In *Grandstaff* the showing of "official policy" was based on the inadequate training of the police officers involved in the shooting.

Sorichetti v. *City of New York* and *Thurman* v. *Torrington,*[d] both in 1985, focused on police failure to protect citizens. For the most part, however, citing the Supreme Court's position on sovereign immunity as stated in *South* v. *Maryland* in 1856,[e] the courts have ruled that state and municipal governments generally may not be held liable for

3. They would provide blacks and other minority group members an avenue of redress, which would help restore their dwindling confidence in the police departments.
4. They would explain police procedures to citizens, review enforcement requirements with police, and initiate a genuine dialogue in place of mutual recrimination.[58]

Civilian review boards: Citizen-controlled boards empowered to review and handle complaints against police officers.

Proposals for **civilian review boards** incensed most police officers, and were bitterly fought by such organizations as the International Association of Chiefs of Police (IACP), the International Conference of

failure to protect individual citizens from harm caused by criminal conduct. However, the courts have also recognized a "special relationship" exception to this rule. In *Sorichetti,* a case in which a woman sued the New York City Police Department for its failure to protect her daughter from the mother's estranged husband, such a "special relationship" existed. Liability was imposed for injuries the father inflicted on his daughter since the police department knew of the father's violent history and of a court order issued against him, but failed to follow up assurances it gave Mrs. Sorichetti that it would investigate the child's welfare. *Thurman* involved a similar circumstance. Tracey Thurman was a battered wife who sued the police for failing to act on her complaints regarding her estranged husband's violations of a stay-away order, which resulted in a severe beating.

One of the more interesting applications of Section 1983 and Monell occurred in *Brandon* v. *Holt* in 1986.[f] In that case, a U.S. District Court ruled that tacit policies that added up to a laissez-faire attitude toward police brutality rendered the city of Memphis, Tennessee, and its police department liable for the retention of an "obviously dangerous man" as a police officer.

The behavior of the officer in question was well known in local police circles. When first hired, a psychiatrist retained to evaluate police recruits warned that he had "difficulty controlling his impulses" and that he should be "watched closely." Subsequently, some twenty complaints were filed against the officer, including charges for the serious abuse of police authority and the use of unnecessary force. On one occasion he had been suspended for beating an inmate at the city jail. The District Court ruling identified four policies that made the city and the police department liable for the assaults perpetrated by the officer. *First,* the city's police director was kept in the dark about police misconduct. *Second,* both rank and file and supervisory officers maintained a "code of silence" about their fellow officers' acts of brutality. *Third,* the police department had an apparently accepted policy against disciplining officers by reassigning them to jobs with less potential for violence. *Fourth,* it appeared that any dismissal based on brutality would be routinely overturned by the city's civil service commission.

The impact of these and other court decisions has been felt at several levels. On the one hand, police agencies have

begun to address the policies and practices that lead to malpractice suits. On the other, losing such cases has been disastrous for some local governments, especially small towns with little or no insurance. The City of South Tucson, Arizona, for example, had to file for bankruptcy in 1984 after the state appellate courts upheld a $3.6 million judgment in a police negligence case. The award was almost $1 million more than the town's entire annual budget.[g]

SOURCES:
a. *Monell* v. *New York City Department of Social Services,* 436 U.S. 658 (1978).
b. *Prior* v. *Woods:* see *National Law Journal,* November 2, 1981, p. 5; also, *New York Times,* May 12, 1985, p. 39.
c. *Biscoe* v. *Arlington:* 80-0766; *National Law Journal,* May 13, 1985, p. 1; *Grandstaff* v. *City of Borger,* CA 5(1985) 37 CrL 1085.
d. *Sorichetti* v. *City of New York,* NY CtApp (1985) 37 CrL 1067; *Thurman v.* Torrington, USDC DConn (1985) 37 CrL 2329; *National Law Journal,* July 15, 1985, p. 6; *USA Today,* June 26, 1985, p. 1A.
e. *South* v. *Maryland,* 59 U.S. 394 (1856).
f. *Brandon* v. *Holt,* USDC W. Tenn, 10/7/86; 40 CrL 2139 (1986).
g. *National Law Journal,* May 13, 1985, p. 36.

Police Associations (ICPA), and the Fraternal Order of Police (FOP). Despite opposition, however, a few cities did establish civilian review boards. The first was set up in Philadelphia, on October 1, 1958, but from its inception its potential for objective judgment was severely compromised. Philadelphia's five-person Police Advisory Board had no investigatory staff of its own and had to rely on the police department's community relations unit to investigate all complaints.

In the years hence, civilian review boards have come and gone in a number of cities, and currently exist in but a few places — Washington,

Sovereign immunity: The principle that the state cannot be sued in its own courts or in any other court without its consent and permission.

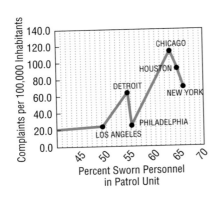

Percent of Sworn Personnel in Patrol Units and Complaints Against Officers per 100,000 Residents in Selected Cities *There is a tendency for those departments with the highest percent of their personnel assigned to patrol to also have the highest number of complaints per capita.*

SOURCE: Police Foundation, 1991

D.C., Berkeley, Calif., New York City, and Dade County, Fla. The likelihood that their numbers will expand to any great extent, however, is unlikely, at least for the present. The experience demonstrated that they had a debilitating effect on morale, that they were viewed by police as a mechanism for appeasing the more radical elements in minority group areas, and according to some police groups, they served only as a wedge between the police and the community. Police researcher James J. Fyfe maintains that civilian review boards may be a good thing when public confidence in police integrity has sunk so low that no internal investigative process can ever be viewed as credible. Over the long haul, however, he sees the solution in the office of the chief of police — if it is honest and open, no review board is needed because the complaint investigation and review process can be demonstrated to work fairly.[59]

Police Control

Control of police misconduct directly from within police departments is generally of two types, preventive and punitive.

Preventive control manifests itself in several areas, all of which involve numerous alterations in the structure and philosophy of a police department. First, the policy of *internal accountability* holds members of a law enforcement agency responsible for their own actions as well as for those of others. It is based on a clear communication of standards to which officers and officials will be held accountable, and an articulation of "who will be responsible for whom." Second, internal accountability becomes workable only under *tight supervision* of police officers by administrators, precinct commanders, and other control staff. Tight supervision involves direct surveillance of officers' work time and work products by field commanders, combined with daily logs documenting officer activity. Third, preventive control can affect areas of police misconduct through an *abolition of corrupting procedures*. Every large police department and many smaller ones have numerous formal procedures that inadvertently encourage corruption. For example, some policies imply levels of productivity that are all but impossible to achieve by legitimate means; others create pressures for financial contributions by officers that they attempt to "earn back" in corrupt ways. Vice investigators and detectives, for instance, often must "purchase" leads from informers, but funds for such purposes may be limited or unavailable. Similarly, criminal investigation work may require the use of personal autos with no provisions for expense reimbursement.

Sociologist Lawrence W. Sherman has noted that subsequent to the police scandals in Oakland during the 1950s and in New York as an outgrowth of the Knapp Commission, preventive controls along these lines were implemented.[60] In both cities, reform executives established policies of internal accountability aimed at diffusing the responsibility for control of misconduct both vertically and horizontally throughout the police departments. Concomitantly, these policies were swiftly enforced. In Oakland, for example, a detective commander lost five days' pay for failing to thoroughly investigate a corruption allegation; a sergeant was suspended for failing to investigate a prisoner's complaint that officers had taken money from him; and another sergeant was suspended for letting one of his patrolmen work while intoxicated. Supervision was tightened, primarily through the extension of decision-making powers to lower levels in the police hierarchy and maintaining a lower ratio of line officers to supervisors.

The reform administration in New York also focused on its many potentially corrupting procedures. "Buy money" for purchasing drugs, and funds for informers, were greatly increased and more rigidly controlled; the cost of using personal autos in surveillance work was reimbursed on a per-mile basis; and the use of arrest quotas to evaluate the productivity of vice investigators was abolished.

Punitive control falls into that area of policing known as internal affairs or *internal policing* — the purview of the so-called "headhunters" and "shoo-fly" cops who investigate complaints against police personnel or other actions involving police misconduct. Internal policing may be the responsibility of a single officer or detective, a small police unit, or an entire division or bureau, depending on the size of a department and its commitment to in-house review. Regardless of size, however, the responsibilities of internal affairs units generally include inquiries into the following:

1. allegations or complaints of misconduct made by a citizen, police officer, or any other person against the department or any of its members
2. allegations or suspicions of corruption, breaches of integrity or cases of moral turpitude from whatever source — whether reported to or developed by internal policing
3. situations in which officers are killed or wounded by the deliberate or willful acts of other parties
4. situations in which citizens have been killed or injured by police officers either on or off duty
5. situations involving the discharging of weapons by officers[61]

Internal policing began during the latter part of the nineteenth century, when headquarters roundsmen made inspections on a city-wide basis and investigated corruption. They became known in New York and a number of other cities as "shoo-flies," a term taken from the argot of the professional underworld. The "shoo-fly" was originally a criminal's spy, who watched for police activity in order to warn the thief.[62] By 1900, detectives were also known as "shoo-flies," because in their nonuniformed investigative roles they spied on criminals.[63] During the tenure of Arthur Woods as commissioner of the New York Police Department which began in 1914, a confidential squad was organized to spy on the activities of police officers.[64] It was at that point that the shoo-fly cop more formally became a part of police argot.

It was not until the mid-1900s, however, that structured bureaus for internal policing came into being.[65] In the wake of a major scandal during the late 1940s, Los Angeles police chief William A. Worton formed the Bureau of Internal Affairs. Within a decade, Boston, Chicago, and Atlanta followed suit, and at the beginning of the 1960s New York City joined the trend when the police commissioner established the Inspection Service Bureau, which brought together several units that had been separately monitoring the integrity and efficiency of the police.

The special internal control units and bureaus, although permanent fixtures in big-city policing, are not without their problems. Police rank and file have always despised the activities of the headhunters and shoo-fly cops. Furthermore, internal affairs officers have sometimes been corrupt themselves, and others have been unwilling to tarnish the reputation of their departments by exposing corruption and incompetence. Finally, citizens have apparently been unwilling to file complaints and

IAD [Internal Affairs Division] investigators are considered by many NYPD officers to be scum. To most cops, they are turncoats, known by various epithets, such as "Cheese-eater," "Ben," and "Willard"— all signifying "rat." Mention the three letters I-A-D, and a cop will instinctively sneer.

— FROM *COP HUNTER*, BY VINCENT MURANO

How Much Police Violence Is Used Against Citizens in Your Community

From what you have read or seen, do you think the Los Angeles police clubbing of a black man was racially motivated?

YES 43%   NO 20%

Should criminal charges be brought against these officers, or should this matter be left to the police for disciplinary procedures?

Criminal charges 67%   Police discipline 17%

How often do you think incidents occur in your community where police use violence against private citizens?

Very often	9%
Fairly often	13%
On occasion	48%
Never	23%

SOURCE: From a telephone poll of 500 American adults taken for TIME/CNN on March 13, 1991 by Clancy Shulman. Sampling error is plus or minus 4.5%. "Not sures" omitted.

officers have been unwilling to testify against one another. The product of such difficulties is an acutely low level of efficiency.

Nevertheless, not all aspects of internal policing have been unsuccessful. Even in the more disorganized and inefficient of departments a certain level of misconduct has been detected and ferreted out. Without any internal control mechanisms, police organization would probably become chaotic.

Attempts to reduce police misconduct should not be limited to efforts by the legislature, review boards, and internal policing. These treat only the symptoms of the problem. More work in the area of police professionalization also seems warranted. However, this too is an area that is problematic, for there are differing conceptions of professionalism in law enforcement. Police understand professionalism to mean more tightly defined rules and regulations, increased central control, strict discipline, and obedience. In every other organization, professionalism means that a large measure of discretion is left to individuals, who respond to situations with a wealth of personal expertise born of long training and experience, which, rather than organizational rules and regulations, guide them in handling various situations. In law enforcement agencies, such professionalism would come from better trained and educated officers, more sophisticated police resources, closer attention to the needs for community service and police–community relations, and more efficient and detailed policies regarding police behavior in contacts with citizens.

Police professionalism: The notion that brutality and corruption are incompetent policing.

Properly understood, **police professionalism** implies that brutality and corruption are incompetent policing. And incompetence may be measured in terms of the following axiom: while the core of the police

role is the right to use force, the skill in policing is the ability to avoid its use. With respect to corruption, professionalism engenders group norms of pride and dignity of occupation that make police intolerant of fellow officers who taint the profession.[66]

There are reports that this notion of professionalism has taken hold in some police agencies. It should be noted, for example, that one of the first officers to publicly go against the police "code of silence" (perhaps better known as the "blue curtain of secrecy") was Frank Serpico of the N.Y.P.D. Serpico's disclosures about police corruption led to the Knapp Commission investigation, which (as mentioned earlier in this chapter) found that more than half of New York City's police officers had taken part in corrupt practices. That was in 1970 and 1971; a decade later, the situation had changed considerably. In 1981, there were 2,319 allegations of police misdeeds in New York City, and almost twenty percent of these reports were submitted by police officers.[67] The trend continued into the 1980s and 1990s, and fellow officers were found to be less willing to cover up such police improprieties as accepting bribes from narcotics dealers, possession and sale of narcotics and cocaine, stealing drugs and money from suspects, and accepting money from business operators in exchange for favors.[68]

SUMMARY

Police misconduct falls primarily into two areas: corruption and the excessive use of violence. Police corruption reflects illegal activities for economic gain, including payment for services that police are sworn to do as part of their law enforcement role. Police violence, in the forms of brutality and the misuse of deadly force, involves the wrongful use of police power.

Police corruption can occur in many ways, but observers and researchers in the field of police behavior agree that it is most manifest in nine specific areas: meals and services, kickbacks, opportunistic theft, planned theft, shakedowns, protection, case fixing, private security, and patronage. Policing is rich in opportunities for corruption — more so than most, of not all, other occupations.

Police violence has been relatively visible throughout American history and has received much attention in recent years by the U.S. Supreme Court and the Kerner Commission. Studies have shown that police violence occurs most often when people show disrespect for officers and when police encounter certain types of offenders, as well as when police try to coerce confessions.

In the past, police brutality was considered to be a practice limited to a few sadistic officers. More recent commentaries suggest that it is not particularly widespread and is an unfortunate consequence of the police role. Police violence also includes the improper use of deadly force — a "shoot-to-kill" doctrine based on common-law principles that persist in a few law enforcement agencies.

Attempts to control police misconduct of all varieties have emanated from the legislature, from civilian review boards, and from police agencies themselves. Perhaps the most effective method is police professionalization, which views brutality as incompetent policing, and corruption as beneath the dignity of effective law enforcement agents.

KEY TERMS

civilian review boards **(298)**
police brutality **(289)**
police corruption **(277)**

"police presence" **(277)**
police professionalism **(302)**

sovereign immunity **(299)**
Tennessee v. *Garner* **(292)**

QUESTIONS FOR DISCUSSION

1. Is the problem of brutality so much a part of the police role that it can never be routed out? Why or why not?
2. In your community, what do you feel would be the best combination of activities for controlling police corruption?
3. Do you feel that corruption is *more* or *less* widespread in the ranks of policing than in other occupations and professions? Why?
4. What kinds of police misconduct have you observed? In each case, were they officer- or citizen-initiated?

FOR FURTHER READING

Edwin J. Delattre. *Character and Cops: Ethics in Policing.* Washington, DC: American Enterprise Institute for Public Policy Research, 1989, 71–78.

Fyfe, James J. "Police Use of Deadly Force: Research and Reform." *Justice Quarterly* 5 (June 1988): 165–205.

Goldstein, Herman. *Police Corruption: A Perspective on its Nature and Control.* Washington, D.C.: The Police Foundation, 1975.

Skolnick, Jerome H., and David H. Bayley. *The New Blue Line: Police Innovation in Six American Cities.* New York: Free Press, 1986.

NOTES

1. A. E. Costello, *Our Police Protectors* (New York: Author's Edition, 1885), pp. 364–365.
2. Herbert Asbury, *The Gangs of New York* (Garden City, N.Y.: Garden City, 1928), p. 235.
3. James F. Richardson, *The New York Police: Colonial Times to 1901* (New York: Oxford University Press, 1970), p. 204.
4. *Report of the Special Committee Appointed to Investigate the Police Department of the City of New York* (Albany: State of New York, Senate Documents, 1895), vol. I, pp. 30–32.
5. Lloyd Morris, *Incredible New York* (New York: Bonanza, 1951), p. 112; Edward Robb Ellis, *The Epic of New York City* (New York: Coward-McCann, 1966), p. 432.
6. Lawrence W. Sherman, *Scandal and Reform* (Berkeley: University of California Press, 1978), p. xxii.
7. Herman Goldstein, *Police Corruption: A Perspective on Its Nature and Control* (Washington, D.C.: Police Foundation, 1975), p. 55.
8. Jonathan Rubinstein, *City Police* (New York; Farrar, Straus and Giroux, 1973), p. 400.
9. *The Knapp Commission Report on Police Corruption* (New York: Braziller, 1972).
10. See, for example, Richard J. Lundman, *Police and Policing* (New York: Holt, Rinehart and Winston, 1980), pp. 142–148; Herman Goldstein, *Policing a Free Society* (Cambridge, Mass.: Ballinger, 1977), pp. 194–195; Thomas Barker and Julian Roebuck, *An Empirical Typology of Police Corruption: A Study in Organizational Deviance* (Springfield, Ill.: Charles C. Thomas, 1973); Rubinstein, *City Police.*
11. This discussion is based on Sherman, *Scandal and Reform; Rubinstein, City Police;* and on personal observations and contacts with police in New York City, Tampa, Philadelphia, Miami, and San Francisco.
12. Personal communication, May 15, 1974.
13. The events described were reported to the author by victims, police officers, and detectives in several cities.
14. *Miami Herald,* October 30, 1982, p. B1; see also, Mike McAlary, *Buddy Boys: When Good Cops Turn Bad* (New York: G. D. Putnam's Sons, 1987).
15. *New York Times,* June 30, 1988, p. B3; *Newsweek,* September 5, 1988, p. 37.
16. Lundman, *Police and Policing,* p. 148; Barker and Roebuck, *Empirical Typology of Police Corruption,* p. 36.
17. James A. Inciardi, *Careers in Crime* (Chicago: Rand McNally, 1975), p. 29.
18. Mike Royko, *Boss: Richard Daley of Chicago* (New York: Signet, 1971), p. 108.
19. Commission to Investigate Allegations of Police Corruption, and the City's Anti-Corruption Procedures, *The Knapp Commission Report on Police Corruption,* August 3, 1972.
20. See, for example, *New York Times,* August 12, 1984, p. 30.
21. Lundman, *Police and Policing,* p. 147.
22. Personal communication, March 1970.
23. Personal communication, July 1988.
24. Goldstein, *Policing a Free Society,* p. 194.
25. Anonymous communication, March 13, 1981.

26. William Safire, *Safire's Political Dictionary* (New York: Random House, 1978), p. 517.

27. Edwin J. Delattre, *Character and Cops: Ethics in Policing* (Washington, DC: American Enterprise Institute for Public Policy Research, 1989), pp. 71–78.

28. Ralph Lee Smith, *The Tarnished Badge* (New York: Arno Press, 1974), pp. 191–192.

29. Arthur Niederhoffer, *Behind the Shield: The Police in Urban Society* (Garden City: Doubleday, 1969), p. 70.

30. Goldstein, *Policing a Free Society*, p. 199.

31. Samual Walker, *The Police in America* (New York: McGraw-Hill, 1983), pp. 180–181.

32. Cited by Albert J. Reiss, Jr., "Police Brutality — Answers to Key Questions," *Trans-Action* 5 (1968): 10.

33. *Brown* v. *Mississippi*, 297 U.S. 278 (1936).

34. *Rogers* v. *Richmond*, 365 U.S. 534 (1961); *Greenwald* v. *Wisconsin*, 390 U.S. 519 (1968); *Georgia* v. *Sims*, 385 U.S. 538 (1968); *Florida* v. *Brooks*, 389 U.S. 413 (1968).

35. *Report of the National Advisory Commission on Civil Disorders* (New York: E. P. Dutton, 1968).

36. William A. Westley, *Violence and the Police* (Cambridge, Mass.: MIT Press, 1970), p. 122.

37. Reiss, "Police Brutality," p. 10.

38. *U.S. News & World Report*, August 27, 1979, pp. 27–8.

39. Wilmington (Delaware) *News-Journal*, October 14, 1983, p. A5; *Time*, May 13, 1985, p. 59; *Newsweek*, May 6, 1985, p. 59.

40. See *Time*, March 25, 1991, pp. 16–18; *New York Times*, March 18, 1991, pp. March 18, 1991, pp. A1, B7 *New York Times*, March 20, 1991, p. A18.

41. James Q. Wilson, *Varieties of Police Behavior* (New York: Atheneum, 1975), pp. 140–171.

42. Lundman, *Police and Policing*, pp. 161–164.

43. Personal communication, May 13, 1981.

44. Personal communication, August 28, 1978.

45. Lundman, *Police and Policing*, p. 163.

46. *Newsweek*, June 23, 1969, p. 92.

47. *Livingston* v. *Browder*, 51 Ala. App. 366, 285 So. 2nd 923 (1973).

48. *Tennessee* v. *Garner*, US SupCt (1985) 36 CrL 3233.

49. James J. Fyfe, "The Split-Second Syndrome and Other Determinants of Police Violence," in Anne Campbell and John Gibbs (eds.), *Violent Transactions* (New York: Basil Blackwell, 1986).

50. *U.S. News & World Report*, August 27, 1979, p. 27; *Time*, January 21, 1980, p. 32; *U.S. News & World Report*, June 2, 1980, pp. 19–22; Arthur L. Kobler, "Police Homicide in a Democracy," *Journal of Social Issues* 31 (Winter 1975): 163–184. Gerald D. Robin, "Justifiable Homicides by Police Officers," *Journal of Criminal Law Criminology and Police Science*, June 1963, pp. 225–231; Ralph Knoohirizen, Richard P. Fahey, and Deborah J. Palmer, *The Police and Their Use of Fatal Force in Chicago* (Evanston, Ill.: Chicago Law Enforcement Study Group, 1972); Betty Jenkins and Adrienne Faison, *An Analysis of 248 Persons Killed by New York City Policemen* (New York: New York Metropolitan Applied Research Center, 1974); David Jacobs and David Britt, "Inequality and Police Use of Deadly Force: An Empirical Assessment of a Conflict Hypothesis," *Social Problems* 26 (April 1979): 403–412; Lennox S. Hinds, "The Police Use of Excessive and Deadly Force: Racial Implications," in *A Community Concern: Police Use of Deadly Force*, ed. Robert N. Brenner and Marjorie Kravitz (Washington, D.C.: U.S. Department of Justice, 1979), p. 7–11; *Miami Herald*, March 27, 1983, p. 18A.

51. Paul Takagi, "A Garrison State in a 'Democratic' Society," *Crime and Social Justice* 1 (Spring–Summer 1974): 27–33; "Death by 'Police Intervention,'" in *A Community Concern*, ed. Brenner and Kravitz, pp. 31–38.

52. Richard Kania and Wade Mackley, "Police Violence as a Function of Community Characteristics," *Criminology* 15 (May 1977): 27–48.

53. Kobler, "Police Homicide in a Democracy." James J. Fyfe, "Police Use of Deadly Force: Research and Reform," *Justice Quarterly*, 5 (June 1988), pp. 165–205.

54. See James A. Inciardi (ed.), *The Drug Legalization Debate* (Newbury Park, CA: Sage, 1991).

55. Arthur I. Waskow, "Community Control of the Police," *Trans-Action* 7 (December 1969): 4–7.

56. Paul Chevigny, *Police Power: Police Abuses in New York City* (New York: Vintage, 1969), p. 260; David H. Bayley and Harold Mendelsohn, *Minorities and the Police: Confrontation in America* (New York: Free Press, 1971), pp. 127–135.

57. Robert M. Fogelson, *Big City Police* (Cambridge, Mass.: Harvard University Press, 1977), pp. 283–284.

58. Fogelson, *Big City Police*, p. 284.

59. Fyfe, James J., "Reviewing Citizens Complaints Against Police," in James J. Fyfe (ed.), *Police Management Today: Issues and Cases*, (Washington, D.C.: International City Management Association, 1985), pp. 76–87.

60. Sherman, *Scandal and Reform*, pp. 120–145.

61. George D. Eastman, ed., *Municipal Police Administration* (Washington, D.C.: International City Management Association, 1969), pp. 203–204.

62. Langdon W. Moore, *His Own Story of His Eventful Life* (Boston: L. W. Moore, 1893), pp. 287–289.

63. Hutchins Hapgood, *The Autobiography of a Thief* (New York: Fox, Duffield, 1903), p. 265.

64. Thomas A. Reppetto, *The Blue Parade* (New York: Free Press, 1978), p. 162.

65. Fogelson, *Big City Police*, p. 179.

66. Egon Bittner, *The Functions of Police in Modern Society* (New York: Jason Aronson, 1975).

67. *New York Times*, April 11, 1982, p. 43.

68. *New York Times*, September 30, 1988, p. B1.

PART

THREE

The Courts

10

This is the House That Justice Built: The Structure of American Courts

---

CITIZEN: *Where's the courthouse?*
POLICE OFFICER: *Which one?*
CITIZEN: *The criminal court, please.*
POLICE OFFICER: *Which one?*
CITIZEN: *Huh?*
POLICE OFFICER: *There's the police court, county court, circuit court, trial court, superior court, and appeals court!*
CITIZEN: *The trial court, I guess.*
POLICE OFFICER: *Which one?*

How to win a case in court?
If the law is on your side, pound on the law.
If the facts are on your side, pound on the facts.
If neither is on your side, pound on the table.

—ANONYMOUS

As America evolved into a nation, the court emerged as an integral part of life in most communities. It was at the local courthouse that celebrations were held and emergencies brought to the attention of the populace. Courthouses provided mustering places during the War of Independence and Civil War, and victories and reverses were first announced by broadsheets posted on their doors. Because they were often built before any churches, they frequently served as meeting places—for religious services, dances, and town council assemblies—as well as fulfilled their primary function, the dispensation of justice. And courthouses were places for exchanging the news and meeting old friends.

In matters of law, the procedure was clear and simple. The courthouse stood at the center of town. There, the local justice of the peace decided on all aspects of civil disputes and minor criminal transgressions. With the more serious issues of crime, law, and justice, the procedure—at least in its more outward aspects—was just as clear. Once each month, on "court day," a judge of some higher authority would visit the community and dispose of these weightier matters.

As towns became cities, the procedures became somewhat less simple, but not by a great deal. Since there were more people, and hence more problems, there were more courts. For civil matters, there were counterparts of the rural justices of the peace; for less serious criminal affairs, there were police and magistrates' courts; and for the serious, pressing problems of law and order, there was a more permanent higher court.[1]

As the nation grew more populous and more mature, so too did its system of courts. By the late nineteenth century, American courts reflected a bewildering mosaic of names, types, structures, and functions. The old courthouse still stood, the rural justices of the peace and the urban magistrates still decided on certain matters of law, and the county courts, night courts, and higher courts still operated. But along with these one could also find mayors' courts, municipal courts, probate courts, chancery courts, superior courts, and various levels of appeals and supreme courts. Some local town and county courts were consolidated into circuits and districts; numerous areas had general sessions and special sessions courts; and legal practitioners spoke in terms of appeals courts and trial courts, higher courts and lower courts, superior courts and inferior courts. And over all was a **dual court system** that had evolved throughout America after the signing of the Declaration of Independence—at the state level and at the federal. Without question, "finding the courthouse," or at least the *right* courthouse, had become a perplexing problem.

Today, the situation is no less knotty, even when the courts handling civil matters exclusively are eliminated from consideration. In fact, it has

Dual court system: Courts at the state and federal levels.

become even more intricate. No two state court systems are identical, and the names of the courts tend to vary regardless of function. The purpose of this chapter is to unravel these complexities of American court configuration and to analyze the roles of the various courts in criminal justice processing.

THE STATE COURTS

This is the house that justice built,
this is the castle of fair play;
this is the place where wise men sit,
for the law and truth they belay.

The drums of crime, of lust and strife,
these are the souls we see;
in the righteous house that justice built,
here on this star-spangled street.

—Anonymous, c. 1980

These few lines of verse, found scribbled on a restroom wall in the basement of the Ross County Courthouse in Chillicothe, Ohio, are expressive of a role that many state courts play in the administration of justice. Exactly what type of justice the author of these words had in mind, however, is only open to speculation, for the particular courthouse in which they appeared houses many different types of courts. The writings are somewhat curious and paradoxical as well. Some of the words and even whole lines seem to have been taken from a Milton MacKaye article published in the *New York Evening Post* half a century earlier on January 10, 1930.[2] The paradox is in the fact that MacKaye's commentary was hardly one that praised the "righteous house that justice built." Rather, as a firsthand description of a busy magistrate's court in New York City, it was part of a series entitled "The Magistrate Racket" and addressed only the dismal aspects of the American court system. Or perhaps the anonymous author's poetic celebrations were written in a

Ross County courthouse, Chillicothe, Ohio

Courts do not exist for the sake of discipline, but for the sake of deciding matters in controversy.
— CROPPER V. SMITH, 1884

Lower courts have often been labeled inferior courts. Some have alleged that this designation comes from the lesser quality of justice and courtroom professionalism apparent in them. The term *inferior*, however, actually refers to the fact that the jurisdiction of these courts is limited.

spirit of sarcasm, for there are thousands of tribunals across the United States — small and large, rural and urban — and a number of them are quite chaotic in their approach to the administration of justice.

State Court Infrastructure

Characteristic of the state court systems are that no two are exactly alike and that the names of the various courts vary widely regardless of function. For example, all states have major trial courts devoted to criminal cases. In Ohio and Pennsylvania, these are called courts of common pleas; in California, they are known as superior courts; in New York, they are supreme courts — a designation typically used elsewhere for appeals courts. Moreover, while Michigan's major trial courts use the label of circuit court, within the corporate limits of the city of Detroit they are called the recorder's court.

The many names, functions, and types that characterize state court structures have resulted from the fact that each state is a sovereign government insofar as the enactment of a penal code and the setting up of enforcement machinery are concerned. Thus, in each of the fifty jurisdictions, the court systems grew differently — sometimes in an unplanned, sporadic way — generally guided by different cultural traditions, demographic pressures, legal and political philosophies, and needs for justice administration. Yet, despite this apparent confusion, there is nevertheless a clear-cut structure within all the state court systems. State judiciaries are divided into three, four, and sometimes five specific tiers, each having separate functions and jurisdictions.

As outlined in Exhibit 10.1, the courts of last resort are at the uppermost level, occupying the highest rung in the judicial ladder. These are the appeals courts. All states have a court of last resort, but depending on the jurisdiction, the specific name will vary — supreme court, supreme court of appeals, or perhaps simply court of appeals. In addition, in states such as Texas and Oklahoma, there are two courts of last resort, one for criminal cases and one for all others.

Immediately below the courts of last resort in more than half the states are the intermediate appellate courts. Located primarily in the more populous states, these courts have been structured to relieve the case-load burden on the highest courts. Like the highest courts, they are known by various names; often the names are similar to those of the courts above them in the hierarchy (appeals courts), as well as below them (superior courts).

The major trial courts are the courts of general jurisdiction, where felony cases are heard. All states have various combinations of these, and depending on the locale, they might be called superior, circuit, district, or some other designation.

The lower courts, often referred to in legal nomenclature as inferior, misdemeanor, minor, or courts of limited jurisdiction, exist in numerous combinations in every state. Variously named county, magistrate, police, municipal, justice of the peace, and justice courts, as well as dozens of other designations, they are the entry point for most defendants being processed through the criminal justice system, and the only level at which infractions and most misdemeanors are processed.

The *jurisdiction* of each court varies by geography, subject matter, and hierarchy. Courts are authorized to head and decide disputes arising within specific political boundaries — a city, borough, township, county, or group of counties. In addition, some courts are limited to

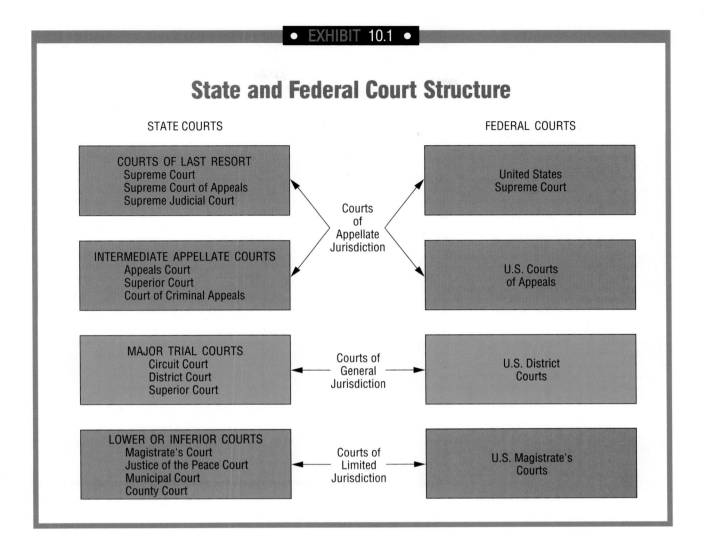

EXHIBIT 10.1

State and Federal Court Structure

STATE COURTS   FEDERAL COURTS

COURTS OF LAST RESORT
Supreme Court
Supreme Court of Appeals
Supreme Judicial Court

United States
Supreme Court

Courts
of
Appellate
Jurisdiction

INTERMEDIATE APPELLATE COURTS
Appeals Court
Superior Court
Court of Criminal Appeals

U.S. Courts
of Appeals

MAJOR TRIAL COURTS
Circuit Court
District Court
Superior Court

Courts of
General
Jurisdiction

U.S. District
Courts

LOWER OR INFERIOR COURTS
Magistrate's Court
Justice of the Peace Court
Municipal Court
County Court

Courts of
Limited
Jurisdiction

U.S. Magistrate's
Courts

specific matters — for example, misdemeanors or civil actions versus all other types of cases. There are family courts that decide on juvenile and domestic relations matters, probate courts whose jurisdiction is limited to the handling of wills and the administration of decedents' estates, and many others. Jurisdiction can also be viewed as limited, general, and appellate:

1. *Courts of limited jurisdiction,* the lower courts, do not have powers that extend to the overall administration of justice, they do not try felony cases, and they do not possess appellate authority.
2. *Courts of general jurisdiction,* the major trial courts, have the power and authority to try and decide any case, including appeals from a lower court.
3. *Courts of appellate jurisdiction,* the appeals courts, are limited in their jurisdiction to decisions on matters of appeal from lower courts and trial courts.

Court systems may be simple or complex in their organizational structure. The state of Florida has a simple four-tier court system of organization (see Exhibit 10.2). The county courts are the courts of

Levels of jurisdiction in state courts

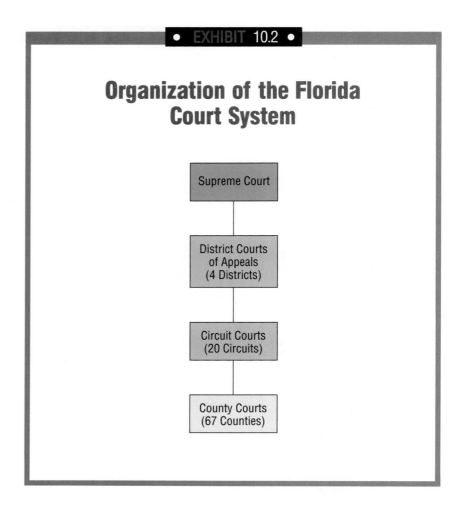

Organization of the Florida Court System

limited jurisdiction and the circuit courts are those of general jurisdiction. The supreme court and the district courts of appeal are two levels of appellate jurisdiction. This system can be contrasted with the complexity of the system in New York State, which also has a four-tier system (see Exhibit 10.3). The two lowermost levels are the courts of limited jurisdiction, which are separated by discrete functions and geography. The supreme courts are the courts of general jurisdiction, and the upper courts, like those of Florida, are the appellate courts.

In the pages that follow, each level of the state court system is examined in more detail. The greatest amount of discussion will be about the lower courts, for it is there that most defendants begin judicial processing. The chief function of the trial court — the criminal trial — is addressed in Chapter 12.

Courts of Limited Jurisdiction

The lower criminal courts represent a stepchild of the American judicial system.

—H. TED RUBIN, 1976

Courts of limited jurisdiction: The entry point for judicial processing, with jurisdiction limited to full processing of *all* minor offenses and pretrial processing of felony cases.

The **courts of limited jurisdiction,** or *lower courts* — more than 13,000 in number across the nation — are the entry point for criminal judicial

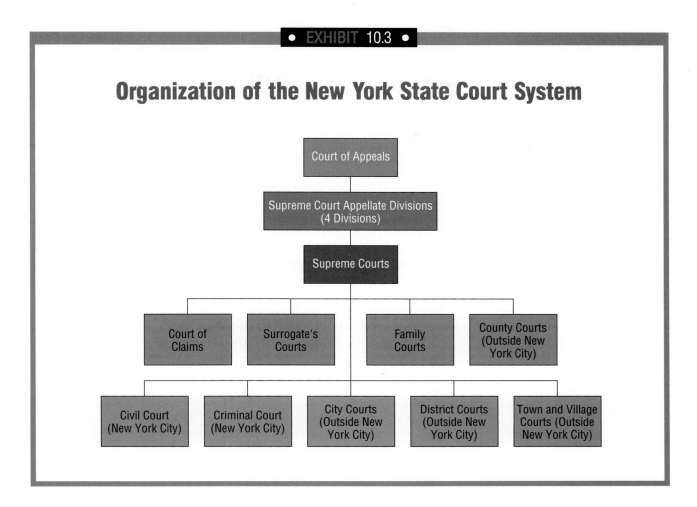

EXHIBIT 10.3

Organization of the New York State Court System

Court of Appeals

Supreme Court Appellate Divisions
(4 Divisions)

Supreme Courts

Court of Claims

Surrogate's Courts

Family Courts

County Courts (Outside New York City)

Civil Court (New York City)

Criminal Court (New York City)

City Courts (Outside New York City)

District Courts (Outside New York City)

Town and Village Courts (Outside New York City)

processing. They handle all minor criminal offenses, such as prostitution, drunkenness, petty larceny, disorderly conduct, and the myriad violations of traffic laws and city and county ordinances. In addition, they hear most civil cases and conduct inquests. For defendants charged with felonies, the lower courts have the authority to hold initial appearances and preliminary hearings, and to make bail decisions.

In matters of minor law violation, the lower court conducts all aspects of the judicial process — from initial appearance to sentencing. Given the large number of felony cases that are initially processed in this part of the state court structure, the lower courts ultimately deal, in one way or another, with more than 90 percent of all ciminal cases.

Historically, the lower courts have been the most significant, yet typically the most neglected, of all the courts. The significance of these courts to the adminstration of justice lies not only in the sheer number of defendants who pass through them, but also in their jurisdiction over many of the offenses that represent the initial stage of an individual's criminal career. As pointed out by the President's Commission on Law Enforcement and Administration of Justice, most convicted felons have prior misdemeanor convictions, and although the likelihood of diverting an offender from a career in crime is greatest at the time of his or her first brush with the law, the lower courts do not deal effectively with those who come before them.[3]

"I'm afraid this is a matter for the lower court . . ."

Drawing by Arnie Levin, National Law Journal.

Trial *de novo:* A new trial, on appeal from a lower court to a court of general jurisdiction.

Justices of the Peace: The judges in many lower courts in rural areas, who are typically not lawyers and are locally elected.

Problems with justice of the peace courts

In 1919, in his address to the members of the New York Bar Association, the late Supreme Court Justice Charles Evans Hughes commented on the proper role of the lower courts:

> The Supreme Court of the United States and the Court of Appeals will take care of themselves. Look after the courts of the poor, who stand most in the need of justice. The security of the Republic will be found in the treatment of the poor and the ignorant; in indifference to their misery and helplessness lies disaster.[4]

Although Justice Hughes might have been better advised to make his reference not only to the poor but also to the millions of others who pass through the lower courts each year, his point was well intentioned and unquestionably correct. But in the decades that followed, few changes in the lower courts seem to have occurred.

In the 1970s, the National Advisory Commission on criminal Justice Standards and Goals echoed the impressions of Hughes, and outlined the three major problems that continued to plague the lower courts: (1) neglect by bar associations, the higher courts, and the government agencies; (2) the volume and nature of their case loads; and (3) the **trial *de novo* system.**[5] (See Exhibit 10.4.)

By the beginning of the 1990s, little had changed with respect to the operations of the lower courts.[6] However, there are some differences in the nature of these enduring problems between rural and urban lower courts.

Justice of the Peace Courts Justice of the peace courts, which are similar to aldermans' and mayors' courts, developed at a time when a lack of effective transportation and communication tended to isolate small communities, thus preventing them from having a quick means for hearing minor criminal cases and for exercising local community authority. The **justice of the peace** was generally not required to be an attorney, and was typically best known as the person who performed marriages. The justice was either appointed or elected and usually had strong community ties. He heard ordinance violations, issued search and arrest warrants, determined bail, arraigned defendants, and processed civil cases involving limited dollar amounts.[7]

The problems with this judicial system were, and still are, numerous. First, justices of the peace, referred to as JPs, not only had minimal, if any, legal training, but in addition dealt with legal matters in saloons and in filling stations where they worked, or in other similarly undignified settings. (See Exhibit 10.5.)

Second, methods of compensation were problematic. In some jurisdictions the JP was paid from the court costs he would assess convicted offenders. If the defendant was acquitted, the JP could assess no costs. Thus it was in the justice's interest to convict as many persons as possible.

In recent years, justice of the peace courts have been eliminated in some states, and have been upgraded in others. But many of the difficulties still persist. For example, although *Tumey* v. *Ohio* in 1927 declared that the practice of paying JPs from costs assessed defendants only when they were convicted was unconstitutional,[8] the President's Commission on Law Enforcement and Adminstration of Justice found the practice to be still current in some areas. Furthermore, as recently as 1977, the U.S. Supreme Court invalidated a Georgia law that provided JPs with a $5 fee for each search warrant they issued to the police.[9]

The lack of legal training among justices of the peace and the undignified nature of their court settings still endures in several jurisdictions.

● EXHIBIT 10.4 ●

The Problems of the Lower Courts

The lower courts of most states share three problems.

The first is their position on the bottom rung of the judicial ladder, which results in neglect by those forces that should be scrutinizing and aiding the level of court performance — bar associations, the state supreme court, the press, government agencies, and citizen groups. The neglect is so severe that members of the legal profession and of the judiciary often are unaware of the number, names, functions, or identity of the judges of the lower courts. The inferior status of the lower courts and the traditional view that their work is ministerial, monotonous, and legally unchallenging also is reflected in the use of part-time support personnel, low salaries, and inadequate facilities. As a result, the lower courts generally tend to attract prosecutors, defense counsel, clerks, and judges of a caliber lower than normally encountered in the courts of general jurisdiction.

The second problem is the volume and nature of the case load. The overwhelming part of the case load of the lower courts consists of traffic violations and public intoxication prosecutions. These cases seldom raise any issue that requires consideration and decision and they encourage perfunctory, summary dispositions, often referred to as assembly-line justice. Assembly-line justice minimizes the likelihood that cases will be heard fully and fairly and virtually precludes any meaningful correctional disposition.

The third problem is the trial *de novo* system. This precludes effective review and monitoring of the work and decisions of the lower courts by appellate tribunals, and enables judges of the lower courts, unlike their general jurisdiction judicial counterparts, to operate with improper procedures and under erroneous assumptions of the substantive law.

SOURCE: National Advisory Commission on Criminal Justice Standards and Goals, *Courts* (Washington, D.C.: U.S. Government Printing Office, 1973), pp. 161–162.

Reports by the *New York Times* and CBS-TV found that in South Carolina and other states, the average JP had only a high school education and some had never opened a law book; their courtrooms included kitchens, barns, and porches; and their dispensing of justice was only a part-time endeavor.[10] Similarly, the Louisiana constitution of 1921, still in effect today, provides that "Justices of the Peace shall be of good moral character, freeholders and qualified electors, able to read and write the English language correctly, and shall possess such other qualifications as may be prescribed by law."[11] Legal training was not considered a prerequisite for dispensing justice.

Conditions that led to the development and growth of justice of the peace courts no longer exist. Modern means of transportation and communication have eliminated the total isolation of even the most remote rural outposts. But as long as JPs can convince the electorate and legislature that their closeness to the community and its interests is advantageous, the justice of the peace court will continue to exist. JP courts persist, for example, throughout Delaware, not only in rural areas but also in the densely populated metropolitan county of New Castle.

Alternatives to the JP courts in rural America are the county courts and their variants, which do not involve the more negative aspects of the justice of the peace system. As lower courts, they handle minor offenses, civil issues, and the pretrial aspects of felony processing. County justices usually have at least some legal training; the dispensing of justice occurs in more formal courts of law staffed by judges, clerks,

• EXHIBIT 10.5 •

The Law West of the Pecos

In history and folklore, Judge Roy Bean of the West Texas frontier is a familiar character. Books have been written about him, and the 1972 Warner Brothers production *The Life and Times of Judge Roy Bean* cast actor Paul Newman as the colorful seat of the rural bench. Although Bean was hardly a Paul Newman lookalike, he was a caricature and exaggeration of everything that could possibly be wrong with a rural magistrate, and his methods of distributing justice were indeed a satirical rendition of the justice of the peace court.

Born in the hills of Mason County, Kentucky, in 1825, Roy Bean's early life hardly reflected the qualities and experiences one would hope to find in a person charged with making decisions in the cause of justice. In 1847 he shot a man in a barroom brawl; several years later, he killed a Mexican army officer in a gun duel over a woman, after which he was hanged (but survived); during the Civil War he operated with Confederate irregulars; and following the war he was a blockade runner in San Antonio.

Bean's career in frontier justice began in 1882 when he drifted across the Pecos River into West Texas, dispensing whiskey from a tent. First at a place called Eagle's Nest on the Rio Grande, and later beside a railroad bed that ran through Dead Man's Canyon just north of the Mexican border, he plied his trade as a saloonkeeper. His saloon was called the "Jersey Lilly," and the spot was Langtry, Texas — both named after actress Lily Langtry, whom Bean idolized but had never met.

The records of Pecos County, Texas, document that Roy Bean was appointed justice of the peace on August 2, 1882, by the county commissioner's court, and that he fully qualified for the position by submitting a $1,000 bond on December 6, 1882.

As a rural magistrate, he dispensed both justice and beer from the same bar, frequently interrupting his court to serve liquor. He knew little of law or criminal procedure, and his methods of handling cases were often bizarre. Once he reportedly fined a dead man $40 for carrying a concealed weapon; on another occasion he threatened to hang a lawyer for using profanity in the courtroom (the attorney had stated that he planned to *habeas corpus* his client). And in one memorable trial Judge Bean freed a man accused of murdering a Chinese railroad worker because he could not find any law that made it a crime "to kill a Chinaman."

Bean's antics became so widely known that passengers passing through Langtry often stopped to look at the "Law West of the Pecos," as the judge called himself. These visits sparked more tales, which encouraged Bean to hand down more of his infamous "decisions." In fact, he spent much of his time working on the diffusion of his own legend.

But the "Law West of the Pecos" was anything but just, for Bean was ignorant, biased, and corrupt. He allowed his jurors (when he had them) to drink profusely before considering a verdict; he pocketed most of the fines he collected; he confiscated money and property from bodies brought to him in his role as coroner; he stuffed ballot boxes to ensure his re-election; and although he could hang a horse thief without batting an eye, when his friends were accused of murder, leniency always prevailed.

Besides his involvement — or lack of involvement — with law and order, Roy Bean spent much of his time worshiping Lily Langtry. As legend tells it, his most precious moment came in the spring of 1888, when the woman whose tattered picture he carried in his pocket played in San Antonio. Free of alcoholic fumes and in a front row seat, Bean watched the woman who had tortured his mind for years. But no one would introduce him to her, and sadly he returned to Langtry and his "Jer-

and other personnel on state or county payrolls; and the trappings of fees for service are absent. But as with all the lower courts, they tend to reflect the shortcomings characteristic of courts of limited jurisdiction.

Municipal Courts The urban counterpart of the justice of the peace and county courts are the municipal courts, also called magistrate's courts. In jurisdictions where the judicial system has formally separated

sey Lilly," thinking only of a love he could never have.

For the next eight years he continued his antics in frontier justice, until he finally overstepped his bounds. In 1896, after a count of votes cast for Bean proved their number to be well in excess of the Langtry population, he was removed from the bench. For the next seven years, until his death in 1903, Bean continued as a saloonkeeper, having failed to achieve his lifelong dream of meeting Miss Langtry. Ironically, only months after his death, she visited his saloon while on a tour through Texas. The Langtry townspeople gave Bean's revolver to Lily, and she kept it until her own death in 1929. Today, Roy Bean's "Jersey Lilly" still stands, and Langtry remains a small town in Texas with a population of some seventy-five persons.

SOURCE: Horace Bell, *On the Old West Coast* (New York: William Morrow, 1930); C. L. Sonnichsen, Roy Bean: *Law West of the Pecos* (Old Greenwich, Conn.: Devin-Adair, 1943).

Judge Roy Bean's combined courthouse and saloon, the "Jersey Lilly," in Langtry, Texas. Named for his idol, the actress Lily Langtry, it was the setting for Bean's wild-west justice from 1882 to 1903.

the processing of criminal and civil cases, these lower courts may be known as criminal courts or police courts.

The functions of the municipal courts are the same as those of the county courts, and many of the problems are similar. But municipal courts have the added difficulty of large case loads and assembly-line justice. Some magistrates, in the face of heavy work loads, exercise wide discretion in ordering certain cases dismissed and in abbreviating the

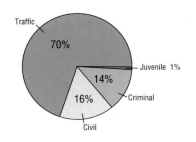

Distribution of Cases Filed in Courts of General and Limited Jurisdiction

SOURCE: Bureau of Justice Statistics, 1990

Conditions in the criminal court in Brooklyn, New York

Too often, when our citizens seek a dignified place of deliberation in which to resolve their controversies, they find instead aesthetic revulsion. They bear witness — not to dignity, but to deterioration, not to actual justice delivered, but to the perception of justice denied or, worse, justice degraded.

— SOL WACHTLER, CHIEF JUDGE, NEW YORK STATE, 1985

law. In addition, with lesser offenses such as prostitution, drunkenness, and loitering, groups of defendants are processed en masse and dispensed with quickly.

During the early 1920s, legal scholars Roscoe Pound and Felix Frankfurter participated in an analysis sponsored by The Cleveland Foundation of criminal justice administration in that midwestern city. Their report included a scathing denunciation of Cleveland's municipal court, noting that it was devoid of any quality and commenting that it was not unlike an early nineteenth-century police court.[12] Some fifty years later, H. Ted Rubin, former judge and assistant executive director of the Institute for Court Management in Denver, Colorado, returned to the Cleveland Municipal Court and described it as follows:

> The Criminal Division of the Cleveland Municipal Court is located in the Police Building at 21st and Payne. The courtroom is well worn, crowded, and noisy. Row on row of benches are peopled with defendants out on bail, witnesses, friends and relatives of defendants, attorneys, social service personnel, and others. Most attorneys sit at the several counsel tables at the front of the room. The judge is flanked by a representative of the clerk's office to his right and two police officers. To his left is his bailiff. An assistant police prosecutor is present on one end of the judge's bench, an assistant county prosecutor on the other. A stenotype reporter was added during April 1971, and sits along the bar in front of the judge immediately next to the defendants and counsel who appear. The arraignments, hearings, and conferences which occur at the bench are largely inaudible beyond the second or third row of the spectator gallery. Witnesses generally testify from standing positions off to the side of the judge. There is little dignity to the setting. Jailed defendants are brought in and out from a door behind the judge and off to his right. People leaving the courtroom go out a door in the front of the room and off to the judge's left, where outside noise enters the courtroom as the door opens and closes.[13]

According to Rubin the situation in the Cleveland Municipal Court in the early 1970s can be considered mild when compared with that in the New York criminal courts of the 1980s and early 1990s. The criminal court in Brooklyn, New York, for example, is a court of limited jurisdiction that handles minor criminal offenses as well as pretrial processing of all felony cases. Observations made during 1980, 1981, and 1990, showed a chaotic system of justice.[14] On one Monday morning in one particular courtroom that dealt almost exclusively with preliminary hearings and arraignments of felony cases, the rows of benches were packed with hundreds of spectators. Presumably, these were the families, friends, and acquaintances of the defendant, together with other interested parties, and possibly sightseers. Although many sat in a dignified manner, attempting to follow the proceedings, others conversed, ate, slept, played cards, read, or attended to other matters. Children played at their mothers' feet; an artist sketched the posture of the magistrate; and a Brooklyn College student read an accounting text while his female acquaintance attempted to solve the mystery of a Rubik's cube.

The rumble of sound made paying attention to the matters of the court impossible. Only those in the first few rows of the courtroom, which were reserved for attorneys, could hear the words of the judge, defendant, prosecutor, bailiff, and defense. An occasional thunderclap of laughter or crying or boisterousness would alert the clerk to remind the crowd that it was a court of law.

Along the aisles, sides, and rear walls of the courtroom were dozens of police, parole, and probation officers. They complained that the docket was crowded again that day, that their case would not be heard for at least three hours: "There goes another day off," said one patrolman. Another responded, "Doesn't pay to make an arrest any more."

Just beyond the rail that separated the bench from the spectators was the quarters of the Legal Aid lawyers. It was a long table piled high with case materials. Court personnel huddled around the table to discuss cases during the proceedings, while defendants, mothers, fathers, spouses, attorneys, police officers, and probation and parole officers hung over the rail to glance at the materials, plead their cases, or otherwise elicit information.

To the left of the magistrate's bench was a door that led to the detention pens where defendants awaited their turn. To the right of the bench, within the courtroom, was another holding area, where the faces of the accused were grim and their hands cuffed.

Justice was swift and to the point. A preliminary hearing in a felony case took only ten minutes, or five, or two. In one hearing, after the charges of robbery, assault, and possession of a deadly weapon were read, the following exchange took place:

MAGISTRATE: Son, do you understand the charges as they have been read?
DEFENDANT: Yes, sir.
MAGISTRATE: How do you plead?
DEFENDANT: Not guilty, sir.
MAGISTRATE: Is the state's case ready?
PROSECUTOR: Yes, your honor.
MAGISTRATE: Is the defense's case ready?
ATTORNEY: Yes, your honor.
MAGISTRATE: Bind him over for trial!

The entire proceeding lasted a total of twenty-seven seconds. In another case:

MAGISTRATE: Where's your lawyer?
DEFENDANT: I don't know, he was supposed to be here.
MAGISTRATE: Postponement.

With that the magistrate rose to his feet, called the court to order, chastised those present for the misdeeds of those who had failed to be in the court, addressed the fact that justice could not be otherwise served, and called a recess.

Other urban courts reflect similar styles of criminal processing. The basic problem stems from case overloads, and the result is often short-hand justice. Defendants may not be accorded the full range of procedural safeguards, and the several millions who appear annually before the urban courts run the risk of conviction and sentence in situations in which constitutional guidelines may not be fully observed.

Major Trial Courts

The major *trial courts,* or **courts of general jurisdiction,** are authorized to try *all* criminal and civil cases. Such courts, numbering in excess of 3,000 across the nation, handle about 10 percent of the defendants originally brought before the lower courts who are charged with felonies and serious misdemeanors (the balance having been already disposed of at the lower court level).

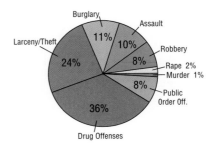

Felony Defendants in Urban Areas by Arrest Charge

SOURCE: Bureau of Justice Statistics, 1990

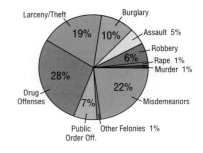

Felony Defendants in Urban Areas by Conviction Offense

SOURCE: Bureau of Justice Statistics, 1990

Courts of general jurisdiction: Courts authorized to try *all* criminal and civil cases.

Judicial circuit: A specific jurisdiction served by a judge or court, as defined by given geographical boundaries.

In terms of nomenclature, distinctions between some types of lower courts and trial courts can often be confusing. They may be called circuit, district, superior courts, or they may have numerous other titles. But there are some exceptions. For example, Indiana has both circuit courts and superior courts, and in Indianapolis the court is simply called "Criminal Court." While many county courts may be part of a state's lower courts, as described earlier, other county courts may actually be circuit or district courts and hence are major trial courts. Also, a given county courthouse may often serve as both a lower court and a trial court. For example, when several counties are politically grouped together in a **judicial circuit,** it is customary for a judge to hold court in each county in turn. The judge moves from county to county within the circuit, and the local county courthouse becomes the circuit court during the judge's term there; the phrase "riding the circuit" derives from this practice.[15]

The administration of criminal justice in the major trial courts tends to be less problematic than it is in the courts of limited jurisdiction. Judges are lawyers and members of the bar, and hence are better equipped to deal with the complex issues of felony cases: most are salaried, full-time justices and are not tarnished by the fee-for-service payment structure; the adjudication process is generally cloaked in the formalities of procedural criminal law and due process; and as courts of original jurisdiction, the trial courts are **courts of record,** which means a full transcript of the proceedings is made for all cases. However, this does not mean that the trial courts are without difficulties. As seen in later chapters, there are procedural problems involving bail, indictment, plea negotiation, sentencing, and judicial discretion that can affect the fairness of trial court justice.

Courts of record: Courts in which a full transcript of the proceedings is made for all cases.

As a final note here, some comment seems warranted to illustrate more fully the separate roles and relationships between the lower and trial courts. The criminal case processing in Colorado's First Judicial Circuit (see Exhibit 10.6), generally reflects what is typical throughout the nation. *All* felonies and misdemeanors begin in the lower court, called the county court in that jurisdiction. While the misdemeanor cases remain in the lower court through sentencing, felony processing shifts to the district court, the major trial court, at arraignment. This is in contrast to jurisdictions in which the *entire* felony process occurs in the trial court. The felony case flow in Indianapolis, Indiana, is an example of this latter type of processing.

Appellate Courts

Appellate jurisdiction: Jurisdiction restricted to matters of appeal and review.

In law and criminal justice, the word *appeal* refers to the review by a higher court of the judgment of a lower court. Thus, **appellate jurisdiction** is restricted to matters of appeal and review; it cannot try cases as in the courts of general jurisdiction. However, this is not to say that the work load of these courts is light. Filings for appeal emerge not only from criminal cases, but from civil matters as well. In fact, the majority of appeals come out of civil suits. In the area of domestic relations alone, for example, the number of appeals filed requesting reviews of decisions rendered in matters of child custody rights, dependent support, alimony, and property settlement runs into the tens of thousands.

Intermediate courts of appeal

As a result, there are *intermediate courts of appeal* in more than half the states. If an attorney complies with the court's rules for appealing a case, the court must hear it. (This assumes that the matter is appealable —an issue discussed in Chapter 13.)

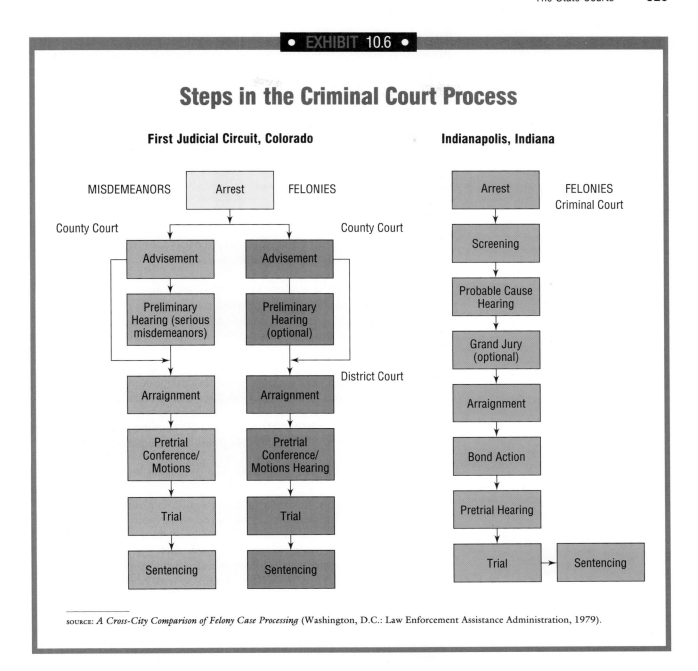

Steps in the Criminal Court Process

First Judicial Circuit, Colorado

MISDEMEANORS   Arrest   FELONIES

County Court   County Court

Advisement   Advisement

Preliminary Hearing (serious misdemeanors)   Preliminary Hearing (optional)

District Court

Arraignment   Arraignment

Pretrial Conference/ Motions   Pretrial Conference/ Motions Hearing

Trial   Trial

Sentencing   Sentencing

Indianapolis, Indiana

FELONIES
Criminal Court

Arrest

Screening

Probable Cause Hearing

Grand Jury (optional)

Arraignment

Bond Action

Pretrial Hearing

Trial → Sentencing

SOURCE: *A Cross-City Comparison of Felony Case Processing* (Washington, D.C.: Law Enforcement Assistance Administration, 1979).

The intermediate courts of appeal serve to relieve the state's highest court from hearing every case. An unfavorable decision from an intermediate appeals court, however, does not automatically guarantee a hearing by the state supreme court, the court of last resort in each state. It has the power to choose which cases will be placed on its docket—a characteristic of the highest court in every jurisdiction.

Reform and Unification of State Courts

The state courts have many problems. There are awkward matters of procedure, but more pertinent to this discussion are problems of organization, structure, and deployment.

For most of the twentieth century, various federal, state, and city commissions and foundations have examined the state courts, and their recommendations for reorganization have remained unchanged through the years:

- unify felony and misdemeanor courts
- create single, unified state court systems
- centralize administrative responsibility
- abolish the justice of the peace courts
- increase judicial personnel
- improve physical facilities

Perhaps the most pressing issue in this regard is the matter of court unification. As a study by the National Advisory Commission on Criminal Justice Standards and Goals emphasized:

> State courts should be organized into a unified judicial system financed by the State and administered through a statewise court administrator or administrative judge under the supervision of the chief justice of the State supreme court.
>
> All trial courts should be unified into a single trial court with general criminal as well as civil jurisdiction. Criminal jurisdiction now in courts of limited jurisdiction should be placed in these unified trial courts of general jurisdiction, with the exception of certain traffic violations. The State supreme court should promulgate rules for the conduct of minor as well as major criminal prosecutions.
>
> All judicial functions in the trial courts should be performed by full-time judges. All judges should possess law degrees and be members of the bar.
>
> A transcription or other record of the pretrial court proceedings and the trial should be kept in all criminal cases.
>
> The appeal procedure should be the same for all cases.[16]

Court unification, however, is more easily recommended than implemented. Some unification has occurred in Arizona, Illinois, North Carolina, Oklahoma, and Washington, and each year other states entertain proposals for a unified system. But few such proposals have been adopted due to the political, philosophical, and pragmatic dimensions involved. Local governments wish to retain control of their local courts; some judges fear that they would lose their status and discretion; nonlawyer judges fear that they would lose their jobs; political parties fear a loss of patronage opportunities; local municipalities fear the loss of revenues derived from court fines and fees; and many lawyers, judges, and prosecutors in all jurisdictions are simply resistive to change.[17]

The problem of overloaded court dockets is even more pervasive than court unification, for the costs that would be involved in expanding staff and facilities are well beyond the resources and willingness of most jurisdictions. Further, it seems that the overloading is only getting worse, principally an outgrowth of the proliferation of drug abuse, drug-related crime, and increased police activity in drug-ridden neighborhoods. The overall result has been greater numbers of drug cases coming to the attention of court systems across the nation. In Chicago, for example, new filings of drug charges increased by 74 percent from 1988 to 1990, while other types of criminal cases rose a more modest 14 percent.[18] Similar increases have been seen in other locales.[19] One response to the crowding and backlogs has been the establishment of special "drug courts" in a number of jurisdictions (see Exhibit 10.7).

● EXHIBIT 10.7 ●

Sidelights on Criminal Matters
The New "Drug Courts"

The label "drug court" is actually a generic term for several different kinds of initiatives designed to cope with the growing number of drug cases. These approaches include special courts or judges, distinctive case management systems, and/or pretrial diversion programs. Many of these new entities function as traditional courts by hearing evidence and adjudicating guilt, while others serve as special "plea bargaining" forums. Many handle only first offenders, with others having no such limitations. The courts established in New York City, Middlesex County (New Brunswick), New Jersey, and Cook County (Chicago), Illinois are examples of the numerous types. Those that function primarily as pretrial diversion initiatives are addressed in Chapter 17.

In New York City, special "crack courts" were established in 1987 to provide defendants with an immediate and one-shot opportunity to plead guilty to a significantly reduced offense. Under the traditional system, every defendant had to be indicted, arraigned, and summoned to repeated hearings

until he or she pleaded guilty or went to trial. Cases would drag on for months, some for more than a year. Under the "crack court" system, if the defendant accepts the plea, he or she is released from jail, generally without posting bail, and a sentencing date is set. No grand jury has to review the case, no police officer testifies, and no judge presides over time-consuming hearings and postponements. There are no trials in these "crack courts." Defendants who do not plead guilty are indicted, and their cases are turned over to other judges. During this new court's first year of operation, 20 percent of the defendants pleaded guilty, 60 percent to felony charges.

In Middlesex County, New Jersey, the court system has implemented a special case management program for the growing number of drug crimes. The program designated a special judge to handle all drug cases, developed a system which segregates all drug cases from the rest of the criminal docket and assigns them to appropriate case processing tracks, each involving special procedures to expedite

their adjudication. In addition, strategies were put in place to ensure that those defendants in need of rehabilitative services actually received them, and that those convicted of serious offenses did not pass through the system unpunished.

In Chicago, an evening drug court was established in October, 1989. Operating in five courtrooms, its purpose was to reduce the disposition time of drug cases. From October 1989 through February 1990, the court disposed of almost 3,000 cases. During that time, almost 10,000 new cases were introduced to the justice system as a whole. However, because of the added help of the drug court, cases were being disposed of faster than new cases were being introduced to the system.

Although many of the new drug courts have been effective in reducing court backlogs by rapidly disposing of cases, a number have been accused being no more that "assembly line justice mills" through which most defendants pass without any fear of incarceration.

THE FEDERAL JUDICIARY

The judicial power of the United States shall be vested in one Supreme Court, and in such inferior courts as the Congress may from time to time ordain and establish.
                    —THE CONSTITUTION OF THE UNITED STATES

Unlike the state court systems, the federal judiciary has a unified structure with jurisdiction throughout the United States and its territories. But the federal court system is also complex. It has a four-tier structure

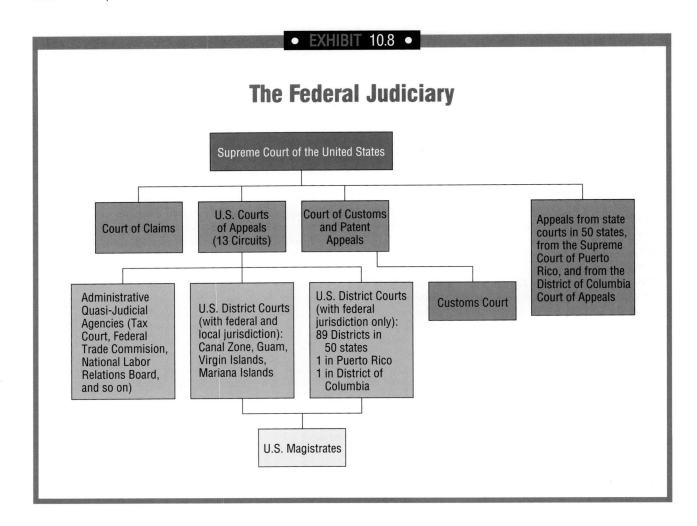

• EXHIBIT 10.8 •

The Federal Judiciary

Supreme Court of the United States

Court of Claims

U.S. Courts of Appeals (13 Circuits)

Court of Customs and Patent Appeals

Appeals from state courts in 50 states, from the Supreme Court of Puerto Rico, and from the District of Columbia Court of Appeals

Administrative Quasi-Judicial Agencies (Tax Court, Federal Trade Commision, National Labor Relations Board, and so on)

U.S. District Courts (with federal and local jurisdiction): Canal Zone, Guam, Virgin Islands, Mariana Islands

U.S. District Courts (with federal jurisdiction only): 89 Districts in 50 states 1 in Puerto Rico 1 in District of Columbia

Customs Court

U.S. Magistrates

similar to that in most of the states (see Exhibit 10.8). Although it handles fewer cases than the states, its scope is considerably greater. It has the responsibility for the enforcement of the following:

1. all federal codes (criminal, civil, and administrative) in all fifty states, U.S. territories, and the District of Columbia
2. local codes and ordinances in the territories of Guam, the Virgin Islands, the Canal Zone, and the Northern Mariana Islands

In addition, the U.S. Supreme Court has ultimate appelate jurisdiction over the federal appeals courts, the state courts of appeal, the District of Columbia Court of Appeals, and the Supreme Court of Puerto Rico.

U.S. Commissioners' and U.S. Magistrates' Courts

Historically, U.S. commissioners occupied positions comparable to justices of the peace in the state court systems. Established by an act of Congress at the beginning of the twentieth century, commissioners had the authority to issue search and arrest warrants, arraign defendants, fix bail, hold preliminary hearings, and try petty offense cases on certain federal reservations. Many of the criticisms leveled at the justice of the peace system, however, were also applicable to the U.S. commissioners'

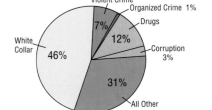

Crimes Referred by the FBI to the Federal Courts

SOURCE: General Accounting Office, 1991

courts. In 1967, the President's Commission on Law Enforcement and Administration of Justice found that 30 percent of the more than 700 commissioners were not lawyers, that all but seven had outside employment due to the part-time nature of the work, that commissioners' private businesses often took precedence over official duties, and that the number of commissioners in many districts had no relation to the number that might be needed. The President's Commission concluded by recommending that the system be either abolished or drastically altered.[20]

On the basis of the commission's findings, together with an examination of the situation by the Senate Judiciary Committee, the federal Magistrate's Act, passed by Congress in 1968, provided for a three-year phasing out of the office of the U.S. commissioner. The act also established **U.S. magistrates**—lawyers whose powers are limited to trying lesser misdemeanors, setting bail in more serious cases, and assisting the district courts in various legal matters. In 1976, their authority was expanded to include the issuance of search and arrest warrants, the review of civil rights and *habeas corpus* petitions, and the conducting of pretrial conferences in both civil and criminal hearings.[21] Magistrates can be both full-time and part-time jurists and all are appointed by the federal district court judges.

The phaseout of U.S. commissioners and the establishment of U.S. magistrates

U.S. magistrates: Federal lower court officials whose powers are limited to trying lesser misdemeanors, setting bail, and assisting district courts in various legal matters.

United States District Courts

The sword of human justice is about to fall upon your guilty head.
— Isaac C. Parker, federal district court judge, 1876

The U.S. district courts were created by the federal Judiciary Act, passed by Congress on September 24, 1789. Originally there were thirteen courts, one for each of the original states, but by the 1980s there were ninety-five—eighty-nine distributed throughout the fifty states, and one each in the District of Columbia, Puerto Rico, Guam, the Canal Zone, the Virgin Islands, and the Northern Mariana Islands.

The **U.S. district courts** are the trial courts of the federal system and the District of Columbia—the courts of general jurisdiction. They have dominion over cases involving violations of federal laws, including bank robbery, civil rights abuses, mail fraud, counterfeiting, smuggling, kidnapping, and crimes involving transportation across state lines. The district courts try cases that involve compromises of national security, such as treason, sedition, and espionage; handle selective service violations, copyright infringements, and jurisdictional disputes; and try violations of the many regulatory codes, such as violations of the Securities and Exchange Acts, the Endangered Species Acts, the Meat and Poultry Inspection Acts, and the Foreign Agent Registration Act, among many others. In addition, district court case loads include numerous civil actions and petitions filed by state and federal prisoners.

Each district court has one or more judges, depending on the case load, with over 500 judgeships authorized by law. In most cases, a single judge presides over trials, and a defendant may request that a jury be present. In complex civil matters, a special three-judge panel may be convened. In addition to U.S. magistrates, each court has numerous other officers attached to it: a U.S. attorney, who serves as the criminal prosecutor for the federal government; several assistant U.S. attorneys; a U.S. marshal's office; and probation officers, court reporters, clerks, and bankruptcy judges.

U.S. district courts: The trial courts of the federal judiciary.

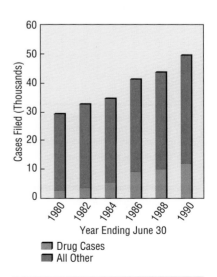

U.S. District Courts Criminal Filings 1980–1990

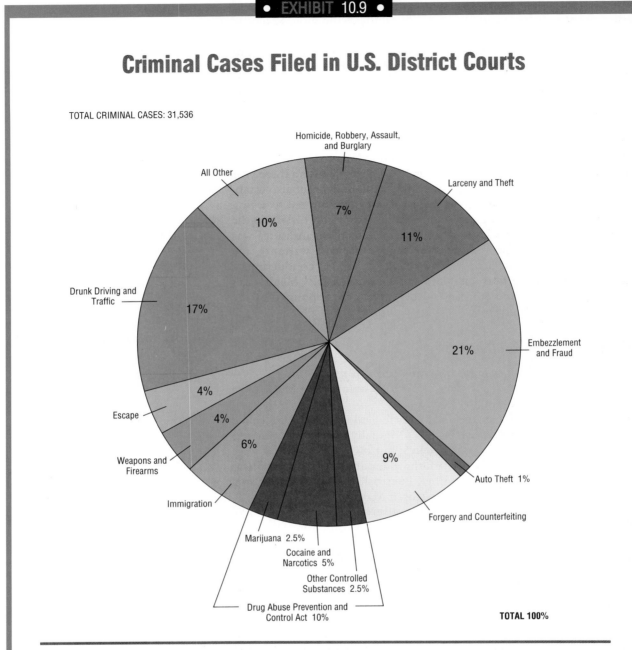

• EXHIBIT 10.9 •

Criminal Cases Filed in U.S. District Courts

TOTAL CRIMINAL CASES: 31,536

Homicide, Robbery, Assault, and Burglary 7%

Larceny and Theft 11%

All Other 10%

Drunk Driving and Traffic 17%

Embezzlement and Fraud 21%

Escape 4%

4%

6%

Auto Theft 1%

9%

Weapons and Firearms

Immigration

Forgery and Counterfeiting

Marijuana 2.5%

Cocaine and Narcotics 5%

Other Controlled Substances 2.5%

Drug Abuse Prevention and Control Act 10%

TOTAL 100%

Note: Figure includes all offenses filed in federal district courts in accordance with reporting changes necessitated by the implementation of provisions of the Speedy Trial Act of 1974 (P.L. 93-619, approved January 3, 1975).

ᵃ Escape from custody, aiding or abetting an escape, failure to appear in court, and bail jumping.

SOURCE: Clerk, Administrative Office of the United States Courts.

Throughout the 1980s, the district courts have had to function under near-crisis conditions. The work load has increased dramatically, from 122,624 cases in 1970 to almost 300,000 by 1986. And although the level of criminal cases has remained relatively stable — from 30,000 to 40,000 filings each year dealing with everything from traffic offenses to significant violations of the U.S. Criminal Code (see Exhibit 10.9) —

the number of district court judges has not been expanded in proportion to the work load. In 1970, there were 331 judges with an average load of 370 cases. In 1986, there were 575 judges with average loads of almost 600 cases, reflecting an increase of some 60 percent of the sixteen-year period.[22] To keep pace with the work load almost 300 new judges would have to be hired, and it is unlikely that there are many highly qualified attorneys in the United States who would be willing to work for the salary offered. By 1986, district court judges were earning $78,700, and by 1991 this figure was almost $100,000.[23] Although this is no trifling salary when compared with the average national income, it is more than 100 percent below that of other people in the legal profession with similar credentials and experience. Yet by contrast, district court judges are already among the highest paid officials in the federal government, and if their salaries were raised significantly, many other federal salaries would have to be raised as well. The public, increasingly disenchanted with government spending and unmanageable budget deficits, probably would not stand for it.

United States Court of Appeals

Appeals from the U.S. district courts move up to the next step in the federal judicial hierarchy, the **U.S. courts of appeals.** There are thirteen of these courts, with more than 150 authorized judgeships. Each court is located in a *circuit* — described earlier in this chapter as a specific judicial jurisdiction served by the court, as defined by geographical boundaries. For example, the U.S. Court of Appeals of the First Circuit is located in Boston and serves the district courts located in Maine, Massachusetts, New Hampshire, Rhode Island, and Puerto Rico (see Exhibit 10.10).

The thirteen courts of appeals hear more than 30,000 cases each year involving both criminal and civil matters.[24] The cases heard are those appealed from the U.S. district courts — *not* those from state supreme or appeals courts. Almost all cases are heard by three-judge panels; a few are heard *en banc,* or "in bank," meaning the full bench of judges authorized for the court considers the appeal. In only three instances can a case appealed from one of the district courts bypass the court of appeals and go directly to the U.S. Supreme Court:

1. when the ruling under appeal was decided by a special three-judge district court hearing
2. when the case involves a federal statute declared unconstitutional by a district court, and the United States is a litigant
3. when the issue under review is deemed to be of such importance that it requires immediate settlement

The United States Supreme Court

We look to the history of the time of framing and to the intervening history of interpretation. But the ultimate question must be, what do the words of the text mean in our time?
— WILLIAM J. BRENNAN, JR., ASSOCIATE JUSTICE, U.S. SUPREME COURT, 1985

The **U.S. Supreme Court,** also known as the Court, High Court, and High Tribunal, is the highest court in the nation. It stands at the apex of the federal judiciary and is truly the court of last resort. The High Court is composed of nine justices: one chief justice and eight associate justices, who serve for life. They are nominated by the president of the United States and must be confirmed by the Senate.

U.S. courts of appeals: The federal courts of appellate jurisdiction.

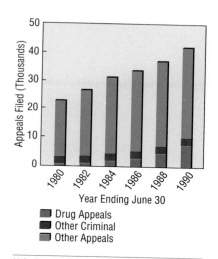

U.S. Courts of Appeals Filings 1980–1990

U.S. Supreme Court: The highest court in the nation and the court of last resort.

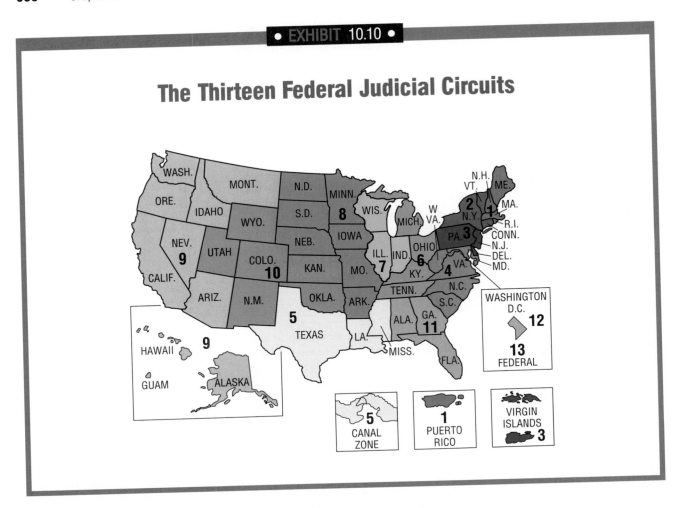

• EXHIBIT 10.10 •

The Thirteen Federal Judicial Circuits

The Origins of the Supreme Court   The Court was provided for by the Constitution, but only in the briefest of terms. Article III placed the judicial power of the United States in a supreme court and inferior federal courts: Section 1 of the article noted that the justices would hold their posts during "good behavior," and Section 2 outlined the range of judicial power. In contrast to Articles I and II of the Constitution, which spell out with considerable detail the powers and prerogatives of the Congress and the executive branch, what was stated for the nation's highest court was no more than a terse outline. Moreover, the Court had a slow start.

On September 24, 1789, President George Washington signed the Judiciary Act, which actually created the Supreme Court, into law, and sent to the Senate for confirmation the names of the first chief justice and five associate justices. However, one of these declined, another accepted but never attended, and three others either resigned or died before the close of the Court's first decade. John Jay of New York, the first chief justice, spent much of his tenure abroad and resigned in 1795. Two other men followed him as chief justice within ten years — John Rutledge of South Carolina, as an unconfirmed recess appointment in 1795, and John Marshall of Virginia in 1801.

The status of the first terms of the Court during the 1790s were also ambiguous and comparatively minor.[25] Only three of the six justices

The people can change Congress, but only God can change the Supreme Court.

— THE LATE GEORGE NORRIS, U.S. SENATOR FROM NEBRASKA

were present for the Court's opening session on February 1, 1790, but there was no business other than the appointment of a clerk. In fact, during the Court's first three years, no judicial decisions were made, and in 1792 Chief Justice John Jay reportedly described the post of a Supreme Court justice as "intolerable." [26]

Although the early terms of the Court saw few significant decisions, the justices themselves were kept busy. When the Judiciary Act of 1789 created the Supreme Court and the thirteen district courts, it also established three judicial circuits, each composed of the geographical areas covered by several of the district courts. Twice annually, within each of the circuits, circuit court sessions were held to handle some of the more serious federal cases. But the Judiciary Act had not provided for a set of judges for the federal circuit courts. Thus, the chief justice and his five associate justices were required to travel throughout the country to hold circuit court where and when necessary, a situation that lasted for almost a full century.

Marbury v. *Madison*   The full establishment of Supreme Court power occurred during the early decades of the nineteenth century under the leadership of John Marshall, chief justice from 1801 through 1835. Just two years after Marshall assumed his post, the Court announced its decision in ***Marbury v. Madison,*** [27] and in so doing it claimed, exercised, and justified its authority to review and nullify acts of Congress that it found to conflict with the Constitution.

Marbury v. *Madison* in 1803 was a dispute over presidential patronage that had escalated into a contest for authority between Congress and the Supreme Court. The case emerged from the bitter presidential

Marbury v. Madison: The Supreme Court decision that established the High Court's power to review acts of Congress and declare invalid those it found in conflict with the Constitution.

Left: Supreme Court chambers, Southampton, New York.
Right: The Supreme Court of the United States.

election of 1800, when Republican Thomas Jefferson defeated Federalist John Adams. Unwilling to relinquish the power they had held since the beginning of the Union, the Federalists sought to entrench themselves in the federal judiciary. John Marshall's appointment had been part of that entrenchment. In addition, the lame duck Congress, just prior to Adam's leaving office as president, approved legislation creating sixteen new district court judgeships. Furthermore, it authorized Adams to appoint as many justices of the peace for the newly created District of Columbia as he deemed necessary, and it reduced the number of Supreme Court justices from six to five at the next vacancy. This latter move was intended to deprive Jefferson of a quick appointment to the bench.

Adams named and Congress confirmed the sixteen district court judges and forty-two justices of the peace. On his last night in office, Adams signed the commissions for the new justices of the peace and had them taken to Marshall, then secretary of state, who was to affix the Great Seal of the United States and deliver them to the appointees. The Seal was affixed, but not all of the commissions were delivered.

William Marbury, an aide to the secretary of the Navy, was one of four men who had not received their commissions. At President Jefferson's request, Secretary of State James Madison refused deliverance of the commissions. Marbury asked the Supreme Court to issue a writ of *mandamus* ordering Madison to give the four men their commissions. A **writ of *mandamus*** is simply a command to perform a certain duty, and the Judiciary Act of 1789 had authorized the Supreme Court to issue such writs to officers of the federal government.

Chief Justice Marshall found himself in a dilemma, with the authority of the Supreme Court at stake. If the High Court ordered delivery of the commission, Madison could refuse to obey the order, which seemed likely, and the Court had no means to enforce compliance. If the Court did not issue the writ, it would mean surrendering to President Jefferson's point of view. Either way, the Court would be conceding its power.

In what has been called a "masterwork of indirection, a brilliant example of Marshall's capacity to sidestep danger while seeming to court it, to advance in one direction while his opponents are looking in the other." [28] the chief justice made a cunning decision. First, he ruled that once the president had signed the commissions and the secretary of state had recorded them, the appointments were complete and valid. Second, he ruled that a writ of *mandamus* was the proper tool to require the new secretary of state to deliver the commissions. These actions served to rebuke Madison, and Jefferson by implication. Marshall then turned to the question of jurisdiction, to whether the High Court had the authority to issue the writ. He concluded that it did not. Marshall stated that the Congress could not expand or contract the jurisdiction of the Supreme Court, and that Congress had acted unconstitutionally and exceeded its power when, in Section 13 of the Judiciary Act of 1789, it had authorized the Court to issue such writs in original cases ordering federal officials to perform particular acts.

Although this matter of jurisdiction served to absolve the Jefferson administration of installing several of President Adam's appointments, the real significance of *Marbury* v. *Madison* was the establishment of the Court's power to review acts of Congress.

The *Marbury* decision is considered by many to have been the most important ruling in Supreme Court history, for without it, the Court may never have summoned itself up from its constitutional vapors.

Writ of *mandamus*: A command issued by a court to perform a certain duty.

In establishing the Court's power to review acts of Congress, *Marbury* v. *Madison* is considered by many constitutional scholars to be the most important ruling in Supreme Court history.

• EXHIBIT 10.11 •

Scorecard of the High Court Appointments
Whites 104, Blacks 2, Men, 105, Women 1

When President George Washington made his nominations for the United States Supreme Court in 1790, his six selections for the Court's first bench reflected the tenor of the times — all were white, male, and Protestant. It would be almost half a century before this barrier would even begin to be breached.

The first Roman Catholic to get a seat on the Supreme Court was Roger Brooke Taney, the son of a Maryland plantation owner. Taney had been nominated by President Andrew Jackson to fill the seat left vacant by the death of Chief Justice John Marshall.

Another eighty years passed before the barrier against Jews was finally breached. In 1916, President Woodrow Wilson filled a vacant seat with Louis Dembits Brandeis, a prominent Boston lawyer and the son of Jewish immigrants from Bohemia. There was vicious opposition to Brandeis's nomination, but he was confirmed nevertheless by a Senate vote of forty-seven to twenty-two.

In 1932, Benjamin Nathan Cardozo was seated on the Supreme Court by President Herbert Hoover. Cardozo's parents were descendants of Sephardic Jews who had settled in New York — one of whom had authored the words at the base of the Statue of Liberty. Cardozo's so-called Jewish seat was successively held by Felix Frankfurter (1939–1962), Arthur Goldberg (1962–1965), and Abe Fortas (1965–1969).

The barrier against blacks fell in 1967, with President Lyndon B. Johnson's appointment of Thurgood Marshall, a former U.S. court of appeals judge.

And after almost two centuries, the barrier against women also finally fell. It came in 1981, with the vacancy left by the retirement of Associate Justice Potter Stewart, who had been a member of the Bench since 1958. The "brethren's" first "sister" was Sandra Day O'Connor, an Arizona court of appeals judge nominated by President Ronald Reagan in fulfillment of a campaign promise.

Currently, the Court has four "minority" members — one woman (Sandra Day O'Connor), one black (Clarence Thomas), and two Catholics (Antonin Scalia and Anthony M. Kennedy). The remaining members, as in 1790, are white, male, and Protestant.

Roger Brooke Taney
1836–1864

Sandra Day O'Connor
1981–

Louis Dembits Brandeis
1916–1939

Benjamin Nathan Cardozo
1932–1938

Thurgood Marshall
1967–1991

The Jurisdictional Scope of the Supreme Court   In the words of the Constitution, the jurisdiction of the Supreme Court is broad but not unbounded. As stated in Article III, Section 2:

> The judicial power shall extend to all cases, in law and equity, arising under this Constitution, the laws of the United States, and treaties made, or which shall be made, under their authority; to all cases affecting ambassadors, other public ministers and consuls; to all cases of admiralty and maritime jurisdiction; to controversies to which the United States shall be a party; to controversies between two or more States; between a State and citizens of another State; between citizens of the same State claiming lands under grants of different States, and between a State, or the citizens thereof, and foreign States, citizens or subjects.

Thus the Constitution outlined eight jurisdictional areas for the Supreme Court, but its main function was as guardian of the Constitution.

As defined by the Constitution and spelled out in the Judiciary Act of 1789, the Supreme Court has two kinds of jurisdiction over cases — general and appellate. The Court's general jurisdiction usually involves suits between two states, issues that test the constitutionality of state laws, and matters relating to ambassadors. In such instances, the Supreme Court can serve as a trial court. In its appellate jurisdiction, the High Court resolves conflicts that raise "substantial federal questions" — typically related to the constitutionality of some lower court rule, decision, or procedure.

The Supreme Court in session in the 1930s. This photograph, by Dr. Erich Salomon, is believed to be the only one ever taken while the justices were actually hearing a case.

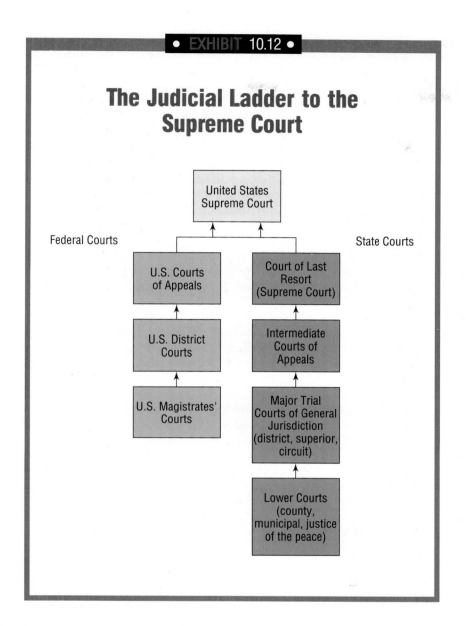

EXHIBIT 10.12

The Judicial Ladder to the Supreme Court

United States Supreme Court

Federal Courts

State Courts

U.S. Courts of Appeals

Court of Last Resort (Supreme Court)

U.S. District Courts

Intermediate Courts of Appeals

U.S. Magistrates' Courts

Major Trial Courts of General Jurisdiction (district, superior, circuit)

Lower Courts (county, municipal, justice of the peace)

Selection of Cases As the final tribunal beyond which no judicial appeal is possible, the Supreme Court has the discretion to decide which cases it will review. However, the Court must grant its jurisdiction in *all* instances in which:

- a federal court has held an act of Congress to be unconstitutional
- a U.S. court of appeals has found a state statute to be unconstitutional
- a state's highest court of appeals has ruled a federal law to be invalid
- an individual's challenge to a state statute on federal constitional grounds is upheld by a state supreme court

In all other instances, as provided by the Judiciary Act of 1925, the Supreme Court decides whether or not it will review a particular case.

The Supreme Court does not have the power and authority to review all decisions of the state courts in either civil or criminal matters. Its jurisdiction extends only to those cases where a federal statute has been interpreted or a defendant's constitutional right has allegedly been violated. Furthermore, a petitioner must exhaust all other remedies before the High Court will consider reviewing his or her case (see Exhibit 10.12). This is, should a matter of "substantial federal question" emerge in a justice of the peace court, for example, the first review would not be in the Supreme Court. Rather it would be heard as a trial *de novo* in the state trial court. Following that would be an appeal to the intermediate court of appeals (in those states where they exist), and then an appeal to the state's highest court. Only then is it eligible for review by the Supreme Court. A similar process occurs with respect to the federal court structure.

Writ of *certiorari*: A writ issued by the Supreme Court ordering some lower court to "forward up the record" of a case it has tried so the High Court can review it.

The High Court's authority to exercise its own discretion in deciding which cases it will hear is known as its *certiorari power,* and comes from the **writ of *certiorari,*** a writ of review issued by the High Court ordering some lower court to "forward up the record" of a case it has tried in order that the Supreme Court can review it.

Prior to this granting of *certiorari,* the potential case must pass the **Rule of Four;** that is, a case is accepted for review only if four or more members of the High Court feel that it merits consideration by the full Court.

Rule of Four: The decision of at least four Supreme Court justices that a case merits consideration by the full Court.

The Supreme Court accepts for review only cases in which its decision might make a difference to the appellant, and as stated earlier, only those of "substantial federal question." It does not operate as a court of last resort to correct the endless number of possible errors made by other courts. Rather, it marshals its time and energy for the most pressing matters. Currently, between 4,000 and 5,000 cases are filed annually for review by the Supreme Court. However, the Court limits itself to deciding less than 200 cases with full opinions each term.

Affirming, Reversing, and Remanding When the Supreme Court affirms a case, it has determined that the action or proceeding under review is free from reversible prejudicial or constitutional error and that the judgment appealed from shall stand. Thus, if a conviction appealed from a lower court is *affirmed,* the conviction remains in force.

A Supreme Court decision that *reverses* or overturns a defendant's conviction or sentence does not necessarily free the appellant or impose a lighter penalty. Rather, it *remands* or returns the case to the court of original jurisdiction for a proper judgment. Upon reversing and remanding, the trial court has several options, depending on the nature of the case. Many of the criminal cases that receive Supreme Court attention revolve around the constitutional issues of illegal search and seizure, illegal confessions, and other matters that might invoke the exclusionary rule. In such instances, the court of original jurisdiction can order a new trial, but cannot introduce the "tainted" evidence. In many of these cases, however, the prosecution may decide that without such evidence the state would have only a weak case, and it dismisses the charges. In other circumstances, the Supreme Court decision may require a *change of venue* because of pretrial publicity or community hostility that resulted in an unfair original hearing. The change of venue requires that any new trial be held in a different county or judicial district. Other Supreme Court reversals have ordered institutional au-

Drawing by D. Fradon © 1967,
The New Yorker Magazine, Inc.

"Can you name all nine Supreme Court justices?"

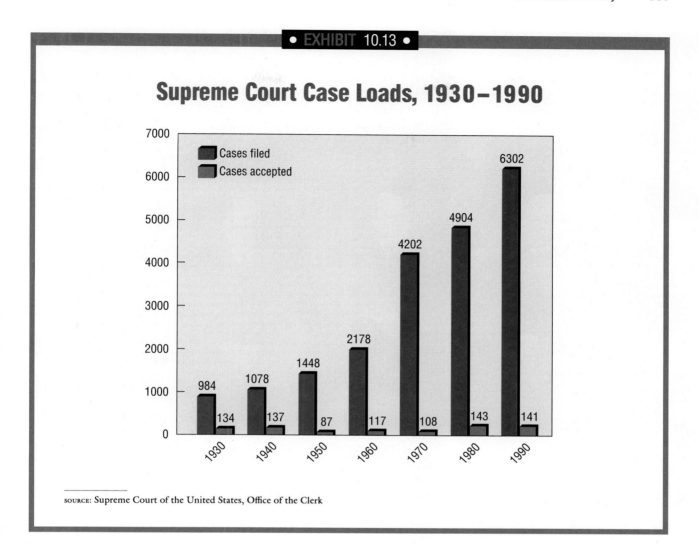

• EXHIBIT 10.13 •

Supreme Court Case Loads, 1930–1990

SOURCE: Supreme Court of the United States, Office of the Clerk

thorities to remedy unconstitutional conditions of incarceration, and have required that trial courts resentence certain defendants on the grounds that the original sentences constituted cruel and unusual punishment.

The Supreme Court's Mounting Problems When the first Supreme Court convened in 1790, its role as guardian of the Constitution had only been recently conceived. At the same time, the country itself was new, with thirteen states and fewer than four million citizens. The work of the High Court in those early days was simple. In its first three years it decided no cases, and during the next two years the six justices ruled on only four matters.

As the United States grew in size, complexity, and maturity, and a greater emphasis was placed on due process, human rights, and civil liberties, more and more cases began to work their way up through the appellate system (see, for example, Exhibit 10.13). By 1991 the number of justices on the Bench had increased by 50 percent, from six to nine. But, in the two centuries since the Court's inception, the population the

The members of the Supreme Court. Standing, from left: David Souter, Antonin Scalia, Anthony M. Kennedy, and the Court's newest member, Clarence Thomas. Seated, from left: John Paul Stevens, Byron R. White, Chief Justice William H. Rehnquist, Harry A. Blackmun, and Sandra Day O'Connor.

Court was serving had expanded by more than 235 million — an increase of about 6,000 percent.

During the term ending in the summer of 1991, more than 4,000 petitions had been received by the Court, a rate of more than seventy each week. With the crush of appeals, the nine justices have been forced to rely more and more on their clerks to review cases, and a greater number of appeals have been rendered without written opinions. Furthermore, the Court has had to become more selective in the cases it chooses to hear; or, as the former dean of Harvard Law School, Erwin N. Griswold, characterized it, the justices have been forced into "rationing justice" — ruling in only a smattering of cases, while leaving citizens without guidance on an array of questions.[29]

The increased Court work load comes not only from the simple mathematics of population growth and from the greater emphasis and awareness of civil liberties, but also from the Supreme Court's very performance. When *Mapp* v. *Ohio* in 1961 extended the exclusionary rule to the states,[30] for example, the Court opened the door to thousands of appeals involving various aspects of illegal search and seizure. Although the *Mapp* decision was clear enough in its spirit and central holding, it offered lower state and federal courts no guidance as to the specific criteria that make a search violative of the Fourth Amendment. For example, *Mapp* shed no light on such important questions as whether searches of automobiles following a traffic arrest were valid, whether search warrants issued on the basis of anonymous tips were justifiable, or whether one spouse could waive the Fourth Amendment rights of the other and consent to a search of the home. Indeed, the Court did not even tell the lower courts if the *Mapp* decision should be regarded as retroactive, that is, applicable to cases where the trial occurred before *Mapp*. In light of the confusion surrounding *Mapp,* then, it is not surprising that research has disclosed that no two state supreme courts have reacted to *Mapp* in the same way. Some state high courts implemented *Mapp* in a very receptive fashion, while others responded to post-*Mapp* legal questions in as restrictive a manner as possible.[31]

Studies of the impact of Supreme Court decisions demonstrate that a similar phenomenon has occurred in the aftermath of every major Supreme Court decision affecting the rights of defendants. Like *Mapp,* decisions such as *Escobedo* v. *Illionois* and *Miranda* v. *Arizona* actually created more legal questions than they answered.[32] In the field of criminal law, as in all areas of law, the Court simply cannot hear enough cases to spell out all of the corollary principles that may derive from its major decisions. The very nature of the Court's work permits the justices to do little more than formulate general policy. The pressures generated by heavy case loads and the necessity to write majority opinions that usually represent a compromise among the divergent viewpoints of individual justices make it highly likely that the Court's decisions will be uncertain and ambiguous.

SUMMARY

The American court system has come to be a bewildering mosaic of names, structures, and functions. There are justice of the peace and municipal courts, county and city courts, superior and inferior courts, trial and appellate courts, plus a host of others. The confusion comes from a variety of sources — no two state court systems are identical, the names of courts vary regardless of function, and there are various levels of jurisdictional authority.

State court structure includes appeals courts, intermediate appellate courts (in more than half the states), major trial courts, and courts of limited jurisdiction. Court jurisdiction varies by geography, subject matter, and hierarchy. The federal judiciary reflects a structure similar to that of the states.

The United States Supreme Court stands at the apex of the federal judiciary and is the highest court in the nation. The Constitution provided the High Court with both original and appellate jurisdiction. Its original jurisdiction covers suits between two states, issues that test the constitutionality of state laws, and matters relating to ambassadors. In its appellate jurisdiction, the Court resolves conflicts that raise "substantial federal questions."

In recent years the Supreme Court has become overburdened by a crush of appeals. This problem has occurred mostly as a result of the greater emphasis on due process, human rights, and civil liberties.

KEY TERMS

appellate jurisdiction **(322)**
courts of limited
   jurisdiction **(314)**
courts of general
   jurisdiction **(321)**
courts of record **(322)**

dual court system **(310)**
judicial circuit **(322)**
justices of the peace **(316)**
Marbury v. *Madison* **(331)**
Rule of Four **(336)**
trial *de novo* **(316)**

U.S. courts of appeals **(329)**
U.S. district courts **(327)**
U.S. magistrates **(327)**
U.S. Supreme Court **(329)**
writ of *certiorari* **(336)**
writ of *mandamus* **(332)**

QUESTIONS FOR DISCUSSION

1. What type of restructuring would be most efficient to unify the state court systems?
2. What are the major problems with the lower courts, and how might these be remedied?

3. What are the similarities and differences between rural and urban lower courts?
4. Is there any solution to the crush of drug cases in America's courts?

FOR FURTHER READING

Feeley, Malcolm M. *The Process Is the Punishment: Handling Cases in a Lower Criminal Court.* New York: Russell Sage, 1979.

Posner, Richard A. *The Federal Courts: Crises and Reform.* Cambridge: Harvard University Press, 1985.

Provine, D. M. *Judging Credentials: Nonlawyer Judges and the Politics of Professionalism.* Chicago: Univeristy of Chicago Press, 1986.

Rehnquist, William H. *The Supreme Court.* New York: William Morrow, 1987.

NOTES

1. For a retrospective overview of the charm of the early American courthouse, see Richard Pare, ed., *Court House* (New York: Horizon Press, 1978).

2. The MacKaye material is reprinted, in part, in Raymond Moley, *Our Criminal Courts* (New York: Minton, Balch, 1930), pp. 5–9. MacKaye's essay included the following:

   This is the house that justice built. This is the castle of fair play. This is the place where wise men shall sit and contemplate our human jealousies, our petty quarrels, our wrong-doings. This, by the grace of God, is a magistrate's court.

      Set squarely down in a backwater street, it is not, for some disappointing reason, impressive. But the spangled parade of a city's life passes here, gaudy and gay, drab and mean. The push of ambition, the drums of crime, the blare of pretension, and keen quiet tragedy . . .

      This, then, is a magistrate's court set down on the backwater street.

3. President's Commission on Law Enforcement and Administration of Justice, *Task Force Report: The Courts* (Washington, D.C.: U.S. Government Printing Office, 1967), p. 29.

4. *Proceedings of the 42nd Annual Meeting of the New York State Bar Association,* 1919, pp. 240–241, as quoted in the President's Commission, *Task Force Report,* p. 29.

5. National Advisory Commission on Criminal Justice Standards and Goals, *Courts* (Washington, D.C.: U.S. Government Printing Office, 1973), pp. 161–162.

6. See *Chicago Tribune,* December 7, 1989, Section 3, p. 3; *Los Angeles Times,* December 16, 1990, pp. A1, A42; *New York Times,* June 23, 1991, pp. 1, 22.

7. H. Ted Rubin, *The Courts: Fulcrum of the Justice System* (Pacific Palisades, Calif.: Goodyear, 1976), p. 49.

8. *Tumey* v. *Ohio,* 273 U.S. 510 (1927).

9. President's Commission, *Task Force Report: The Courts,* p. 34; *Connally* v. *Georgia,* 429 U.S. 245 (1977).

10. *New York Times,* June 2, 1975, p. 16; "60 Minutes," CBS-TV, February 22, 1976.

11. Rubin, *The Courts,* p. 51.

12. The Cleveland Foundation, *Criminal Justice in Cleveland* (Cleveland: The Cleveland Foundation, 1922), pp. 627–641.

13. H. Ted Rubin, *The Felony Processing System, Cuyahoga County, Ohio* (Denver: Institute for Court Management, 1971), pp. 16–17.

14. These observations were made by the author.

15. Murray S. Stedman, *State and Local Governments* (Cambridge, Mass.: Winthrop, 1979), p. 156.

16. National Advisory Commission, *Courts,* p. 164.

17. David W. Neubauer, *America's Courts and the Criminal Justice System* (North Scituate, Mass.: Duxbury, 1979), pp. 65–66.

18. *Chicago Tribune,* Feburary 22, 1990, Section 1, pp. 1, 2; *Chicago Tribune,* November 20, 1990, Section 2, p. 2.

19. *New York Times,* June 23, 1991, p. A1; *Los Angeles Times,* January 16, 1990, p. A1; Paul Nussbaum, "Crime and Punishment," *Philadelphia Inquirer Magazine,* May 5, 1991, pp. 10, 20, 36–40.

20. President's Commission, *Task Force Report: The Courts,* p. 36.

21. See *U.S.* v. *Ford,* 41 CrL 2421 (1987).

22. *Annual Report of the Director of the Administrative Office of the United States Courts* (Washington, D.C.: Government Printing Office, 1990).

23. *New York Times,* August 6, 1991, p. B1.

24. *Annual Report of the Director of the Administrative Office of the United States Courts* (Washington, D.C.: Government Printing Office, 1990).

25. See Robert G. McCloskey, "James Wilson," in *The Justices of the United States Supreme Court, 1789–1969: Their Lives and Major Opinions,* 4 vols., ed. Leon Friedman and Fred L. Israel (New York: Chelsea House and R. R. Bowker, 1969), vol. 1, p. 93.

26. Charles Warren, *The Supreme Court in United States History,* 2 vols. (Boston: Little, Brown, 1926), vol. 1, p. 89.

27. *Marbury* v. *Madison,* 1 Cr. 138 (1803).

28. Robert G. McCloskey, *The American Supreme Court* (Chicago: University of Chicago Press, 1960), p. 40.

29. *U.S. News & World Report,* March 26, 1979, p. 33.

30. *Mapp* v. *Ohio,* 367 U.S. 643 (1961).

31. See Bradley C. Canon, "Reactions of State Supreme Courts to a U.S. Supreme Court Civil Liberties Decision," *Law and Society Review,* vol. 8, no. 1 (Fall 1973): 109–134.

32. *Escobedo* v. *Illinois,* 378 U.S. 478 (1964); *Miranda* v. *Arizona,* 384 U.S. 436 (1966). See Stephen L. Wasby, *The Impact of the United States Supreme Court* (Howard, Ill.: Dorsey, 1970); and Theodore L. Becker and Malcolm M. Feeley, eds., *The Impact of Supreme Court Decisions,* 2nd ed. (New York: Oxford University Press, 1973).

Judges, Prosecutors, and Other Performers at the Bar of Justice

Justice is the great interest of man on earth.
—DANIEL WEBSTER, 1845

Injustice is relatively easy to bear; what stings is justice.
—H. L. MENCKEN, 1922

Everyone loves justice in the affairs of others.
—ITALIAN PROVERB

Judge: A law student who marks his own examination papers.
—H. L. MENCKEN, 1943

Does America really need 70 percent of the world's lawyers?
—VICE PRESIDENT DAN QUAYLE, 1991

In most media presentations of criminal court processing, the judicial encounter is portrayed as a drama staged in four acts: in Act One, the accused is brought into the halls of equity and before the bar of justice; in Act Two, the facts are presented and the testimony is argued before a jury of mirthless souls; in Act Three, the evidence is considered and a judgment is unequivocally rendered; and in Act Four, either a sentence is pronounced or the defendant is released. Furthermore, the cast of characters in such imaginary proceedings is small — there is the accused, represented by a defense attorney who, in turn, is pitted against an aggressive state prosecutor; and there is a judge, a jury, and a small parade of witnesses. In short, the ceremony of the court is usually limited to the pageant of the criminal trial, and to the trial alone — not to the earlier stages of judicial processing or to the other persons crucial to the functioning of judicial proceedings.

Unquestionably, the processing of criminal cases through the American courts is not without dramatic moments and characters. There are the many forms of modern legal magic that put together the words and music of legislation and judicial interpretation; there are courtroom lawyers and wizards who dissect the reason and confusion of legal axioms and ideals; there are procedural practitioners who use justice and emotion to remake legal science into legal engineering; and there is the compromised unblinding of justice, which forces the spirit of fair-minded legal reasoning into states of judicial chaos. All of these reflect the melodrama and romanticism of the judicial process. At the same time, there are also the little-known figures in the judiciary process who, together with the many other components of the court process, represent the backbone of the American court system. This chapter examines the full spectrum of players in the judicial process in order to demonstrate the importance of each to a more unified system of criminal justice.

Spending time in criminal court is like being inside a giant liver. Dark, liver-colored paneling lines the courtrooms. Recessed fluorescent lighting makes jail-pale defendants look that much more like impure particles, there only to be disposed of. Day after day in these courtrooms, the system gets flushed.

Through this huge filtering mechanism pass the accused drug dealers, murderers, home invaders, crackheads, bad-check passers, and killer drunk drivers. Striving to keep the sludge moving are the judges of the criminal courts.

— AUTHOR LONA O'CONNOR IN *SOUTH FLORIDA* MAGAZINE, SEPTEMBER 1991

THE COURTROOM WORK GROUP

The major participants in the criminal judicial process in the United States are the judge, the prosecutor, the defense attorney, and the accused. However, there may be many others present, depending on the particular phase of the process, the type of case, and the level of the court. For example, there may be police officers and witnesses to contribute evidence of innocence or guilt; there may be grand juries and trial juries to consider the nature and importance of the evidence and to render judgment; and there may be certain officers of the court, such as bailiffs, clerks, and reporters, who attend to certain administrative matters. Finally, there are others with only quasi-judicial functions, such as coroners and medical examiners, whose testimony and judgment may be required in specific kinds of cases. Each of these participants has a specific role in criminal court processing, and without them various phases in the judicial system would not be fully possible.

Judges

It is upon the judge's wisdom that we must rely.
>—Justice Charles Evans Hughes, 1907

Judges are apt to be naive, simple-minded men.
>—Justice Oliver Wendell Holmes, Jr., 1913

Although there are many high-ranking officials at all levels of the criminal justice process, none have the prominence and the prestige of **judges,** or justices. The courtroom is their eminent domain, and it is there that they are fully responsible for the honest, impartial, and equitable administration of justice. To most observers, they are the ultimate arbiters and symbols of law and order. When they enter a courtroom, everyone rises; when they speak, others listen. Although at times their power to decide a case may be assigned to a jury, it is the judges alone who have the authority to interpret the rules that govern the court proceedings.

Roles and Responsibilities The roles and responsibilities of judges are numerous—in fact, in a monograph prepared by the American Bar Association during the 1970s, it took some 100 pages to describe them only briefly.[1] At the most general level, judges are both arbiters and administrators. As arbiters, it is their responsibility to safeguard the rights of the accused as well as the interests of the public in the administration of criminal justice. As administrators, judges must control the flow of cases through the courts and oversee such ancillary duties as the appointment and evaluation of court personnel, record keeping, and budget requests.

Judges: Public officers who preside over courts of law.

Nobody outside of a baby carriage or a judge's chamber can believe in an unprejudiced point of view.
>—Lillian Hellman

I think a judge should be looked on rather as a sphinx than as a person—you shouldn't be able to imagine a judge having a bath.
>—Judge H. C. Leon

Generally, these roles and responsibilities fall to the justices of all trial courts, whether they are magistrates in urban municipal courts, rural county courts, or state trial courts. Even justices of the peace at the local level have similar duties as they preside over minor offenses. However, there are variations depending on the size and complexity of a particular jurisdiction. County judges are more often saddled with administrative housekeeping duties — securing funds to operate the court, hiring personnel, and purchasing supplies — than are members of the bench on the higher rungs of the judicial ladder. Conversely, justices in the urban municipal courts or the state trial courts are likely to have more work managing the court case flow than those in less populated areas, simply because they have more defendants.

At the appellate level, the responsibilities of judges vary widely from those of judges presiding in the lower and felony courts. In appeals, there are no witnesses or juries present, and the managerial aspects of criminal processing do not emerge. Rather, issues are dealt with through written briefs or oral arguments, and in the latter case the participants are the counsels for the defense and the prosecution. The responsibilities of the appeals judge(s), then, are as follows:

1. determining whether the proper procedures have been followed in the presentation of the appeal
2. examining the written brief, the trial record, or other materials that may have been filed
3. presiding over any oral arguments
4. weighing the facts of the case and the nature of the appeal in order to arrive at a decision
5. negotiating a decision through vote, persuasion, or compromise in instances where more than one judge hears the appeal
6. preparing an *opinion* that details the logic and reasons for the decision

Beyond these duties and responsibilities, judges also have influence over other aspects of the criminal justice process that are related directly and sometimes indirectly to the court. In some jurisdictions, for example, service agencies such as probation and release-on-recognizance programs are under the administrative control of the court. In others, where these are separate county or state agencies, their functioning is nevertheless influenced by the attitudes and judicial policies of the local chief magistrate. Similarly, police and prosecutors are influenced by the judge, for his or her discretion in the acceptance of evidence and pleas and in sentencing clearly has an impact on the arrest and charging processes.

Judicial Selection Although judges, justices, and magistrates have the highest authority in the criminal justice process, they are not always the most qualified or best trained. In many of the lower courts, neither a college nor a law degree is required, and as noted in Chapter 10 some justices of the peace have no legal training whatsoever. This situation has evolved from both the manner in which judges are recruited and the methods through which they are trained. Judges are either *elected* or *appointed,* and both mechanisms are beset with a variety of pitfalls.

In jurisdictions where judges are elected, political connections are typically important. To win a judgeship, the candidate must first secure the party nomination, and then campaign on the party ticket. Thus, the potential judge becomes embroiled in the same type of partisan politics that is apparent in the election of presidents, governors, legislators, and other government officials. This system generally results in the election of the most politically active, and not necessarily the most qualified candidates. In jurisdictions where judgeships occur through appointment, partisan politics again can play a role, but the degree of influence over specific selections can vary by state and by level in the judicial hierarchy.

All federal judges are nominated by the president and must be confirmed by the Senate. The Constitution of the United States specifies this for Supreme Court justices, and the Judiciary Act of 1789 adopted the same procedure for other federal judgeships.

Since all federal judges hold their offices "during good behavior" —that is, for life—the appointments are extremely important and they seem to give the president almost unlimited power to shape the direction of federal judicial policy. This is unquestionably the case with respect to the United States Supreme Court. Generally, although senatorial confirmation of a presidential nominee to the High Court seems to be little more than a formality, it is a process the Senate takes seriously and that has resulted in some rugged battles. Nevertheless, on only six occasions during the current century, and on twenty-one others since the founding of the Union, has the Senate failed to confirm a presidential choice. Furthermore, the margins of confirmation have been wide, with more than two-thirds of the nominees receiving unanimous Senate approval. Finally, the presidential prerogatives have also been apparent in the limited number of nonpartisan appointments. Of the 106 Supreme Court justices, only twelve were not affiliated with the political party of the incumbent president. Thus, a chief executive has always been able to leave the imprint of his administration on the country, sometimes for more than a generation.

In the other federal courts, there has been some erosion of presidential influence in selecting judges over the years.[2] Senators use appointments to the U.S. district courts and U.S. courts of appeal as political patronage. Although the president makes the nomination, most senators sponsor specific candidates and expect them to receive the appointment, unless some grave misdeed clouds a candidate's past. Senators enforce their demands in specific ways. They can threaten to withdraw their support for certain bills that are important to the president's legislative program, or they can block the appointment of anyone else to the post by involving the rule of "senatorial courtesy." This unwritten rule states that if a senator of the president's party declares that any appointee who is to serve in his home state is "personally obnoxious" to him or her, the Senate must refuse to confirm the nomination.[3] During the 1980s, however, the Reagan administration resurrected a stronger role for the presidency in federal judicial selection. One tactic, for example, was to have Republican home state governors offer two or three names for judicial vacancies as opposed to only one. This preserved some role for the senator but let the President pick the judge who seemed most ideologically suited to Reagan's conservative justice agenda.[4]

In state judicial systems where judges are appointed, governors appear to have more freedom than the president in making selections. Generally, gubernatorial appointments are made to the courts of appeals and sometimes the major trial courts. In both instances, party connections and service in the state legislature play important roles in the nomination process.

At the lower levels of the judicial hierarchy, partisan politics are almost always present in the selection of judges. Appointments to the

Federal judges hold their offices for life.

That judges of important causes should hold office for life is a disputable thing, for the mind grows old as well as the body.

—Aristotle

Judges are the weakest link in our system of justice, and they are also the most protected.

—Alan M. Dershowitz, 1978

The Missouri Plan: A method of selecting judges in which the governor, the bar association, and the voters all participate in the process.

Judge Hampton has a reputation for fairness and impartiality and has never exhibited bias or prejudice toward any group, class, or individual.
—FROM A 1989 REPORT INVESTIGATING MISCONDUCT ACCUSATIONS AGAINST DALLAS DISTRICT COURT JUDGE JACK HAMPTON, WHO CALLED TWO MURDER VICTIMS "QUEERS" AND TOLD REPORTERS THAT THEIR HOMOSEXUALITY WAS A MITIGATING FACTOR IN SENTENCING THEIR KILLER

I'm not talking to reporters anymore.
—JUDGE HAMPTON, AFTER THE REPORT WAS RELEASED

bench in the municipal and justice of the peace courts are typically made by mayors, county managers, or town councils, and strong support for a position on the local bench often occurs through friendship, kinship, party affiliation, and the political spoils system.

In an attempt to overcome the shortcomings of judicial selection through appointment or election, the American Bar Association (ABA) has long advocated a hybrid appointment and election system called the **Missouri Plan.**[5] Known as the ABA Plan or "merit selection," it calls for a gubernatorial appointment to be made from a list of nominees drafted by a commission of lawyers, members of the lay electorate, and an incumbent judge. The appointee then serves one or more years, or until the next election, and then must be confirmed by the people in a *plebiscite* (vote of the people). The voters are asked, "Shall Judge ———— be retained in office?" If the incumbent is supported, he or she serves a full term until the next such "election." If not, another appointee ascends to the bench through the same procedure. The Missouri Plan is, then, a mechanism through which the governor, the bar association, and the people participate in judicial selection, as well as an avenue through which the voters can reject a sitting judge.

By the 1980s, the Missouri Plan or comparable forms of merit selection of judges had been established in thirty-one states and the District of Columbia.[6] More recently, however, it appears that the Missouri Plan may be running into some trouble. In Missouri, where the plan originated in 1940 as a cure for widespread patronage appointments, there have been allegations that the merit selection process once again has become politically influenced. Moreover, studies are beginning to suggest that when comparing the Missouri plan of selection with partisan-election systems, the characteristics of the judges selected under the two alternative processes tend to be similar in both background and legal experience.[7] By the latter half of the 1980s, the popularity of merit selection had declined, with the majority of states determining judges through *partisan* (using political parties) or *nonpartisan* (without party politics) elections. (See Exhibit 11.1.)

Judicial Training Although the various judges, justices, and magistrates in the United States find their way to a courtroom bench through various political mechanisms, this should not suggest that all are unqualified to serve. There are, to be sure, no constitutional or statutory qualifications for serving on the U.S. Supreme Court—there is no age limitation, no requirement that the justices be native-born citizens, nor even the obligation that appointees have a legal background. However, informal criteria for membership in the High Court naturally exist, and *every nominee in history has been a lawyer.* Curiously, however, it was not until 1957 that the Court was composed, for the first time, entirely of law school graduates.*

All of the current members of the Supreme Court Bench have extensive legal backgrounds, primarily in the federal judicial system. Justice Anthony M. Kennedy, for example, nominated by President Ronald Reagan in 1988, graduated from Harvard Law School, and practiced law for more than two decades, was a part-time professor at the McGeorge School of Law, a member of the United States Tax Court bar, and

---

* Until only recently, many people became lawyers through apprenticeships with practicing attorneys without ever having attended or graduated from law school.

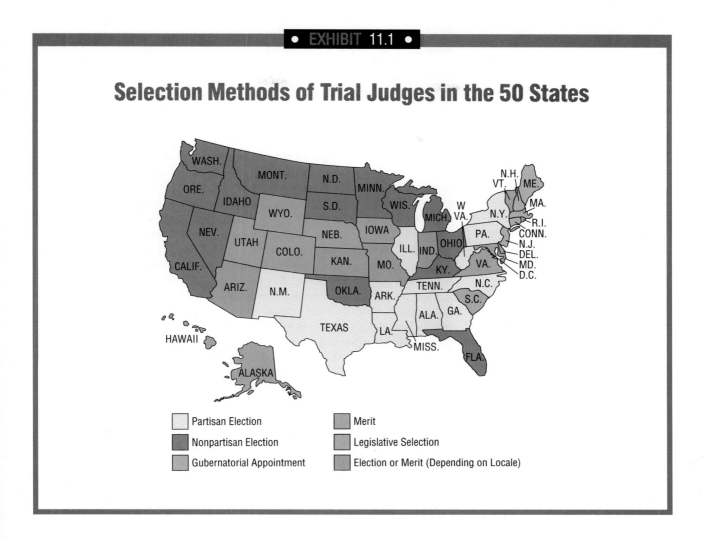

• EXHIBIT 11.1 •

Selection Methods of Trial Judges in the 50 States

Partisan Election

Nonpartisan Election

Gubernatorial Appointment

Merit

Legislative Selection

Election or Merit (Depending on Locale)

ultimately served as a U.S. court of appeals judge. U.S. district and appeals court judges have similar backgrounds, and more than 90 percent are law school graduates.[8]

At the state level, the vast majority of trial and appellate judges have law education and training, but in the courts of limited jurisdiction there are many with little or no exposure to law prior to their appointments. This problem seems to be more prevalent in the county court systems, and almost universal in the justice of the peace courts. Within the larger urban municipal court structures, however, some changes have emerged in recent years. The New York City Criminal Court Act, for example, requires that

> each of the judges of the court shall be a resident of the city. No person, other than one who holds such office on the first day of September, nineteen hundred sixty-two, may assume the office of judge of the court unless he has been admitted to practice law in this state at least ten years.[9]

The New York law, established in 1962 and adopted by numerous other jurisdictions since then, was designed to prevent the appointment of inexperienced legal practitioners. Although it did not require law school graduation, it did mandate admittance to the bar—that is, passing the state bar examination. Furthermore, the wording of the act also implied some ten years' experience in the practice of law, which in effect set a minimum age requirement of thirty to thirty-five years.

Yet, even with the various changes in judicial selection practices and requirements for legal education, the matter of training for judges remains a problem. Trial judges in the courts of original jurisdiction are the most crucial actors in criminal justice processing, but few have any formal training or apprenticeship in the judicial function. They generally assume their positions on the bench with no knowledge of the art of judging other than perhaps some experience as trial lawyers—experiences that *rarely* include extensive criminal practice.

The idea that judges should go back to school for training seminars has never been a popular one, but since the 1960s some programs have been developed through the efforts of the American Bar Association. Currently, the National College of the State Judiciary conducts two- and four-week summer courses for trial judges, and the Federal Judicial Center conducts seminars for newly appointed federal judges as well as continuing education for veteran judges. Yet in the main, only a minority of the nation's jurists have exposure to such judgeship training, and the possibility of structuring apprenticeships for those wishing to pursue judicial careers—an educational mechanism that exists in most European countries—remains a moot issue.

Prosecutors

In truth, there is a tremendous ambivalence—almost a schizophrenia—that the quasi-judicial role of a prosecutor imposes. On the one hand, he is a trial advocate, expected to do everything in his power to obtain convictions. On the other hand, he is sworn to administer justice dispassionately, to seek humane dispositions rather than to blindly extract every last drop of punishment from every case.

— Steven Phillips, former assistant district attorney, Bronx County, New York

The **prosecutor,** also known as the district attorney, the county attorney, the state attorney, or the U.S. attorney—depending upon the jurisdiction of his or her office—is a government lawyer and the chief law enforcement authority of a community. As an elected or appointed public official, the prosecutor occupies a pivotal and crucial position in criminal justice processing. It is the prosecutor who determines how cases brought by the police will be disposed of; it is the prosecutor who decides which cases will be pursued through the courts; it is the prosecutor who decides whether the original charges against an accused may be reduced to some lesser offense; and in many jurisdictions, it is the prosecutor who prepares and approves arrest and search warrants before they are formally issued by a magistrate.

Roles and Responsibilities At the most general level, the responsibilities of the prosecutor are threefold:

1. enforcing the law
2. representing the government in matters of law
3. representing the government and the people in matters of legislation and criminal justice reform

---

It's all in a day's work.
— New York State Supreme Court Judge Abraham Levy, in 1987, after a woman barged into his office, announced, "I'm going to blow you away," and fired two shots at him, missing both times

Prosecutor: A government attorney who instigates the prosecution of an accused and represents the state at trial.

The prosecutor functions at each step in the criminal justice process.

As such, the functions of the prosecutor are extremely broad and considerably more diverse than the commonly perceived role of the state's trial lawyer. Furthermore, the specifics of the prosecutorial role are sometimes difficult to grasp fully, as legal scholar Wayne R. LaFave has suggested:

> Appraisal of the role of the prosecutor is made difficult because that role is inevitably more ambiguous than that of the police or the trial court. It is clear that the police are concerned with the detection of crime and the identification and apprehension of offenders; it is likewise apparent that courts must decide the issue of guilt or innocence. A prosecutor, however, may conceive of his principal responsibility in a number of different ways. He may serve primarily as trial counsel for the police department, reflecting the views of the department in his court representation. Or, he may serve as a sort of "house counsel" for the police, giving legal advise to the department on how to develop enforcement practices which will withstand challenge in court. On the other hand, the prosecutor may consider himself primarily a representative of the court, with the responsibility of enforcing rules designed to control police practices and perhaps otherwise acting for the benefit of persons who are proceeded against. Another possibility is that the prosecutor, as an elected official . . . will try primarily to reflect community opinion in the making of decisions as to whether to prosecute.[10]

At the very least, the prosecutor is all of these things, for unlike any other player in the administration of justice, the roles of the prosecutor span the entire criminal justice process. At each step of the process the prosecutor has an important function.

Investigation: During the investigation phase of the criminal justice process, prosecutors prepare search and arrest warrants and work with police in ensuring that investigation reports are complete. In some circumstances, either through citizen complaints or suspicions of alleged criminal acts, prosecutors will initiate their own investigations, which may be independent of police activity.

Arrest: Subsequent to arrest, prosecutors screen cases to determine which should be prosecuted and which should be dropped.

Initial appearance: During the first court appearance, prosecutors ensure that all defendants are notified of the charges against them. In addition, prosecutors serve as the government's attorneys at summary trials in minor cases, and participate in bail decisions. Importantly, prosecutors can also discontinue a prosecution through a *nolle prosequi.* The *nolle prosequi,* also referred to as *nol. pros.* or simply *nolle,* is a formal entry of record declaring an unwillingness to prosecute a case. As such, it is an agreement not to proceed further in a particular case.

Preliminary hearing: Prosecutors have two functions at preliminary hearings: to establish probable cause and to *nol. pros.* cases when appropriate. In jurisdictions that have no initial appearance but proceed directly to the preliminary hearing, prosecutors have the additional tasks of giving formal notice of charges and participating in bail decisions.

Information and indictment: Prosecutors prepare the *information* report that establishes probable cause and binds an accused over for trial. In jurisdictions that use the indictment rather than the "information," prosecutors establish probable cause before the grand jury.

Arraignment: Here, prosecutors arraign felony defendants; that is, they bring the accused to the court to answer to matters charged in the information or indictment. Prosecutors also participate in **plea negotiation,** that is, allowing defendants to plead guilty to a reduced charge or charges.

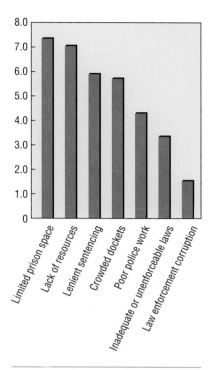

Prosecutors' Biggest Complaints *On a scale of 1 to 10, prosecutors rated how seriously the following factors hamper their efforts.*
SOURCE: *National Law Journal,* August 8, 1988

Plea negotiation: The negotiation of an agreement among the prosecutor, the judge, and the accused's attorney as to the charge(s) and sentence imposed if the accused pleads guilty.

Pretrial motions: As representatives of the state, prosecutors initiate and participate in the argument of any pretrial motions.

Trial: Prosecutors are the government trial lawyers, and as such, argue to prove guilt beyond a reasonable doubt.

Sentencing: Prosecutors make recommendations to the bench, arguing for rigid or lenient sentencing dispositions.

Appeal: Through written or oral debate, prosecutors argue that convictions were obtained properly and should not be reversed.

Parole: In some jurisdictions, prosecutors make recommendations for or against parole for all inmates up for review. In most instances, however, prosecutors typically limit themselves to opposing the early parole release of serious offenders.[11]

Of these many functions and roles, those with the greatest impact on criminal justice processing are the ones involving *prosecutorial discretion* — the decision to prosecute, the *nol. pros.* of cases, and plea bargaining.

The Decision to Prosecute Prosecutorial discretion typically begins after arrest, when police reports are forwarded to the county or state attorney for review. At that point, the prosecutor screens and evaluates the evidence and the details of the arrest, and decides whether to accept or reject the case for prosecution. In this decision-making process, the prosecutor has, in theory, absolute and unrestricted discretion to choose who is prosecuted and who is not. The prosecutor's decision in this behalf is called "selective prosecution." The justifications for such a practice are not unlike those for selective enforcement of the criminal law by police, including ambiguity in the penal codes, seriousness of the offense, work load size, and the need to individualize justice.

> The prosecutor has, at least in theory, absolute and unrestricted discretion to choose who is prosecuted and who is not.

The legitimacy and necessity of the prosecutor's discretion in pressing charges has long been recognized. As the President's Commission on Law Enforcement and Administration of Justice pointed out some years ago:

> There are many cases in which it would be inappropriate to press charges. In some instances, a street fight for example, the police may make lawful arrests that are not intended to be carried forward to prosecution. When the immediate situation requiring police intervention has passed, the defendant is discharged without further action. Often it becomes apparent after arrest that there is insufficient evidence to support a conviction or that a necessary witness will not cooperate or is unavailable; an arrest may be made when there is probable cause to believe that the person apprehended committed an offense, while conviction after formal charge requires proof of guilt beyond a reasonable doubt. Finally, subsequent investigation sometimes discloses the innocence of the accused.[12]

> *Far more than in any other democracy, American prosecutors have almost unfettered authority to decide whom to charge, what crimes to identify, what penalties to seek, what bail to urge, what evidence to present, what persons to give immunity from prosecution, what plea bargains to make, and what sentences to negotiate.*
> —*New York Times* law correspondent Stuart Diamond, July 22, 1988

Beyond these contingencies, there may be tactical matters and law enforcement needs that make it inadvisable to press charges, such as conserving resources for more serious cases, or perhaps dropping a charge in exchange for information about more menacing crimes. Similarly, invoking the criminal process against marginal offenders may accomplish more harm than good. Attaching a criminal label to a one-time petty offender can conceivably set in motion a course of events that might initiate a career in serious crime. In addition, a large proportion of the arrests across the nation involve annoying and offensive behavior — drunkenness, vagrancy, disorderly conduct — rather than dangerous crime. Persecution in all these instances would cause undue hardships on both the defendants and the judicial process.

Other types of cases in which prosecutors commonly appear disinclined to seek criminal penalties are domestic disturbances; assaults and petty thefts in which the victim and the offender are in the same family or have some social relationship; statutory rape when both parties are young; first offense car thefts that involve teenagers taking a short joyride; checks that are drawn on insufficient funds; shoplifting by first offenders, particularly when restitution is made; and criminal acts that involve offenders suffering from emotional disorders.

In instances when the accused presents a serious threat to the welfare of a community — or conversely, when the offense involves only a minor breach of the criminal law — the decision to prosecute or not to prosecute is an easy one to make. In many circumstances, however, the offense and its related elements fall somewhere between these extremes, and the prosecutor must decide whether the benefit to be derived from prosecution would outweigh the costs of such an action. In practice, however, the prosecutor's office is the focal point in an exchange system in which numerous marketlike relationships influence the allocation of justice. Political scientist George F. Cole's examination of prosecutorial decision making in Seattle, for example, demonstrated that in actuality, prosecuting attorneys had only a limited degree of discretion when deciding whether or not to bring formal criminal charges against those arrested for violating the law.[13] Cole found that police, court personnel, defense attorneys, and community leaders often managed to affect prosecutorial behavior:

Pressures on prosecutorial discretion

- Police can apply pressure on a district attorney's office not to prosecute a certain offender because of information the suspect is willing to provide regarding other more serious criminals. In exchange, the police may offer greater investigation resources for a case that the prosecutor is especially interested in.
- Within the courts, pressures from the wardens of overcrowded prison systems affect judges' decisions to convict, which decisions, in turn, have an impact on the behavior of the prosecutor. Court backlog also influences the decision to prosecute.
- Defense attorneys, too, have exchange relationships with prosecutors. Both prosecutor and defense counsel are interested in a speedy solution to criminal cases. This common interest results in decisions not to prosecute certain defendants in exchange for the defense's cooperation in prosecuting others.
- Community leaders, as well, can apply pressure on the prosecutor's office. County, district, and state attorneys are appointed or elected to their posts, and all are vulnerable to public criticism. In an effort to appease the concerns of a community and its influential representatives, prosecutors tend to ignore certain types of offenders and offenses in favor of others. In other instances they may overplay their roles, as was the situation in a Florida case in 1991, when a prosecutor tried to use the state's car seat law to win a homicide verdict (see Exhibit 11.2).

Nolle Prosequi

Once prosecution has formally begun and the case is a matter of court record, the prosecutor can terminate any further processing through the *nolle prosequi*. As noted earlier, the *nolle prosequi* or *nol. pros.* is a formal entry in the record by which the prosecutor declares that he or she "will no further prosecute" the case, either (1) as to some of the counts, (2) as to some of the defendants, or (3) altogether.

Nolle prosequi: A formal entry in the record by which the prosecutor declares that he or she "will no further prosecute" the case.

● EXHIBIT 11.2 ●

Sidelights on Criminal Matters
Can Two Misdemeanors Equal One Felony?

Remember that old trick with algebra where you could make 2 equal 1? The equations went something like this:

STEP 1. If $a = 1$ and $b = 1$, therefore $a = b$.

STEP 2. Multiplying both sides by (a) yields $a^2 = ab$.

STEP 3. Subtracting (b^2) from both sides yields
$a^2 - b^2 = ab - b^2$

STEP 4. Factoring the equation yields
$(a + b)(a - b) = b(a - b)$

STEP 5. Dividing both sides by $(a - b)$ yields
$a + b = b$, or $2 = 1$.

Although it would appear that 2 might equal 1 here, there is a fallacy. Step 5 called for dividing both sides of the equation by $(a - b)$, which is "zero" in this case, and you may not divide by zero in any branch of mathematics.

The legal parallel to this example occurred in a Florida courtroom during the early months of 1991. The case revolved around Ramiro de Jesus Rodriguez and a parent's worst nightmare. When his car hit an oncoming van at a suburban intersection, his three-year-old daughter pitched from her mother's arms into the windshield, suffering fatal head injuries. Theoretically, it would appear that Mr. Rodriguez had committed two crimes: failing to secure his child in a car seat—a misdemeanor punishable in Florida by a $37 fine; and failure to yield the right of way when making a left turn—a traffic infraction. The prosecution interpreted the failure to yield as "reckless driving," and elevated the charge to vehicular homicide.

The case against Rodriguez —a Nicaraguan immigrant who spoke no English and couldn't believe what was happening to him—was so wrenching and so sad that many potential jurors expressed outrage that he was even being put on trial. After the prosecution rested its case, however, the judge dismissed the charge, ruling that "failure to yield" does not automatically mean "recklessness." In the end, like the mythical $2 = 1$, the prosecutor's legal equation had a fallacy of its own.

SOURCES: *New York Times,* May 4, 1991, pp. 1, 8; *Time,* May 13, 1991, p. 54.

This right of the prosecutor *not* to prosecute further, even in the face of sufficient evidence, is one of the most powerful examples of discretionary authority in the criminal justice system. The reasons for a *nol. pros.* are numerous. The prosecutor may decide, once the judicial process has begun, that the evidence after all is not sufficient for conviction or that it is inadmissible. Alternatively, the decision may rest on aspects of the plea negotiation process, or even on leniency.[14] Although this aspect of the prosecutor's discretionary powers has been heavily criticized,[15] it has been repeatedly upheld in the appellate courts. For example, in

United States v. *Cowen*,[16] a U.S. attorney negotiated a plea agreement whereby the accused would plead guilty to one count of bribery and would cooperate with the Watergate investigation. In exchange, another indictment against the defendant pending in Texas would be dismissed through a *nol. pros.* At trial, the presiding judge denied the U.S. attorney's motion to dismiss, yet on appeal to the Fifth Circuit of the U.S. Court of Appeals the prosecutor's "absolute power" to dismiss proceedings was fully upheld.

The *nol. pros.* is not without problems, for it can lend itself to corruption, favoritism, nepotism, and discrimination. Nevertheless, some form of this discretionary process seems necessary, if only to screen out the trivial, to eliminate false accusations, and to remove cases in which the accused may indeed be guilty but the prosecution is almost certain to lose — thus wasting the court's time and resources.

Plea Negotiation In *United States* v. *Cowen*, already noted in the previous section, two aspects of prosecutorial discretion were involved: the *nol. pros.* and plea negotiation. More commonly referred to as "plea bargaining," it is one of the most commonly accepted practices in criminal justice processing. Furthermore, it is generally believed that more than 90 percent of criminal convictions result from negotiated pleas of guilty (see Exhibit 11.3).

Plea bargaining takes place between the prosecutor and the defense counsel or the accused, and involves discussions that aim toward an agreement under which the defendant will enter a plea of guilty in exchange for some prosecutorial or judicial concession (see Exhibit 11.4). These concessions are of four possible types:

1. The initial charges may be reduced to some lesser offense, thus ensuring a reduction in the sentence imposed.
2. In instances of multiple criminal charges, the number of counts may be reduced.
3. A recommendation for leniency may be made by the prosecutor, thus reducing the potential sentence from one of incarceration to probation.
4. In instances where the charges involve a negative label, such as child molesting, the complaint may be altered to a less repugnant one, such as assault.[17]

The widespread use of negotiated pleas of guilty comes about as a result of overcrowded case loads in U.S. criminal courts. Proponents of the plea bargaining process maintain that it is beneficial to both the accused and the state. For the accused, plea bargaining has three advantages:

The advantages of plea bargaining to the state and to the accused

1. It reduces the possibility of detention during extensive pretrial and trial processing.
2. It extends the potential for a reduced sentence.
3. It reduces the financial costs of legal representation.

For the state, plea bargaining has its own advantages:

1. It reduces the overall financial costs of criminal prosecution.
2. It improves the administrative efficiency of the courts by having fewer cases go to a full and time-consuming trial.
3. It enables the prosecution to devote more time and resources to cases of greater importance and seriousness.

• EXHIBIT 11.3 •

The Prevalence of Guilty Pleas

It has generally been held that more than 90 percent of all criminal convictions result from negotiated pleas of guilt. Yet for the most part, this figure has been accepted as an article of faith with little empirical evidence to support it. As part of an in-depth study of felony case processing, the U.S. Department of Justice addressed this issue in a 1990 analysis of felony cases that reached final disposition during 1987. The data indicated that for every one hundred felony arrests made by the police, eighteen were rejected by the prosecutor at screening and another twenty were later dismissed. Of the remaining fifty-seven cases carried forward, fifty-six resulted in convictions—two through guilty verdicts and fifty-four through guilty pleas. As such, some 98 percent of the convictions were the result of pleas of guilty.

SOURCE: U.S Department of Justice, Bureau of Justice Statistics, *The Prosecution of Felony Arrests* (Washington, D.C.: U.S. Government Printing Office, 1990).

```
                          ┌──────────────┐
                          │     100      │
                          │   Arrests    │
                          └──────────────┘
          ┌───────────────────┼───────────────────┐
   ┌────────────┐      ┌────────────┐      ┌────────────┐
   │ 5 Diverted │      │ 77 Accepted│      │ 18 Rejected│
   │ or Referred│      │ at Initial │      │ at Initial │
   │            │      │ Screening  │      │ Screening  │
   └────────────┘      └────────────┘      └────────────┘
                       ┌──────┴──────┐
                ┌────────────┐   ┌────────────┐
                │ 57 Carried │   │20 Dismissed│
                │  Forward   │   │by Prosecutor│
                │            │   │  or Court  │
                └────────────┘   └────────────┘
             ┌───────┴───────┐
       ┌────────────┐   ┌────────────┐
       │ 54 Guilty  │   │  3 Trials  │
       │   Pleas    │   │            │
       └────────────┘   └────────────┘
                     ┌──────┴──────┐
               ┌────────────┐  ┌────────────┐
               │ 2 Guilty   │  │1 Acquittal │
               │ Verdicts   │  │            │
               └────────────┘  └────────────┘
```

21 Sentenced
to Incarceration
of less than
1 year

13 Sentenced
to Incarceration
of more than
1 year

56 Convicted
of Felony or
Misdemeanor

22 Given
Probation or
Other Alternative
to Incarceration

Outcome of 100 Typical Felony Arrests

The problems with plea bargaining

While plea negotiation is common, it is also highly controversial. First, it encourages an accused to waive the constitutional right to trial. Second, it enables the defendant to receive a sentence generally less severe than he or she might have otherwise received. In the eyes of the public, the criminal has "beaten the system" and the judicial process becomes even further tarnished. Third, it sacrifices the legislative policies reflected in the criminal law for the sake of tactical accommodations between the prosecution and defense. Fourth, it ignores the correctional needs of the bulk of offenders, for in many instances the accused may ultimately plead guilty to a charge far removed from that of the original crime. Fifth, it raises the danger that an innocent person, fearing a determination of guilt and a harsh sentence if the case goes to trial, will accept conviction of a crime if convinced that a guilty plea will result in lighter treatment. For example, there is the problematic case of Harry Seigler, a thirty-year-old man tried in a Virginia court in 1982 for robbery and murder. Having pleaded not guilty, he was waiting for the jury to return a verdict. With three convictions of robbery already to his credit, he was nervous. His two lawyers had disagreed on his chances of being found innocent, there was the possibility of his being convicted of capital murder, and a man by the name of Frank J. Coppola had just been executed in Virginia's electric chair. The prosecutor in the case offered Seigler's attorneys a deal: their client would plead guilty to first-degree murder and robbery and receive a sixty-year prison term, with twenty years suspended. Seigler accepted the deal, and so did the judge. As Seigler was led away, the judge was informed that the jury had finally reached a verdict: *not guilty.*[18]

Perhaps the strongest statement against the negotiated plea came from the National Advisory Commission on Criminal Justice Standards and Goals in 1973:

> As soon as possible, but in no event later than 1978, negotiations between prosecutors and defendants—either personally or through their attorneys—concerning concessions to be made in return for guilty pleas should be prohibited. In the event that the prosecution makes a recommendation as to sentence, it should not be affected by the willingness of the defendant to plead guilty to some or all of the offenses with which he is charged. A plea of guilty should not be considered by the court in determining the sentence to be imposed.[19]

Clearly, the commission's recommendation never came to pass, for plea bargaining is no less common now than in 1973.* Furthermore, it has received the blessing of the Supreme Court. The High Tribunal once commented that although there may be neither a constitutional nor a statutory basis for plea bargaining, the practice can nevertheless serve the interest of both the accused and the court. This formal recognition of the previously unacknowledged custom of plea negotiation, however, occurred only in 1970. In ***Brady v. United States,***[20] the Court upheld the use of plea negotiation, advising that it provided a "mutuality of advantage" for the state and for the defendant. In later declarations, the Supreme Court also built a number of safeguards into the bargaining process. In 1971, it maintained that the promise of a prosecutor made during plea negotiations must be kept;[21] and in 1976, the Court ruled that to be valid, a guilty plea had to be *voluntarily* made and entered with full knowledge of its implications.[22]

In defense of the state's position in plea bargaining, the United States Supreme Court has also made its position clear. In the 1970 case of *North Carolina* v. *Alford,*[23] for example, the Court ruled that a judge may accept a guilty plea from a defendant *who maintains his innocence* if (1) the plea is made voluntarily and understandably and (2) there is

The typical method of conviction is by the accused's plea of guilty. Mostly, therefore, the system of administering criminal justice in the United States is a system of justice without trial.
— JEROME H. SKOLNICK, 1966

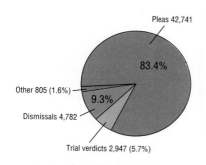

Outcome of Felony Indictments in New York City in 1990
SOURCE: New York State Office of Court Administration

Brady* v. *United States: The Supreme Court ruling that upheld the use of plea negotiations.

---

* Alaska, however, has abolished plea bargaining.

• EXHIBIT 11.4 •

Players in the Plea Bargaining Process

Discussions about plea bargaining generally revolve around two issues: the advantages and disadvantages of the practice, and Supreme Court decisions that have attempted to regulate the proper conduct of the negotiations. But who are the principal players in the process and what are their roles in the negotiation of a plea?

The Prosecutor

Without question, it is the prosecutor who plays the major role in plea negotiation. On a case-by-case basis, the prosecutor determines the concessions to be offered. Some jurisdictions have guidelines to provide consistency in plea bargaining cases, but in most there are no procedures to control the discretion of the prosecutor. Thus, such competing alternatives and factors as the seriousness of the crime, the attitude of the victim, the content of the police report, the applicable sentencing provisions, the strength of the state's case, the presiding judge's attitudes toward plea bargaining, the court case load, and the pressures exerted by the police and the community all represent input to the prosecutor's decision.

The Defense Counsel

The defense, whether a private attorney, assigned counsel, or a public defender, has a very explicit role in the plea bargaining process. First, the counsel for the defense interacts directly with the prosecutor in the nego-

tiation of the plea. Second, once a plea has been initially "bargained," there are well-established guidelines — both from the U.S. Supreme Court and the American Bar Association — as to the defense attorney's actions. It is the responsibility of the defense to make certain that his or her client understands both the bargaining process and the plea. That is, the attorney must explain to the accused the facts of the various charges, the sentencing provisions of the alternative charges, and that he or she is waiving certain rights by pleading guilty. Thus, the defense acts in an advisory role and is required to inform the client of all the discussions and negotiations throughout the bargaining process.

The Accused

Although it is the accused whose future is at stake, he or she has only a small role in the plea bargaining process. The accused rarely takes part in direct negotiations, the exceptions involving defendants who may have some information to offer a prosecutor about other cases in return for further concessions. In general, however, the accused's role is limited to an acceptance or a rejection of the prosecutor's offer.

The Judge

Judicial participation by federal judges in plea negotiations is prohibited by the federal rules of

criminal procedure. At the state level, some jurisdictions formally prohibit the practice while others encourage it. Some argue that judicial participation in plea negotiations would regulate the practice, ensure greater fairness, and make sentencing more uniform. However, opponents claim that such participation lessens the objectivity of the judge in determining the voluntariness of the plea, is inconsistent with the purposes of the presentence investigation report, and suggests to the defendant that he or she may not receive a fair trial. While the debates continue over the appropriateness, fairness, and efficacy of plea bargaining, the practice persists. Furthermore, since most of the negotiations take place in the judges' chambers, in prosecutors' offices, in courtroom hallways and restrooms, and even in the barrooms adjacent to the courthouse, it remains difficult either to fully assess the actual roles played by all of the participants or to more effectively regulate the level of their conduct and involvement.

sources: National Institute of Law Enforcement and Criminal Justice, *Plea Bargaining in the United States* (Washington, D.C.: U.S. Government Printing Office, 1978); Arthur Rosett and Donald R. Cressey, *Justice by Consent: Plea Bargains in the American Courthouse* (Philadelphia: J. B. Lippincott, 1976); Advisory Committee on the Judge's Function, *The Function of the Trial Judge* (New York: American Bar Association, 1972); N. Gary Holton and Lawson L. Lamar, *The Criminal Courts: Structures, Personnel, Processes* (New York: McGraw-Hill, 1991).

strong factual evidence of the defendant's guilt. And in *Bordenkircher* v. *Hayes*,[24] decided in 1978, the Court ruled that a defendant's due process rights are not violated when a prosecutor threatens to reindict the accused on more serious charges if he or she does not agree to plead guilty to the original charge.

In the final analysis, plea bargaining will necessarily endure. It is a great safety valve, perhaps the only factor that stands between the administration of justice and utter chaos. Without this practice, every defendant charged with an offense, however serious or benign, would have to go to trial. As it is, millions of cases are processed in the felony and misdemeanor courts each year. With existing resources, a person arrested today might have to wait a quarter of a century for his or her case to come up. Aside from expediency, however, the "virtue" of plea bargaining for both the defense and the prosecution is that it eliminates uncertainty — all sides generally prefer to opt for a "sure thing." For the defendant charged with murder, it can remove the possibility of a life sentence, or even death; for the prosecutor, it precludes any possibility of having a serious offender escape justice because of some real or imagined weakness in the case. On the negative side, however, there are individuals innocent of any offense who would rather plead guilty to a negotiated offense than face the possible consequences of an adverse verdict; these are people caught in a web of circumstances that have made them appear guilty. There is no way of knowing how many totally innocent defendants have chosen this course and have spent weeks, months, or even years in prison.

Alternatively, with the increased emphasis on drug control in recent years and the greater number of drug-related cases reaching the courts, some observers argue that plea negotiation is being misused. More specifically, it is claimed that in a number of jurisdictions an overuse of plea negotiation to relieve court backlogs has resulted in a near decriminalization of certain crimes. In New York, Los Angeles, and numerous jurisdictions, for example, although prosecutors can boast high conviction rates, the majority of felony cases result in reduction to misdemeanors and/or sentences of one year or less.[25]

Defense Attorneys

The defendant in a criminal trial wants to hide the truth because he's generally guilty. The defense attorney's job is to make sure that the jury does not arrive at that truth.

—ALAN M. DERSHOWITZ, 1982

The right of a criminal defendant to be represented by counsel is fundamental to the American system of criminal justice. The reason for this right is the need to protect individual liberties. Defendants facing criminal charges require the assistance of counsel to protect their interests at every phase of the adversary process and to help them understand the nature and consequences of the proceedings against them. Furthermore, courtroom operations are highly technical, and even the most informed of defendants are ill-equipped to represent themselves tactically in the face of the complexities of criminal law and criminal procedure.

The Functions of the Defense Counsel As the advocate for the accused, the defense counsel can perform many functions while

Alan M. Dershowitz—criminal defense lawyer and professor of law at Harvard University, and perhaps the most well-known appellate attorney in the United States. Dershowitz was born in 1938 in Brooklyn, New York, earned his law degree at Yale University, and became the youngest tenured professor at Harvard Law School, at age 28. His clients have included such notables as Jim Bakker, Leona Helmsley, and Claus von Bulow. The film Reversal of Fortune, *about the von Bulow case, cemented his reputation as the "lawyer of last resort."*

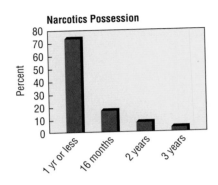

Narcotics Possession

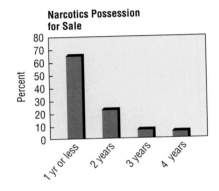

**Narcotics Possession
for Sale**

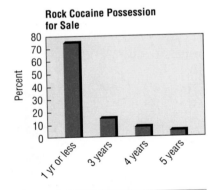

**Rock Cocaine Possession
for Sale**

Sentences for Drug Felonies A large percentage of felony drug sentences in Los Angeles County are for jail time rather than prison terms as prescribed by law.

SOURCE: *Los Angeles Times,* 1990

Motion: An application made to the court or the judge requesting an order or ruling in favor of the applicant.

Some of the advantages of pretrial motions

representing a defendant in the criminal process. Such functions generally include the following:

1. representing the accused immediately after arrest to provide advice during interrogation and to ensure that constitutional safeguards during pretrial procedures are not violated
2. reviewing police reports and further investigating the details of the offense
3. interviewing the police, the accused, and the witness, and seeking out additional evidence and witnesses in behalf of the defendant
4. discussing the offense with the prosecutor to gain initial insight into the strength of the state's case
5. representing the accused at bail hearings and during plea negotiations
6. preparing, filing, and arguing various pretrial motions
7. preparing the case for trial
8. participating in jury selection
9. representing the accused at trial
10. providing advice and assistance at sentencing
11. determining and pursuing the appropriate bases for appeal
12. presenting written or oral arguments at appeal[26]

In actual practice, few defense attorneys participate in all of these activities. As noted earlier, a number of cases are "screened out" of the justice system through the prosecutor's decision not to prosecute, and most of the remaining cases are disposed of through guilty pleas. Thus, the defense attorney's activities are usually limited to those involved with the pretrial phases of the judicial process. Furthermore, studies have indicated that most defense lawyers have their initial contacts with their clients only after they have been placed on bail or released on some type of recognizance program.[27]

Since more and more government attorneys are selecting for prosecution only those cases in which the potential for conviction is high, the defense counsel's most intensive efforts take place at the beginning of the discretionary screening process. During this period, which can last up to two weeks in urban areas where arrest rates are high, the defendant's lawyer has the opportunity to gather background material on the client and the case. If this preliminary investigation suggests that the offense was a minor one, that the arrest was weak or questionable, or that there were some irregularities in the arresting officer's behavior (such as illegal search and seizure), the defense counsel can exert pressure on the prosecutor to dismiss the case or begin plea negotiations.

A second level of defense attorney activity involves the process of pretrial motions. A **motion** is an application made to the court or the judge requesting an order or ruling in favor of the applicant. Motions can be of various types, but most common at the pretrial proceedings are those that seek to learn something about the prosecutor's case or that seek to suppress certain types of evidence. Prominent Houston attorney Anthony C. Friloux noted that the aggressive use of pretrial motions can have numerous advantages for the defense:

1. It forces a partial disclosure of the prosecutor's evidence at an early date.
2. It puts pressure on the prosecutor to consider plea bargaining, early in the proceeding.

3. It forces exposure of primary state witnesses at an inopportune time for the prosecution.
4. It raises before the trial judge early in the proceedings matters the defense may want called to his attention.
5. It forces the prosecutor to make decisions prior to his final case preparation.
6. It allows the defendant to see his defense counsel in action, which has salutary effect on the client – attorney relationship.[28]

This use of motions is also in part a bluffing game to determine how the court will react and how many rulings a judge will make. Nevertheless, it tends to wear down many prosecutors. In some heavily populated jurisdictions, it is not unusual for a prosecutor to be carrying fifty to sixty cases at any given time. With this heavy work load it is generally easier for the prosecutor to negotiate a guilty plea or drop the case altogether than to continue in a time-consuming struggle to answer all of his adversary's petitions.

Retained Counsel The idea of a "criminal lawyer" may conjure up images of people such as Alan Dershowitz, F. Lee Bailey, the fictional Perry Mason, or even the attorneys in television's "L.A. Law." But these are only the most visible of the profession. They accept only the most sensational and dramatic of cases, or ones that will ensure them substantial fees for their expertise. In contrast, the average criminal lawyer deals with the more mundane crimes and occupies a less prestigious sector of the profession.

Criminal law is a field few attorneys actively choose. The greatest financial rewards go to lawyers who devote their professional lives to the litigation of major civil suits and to advising the businesses and

Defending people accused of a crime is the most distasteful function performed by lawyers.

—F. Lee Bailey

A frontier lawyer awaits clients in his "office" during the Oklahoma land rush of 1889.

Criminal law seems to be a calling that few attorneys actively choose.

The terms *shyster, schlock,* and *schnorrer* are Yiddish colloquialisms, present in American slang since the nineteenth century. A *shyster* is someone dishonest, unprofessional, or both; *schlock* is something that is defective, cheap and gaudy, or of poor workmanship; a *schnorrer* is a beggar or chiseler.

The "lawyer–client confidence game"

corporations that chart the course of American economic life. Thus the best trained and most highly skilled attorneys are drawn to the corporate, large-scale, bureaucratic types of practice. The criminal lawyer, on the other hand, exists in an environment characterized by long hours in overcrowded, physically unpleasant courts, generally dealing with people who are educationally, economically, and socially underprivileged. Furthermore, published studies have demonstrated that criminal work is most often undertaken by that legion of small-time lawyers operating as individual practitioners. Their roots are often found in working-class America, and many went to law school on a part-time basis.[29] Known in New York as "Barter's bar," in the District of Columbia as the "Ffith Streeters," in Chicago as the "State Street bar," and almost everywhere as "the courthouse gang" or the night school "schlocks," these are the attorneys at the lower end of the legal profession. They do the "dirty work" of the bar — not only criminal cases, but personal injury, divorce, and collections as well.

The "Court Street lawyers" of Brooklyn, New York, are typical of this group. Referred to locally as "ambulance chasers" and as "shysters," "schlocks," and "schnorrers," many operate from small, one-person, store-front offices along the commercial streets near the various court buildings. The front doors and windows of their business premises are filled with notices of the various related services they perform: real estate and insurance sales, tax preparation, and notary work. They are readily found roaming the hallways, galleries, and restrooms of the courts, searching for clients who can pay them a modest fee.

As to the role of defense counsel in the typical criminal case, lawyer-sociologist Abraham S. Blumberg has referred to it as a "lawyer–client confidence game," in which the mission of these attorneys is the fixing and collection of fees.[30] At the outset, the criminal defense attorneys who are members of the local "courthouse gangs" make it clear to their clients that there is a firm connection between fee payment and the zealous exercise of professional expertise, "inside" knowledge, and organizational connections in their behalf. Thus, there exists a relationship between the fee and the accused's extrication from difficulties. The attorney then manipulates the client and stage-manages the case so that legal service at least has the appearance of being rendered. This is accomplished through a certain amount of sales puff, combined with the implication of access to secret legal knowlege and connections with the seat of judicial power.

For Blumberg, the lawyer–client relationship represents a confidence game in that throughout his performance the criminal defense attorney is a "double agent" who works not only for the accused, but for the court organization as well. Both principals are anxious to terminate the litigation with a minimum of time, expense, and damage. The attorney collects his fees in advance, emphasizes to his client how difficult the case is and prepares him for defeat, speaks of his "connections" within the court system and assures the client that he can do "something," negotiates a lesser plea that is in the interests of the prosecutor, and ultimately "cools out" the client by telling him that his lesser sentence on the reduced charge was actually a victory. Furthermore, as Professor Blumberg emphasized, "as in a genuine confidence game, the victim who has participated is loath to do anything that will upset the lesser plea which his lawyer has 'conned' him into accepting."[31] And the con game is *complete,* since the defendant is invariably separated from the spoils he

• EXHIBIT 11.5 •

On Lawyers

Lawyer: a person learned in the law.
— BLACK'S LAW DICTIONARY

Lawyers are operators of the toll bridge across which anyone in search of justice must pass.
— JANE BRYANT QUINN

To some lawyers all facts are created equal.
— JUSTICE FELIX FRANKFURTER

A lawyer starts life giving five hundred dollars' worth of law for five dollars, and ends giving five dollars' worth for five hundred dollars.
— BENJAMIN H. BREWSTER

A lawyer is a man who helps you get what is coming to him.
— JEAN GIRAUDOUX

A lawyer is a man who prevents someone else from getting your money.
— WILL ROGERS

If there were no bad people there would be no good lawyers.
— CHARLES DICKENS

I don't want a lawyer to tell me what I cannot do; I hire him to tell me how to do what I want to do.
— J. PIERPONT MORGAN

Accuracy and diligence are much more necessary to a lawyer than comprehension of mind or brilliancy of talent.
— DANIEL WEBSTER

My lawyer is the epitome of brilliance and logic.
— ANONYMOUS

My lawyer is a cocaine freak.
— ANONYMOUS

The minute you read something you can't understand, you can almost be sure it was drawn up by a lawyer.
— WILL ROGERS

Lawyers spend a great deal of their time shoveling smoke.
— JUSTICE OLIVER WENDELL HOLMES, JR.

Lawyers and painters can soon change white to black.
— DANISH PROVERB

A peasant between two lawyers is like a fish between two cats.
— SPANISH PROVERB

The bad image and reputation lawyers have are earned in part, and part is the nature of the business, which is filled with controversy. It is a business in which, at a minimum, each lawyer makes somebody unhappy either by beating him, embarrassing him, or tying him in knots.
— F. LEE BAILEY

How do you know when a lawyer is lying? When you see his lips moving.
— ELLIS RUBIN, MIAMI ATTORNEY

may have acquired from his illicit activities. Not infrequently, the returns from a larceny are sequestered (seized) by a defense lawyer in payment of fee.

This lawyer–client confidence game is played not only by many of the "courthouse gang," but also by some of the larger and more prestigious operations as well:

> The large-scale law firm may not speak as openly of its "contacts" and "fixing" abilities as does the lower-level lawyer. It trades instead upon the facade of thick carpeting, walnut paneling, genteel low pressure, and superficialities of traditional legal professionalism. But even the large firm may be challenged because the services rendered or results obtained do not appear to merit the fee asked. Thus there is a recurrent problem in the legal profession in fixing the fee and justifying it.[32]

Whether the defense counsel is truly representing the interests of the client, or is operating from the posture of the lawyer–client confidence game, the general impression given to the public at large is that the attorney is helping the criminal to "beat the rap." To most Americans

Too Many Lawyers?

When Vice President Dan Quayle commented before the American Bar Association in 1991 that the United States had too many lawyers, he was not exaggerating. For example:

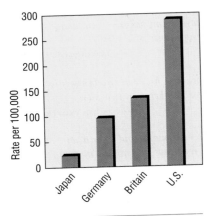

No. of Lawyers per 100,000 Population

SOURCE: President's Council on Comprehensiveness (*Agenda for Civil Justice Reform in America*)

And too, the number of lawyers keeps increasing.

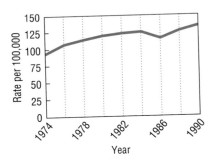

SOURCE: American Bar Association

this seems a perversion of justice. It especially appears to be so when all evidence suggests that the accused is clearly guilty but, through a lawyer's skillful maneuverings, is set free on a legal technicality.

Many people also question the ethics of an attorney who defends a client that he or she knows is guilty. However, both the code of the legal profession and the principles of American jurisprudence demand such an action. The doctrine of fairness in the adversary system of American law recognizes that those accused of criminal offenses are entitled to use every resource at their disposal to defend themselves. The function of the defense attorney is *not* to decide the innocence of the accused, but to give the client the best possible advice within the limits of the law and the ethics of the legal profession. The rights of the accused were designed to protect the innocent, and if the guilty are freed as the result of some technical issue, then that is the price that must be paid in order to ensure that the scales of justice remain in balance. Thus, defense attorneys should not be seen as legal technicians who are attempting to "get criminals off," but rather as counselors who are protecting the entire system. As one legal commentator put it:

> If attorneys refuse to represent defendants who they believe are guilty, the right of a defendant to be represented by counsel is eliminated and with it the entire traditional trial.[33]

This difficulty is often faced by public defenders, who represent a large segment of the defendants in criminal proceedings. But whether counsel is a private attorney or a public defender, he or she is an advocate whose role is to obtain an acquittal for the client. Of course, a defense lawyer is not permitted under ethical and legal codes to mount a dishonest defense; he should not arrange for witnesses that he knows will lie, for example. Aside from that, the lawyer's only obligation is to his or her client.

Bailiffs, Clerks, and Other Regulars in the American Courthouse

In addition to the principal actors in the courtroom work group—judges, prosecutors and defense attorneys—there are other persons who play a role in criminal proceedings.

Bailiffs and Sheriffs Each courtroom is assigned a *bailiff* or *sheriff,* whose formal duties are to announce the arrival and departure of the judge and to maintain order in the courtroom. In addition, as local custom may dictate, they serve as messengers for lawyers and other court officials; they keep track of prosecutors, atorneys, and witnesses in order that they be present when their cases come up; and in some instances, they serve as information sources for defendants—advising them which court they belong in, where their attorney might be found, and if asked, what the outcome of the case might be.[34]

The Court Clerk Every court has a clerk, whose responsibilities include "calling the calendar" (calling up the next case before the judge), updating the defendants' files, exercising control over the court's files, and ensuring the security of evidence that is in the custody of the court. In the small lower courts, there may be only one clerk for the entire courthouse. In larger jurisdictions, each courtroom may have its own *court clerk,* plus several courthouse file clerks who help maintain the court's records, collect any fines and court costs imposed, and prepare the daily calendars.

Although the title may convey otherwise, the court clerk occupies a position of considerable importance, especially the chief clerk of a large court system. Often the clerk's post is occupied by young attorneys who use it as a stepping-stone to the prosecutor's office. Not only does it give the incumbent exposure to the routine of the courthouse, but it also provides experience in some areas of law, since many clerks are empowered to prepare formal writs and process documents issued by the court.

Court Reporters and Court Stenographers A *court reporter* or *court stenographer* is present at almost every judicial proceeding to report and (perhaps) transcribe matters of record. The mechanics of court reporting have changed considerably over time. In years past most reporters were expert stenographers who used a manual shorthand system to fashion verbatim accounts (transcripts) of proceedings. Manual shorthand writers are almost extinct, having been replaced by machine writers. Machine writers use a device that resembles a small typewriter with which to imprint coded letters on a tape. The tape may be translated visually, or it may be optically scanned. Alternatively, the keystrokes may be used to create a cassette from which a computer is instructed to transcribe.

Enormous sums have been spent on installing electrical equipment with which to record judicial proceedings, and some courtrooms are even designed to accommodate such systems. Although cost effective when compared to live reporter costs — some reporters earn as much as $300 a day or more — the product has proved cost defective. Objectionable comments of witnesses and counsel, extraneous noises, and privileged communications are regularly recorded — none of which is easily edited. More importantly, there is no court reporter present to interrupt proceedings when language is unclear, garbled, or barely audible.

Computer-assisted reporting and transcription have revolutionized the profession. Not only are transcripts more accurate; but preparation and delivery times have been reduced appreciably. Today's court reporter must be a computer-compatible writer, a far cry from the Scribes of Israel.

Witnesses Almost all criminal proceedings have witnesses — one or more of three principal types: the police witness, the lay witness, and the expert witness.

A *police witness* is generally an arresting officer who has some knowledge of the facts of the case through his or her presence at the scene of the crime during or soon after its commission. The police witness would be called to testify if the officer had observed some part of the offense (for example, having seen the accused perpetrating the crime), or pertinent events in its aftermath (for example, having observed the accused fleeing from the scene of the crime). Police also serve as witnesses when they present the results of an investigation that led to the arrest of the defendant.

The *lay witness* is a citizen bystander or victim who has some personal knowledge relevant to the case. The lay witness is permitted to testify only on facts directly ascertained through sensory perception. Thus, the citizen cannot be a witness if his or her knowledge of the case is based on conjecture or opinion.[35]

Can you imagine a world without rats, roaches, lawyers, and smokers?

— ANONYMOUS NON-SMOKING CHARLESTON, SOUTH CAROLINA, COURT CLERK, 1990

The police witness

The lay witness

The expert witness

The *expert witness* is called into court to provide technical information and opinions about matters of which the judge or jury may have no knowledge. To qualify as an expert, the witness must offer testimony in an area in which the general public has little or no understanding, and must have established qualifications and authority in that area. The decision whether someone qualifies as an expert witness is made by the trial judge. A psychiatrist, for example, may serve as an expert witness to testify as to the accused's mental competency to stand trial; an authority on ballistics may serve as an expert witness to comment on whether a bullet was fired from a certain weapon; or a specialist in earth science may serve as an expert to establish whether the soil on an accused's clothing matches that where a murder victim was found. There are also experts on fiber evidence, DNA evidence, and eye witness testimony. The expert witness role is also the subject of debate, however, with concerns about "hired guns" and specialists in "junk science" who advertise that they will testify in any court to almost any theory as long as they are well paid.

The coroner's role

Coroners and Medical Examiners   The *coroner* is an appointed or elected county official whose chief function is to investigate the cause of all deaths that have occurred in the absence of witnesses, where there has been evidence of violence, or that have occurred under any suspicious circumstances. The office of coroner is an English invention dating from the twelfth century, when the entire realm was considered to be the property of the king. The term derives from *corona,* meaning crown, and the coroner was second only to the king in power and dignity. He was a man of substance who was considered to be capable of mature judgment; his duties included adjudicating not only on matters of violent and suspicious death but also on questions of property ownership.[36]

The American coroner system is a relic of its early English counterpart. Currently, the office of coroner in most communities is a political position like that of mayor or sheriff, and the potential incumbent needs no qualification other than that of eligibility to run on the predominant party ticket. To perform his duties, the coroner appoints a number of deputies, a forensic pathologist — sometimes with an assistant who specializes in toxicology or ballistics — and a scattering of part-time physicians.

The coroner does not hold a judicial position in the strictest sense, but quasi-judicial functions are nevertheless present. The coroner is authorized, for instance, to conduct *inquests,* which are legal inquiries into deaths where accident, foul play, or violence is suspected. The inquest in many ways is similar to a trial, although it is not governed by the precise procedure. The coroner conducts the inquest, subpoenas witnesses and documents, cross-examines witnesses under oath, introduces evidence, and receives testimony — all with a jury present. Should the inquest suggest "just cause" and a suspect exists, the coroner issues an arrest warrant or moves for the prosecutor to request a warrant from a magistrate.

Criticisms of the coroner system

The coroner system in the United States has been heavily criticized for both corruption and incompetence. The coroner has often been the recipient of a patronage position, either through direct appointment or placement on the ballot. Coroners usually have no background in either medicine or law; the physicians who work as adjuncts to the office are not necessarily required to have any medico-legal training; and if a forensic pathologist is appointed as a coroner's deputy, he or she is generally a newly qualified medic with little experience.

As a result, many jurisdictions have abolished the office of coroner and substituted the office of *medical examiner,* thus divorcing the system from political control and influence. The medical examiner is a licensed physician with training in forensic pathology who is appointed by government authority on a nonpartisan basis. He or she carries out only the medical aspects of any investigation, not the quasi-judicial functions, which are handled by the courts.[37]

The medical examiner is free from political control and is a forensically trained physician.

The medical examiner system was first installed in Massachusetts as early as 1877 and is currently used in almost half the states. It also functions in the metropolitan areas of some states where the coroner system still persists. And in addition, some jurisdictions, such as Los Angeles County, have medical examiner – coroner systems, in which the coroner's office is headed by a medical examiner.[38]

Auxiliary Court Personnel Depending on the jurisdiction, the size of the court, and the traditions of a given legal community, a range of additional figures may provide support services for the criminal judicial process. Both the prosecutor's and public defender's offices may have a number of *secretaries, aides,* and *investigators,* who assist in the collection of evidence and the preparation of cases. There are *court officers,* or perhaps *police officers assigned to the court,* or *correction officers* who maintain custody over detainees who are making court appearances. Also, since many courts have various types of pretrial diversion programs, there may be any number of *pretrial service representatives.* Or similarly, since pretrial release often occurs, *bail bondsagents* are also visible in the court process.

Finally, there are a number of highly significant figures in the court process that have not yet been mentioned, primarily because they are discussed in detail in later chapters. These are *probation officers, grand juries,* and *trial juries.*

THE RIGHT TO COUNSEL

. . . in all criminal prosecutions, the accused shall enjoy the right . . . to have the assistance of counsel for his defense.

—FROM THE SIXTH AMENDMENT

Despite the rather unambiguous language of the *Sixth Amendment,* for almost a century and a half after the framing of the Constitution only persons charged with federal crimes punishable by death were guaranteed the right to counsel. The right of all other defendants — both federal and state — to have the help of an attorney typically depended on their ability to retain their own defense lawyer. Beginning in the 1930s, however, all of this began to change.

The Sixth Amendment

Powell v. Alabama

On March 25, 1931, a group of nine young blacks, ranging in age from thirteen to twenty-one years, were riding in an open gondola car aboard a freight train as it made its way across the state of Alabama. Also aboard the train were seven other boys and two young women, all of whom were white. At some point during the journey, and for whatever reason, a fight broke out between the two groups, during the course of which six of the white boys were thrown from the train. A message was relayed ahead reporting the incident and requesting that all of the blacks be taken from the train. As it pulled into the station at Paint Rock, a small town in northeast Alabama, a sheriff's posse was waiting. The two white women, Victoria Price and Ruby Bates, claimed that they had been raped by a number of the black youths. All nine blacks were immediately taken into custody. Amidst the hostility of a growing crowd, the youths were taken some twenty miles east and placed under military guard in the local jail at Scottsboro, the seat of Jackson County, Alabama.

The "Scottsboro boys"

The "Scottsboro boys," as they became known to history, were indicted on March 31, arraigned on the same day, and entered pleas of not guilty. Until the morning of the trial, no lawyer had been designated by name to represent any of the defendants. On April 6, a visiting lawyer from Tennessee expressed an interest in assisting any counsel the court might designate for the defense. And a local Scottsboro attorney offered a reluctant willingness to represent the defendants, whereupon the proceedings immediately began.

Of the nine youths arrested, one had not been indicted because he was only thirteen years old. The remaining eight were joined into three groups for separate trials, each lasting only a single day. Medical and other evidence was presented which established that the two women, who were alleged to be prostitutes, had *not* been raped. Nevertheless, the eight Scottsboro boys were convicted of rape. Under the existing Alabama statute, the punishment for rape was to be fixed by the jury—anywhere from ten years' imprisonment to death. The jury chose death for all eight defendants.[39]

The trial court overruled all motions for new trials and sentenced the defendants in accordance with the jury's recommendation. Subsequently, the supreme court of Alabama reversed the conviction of one

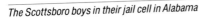

The Scottsboro boys in their jail cell in Alabama

defendant, but affirmed the convictions of the remaining seven. Upon appeal to the U.S. Supreme Court, the Scottsboro defendants, in *Powell v. Alabama*,[40] alleged a denial of Fourteenth Amendment due process and equal protection of the laws because (1) they had not been given a fair trial, (2) they had been denied the right to counsel, and (3) they had been denied a trial by an impartial jury since blacks were systematically excluded from jury service.

In reversing the rape convictions, the Supreme Court observed that Powell and his codefendants were denied their right to the effective assistance of legal counsel and, in turn, that this denial contravened the due-process clause of the Fourteenth Amendment. In the Court's 7-to-2 majority opinion, Justice George Sutherland made the following comments:

> It is hardly necessary to say that . . . a defendant should be afforded a fair opportunity to secure counsel of his own choice. Not only was that not done here, but such designation of counsel as was attempted was either so indefinite or so close upon the trial as to amount to a denial of effective and substantial aid in that regard.

And further:

> In the light of the facts outlined . . . —the ignorance and illiteracy of the defendants, their youth, the circumstances of public hostility, the imprisonment and the close surveillance of the defendants by the military forces, the fact that their friends and families were all in other states and communication with them necessarily difficult, and above all that they stood in deadly peril of their lives—we think the failure of the trial court to give them reasonable time and opportunity to secure counsel was a clear denial of due process.

The decision in *Powell* was a very narrow ruling, for it limited its application to defendants who were indigent, accused of a crime for which the death penalty could be imposed, and incapable of defending themselves because of low intelligence, illiteracy, or some similar handicap. Nevertheless, *Powell* was the first in a series of Supreme Court cases that would extend the Sixth Amendment right to counsel.[41] (For more about the Scottsboro youths and the disposition of their cases, see Exhibit 11.6.)

Extending the Sixth Amendment Right

Six years after *Powell,* the High Court's decision in *Johnson* v. *Zerbst* held that all indigent *federal* defendants facing felony charges were entitled to the assistance of a government-supplied attorney.[42] Johnson, a U.S. Marine charged with passing counterfeit money, had been convicted, but without the aid of a defense attorney. He challenged his conviction, and won a reversal from the Supreme Court. But *Johnson,* with its emphatic declaration of the right of federal defendants to have an attorney, provided no relief to state defendants. *Powell* had extended this right to those charged with capital offenses, and *Townsend* v. *Burke* extended the Sixth Amendment right to defendants in state cases at the time of sentencing,[43] but the Court continued to withhold such aid in all other state cases. In 1942 the Supreme Court reaffirmed its early traditional position on the matter in *Betts* v. *Brady,*[44] ruling that in noncapital crimes, "appointment of counsel is not a fundamental right" for state felony defendants, unless "special" or "exceptional" circumstances such as "mental illness," "youth," or "lack of education" were present. In the

Powell v. *Alabama:* The Supreme Court ruling that an indigent charged in a state court with a capital offense has the right to the assistance of counsel at trial under the due process clause of the Fourteenth Amendment.

The ruling in *Powell* was the first in a series of Supreme Court decisions that would extend the Sixth Amendment right to counsel.

Johnson v. *Zerbst:* The Supreme Court ruling that the Sixth Amendment right to counsel applies to all felony defendants in federal prosecutions.

Betts v. *Brady:* The Supreme Court ruling that the Fourteenth Amendment's due process clause does not require states to supply defense counsel to defendants too poor to employ their own attorney.

years that followed *Betts,* the Court slowly expanded the scope of the Sixth Amendment.[45] At the same time, however, there were many cases in which the states failed to appoint counsel in compliance with *Betts,* thus leading to the most important Sixth Amendment ruling in the High Court's history.

Gideon v. *Wainwright*

Gideon v. *Wainwright:* The Supreme Court ruling that an indigent defendant charged in a state court with any noncapital felony has the right to counsel under the due process clause of the Fourteenth Amendment.

Among the Court's most significant decisions was **Gideon** v. **Wainwright** in 1963,[46] for not only did it extend the right to counsel to all state defendants facing felony trials, but it also dramatically demonstrated that even the least influential of citizens could persuade those in charge to reexamine the premises of justice in America.

Clarence Earl Gideon was charged with breaking and entering into the Bay Harbor Pool Room in Panama City, Florida, with the intent of committing a misdemeanor — a case of petty larceny which, under Florida law, is considered a felony. The year was 1961, and Gideon was a fifty-one-year-old white man who had been in and out of prisons much of his life. He was not a violent man, but he had served time for four previous felonies. He was a drifter who never seemed to settle down, making his way through life by gambling and occasional thefts. He also bore the marks of a difficult life: a wrinkled, prematurely aged face, a voice and hands that trembled, a frail body, and white hair. Those who knew him, even the officers who had arrested him considered Gideon a harmless and rather likeable human being, but one tossed aside by life.[47]

On August 4, 1961, Clarence Earl Gideon was tried on the breaking and entering in the Bay County, Florida, Circuit Court before Judge Robert L. McCrary, Jr., and the hearing began as follows:

THE COURT:	The next case on the docket is the case of the state of Florida, Plaintiff, versus Clarence Earl Gideon, defendant. What says the state, are you ready to go to trial in this case?
MR. HARRIS:*	The state is ready, your honor.
THE COURT:	What says the defendant? Are you ready to go to trial?
THE DEFENDANT:	I am not ready, your honor.
THE COURT:	Did you plead not guilty to this charge by reason of insanity?
THE DEFENDANT:	No sir.
THE COURT:	Why aren't you ready?
THE DEFENDANT:	I have no counsel.
THE COURT:	Why do you not have counsel? Did you not know that your case was set for trial today?
THE DEFENDANT:	Yes sir, I knew that it was set for trial today.
THE COURT:	Why, then, did you not secure counsel and be prepared to go to trial?

(The defendant answered the court's question, but spoke in such low tones that it was not audible.)

THE COURT:	Come closer up, Mr. Gideon, I can't understand you, I don't know what you said, and the reporter didn't understand you either.

(At this point the defendant arose from his chair where he was seated at the counsel table and walked up and stood directly in front of the bench, facing his honor, Judge McCrary.)

THE COURT:	Now tell me what you said again, so we can understand you, please.
THE DEFENDANT:	Your honor, I said: I request this court to appoint counsel to represent me in this trial.

---

* William E. Harris, assistant state attorney.

THE COURT:	Mr. Gideon, I am sorry, but I cannot appoint counsel to represent you in this case. Under the laws of the state of Florida, the only time the court can appoint counsel to represent a defendant is when that person is charged with a capital offense. I am sorry, but I will have to deny your request to appoint counsel to defend you in this case.
THE DEFENDANT:	The United States Supreme Court says I am entitled to be represented by counsel.

Gideon, of course, was wrong, for the High Court had *not* said that he was entitled to counsel. In *Betts* v. *Brady,* some twenty years earlier, the Supreme Court had stated quite the opposite. The decision in *Betts* had actually *denied* free legal counsel to indigent felony defendants in state courts, unless "special circumstances" were present.

Judge McCrary apologetically informed Gideon of his mistake. Put to trial before a jury, Gideon heroically conducted his own defense as best as he could. He made an opening statement to the jury, cross-examined the state's witnesses, presented witnesses in his own defense, declined to testify himself, and made a short closing argument emphasizing his innocence to the charge. But Gideon's defense had been ineffective, for he was found guilty and sentenced to serve five years in state prison.

In the morning mail of January 8, 1962, the U.S. Supreme Court received a large envelope from Clarence Earl Gideon, prisoner number 003826, Florida State Prison, P.O. Box 211, Raiford, Florida. Gideon's petition was *in forma pauperis* — in the form of a poor man. It was prepared in pencil, with carefully formed printing on lined sheets provided by the Florida prison. Printed at the top of each sheet, under the heading Correspondence Regulations, was a set of rules ("Only 2 letters each week . . . written on one side only . . . letters must be written in English . . ."), and the warning: "Mail will not be delivered which does not conform to these rules." [48]

Certiorari was ultimately granted to Gideon's petition. The Supreme Court assigned Washington, D.C., attorney Abe Fortas, who was later appointed to the Supreme Court by President Lyndon B. Johnson, to argue Gideon's claim. Fortas contended that counsel in a criminal trial is a fundamental right of due process enforced on the states by the Fourteenth Amendment. The Court's decision was unanimous, and in overturning *Betts,* Justice Black wrote:

> Any person haled into court, who is too poor to hire a lawyer, cannot be assured a fair trial unless counsel is provided for him. This seems to us an obvious truth.

This ruling of the Supreme Court on March 18, 1963, after Gideon had served almost two years in prison, entitled Gideon to a new trial. He was immediately retried in the same courtroom and by the same judge as in the initial trial, but this time he was represented by counsel and was acquitted. Gideon was set free, as were thousands of other prisoners in Florida and elsewhere because they had been tried unrepresented by an attorney. [49] (For later events in Gideon's life, see Exhibit 11.6.)

Argersinger v. Hamlin

In extending the right to counsel to all state defendants facing felony trials, *Gideon* also represented the beginning of a trend that would ultimately expand Sixth Amendment rights to most phases of criminal

In forma pauperis: The characterization of an appeal by a poor person.

Forma pauperis *means in the character of a poor person — a method by which a litigant without money for lawyers is considerably permitted to lose his case.*

—AMBROSE BIERCE, *THE DEVIL'S DICTIONARY,* 1911

● EXHIBIT 11.6 ●

Whatever Happened to . . .

The Scottsboro Boys

For the nine Scottsboro boys—Clarence Norris, Olen Montgomery, Ozie Powell, Haywood Patterson, Willie Roberson, Charlie Weems, Eugene Williams, Roy Wright, and Andrew Wright—the decision in *Powell* v. *Alabama* was but a shallow victory. They were retried in the Alabama courts and reconvicted. At one point, Ruby Bates recanted her earlier testimony, stating that neither she nor Victoria Price had ever been raped, but had concocted the charge in an attempt to avoid being arrested for vagrancy. This, combined with the lack of any medical evidence of rape, would suggest that the convictions had been gross miscarriages of justice. Victoria Price, however, did not fully agree with the statements of Bates, but Price did concede that she had been raped by only six of the defendants. Thus, at least one, *and likely all,* of the Scottsboro boys had to have been innocent of active participation in the alleged crime.

The cases were appealed and retried again, but with little success. In a series of trials held in 1936 and 1937, four of the original nine defendants were, for the third time, convicted of rape by all-white juries. Their sentences ranged from seventy-five to ninety-nine years to electrocution.

- On July 24, 1937, the rape charges against *Olen Montgomery, Willie Roberson,* and *Eugene Williams* were dropped. A year after their release, the three made a personal appearance at New York's Apollo theater, but subsequently fell into obscurity.

- *Roy Wright* was released along with Montgomery, Roberson, and Williams in 1937. On August 17, 1959, amidst a jealous rage, Wright stabbed his wife to death and subsequently took his own life.

- The rape charges against *Ozie Powell* were dropped in 1937. However, on January 24, 1936, Powell had attacked a deputy sheriff by shooting him in the head. He was convicted of assault and sentenced to twenty years' imprisonment. Powell was paroled in 1946 and quickly fell into obscurity.

- *Charlie Weems* was convicted on the rape charges in 1937 and sentenced to seventy-five years. He was paroled in 1943 and retired to an anonymous existence.

- *Andrew Wright* was convicted on the rape charges in 1937 and drew a sentence of ninety-nine years. He was paroled in 1944 but was returned to prison almost immediately, having been charged with parole violation for leaving Alabama. He was paroled again in 1947 but returned to prison when his employer learned that he was a Scottsboro boy and fired him. Wright was released for a third time in 1950 and moved to Albany, New York. Since that time, his name surfaced publicly only once. On July 12, 1951, he was arrested for the rape of a thirteen-year-old girl. He was found innocent and released.

- On January 23, 1936, *Haywood Patterson* was convicted on the rape charges and sentenced to seventy-five years. In 1948, however, he escaped from prison and fled Alabama. On January 25, 1951, Patterson was convicted of manslaughter and sentenced to fifteen to twenty years by a Michigan court. Less than a year later, however, he died of lung cancer.

Douglas v. California

justice proceedings. On the same day as *Gideon,* the Court also delivered its opinion in *Douglas* v. *California,*[50] which required that indigent felons were entitled to counsel, if requested, to argue their cause at the first appeal proceedings. The ruling in *Douglas* was doubly significant. Most of the Supreme Court decisions related to the Sixth Amendment right to counsel had addressed only the due process clause of the Fourteenth Amendment; *Douglas* was the first case to reference both the due process and equal protection clauses. In delivering the Court's opinion, Justice William O. Douglas wrote the following:

There is lacking that equality demanded by the Fourteenth Amendment where the rich man, who appeals as of right, enjoys the benefit of counsel's examination

• *Clarence Norris* was convicted on the rape charge in 1936 and sentenced to death. In 1938, the death sentence was commuted to life imprisonment, and he was paroled in 1944. Norris immediately left Alabama in violation of his parole, was captured, and returned to prison. He was paroled again in 1946, but left the state just three days later and was declared delinquent as a parole violator. Norris remained at large in New York City for many decades. In 1976, Alabama's attorney general recommended Norris's pardon, declaring that studies of the case indicated that this last of the Scottsboro boys was innocent of the rape with which he had been charged some forty-five years earlier. The pardon was granted by Alabama governor George Wallace. In 1977, a bill to compensate Norris for his wrongful conviction and imprisonment was defeated by an Alabama legislative committee. Regarding the decision, Norris's attorney, Donald Watkins, commented: "The mentality of the 1930s is alive and well in the 1970s." On January 23, 1989, Clarence Norris, the last of the Scottsboro boys, died of natural causes at the age of 76.

Clarence Earl Gideon

After the Supreme Court's *Gideon* v. *Wainwright* ruling in 1963, Clarence Earl Gideon was granted a new trial. Represented by counsel, he was found not guilty and set free. Once again he became a drifter, a style of life he had embarked upon in 1925

Clarence Earl Gideon

when, at age fourteen, he left school and ran away from home.

The year 1965 found him in a Louisville courtroom. He had traveled to that part of the country to attend the Kentucky Derby. But out of work and having picked a losing horse, he was arrested on a charge of vagrancy. At the trial, the judge recognized Gideon's name and offered to jail him long enough so that he could appeal for the right to counsel in petty trials. That was several years prior to the High Court's decision in *Argersinger*. But Gideon declined, telling the judge he'd just as soon plead guilty and walk away.

On January 18, 1976, Clarence Earl Gideon passed away at the age of sixty-one in a Fort Lauderdale medical center. Although he had been the key figure in a Supreme Court decision immortalized in hundreds of legal essays, a major book (*Gideon's Trumpet* by *New York Times* correspondent Anthony Lewis in 1964), and a Hollywood production (Samuel Goldwyn Studios' *Gideon's Trumpet* in 1979, with actor Henry Fonda in the leading role), Gideon died as an obscure man — cast aside by life, without money or influence.

into the record, research of the law, and marshalling of arguments on his behalf, while the indigent, already burdened by a preliminary determination that his case is without merit, is forced to shift for himself. The indigent . . . has only the right to a meaningless ritual, while the rich man has a meaningful appeal.

Following *Gideon* and *Douglas* in 1963, the Court continued its trend with *Massiah* v. *United States, Escobedo* v. *Illinois, Miranda* v. *Arizona,* and *United States* v. *Wade,* which applied the right of access to counsel at indictment, interrogation, and postindictment lineups.[51] In the 1970 decision of *Coleman* v. *Alabama,*[52] the Court ruled that the preliminary hearing was a "critical stage" in a criminal prosecution, at which time the "guiding hand of counsel" is essential.

Argersinger v. *Hamlin:* The Supreme Court ruling that a defendant has the right to counsel at trial whenever he or she may be imprisoned for any offense, even for one day, whether it is classified as a felony or as a misdemeanor.

Ever since the Supreme Court's ruling in *Gideon* v. *Wainwright,* there had been some question whether or not the constitutional right to be represented by counsel should apply not only to felony cases, but to misdemeanors as well. *Argersinger* v. *Hamlin* in 1972 addressed this issue.[53] In *Argersinger,* the defendant was an indigent charged in Florida with carrying a concealed weapon, the potential punishment for which was up to six months' imprisonment and/or a $1,000 fine. At the trial, the defendant was not represented by counsel but was convicted and sentenced to serve ninety days in jail. In a *habeas corpus* petition to the Florida Supreme Court, the defendant argued that because he was but a poor man and had not been provided with counsel, the charge against him could not effectively be defended. The Florida appellate court rejected the claim, and the United States Supreme Court granted *certiorari*.

In a unanimous decision, the Court ruled that the right to counsel applied not only to state defendants charged with felonies, but in all trials of persons for offenses serious enough to warrant a jail sentence. Speaking for the Court, Justice William O. Douglas recalled both *Powell* v. *Alabama* and *Gideon* v. *Wainwright:*

> Both *Powell* and *Gideon* involved felonies. But their rationale has relevance to any criminal trial, where an accused is deprived of liberty. *Powell* and *Gideon* suggest that there are certain fundamental rights applicable to all such criminal prosecutions.
>
> The requirement of counsel may well be necessary for a fair trial even in a petty offense prosecution. We are by no means convinced that legal and constitutional questions involved in a case that actually leads to imprisonment even for a brief period are any less complex than when a person can be sent off for six months or more. . . .
>
> Under the rule we announce today, every judge will know when the trial of a misdemeanor starts that no imprisonment may be imposed, even though local law permits it, unless the accused is represented by counsel.

Restrictions on the Sixth Amendment Right

While *Powell, Zerbst, Gideon,* and *Argersinger* served to guarantee the right to counsel to all federal and state defendants facing trials on charges where sentences of death or imprisonment could be imposed, the Court also took steps that, in its opinion, would not overliberalize the Sixth Amendment right. For example, in *McMann* v. *Richardson,*[54] the Court declared that defendants must assume a certain degree of risk that their attorneys would make some "ordinary error" in assessing the facts of their case and the law that applied, and that such error was not a basis for reversing a conviction.

In *Ross* v. *Moffitt,*[55] the Court held that the state's constitutional obligation to provide appointed counsel for indigents appealing their convictions did not extend beyond the first appeal.

In *Scott* v. *Illinois,*[56] the Court decided that a criminal defendant charged with a statutory offense for which imprisonment upon conviction is authorized but not imposed does not have the right to appointed counsel.

In *Pennsylvania* v. *Finley,*[57] the Court ruled that there is no constitutional right to counsel in state postconviction proceedings.

In *Strickland* v. *Washington,*[58] the Court addressed the issue of the right to "effective" counsel, holding that in order to prevail on a Sixth Amendment claim of ineffective assistance, the defendant must prove that his or her attorney's performance was deficient, that the deficiency prejudiced the case, and that there was a reasonable probability that if it

In *Strickland* v. *Washington,* the Court held that a convicted person alleging ineffectiveness of counsel must satisfy that the defense counsel's representation fell below an objective standard of reasonableness and that the ineffectiveness actually prejudiced the defendant.

were not for the unprofessional errors, the result would have been different. It should be added here that this is a difficult standard to meet, as pointed out by Justice Thurgood Marshall in his vigorous dissenting opinion. The effect of *Strickland* was to uphold a death sentence even though the defense attorney had failed to investigate and present several potentially important mitigating factors at the penalty phase of the trial.

Currently, there remain several areas in criminal processing—from arrest to appeal—where the courts do not mandate the assistance of counsel for the accused, including (1) preindictment line-ups, (2) booking procedures, (3) grand jury investigations, and (4) appeals beyond the first review. Decisions that address the right to counsel regarding parole and correctional matters are discussed in Chapter 17. (For a summary of court decisions extending the right to counsel, see Exhibit 11.7. Exhibit 11.8 discusses the right *not* to have counsel.)

LEGAL AID, ASSIGNED COUNSEL, AND PUBLIC DEFENDERS

Legal services for the indigent come from three primary sources: voluntary defender programs sponsored by numerous charitable and private organizations; assigned counsel systems through which a presiding judge can call upon a local practicing attorney to defend a case; and public defenders, who are salaried by the courts to represent criminal defendants.

Prior to *Gideon,* the availability of legal defense help for indigent defendants was notably limited. In 1961, for example, public defender systems existed in only 3 percent of the nation's counties, serving 25 percent of the U.S. population.[59] The balance relied on assigned counsel programs, which were generally rare due to the organized bar's indifference to the need for defense assistance and to private attorneys' lack of interest in practicing criminal law. Furthermore, since the right to counsel was not yet a Supreme Court mandate, most jurisdictions did not make any arrangements for the defense of indigents charged with criminal offenses. However, with *Gideon* in 1963 and *Argersinger* in 1972, the criminal justice system was forced to meet the needs of the indigent, which comprise some two-thirds of all felony defendants. By 1980, public defender services were available in more than 1,000 counties to serve some 68 percent of the base population.[60] Since then, even more public defender programs have been established, assigned counsel systems have been improved, and voluntary defender programs have become more visible.

Eligibility for these forms of supported defense varies. Some judges apply stringent *"indigency standards"* before appointing counsel. In some jurisdictions, for example, if the defendant owns a home, is employed full-time, or has the resources to meet the monetary bond that has been established, he or she is not considered indigent. Others require the filing of tax returns or affidavits that document resources. Some presiding judges simply ask the defendant: "Can you afford a lawyer?" A simple yes or no in such cases determines eligibility.

Some courts apply "indigency standards" for the appointment of defense counsel.

Voluntary Defender Programs

Many private organizations across the country provide legal assistance to indigents. The most numerous are the legal aid societies, which are

● EXHIBIT 11.7 ●

Major Supreme Court Decisions Extending the Sixth Amendment Right to Counsel

Defining the scope of the constitutional right to counsel has occupied the courts since 1789, and efforts to expand this right have led to a variety of questions:

- In what kinds of cases should the right to counsel exist?

- When does the right begin in a case?
- What does the assistance of counsel include?
- Can there be two standards for legal assistance — one for the rich and another for the poor?

Case	Ruling
Powell v. *Alabama,* 287 U.S. 45 (1932)	An indigent defendant charged in a state court with a capital offense has the right to the assistance of counsel at trial under the due process clause of the Fourteenth Amendment.
Johnson v. *Zerbst,* 304 U.S. 458 (1938)	The Sixth Amendment right to counsel applies to all defendants in federal prosecutions.
Townsend v. *Burke,* 334 U.S. 736 (1948)	A convicted offender has the right to counsel at the time of sentencing.
Uveges v. *Pennsylvania,* 335 U.S. 437 (1948)	Counsel must be appointed to represent an indigent defendant whether he or she elects to stand trial or to plead guilty, where the seriousness of the crime and other factors would otherwise render the proceedings fundamentally unfair.
Moore v. *Michigan,* 355 U.S. 155 (1957)	A defendant has a right to counsel when submitting any guilty plea to the court.
Hamilton v. *Alabama,* 368 U.S. 52 (1961)	The denial of the right to counsel during arraignment, even if the offense charged is a noncapital felony, is a violation of due process of law.
Carnley v. *Cochran,* 369 U.S. 506 (1962)	Trial judges must inform defendants of their right to counsel prior to accepting guilty pleas, and a defendant's failure to request counsel does not constitute a waiver of his or her right to counsel.
Gideon v. *Wainwright,* 372 U.S. 355 (1963)	An indigent defendant charged in a state court with any noncapital felony has the right to counsel under the due process clause of the Fourteenth Amendment.
Douglas v. *California,* 372 U.S. 353 (1963)	If state appellate review is statutorily required in criminal cases, an indigent felon is entitled to counsel, if requested, on the first appeal following a felony conviction.
Massiah v. *United States,* 377 U.S. 201 (1964)	In federal cases, the right to counsel becomes applicable upon indictment.

financed by state and private contributions and staffed by full-time attorneys who earn their living representing the poor. In addition, there are legal aid bureaus attached to charitable organizations, bar association legal aid offices, and law school clinics that provide legal assistance.

During the mid-1960s, federally supported legal assistance programs were started as part of the Johnson adminstration's war on pov-

Since the 1930s, the U.S. Supreme Court has repeatedly examined these issues. The following decisions, listed chronologically, reflect the Court's rulings on matters of criminal procedure from arrest through appeal. The Court's purpose in extending the right to counsel at arrest was to prevent improper police practices that could result in involuntary confessions. Its purpose in extending this right to postarrest proceedings was to guarantee a fair trial and access to appeal.

Case	Ruling
Escobedo v. *Illinois,* 378 U.S. 478 (1964)	A defendant has the right to counsel during the course of any police interrogation.
Miranda v. *Arizona,* 384 U.S. 694 (1966)	The guarantee of due process requires that suspects in police custody be informed — before any questioning can permissibly take place — of their right to remain silent, that anything they say may be used against them, and that they have the right to counsel.
United States v. *Wade,* 388 U.S. 218 (1967) *Gilbert* v. *California,* 388 U.S. 263 (1967)	A defendant in a line-up for identification purposes has the right to the assistance of counsel. (*Wade* applied to federal defendants; *Gilbert* applied to state defendants.)
Coleman v. *Alabama,* 399 U.S. 1 (1970)	The preliminary hearing can be a critical stage in a criminal prosecution; thus, a state's failure to provide counsel at that stage may be a violation of the Sixth Amendment.
Argersinger v. *Hamlin,* 407 U.S. 25 (1972)	A defendant has the right to counsel at trial whenever he or she may be imprisoned for any offense, even one day, whether it is classified as a felony or as a misdemeanor.
Kirby v. *Illinois,* 406 U.S. 682 (1972)	Counsel is required only at those line-ups that take place after indictment or other "adversary criminal proceedings" (thus limited both *Wade* and *Gilbert*).
Moore v. *Illinois,* 434 U.S. 220 (1977)	A defendant has a right to counsel during an in-court identification at a preliminary hearing after a criminal complaint has been initiated.
Brewer v. *Williams,* 430 U.S. 387 (1977)	Once any adversary proceedings have begun against a defendant, he or she has the right to the assistance of counsel.
United States v. *Henry,* 100 S. Ct. 2183 (1980)	A defendant's Sixth Amendment right to counsel is violated when government agents are used to covertly solicit statements from him or her on his or her pending charge, and such statements are introduced at trial.

erty. Originally funded by the Office of Economic Opportunity (OEO) and restructured in 1974 as the Legal Services Corporation when OEO was disbanded, these offices were established in many of the poorest urban neighborhoods and centers of rural poverty. By 1967, shortly after the program became fully operational, there were 299 legal assistance offices handling almost 300,000 cases annually.[61] These federally

• EXHIBIT 11.8 •

The Right *Not* to Have Counsel

The case of *Faretta* v. *California* (422 U.S. 806), decided by a 6-to-3 majority in 1975, seemed to turn inside out the Supreme Court's series of rulings expanding the Sixth Amendment right to counsel in state proceedings.

The defendant, Anthony Faretta, had been accused of grand theft. At his arraignment the presiding judge assigned a local public defender to represent him. Well in advance of his trial, Faretta requested that he be permitted to represent himself. He argued that he had represented himself in a previous prosecution, and that the public defender's case load was far too heavy to allow the defender the time to prepare an effective defense. The judge approved the request, at least tentatively, but warned the defendant that he was "making a mistake."

Several weeks later, still in advance of the trial date, the judge questioned Faretta about various issues in criminal procedure to inquire into his ability to conduct his own defense. On the basis of Faretta's answers and demeanor, the judge ruled that the defendant had not made a knowing and intelligent waiver of his right to counsel and that he did not have a constitutional right to conduct his own defense. Over Faretta's objections, a public defender was appointed, and the trial led to a conviction and sentence of imprisonment.

Upon review, the United States Supreme Court ruled in Faretta's favor. Writing for the majority, Justice Potter Stewart commented:

The Sixth Amendment does not provide merely that a defense shall be made for the accused; it grants to the accused personally the right to make his defense. It is the acccused, not counsel, who must be "informed of the nature and cause of the accusation," and who must be "confronted with the witnesses against him," and who must be accorded "compulsory process for obtaining witnesses in his favor." Although not stated in the Amendment in so many words, the right to self-representation—to make one's own defense personally—is thus necessarily implied by the structure of the Amendment. The right to defend is given directly to the accused; for it is he who suffers the consequences if the defense fails.

In a dissenting opinion, however, Justice Harry A. Blackmun argued that the decision in *Faretta* left open a host of other procedural issues:

Must every defendant be advised of his right to proceed *pro se?* If so, when must that notice be given? Since the

---

funded service centers endured throughout the 1970s and into the early 1980s, but when the Reagan administration's budget cuts began in 1981, funding for the Legal Services Corporation was sharply reduced, thus opening a gap in legal services for the poor.[62]

Other voluntary legal services come from individual attorneys and some private agencies that actively seek out specific kinds of court cases. The noted activist lawyer William M. Kunstler, for example, working in conjunction with the Law Center for Constitutional Rights, devotes much of his time to cases involving constitutional rights and civil liberties.

The American Civil Liberties Union (ACLU) is the best-known of the voluntary legal services.

The best known practitioner of this type of service, however, is the *American Civil Liberties Union (ACLU).* Founded in 1920 as a nonpartisan organization devoted to the preservation and extension of the basic rights set forth in the U.S. Constitution, the American Civil Liberties Union was an outgrowth of earlier groups that had defended the rigths of conscientious objectors during World War I. Its focus is on three areas of American civil liberties: (1) *inquiry and expression,* including freedom of speech, press, assembly, and religion; (2) *equality before the law,* for everyone, regardless of race, nationality, political opinion, or religious belief; and (3) *due process of law* for all persons.[63]

The various voluntary defender programs have a number of serious weaknesses and shortcomings that have an impact on their usefulness for criminal defendants. For example, the uncertainty of their continuing

right to assistance of counsel and the right to self-representation are mutually exclusive, how is the waiver of each right to be measured? If a defendant has elected to exercise his right to proceed *pro se,* does he still have a constitutional right to assistance of standby counsel? How soon in the criminal proceeding must a defendant decide between proceeding by counsel or *pro se?* Must he be allowed to switch in midtrial? May a violation of the right to self-representation ever be harmless error? Must the trial court treat the *pro se* defendant differently than it would professional counsel? . . . Many of these questions . . . such as the standards of waiver and the treatment of the *pro se* defendant, will haunt the trial of every defendant who elects to exercise his right to self-representation. The procedural problems spawned by an absolute right to self-representation will far out-weigh whatever tactical advantage the defendant may feel he has gained by electing to represent himself.

Without question, *Faretta* did raise a number of problematic issues. Most critical is the potential "catch-22" that could emerge whereby a judge attempts to carry out the *Faretta* mandate, and at the same time knowingly allows a defendant to make a mockery of his own defense or antagonize the court. In this regard, one can only recall the case of Caryl Chessman, the infamous "Red Light Bandit." On January 23, 1948, Chessman was arrested in Los Angeles and charged with eighteen counts of robbery and rape, committed in a local "lover's lane" during the previous year. At least two of the victims identified Chessman as the man who had approached a parked car, flashed a red light on its occupants, and at gunpoint

robbed the driver and compelled the women to engage in sexual acts. Chessman was convicted and sentenced to death. He lodged thirty-nine appeals and his execution date was deferred eight times. But finally he died in San Quentin's gas chamber on May 2, 1960, some eleven years and two months after his arrest. Chessman had conducted his own defense, and his abrasive demeanor tended to anger the court. There are those who have maintained that the evidence against Chessman was not overwhelming, that he was innocent, and that his conviction came solely from the biases against him that were generated by the condescending and irritating manner in which he defended himself.

financial support is a crucial problem, and, as with the Legal Services Corporation, can lead to termination of services. More importantly, however, the voluntary programs accept few criminal cases. With a small number of exceptions, the legal aid societies, federal assistance centers, bar association progams, law school clinics, and other service groups concentrate their efforts primarily on family and civil issues. The cases they most readily accept are ones involving divorce and child support, housing problems, conflicts with welfare agencies, and consumer credit disputes. However, organizations such as the Law Center for Constitutional Rights and the American Civil Liberties Union do handle some criminal matters. In recent years, for example, the ACLU has placed considerable emphasis on such due process issues as a prisoner's rights, police arrest behavior, and cruel and unusual punishment. More often than not, though, the individuals defended by ACLU lawyers are involved in test cases, and routine criminal trials are only rarely handled.

Assigned Counsel Systems

The assigned counsel system is unquestionably the oldest and most widely used method for the representation of indigent criminal defendants. Lawyers represent defendants on a case-by-case basis. Appointments are made by a presiding judge from a list that may consist of *all* the practicing attorneys in the jurisdiction, or only those who have

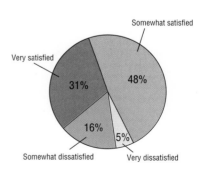

How Satisfied Are Lawyers With Their Careers?

SOURCE: *National Law Journal,* May 28, 1990

The drawbacks of the assigned counsel system

volunteered to defend indigents. The attorneys, in turn, contribute their time as part of their responsibility to the profession and the community.

The assigned counsel system, however, has some very serious drawbacks:

- In the majority of jurisdictions, assigned counselors are either novices or "has beens"; that is, they are either recent law school graduates who desire courtroom experience or older nonprestigious members of the bar who need numerous appointments to make a living.

- Even when appointments are rotated among all members of the practicing bar, there is no guarantee that the counsel assigned is qualified to handle the complexities of criminal law and procedure. Through the luck of the draw, the defendant's lawyer may be the best tax or probate attorney in the area but have virtually no experience in criminal cases.

- Many jurisdictions neither pay attorneys for representing indigents nor reimburse the assigned counsel for out-of-pocket expenses. Where court-appointed lawyers are paid, compensation is only minimal. This serves not only to discourage qualified attorneys who might otherwise serve, but it also pressures attorneys to dispose of cases quickly in order to devote more time to fee-paying clients.

- Assigned counsel systems seldom provide funds to hire investigators or secure the service of expert witnesses, further decreasing the likelihood of a thorough and adequate defense.

- Attorneys who are dependent on the assigned counsel system for a livelihood may be concerned more with pleasing the court than with helping the client. Such counselors may avoid arguing for lower bail, filing a greater number of pretrial motions, objecting to court rulings, or using other tactics in the client's defense in order not to anger the court.[64]

"*This trial has had a court-appointed lawyer and a court-appointed psychiatrist. Now, for a change of pace, I'd like to introduce a court-appointed stand-up comic.*"

Despite these considerable weaknesses, however, advocates support the assigned counsel system because it disperses the responsibility for defending indigents among a wide spectrum of practicing lawyers:

> Many problems in the administration of criminal justice, both at the federal and state levels, result from the absence of involvement of most lawyers in the practice of criminal law. An almost indispensable condition to fundamental improvement of American criminal justice is the active and knowledgeable support of the bar as a whole. There is no better way to develop such interest and awareness than to provide wider opportunities for lawyers to participate in criminal litigation at reasonable rates of compensation.[65]

There is an additional advantage to the assigned counsel system. Criminal defendants potentially have attorneys with fresh perspectives to represent them. *Not* being a member of the courtroom workgroup can lead to a more vigorous defense. Moreover, many an accused will argue that he or she does not like being represented by the public defender, feeling far more confident in an assigned counsel.

Public Defenders

The public defender is a part- or full-time county, state, or federal government employee who earns a fixed salary and specializes in representing indigent criminal defendants. The first public defender office was established in Los Angeles County in 1914. Today, public defender systems exist in most urban areas and are increasingly being adopted in many small and medium-sized jurisdictions. The systems, however, vary widely in size. In Los Angeles, for example, there are many hundreds of public defenders on staff to serve the population of indigent defendants, while in other areas there is only a single such counsel, who is responsible for the criminal case load of an entire county.

With few exceptions, defendants who are represented by public defenders are generally more fortunate than those receiving the services of an assigned counsel or a volunteer from a local legal aid society. First, defender offices are staffed by attorneys who are as skilled and specialized as those on the corresponding prosecutor's staff. Second, the public defender system attracts attorneys of generally greater ability than those in assigned counsel systems, for it provides a regular means of income and the experience necessary for advancement. Third, most defender offices have some funds available for investigations, and the opportunity to conduct an independent investigation permits the undertaking of a more vigorous defense. Fourth, since the income of the assigned public defender continues regardless of whether the case goes to trial, the attorney is less likely to force the plea negotiation process where it may not be appropriate.

On the other hand, the defender system does have problems. The salaries paid to public defenders are not competitive with those paid to other attorneys with similar experience; hence turnover tends to be high. In many jurisdictions, case loads are extremely heavy, restricting the amount of time available for each case. Public defender offices lack community support; citizens are often hostile to the system because it represents "criminals" with tax dollars. Too, although some chief public defenders are elected, most are appointed either by the governor or the court. This creates the potential for patronage and favoritism, and the divided allegiance of the defense. Finally, like many attorneys in the assigned counsel system, many public defenders may not wish to anger the court through the vigorous use of motions, demands for jury trials, and appeals.

"Objection your honor, counsel for the defense is leading the witness!"

Contract Systems

Relatively new to the spectrum of indigent defense is the contract system, in which individual attorneys, bar associations, or private law firms contract to provide services for a specified dollar amount. Contract awards are generally made on the basis of competitive bidding, with selection criteria including cost, qualifications of bidders, and their proposed methods of representation. Currently, only a minimal number of counties in the United States use some form of the contract system, and this system is the dominant form of indigent representation in only six states. (See Exhibit 11.9.) Moreover, while the contract system appears to be growing, it has tended to concentrate in the less populated areas and on cases for which other forms of indigent defense were unavailable.[66]

ISSUES IN JUDICIAL CONDUCT

For most of this century, discussions of corruption and other forms of misconduct in criminal justice processing have focused on police behavior. Increasingly, however, problems within the legal and judicial sectors

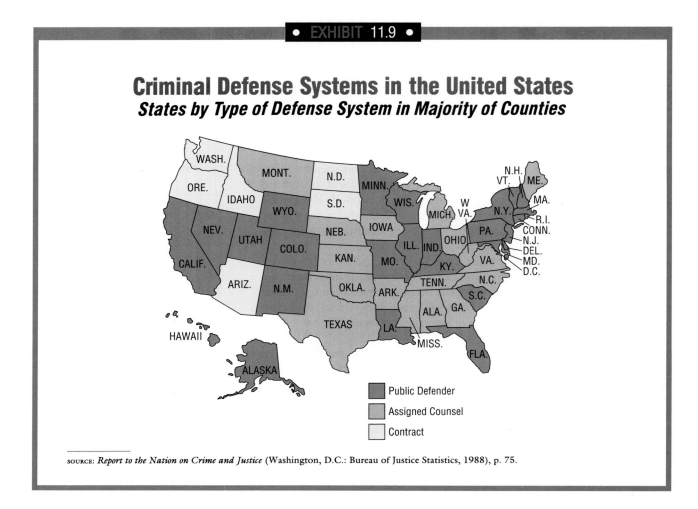

• EXHIBIT 11.9 •

Criminal Defense Systems in the United States
States by Type of Defense System in Majority of Counties

Public Defender

Assigned Counsel

Contract

SOURCE: *Report to the Nation on Crime and Justice* (Washington, D.C.: Bureau of Justice Statistics, 1988), p. 75.

have become more visible. Furthermore, a variety of charges have been aimed at all practitioners in the courtroom work group. There have been charges of dishonesty — a growing number of judges, lawyers, and prosecutors are being accused of conflicts of interest, defrauding clients, or participating in other misdeeds that reflect a total contempt for professional ethics. There have been charges of greed — lawyers are being faulted with charging fees that go far beyond what is justified by the work involved. And there have been charges of incompetence — various legal practitioners are being cited for costly mistakes and inexcusable errors during trials.

High-ranking members of the American Bar Association maintain that of the more than 600,000 lawyers across the nation (including judges), only a small minority are either inept, greedy, or corrupt. However, former Chief Justice of the Supreme Court Warren Burger maintained over the years that up to half of the nation's trial lawyers are unfit to appear in court.

At the same time, the National Legal Aid and Defender Association has estimated that some 1,000 cases each year claim ineffective representation by defense attorneys.[67] For some of those defendants, the quality of the legal assistance received can be a matter of life and death. This was certainly the case for Elvin Myles, convicted and sentenced to death for the 1977 slaying of a Louisiana department store clerk. The claim of ineffective counsel was based on the lawyer's failure to ask the jury to spare Myles from electrocution. The Louisiana Supreme Court deter-

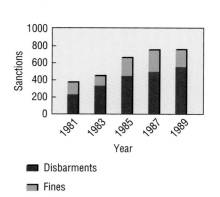

Disbarments

Fines

Sanctions Imposed on Lawyers by State Courts 1981–1989

SOURCE: American Bar Association

mined that the defense counsel had acted more like a "neutral observer" than an advocate, and ordered a new sentencing hearing.[68]

For Elvin Myles, the decision was a fortunate one, for it is the position of both the federal and state courts that legal representation can be deemed poor and "ineffective" only when there is proof that it prejudiced the proceedings.

In an effort to remedy the problems generated by incompetence, corruption, or unethical practices within the courtroom work group, a number of programs have been instituted. Judges are now answerable to the various judicial discipline commissions that exist in more than two-thirds of the states. The first of these was California's Commission on Judicial Performance, established in 1960. Composed of judges, lawyers, and citizens, its authority extends to investigating complaints against members of the bench, demanding explanations from any judges charged with misconduct, and recommending disciplinary measures to the California Supreme Court. This court-watching program has had an impact, for it has induced the resignations and retirements of many judges and has been responsible for the censure of numerous others.[69] New York State's Commission on Judicial Conduct is similar to the one in California, and disciplines judges with measures ranging from "admonishment," which amounts to a public criticism, to outright removal from the bench.[70]

The disciplining of lawyers is handled by the American Bar Association as well as local bar associations and the courts, and measures range from censure to actual disbarment. Allegations of attorney misconduct and incompetence are investigated by the National Legal Aid and Defender Association. At the local level, investigations are undertaken that aim at protecting the indigent from unfit and unscrupulous attorneys.

SUMMARY

The criminal judicial process in the United States has many participants. First, in the courtroom work group are the judge, who serves at the head of the court; the prosecutor, who argues the state's case; the defense attorney, who argues in behalf of the accused; and the accused. Second, there are many others who are significant to the process, depending on the nature of the proceeding, the type of case, and the level of the court. These include police officers, witnesses, victims, grand juries and trial juries, and various officers of the court. Third, there are those with quasi-judicial functions, such as coroners and medical examiners. Each of these participants has a specific role in the criminal court process, without which given phases in the judicial sytem would not be fully possible.

It is generally believed that more than 90 percent of criminal convictions result from negotiated pleas of guilty. Plea bargaining takes place between the prosecutor and the defense counsel or the accused, and involves discussions looking toward an agreement under which the defendant enters a plea of guilty in exchange for some prosecutorial or judicial concession. Plea bargaining has both advantages and disadvantages, and its abolition has been called for. Its use continues, however, for without it the courts would become even more backlogged than they are now.

The Sixth Amendment holds that in all criminal prosecutions the accused shall enjoy the right to have assistance of counsel for his defense.

Bare Justice

A Hammond, Indiana, judge was charged with professional misconduct after he mooned several people in his office. According to the complaint filed with the Indiana Commission on Judicial Qualification, Judge Peter Katic invited a woman into his office on Feb. 14, along with another employee and a city police officer. He then "turned his back to the female employee and without invitation or forewarning pulled down his pants, entirely revealing his bare buttocks."

The judge says it was just a practical joke to show off some colorful, extremely skimpy underwear.

The complaint says Katic violated three canons of the Code of Judicial Conduct: Canon 1, which calls for a high standard of official conduct; Canon 2, which calls for judges to promote public confidence and integrity; and Canon 3a3, which says that a judge "should be dignified and courteous to persons with whom he deals in his official capacity."

The commission is awaiting a response from Katic, who has claimed that political rivals reported the incident in an effort to discredit him personally and professionally during his reelection bid.

SOURCE: *Insight,* August 19, 1991

Despite this guarantee, for almost a century and a half after the framing of the Constitution only persons charged with capital federal crimes enjoyed the right to counsel. This situation began to change in the 1930s with the Scottsboro case. *Gideon* v. *Wainwright* in 1963 extended the right to virtually all felony defendants. *Argersinger* v. *Hamlin* in 1972 extended the right to misdemeanor cases if imprisonment was a possible penalty. Additional Supreme Court decisions have affected this right to counsel as it relates to stages of the criminal justice process other than trial.

Legal services for the indigent come from several sources—legal aid, assigned counsel, and public defenders. All of these means suffer from a variety of problems with the consequence that the poor do not always receive adequate representation.

KEY TERMS

Argersinger v. *Hamlin* **(374)**
Betts v. *Brady* **(369)**
Brady v. *United States* **(357)**
in forma pauperis **(371)**

Gideon v. *Wainwright* **(370)**
Johnson v. *Zerbst* **(369)**
judges **(345)**
Missouri Plan **(348)**

nolle prosequi **(353)**
plea negotiation **(351)**
Powell v. *Alabama* **(369)**
prosecutor **(350)**

QUESTIONS FOR DISCUSSION

1. In *McMann* v. *Richardson* and *Strickland* v. *Washington*, the U.S. Supreme Court addressed the issue of incompetent counsel. In *Faretta* v. *California*, the Court tackled the issue of a defendant's right *not* to have counsel. How might these two decisions affect one another?
2. What kinds of problems have the decisions in

Gideon and *Argersinger* created for the processing of cases in criminal courts?
3. Comparing the roles of police and prosecutors, who has more discretion and who has the greater potential for the abuse of that discretion? Why?
4. Should plea bargaining be abolished? Why or why not?

FOR FURTHER READING

Lewis, Anthony. *Gideon's Trumpet.* New York: Vintage, 1966.

Loftus, Elizabeth, and E. Ketcham. *For the Defense.* New York: St. Martin's Press, 1991.

Sanborn, Joseph B. "A Historical Sketch of Plea Bargaining," *Justice Quarterly* 3 (June 1986), pp. 111–137.

Schmidhauser, John R. *Judges and Justices: The Federal Appellate Judiciary.* Boston: Little, Brown, 1979.

NOTES

1. Advisory Committee on the Judge's Function, *The Function of the Trial Judge* (New York: American Bar Association, 1972).
2. Herbert Jacob, *Justice in America: Courts, Lawyers, and the Judicial Process* (Boston: Little, Brown, 1972), p. 100.
3. For a more detailed discussion of the selection of federal judges, see Jacob, *Justice in America,* pp. 98–107; Richard J. Richardson and Kenneth N. Vines, *The Politics of Federal Courts* (Boston: Little, Brown, 1970).
4. Sheldon Goldman, "Reagan's Judicial Legacy: Completing the Puzzle and the Summing Up," *Judicature,* 27 (April–May 1989), pp. 318, 322, 324–325.

5. See Richard W. Watson and Ronald G. Downing, *The Politics of the Bench and the Bar* (New York: Wiley, 1969).
6. Larry Berkson, Scott Beller, and Michele Grimaldi, *Judicial Selection in the United States: A Compendium of Provisions* (Chicago: American Judicature Society, 1980); N. Gary Holton and Lawson L. Lamar, *The Criminal Courts: Structures, Personnel, Processes* (New York: McGraw-Hill, 1991).
7. *National Law Journal,* May 27, 1985, pp. 1, 26–28.
8. John R. Schmidhauser, *Judges and Justices: The Federal Appellate Judiciary* (Boston: Little, Brown, 1979), p. 75.

9. New York City Criminal Court Act, Laws of 1962, Chapter 697, Section 22 (1).

10. Wayne R. LaFave, *Arrest: The Decision to Take a Suspect into Custody* (Boston: Little, Brown, 1965), p. 515.

11. Advisory Committee on the Prosecution and Defense Functions, *The Prosecution Function and the Defense Function* (New York: American Bar Association, 1970), pp. 17–134.

12. President's Commission on Law Enforcement and Administration of Justice, *Task Force Report: The Courts* (Washington, D.C.: U.S. Government Printing Office, 1967), p. 5.

13. George F. Cole, "The Decision to Prosecute," *Law and Society Review* 4, no. 3 (1970): 331–343. See also Eric D. Poole and Robert H. Regoli, "The Decision to Prosecute in Felony Cases," *Journal of Contemporary Criminal Justice* 2 (March 1983): 18–21.

14. See Joan E. Jacoby, *The Prosecutor's Charging Decision: A Policy Perspective* (Washington, D.C.: U.S. Department of Justice, 1977).

15. Kenneth C. Davis, *Discretionary Justice* (Baton Rouge: Louisiana State University Press, 1969), p. 170.

16. *United States* v. *Cowen*, 524 F. 2d 785 (1975).

17. See Arthur Rosett and Donald R. Cressey, *Justice by Consent: Plea Bargains in the American Courthouse* (Philadelphia: J. B. Lippincott, 1976).

18. *Miami Herald*, August 22, 1982, p. 11A; *Time*, August 30, 1982, p. 22.

19. National Advisory Commission, *Courts*, p. 46.

20. *Brady* v. *United States*, 397 U.S. 742 (1970).

21. *Santobello* v. *New York*, 404 U.S. 257 (1971).

22. *Henderson* v. *Morgan*, 426 U.S. 637 (1976).

23. *North Carolina* v. *Alford*, 400 U.S. 25 (1970).

24. *Bordenkircher* v. *Hayes*, 434 U.S. 357 (1978).

25. *Los Angeles Times*, December 18, 1990, p. A33: *New York Times*, June 23, 1991, pp. 1, 22.

26. See Advisory Committee, *Prosecution Function and the Defense Function*, pp. 141–309; Paul W. Wice, *Criminal Lawyers: An Endangered Species* (Beverly Hills: Sage, 1978).

27. Wice, *Criminal Lawyers*, p. 143.

28. Anthony C. Friloux, "Motion Strategy—The Defense Attack," Speech before the National College of Criminal Defense Lawyers, Houston, Texas, 1975, cited by Wice, *Criminal Lawyers*, p. 148.

29. For example, see Jack Ladinsky, "Careers of Lawyers, Law Practice, and Legal Institutions," *American Sociological Review* 27 (February 1963, pp. 47–54).

30. Abraham S. Blumberg, *Criminal Justice: Issues and Ironies* (New York: New Viewpoints, 1979), pp. 242–246.

31. Blumberg, *Criminal Justice*, p. 245.

32. Blumberg, *Criminal Justice*, p. 243.

33. Murray A. Schwartz, quoted in John Kaplan, *Criminal Justice* (Mineola, N.Y.: Foundation Press, 1973), p. 261.

34. Malcolm M. Feeley, *The Process Is the Punishment: Handling Cases in a Lower Criminal Court* (New York: Russell Sage, 1979), p. 121.

35. See Delmar Karlen, *The Citizen in Court* (Hinsdale, Ill.: Dryden, 1964).

36. Frank Smyth, *Cause of Death* (New York: Van Nostrand Reinhold, 1980), pp. 32–34.

37. William J. Curran, A. Louis McGarry, and Charles S. Petty, *Modern Legal Medicine, Psychiatry, and Forensic Science* (Philadelphia: F. A. Davis, 1980), pp. 51–56.

38. Curran et al., *Modern Legal Medicine*, p. 55.

39. The full story of the Scottsboro boys can be found in Dan T. Carter, *Scottsboro: A Tragedy of the American South* (New York: Oxford University Press, 1969).

40. *Powell* v. *Alabama*, 287 U.S. 45 (1932).

41. See Howard N. Meyer, *The Amendment That Refused to Die* (Boston: Beacon, 1978).

42. *Johnson* v. *Zerbst*, 304 U.S. 458 (1938).

43. *Townsend* v. *Burke*, 334 U.S. 736 (1948).

44. *Betts* v. *Brady*, 316 U.S. 455 (1942).

45. See *Uveges* v. *Pennsylvania*, 335 U.S. 437 (1948); *Moore* v. *Michigan*, 355 U.S. 155 (1957); *Carnley* v. *Cochran*, 369 U.S. 506 (1962); *Hamilton* v. *Alabama*, 368 U.S. 52 (1961).

46. *Gideon* v. *Wainwright*, 372 U.S. 335 (1963).

47. Anthony Lewis, *Gideon's Trumpet* (New York: Vintage, 1966), pp. 5–6.

48. Lewis, *Gideon's Trumpet*, p. 4.

49. See Meyer, *Amendment That Refused to Die*.

50. *Douglas* v. *California*, 372 U.S. 353 (1963).

51. *Massiah* v. *United States*, 377 U.S. 201 (1964); *Escobedo* v. *Illinois*, 378 U.S. 478 (1964); *Miranda* v. *Arizona*, 384 U.S. 694 (1966); *United States* v. *Wade*, 388 U.S. 218 (1967).

52. *Coleman* v. *Alabama*, 399 U.S. 1 (1970).

53. *Argersinger* v. *Hamlin*, 407 U.S. 25 (1972).

54. *McMann* v. *Richardson*, 397 U.S. 759 (1970).

55. *Ross* v. *Moffitt*, 417 U.S. 600 (1974).

56. *Scott* v. *Illinois*, 440 U.S. 367 (1979).

57. *Pennsylvania* v. *Finley*, 107 S. Ct. 1990 (1987).

58. *Strickland* v. *Washington*, 466 U.S. 668 (1984).

59. Lawrence A. Benner and Beth Lynch Neary, *The Other Face of Justice* (Chicago: National Legal Aid and Defender Association, 1973), p. 13.

60. *Criminal Defense Systems*, Bureau of Justice Statistics Special Report, August 1984.

61. Harry P. Strumpf, "Law and Poverty: A Political Perspective," *Wisconsin Law Review* (1968): 698–699.

62. *Time*, October 3, 1983, p. 83; *U.S. News & World Report*, October 31, 1983, pp. 66–67.

63. See Charles L. Markmann, *The Noblest Cry: A History of the American Civil Liberties Union* (New York: St. Martin's Press, 1965).

64. See Michael Moore, "The Right to Counsel for Indigents in Oregon," *Oregon Law Review* 44(1965): 255–300; Lee Silverstein, *Defense of the Poor* (Chicago: American Bar Association, 1965).

65. *Report of the Attorney General's Committee on Poverty and the Administration of Federal Criminal Justice* (Washington, D.C.: U.S. Government Printing Office, 1963), p. 40.

66. *Criminal Defense Systems*, supra note 65.

67. *The National Law Journal*, October 5, 1981, p. 1.

68. *State* v. *Myles*, 389 So. 2d 12 (1981).

69. *U.S. News & World Report*, March 13, 1978, p. 63.

70. *New York Times*, July 19, 1981, p. 20.

12

The Business of the Court: From First Appearance Through Trial

Courtroom: a place where Jesus Christ and Judas Iscariot would be equals, with the betting odds in favor of Judas.
—H. L. MENCKEN

The task of the trial court is to reconstruct the past from what are at best second-hand reports of the facts.
—JEROME FRANK, U.S. COURT OF APPEALS JUDGE

Laws are a dead letter without courts to expound and define their true meaning and operation.
—ALEXANDER HAMILTON

common theme in the discussions of many social critics and legal reformers is the chaotic state of criminal justice in the United States. They often refer to the organization and administration of justice as a "nonsystem," because the police, the courts, and the correctional process have no common goals, cooperative attitudes, or central direction. They claim that America's courts are at the brink of disaster: backlogs are colossal, work loads are always increasing, and the entire design is misshapen and understaffed. Furthermore, it is often argued that the administration of criminal justice has underscored the notions of due process and defendants' rights to such an exaggerated degree that criminals are all too quickly and easily dispersed to again prey on law-abiding citizens.

Of course, to suggest that the legal process is not working is clearly absurd. After all, each year millions of offenders are arrested and convicted, and a significant number are incarcerated. Others are dismissed or exonerated, presumably because of lack of evidence or because of their innocence, but dismissing and releasing the arrested under such circumstances is unquestionably a legitimate function of the court.

When the serious observer takes the time to examine what actually happens in the criminal courts, what is remarkable is not how badly they seem to function, but how well. As inefficient and unjust as it may appear, courthouse justice generally does an effective job of separating the innocent from the guilty. Although most of those who are guilty of crimes are never arrested, most of those coming to the courts who should be convicted *are* convicted, and most of these who should be punished *are* punished. Further, there is no evidence to support the contentions that repealing the exclusionary rule, eliminating plea bargaining, legislating mandatory prison terms for serious offenders, or reducing judges' freedom to determine length of sentences would produce any significant reduction in the rate of crime in the streets. On this point, journalist Charles E. Silberman has argued persuasively:

- It is *not* true that the courts have been hamstrung by the exclusionary rule or other decisions of the Warren Court; except for drug cases, few convictions are lost because "tainted" evidence is excluded from court.

- It is *not* true that the courts are more lenient than they used to be; the available data indicate that a larger proportion of felons are incarcerated now than in the 1920s.

- It is *not* true that disparate sentencing practices undermine the deterrent power of the criminal law. Within any single court system, the overwhelming majority of sentences — on the order of 85 percent — can be predicted if one knows the nature of the offense and of the offender's prior record.

- It is *not* true that plea bargaining distorts the judicial process. Contrary to popular impression, plea bargaining is not a recent innovation, nor is it the product of heavy case loads; it has been the dominant means of settling criminal cases for the last century.

- Most important of all, it is *not* true that the guilty escape punishment; when charges are dropped, it usually is because the victim refuses to press charges, or because the prosecutor lacks the evidence needed to sustain a conviction.[1]

This should not suggest that the administration of justice in the United States, and particularly the processing of defendants through the criminal courts, have no problems. The courts indeed *are* overcrowded and understaffed, plea bargaining *does* result in lighter sentences for many offenders and in guilty records for some innocents, and the rigid adherence to constitutional safeguards *does* allow some dangerous criminals to return to freedom. But it is important to keep in mind that many of these phenomena are the direct result of the U.S. Constitution's regard for individual rights and civil liberties. On the one hand, perfect protection of the accused does mean imperfect protection of society. On the other, a system of justice that has no miscarriages is not a workable one; a system that automatically checkmates every defendant seeking equity and justice is hardly fair-minded and dispassionate. Speaking before the House of Commons in 1947, Sir Winston Churchill remarked: "Democracy is the worst form of government except all those other forms that have been tried from time to time." So it might also be argued about a system of justice based on the adversary process and grounded in "due process of law."

Perhaps the greatest difficulties with criminal judicial processing come from its very complexity. Defendants are arrested and booked. There is an initial appearance, with or without preliminary hearing, at which point pretrial release is considered and "probable cause" is determined. Through an information or indictment the charges are formalized. Should the evidence warrant it, defendants then face arraignment. There, before the presiding magistrate, the charges are read and a plea is entered. And perhaps throughout these pretrial phases plea negotiation has been discussed. Taking the process further, there are pretrial motions, jury selection, and the drama of the criminal trial. At its conclusion there is a verdict, posttrial motions, sentencing, and perhaps an appeal. In all, it is a complex of proceedings with due-process safeguards at every juncture. It is hardly a speedy process. But its very lack of speed is relevant because determining the innocence or guilt of the accused is important to ponder — and to ponder at length. As distinguished attorney and legal writer Charles Rembar has poignantly remarked: "Speedy justice is not the ultimate aim; just justice is."[2]

The courts are the final strongholds of feudalism in the United States.
—HARVEY A. SIEGAL, 1983

It is as important to keep out of court as it is to keep out of debt.
—E. W. HOWE, 1911

BAIL AND PRETRIAL RELEASE

Excessive bail shall not be required. . . .

— FROM THE EIGHTH AMENDMENT

For a defendant, bail is the bottom line of a criminal case.
— STEVEN PHILLIPS, FORMER ASSISTANT DISTRICT ATTORNEY, BRONX COUNTY, NEW YORK

Bail: Security posted guarantee that a defendant in a criminal proceeding will appear and be present in court as required.

Bail is a form of security guaranteeing that a defendant in a criminal proceeding will appear and be present in court at all times as required. Thus, bail is a guarantee: in return for being released from jail, the accused guarantees his or her future appearance by posting funds or some other form of security with the court. When the defendant appears in court as required, the security is returned; if he fails to appear, the security is forfeited.

The bail system as we know it today has its roots deep in English history, well before the Norman Conquest in 1066. It emerged at a time when there were few prisons, and the only places secure enough to detain an accused awaiting trial were the dungeons and strong rooms in the many castles around the countryside. Magistrates often called upon respected local noblemen to serve as jailers, trusting them to produce the accused on the day of trial. As the land became more populated and the castles fewer in number, magistrates were no longer able to locate jailers known to them. Volunteers were sought, but to ensure that they would be proper custodians, they were required to sign a bond. Known as private sureties, these jailers would forfeit to the king a specified sum of money or property if they failed to live up to their obligations of keeping defendants secure and producing them in court on the day required.[3] As the system was transferred to the New World, it shifted from a procedure of confinement to one of freedom under financial control. In current practice, it is the accused that posts the bond, or has some third party—a **surety**—post it in his or her behalf.

Surety: A third party who posts a bond for an accused.

The Right to Bail

The Eighth Amendment to the United States Constitution clearly specifies that "excessive bail shall not be required," but the extent to which the accused have any "right" to bail is a matter still under contention. The statutory right of federal defendants to have bail set in all but capital cases was established by the Judiciary Act of 1789. Furthermore, the Supreme Court held in *Hudson* v. *Parker* that a presumption in favor of granting bail exists in the Bill of Rights. Justice Horace Gray wrote in 1895:

> The statutes of the United States have been framed upon the theory that a person accused of crime shall not, until he has been fully adjudged guilty in the court of last resort, be absolutely compelled to undergo imprisonment or punishment, but may be admitted to bail, not only after arrest and before trial, but after conviction and pending a writ of error.[4]

But Justice Gray's words carried no firm guarantees for all criminal defendants seeking release on bail. Only one year before, the Court had ruled in *McKane* v. *Durston* that the Eighth Amendment's bail provision placed limits only on the federal courts, and did not apply to the states.[5] Since that time, the Supreme Court has decided relatively few cases involving bail, mainly because it is an issue that is moot by the time the case reaches the appellate stage of the criminal process. At the state level, the vast majority of state constitutions grant an absolute right to bail in noncapital cases.[6] However, constitutional or statutory rights to have bail set have never in practice meant an absolute right to freedom before trial. In years past, judges invariably insisted on cash bail or a surety bond from a bail bondsman. If the defendant could not afford it, he or she remained in jail awaiting trial—for days, months, and sometimes even years.

In its principal bail ruling, *Stack v. Boyle* in 1951,[7] the Supreme Court left unsettled the constitutional status of a defendant's *right* to bail. But the Court did address the issue of "excessive bail," ruling that the fixing of bail must be based on standards relevant to the purpose of ensuring the presence of the defendant at trial. One year later, in *Carlson v. Landon*,[8] however, the Court held that inasmuch as the Eighth Amendment fails to state that all offenses are bailable, Congress may define the classes of *federal* offenses in which bail shall be allowed.

Discretionary Bail Setting

In theory, the purpose of bail is to ensure that the accused appear in court for trial. With this in mind, the magistrate is required to fix bail at a level calculated to guarantee the defendant's presence at future court hearings. This view has grown out of the historical forms of bail, as well as from the adversarial premise that a person is innocent until proven guilty and therefore ought not suffer confinement while awaiting trial. At the same time, however, there is the belief that more important than bail is the matter of societal protection. Should potentially dangerous defendants who might commit additional crimes be free to roam the community prior to trial? Judges often answer this problem by setting bail so high for some defendants that in practice, bail becomes a mechanism for preventive detention.

In most jurisdictions, those arrested for minor misdemeanors can be released almost immediately by posting bail at the police station where they are booked. In these cases, there are fixed bail schedules and the size of the bond is relatively small. For serious misdemeanors and felonies, the amount of bail required is left to the discretion of the judge. Research has demonstrated, however, that decisions determining the size of bail are neither random nor arbitrary.

By the statutory and case law, most jurisdictions have certain criteria that need to be considered in determining bail. In practice, however, there are typically only three factors that are considered in bail setting. By far, the most important is the *seriousness of the crime;* the assumption is that the more severe the offense the greater the likelihood of forfeiture of bail. The second factor is the defendant's *prior criminal record;* the rationale for this is that recidivists (repeat offenders) have a higher probability of forfeiting bond. In conjunction with these two factors is the *strength of the state's case.* Here the premise is that the greater the chance of conviction, the stronger the accused's interest in fleeing.[9]

Thus, if the state has a strong case against an accused with a prior felony record, and the current offense was a dangerous crime, then unquestionably, the bail set would be high.

The Bail Bond Business

Once bail has been set, there are three ways it can be exercised. First, the accused may post the full amount of the bond in cash with the court. Second, many jurisdictions allow a defendant (or family and friends) to put up property as collateral and, thus, post a property bond. In either case, the money or property is returned when all court appearances are satisfied, or they are forfeited if the defendant fails to appear.

Neither cash bail nor property bonds are commonly used, however. Most defendants seldom have the necessary cash funds to meet the full bond, and the majority of courts require that the equity in the property

Stack v. Boyle: The Supreme Court ruling that bail set at a figure higher than an amount reasonably calculated to assure the presence of the accused at trial and at the time of final submission to sentence is "excessive" under the Eighth Amendment.

Statutory Bailing Considerations

1. The principal's character, habits, reputation, and mental condition;
2. His employment and financial resources;
3. His family ties and the length of his residence, if any, in the community;
4. His criminal record, if any;
5. His previous record, if any, in responding to court appearances when required or with respect to flight to avoid criminal prosecution;
6. The weight of the evidence against him in the pending criminal action and any other factor indicating probability or improbability of conviction;
7. The sentence which may be imposed upon conviction.

SOURCE: *New York State Criminal Procedure Law,* Section 510.30.

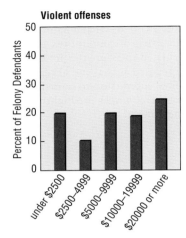

Violent offenses

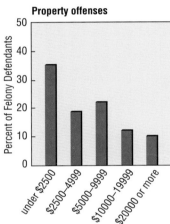

Property offenses

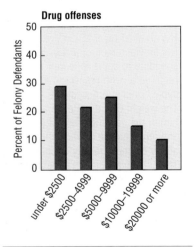

Drug offenses

Bail Amounts for Felony Defendants

SOURCE: Bureau of Justice Statistics *National Update*, July 1991

held as collateral be at least double the amount of bond. Thus the most common method—the third alternative—is to use the services of bail bondsmen.

Clustered around urban courthouses across the nation are the storefront offices of the bail bondsmen. Often aglow with bright neon lights, their signs boldly proclaim: BAIL BONDS—24-HOUR SERVICE. Or sometimes, during the late night hours on local television, the viewer is confronted with the most unlikely of commercials: "Are you in trouble? Call ————, twenty-four-hour bail bond services!" In either case, the message is quite clear, that freedom is available—for a price.

Bail bondsmen, also referred to as commercial bondsagents, are essentially small business entrepreneurs who serve as middlemen with the courts. For a nonrefundable fee, they post a surety bond with the court, and if the defendant fails to appear at trial, the bondsagent is responsible for the full amount of the bond.

Defendants without the funds or property necessary to meet the full amount of bail seek out a bondsman, for the actual out-of-pocket costs usually amount to only 10 percent of the established bail. Furthermore, in actual practice the bondsman rarely posts a cash surety with the court. Let us assume, for example, that defendant Smith's bail is set at $10,000. His bondsman charges him a nonrefundable fee of $1,000, since 10 percent is the prevailing rate. The bondsman then purchases a surety bond from an insurance company, which typically costs 30 percent of the fee collected. Smith's cost for pretrial freedom is $1,000, of which $700 becomes the property of the bondsman—whether or not Smith ever appears in court again. If Smith should "jump bail," the insurance company, in theory, pays the forfeiture.

Smith's case, however, is an idealized typical one, and would proceed smoothly as described only if he was considered a good bail risk. If he were not, it is unlikely that the insurance company would provide a bond, or that the bondsman would even accept him as a client. In general, the bondsagent views four types of defendants as poor risks:

1. *first felony offenders,* because they are likely to panic and leave the community
2. *recidivists* whose new offenses are more serious than previous ones
3. *violent offenders,* because they can represent a personal threat to the bondsagent
4. *those whose bail has been set at a high level,* because forfeiture would result in large financial losses, as well as damage to the agent's reputation with the insurance companies

In assessing a client's reliability, the bondsman inquires into his or her criminal record, family situation, employment history, roots in the community, and anything else that would suggest that the defendant has some type of "investment" in the social system. If the client is considered a bad risk, he will be rejected; if he is a marginal risk, the bondsman may require him to post collateral—such as his house, car, or some other resource—in addition to the fee.

Criticisms of the Bail System

For decades, the bail system has been the subject of continuing criticism. In 1931, the National Commission on Law Observance and Enforcement launched a strong attack on bail procedures, noting that the amount of bail set was arbitrarily determined; that bondsmen were unreliable and sometimes corrupt, and that they played too important a role in the administration of justice; and that bonds were easily forfeited, but in only a small portion of the cases were the forfeitures ever collected.[10] The findings and overall sentiments of the commission were not unlike those of the Cleveland Foundation's analysis of crime and justice in 1922, The Missouri Crime Survey in 1926, the Survey of the Administration of Criminal Justice in Oregon in 1932, and other governmental commissions in the years hence.[11]

Criticisms of the bail system continue, although they vary from one jurisdiction to the next. First, bail tends to discriminate against the poor. When cash bail is set at a high level, it results in the pretrial confinement of many "low risk" defendants who do not have the funds either to post bond or retain a bondsman. Second, despite the Eighth Amendment safeguard against excessive bail, bail setting is totally discretionary on the part of the judge; many courts set bail at unreasonably high levels. Third, since bail is generally determined at the initial appearance, the court has little time to investigate the background of the accused and, hence, cannot adequately determine the nature of risk. Fourth, bail is often manipulated into an instrument for preventive detention. As a measure of community protection against offenders who are viewed by the courts as risks to the social welfare and safety, bail is set so high that it can rarely be met.[12]

As to the criticisms leveled against the bail bond industry decades ago, most still apply today. First, as with the bail system in general, commercial bail bond operations also discriminate against the indigent. As a penalty for being poor, the defendant is forced to buy his freedom for a fee, which is nonrefundable—whether or not he appears for trial, and whether or not he is completely exculpated.

Second, the very structure of bail bonding serves to defeat the basic asumption that underlies the cash bail system. In current practice, most defendants pay a 10 percent fee to the bondsagent, who then secures a bond from an insurance company. The financial risks of forfeiture are transferred to the agent and the insurance company, eliminating the defendant's financial penalty. The fact that the bondsman's fee is not returnable under any circumstances further reduces any incentives to appear.

Third, the bondsman is in effect an agent of the court and plays a crucial role in determining who will receive pretrial release. Even though it is the judge who sets bail, in the reality of many defendants the court makes a determination of "bail eligibility." The bail bondsman's right to deny his services, to set his fee, to raise premiums, and to require collateral gives him the power to veto the court's bail decision.

Fourth, the bail bond industry tends to promote corruption. Clients are secured through advertising and referrals, and the referral network produces a situation ready-made for unscrupulous practices. Some bondsmen enter into collusive agreements with lower-level judges to set unnecessarily high bail or to increase the bondsagent's bail fee. For his part, the magistrate may receive a kickback or an illegal "gift" from the bondsman. At the same time, the magistrate returns the favor, granting to a favored few bonding firms permission to solicit clients at local lockups. Furthermore, through the magistrate–bondsman arrangement, the charging of illegal fees is both encouraged and protected.

Fifth, although many surety bonds are secured through insurance and are fortified by collateral, most bondsmen suffer no direct financial losses if the defendant fails to appear at trial. Nevertheless, it is in a bondsman's best interests that his clients do appear; otherwise, relation-

Bail tends to discriminate against the poor.

A bondsman is a fool who, having property of his own, undertakes to become responsible for that entrusted by another to a third.

—AMBROSE BIERCE, *THE DEVIL'S DICTIONARY, 1911*

Deficiencies in the bail bond industry

Bench warrant: A written order, issued by the court, authorizing a defendant's arrest.

ships with the court and insurance carriers will weaken. The methods used by some bondsmen to insure appearance have been both unethical and illegal, including threats, violence, and abduction.

Sixth, the requirement to pay high fees for bonding has led many defendants to commit new crimes while out on bail.

Seventh, bail bondsmen have extraordinary legal powers over bailed defendants who "jumped bond" and flee. When a bond is issued, the client is required to sign a contract waiving the right to extradition and allowing the *bondsman* — or his agent or deputy — to retrieve him from wherever he has fled. This results in law enforcement powers that exceed those of police officers. Bondsmen need no warrants, nor are they prevented from taking bond jumpers across state lines. Worse, since most bondsmen are ill equipped to seek out bond jumpers personally, they use professional "skip tracers," who are essentially armed bounty hunters (see Exhibit 12.1).

Eighth, and finally, failure to appear in court means that the entire amount of the bond is forfeited. Yet in many jurisdictions, forfeited bonds regularly go uncollected. The reason for this is the judge's discretionary power to vacate outstanding bonds, and it is often in the court's best interests to "go easy" on the bondsmen. Without the bail bond industry, the courts would be faced with a large jail population, and costs for pretrial detention would be prohibitive. The courts tend to do what they can to keep the bail system healthy. In Philadelphia, for example, in some cases where the accused cannot afford to post bail, the city pays the bill, just to keep from filling up another jail bunk.[13]

In addition to forfeiture of bail, failure to appear in court as required entails other consequences. A *capias,* or *bench warrant,* is issued by the court authorizing the defendant's arrest. Furthermore, bail jumping represents a new offense and carries criminal penalties. In Maryland, for example, which is typical of most jurisdictions, "failure to surrender after forfeiture of bail" can result in a new felony charge with penalties of five years' imprisonment with or without a $5,000 fine:

> Any person who has been admitted to bail . . . in any criminal case in this State who forfeits the bail . . . and willfully fails to surrender himself within thirty days following the date of forfeiture shall be sentenced as provided herein. If the bail . . . was given in connection with a charge of felony or pending an appeal *certiorari, habeas corpus,* or post conviction proceeding after conviction of any offense, the person shall be fined not more than $5,000 or imprisoned in the penitentiary for not more than five years or both. If the bail . . . was given in connection with a charge of committing a misdemeanor, the person shall be fined not more than $1,000 or imprisoned for not more than one year, or both.[14]

Pretrial Detention

For defendants, the principal difficulty with the bail system is its relationship to financial well-being. Although most bail premiums paid to bondsmen are 5 to 10 percent of the face amount of the bond, rates as high as 20 percent have been reported. When bail is set at $1,000 or more, premiums of $100 to $500 become more than many defendants can afford. In a 1988 study of felony defendants in the nation's seventy-five largest counties, for example, 22 percent failed to make bail set under $2,500, 28 percent failed at $2,500 to $4,999, and 45 percent failed at $5,000 to $9,999.[15] The result of bail, then, has been the arbitrary punishment of hundreds of thousands of persons, many of whom were innocent of any crimes. Here are some examples:

● EXHIBIT 12.1 ●

From Bounty Hunters to "Skip Tracers"

It is noon. The sun blazes down on a deserted, dusty street. Two men step casually from the shadows to face each other. Both are unshaven and a bit disheveled; their lips are drawn back in a sneer, and they walk arrogantly forward looking neither to the right nor the left. Suddenly, hands flash down, and there is a thunderous roar of gunfire. When the smoke clears, one man stands alone, gun in hand. The other lies dead in the street. It is a scene often depicted in films of the American West. Sometimes the victor is Wyatt Earp, Wild Bill Hickok, or John Wesley Hardin. But often it is the bounty hunter, charged with bringing back his quarry "dead or alive."

There is a modern counterpart to the story. It is a rainy Sunday afternoon in Manhattan. The streets are deserted, except for a late-model Ford LTD parked at the end of the block. Inside sits a heavy-set man in his early fifties. He wears jeans, black boots, a wool shirt, and a hunting jacket whose pockets are filled with cigars. He is armored with a bulletproof vest and has a shotgun at his side. The man is Stan Rivkin, and he is watching the door of a tenement house halfway down the block. Somewhere inside the building is another man — wanted for drug-dealing and the attempted murder of a police officer. He is also wanted for jumping bail in California, and there is a price on his head. That is why Stan Rivkin sits, waits, and watches. Rivkin is a *"skip tracer,"*[a] a modern-day bounty hunter working for a bail bondsagent. In capturing bail-jumpers Rivkin has more authority than any law enforcement officer in the

Modern-day bounty hunters like Stan Rivkin, shown here with his shotgun and Duke, his Doberman, have legal powers of arrest that surpass those of any law officer in the United States.

United States. He can enter a house without a warrant; he can arrest a bail-jumper in any state and return him to court without the formalities of extradition. The Constitution has been suspended for him.

Stan Rivkin's extraordinary powers of arrest come from a century-old Supreme Court decision. In *Taylor* v. *Taintor,*[b] argued in 1873, the court described the common law power of the bondsagent:

When bail is given, the principal is regarded as delivered to the custody of his sureties. Their dominion is a continuance of the original imprisonment. Whenever they choose to do so, they may seize him and deliver him up to their dis-

charge; and if it cannot be done at once, they may imprison him until it can be done. They may exercise their rights in person or by agent. They may pursue him into another state; may arrest him on the Sabbath; and if necessary, may break and enter his house for that purpose. The seizure is not made by virtue of due process. None is needed.

In place now for more than a century in the United States, the powers of pursuit and arrest held by bail bondsagents, and their designated skip tracers, has neither been revoked nor altered by the Supreme Court.

SOURCES:
[a] *Parade,* August 5, 1984, p. 11.
[b] *Taylor* v. *Taintor,* 83 U.S. 66 (1873).

- A man was jailed on a serious charge. . . . He could not afford bail and spent 101 days in jail until a hearing. Then the complainant admitted the charge was false.
- A man could not raise $300 bail. He spent fifty-four days in jail waiting trial for a traffic offense, for which he could have been sentenced to no more than five days.
- A man spent two months in jail before being acquitted. In that period, he lost his job, and his car, and his family split up.[16]

Then there was the Charlottesville, Virginia, case in which a man was jailed for fourteen days because he could not raise $250 for bail. The only difficulty was that he had been arrested for abusive and insulting language, a misdemeanor offense that carried no jail sentence.[17]

In addition to depriving a defendant of freedom, *pretrial detention* prevents the accused from locating evidence and witnesses, and from having more complete access to counsel. It disrupts employment and family relations. It coerces defendants into plea negotiation in order to settle the matter more rapidly. Most importantly, however, pretrial detainees are confined in city and county jails — the worst penal institutions in the country. They are overcrowded, unsanitary, and poorly equipped. Few have sufficient space for inmates to confer with counsel or visit with families. Defendants awaiting trial are indiscriminately mixed with convicted felons, with a result, as the late Supreme Court Justice William O. Douglas once remarked, "equivalent to giving a young man an M.A. in crime."[18] Finally, jails are populated by many violent offenders, and scores of detainees each year are beaten, raped, and murdered.

Preventive Detention

Stack v. *Boyle* in 1951 made it explicitly clear that the purpose of bail is "to assure the defendant's attendance in court when his presence is required." At the same time, the Supreme Court also noted that bail is not "a means for punishing defendants nor protecting public safety." In these words, the High Court has made its position on *preventive detention* unmistakable, at least by implication; at the same time, however, it has not ruled whether the practice is constitutionally impermissible. As a result, many magistrates use bail as a mechanism for preventive detention. For those who are considered dangerous offenders or where there is a likelihood of repeated crimes during the pretrial period, prohibitively high money bail is set for the ostensible purpose of insuring an accused's appearance in court. In fact, despite the implication in *Stack* v. *Boyle,* as of 1985 the District of Columbia, the entire federal system, and thirty-two states had laws permitting judges to consider an accused's danger to the community in setting pretrial release conditions.[19] In the federal system, this was promulgated by the new Bail Reform Act of 1984 (see Exhibit 12.2).

The legal consequences of pretrial detention, whether preventive or otherwise, can be disastrous. Research has demonstrated repeatedly that detainees are more likely to be indicted, convicted, and sentenced more harshly than released defendants. Furthermore, in its work on pretrial release the American Bar Association noted that studies in Philadelphia, New York, and the District of Columbia all indicated that the conviction rate for jailed defendants materially exceeded that of bailed defendants.[20] In terms of the sentence imposed on those convicted, the bailed defendant was far more likely to receive probation; his jailed counterpart, having been unable to confer more fully with his counsel, seek out witnesses and evidence in his own behalf, and most importantly, prevented from demonstrating his reliability in the community, went to prison more frequently.

The legal consequences of pretrial detention

There are some factors, such as strong evidence of guilt or a serious prior criminal record, that necessarily lead to high bail and hence detention. These factors, of course, and not just pretrial detention, can also cause a court to find a defendant guilty and sentence him to prison rather than give him probation. However, one study that took these factors into consideration as well still found a strong relationship between detention and unfavorable disposition.[21] Moreover, in an experimental mock jury study of criminal trial judgments, it was found that "jurors" were more likely to convict "defendants" who had been kept in jail prior to trial than those who had been released.[22]

● EXHIBIT 12.2 ●

U.S. v. *Salerno* and the Bail Reform Act of 1984

During early 1983, President Ronald Reagan sent a forty-four-point crime package to Congress as part of his commitment to engineer changes in the American system of justice. The result was the Comprehensive Crime Control Act of 1984 (CCCA), legislation which Reagan hoped would shift the balance away from suspects toward victims and the state.[a] Although CCCA contained provisions that brought about numerous changes in federal criminal law, what had an immediate impact was its opening chapter, the Bail Reform Act of 1984.

Under the new bail law, federal judges could assess an accused's danger to other persons and the community in making temporary release decisions. Moreover, pursuant to the findings of a detention hearing, bail could be denied outright to defendants if there was an indication that they would not show up for trial. As such, certain aspects of the act represented an endorsement of preventive detention.

A key feature of the act was its establishment of a "no-bail

presumption" in certain types of cases. In other words, the court could deny bail on the presumption that certain kinds of defendants, such as drug traffickers, were unlikely to appear for trial. Furthermore, when this presumption was triggered, the burden of rebuttal fell on the accused. This provision was especially welcomed by federal prosecutors in South Florida who had been plagued with repeated instances of bail jumping in cocaine trafficking cases. Known in the Miami courts as the "Colombian dismissal," it was not uncommon for a trafficker to put up $1 million in cash bail, then go to Miami International Airport and take a one-way flight to Bogota.[b]

Almost immediately after the Bail Reform Act was put into force, its pretrial detention aspect was challenged in the courts. It was argued that the "no-bail presumption" denied substantive due process because it authorized punishment before trial. The challenges worked their way up the judicial ladder, culminating with *U.S.* v. *Salerno* before the United States Su-

preme Court in 1987.[c] The High Court ruled:

The 1984 Bail Reform Act provision, which authorizes pretrial detention of arrestees who are charged with certain serious felonies and who are found, after adversary hearing, to pose threat to the safety of individuals or to the community that no combination of release conditions can reasonably dispel, does not, on its face, violate either the Fifth Amendment's Due Process Clause or the Eighth Amendment's prohibition of excessive bail.

In making this decision, the Court explained that the statute was *not* punitive. Writing for the majority, Chief Justice Rehnquist commented: "The legislative history clearly shows that Congress formulated the Bail Reform Act to prevent danger to the community—a legitimate regulatory goal—rather than to punish dangerous individuals."

SOURCES:
[a] *Comprehensive Crime Control Act of 1984.* Public Law 98–473, October 12, 1984.
[b] James A. Inciardi, *The War on Drugs: Heroin, Cocaine, Crime, and Public Policy* (Palo Alto, Calif.: Mayfield, 1986).
[c] *U.S.* v. *Salerno,* 55 USLW 4663 (1987).

There is an additional problem with preventive detention. Some courts have used it as a method of punishing defendants for the crimes for which they were charged. This is a serious abuse of judicial discretion, for punishment without conviction is patently illegal. Nevertheless, there are differing opinions on the matter. On the other side, a South Carolina justice of the peace remarked not too many years ago, "It is for violation and a good reminder not to do it again." [23] More to the point, from New York City comes this remark:

THE COURT: Now, these boys, as I see it, have gone beyond children's acts. This is something that shows they don't know when to stop. Maybe a couple of days in jail may solve the problem. I'm going to set $5,000 bail on each. Now, I'm leaving word that if a bond is presented, the matter is to be sent back to me, and

I'll tell you right now, if they put up $5,000 bail, I'll make it $10,000, and if they put up ten, I'll make it $25,000. I want these boys to spend one or two nights in jail. Maybe that is the answer.[24]

Release on Recognizance

At the beginning of the 1960s, increasing dissatisfaction with the bail bond system led to experimentation with alternative forms of pretrial release. Early in the decade, New York industrialist Louis Schweitzer's concern for youths who were detained while awaiting trial led to his establishment of the Vera Foundation (named after Schweitzer's mother). The foundation, later called the Vera Institute of Justice,[25] conducted an experiment with pretrial release based on the notion that "more persons can successfully be released . . . if verified information concerning their character and roots in the community is available to the court at the time of bail determination."[26] Known as the Manhattan Bail Project and begun in 1961, the effort was made possible through the cooperation of the New York criminal courts and law students from New York University. The students interviewed defendants, looking for information that would support a recommendation for pretrial release: (1) present or recent residence at the same address for six months or more; (2) current or recent employment for six months or more; (3) relatives in New York City with whom the defendant was in contact; (4) no previous conviction of a crime; and (5) residence in New York City for ten years or more. For those who met the criteria, the students would recommend

The Manhattan Bail Project

A holding cell in New York City's infamous Manhattan House of Detention, known as the "Tombs"

Release on recognizance (ROR): The release of an accused on his or her own obligation rather than on a monetary bond.

10 percent cash bond plans

Criminal Offenses and I-Bond Releases in Cook County, Illinois

Release permitted in cases of:
aggravated assault
battery
burglary
drug possession and delivery
forgery
gambling
prostitution
theft
weapons use

Release prohibited in case of:
armed violence
arson
child pornography
home invasion
kidnapping
murder
residential burglary
robbery
sexual assault

Drug defendants now typically have no fear of the criminal justice system. They view the system as ineffective and perceive the possibility of arrest as an acceptable risk since they are reasonably certain of a swift release, without even the necessity of posting bail, and because they know that the system lacks the ability to compel their appearance in court.
— PROSECUTING ATTORNEY GALEN CLEMENTS OF PHILADELPHIA'S DANGEROUS DRUG OFFENDER UNIT, 1991

release on recognizance (ROR) to the judge. ROR simply meant that the defendant would be released on his or her own obligation without any requirement of money bail. The obligation was one of record entered into before the court with the condition to appear as required. If the judge agreed with the project's recommendation, the accused was released, subject to some follow-up contacts to ensure that the defendant knew when he or she was due to make a court appearance. Not all defendants were eligible for ROR. Those arrrested for such charges as murder, robbery, rape, and other serious crimes were excluded, as were defendants with long criminal histories.

The Vera Institute's pioneer effort in release on recognizance was an immediate success in that four times as many defendants were released. Follow-up studies demonstrated that few released defendants defaulted on their obligation, and the ROR programs modeled after the Manhattan Bail Project were also deemed successful. In the years hence, ROR programs have expanded dramatically, and other forms of pretrial release have emerged as well. Under the *10 percent cash bond plans,* for example, the court sets bail as it normally would. However, the accused is permitted to deposit 10 percent of the bond directly with the court, eliminating the need for a bondsagent. When the accused appears for trial, 90 percent of the deposit is returned, with the remainder held to support the operating costs of the program.[27] For example, should the bail be set at $2,000, the defendant deposits a $200 cash bond with the court; when he or she appears for trial, $180 is returned. In this way, the financial incentive to appear shifts from the bondsagent to the accused.

The size of the deposit and the proportion that is returned varies from one jurisdiction to another. Some require only a 5 percent deposit; others, such as Atlantic City, New Jersey, return the entire deposit upon appearance. Whatever the arrangement, the purposes were to make bail possible for those who were not eligible for ROR and at the same time to eliminate the bondsman from the administration of bail.

Both the 10 percent cash bond and the ROR programs have been successful, and a larger portion of defendants are released who might otherwise have awaited trial in detention facilities. Nevertheless, there have been difficulties. A case in point is Cook County (Chicago), Illinois' *no-cash* "I-bond" program. The I-bond procedure was established during the mid-1980s when a U.S. District Court judge found local jail officials to be in contempt of a 1982 federal court order requiring that a bed be available for each inmate. When jail officials couldn't reduce the crowding, the judge ordered that defendants be released on bonds requiring no cash. During the late 1980s and early 1990s, with tens of thousands of drug arrests in the county each year, use of the I-bond program became widespread and indiscriminate. The result was that one in every four defendants freed from the Cook County Jail on the no-cash bond system was rearrested on new charges at least once within the following six months.[28] A similar problem became apparent in Philadelphia, again a result of city's problems with drugs and drug-related crime. Not only were high risk cases receiving no-cash bonds, but significant numbers were failing to appear when required. During 1990 and 1991, for example, one-third of the suspects in criminal court cases were failing to appear, and bench warrants were not being served. At the beginning of 1991, specifically, there were almost 40,000 outstanding bench warrants, with only twenty-eight investigators to enforce them.[29] In effect, the combination of increased drug enforcement, and crowded jails and courts, along with the widespread use of no-cash bonds served to practically decriminalize such offenses as burglary, prostitution, and drug sales.

THE GRAND JURY

It must be remembered that a proceeding before a grand jury is an inquest and not a trial. If defendants are treated as having any right to be heard, the whole affair is likely to cease to be an ex parte *proceeding resulting in a charge which can be fully met at the trial, but to become a litigation in which each side has the right to offer evidence, and an indictment can only be found if the evidence on the whole case preponderates against the defendants. Such it is believed was never the function of the Grand Inquest.*
—JUDGE AUGUSTUS HAND, 1922

Following the initial court proceedings, prosecution is instituted by an information, indictment, or presentment. The **information** is a document filed by the prosecutor that states the formal charges, the statutes that have been violated, and the evidence to support the charges. The filing of the information generally occurs at the preliminary hearing and the judge determines whether there is "probable cause" for further processing. The **indictment** is a formal charging document returned by a grand jury, based on evidence presented to it by the prosecutor. Slightly different from the indictment is the **presentment,** which is a written notice of accusation issued by a grand jury. The presentment comes not from evidence and testimony provided by the prosecution, but rather from the initiative of the grand jury, based on its own knowledge and observation. In actual practice, however, the terms *indictment* and *presentment* have come to be substantially interchangeable.

The **grand jury** system apparently originated in England in 1166, when King Henry II required knights and other freemen drawn from rural neighborhoods to file with the court accusations of murder, robbery, larceny, and harboring of known criminals. In time, as the common law developed, the English grand jury came to consist of not fewer than twelve or more than twenty-three men. Furthermore, not only did they tender criminal accusations, but they considered them from outsiders as well. The jurors heard witnesses and, if convinced that there were grounds for trial, returned an indictment.[30] Historically, therefore, the purposes of the grand jury were to serve as an investigatory body and to act as a buffer between the state and its citizens in order to prevent the Crown from unfairly invoking the criminal process against its enemies.

After the American Revolution, the grand jury was incorporated into the Fifth Amendment to the Constitution, which provides that "no person shall be held to answer for a capital or otherwise infamous crime, unless on a presentment or indictment of a grand jury." Despite this Fifth Amendment guarantee, however, the Supreme Court ruled in *Hurtado v. California* more than a century ago that the grand jury was merely a form of procedure that the states could abolish at will (see Exhibit 12.3).[31]

The American grand jury has retained the common law size from twelve to twenty-three persons, and the jury's purposes remained unchanged: to investigate and to protect citizens from unfair accusations. Currently, most of the states and the federal system use grand juries, and

Information: A formal charging document drafted by a prosecutor and tested before a magistrate.

Indictment: A formal charging document returned by a grand jury, based on evidence presented to it by the prosecutor.

Presentment: A written notice of accusation issued by a grand jury, based on its own knowledge and observation.

Grand jury: A body of persons who have been selected according to law and sworn to hear the evidence against accused persons and determine whether there is sufficient evidence to bring those persons to trial, to investigate criminal activity generally, and to investigate the conduct of public agencies and officials.

Hurtado v. California: The Supreme Court ruling that the due process clause of the Fourteenth Amendment does not require states to use grand jury indictments or presentments in capital cases.

• EXHIBIT 12.3 •

Hurtado v. California

In the early days of the Republic, due process was construed not as compliance with the fundamental rules for fair and orderly legal proceedings, but more simply as a limitation on governmental procedure. In terms of criminal procedure, it was presumed to be the procedures spelled out in the Bill of Rights. In the 1878 case of *Davidson* v. *New Orleans* (96 U.S. 97), however, the Supreme Court rejected the notion that due process required adherence to a fixed list of prescribed procedures. Rather, it explained that the meaning of due process would be determined "by the gradual process of judicial inclusion and exclusion." Furthermore, the Court had already decided in 1856 in *Murray's Lessee* v. *Hoboken Land and Improvement Co.* (18 How. 272) that "due" process did not necessarily mean "judicial" process. But if due process procedures were not nec-

essarily "judicial," shouldn't they not then be the common law procedures listed in the Bill of Rights? This was the argument in *Hurtado* v. *California*.*

In 1882, Joseph Hurtado was accused of killing a man named José Stuardo. In a California court, Hurtado was convicted and sentenced to hang. Some years earlier, in 1879, California's constitution had dropped the grand jury system, substituting the prosecutor's information in its place. Hurtado's attorneys objected, claiming that their client was forced to trial without having been indicted and thus denied "due process of law."

The Supreme Court upheld Hurtado's conviction and death sentence stating that the grand jury is merely a form of procedure the states can abolish at will. Furthermore, the Court ruled, the due process clause of the Fourteenth Amendment did not encompass any of the funda-

mental rights that were enumerated in the first ten amendments.

Thirteen years later in the 1897 case of *Chicago, Burlington & Quincy Railroad Co.* v. *City of Chicago* (167 U.S. 226), the Court held that it had been narrow-sighted in *Hurtado,* nullifying the justification for its holding in that decision. However, it never overturned *Hurtado,* and states that joined the Union later failed to adopt the grand jury system, doing so without Supreme Court interference.

As if to disregard its belief that grand juries serve a useless purpose in the administration of justice, the Supreme Court has followed a path of almost complete noninterference with grand jury actions.

———

* *Hurtado* v. *California,* 110 U.S. 516 (1884).

members are generally selected from voting registers. However, many of the territories west of the Mississippi that achieved statehood late in the nineteenth century did not adopt the grand jury system, choosing instead the prosecutor's information.

Operation of the Grand Jury

Investigatory and accusatory grand juries

There are essentially two types of grand juries: *investigatory* and *accusatory.* The investigatory grand jury (which must be specially impaneled as such) looks into general allegations of unlawful activity within its jurisdiction in an effort to discover if there is enough information to justify initiating criminal prosecutions against anyone. An investigatory grand jury may sit for as little as one month and as many as eighteen months, and most often examines suspicions and allegations regarding organized crime and official corruption. More common is the accusatory grand jury, a body impaneled for a set period of time — generally three months — that determines whether there is sufficient evidence against persons already charged with particular crimes to warrant criminal trials. It is the

Grand juries, gentlemen, are in reality, the only censors of this nation.
— HENRY FIELDING, 1749

indictment by the accusatory grand jury that parallels the prosecutor's filing of an information, and it is the accusatory grand jury that serves as a screening body to decide whether cases already in the early stages of the criminal justice process are worthy of being tried.

Since grand juries are either investigating or accusing bodies, and do not determine guilt or innocence, many of the elements of due process are absent. For example:

- Grand jury sessions are private and secret.
- Witnesses, having been subpoenaed by the prosecutor, are sworn and heard one by one, and excused as soon as they are finished testifying.
- Ordinarily the accused is not present, unless compelled to testify or invited to serve as a witness.
- In most jurisdictions, the defense counsel has no right to be present; if present, the defense counsel has no right to cross-examine witnesses.
- In some jurisdictions, written transcripts are not required.

When the members of a grand jury agree that an accused should be tried for a crime, they issue a **true bill.** That is, they endorse the validity of the charge or charges specified in the prosecutor's bill, thus returning an indictment. When they fail to find probable cause, they issue a *no bill* and the accused is released. Since the grand jury proceeding is not a trial, only a majority vote — not a unanimous one — is required for a true bill.

True bill: A grand jury's endorsement of the charge or charges specified in the prosecutor's bill.

Grand Jury Procedure and the Supreme Court

Prosecutors have wide discretion in the conduct of grand jury proceedings. They may introduce almost any evidence to support their cases, for the Supreme Court has generally refused to impose substantive limits on a grand jury's exercise of discretion. One exception to this course occurred in 1906, in *Hale* v. *Henkel.*[32] In this decision, the Court ruled that "a grand jury may not indict upon current rumors or unverified reports." At the same time, however, the justices did agree that indictments could be based on other information — however unreliable — as long as it was not called "rumor." The Court's position on this latter point became more explicit half a century later in the 1956 case of *Costello* v. *United States.*[33]

The principal in the case was Frank Costello, a member of organized crime. Costello was well known to the federal judiciary — he was an associate of such underworld figures as Charles "Lucky" Luciano and Vito Genovese, and had been the star witness in the Kefauver Committee hearings in 1951. Furthermore, as a syndicate racketeer who had consolidated gambling interests throughout the United States during the 1930s, he had the continuous attention of the Internal Revenue Service.

Early in the 1950s, Frank Costello was indicted by a federal investigatory grand jury for willfully attempting to evade payment of federal income taxes for the years 1947 through 1949. The indictments, however, were based on hearsay evidence. Three FBI agents who had no personal knowledge of Costello's finances appeared before the grand jury and "summarized his net worth on the basis of witnesses who were not called to testify." The agents produced "exhibits," which included newspaper stories about Costello's activities. They also made "computa-

In *Hale* v. *Henkel,* the Supreme Court warned that the grand jury may not base an indictment "upon current rumors and unverified reports."

In *Costello* v. *United States,* the Supreme Court concluded that indictments based entirely upon hearsay evidence are not necessarily fatally defective, despite the admonition in *Hale.*

tions" based on the "exhibits" to demonstrate that Costello and his wife had received a far greater income during those years than they had reported.

After a trial in which 144 witnesses testified and 368 exhibits were introduced, Costello was convicted. The Supreme Court upheld the indictments against Costello, and in so doing, established a precedent that grand juries may issue indictments based on hearsay evidence — evidence learned through others and not within the personal knowledge of the witness offering it as testimony. In delivering the Court's opinion in *Costello,* Justice Hugo L. Black wrote the following:

> Neither the Fifth Amendment nor any other constitutional provision prescribes the kind of evidence upon which grand juries must act. The grand jury is an English institution, brought to this country by the early colonists and incorporated in the Constitution by the Founders. There is every reason to believe that our constitutional grand jury was intended to operate substantially like its English progenitor. The basic purpose of the English grand jury was to provide a fair method for instituting criminal proceedings against persons believed to have committed crimes. Grand jurors were selected from the body of the people and their work was not hampered by rigid procedural or evidential rules. In fact, grand jurors could act on their own knowledge and were free to make their presentments or indictments on such information as they deemed satisfactory. . . .
>
> If indictments were to be held open to challenge on the ground that there was inadequate or incompetent evidence before the grand jury, the resulting delay would be great indeed. The result of such a rule would be that before trial on the merits a defendant could always insist on a kind of preliminary trial to determine the competency and adequacy of the evidence before the grand jury. This is not required by the Fifth Amendment.

United States v. Calandra: The Supreme Court ruling that refused to extend the exclusionary rule to grand jury questions based on illegally seized evidence.

In ***United States*** v. ***Calandra,***[34] almost two decades later, the Court addressed the role of the exclusionary rule in grand jury proceedings. The case involved the search of John Calandra's place of business in Cleveland, Ohio. Federal agents, armed with a valid search warrant, were seeking evidence of bookmaking records and gambling paraphernalia. They found none, but during the course of the search they did discover evidence of a loan-sharking operation. Subsequently, a special federal grand jury was convened and Calandra was subpoenaed to answer questions based on the evidence seized. Calandra refused on Fifth Amendment grounds, as well as on the basis that the search and seizure exceeded the scope of the warrant and was in violation of the Fourth Amendment. The district court ordered the evidence suppressed and the U.S. court of appeals affirmed, holding that the exclusionary rule may be invoked by a witness before a grand jury to bar questioning based on illegally obtained evidence.

On an appeal to the United States Supreme Court brought by the prosecution, the lower court ruling was reversed. The Court based its decision to allow the evidence to be used upon what it found to be the purpose of the exclusionary rule: "The rule is a judicially-created remedy designed to safeguard Fourth Amendment rights generally through its deterrent effects rather than a personal constitutional right of the party aggrieved."

> In deciding whether to extend the exclusionary rule to grand jury proceedings, we must weigh the potential injury to the historic role and functions of the grand jury against the potential benefits of the rule as applied in this context. It is evident that this extension of the exclusionary rule would seriously impede the grand jury. Because the grand jury does not finally adjudicate guilt or innocence, it has tradi-

tionally been allowed to pursue its investigative and accusatorial functions unimpeded by the evidentiary and procedural restrictions applicable to a criminal trial. Permitting witnesses to invoke the exclusionary rule before a grand jury would precipitate adjudication of issues hitherto reserved for the trial on the merits and would delay and disrupt grand jury proceedings. . . .

Grand Juries on Trial

Historically, the grand jury was created to stand between government and the citizen as a protection against unfounded charges and unwarranted prosecutions. Critics maintain, however, that the grand jury process has now become an instrument of the very prosecutorial misconduct it was intended to buffer the citizen against.

One complaint concerns the *ex parte* nature of grand jury proceedings. An ex parte is a "one-party" proceeding, meaning that the accused and his or her attorney are not permitted to be present during the grand jury hearing. Under this circumstance, the accused cannot cross-examine witnesses, or object to testimony or evidence.

Ex parte proceedings

Criticisms leveled against grand juries also suggest abuses of their power as they relate to the granting of "immunity." The Fifth Amendment protects individuals against self-incrimination. Traditionally, the government could compel a witness to testify and still protect his or her Fifth Amendment privilege by providing **transactional immunity.** This meant the witness was granted immunity against prosecution in return for testifying. Pursuant to a federal statute in 1970, however, the government adopted a new form of immunity, **use immunity.** This is a limited immunity that prohibits the government only from using a witness's compelled testimony in a subsequent criminal proceeding. If a grand jury witness has been granted use immunity, his compelled testimony cannot be used against him as direct evidence or as an "investigatory lead" in a subsequent criminal proceeding. At the same time, the prosecutor has an affirmative duty to prove that the evidence he or she proposes to use against the immunity-granted witness was derived from a source wholly independent of the compelled testimony. However, as supported by the Supreme Court's 1972 decision in *Kastigar* v. *United States,*[35] a witness can be indicted on the basis of evidence gathered because of, but "apart" from, his testimony. For example, if a grand jury witness has been given use immunity and his compelled testimony reveals that he was a participant in a bank robbery, the witness may nevertheless be prosecuted for that crime *if* the prosecution is able to produce at trial evidence wholly independent of the witness's grand jury testimony. In the final analysis, then, use immunity is not total immunity.

Transactional immunity: Immunity against prosecution given to a grand jury witness in return for testifying.

Use immunity: A limited immunity that prohibits the government only from using a grand jury witness's compelled testimony in a subsequent criminal proceeding.

In *Kastigar* v. *United States,* the Supreme Court ruled that in any subsequent prosecution of an immunized witness, the government must demonstrate that evidence presented is derived from sources independent of testimony given under a grant of immunity.

Grand juries also posses *contempt power,* which can be used to compel witnesses to provide testimony needed for criminal investigations. Witnesses who refuse to testify can be jailed for an indefinite period of time until they "purge" themselves of contempt by providing the requested information.* This would seemingly result in the abridgement of certain constitutional guarantees. However, the Supreme Court's decision in *Branzburg* v. *Hayes* in 1972 forced journalists to testify before a grand jury when subpoenaed.[36] Some journalists have gone to jail, rather than reveal their confidential sources because they believe that to do so would erode the freedom of the press, protected by the First Amendment.

Contempt power of grand juries

---

* Although the jailing for contempt can be indefinite, it is usually limited to the period that the grand jury is in session, and to eighteen months in the federal jurisdiction.

Furthermore, some critics have maintained that the grand jury's contempt power has been used to intentionally punish political dissidents. Activist Anne Strick has argued this point:

> The grand jury, in other words, strips the citizen of almost all constitutional protection; denies him almost all reasonable aid; and then confronts him with the investigatory resource and prestige of an entire state or federal government. Far from protecting the innocent, the grand jury more often offers the innocent no chance to protect themselves from their accusers no matter how false the evidence may be. The witness who resists goes to jail.[37]

THE PLEA

After the formal determination of charges through either the information or indictment the defendant is arraigned, at which time he or she is asked to enter a plea. The four basic pleas, as noted in Chapter 5, are not guilty, guilty, *nolo contendere,* and standing mute. There is also the special plea of not guilty by reason of insanity.

Plea of Not Guilty

The plea of not guilty, the most common entry at arraignment, places the full burden on the state to move ahead and prove beyond a reasonable doubt the case charged against the defendant. Under the principles of American jurisprudence, even the "guilty" are morally and legally entitled to make such a plea. In the adversary system of justice, it is the right of everyone charged with a crime to rely on the presumption of innocence. *Standing mute* at arraignment by failing or refusing to enter a plea is presumed to be an entry of not guilty.

Guilty Plea

The guilty plea, whether negotiated or not, has several consequences, as pointed out by the National Advisory Commission on Criminal Justice Standards and Goals:

> Such a plea functions not only as an admission of guilt but also as a surrender of the entire array of constitutional rights designed to protect a criminal defendant against unjustified conviction, including the right to remain silent, the right to confront witnesses against him, the right to a trial by jury, and the right to be proven guilty by proof beyond a reasonable doubt.[38]

As such, the entry of a plea of guilty serves to surrender numerous constitutional rights, including those guaranteed under the Fifth and Sixth Amendments.

Nolo Contendere

Nolo contendere: A plea of "no contest" or "I do not wish to contest," with the same implication as a guilty plea.

The *nolo contendere* plea, which means "no contest," or, more specifically, "I will not contest it," is essentially a guilty plea. It carries with it the surrendering of certain constitutional rights, and conviction is immediate. However, there is one important difference between a *nolo contendere* and a guilty plea. With *nolo contendere,* there is technically no admission of guilt, which protects the accused in civil court should the victim subsequently sue for damages. In a 1977 case, for example, the noted motorcycle daredevil Evel Knievel entered such a plea after being charged with assaulting his former press agent. Knievel's conviction,

"While it's true that I did swear to tell the truth and nothing but the truth, I think you should know I'm saddled with a highly selective memory."

then, could not automatically be used against him if the agent later sued for injuries and any lost income resulting from the assault.[39]

The *nolo contendere* plea is not an automatic option at arraignment. It is acceptable in the federal courts and in about half the states, and may be entered only at the discretion of the judge and the prosecutor. Generally, this plea is entered for the benefit of the accused, but in at least one instance, it carried an unintended consequence for perhaps the whole nation. On August 7, 1973, the *Wall Street Journal* reported that Spiro T. Agnew — at the time vice president of the United States under Richard Nixon — was the target of an investigation by U.S. Attorney George Beall in Maryland concerning allegations of kickbacks by contractors, architects, and engineers to officials of Baltimore County. The alleged violations of conspiracy, extortion, bribery, and tax statutes were supposed to have extended from the time Agnew was a Baltimore County executive in 1962 through his years in the vice presidency. After several sessions of plea negotiation between Agnew's attorneys and the Justice Department, it was agreed that Agnew would resign the vice presidency and plead *nolo contendere* to a single charge of income tax evasion. In return, the Justice Department would not proceed with indictment on the other charges. On October 10, 1973, Agnew announced his resignation and entered his plea. It was accepted by Federal District Judge Walter Hoffman, and Agnew received a $10,000 fine and three years' unsupervised probation.

Seven years later, Judge Hoffman recalled the case and remarked that accepting Agnew's plea had been a "wise decision." Had he not accepted the plea, Agnew would have been indicted, tried, and, upon conviction, probably would have appealed. This would have meant that the case would still have been pending when President Nixon resigned from the presidency on August 9, 1974. As Hoffman put it, "When Nixon resigned, Agnew would automatically have been President of the United States." [40]

Insanity Plea

The plea of not guilty by reason of insanity is generally not to the advantage of the accused, for it is an admission of guilt with the contention that the commission of the crime is not culpable in the eyes of the law because of the insanity of the defendant at the time he or she committed the act. More typically, a dual plea of not guilty *and* not guilty by reason of insanity is entered, which implies, "the burden is on the government to prove that I did the act upon which the charge is based, and, even if the government proves that at trial, I still claim I am not culpable because I was legally insane at the time." [41]

Not all jurisdictions have a separate insanity plea, nor do all have the dual plea of not guilty–not guilty by reason of insanity. In these instances, a plea of not guilty is entered and it is the burden of the defense to raise the issue of insanity. However, even in jurisdictions where the statutes allow the insanity plea, the accused and his or her counsel must present an *affirmative defense*. In law, this defense amounts to something more than just a mere denial of the prosecution's allegations. Thus, while the burden of proving the guilt of the accused is on the state, evidencing insanity at the time of the commission of the offense generally rests with the defendant.

Since the early 1970s, there has been considerable opposition to the insanity plea, and courts and legislatures have been pressured to limit, redefine, and even abolish the insanity defense. The opposition is based on the belief that such a plea and defense is an easy route by which defendants in grisly murders, bizarre sex crimes, and attempts on the lives of national figures can hope to avoid punishment. During the fall of 1981, for example, an Associated Press–NBC News poll demonstrated that 87 percent of the public felt that too many murderers were using insanity pleas to avoid a prison sentence, and almost 70 percent would have banned insanity defenses altogether in murder cases. [42] This sentiment was an outgrowth of the assassination attempt on President Ronald Reagan in 1980 by John W. Hinckley, Jr., an event that, as noted earlier in Chapter 2, led to the enactment of "guilty but mentally ill" statutes. Under these regulations, which other states are considering, defendants found guilty but mentally ill go to prison. If they require psychiatric treatment, they receive it in the penitentiary.

On the other hand, studies suggest that the general public drastically overestimates the incidence of successful insanity pleas, primarily because the insanity cases are among the most highly publicized. In reality, comparatively few defendants enter pleas of not guilty by reason of insanity. Furthermore, the insanity defense rarely wins. Of the millions of criminal cases disposed of each year in state and federal courts, less than one-tenth of one percent involve insanity pleas, only one in four of such pleas lead to acquittals, and the majority of these involve misdemeanor charges.[43]

Pleas of Statute of Limitations

Every state has laws known as "statutes of limitations," which bar prosecution for most crimes after a certain amount of time has passed; that is, the suspect must be accused within a reasonable period of time after the offense was committed. The reasons for these statutes are numerous. After the passage of time, for example, defendants may be unable to establish their whereabouts at the time of the crime, or evidence or witnesses supporting their innocence might be lost. Similarly, after long periods of time, those guilty of crimes may be unable to gather evidence to support their defense or to mitigate their conduct. Furthermore, during the long period of time since the offense the offender may have become a law-abiding citizen who presents no further threat to the community, and conviction and sentencing would serve little purpose.

Statutes of limitations can be quite complex. Generally, such statutes do not apply to murder prosecutions. Furthermore, statutes for other offenses may be *tolled* (suspended) by reason of numerous circumstances, such as the defendant's absence from the state. And finally, in most jurisdictions the plea of statute of limitations must be entered at arraignment, otherwise the accused will be deemed to have waived that particular defense.[44]

Double Jeopardy

To restrain the government from repeatedly prosecuting an accused for one particular offense, the prohibition against **double jeopardy** — two trials for one offense — was included in the Constitution. The Fifth Amendment provides in part: "Nor shall any person be subject for the same offense to be twice put in jeopardy of life or limb."

The Supreme Court has held that this guarantee protects the accused against both multiple prosecutions for the same offense and multiple punishments for the same crime. However, to whom and when the Fifth Amendment guarantee applies are matters that have taken the Supreme Court almost two centuries to clarify.

United States v. *Perez* in 1824 denied double jeopardy protection in cases where a jury failed to agree on a verdict.[45] In 1896, the Court ruled in *United States* v. *Ball* that if a conviction is set aside for some reason other than insufficient evidence, the defendant may be tried again for the same offense.[46] *Wade* v. *Hunter* in 1949,[47] following a similar line, declared that the double jeopardy clause did not apply in certain circumstances of mistrial.

In the 1922 case of *United States* v. *Lanza*,[48] the Court addressed the issue of double jeopardy and dual sovereignty. In *Lanza*, the defendant had been convicted of violating Washington state's prohibition law. He had then been indicted on the same grounds for violating the federal prohibition law. In a 6-to-3 vote, the Court ruled that the Fifth

Double jeopardy: The Fifth Amendment protects an accused from both multiple prosecutions for the same offense and multiple punishments for the same crime.

In *United States* v. *Lanza*, the Supreme Court ruled that where both federal and state jurisdictions make the same act a crime, the double jeopardy guarantee of the Fifth Amendment does not prohibit a federal prosecution and a state prosecution of the same defendant for the same crime.

Palko v. *Connecticut:* The Supreme Court ruling that the due process clause of the Fourteenth Amendment does not require the states to observe the double jeopardy guarantee of the Fifth Amendment.

Benton v. *Maryland:* The Supreme Court ruling that overruled *Palko* and extended the double jeopardy protection to state actions.

Downum v. *United States:* The Supreme Court ruling that double jeopardy begins at the point where the second trial jury is sworn in.

Amendment double jeopardy clause protected only against repeated prosecutions by a single sovereign government. The Court's opinion, which approached the state of Washington and the federal government as separate sovereignties deriving power from different sources, was that the second indictment had been a valid one. The *Lanza* rule was reaffirmed in the 1959 case of *Abbate* v. *United States,*[49] but in *Waller* v. *Florida* eleven years later,[50] the Court ruled that a city and a state were not separate sovereignties.

As noted earlier in some detail in Chapter five, the application of the double jeopardy clause to state criminal trials wes rejected by the Supreme Court in the 1937 case of **Palko v. Connecticut.**[51] Some three decades later, however, in **Benton v. Maryland** — the last announced decision of the Warren Court — the majority opinion declared that the double jeopardy clause applied to the states through the due process clause of the Fourteenth Amendment.[52] Finally, in **Downum v. United States,**[53] the Court declared that double jeopardy begins at the point when the second trial jury is sworn in.

Under state statutes, pleas of not guilty on double jeopardy grounds can be of two types: *autrefois* acquit and *autrefois* convict.[54] The accused can plead *autrefois acquit* (formerly acquitted) if he or she was acquitted of the identical charge involving the same set of facts on a previous occasion before a court of competent jurisdiction. Or the accused can plead *autrefois convict* (formerly convicted) if he or she was convicted of the identical charge involving the same set of facts on a previous occasion before a court of competent jurisdiction.

PRETRIAL MOTIONS

Motion: A formal application or request to the court for some action.

All pleas of not guilty (other than those dismissed on statute of limitations or double jeopardy grounds) result in the setting of a trial date. Prior to the actual commencement of the trial, however, and sometimes prior to arraignment, both the defense and the prosecution may employ a number of motions. A **motion** is a formal application or request to the court for some action, such as an order or rule. The purpose of motions is to gain some legal advantage, and most are initiated by the defense. The number and type of motions vary by the nature and complexity of the case, and it is the court's role to decide whether each should be granted or denied. Without question, the court's decision in these matters can have a considerable impact on the outcome of a proceeding.

Motion for Discovery

It is always in the best interests of the defense to know in advance what witnesses and kinds of evidence the prosecution plans to introduce at trial. The *motion for discovery* is a request to examine the physical evidence, evidentiary documents, and lists of witnesses in the possession of the prosecutor. Although some jurisdictions may resist such a motion, discovery is a matter of constitutional law. The Supreme Court's decision in the 1963 case of *Brady* v. *Maryland* held that a prosecutor's failure to disclose evidence favorable to the accused upon request violates due process.[55] However, in *Moore* v. *Illinois* some years later,[56] the Court also ruled that there was no constitutional requirement for the prosecution to fully disclose the entire case file to the defense.

Motion for Change of Venue

Venue, from the Latin meaning "neighborhood," refers to the county or district—not the jurisdiction—wherein a case is to be tried. A *motion for a change of venue* is a request that the trial be moved from the county, district, or circuit in which the crime was committed to some other place. The jurisdiction does not change; the original trial court simply moves if the motion is granted.

Either the defense or the prosecution can introduce such a motion. Typically, however, it is a move made by the defense in the case of sensational or highly publicized crimes when it is felt that the accused cannot obtain a fair trial in the particular locale of the court.[57]

Motion for Suppression

Mapp v. *Ohio, Escobedo* v. *Illinois,* and *Miranda* v. *Arizona* collectively served to make suppression one of the most common of pretrial motions in criminal cases.[58] The *motion for suppression* is a request to have evidence excluded from consideration. Typically, it is filed by the defense to prohibit evidence that was obtained as the result of an illegal search and seizure or wiretap, or to challenge the validity of a confession.

"Most extreme change of venue I've ever seen."

Motion for a Bill of Particulars

A *bill of particulars* is a written statement that specifies additional facts about the charges contained in the information or indictment. As a motion filed by the defense, it is a request for more details from the prosecution. The motion is not made for the purpose of discovering evidence or of learning exactly how much the prosecution knows, and it is not designed to suggest an insufficient indictment. Rather, the *motion for a bill of particulars* asks for details about what the prosecution claims in order to give the accused fair notice of what must be defended. For example, if a neighborhood bookie who operates illegal lotteries and off-track betting schemes is charged with possession of gambling paraphernalia, the defense might wish to know which of the confiscated materials (policy slips, betting cards, and so on) the prosecutor intends to use as the basis of his or her action.

A bill of particulars is a written statement that specifies additional facts about a charge.

Motion for Severance of Charges or Defendants

Many legal actions involve multiple charges against one defendant. The accused may have been arrested, for example, for a number of different crimes resulting from a single incident—an auto theft, for example, followed by destruction of property, resisting arrest, and assault upon a police officer. Or the accused may be charged with multiple counts of the same offense—perhaps several sales of dangerous drugs during a given period of time. In both instances, and for the sake of expediency, the prosecution may consolidate these multiple charges into a single case. The defense, however, may feel that different tactics are required for dealing with each charge. Thus, the *motion for severance of charges* requests that each specific charge be tried as a separate case.

Similarly, many proceedings involve more than one person charged with participation in the same crime—perhaps four codefendants in a bank robbery. There are times when the best interests of one or more of the accused are served by separate trials. Defendant Smith, for example, may wish a trial by jury; defendant Jones may wish to place the blame on his codefendants. Thus, the *motion for severance of defendants* requests that one or more of the accused be tried in separate proceedings.

It should be pointed out here that recent research has demonstrated that *joinders* (of charges and/or defendants) may have prejudicial effects. In several mock jury experiments, for example, "jurors" were presented with cases in which "defendants" were charged with individual or multiple charges. When defendants had joined trials, there was a greater tendency to convict. When charges were joined, jurors confused the evidence among the charges and made more negative inferences about the character of the defendant.[59]

Joinders may have prejudicial effects on the outcome of a trial.

Motion for Continuance

The *motion for continuance* requests that the trial be postponed to some future date. Such a motion is filed by the defense or the prosecution on the grounds that there has not been sufficient time to prepare the case. There may, for example, have been difficulty in gathering evidence or locating witnesses. This motion is used by some defense attorneys as a stalling tactic to enhance the accused's chances. As one of Brooklyn, New York's "Court Street lawyers" commented:

The witness stand in the Edgefield County courthouse, Edgefield, South Carolina.

If you can delay a case long enough, victims' memories begin to fail, witnesses begin to lose interest, and the court wants to move on to other things. Sometimes you end up working out a better plea, and on two separate occasions we actually managed to get the cases dismissed because of lack of witnesses.[60]

Motion for Dismissal

As a matter of common practice, at arraignment, defense attorneys make a *motion for dismissal* of charges on the grounds that the prosecution has failed to produce sufficient evidence to warrant further processing. Justified or not, this is an almost automatic motion filed by most defense attorneys. In practically all instances, however, such a motion is denied by the judge. There are other situations, though, where the motion for dismissal is fully warranted and is granted by the presiding magistrate. A previously granted motion for suppression, for example, may have weakened the state's case. Here it could be the defense *or* the prosecution who files the motion. Furthermore, in jurisdictions where prosecutors do not have full authority to issue a *nolle prosequi,* the dropping of charges must be sought through a judicial dismissal.

Other pretrial motions may include requests to inspect grand jury minutes, to determine sanity, or to discover statements made by prosecution witnesses. By far, however, the most common are the motions for suppression and dismissal.

It should be emphasized here that if a motion by the defense results in the dismissal of a case, the prosecution has the legal authority to reinstate the case. Charges can be filed, dismissed, and refiled, for there is no double jeopardy connected with the pretrial process. As noted in *Downum* v. *United States* and reaffirmed by the Supreme Court in *Serfass* v. *United States,*[61] in a jury trial, jeopardy attaches when the jury is impaneled and sworn; in a bench trial, jeopardy attaches when the court begins to hear evidence.

SPEEDY AND PUBLIC TRIAL

In all criminal prosecutions, the accused shall enjoy the right to a speedy and public trial. . . .

— FROM THE SIXTH AMENDMENT

It is no surprise that the right to a **speedy trial** appears in the Constitution of the United States. Without it, persons accused of crimes would have no protection against indefinite incarceration prior to coming to trial. Like all other provisions in the Bill of Rights, the guarantee of a speedy trial is a measure devised solely to ensure the rights of individual defendants, rather than to protect the state from delays that might be caused by the accused.

Putting the speedy trial clause of the **Sixth Amendment** into practice, however, has been difficult. *First,* since the early days of the Constitution, the criminal justice system has become more complex. Many procedural steps have been added to criminal proceedings in order to guarantee a fair hearing for the accused. *Second,* more persons are accused of violations of the law each year, making delays inevitable. Furthermore, in many metropolitan areas where crime rates are high, it is difficult for some defendants to receive any trial at all, not to mention a speedy one. *Third,* the criminal law has become more detailed and elabo-

Speedy trial: The Sixth Amendment guarantee that protects an accused from indefinite incarceration prior to coming to trial.

Sixth Amendment: The right to:

- A speedy and public trial, by an impartial jury, in the district where the offense was committed;

- notice of charges;

- confrontation with witnesses;

- compulsory process for obtaining witnesses; and

- assistance of counsel.

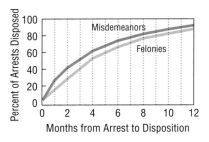

Time From Arrest to Disposition in State Court Cases

SOURCE: Bureau of Justice Statistics, October 1990

The Constitution offers no clues as to what its framers had in mind when they incorporated the concept of "speedy trial" into the Bill of Rights.

In *Barker* v. *Wingo*, the Supreme Court rejected the view "that a defendant who fails to demand a speedy trial forever waives his right."

rate. Some state statutes have become so highly specific that the evidence-gathering process in many cases has evolved into a time-consuming task. *Fourth,* the requirement that the judicial contest be conducted with promptness must be balanced against the right of an accused as well as of a prosecutor to have ample time to prepare their cases before going to trial. *Fifth,* some trials are inexcusably delayed by either the prosecution or the defense for the purpose of achieving their own objectives. A prosecutor, for example, may seek several continuances, hoping to put off a trial until an accused's codefendant is convinced to "strike a deal" and become a witness for the state. A defense attorney may employ the same delaying tactics in anticipation of witnesses' loss of interest in the case. *Sixth,* some delays result from little more than prosecutors' apathy or lack of concern for defendants' rights and humanity. A case that received national publicity involved a New York truck driver awaiting trial on charges of two counts of vehicular homicide. After spending some fourteen months in jail, he was finally freed when it was disclosed that two assistant district attorneys had known for the entire period that eyewitnesses corroborated the accused's claim that he was not the driver of the vehicle in question.[62] And *seventh,* there is no consensus among the states as to the meaning of "speedy trial." Statutory time limits vary by jurisdiction and by the nature of the offense charged. Here are three examples:

- In California, the period between arraignment and trial must not exceed fifty-six days.[63]

- In Alabama, the time limit between arrest and trial is set at twelve months for misdemeanors, three years for all felonies — except capital offenses, for which there is no limit.[64]

- In Maine, there is a flexible standard of "unnecessary delay" — whatever that might mean.[65]

The Supreme Court and Speedy Trial

The Constitution offers no clues as to what its framers had in mind when they incorporated the concept of "speedy trial" into the Bill of Rights. As a result, the Supreme Court has attached a standard of *reasonableness* to the right, which represents an attempt at a balancing of interests — weighing the effects of delays against their causes and justifications. The Court emphasized this posture, as early as 1905, when in *Beavers* v. *Haubert* it ruled that the right to a speedy trial was only a "relative" matter "consistent with delays and dependent on circumstances."[66]

In many of the Court's subsequent decisions, the particulars of individual cases seem to have been addressed rather than more encompassing policy issues. With the onset of the 1970s, however, the Supreme Court rulings in a series of cases did provide some guidelines for trial courts. The first of these was *Barker* v. *Wingo,*[67] decided in 1972. Until that time, both federal and state courts operated under the assumption that an accused's failure to demand a speedy trial meant that he was essentially unopposed to any accumulating delays. In *Barker,* the Court rejected this thesis, holding that passive compliance does not amount to a waiver of the Sixth Amendment right. Furthermore, although the Court was unwilling to announce any specific time frame for what would constitute delay, it did identify a variety of factors that trial courts should examine in determining whether the right to a speedy trial had been denied: the length of the delay, the reason for the delay, the defendant's assertion of his right, and prejudice to the defendant.

The following year, in *Strunk* v. *United States,*[68] the Supreme Court unanimously held that if a defendant is denied a speedy trial, "the only possible remedy" is for the charges to be dismissed. Later in the decade, in *United States* v. *Lovasco,*[69] the Court made clear that the Sixth Amendment right did not apply to delays before a person is accused of a crime, but rather, only to the interval between arrest and trial.

Strunk v. *United States*

United States v. *Lovasco*

Speedy Trial and the States

Speedy trial, a constitutional guarantee since the framing of the Bill of Rights, was not made applicable to the states until recently. The vehicle was **Klopfer v. North Carolina,**[70] decided in 1967.

The petitioner in this somewhat unusual case was Peter H. Klopfer, a professor of zoology at Duke University. Klopfer had been indicted by the state of North Carolina for criminal trespass as the result of a sit-in at a segregated motel and restaurant. At trial, however, the jury failed to agree on a verdict. This resulted in a mistrial, thus necessitating a new trial. But after a year had passed and the second trial had not been ordered, Professor Klopfer demanded that his case either be tried immediately or dismissed. Rather than complying with the petitioner's demands, the presiding judge instead granted the prosecutor's request for a *nolle prosequi.* At the time, this allowed the prosecutor to place the indictment in an inactive status without bringing it to trial — and thus retaining it for use at *any* time in the future. On appeal to the North Carolina Supreme Court, Klopfer argued that the trial judge's action denied his Sixth Amendment right, which he regarded as applicable to the states. The Carolina appeals court ruled that a defendant's right to a speedy trial did not encompass "the right to compel the state to prosecute him." Thus, still in limbo with his "suspended" trespass indictment, Klopfer petitioned the United States Supreme Court.

The Court ruled in favor of Professor Klopfer, and more. First, it unanimously struck down the recalcitrant North Carolina law that allowed indefinite postponement of a criminal prosecution without dismissal of an indictment. And second, Chief Justice Earl Warren explained that the North Carolina procedure

> clearly denies the petitioner the right to a speedy trial which we hold is guaranteed to him by the Sixth Amendment. . . . We hold here that the right to a speedy trial is as fundamental as any of the rights secured by the Sixth Amendment.

In so stating, the Court extended the speedy trial clause to the states.

Klopfer v. North Carolina: The Supreme Court ruling that the Sixth Amendment right to a speedy trial applies in state as well as federal proceedings.

A trial is a formal inquiry designed to prove and put upon record the blameless characters of judges, advocates, and jurors.
— AMBROSE BIERCE, *THE DEVIL'S DICTIONARY, 1911*

The Speedy Trial Act of 1974

The ruling in *Barker* v. *Wingo* prompted Congress — against the advice of both the Justice Department and the federal judges — to pass the **Speedy Trial Act** of 1974 in an effort to demand a reduction in delays in *federal* trials. Under the sponsorship of Senator Sam J. Ervin of North Carolina, the act established a 100-day deadline between arrest and trial.

The Speedy Trial Act was phased in gradually, not becoming fully effective until June 30, 1980. Currently, under its mandate, failure to bring a case to trial within the 100 day deadline — except in a few rigidly defined situations — results in dismissal of charges.

Speedy Trial Act: A Congressional measure that established a 100-day deadline between arrest and trial in federal cases.

The Right to a Public Trial

The Sixth Amendment right to a public
trial derives from English common law.

The Sixth Amendment provides not only for a speedy trial, but for a
public trial as well — a guarantee with its roots in our heritage of English
common law.

The traditional Anglo-American distrust for secret trials evolved
from the notorious use of the practice by the Spanish Inquisition, the
English Star Chamber court,* and the French monarchy's use of the
lettre de cachet.† In the hands of despotic groups, these institutions
became instruments of political and religious suppression through their
ruthless disregard of the accused's right to a fair trial.

Although all jurisdictions have adopted the Sixth Amendment right
to a public trial through state constitutions, by statute, or by judicial
decisions, there have been exceptions in the recent past. *In re Oliver*,[71]
decided in 1948, was one of the very few cases addressed by the Supreme
Court on the right to a public trial. The issue in *Oliver* stemmed from the
actions of a Michigan judge serving in the role of a one-person grand
jury. The judge's actions were described in the High Court's opinion:

In re Oliver

> In the case before us, the petitioner was called as a witness to testify in secret
> before a one-man grand jury conducting a grand jury investigation. In the midst of
> petitioner's testimony the proceedings abruptly changed. The investigation be-
> came a "trial," the grand jury became a judge, and the witness became an ac-
> cused charged with contempt of court — all in secret. Following a charge, convic-
> tion, and sentence, the petitioner was led away to prison — still without any break
> in the secrecy. Even in jail, according to undenied allegations, his lawyer was de-
> nied an opportunity to see and confer with him. And that was not the end of the
> secrecy. His lawyer filed in the state supreme court this *habeas corpus* proceed-
> ing. Even there, the mantle of secrecy enveloped the transaction and the state su-
> preme court ordered him sent back to jail without ever having seen a record of
> his testimony, and without knowing all that took place in the secrecy of the
> judge's chambers. In view of this nation's historic distrust of secret proceedings,
> their inherent dangers to freedom, and the universal requirement of our federal
> and state governments that criminal trials be public, the Fourteenth Amendment's
> guarantee that no one shall be deprived of his liberty without due process of law
> means that at least an accused cannot be thus sentenced to prison.

The Court further held that the failure to give the accused a reasonable opportunity to defend himself against the contempt charge was a
denial of due process of law. Yet curiously, despite the justice's pro-
nouncement in behalf of the petitioner, *Oliver* did not expressly incorporate the Sixth Amendment right to a public trial within the meaning of
the Fourteenth Amendment. This did not occur until thirty years later,
in a footnote to *Duncan* v. *Louisiana*,[72] discussed in the next section.

---

* In England during the Middle Ages, the Star Chamber was a meeting place of the King's counselors in
the palace of Westminster — so called from the stars painted on its ceiling. The Court of the Star
Chamber developed from the proceedings traditionally carried out by the king and his council, and
typically dealt with equity matters. In the fifteenth century under the Tudors, the jurisdiction of the
court was extended to criminal matters. Faster and less rigid than the common law courts, Star Chamber
proceedings tended to be harsh at times, and they were ultimately abolished by Parliament in 1641. (It
was from this court that the 20th Century-Fox film *Star Chamber,* in 1983, drew its title.)

† A part of seventeenth-century French law, the *lettre de cachet* was a private, sealed document issued as a
communication from the king which could order the imprisonment or exile of an individual without
recourse to the courts.

THE JURY

As a criminal prosecution approaches the trial date, a pretrial hearing is held, at which point the pretrial motions are heard and dealt with by the judge. At the same time, the court also asks whether the accused wishes a trial by judge or a trial by jury.

The trial by judge (or judges), more commonly referred to as a *bench trial,* is one in which the decision of innocence or guilt is made by the presiding judge. In some jurisdictions the decision regarding trial by judge may be dictated by state requirements. Under Tennessee statutes, for example, the accused is not prevented from waiving his right to a trial by jury;[73] in Idaho, however, this waiver is permitted only in nonfelony cases.[74]

Bench trials

When defendants are in a position to exercise a choice, there are several circumstances under which the bench trial would probably be more desirable. For example, the crime may be so reprehensible or so widely publicized that finding a neutral jury could be difficult if not impossible. Or the nature of the defense may be too complex or technical for persons untrained in law to fully comprehend. Also, the presiding judge may have a previous record of favorable decisions in like cases. In addition, there is the possible effect of the defendant's appearance and past record on the jury:

> The general appearance of the defendant may be such that a jury may become more prejudiced against him. The defendant may have a serious past criminal record subjecting him to possible impeachment should he take the witness stand in his own defense, and the probability of the jury convicting the defendant on his past record rather than on the evidence contended in the present charge is great. Or the defendant may be a part of an organized criminal syndicate, or minority group of which local feeling is against, and the jury may convict the accused by association rather than on the facts of the case. A judge is considered less inclined to be affected by any of these situations than a jury.[75]

The reasons for selecting a trial by jury are perhaps even more compelling. The jury serves as a safeguard against overzealous prosecutors and biased judges, and it affords the accused the benefit of commonsense judgment as opposed to the perhaps less sympathetic reactions of a single magistrate.

The Right to Trial by Jury

The trial by jury is a distinctive feature of the Anglo-American system of justice, dating back more than seven centuries. When the Magna Carta was signed in the year 1215, it contained a special provision that no freeholder would be deprived of life or property except by judgment of his or her peers. This common law principle was incorporated into the Constitution of the United States. Article III contains this simple and straightforward statement: "The trial of all crimes, except in cases of impeachment, shall be by jury." Article III is reaffirmed by the Sixth Amendment, which holds that "in all criminal prosecutions, the accused shall enjoy the right to a speedy and public trial by an impartial jury."

In federal cases, where Article III applies directly, the Supreme Court has been unrelenting in its view that a jury in criminal cases must contain twelve persons and reach a unanimous verdict.

Duncan v. Louisiana: The Supreme Court's ruling that the Fourteenth Amendment's guarantee of due process requires states to provide trial by jury to persons accused of serious crimes.

Curiously, however, for almost two centuries after the framing of the Constitution, the right to a trial by jury "in all criminal prosecutions" was not fully binding in state trials. Despite Article III and the Sixth Amendment, some state statutes denied the right to many defendants. What ultimately brought the right to a jury trial to the states was *Duncan v. Louisiana,*[76] decided in 1968.

The setting was Plaquemines Parish, Louisiana, an oil-rich community some fifty miles northwest of New Orleans. At the time, Plaquemines Parish had long been bossed by the skillful political leader Leander H. Perez, a virulent segregationist whose philosophies and opinions seemingly influenced local folkways. Gary Duncan, a nineteen-year-old black, had been tried in the local court on a charge of simple battery—a misdemeanor punishable by a maximum of two years' imprisonment and a $300 fine. His crime had involved no more than slapping the elbow of a white youth. He was convicted, fined $150, and sentenced to sixty days in jail. Duncan had requested a trial by jury, but this was denied on the authority of the Louisiana constitution, which granted jury trials only in cases where capital punishment or imprisonment at hard labor could be imposed. Duncan appealed to the U.S. Supreme Court, contending that his right to a jury trial was guaranteed by the Sixth and Fourteenth Amendments.

In a 7-to-2 decision, the Court ruled in favor of Duncan, thus incorporating the Sixth Amendment right to a jury into the due process clause of the Fourteenth Amendment. In the words of Justice Byron White:

> Because we believe that trial by jury in criminal cases is fundamental to the American scheme of justice, we hold that the Fourteenth Amendment guarantees a right of jury trial in all criminal cases which—were they to be tried in federal court—would come within the Sixth Amendment's guarantee. Since we consider the appeal before us to be such a case, we hold that the Constitution was violated when appellant's demand for jury trial was refused.

In spite of this holding, the matter was not fully resolved—not for Gary Duncan and not for thousands of defendants who would be requesting jury trials. The Supreme Court's ruling in *Duncan* had reversed the Louisiana trial court's conviction of Gary Duncan. This mandated either a dismissal of the simple battery charge or a new trial. But the Louisiana court refused to comply with either alternative, thus leaving Duncan under a continuing threat of further prosecution. His situation remained unchanged for three years, until the federal courts could effectively command Plaquemines Parish to dispose of the case.[77]

The other unresolved issue related to a segment of Justice White's opinion in *Duncan.* He had pointed out that so-called petty offenses were traditionally tried without a jury. That would continue to be so, but beyond that, he offered no distinction between serious and petty offenses in state cases. Two years later the Court brought this matter to rest in *Baldwin v. New York,*[78] when it defined a petty offense as one carrying a maximum sentence of six months or less.

Baldwin v. New York

Jury Selection

Petit juries

Williams v. Florida

Historically, trial juries—sometimes referred to as *petit juries* to differentiate them from grand juries—have typically consisted of twelve jurors. In all federal prosecutions twelve-member juries are required, but not in all state prosecutions (see Exhibit 12.4). In *Williams v. Florida,*[79] decided in 1970, the Court ruled that it was proper for states to use juries

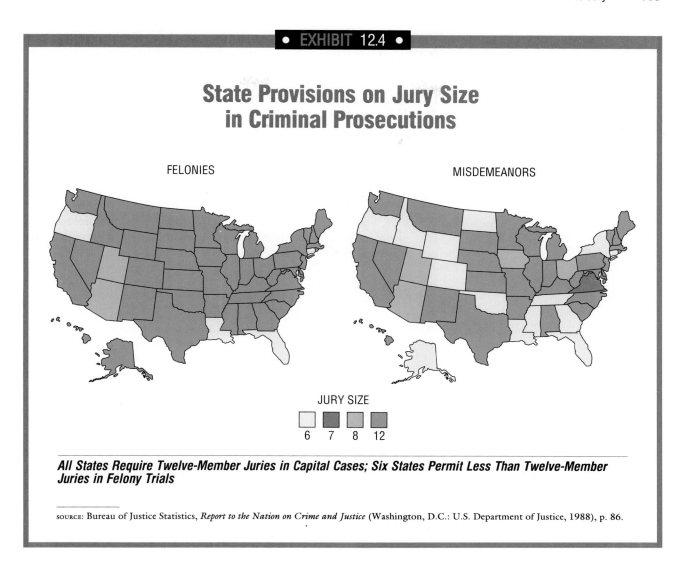

• EXHIBIT 12.4 •

**State Provisions on Jury Size
in Criminal Prosecutions**

FELONIES   MISDEMEANORS

JURY SIZE

6   7   8   12

*All States Require Twelve-Member Juries in Capital Cases; Six States Permit Less Than Twelve-Member
Juries in Felony Trials*

SOURCE: Bureau of Justice Statistics, *Report to the Nation on Crime and Justice* (Washington, D.C.: U.S. Department of Justice, 1988), p. 86.

composed of as few as six persons, at least in noncapital cases, and some
eight years later it reaffirmed this decision when it rejected the use of a
five-person jury in the state of Georgia.[80]

Jury selection involves a series of procedural steps, beginning with
the preparation of a master list of eligible jurors. Eligibility requirements
generally include citizenship and literacy. In addition, there are restrictions against minors, persons with serious felony convictions, and occupational groups such as physicians, attorneys, police officers, legislators,
the clergy, and several others, depending on the rules of the jurisdiction.
Others, such as the aged, disabled, mothers with young children, and
persons whose employers will not allow it, may be exempted from jury
service on the basis of hardship. Not too many exemptions can be allowed, in preparing the master list, however, because an "impartial" jury
in constitutional terms means a representative cross-section of a community's citizens. This is why the Supreme Court in 1975 struck down a
Louisiana law that barred women from juries unless they specifically
requested, in writing, to participate.[81]

The steps in jury selection

In current practice, the basis of the master list in many communities is the local voter registration roll. This source, at least in theory, is considered to be representative of the population, and it is readily available. However, studies of voting behavior have demonstrated that registration lists are highly biased as sources of jury pools. From 30 percent to 50 percent of those eligible in various jurisdictions do not register to vote. Furthermore, one study undertaken during the late 1970s found the registration rates for persons with incomes of less than $3,000 to be only 61.2 percent, compared to 85 percent for those earning over $15,000.[82] Similarly, members of racial minorities, young people, and the poorly educated more frequently ignore the electoral process, or have been excluded from it by legal or extralegal means. To mitigate this difficulty, some communities have initiated the use of multiple-source lists, supplementing voter registration lists with names drawn from rosters of licensed drivers and telephone directories.

A fox should not be on the jury at a goose's trial.
—Thomas Fuller, 1732

The *Venire*

Venire: A writ that summons jurors.

From the master list of eligible jurors, names are randomly selected for the *venire.* The *venire,* or *venire facias,* is the writ that summons jurors. More commonly, however, the *venire* refers to the list of potential jurors who are eligible for a given period of service. These summoned jurors become members of a jury pool, and they are interviewed to confirm their eligibility and availability. Those who remain in the pool are paid for their time; the current nationwide average rate is $15 per day.

The procedure through which members of the jury pool become actual trial jurors begins with the selection of a jury *panel.* In a felony prosecution that requires twelve jurors, as many as thirty are selected for the panel. Their names are drawn at random by the clerk of the court, and from there they move on to the *voir dire* examination.

The *Voir Dire*

Voir dire: An oath sworn by a juror regarding his or her qualifications.

A *voir dire,* meaning "to speak the truth," is an oath sworn by a prospective juror regarding his or her qualifications as a juror. The *voir dire* examination involves questioning by the prosecutor, defense attorney, and sometimes the judge in order to determine a candidate's fitness to serve as a juror. The inquiry focuses on the person's background, familiarity with the case, associations with persons involved in the case, attitudes about certain facts that might arise during the trial, and any other matters that may reflect upon his or her willingness and ability to judge the case fairly and impartially.

A potential juror who is deemed unacceptable to either the prosecutor or the defense is eliminated through either the challenge for cause or the peremptory challenge.

Challenge for cause

The *challenge for cause* means that there is a sound legal reason to remove a potential juror, and whoever makes such a challenge—either the defense attorney or the prosecutor—must explain to the judge the nature of the concern. Typically, challenges for cause allege that the prospective juror would be incapable of judging the accused fairly. Such challenges are controlled by statute, and the decision to remove a juror is vested with the court. Also, there is technically no limit on the number of challenges for cause that may be made.

Peremptory challenge

A *peremptory challenge* is an objection to a prospective juror for which no reason must be assigned. It can be made for any reason or no reason at all and is totally within the discretion of the attorney making it. Peremptory challenges generally reflect the biases and strategies of the defense and the prosecution. Clarence Darrow, perhaps the greatest defense attorney of the twentieth century, once advised his colleagues to avoid affluent jurors, "because, next to the Board of Trade, the wealthy consider the penitentiary to be the most important of all public buildings."[83] In contrast is an excerpt from a training manual for Texas district attorneys:

WHAT TO LOOK FOR IN A JUROR

A. Attitudes

(1) You are not looking for a fair juror, but rather a strong biased, and sometimes hypocritical individual who believes that defendants are different from them in kind, rather than degree.

(2) You are not looking for any member of a minority group which may subject him to oppression — they almost always empathize with the accused.

(3) You are not looking for the free thinkers and flower children. . . .[84]

During the 1974 trial of James Richardson, a black man charged with the murder of a white police officer in New York City, the noted defense attorney William M. Kunstler used most of his peremptory challenges to eliminate from the jury as many whites as possible. At the same time, assistant district attorney Steven Phillips used his peremptory challenges in an effort to stack the jury with a large number of conservative, law-and-order black jurors. In addition, Phillips eliminated one juror solely on the basis that he was a longtime admirer of Kunstler's flamboyance and apocalyptic rhetoric.[85]

In short, many attorneys use these challenges to try to obtain partial jurors, not impartial ones; they hope to impanel jurors sympathetic to their side. This was certainly the case in the late 1960s trial of Black Panther Warren Wells, charged with the murder of a police officer. Wells's first two trials resulted in hung juries: 10-to-2 and 11-to-1 for acquittal. At his third trial, however, he was convicted. The guilty verdict was reached by an all-white jury put together by the district attorney by using all of his peremptory challenges to eliminate blacks from the jury.[86] The practice of systematically excluding minorities from juries has been sanctioned by the Supreme Court in 1965 through its ruling in *Swain* v. *Alabama*.[87] In 1986, the Supreme Court overruled *Swain* in part, holding that prosecutors may not exclude blacks from juries because of concern that they will favor a defendant of their own race. The case was *Batson* v. *Kentucky*,[88] in which the prosecutor, in the trial of a black man, used his peremptory challenges to strike all four black persons on the venire, and a jury composed of only white persons was selected. The defendant was convicted. On appeal to the U.S. Supreme Court, it was held that the equal protection clause of the Fourteenth Amendment is violated when a defendant is put on trial before a jury from which members of his or her race have been purposely excluded. The High Court reasoned that although a defendant has no right under the equal protection clause to a jury composed in whole or part of persons of his or her own race, the clause forbids the prosecutor from challenging potential jurors *solely* on account of their race or on the assumption that black jurors as a group will be unable impartially to consider the state's case.

Cat Mousam, who was listed as an occupant on her owners' door, was duly counted by the Boston census taker and later summoned for jury duty. Her owners, social workers wise to bureaucratic ways, used the portion of the summons set aside for reasons to decline to serve to declare that "Cat Mousam is not qualified to serve as a juror because she is a cat." Accordingly, notice came back from the Massachusetts jury commissioner that Cat Mousam would indeed be excused from duty. Reason: "Language."

The jury consists of twelve persons chosen to decide who has the better lawyer.
— ROBERT FROST

Batson v. Kentucky: The Supreme Court's ruling that a prosecutor's use of peremptory challenges to exclude from a jury members of the defendant's race solely on racial grounds violates the equal protection rights of the defendant.

The *voir dire* examination continues until the required number of jurors has been selected. In many jurisdictions where the twelve-person jury is used, as many as fourteen may be accepted. The additional two jurors serve as alternates. They sit through the entire trial and are available to take the place of a regular jury member should he or she become ill, be forced to withdraw, or become disqualified while the trial is in process. Potential jurors who are successfully challenged return to the original jury pool, and new ones are drawn from the panel and subjected to *voir dire* (see Exhibit 12.5). Those ultimately selected are sworn in and become the trial jury.

The *voir dire* can be brief or it can be time-consuming. In prosecutions of misdemeanors and many felonies where there has been little pretrial publicity and trial proceedings are anticipated to be fairly routine, there may be few challenges and the *voir dire* may last only a few hours or even less. In other cases, the examination can continue for days, weeks, or even months. When Black Panthers Bobby Seale and Ericka Huggens were tried in a New Haven, Connecticut, courtroom in 1971 on a charge of murdering a fellow Panther, the process was even more time consuming. The *voir dire* lasted for more than four months, and a total of 1,035 prospective jurors were interrogated.[89]

It is the challenges for cause that lengthen the *voir dire* proceedings. Any and every potential juror can be thus challenged. Peremptory challenges, on the other hand, are controlled by statute. In New York, for example, the maximum permitted is three, except in such serious cases as murder, where as many as twenty are allowed, and where there are multiple defendants.

The *voir dire* can be crucially important part of a criminal proceeding. Its purpose is to do more than merely choose a fair and impartial jury — as significant as this may be. Its primary functions are to educate the citizen as to the role of the juror and to develop jury–attorney rapport. Moreover, the *voir dire* provides the defense and the prosecution with the opportunity to attempt to influence jurors' attitudes and perhaps their later vote. One prosecutor put it this way:

Drawing by Lorenz. © 1977, The New Yorker Magazine, Inc.

"The jury will disregard the witness's last remarks."

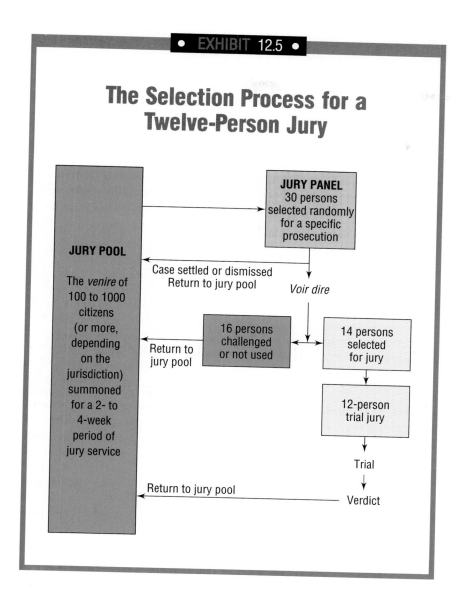

• EXHIBIT 12.5 •

The Selection Process for a Twelve-Person Jury

JURY PANEL
30 persons selected randomly for a specific prosecution

JURY POOL

The *venire* of 100 to 1000 citizens (or more, depending on the jurisdiction) summoned for a 2- to 4-week period of jury service

Case settled or dismissed
Return to jury pool

Voir dire

16 persons challenged or not used

Return to jury pool

14 persons selected for jury

12-person trial jury

Trial

Return to jury pool

Verdict

There is much more to a *voir dire* than the simple process of questioning and selecting jurors. In addition to the gamesmanship and psychology, a *voir dire* is an opportunity for the attorneys to educate their juries about the theories of their cases. It is also an opportunity to plant seeds of doubt that they hope will produce a favorable verdict. It is a chance to predispose jurors to be receptive to the attorney's case.[90]

THE CRIMINAL TRIAL

I'll be judge, I'll be jury, I'll try the whole cause and condemn you to death.
—FROM LEWIS CARROLL'S *ALICE'S ADVENTURES IN WONDERLAND*, 1865

The trial is the climax of the criminal proceeding and it begins as soon as the jury is sworn in. The only matter that remains in doubt before commentary and testimony can begin is the judge's decision as to

Sequestration: The removal of the jurors (and alternates, if any) from all possible outside influences.

COUNSEL: Have you any idea of what your defense is going to be?
DEFENDANT: Well, I didn't do it sir.
COUNSEL: Yes, well, er, I think we can afford to fill that out a little. It's not in itself a cast iron defense.
DEFENDANT: Well I didn't do it sir! I didn't do it! And if I did it, may God strike me dead on the spot, sir!
COUNSEL: Well, we'll just give him a moment or so, shall we. . . .
— ALAN BENNETT, BBC-TV, 1966

whether or not to sequester the jurors for the entire trial. **Sequestration** involves removal of the jurors (and alternates, if any) from all possible outside influence. They are housed in a hotel or motel for the duration of the trial; they are forbidden all visitors; and the newspapers they read, as well as the television programs they watch, are fully censored.

Few juries are sequestered for an entire trial, for most criminal prosecutions fail to generate a line of newspaper copy or even a second of television news time. Only if there is continuing media coverage that has the potential for influencing a juror's decision is sequestration ordered. If the judge does so rule, however, sequestration places a tremendous hardship on the jury members. One recent commentator spoke of the total isolation resulting from sequestration:

> Jurors were driven to their homes on January 15, the first evening after they had been selected to serve, so that they could get a week's worth of clothing. They were returned to their homes for clean clothing on January 20 and January 27. . . . Each juror was accompanied by a marshal on each trip . . . and even the windows of the vans [were] covered with paper so a juror [could not] see a newspaper headline at a newsstand. The jurors also were escorted by marshals to two theater productions and to one dinner at a restaurant away from their hotel. . . . The jurors were allowed no visits by relatives and were allowed telephone conversations only after a deputy marshal dialed the number, cautioned the answering party against discussing the case, and listened in on a second telephone that had a cut-off button to be used if either party violated the restrictions.[91]

The procedures used in criminal trials are for the most part the same throughout the United States, and the process consists of the following steps:

- opening statements
- presentation of the state's case
- presentation of the defense's case
- rebuttal and surrebuttal
- closing arguments
- charging the jury
- deliberation and verdict

In bench trials, this process is altered only minimally. First, those steps involving the jury are eliminated. Second, the tactics and strategies of the defense and prosecuting attorneys are simplified and much of the dramatic effect is removed.

Opening Statements

The first step in a trial proceeding is the reading of the criminal complaint by the court clerk, followed by opening statements—first by the prosecution and then by the defense.

The prosecutor's statement is an attempt to provide the jury with an outline of the case and how the state intends to prove, beyond a reasonable doubt, that the defendant did indeed commit the crime or crimes charged in the indictment. This outline generally includes a description of the crime, the defendant's role in it, and a discussion of the evidence and witnesses to be presented. In addition, the prosecutor is likely to address the meaning of "beyond a reasonable doubt." Reasonable doubt is fair doubt based upon reason and common sense and growing out of the testimony of the case; it is doubt arising from a candid and impartial investigation of all the evidence and testimony presented. The purpose of the prosecutor's analysis here is to distinguish between reasonable doubt and vague apprehension, and at the same time to emphasize that the state's object is to prove guilt beyond a *reasonable* doubt — not beyond *all* doubt.

Although the prosecutor has considerable freedom as to what is said in the opening statement, no references may be made to evidence that is known to be inadmissible, and no comment may be made concerning the defendant's prior criminal record (if any exists). To make such a comment would be considered a *prejudicial error* — an error of such substance that it compromises the rights of the accused. Prejudicial errors that cannot be corrected by any action by the court are often the bases for appeals. Furthermore, they can result in a **mistrial,** a discharging of the jury without a verdict. A mistrial is the equivalent of no trial at all.*

The defense attorney's opening statement is an address to the jury that focuses on how the defense will show that the state has a poor case, and that proof of guilt beyond a reasonable doubt cannot be demonstrated. It is not uncommon for defense attorneys to stress that the accused is innocent until proven guilty, and that the burden of proof is fully on the prosecution.

Defense attorneys and prosecutors often vary their strategies for opening statements, as dictated by the nature of the case, evidence, and witnesses. One approach is to keep opening remarks short and vague, letting the particulars of the case emerge during the course of the trial. Such a tactic makes few promises to the jury, but it allows flexibility. Such flexibility can be important because it enables the attorney, during the final summation, to structure an argument uncompromised by promises that he or she could not deliver. An alternative is a detailed opening statement, eloquently expressed and forcefully presented, that conditions the jury to accept the evidence that is ultimately delivered. This can be a risky technique, but it is highly rewarding if the promises made can be kept during the course of the trial.[92]

In a jury trial, the prosecutor always delivers an opening statement. Without it, the jurors would have no framework within which to consider the evidence and testimony. The defense attorney, however, may choose to make no statement at all — out of necessity perhaps, if the defense strategy cannot be determined until the content of the state's case is revealed; or as part of the strategy, which is not to be revealed until the proper time. Opening statements are infrequently used in bench trials; they are less effective, since the seasoned judge has handled perhaps hundreds of similar cases in the past.

Prejudicial errors can result in judicial action, appeals, or a mistrial.

Mistrial: A trial that has been terminated without a verdict and declared invalid by the court because of some circumstance that creates a substantial and uncorrectable prejudice to the conduct of a fair trial.

---

* It should be noted that it is not only the prosecutor who can make prejudicial errors resulting in a mistrial. In a 1981 Washington, D.C., rape case, a mistrial was declared when the judge learned that two jurors had been drinking heavily during the trial arguments (*Time,* May 18, 1981, p. 29). In a 1983 narcotics case, also in the District of Columbia, trial proceedings were terminated when it became apparent that one of the jurors was deaf and had heard none of the testimony (*National Law Journal,* December 5, 1983, p. 43). In a 1984 Ohio capital murder trial, the presiding county court judge ordered a mistrial when one juror had grabbed and frightened two others during deliberations (*National Law Journal,* March 5, 1984, p. 10). The failure to order a mistrial when warranted is grounds for appeal (see Chapter 13).

Presentation of the State's Case

In order to give the accused the opportunity to provide an informed defense, it is the state that presents its case first in the adversary system of justice. The prosecutor begins by presenting evidence and questioning witnesses.

Evidence: Any species of proof, through the medium of witnesses, records, documents, concrete objects, and circumstances.

The Rules of Evidence Generally, **evidence** is any species of proof, through the medium of witnesses, records, documents, concrete objects, and circumstances. Specifically, evidence is of four basic types:

1. *Real evidence* is physical objects, such as a murder weapon, stolen property, fingerprints, the physical appearance of the scene of the crime, the physical appearance of a person when exhibited to the jury, wounds, or other items. Real evidence may be the original objects, or facsimile representations, such as photographs, models of the crime scene, tire tracks, or other duplicates of objects that are either unavailable or unusable in their original form.
2. *Testimonial evidence* is the sworn, verbal statements of witnesses. All real evidence is accompanied by testimonial evidence, in that objects presented in evidence are explained by someone qualified to discuss them. Conversely, however, not all testimonial evidence is accompanied by real evidence.
3. *Direct evidence* is eyewitness evidence. Testimony that a person was seen painting a fence, for example, is direct evidence that the person painted a fence.
4. *Circumstantial evidence,* or indirect evidence, is evidence from which a fact can be reasonably inferred. Testimony that a person was seen with paint and a paint brush in the vicinity of a newly painted fence is circumstantial evidence that the person painted the fence.

That's what's wrong with our legal system, ya need evidence!
—ARCHIE BUNKER, 1982

All evidence must be competent, material, and relevant.

These four types necessarily overlap, since all are ultimately presented through testimony. Furthermore, *all* evidence must be competent, material, and relevant. Evidence is *competent* when it is legally fit for admission to court. The testimony of an expert witness on a scientific matter is deemed competent, for example, if the court accepts his or her credentials as a reflection of proficiency in the subject area. In contrast, testimonial evidence on ballistics presented by an automobile mechanic would be considered incompetent; or an individual who has been convicted of perjury might be considered incompetent to testify. In common law, a person was considered to be "incompetent" to testify against his or her spouse, under the theory that by being compelled or even allowed to do so would undermine the marriage and thus be detrimental to the public welfare. In 1980, however, the Supreme Court ruled in *Trammel* v. *United States* that a criminal defendant could no longer invoke the "privilege against adverse spousal testimony," as long as the testimony is voluntary and does not compromise a confidential marital communication.[93]

There is one way to find out if a man is innocent—ask him. If he says yes, you know he is guilty.
—GROUCHO MARX

Evidence can be deemed incompetent if it is based on hearsay. Under most circumstances the hearsay rule prohibits a witness from testifying about statements not within his or her personal knowledge—that is, about secondhand information. There are two exceptions to this rule. The first is an admission of criminal conduct made by the defendant to the witness. Such hearsay testimony is allowed because the accused is

present in court to challenge it. The other exception is the "dying decla-ration" of a crime victim that has been told to or overheard by the witness; it is based on the presumption that a person who is about to die will not lie.[94]

To be admissible in a court of law, evidence must also be material and relevant, and there is only a slight distinction between the two. Evidence is *material* when it has a legitimate bearing on the decision of the case. Evidence is *relevant,* when it is applicable to the issue in ques-tion. For example, evidence of a defendant's bad character on previous occasions is immaterial (unless he is submitting his good character in evidence). By contrast, the fact that an accused has stolen property in the past is irrelevant to whether or not he has murdered someone (assuming, of course, that he is not being tried on multiple charges of theft and murder).

Examination of Witnesses   The state's presentation begins with the *direct examination* of witnesses. This consists only of eliciting facts from the witness in some chronological order. The first witness called is gen-erally one who can establish the elements of the crime. Subsequent witnesses introduce physical, direct, and indirect evidence, and expert testimony.

After the prosecutor has completed his interrogation of a witness through direct examination, the defense is permitted (but not required) to cross-examine the witness. The purpose of *cross-examination* is to discredit the testimony, by either teasing out inconsistencies and contra-dictions or attacking the credibility of the witness. The prosecution can ask further questions of the witness through a *redirect examination,* as can the defense with a *recross-examination*. This examination procedure continues until all of the state's witnesses have been called and evidence presented.*

Objections During the examination of any witness, whether it be by the prosecutor or the defense counsel, the opposing attorney can *object* to the introduction of evidence or testimony that he or she considers to be incompetent, immaterial, or irrelevant. Objections can also be made to "leading questions" (ones that inherently instruct or at least suggest to the witness how to answer), to eliciting witness's opinions and conclusions, to being argumentative, and to "badgering" (abusing) a witness.

If the objection is *sustained* (consented to), the examiner is ordered to withdraw the question or cease the mode of inquiry, and the jury is instructed to disregard whatever was deemed inappropriate. If the objection is *overruled* (rejected), the examining attorney may continue with the original line of questioning.

Motion for Directed Verdict

Following the presentation of the state's case, it is not uncommon for the defense attorney to enter a motion for a *directed verdict*. With this, the defense moves that the judge enter a finding of acquittal on the grounds that the state failed to establish a *prima facie* case of guilt against the accused. If the judge so moves, he directs the jury to acquit the defendant. Even in the absence of a motion by the defense, the trial judge can order a directed verdict. Furthermore, the judge can do so not only on the grounds that the state failed to prove its case, but also because the testimony of the prosecution witnesses was not credible or because the conduct of the prosecutor was not proper. Conversely, *a judge cannot direct the jury to convict the accused.*

Presentation of the Defense's Case When the U.S. Supreme Court spoke of "the dead hand of the common law rule of 1789" many decades ago,[95] it was referring to a provision of the Judiciary Act of 1789 which noted that codefendants were not entitled to testify in each other's behalf. The provision seemingly was a remnant of a pre-eighteenth-century English common law principle that denied defendants charged with treason or felonies the right of having witnesses testify in their defense. This restriction in the Judiciary Act, however, seemed to contradict a component of the Sixth Amendment providing that in all criminal prosecutions the accused shall enjoy the right "to have compulsory process for obtaining witnesses in his favor." *Compulsory process* refers to the subpoena power that can force a witness into court to testify. In 1918, the Supreme Court extended the compulsory process clause, without limitation, to federal defendants.[96] In *Washington* v. *Texas,*[97] decided in 1967, the Court extended the right to the states.

This compulsory process clause rests at the foundation of the presentation of the defense's case. During this presentation the counsel for the accused calls witnesses to testify in support of the not-guilty plea. It is also at this point that the counsel for the accused has the opportunity to offer **evidence in chief**—that is, the first or direct examination of a witness.

Prima facie case is one supported by sufficient evidence to warrant submission to the jury for the rendering of a verdict.

Evidence in chief: The first or direct examination of a witness.

---

* Redirect examinations and recross-examinations are limited—redirect only to matters emanating from the cross, and recross only to matters emanating from the redirect.

At the outset, the defense attorney has the option of presenting many, some, or no witnesses or evidentiary elements on behalf of the accused. In addition, the defense must decide whether the accused will testify on his or her own behalf. The Fifth Amendment right against self-incrimination does not require it, but if the defendant does so choose, the prosecution then has the option of cross-examination.

Once these matters are decided, the defense's presentation follows the procedures outlined for the state's presentation: direct examination, cross-examination, redirect examination, and recross-examination. In addition, the rules of evidence and right to make objections apply equally to the defense as to the prosecution.

It is a common misconception that during this stage of the trial the burden of proof shifts to the defense. *This is not so.* The responsibility of proving guilt beyond a reasonable doubt always remains with the prosecution. What shifts to the defense is the "burden of going forward with the evidence." [98] This means that since the prosecution has presented its suit to the jury, it becomes the defense's responsibility to offer its own argument for the jury to consider.

> The responsibility of proving guilt beyond a reasonable doubt always rests with the prosecution.

Rebuttal and Surrebuttal

When the defense "rests" (concludes its presentation), the prosecutor may elect to introduce new witnesses or evidence in an effort to refute the defense's case. Known as the *prosecutor's rebuttal,* the same format of examination and cross-examination, redirect and recross-examination is followed. In turn, the counsel for the accused may put forth a *surrebuttal,* which is a rebuttal of the prosecutor's rebuttal.

Closing Arguments

The *summation,* or closing arguments, gives each side the opportunity to recapitulate all the evidence and testimony offered during the trial. The arguments are made directly to the jury, and the defense emphasizes a posture of innocence while the state proffers the opposite view.

The summation ceremonies begin with the defense attorney, who points out any weaknesses or flaws in the prosecutor's theory and evidence. Counsel for the accused argues that proof "beyond a reasonable doubt" has not been established, and reminds the jurors that they will have to live with their decision and consciences for the rest of their lives. Since the burden of proof rests with the state, the prosecutor is entitled to the final argument. For both the defense and the prosecution, perhaps the most vital element to be offered is *persuasion*. One prosecutor made just this point:

> Summing up in a criminal trial is a throwback to an earlier age. It is one of the few arts left in which time is of no consequence. Standing before twelve people, a lawyer can be brief or lengthy—the choice is his own; there are no interruptions, and a captive audience. All that matters are those twelve people; they must be persuaded, or everything that has gone before is in vain. Summation is the one place where lawyers do make a difference; if an attorney can be said to "win" or "lose" a case, the chances are that he did so in his closing argument to the jury.
>
> The appeal of a summation may be to the heart, the intellect or the belly—or to all of them. There are as many different ways of summing up as there are trial lawyers, and there is no one correct way to deliver a summation, or to learn how to give one. It is largely a matter of instinct and of experience. Either you are able to reach out and move people with your words or you are not, and that is all there is to it.[99]

Charging the Jury

Charging the jury: An order by the judge directing the jurors to retire to the jury room, consider the facts of the case and the evidence and testimony presented, and from their deliberations return a just verdict.

Charging the jury involves an order by the judge that directs the jurors to retire to the jury room, consider the facts of the case and the evidence and testimony presented, and from their deliberations return a just verdict. Regarded by many as the single most important statement made during the trial, it includes instructions as to the possible verdicts, the rules of evidence, and the legal meaning of "reasonable doubt." The instructions contained in the charge, furthermore, are often arrived at through consultation by the defense and the prosecution with the judge, and from statutory instructions as contained in the jurisdiction's code of criminal procedure.

In some states, the judges are permitted to review thoroughly all the evidence that has been presented to the jury. They are free to summarize, for example, the testimony of each witness. This can be useful to jurors, especially if the trial has been long and complex. But it also can be hazardous, for a judge has opinions about innocence and guilt, and these can inadvertently influence the jury.

In North Carolina, for example, although the statute governing instructions to the jury does not require the judge to state the evidence, it does not prohibit it either:

> In instructing the jury, the judge must declare and explain the law arising on the evidence. He is not required to state the evidence except to the extent necessary to explain the application of the law to the evidence.[100]

The rule goes on to forbid the judge from expressing opinions as to the accused's culpability, the strengths and weaknesses of evidence, and whether or not some fact was proven. Any violations of this rule could result in a mistrial. Clearly, it would have tremendous impact on the jury if the judge were to state the following, for example:

> The jury should bear in mind that while the accused has maintained that he was at a neighborhood cocktail party at the time of the offense, it seems strange that he cannot remember the name of a single person—*not one*—who was also at the party, or where the party even took place.

Such a statement would be highly prejudicial in any jurisdiction and would likely result in a mistrial. Nevertheless, the North Carolina statute, like similar ones in many other jurisdictions, gives the judge tremendous latitude for expression. If the judge believes the defendant is guilty, he or she might give more time and emphasis to the most damaging evidence; if the judge views the accused as innocent, he or she might give more consideration to the testimony of defense witnesses. As a result, complete objectivity can be difficult to achieve.

Even more difficult to present seems to be instructions that juries can fully understand. Because the nuances of the law are so complex the instructions can take hours to deliver. In a Justice Department study conducted in 1981, moreover, it was found that in half the cases jurors had been confused by the judges' instructions.[101]

Finally, the members of the jury are instructed that they cannot communicate with anyone as to the facts of the case. Further sequestration might be ordered, which would place the jurors under the supervision of a court officer until a verdict is reached.

Jury Deliberations

Every jury has a *foreman* or *forewoman,* who serves as the nominal leader of the group. He or she is chosen by the jurors during the trial or after

The Criminal Trial 431

● EXHIBIT 12.6 ●

Sidelights on Criminal Matters
A Most Unpredictable Jury

Some years ago, a man was tried in a California court for the murder of his wife. The state's case was quite convincing, but one thing was missing—the victim's body. This was the basis of the defense's case, and no evidence or testimony was presented on behalf of the accused.

In a dynamic summation performance, the counsel for the defense soared to eloquent heights of oratory, repeating that with the absence of the body of the alleged victim, it could not be proven that a crime had been committed. "You must find my client innocent for one simple reason," he shouted. Then, dropping to a breathless whis-per, he added, "His wife is still alive. In fact—she just walked into the courtroom!"

At once, the heads of all the jurors and spectators turned only to see that not a soul had entered the chambers. But the attorney had made his point. How could proof beyond a reasonable doubt be concluded if the jurors suspected that the defendant's wife might still be alive.

Everyone agreed that it was a brilliant ploy, and after less than an hour's deliberation, the jury returned with a verdict. Yet, to the amazement and disbelief of all those present, the jury had found the accused guilty of murder.

When the trial was over and the jury dismissed, the bewildered defense counsel confronted the first few jurors he saw. "How," he asked, "could you find a man guilty when you weren't even sure his wife was dead? Hadn't everyone turned to look for her in the back of the courtroom?"

"Yes," answered one of the jurors, "everybody except your client."

source: Based on a story in Melvyn Bernard Zerman, *Beyond a Reasonable Doubt: Inside the American Jury System* (New York: Crowell, 1981), pp. 10–13.

---

retirement to the jury room. In New York the first juror selected in the *voir dire* becomes the leader. Whether this person becomes the *actual* leader is another matter, depending on personality factors and the dynamics of group interaction.

Once the jury has retired, it is traditional for the foreman to sit at the head of the table and call for a vote. With the exceptions of Oregon and Louisiana, unanimous verdicts are required by law. If such a verdict is acquired, the deliberations are finished. Typically, however, it is not that simple. In one study undertaken by the University of Chicago, for example, one vote was all that was necessary to reach a unanimous verdict in only 30 percent of the cases.[102]

Should deliberations fail to generate a unanimous decision, the dilemma is referred to as a deadlocked or "hung" jury. There are several consequences of such a situation: the jury is dismissed in open court, the judge declares a mistrial, and the prosecution can either retry the case or dismiss the charges. Deadlocked juries result from differences of opinion over the strengths and weaknesses of evidence, varying perceptions of innocence and guilt, and the meaning of "reasonable doubt." The deadlocked jury is not a common occurrence. Reports indicate that only 6 percent of all criminal trials end with a hung jury,[103] with most resulting in a negotiated consensus.[104]

The "hung" jury

Verdict and Judgment

When the jury reaches a verdict, it returns to the courtroom to announce its decision: "We, the jury, duly impaneled and sworn, find the defend-

The refusal or marked reluctance on the part of a jury to convict, because of the severe nature of the sentence involved.

ant guilty [or not guilty] as charged." In cases involving multiple counts, the jury may find the accused guilty of some and innocent of others.

One of the more enduring issues in criminal trials is the problem of **jury nullification.** It occurs when juries do not follow the court's interpretation of the law in every instance, disregard what they have been told about the law or certain aspects of evidence, consider the application of certain laws to be unjust, refuse to convict because they consider the penalties too severe, or otherwise "nullify" or suspend the force of strict legal procedure. Instances of jury nullification have occurred in cases of battered spouses who kill, political crimes, and mercy killings.

Jury nullification can be both inadvertent or by design. If a verdict of guilty is returned and it is the court's opinion that it is an erroneous decision, the judge can refuse to abide by it. He or she can *direct* the jury to acquit, or "arrest" the guilty verdict and enter a judgment of acquittal. However, a trial judge does *not* have the authority to direct a jury to convict or enter a judgment arresting a verdict of not guilty.

Polling the jury

Lastly, jurors can be *polled.* At the request of the defense or the prosecution, the judge (or the bailiff) asks each juror if the verdict announced is his or her individual verdict. Polling the jury is done to determine whether any juror has been pressured by fellow jury members into voting a particular way.

Posttrial Motions

With a judgment of not guilty, the defendant is immediately released — unless other charges are still pending. With a guilty verdict, most jurisdictions allow the defense to file motions to set aside the judgment or to file motions for a new trial.

Motion in arrest of judgment

The *motion in arrest of judgment* asks that no judgment be pronounced because of one or more defects in the record of the case. Possible defects include the following: (1) The trial court had no jurisdiction over the case; (2) the verdict included conviction on a charge that was not tested in the indictment or information; or (3) there was error "on the face of the record." This last term refers to any faults of procedure that may have occurred during the pretrial process.

Motion for a new trial

The *motion for a new trial,* which can be made only by the defense, can be based on numerous grounds: (1) The jury received evidence outside of the courtroom; (2) the jury was guilty of misconduct during deliberations; (3) the court erred in overruling an objection or permitting the introduction of certain evidence; (4) the jury charge was made improperly; (5) the prosecution was guilty of misconduct; (6) there is a suspicion of *jury tampering* (bribes or threats made to a juror to influence his or her vote); and (7) newly discovered evidence is available for review.

Jury tampering

If either motion is sustained, new proceedings will be initiated. Any new trial that results, however, does not represent double jeopardy, for the defendant's motion is an allegation that the proceedings should be declared utterly invalid.

SUMMARY

The movement of defendants through the criminal courts is complex. The process is characterized by many stages and checks and balances while beset with numerous difficulties. Early in the process is the matter of pretrial release. Bail has been the traditional mechanism of temporary release. The amount of bail set is determined by a number of factors, including the seriousness of the crime, the defendant's prior criminal record, and the strength of the state's case. The bail system has been heavily criticized on the grounds that it discriminates against the poor and that the bail bond industry promotes inequity and corruption.

Stack v. *Boyle* noted that bail was not a means for punishing defendants or protecting society, but rather of assuring the accused's attendance in court. Nevertheless, high bail is often set for the purposes of preventive detention. Moreover, for those who cannot make bail, pretrial detention has negative effects on their criminal processing. Release on recognizance has become a popular alternative to bail and has been generally effective.

Following the initial court proceedings, an information or indictment initiates prosecution. The indictment is handed down by a grand jury, whose purpose is to investigate and to protect citizens from unfair accusations. Since grand juries do not determine guilt or innocence, many of the elements of due process are absent. The Supreme Court has generally refused to impose substantive criteria on the grand jury's exercise of discretion.

After the formal determination of charges, the defendant is arraigned, at which time he or she is asked to enter a plea. The basic pleas are those of guilty, not guilty, *nolo contendere,* and standing mute. In addition, there are the insanity plea, pleas of statute of limitations, and the issue of double jeopardy.

Prior to the actual trial a number of motions can be filed by the defense or prosecution: discovery, change of venue, suppression, bill of particulars, severance, continuance, and dismissal. Then there is the matter of a "speedy trial" as guaranteed by the Sixth Amendment. There are many legitimate reasons for delays in formally trying a defendant, but the Supreme Court has held that if a defendant is denied a speedy trial, the remedy is dismissal of the charges.

Criminal defendants have a constitutional right to a trial by jury, a right extended to the states through *Duncan* v. *Louisiana* in 1968. Potential jurors are selected from voter registration rolls or multiple source lists. The *voir dire* examination functions to determine a candidate's fitness to serve, and jurors can be eliminated through challenges by the defense and prosecution.

The criminal trial has many steps: opening statements, presentation of the state's and defense's case, rebuttal and surrebuttal, closing arguments, charging the jury, and deliberation and verdict. There may be posttrial motions for arrest of judgment or for a new trial.

KEY TERMS

bail (**390**)
Batson v. *Kentucky* (**421**)
Benton v. *Maryland* (**410**)
charging the jury (**430**)
double jeopardy (**409**)
Downum v. *United States* (**410**)
Duncan v. *Louisiana* (**418**)
evidence (**426**)
evidence in chief (**428**)
grand jury (**401**)
Hurtado v. *California* (**401**)
indictment (**401**)

information (**401**)
jury nullification (**432**)
Klopfer v. *North Carolina* (**415**)
mistrial (**425**)
motion (**410**)
nolo contendere (**406**)
Palko v. *Connecticut* (**410**)
presentment (**401**)
release on recognizance
  (ROR) (**400**)
sequestration (**424**)
Sixth Amendment (**413**)

Speedy Trial Act (**415**)
speedy trial (**413**)
Stack v. *Boyle* (**391**)
surety (**390**)
transactional immunity (**405**)
true bill (**403**)
United States v. *Calendra* (**404**)
use immunity (**405**)
venire (**420**)
voir dire (**420**)

QUESTIONS FOR DISCUSSION

1. Do Justice Gray's remarks in *Hudson* v. *Parker* at least imply (1) that all defendants have a right to bail, and (2) that defendants have some right to remain at liberty until all mechanisms of appeal have been exhausted? Why?
2. How might a bench trial versus a jury trial alter the opposing attorneys' strategies and tactics?
3. Given the respective roles of the defense and the prosecution, is the deliberate seeking of biased jurors legal or ethical?
4. Should the concept of "due process of law" be extended to grand jury proceedings?
5. What are the potential consequences of a defendant's waiver of rights?

FOR FURTHER READING

Frankel, Marvin E., and Gary P. Naftalis. *The Grand Jury: An Institution on Trial.* New York: Hill and Wang, 1977.

Hans, Varlerie P., and Neil Vidmar. *Judging the Jury.* New York: Plenum, 1986.

McConahay, John B., Courtney J. Mullin, and Jeffrey Frederick. "The Uses of Social Science in Trials with Political and Racial Overtones: The Trial of Joan Little," *Law and Contemporary Problems* 41. Winter, 1977, pp. 205–229.

Phillips, Steven. *No Heroes, No Villains: The Story of a Murder Trial.* New York: Vintage, 1978.

Wice, Paul. *Freedom for Sale.* Lexington, Mass.: Lexington, 1974.

Zerman, Melvyn B. *Beyond a Reasonable Doubt: Inside the American Jury System.* New York: Crowell, 1981.

NOTES

1. Charles E. Silberman, *Criminal Violence, Criminal Justice* (New York: Random House, 1978), pp. 254–255.
2. Charles Rembar, *The Law of the Land: The Evolution of Our Legal System* (New York: Simon and Schuster, 1980), p. 95.
3. See Luke Owen Pike, *A History of Crime in England,* vol. 1 (London: Smith, Elder, 1873–1876), pp. 57–60; Ernst W. Puttkammer, *Administration of Criminal Law* (Chicago: University of Chicago Press, 1953), pp. 99–100.
4. *Hudson* v. *Parker,* 156 U.S. 277 (1895).
5. *McKane* v. *Durston,* 153 U.S. 684 (1894).
6. Patricia M. Wald, "The Right to Bail Revisited: A Decade of Promise Without Fulfillment," in *The Rights of the Accused,* ed. Stuart S. Nagel (Beverly Hills, Ca.: Sage, 1972), pp. 175–205.
7. *Stack* v. *Boyle,* 342 U.S. 1 (1951).
8. *Carlson* v. *Landon,* 342 U.S. 524 (1952).
9. See Paul Wice, *Freedom for Sale* (Lexington, Mass.: Lexington, 1974); Frederick Suffet, "Bail Setting: A Study of Courtroom Interaction," *Crime and Delinquency* (October 1966): 318–331. See also, John S. Goldkamp and Michael R. Gottfredson, "Bail Decision Making and Pretrial Detentions," *Law and Human Behavior,* 3 (1979), pp. 227–249; Ilene H. Nagal, "The Legal/Extra-Legal Controversy: Judicial Decisions in Pretrial Release, *"Law and Society Review,"* 17 (1983), pp. 481–515.
10. National Commission on Law Observance and Enforcement, *Report on Prosecution* (Washington, D.C.: U.S. Government Printing Office, 1931), pp. 89–92.
11. The Cleveland Foundation, *Criminal Justice in Cleveland* (Cleveland: Cleveland Foundation, 1922); Missouri Association for Criminal Justice, *The Missouri Crime Survey* (New York: Macmillan, 1926); Wayne L. Morse and Ronald H. Beattie, *Survey of the Administration of Criminal Justice in Oregon* (Eugene: University of Oregon Press, 1932); President's Commission on Law Enforcement and Adminstration of Justice, *Task Force Report: The Courts* (Washington, D.C.: U.S. Government Printing Office, 1967).
12. See Frederick Suffet, "Bail Setting"; Wice, *Freedom for Sale.*
13. *New York Times,* August 15, 1990, p. A1.
14. *Annotated Code of Maryland,* Article 27, Section 12B.
15. *Pretrial Release of Felony Defendants.* (Washington, D.C.: Bureau of Justice Statistics, 1991).
16. President's Commission, *Task Force Report: The Courts,* p. 38.
17. *National Law Journal,* June 29, 1981, p. 9.
18. *New York Times,* April 4, 1963, p. 37.
19. *National Law Journal,* July 8, 1985, p. 20.
20. Advisory Committee on Pretrial Release, *Standard Relating to Pretrial Release* (New York: American Bar Association, 1968), p. 3. See also *Pretrial Release of Felony Defendants.*
21. Anne Rankin, "The Effect of Pre-Trial Detention," *New York University Law Review* 39 (June 1964):641.
22. P. Koza, and A. N. Doob, "The Relationship of Pretrial Custody to the Outcome of a Trial," *Criminal Law Quarterly,* 17 (1975), pp. 391–400.
23. *New York Times,* June 2, 1975, p. 16.
24. Ronald Goldfarb, *Ransom: A Critique of the American Bail System* (New York: Harper & Row, 1965), p. 47.
25. For more on the Vera Foundation and the Vera Institute of Justice, see its ten-year report, 1961–1971, *Programs in Criminal Justice Reform* (New York: Vera Institute, 1972); and *Further Work in Criminal Justice* (1977), its later five-year report.
26. Charles E. Ares, Anne Rankin, and Herbert Sturtz, "The Manhattan Bail Project," *New York University Law Review* 38 (January 1963):68.
27. Tyce S. Smith and James W. Reilley, "The Illinois Bail System: A Second Look," *John Marshall Journal of Practice and Procedure,* Fall 1972, p. 33.
28. *Chicago Tribune,* September 2, 1990, pp. 1, 10; September 3, 1990, pp. 1, 2; September 4, 1990, pp. 1, 10.
29. Paul Nussbaum, "Crime and No Punishment," *Philadelphia Inquirer Magazine,* May 5, 1991, pp. 19–20, 36–38, 40.

30. Marvin E. Frankel and Gary P. Naftalis, *The Grand Jury: An Institution on Trial* (New York: Hill and Wang, 1977), pp. 3–17.

31. *Hurtado* v. *California,* 110 U.S. 516 (1884).

32. *Hale* v. *Henkel,* 201 U.S. 43 (1906).

33. *Costello* v. *United States,* 350 U.S. 359 (1956).

34. *United States* v. *Calandra,* 414 U.S. 338 (1974).

35. *Kastigar* v. *United States,* 406 U.S. 441 (1972).

36. *Branzburg* v. *Hayes,* 408 U.S. 665 (1972).

37. Anne Strick, *Injustice for All* (New York: Penguin, 1978), p. 175.

38. National Advisory Commission on Criminal Justice Standards and Goals, *Courts.* (Washington, D.C.: U.S. Government Printing Office, 1973), p. 13.

39. *New York Times,* December 9, 1977, p. D1.

40. *New York Times,* October 5, 1980, p. 33.

41. Thomas C. Marks and J. Tim Reilly, *Constitutional Criminal Procedure* (North Scituate, Mass.: Duxbury, 1979), p. 136.

42. *National Law Journal,* May 3, 1982, p. 11.

43. *National Law Journal,* May 3, 1982, p. 11.

44. David A Jones, *The Law of Criminal Procedure* (Boston: Little, Brown, 1981), p. 398.

45. *United States* v. *Perez,* 9 Wheat. 579 (1824).

46. *United States* v. *Ball,* 163 U.S. 662 (1896).

47. *Wade* v. *Hunter,* 336 U.S. 684 (1949).

48. *United States* v. *Lanza,* 260 U.S. 377 (1922).

49. *Abbate* v. *United States,* 359 U.S. 187 (1959).

50. *Waller* v. *Florida,* 397 U.S. 387 (1970).

51. *Palko* v. *Connecticut,* 302 U.S. 319 (1937).

52. *Benton* v. *Maryland,* 395 U.S. 784 (1969).

53. *Downum* v. *United States,* 372 U.S. 734 (1963).

54. See, for example, *Code of Alabama,* 1975, Title 15, Section 15-4.

55. *Brady* v. *Maryland,* 363 U.S. 83 (1963).

56. *Moore* v. *Illinois,* 408 U.S. 786 (1972).

57. For some interesting details about defense team efforts to move a trial, see John B. McConahay, Courtney J. Mullin, and Jeffrey Frederick, "The Uses of Social Science in Trials with Political and Racial Overtones: The Trial of Joan Little," *Law and Contemporary Problems,* 41 (Winter, 1977), pp. 205–229.

58. *Mapp* v. *Ohio,* 367 U.S. 643 (1961); *Escobedo* v. *Illinois,* 368 U.S. 478 (1964); *Miranda* v. *Arizona,* 384 U.S. 436 (1966).

59. See Sarah Tanford, Steven Penrod and Rebecca Collins, "Decision Making in Joined Criminal Trials: The Influence of Charge Similarity, Evidence Similarity, and Limiting Instructions," *Law and Human Behavior,* 9 (1985), pp. 319–337; Kenneth S. Bordens and Irwin A. Horowitz, "Joinder of Criminal Offenses," *Law and Human Behavior,* 9 (1985), pp. 339–353.

60. Personal communication, September 15, 1971.

61. *Serfass* v. *United States,* 420 U.S. 377 (1975).

62. *New York Times,* May 21, 1975, p. 1.

63. *California Penal Code,* Section 1382 (1).

64. *Code of Alabama,* Title 15, Section 3-1.

65. *State* v. *Brann,* 292 A. 2d 173 (Me. 1972).

66. *Beavers* v. *Haubert,* 198 U.S. 77 (1905).

67. *Barker* v. *Wingo,* 407 U.S. 514 (1972).

68. *Strunk* v. *United States,* 412 U.S. 434 (1973).

69. *United States* v. *Lovasco,* 431 U.S. 783 (1977).

70. *Klopfer* v. *North Carolina,* 386 U.S. 213 (1967).

71. *In re Oliver,* 333 U.S. 257 (1948).

72. *Duncan* v. *Louisiana,* 391 U.S. 145 (1968).

73. *Tennessee Code Annotated,* Title 40-2504.

74. *Idaho Code,* Title 19-1902.

75. Gilbert B. Stuckey, *Procedures in the Criminal Justice System* (Columbus, Ohio: Merrill, 1976), p. 91.

76. *Duncan* v. *Louisiana,* 391 U.S. 145 (1968).

77. *Perez* v. *Duncan,* 404 U.S. 1071, *certiorari* denied (1971).

78. *Baldwin* v. *New York,* 399 U.S. 66 (1970).

79. *Williams* v. *Florida,* 399 U.S. 78 (1970).

80. *Ballew* v. *Georgia,* 435 U.S. 223 (1978).

81. *Taylor* v. *Louisiana,* 419 U.S. 522 (1975).

82. Laura Rose Handman, "Underrepresentation of Economic Groups in Federal Juries," *Boston University Law Review* 57 (January 1977): 198–224.

83. Melvyn B. Zerman, *Beyond a Reasonable Doubt: Inside the American Jury System* (New York: Crowell, 1981), p. 181.

84. Zerman, *Beyond a Reasonable Doubt,* p. 181.

85. Steven Phillips, *No Heroes, No Villains: The Story of a Murder Trial* (New York: Vintage, 1978), pp. 132–138.

86. Ann Fagan Ginger, *Minimizing Racism in Jury Trials* (Berkeley, Calif.: National Lawyers Guild, 1969), pp. 157–160.

87. *Swain* v. *Alabama,* 380 U.S. 202 (1965).

88. *Batson* v. *Kentucky,* 106 S. Ct. 1712 (1986).

89. *New York Times,* March 12, 1971, p. 1.

90. Phillips, *No Heroes, No Villains,* pp. 136–137.

91. Noted by Zerman, *Beyond a Reasonable Doubt,* pp. 147–148.

92. See, for example, Phillips, *No Heroes, No Villains;* Seymour Wishman, *Confessions of a Criminal Lawyer* (New York: Times Books, 1981).

93. *Trammel* v. *United States,* 445 U.S. 40 (1980).

94. Jones, *Law of Criminal Procedure,* p. 475.

95. *Rosen* v. *United States,* 245 U.S. 467 (1918).

96. *Rosen* v. *United States,* 245 U.S. 467 (1918).

97. *Washington* v. *Texas,* 388 U.S. 14 (1967).

98. Marks and Reilly, *Constitutional Criminal Procedure,* p. 147

99. Phillips, *No Heroes, No Villains,* pp. 196–197.

100. *General Statutes of North Carolina,* Laws of 1977, Chapter 15A–1232.

101. *New York Times,* June 7, 1981, p. 25.

102. D. W. Broeder, "The University of Chicago Jury Project," *Nebraska Law Review* 38 (May 1959): 744–760.

103. Zerman, *Beyond a Reasonable Doubt,* p. 102.

104. See Kalven and Zeisel, *American Jury.*

13

Sentencing, Appeal, and the Judgment of Death

All I can say is, forgive them, Father, for in their ignorance they know not what they do.
—Convicted murderer Anthony Antone, moments before his execution in Florida's electric chair in 1984

I'm not kidding. Capital punishment may not be much of a deterrent against murder, but the sight of a few corpses swinging from a scaffold might work with drug dealers.
—*Newsweek* columnist James J. Kilpatrick, 1986

Death row is noticeably quieter.
—Louisiana State Penitentiary Warden Hilton Butler in 1987, after three executions at his institution in just one week

It's one of the few times in my life I ever got what I wanted.
—Confessed murderer Lloyd Hampton in 1990, who supports the death penalty as a deterrent, after an Illinois court sentenced him to death

fter conviction, the business of the court is not complete. First there is the matter of sentencing, and second there is the potential for appellate review.

What makes both sentencing and appeal significant is that in all prior phases of justice administration the purpose is to establish, beyond a reasonable doubt, the criminal liability of the defendant. The adversary system of American jurisprudence, grounded in due process of law, is structured from arrest through trial on the premise that the accused is innocent until proven guilty. Upon conviction, of course, the accused *has* been proven guilty. At sentencing, the court's obligation to criminal law and judicial procedure suddenly shifts from impartial and equitable litigation to the determined imposition of sanctions. On appeal, the court also deals, at least in most circumstances, with those who have been proven guilty, but who are requesting decisions on errors they claim were made in procedure or judgment.

In either case, the court's position is arduous and challenging. It must mediate among the functions of justice, the statutory authority of law, the assurances of due process, the needs for correctional application, the burdens of a congested justice system, the urgency of political realities, the essentials of legal ethics, and the demands for community protection.

Without question, sentencing is the most controversial aspect of criminal justice processing. Appellate review, although somewhat less visible, can also generate considerable controversy. And perhaps of greatest concern is the judgment of death, a criminal sanction that cuts across both sentencing and appellate decision making.

I listened to the testimony. Your version of what happened was so far out in space that it could not be believed.
—JUDGE JEROME O. HERLIHY OF WILMINGTON, DELAWARE, IN 1991, AS HE SENTENCED A TWENTY-THREE-YEAR-OLD MAN TO TWENTY-FOUR YEARS IN PRISON FOR MULTIPLE COUNTS OF KIDNAPPING, RAPE, ASSAULT, AND WEAPONS VIOLATIONS

SENTENCING

Life for life, eye for eye . . .

—EXODUS 21:22–23

What should be done with criminal offenders after they have been convicted? The answer is a difficult one for a sentencing judge, because the administration of justice has a variety of conflicting goals: the rehabilitation of offenders, the discouragement of potential lawbreakers, the isolation of dangerous criminals who pose a threat to community safety, the condemnation of extralegal conduct, and the reinforcement of accepted social norms. Objectives as varied as these tend to generate such contradictory suggestions as the following:

"The punishment should fit the crime."
"The public demands a prison sentence."
"The purpose of justice is individualized sentencing."
"The sentence should be a warning to others."
"Rehabilitate the offender so he can be returned to society."
"Lock him up and throw away the key."

The burden of the judge is to choose among one or more of these various goals while subordinating all others.

Sentencing Objectives

Throughout the history of the United States, there has been no single and clearly defined rationale to serve as a guiding principle in sentencing. For over 200 years, the public has alternated between revulsion at inhumane sentencing practices and prison conditions on the one hand, and overly compassionate treatment on the other. While the former practices are denounced as "barbaric" and "uncivilized" and the latter as "coddling criminals," the fate of convicted offenders has repeatedly shifted according to prevailing national values and current perceptions of danger and fear of crime. As a result, sentencing objectives are based on at least five competing philosophies: retribution, vengeance, isolation, deterrence, and rehabilitation.

Retribution   To use a 200-year-old definition once offered by classical scholar Cesare Beccaria, **retribution** is an effort "to make the punishment as analogous as possible to the nature of the crime." In more modern terminology, retribution involves creating an equal or proportionate relationship between the offense and the punishment. It is concerned exclusively with making the punishment fit the crime and is as old as recorded history. It can be found in Genesis (27:45), Exodus (21:23–25), and Leviticus (25:17–22), with such prescriptions as "When one man strikes another and kills him, he shall be put to death," and "Eye for eye, tooth for tooth, hand for hand, foot for foot, burning for burning, wound for wound . . ." Retribution was also the basis of punishment under Mosaic law—that there should fall upon the offender what he had done to his neighbor.

Retribution rests on the notion that criminals are wicked, evil people who are responsible for their actions and deserve to be punished. At the same time, however, it asserts that the *state* shall act as the instrument of the community's collective response, thus incorporating the idea that the victims of crime cannot make reprisals against the offending parties.

As a sentencing philosophy, retribution presents an ethical dilemma. In a democratic society built on the principles of individual rights and civil liberties, criminal penalties based on "getting even" represent a contradiction in values. Furthermore, many libertarian ideals in modern society foster the notion that "making criminals suffer for the sake of suffering" is barbaric and uncivilized. As a result, there have been few twentieth-century advocates of the retribution theory of punishment. Most recently, however, there has been a resurgence of this posture, referred to as a "just deserts" philosophy. Stated simply, the philosophy is that criminal sanctions should be imposed because the offender "deserves" them. "Just deserts" implies retribution, but with its current label the theme has been receiving wider attention since—at least semantically—it is less emotion laden.[1]

A criminal is executed by an elephant at Baroda, India.

Retribution: A sentencing philosophy seeking to create an equal or proportionate relationship between the offense and the punishment.

"Just deserts"

Vengeance: A sentencing philosophy seeking satisfaction from knowing or seeing that offenders are punished.

In *Payne* v. *Tennessee,* the Supreme Court permitted the use of victim impact evidence in the penalty phase of capital trials.

Victim impact statements

Isolation: A sentencing philosophy seeking to remove the offender from society.

Deterrence: A sentencing philosophy seeking to prevent criminal acts by making an example of persons convicted of crimes

Vengeance   In contrast with retribution, **vengeance** is the desire to punish criminals because society gains some measure of satisfaction from seeing or knowing that they are punished.[2] Like retribution, vengeance also presents an ethical dilemma. Should it be accepted as a valid rationale for punishment? The U.S. Supreme Court's recent decision in *Payne* v. *Tennessee* suggests that it may already have been.[3] In *Payne,* decided in 1991, the Court held that at a capital sentencing proceeding, the Constitution does not forbid the admission of evidence or prosecutorial argument concerning the personal characteristics of the victim or the impact of the crime on the victim's family. In other words, the decision permitted *"victim impact statements"* at sentencing hearings, or as Chief Justice Rehnquist put it: "victim impact evidence is simply another form or method of informing the sentencing authority about the harm caused by the crime in question." One could reasonably argue that by permitting the victim, or members of the victim's family, to testify at sentencing as to the personal harm the offender has caused is tantamount to eliciting requests for vengeance from a sentencing judge or jury.

Isolation   Unlike retribution, **isolation** is simply the removal of dangerous persons from the community.[4] Also referred to as the "restraint" or "incapacitation" philosophy, its object is community protection rather than revenge. By removing the offender from society through execution, imprisonment, or exile (as is the case with the *deportation* of foreign nationals upon conviction of certain crimes), the community is thus protected from further criminal activity. (See Exhibit 13.1.)

As with retribution, isolation as a punishment philosophy is problematic. If the goals are crime prevention and community protection, then the sanctions would have to be quite severe to be effective. Regardless of the offense, life imprisonment with no parole and execution are the only forms of restraint that can guarantee the elimination of future offenses against the community. The alternative — temporary incarceration until such times as the community can be reasonably assured the offender will no longer commit crimes — is impossible to predict. In addition, there is an economic dimension. As the guiding principle of sentencing, isolation would require the costly construction of many more prison facilities, plus the annual costs of supporting an expanded population of inmates, combined with the increased expense of new custodial personnel.

In current practice, isolation as a premise for sentencing is not uncommon. The National Advisory Commission on Criminal Justice Standards and Goals has noted the following, however, about prisons as vehicles for offender restraint:

> They protect the community but that protection is only temporary. They relieve the community of responsibility by removing the offender, but they make successful reintegration of the offender into the community unlikely.[5]

Deterrence   The most widely held justification for punishment is reducing crime. Thus, as a sentencing philosophy, **deterrence** refers to the prevention of criminal acts by making examples of persons convicted of crimes. Deterrence can be both general and specific. *General deterrence* seeks to discourage would-be offenders from committing crimes; *specific deterrence* is designed to prevent a particular convicted offender from engaging in future criminal acts.

● EXHIBIT ·13.1 ●

The Isolation of Habitual Offenders and Sexual Psychopaths

Isolation of a relatively permanent nature evolved during the early part of this century under what has often been referred to as the "Baumes laws." In 1926, restrictive penal legislation was sponsored by a New York State penal committee headed by Senator Caleb H. Baumes. The laws provided for an increase in penalty with each successive felony offense and an automatic life sentence for the fourth offense. The term *Baumes laws* became widely applied to similar *habitual offender laws* passed in other states. Virtually all jurisdictions in the United States now have some form of habitual offender laws. Most have statutes similar to the New York codes, which now can provide for life imprisonment for a third felony offense. Some states go one step further; in Texas, for example, a sentence of up to ninety-nine years may be mandated for some second felony offenders.

Comparable to the habitual offender laws are the sexual psychopath laws and sex offender acts, which also call for sentences of extended isolation. Such legislation came into being as the result of alarm over widely publicized sex crimes. The first of these laws appeared in Michigan in 1935, and by the 1950s they were apparent in many jurisdictions. They allowed prosecutors to initiate proceedings against a defendant to have him placed in an institution for an indeterminate length of time if there was sufficient reason to believe that he was sexually dangerous. The indeterminate period, furthermore, could range anywhere from one day to life, and some did not even require proof that a crime had been committed.

The sexual psychopath laws were ultimately deemed to have little value, primarily because they were enacted out of hysteria and provided little community protection. The vicious acts of child molesting and sadomasochistic rape that they targeted were behavior that could be neither predicted nor prevented, and many offenders rarely repeated their crimes. Over time, the laws were either revoked or ignored, but in some jurisdictions they nevertheless remain in force. In Illinois, for example, the Sexually Dangerous Persons statute currently reads:

All persons suffering from a mental disorder, which mental disorder has existed for a period of not less than one year, immediately prior to the filing of the petition hereinafter provided for, coupled with criminal propensities to the commission of sex offenses, and who have demonstrated propensities toward acts of sexual assault or acts of sexual molestation of children, are hereby declared sexually dangerous persons.

SOURCES: State of New York, Penal Law, 40–70.10; Texas Penal Code, Section 12.42; Illinois Codes, 38-105-3; Alan H. Swanson, "Sexual Psychopath Statutes: Summary and Analysis," *Journal of Criminal Law, Criminology and Police Science* 51 (July–August 1960): 215–235.

The notion of punishment as a deterrent is best illustrated in the words of an eighteenth-century judge who reportedly stated to a defendant at sentencing, "You are to be hanged not because you have stolen a sheep but in order that others may not steal sheep."[6] Belief in the efficacy of deterrence, however, seems mainly based on conjecture, faith, and emotion, and there is overwhelming evidence to suggest that the deterrent effect of punishment is, at best, weak.[7] Increased crime rates in the nation's cities as well as high levels of recidivism among many offender populations are ample evidence of this. On the other hand, the philosophy of specific deterrence does seem to have an impact on the behavior of many white-collar criminals and first-time misdemeanants whose arrests and convictions cause them embarrassment and public disgrace, and threaten their careers and family life. General deterrence can be applied to similar populations for certain types of criminal activity. For example, when many jurisdictions made it a misdemeanor to patronize a prostitute, a U.S. Department of Justice employee commented:

> Almost every weekend I'd go to downtown D.C., to Atlantic City, or Times Square and shack up with some sleazy hooker. . . . No more, babe! That's all I need, getting busted for sleeping with a whore. . . . So much for a career in Justice.[8]

Rehabilitation: A sentencing philosophy seeking to reintegrate the offender into society.

Rehabilitation From a humanistic point of view, the most appealing basis for sentencing and justification for punishment is that future crime can be prevented by changing the offender's behavior. The **rehabilitation** philosophy rests on the premise that persons who commit crimes have identifiable reasons for doing so, and that these can be discovered, addressed, and altered. Rehabilitation suggests to the offender that "crime does not pay" and that "there is a better way." Its aim is to modify behavior and reintegrate the lawbreaker into the wider society as a productive citizen.

The goal of rehabilitation has wide support, for in contrast with other sentencing philosophies, it takes a positive approach to eliminating offense behavior. Unlike the false hope of deterrence or the temporary measures of retribution and isolation, proponents argue that rehabilitation is the only humanitarian mechanism for altering the criminal careers of society's casualties.

Yet the efficacy of rehabilitation has been seriously questioned. Some suggest that since the causes of crime are not fully understood, efforts at behavioral change are of questionable value. Others maintain that since the availability of rehabilitative services in many institutions and community-based programs is either minimal or nonexistent, then "correction" as such has only little limited practical potential. Still a third group espouses a "nothing works" philosophy, arguing that rehabilitation has not demonstrated and never will demonstrate its ability to prevent or reduce crime.[9]

Statutory Sentencing Structures

Regardless of the sentencing philosophy of the presiding judge, the actual sentence imposed is influenced to some degree by the statutory alternatives that appear in the penal codes, combined with the facilities and programs available in the correctional system. Thus, the competing objectives of retribution, vengeance, isolation, deterrence, and rehabilitation may be diluted to some degree since the judicial sentencing responsibility must be carried out within the guidelines provided by legislative sentencing authority.

Statutory sentencing guidelines provide a range of sentencing alternatives.

The *statutory sentencing guidelines,* which have generally evolved over long periods of time and often reflect the changing nature of legislative philosophy, appear in each state's criminal code. No two state codes are quite alike — the punishments they designate for specific crimes vary, and the methods establishing the parameters for sentencing can also differ. Furthermore, some statutes give judges wide latitude in sentencing, while others do not. In some states — Tennessee, for example — the penal code designates the range of punishments for each specific crime. Others, such as Idaho, follow the Tennessee model for some crimes, but extend almost total discretion to the judge for others. And in other states, such as New York, crimes are first classified according to their severity (for example, rape in the first degree is a class B felony, while incest is a class E felony) and then assigned punishments according to their felony or misdemeanor class.

Although statutory guidelines provide a range of sentencing alternatives, judges also have discretion in many instances to deviate from the legislative norm, on the premise that sentences should be individualized. Conversely, there are situations in which sentencing discretion can be taken away from the judge. For example, a person convicted of rape in the first degree in the state of New York faces a statutory period of imprisonment of no less than six years and no more than twenty-five years, since the crime is a class B felony. Assume that the judge imposes the maximum of eight to twenty-five years, his or her philosophy being that the defendant is a dangerous criminal from which society must be protected for as long as is legally possible. Under Section 70.40 of the New York penal law, however, this offender can be released on parole after serving the minimum sentence — six years. In addition, under Section 241 of the New York correction law, the governor always has the

Executions by beheading — a potent deterrent — took place in China at the turn of the century.

Two Words that Helped to Lengthen a Sentence

In 1984, defendant Harold Coleman was facing thirty-five years in prison after convictions of burglary, theft, and being a habitual criminal. However, following an outburst at his sentencing hearing during which he called the presiding judge a "prick" and an "asshole," another seven years was added to his sentence. The judge remarked that "he called me a few choice names that didn't reflect well on the judiciary, and you can't let them get by with this." Coleman's attorney commented that "I don't think it was worth the satisfaction my client got."

SOURCE: *National Law Journal*, September 3, 1984 p. 11.

power to reduce a sentence or grant a pardon. Although these contingencies are highly unlikely with a violent crime such as forcible rape, they have occurred with less serious felonies, countermanding the original designs of the sentencing judge.

A judge's authority and discretionary power to determine a sentence is, in a few jurisdictions, delegated by statute to the jury — but only for certain types of crimes. North Carolina, for example, is one of several southern states in which the jury makes the sentencing decision in capital cases. In addition, thirteen jurisdictions provide for jury-determined sentences in some noncapital cases. The wisdom of this practice, however, has been called into serious question. Author Melvyn Zerman has commented that the sentencing decision is the most formidable demand that can be made of a jury, and that it often occurs at a time when the jurors are both mentally and physically weak.[10] Even more to the point, the National Advisory Commission on Criminal Justice Standards and Goals has argued:

> The practice has been condemned by every serious study and analysis in the last half century. Jury sentencing is nonprofessional and is more likely than judge sentencing to be arbitrary and based on emotions rather than the needs of the offender or society. Sentencing by juries leads to disparate sentences and leaves little opportunity for development of sentencing policies.[11]

Sentencing Alternatives

Whatever theory of sanctions ultimately guides the sentencing of the defendant, and depending on the statutory requirements of the jurisdiction, the alternatives for the presiding judge include fines, probation or some other community-based program, imprisonment, or the death penalty.

Fines Fines are imposed either in lieu of or in addition to incarceration or probation. They are the traditional means of dealing with most traffic infractions and many misdemeanors, and the sentence "$30 or thirty days" has often been heard in courtrooms across America over the years. The following illustrate the use of fines in contemporary statutes:

- In Maryland, larceny of goods valued at less than $300 — a misdemeanor — calls for (1) return of the goods stolen or repayment of their full value to the owner, and (2) a fine of not more than $300, and/or (3) imprisonment of not more than eighteen months.[12]

- In New York, exposure of a female — a "violation" with the curiously worded definition of "clothed in such a manner that the portion of her breast below the top of the areola is not covered" — calls for (1) a fine not to exceed $250, or (2) imprisonment of not more than fifteen days.[13]

Fines can also be imposed for felonies, instead of or in addition to some other sentence. They can involve many thousands of dollars, and sometimes twice the amount of the defendant's gain from the commission of the crime. However, since *Williams* v. *Illinois* in 1970 and *Tate* v. *Short* the following year,[14] the use of fines has been curtailed somewhat. In *Williams,* the Supreme Court ruled that no jurisdiction could hold a person in jail or prison beyond the length of the maximum sentence merely to work off a fine they were unable to pay — a practice that was allowed at that time in forty-seven states. In *Tate,* the Court held that the historic *"$30 or thirty days"* sentence was an unconstitutional denial of equal protection. The Court's unanimous decision maintained that limiting punishment to a fine for those who could pay, but expanding punishment for the same offense to imprisonment for those who could not, was a violation of the Fourteenth Amendment. More recently, in *Bearden* v. *Georgia,*[15] decided in 1983, the Supreme Court ruled that a sentencing court may not automatically revoke a defendant's probation solely because he or she could not pay a fine that was a condition of probation.

A criminal court in New York City initiated an experiment in 1988 intended to make fines a more meaningful sentencing option. Judges have been adjusting fines to account for the financial means of the offender as well as the seriousness of the crime. These fines, furthermore, are referred to as *"day fines"* because they are figured as multiples of the offender's daily net income.[16]

For a convicted offender who receives a sentence of imprisonment, there are numerous types of sentence on the statute books; some have elicited considerable controversy. Sentences can be *indeterminate, determinate, definite, "flat," "fixed," indefinite, intermittent,* or *mandatory,* plus a host of other names, many of which have been confused and mislabeled in the literature. In practice, there are three major types: the indeterminate, the determinate, and the definite sentence.

The Indeterminate Sentence The most common sentence is the **indeterminate sentence,** which has a fixed minimum and a fixed maximum term for incarceration, rather than a definite period. The actual amount of time served is determined by the paroling authority. Sentences of one to five years, seven and one-half to fifteen years, ten to twenty years, or fifteen years to life are indeterminate.

The statutory sentencing guidelines for forcible rape in New York, are truly indeterminate. For example, the crime of rape in the first degree calls for a period of incarceration of not less than six years and not more than twenty-five years, with the minimum fixed at one-third of the maximum. Within those guidelines, the judge can impose a sentence, for example, of seven to twenty-one years. Thus, the offender must serve at least seven years, after which the paroling authority may release him at *any* time prior to the completion of his maximum sentence.

The philosophy behind the indeterminate sentence is based on a purely correctional model of punishment, the underlying premise being that the sentence should meet the needs of the defendant. After incarceration begins, at least in theory, the rehabilitation process is initiated, and the inmate should be confined until there is substantial evidence of "correction." At that point, it becomes the responsibility of the paroling authority to assess the nature and extent of such rehabilitation, and release the defendant if the evidence so warrants it. Thus, the indeterminate sentence rests on the notion that the length of imprisonment should be based on progress toward rehabilitation:

1. Criminals are personally or socially disturbed or disadvantaged and therefore their commission of crime cannot be considered a free choice. If this is the case, then setting terms commensurate with the severity of the crime is not logical.
2. Indeterminate sentences allow "effective" treatment to rectify socio-psychological problems, which are the root of crime.
3. Readiness for release varies with the individual and can only be determined when the inmate is in the institution, not before.[17]

$30 or thirty days

Bearden v. *Georgia*

"Day fines"

Indeterminate sentence: A sentence of incarceration having a fixed minimum and a fixed maximum term of confinement.

(All of these contentions are disputable and are not widely held in penological and criminological circles.)

In its purest form, the indeterminant sentence would involve a term of one day to life, but this is rarely found in current statutes. Confusion emerges in that some refer to this last example as the "indefinite" sentence, while others use the terms *indefinite* and *indeterminate* interchangeably.

In recent years, the practice of indeterminate sentencing has received considerable criticism. For example, the following arguments have been made against this form of sentencing:

Criticisms of indeterminate sentencing

- Since the causes of crime and criminal behavior are not readily understood, they cannot be dealt with under the premise of indeterminate sentencing.
- Rehabilitation cannot occur within the prison setting, regardless of the nature of the sentencing.
- The indeterminate sentence is used as an instrument of inmate control, put into practice through threats of disciplinary reports and hence, extended sentences.
- Sentences within the indeterminate model can vary by judge and by jurisdiction, resulting in unfair and disparate terms of imprisonment.
- An offender's uncertainty as to how long his or her prison term may endure can lead to frustration, violence, and riot.[18]

The Determinate Sentence   The growing concerns over indeterminate sentencing have generated considerable interest in the **determinate sentence.** Known also as the "flat," "fixed" or "straight" sentence, it has no set minimum or maximum, but rather, a fixed period of time. The term of the determinate sentence is established by the legislature — say, fifteen years — thus removing the sentencing discretion of the judge. However, under determinate sentencing guidelines, the court's discretion to choose between prison, probation, a fine, and some other alternative is not affected. Only the length of the sentence is taken away from judicial discretion, if the judge imposes imprisonment.

Determinate sentence: A sentence of incarceration for a fixed period of time.

In some instances, the determinate sentence can, in effect, become an indeterminate sentence. Under determinate sentencing statutes, inmates are still eligible for parole after a portion of their terms have been served. Thus, in a state where parole eligibility begins after one-half of the term has expired, a determinate sentence of ten years really ranges from a minimum of five years to a maximum of ten.

The Definite Sentence   The first application of indeterminate sentencing policies in the United States appeared in 1924 at New York's House of Refuge.[19] Prior to that time, a regular feature of incarceration was the **definite sentence** — one having a fixed period of time with no reduction by parole. This type of sentence fell out of favor, however, because those interested in rehabilitation found it to be too rigid and insensitive to defendants' individual characteristics and needs.

Definite sentence: A sentence of incarceration having a fixed period of time with no reduction by parole.

In contemporary statutes, the definite sentence is occasionally seen with respect to punishments for minor misdemeanors. It is rarely imposed with felonies, however, although life sentences with no eligibility for parole are in a sense definite sentences. For example, in Delaware,

> any person who is convicted of first-degree murder shall be punished by death or by imprisonment for the remainder of his or her natural life without benefit of probation or parole or any other reduction.[20]

The diminished appeal of the indeterminate sentence in recent years, combined with the growing concerns over street crime and the "coddling of criminals," has led to renewed interest in definite sentencing guidelines. In 1975, Maine became the first state to abandon the indeterminate sentencing system. At the same time, it also abolished parole. Under its new "flat" sentencing laws, terms of imprisonment are, in effect, definite sentences.

Other Sentencing Variations   In addition to the three basic sentences of imprisonment — the indeterminate, the determinate, and the definite — a number of variations and adaptations have been receiving increased attention in recent years.

In New York and several other jurisdictions there is the sentence of intermittent imprisonment. Under the New York statute, the **intermittent sentence** is a term to be served on certain days or periods of days as specified by the court.[21] For example, a defendant who pleaded guilty to the felonious possession of seventy-four pounds of marijuana was sentenced to an intermittent term of sixty days, to be served on consecutive weekends, followed by five years' probation.[22] It is a sanction used in instances where the nature of the offense warrants incarceration, but where the defendant's characteristics and habits suggest full-time imprisonment to be inappropriate. It should also be noted that a sentence of intermittent imprisonment is *revocable.* That is, should the offender

Intermittent sentence: A sentence to periods of confinement interrupted by periods of freedom.

● EXHIBIT 13.2 ●

Castrating the Rapist

Since violent people beget other violent people, castration would prevent a second generation.
— Woody Aydlette, 1983

Drawing by David Seavey, USA Today, December 5, 1983, p. 10A.

Castration involves the removal of the testicles, thus depriving a male of his sexual vitality. One may think of castration as a penalty for rape to be associated with the unusual punishments of antiquity, but it has a recent history in the United States. Scores of sex offenders were castrated in California during the 1930s and 1940s. Moreover, in the early 1970s a Colorado man facing a forty-year term for rape and child molestation volunteered for and underwent surgical castration, with a prior agreement with the judge that probation would be granted in exchange.

More recently, however, the issue became an emotional and legal debate of national proportions following a trial in the small town of Anderson, South Carolina. In April 1983, three men committed what was described as a heinous crime. They had raped a twenty-three-year-old woman in a motel room for six hours, tortured her with a cigarette lighter, and photographed her in the various sex acts into which she was forced. The victim lost a total of four pints of blood; her hospitalization lasted several days; and it is

probable that she will suffer emotional scars for the rest of her life. After their conviction in 1983, presiding judge C. Victor Pyle gave the defendants — ages twenty-seven, twenty-one, and nineteen — a shocking choice: accept a thirty-year prison sentence, or submit to surgical castration and go free.

Immediately, there were moral, legal, ethical, medical, and constitutional questions and arguments raised. Judge Pyle's sentence also became the center of an emotional debate. There was considerable support for the idea of castrating rapists; many people even held that castration alone was not a severe enough

punishment. Representative Woody Aydlette of South Carolina put it, "In my humble opinion, Judge Pyle's sentence was a masterful piece of creativity and imagination." Yet many people were opposed to the idea. Physicians held that while castration might prevent a rapist from having children, it might not prevent intercourse. For after all, male hormones which restore both libido and potency are available in artificial form by pill or injection.

Criminologists and women's rights advocates had long since argued that castration does not even begin to solve the problem of rape, a crime that is a sexual

---

fail to report to the institution on the days specified, he or she can be returned to court and resentenced to a more traditional term of imprisonment.

Mandatory sentence: A statutory requirement that a certain penalty shall be set and carried out in all cases upon conviction for a specified offense or series of offenses.

Also, a variety of determinate sentence known as the **mandatory sentence** has been the subject of extensive discussion since the middle of the 1970s. Mandatory sentences limit judicial discretion; they are penal code provisions that require the judge to sentence persons convicted of certain specified crimes to prison terms. Under these statutes, which are

expression of aggression, not an aggressive expression of sexuality. And there was support for this position in the very case that initiated the debate. The motive behind the rape, at least in part, was a kind of blackmail: the victim had brought a paternity suit against one of the men, and he was trying to pressure her, with the help of his friends, to drop the suit.

Professor Alan Dershowitz of Harvard Law School commented on a different aspect of the debate:

When Judge C. Victor Pyle recently gave three convicted rapists the "choice" between thirty years' imprisonment and surgical castration, he was acting more like a mikado* than an American judge. . . .

Supporters of Judge Pyle will argue that castration was not the *sentence* imposed. The defendants were given a *choice* between imprisonment and castration.

But the illusion of choice should not salvage the constitutionality of the sentence. Were judges permitted to circumvent the Constitution by allowing choices, it would be a simple matter for an American mikado to achieve his "object all sublime." He would impose severe traditional sentences and then give the defendant the "choice" of accepting less severe, but unconstitutional, alternate punishments that "fit the crime."

The possibilities are limitless: ten years imprisonment or convert to Baptism; five years or move to another state; three years or sixty lashes; one year or quit the National Organization for Women; six months or vote Republican.

In the aftermath of the sentence, all three defendants filed appeals. However, Roscoe Brown, the oldest of the three, quickly dropped his appeal and asked to be castrated so as to get out of prison. Judge Pyle delayed ruling on the matter until the final disposition of the other defendants' appeals. Roscoe Brown then filed a petition for a writ of *mandamus* with the South Carolina Supreme Court to force the judge to carry out the sentence. Later, the other two defendants asked that their appeals be dismissed so they also could choose castration. On February 13, 1985, after hearing oral arguments on the *mandamus* request, the justices of the South Carolina Supreme Court voided the entire sentence on grounds that it violated the Eighth Amendment ban on cruel and unusual punishment, and remanded the case for resentencing.

Despite the South Carolina ruling, the idea of castrating rapists has remained in the news. In 1990, for example, the state of Washington received brief international attention when its Republican-controlled Senate approved a bill allowing sex offenders to reduce their prison sentences by up to 75 percent by voluntarily undergoing surgical castration. The legislation was in part a reaction to a recent series of rapes, including the sexual mutilation of a seven-year-old Tacoma child. The bill was ultimately defeated in a House committee. In 1992, a Houston man charged with sexually assaulting a thirteen-year-old girl won judicial approval to undergo surgical castration in lieu of a prison sentence, but it never came to pass. Aside from the Eighth Amendment arguments that quickly emerged, no surgeon could be found who was willing to perform the operation. Nevertheless, castration continues to be a hotly debated possible punishment for repeat sex offenders.

---

* A Japanese emperor.

SOURCES: *Brown* v. *State,* SC SupCt (1983) 36 CrL 2463; *Newsweek,* September 5, 1983, p. 69; Wilmington (Delaware) *News-Journal,* November 27, 1983, p. A17; *New York Times,* December 11, 1983, p. 35; *Time,* December 11, 1983, p. 70; Philadelphia *Inquirer,* January 1, 1984, pp. 1A, 2A, 14A; *USA Today,* December 5, 1983, p. 10A; *National Law Journal,* March 4, 1985, p. 9; *New York Times,* February 14, 1991, p. A21; *Christian Science Monitor,* March 6, 1990, p. 7.

intended to guarantee that recidivists, violent offenders, and other serious criminals face the strictness and certainty of punishment, neither probation nor other alternative sentences are permitted.

Although some people would argue that mandatory sentences could be construed as cruel and unusual punishment in violation of the Eighth Amendment, more and more states are adopting mandatory sentencing provisions in their penal laws, particularly with regard to cocaine and crack possession and trafficking offenses.

Finally, there have been some unique variations in sentencing imposed by judges across the country on the basis of "letting the punishment fit the crime." For example:

- In 1984, a Tennessee farmer who had assaulted his mistress was sentenced to buy a new car—*for his wife*.[23]
- In 1981, a San Francisco judge sentenced a local prostitute to spend ninety days in a convent with the Sisters of the Good Shepherd.[24]
- For first-time shoplifters, an East Brunswick, New Jersey, magistrate imposes a $300 fine and four and one-half hours of lectures by a supermarket manager.[25]
- In Florida, Virginia, and Texas during 1982, several sentencing judges invoked the "law of the old West," when they offered several convicted defendants the choice of either incarceration or "getting out of town."[26]
- In 1987, a seventy-seven-year-old-man who had killed his wife and tried to kill himself was ordered to watch the movie classic "It's a Wonderful Life" as part of his sentence.[27]
- In 1988, a Brooklyn, New York, judge ordered a drug dealer to pay more than $2 million to treat persons who became addicted to the heroin he sold.[28]

And then there is a most controversial sentence for convicted rapists—castration (see Exhibit 13.2).

Disparities in Sentencing

Sentencing disparities have long since been a major problem in criminal justice processing. The basis of the difficulty is threefold:

1. the structure of indeterminate sentencing guidelines
2. the discretionary powers of sentencing judges
3. the mechanics of plea bargaining

The statutory minimum and maximum terms of imprisonment combined with fines, probation, or other alternatives to incarceration create a number of sentencing possibilities for a specific crime. With judicial discretion in sentencing, sanctions can vary widely according to the jurisdiction, the community, and the punishment philosophy of a particular judge. The dynamics of plea bargaining enable various defendants accused of the same crime to be convicted and sentenced differentially. These problems exist, furthermore, both within an individual court and across jurisdictions, since sentencing statutes can differ drastically from one state to the next.

Consider, for example, the range of sentences possible for conviction of burglary in the first degree (or its equivalent) in the following states:

- *Idaho:* imprisonment for not less than one year nor more than fifteen years, or probation[29]
- *New York:* imprisonment for not less than three years and not more than twenty-five years, or probation, or a fine[30]
- *West Virginia:* imprisonment for not less than one year nor more than ten years, or probation (for a first felony conviction)[31]

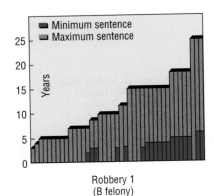

Robbery 1
(B felony)

Disparate Sentencing In a study of forty-one New York judges from across the state, the judges were asked to review files on actual cases and then indicate the sentences they would impose.

In this case, an elderly man was robbed at gunpoint by a heroin addict. The defendant was convicted of first-degree robbery. He was unemployed, lived with his pregnant wife, and had a minor criminal record. Each bar in the figure represents one judge's hypothetical sentence. (His actual sentence was 0–5 years.)

SOURCE: *New York Times*, March 30, 1979, p. B3.

- *Delaware:* three to thirty years' imprisonment, or a suspended sentence, or probation, or a fine (payable in installments)[32]
- *Maryland:* imprisonment for not more than twenty years, or probation[33]
- *Alabama:* imprisonment for not less than ten years, or probation[34]

Just within these few jurisdictions, the potential for disparate sentences is obvious. In Delaware, for example, the sentence imposed upon conviction for first-degree burglary can range from a fine to thirty years' imprisonment. Minimum terms of imprisonment extend from a low of one year in Idaho to a high of ten years in Alabama. And the maximum term allowable can range from ten years (West Virginia) to thirty years (Delaware), to perhaps even life (Alabama).

Statistical comparisons of sentencing tendencies in various jurisdictions demonstrate that disparities are indeed widespread. In the Detroit Recorder's Court, for example, sentencing dispositions were sampled from ten judges over a twenty-month period. It was found that one judge imposed prison terms upon as many as 90 percent of the defendants he sentenced, while another ordered such sentences in only 35 percent of his cases. Another magistrate consistently imposed prison sentences twice as long as those of the most lenient judge; and judges who were the most severe for certain crimes were the most lenient in others.[35] Similarly, forgers sentenced by federal judges in the Southern District of New York (Manhattan) received sentences that were an average of twenty months longer than those imposed in the Eastern District of New York (Brooklyn and Long Island).[36] Recent analyses have also demonstrated that a conviction for automobile theft in West Virginia will result in more time in prison than a rape conviction in sixteen other states, and that South Carolina prisoners sentenced for armed robbery end up doing more time in the penitentiary than convicted murderers in six other states.[37] For example, a Miami woman shot and killer her lover in 1984 after he slapped her in the face. After being charged with murder, she pleaded guity to manslaughter and was placed on probation.[38] By contrast, there was the case of Roger Trenton Davis, convicted in Virginia in 1973 for "possession with intent to distribute" nine ounces of marijuana. The judge imposed a term of forty years — a sentence which the Supreme Court upheld in 1982.[39]

With the examples of sentencing disparity noted here, it might be argued that the judges might have been dealing with crimes of varying degrees of seriousness and with offenders who were deserving of more or less punishment; but other data tend to contradict such an argument. In one study, conducted by the Federal Judicial Center during 1974, each of fifty federal judges from the Second Circuit were given twenty identical presentence reports drawn from actual cases, and asked to render sentences. The outcome clearly indicated disparate sentencing. In one case involving a defendant convicted of extortion, the sentences ranged from three years' imprisonment, at one end, to twenty years plus a $65,000 fine, at the other.[40] Later during the 1970s, forty-one New York judges drawn from across the state participated in a similar experiment, and the results further confirmed disparate sentencing practices.[41] During the 1980s, a similar study was conducted by the Justice Department with 264 federal judges. A major highlight of the finding was that for the same hypothetical offense, the recommended sentences ranged from probation to twenty years' imprisonment.[42]

The consequences of disparate sentencing

The consequences of disparities in sentencing can be significant, and not only for the convicted, but also for the court and correctional systems and the entire administration of justice. First, the wide variations in sentencing make a mockery of the principle of evenhanded administration of the criminal law, thus calling into question the very philosophy of justice in America. Second, disparities have a rebound effect on plea bargaining and court scheduling. On the one hand, defendants may opt for a negotiated plea rather than face trial before a judge known to be severe. On the other, substantial delays often result from the granting of continuances sought by defense attorneys who hope that numerous reschedulings will ultimately bring their cases before lenient judges. Known as "judge-shopping," the practice is so widespread that at one time in the District of Columbia court of general sessions, giving a defendant the judge of his or her choice became part of the plea negotiation arrangements.[43] Third, prisoners compare their sentences, and an inmate who believes that he or she received an unfair sentence or was the victim of judicial prejudice often becomes hostile, resistant to correctional treatment and discipline, and even riot-prone. Fourth, the image of the courts and of the process of justice is even further denigrated. (See Exhibit 13.3.)

Sentencing Reform

There have been a number of strong criticisms on the matter of sentencing disparities. Decades ago, U.S. attorney general Robert H. Jackson commented:

> It is obviously repugnant to one's sense of justice that the judgment meted out to an offender should be dependent in large part on a purely fortuitous circumstance: namely, the personality of the particular judge before whom the case happens to come for disposition.[44]

More recently, federal judge Marvin E. Frankel of the Southern District of New York commented:

> The sentencing powers of the judges are, in short, so far unconfined that, except for frequently monstrous maximum limits, they are effectively subject to no law at all. Everyone with the least training in law would be prompt to denounce a statute that merely said the penalty for crimes "shall be any term the judge sees fit to impose." A regime of such arbitrary fiat would be intolerable in a supposedly free society, to say nothing of being invalid under our due-process clause. But the fact is that we have accepted unthinkingly a criminal code creating in effect precisely that degree of unbridled power.[45]

The criticisms of both Attorney General Jackson and Judge Frankel, as well as those of numerous others, are directed not only toward judicial discretion, but also toward the penal statutes that make far-reaching discretion possible. Criminal laws that allow jurists to impose terms of "not more than" five years, or ten years, or thirty years proclaim, in effect, that sentencing judges are answerable only to their consciences. The measures that have been proposed or adopted in various jurisdictions to remedy the problem of sentencing disparities remove that key phrase "not more than" from the penal laws, reducing judicial discretion. Mandatory sentencing statutes, with their stipulations of fixed penalties, are in part the result of calls for better community protection, but they also clearly decrease the court's discretion. Mandatory sentence

● EXHIBIT 13.3 ●

Sidelights on Criminal Matters
A Consequence of Sentencing Disparity?

One of the more celebrated cases of disparate sentencing practices involved the conviction of a twenty-year-old youth on charges of conspiracy to commit a felony and assault with the intent to rob. The year was 1924, and the youth, although AWOL from the U.S. Navy, had no prior criminal record. His co-defendant, Edgar Singleton, was a thirty-one-year-old former convict and umpire for a local baseball team.

The two had collaborated to rob a grocery store in Mooresville, Indiana, but the victim resisted, the attempt was thwarted, and both were quickly arrested.

Fearing the strictness and certainty of punishment handed down at the county court in Martinsville, Indiana, Singleton obtained a change of venue, received a term of two to ten years, and was paroled after less than two years. The youth, however, threw himself on the mercy of the local court, but nevertheless received sentences of two to fourteen years and ten to twenty years.

Embittered by unequal justice and the inequitable sentence, the youth rebelled against his warders at the Indiana State Reformatory. He attempted escape on three occasions, was charged with numerous disciplinary violations, and as a result was denied parole when first eligible in 1929. Later that year, he was transferred to Indiana State Prison, where he met a score of experienced criminals who taught him the fine art of bank robbery.

On May 22, 1933, just a few days before his thirtieth birthday, after having spent his entire young adult life in prison, he was finally paroled. Based on the tutelage provided by his inmate associates, he began a professional career in bank robbery. During the next thirteen months, he engineered a score of armed holdups at banks and stores across the Midwest. His efforts netted him many hundreds of thousands of dollars, but in the process he killed at least fifteen people. On July 2, 1934, as a young man of only thirty-one years, FBI agents shot him to death as he exited a theater in Chicago, Illinois. His name was John Dillinger.

SOURCES: L. L. Edge, *Run the Cat Roads* (New York: December, 1981); J. Edgar Hoover, *Persons in Hiding* (Boston: Little, Brown, 1938); Jay Robert Nash, *Bloodletters and Badmen* (New York: M. Evans, 1973); John Toland, *The Dillinger Days* (New York: Random House, 1963).

statutes, however, are not a panacea for either crime control or sentencing disparities, for they can easily increase prosecutorial discretion, court delays, and overcrowded prison conditions. Furthermore, they almost totally eliminate the rehabilitative goals of individualized justice.

A less extreme model for eliminating the abuses of discretion is the *presumptive fixed sentence,* now under consideration in several jurisdictions. The objectives of presumptive sentencing are (1) to reduce

Presumptive sentencing

disparities by limiting judicial discretion without totally eliminating it, and (2) to increase community protection by imposing a sentence the offender is required to serve.

More stringent than the indeterminate sentence but less rigid than the determinate sentence, the presumptive fixed sentence is a good combination of the two. A state legislature would set a minimum and maximum term, with a limited range, for a particular crime. The judge would impose a fixed determinate sentence within that range, decided on the bases of mitigating circumstances and the offender's characteristics. This sentencing scheme also eliminates the need for parole.[46]

For example, a presumptive sentence for the crime of burglary in the first degree might have a lower legislative limit of three years and an upper limit of ten, with a fixed sentence of five years as set by the judge. Through this model, imprisonment becomes mandatory, a defined range of terms is established by statute, and a degree of judicial discretion remains. At the same time, such disparity-producing guidelines as Delaware's three to thirty years' imprisonment for the same crime, or Alabama's imprisonment "for not less than" ten years, or other terms "as the judge sees fit to impose" would be eliminated.

Sentencing institutes, councils, and guidelines also have been introduced in the hope of influencing judicial discretion. *Sentencing institutes,* initiated at the federal level in 1958, are designed to generate interest in formulating policies and criteria for uniform sentencing procedures. Periodically convened in the form of one- and two-day workshops, they typically involve mock sentencing experiments followed by discussions of any observed disparities. *Sentencing councils,* which were started in 1960 in the federal court for the Eastern District of Michigan, are also intended to reduce disparities. The council includes three judges who examine the cases awaiting sentence and make recommendations to the sentencing judge. *Sentencing guidelines* are based on the actual sentencing behavior of judges. Statistical tables are constructed that reflect the average sentences imposed by judges in a specific jurisdiction, broken down by the seriousness of the crime and the characteristics of the offender. These guideline tables make it possible for a judge to know in advance of sentencing a case what his or her peers have done in similar circumstances. Such tables are intended to curb disparities by structuring discretion on the judges' common experience.

None of these approaches, however, has been particularly effective.[47] The institutes are poorly attended, the councils have been only rarely adopted, and the guidelines are cumbersome and have appeared only periodically in a few jurisdictions. The reason for the limited attendance and adoption is, for the most part, judicial opposition. Sentencing is the one area of court processing where judges are in total command and can freely exercise their power and authority — capacities they are not likely to relinquish easily. One judge expressed his opposition this way: "To do away with judicial sentencing is to improperly delegate a responsibility that is rightfully and inherently a part of the judiciary."[48]

Sentencing institutes

Sentencing councils

Sentencing guidelines

Federal Sentencing Guidelines

In an attempt to reduce disparities at the federal level, in 1985 Congress created the Federal Sentencing Commission. It was a nine-member committee whose task was to establish sentencing guidelines that would reduce judicial discretion and thereby ensure more equal punishments. After some two years of work, the new guidelines were put into force effective November 1, 1987. They promulgated the greater uniformity that was hoped and at the same time tended to send more defendants to prison (although for shorter periods of time). For example, the following table shows the case for first offenders.

Crime	Average Time Served Prior to Guidelines	Sentences Under New Guidelines
Kidnapping	7.2 to 9 years	4.2 to 5.2 years
First-degree murder	10 to 12.5 years	30 years to life in all cases
Income tax evasion ($5,000 or less)	4 to 10 months for the only 30% who serve time	Virtually all are subject to some confinement for 1 to 7 months
Drug dealing (1 oz. of cocaine)	21 to 27 months for the only 33% who serve time	Virtually all serve 21 to 27 months

Note: Comparisons apply only to the 15% of federal defendants who go to trial, plea negotiations not included.
SOURCE: *Sentencing Guidelines and Policy Statements for the Federal Courts*, 41 CrL 3087 (1987).

Although the new federal guidelines held the promise of sentence reform, they were attacked immediately because of the way that the U.S. Sentencing Commission had been formed. The commission was an independent body within the judicial branch of government, but it was argued that the act of writing the guidelines was essentially legislative. As such, this represented an unconstitutional delegation of authority by Congress and a violation of the separation-of-powers doctrine. The **separation-of-powers doctrine** is a major principle of American government whereby power is distributed among three branches of government—the legislative, the executive, and the judicial. The officials of each branch are selected by different procedures, have different terms of office, and are independent of one another. The separation is not complete, however, in that each branch participates in the functions of the other through a system of checks and balances. Yet most importantly, the doctrine serves to ensure that the same person or group will not make the law, interpret the law, and apply the law.

By early 1988, hundreds of federal judges had faced the question of the guidelines' constitutionality. Slightly more than half had struck them down, in most instances on separation-of-powers grounds. It was at that point that the U.S. Supreme Court agreed to hear the case. In 1989, decided by an 8-to-1 majority, the Court ruled that the creation of the Federal Sentencing Commission was neither an unconstitutional delegation of legislative discretion nor a violation of the separation of powers doctrine.[49]

The Sentencing Process

Sentencing is generally a collective decision-making process that involves recommendations of the prosecutor, the defense attorney, the judge, and sometimes the presentence investigator. In jurisdictions where sentence bargaining is part of the plea negotiation process, the judge almost invariably imposes what has been agreed upon by the prosecution and the defense.

In the federal system and the majority of state jurisdictions, a **presentence investigation** may be conducted prior to actual sentencing. This is undertaken by the court's probation agency or presentence office,

Separation-of-powers doctrine: The principle that power is distributed among three branches of government—the legislative, the executive, and the judicial—for the purpose of ensuring that no one person or group will make the law, interpret the law, and apply the law.

Presentence investigation: An investigation into the background and character of a defendant that assists the court in determining the most appropriate sentence.

and the resulting report is a summary of the defendant's present offense, previous criminal record, family situation, neighborhood environment, school and educational history, employment record, physical and mental health, habits, associates, and participational activities. The report may also contain comments as to the defendant's remorse, and recommendations for sentencing by the victim, the prosecutor, and the officer who conducted the investigation.

Presentence reports vary in detail and length depending on the resources and practices of the jurisdiction. The statutes requiring the use of such reports are of three basic types:

1. those that make it a matter of judicial discretion;
2. those that make it mandatory for certain types of cases — such as felonies, or where the defendant is a recidivist, or where the offense is punishable by a year or more imprisonment; and,
3. those that make it mandatory if probation is to be the disposition.[50]

The value of presentence reports

Although presentence investigations are not mandatory in all jurisdictions, the American Bar Association has recommended that they be used for every criminal case.[51] Furthermore, as noted by the Administrative Offices of the U.S. Courts, the value of presentence reports goes well beyond their use in determining appropriate sentences. For example:

- They aid probation and parole officers in their supervision of offenders.
- They aid correctional personnel in their classification, treatment, and release programs.
- They furnish parole boards with useful information for release decision making.
- They can serve as a data base for systematic research.[52]

Following the submission of the presentence report to the judge, a sentencing hearing is held. In common law, and in most jurisdictions, a convicted offender has the right to address the court personally prior to the imposition of sentence. Known as **allocution,** this practice is available so that the court can identify the defendant as the person judged guilty, the defendant can be given the opportunity to plead a pardon, move for an arrest of judgment, or indicate why judgment ought not be pronounced. The specific matters a defendant might state at the allocution are limited and would not include attempts to reopen the question of guilt. Rather, some of the claims included in allocutions have been that the offender has become insane since the verdict was rendered,* that he or she has received a pardon for the offense in question, that the defendant is not the person against whom there was a finding of guilt, and in the case of a woman, especially if a death sentence is to be pronounced, that the punishment be adjusted or deferred because of a possible pregnancy.[53]

Allocution: The right of a convicted offender to address the court personally prior to the imposition of sentence.

Under Rule 32(a) of the Federal Rules of Criminal Procedure, allocution is required. However, the failure of a federal judge to allow a defendant to address the court under Rule 32(a) is not considered an error of constitutional dimension.[54] Such a denial might result only in a remanding of the case for resentencing. Allocution only rarely produces a deferral of punishment.

---

* Under the system of due process, the law will not punish a person who is unable to understand why he or she is being punished. If such is the case, the sentence must be deferred until understanding and reason have returned.

The presiding judge then imposes the sentence. As noted earlier, the most typical sanctions include fines, imprisonment, probation, or some combination thereof, or death. In instances where the defendant receives multiple sentences for several crimes, the judge may order that terms of imprisonment be served concurrently or consecutively. *Concurrent sentences* are those that are served simultaneously. For example, if the defendant is convicted of both burglary and assault, and is given two terms of five years' imprisonment to be served concurrently, both terms are satisfied after five years. *Consecutive sentences* are successive — one after another.

Concurrent and consecutive sentences

As noted earlier in the discussions of bail and pretrial detention, it often happens that a defendant comes before a judge for sentencing having already spent weeks, months, and sometimes even years in a local jail or detention facility awaiting trial. This period of detention, referred to as *"jail time,"* is generally deducted from the period of imprisonment imposed. When the conviction is for a misdemeanor or minor felony and the period of pretrial detention closely matches the probable term of imprisonment, the judge may impose a sentence of "time served." That is, the accumulated jail time represents the sentence, and the defendant is released. When the jail time spent awaiting trial is not counted as part of the final sentence, it is commonly referred to as "dead time."

"Jail time"

THE DEATH PENALTY IN THE UNITED STATES

Death cases are indeed different in kind from all other litigation. The penalty, once imposed, is irrevocable.

—Justice John Paul Stevens, 1981

For the greater part of U.S. history, the death penalty was used as a punishment for crime, with little thought given to its legitimacy or justification. It was simply accepted as an efficient mechanism for dealing with criminal offenders. When the framers of the Constitution created the *Eighth Amendment ban* against cruel and unusual punishment, the death penalty itself was apparently not an issue. From the earliest days of the colonial experience, capital punishment was considered neither cruel nor unusual. Under the criminal codes of 1642 and 1650 enacted for the New Haven colony, for example, a total of eleven offenses — some of which do not even appear as misdemeanors in contemporary statutes — called for the death sentence:

The Eighth Amendment ban against cruel and unusual punishment

1. If any person within this Government shall by direct, express, impious or presumptuous ways, deny the true God and His attributes, he shall be put to death.
2. If any person shall commit any wilful and premeditated murder he shall be put to death.
3. If any person slayeth another with a sword or dagger who hath no weapon to defend himself; he shall be put to death.
4. If any man shall slay, or cause another to be slain by lying in wait privily for him or by poisoning or any other such wicked conspiracy; he shall be put to death. . . .
5. If any man or woman shall lie with any beast or brute creature by carnal copulation they shall be put to death, and the beast shall be burned.

What's one less person on the face of the earth, anyway?
—Serial murderer Ted Bundy, 1986

The infamous electric chair, also referred to in underworld lingo as the "hot seat," "hot chair," "hot shot," "Old Sparky" (in Florida), "Gruesome Gertie" (in Louisiana), or simply, the "chair"

6. If any man lieth with mankind as he lieth with a woman, they shall be put to death, unless the one party were forced or be under fourteen years of age, in which case he shall be punished at the discretion of the Court of Assizes.
7. If any person forcibly stealeth or carrieth away any mankind; he shall be put to death.
8. If any man bear false witness maliciously and on purpose to take aways a man's life, he shall be put to death.
9. If any man shall traitorously deny his Majesty's right and titles to his Crowns and Dominions, or shall raise armies to resist his authority, he shall be put to death.
10. If any man shall treacherously conspire or publickly attempt to invade or surprise any town or towns, fort or forts, within this Government, he shall be put to death.
11. If any child or children, above sixteen years of age, and of sufficient understanding, shall smite their natural father or mother, unless thereunto provoked and forced for their self-protection from death or maiming, at the complaint of said father and mother, and not otherwise, there being sufficient witnesses thereof, that child or those children so offending shall be put to death.[55]

Within such a context, execution upon conviction of numerous crimes was indeed quite usual. The definition of what was cruel punishment similarly eluded rigid guidelines. Consider, for example, the punishment for treason under the English common law — the very sanction that the leaders of the American Revolution risked by signing the Declaration of Independence:

That you and each of you, be taken to the place from whence you came, and from thence be drawn on a hurdle to the place of execution where you shall be hanged by the neck not till you are dead; that you be severally taken down, while yet alive, and your bowels be taken out and burned before your faces—that your heads be then cut off, and your bodies cut into four quarters, to be at the king's disposal. And God have mercy on your souls.[56]

What the framers likely had in mind, however, were the many more grisly forms of execution that had periodically appeared throughout human history. Down through the ages criminals have been burned at the stake, crucified, boiled in flaming oil, impaled, and flayed, to name only a few. Or, take the case of Mithridates of ancient Persia:

He was encased in a coffin-like box, from which his head, hands, and feet protruded, through holes made for that purpose; he was fed with milk and honey, which he was forced to take, and his face was smeared with the same mixture; he was exposed to the sun, and in this state he remained for seventeen days, until he had been devoured alive by insects and vermin, which swarmed about him and bred within him.[57]

The Death Sentence, 1864–1967

On January 20, 1864, William Barnet and Sandy Kavanagh were executed in the Vermont State Prison for the crime of murder. During the slightly more than 100 years that followed, through 1967, there were a total of 5,707 state-imposed death sentences carried out across the country.[58] Few of these executions (less than 1 percent) occurred prior to 1890, but the number then began to grow rapidly. The imposition of the

A Frontier Judge Imposes Death
Judicial Candor or Racial Discrimination?

Jose Manuel Miguel Xaviar Gonzales, in a few short weeks it will be spring. The snows of winter will flee away. The ice will vanish. And the air will become soft and balmy. In short, Jose Manuel Miguel Xaviar Gonzales, the annual miracle of the years will awaken and come to pass, but you won't be there.

The rivulet will run its soaring course to the sea. The timid desert flowers will put forth their tender shoots. The glorious valleys of this imperial domain will blossom as the rose. Still, you won't be here to see.

From every tree top some wild woods songster will carol his mating song. Butterflies will sport in the sunshine. The busy bee will hum happy as it pursues its accustomed vocation. The gentle breeze will tease the tissels of the wild grasses, and all nature, Jose Manuel Miguel Xaviar Gonzales, will be glad but

you. You won't be here to enjoy it because I command the sheriff or some other officers of the county to lead you out to some remote spot, swing you by the neck from a knotting bough of some sturdy oak, and let you hang until you are dead.

And then, Jose Manuel Miguel Xaviar Gonzales, I further command that such officer or officers retire quickly from your dangling corpse, that vultures may descend from the heavens upon your filthy body until nothing shall remain but bare, bleached bones of a cold-blooded, copper-colored, blood-thirsty, throat-cutting, chili-eating, sheep-herding, murdering son-of-a-bitch.

SOURCE: From the judge's decision in *United States* v. *Gonzales* (1881), United States District Court, New Mexico Territory Sessions.

death penalty reached its peak during the 1930s, with more than 1,500 executions during that decade alone. The numbers then began to decline, from 1,174 during the 1940s to less than 200 by the 1960s.

This extensive use of the death penalty is explained, at least in part, by the number of states with capital statutes in their penal codes and the proportion of offenses that were punishable by death. In 1961, for example, of fifty-four jurisdictions (including the fifty states, the District of Columbia, Puerto Rico, and the federal civil and military authority), forty-eight carried capital statutes; for homicide in forty-seven jurisdictions; for kidnapping in thirty-seven; for treason in twenty-five; for rape in twenty; for carnal knowledge in sixteen; for robbery in ten; for perjury (in a capital case) in nine; for bombing in seven; for assault (by a life-term prisoner) in five; for train robbery, burglary, or arson in four; for train wrecking in three; and for espionage in two.[59] In addition, nineteen jurisdictions carried a variety of special statutes whereby the death sentence could be imposed for such offenses as aiding a suicide and forcing a woman to marry (in Arkansas), performing an abortion and advising abortion to a woman (in Georgia), lynching (in Kentucky), attempt or

Executions Under State Authority, 1860s–1960s

DECADE	NUMBER OF EXECUTIONS	%
1850s–1860s	12	0.2
1870s	18	0.3
1880s	26	0.5
1890s	154	2.7
1900s	275	4.8
1910s	625	11.0
1920s	1,030	18.0
1930s	1,520	26.6
1940s	1,174	20.6
1950s	682	12.0
1960s	191	3.3
Total	5,707	100.0

conspiracy to assault a chief of state (in New Jersey), use of a machine gun in a crime of violence (in Virginia), and child stealing (in Wyoming), to name but a few. In addition, the death penalty was the mandatory sentence for some offenses (typically homicide and treason) in twenty-seven jurisdictions.

Statutes calling for the death penalty varied widely from one jurisdiction to the next. In the District of Columbia, Connecticut, Delaware, Massachusetts, and New Hampshire, for example, capital punishment could be imposed only in the case of murder. In Rhode Island the death penalty was restricted even further to the crime of murder when committed by a prisoner serving a life sentence. In contrast, there were twenty-two capital statutes in the federal criminal codes, and a dozen or more in the states of Alabama and Arkansas.

Capital Punishment and Discrimination

In 1967, the President's Commission on Law Enforcement and Administration of Justice commented that the death penalty "is most frequently imposed and carried out on the poor, the Negro, and the members of unpopular groups."[60] Such an observation was no surprise to those who had watched closely the pattern of the imposition of capital punishment over the years, or to the many blacks, especially in the South, who had been systematically victimized by death sentences for well over a century and a half. In Virginia during the 1830s, for example, there were five capital crimes for whites but at least seventy for blacks.[61] In 1848 the Virginia legislature required the death penalty for any offense committed by a black for which three or more years' imprisonment might be imposed as punishment for a white.[62] Pursuant to the South Carolina Black Codes in 1825, burning at the stake was permitted and even carried out — a punishment that had originally been reserved for executing heretics in medieval Europe.[63] And from 1882 through 1903 at least 1,985 blacks were hanged or burned alive by the Ku Klux Klan and other southern lynch mobs — often when there was no offense at all or the mere suspicion of one. (See Exhibit 13.5.)

Even the most superficial analysis of executions under civil authority reflects a clear overrepresentation of blacks. In 1965, for example, sociologist Marvin E. Wolfgang and law professor Anthony Amsterdam began a study to determine the relationship between ethnicity and sentencing for rape in eleven southern and border states where rape was a capital offense. Their findings supported the notion that blacks were treated with undue severity:

> Among the 823 blacks convicted of rape, 110, or 13 percent, were sentenced to death; among the 442 whites convicted of rape, only 9, or 2 percent, were sentenced to death. *The statistical probability that such a disproportionate number of blacks could be sentenced to death by chance alone is less than one out of a thousand.*[64]

There were 3,859 prisoners executed under civil authority in the United States from 1930 through 1967. When these cases are studied, it becomes even more evident that capital punishment was used as an instrument for racial discrimination. In this period, some 55 percent of those executed for all crimes were either black or members of some other minority group. Of the 455 executed for rape alone, 90 percent were nonwhite.

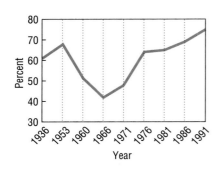

Support for the Death Penalty (for murder) in the United States   *Percent responding "yes."*

SOURCE: The Gallup Poll

Cruel and Unusual Punishment

Historically, the Supreme Court's position on the death penalty has been grounded in the broader issue of "cruel and unusual" punishment as prohibited by the Eighth Amendment. When adopting the Eighth Amendment ban, it is likely that the framers of the Constitution had intended to outlaw punishments that were outside both the mainstream of penalties typically imposed in the new nation and the moral judgments of the people. Thus the purpose of the amendment may have been to prevent any return to the screw and the rack, rather than to outlaw any sanctions then in common use. But this can be viewed only as conjecture, for the High Court itself, for more than a century, offered little as to the nature and scope of the ban.

The basic thrust of the Eighth Amendment is to outlaw punishments which are outside the mainstream of penalties in our country and the moral judgments of the people.
— ROBERT H. BORK, 1976

The notion that punishment *could* be cruel and unusual was argued by at least one of the justices in 1892. The case was *O'Neil* v. *Vermont*,[65] in which the petitioner stood to serve 19,915 days (almost fifty-five years) in jail for 307 separate illegal sales of liquor. The Court found that since the Eighth Amendment did not limit the states, no federal question was involved, and the sentence imposed by the Vermont court was affirmed. However, in a strong dissenting opinion, Justice Stephen J. Field argued that punishment would necessarily be cruel and unusual when it did not fit the crime to which it was attached.

After *O'Neil,* the issue remained dormant for almost two decades until ***Weems* v. *United States*,**[66] decided in 1910. The case was significant for the Eighth Amendment ban, for in its ruling the Court struck down a sentence involving a heavy fine, fifteen years at hard labor, the wearing of chains, the lifelong loss of certain rights, plus several other sanctions — all for the offense of making false entries in official records. The High Court had found the sentence disproportionate to the offense, and as such, *Weems* was the first case decided on Eighth Amendment grounds.

Weems* v. *United States: The Supreme Court ruling that a sentence disproportionate to the offense is in violation of the Eighth Amendment ban against cruel and unusual punishment.

By 1958, the Court had agreed that the constitutional prohibition could have no fixed and unchanging meaning. Rather, any challenges brought to the Court must necessarily be viewed in terms of "evolving standards of decency":

> The exact scope of the constitutional phrase "cruel and unusual" has not been detailed by this Court. . . . The basic concept underlying the Eighth Amendment is nothing less than the dignity of man. While the State has the power to punish, the Amendment stands to assure that this power be exercised within the limits of civilized standards. Fines, imprisonment and even execution may be imposed depending upon the enormity of the crime, but any technique outside the bounds of these traditional penalties is constitutionally suspect. . . . The Court [has] recognized . . . that the words of the Amendment are not precise, but that their scope is not static. The Amendment must draw its meaning from the evolving standards of decency that mark the progress of a maturing society.[67]

Death and the Supreme Court

On the issue of capital punishment per se, the Supreme Court's interpretation of the Eighth Amendment has remained flexible. As to the method of execution, the Court offered some preliminary guidelines more than a century ago. In *Wilkerson* v. *Utah*,[68] decided in 1878, the justices agreed that public shooting was neither cruel nor unusual. At the

• EXHIBIT 13.5 •

Squire Birch, Judge Lynch, and the American "Necktie Party"

In both history and folklore, "lynch law" was primarily an American custom. It was the practice of summary judgment and punishment for real or alleged crimes without due process of law, and it seems to have begun in the South Carolina back country about a decade before the Revolutionary War.

Well into the nineteenth century, lynch law generally meant the infliction of corporal punishment. In its most common form, the accused received thirty-nine lashes with a birch rod, a whip, a hickory withe, or any readily available instrument. The man who laid on the lash became known as Squire Birch, and his tribunal was established under a tree in an open meadow or nearby woods. By the middle of the nineteenth century, lynch law had come to be synonymous with killing, usually by hanging, as a frontier approach to law and order.

The origins of the infamous Judge Lynch have been obscured to some degree by legend-makers, for a journey through American history and folklore points to several conflicting fables. The court of Judge Lynch is reputed to have derived its name from James Lynch Fitz-Stephen, a sixteenth-century Irishman who, while engaged as the warden of Galway Jail, was alleged to have hanged his own son for murder. It has also been attributed to a Virginia farmer named Joseph Lynch, who was reported to have executed numerous blacks with reckless abandon during the 1780s.

From the adventures of the infamous "Judge Lynch": A group of masked horsemen ride away from a hanging body.

Upon closer analysis, however, history has documented that there was indeed a *Judge* Lynch and an act of the Virginia legislature known as *Lynch's Law*. The real Judge Lynch, who was to give his name to a form of jurisprudence that he never practiced and would never have tolerated, was the confirmed Quaker Charles Lynch, born in Bedford County, Virginia, in 1736 where the city of Lynchburg now stands.

During the Revolutionary War, he was a Colonel in the Virginia Militia at a time when the war effort had created a desperate need for horses on both sides of the conflict. The prices being paid for the animals were so high that gangs of rustlers sought to cash in on the lucrative trade. Most of the thieves were Tories (Americans who upheld the cause of the British Crown), and Colonel Lynch sought to restore order and security in the Virginia community.

As a temporary war-time measure, the locals appointed Lynch as a presiding justice, along with three of his neighbors — Captain Robert Adams, Colonel James Callaway, and William Preston — to serve as associate justices. Lynch's home became the local courthouse to which the accused were brought.

Colonel Lynch's court reflected some manner of due process. The accused was permitted to testify, and he could summon witnesses on his own behalf. If found innocent, he was released, with apologies, and with his right to sue for false arrest intact. If judged guilty, he was given thirty-nine lashes and strung up by the thumbs until he shouted "liberty forever." The method was effective and gave rise to the once patriotic song:

Hurrah for Colonel Lynch,
Captain Bob and Callaway!
They never turned a Tory loose,
Until he cried out "Liberty."

After the war, Tories who had suffered at the hands of Lynch threatened to prosecute him. He laid the matter before the Virginia legislature, which in 1782 passed an act that indemnified the actions of Colonel Lynch and his associates.

That was the *real* Judge Lynch. In the years that followed, however, the *legendary* Judge Lynch emerged as a sordid American saga. He took over the bench filled by Squire Birch, placing the law in his own hands

with promptness and certitude. He gave birth to lynch mob violence, and it is estimated that through January 1938, "lynch law" took the lives of no less than 5,000 victims.

Lynching was practiced most predominantly in the South, with blacks the primary targets. From 1882 through 1903, more than 2,000 blacks were either hanged or burned alive — in many instances where there was neither an offense or even the suspicion of one. In the West, the ephemeral "necktie party" was often gathered for the summary disposal of murderers, robbers, horse thieves, rustlers, and sometimes sheep herders and squatters.

Lynch law executions had reached their peak during the early 1890s, with a peak of 235 victims in 1892. With the onset of the twentieth century, lynching declined rapidly, but it persisted to some extent in the South and was still directed against blacks. During the 1930s, the number of known executions averaged as few as fifteen per year, but almost 90 percent of these victimized were Southern blacks.

Currently, lynch law is not unknown, although the executions that do take place rarely reflect the organization and flamboyance of years past. A case in point was the recent vigilante slaying of Kenneth McElroy in Skidmore, Missouri. McElroy was the town bully, and most of Skidmore's 440 residents lived in daily fear of him. Although his activities in-

Kenneth R. McElroy, shot to death in a vigilante-style slaying

cluded rape, arson, theft, and killing, he managed to stay on the streets through either bail or the intimidation of witnesses or victims. However, in July 1981, while free on bond pending an appeal of a homicide conviction, Skidmore put an end to McElroy's reign of terror. As sixty townspeople looked on, someone aimed a high-powered rifle into his pickup truck and pumped at least three bullets into his chest, killing him almost instantly. Curiously, other than McElroy's wife, no eyewitnesses reported seeing the shooting, and the local coroner's jury placed the responsibility on "person or persons unknown."

SOURCES: James Elbert Cutler, *Lynch-Law* (New York: Longmans, 1905); Frank Shay, *Judge Lynch: His First Hundred Years* (New York: David McKay, 1938); Hugh Davis Graham and Ted Robert Gurr (eds.), *Violence in America* (Beverly Hills, Calif.: Sage, 1979); *Newsweek*, August 3, 1981, p. 33.

In re Kemmler

The first execution by electrocution took place at Auburn Prison, Auburn, New York, on August 6, 1890. The prisoner, William Kemmler, was executed for murder.

Witherspoon v. Illinois: The Supreme Court ruling that states cannot exclude from juries in capital cases *all* persons opposed to the death penalty.

McGautha v. *California*

same time, however, it was noted that the constitutional amendment would oppose such punishments as drawing and quartering, burning alive, and other punishments of torturous death. *In re Kemmler,*[69] decided in 1890, held that death by electrocution reflected humane legal intentions, and hence did not offend the Eighth Amendment.

Subsequent to *Kemmler,* the Court remained essentially silent on the constitutionality of capital punishment for almost eight decades. In *Trop* v. *Dulles,*[70] decided in 1958, a plurality of four justices held that expatriation was a cruel and unusual punishment, but noted that this holding did not necessarily apply to the death penalty.

Meanwhile, throughout the 1950s and well into the 1960s, the NAACP Legal Defense and Education Fund combined its efforts with those of the American Civil Liberties Union (ACLU) to wage an all-out legal attack against capital punishment. The two organizations came to the aid of many prisoners who had been sentenced to death. Briefs were prepared, appeals were filed, and data on the disproportionate use of the death penalty for black offenders were collected. And the courts reflected an increasing willingness to review capital cases and to reverse lower court decisions, with the result that many state authorities became reluctant to schedule and perform executions.

In 1963, Justice Arthur J. Goldberg suggested that capital punishment may be a *per se* violation of the Eighth Amendment. Although he was not speaking for the majority of the Court at the time, his statement, combined with mounting pressure for a decision on the constitutionality of the death penalty, served to further NAACP–ACLU effort. The penalty was ultimately challenged on a variety of legal grounds, and on June 3, 1967, the impending execution of more than 500 condemned prisoners throughout the country came to a halt, while courts and governors waited to see what the High Court would decide.

Witherspoon v. Illinois

The first of these challenges reached the Supreme Court in *Witherspoon* v. *Illinois,*[71] and the decision in 1968 was the first indication that the death penalty might be in trouble. In *Witherspoon,* an Illinois court had permitted a verdict of guilty and a sentence of death to be handed down by a jury from which the state had deliberately and systematically excluded all persons who had any scruples against capital punishment. The Court sustained Witherspoon's challenge, ruling that the "death-qualified jury" was indeed unconstitutional. Coming at almost the same time was the High Court's decision in *United States* v. *Jackson,*[72] which invalidated the death penalty provisions of the Federal Kidnapping Act (better known as the Lindbergh Law).

McGautha v. California

Witherspoon had not been a total victory for those opposed to capital punishment. They remained firmly optimistic, however, and the moratorium on executions continued as other challenges were prepared for Supreme Court review. The abolition movement eagerly awaited the ruling in *McGautha* v. *California,*[73] a case that argued that leaving the choice between life imprisonment or death to the total discretion of a jury was a violation of the due-process clause of the Fourteenth Amendment. Decided in 1971, the Court held in *McGautha:*

In light of history, experience, and the present limitations of human knowledge, we find it quite impossible to say that committing to the untrammeled discretion of the jury the power to pronounce life or death in capital cases is offensive to anything in the Constitution.

McGautha seemed to be a fatal blow to the movement dedicated to the abolition of capital punishment, and it was widely viewed as the Supreme Court's final word on the death penalty. Furthermore, with no new cases pending before the Court on the issue, and with the right of juries to discretionarily impose the death sentence firmly guaranteed, it appeared unlikely that any Eighth Amendment argument could prevail. However, as the states began preparations for executing the more than 600 prisoners that had accumulated on death row, the Court suddenly announced that it would hear a group of cases involving the Eighth Amendment ban on cruel and unusual punishment.

Furman v. Georgia

In the fall of 1971, *Furman* v. *Georgia, Jackson* v. *Georgia,* and *Branch* v. *Texas* were brought before the High Court on the challenge that the death sentences ordered were "cruel and unusual" because of the arbitrary and discriminatory manner in which such sanctions had been imposed in the past for the crimes of murder and rape. The leading case was *Furman* v. *Georgia,*[74] which involved the death sentence following William Furman's conviction for a murder that had occurred during the course of a burglary attempt. The decision as to whether Furman's sentence should be life or death had been left to the jury, and his conviction and sentence had been affirmed by all of the Georgia courts.

The Supreme Court's *Furman* decision on June 29, 1972, was a most complex one. It was announced in a nine-opinion *per curium* (unsigned) opinion that summarized the narrow argument of the five justices in the majority. In addition, each of the nine justices issued a separate concurring or dissenting opinion. Only Justices Brennan and Marshall were willing to hold that capital punishment was unconstitutional per se. Justices Douglas, Stewart, and White adopted a more narrow view, arguing that the state statutes in question were unconstitutional because they offered judges and juries no standards or guidelines to consider in deciding between life and death. As Justice Stewart put it, the result was that the punishment of death was tantamount to being "struck by lightning." In other words, all state and federal death penalty statutes were deemed too arbitrary, capricious, and discriminatory to withstand Eighth Amendment scrutiny. The position taken by Justice Douglas, Stewart, and White represented the common ground of agreement with Justices Brennan and Marshall, thus constituting the five-justice majority.

The four dissenting justices were Burger, Blackmun, Powell, and Rehnquist—all appointed to the High Court by President Richard Nixon. All four dissenting opinions emphasized the view that in a democracy, issues such as capital punishment should be decided by the legislative branch of government—the people's representatives—and not by the courts. Chief Justice Burger also accused the justices in the majority of "overruling *McGautha* in the guise of an Eighth Amendment adjudication." He also asked rhetorically whether those in the majority would be willing to sanction mandatory death penalty laws on

The death penalty is the final resort to truly evil crime.
—Texas prison guard, 1981

Furman v. Georgia: The Supreme Court ruling that statutes which leave arbitrary and discriminatory discretion to juries in imposing death sentences are in violation of the Eighth Amendment.

Whatever can be said about the death penalty, it cannot be said that it causes otherwise unavoidable death.
—Ernest van den Haag, 1983

● EXHIBIT 13.6 ●

If at First You Don't Succeed . . .
The Strange Case of Willie Francis

A small note in contemporary American folklore suggests that if the state bungles its attempt to electrocute a convicted killer, it can't try again and the prisoner gets to go free. True or false? For the answer, check out the case of Willie Francis.

The story began in November 1944 with the killing of Andrew Thomas, a pharmacist from St. Martinsville, Louisiana. Thomas was shot five times, and when his body was found by the police, a watch and a wallet containing $4 were missing.

While the quest for Thomas's killer was under way in Louisiana, an unrelated search was in progress some 200 miles southwest, in Port Arthur, Texas. The Texas case involved narcotics, and during the course of the investigation a fifteen-year-old black youth named Willie Francis was arrested — mistakenly thought to be the accomplice of a suspected drug dealer.

During interrogation by Port Arthur police, Francis admitted to the murder of Andrew Thomas. Francis was then turned over to Louisiana author-

ities and tried for murder. Although there were no witnesses to the crime and the murder weapon was lost, the prosecution's case was strong. Francis had confessed twice, and a dozen witnesses testified that his confessions had been voluntary. And Francis's case was weak. His two court-appointed attorneys called no witnesses in his behalf.

The trial lasted only three days, and the jury found the defendant guilty of murder. No transcript of the trial had been taken, no request for a change of venue had been made, no motion for a new trial had been entered, and no appeal had been filed. On the very next day Francis was sentenced to death, with his electrocution set for several months from then.

On May 3, 1946, Francis, now age seventeen, was strapped into the electric chair that had been trucked to St. Martinsville the previous night. Captain E. Foster of the Louisiana State Penitentiary, formally in charge of the execution, checked his dials, bid Francis goodbye, and threw the switch.

For a fraction of a second nothing happened. Then Francis jumped; he strained against the straps, and then groaned. But he didn't die! Frantically, Foster threw the switch again and again. For two minutes the procedure was repeated before a panel of horrified spectators.

The electrodes were then removed from Francis's body, and everyone in the jailhouse breathed a sigh of relief. He managed to get to his feet, and later said that he had felt only a small current of electricity.

Whatever miracle had saved Willie Francis from death caught the public's imagination. The story made headlines across the country, and the governor of Louisiana was engulfed with letters imploring him not to send the youth through the experience again.

Francis appealed to the United States Supreme Court, asking them to forbid the state a second execution attempt because it would constitute "cruel and unusual punishment" in violation of the Eighth Amendment.

the grounds that such laws would eliminate the harmful effects of excessive jury discretion. Although the chief justice may have scored some debating points, the effect of *Furman* was nevertheless to invalidate every death penalty statute in the United States.

Where the Court had rejected a Fourteenth Amendment due process challenge to jury imposition of the death sentence in *McGautha,* it upheld an Eighth Amendment argument in *Furman.* What represented a majority opinion in *Furman* was neither a statement against capital punishment nor an argument against a jury's authority to decide upon the death sentence. Rather, it was an attack on state statutes that allowed a jury to find an accused guilty and then, in the absence of any guidance or direction, decide on whether that person should live or die.

Speaking for the majority opinion, Justice Stanley F. Reed commented:

> The fact that petitioner has already been subjected to a current of electricity does not make his subsequent execution any more cruel in the constitutional sense than any other execution. The cruelty against which the Constitution protects a convicted man is cruelty inherent in the method of punishment, not the necessary suffering involved in any method employed to extinguish life humanely. The fact that an unforeseeable accident prevented the prompt consummation of the sentence cannot, it seems to us, add an element of cruelty to a subsequent execution.

On May 9, 1946, Willie Francis was again strapped into the electric chair. The switch was thrown, and on this occasion his coffin could be used, and the crowd was not disappointed.

Willie Francis

SOURCES: *Louisana ex. rel. Francis v. Resweber,* 329 U.S. 459 (1947); Barrett Prettyman, *Death and the Supreme Court* (New York: Harcourt, Brace & World, 1961).

Gregg v. Georgia

By effectively invalidating all existing state death penalty statutes, *Furman* also served to remove over 600 persons from death row. But the Court's decision in *Furman* did provide two avenues by which states could enact new capital punishment laws. First, they could establish a two-stage procedure: a trial at which the question of culpability could be determined, followed by an additional proceeding for those found guilty, during which evidence might be presented to make the decision for death or life more informed and procedurally sound. Second, states could remove the discretion from the jury by making death the mandatory punishment for certain crimes.

Have you noticed that right-to-life people are in favor of capital punishment?

—GORE VIDAL, 1979

Gregg v. Georgia: The Supreme Court ruling that (1) the death penalty is not, in itself, cruel and unusual punishment; and (2) a two-part proceeding—one for the determination of innocence or guilt and the other for determining the sentence—is constitutional and meets the objections noted in *Furman* v. *Georgia.*

The death penalty is a fact of life, if that isn't an oxymoron.
—Gara LaMarche of the ACLU, 1986

Woodson v. North Carolina

In the wake of *Furman,* thirty-five states passed new capital statutes. Ten chose the mandatory route while twenty-five selected the two-stage procedure. By 1976, both approaches were brought before the Supreme Court, and the constitutionality of the death penalty was again argued.

The issue in *Gregg* v. *Georgia*[75] was Georgia's new bifurcated trial structure: following a conviction of guilt in first-degree murder cases, the nature of punishment was decided in a separate proceeding. The Georgia statute required the judge or jury to consider any aggravating or mitigating circumstances in the life-or-death decision, including the following conditions:

- The defendant had a prior conviction for a capital felony or a substantial history of serious assaultive criminal convictions.
- The murder was committed during the course of a rape, an armed robbery, a kidnapping, a burglary, or arson.
- The defendant created a grave risk of death to more than one person.
- The defendant killed for profit.
- The victim was a judicial officer or a prosecutor killed during or because of his exercise of official duty.
- The victim was a police officer, corrections employee, or fireman who was engaged in the performance of his duties.
- The defendant directed another person to kill as his agent.
- The murder was committed in a wantonly vile, horrible, or inhumane manner because it involved torture, depravity of mind, or an aggravated battery.
- The defendant was a prison escapee.
- The murder was committed in an attempt to avoid arrest.[76]

By a 7-to-2 majority, the decision in *Gregg* upheld the Georgia law, reasoning that

the new Georgia sentencing procedures, by contrast, focus the jury's attention on the particularized nature of the crime and the particularized nature of the individual defendant. While the jury is permitted to consider any aggravating or mitigating circumstances, it must find and identify at least one statutory aggravating factor before it may impose a penalty of death. In this way is the jury's discretion channeled. No longer can a jury wantonly and freakishly impose the death sentence; it is always circumscribed by the legislative guidelines.

In two companion cases the Court also upheld similar procedures adopted by Florida and Texas (and presumably twenty-two additional states), thus declaring capital punishment laws constitutional as long as they provided judges and juries with clear and fair criteria when deciding whether to sentence an offender to death.[77] However, in *Woodson* v. *North Carolina,*[78] decided on the same day, the Court struck down state laws that made death the mandatory penalty for first-degree murder. The Court's position was that mandatory death penalty statutes "simply papered over the problem of unguided and unchecked jury discretion" and failed to allow for differences in individual defendants and crimes.

Post-*Gregg* Developments

During the years following the decision in *Gregg,* the Supreme Court continued in its refusal to hold categorically that the death penalty per se constituted cruel and unusual punishment. However, in a series of rulings from 1977 through 1980, the Court did place limitations on the imposition of capital sentences. In **Coker v. Georgia,**[79] decided in 1977, it was held that the death sentence could not be imposed for rape, because such punishment was grossly disproportionate to the injury caused the victim. And without expressly stating so, the Court strongly implied in *Coker* that a death sentence was inappropriate except as punishment for murder. In a series of Ohio cases, decided in 1978, the Court ruled against a state statute that required jury consideration of aggravating circumstances, but not mitigating circumstances, in the imposition of capital sentences.[80]

Coker v. Georgia: The Supreme Court ruling that the sentence of death for the crime of rape is an excessive and disproportionate penalty forbidden by the Eighth Amendment.

In *Godfrey* v. *Georgia,*[81] decided in 1980, the High Court continued to clarify its holding in *Gregg.* In *Godfrey,* the petitioner had murdered his wife and mother-in-law in the presence of his daughter. The killings had occurred as the result of "heated arguments" that Godfrey felt had been induced by his mother-in-law, and stemmed from a host of marital differences of opinion. Immediately after the homicides, Godfrey telephoned the local sheriff, confessed to the crimes, led authorities to the slain bodies, and stated that the scene was "hideous." Godfrey was convicted, and pursuant to the revised Georgia law as tested in *Gregg,* both murders were found to be accompanied by one of the "aggravating circumstances": the killings were committed in a "wantonly vile, horrible, or inhumane" manner because they involved "depravity of mind." Thus, the jury imposed a death sentence.

Godfrey v. *Georgia*

Upon Court review, Godfrey's death sentence was vacated on grounds that the jurors were given too much discretion under the state's statutory guidelines for capital cases. A plurality of justices maintained, specifically, that Georgia statute had been interpreted too broadly, that the "depravity of mind" clause was a "catch all" phrase for cases that did not fit other statutory circumstances. Finally, although Justices Marshall and Brennan concurred with the ruling, they reiterated their minority view that the death penalty was unconstitutional under all circumstances and remarked that *Gregg* was doomed to failure.

The Return of Capital Punishment

On June 2, 1967, Luis José Monge was put to death in Colorado for the crime of murder. He was the last person to be executed in the United States prior to the suspension of capital punishment later that year, and for a full decade capital punishment ceased to exist throughout the United States. With the decision of *Gregg,* however, made on the eve of the nation's two-hundredth birthday, the Supreme Court upheld the constitutionality of capital punishment. By 1977, more than 400 persons were on death row, with the first execution occurring during the early weeks of that year.

The prisoner was Gary Mark Gilmore, a convicted murderer who had been sentenced to death by a Utah court. The Gilmore case attracted national headlines, not only because it was the first probable execution in a decade, but also because of the many bizarre events associated with it. The initial sensation came late in 1976 when Gilmore fired his attorneys, abandoned his appeal, and requested that his execution be carried out at the earliest possible date. He even appeared before the justices of the U.S. Supreme Court to argue that he had a "right to die."

Attorneys then petitioned the Utah courts, indicating that Gilmore was insane, that he was incapable of representing himself, and that his

Gary Gilmore

If they are serious about using the death penalty as a deterrent, they should let the people see it. Televise it on the networks.

— James Autry, executed in Texas in 1984

The gallows at Washington State Penitentiary, Walla Walla. The noose into which the prisoner's head is placed hangs over a trap door. The prisoner is strapped to the board at left, and then the trap door is sprung.

It is sweet to dance to violins
  When love and life are fair;
To dance to flutes, to dance to lutes
  Is delicate and rare;
But it is not so sweet with nimble feet
  To dance upon the air.

— Oscar Wilde

"death wish" was "tantamount to suicide." But the state court rejected this argument, and all pending appeals were dismissed. Gilmore's mother then petitioned the U.S. Supreme Court, maintaining that her son was incompetent to waive his right to appeal. The stay of execution she requested was denied, however, on the basis that she had no legal standing to seek relief for her son.

The case of Gary Mark Gilmore then began to take on a tragically comic air. On the morning of November 16, 1976, Gilmore attempted suicide by taking an overdose of sedatives. At almost the same moment, some forty miles south of the prison in a small apartment just outside Provo, Utah, twenty-year-old Nicole Barrett also took an overdose of drugs. The "suicide pact" had been arranged as part of a pathetic love affair that Gilmore had been carrying on with the young mother of two. But Gilmore survived the ordeal, as did Ms. Barrett.

Counsel was then appointed to help Gilmore secure an execution date. It was later revealed that this attorney had a financial interest in Gilmore's death, having secured the exclusive right to act as the condemned man's biographer and agent; a six-figure contract had been negotiated for publication and motion picture rights to the story of Gilmore's life and death. GARY GILMORE T-shirts also appeared, and the media "bidding wars" began for exclusive interviews and stories.

Independent legal groups challenged the courts with collateral legal suits, but angered over the new delays, Gilmore staged yet another unsuccessful suicide attempt. The Supreme Court elected not to intervene in any further litigation, and an execution date was finally set. As the day approached, the media and pro- and anti-death groups began a death watch outside the walls of the prison. During his final hours, Gilmore refused any interviews. There was another stay of execution, but it lasted only a few short hours. Gilmore was scheduled to die before a firing squad, and while he was being led to the execution chamber, mobile television crews attempted to position themselves to record the gunshots signaling Gilmore's demise. When asked by Warden Samuel W. Smith if he had any last words, Gilmore offered nothing philosophical or dramatic — simply, "Let's do it!" Finally, just after dawn on January 17, 1977, Gilmore was strapped to a wooden chair in a cold and shadowy prison warehouse. At 8:07 A.M., a signal was given to marksmen hidden behind a cubicle thirty feet from the prisoner. Four .30-caliber bullets ripped through his chest, and Gary Mark Gilmore became the first person to be executed in an American prison in almost a decade.[82]

Methods of Execution

In a series of decisions spanning the period 1878 through 1953, the Supreme Court has upheld as constitutional such methods of execution as hanging, shooting, electrocution, and the use of lethal gas.

As of 1992, thirty-six states had a death penalty in force (see Exhibit 13.7). A number of states allowed for more than one mode of execution, including lethal gas. While electrocution is generally instantaneous, the use of cyanide gas is considered by many to be more humane. The well-known "gas chamber," however, also seems to be a grim process. An eyewitness described the execution of Luis José Monge in 1967:

According to the official execution log unconsciousness came more than five minutes after the cyanide splashed down into the sulphuric acid. Even after unconsciousness is declared officially, the prisoner's body continues to fight for life. He coughs and groans. The lips make little pouting motions resembling the motions made by a goldfish in a bowl. The head strains back and then slowly sinks down to the chest. And in Monge's case, the arms, though tightly bound to the chair, strained through the straps and the hands clawed torturously as if the prisoner were struggling for air.[83]

In four states — Delaware, Montana, New Hampshire, and Washington — the official methods of execution include hanging. In Delaware, many a defense attorney has vividly described execution via the hangman's noose in an attempt to sway jurors away from imposing a death sentence. This was most effectively done in the case of Mark McKinney, convicted of a 1980 homicide:

He will walk thirteen steps to the gallows. He will stand, and a hood, black in color, will be placed over his head. A noose with thirteen knots will be dropped over his shoulders and pulled around his neck. There will be an executioner, whom we do not know, who will stand removed, and Mark will stand over a trap door. The executioner will push a button which will cause the trap door to spring open, and Mark will drop between four to six feet. The rope will constrict around his neck, causing him to die.[84]

For inmates sentenced to death under federal statutes, the method of execution is governed by the law of the state in which the punishment is to be carried out.

"The Ultimate High" Among the most virulent arguments regarding the nature of execution emerged in 1977 when a number of states enacted statutes that put to rest their electric chairs, gas chambers, and gallows. In their place was death by lethal injection, referred to by many death row inmates as "the ultimate high."

Proponents of the new process argued that it would be a more palatable way of killing — it would be instantaneous, and the prisoner would simply fall asleep.[85] Opponents denied its humanity, arguing that sticking a needle into a vein can be tricky, with the prospect of repeated attempts upon a struggling prisoner posing "a substantial threat to tortuous pain."[86] The American Medical Association also took a stand on the matter, instructing its members not to take part in such executions, arguing that the role of the physician was to protect lives, not take them.[87]

Despite the arguments, the new method of execution went forward. On December 7, 1982, Charles Brooks, Jr., was put to death in Huntsville, Texas, becoming the first person to die by a state-sanctioned lethal injection. First a catheter was placed into the vein of his left arm through which a saline solution flowed — a sterile salt water used routinely as a medium for drug injections. Brooks was then given doses of barbiturates and potassium chloride, which paralyzed him, stopped his breathing, and guaranteed his death.[88] Ironically, on Brooks's arm above the catheter through which the deadly concoction flowed was a tattoo that read, "I was born to die."

By the middle of the 1980s, the debate over the humanity of lethal injections quelled, while others argued against the brutal nature of electrocution (see Exhibit 13.8). By the beginning of the 1990s, however, injection had become the primary mechanism, followed immediately by electrocution.

A hangman is an officer of the law charged with duties of the highest dignity and utmost gravity, and held in hereditary disesteem by a populace having a criminal ancestry. In some of the American States his functions are now performed by an electrician, as in New Jersey, where executions by electricity have recently been ordered.
— AMBROSE BIERCE, *THE DEVIL'S DICTIONARY*, 1911

Hanging someone wasn't really something in our knowledge base.
— VELTRY JOHNSON OF THE WASHINGTON STATE CORRECTIONS DEPARTMENT IN 1989, ON TRYING TO FIND A COMPETENT HANGMAN IN A STATE WHERE NO ONE HAD BEEN EXECUTED IN ALMOST THREE DECADES

The switch for Georgia's electric chair

• EXHIBIT 13.7 •

Inmates on Death Row, Total Executed since 1976, and Methods of Execution

State	Number of Inmates	Number Executed	Method
Alabama	112	8	Electrocution
Alaska	No death penalty		
Arizona	101	0	Gas
Arkansas	35	2	Injection, electrocution
California	308	0	Gas
Colorado	3	0	Injection
Connecticut	4	0	Electrocution
Delaware	7	0	Hanging, injection
District of Columbia	No death penalty		
Florida	314	27	Electrocution
Georgia	111	15	Electrocution
Hawaii	No death penalty		
Idaho	21	0	Injection, firing squad
Illinois	141	1	Injection
Indiana	53	2	Electrocution
Iowa	No death penalty		
Kansas	No death penalty		
Kentucky	28	0	Electrocution
Louisiana	37	20	Electrocution
Maine	No death penalty		
Maryland	15	0	Gas
Massachusetts	No death penalty		
Michigan	No death penalty		
Minnesota	No death penalty		
Mississippi	51	4	Gas
Missouri	78	6	Injection
Montana	6	0	Injection, hanging

The Death Penalty Debate

The arguments for or against capital punishment historically have revolved around the issues of economics, retribution, public opinion, community protection, deterrence, irreversibility, discrimination, pro-

State	Number of Inmates	Number Executed	Method
Nebraska	12	0	Electrocution
Nevada	61	5	Injection
New Hampshire	0	0	Hanging
New Jersey	11	0	Injection
New Mexico	1	0	Injection
New York	No death penalty		
North Carolina	102	4	Gas, injection
North Dakota	No death penalty		
Ohio	102	0	Electrocution
Oklahoma	125	1	Injection
Oregon	17	0	Injection
Pennsylvania	140	0	Injection
Rhode Island	No death penalty		
South Carolina	44	4	Electrocution
South Dakota	0	0	Injection
Tennessee	95	0	Electrocution
Texas	345	42	Injection
Utah	12	3	Firing squad, injection
Vermont	No death penalty		
Virginia	47	13	Electrocution
Washington	11	0	Hanging, injection
West Virginia	No death penalty		
Wisconsin	No death penalty		
Wyoming	2	0	Injection
Federal jurisdictions	7		Injection
Total	2,559	157	

Note: Number of inmates on death row as of January 1, 1992.

SOURCE: Bureau of Justice Statistics; NAACP Legal Defense and Educational Fund, Inc.

tection of the criminal justice system, brutalization, and cruel and unusual punishment.

The *economic argument* for capital punishment holds that execution is far less expensive than maintaining a prisoner behind bars for the remainder of his or her natural life. Death sentences are invariably

If there were a death penalty, more people would be alive.

—NANCY REAGAN, 1982

● EXHIBIT 13.8 ●

"Enough Electrical Energy to Light 800 Lights in the Average Home"

The condemned prisoner undergoing electrocution at Sing Sing Prison is given one shock of . . . alternating current at an average starting potential of approximately 2,000 volts. This voltage is immediately reduced at the end of three seconds to the neighborhood of 500 volts where it is held for an additional period of 57 seconds. . . .

The initial force sends a starting current of eight to ten amperes through the human body, which causes instantaneous death and unconsciousness by its paralysis and destruction to the brain. The current is then cut down under the lower voltages to from three to four amperes in order to avoid burning the body and at the same time to hold paralysis of the heart, respiratory organs, and brain at

a standstill for the remaining period of execution. This insures complete destruction of all life.

As the switch is thrown into its socket there is a sputtering drone, and the body leaps as if to break the strong leather straps that hold it. Sometimes a thin gray wisp of smoke pushes itself out from under the helmet that holds the head electrode, followed by the faint odor of burning flesh. The hands turn red, then white, and the cords of the neck stand out like steel bands. . . .

If temperatures are taken during and immediately after an application of electricity it will be found that the electrodes making the contact may reach a temperature high enough to melt copper . . . and that the average body temperature will be in

the neighborhood of 140 degrees . . . and that the temperature of the brain itself approaches the boiling point of water. . . .

Although it would be absolutely impossible to revive any person after electrocution in Sing Sing's death chair, an autopsy is immediately performed as provided by law. Thus justice grinds out its grist; the hand of the law drops a living man or woman into the death-house hopper, where the chair and the surgeons' knives and saws convert it into the finished product —a grisly corpse.

SOURCE: Lewis E. Lawes, *Life and Death in Sing Sing* (Garden City, N.Y.: Garden City, 1928), pp. 170–171, 188–190.

Capital punishment is our society's recognition of the sanctity of human life.
— UTAH SENATOR ORRIN HATCH, 1988

We are all sentenced to death—it is part of our life sentence. . . . But execution is probably less painful than most natural ways of dying.
— ERNEST VAN DEN HAAG, 1983

appealed, and these too can be costly. One estimate of California's expense in the case of Caryl Chessman, who was eventually executed, totaled more than half a million dollars.[89] For Gary Gilmore, the seventy-eight days preceding his death cost the state of Utah, in addition to food, clothing, and supervision, at least $98,568—over $60,000 to keep him alive during his suicide attempts and another $18,330 for convalescent care, $19,000 in overtime payments for secretaries and deputies on execution day, $513 for a charter flight to Denver where a last-minute stay of execution was overturned, and $725 to pay for the six-man firing squad.[90] And not only was *Gilmore* a case in which the death penalty was imposed, but one in which the condemned argued for his "right to die." Moreover, every available quantitative study of this argument demonstrates that because of all of the additional appeals and other procedural safeguards that are constitutionally required in capital cases, the death penalty costs taxpayers substantially more than life imprisonment.[91]

The *retribution argument* asserts that the kidnapper, murderer, and the rapist, as vile and despicable human beings, deserve to die. This is simply a matter of individual opinion, and differences in philosophy appear even within the Supreme Court. In *Furman,* Justice Thurgood

Marshall spoke against this position. At the same time, however, the Court stated that while retribution was no longer a dominant objective, "neither is it a forbidden objective nor one inconsistent with our respect for the dignity of men."

Public opinion has been a motivating factor in the recent reenactment of death penalty statutes. When the California Supreme Court declared the state's death penalty law unconstitutional in February 1972, letters and telegrams opposing the decision poured into the legislature and governor's office. In a referendum held later that year, five months after *Furman,* California voters overwhelmingly approved an amendment to the state constitution that made capital punishment mandatory for selected crimes.[92] In the years hence, throughout the United States, every poll conducted on the matter found the vast majority of Americans to favor the death penalty for murder.[93]

The *community protection argument* made by supporters of the death penalty maintains that such a "final solution" is necessary to keep the murderer from further ravaging society. Counter to this position is the claim that life imprisonment could achieve the same goal. Yet, as has been pointed out by the President's Commission on Law Enforcement and the Administration of Justice and others, paroled murderers have lower rates of recidivism than other classes of offenders.[94]

Related to this is the *deterrence argument,* held by retentionists, that capital punishment not only prevents the offender from committing additional crimes, but deters others as well. With respect to deterrence in general, the work of Franklin E. Zimring and Gordon J. Hawkins demonstrated that punishment is an effective deterrent for those who are not predisposed to commit crimes, but a questionable deterrent for those who are criminally inclined.[95] A number of studies have also been done on the deterrent effects of capital punishment. One research strategy for such studies has been to compare the homicide rates in states that have death penalty provisions with states that do not. Another has been to examine murder rates in given areas both before and after an execution. And still a third approach has been to analyze crime rates in general as well as murder rates in particular in jurisdictions before and after the abolition of capital punishment. Regardless of the nature and logic of the inquiry applied, the studies have consistently produced no evidence that the death penalty deters homicide.[96]

The *irreversibility argument* put forth by those opposed to the death penalty contends that there is always the possibility that an innocent person might be put to death. Retentionists maintain that although such a risk might exist, there are not documented cases of such an occurrence in recent years. But as Roy Calvert, the leading figure in the English abolition movement during the 1930s, has noted, "The fact that few errors of justice come to light in connection with capital offenses should not lead us to suppose that such mistakes do not occur."[97]

In fact, there have been numerous errors of justice of this type. Michael Radelet and Hugo Adam Bedau, prominent researchers on this topic, recently completed the most comprehensive study ever conducted on miscarriages of justice in capital (and potentially capital) cases.[98] Their research focused only on cases of factual innocence, and they located and documented twentieth century cases involving 350 defendants who were either erroneously convicted of a capital crime or who were convicted of crimes that never occurred — such as seven cases in which the "murder victim" showed up alive after a conviction had been handed down.

The needle used in Texas for executions by injection. Murderer Charles Brooks, Jr., was the first in the United States to be executed by this method, on December 7, 1982.

Common sense tells us that the death penalty does operate as an effective deterrent for some crimes.
—LOWELL JENSEN, U.S. DEPT. OF JUSTICE, 1981

I believe capital punishment to be an appropriate remedy for anyone who does me injury, but under no other circumstances.
—F. LEE BAILEY, 1977

Those who assert that capital punishment is wrong because the state should not itself take on the guilt of murder completely miss the point. For by failing to take the life of those who murder their fellow men, the state becomes a passive accessory after the fact.
—NETTIE LEEF, 1975

Race of victim in all murder cases

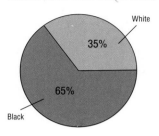

White 35%

Black 65%

Race of victim in all murder cases where district attorney sought death penalty:

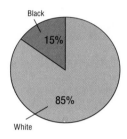

Black 15%

White 85%

Percentage of cases where death penalty was sought, by race of defendant and victim:

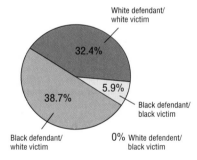

White defendant/ white victim 32.4%

Black defendant/ black victim 5.9%

Black defendant/ white victim 38.7%

White defendent/ black victim 0%

The Death Penalty and Accusations of Racial Bias: The Chattahoochee Study A look at prosecution for the death penalty since 1973 in Chattahoochee judicial district which covers six counties in western Georgia, and includes Columbus, the state's second largest city.

SOURCE: Death Penalty Information Center and Southern Christian Leadership Council

There is no great difficulty to separate the soul from the body, but is not so easy to restore life to the dead.
—MUSHARRIF-UDDIN, 1258

One could readily argue that since most of the convictions were ultimately reversed and the defendant's life spared, the moral is easily dodged. Yet the very same reasoning can be used to support the irreversibility argument — that wrongful convictions do indeed happen, and only through luck and circumstance have many of the victims managed to escape death. An illustration of this is the case of Isidore Zimmerman.

On June 5, 1937, at age nineteen, Zimmerman was arrested along with serveral other youths for the crime of murder in the first degree. Ten months later he was convicted and sentenced to death. From April 1938 through January 1939, Zimmerman lived on Sing Sing's death row. During that time thirteen men were electrocuted, including one of his codefendants. Only two hours before his scheduled execution, New York's Governor Herbert H. Lehman commuted the sentence to life imprisonment. For the next twenty-three years, Zimmerman was simply a number in New York's maximum-security prison population. During a three-year stay at Attica State Prison, from 1947 through 1950, he spent eight months in solitary confinement.

In February 1962, Zimmerman was released from prison upon a ruling of the state appeals court granting a writ of *coram nobis,** setting aside his original conviction and directing a new trial. On March 13, 1967, almost thirty years after his arrest on the murder charge, the indictment was dismissed, the original conviction having been obtained on the basis of suppressed evidence and perjured testimony.[99] And to the Zimmerman story it should be noted that the Radelet-Bedau research discovered compelling evidence that since 1900, at least twenty-three innocent defendants went to their deaths knowing all too well that no system of justice is perfect.

The *discrimination argument* against capital punishment contends that the death penalty is a lottery system, with the odds stacked heavily against those less capable of defending themselves. As Justice Thurgood Marshall wrote in his concurring opinion in *Furman* v. *Georgia:*

> It also is evident that the burden of capital punishment falls upon the poor, the ignorant, and the underprivileged members of society. It is the poor, and the members of minority groups who are least able to voice their complaints against capital punishment. Their impotence leaves them victims of a sanction which the wealthier, better-represented, just-as-guilty person can escape. So long as the capital sanction is used only against the forlorn, easily forgotten members of society, legislators are content to maintain the status quo, because change would draw attention to the problem and concern might develop. Ignorance is perpetuated and apathy soon becomes its mate, and we have today's situation.

The most recent statistics available on the social characteristics of death row inmates suggest that the death penalty continues to be administered in a selective and discriminatory manner. As of August 1, 1988, over 40 percent of those under the sentence of death were black, and nearly all of those on death rows across the United States were indigents — too poor to afford private counsel — who had to rely on a state-supplied attorney.[100] The federal courts have rejected this claim, however, even when arguments have been grounded in precise statistical studies. In *McCleskey* v. *Zant,*[101] a 1984 Georgia case, the U.S. district court held that statistical data "are incapable of producing evidence on whether racial factors play a part in the imposition of the death penalty in any particular case."

---

* *Coram nobis* is a writ used to obtain review of a judgment for the purpose of correcting errors of fact.

The *protection of the criminal justice system argument* against capital punishment holds that equity in the administration of justice is hindered by the very bearing of capital statutes. As noted by the President's Crime Commission:

> Whatever views one may have about the efficacy of the death penalty as a deterrent, it clearly has an undesirable impact on the administration of justice. The trial of a capital case is a stirring drama, but that is perhaps its most dangerous attribute. Selecting a jury often requires several days; each objection or point of law requires excessive deliberation because of the irreversible consequences of error. The jury's concern with the death penalty may result in unwarranted acquittals and there is increased danger that public sympathy will be aroused for the defendant, regardless of his guilt of the crime charged.[102]

The *brutalization argument* holds that executions actually *cause* homicides, rather than deter them. In this behalf, William J. Bowers has extensively analyzed numerous studies of both the short-term and long-term effects of executions on homicide rates. He demonstrated that executions cause a slight but discernible increase in the murder rate. This "brutalizing effect," he added, typically occurs within the first two months after an execution and dissipates thereafter. Bowers' explanation is that the effect is most likely to occur among those who have reached a state of "readiness to kill"—a small subgroup of the population composed of individuals on the fringe of sanity for whom the suggestive or imitative message of the execution is that it is proper to kill those who betray, disgrace, or dishonor them.[103]

And finally, the *cruel and unusual punishment argument* maintains that the death penalty is a violation of the constitutional right guaranteed by the Eighth Amendment. Abolitionists and retentionists differ, however, in their interpretations of the "cruel and unusual punishment" clause. The former hold that capital punishment *in all circumstances,* is cruel and unusual. The latter insist that a sentence of death is forbidden by the Eighth Amendment only when it is a disproportionate

I go to sleep and I dream of me sitting down in that chair. I mean it's such a fearful thought. Me walking down the tier, sitting down in it, them hooking it up and turning it on. . . . I can wake up, my heart's beating fast, I'm sweating like hell, just like I'd rinsed my head in water. . . . I feel I'm gonna have a heart attack.
—ALABAMA DEATH ROW PRISONER, 1978

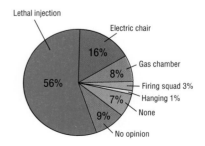

Apart from your opinion about the death penalty, what form of execution do you consider to be the most humane?

SOURCE: The Gallup Poll, 1991

• EXHIBIT 13.9 •

Quotes from the Death Penalty Debate

"He is one of the most remorseless and dangerous individuals I have come across in twenty-four years of practice."
— JUDGE ROBERT ALTMAN, WHO SENTENCED MICHAEL HAGEN

"I wish they had sentenced him to death."
— IRENE MOSIER, THE VICTIM'S MOTHER

"One day I'll be back on the streets, and I'm gonna be hard, hard, hard — one mean son of a bitch ready for action."
— MICHAEL HAGEN

Los Angeles gang member Michael Hagen, sentenced in 1987 to the maximum term of twenty-seven years to life for the killing of seventeen-year-old Kellie Mosier.

punishment for the crime committed. These conflicting views were the bases for the Supreme Court's rulings in both *Furman* and *Gregg*.

Capital Punishment in the 1980s

By the end of 1980, a total of 714 persons were under the sentence of death in the United States, and during the following year the death row population increased to over 900. By the beginning of 1992, this figure had climbed to more than 2,500 (see Exhibit 13.10). And as the growing number of offenders awaiting death increased, so too did the number of executions. During the first six years after the reinstatement of capital punishment in 1976, there were only six executions. Then, there were five in 1983, twenty-one in 1984, eighteen in 1985, seventy from 1986–1989, and a grand total of 152 through late 1991. It might be argued that during the 1990s the number of executions may increase for a variety of reasons. *First,* many of the residents of America's death rows have exhausted their appeals. *Second,* during the first half of the 1980s the Supreme Court decided on one case that served to curtail an avenue for appeal and on another that clamped down on the lengthy appeals process. In *Pulley* v. *Harris,*[104] decided by the Court in 1984, petitioner Robert Alton Harris had claimed that California's capital punishment statute was invalid under the constitution because it failed to require the California Supreme Court to compare his sentence with others imposed in similar capital cases and thereby determine whether they were proportionate. The U.S. Supreme Court held that Harris's claim was without merit, ruling that the Eighth Amendment ban against cruel and unusual

Killing human beings is an act so awesome, so destructive, so irremediable that no killer can be looked upon with anything but horror, even when that killer is the state.
— HENRY SCHWARZSCHILD, AMERICAN CIVIL LIBERTIES UNION, 1981

I'm pro-death. I believe in the death penalty. Let's get on with it.
— CHICAGO MAYOR RICHARD M. DALEY, ON THE SEPTEMBER 1990 EXECUTION OF CONVICTED MURDERER CHARLES WALKER

punishment does not require, as an invariable rule in every case, comparative proportionality review of capital sentences by an appellate court. In *Barefoot* v. *Estelle*,[105] decided a year earlier, the Court said, in effect, that federal appeals courts may compress the time they take to consider appeals as long as all the issues are covered adequately and on their merits. While the ruling in *Barefoot* mandated nothing, it suggested to federal

To many, Theodore Bundy was the ultimate serial killer—thirty-one killings, nine states, young women terrorized, raped, strangled, and then raped again even after they died. Shortly before his death, Bundy was video-taped talking extensively about his life. When Bundy was finally executed in late January 1989, he received a raucous send-off from Florida State University students. Presumably they were seeking retribution for the 1978 deaths of two sorority sisters, for whose brutal murder (along with that of a twelve-year-old Lake City, Florida girl) he had been sentenced to die. Nearly three hundred students arrived in cars bearing such slogans as "Thank God, It's Fryday," "Bundy BBQ," and "Roast in Peace."

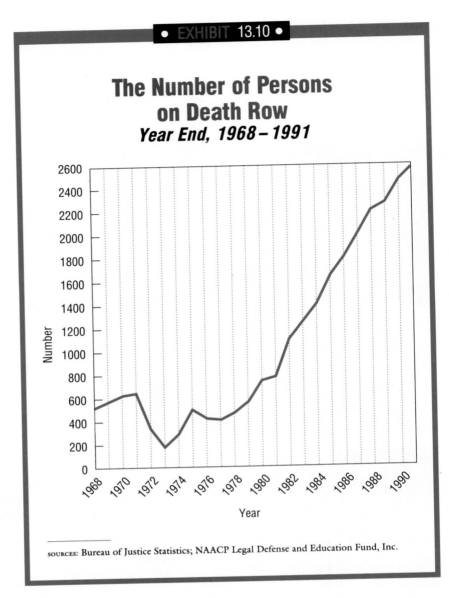

• EXHIBIT 13.10 •

The Number of Persons on Death Row
Year End, 1968–1991

SOURCES: Bureau of Justice Statistics; NAACP Legal Defense and Education Fund, Inc.

appeals courts the adoption of rules under which stays of execution could be granted. Moreover, it noted that stays of execution were not automatic upon filing petitions of *certiorari*.

And finally, the second half of the 1980s and the early 1990s witnessed other High Court decisions that served to reaffirm that capital punishment would remain a visible part of American justice. For example:

Lockhart v. McCree: The Supreme Court ruling that a prosecutor's removal for cause, at the start of the guilt phase of a capital trial, of prospective jurors so opposed to the death penalty as to be unable to perform their duties at sentencing, is not a violation of the Fifth Amendment.

- In *Lockhart v. McCree,*[106] decided in 1986, the Court asserted that even if death-qualified juries are "conviction prone," this in itself does not violate any constitutional provisions. (See Exhibit 13.11.)

- In *McCleskey v. Kemp,*[107] decided in 1987, the Court held that statistical evidence of racial discrimination in death sentencing cannot, in and of itself, establish a violation of the Eighth and/or Fourteenth Amendments. The Court further held that to

• EXHIBIT 13.11 •

Lockhart v. McCree

In *Witherspoon* v. *Illinois,* decided in 1968, the U.S. Supreme Court held that in capital cases states cannot exclude from juries *any* persons opposed to the death penalty. To do so, the Court argued, would result in a jury that could not speak for the community. Constituted as such, a jury would be "death-qualified" and thus represent a violation of due process. But the justices held that jurors could be excluded for cause if their scruples against the death penalty were so strong that they would automatically vote against the imposition of capital punishment *regardless of the evidence.* Such jurors have become known as "*Witherspoon* excludables." Moreover, the ruling applied only to juries involved in sentencing decisions, leaving open the question of whether "death qualification" tainted a guilty or not-guilty verdict. *Lockhart* v. *McCree,* decided by the Court in 1986, addressed this latter issue.

In 1978, Ardia McCree had been charged with capital felony murder. In accordance with Arkansas law, the trial judge at *voir dire* removed for cause, over McCree's objections, those prospective jurors who stated that they could never vote for the imposition of the death penalty. McCree was convicted, and although the prosecution had requested a capital sentence, the jury set the punishment at life imprisonment without the possibility of parole. On appeal before the Eighth Circuit Court of Appeals,[a] McCree argued two points. First, he claimed that the removal for cause of the "*Witherspoon* excludable" prospective

jurors violated his right under the Sixth and Fourteenth Amendments to have his guilt or innocence determined by an impartial jury selected from a representative cross-section of the community. Second, McCree maintained that the absence of the "*Witherspoon* excludables" slanted the jury in favor of conviction. He produced the findings of a variety of studies which suggested that the juries in question were indeed conviction-prone.

When the court of appeals ruled in favor of McCree, sending the matter to the U.S. Supreme Court, *Lockhart* suddenly became the most important death penalty case of the 1980s. Only days before the Court finally released its opinion on May 5, 1986, there were more than 1,700 inmates housed on death rows nationally, most of whom had been convicted by "death-qualified" juries. An affirmation of the circuit court decision would have meant new trials for several hundred inmates awaiting execution.

To the bewilderment of civil libertarians, the Court ruled against McCree by a 6-to-3 majority. It was the opinion of the Court that the "death qualification" process does not cast doubt on the impartiality of anyone chosen to be on a jury, and that the Constitution does not require that a trial jury hold a balance of viewpoints or attitudes.

At the heart of the Court's decision was the issue of whether the Sixth Amendment required that a jury represent a fair cross-section of a community:

The essence of a "fair cross-section" claim is the systematic exclusion of a "distinctive" group in the community.

In our view groups defined solely in terms of shared attitudes that would prevent or substantially impair members of the group from performing one of their duties as jurors, such as the "*Witherspoon* excludables" at issue here, are not "distinctive groups" for fair cross-section purposes.

"Death qualification," unlike the wholesale exclusion of blacks, women, or Mexican-Americans from jury service, is carefully designed to serve the state's concededly legitimate interest in obtaining a single jury that can properly and impartially apply the law to the facts of the case at both the guilt and sentencing phases of a capital trial.

As to the many studies that addressed the purported conviction-prone nature of "death-qualified" juries,[b] the Court had examined them closely. But, said Justice Rehnquist:

We have serious doubts about the value of these studies in predicting the behavior of actual jurors. In addition, two of the three "new" studies did not even attempt to simulate the process of jury deliberation, and none of the "new" studies was able to predict to what extent, if any, the presence of one or more "*Witherspoon* excludables" on a guilt-phase jury would have altered the outcome. . . .

We will assume . . . that "death qualification" in fact produces juries somewhat more "conviction-prone" than "non-death-qualified" juries. We hold, nonetheless, that the Constitution does not prohibit the States from "death qualifying" juries in capital cases.

SOURCES:

a. *Lockhart* v. *McCree,* 39 CrL 3085 (1986).

b. Brief for *Amicus Curiae,* American Psychological Associatioin in Support of Respondent, *Lockhart* v. *McCree,* on Writ of *Certiorari* to the United States Court of Appeals for the Eighth Circuit.

• EXHIBIT 13.12 •

Enmund, Tison, and the "Nontriggerman" Defense Against Capital Punishment

In *Enmund* v. *Florida,* decided by the Supreme Court in 1982, a murder had been committed during the course of a robbery. The appellant in the case, who had aided and abetted the robbery, was convicted of murder in the first degree and sentenced to death. The Supreme Court held that the Eighth Amendment ban against cruel and unusual punishment does not permit the death penalty on a defendant who aids and abets a felony in the course of which a murder is committed by others where a showing that the defendant attempted to kill or intended to kill was absent. The Court reasoned that the identical treatment of a robber and his accomplice, and the attribution of culpability of one to the other in these circumstances, is unconstitutional.

The decision in *Enmund* was modified by *Tison* v. *Arizona,* decided in 1987. Specifically, brothers Ricky Tison and Raymond Tison, along with other members of their family,

The three Tison brothers

planned and effected the escape of their father, Gary Tison, from prison where he was serving a life sentence for having killed a guard during a previous escape. Ricky and Raymond Tison, as well as a third brother (Donald), entered the prison with an ice chest filled with guns, armed their father and another convicted murderer, later helped to abduct, detain, and rob a family of four, and watched their father

and the other convict murder the members of that family with shotguns. Although they later stated that they were surprised by the shooting, neither of the Tison brothers made any effort to help the victims, but drove away in the victims' car with the rest of the escape party. After the Arizona Supreme Court affirmed individual convictions for capital murder under the state's felony murder and ac-

Tison v. Arizona: The Supreme Court ruling that a "nontriggerman" who does not intend to commit murder may be executed when he or she participates in a felony that leads to murder and is found to have exhibited "reckless indifference" for human life.

obtain relief, a defendant must prove either (1) that decision makers in his or her case acted with discriminatory purpose, or (2) that the legislature enacted or maintained the death penalty statute *because* of an anticipated racially discriminatory effect.

- In ***Tison v. Arizona,***[108] also decided in 1987, the Court held that a defendant who does not intend to commit murder and who does not actually commit murder may be executed when he or she participates in a felony that leads to murder and is found to have exhibited "reckless indifference" for human life. (See Exhibit 13.12.)

- In *Penry v. Lynaugh,*[109] decided in 1989, the Court ruled, in effect, that the death penalty could be imposed on mentally retarded defendants.

complice liability statutes, the Tisons collaterally attacked their death sentences in state postconviction proceedings, alleging that *Enmund* v. *Florida* required reversal.

The Arizona Supreme Court determined that the Tison brothers should be executed, holding that *Enmund* requires a finding of "intent to kill" and interpreting that phrase to include situations in which the defendant intended, contemplated, or anticipated that lethal force would or might be used or that life would or might be taken in accomplishing the underlying felony. Despite finding that the Tisons did not specifically intend that the victims die, plan the homicides in advance, or actually fire the shots, the court ruled that the requisite intent was established by evidence that they played an active part in planning and executing the breakout and in the events that led to the murders, and that they did nothing to interfere with the killings nor to disassociate them-

selves from the killers afterward. Although only *one* of the Tison brothers testified that he would have been willing to kill, the court found that both of them could have anticipated the use of lethal force.

The High Court ruled against the Tisons, holding that although they neither intended to kill the victims nor inflicted the fatal wounds, the record might support a finding that they had the culpable mental state of reckless indifference to human life. The Court explained that the Eighth Amendment does not prohibit the death penalty as disproportionate in the case of a defendant whose participation in a felony that results in murder is major and whose mental state is one of reckless indifference. A survey of state felony murder laws and judicial decisions after *Enmund* indicates a societal consensus that this combination of factors may justify the death penalty even without a specific "intent to kill." Reckless disregard for human life also repre-

sents a highly culpable mental state that may report a capital sentencing judgment in combination with major participation in the felony resulting in death. According to the High Court, the Arizona Supreme Court correctly affirmed the death sentences upon a finding that the defendants "intended, contemplated, or anticipated that lethal force would or might be used or that life would or might be taken."

As for Donald Tison, the third brother involved in the escape, he was killed during a shootout at a police roadblock a few days after the prison break. Gary Tison evaded the police and escaped into the desert, but subsequently died of exposure.

SOURCES: *Enmund* v. *Florida*, 458 U.S. 782 (1982); *Tison* v. *Arizona*, 41 CrL 3023 (1987); James W. Clarke, *Last Rampage: The Escape of Gary Tison* (Boston: Houghton Mifflin, 1988).

- In *Blystone* v. *Pennsylvania*,[110] decided in 1990, the Court upheld a state statute requiring sentencing juries to impose a death sentence if they found at least one aggravating circumstance and no mitigating circumstances.

- In *Coleman* v. *Thompson*,[111] decided in 1991, the Court asserted that death row inmates (and other state prisoners) forfeit their ability to bring even an initial federal habeas corpus petition if, through their attorney's miscalculation or some other procedural error, they have failed to present their appeal properly in the state courts.

Yet these decisions in no way indicated that the High Court had made up its mind on the death penalty. Quite the contrary. As public

Jimmy Lee Gray in his death row cell in Mississippi State Prison. Executed on September 2, 1983, Gray had been convicted of kidnapping and raping a three-year-old girl and murdering her by suffocation in mud. At the time of the kidnapping, Gray was on parole from an Arizona prison, where he had served seven years of a twenty-year sentence for the 1968 slaying of his sixteen-year-old fiancée. Ironically, Gray, whose mother even urged her son's execution, died through suffocation by lethal gas .

sentiment pushed for a more rapid imposition of the death penalty, the Justices argued among themselves about the merry-go-round of litigation that had come to characterize capital punishment cases. And too, although the pace of executions had at first increased and then ebbed, the American death house remained a warren of segregated convicts preparing briefs while rehearsing the day of their final judgment and ceremony of death.

APPELLATE REVIEW

An appeal is when you ask one court to show its contempt for another court.
— FINLEY PETER DUNNE

Appeal: A complaint to a superior court of an injustice done or an error committed by a lower court, whose judgment or decision the higher tribunal is called upon to correct or reverse.

This brief utterance from the essays of the early twentieth-century American journalist and humorist Finley Peter Dunne, although cynical and irreverent in tone, is essentially what an appeal is all about. More accurately, an **appeal** is a complaint to a superior court of an injustice done or error committed by a lower court, whose judgment or decision the higher tribunal is called upon to correct or reverse.

Despite the fact that appellate procedures exist throughout the federal and all of the state court structures, the right of appeal was unknown in common law, and such a right was not incorporated into the Constitution. Furthermore, the constitutionality of a state's denial of appellate review has never been decided by the United States Supreme Court, and the High Court has often noted, *in dicta,** on many occasions that such review is not constitutionally required.[112]

The Defendant's Right to Appeal

At the appellate stage, the presumption of innocence has evaporated, and it becomes the defendant's obligation to show why a conviction should be overturned. Thus the nature of the adversary system changes, the burden of proof shifting from the prosecution to the defense.

All jurisdictions have procedural rules requiring that objections to the admission (or exclusion) of evidence, or to some other procedure, be made by the defense either at a pretrial hearing or at the time evidence or other procedure becomes an issue at trial. Failure to make a timely objection results in an automatic forfeiture of the claim for appeal purposes. Such a requirement has been instituted in order that trial judges can make rules and develop facts that will appear in the record and thus enable the appeals court to conduct an adequate review.

The Plain Error Rule   The notable exception to the timely objection requirement is the *plain error rule,* incorporated into *Federal Rules of Criminal Procedure* and with an equivalent in all state jurisdictions. Under this rule, "plain errors or defects affecting substantial rights" of defendants become subject to appellate review even though they may not have been properly raised at trial or during some prior appeal.[113] Thus, a denial of the right to counsel at trial, the admission of an involuntary confession, or the negation of some other constitutional guarantees — even in the absence of a timely objection — are considered "plain errors" and hence appealable.

Plain errors are subject to appellate review.

The Automatic Reversal Rule   On numerous occasions, The Supreme Court has held that certain constitutional errors are of such magnitude that they require *automatic reversal* of a conviction: hence the *automatic reversal rule.* The Fourteenth Amendment guarantee of due process, for example, ensures the defendant a fair trial before an impartial judge. Pursuant to this guarantee, the Court ruled in *Tumey* v. *Ohio,*[114] decided in 1927 by a unanimous vote, that an accused is denied due process when tried before a judge with a direct, personal, pecuniary interest in ruling against him. At issue in *Tumey* was the fact that the petitioner had been tried in a city court, whose judge was the mayor, and from which fines were deposited in the city treasury. The High Court found the lower court's error to be of such significance that it mandated an automatic reversal of Tumey's conviction. Similarly, the Court considers as automatically reversible such *plain* errors as the use of an involuntary confession at trial, and the denial of counsel at trial in violation of its holding in *Gideon* v. *Wainwright.*[115]

Certain constitutional errors are subject to automatic reversal.

* *In dicta* are expressions in an opinion of the court that do not necessarily support the decision.

A denial of a constitutional right can at times be a harmless error not subject to reversal on appeal.

The Harmless Error Rule In *Chapman* v. *California*,[116] decided in 1967, the Supreme Court established the *harmless error rule,* holding that a denial of a federal constitutional right can at times be of insufficient magnitude to require a reversal of a conviction on appeal. Known also as the *Chapman* rule, the "harmless error" doctrine has been applied by the Supreme Court and other appellate courts in numerous areas of constitutional dimension: evidence seized in violation of the Fourth Amendment, denial of counsel at a preliminary hearing, in-court identifications based on invalid pretrial identification procedures, and obtaining a confession from a defendant after indictment without expressly informing the defendant of his right to counsel.[117] When a court considers an error to be harmless, it is indicating that the mistake was not prejudicial to the rights of the accused and thus made no difference in the subsequent conviction or sentence.

On appeal or review, the defense cannot use an erroneous ruling it has requested the court to make.

The Invited Error Rule Although uncommon, there have been instances where during the course of a proceeding, the defense requests the court to make a ruling that is actually erroneous, and the court does so. Under the *invited error rule,* the defense cannot take advantage of such an error on appeal or review.[118]

The Prosecution's Right to Appeal

Neither the federal government nor the states may appeal the acquittal of a defendant. Nor can the prosecution appeal the conviction of some lesser offense (say, murder in the second degree or manslaughter) when the original indictment was for a greater one (murder in the first degree). In either case, such an action is barred by the double jeopardy clause of the Fifth Amendment. However, there are two instances in which the prosecution may initiate appellate review. Should a defendant successfully appeal and his or her conviction is reversed on some matter of law, the prosecution may contest the correctness of that legal ruling to the next higher court or even to the United States Supreme Court. Such was the case in *Delaware* v. *Prouse*,[119] which involved a seizure of marijuana following a random "spot check" of the defendant's driver's license and vehicle registration. Upon conviction, the defendant appealed to the Delaware Supreme Court, which overturned the lower court ruling on the basis of illegal search and seizure. The prosecution then appealed to the United States Supreme Court, to argue the constitutionality of the state's random license check practices. (See Chapter 8.)

Alternatively, some jurisdictions permit the prosecution to initiate appeals from both convictions *and* acquittals, solely for the purpose of correcting any legal errors that may have occurred during trial.[120]

Appellate Review of Sentences

Although appeals are commonly filed to review either real or imagined errors in court procedure, sentences, for the most part, are unappealable. This is so because each jurisdiction has statutes that mandate a range of penalties for each specific crime. Although a convicted offender might consider the sentence imposed to be unfair, as long as it falls within statutory guidelines, it is *legal.*

There are, however, a number of circumstances under which sanctions have been appealed and reversed, including when: (1) the sentence was not authorized by statute and thus was illegal; (2) the sentence was based on sex, ethnicity, or socioeconomic status and was, therefore, a violation of due process; (3) the sentence had no relationship to the purposes of criminal sanctions; and (4) the sentence was cruel and unusual. Note that in these four potential instances, the bases for appeal are not simply issues of sentencing "excess," but rather, straightforward matters of constitutional rights.

It has been argued for many decades that all sentences should be subject to some form of appeal. The fact that sentences are discretionary within a jurisdiction's statutory guidelines and, as such, are lawful should not automatically suggest that they are therefore unappealable. Discretion, after all, can be abused. Furthermore, as Judge Marvin E. Frankel has maintained:

> The contention that sentencing is not regulated by the rules of "law" subject to appellate review is an argument for, not against, a system of appeals. The "common law" is, after all, a body of rules evolved through the process of reasoned decision of concrete cases, mainly by appellate courts. English appellate courts and some of our states have been evolving general, legal "principles of sentencing" in the course of reviewing particular sentences claimed to be excessive. One way to begin to temper the capricious unruliness of sentencing is to institute the right of appeal, so that appellate courts may proceed in their accustomed fashion to make law for this grave subject.[121]

Appeal, verb. In law, to put the dice into the box for another throw.
—AMBROSE BIERCE, *THE DEVIL'S DICTIONARY,* 1911

Currently, only about fourteen states have appellate bodies that generally review a term handed down by a sentencing judge. State appeals courts, on the other hand, are generally reluctant to review sentences. Not wishing to "second guess" the sentencing judge, these higher courts feel that the magistrate who presided at the trial and pronounced the sentence had the most information available and was in the most qualified position to determine the penalty.

Finally, although the U.S. Supreme Court has reviewed many sentences where the issue at stake was of constitutional magnitude, only once did the justices require a sentencing judge to explain the bases of the penalty imposed. The case was *North Carolina* v. *Pearce,*[122] in which the defendant, who was retried by the same judge after his original conviction was reversed, was reconvicted and sentenced more severely than he was after the first conviction. The Court ruled that in such circumstances, the reasons for the more severe sentence must be placed in the record, the logic being that the due-process clause of the Fourteenth Amendment forbids the imposition of a harsher sentence for the purpose of discouraging defendants from exercising their rights of appeal.

The Appeal Process

After conviction, appeals are not automatic. There are specific procedural steps that must be followed. First, within a specified period of time (from thirty to ninety days) subsequent to conviction, the petitioner must file with the court a notice of appeals. Second, and again within a specified period of time, the petitioner must submit an "affidavit of errors" setting forth the alleged errors or defects in the trial (or pretrial) proceedings that are the subjects of the appeal. If these requirements are followed, the higher court must review the case.[123] Appeals are argued on the basis of the affidavit of errors, and sometimes through oral argument. In either case, the subject matters of the appeal must be limited to the contents of the original proceeding. Thus, no new evidence or testimony can be presented, for an appeal is not a trial. However, if new evidence is discovered that was unknown or unknowable to the defense at the time of the trial, that can be made the *basis* of an appeal.*

SUMMARY

After the verdict, the business of the court is not complete. First there is the matter of sentencing. Throughout American history, there has been no single and clearly defined rationale to serve as a guiding principle in sentencing. As a result, even contemporary sentencing objectives are seemingly based on at least four competing philosophies: retribution, isolation, deterrence, and rehabilitation. Sentencing alternatives include fines, probation or some other community-based program, imprisonment, or the death penalty.

The death penalty is the most terminal form of punishment. When the framers of the Constitution incorporated the Eighth Amendment ban against cruel and unusual punishment, the death penalty was apparently not at issue. Under colonial philosophy, capital punishment was considered neither cruel nor unusual.

The Supreme Court's interpretation of the Eighth Amendment has been flexible. The Court has ruled on various forms of punishment but has generally been silent regarding the constitutionality of capital punishment. *Furman* v. *Georgia* in 1972 invalidated state death penalty statutes on Eighth Amendment grounds, but it enabled the states to enact new capital punishment laws. Executions resumed, and the number of persons on death rows across the nation began to grow. Meanwhile, the death penalty debate continues, with arguments for and against capital punishment revolving around issues of economics, retribution, public opinion, community protection, deterrence, irreversibility, discrimination, and cruel and unusual punishment.

At the appellate stage of the criminal justice process, the presumption of innocence has evaporated with the finding of guilt. It then becomes the defendant's obligation to show why a conviction should be overturned. There are grounds on which the defense can initiate an appeal, but the prosecution cannot appeal the acquittal of a defendant because of the double jeopardy clause of the Fifth Amendment. However, should an accused successfully appeal and have his conviction reversed on some matter of law, the prosecution may contest the correctness of that legal ruling to the next highest court or even to the U.S. Supreme Court.

---

* There are other mechanisms through which cases can be reviewed, such as collateral review proceedings and writs of *habeas corpus*. These are generally initiated after the defendant's sentence has commenced. They are discussed in Chapter 16, under prisoners' rights and postconviction remedies.

KEY TERMS

allocution (**456**)
appeal (**484**)
Coker v. *Georgia* (**469**)
definite sentence (**447**)
determinate sentence (**447**)
deterrence (**440**)
Furman v. *Georgia* (**465**)
Gregg v. *Georgia* (**468**)

indeterminate sentence (**445**)
intermittent sentence (**447**)
isolation (**440**)
Lockhart v. *McCree* (**480**)
mandatory sentence (**448**)
presentence investigation (**455**)
rehabilitation (**442**)
retribution (**439**)

separation-of-powers
   doctrine (**455**)
Tison v. *Arizona* (**482**)
Weems v. *United States* (**461**)
Witherspoon v. *Illinois* (**464**)
vengeance (**440**)

QUESTIONS FOR DISCUSSION

1. Should vengeance be accepted as a rationale for punishment?
2. How might mandatory sentencing statutes lead to increased prosecutorial discretion and court delays?
3. What argument in favor of capital punishment seems most valid? Should capital punishment be abolished? Will it be?
4. Would mandatory sentencing statutes make the certainty of punishment more realistic? Would such sentences affect the crime problem?

FOR FURTHER READING

Haas, Kenneth C., and James A. Inciardi (eds.). *Challenging Capital Punishment: Legal and Social Science Approaches.* Newbury Park, CA: Sage Publications, 1988.

Marquart, James W., and Jonathan R. Sorensen. "Institutional and Postrelease Behavior of Furman-Committed Inmates in Texas," *Criminology,* 26 (November 1988), pp. 677–693.

van den Haag, Ernest, and John P. Conrad. *The Death Penalty: A Debate.* New York: Plenum Press, 1983.

Wiliams, Charles J. "The Federal Death Penalty for Drug-Related Killings," *Criminal Law Bulletin,* 27 (Sept.–Oct. 1991), pp. 387–415.

Zimring, Franklin E., and Gordon J. Hawkins. *Deterrence.* Chicago: University of Chicago Press, 1973.

NOTES

1. See Andrew von Hirsch, *Doing Justice: The Choice of Punishments* (New York: Hill and Wang, 1976), pp. 45–55, 143–149.
2. Paul Boudreaux, "*Booth* v. *Maryland* and the Individual Vengeance Rationale for Criminal Punishment," *Journal of Criminal Law and Criminology,* 80 (Spring 1989), pp. 177–196.
3. *Payne* v. *Tennessee,* 49 CrL 2325 (1991).
4. Paul W. Tappan, *Crime, Justice and Correction* (New York: McGraw-Hill, 1960), p. 255.
5. National Advisory Commission on Criminal Justice Standards and Goals, *Corrections* (Washington, D.C.: U.S. Government Printing Office, 1973), p. 1.
6. Quoted in Sanford H. Kadish and Monrad G. Paulsen, *Criminal Law and Its Processes* (Boston: Little, Brown, 1969), p. 85.
7. See Franklin E. Zimring and Gordon J. Hawkins, *Deterrence* (Chicago: University of Chicago Press, 1973).
8. Personal communication, January 6, 1978.
9. The issues for and against the rehabilitative approach are discussed at greater length in Part 4 of this text.
10. Melvyn Bernard Zerman, *Beyond a Reasonable Doubt: Inside the American Jury System* (New York: Crowell, 1981), p. 170.
11. National Advisory Commission on Criminal Justice Standards and Goals, *Courts* (Washington, D.C.: U.S. Government Printing Office, 1973), p. 110.
12. *Code of the Public General Laws of Maryland,* Article 27, Section 341.
13. State of New York, *Penal Law,* 40-70.15, 80.05, 245.01.
14. *Williams* v. *Illinois,* 399 U.S. 235 (1970); *Tate* v. *Short,* 401 U.S. 395 (1971).
15. *Bearden* v. *Georgia,* 33 CrL 3103 (1983).
16. *Criminal Justice Newsletter,* September 1, 1988, p. 4.
17. Walter S. Carr, "Sentencing Practices, Problems, and Remedies," *Judicature* 53 (1969): 14.
18. See Marvin E. Frankel, *Criminal Sentences: Law Without Order* (New York: Hill and Wang, 1973); Karl Menninger, *The Crime of Punishment* (New York: Viking, 1968); von Hirsch, *Doing Justice;* Nigel Walker, *Sentencing in a Rational Society* (London: Penguin, 1972).
19. Harry Elmer Barnes, *The Repression of Crime* (New York: George H. Doran, 1926), p. 220.
20. *Delaware Code,* Title 11, Section 4209.
21. State of New York, *Penal Law,* 40-85.
22. *People* v. *Warren,* 79 Misc 2d 777, 360 NYS 2d 961 (1974).
23. *National Law Journal,* November 19, 1984, p. 47.
24. *People,* January 1, 1981, p. 86.
25. *New York Times,* November 4, 1984, p. 57.
26. *National Law Journal,* March 29, 1982, p. 47.
27. *National Law Journal,* December 28, 1987, p. 43.
28. *Drug Abuse Report,* April 4, 1988, p. 6.
29. *Idaho Code,* 18-1403, 19-2601.
30. State of New York, *Penal Law,* 40-70.00, 80.00, 140.30.
31. *West Virginia Code,* Chapter 61, Section 3-11; Chapter 62, Section 12-2.
32. *Delaware Code,* Title 11, Sections 826, 4204-5.
33. *Code of the Public General Laws of Maryland,* Article 27, Sections 29, 641.
34. *Code of Alabama,* 13-2-40, 15-22-50.
35. President's Commission on Law Enforcement and Administration of Justice, *The Courts* (Washington D.C.: U.S. Government Printing Office, 1967), p. 23.
36. William Zumwalt, "The Anarchy of Sentencing in the Federal Courts," *Judicature* 57 (October 1973): 96–104.
37. *New York Times,* February 15, 1981, p. 43.
38. *Miami Herald,* January 13, 1984, p. 1D.

39. *Hutto* v. *Davis*, 454 U.S. 372 (1982). See also *High Times*, July 1983, pp. 32–37.

40. *National Observer*, September 14, 1974, p. 5.

41. *New York Times*, March 30, 1979, p. B3.

42. *National Law Journal*, April 5, 1982, p. 3.

43. President's Commission, *Courts*, p. 24.

44. President's Commission, *Courts*, p. 23.

45. Frankel, *Criminal Sentences*, p. 8.

46. Marvin Zalman, "The Rise and Fall of the Indeterminate Sentence," *Wayne Law Review* 24 (1978): 857.

47. See, for example, Frankel, *Criminal Sentences*.

48. Joseph Mattina, "Sentencing: A Judge's Inherent Responsibility," *Judicature* 57 (October 1973): 105.

49. *Mistretta* v. *U.S.*, 44 CrL 3061 (1989).

50. National Advisory Commission, *Courts*, p. 326.

51. Advisory Committee on Sentencing and Review, *Standards Relating to Probation* (New York: American Bar Association, 1970), p. 32.

52. Administrative Offices of the U.S. Courts, Division of Probation, "The Selective Presentence Investigation Report," *Federal Probation* 38 (December 1974): 48.

53. Ernest W. Puttkammer, *Administration of Criminal Law* (Chicago: University of Chicago Press, 1953), p. 215.

54. *Hill* v. *California*, 368 U.S. 424 (1962).

55. Barnes, *Repression of Crime*, pp. 44–45.

56. George Ryley Scott, *The History of Capital Punishment* (London: Torchstream, 1950), p. 179.

57. Cited by Harry Elmer Barnes, *The Story of Punishment: A Record of Man's Inhumanity to Man* (Montclair, N.J.: Patterson Smith, 1972), p. 232.

58. Negley K. Teeters and Charles J. Zibulka, "Executions Under State Authority: 1864–1967," in *Executions in America*, ed. William J. Bowers (Lexington, Mass.: D. C. Heath, 1974), pp. 200–401.

59. Hugo Adam Bedau, *The Death Penalty in America* (Chicago: Aldine, 1964), p. 46.

60. President's Commission, *Courts*, p. 28.

61. C. Spear, *Essays on the Punishment of Death* (London: John Green, 1844), pp. 227–231.

62. David A. Jones, *The Law of Criminal Procedure* (Boston: Little, Brown, 1981), p. 543.

63. Jones, *Law of Criminal Procedure*, p. 544.

64. Marvin E. Wolfgang and Marc Riedel, "Race, Judicial Discretion, and the Death Penalty," *Annals of the American Academy of Political and Social Science* 407 (May 1973): 129.

65. *O'Neil* v. *Vermont*, 114 U.S. 323 (1892).

66. *Weems* v. *United States*, 217 U.S. 349 (1910).

67. *Trop* v. *Dulles*, 356 U.S. 86 (1958).

68. *Wilkerson* v. *Utah*, 99 U.S. 130 (1878).

69. *In re Kemmler*, 136 U.S. 436 (1890).

70. *Trop* v. *Dulles*, *supra* note 66.

71. *Witherspoon* v. *Illinois*, 391 U.S. 510 (1968).

72. *United States* v. *Jackson*, 390 U.S. 570 (1968).

73. *McGautha* v. *California*, 402 U.S. 183 (1971).

74. *Furman* v. *Georgia*, *Jackson* v. *Georgia*, *Branch* v. *Texas*, 408 U.S. 238 (1972).

75. *Gregg* v. *Georgia*, 428 U.S. 153 (1976).

76. *Georgia Code*, 26-1101, 1311, 1902, 2001, 3301 (1972).

77. *Profitt* v. *Florida*, 428 U.S. 325 (1976); *Jurek* v. *Texas*, 428 U.S. 262 (1976).

78. *Woodson* v. *North Carolina*, 428 U.S. 280 (1976).

79. *Coker* v. *Georgia*, 433 U.S. 583 (1977).

80. *Lockett* v. *Ohio*, 438 U.S. 586 (1978); *Bell* v. *Ohio*, 438 U.S. 637 (1978).

81. *Godfrey* v. *Georgia*, 446 U.S. 420 (1980).

82. This account on the Gilmore case is based on Louis R. Katz, *The Justice Imperative* (Cincinnati: Anderson, 1980); pp. 348–349; *New York Times*: January 18, 1977, pp. 1, 21; January 12, 1977, pp. 1, 12; January 11, 1976, pp. 1, 14; January 16, 1977, p. 1, 48; December 1, 1976, p. 18; January 17, 1976, pp. 1, 24.

83. Quoted in Austin Sarat and Neil Vidmar, "Public Opinion, The Death Penalty, and the Eighth Amendment: Testing the Marshall Hypothesis," *Wisconsin Law Review* (1976): 206.

84. Wilmington (Delaware) *News-Journal*, February 17, 1985, p. A16.

85. *New York Times*, December 9, 1979, p. 73.

86. *National Law Journal*, September 14, 1981, p. 5.

87. *American Medical News*, July 11, 1980, p. 13.

88. *Time*, December 20, 1982, pp. 28–29. See also, *Texas Monthly*, February 1983, pp. 100–105, 170–176, 182.

89. Cited by Sue Titus Reid, *Crime and Criminology* (New York: Holt, Rinehart and Winston, 1979), p. 566.

90. *New York Times*, January 31, 1977, p. 12C.

91. See, M. Garey, "The Cost of Taking a Life," *University of California–Davis Law Review*, 18 (1985), pp. 1221–1270.

92. *National Observer*, November 18, 1972, p. 2.

93. James O. Finckenauer, "Public Support for the Death Penalty: Retribution as Just Deserts or Retribution as Revenge?" *Justice Quarterly*, 5 (March 1988), pp. 81–100.

94. President's Commission, *Courts*, p. 27.

95. Zimring and Hawkins, *Deterrence*.

96. See Thorsten Sellin, ed., *Capital Punishment* (New York: Harper & Row, 1967); Karl F. Schuessler, "The Deterrent Influence of the Death Penalty," *Annals of the American Academy of Political and Social Science* 284 (November 1952): 54–62; Hugo Adam Bedau and Chester M. Pierce, eds., *Capital Punishment in the United States* (New York: A M S Press, 1976), pp. 299–416.

97. Roy E. Calvert, *Capital Punishment in the Twentieth Century* (New York: G. P. Putnam's, 1936), p. 125.

98. Michael L. Radelet and Hugo Adam Bedau, "Fallibility and Finality: Type II Errors and Capital Punishment," in Kenneth C. Haas and James A. Inciardi (eds.), *Challenging Capital Punishment: Legal and Social Science Approaches* (Newbury Park, CA: Sage, 1988), pp. 91–112.

99. Isidore Zimmerman, *Punishment Without Crime* (New York: Manor, 1973).

100. William J. Bowers and Glenn L. Pierce, "Arbitrariness and Discrimination under Post-*Furman* Capital Statutes," *Crime and Delinquency* 26 (October 1980), pp. 563–635; Kenneth C. Haas, "Reaffirming the Value of Life: Arguments Against the Death Penalty," *Delaware Lawyer* 3 (Summer 1984), pp. 12–20; *USA Today*, August 26, 1985, p. 2A; NAACP Legal Defense and Education Fund, *Death Row, U.S.A.*, August 1, 1988.

101. *McCleskey* v. *Zant*, 34 CrL 2429 (1984).

102. President's Commission, *Courts*.

103. See William J. Bowers, "The Effect of Executions is Brutalization, Not Deterrence," in Kenneth C. Haas and James A. Inciardi (eds.), *Challenging Capital Punishment: Legal and Social Science Approaches* (Newbury Park, CA: Sage Publications, 1988), pp. 49–89.

104. *Pulley* v. *Harris*, U.S. Sup Ct (1984) 34 CrL 3027.

105. *Barefoot* v. *Estelle*, 103 S.Ct. 3383 (1983).

106. *Lockhart* v. *McCree*, 39 CrL 3085 (1986).

107. *McCleskey* v. *Kemp*, 41 CrL 4107 (1987).

108. *Tison* v. *Arizona*, 41 CrL 3023 (1987).

109. *Penry* v. *Lynaugh*, 45 CrL 3188 (1989).

110. *Blystone* v. *Pennsylvania*, 46 CrL 2147 (1990).

111. *Coleman* v. *Thompson*, 48 CrL 3059 (1991).

112. For example, in *McKane* v. *Durston,* 153 U.S. 684 (1894); *Griffin* v. *Illinois,* 351 U.S. 12 (1956).

113. *Federal Rules of Criminal Procedure,* Rule 52 (b).

114. *Tumey* v. *Ohio,* 273 U.S. 510 (1927).

115. *Gideon* v. *Wainwright,* 372 U.S. 335 (1963).

116. *Chapman* v. *California,* 386 U.S. 18 (1967).

117. See Peter W. Lewis and Kenneth D. Peoples, *The Supreme Court and the Criminal Process* (Philadelphia: W. B. Saunders, 1978), p. 515.

118. *Gresham* v. *Harcourt,* 93 Tex. 149, 53 S. W. 1019.

119. *Delaware* v. *Prouse,* 440 U.S. 648 (1979).

120. Katz, *Justice Imperative,* p. 315.

121. Frankel, *Criminal Sentences,* p. 84.

122. *North Carolina* v. *Pearce,* 395 U.S. 711 (1969).

123. *Gilbert Criminal Law and Procedure* (New York: Matthew Bender, 1979), p. 460.10.

PART

FOUR

Corrections

CHAPTER

From Walnut Street to Alcatraz: The American Prison Experience

The mood and temper of the public with regard to the treatment of crime and criminals is one of the unfailing tests of the civilization of any country.
—WINSTON CHURCHILL, 1910

Prison of course is the school of crime par excellence. Until one has gone through that school, one is only an amateur.

—HENRY MILLER, 1945

The public will grow increasingly ashamed of its cry for retaliation, its persistent demand to punish. This is its crime, our crime against criminals.
—KARL MENNINGER, 1968

Punishment—if not the only, or the first, or even the best means of making people obey laws—is ultimately indispensable.

—ERNEST VAN DEN HAAG, 1975

I learned some great new skills in jail, like gambling, raping a faggot, sharpening a pork chop bone into a knife, and hiding a razor blade above my gums.
—A NEW YORK CITY JAIL INMATE, 1990

istorically and cross-culturally, the range of punishments imposed by societies has been vast. Over the centuries, the sanctions for even less serious crimes were exceedingly harsh, and the litany of punishments down through the ages has often been referred to as the story of "man's inhumanity to man."[1]

In early societies the death penalty was a universal form of punishment. It was commonly applied both as a deterrent and a means for removing an offender from the community. Criminal codes from the ancient East to the modern West included capital statutes for offenses as trivial as adultery and petty theft. As recently as the early nineteenth century in England there were 200 capital crimes—ranging from murder and rape to larceny and disturbing the peace. The methods of execution went well beyond the diabolical and macabre, and they were often performed in public.[2]

Corporal punishment, in the form of mutilation, branding, whipping, and torture, was also commonplace for a variety of punitive purposes. Mutilations were attempts to "let the punishment fit the crime": thieves and robbers lost their hands, perjurers and blasphemers had their tongues cut out or pierced with hot irons, and rape was punished by castration. Branding and whipping were noncapital sanctions to preserve discipline and to deter would-be offenders. Torture, a popular means for exacting confessions, included measures of gruesome ingenuity. The torture devices of medieval Europe, for example, were often monstrous. They included the *rack,* which stretched its victims, and the "Scavenger's Daughter," which rolled them into a ball:

> On the rack the prisoner seemed in danger of having the fingers torn from his hands, the toes from his feet, the hands from the arms, the feet from the legs, the forearms from the upper arms, the legs from the trunk. Every ligament was strained, every joint loosened in its socket; and if the sufferer remained obstinate when released, he was brought back to undergo the same cruelties with the added horror of past experience and with a diminished fortitude and physical power. In the Scavenger's Daughter, on the other hand, the pain was caused by an ingenious process of compression. The legs were forced back to the thighs, the thighs were pressed onto the belly, and the whole body was placed within two iron bands which the torturers drew together with all their strength until the miserable human being lost all form but that of a globe. Blood was forced out of the tips of the fingers and toes, the nostrils and mouth; and the ribs and breastbone were commonly broken in by the pressure.[3]

Banishment and transportation were alternatives to capital punishment. Banishment served to rid the community of undesirables, who were never to return, under penalty of certain death. The most systematic form of banishment occurred in several European countries during the sixteenth through nineteenth centuries under a program of transpor-

Corporal punishment: Punishment applied to the body such as whipping or branding.

tation to far-removed lands. England led the world in this practice, which it used to eliminate convicts from its shores as well as colonize what were considered inhospitable territories. From 1606 through 1775, tens of thousands of vagrants and thieves were shipped to the American colonies in the West Indies, and then to Australia following the discontinuance of transportation to the American colonies after the American Revolution.[4] In its most modern form, banishment has appeared as "deportation" of alien criminals, with examples including mobster Charles "Lucky" Luciano and prostitute Xaviera Hollander ("the Happy Hooker")—both forced out of the United States after convictions on "morals" charges.

Other punishments have included forced labor, sterilization, excommunication from the church, loss of property and inheritance rights, disfigurement, and imprisonment.

THE ROOTS OF AMERICAN CORRECTIONAL PHILOSOPHY

With the growth of the American colonies, many of the punishments that had been common throughout medieval Europe found their way to the New World. Capital statutes endured for numerous offenses, as did banishment, and corporal punishments in the form of branding, flogging, and mutilation persisted.

Colonial Punishments

A curious variety of sanctions appeared in colonial tradition: the ducking stool, the stocks and pillory, the brank, the scarlet letter, and the bilboes. They were imposed for minor offenses, and although they are generally associated with early American life, most had originated in Western Europe as means to shame and humiliate offenders.[5]

The *ducking stool,* as its name implies, was a chair fastened to a long lever and situated at the bank of a river or pond. The victim, generally a village gossip or scold, was repeatedly submerged in the water before a jeering crowd. The *stocks and pillory,* common in almost every early New England community, were wooden frames with holes for the head, hands, and feet. They were located in the town square, and the culprit—generally a wife beater, petty thief, vagrant, Sabbath-breaker, drunkard, adulterer, or unruly servant—would be open to public scorn. Confinement in the stocks or pillory often resulted in much more than simple humiliation. The offenders were often whipped or branded while being detained, and most were pelted by passersby. Some were even stoned to death. Those secured to the pillory generally had their ears nailed to the frame, and were compelled to tear themselves loose (or have their ears cut off) when their period of detention concluded.

The *brank,* also called the "gossip's helm" and the "dame's bridle," was a cage placed about the head. It had a spiked plate or flat dish of iron that was placed in the mouth over the tongue thus inflicting severe pain if the offender spoke. As the structure of the device would suggest, it had been designed for gossips, perjurers, liars, and blasphemers, but in colonial New York it was also used for husband beaters and village drunkards.

The *scarlet letter,* made famous by Nathaniel Hawthorne's novel of the same name, was used for a variety of offenses. The adulterous wife

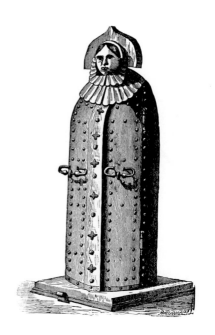

The pillory is a mechanical device for inflicting personal distinction.
—AMBROSE BIERCE, *THE DEVIL'S DICTIONARY,* 1911

• EXHIBIT 14.1 •

Sidelights on Criminal Matters
The Scarlet Letter *Revisited*

We've lost our sense of shame in this country, and humiliation as punishment is valid.

— JUDGE BECKY TITUS, SARASOTA, FLORIDA

It's like having my client pilloried in the courtyard every Tuesday from noon to five.

— SARASOTA DEFENSE ATTORNEY PHILIP PROSCH

Nathaniel Hawthorne's *The Scarlet Letter,* published in 1850, is a story of Puritanism and pariahs in seventeenth century Boston. Hester Prynne, having given birth to an illegitimate daugher, is scorned by her neighbors and forced by her church to wear a scarlet A — signifying "adultress" — as a token of her sin.

Throughout the 1980s, well over a century since Hawthorne's writing and even further removed from the era of Boston Puritanism, courts across the United States are using similar "public" announcements in an effort to deter modern day crime and "sin."

In New York City, former Mayor Ed Koch once announced on the radio the names of "johns" arrested on charges of soliciting prostitutes. In Newark, New Jersey, and Washington, D.C., photographs are taken of drivers who pull over to solicit prostitutes, and then mailed to the home addresses corresponding to the license plates.

In Sarasota County, Florida, persons convicted of "driving under the influence" (DUI) of alcohol in the court of Judge Becky Titus face an even more visible form of public humiliation. They are required to put red stickers on their cars' rear bumpers that read CON-VICTED DUI.

Perhaps the most controversial case of this nature involved a forty-seven-year-old Oregon man named Richard James Bateman who had been sentenced to prison in 1988 for sexually molesting two minor children. But because of overcrowding in Oregon Prisons that might have prompted an early release, District Judge Dorothy Baker placed Bateman on probation. One of her stipulations, however, quickly drew both praise and condemnation. Mr. Bateman

wore an *A*, cut from scarlet cloth and sewn to her upper garments. The blasphemer wore a *B*, the pauper a *P*, the thief a *T*, and the drunkard a *D* (see Exhibit 14.1).

And finally there was the *bilboes,* wherein the citizen convicted of slander and libel was shackled by the feet to a wooden stake.

Punishment versus Reformation

Throughout English and American history, scholars and kings, philosophers and reformers, and legislators and statesmen have argued the merits of punishment versus reformation in the management and control of criminal offenders. Their views were shaped by the evolution of

The object of punishment is the reformation of the sufferer, and that of revenge, the gratification of the agent.

— ARISTOTLE

was required to post signs on the front door of where he lived, and on both sides of any vehicle he drove, that read: "Dangerous Sex Offender, No Children Allowed," in bold letters three inches high.

The probation also required that Mr. Bateman not visit zoos, parks, schools, and anywhere else that children are likely to be found and that he enter a treatment program for sex offenders. The unusual sentence had been conceived on the grounds that Bateman had been convicted of abusing children in both his home and car in the past, that he was diagnosed as a likely repeat offender, and that he had never acknowledged his crimes.

The ensuing debate focused on the appropriateness of various punishments for child molesters and the usefulness of novel sentences. Critics charged that the signs were unconstitutional because they were a form of branding. Others agreed with Judge Baker, that signs would alert the community of an offender in their midst. And as the controversy endured, other courts adopted the tactic. Shortly after Bateman's probation went into effect, a Seattle judge ordered a similar punishment for nineteen-year-old Julia Gilbert. Rather than spending thirty days in jail for sexual contacts with two young girls, Gilbert was ordered to wear a sign for sixty days which read: "I've been convicted of communicating with a minor for immoral purposes."

Finally, the most recent version of the "scarlet letter" is to publish the names and photographs, in local newspapers, of persons arrested on drug charges.

SOURCES: *Time,* June 17, 1985, p. 52; *National Law Journal,* March 14, 1988, p. 23; *USA Today,* April 1, 1988, p. 3A; *New York Times,* April 9, 1990, p. B2; *Newsweek,* February 18, 1991, p. 75.

criminal law, alternative conceptions of justice, and changing social attitudes toward what might be appropriate responses to lawbreaking. The varying ideas and practices, however, all shared similar goals — the taking of vengeance, the reduction of crime, and the protection of self and society. Criminal sanctions focused on retribution, banishment, isolation, and death, and were based on the reasoning that offenders were enemies of society, that they deserved punishment, and that severe approaches would eliminate their potential for future crime. This *punishment ideology* has endured throughout recorded history.

During the eighteenth century — the Age of Enlightenment — a new ideology began to emerge. It was a reform movement that stressed the dignity and imperfections of the human condition; it recognized the harshness of criminal law and procedure; and it fought against the cruelty of many punishments and conditions of confinement. Among the leading European thinkers in the reform movement were Charles Montesquieu, François Voltaire, and Denis Diderot in France; Cesare Beccaria in Italy; and Jeremy Bentham, John Howard, Samuel Romilly, and Robert Peel in England (see Exhibit 14.2).[6]

The Classical School of Criminology

The principles of Montesquieu, Voltaire, and other Englightenment philosophers with regard to criminal law and the administration of justice merged during the middle of the eighteenth century into what has become known as the **classical school of criminal law and criminology.** It has been called "classical" because of its historical significance as the first body of ideas before modern times that was coherently formulated to bring about changes in criminal law and procedure. At the basis of the classical tradition were the ideas that man was a self-determining being, acting on reason and intelligence, and therefore responsible for his behavior.

The classical school began as an outgrowth of the acquaintanceship between the young Italian economist **Cesare Beccaria** and Alessandro Verri, a prison official in Milan. Beccaria's numerous visits to Verri exposed him to the existing policies of criminal justice procedure. He found judges to be applying capricious and purely personal justice; he found criminal sanctions to be almost totally discretionary; he saw many magistrates exercising their power to add to the punishments nebulously prescribed by law; and he witnessed such tyrannical and brutal punishments as having criminals branded, mutilated, torn limb from limb, fed to animals, slowly starved, scalded, burned, hanged, enslaved, crucified, and stoned or pressed to death.

Outraged by the experience, Beccaria, at age twenty-four, began writing what became one of the most significant books of his time. Two years later, in 1764, his *Dei delitti et delle pene (An Essay on Crimes and Punishments)* was published. It outlined a liberal doctrine of criminal law and procedure, and highlighted the following points:

1. Since the criminal law placed restrictions on individual freedom, the law should be limited in scope. The function of the law as to serve the needs of a given society, not to enforce moral virtue, and as such, to prohibit an action necessarily increases rather than decreases crime.
2. In the administration of justice, the presumption of innocence should be the guiding factor, and at all stages in the criminal justice process the rights of the suspected, the accused, the convicted, and the sentenced should be protected.
3. The criminal law should define in advance both the offenses and their punishments. Thus there should be a complete written code of criminal law.
4. Punishment should be retributive: "Everyone must suffer punishment so far to invade the province of his own rights as the crime he has committed has penetrated into that of another."
5. The severity of punishment must be limited; it should be proportionate to the crime; it should not go beyond the point that already prevents the offender from further injuring others or beyond the point that already deters others.

Classical school of criminal law and criminology: A body of ideals from Enlightenment philosophers and reformers for transforming criminal law and procedure.

Cesare Beccaria: The founder of the classical school of criminal law and criminology.

Care should be taken that the punishment should not be out of proportion to the offenses.

—Cicero

Leading Figures in the Classical School

Montesquieu (1689–1755)

Charles-Louis de Secondat, Baron de La Brède et de Montesquieu, the French lawyer, philosopher, and man of letters, epitomized the Enlightenment's concern for the rights of humanity. His book, *The Spirit of the Laws,* and essay, "Persian Letters," condemned the barbarous injustice of the French penal code and advocated reforms that would make punishments less severe and more adapted to the crimes for which they were imposed.

Voltaire (1694–1778)

François-Marie Arouet, or Voltaire, the French humanist and satirist, was also the most versatile of the eighteenth-century philosophers. In his writings, he condemned the arbitrary powers of judges, the secret trial, and the use of torture, and he demanded that the purpose of the law be the protection of the citizen and that all persons should be equal before the law.

Diderot (1713–1784)

Denis Diderot, the French encyclopedist, novelist, dramatist, and art critic, was also a philosopher who attacked the orthodoxy of his time. He revolted against the unquestioning acceptance of tradition and authority, and in many of his works he heavily criticized the chaos and corruption in political institutions as well as the superstition and cruelty that pervaded penal practices.

Beccaria (1738–1794)

Cesare Bonesana, Marchese di Beccaria, the Italian economist and jurist, proposed a whole new concept for the administration of justice. His major work, *An Essay on Crimes and Punishments,* became the manifesto of the liberal approach to criminal law. It condemned capital punishment and torture, suggested that the law should be specific, and advocated the prevention of crime and rigid rules of criminal procedure.

Bentham (1748–1832)

Jeremy Bentham, the English jurist and philosopher, was the leader of English criminal law reform. He believed that punishment should be a deterrent. His "hedonistic calculus" argued that if punishments were designed to negate whatever pleasure or gain the criminal derived from crime, the crime rate would to down. This ethical doctrine was founded on the notion that the morality of actions is determined by utility, and appeared in his major work on the administration of justice, *Introduction to the Principles and Morals of Legislation.*

Howard (1726?–1790)

The name of John Howard, High Sheriff of Bedfordshire for almost two decades, became synonymous with English prison reform. His work, *State of Prisons,* was based on observations of prison conditions throughout England and continental Europe, and influenced the passage of the Penitentiary Act of 1779. This legislation resulted in England's first penitentiary, one that incorporated many principles of basic prison reform.

Romilly (1757–1818)

Sir Samuel Romilly, the English lawyer and law reformer, devoted his energies to changes in the harsh criminal codes. His efforts secured the repeal of many Elizabethan capital statutes and numerous other harsh and irrational laws. He also influenced the construction of the first modern English prison.

Peel (1788–1850)

Sir Robert Peel, the English statesman, member of Parliament, and prime minister, influenced legislation that reformed the criminal law. He established the Irish constabulary (called the "Peelers"), and pushed the legislation that created the London metropolitan police (the "bobbies")—both named after him.

6. The nature of the punishment should correspond with the nature of the offense; a fine would be appropriate for simple thefts, but corporal punishment and labor would satisfy crimes of violence.

7. There must be certainty of punishment; penalties must be applied with speed and certainty.

8. Punishment should not be used to make an example of the offender for society, nor should the punishment include reformatory measures, since enforced reformation by its very nature is of little use. Furthermore, the punishment should be based on the objective criterion of the crime, and not varied to suit the personality of the offender.

9. "It is better to prevent crimes than to punish them" and prevention consists in a clear and limited code of laws, supplemented by the rewarding of virtue.[7]

Beccaria's reformist views were highly praised, for they appeared at a time when European jurists were ready to hear and implement the kinds of changes he had proposed. His arguments were incorporated into both English and French criminal codes, and among those inspired by Beccaria's work were the framers of the United States Constitution.

The "bloody codes"

The classical school was not limited to the writing and influence of Cesare Beccaria. In England, such classicists as Jeremy Bentham, Samuel Romilly and John Howard sought to reform the infamous *"bloody codes"* —a system of laws that permitted execution for pickpocketing, cutting down trees on government parklands, setting fire to a cornfield, escaping from jail, and shooting a rabbit.

The pleasure–pain principle

However, the doctrine of free will, which dominated classical thinking, also served to generate weaknesses in its perspective. Its proponents argued that all behavior was based on *hedonism,* the *pleasure–pain principle.* People chose those courses of action that would give them the most pleasure and avoided those that would bring pain. Thus behavior was purposive, and punishment, they reasoned, should result in more pain than the pleasure received from the forbidden act. Moreover, this view applied equally to all citizens with no allowances for aggravating or mitigating circumstances. In spite of this flaw, the classical school did make contributions. It was instrumental in making the law impartial, in reducing the harshness of penalties, and with replacing the arbitrary powers of judges with a specified range of criminal sanctions.

AMERICAN PRISONS IN PERSPECTIVE

William Penn

The American prison system had its beginnings during the second half of the seventeenth century in Philadelphia. In 1682, *William Penn,* a religious reformer and the founder of Pennsylvania, made sweeping changes in the administration of justice in the territory under his control. He limited the death penalty in Pennsylvania to cases of murder, called for fines and imprisonment as penalties for most offenses, and urged flogging for adultery, arson, and rape. These were mild sanctions compared to the executions, brandings, mutilations, and other severe punishments that existed throughout the other colonies. Penn also influenced the construction of county jails, which were designed to be workhouses for convicted felons. The first of these was the High Street

Jail in Philadelphia erected in 1682; others appeared in the decades that followed. But even before Penn's death in 1718, the workhouse idea failed due to overcrowding and inadequate conditions. As one observer described the situation:

> What a spectacle must this abode of guilt and wretchedness have presented, when in one common herd were kept by day and night prisoners of all ages, colors and sexes! No separation was made of the most flagrant offender and convict, from the prisoner who might, perhaps be falsely suspected of some trifling misdemeanor; none of the old and hardened culprits from the youthful, trembling novice in crime; none even of the fraudulent swindler from the unfortunate and possibly the most estimable debtor; and when intermingled with all these, in one corrupt and corrupting assemblage were to be found the disgusting object of popular contempt, besmeared with filth from the pillory—the unhappy victim of the lash, streaming with blood from the whipping post—the half-naked vagrant—the loathsome drunkard—the sick, suffering from various bodily pains, and too often the unaneled* malefactor, whose precious hours of probation had been numbered by his earthly judge.[8]

The Walnut Street Jail

During the eighteenth century, the Quakers of Pennsylvania placed their commonwealth in the forefront of correctional history. In 1787, they formed the Philadelphia Society for Alleviating the Miseries of Public Prisons and quickly addressed the conditions of their local jails. In 1776, a new prison-workhouse opened on Philadelphia's Walnut Street to receive prisoners from the overcrowded High Street Jail. In 1790, influenced by the work of John Howard, the society transformed the new structure on Walnut Street into the first American penitentiary.

The **Walnut Street Jail** was both a prison and a workhouse, and covered some two acres of ground. Those convicted of the most serious crimes were confined without labor in sixteen solitary cells, each six feet wide and eight feet long, with an inner iron door, an outer wooden door, and wire across the single window. The prisoners were fed the rather peculiar diet of pudding made of molasses and maize. A large pipe extending from each cell to a sewer served as a toilet, while a stove in the corridor provided heat. Offenders confined for less serious crimes were lodged together in rooms eighteen by twenty feet in size. Together they worked in a large stone structure at shoemaking, carpentry, weaving, tailoring, and nailmaking. Women worked at spinning cotton, preparing hemp and wool, washing, and mending. Vagrants and unskilled prisoners beat hemp or picked moss and oakum (jute fiber used for caulking ships). Male prisoners were credited with the prevailing wage but were charged the costs of their trials, fines, and maintenance. Women were not given wages, nor were they charged for their maintenance. No irons or guard weapons were permitted. Except for women prisoners, silence was enforced in the shops and at meals, but some low-toned conversation was permitted in the night quarters before bedtime. Religious instruction and weekly services were offered.[9]

Throughout the 1790s, the Walnut Street Jail was considered a model prison. Officials from other states and from throughout Europe visited to observe its cellular confinement pattern and workhouse program, returning to their homes to praise its design and procedures. By

Walnut Street Jail: The first American penitentiary.

---

* Not having received the last rites of the church.

In some prisons, the most dangerous prisoners are not only kept in separate cells—their outdoor recreation is solitary, too.

The history of correction is a graveyard of abandoned fads.
— ROBERT MARTINSON, 1976

Stone walls do not a prison make, nor iron bars a cage.
— RICHARD LOVELACE, 1649

Separate system: Solitary confinement in an isolated cell for the purpose of eliminating evil association in congregate quarters.

Prison, n. *A place of punishment and rewards. The poet assures us that—"Stone walls do not a prison make," but a combination of the stone wall, the political parasite and the moral instructor is no garden of sweets.*
— AMBROSE BIERCE, *THE DEVIL'S DICTIONARY,* 1911

the beginning of the nineteenth century, however, Philadelphia's acclaimed jail had begun to deteriorate, primarily due to overcrowding. Work activity had become impossible to continue, discipline had become difficult, and riots were common.

The Separate System

The solitary confinement of hardened offenders in the Walnut Street Jail was based on the notion that recidivism could be prevented and offenders reformed by eliminating evil association in congregate prison quarters. Confinement in an isolated cell would give the convict an opportunity to contemplate the evils of his past life, thereby leading him to resolve "in the spiritual presence of his Maker" to reform his future conduct.[10] More specifically, the defenders of this **separate system** argued, it possessed a number of wholesome virtues:

- the protection against possible moral contamination through evil association
- the invitation to self-examination and self-reproach in solitude
- the impossibility of being visited by anyone (other than an officer, a reformer, or members of the clergy)
- the great ease of administration of discipline
- the possibility of a great degree of individuality of treatment
- the minimal need for disciplinary measures
- the absence of any possibility of mutual recognition of prisoners after discharge
- the fact that the pressures of loneliness would make convicts eager to engage in productive labor, during which time they could be taught a useful trade[11]

Such was the basis for the construction of Western Penitentiary near Pittsburgh in 1826, and Eastern Penitentiary near Philadelphia in 1829. Eastern Penitentiary (pictured on the cover of this text) epitomized the Pennsylvania correctional philosophy, and its architecture was adapted to the principle of solitary confinement.[12] It had seven wards housing 844 individual cells, all radiating from a common center like the spokes of a wheel. To each individual cell on the lower floor of each ward was attached a small exercise yard, which the prisoner could visit twice daily for short periods of time. In the interim, he washed, ate, and slept in his cell, seeing no one other than the prison officials and reformers from the outside community. Massive walls surrounded the entire institution and divided its parts so as to eliminate all contact and make escape impossible.

Visitors from almost every nation in the Western world marveled at the construction and plan of Eastern Penitentiary, and recommended that the model be adopted in their home countries. In 1833, French writers Gustave de Beaumont and Alexis de Tocqueville commented on the reformative effects of the absolute solitude that Pennsylvania's separate system provided for its confined offenders:

> Generally, their hearts are found ready to open themselves, and the facility of being moved renders them also fitter for reformation. They are particularly accessible to religious sentiments, and the remembrance of their family has an uncommon power over their minds. . . . Nothing distracts, in Philadelphia, the mind of the convicts from their meditations; and as they are always isolated, the presence of a person who comes to converse with them is of the greatest benefit. . . . When we visited this penitentiary, one of the prisoners said to us: "It is with joy that I perceive the figure of the keepers, who visit my cell. This summer a cricket came into my yard; it looked like a companion. When a butterfly or any other animal happens to enter my cell, I never do it any harm."

(Below) Eastern Penitentiary, Philadelphia, Pennsylvania, as it appeared in its early years; (above) its dilapidated interior today.

However, the abominable simplicity of the separate system was also a dehumanizing experience. As one commentator described it:

> He was given a hot bath, and a prison uniform. Then his eyes were bandaged, and he was led blindfolded into the rotunda, where, still not seeing, he heard the rules of the house explained by the superintendent. And still blindfolded, he was led to his living grave. The bandage was taken from his eyes. He saw a cell less than twelve feet long, less than eight feet wide, and if he was to live on the ground floor, he saw a little courtyard, the same size, highly walled, opening out of it, in which he sometimes might exercise. In that cell, and that courtyard, he stayed, without any change, for three, ten, twenty years or for life. He saw only the guard who brought his food to him, but who was forbidden to speak to him. He got no letters, saw none of his family. He was cut off from the world. When the cholera raged in Philadelphia in 1843, it was months before the prisoners got a hint that an epidemic had visited the city. After the slave had been three days in his cell, he was allowed to work, if he wished, and the fact that nearly all prisoners asked for something to do proved to the inspectors that reform was beginning. If they did not choose to work they might commune with their corrupt hearts in a perfectly dark and solitary punishment cell.[14]

Despite its attractiveness to Europeans, the Pennsylvania plan never gained widespread popularity in the United States. It was the basis of temporary experimentation in New Jersey and Rhode Island, but by the latter part of the nineteenth century it had been abandoned, even in Pennsylvania.

The Silent System

The demise of the separate system was due not so much to the destructive effects of long-term solitary confinement as to the emergence of a different pattern of prison administration in New York State. Known as the **silent system** and established at Auburn Prison in 1823, it was considered to be the most economically sound of penitentiary programs (see Exhibit 14.3). As opposed to the outside cells with individual exercise

Inside cells at Auburn Prison yesterday (right) and today (below). Under Auburn's silent system, proponents claimed, such prisons were cheaper to build and run, gave prisoners vocational training, and produced more state revenue. Defenders of the separate system, on the other hand, held that institutions such as Pennsylvania's Eastern Prison prevented "contamination" by completely separating prisoners from one another, hence promoting the best chance for repentance. The silent system eventually won out, even in Pennsylvania, due to its economic advantages.

• EXHIBIT 14.3 •

A Day at Auburn Prison

At Auburn we have a more beautiful example still of what may be done by proper discipline, in a prison well constructed. It is not possible to describe the pleasure which we feel in contemplating this noble institution, after wading through the fraud, and the material and moral filth of many prisons. We regard it as a model worthy of the world's imitation. We do not mean that there is nothing in this institution which admits of improvement; for there have been a few cases of unjustifiable severity in punishments; but, upon the whole, the institution is immensely elevated above the old penitentiaries.

The whole establishment, from the gate to the sewer, is a specimen of neatness. The unremitted industry, the entire subordination and subdued feeling of the convicts, has probably no parallel among an equal number of criminals. In their solitary cells they spend the night, with no other book but the Bible, and at sunrise they proceed, in military order, under the eye of the turnkeys, in solid columns, with

the lock march, to their workshops; thence, in the same order, at the hour of breakfast, to the common hall, where they partake of their wholesome and frugal meal in silence. Not even a whisper is heard; though the silence is such that a whisper might be heard through the whole apartment. The convicts are seated, in single file, at narrow tables, with their backs towards the center, so that there can be no interchange of signs. If one has more food than he wants; he raises his left hand; and if another has less, he raises his right hand, and the waiter changes it. When they have done eating, at the ringing of a little bell, of the softest sound, they rise from the table, form the solid columns, and return, under the eye of the turnkeys, to the workshops. From one end of the shops to the other, it is the testimony of many witnesses, that they have passed more than three hundred convicts, without seeing one leave his work, or turn his head to gaze at them. There is the most perfect attention to business from morning

till night, interrupted only by the time necessary to dine, and never by the fact that the whole body of prisoners have done their tasks, and the time is now their own, and they can do as they please. At the close of the day, a little before sunset, the work is all laid aside at once, and the convicts return, in military order, to the solitary cells, where they partake of the frugal meal, which they were permitted to take from the kitchen, where it was furnished for them as they returned from the shops. After supper, they can, if they choose, read Scripture undisturbed and then reflect in silence on the errors of their lives. They must not disturb their fellow prisoners by even a whisper.

SOURCE: From a letter by Lewis Dwight, founder of the Boston Prison Discipline Society, written shortly after the full implementation of the "silent system" at Auburn in 1823; cited by Harry Elmer Barnes, *The Story of Punishment: A Record of Man's Inhumanity to Man* (Montclair, N.J.: Patterson Smith, 1972), pp. 136–137.

---

yards at Eastern Penitentiary, prisoners at Auburn were confined in banks of inside cells each measuring only seven feet by three and one-half feet. Inmates were employed in congregate shops during the day under a rigid rule of absolute silence at all times, and with solitary confinement only at night. Hard labor was considered essential to the reformation of character and to the economic solvency of the prison. Perpetual silence was seen as mandatory while inmates were in close proximity in order to avoid their corruption of one another and to reduce any opportunities for the hatching of plots for insurrection, escape, or riot. Furthermore, all prisoners were totally separated from the outside world; communication with relatives and friends was forbidden.[15]

The attractiveness of the silent system was primarily due to its economic advantages. Small inside cells were cheaper to construct. Also, industrial production within a setting of large congregate work areas was

Silent system: Confinement under a rigid rule of absolute silence at all times.

Prisoners marching in lock-step at Joliet Penitentiary, Illinois, in 1900

far greater and more efficient than the limited output possible under the Pennsylvania plan of handicraft construction in separate confinement. The hard and unremitting labor, perpetual silence, and unquestioning obedience were maintained by severe corporal punishments such as flogging, the "douche," and the "water cure." Flogging was considered the most effective method of gaining compliance, and was generally done with a rawhide whip or a "cat" made of wire strands. The "douche" involved the continuous dumping of frigid water from a great height onto the body of the prisoner. The "water cure" was of several varieties. At times it consisted of a strong fine stream of water turned onto sensitive parts of the prisoner's body; on other occasions, water came only one drop at a time onto the prisoner's head, the process sometimes lasting for days. These were common punishments for breaking the silence rule. The technique of talking out of the side of one's mouth — often depicted in the gangster movies of the 1930s and 1940s — had its origin in "silent" prisons, where it was a means of getting around the silence rules.

Prison stripes and the *lock-step* were also features of prison life devised at Auburn. Striped uniforms served to degrade convicts and to make them conspicuous should they escape. The lock-step, which was originated for the purpose of making supervision easier, was a bizarre marching formation. Prisoners were required to line up behind one another, with their hands on the shoulders or under the arms of the person in front. The line then moved rapidly toward its destination as the prisoners shuffled their feet in unison, without lifting them from the ground with their eyes focused on the guard. Another feaure of Auburn was the "prison-within-a-prison," or "hole," which was an area where prisoners were put into total isolation for violation of some institutional rule.

Prison Industries

The Auburn model became the major pattern of prison administration for the rest of the nineteenth century. Sing Sing Prison in New York followed the Auburn plan in 1825, and more than thirty other states built similar institutions in the years that followed. However, the rule of absolute silence was soon relaxed, for conditions within most penitentiaries made it impractical. Not only had most of the institutions become overcrowded, but more importantly, the Industrial Revolution had arrived and factory workshop production had been introduced to exploit cheap inmate labor and to make the penitentiaries self-sustaining. Production became the paramount goal of prisons, and the necessity for communication within the industrial shops served to make the perpetual silence rule counterproductive.[16]

Contract labor and the piece-price system were the earliest forms of prison industry. Under the **contract system,** the labor of the inmates was leased to an outside contractor, who furnished the machinery and raw materials and supervised the work. The only responsibility of the prison administration under such an arrangement was to guard the convicts. The **piece-price system** was a variation on this. Under this plan, the contractor supplied the raw material and received the finished product, paying the prison a specified amount for each unit produced. Under both plans the prisoners were invariably exploited, overworked, and otherwise abused. Contractors often shortchanged convicts in their work tallies, and prison officials were known to force inmates to work long hours, under deplorable conditions, and for little or no pay. Recalling his experiences at Michigan's Ionia Reformatory in 1889, an inmate at Illinois State Penitentiary wrote some four decades later:

> During my stay at this time there was a great deal of fighting, especially in the Cigar Shop, owing to the fact that the boys were continuously stealing cigars from each other to complete the task set them by the Contractors, as it was almost impossible to do what they demanded. In the Shoe Shop things were about the same, and a friend of mine, Tiny Prince, tried to cut off his finger in full view of all of us. Another man on the Shoe Contract took a hatchet and cut off his thumb because he was unable to do his task.

Contract system: A form of prison industry in which the labor of inmates was leased to an outside contractor, who furnished the machinery and raw materials and supervised the work.

Piece-price system: A variation of the contract system of prison industry in which the contractor supplied the raw material and received the finished product, paying the prison a specified amount for each unit produced.

Warden T. M. Osborne and jailers in a cell block at Sing Sing, 1915

Here I will make a confession I have never made in my life before. The first finger of my left hand is gone. I have always let people think it got cut off accidentally in a machine. Well, it didn't. I cut if off myself like these other men did, in order to cripple myself so I could escape for a little while from the hell of that contract labor at Ionia. I did it by bracing a knife blade against my finger and pounding it with my shoe. That was how bad some of us hated the contract system.[17]

Lease system: A form of prison industry under which contractors assumed complete control over prisoners.

Even more vicious was the **lease system,** under which contractors assumed complete control over the prisoners, including their maintenance and discipline. Convicts were taken from the institutions and employed in agriculture, quarrying, bridge and road construction, mining, and in turpentine camps or sugar cane plantations. The forced labor resembled slavery, and prisoners received little, if any compensation for their work.[18]

State account system: A form of prison industry in which inmate production was directed by prison officials, goods were sold on the open market, and inmates received a share of the profits.

Alternatives to the contract labor practices were the **state account** and **state-use systems.** Under the state account plan, inmate production was directed and supervised by prison officials, the manufactured goods were sold on the open market, and the convicts received a small share of the profits. The state-use plan produced articles in prison that were subsequently used in state-supported institutions and bureaus. Related to these was the public works system of prison labor, under which inmates were employed in the construction and repair of public streets, highways, and structures. The well-known Sing Sing Prison, for example, from which came such terms as the "big house" and "up the river," * was constructed by a team of 100 inmates from Auburn under the public works system.[19]

State-use system: A form of prison industry in which inmate-produced goods were used in state institutions and bureaus.

Most nineteenth-century prisons also included farming as a form of prison labor. As a separate form of the state-use philosophy, prison agriculture was viewed as a necessary part of institutional procedure. The raising of crops and vegetables was a means of hard inmate labor, while at the same time it reduced the cost of inmate maintenance (see Exhibit 14.4).

The Reformatory Era

From the institutional backwater of the mid-nineteenth century emerged a *treatment* philosophy of corrections. This was an ideology that viewed many forms of offense behavior as manifestations of various social "pathologies," psychological "maladies," and inherited "predispositions" that could be "corrected" by some form of therapeutic or rehabilitative intervention. This new treatment ideology led to the *reformatory era* in American corrections, which endured from 1870 through 1910. The influences that led to the reformatory idea came from numerous theorists and practitioners in many parts of the world, but the movement was affected most directly by the work of Captain Alexander Maconochie in Australia and Sir Walter Crofton in Ireland.

The reformatory era in American corrections

Alexander Maconochie

In 1840, Captain *Alexander Maconochie,* a geographer with England's Royal Navy, was placed in charge of Norfolk Island, a penal colony for habitual felons located 1,000 miles off the coast of Australia. Conditions were so bad at Norfolk that it has been said that "men who were reprieved wept with sorrow that they had to go on living, and those doomed to die fell on their knees and thanked God for the release that was to be theirs." [20] Maconochie eliminated the brutality of the system and implemented a correctional scheme that rested on five postulates:

* Sing Sing, for a short time known as Ossining Correctional Facility, is located on the eastern shore of the Hudson River, thirty miles north of New York City.

1. Sentences should not be for a period of time, but for the performance of a determined and specified quantity of labor; in brief, time sentences should be abolished, and task sentences substituted;

2. The quantity of labor a prisoner must perform should be expressed in a number of "marks" which he must earn, by improvement of conduct, frugality of living, and habits of industry, before he can be released;

3. While in prison he should earn everything he receives; all sustenance and indulgences should be added to his debt of marks;

4. When qualified by discipline to do so he should work in association with a small number of other prisoners, forming a group of six or seven, and the whole group should be answerable for the conduct and labor of each member of it;

5. In the final stage, a prisoner, while still obliged to earn his daily tally of marks, should be given a proprietary interest in his own labor and be subject to a less rigorous discipline in order to prepare him for release into society.[21]

This "apparatus," as Captain Maconochie called it, removed the "flat" term of imprisonment, and replaced it with a **"mark system,"** whereby an inmate could earn early release by hard work and good behavior. But the scheme was not looked upon favorably by Maconochie's superiors. He was removed as administrator after only a brief time, his accomplishments were disclaimed, and the colony quickly returned to its former brutalizing routine.

But what had occurred at Norfolk Island had not gone unnoticed. Drawing upon Maconochie's notion that imprisonment could be used to prepare a convict for eventual return to the community, Sir Walter Crofton of Ireland implemented what he called his "indeterminate system." Also known as the *"Irish system,"* it called for four distinct stages of treatment: solitary confinement at monotonous work for two years, followed by congregate labor under a marking system that regulated privileges and determined the date of discharge, then by an intermediate stage during which inmates were permitted to work on outside jobs, and finally conditional release under a **"ticket-of-leave."** [22] This ticket, which could be revoked if the convict failed to live up to the conditions of his temporary release, was the first attempt at what has come to be known as *parole.*

Maconochie's "mark system" and Crofton's "Irish system" were overwhelmingly endorsed at the American Prison Congress in 1870. The result was the opening of the first reformatory in the United States in 1876, at Elmira, New York, as an institution for youths and young adults serving their first term of imprisonment. Zebulon Brockway, the first superintendent of Elmira, listed the essentials of a successful reformatory system:

1. The material structure establishment itself. . . . The general plan and arrangements should be those of the Auburn System plan, modified and modernized; and 10 percent of the cells might well be constructed like those of the Pennsylvania System structures. The whole should be supplied with suitable modern sanitary appliances and with abundance of natural and artificial light.

2. Clothing — not degradingly distinctive but uniform, yet fitly representing the respective grades or standing of the prisoners. . . . Scrupulous cleanliness should be maintained and the prisoners appropriately groomed.

3. A liberal prison dietary designed to promote vigor. Deprivation of food, by a general regulation, is deprecated. . . .

"Mark system": Started by Alexander Maconochie at Norfolk Island, a system by which inmates could earn early release by hard work and good behavior.

Sir Walter Crofton's "Irish system"

"Ticket-of-leave": Started by Sir Walter Crofton of Ireland, a system of conditional release from prison that represented an early form of parole.

• EXHIBIT 14.4 •

Contract Prison Labor in the Post-Civil War South

After the Civil War had shattered both the social structure and economy of the South, maintaining adequate prison systems tended to have only minimal priority for state officials. Approaches were sought for making prisons at least self-supporting, and perhaps even profit making. The obvious solution was to lease prisons and convicts to private contractors, and by 1875 almost every southern state had some sort of a contract labor policy.

As in some Northern jurisdictions, however, many southern prison lease systems quickly evolved into varieties of penal servitude. Although state inspectors were assigned to monitor such arrangements, inmates typically lived and worked under conditions of poor hygiene and excessive brutality, often spending much of their time shackled to heavy iron balls. A late nineteenth-century commentary on contract labor conditions in Mississippi reported this:

Those on farms and public works have been subjected to indignities without authority of law and contrary to civilized humanity. Often subleasers resort to "pullin" the prisoner until he faints from the lash on his naked back, while the sufferer was held by four strong men holding each a hand or foot stretched out on the frozen ground or over stumps or logs—often over 300 **stripes** [lashes] at a time, which more than once, it is thought, resulted in the death of a convict. Men unable to work have been driven to their death and some have died fettered to the chain gang. . . . When working in the swamps or fields they were refused pure water and were driven to drink out of sloughs or plow furrows in the fields in which they labored. . . . Some were placed in the swamp in water ranging to their bare knees, and in almost nude state they spaded caney and rooty ground, their bare feet chained together by chains that fretted the flesh.

Convicts at a southern prison farm in the 1940s and the 1990s

They were compelled to attend to the calls of nature in line as they stood day in and day out, their thirst compelling them to drink the water in which they were compelled to deposit their excrement.

The brutal conditions of the lease system received such widespread criticism and legislative focus that contract labor as such became obsolete throughout the South by 1920. In its place emerged public works systems and their well-known *chain gangs.* In South Carolina, Florida, and Georgia, for example, all able-bodied prisoners were sentenced, as an alternative to the state penitentiary, to the county to perform road and bridge work. Although public works systems tended to be less exploitive of inmates than leas-

ing, life on a chain gang was anything but pleasant. "Whipping bosses" maintained discipline through severe punishments, and brutality was not uncommon. The use of the chain gang was so widespread that, with time, its inmates in striped uniforms and chains doing roadwork under the watchful eyes of a gun-toting boss came to symbolize Southern corrections.

By contrast, Texas, Louisiana, Arkansas, and Mississippi replaced leasing with the *plantation prison system.* Legislatures in these jurisdictions had stressed self-sufficiency. Too, turning old plantations into productive prison farms appeared to be a solution to the burgeoning black prisoner population of the post-Civil War period. It was the

opinion of many whites during these years that former slaves were still fieldhands that could not be reformed.

A hallmark of the Southern plantation prisons was the *trusty* model of inmate control — closely akin to the slave driver system on antebellum planta-tions. As a mechanism of deal-ing with limited institutional budgets, select groups of con-victs were chosen to watch over their inmate peers. They were housed separately and typically had far more privileges than other prisoners. Convict guards in Arkansas, Louisiana, and Mississippi, generally called "shooters," herded over their quarry with loaded shotguns — an arrangement that endured well into the twentieth century. The Texas counterpart to the

trusty was the *building tender.* In contrast to trusties, building ten-ders were unarmed and lived in the same quarters as other in-mates, but watched them never-theless. The building tender sys-tem survived in Texas until the 1980s, finally crumbling in the aftermath of the *Ruiz* v. *Estelle* prison conditions case (see Chapter 16).

sources: Edward L. Ayers, *Vengeance and Justice: Crime and Punishment in the 19th Century American South* (New York: Ox-ford University Press, 1984); Mark T. Carleton, *Politics and Punishment: The History of the Louisiana State Penal System* (Baton Rouge: Louisiana State University Press, 1971); James W. Marquart and Ben M. Crouch, "Co-opting the Kept: Using Inmates for Social Control in a Southern Prison," *Justice Quarterly,* 1 (1984), pp. 491–509; *Ruiz* v. *Estelle,* F. 2d 115 (5th. Cir. 1982).

Elmira Reformatory

4. All the modern appliances for scientific physical culture; a gymnasium completely equipped with baths and apparatus; and facilities for field athletics.

5. Facilities for manual training sufficient for about one-third of the population. . . . This special manual training covers, in addition to other exercises in other departments, mechanical and freehand drawing; cardboard constructive form work; clay modeling; cabinet making; clipping and filing; and iron molding.

6. Trade instruction based on the needs and capacities of individual prisoners.

7. A regimental military organization with a band of music, swords for officers and dummy guns for the rank and file of prisoners.

8. School of letters with a curriculum that reaches from an adaptation of the kindergarten . . . up to the usual high school course; and, in addition, special classes in college subjects. . . .

9. A well-selected library for circulation, consultation and, for occasional semi-social use.

10. A weekly institutional newspaper, in lieu of all outside newspapers, edited and printed by the prisoners under due censorship.

11. Recreating and diverting entertainments for the mass of the population, provided in the great auditorium; not any vaudeville or minstrel shows, but entertainments of such a class as the middle cultured people of a community would enjoy. . . .

12. Religious opportunities . . . adapted to the hereditary, habitual, and preferable denominational predilection of the individual prisoners.

13. Definitely planned, carefully directed, emotional occasions; not summoned, primarily, for either instruction, diversion, nor, specifically, for a common religious impression, but, figuratively, for a kind of irrigation.[23]

The program established at Elmira quickly spread to other states, but the reformatory movement as a whole proved to be a relative failure and disappointment for its advocates. Many of Brockway's principles were never put into effect; prison employees were too conditioned to the punishment ideology to support the new concepts; safe and secure custody continued to be regarded as the most important institutional activity; the reformatories quickly became overcrowded and staff shortages prevented the development of academic programs; and, hard-core offenders were housed in the new structures, thus turning them into the more typical penal environments.[24]

By 1910 the reformatory experiment was abandoned. Nevertheless, it left an important legacy for corrections in the years to come. The indeterminate sentence, conditional release, educational programs, vocational training, and the other rehabilitative ideals fostered by the reformatory became fully a part of the correctional ideology of later decades.

The Twentieth-Century Industrial Prison

By the early years of the twentieth century, the American prison system had evolved into a growing number of Sing Sing and Auburn-type institutions. With many reflecting the architecture of medieval dungeons and Gothic castles, they were fortresslike structures, operated on the principles of mass congregate incarceration and rigid discipline and security. Their most distinctive feature, furthermore, was the use of inmate labor for the production of industrial goods for sale on the open market. This practice was widely encouraged not only because of the belief in hard labor as a correctional tool, but also because of the economics of creating a self-sustaining prison system.

Yet as the industrial prison was developing into a prudent financial operation, so too was *opposition to inmate labor*. Prison industries under the contract, piece-price, lease, and state account systems were seen as threats to free enterprise. With the formation of the American Federation of Labor in 1880, labor and its political lobbyists organized a formal attack on the industrial prison. The culmination of the assault came during the years of the Great Depression with the passage of numerous federal and state statutes.[25] Even before the economic strains of the depression occurred, the *Hawes-Cooper Act* of 1929 disallowed certain prison-made goods from being shipped to other states. Put into force on January 1, 1934, the act, in effect, barred these products from interstate commerce. At the same time, thirty-three states produced legislation that prohibited the sale of prison goods on the open market. The *Ashurst-Sumners Act* in 1935 banned transportation companies from accepting inmate products for shipment into states where the local laws prohibited their sale. And the *Walsh-Healy Act,* signed into law by President Franklin D. Roosevelt on October 14, 1940, excluded almost all prison-made products from interstate commerce.

Humanitarian concerns as well aided in the demise of the prison industrial complex. Contract labor systems were often no more than exploitation motivated by corruption and greed. Although the philosophy of the time supported the notion that offenders needed discipline and hard labor to teach them the lessons of deterrence and salvation, reformers nevertheless opposed the misuse of convict workers.

The abolition of contract labor was in many ways desirable, but there was little to take the place of free-market prison enterprise. State use and public works programs survived, but a majority of convicts were left idle. The reduction in institutional self-support and maintenance led to the gradual decay of prison structures and conditions. Eventually many state penitentiaries began shifting back to their original purposes of punishment and custody.

After the depression years, through World War II, and into the second half of the twentieth century, there was great turmoil within state

Opposition to inmate labor

Hawes-Cooper Act

Ashurst-Sumners Act

Walsh-Healy Act

Wages Paid in Selected States for Inmate Labor During 1990 for Prison Construction

STATE	HOURLY RATE
Alabama	$.15 to .25
California	.30 to .90
Delaware	.50 to 3.00
Indiana	.65 to 1.25
Louisiana	.03 to .20
Michigan	.50 to 5.00
Oklahoma	.18 to .45
Wisconsin	.08 to .47

SOURCE: U.S. Dept. of Justice

prison systems. Referred to as the "period of transition" in American corrections,[26] it was a time when clinicians and reformers were introducing new treatment ideas against a backdrop of growing apathy and decaying institutions. Some segments of the public subscribed to the rehabilitative goals of correctional ideology; others wished prisons to be no more than secure places to house criminal offenders.

The 1960s and 1970s reflected even greater contrasts. Emphasis was placed more on the needs of individual prisoners, and many of the ideas generated during the reformatory era were put into place. Academic and vocational programs were established; social casework and psychiatric treatment approaches were designed and implemented; many prison facilities were expanded; special institutions were built and equipped for youthful offenders; more concern was demonstrated for the separation of hard-core from amateur criminals; a variety of changes made prison life somewhat more humane and productive; and, state and federal judges reflected a greater awareness of prisoners' rights by providing easier access to the courts for those seeking remedies against cruel and unusual punishment. At the same time, however, there was growing unrest within the nation's institutions. The majority of state penitentiaries were still the walled fortresses of decades past — solemn monuments to the ideas of nineteenth-century penology. Prison administrators were faced with the contradictions of "rehabilitation" within a context of mass overcrowding, personnel shortages, and demands for better security. It was also a time of militancy and violence within the nation's correctional institutions. The awareness of prisoners' rights under conditions that seemed to be getting worse instead of better led to riots — in the East, the Midwest, the South, and the far West.

Throughout the 1980s and into the 1990s, the future of the American prison system still remained unclear. Diagnosticians, reformers, social scientists, and civil libertarians continued their efforts to make prisons more humane, structured for the rehabilitation of offenders. Yet the growing "law and order" approach toward offenders combined with perceptions of inefficiency within the criminal justice system served only to harden public attitudes toward the treatment of criminals.

THE FEDERAL PRISON SYSTEM

The most diversified prison system in the United States emerged at the federal level, and many of the reforms and rehabilitative measures that were introduced in state institutions following the depression years were modeled after federal practices. The federal system is also the most recently developed, although its roots date back to the signing of the Declaration of Independence.

Beginning in 1776 and for more than a century, all federal offenders were confined in state and territorial institutions. The criminal law of the United States government was not particularly well developed at that time, and the few federal prosecutions there were limited to the areas of counterfeiting, piracy and other crimes on the high seas, and felonies committed on Indian reservations. By the 1880s, however, the number of federal prisoners in state penitentiaries numbered over 1,000 with an additional 10,000 housed in county jails. This situation created pressure on federal authorities to take a more active role in the field of corrections.[27]

Don't do the crime if you can't stand the time.
—OLD PRISON SAYING

Snitches get stitches.
—OLD PRISON SAYING

Eric: *I'll never forget my mother's words to me when I first went to jail.*
Ernie: *What did she say?*
Eric: *Hello, son.*
—ERIC MORCAMBE AND ERNIE WISE, 1979

The first federal penitentiaries were authorized by Congress in 1891, and by 1905 institutions were opened in Atlanta, Georgia, and Leavenworth, Kansas. In 1919, McNeil Island in Puget Sound off the coast of Washington State was designated as a federal facility; in 1924, a women's reformatory was constructed at Alderson, West Virginia, and during the following year a men's reformatory was authorized at the military reservation at Chillicothe, Ohio.

As a result of the Mann Act (1910), which prohibited the transportation of women in foreign and interstate commerce for immoral purposes; the Harrison Act (1914), which regulated the distribution and sale of narcotics; the Volstead Act (1919), which prohibited the manufacture, transportation, and sale of alcoholic beverages; and the National Motor Vehicle Theft Act (1919), which controlled the interstate transportation of stolen vehicles, the number of persons convicted of federal crimes during the 1920s grew rapidly. The result was the creation of the *Federal Bureau of Prisons,* signed into law on May 14, 1930. It called for the "proper classification and segregation of Federal prisoners according to their character, the nature of the crimes they have committed, their mental condition, and such other factors as should be taken into consideration in providing an individualized system of discipline, care, and treatment." [28]

The creation of the Federal Bureau of Prisons

Subsequently, the bureau established a graded system of institutions including maximum-security penitentiaries for the close custody of the most serious felons, medium-security facilities for the better rehabilitative prospects, reformatories for young and inexperienced offenders, minimum-security open camps for those requiring little custodial control, detention centers for those awaiting trial and disposition, and a variety of halfway houses and community treatment centers. Despite the many negative opinions about its fortresslike *Alcatraz Island Penitentiary* (see Exhibit 14.5), the bureau evolved into the acknowledged leader in American correctional practice. By the early 1990s, the bureau had grown to the point where it operated an integrated system of ninety-two adult and juvenile correctional facilities nationwide. [29]

Alcatraz Island Penitentiary

JAILS AND DETENTION CENTERS

JAIL: An unbelievably filthy institution in which are confined men and women serving sentences for misdemeanors and crimes, and men and women not under sentence who are simply awaiting trial. . . . A melting pot in which the worst elements of the raw material in the criminal world are brought forth blended and turned out in absolute perfection.
— JOSEPH F. FISHMAN, INSPECTOR OF PRISONS, UNITED STATES GOVERNMENT, 1923

The jail is for the poor, the street is for the rich.

— NOAH POPE, JAIL INMATE

A jail is not a prison. **Prisons** are correctional institutions maintained by the federal and state governments for the confinement of convicted felons. **Jails** are facilities of local authority for the temporary detention of defendants awaiting trial or disposition on federal or state charges, and of convicted offenders sentenced to short-term imprisonment for minor crimes. Historically, however, jails have been somewhat more

Prisons: Correctional institutions maintained by federal and state governments for the confinement of convicted felons.

Jails: Local facilities for temporary detention.

than this — they have been used for the holding of many types of outcasts, suspects, and offenders.

Gaols, Hulks, and the Origins of American Jails

The jail is the oldest institution for incarcerating offenders, dating to perhaps as early as fourth-century England, when Europe was under the rule of the Roman Empire. But little is known of the jails of that period other than that they were places for the accused and that there were separate quarters for women and men.

Hulks

Even more wretched were the notorious hulks of eighteenth- and nineteenth-century England. In 1776, when transportation to the American colonies was terminated, a series of acts passed by George III ordered that the excess prison populations be placed in *hulks,* abandoned or unusable sailing vessels, generally of the man-of-war (warship) variety, permanently anchored in rivers and harbors throughout the British Isles. Within, they were similar to prisons and other places of detention. For security, inmates were often chained in irons. Like the gaols, hulks were overcrowded and dirty, and they quickly degenerated into human garbage dumps.

The American jail as we know it today is more likely rooted in the twelfth century, when places of detention had to be provided for prison-

Prison barges of the early nineteenth century (top); modern-day floating jail in Manhattan's East River (bottom).

ers awaiting trial in the English courts. Known as *gaols* (pronounced "jails"), they were often only a single room or two in a castle, market house, or the gaoler's own dwelling. The inmates were known as *gaol-birds* (jailbirds), from the large cagelike cells often used to confine groups of the prisoners like "birds in a cage."

By the seventeenth century, England's jails had come to house both accused and convicted criminals. In addition to those awaiting trial, the jails held minor offenders sentenced to short-term imprisonment; debtors who were detained until they paid their creditors; vagrants, beggars, and other rogues and vagabonds who were considered public nuisances; and prisoners awaiting transportation to the colonies, execution, mutilation, branding, or placement in the stocks or pillory. The conditions were abominable, and inmates were abused and exploited by their keepers. Furthermore:

> Devoid of privacy and restrictions, its contaminated air heavy with the stench of unwashed bodies, human excrement, and the discharges of loathsome sores, the gaol bred the basest thoughts and the foulest deeds. The inmates made their own rules, and the weak and the innocent were exposed to the tyranny of the strong and the vicious. Prostitutes plied their trade with ease, often with the connivance and support of the gaolers, who thus sought to supplement their fees. Even virtuous women sold themselves to obtain food and clothing, and frequently the worst elements of the town used the gaol as they would a brothel. Thus, idleness, vice, perversion, profligacy, shameless exploitation, and ruthless cruelty were compounded in hotbeds of infection and cesspools of corruption. These were the common goals of England.[30]

The English jail tradition came with the colonists to the New World. Jails first appeared in the Virginia colony in 1626, and were established in Pennsylvania as promulgated by the *Charter and Laws* of the Duke of York on September 25, 1676.

> Every town shall provide a pair of stocks for offenders, and a pound for the impounding of cattle; and prisons and pillories are likewise to be provided in these towns where the several courts of sessions are to be holden.

Thus, the conventional English detention jail was introduced into America. The city and county jails in the colonies, and later in the states, maintained the characteristics of their prototypes. They were overcrowded and poorly maintained, prisoners were exploited by their warders, and both suspected and convicted offenders were kept unsegregated within their walls. It was not until the conversion of Philadelphia's Walnut Street Jail into a prison in 1790 and the development of the penitentiary system during the following century that jails and prisons across America became distinct custodial entities.

Contemporary Jail Systems

Jails, in current terminology, include a variety of facilities and structures. Depending on the jurisdiction and locale, they might be called "lockups," workhouses, detention centers, stockades, or town, city, and county jails. Regardless of the particular nomenclature, however, all are institutions of temporary or short-term detention. Some are small and able to hold only a few inmates; others can house many hundreds, even thousands, of prisoners.

Jail systems vary widely in terms of organization and jurisdictional authority. There are county jails under the jurisdiction of the local

Gaols

To describe contemporary jails is to give a monotonous repetition of rotten plumbing, horrible overcrowding, damp, dark, and indescribably dirty caverns, and other conditions the description of which are not printable, all bespeaking a callous and brutal disregard of the most elementary rules of hygiene and sanitation.
—J. F. FISHMAN, CRUCIBLES OF CRIME, 1923

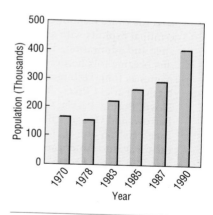

American Jail Population (Average Daily Census) 1970–1990
SOURCE: Bureau of Justice Statistics, 1991

• EXHIBIT 14.5 •

The "Rock"
Alcatraz Island Penitentiary

Would it not be well to think of having a special prison for racketeers, kidnappers, and others guilty of predatory crimes. . . . It would be in a remote place—on an island. . . .

—HOMER S. CUMMINGS, U.S. ATTORNEY GENERAL, AUGUST 1, 1933

During the early years of the Great Depression, an unusual crime wave spread across the American Midwest. Banks that had weathered the Crash of 1929 were being robbed at the rate of two a day. The outlaws operated with flair and skill. Armed with machine guns, they recreated a frontier pattern of rapid assault followed by elusive retreat. The millions of citizens caught in the drab round of idleness and poverty that characterized the times responded to the criminal exploits with acceptance and admiration. The bandits became folk heroes and such names as John Dillinger, Frank Nash, Charles "Pretty Boy" Floyd, Bonnie Parker, Clyde Barrow, and George "Baby Face" Nelson quickly found their way into American folklore. But to the Federal Bureau of Investigation they were "public enemies"; to FBI Director J. Edgar Hoover they were "public rats," "the lowest dregs of society," "vermin in human form," "slime," "vermin spewed out of prison cells," and "scum from the boiling pot of the underworld."

The crime wave, the public enemies, and the vibrant rhetoric ushered in a new phase in twentieth-century penology. It was a thesis built on the belief that some criminals were so in-

corrigible that they should be repressed and disciplined with absolute inflexibility. As U.S. Attorney General Homer S. Cummings announced during a national radio address on October 12, 1933:

For some time I have desired to obtain a place of confinement to which could be sent our more dangerous, intractable criminals. You can appreciate, therefore, with what pleasure I make public the fact that such a place has been found. By negotiation with the War Department we have obtained the use of Alcatraz Prison, located on a precipitous island in San Francisco Bay, more than a mile from shore. The current is swift and escapes are practically impossible. Here may be isolated the criminals of the vicious and irredeemable type.

Originally named by eighteenth-century Spanish explorers Isla de los Alcatraces (Island of Pelicans) after the birds that then roosted there, Alcatraz has an area of twelve acres and rises steeply to 136 feet above the bay. In 1859 a U.S. military prison was built on the island, and in March 1934 it was taken over by the Federal Bureau of Prisons.

Alcatraz became the most repressive maximum security facility in the nation. Its six guard towers, equipped with .30-caliber carbines and high-powered rifles, could observe every square foot of the island. Barbed-wire barriers dotted the shorelines, and each entrance to the cell house had a three-door security system.

There were 600 one-man cells, built into three-tiered cell blocks. Measuring eight feet by four feet, each cell contained a

fold-up bunk hooked to the wall, fold-up table and chair, shelf, wash basin, toilet, and shaded ceiling light. Cell block D was the disciplinary barracks—solitary confinement for the more difficult offenders. It included "the Hole," a series of smaller cells with solid steel walls, floors, and doors; there were no furnishings and its inmates were locked into total darkness.

Each day at Alcatraz began at 6:30 A.M. with the clanging of a bell and a burst of electric light. Inmates had twenty minutes to dress and make their beds. At 6:50 the bell sounded again and the guard counted the prisoners. A third bell signaled that the count was "right"—all prisoners accounted for. No inmate could wear a watch. Bells told the time. Fourth bell. Breakfast. 7 A.M. Bell, workshops. Midmorning. Bell. Recess. Bell. Work. 11:30. Bell. Count. Bell. Noon. Bell. Lunch. 1 P.M. Bell. Work. Midafternoon. Bell. Recess. Bell. Work. 4:30. Bell. Count. Bell. Supper. Bell. Back to cell. Bell. Count. Bell. 6:30. Bell. Lockup. 9:30. Bell. Lights out!

Recreation was limited to an exercise yard and a small library. There was no commissary. Prisoners were allowed three packs of cigarettes each week. Newspapers and radio were denied in order to intensify the sense of isolation. One letter could be written each week and three could be received, but with severe restrictions: Correspondence could not be carried on with nonrelatives, and the content was restricted to family

Alcatraz Island Penitentiary

matters. One visit per month, from a family member or attorney, was permitted. Work was limited to cooking, cleaning, maintenance, and laundry. Security was rigid, with one guard for every three inmates.

With its policy of maximum security combined with minimum privileges and total isolation for America's "public enemies," Alcatraz did have a number of underworld aristocrats and spectacular felons: Arthur "Doc" Barker, last surviving son of Ma Barker's murderous brood; kidnappers George "Machine Gun" Kelly,

Albert Bates, and Harvey Bailey; train bandit and escape artist Roy Gardner; Alvin Karpis, the most evasive bank robber of the 1930s; and bootlegger, murderer, and syndicate boss Al "Scarface" Capone. But for the most part, comparatively few big-time gangsters ever went to Alcatraz; many of the island's inmates were actually first offenders.

From its earliest days, the concept behind Alcatraz had generated considerable opposition from social scientists and prison administrators. It was closed in 1963 because it was

too costly to operate and too typical of the retributive justice that no longer had any stature in the federal prison system. Today, Alcatraz Island Penitentiary is part of the Golden Gate National Recreation Area, having shifted over a four-decade period from a dead-end prison to a public tourist attraction.

SOURCES: E. E. Kirkpatrick, *Voices from Alcatraz* (San Antonio: Naylor, 1947); James A. Johnston, *Alcatraz Island Prison* (New York: Scribner's, 1949); John Kobler, *Capone: The Life and World of Al Capone* (New York: G. P. Putnam's, 1971); L. L. Edge, *Run the Cat Roads* (New York: Dembner, 1981).

The "lockup"

sheriff, and city jails under the authority of the chief of police. There are often independent units and not tied to any jail "system" as such. In some large communities, there are complex arrangements of authority between several segments of local government. In many urban areas, for example, each police precinct has its own *"lockup,"* which holds suspects during the questioning and booking stages of processing. In this phase, the jailing authority is in the hands of the precinct captain and the city police commissioner. Prisoners are then shifted to one of many city or county jails or detention centers. There are also statewide systems, such as in Alaska, Connecticut, Delaware, Rhode Island, and Vermont, where all jails fall under the authority of a single state agency. Finally, there is the federal system, with its numerous detention centers throughout the United States under the jurisdiction of the Federal Bureau of Prisons.

The Jail Population

The jail is the portal of the criminal justice system. Except for defendants who are bailed while still in initial police custody, most arrestees are placed in jail, even if only for a short period of time.

According to a recent survey conducted by the Department of Justice, as of June 29, 1990 there were more than 3,500 jails across the nation holding an estimated 405,320 inmates.[31] Of this population, 91 percent were men and about one-half of 1 percent were juveniles. The survey data reflects the traditional, two-fold function of the jail: a place

for the temporary detention of the unconvicted and a confinement facility where many convicted persons, primarily misdemeanants, serve out their sentences. As of June 29, 1990, some 51 percent of the jail inmates were unconvicted, either not arraigned or arraigned and awaiting trial. The balance were either sentenced offenders or convicted offenders awaiting sentence.

Noah Pope's contention, noted at the beginning of this section, that "jail is for the poor, the street is for the rich" [32] was borne out in a jail survey conducted in 1978, for which more data were made available. At that time, although the majority of the jail inmates were employed prior to their arrest, their earnings were minimal. The median annual income of the surveyed inmates was $3,714—well below the poverty level. Including those with no sources of funds, some 46 percent had incomes below $3,000, 68 percent had incomes below $6,000, and 82 percent had incomes below $10,000. Only 13.5 percent of the jail inmates reported earnings of $10,000 or more annually. Combining these figures with the facts that most had less than a high school education and were under age thirty, it becomes clear that the U.S. jail population includes primarily the poor who are both young and uneducated. [33]

Jail Conditions

For more than two centuries, jails have been described as "cesspools of crime," the "ultimate ghetto," "dumping grounds," and "festering sores in the criminal justice system." And what was said about American jails in the 1780s still applies in the 1990s. [34] Most jails were, and are still, designed to allow for a minimum of staff while providing secure confinement for inmates. Most cells are large, cagelike rooms that hold significant numbers of prisoners at any given time. Although some structures have separate quarters for violent offenders, "drunk tanks" for the intoxicated, and alternative facilities for youthful offenders, many maintain all inmates in common quarters. The only exception here is the separation of sexes, which is almost universal.

Sanitary facilities are often poor and degrading, especially in older jails. Common open toilets prevent personal privacy; the large percentage of drunks and others who spew vomit and urine on the toilets and floors make for unhealthy and unwholesome circumstances; poor plumbing often results in repeated breakdowns and clogged facilities; and the inadequate availability of showers and washrooms inhibits personal cleanliness. To add to these potential health problems, many jails fail to provide appropriate medical care or even a physical examination at admission, thus increasing the possibility of disease.

Jails are poorly staffed. Whatever personnel is available is often untrained. This can result in a lack of attention to inmate needs and mistreatment by other prisoners or guards. As one offender in the Manhattan House of Detention—the infamous New York "Tombs"—reported some years ago:

> As they took me into the Tombs I asked to see a doctor. "I have a bad case of piles [hemorrhoids]," I said. The guard tells me to turn around, and then he just kicks me in the ass. [35]

Most jail inmates have little to do with their time. Some of the larger detention centers have libraries and exercise areas, but in the main, recreational and academic facilities are not provided. Furthermore, the concepts of "treatment" and "rehabilitation" are not part of the

	American Jail Inmates and Drugs	
TYPE OF DRUG	PERCENT WHO EVER USED DRUGS	% WHO USED IN MONTH BEFORE ARREST
Any drug	77.7%	43.9%
Major drug		
Cocaine or crack	50.4	23.6
Heroin	18.2	7.0
LSD	18.6	1.6
POP	13.9	1.7
Methadone	4.8	.6
Other drug		
Marijuana	70.7	31.3
Amphetamines	22.1	5.4
Barbiturates	17.2	3.3
Methaqualone	14.7	.8
Other drugs	11.0	2.4

SOURCE: Bureau of Justice Statistics, 1991

The jail has often been described as the "ultimate ghetto" of the American criminal justice system.

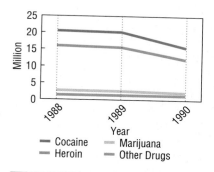

Retail Value of Illegal Drugs Consumed by Those Who Come in Contact With the Criminal Justice System (in $ billions)
SOURCE: Office of National Drug Control Policy, 1991

• EXHIBIT 14.6 •

The Raymond Street Jail
Brooklyn's Gothic Horror

Six o'clock in the morning,
the waiter comes around;
a slice of bread and butter,
that weighs a half a pound.

The coffee's like tobacco java,
the bread is hard and stale,
and that's the way they treat the boys
in Raymond Street's nice jail.

This short chorus, sung to the melody of the Irish patriotic and revolutionary song *The Wearing of the Green,* was periodically heard on the streets of Brooklyn, New York, during the early years of the twentieth century. But it never fully described the conditions that existed in the Raymond Street Jail for more than eighty years. Officially known as Kings County Jail, this grim "gothic castle" was erected in 1879 and immediately received criticism for the barbaric circumstances within its walls.

My first visit to Raymond Street Jail was in 1962. I was a newly assigned parole officer, directed to interview a parole violator who was being detained there. After I entered the jail's massive doors, my attention was immediately drawn to a series of brown paper bags, carefully hung from a ceiling pipe by long strands of wire. I later learned that the bags contained the guards' lunches, positioned like that to keep them out of reach of vermin.

As I moved to the interior of the facility, being escorted to the cell where the parolee was quartered, I was reminded of the medieval dungeons of the old Robin Hood movies. The jail was like a gloomy cave; the air was stale, thick with the smell of urine, sweat, and excrement; and the walls and floors were damp. The environment seemed more suitable for snakes, bats, and owls than for people, for in competition with the inmates for space was a noticeable population of healthy mice, roaches, and other small creatures.

After being led through the bowels of Raymond Street Jail, I was finally brought to the person I had requested to see. His name was Bernard. "Benny," as the guards called him, was thirty-three years old. In 1951, he had been arrested for opening a garage door and stealing a bicycle. Charged with breaking and entering and grand larceny, he was convicted the following year, sentenced to seven and one-half to fifteen years, and transferred to Sing Sing Prison. Not only had it been his first conviction, but his first arrest as well.

At Sing Sing, Benny had hardly been a model prisoner. His long record of minor disciplinary reports served to deny him early parole. After nine years he ultimately earned his release, but within three weeks he was cited for parole violation, arrested, and returned to Sing Sing. He was released after nine more months, again to be cited for violation of parole within only a short period. On this occasion he was arrested for disorderly conduct and resisting arrest — that was what I was there to find out about. As a parolee under the supervision of the state, Benny had had a parole violation warrant lodged against him, so he could not be bailed.

Benny's cell looked like a small cave. The door was of strap iron, which ran both up and down and side to side, leaving openings of only about one square inch, and providing little fresh air to breathe or light for seeing. We spoke in an adjacent room. He told me his story. I related that the parole board would make a decision after he was tried on the new charges.

Thirty-eight days later he entered a plea of guilty and was sentenced to time served. Then his violation report went to the parole board, and they ordered him to be released. I returned again to Raymond Street to remove the warrant on Benny. As we walked out together, he told me that he would rather die than go back to Raymond Street. He had spent 1,512 hours in that dark, cramped, slimy, smelly, vermin-infested jail with no fresh air, exercise, or recreation, "all for calling a cop a son of a bitch."

In 1963, Raymond Street Jail was ordered closed, bringing an end to what was considered the worst jail in New York's history. The following year the building was razed. The site is now occupied by Brooklyn Hospital. As for Benny, his fate was no better than that of the Raymond Street Jail. In 1966 he was arrested for petty theft. Unable to make bail, he was detained in the New York Tombs, where he hanged himself.

SOURCE: James A. Inciardi.

New York's Raymond Street Jail, officially known as King's County Jail, was for more than eighty years an example of desperately poor conditions in a fortress-like setting. Considered the worst jail ever built in New York, Raymond Street's damp, cavelike cells smelled of human waste and provided no fresh air, little light, and a haven for the vermin that lived side by side with the prisoners. Although these conditions are an extreme example of those in jails generally, they are found to some degree in many jails nationwide; warehousing replaces recreation and rehabilitation as the guiding philosophy of most jails.

Inmates in the cafeteria at Pima County Jail in Arizona

Rikers Island Penitentiary

It reminds me of a television program I once saw with rats running around a large cage, looking happy. When you put them in a smaller cage, they start killing each other.
— A CORRECTIONAL COUNSELOR
REFLECTING ON THE SITUATION AT
RIKERS ISLAND, 1990

We're literally dealing with the scum of the earth here. They're just not normal human beings like you and me, and it doesn't make sense to treat them that way.
— A RIKERS ISLAND CORRECTION OFFICER, 1990

I've never been somewhere where someone can live or die over a carton of cigarettes.
— A RIKERS ISLAND INMATE, 1990

If invention is born of idleness, it is also born of necessity, and in Rikers, having a weapon of some sort is very much a necessity.
— A RIKERS ISLAND INMATE, 1991

American jail tradition. New York City's *Rikers Island Penitentiary* is the largest penal colony in the nation. It consists of six facilities, each holding a separate population of offenders and a total daily inmate count of some fourteen thousand. Built in 1933 to house sentenced offenders, some of its cell blocks are the length of a football field. One of its facilities is a house of detention for men. With respect to both the detainees and the inmates serving time, an official at Rikers made the following comment about rehabilitative treatment:

> This is neither a country club, a finishing school, nor a psychiatric facility. It's a prison, and that's all. The people here won't and can't be rehabilitated. They just get three "squares" [meals] a day, a clean place to shit, and a chance to do their time . . . nothing more, but nothing less.[36]

Yet even this was an overstatement, or perhaps an understatement. Inquiries into disturbances that occurred at Rikers Island in 1990 found that the institution was alarmingly unsafe. Slashings, stabbings, and assaults had become commonplace, there were constant struggles for control both among inmates and between officers and prisoners, and there were fights over almost everything — from time on the telephones to channels on the television sets.[37]

In fairness to those sheriffs, police chiefs, wardens, and other jail administrators who have made attempts to upgrade the personnel and conditions in the facilities under their authority, it must be stated here that not all detention centers across America suffer from all of these deficiencies. There are many jurisdictions that have provided the funds for the construction of modern, humane jails. Recent court decisions have legislated change in others. And too, there are independent jailers and wardens who have extended themselves to make the best of what otherwise might have been intolerable situations.

There have been numerous suggestions for improving local jails, including state inspection; the provision of social casework services; the development of educational, medical, and drug treatment programs; the use of volunteers to structure and supervise recreational services; and reorganization and cost sharing by state and local governments.[38] Some of these approaches are beginning to be implemented.

In the final analysis, most of the problems of jails stem from overcrowding. It was once estimated that the daily population of American jails could be reduced by 50 percent, without endangering the public, by making the following changes:

1. the wider use of release on recognizance
2. preferential trial scheduling for those in jail
3. the use of citations rather than jail terms for more offenses
4. the creation of installment plans for those who go to jail because they cannot pay their fines
5. the use of work-release for jail inmates[39]

Although these alternatives have been implemented widely in many jurisdictions, apparently they have not been enough. The jail population of 405,320 inmates in 1990 represented a 57 percent increase since 1985, up some 250,000 inmates. Perhaps in years to come, the jail population will begin to decline as a result of the popular detention innovation—the electronic jail (see Exhibit 14.7).

New York's famous City Prison, "The Tombs," was of Egyptian style and made of solid granite. This illustration of the building dates from 1850.

• EXHIBIT 14.7 •

Home Incarceration as a Correctional Tool
by Patricia K. Loveless

Although house arrest has been in existence since the first Neanderthal adolescent was confined to the cave by angry parents, its use as an official sanction for criminal behavior in the United States flourished during the 1980s, due to the convergence of two factors: increased crowding of correctional facilities and the development of electronic monitoring equipment. House arrest for many years was not considered a feasible alternative to incarceration because, short of twenty-four-hour surveillance by police or probation officers, there was no way to insure total compliance with the court's directives. It was also believed that an offender's ability to "beat the system" and leave home undetected would encourage further antisocial behavior. That changed with the advent of electronic monitoring equipment.

Although a judge in Albuquerque, New Mexico claims to have invented electronic monitoring after reading a "Spiderman" comic in 1977, Harvard Law Professor Ralph Schwitzgebel reported the development of small radio transmitters operating on CB frequencies as early as 1964, and in 1969 described the results of a field test on sixteen offender and non-offender volunteers. Not until the 1980s did electronic monitors become suf-

ficiently small in size and reliable to be used for home incarceration purposes. In December 1986 there were at least forty-six home incarceration programs active in the United States, and more than a dozen manufacturers of electronic monitoring equipment. By the end of the decade, few medium- or large-sized metropolitan jurisdictions were without an electronic monitoring program.

The two types of electronic monitoring systems available are generally referred to as "active" and "passive" systems. In active systems, a transmitter is affixed to an offender by means of an ankle or wrist strap. The transmitter gives off a signal which is received by a monitor attached to the offender's telephone line. When the offender strays more than a prescribed distance from the monitor, it signals a central computer that the offender is out of range. Passive systems rely on computer-generated random or pre-programmed telephone calls to the offender's home. When the person being monitored answers the telephone, his/her voice is electronically matched with a voice template on file in the computer's memory. Some passive systems even test offenders for drug and alcohol use over the telephone lines.

Arguments For and Against

Although readily embraced by harried corrections officials pressed by inadequate facilities and demands that more criminals be locked up for longer periods of time, home incarceration with electronic monitoring has not been accepted in all legal and criminal justice circles. Arguments against home incarceration are primarily philosophical, while arguments in its favor are primarily pragmatic.

The primary argument for home incarceration is that it saves money, in a time when governments are faced with conflicting public demands for tax relief and stiffer criminal penalties. Not only is the daily per-offender cost of leasing or purchasing electronic monitoring equipment considerably less than that of maintaining an offender in a correctional institution, most jurisdictions require offenders who are employed to pay at least part of the cost of supervision. It is also argued that home incarceration can reduce correctional facility crowding. Although no such programs appear to have had any effect on jail populations at the county level, where the sentencing judge decides whether to place an offender on home incarceration, they can be effective devices for

SUMMARY

Throughout history, the range of punishments has been vast. At one time, the death penalty was an almost universal form of punishment. Corporal punishment, particularly in the forms of whippings and torture, was also widespread. During the Age of Enlightenment a new

controlling prison populations if release decisions are made by correctional officials. In addition, home incarceration is perceived, at least by some correctional officials and judges, as more humane than confinement in jail or prison.

According to criminologist Gilbert L. Geis, "the idea that a man's and a woman's house is their castle—their sanctuary, not their prison—seems to lie particularly close to the heart of concerns about house arrest." This ancient legal doctrine, first enunciated in the Justinian Code (c. 533 A.D.), became part of the English common law upon which part of the American legal tradition is based. However, the privilege of persons to be secure from government intrusion in their homes was never absolute; the Fourth Amendment to the Constitution of the United States, for example, prohibits only **unreasonable** searches and seizures and prescribes the proper procedures.

Although some who question home incarceration believe that it represents the "coddling" of criminals who should be incarcerated, most critics come from the other end of the political spectrum. Such radical critics as Gary Marx have described home incarceration as another move toward repression in the form of

"humanitarianism," and denounced turning a person's home into his/her prison as the ultimate audacity of the political state. Others are uncomfortable with the idea of house arrest because of its history of use in totalitarian nations to silence political dissent.

Criminal justice theoreticians and professionals are concerned about the potential net-widening effect if persons are placed on home incarceration who would otherwise receive sentences of probation. This is a real threat, as illustrated by the new Federal Sentencing Guidelines, which explicitly reject home incarceration as an alternative to prison, approving it for use only with offenders who are granted probation or some other form of conditional release.

Although no successful legal challenge to home incarceration has yet been mounted, probably because most programs are limited to volunteers, some scholars believe that home incarceration may be vulnerable to challenge on various constitutional grounds. First and foremost, home incarceration might be considered to violate the constitutionally protected right to privacy. Arguments have also been advanced that home incarceration represents an illegal search and seizure, in violation of the

Fourth Amendment; that data gathered through electronic monitoring could be considered a form of self-incrimination, in violation of the Fifth Amendment; that home incarceration may constitute cruel and unusual punishment, in violation of the Eighth Amendment; and that it denies equal protection of the laws (Fourteenth Amendment) to persons who cannot afford permanent homes in which to be incarcerated and telephones for monitoring purposes.

SOURCES: Richard A. Ball, C. Ronald Huff, and J. Robert Lilly, *House Arrest and Correctional Policy: Doing Time at Home* (Newbury Park CA: Sage Publications, 1988); Richard A. Ball and J. Robert Lilly, "A Theoretical Examination of Home Incarceration," *Federal Probation* 50 (March 1986): 17–24; Paul J. Hofer and Barbara S. Meierhoefer, *Home Confinement: An Evolving Sanction in the Federal Criminal Justice System* (Washington, D.C.: Federal Judicial Center, 1987); J. Robert Lilly and Richard Ball, "A Brief History of House Arrest and Electronic Monitoring," *Northern Kentucky Law Review* 13 (1987): 343–74; "Probation 'Bracelets': The Spiderman Solution," *Corrections Magazine,* June 4, 1983, 4; Ralph Schwitzgebel, "Development of an Electronic Rehabilitation System for Parolees," *Law and Computer Technology* 2 (March 1969): 9–12; Ralph Schwitzgebel, Robert Schwitzgebel, Walter N. Pahnke, and William Hurd, "A Program of Research in Behavioral Electronics," *Behavioral Science* 9 (July 1964): 233–38.

ideology began to emerge in a reform movement spirited by the work of Montesquieu, Voltaire, Diderot, Beccaria, Bentham, Howard, Romilly, and Peel. Particularly influential was Beccaria's liberal doctrine of criminal law and procedure, which emphasized the principle of free will.

The American prison experience began during the eighteenth century in Philadelphia. The Walnut Street Jail was the nation's first penitentiary. Throughout the 1790s its structure and separate system characterized it as a model prison. This was subsequently rivaled by New York's silent system as it emerged at Auburn Prison in 1823.

The work of Alexander Maconochie in Australia and Sir Walter Crofton in Ireland influenced America's reformatory era. The first reformatory was at Elmira, New York, but by 1910 this correctional experiment was abandoned. As corrections moved from the mid-1800s into the early years of this century, the American prison system had evolved into an expanding hoard of maximum-security institutions. This period first witnessed active prison industries, then idle convict populations. Following the depression years, new treatment ideas were introduced against a backdrop of growing apathy and decaying institutions. The 1960s through 1990s saw even greater contrasts—an emphasis on individual prisoners' needs and rights in settings of unrest and mass overcrowding.

KEY TERMS

Cesare Beccaria (**500**)
classical school of criminal law and criminology (**500**)
contract system (**509**)
corporal punishment (**496**)
jails (**518**)

lease system (**510**)
"mark system" (**511**)
piece-price system (**509**)
prisons (**517**)
separate system (**504**)

silent system (**507**)
state account system (**510**)
state use system (**510**)
"ticket-of-leave" (**511**)
Walnut Street Jail (**503**)

QUESTIONS FOR DISCUSSION

1. How did the Industrial Revolution affect the evolution of prisons in the United States?
2. Could the purposes of Alcatraz, as stated by Attorney General Cummings, be achieved by some other penal policies?
3. Which of Beccaria's ideas are reflected in current conceptions of due process?
4. How might the alternative conceptions of bail reform affect the jail problem?
5. Is "the scarlet letter" an appropriate form of punishment?

FOR FURTHER READING

Ball, Richard A., C. Ronald Huff, and J. Robert Lilly. *House Arrest and Correctional Policy.* Newbury Park, CA: Sage, 1988.
Goldfarb, Ronald. *Jails: The Ultimate Ghetto of the Criminal Justice System.* Garden City, N.Y.: Anchor, 1976.

McKelvey, Blake. *American Prisons: A History of Good Intentions.* Montclair, N.J.: Patterson Smith, 1977.
Thompson, Joel A., and G. Larry Mays (eds.). *American Jails: Public Policy Issues.* Chicago: Nelson-Hall, 1991.

NOTES

1. Harry Elmer Barnes, *The Story of Punishment: A Record of Man's Inhumanity to Man* (Montclair, N.J.: Patterson Smith, 1972).
2. The public execution endured into the twentieth century, even in the United States. The last such event, at least in this country, occurred with the hanging of twenty-two-year-old Ramsey Bethea in Owensboro, Kentucky, on August 14, 1936. News dispatches stated that some 20,000 spectators witnessed the execution. See Negley K. Teeters, "Public Executions in Pennsylvania, 1682 to 1834," *Journal of the Lancaster County Historical Society* (Spring 1960): 117.
3. Luke Owen Pike, *A History of Crime in England,* vol. 2 (Montclair, N.J.: Patterson Smith, 1968), pp. 87–88.

4. See George Rusche and Otto Kirchheimer, *Punishment and Social Structure* (New York: Columbia University Press, 1939).

5. See Alice Morse Earle, *Curious Punishments of Bygone Days* (Montclair, N.J.: Patterson Smith, 1969).

6. For a discussion of the leading thinkers in the eighteenth-century reform movement, see Leon Radzinowicz, *Ideology and Crime* (New York: Columbia University Press, 1966).

7. George B. Vold, *Theoretical Criminology* (New York: Oxford University Press, 1958), pp. 14–18; Radzinowicz, *Ideology and Crime*, pp. 6–14.

8. Cited by Harry Elmer Barnes, *The Evolution of Penology in Pennsylvania* (Indianapolis: Bobbs-Merrill, 1927), p. 64.

9. Orlando F. Lewis, *The Development of American Prisons and Prison Customs, 1776–1845* (Albany: Prison Association of New York, 1922), pp. 26–28.

10. Harry Elmer Barnes, *The Repression of Crime* (New York: George H. Doran, 1926), p. 162.

11. Barnes, *Repression of Crime*.

12. See Negley K. Teeters and John D. Shearer, *The Prison at Philadelphia: Cherry Hill* (New York: Columbia University Press, 1957); William Crawford, *Report on the Penitentiaries of the United States* (Montclair, N.J.: Patterson Smith, 1969), pp. 1–2.

13. Gustave de Beaumont and Alexis de Tocqueville, *On the Penitentiary System in the United States and Its Application to France* (Carbondale: Southern Illinois University Press, 1964), p. 83.

14. Margaret Wilson, *The Crime of Punishment* (New York: Harcourt, Brace, 1931), pp. 219–220.

15. Lewis, *Development of American Prisons*, pp. 80–95.

16. See Blake McKelvey, *American Prisons: A History of Good Intentions* (Montclair, N.J.: Patterson Smith, 1977), pp. 116–149.

17. Charles L. Clark and Earle Edward Eubank, *Lockstep and Corridor: Thirty-five Years of Prison Life* (Cincinnati: University of Cincinnati Press, 1927), p. 30.

18. See J. C. Powell, *The American Siberia* (Chicago: H. J. Smith, 1891).

19. McKelvey, *American Prisons*, p. 14.

20. John V. Barry, "Alexander Maconochie," *Journal of Criminal Law, Criminology, and Police Science* 47 (July-August 1956): 145–161.

21. John V. Barry, "Captain Alexander Maconochie," *The Victorian Historical Magazine* 27 (June 1957), p. 5.

22. McKelvey, *American Prisons*, p. 37.

23. Zebulon Brockway, *Fifty Years of Prison Service* (Montclair, N.J.: Patterson Smith, 1969), pp. 419–423.

24. Harry Elmer Barnes and Negley K. Teeters, *New Horizons in Criminology* (Englewood Cliffs, N.J.: Prentice-Hall, 1959), p. 428.

25. Frank Flynn, "The Federal Government and the Prison Labor Problem in the States," *The Social Science Review* 24 (March, June 1950), pp. 19–40, 213–236.

26. Harry E. Allen and Clifford E. Simonsen, *Corrections in America* (New York: Macmillan, 1981), pp. 51–53.

27. Paul W. Tappan, *Crime, Justice, and Correction* (New York: McGraw-Hill, 1960), p. 619.

28. 18 *U.S. Code 907*, cited by Tappan, *Crime, Justice and Correction*, p. 620.

29. U.S. Department of Justice, Bureau of Justice Statistics, *Justice Agencies in the United States* (Washington, D.C.: U.S. Government Printing Office, 1980).

30. Robert G. Caldwell, *Criminology* (New York: Ronald Press, 1965), p. 495.

31. *Jail Inmates 1990,* Bureau of Justice Statistics Bulletin, June 1991.

32. Cited by Ronald Goldfarb, *Jails: The Ultimate Ghetto of the Criminal Justice System* (Garden City, N.Y.: Anchor, 1976), p. 3.

33. Federal Bureau of Prisons, Office of Research and Evaluation, *Population Report,* August 29, 1991.

34. See Goldfarb, *Jails:* George Ives, *A History of Penal Methods* (Montclair, N.J.: Patterson Smith, 1970); Joseph F. Fishman, *Crucibles of Crime: The Shocking Story of the American Jail* (Montclair, N.J.: Patterson Smith, 1969); *Newsweek,* August 18, 1980, pp. 74, 76; *New York Times,* August 14, 1987, pp. B1, B3; *New York Times,* August 30, 1990, pp. A1, B2; Wayne N. Welsh, Henry N. Pontell, Matthew C. Leone, and Patrick Kinkade, "Jail Overcrowding: An Analysis of Policy Makers' Perceptions," *Justice Quarterly,* 7 (June 1990), pp. 341–370; Joel A. Thompson and G. Larry Mays (eds.), *American Jails: Public Policy Issues* (Chicago: Nelson-Hall, 1991).

35. Personal communication, August 1974.

36. Personal communication, June 1966. See also, *New York Times,* August 10, 1990, p. A1.

37. *New York Times,* September 1, 1990, pp. 1, 22.

38. C. Ronald Huff, *The Baltimore Jail Project: An Experiment in the Coordination of Legal Services* (Washington, D.C.: American Bar Association, 1978); Benedict S. Alper, *Prisons Inside-Out: Alternatives in Correctional Reform* (Cambridge, Mass.: Ballinger, 1974); Hans Mattick, "The Contemporary Jails of the United States: An Unknown and Neglected Area of Justice," in *Handbook of Criminology,* ed. Daniel Glaser (Chicago: Rand McNally, 1974), pp. 777–848.

39. Richard A. McGee, "Our Sick Jails," *Federal Probation* 35 (March 1971), pp. 4–5.

15

Penitentiaries, Prisons, and Other Correctional Institutions: A Look Inside the Inmate World

A prison is a house of care,
*   a place where none can thrive;*
A touchstone true to try a friend
*   a grave for one alive.*
Sometimes a place of right,
*   sometimes a place of wrong.*
Sometimes a place of rogues and thieves
*   and honest men among.*
— INSCRIPTION ON TOLBOOTH PRISON,
        EDINBURGH, SCOTLAND, 1817

One learns patience in prison.
— FYODOR DOSTOYEVSKI, 1861

Each wretched cell in which we dwell
Is a foul and dank latrine:
And the fetid breath of living death
*   Chokes up each grated screen;*
And all, but Lust, is turned to dust
In Humanity's Machine
— OSCAR WILDE

Total institutions: Places that furnish barriers to social interchange with the world at large.

The "Dark Figure" of Crime

1,000,000 Part I Crimes

260,000 Arrests

190,000 Available for Prosecution

63,000 Formal Felony Complaints

57,000 Sentences

22,000 Sent to Prison

The Criminal Justice Funnel

Maximum-security prisons: Correctional institutions designed to hold the most aggressive and incorrigible offenders.

Total institutions are places that furnish barriers to social interchange with the world at large.[1] In total institutions, large groups of persons live together, day and night, in a fixed area and under a tightly scheduled sequence of activities imposed by a central authority. In total institutions there are "subjects" and "managers." Subjects are the large class of individuals who have restricted contact with the world outside the walls. Managers, who are socially integrated into the outside world, are the small class that supervise the subjects. In total institutions the social distance between subjects and managers is great and communication is restricted. Each group conceives of the members of the other in terms of narrow, hostile stereotypes, resulting in the development of alternative social and cultural worlds that remain in continuous conflict with one another. In total institutions there is an elaborate system of formal rules intended to achieve the organization's official aim and to maintain the distance between subjects and managers. Correctional institutions are total institutions organized to protect the community against what are conceived to be intentional dangers to it. Correctional institutions include penitentiaries and reformatories, as well as a multitude of training schools, ranches, farms, and camps. Regardless of the designations, however, all are generally referred to as "jails" or "prisons" — two words that have quite distinct meanings for the professional, although probably not for the lay public.

TYPES OF PRISONS

It has been traditional in the United States to divide correctional institutions into three or more levels of custody, according to their construction and measures of custody and control.

Maximum-Security Prisons

The best-known prisons in the United States are likely Sing Sing, Attica, San Quentin, Leavenworth, Joliet, and the now-closed Alcatraz Island Penitentiary. These are **maximum-security prisons.** They are walled fortresses of concrete and steel and house the most serious, most aggressive, and most incorrigible of offenders.

Most maximum-security prisons have a common design. Housing anywhere from many hundreds to several thousands of inmates, secure custody and control are the guiding principles. They are enclosed by massive concrete walls, sometimes as high as thirty feet, or by a series of double or triple perimeter fences topped with barbed wire or razor ribbon, and often electrically charged. Located along the outer-perimeter

walls are well-protected guard towers, strategically placed to provide guards with open fields of fire and observation of prison yards and the outside areas surrounding the prison. New York's Green Haven Correctional Facility (called Green Haven Prison until 1970, when the state legislature decreed that "prisons" henceforth would be "correctional facilities," "guards" would be "correction officers," and "wardens" would be "superintendents") is typical, if not an exaggeration, of this high-control design. Built as a military prison during World War II and acquired by New York in 1949, Green Haven was designed to be an "escape-proof" institution. Its outer wall of reinforced concrete is thirty feet high, almost three feet thick, and is said to go thirty feet below the ground. Its twelve towers, reaching to forty feet above the ground, are evenly positioned along the mile-long wall around the perimeter of the prison. Tower guards, armed with an array of shotguns, rifles, and tear gas guns, have a sweeping view of both sides of the wall. The towers also provide focused surveillance of "no man's land," a 100-foot-wide stretch of open space between the inner and outer walls of the prison across which nothing and no one can pass unobserved. No one has ever managed to escape over the wall at Green Haven.[2]

A characteristic feature of the maximum-security prison is the inside cell block. **Inside cells** are constructed back to back, with corridors running along the outside shell of the cell house. In contrast to *outside cells,* which are affixed to the outside walls of the cell house, inside cells are considered more secure. Whereas escape through the window or wall of an outside cell would place an inmate in the prison yard, such escape from an inside cell would leave the prisoner still within the cell block.

Inside cells: Cells constructed back to back, with corridors running along the outside shell of the cell house.

Prison is the only garbage dump we have that is so repulsive we encircle it with barbed wire and a stone wall.

— BRUCE JACKSON, 1971

To refer to jail and prison as "unpleasant" . . . is like referring to the Nazi torture of the Jews as "unkind."

— KARL MENNINGER, 1966

Medium-security prisons often feature outside cells and a system of fences.

Prisons are built with stones of law; brothels with bricks of religion.

— WILLIAM BLAKE, 1790

Minimum-security prisons hold low-risk inmates in dormitory quarters.

Each tier of cells is called a *cell block* and the cell house may contain as many as ten such blocks. The cell blocks are self-contained security enclosures, often partitioned off from one another by a series of gates and pens. This creates a complex of miniature prisons within the penitentiary, thus enhancing the overall security. Such a pattern is double effective since each cell house is similarly separated from all others.

The emphasis on escape-proof measures in these institutions also includes tool-proof steel construction, multiple lock devices, frequent *shakedowns* (searches) and counts, infrared sensing devices, and closed-circuit TV. More modern maximum-security prisons are beginning to move away from the construction of these double and triple security patterns, and particularly the massive outside walls, due to their prohibitive cost. In their place, they are increasing the use of sophisticated technological intrusion devices.

Medium-Security Prisons

While reproducing the basic pattern of maximum-security prison, there is somewhat less emphasis on internal fortification in the *medium-security* facilities. They are rarely fortresslike structures with high stone walls. Rather, the perimeters are marked by a series of fences and enclosures with fewer guard towers. Outside cells are characteristic, and in the newer structures, banks of dormitories and other congregate living quarters are becoming common.

The inmates placed in medium-security institutions are those who are considered less dangerous and escape-prone than those in the more security-oriented institutions. Their internal movements within the facility are less controlled, and surveillance is less vigilant. However, these prisons generally do have a maximum-security unit, available for those inmates who become custodial problems or threats to the safety of other prisoners.

Minimum-Security Prisons

Correctional institutions of *minimum-security* design operate without armed guards, without walls, and sometimes even without perimeter fences. The inmates of these facilities are considered to be low security risks: the most trustworthy and least violent offenders, those with short sentences, and white-collar criminals. A great deal of personal freedom is allowed, dormitory living is the common practice, educational release is encouraged, and the level of surveillance is low.

Some of the newest of the minimum-security prisons fully reflect a shift away from the oppressive rigors of confinement. They are replacing the stifling nature of the traditional prison compound with a more villagelike atmosphere:

> One remarkable minimum-security correctional center was opened in 1972 at Vienna, Ill., as a branch of the Illinois State Penitentiary. Although a large facility, it approaches the quality of the nonpenal institution. Buildings resembling garden apartments are built around a ''town square'' complete with churches, school, shops, and library. Paths lead off to ''neighborhoods'' where ''homes'' provide private rooms in small clusters. Extensive provision has been made for both outdoor and indoor recreation. Academic, commerical, and vocational education facilities equal or surpass those of many technical high schools.[3]

Minimum-security facilities such as this one in Illinois and others that cater to white-collar criminals, built on what has become known as the "cottage plan," have often been criticized as being more like country clubs than prisons. Yet despite the attractiveness of their physical layout and resources, they are nevertheless "total institutions" and serve as effective barriers to the outside world.

The "cottage plan"

Open Institutions

As a departure from the traditional maximum-, medium-, and minimum-security prisons, which are essentially closed institutions, there are variations in the minimum-security plan that serve as "prisons without walls." These are the prison farms, camps, and ranches, the vocational training centers, and the forestry settlements that are relatively recent innovative reforms. The modern counterpart of the nineteenth-century reformatory for youthful offenders and young adult felons, they provide instructive work for inmates within an environment more conducive to behavioral change.

These **open institutions** have numerous advantages over the more traditional correctional facilities. They relieve the problem of over-crowding in other types of institutions; they are less costly to construct and maintain; and they enable various types of prisoners to be separated, thus reducing the opportunities for contamination of attitudes. Furthermore, they have economic and community service advantages. Prisoners in the open camps produce crops and dairy products for use in the state correctional system and other government facilities. Ranches employ inmates in cattle raising and horse breeding. Forestry camps are used to maintain state parks, fight forest fires, and aid in reforestation. Finally, these camps and farms avoid many of the drawbacks of the traditional total institutions, for regulation and regimentation is more relaxed and greater freedom of movement is possible.

Open institutions: "prisons without walls," such as correctional camps, farms, and ranches.

Women's Institutions

Historically, there have been few women prisoners. Prior to the beginning of the twentieth century, women represented less than 1 percent of the adult felon prison population. This changed somewhat over the years, and from 1970 through the early 1990s the proportion of women in state and federal correctional institutions increased from 2.9 percent to almost 6 percent.[4] This low population of women has resulted, for most of the past 200 years of U.S. history, in a series of rather disjointed and arbitrary policies for the incarceration of female offenders.

Not until 1873, in Indianapolis, Indiana, was the first separate prison for women opened in the United States. Prior to that time, women were confined in congregate quarters with men, or held in isolation within small sections of men's penitentiaries and supervised by male warders.[5] During the last fifty years, and especially in the past two decades, the number of correctional facilities for women has increased dramatically. And, in spite of considerable progress, these institutions reflect both the best and the worst elements of the American prison system.

Today, although they are often referred to as reformatories and state farms, women are confined in separate maximum- and medium-security prisons, in isolated wings of men's penitentiaries, in coeducational facilities (discussed later in this chapter), and in open institutions. *Some states*

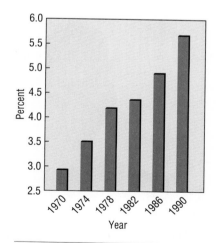

Proportion of Female Inmates in State and Federal Correctional Institutions, 1970–1990
SOURCE: Bureau of Justice Statistics

have no correctional facilities for women, using in their place, under a contract arrangement, the institutions of other jurisdictions.

Most women prisoners are incarcerated in facilities designed under the cottage plan, a situation that has had both positive and negative consequences for the female offender. These minimum-security and open institutions have insulated women from the isolation, deprivation, and hard labor characteristic of the walled penitentiaries. However, the philosophy underlying the construction of cottage prisons for women has resulted in a benign neglect of the needs of female offenders. Typically, correctional administrators express the philosophy — one which seems characteristic of social institutions in general — that the dominant status or role of women is mother and homemaker. It is therefore argued that female inmates need a homelike setting and instruction in caring for children. Furthermore, women are alleged to be undermotivated, to have particular difficulties in handling confinement experiences, and to raise special medical problems. Such a conception of women as being more dependent and less self-reliant than males has severely limited the variety of academic, vocational, and industrial programs available to them. Sewing and laundry have been the dominant commercial operations in female institutions; vocational training, when present, has focused on food service, cosmetology, and typing; and recreation has stressed sitting and walking to the exclusion of vigorous athletic experiences.[6]

As the general population of prison inmates has expanded, so too has the number of women inmates (see Exhibit 15.1). Among the special problems that this creates is the number of young children separated

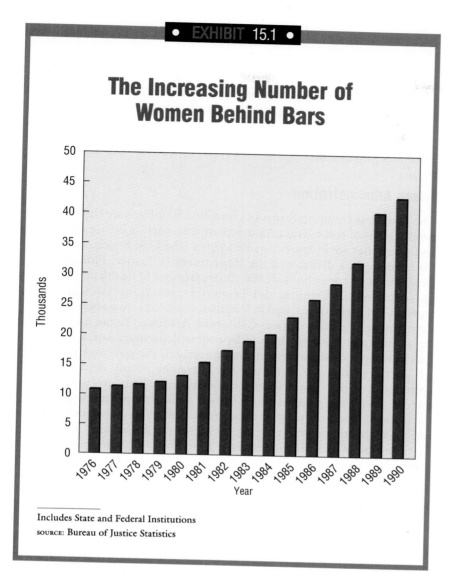

● EXHIBIT 15.1 ●

The Increasing Number of Women Behind Bars

Includes State and Federal Institutions
SOURCE: Bureau of Justice Statistics

from their mothers. Many states are now adjusting to this situation, revising alternatives to incarceration for women offenders that address the issues of "correction," community protection, and maternal bonding.

CORRECTIONAL ORGANIZATION AND ADMINISTRATION

The central administration of correctional systems in the United States reflects a wide diversity of organizational patterns within complex state power structures. But it was not always this way. Until the beginning of the twentieth century, prisons were administered by state boards of charities, boards of inspectors, state prison commissions, boards of control made up of "prominent citizens," or individual prison keepers.[7] Generally, however, most prisons in most states operated as independent

Girls pick up all sorts of things in prison. We can hardly expect her to be honest.

—JOHN GALSWORTHY, 1922

Most women inmates are pretty hard when they arrive here. When they leave . . . forget it. Now you're really talkin' tough.

— ANONYMOUS FEMALE CORRECTIONAL
COUNSELOR, NEW JERSEY, 1991

Black men born in the U.S. and fortunate enough to live past the age of eighteen are conditioned to accept the inevitability of prison. For most of us, it simply looms as the next phase in a sequence of humiliations.

— GEORGE JACKSON, 1970

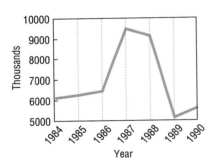

Assaults on Prison Staff by Inmates, 1984–1990

SOURCE: *Corrections Compendium*, June 1991

Prison wardens

fiefdoms. Few jurisdictions had a state department of corrections. Individual wardens received their appointments directly from governors through the system of political patronage, and institutional staff held their positions by virtue of their political connections. While governors made hiring and budgetary decisions, the leadership roles and the administrative procedures of individual institutions were under the absolute control of the wardens. Today, every state has some form of centralized department of corrections that establishes policy for all institutions within its jurisdiction.

Prison Administration

The two most common forms of correctional systems are those that are subdivisions of some larger state department, such as justice or welfare, and those that are independent structures. The U.S. Bureau of Prisons, for example, is a division of the Department of Justice; Florida has its department of corrections within its department of health and rehabilitative services; in Vermont and Tennessee corrections falls under a department of institutions; and in Virginia, corrections is a segment of the department of public welfare. California, Arkansas, Texas, and numerous other states, however, have independent departments of corrections, that have lines of authority running directly to the governor's office.

At the top of the administrative hierarchy of any department of corrections is the commissioner of corrections. This executive works directly under the governor to establish policy, shape the direction of institutional procedures, negotiate annual budgetary allotments for the various institutions, and make major personnel decisions.

The head of each prison, generally appointed by the commissioner of corrections, is a warden, director, principal keeper, or superintendent, depending on state nomenclature. In decades past, the position of warden was one of great power, but also of questionable reputation because of its association with the political "spoils system":

> In many jurisdictions the administrative framework of institutional correction is a basic barrier to [the] establishment of collaborative regimes focused on reintegration of offenders into the community. The position of warden in state prisons too often has been a political reward. It has carried numerous fringe benefits, such as a lavish residence, unlimited inmate servants, food and supplies from institutional farms and warehouses, furnishings, and a large automobile. Furthermore, for anyone who enjoyed power, the warden's position was most attractive, for his control over both inmates and staff tended to be quite autocratic.[8]

Although systems like this continue to persist in a few jurisdictions, most wardens and superintendents are civil service employees who have earned their positions on a seniority or merit basis and who receive no more fringe benefits than other state employees. One monument to the "old ways" can be found on Spring Street in Ossining, New York: the old warden's mansion at Sing Sing Prison. The old mansion now serves as office space for corrections personnel, and recent superintendents of that institution live in their own homes, struggling against rush-hour traffic as do all the other commuters in the area.

The duties of the warden or superintendent are to manage the prison. In the larger institutions, the warden may be assisted by one or more associates: a deputy warden in charge of discipline, security, inmate movement and control, and prison routine; a second deputy in charge of prison programs, records, library services, mail and visitation, recreation, and release procedures; an industries manager in charge of prison industries, farms, production, and supplies; and a medical supervisor in charge of prison health services and sanitation.⁹

The management of a prison is a major task, rivaling that of many large businesses and industries in its complexity of administrative functions. Historically, however, the majority of prison wardens lacked the educational, managerial, and experiential qualifications appropriate for effective and humanitarian leadership of large institutions. Appointments through political patronage rarely considered the candidate's preparedness for a wardenship. With the establishment of state departments of corrections and the growth of civil service in the twentieth century, however, a newer recruitment pattern emerged. On the basis of merit and longevity of service, prison guards worked their way "up through ranks" to the warden's office. This pattern has produced many capable wardens over the years, but it also has had serious drawbacks. Many such wardens have had minimal education, limited administrative exposure, and a socialization to the correctional process limited to a setting where custodial issues were often the only concern. These circumstances served to generate attitudes among prison administrators that were hardly conducive to effective correctional treatment. Consider, for example, the following statement made by an official in Michigan's Jackson Prison:

> These cons are all alike. They lie, steal, cheat, plot, and kill. You've got to watch them all the time and you can't change them. All they're good for is sitting in the cell like the animals they are.¹⁰

Over the last two decades a new pattern of recruitment has begun to evolve, one that draws upon capable administrators with long careers in corrections but not necessarily from the ranks of prison custodial personnel. In a number of jurisdictions, selection processes are drawing more on people who have varied and intensive education and experience, and who are more likely to be wardens sensitive not only to the complexities of prison security and administration, but to inmates' needs as well.

Prison Personnel

In addition to wardens, their deputies, and other administrators, prison personnel includes both professional and custodial staff. The *professional staff* is the physicians, nurses, dentists, chaplains, psychiatrists, psychologists, clerks and secretaries, teachers, counselors, and dieticians who deal with the institutional paperwork and serve the medical, spiritual, and treatment needs of the offender population. The size of the professional staff varies with that of the institution and with its particular orientation (custody versus rehabilitation). In larger prisons, professionals constitute about one-third of the work forced. The *custodial staff* is made up of the guards and their supervisors, whose functions fall into the areas of inmate security, movement, and discipline. Invariably, however, their roles go considerably further.

Prison *guards,* more currently referred to as correction or custodial officers, work in a maligned profession. Guarding is considered a tainted occupation because people find the surveillance and repression that are characteristic of prison life to be repugnant. The popular media is in large part responsible for creating and sustaining this image. Contemporary cinema and television dramas have portrayed the correction officer as evil and savage. Late-night TV movies such as *The Big House* (1930), *White Heat* (1949), *Inside the Walls of Folsom Prison* (1951), *Birdman of*

Guards do not possess the reformer's zeal.

—DONALD CLEMMER, 1940

Alcatraz (1962), *Cool Hand Luke* (1967), and *Chain Gang Women* (1971), to name but a few, have shown prison guards as bigoted, corrupt, brutal, and morally base. More recently, the Earle Owensby films of the 1970s and *Escape from Alcatraz* in 1978, have continued the tradition. Segments of the prison literature, particularly those that have appeared as emotional statements against the prison system — such as Eldridge Cleaver's *Soul on Ice* and George Jackson's *Soledad Brother* — have also presented the prison guard in a most negative way.[11]

Without question, there are many corrupt and brutal prison guards. But to put them all in a common mold would be no more accurate than suggesting that "all convicts are evil," "all police are dishonest," or "all politicians are criminals." In fact, if the popular image of the guard were accurate, most prisons would not function.

The guard's duties are onerous and difficult, and they must be performed under the most unpleasant of circumstances. His career unfolds while he is locked up in an unattractive and depressing environment. Outnumbered by a legion of hostile, restless, and sometimes desperate and violent inmates, he must always be watchful and always appear vigilant, alert, strong, competent, and self-confident. Moreover, as the eminent criminologist Robert G. Caldwell once described the prison guard:

> The guard . . . occupies a pivotal and strategic position in the prison. Upon his competence and loyalty, upon his resourcefulness and skill, depend both the safety of the prison and the spirit of the inmates. He is the first line of attack in case of escapes and the most immediate instrument for the proper handling of the prisoners. He must enforce the rules and regulations. He must be on the alert

to detect signs of uprisings and to prevent the introduction of contraband into the prison and its circulation among the inmates. He must count the prisoners under his charge several times a day. He must patrol his gallery and periodically inspect the cells there. He must administer to the inmates' needs and make reports regarding their condition and behavior. During the day he must supervise the prisoners while they are at work and play and as they march from place to place. At night he must lock them in, see that the lights are out, and make certain that all is secure.[12]

Within such a setting, "a closed and timeless world where days, weeks, and months have little to distinguish them," [13] and faced with few means for carrying out their custodial duties, guards must resort to a number of unconventional mechanisms for maintaining the internal order of the prison. Some become brutal and sadistic. A few become indispensable to the inmate black market, providing illegal services and contraband or serving as "mules" to carry drugs into the prison. And still others develop a system of punishments and rewards to exact inmate compliance. Most prison guards, however, use the spirit of compromise to accomplish their mission. They overlook a number of infractions. Inmates may be allowed to remain out of their cells without authorization, to pass letters back and forth, to cook food stolen from the prison kitchen, to smoke in unauthorized areas, or to possess trivial contraband items. In return, they are expected to refrain from violence, to perform their assigned tasks, and to be civil toward the guards.[14] As one officer from a New Jersey prison put it:

> You could write these guys up [prepare a disciplinary report] every day of the week. They're all into something. . . . But you have to bend some if you want to get your job done. . . .
>
> Yesterday I caught this one with a "dropper" [a wire device connected to the light socket, used for boiling water]. It's not allowed because you could electrocute yourself, but he's smart enough not to do that. I could have taken it and cited him, but I just told him to take it down. He'll remember. . . . Next time I tell him to get in line he'll move. . . . It's like the old saying, "grease the floor and you slide easier." [15]

Most guards have nothing to do but stand guard; they do not use inmates productively any more than they themselves are used productively by prison managers.
—Donald R. Cressey, 1965

INSTITUTIONAL ROUTINES

When they locked me in my cell that very first day it suddenly hit me all at once. "This is it, asshole," I said to myself, "you're gonna die in this place." I was scared, lonely, and depressed and really feeling sorry for myself. But I didn't die. I became just like all the other shitheads, pissholes, and zombies—playing the games, doing the time, falling into the routine . . . sleep, eat, work, sleep, eat, work, "yes sir," "no sir," "I'm sorry sir," "I must have been mistaken sir. . . ."
— Former inmate, Leavenworth Penitentiary

At the beginning of 1991, there were almost 800,000 persons housed in federal and state correctional institutions in the fifty states, the District of Columbia, and the U.S. territories.[16] The institutions in which these prisoners were being held included the full range of correctional facilities—from maximum-security walled fortresses, to minimum-security cottages and reformatories, to "open" forestry camps and ranch settlements. The physcial conditions of these institutions also covered

Change is a rare occasion in prison— sameness is the law. The same people with the same crime, the same colored clothes with the same stripe, the same brown-suited guards with the same orders, the same food on the same day, the same disciplinary slips with the same verdicts (guilty), the same bed in the same cell night after night.
—Anonymous prison inmate, 1971

Manning the cell-block watch station

the entire range of alternatives — from the best to the worst that the American prison system has to offer. Although many new correctional facilities have been built over the years, the majority are old and in varying stages of decay, with conditions that are often appalling.

Prison Facilities

America's ancient correctional institutions

In 1975, studies by the Federal Bureau of Prisons revealed that of the hundreds of state institutions in operation at that time, 47 percent had been built since 1949, 32 percent dated from the period 1924–1948, and the balance had been put into operation during 1923 or earlier.[17] Furthermore, twenty-four of the prisons — most of them large maximum-security facilities — had been in continuous use since before 1874. By the early 1990s, with proper upkeep of the institutions difficult, further deterioration had become apparent. Today, Clinton Prison in New York, Joliet in Illinois, and California's San Quentin are more than 125 years old; Michigan's Jackson Prison and Pennsylvania's Eastern Penitentiary have been housing inmates for over a century and a half; and if current trends in prison use continue, both Auburn and Sing Sing in New York may celebrate their bicentennials as still-operational institutions. All of these ancient institutions have made improvements over the years: many of the original cell blocks have been abandoned or modernized, new structures have been added, and sanitary and other facilities have been renovated to reflect more humanitarian standards. Nevertheless, in their basic order and design, the more than 100 correctional institutions built during the nineteenth and early twentieth centuries, together with the many more built during the 1920s and 1930s, continue to operate as grim monuments to the penal philosophy of the unyielding past.[18]

Classification

The prison experience generally begins with classification. In its broadest sense, **classification** is the process through which the educational, vocational, treatment, and custodial needs of the offender are determined. At least theoretically, it is the system by which a correctional agency reckons differential handling and care, and fits the treatment and security programs of the institution to the requirements of the individual.

The most rudimentary forms of correctional classification were seen when the practice developed of imprisoning people after conviction. Separating the guilty from the not-guilty was itself a process of classifying those accused of criminal behavior. The separation of debtors from criminals was a type of classification by legal status. Early forms of classification included the separation of men from women, youth from adults, and first offenders from habitual criminals. The reformatory movements of the late nineteenth century, the differentiation between maximum- versus medium- and minimum-security prisons, and the designation of Alcatraz as a superpenitentiary for the most incorrigible felons were all examples of rudimentary classification schemes. As correctional systems continued to evolve, the separation of the feeble-minded, the tubercular, the venereally diseased, the sexually perverted, the drug addicted, and the aged and crippled from the general prison population or into special institutions was also based on the principle of classification.

Currently, classification goes beyond the mere separation of offenders on the basis of age, sex, custodial risk, or some other factor. It is now based on diagnostic evaluation and treatment planning, followed by placement into the recommended institutional programs or one type of correctional facility as opposed to another. The extent to which classification schemes are used tends to vary, however, not only from state to state but also among institutions within the same jurisdiction. Furthermore, there are numerous different organizational structures within which classification may occur: reception and orientation units, classification committees, and reception-diagnostic centers.

Reception and Orientation Units   Some jurisdictions have reception units or *classification clinics* within the institutions. Staffed by psychologists, social workers, or other professionals, these units carry out a series of diagnostic studies and make recommendations to institutional authorities regarding the custodial, medical, vocational, and treatment needs of each incoming inmate. Classification clinics also provide orientation programs for new prisoners, providing them with an overview of institutional life, routine, rules and regulations, and custodial and correctional expectations.

The reception unit system, although generally characterized by high-quality diagnostic work, suffers from a number of defects, which have called its usefulness into serious question.[19] Reports submitted to administrative authorities are often ignored and recommendations are not followed. There are rarely effective linkages between these units and the institutional program components; this results in discrepancies

Classification: The process through which the educational, vocational, treatment, and custodial needs of the offender are determined.

Early classification schemes

Prisons give those outside a resting period from town bullies and horrible characters, and for this we should be very grateful.

—ROY KERRIDGE, 1984

between classification and placement. Furthermore, these units generally lack research personnel, thus preventing follow-up to determine whether the classification process is actually working.

Classification Committees Whereas the reception unit operates autonomously and its recommendations are not binding on institutional authorities, classification committees, composed of both professional and administrative personnel, have emerged as integrated classification systems. A classification committee may be chaired by the warden or deputy warden and may include institutional social workers, psychologists, chaplains, medical officers, teachers, vocational and recreational supervisors, and others. The decisions of the committee are binding on the administration, and any changes in the recommended program must be approved by the committee.[20]

The integrated committee is the most widely used classification system in contemporary institutions. Its important advantages are that it permits professional and administrative personnel to work together in determining inmate needs, and at the same time it allows each group of personnel to gain some understanding of the problems the other faces. Even this integrated committee structure, however, has problems. The classification committee processes *all* inmates, and time constraints restrict the discussion of issues and interactions with individual inmates. Since committee members drawn from administrative and program personnel have other duties and responsibilities, their commitment to the classification process is segmented. These time and work load pressures combine to overroutinize the classification process, resulting in recommendations based overwhelmingly on case-file material, with little or no personal contact with the inmates under review. The National Advisory Commission on Criminal Justice Standards and Goals summarized the problem:

> The demands of time, program routine, and workload—and the institutionalization of personnel themselves—prevent effective performance of service. The result is that a large number of ranking institutional personnel are tied up in a process that accomplishes very little in effective programming for the individual inmate.[21]

Reception center: A central receiving institution where all felony offenders sentenced to a term of imprisonment are committed for orientation and classification.

Reception Centers The **reception center,** or diagnostic center, is a central receiving institution where all felony offenders sentenced to a term of imprisonment are committed for orientation and classification. These specialized facilities are relatively new in American corrections, dating from the 1940s when they were established in New York, California, and the federal system.

The purpose of these centers is to delegate the responsibility of classification to the authority of the correctional system, rather than to a specific institution. This standardizes the classification process statewide and provides for a facility and staff whose sole functions are classification and orientation. Furthermore, as a mandate of the state's correctional policy, it makes the diagnostic recommendations binding on the authorities of the individual institutions to which the classified inmates are ultimately sent. At the reception center, the newly sentenced inmates are intensively studied for a period of twenty to perhaps ninety days. The ensuing recommendations include not only custodial and treatment plans, but also a statement as to which correctional facility the inmates should be sent.

Critical reactions to and opinions of the reception center concept have been mixed. In 1973, the National Advisory Commission on Criminal Justice Standards and Goals maintained that reception-diagnostic centers were obsolete and urged that they be discontinued, for the following reasons:

1. They started prisoners in the most confining, most severe, and most depressing part of the state's correctional system;
2. they employed an impersonal assembly-line procedure;
3. they produced excessive information that was often not used after custodial placement;
4. they kept prisoners for too long; and,
5. they drained the state's correctional system of its best professional personnel to staff the centers, therefore placing a premium on diagnosis rather than on treatment.[22]

In contrast, the American Correctional Association has strongly endorsed the reception-diagnostic center concept, urging that it be established in all fifty states.[23] The association feels that only by using this system can a good diagnosis and treatment plan be developed for each inmate. In its view, the system's pivotal position within a state's correctional structure helps to ensure that the diagnostic recommendations will be implemented at the receiving institutions.[24]

The Classification Process Three factors generally combine to dictate how intensive the classification process will be: the personnel available; the inmate workload; and whether it occurs in a reception and orientation unit of a prison facility, through an integrated classification committee, or at a separate reception-diagnostic center. The procedure may range from a physical examination and a single interview to an extensive

Nobody wants literate people to go to prison — they have a distressing way of revealing what it's actually like and destroying our illusions about training and rehabilitation with nasty stories about sadism and futility and buckets of stale urine.
— DAVID FROST, 1968

A nineteenth-century convict transportation cage

Sex

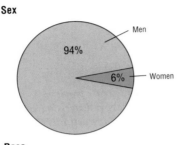

Race

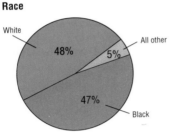

Age

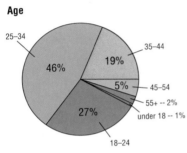

Commitment Offense

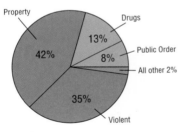

Education

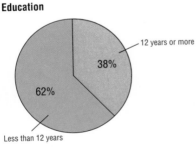

The U.S. Prison Population

SOURCE: Bureau of Justice Statistics, 1991

series of psychiatric and psychological tests, academic and vocational evaluations, orientation sessions, medical and dental checkups, and numerous personal interviews. Some classification programs may also include analyses of athletic abilities and recreational interests, and contacts with religious advisors.

Subsequent to the testing and interview period, reports are prepared by the various diagnosticians and incorporated into the inmate's case file. Summaries of the prisoner's social and family background, work history, criminal record, prior institutionalization (if any), current offense, and any other relevant background data are also included. A classification board or committee then evaluates the case, and makes its recommendations. This board can range from one counselor or social worker to as many as fifteen persons, including teachers, psychologists, physicians, researchers, members of the administrative and custodial staffs, and persons from numerous other fields. This board then integrates and discusses the various data, and plans the inmate's correctional career. It also takes responsibility for *reclassification* should the inmate's needs or situation change.

Trends in Classification During recent decades, there have been experiments with new approaches to classification. The *treatment team concept,* begun in 1958 at the Air Force Retraining Facility at Amarillo, Texas, and used later at the Federal Correctional Institution at Ashland, Kentucky, provides for the continuity of care that is lacking in traditional classification and treatment planning. In the team approach, a counselor, a teacher, and a custodial officer become a "team" for each individual inmate. The team takes over the duties of classification, coordinates the treatment plan, and handles disciplinary problems. The same team may be assigned to all the inmates in a particular dormitory or cell block. Its major benefit has been to make academic and custodial staff more treatment-oriented, and counseling staff more sensitive to custodial issues by virtue of their collective involvement in the correctional and prison management processes.[25]

Contract classification has been reported by Warden A. J. Murphy of the Oklahoma State Penitentiary at McAlester as gaining favor among both inmates and staff.[26] The basic process is similar to other forms of classification, but the recommendations are in the form of a contract signed by the inmate and the chair of the classification committee. Inmate "needs" and requirements are spelled out in the document, and when these are achieved, such benefits as lower security, additional privileges, and recommendation for early parole are awarded.

With the exploding growth of technological literacy across the United States, *computerized classification* has recently been introduced as a diagnostic tool. First implemented by the U.S. Bureau of Prisons during the late 1960s,[27] and later refined in Kentucky, the process is based on a "screening" system designed to measure an inmate's potential for aggressive behavior, depression and suicidal tendencies; intellectual status, vocational skills and interests, socialization, criminal sophistication, and physical and mental health. As explained by its designers:

The new system consists of a twenty-minute, structured caseworker interview and a series of questionnaires, checklists, and interest and ability tests requiring approximately two hours for completion. These data are optically scanned and computer processed, and a detailed printout comparing each inmate with the total population of inmates that have been previously classified is provided.[28]

Prison Programs

Institutional programs include a variety of activities, all of which can have an impact, either directly or indirectly, on the rehabilitation of offenders and their successful reintegration into the free community. There are *treatment programs,* for example, which focus on behavioral change. These attempt to remove what are often considered "defects" in an inmate's socialization and psychological development and that are necessarily responsible for some lawbreaking behaviors. There are *academic and vocational programs,* which attempt to provide inmates with the skills necessary for adequate employment after release. There are *recreational programs,* which have humanitarian, medical, social-psychological, and custodial motives; they are structured to ease the pressures of confinement, making inmates more receptive to rehabilitation and less depressed, hostile, and asocial. There are *work programs,* which serve many of the humanitarian and rehabilitative needs of the offender, yet at the same time are related to the successful economic functioning of the institution. And finally, there are *medical and religious programs,* which also have implications for institutional management and reintegration of the offender into the community.

Health and Medical Services

The number and types of programs and services available to inmates vary widely by both jurisdiction and institution. Every prison has some form of health and medical program, although some are quite rudimentary. All reception centers have comprehensive medical facilities, with separate hospital units and some with well-equipped operating rooms. Similar facilities are also present in the larger prisons and reformatories.

Smaller institutions use a range of medical and health alternatives. Some have small hospital units with a full-time physician or nurse, and paraprofessionals who are on hand for the day-to-day care of minor illnesses and injuries. Where a physician is not a full-time member of the institutional staff, one is drawn from the local community to visit on a routine basis. All but the largest prisons and reception centers contract out for the services of dentists and opticians.

The importance of sufficient medical care for prison inmates cannot be overstated. Poor diet, alcoholism and drug abuse, and histories of inadequate medical attention are disproportionately evident among those entering the nation's correctional system. There is also the increasing problem of AIDS (see Exhibit 15.2). Furthermore, the potential for the rapid spread of even the most minor illnesses is high within a population that is confined in such close quarters. The prison medical unit also has responsibility for monitoring sanitary conditions and inmate dietary needs, for these too are directly related to the well-being of the institution as a whole.

Religious Programs

The availability of spiritual services to prison inmates has a long history in American corrections. Solitary meditation was the theoretical basis of reform in Philadelphia's Walnut Street Jail almost two centuries ago, and penitence was encouraged by frequent visits by missionaries and local clerics. Over the years, various Christian denominations and other

I understand church attendance is up dramatically.
—BUDDY DALLAS, ATTORNEY FOR SINGER JAMES BROWN, WHO COACHED THE CHOIR IN THE SOUTH CAROLINA PRISON WHERE HE WAS INCARCERATED

● EXHIBIT 15.2 ●

Prisoners and AIDS

AIDS (acquired immune deficiency syndrome) is likely the most publicized disease of the twentieth century. It is best defined as a severe late manifestation of infection with *HIV (human immunodeficiency virus),* a virus that destroys or incapacitates components of the immune system. The actual causes of death among AIDS victims include a variety of rare infections and other diseases that an otherwise healthy immune system can effectively cope with.

HIV is transmitted when virus particles or infected cells gain direct access to the bloodstream. This can occur during all forms of sexual intercourse that involve the transmission of body fluids, as well as oral/genital intercourse with an infected partner. Other major routes of transmission include the sharing of needles among intravenous (IV) drug users, the passing of the virus to unborn or newborn children by infected mothers,

and through transfusions from an infected blood supply. As indicated in the following table, the highest rates of AIDS in the United States are among homosexual and bisexual men, followed by intravenous drug users.

The "heterosexual" cases include those who have had heterosexual contact with a person with AIDS or at high risk for AIDS.

Because of how the HIV infection is transmitted, AIDS has

An AIDS patient in an isolation cell at New York's Sing Sing Prison

AIDS Cases in the United States Reported to the Centers for Disease Control Through February 1992		
Transmission Category	**Number**	**%**
Men who have sex with men	122,405	57
Injecting drug use	47,309	22
Men who have sex with men *and* inject drugs	13,456	6
Hemophilia/other transfusion cases	6,251	3
Heterosexual cases	12,510	6
Undetermined	8,022	4
Pediatric	3,598	2
Total	213,641	100

SOURCE: Centers for Disease Control, *HIV/AIDS Surveillance*, March 1992

become a special problem in contemporary prison settings. Homosexual and bisexual men account for the vast majority who contract AIDS, but they are not particularly associated with the types of crimes that result in a prison sentence. On the other hand, IV drug users *are,* and their proportion among all known AIDS cases is increasing.

Although prison health care personnel are uncertain about how quickly AIDS can be transmitted in a prison setting—whether through drug use or sexual activity—they believe that the incubation period can be in excess of ten years. This suggests that the extent of the problem might not be known for many years. And there are many other variables. As of October 1989, some 5,500 correctional inmates in the United States were diagnosed as having AIDS—a rather small proportion of the total number of inmates in state and federal correc-

tional facilities. This figure, however, includes only those diagnosed as already having AIDS. It does *not* include those carrying the HIV infection, which can be transmitted through sexual activity and needle sharing. The number of inmates in this latter category may be considerable. Studies indicate that in some areas as many as 70 percent of all IV heroin and cocaine users are already infected with HIV, and many of these eventually end up in correctional institutions.

Correctional administrators have used a number of options in treating and placing inmates with AIDS, ARC, and HIV infections. As indicated in the following table, of the fifty-one jurisdictions that comprise state and federal corrections, most separate inmates with AIDS from the rest of the population through segregation, or at least place restrictions on their contact with other inmates. In either

case, they become the pariahs of the prison system. Known HIV-infected inmates, on the other hand are typically left in the general population. This suggests that a clear potential remains for the spread of AIDS in prison populations. AIDS education programs for inmates are widespread in American corrections. However, only a few prisons offer condoms to inmates for the prevention of infection; the balance of jurisdictions resist the practice on the grounds that it would condone or even encourage prohibited behavior.

SOURCES: Centers for Disease Control, *HIV/AIDS Surveillance,* August 1991; Duane C. McBride and James A. Inciardi, "AIDS and the IV Drug User in the Criminal Justice System," *Journal of Drug Issues,* 20 (Spring 1990), pp. 267–280; National Institute of Justice, *AIDS in Correctional Facilities,* May 1990.

Management Policies for Inmates with AIDS and Known HIV Infection

Policy	Jurisdictions Following this Policy			
	AIDS		ASYMPTOMATIC HIV INFECTION	
	NUMBER	%	NUMBER	%
Maintain in general population	9	17	34	67
Maintain in general population with special restrictions[a]	10	20	10	20
Administrative segregation/separation[b]	16	31	4	8
Case-by-case determination	12	24	3	6
No policy or no data	4	8	—	—

[a] This category includes single-celling.
[b] This category includes housing inmate in medical units for administrative reasons. This policy is generally intended to protect affected inmates from other inmates and/or to facilitate their supervision.

religious organizations have devoted their time to the spiritual needs of inmates and have provided ongoing programs of religious instruction.

Contemporary institutions generally retain Protestant, Roman Catholic, and sometimes Jewish chaplains, or at least a nondenominational cleric, on a full- or part-time basis, for religious counseling and worship services. In some small institutions where there are no educational programs or rehabilitative services, the prison chaplain represents the only available treatment component.

Opinions as to the usefulness of religious programs in prisons are decidedly mixed. They have been praised by wardens as anchors of law and order, by chaplains as powerful treatment forces, and by some inmates as sources of inspiration and cushions against despair. At the same time, however, they have been heavily criticized. Many prison administrators view religious counseling as useless and the cause of trouble and dissension; inasmuch as some jurisdictions prohibit the searching or questioning of the clergy, chaplains have also been viewed as potential security risks. Many chaplains look on their own programs as dull and unrealistic, and given the remote locations of many correctional facilities the prison chaplaincy has become one of the positions least sought after by ministers. Inmates often consider the programs to be empty, insincere, stale, and platitudinous; as a result, few make use of them.[29] As one inmate expressed it: "If there is a God, he sure as hell was not on my side."[30] Many of these issues have become further complicated by the current conflicts within organized religion.[31] As more and more members of the clergy drift from the conservative pastures of orthodox theology and its uncompromising acceptance of tradition, the role of the prison chaplain has become a frustrating one. Recognizing the inequities of institutional life, many wish to act on behalf of inmates' legitimate interests. Yet the domination of correctional policies that see prisons as coercive environments have thwarted the hopes of numerous chaplains to serve as activist ministers of dissent.

Education Programs Most Americans have confidence in education as a mechanism for upgrading skills and understanding, for shaping attitudes, and for promoting social adjustment. It is not surprising then that academic education and vocational training are regarded as the primary programs in correctional institutions.

In *academic education* programs, the emphasis is on the acquisition of basic knowledge and communicative skills. Most institutions have some sort of prison school, and in most state correctional systems education for inmates is a matter of legislative mandate. Courses of instruction vary from one institution to the next, ranging from literacy programs to high school equivalency studies to college level learning with degree-awarding curricula.[32]

Prison schools, however, are beset with numerous difficulties. Many institutions are short on classroom facilities and useful teaching aids; there is a lack of qualified instructors, which forces a reliance on rejects from the public school system and on inmate teachers, scores of whom are undereducated; many inmates lack motivation, which results in teachers being pressured to make the classes effortless and to complete false reports on inmate progress; and the realities of prison discipline and security often interfere with inmates' courses of instruction or curtail enrollments. And in addition to these issues there is another problem:

The classes held in most institutions are conventional and relatively old fashioned, in contrast to the learning innovations available to students at all levels on the outside. Most prisoners have had little formal education and probably resisted whatever teaching they were exposed to. Material that bored them as children or as truant teenagers is not likely to hold them enthralled as adults. What these mature felons do not need are "Dick and Jane" readers or other textbooks designed for children. But because of the low priority and minimal funds assigned to education in most institutions, it is these useless texts that prisoners are offered, often by public schools that no longer use them. Small wonder that most prison programs are neither accredited nor enthusiastically supported by inmates. The surprising fact is that some educational services not only survive, but even contribute to inmate rehabilitation.[33]

Vocational training programs focus on preparing inmates for meaningful postrelease employment. Most of the larger institutions and many small ones have a number of such programs, including automobile repair and maintenance, welding, sheet metal work, carpentry and cabinet making, plumbing and electricity, and radio and television repair. As with academic programs, these too have some problems. Many prison shops are poorly equipped and lack the appropriate technical staff; in others the machinery and fittings have long since become outmoded; and in still a third group, the training is in fields where work is unavailable in the outside world. Furthermore, inmates acquiring skills in such areas as plumbing, electrical work, carpentry, and masonry are often barred upon release from joining unions because of their criminal records. Even more frustrating is the fact that some institutional programs continue to train inmates in spheres that have virtually no relevance to the job market.[34] One inmate remarked not long ago:

> I came in here a laborer and I will go out a laborer. They taught me how to make [license] tags, but where else can I go to make tags? I got news for you, baby. In six months you'll have me back makin' those tags.[35]

Print shop at the State Penitentiary of New Mexico at Santa Fe

Despite the many difficulties, the profile of academic education and vocational training programs in contemporary corrections is not entirely bleak. The administrators of many institutions have encouraged community volunteers and local school districts to aid in tutoring the more motivated inmates; prison routines have been more flexible for those wishing to attend classes; federal funds have been allocated for the upgrading of many prison schools; self-taught programmed courses of instruction in elementary and secondary school subjects have become more available; and a growing number of prison systems are introducing college degree-granting programs. Futhermore, the need for more relevant vocational education has also been recognized. Numerous correctional facilities are upgrading prison shop equipment; others are implementing new programs in more timely fields such as graphic communications and computer operation and technology.

Prison Labor and Industry

Closely related to vocational training in correctional institutions are the prison work and industrial programs. At least in theory, these can provide numerous opportunities for inmates

- to earn wages while serving their terms
- to develop regular work habits
- to gain experience in machine operation, manufacturing, and other specialized skills
- to ease the boredom of institutional confinement

Despite these praiseworthy possibilities, most prison work programs generally fail to provide most, if not all, of these opportunities. First, many penitentiaries and other correctional institutions have no such programs. Those that do are open to less than 25 percent of the prison population and they provide wages that are extremely low. Second, the jobs made available to inmates in many jurisdictions are typically dull and irrelevant. The major industries include printing and the production of auto tags, road signs, brooms, clothing, and similar articles. Furthermore, many nonindustrial prison jobs are restricted to such meaningless tasks as cleaning, laundry, and other simple maintenance work.

There are many reasons for this situation. First, state use is the chief outlet for prison-made products. As noted in Chapter 14, this situation is the result of state and federal legislation that barred prison industrial production from competing with private enterprise. Second, prison industrial plants are costly to construct, equip, maintain, and keep up to date. And third, to house an inmate in a correctional institution is prohibitively expensive, from the annual expenditures per inmate to $10,000 annually per inmate in some jurisdictions and to as much as $25,000 in others, with the national averages set at $16,500.[36] This rebounds on prison inmates in that their wages are kept low, with most of the profits going into state treasuries.

On the more optimistic side, not all states and institutions suffer equally from these problems. A number of prisons have modernized their industrial plants or constructed totally new ones in an effort to make inmate work more instructive, meaningful, and efficient. Florida's Union Correctional Institution, for example, has its own inmate-operated slaughterhouse and cement block plant. In Texas, where local laws do not prohibit the sale of its prisons' products in markets within the state, prison industries have moved into some highly technical areas and generate many millions of dollars each year.

Former Supreme Court Chief Justice Warren E. Burger repeatedly argued throughout the first half of the 1980s, that as an alternative to the present system, prisons should be changed from "warehouses" for criminals to "factories with fences":

> Most prison inmates, by definition, are maladjusted people. Place that person in a factory, whether it makes ballpoint pens, hosiery, cases for watches, parts of automobiles, lawn mowers, computers, or parts of other machinery; then pay that person some reasonable compensation, and charge something for room and board and keep, and we will have a better chance to release from prison a person able to secure gainful employment.[37]

To put people behind walls and bars and do little or nothing to change them is to win a battle but lose a war. It is wrong. It is expensive. It is stupid.
—CHIEF JUSTICE WARREN BURGER, 1984

The Chief Justice also noted, however, that achieving such a goal would require the conversion of prisons into places of education and training and into factories for production, and in the process, repealing laws that limit prison industry production, limiting any form of discrimination against prison products, and working to change the attitudes of organized labor and business leaders toward the use of prison inmates to produce goods or parts. Given the ever-changing economic scene, however, combined with the already highly competitive markets brought about by increasing foreign imports, it is questionable whether such drastic changes will actually be made.

On the other hand, faced with the costly challenges of increasing prison populations throughout the 1980s and into the 1990s, many states have begun shifting from the nineteenth-century legacy of rock-busting, ditch-digging, and license plate-stamping to highly profitable prison labor programs. In at least twenty jurisdictions, inmates work behind bars for private companies. They take hotel reservations in Arizona, make designer underwear in Washington, construct stretch limousines in Nevada, and fashion belt buckles in Idaho.[38] In the federal system during late 1990, inmates were assembling parts for Air Force fighter jets destined for Operation Desert Shield/Desert Storm in the Middle East.[39] It is estimated that in all, the new genre of prison industries has evolved into a $600 million plus enterprise involving some 52,000 inmates in all fifty states.[40]

Clinical Treatment Programs   Academic education and vocational training are often viewed as the primary rehabilitative tools a correctional institution has to offer. It is felt that if inmates can learn the necessary skills and training to secure and maintain gainful employment after release, then their need to return to careers in crime will be eliminated, or at least reduced. In this sense, academic and vocational programs can also be viewed as treatment programs, for correctional treatment has generally meant the explicit activities designed to alter or remove conditions operating on offenders which are responsible for their behavior.[41] In a more clinical sense, however, institutional treatment programs are those efforts specifically oriented towards helping inmates resolve those personal, emotional, and psychological problems that are related to their lawbreaking behavior.

Counseling, social casework, psychological and psychiatric services, and *group therapy* represent the core of clinical treatment programs in prisons. Counseling refers to the relationship between the counselor and the prisoner-client in which the counselor attempts to understand the prisoner-client's problems and to help him or her solve the problems by discussing them together, rather than by giving advice or admonition.[42] Social casework is a process of professional services that (1) develops the prisoner-client's case history, (2) deals with immediate problems involving personal and familial relationships, (3) explores long-range issues of social adjustment, and (4) provides supportive guidance for any anticipated plans or activities.[43] Psychological and psychiatric services provide more intensive diagnosis and treatment aimed at (1) discovering the underlying causes of individual maladjustments, (2) applying psychiatric techniques to effect improved behavior, and (3) providing consultation to other staff members.[44]

These three modes of treatment involve direct interaction between clinician and prisoner-patient on an individual, one-to-one basis. Treatment in a group setting includes one or more clinicians plus several prisoner-patients. Group treatment programs have been variously referred to as "group psychotherapy," "group therapy," "group guided interaction," "group counseling," and numerous other terms that are often used interchangeably. However, only two basic kinds of therapy are actually involved when the "group" label is used: group psychotherapy, which is individual therapy in a group setting; and "group" therapy in its truest sense, which is designed to change groups, not individuals.

The more common of the two in the prison setting is "group" therapy. In terms of its underlying approach and philosophy:

> This treatment stratagem focuses on groups as the "patient." It assumes that specific persons exhibit unfavorable attitudes, self-images, and the like because of the associational network in which they are involved. Because the person's interactional associates are extremely meaningful to him, any attempt to change the

I would say there are two basic complaints by prisoners about prison. First: the monotony of prison routine. Second: the numerous ways you are made to feel you are finished as a man.
—WILLIAM R. COONS, 1971

Clinical treatment programs

person without altering those groups with which he associates is likely to fail. Accordingly, group therapy proceeds on the premise that entire groups of persons must be recruited into therapy groups and changed. In addition, it is argued that treatment in which an individual's close associates are participants is likely to have more impact upon a specific person than some other form of treatment. *Group therapy encourages the participants to put pressure on each other for behavioral change and to get the group to define new conduct norms. In a real sense, individual participants in group therapy are at the same time patients and therapists.*[45] [emphasis added]

These four models of clinical treatment—counseling, casework, psychological and psychiatric services, and group therapy—are employed to deal with the general issues associated with criminality and to bring about behavioral change. They are also used to address the problems of specific kinds of offenders, such as sexual deviates and substance abusers. However, these clinical treatment services are not available in most institutions, and only a modest number of prisons have a resident psychiatrist. Furthermore, in reception centers, where there are a significant number of psychologists, social workers, and other clinicians, the primary activities of these professionals are in the area of diagnosis rather than treatment. More common in contemporary correctional facilities are counselors. These, however, generally deal with inmates' confrontations with the day-to-day pressures of institutional life rather than with any long-term treatment goals. Counselors, moreover, rarely have any clinical training or experience. The position of correctional counselor is an entry point to a criminal justice career, and for most counselors, it is their first job after college graduation.

Drug Abuse Treatment As noted elsewhere in this textbook, much of the increased activities and backlogs in the criminal justice system are an outgrowth of the nation's war on drugs. This is particularly apparent in correctional agencies and facilities. In New York, for example, some 33 percent of the state's 56,000 prison inmates were initially arrested for drug-related offenses.[46] In Florida, prison admissions increased by 250 percent from 1980 to 1990, with those for drug-related crimes swelling by almost 2,000 percent.[47] And nationally, it would appear that perhaps three-fourths of all inmates have histories of substance abuse.[48]

One approach to the phenomenon has been to increase prison capacity. During 1989–1990, for example, almost $7 billion was allocated across the nation to construct 128,000 new prison beds.[49] The other approach has been to expand drug abuse treatment services. As of 1990, with the exception of Kentucky, all of the states and the federal system had some sort of drug treatment services for inmates.[50] Furthermore, most were expanding the capacities of existing programs as well as implementing new ones.

The therapeutic community

In addition to the four models of clinical treatment described earlier, prison-based drug rehabilitation strategies also include the *therapeutic community*. More commonly referred to as a "TC," the therapeutic community is a total treatment environment established in a separate residential unit of a prison. TC participants are kept removed from other inmates and are assigned to separate work, school, and recreational programs as well. The purpose is to create a partnership between prisoner-clients and clinicians. The work supervisors, teachers, counselors, correction officers, and other staff members involved with TC inmates become part of the treatment regimen and are regarded as agents of behavioral change. Group therapy is the core treatment model, but the peer pressure characteristic of the therapy sessions appears during other daily routines as well.

The therapeutic community concept was developed during the 1940s by English psychiatrist Maxwell Jones. He introduced it at a hospital for war veterans who were experiencing difficulties in finding and keeping jobs.[51] In 1958, the approach was adopted in the San Francisco Bay area for the treatment of narcotics addicts by ex-alcoholic Charles Dederich, thus giving birth to the internationally known Synanon drug treatment program.[52] In the years that followed, other therapeutic communities appeared—Daytop Village, Phoenix House, Odyssey House—and in 1966 the approach was introduced at New York's Clinton Prison and at the Federal Correctional Facility at Danbury, Connecticut.[53]

Currently, the therapeutic community is among the most popular —and the most controversial—approaches for the treatment of drug abuse. Its application within the prison setting has been primarily for substance abusers, although some non-drug-abusing offenders are also involved. However, few correctional institutions have therapeutic communities due to the lack of special facilities as well as staff shortages and a concentration of efforts on custodial issues—concerns that tend to limit all varieties of institutional treatment. During the closing years of the 1980s, however, funding from the Bureau of Justice Assistance rekindled the interest in TCs in correctional environments, creating a movement that is expected to continue well into the 1990s (see Exhibit 15.3).

Shock Incarceration

Among the more recent innovations in correctional treatment is what some jurisdictions refer to as "shock incarceration" and others call

An inmate of a "shock incarceration" boot camp makes an obscene gesture at his commanding officer while the officer turns his back to yell at another inmate. The inmate was kicked out of the program a week later.

• EXHIBIT 15.3 •

Therapeutic Communities in Prisons

There are many phenomena in the prison environment that make rehabilitation difficult. Not surprisingly, the availability of drugs is a problem. In addition, there is the violence associated with inmate gangs, often formed along racial lines for the purposes of establishing and maintaining status, "turf," and unofficial control over certain sectors of the prison for distributing contraband and providing "protection" for other inmates. And finally, there is the prison subculture—a system of norms and values that, among other things, hold that "people in treatment are faggots," as one Delaware inmate put it in 1988.

In contrast, the therapeutic community (or simply, "TC") is a total treatment environment isolated from the rest of the prison population—separated from the drugs, the violence, and the norms and values that

militate against treatment and rehabilitation. The primary clinical staff of the TC are typically former substance abusers who themselves were rehabilitated in therapeutic communities. The

treatment perspective is that drug abuse is a disorder of the whole person—that the problem is the *person* and not the drug, that addiction is a *symptom* and not the essence of the dis-

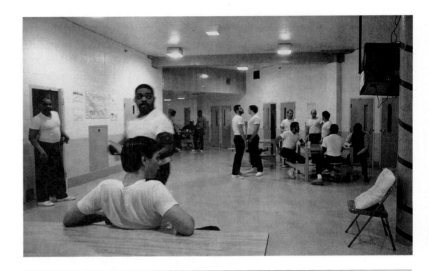

A view of "The Key," Delaware's prison-based therapeutic community

---

Shock incarceration: A three- to six-month regimen of military drill, drug treatment, physical exercise, hard labor, and academic work in return for having several years removed from an inmate's sentence.

We've got three months,
  you've got years.
We'll be gone,
  when you're still here!
— A SHOCK INCARCERATION DRILL CHANT,
    1988

"boot camp." **Shock incarceration** is a three- to six-month regimen of military drill, drug treatment, physical exercise, hard labor, and academic work in return for having several years removed from an inmate's sentence. Available to young nonviolent offenders, the idea is to "shock" budding felons out of careers in crime by imposing large amounts of rigor and order in what appear to be chaotic and otherwise purposeless lives.

For the young offenders in a shock incarceration boot camp, days are sixteen hours long, with two-mile runs, calisthenics, and orders shouted in their faces as daily staples. Like Parris Island, there are military fatigues, rising before dawn to march in platoon formation, and spit-shine discipline.

Since 1984, boot camp correctional programs have been established in twenty-four states and the federal system, and other states are considering them. Although there have been no formal evaluations, the reviews tend to be mixed. While some observers argue that the approach teaches discipline and builds self-esteem, others claim that marching and chanting can never deal with the behavioral disorders that result in criminal careers.[54]

order. In the TC's view of recovery, the primary goal is to change the negative patterns of behavior, thinking, and feeling that predispose drug use. As such, the overall goal is a responsible drug-free lifestyle.

Recovery through the TC process depends on positive and negative pressures to change, and this is brought about through a self-help process in which relationships of mutual responsibility to every resident in the program are built. Or as TC researcher George De Leon once described it:

> The essential dynamic in the TC is mutual self-help. Thus, the day-to-day activities are conducted by the residents themselves. In their jobs, groups, meetings, recreation, personal, and social time, it is residents who continually transmit to each other the main messages and expectations of the community.

In addition to individual and group counseling, the TC process has a system of explicit rewards that reinforce the value of earned achievement. As such, privileges are *earned*. In addition, TCs have their own specific rules and regulations that guide the behavior of residents and the management of their facilities. Their purposes are to maintain the safety and health of the community and to train and teach residents through the use of discipline. TC rules and regulations are numerous, the most conspicuous of which are total prohibitions against violence, theft, and drug use. Violation of these cardinal rules typically results in immediate expulsion from a TC.

Although prison-based TCs are few in number, preliminary evaluations have been positive. Moreover, inmates in TCs see them as safe places to finish their time and learn positive values.

As a resident of Delaware's TC commented: "This may be my last chance to save my life." In addition to their potential for treatment, correctional administrators view TCs as excellent tools for prison management. A Delaware official noted in this behalf:

> Not only has there been no fights or disturbances or write-ups in that sector since the program started, but it's the cleanest part of the whole damn joint. In fact, their bathroom floor is cleaner than my kitchen table!

SOURCES: George De Leon and James T. Ziegenfuss, *Therapeutic Communities for the Addictions* (Springfield, Ill.: Charles C. Thomas, 1986; Douglas S. Lipton and Harry K. Wexler, "Breaking the Drug–Crime Connection," *Corrections Today*, August 1988, pp. 144, 146, 155; Dan Gursky, "Innovative Drug Treatment in Delaware," *Corrections Today*, July 1988, pp. 49, 79.

PRISON DISCIPLINE

It was rough doing time, and there was a lot of petty rules, and if the rules all said you can't have your shirttail out, then you would get busted for that, and you would get written up and go to court, and as far as I am concerned this is insanity, and there is no sense to it.

—ANONYMOUS[55]

Upon entering Connecticut State Prison in 1830, the inmate would be presented with a list of six rules and regulations:

1. Every convict shall be industrious, submissive, and obedient, and shall labor diligently and in silence.
2. No convict shall secrete, hide, or carry about his person, any instrument or thing with intent to make his escape.
3. No convict shall write or receive a letter to or from any person whatsoever, nor have intercourse with persons within the prison, except by leave of the warden.

I would rather be caught with a knife by a guard than be caught without one by another inmate.

—A PRISONER, 1976

4. No convict shall burn, waste, injure, or destroy any raw materials or article of public property, nor deface or injure the prison building.

5. Convicts shall always conduct themselves toward officers with deference and respect; and cleanliness in their persons, dress, and bedding, is required. When they go to their meals or labor, they shall proceed in regular order and in silence, marching in the lock step.

6. No convict shall converse with another prisoner, or leave his work without permission of an officer. He shall not speak to, or look at visitors, nor leave the hospital when ordered there, nor shall he make any unnecessary noise in his labor, or do any thing either in the shops or cells, which is subversive of the good order of the institution.[56]

Over the years, lists of inmate rules have grown longer, reaching far into every aspect of inmate life. Regulations in South Dakota prisons, for example, number well into the hundreds. Some rules are of a general nature, pertaining to the orderly operation and safety of the institution:

Orders shall be obeyed promptly. . . .

Fighting is prohibited. . . .

Locking devices will not be tampered with. . . .

Prison guard with confiscated tools and weapons

Others are of questionable value:

> Longed sleeved sweat shirts will not be worn under a short sleeved shirt. . . .
> Only one cribbage board per man. . . . [57]

In Attica, there is even a regulation governing the number of times an inmate may kiss a visitor:

> They have locked up guys in the place for felonious kissing in the visiting room. If a guy kisses his wife six times it is felonious kissing. . . . [58]

Although one may consider the rules to be too numerous and many quite trivial, they found their way into inmate handbooks for very specific reasons. Some were designed to prevent disturbances, violence, and escapes; others serve to ensure the health and safety of both inmates and staff; a third group was imposed to maintain the orderly movement of prisoners and the flow of institutional life and procedure. Many regulations, however, are punitive in nature or, as in the military, are deemed necessary to provide regimentation, to further preserve order, and to define the boundaries of inmate status. Conversely, a variety of regulations have evolved with the idea of creating a self-respecting prison community and inculcating standards that will contribute to successful adjustment after release. Finally, as corrections specialists Harry Allen and Clifford Simonsen have suggested, many rules have resulted from the *"convict bogey"* syndrome — an exaggerated fear of prisoners requiring unnecessarily severe discipline. [59]

A major issue in inmate regulation is *prison contraband.* Contraband is officially defined as any item that can be used to break a rule of the institution or to assist in escape. [60] Such articles as drugs, knives, guns, bombs, and vaulting poles are contraband. In practice, however, contraband becomes *anything* that the custodial staff designates as undesirable, and the banning power is unrestricted. For example:

> Any item that is not issued or not authorized in the jail is contraband. Control of contraband is necessary for several reasons:
>
> 1. To control the introduction of articles that can be used for trading and gambling
> 2. To control the collecting of junk and the accumulation of items that make housekeeping difficult
> 3. To identify medications and drugs and items that can be used as weapons and escape implements
>
> Controlling contraband requires a clear understanding of what contraband is, of regulations that are designed to limit its entry into the jail, and of effective search procedures. The definition of contraband given above is simple and clear. However, this definition can become useless if the jail attempts to supplement it with a long list of approved items. If the jail permits prisoners to have packages, the problem of contraband control will be made difficult, since the list of authorized items may grow long. [61]

Contraband is uncovered by periodic searches of prisoners and their cells or dormitories, and rule breaking is either observed or discovered directly by a custodial officer or indirectly through inmate informers. In many instances, the violations are more or less ignored; sometimes the guard will simply give the inmate a warning and, if minor contraband is involved, confiscate it. In more serious cases, there are formal disciplinary proceedings with many due-process safeguards.

The major violations in prisons, at least those that result in disciplinary hearings, involve drugs, gambling, sex, fighting, stealing, and

If you seek violence, we will put you in jail.
— FORMER NEW YORK CITY MAYOR
ED KOCH, 1985

The "convict bogey"

Prison contraband

In prison, those things withheld from and denied to the prisoner become precisely what he wants most of all.
— ELDRIDGE CLEAVER, 1968

refusing to work. Most inmates are fairly sophisticated when it comes to hiding serious contraband items such as drugs or weapons. Penalties for violations include solitary confinement, temporary loss of privileges, temporary "keeplock" (being locked in the cell during recreation periods), or loss of "good time" (time off for good behavior). Numerous disciplinary violations can also affect an inmate's parole date, since institutional conduct is a factor taken into account in parole release decisions.*

Without question, the structure of rules and regulations and their enforcement creates resentment. One inmate remarked:

> I understand why there is riots all of the time, because they treat us like babies, and anything that you do is wrong. . . . It makes you angry inside.[62]

SEX IN PRISON

A prisoner has no sex. He is God's own private eunuch.
— HENRY MILLER, 1945

Inmate 1: Charley, what's the first thing you're gonna do when you get out? Find yourself some fox and make it with her?

Inmate 2: No man! I been gettin' off here in my cell every night. First thing is gonna be a good steak, cooked just right, in some fine restaurant.
— TWO DELAWARE INMATES, 1985

I remember the first time I forgot what it was like to fuck a woman. That day, man, was a helluva day. I lay there all night trying to remember. I couldn't remember how it was like. And that was a year and a half ago. That's a helluva experience, man — to forget.
— A CALIFORNIA PRISON INMATE[63]

Aside from the loss of liberty itself, perhaps the most obvious area of deprivation associated with prison life is heterosexual activity. Isolation from the opposite sex implies a frustration of sexual desires and drives at a time when, for many inmates, those impulses are quite strong. Some prisoners remain abstinent, or rely wholly on sexual fantasies and masturbation, while others partake in voluntary or involuntary homosexual contacts or rape. However, the data on these activities are only fragmentary, and any conclusions are at best tentative.

Homosexuality

Several decades ago, lawyer-sociologist Paul W. Tappan commented that homosexual behavior is a universal concomitant of sex-segregated living; that it is a perennial problem in camps, boarding schools, one-sexed colleges, training schools, and correctional facilities; and that from a biological point of view homosexuality is normal behavior in the distorted institutional environments that characterize our nation's prisons.[64] Whether Tappan's argument can be applied equally to all sex-segregated environments is difficult to document. Within the prison setting, however, homosexual contacts seem to be relatively common, although perhaps not to the extent that popular images would suggest.

Based on the few studies that have examined the question of homosexual behavior among prison inmates, estimates can be made that between 30 and 45 percent of inmates have experienced homosexual be-

---

* In 1984, officials at the state prison in Florence, Arizona, came up with a new weapon to use against misbehaving inmates. It was "meat loaf." Prisoners who had infractions of the institutional rules for five straight days were subjected to a week of meat loaf — breakfast, lunch, and dinner. Moreover, the "meat loaf" contained no meat. Although the Arizona Civil Liberties Union filed a petition in the local district court maintaining the practice was "cruel and unusual," the presiding judge denied the injunction. As for one inmate who had forty-two consecutive servings of meat loaf, his only comment was: "Where's the beef?" (See *USA Today*, March 15, 1984, p. 1A; *National Law Journal*, April 16, 1984, p. 43.)

havior, with the variations associated with the intensity of custodial surveillance, the characteristics of the inmate population, and the average length of confinement in a given prison.[65]

The patterns of homosexual practices tend to differ, however, between male and female inmates. Among males, homosexuality seldom involves a close relationship between the parties; rather, it is often a response to physical needs. Prostitution is a frequent type of male homosexual association. Also, there are cases in which a male who is particularly vulnerable to homosexual attacks will enter into a relationship with another male who agrees to "protect" him from the assaults of others.[66] Among the females, homosexuality appears to develop out of mutual interest. The relationships attempt to simulate the "family" found outside the institution and are not primarily for sexual gratification. Many women form a relationship that is recognized as a "marriage"—a pseudo-family that serves to compensate for the lack of the close family environment that exists on the outside. Within the pseudo-family the opportunity for homosexual contact can develop.[67]

The most readily observable difference between male and female homosexual behavior in prisons is the nature of the physical contact. Among males it is usually manifested in direct sexual actions—oral and anal sex, and mutual masturbation. For women, there may be only a strong emotional relationship with some body contact, such as embracing or holding hands. Some women do, however, engage in more serious sexual unions, such as deep kissing, oral-genital stimulation, and body contact that attempts to simulate heterosexual intercourse.[68]

Despite the data that suggest that one-third of prison inmates engage in homosexual practices, whether regularly or at least periodically, both inmates and institutional personnel agree that the most frequently observed form of sexual release is solitary masturbation. As one commentator remarked:

Nobody—inmate, staff, or visitor—is in a prison very long before seeing an inmate masturbating in a toilet, shower, or cell.[69]

In recent years, considerable attention has been given to the matter of *homosexual rape* in correctional institutions. It is generally believed that sexual attacks are quite common in men's prisons. For example:

Sexual assaults are epidemic in some prison systems. Virtually every slightly built young man committed by the courts is sexually approached within a day or two after his admission to prison. Many of these young men are overwhelmed and repeatedly "raped" by gangs of inmate aggressors.[70]

Yet the data on this are only fragmentary, and some people have argued that the impressions that behind prison walls the incidence of homosexual rape is high, and that sexual assault is the most characteristic form of prison homosexuality, are essentially unfounded assumptions.[71]

While the research on the incidence of rape in prison remains tentative, there seems to be agreement that such attacks are more often power plays than sources of sexual release. In *Against Our Will*, Susan Brownmiller argues that homosexual rape in a male prison can be compared to sexual assaults on women by men in open society. Both result from needs to control and conquer:

Prison rape . . . is an acting out of power roles within an all-male, authoritarian environment in which the younger, weaker inmate, usually a first offender, is forced to play the role that in the outside world is assigned to women.[72]

In the latter months of 1985, one of the most voracious homosexuals in the federal prison system violated parole in Florida and was returned to the men's maximum security prison at Lompoc [California] to finish his sentence. This one was so predatory that the cons had long ago nicknamed him "Honey Bear." Honey Bear was known to shoot a load of "crank" [methamphetamine] and go walking down a tier advertising favors at every cell he passed; he would enter at the beck and call of anyone who was interested. If there happened to be two men in the cell, appropriate adjustments could be made. The Honey Bear was an accommodating soul. No one seemed to notice the little sores on the back of Honey Bear's neck, although quite a few of his "clients" had an intimate view of them. Early in 1986, the sores got out of hand, and he was having other health problems. Honey Bear went to the doctor and was soon diagnosed as having AIDS.

—San Francisco Chronicle, August 3, 1986

Sexual assault in prisons

Freelancing homosexuals, yeah, fags, keep down rapes. It keeps down rapes, and a whole lot of other things too! If there's enough homosexuals, an attractive inmate don't have to worry when he see dudes like us looking at him.

—California inmate

Similarly, Leo Carroll's analysis of interracial rape in male prisons suggests blacks often sexually assault whites in retaliation for 300 years of social oppression and to demonstrate their manhood and dominance. As one of Carroll's informants explained it:

> To the general way of thinking it's 'cause we're confined and we've got hard rocks. But that ain't it at all. It's a way for the black man to get back at the white man. It's one way he can assert his manhood. Anything white, even a defenseless punk, is part of what the black man hates. It's part of what he's had to fight all his life just to survive, just to have a hole to sleep in and some garbage to eat . . . It's a new ego thing. He can show he's a man by making a white guy into a girl.[73]

As a final note, there is evidence that homosexual rape does occur in women's institutions, but that it is comparatively rare.[74]

Conjugal Visitation

Conjugal visitation: The practice of permitting inmate and spouse to spend time together in private quarters on prison grounds, during which time they may engage in sexual relations.

Conjugal visitation has been promoted as a means of reducing homosexuality in prison, as well as of raising inmate morale and maintaining family ties. During the conjugal visit, inmate and spouse are permitted to spend time together in private quarters on prison grounds, during which they may engage in sexual relations.

Conjugal visitation has been well known in European and Latin American countries for quite some time, and it has likely always occurred in some American prisons although on an informal and haphazard basis. As an official correctional program, however, its first appearance, in the United States was in 1900 at the Mississippi State Penitentiary at Parchman. In 1968, conjugal visiting began as an experiment of California's Tehachapi facility, and was later expanded to other California institutions. More recently, New York, New Jersey, North Carolina, and Texas have also introduced conjugal visitation on an experimental basis. Reports on both the Mississippi and California programs have been positive.[75]

Those who favor conjugal visiting argue that it decreases homosexuality within the prison, that it helps to preserve marriages, and that it strengthens family relationships.[76] Yet there has been opposition to conjugal visiting; opponents argue that such visits can serve only the minority of inmates who have wives, thus raising the question of fairness; appropriate visitation facilities are typically lacking; children may be born to men who cannot support them, and there are potential security risks.[77]

In recent years, two factors have served to refocus correctional thinking about conjugal visitation. The first issue relates to women. Historically, the majority of programs in the United States have been available only to male inmates, the idea that the same heterosexual opportunities should be extended to women inmates was to some a "shocking" idea.[78] An early exception to this pattern has been New York State's Family Reunion Program, begun in 1976 and established at Bedford Hills Correctional Facility for women the following year. The program allows overnight visits for selected inmates and members of their immediate families. The "family member" is typically a spouse, but can include parents and children.

Fueled by the growing number of incarcerated women over the last decade and a half, many more correctional systems have developed structured arrangements whereby women inmates can have meaningful visits with family members in general, and with their children in particular. In Massachusetts, for example, where the majority of women inmates are mothers with young children, a program established in 1985 permits overnight visits with children.[79] Even more significant is Michigan's Children's Visitation Program, established at the close of the 1980s for the purpose of restoring the bonds between children and their incarcerated mothers (see Exhibit 15.4).

The second issue to have an impact on conjugal visitation involves HIV and AIDS. The focus has been on New York, the state with the most AIDS cases not only in the general population, but in the prison population as well. In *Doe* v. *Coughlin,*[80] decided by the New York Court of Appeals in 1987, it was held that an inmate with AIDS could not participate in conjugal visitation. Although the inmate and his wife jointly argued that their right to marital privacy had been violated by the ban, the court agreed with state correctional officials that the prohibition was in the interests of halting the spread of AIDS. In 1991, however, New York suddenly reversed its position, making it the first state with a large population of prisoners with AIDS to permit such visits. Under its new policy, inmates who are infected with HIV or are symptomatic for AIDS are permitted conjugal visits as long as prison officials can ascertain that their condition has been disclosed and that both partners have received safe sex counseling.[81] The logic behind the decision was to encourage the state's many thousands of married prisoners to be tested for HIV infection. Of New York's 56,000 prisoners, about 15 percent, or 8,500, were believed to be HIV-positive. Yet only 2,500 cases were known, because most inmates refuse testing. Hence, increased testing in the long run might reduce the spread of the disease.

Coeducational Prisons

Since 1973, prisons housing both men and women have proliferated throughout the United States. Coeducational facilities currently operate in a number of states and the federal system. In these institutions, inmates eat, study, and work together, and associate with each other generally, except with regard to sleeping arrangements.

The philosophy behind the establishment of these institutions was that men tend to behave better in the presence of women, have fewer fights, take more pride in their appearance, and are less likely to engage in homosexual contacts. Furthermore, it was felt that for both male and female prisoners, the more normal social environment hastens community reintegration.[82] Preliminary study and the testimony of coed facility administrators suggest that these expectations have been met. Both violence and forced homosexuality have declined, attendance in work and education programs has increased, and inmates seem to return home with more self-esteem and higher expectations.[83]

When coed prisons were first opened, some feared that they would become X-rated nightmares with the worst scenarios of rape, love feasts, and general sexual debauchery. But these never came to pass.[84] There are strict sexual codes, pregnancies have been infrequent, and sexual misbehavior generally results in return to a sex-segregated facility. Furthermore, male candidates are heavily screened — they must be minimum-security risks and near their parole eligibility dates.

Yet not everyone has been thrilled about the coeducational experiments. The coed program at Oklahoma's Jess Dunn Correctional Center, which began in 1986, was ended after only two years as the result

A man visits an inmate at the Massachusetts Correctional Institution.

America has the largest prison sentences in the West, yet the only condition long sentences demonstrably cure is heterosexuality.

— BRUCE JACKSON, 1968

Family ties are a major factor in reducing the number of inmates who come back to prison.

— CHARLOTTE NESBITT, AMERICAN CORRECTIONAL ASSOCIATION, 1985

• EXHIBIT 15.4 •

Michigan Program Makes Children's Visits Meaningful
by Christina Jose-Kampfner, Ph.D.

Most incarcerated mothers have great concerns for their children and want to play a positive role in their lives. The prevailing policies and attitudes in many correctional agencies, however, tend to undermine inmates who want to be good parents, instead of using the bond with their children to benefit prison discipline, inmate morale and the children's psychological health.

Corrections officials should take advantage of women's desires to see their children to create an environment conducive to inmates' self-improvement. The Children's Visitation Program, or CVP, at the Huron Valley Correctional Facility in Ypsilanti, Michigan, is an example of how this can be done.

Regular Visits vs. CVP Visits

The Children's Visitation Program began in October 1988 and has served more than 100 children and fifty mothers. The program has served not only to restore the bonds between mothers and children, but also to greatly improve discipline at the institution.

Most prison visiting rooms are not ideal places for intimacy between mothers and children. Correctional officers, of course, are more concerned with security and the detection of contraband than the quality of the visit. Young children must be accompanied by adults, the rooms often are noisy, and people are seated so close to each other that privacy is limited. Children must adhere to strict rules forbidding them from putting their feet on chairs or even standing. Mothers must make sure their children do not disrupt others' visits.

In the CVP, we designed special visits that allow for more natural interaction between mothers and children. Children are not accompanied by other adults, ensuring that they get to spend time alone with their mothers. Mothers are free to move around the room, allowing them to tend to their children's needs, such as styling their hair and taking them to the bathroom. Children also are free to move around the room and play with other children.

There are no uniformed officers present; instead, a nonuniformed Department of Corrections staff member helps with the visit. Not having a uniformed officer in the room is very important to the mothers and children. As one child put it, "Without an officer there telling us what to do and looking at us all the time, it's just like we were ordinary mothers and children playing together and having a good time."

Visits last about three hours and take place in the regular visiting room, which is temporarily converted into a playroom. When the weather is good, visits are moved outside to the prison yard. Aside from group activities, such as singing and reading stories at the beginning and the end of each visit, mothers and their children are free to spend their time as they choose. Toys and games, as well as art, reading and other educational materials, also are provided.

Some of the children have been part of the same visiting group for more than two years. They develop friendships and are comforted by sharing their problems with others who understand and identify with them.

Transportation has been one problem we have had to work to overcome. Some children are forced to travel as much as six hours to see their mothers. Since a disproportionate number of the women are poor, their families are often unable to afford the trip. Even the families that live within an hour of the prison often must spend as much as $50 in bus or taxi fare for three people to come to the prison.

To address this problem, a network of community volunteers provides transportation for children who live far away and have no means of getting to see their mothers. The children are divided into four groups according to where they live. The same group of children come one Saturday each month.

This community involvement helps the public become aware of the problems the women and their children face. People learn that maintaining family relationships can be one of the most effective sources of rehabilitation and a way to prevent recidivism. Community involvement also helps the women feel less isolated.

At the end of each visit, the children get together to discuss their feelings about the experience. When possible, they are divided into two groups — infants to nine-year-olds and ten- to eighteen-year-olds. The mothers also have a small debriefing inside as a forum for discussing their feelings.

Improved Discipline

The main governing body of the program is a committee of ten inmates who are elected by other inmates for two-year terms. Committee members, who make decisions on changes in the room's decor and discipline inmates who violate the program's rules, learn organizational, record-keeping and conflict-resolution skills they are not normally exposed to. Through active participation and decision making, these skills become an integral part of their behavior. This in itself is rehabilitation.

According to a questionnaire filled out by the mothers, 90 percent said they would think twice before engaging in an activity that might mean the loss of a special Saturday visit. Seventy-five percent said the visits have effectively prevented them from engaging in misconduct. Common answers to the question, "Has fear of losing your visit affected your behavior in prison?" were: "Now that I have this visit to be looking forward to, my behavior is fantastic," and "I refuse to allow my behavior to jeopardize seeing my son."

The women constantly remind each other of the consequences of not getting along in the visiting room. As one woman told a group of fellow inmates, "Whatever problems you have, leave them outside the room, because in here we are all mothers trying to mother our children."

In the twenty-seven months the program has been in existence, no contraband has been introduced through the children's visits. On the contrary, the women are very protective of the children and would do nothing to endanger them or jeopardize the program. The subject of bringing in contraband is discussed periodically at the group meetings before each visit. The inmates clearly understand the consequences of such an action and willingly take all necessary preventive measures against it.

Benefits for the Children

This program has an equally important impact on the children, who are greatly affected by their mothers' incarceration but in many cases are not able to express their pain in their family or peer group. They are often teased at school. They worry about their mother's well being. As one child said, "I am afraid for my mother. Coming here helps me know it is OK. I worry about what it is like for her here."

Through this program we have learned that many of the children are suffering from post-traumatic stress disorders, particularly those children who were present during their mothers' crimes or arrests. PTSDs are characterized by numbing or reduced involvement with the world and symptoms such as hyperalertness, sleep disturbances, guilt and impaired memory and concentration.

The CVP has helped us begin to realize how important it is to treat children with problems related to being separated from their mothers.

Teenagers have an especially difficult time when their mothers are incarcerated because they are dealing with their own identity formation. We have seen an alarming number of cases where thirteen- or fourteen-year-old teenagers get pregnant within months of their mothers' incarceration.

A significant number of the children in the program have already had contact with the criminal court system. This pattern was cited in two recent studies published by the Center for the Study of Youth Policy at the University of Michigan which found that more than half of the youths in custody had an immediate family member in prison.

This program has helped these high-risk children; it allows

their mothers to discuss their crimes with them and possibly discourage them from further criminal activity. Also, being able to laugh and cry with their mothers can help them sort out conflicting feelings. These are important elements in the healing process for both parties.

In addition to the visits and debriefing sessions, a clinical psychologist in charge of the visiting room also provides family therapy. This has been very successful in helping children and teenagers stop disruptive behaviors such as fighting in school.

Expanding Children's Programs

Children's visitation programs can be put in place in prisons at almost no cost. They must, however, involve the inmates, the institution and the community. In addition to re-establishing mother-child relationships, a well-designed program helps participants learn skills necessary for successful living and creates a network of community volunteers conscious of the problems of this neglected population. Trained professionals, such as psychologists and social workers with experience working with women in prison, should be involved to ensure success.

As many as 80 percent of incarcerated women have children. Separation from them and a denial of maternal responsibility should not be part and parcel of the punishment these women receive for their crimes. On the contrary, contact with their children is an instrumental part of their rehabilitation. Effective visitation programs can help the inmates and, in addition, help the innocent victims of the system, the children.

SOURCE: Reprinted from *Corrections Today,* August 1991, pp. 130–134. Copyright 1991 by American Correctional Association.

of jealousies over certain male and female inmates pairing off, as well as for the six pregnancies that occurred during that period.[85] For similar reasons, male and female inmates have been separated at the California Youth Authority's Camarillo coeducational compound. Under regulations promulgated in mid-1990 coed activities became limited to school and Sunday worship, with strict separation at all other times.[86]

As for the future of coeducational custody, it is difficult to predict. Expansions are necessarily restricted, however, since women represent such a small proportion of the federal and state correctional populations.

THE INMATE SOCIAL SYSTEM

The psychological milieu is even more depressing than the physical. What to do with oneself, how to put in the long, dragging hours, becomes a problem. One can sleep only so many hours.

— NATHAN F. LEOPOLD, JR., 1957

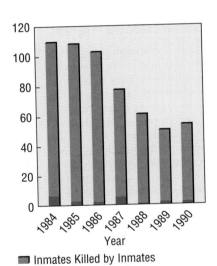

120
100
80
60
40
20
0

1984 1985 1986 1987 1988 1989 1990

Year

■ Inmates Killed by Inmates
■ Staff Killed by Inmates

Prison Violence in the United States, 1984–1990

SOURCE: *Corrections Compendium*, June 1991

The primary task of prisons, despite any arguments to the contrary, is custody. The internal order of the prison is maintained by strictly controlling the inmates and regimenting every aspect of their lives. In addition to their loss of freedom and basic liberties, goods and services, heterosexual relationships, and autonomy, they are deprived of their personal identities. Upon entering prison, inmates are stripped of their clothing and most of their personal possessions; and they are examined, inspected, weighed, documented, and given a number. Thus, prison becomes painful, both physically and psychologically:

> Unable to escape either physically or psychologically, lacking the cohesion to carry through an insurrection that is bound to fail in any case, and bereft of faith in peaceful innovation, the inmate population might seem to have no recourse but the simple endurance of the pains of imprisonment. *But if the rigors of confinement cannot be completely removed, they can at least be mitigated by the patterns of social interaction established among the inmates themselves.*[87]

The rigors and frustrations of confinement leave but a few paths open to inmates. They can bind themselves to their fellow captives in ties of mutual aid and loyalty, in opposition in prison officials. They can wage a war against all, seeking their own advantage without reference to the needs and claims of others. Or they can simply withdraw into themselves. Ideally these alternatives exist only in an abstract sense, and most inmates combine characteristics of the first two extremes:

> The population of prisoners does not exhibit a perfect solidarity yet neither is the population of prisoners a warring aggregate. Rather, it is a mixture of both and the society of captives lies balanced in an uneasy compromise.[88]

It is within this balance of extremes that the inmate social system functions.

Prisonization

Prisonization: The socializing process by which the inmate learns the rules and regulations of the institution and the informal rules, values, customs, and general culture of the penitentiary.

Exposure to the social system of the *prison community* is almost immediate, for all new inmates become quickly aware of the norms and values that are shared by their fellow captives. The internalization of the prison norms and values has been described as **prisonization:**

Every man who enters the penitentiary undergoes prisonization to some extent. The first and most obvious integrative step concerns his status. He becomes at once an anonymous figure in a subordinate group. A number replaces a name. He wears the clothes of the other members of the subordinate group. He is questioned and admonished. He soon learns that the warden is all-powerful. He soon learns the ranks, titles, and authority of various officials. And whether he uses the prison slang and argot or not, he comes to know its meanings. Even though a new man may hold himself aloof from other inmates and remain a solitary figure, he finds himself within a few months referring to or thinking of keepers as "screws," the physician as the "croaker," and using the local nicknames to designate persons. He follows the examples already set in wearing his cap. He learns to eat in haste and in obtaining food he imitates the tricks of those near him.

After the new arrival recovers from the effects of the swallowing-up process, he assigns a new meaning to conditions he had previously taken for granted. The fact that food, shelter, clothing, and a work activity had been given him originally made no especial impression. It is only after some weeks or months that there comes to him a new interpretation of these necessities of life. This new conception results from mingling with other men and it places emphasis on the fact that the environment should administer to him. This point is intangible and difficult to describe in so far as it is only a subtle and minute change in attitude from the taken-for-granted perception. Exhaustive questioning of hundreds of men reveals that this slight change in attitude is a fundamental step in the process we are calling prisonization.[89]

Thus, prisonization refers to the socializing process by which the inmate learns the rules and regulations of the institution and the informal rules, values, customs, and general culture of the penitentiary.

The concept of prisonization comes from Donald Clemmer, who was a staff sociologist at Menard Penitentiary in Chester, Illinois, and is based on his studies of the male prison subculture during the 1930s. His thesis maintains that prisoners share the common experience of enforced confinement, and from this comes many influences that tend to draw them together in a common cause against their keepers. The close physical proximity in which inmates must live destroys much, if not all, of their privacy; prison regulations and routine press them toward conformity; and their isolation limits their range of experience. Furthermore, institutional life fosters a monotonous equalitarianism among inmates. Prisoners occupy similar cells; they wear the same clothes and eat the same food; and they do the same thing at the same time and according to the same rules, regulations, and potential for disciplinary punishment. Within such a setting, prison life holds little for inmates, but what it does offer they share in common. And all of this happens under the same structure of authority — one that is direct, immediate, inescapable, and sometimes brutal. Everything that prisoners have, or fail to have, is traceable to that structure. Food and clothing, rules and regulations, pleasures and pains, sorrows and cruelties, and indignities and brutalities — all seem to come from the same source. The inmate community, then, has a common hatred — the prison administration — against which it can direct its hostilities.

In presenting this notion of prisonization, Clemmer maintains that prison values could be taken on to a greater or lesser degree. Once they were internalized, however, the prisonized inmate became immune, for the most part, to the influences of conventional value systems. This suggests that the process of prisonization transforms the novitiate inmate into a fully accredited convict; it is a *criminalization* process that militates against any reform or rehabilitation.

The prison is a community with its own norms and values, the internalization of which is called prisonization.

Prison is a place where all sorts of things are not there.
— BRUCE JACKSON, 1971

Prisonization as "criminalization"

Some people have argued against Clemmer's thesis. They point to evidence that suggests that inmates are first prisonized and then "deprisonized" immediately prior to release; others hold that prisonization itself is a myth.[90] Most observers agree, however, that some form of prisonization process does indeed occur, but that it is affected by an inmate's priority, duration, frequency, and intensity of contact with the prison subculture and the values of varying segments of the inmate population. This point of view is most likely correct, for circumstances, regulations, population characteristics, and administrative authority structures vary widely from one institution to the next. Furthermore, socialization into the inmate worlds of the more repressive maximum-security prisons across the nation seems to most closely resemble what Clemmer originally described as "prisonization."

The Inmate Code

Regardless of the degree of prisonization experienced by an inmate, every correctional institution has a subculture. Every prison subculture has its system of norms that influence prisoners' behavior, typically to a greater extent than the institution's formally prescribed rules. These subcultural norms are informal, unwritten rules, but their violation can evoke sanctions from fellow inmates ranging from ostracism to physical violence or death. The informal rules, furthermore, are referred to as the **inmate code,** and generally include at least the following:

Inmate code: The unwritten rules of the prison subculture, which, if violated, can result in sanctions ranging from ostracism to death.

1. *Don't interfere with the interests of other inmates.*   Concretely, this means that inmates "never rat on a con," or betray each other. It also includes these directives: "Don't be nosy," "Don't put a guy on the spot," and "Keep off a man's back." There are no justifications for failing to comply with these rules.

2. *Keep out of quarrels or feuds with fellow inmates.* This is expressed in the directives, "Play it cool," "Do your own time."
3. *Don't exploit other inmates.* Concretely, this means, "Don't break your word," "Don't steal from the cons," "Don't welsh on debts," and "Be right."
4. *Don't weaken; withstand frustration or threat without complaint.* This is expressed in such directives as, "Don't cop out" (cry guilty), "Don't suck around," "Be tough," and "Be a man."
5. *Don't give respect or prestige to the custodians or to the world for which they stand.* Concretely, this is expressed by "Don't be a sucker," and "Be sharp."[91]

Although the inmate code is violated regularly, most prisoners adhere to its major directives. But they do so not because it represents a "code of honor," but for other, more serious considerations — the very same reasons why professional thieves follow the underworld code:

> Honor among thieves? Well — yes and no. You do have some old pros who might talk about honor, but they're so well heeled and well connected that they can afford to be honorable. But for most people, it's a question of "do unto others" — you play by the rules because you may need a favor someday, or because the guy you skip on, or the guy you rap to the cops about — you never know where he'll turn up. Maybe he's got something on you, or maybe he ends up as your cell-mate, or he says bad things about you — you can't tell how these things could turn out.[92]

The Sources and Functions of the Inmate Social System

There is little consensus as to how the inmate subculture evolves behind prison walls. One explanation for it has been the *deprivation model;* that is, upon entering prison, inmates are faced with major social and psychological problems resulting from the loss of freedom, status, possessions, dignity, autonomy, security, and personal and sexual relationships. The inmate subculture emerges through prisoners' attempts to adapt to the deprivations imposed by incarceration. The subculture is a mechanism — through mutual cooperation — for reducing the pains of isolation, obtaining and sharing possessions, regaining dignity and status, developing meaningful relationships, and enjoying some personal security.

The deprivation model

Another model, the *importation model,* views inmates as doing considerably more than simply responding to immediate, prison-specific problems. Cultural elements are "imported" into the prison from the outside world. Prisoners bring with them their values, norms, and attitudes, and these become the content of the inmate subculture.[94]

The importation model

Both models seem to be crucial to the inmate subculture. On the one hand, the deprivation thesis serves to explain the emergence and persistence of the subculture. The pains and deprivations of imprisonment represent the stimulus for the formation of a social system that provides status, security, and solidarity. On the other, much of the richness of the subculture comes from the norms of the various underworlds and the experiences of inmates within other, outside criminal subcultures. (See Exhibit 15.5.)

Whether its sources are deprivation, importation, or both, the inmate social system functions not only for its members, but for the prison as a whole. More specifically, the inmate social system is a mechanism for

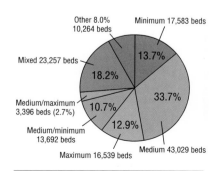

Security Level of New Prison Beds, 1991–1992

SOURCE: *Corrections Compendium,* February 1991

● EXHIBIT 15.5 ●

Sidelights on Criminal Matters
Social Roles and Prison Argot

Prisoners' relationships to the inmate social system are reflected in the roles they take on in the institution and are reflected in the labels they are given by their peers. These labels are part of the general prison argot.

Like other groups that are devoted to specialized activities or purposes separate from those of the wider society, prisoners' communication patterns include the verbal camouflage and symbolism of argot. This artificial language expresses the specific behavioral orientations of the prison community. It emphasizes the attitudes and values of the inmate world while downgrading those of the prison administration and of "straight" society. Furthermore, it represents a means for expressing feelings not normally communicated by traditional language. Perhaps most importantly, prison argot is also a distinguishing system serving to designate the social roles played by the various members of the inmate world. In every prison community, for example, there are:

Rats and **squealers** Those who deny the primary value of inmate cohesion by betraying fellow prisoners.

Center-men Inmates who take on the attitudes and opinions of the official; they are named after the "center," which is the official seat of government of the institution.

Gorillas Prisoners who increase their material goods in prison by the use of force.

Merchants Inmates who refuse to share their scarce goods; they exploit the needs of their peers by selling instead of giving.

Wolves, punks, and **fags** Labels that refer to the various homosexual roles. *Wolves* play the masculine role in homosexual relations while *fags* play the female role and have given up their claims to masculinity; *punks* are masculine except during the sex act, taking on the feminine role out of fear ("punks are made but fags are born").

Ball busters Inmates who openly defy guards. "Toughs" and "hipsters": Among those who frequently fight with other inmates, *toughs* are admired masculine types who fight both the weak and the strong, while *hipsters* are generally bullies.

Real men Those who endure the rigors of imprisonment with dignity.

Square Johns Inmates with only minimal, if any, involvement in systematic crime; they actively participate in prison treatment programs and identify with conventional norms.

Right guys Inmates who avoid contact with staff or treatment programs; they aspire to crimi-

nal vocations, and they fully ascribe to illegitimate standards.

Politicians Sophisticated criminals who use skill and wit to manipulate other inmates and staff.

Outlaws Criminals who confront their victims and always emphasize force.

Dings Inmates whose concerns and behaviors lack the consistency necessary to be assigned to one of the above roles.

In addition, guards are known as "hacks" and "screws," inmates who submit to hard work are "suckers," and the place where prisoners talk about the world of crime and penitentiary life is called the "yard." There are hundreds more.

Although most, if not all, of these social roles emerge within every correctional institution, the specific labels — "rats," "wolves," "dings" — vary from place to place and change over time.

SOURCES: Peter G. Garabedian, "Social Roles and Processes of Socialization in the Prison Community," *Social Problems* (Fall 1963): 139–152; James A. Inciardi, *Careers in Crime* (Chicago: Rand McNally, 1975), p. 56; Gresham M. Sykes, *The Society of Captives: A Study of a Maximum Security Prison* (New York: Atheneum, 1965), pp. 84–105.

controlling the behavior of prisoners. Without it, the custodial administration could not fully maintain order. Within most correctional institutions, both guards and inmates play specific roles. Guards provide inmates with illegitimate opportunities for obtaining needed goods and services. In return, inmates exercise control over their peers. Thus a level of accommodation develops, and each becomes captive and captor to the other. Guards play their roles of accommodation in order to avoid disruptions in prison order and routine. The inmate social system polices its members so that custodial accommodation will not be withdrawn.[95]

The Social Order of Women's Prisons

Most studies of prison communities and inmate social systems have been undertaken in men's institutions, and the findings are not fully applicable to women's prisons. Fewer women are convicted of crimes, and a greater proportion of these who are found guilty are placed on probation. Those who do receive terms of imprisonment have typically been convicted of homicide, aggravated assault, check forgery, shoplifting, and violations of the drug laws, with few serving time for burglary and robbery. Women's prisons have an even greater proportion of minority group members than have institutions for men, but fewer women have had prior prison experiences. Finally, the cottage system is the model more typically followed in women's prisons. Although few women inmates are confined in cells, the more "open" nature of the women's institution often requires more frequent security checks and, hence, close custodial supervision. All of these factors combine to affect the character of the social order of female correctional institutions.

In some ways, the social system in women's prisons is similar to that in the all-male penitentiary. There are social roles, argot, an inmate code, and accommodation between captive and captor. But in other ways the social system of women inmates is not as clearly defined, for it is a microsociety made up to four main groups.[96] There are the "squares" from conventional society, who are having their first experience with custodial life. Many of these are members of the middle class. They see themselves as respectable persons and view prisons as places to which only "criminals" go. Their convictions have generally been for embezzlement or situational homicides. There are the "professionals," who are career criminals and who view incarceration as an occupational hazard. Expert shoplifters fall into this group. They adopt a "cool" approach to prison life that involves taking maximum advantage of institutional amenities without endangering their chances for parole or early release. The third group, and perhaps the largest is made up of habitual criminals, who have had numerous experiences with prison life since their teenage years. Some are prostitutes who have assaulted and robbed their clients, many are thieves, and others are chronic hard drug users and sellers. For them, institutional life provides status and familial attachments. Finally, there is the custodial staff, which reflects the same values and attributes as in men's institutions.[97]

This microsociety seems to be changing. The growth of coeducational institutions over the last decade has served to remove many of the less serious offenders from sex-segregated women's prisons. Furthermore, with the emancipation of women since the 1970s and early 1980s, more are engaging in "male-type" crimes, a larger number are being arrested and convicted, and a greater proportion are being sentenced to terms of imprisonment.[98]

THE EFFECTIVENESS OF CORRECTIONAL TREATMENT

What works?

—ROBERT MARTINSON, 1974

With few and isolated exceptions, the rehabilitative efforts that have been reported so far have no appreciable effect on recidivism.

—MARTINSON, 1974

Is it treatment or our evaluation methods which have failed?

—SUSAN B. LONG, 1979

The treatment approach to the management and control of criminal offenders was used in the United States early in its history, and by the middle of the twentieth century the idea of "changing the lawbreaker" had become a dominant force in correctional thinking. Most offenders were still "punished," but at the same time classification exercises assigned them to "programs" and "supervision" designed for their "reintegration" into law-abiding society.

Yet throughout the history of corrections in America there has also been a tendency among advocates of both the punishment and treatment philosophies to commit themselves to unproven techniques. Correctional and reform approaches were often founded on intuition and sentiment, rather than on an awareness of prior success or failure. This began to change, however, when the rehabilitative ideal emerged as a strong force in correctional thinking. Attempts were made not only to test the efficacy of existing programs, but also to design and evaluate experimental and innovative approaches. Research strategies were devised, outcome measures were specified, data were prudently collected and judiciously analyzed, and the findings were invariably circulated.

Throughout the 1950s and for the better part of the 1960s, a vast body of literature began to accumulate offering testimony on the successes and failures of therapeutic approaches. In the main, however, they projected a rather gloomy outlook for the rehabilitative ideal. One of the early disappointments, for example, was the well-known Cambridge-Somerville Youth Study. Begun in 1935 and often described as the most energetic experiment in the prevention of delinquency, it attempted to test the impact of intensive counseling on young male delinquents. For ten years the research continued, using an experimental group of youths who had access to counseling and a control group who did not. When the findings of the experience were published in 1951, it was learned that there were no significant differences between the outcomes of the treatment and the control groups. This led the evaluators to the natural conclusion that there was no evidence that counseling could make a positive contribution to the rehabilitation of delinquents.[99] In subsequent years, numerous researchers in Europe and the United States surveyed the field of correctional evaluation. Their conclusions were overwhelmingly negative—that the treatment of offenders had questionable results.[100] But still, the focus on treatment continued and the findings of the studies were ignored by all but the social-behavioral research communities.

This apparent disregard of negative results could be readily understood. The research had typically been carried out by members of the academic community. The findings were prepared in a technical format,

The Cambridge-Somerville Youth Study

Prisons don't rehabilitate, they don't punish, they don't protect, so what the hell do they do?

—JERRY BROWN, 1976

and, perhaps more importantly, they appeared almost exclusively in professional and scientific journals, government reports, academic symposia, and books published by university presses. For the general public and the nation's legislators and opinion makers, these sources of information were as remote as medieval parchments hidden in the cellars and garrets of some ancient moated castle. And too, many of the more pessimistic pronouncements were published during the enthusiasm of the 1960s — amidst the vigor of John F. Kennedy's "American Camelot" and the optimism of the Great Society years.

"Camelot" was a reference to the glamour of the Kennedy years. The White House image was that of the legendary court, complete with its handsome king and beautiful queen, and its shining knights, its feudal lords, and its courtiers and fools. At the same time, as a reflection of this, the nation seemed to be asserting itself in a new era under the protectorship of its revered charismatic leader. Even more important, however, were the Great Society years of President Lyndon B. Johnson, who had declared in 1964: "We have been called upon — are you listening? — to build a great society of the highest order, a society not just for today or tomorrow, but for three or four generations to come." The Great Society, the President explained, rested on abundant liberty for all, and it demanded an end to poverty and racial injustice.

But all of this began to fade quickly, followed by a series of events that turned the nation's attention to the effectiveness of correctional treatment.

The Martinson Report

During the late 1960s and early 1970s, the Great Society image began to tarnish. The programs to abolish poverty and racial injustice had not lived up to their expectations. There were riots, many were angered over American involvement in Vietnam, and crime rates were increasing at a rapid pace. Furthermore, there was growing opposition to the many Supreme Court decisions that some claimed, and others denied, were "handcuffing police" and "coddling criminals." During much of this period, researchers in New York had been undertaking a massive evaluation of prior efforts at correctional intervention.

The idea for the research went back to early 1966, when the New York State Governor's Special Committee on Criminal Offenders decided to commission a study to determine what methods, if any, held the greatest promise for the rehabilitation of convicted offenders. The findings of the study were to be used to guide program development in the state's criminal justice system. The project was carried out by researchers at the New York State Office of Crime Control Planning, and for years they analyzed the literature on hundreds of correctional efforts published between 1945 and 1967.

The findings of the project were put together in a massive volume that was published in 1975.[101] Prior to the appearance of the in-depth report, an article by one of the researchers, Robert Martinson, was published in *The Public Interest* entitled "What Works? — Questions and Answers About Prison Reform."[102] In it he reviewed the purpose and scope of the New York study and implied that with few and isolated exceptions, *nothing works!*

There was little that was really new in Martinson's article. In 1966, Professor Walter C. Bailey of the City University of New York had published the findings of a survey of 100 evaluations of correctional

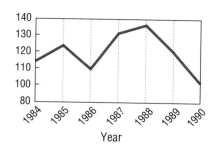

Inmate Suicides, 1984–1990
SOURCE: *Corrections Compendium,* June 1991

We should not fool ourselves that the "hard rocks" will emerge from the cesspools of American prisons willing or able to conduct law-abiding lives.
— DAVID BAZELON, FEDERAL JUDGE, 1985

"What works?"

treatment programs with the final judgment that "evidence supporting the efficacy of correctional treatment is slight, inconsistent, and of questionable reliability."[103] The following year, Roger Hood in England completed a similar review that concluded that the different ways of treating offenders lead to results that are not very encouraging.[104] And in 1971, James Robison and Gerald Smith's analysis of correctional treatment in California asked the questions: "Will the clients act differently if we lock them up, or keep them locked up longer, or do something with them inside, or watch them more closely afterward, or cut them loose officially?" Their conclusion was a resounding "Probably not!"[105]

But the Martinson essay created a sensation, for it appeared in a visible publication and attracted popular media attention at a time when politicians and opinion makers were desperately searching for some response to the widespread public fear of street crime. Furthermore, as Harvard University's James Q. Wilson explained:

> Martinson did not discover that rehabilitation was of little value in dealing with crime so much as he administered a highly visible *coup de grace.* By bringing out into the open the long-standing scholarly skepticism about most rehabilitation programs, he prepared the way for a revival of an interest in the deterrent, incapacitative, and retributive purposes of the criminal justice system.[106]

In a prison rehabilitation program, this participant is constructing doll houses from old magazines.

Martinson also created a sensation within the research and treatment communities — mostly negative. He was criticized for bias, major distortions of fact, and gross misrepresentation.[107] And for the most part, his critics were correct. Martinson had failed to include all types of treatment programs; he tended to ignore the effects of some treatment programs on some individuals; he generally concentrated on whether the particular treatment method was effective in *all* the studies in which it was tested; and he neglected to study the new federally funded treatment programs that had begun after 1967.

In all fairness to Martinson, though, his work cannot be overlooked. While he may have been guilty of overgeneralization, most correctional treatment programs *were* demonstrating little success, and indeed, many were *not* working. Furthermore, his essay had an impact in other ways. It pushed researchers and evaluators to sharpen their analytical tools for the measurement of success and failure. Yet simultaneously, it ushered in an "abolish treatment" era characterized by a "nothing works" philosophy.

The "nothing works" philosophy

The Value of Correctional Treatment

Going beyond the "what works" and "nothing works" rhetoric of the 1970s and early 1980s, questions still remain as to how effective correctional treatment really is. Probably no one actually knows.

Several years ago, sociologist Susan B. Long began looking at the matter in another way by questioning whether it was "treatment" or "evaluation methods" that were failing.[108] This, furthermore, is a question that clinicians in the drug abuse field have been asking for years.[109]

In all likelihood, Long is more correct in her question than Martinson and his critics were in their evaluations. Most realistically, an overview of the various approaches to correctional treatment suggests that *everything is working and everything is failing*. By that it meant that all correctional strategies — whether they be vocational training, academic education, penitence through prayer, recreation, group therapy, or whatever — seem to be working for somebody. However, correctional, therapeutic, and research technologies do not seem to be capable of accurately determining what rehabilitative approach is most effective for whom. Perhaps, then, the greatest problem is in the selection of offenders for delivery of particular correctional services. The poorest achievements may not be in the design of programs, but rather, in (1) the screening of offenders into treatment, (2) the focusing of the most appropriate programs upon those who need them most, (3) the failure to admit that there are persons who cannot be helped, and (4) the determination of when an offender has received the maximum benefits from any given technique.

Obstacles to Effective Correctional Treatment

Despite any advances in correctional techniques and program services, there are numerous obstacles that prevent most prisons from becoming effective agencies of rehabilitation:

1. Many institutions are old and antiquated.
2. Maximum-security prisons are, for the most part, too large or overcrowded.

3. Prison cells and many medium-security dormitories are unsuitable for human habitation.
4. Correctional institutions are typically understaffed and personnel often lack proper training.
5. The proper segregation of inmates is not widely enforced.
6. Inmate unemployment is common, and too many prisoners are assigned to what has become known as "idle company."
7. Institutional discipline is often too rigid.
8. Prison life tends to be monotonous and oppressive.
9. Parole policies are sometimes unfair or inefficient.
10. Comprehensive classification and program strategies are not universally available.
11. The prisonization and criminalization processes apparent in many correctional facilities bar many inmates from achieving any motivation for treatment.

By the early 1990s, attempts at prison reform had accomplished little to remove these obstacles. Moreover, given the fiscal constraints on state and local governments, combined with sentencing philosophies that serve to increase the already overpopulated prisons, it would appear that the American penitentiary of the 1990s will resemble that of the 1970s and 1980s.

SUMMARY

Total institutions such as prisons are places that furnish barriers to social interchange with the world at large. There are a variety of types of prisons differentiated by their level of security. Prisons are administratively structured like other large organizations. The physical facilities of correctional institutions vary from one place to another. Most prisons, however, are rather old, and many are deteriorated. As a result, upkeep tends to be difficult.

The prison experience begins with classification, a process through which the educational, vocational, treatment, and custodial needs of offenders are determined. Prison programs focus on health and medical services, religious needs, academic education and vocational training, labor and industry, recreation, and clinical treatment.

Aside from the loss of liberty itself, perhaps the most obvious deprivation associated with prison life is the loss of heterosexual activity. As a result, homosexual relationships and sexual assaults are not uncommon behind prison walls. The conjugal visit has been promoted as a means for reducing sexual frustrations in correctional institutions. Furthermore, coeducational facilities are being experimented with for the purpose of reducing both homosexuality and violence.

Every prison has an inmate social system, characterized by a specialized argot, social roles, and an inmate code. Exposure to the social system of the prison community begins almost immediately after the prisoner enters an institution. All new inmates become quickly aware of the norms and values that are shared by their fellow inmates. The internalization of these prison norms and values is known as prisonization.

Evaluative studies of correctional treatment programs have not been favorable to the notion of rehabilitation. Research findings during the 1960s and early 1970s resulted in a "nothing works" and "abolish treatment" era in corrections. By and large, however, every type of treatment program seems to work for someone. Research methodologies just cannot determine what treatment is most appropriate for whom.

KEY TERMS

classification **(545)**
conjugal visitation **(564)**
inmate code **(570)**
inside cells **(535)**

maximum-security
  prisons **(534)**
open institutions **(537)**
prisonization **(569)**

reception center **(546)**
shock incarceration **(558)**
total institutions **(534)**

QUESTIONS FOR DISCUSSION

1. In what ways is life in prison similar to that in the military or on the college campus?
2. What are the general characteristics of prison life?
3. Without making prisons into bordellos, what could be done to ease the sexual frustrations of prison life?
4. What steps should be taken to change prison into environments more suitable for rehabilitation and reform?

5. What impact might the changing nature of female crime have on the social order of women's prisons?
6. What kinds of parallels are there between the prison community and certain groups in the outside world?
7. What is your opinion of the "shock incarceration" programs?

FOR FURTHER READING

Clemmer, Donald. *The Prison Community.* New York: Rinehart, 1958.

Fleisher, Mark S. *Warehousing Violence.* Newbury Park, CA: Sage Publications, 1989.

Giallombardo, Rose. *Society of Women: A Study of a Women's Prison.* New York: Wiley, 1966.

Goffman, Erving. *Asylums.* Garden City, N.Y.: Anchor, 1961.

Johnson, Robert. *Hard Time: Understanding and Reforming the Prison.* Monterey, CA: Brooks/Cole, 1987.

Sherman, Michael, and Gordon Hawkins. *Imprisonment in America.* Chicago: University of Chicago Press, 1981.

NOTES

1. Erving Goffman, *Asylums* (Garden City, N.Y.: Anchor, 1961), pp. 1–8.
2. For a description of inmate life in Green Haven, see Susan Sheehan, *A Prison and a Prisoner* (Boston: Houghton Mifflin, 1978).
3. National Advisory Commission on Criminal Justice Standards and Goals, *Corrections* (Washington, D.C.: U.S. Government Printing Office, 1973), p. 345.
4. U.S. Department of Justice, Bureau of Justice Statistics, *Prisoners in 1990* (Washington, D.C.: U.S. Government Printing Office, 1991).
5. Paul W. Tappan, *Crime, Justice, and Correction* (New York: McGraw-Hill, 1960), p. 653.

6. See Rose Giallombardo, *Society of Women: A Study of a Women's Prison* (New York: Wiley, 1966); Clarice Feinman, "Sex Role Stereotypes and Justice for Women," *Crime and Delinquency* 25 (January 1979): 87–94.
7. Blake McKelvey, *American Prisons: A History of Good Intentions* (Montclair, N.J.: Patterson Smith, 1977), pp. 150–196.
8. President's Commission on Law Enforcement and Administration of Justice, *Task Force Report: Corrections* (Washington, D.C.: U.S. Government Printing Office, 1967), p. 59.
9. *Manual of Correctional Standards* (College Park, Md.: American Correctional Association, 1966), p. 319.
10. Personal communication, October 29, 1972.

11. Eldridge Cleaver, *Soul on Ice* (New York: McGraw-Hill 1968); George Jackson, *Soledad Brother: The Prison Letters of George Jackson* (New York: Bantam, 1970).

12. Robert G. Caldwell, *Criminology* (New York: Ronald Press, 1965), p. 576.

13. James B. Jacobs and Harold G. Retsky, "Prison Guard," *Urban Life* 4 (April 1974): 5–29.

14. Jacobs and Retsky, "Prison Guard"; Gresham M. Sykes, *The Society of Captives: A Study of a Maximum Security Prison* (New York: Atheneum, 1965), pp. 40–62; Edgar May, "Prison Guards in America: The Inside Story," *Corrections Magazine* 2 (December 1976): 3–5, 40, 45.

15. Personal communication, April, 1978.

16. U.S. Department of Justice, *Prisoners in 1990*.

17. U.S. Department of Justice, *Census of State Correctional Facilities, 1974* (Washington, D.C.: U.S. Government Printing Office, 1975).

18. U.S. General Accounting Office, *Federal, District of Columbia, and States Future Prison and Correctional Institution Populations and Capacities* (Washington, D.C.: General Accounting Office, February 27, 1984).

19. National Advisory Commission, *Corrections*, p. 206.

20. John Hepburn and Celesta A. Albonetti, "Team Classification in State Correctional Institutions: Its Association with Inmate and Staff Attitudes," *Criminal Justice and Behavior* 5 (March 1978): 63–73.

21. National Advisory Commission, *Corrections*.

22. National Advisory Commission, *Corrections*, p. 207.

23. American Correctional Association, *Handbook on Correctional Classification* (Cincinnati, Ohio: Anderson, 1978), p. 67.

24. For a bibliography of studies of reception centers, see American Correctional Association, *Handbook*, pp. 81–83.

25. Vernon Fox, *Introduction to Corrections* (Englewood Cliffs, N.J.: Prentice-Hall, 1977), pp. 209–210.

26. Cited by Sue Titus Reid, *Crime and Criminology* (New York: Holt, Rinehart and Winston, 1982), p. 546.

27. *United States Bureau of Prisons Policy Statement on the Case Management System* (Washington, D.C.: U.S. Bureau of Prisons, 1969).

28. Robert A. Baker et al., "A Computerized Screening System for Correctional Classification," *Criminal Justice and Behavior* 6 (September 1979): 270.

29. A. E. Kannewischer, "The Role of the Protestant Chaplain in Correctional Institutions," *American Journal of Correction* 19 (January–February 1957); *Final Report: Task Force Report on the Role of the Chaplain in New York City Correctional Institutions* (New York: New York City Correction Board, 1972).

30. Fox, *Introduction to Corrections*, p. 219.

31. Stuart D. Johnson, "The Correctional Chaplaincy: Sociological Perspectives in a Time of Rapid Change," *Canadian Journal of Criminology and Corrections* 14 (April 1972): 173–180.

32. See Benedict Alper, *Prisons Inside-Out* (Cambridge, Mass.: Ballinger, 1974), pp. 43–94.

33. Harry E. Allen and Clifford E. Simonsen, *Corrections in America* (New York: Macmillan, 1981), p. 392.

34. John Irwin, *Prisons in Turmoil* (Boston: Little, Brown, 1980), p. 46; Gordon Hawkins, *The Prison: Policy and Practice* (Chicago: University of Chicago Press, 1976), pp. 116–118.

35. Neil M. Singer, "The Value of Inmate Power," *Journal of Research in Crime and Delinquency* (January 1976): 3–4.

36. Edwin W. Zedlewski, "Making Confinement Decisions," *Research in Brief, National Institute of Justice* (July 1987); *Christian Science Monitor*, February 6, 1989, p. 7.

37. *New York Times*, December 17, 1981, p. B16. See also *Miami Herald*, June 25, 1984, p. 13A.

38. *Christian Science Monitor*, September 6, 1989, p. 7.

39. *Washington Post*, November 12, 1990, p. A1.

40. *Washington Post*, September 17, 1989, p. H2.

41. Don C. Gibbons, *Changing the Lawbreaker: The Treatment of Delinquents and Criminals* (Englewood Cliffs, N.J.: Prentice-Hall, 1965), p. 136.

42. *Manual of Correctional Standards* (Washington, D.C.: American Correctional Association, 1969), p. 422.

43. *Manual of Correctional Standards*, p. 423.

44. *Manual of Correctional Standards*, p. 423.

45. Gibbons, *Changing the Lawbreaker*, p. 151.

46. *DOCS Today* (New York State Department of Correctional Services, August 1990).

47. *Drug Enforcement Report*, August 23, 1991, p. 6; *Alcoholism and Drug Abuse Week*, September 11, 1991, p. 3.

48. *Sourcebook of Criminal Justice Statistics* (Washington, D.C.: Bureau of Justice Statistics, 1991), pp. 617–618.

49. *Corrections Compendium*, September–October 1989, p. 10.

50. *Corrections Compendium*, August 1990, p. 5.

51. Maxwell Jones, *The Therapeutic Community: A New Treatment Method in Psychiatry* (New York: Basic Books, 1953).

52. Lewis Yablonsky, *The Tunnel Back: Synanon* (New York: Macmillan, 1965).

53. For Clinton Prison, see Bruno M. Cormier, *The Watcher and the Watched* (Plattsburgh, N.Y.: Tundra, 1975): for the facility at Danbury; see Louis P. Carney, *Corrections: Treatment and Philosophy* (Englewood Cliffs, N.J.: Prentice-Hall, 1980), p. 203.

54. *New York Times*, March 4, 1988, pp. B1, B4; *USA Today*, May 21, 1987, p. 3A; Doris Layton MacKenzie and Claire C. Souryal, "Boot Camp Survey," *Corrections Today* (October 1991): 90–96.

55. From Hans Toch, *Living in Prison: The Ecology of Survival* (New York: Free Press, 1977), p. 99.

56. Gustave de Beaumont and Alexis de Tocqueville, *On the Penitentiary System in the United States and Its Application in France* (Carbondale: Southern Illinois University Press, 1964), p. 173.

57. Leonard Orland, *Justice, Punishment, Treatment* (New York: Free Press, 1973), pp. 263–269.

58. Toch, *Living in Prison*, p. 100.

59. Allen and Simonsen, *Corrections in America*, pp. 57, 375.

60. Allen and Simonsen, *Corrections in America*, pp. 57, 375.

61. Nick Pappas, *The Jail: Its Operation and Management* (Lompoc, Ca.: Federal Prison Industries, 1971), p. 23.

62. Toch, *Living in Prison*, p. 104.

63. Cited by Tom Wicker, *A Time to Die* (New York: Ballantine, 1975), p. 110.

64. Tappan, *Crime, Justice and Correction*, pp. 678–679.

65. Joseph Fishman, *Sex in Prison* (New York: National Library Press, 1934); Donald Clemmer, *The Prison Community* (New York: Rinehart, 1958), pp. 249–273; Sykes, *Society of Captives*; Peter C. Buffum, *Homosexuality in Prisons* (Washington, D.C.: U.S. Government Printing Office, 1972); John H. Gagnon and William Simon, "The Social Meaning of Prison Homosexuality," *Federal Probation* 32 (March 1968): 23–29.

66. Sykes, *Society of Captives*, pp. 95–99; Clemmer, *The Prison Community*; Leo Carroll, *Hacks, Black, and Cons: Race Relations in a Maximum Security Prison* (Lexington, Mass.: Heath, 1974).

67. Giallombardo, *Society of Women*; David Ward and Gene Kassebaum, *Women's Prisons* (Chicago: Aldine, 1965), pp. 80–101; Gagnon and Simon, "Social Meaning of Prison

Homosexuality"; Reid, *Crime and Criminology*, pp. 588–599.

68. *Ibid.*

69. Gene Kassebaum, "Sex in Prison," *Psychology Today*, January 1972, p. 39.

70. "Sexual Assaults in Prison," from *Report on Sexual Assaults in a Prison System and Sheriffs Vans* (1968), cited in *Crime and Justice: The Criminal Under Restraint*, ed. Leon Radzinowicz and Marvin E. Wolfgang (New York: Basic Books, 1977), p. 223. See also Susan Brownmiller, *Against Our Will: Men, Women, and Rape* (New York: Simon and Schuster, 1975), pp. 257–268; Ted Morgan, "Entombed," *The New York Times Magazine*, February 17, 1974, p. 19; Jared Stout, "Quaker Tells of Rape in D.C. Jail," *Washington Star-News*, August 25, 1973; David L. Aiken, "Ex-Sailor Charges Jail Rape, Stirs Up Storm," *The Advocate*, September 26, 1973, p. 5.

71. Daniel Lockwood, "Issues in Prison Sexual Violence," in Michael Braswell, Steven Dillingham, and Reid Montgomery (eds.), *Prison Violence in America* (Cincinnati, Oh.: Anderson, 1985), pp. 89–96; Buffum, *Homosexuality in Prisons*, pp. 2–3; Allen and Simonsen, *Corrections in America*, pp. 182–183.

72. Brownmiller, *Against Our Will*, p. 258.

73. Leo Carroll, "Humanitarian Reform and Biracial Sexual Assault in a Maximum Security Prison," *Urban Life* 5 (January 1977): 422.

74. Brownmiller, *Against Our Will*, p. 268.

75. Columbus B. Hopper, *Sex in Prison* (Baton Rouge: Louisiana State University Press, 1968); *Time*, August 18, 1967, p. 49; *Time*, August 9, 1968, p. 68.

76. Pauline Morris, *Prisoners and Their Families* (New York: Hart, 1965), p. 90.

77. Donald Johns, "Alternatives to Conjugal Visits," *Federal Probation* 35 (March 1971): 48.

78. Norman S. Hayner, "Attitudes Toward Conjugal Visits for Prisoners," *Federal Probation* 36 (March 1972): 43.

79. *USA Today*, February 7, 1985, p. 3A; *New York Times*, September 18, 1988, p. 28.

80. *Doe v. Coughlin*, NY CtApp, No. 219, November 24, 1987; 42 CrL 2227 (1987).

81. *New York Times*, August 5, 1991, pp. B1, B3.

82. J. G. Ross, E. Heffernan, J. R. Sevick, and F. T. Johnson, *Assessment of Coeducational Corrections* (Washington, D.C.: U.S. Government Printing Office, 1978).

83. *Newsweek*, January 11, 1982, p. 66.

84. *Newsweek*, January 11, 1982, p. 66; *Corrections Digest*, September 18, 1974, p. 2; Sue Mahan, "Co-Corrections: Doing Time Together," *Corrections Today*, August 1986, pp. 134, 136, 138, 164–165; *New York Times*, June 1, 1987, p. A12.

85. *New York Times*, November 15, 1988, p. A16.

86. *Los Angeles Times*, July 24, 1990, p. A3; *Los Angeles Times*, July 29, 1990, p. A29.

87. Sykes, *Society of Captives*, p. 82.

88. Sykes, *Society of Captives*, p. 83.

89. Clemmer, *The Prison Community*, p. 299.

90. For a review and commentary of the various studies and points of view of prisonization, see Hawkins, *The Prison*, pp. 56–80.

91. Gresham M. Sykes and Sheldon L. Messenger, "The Inmate Social System," in *Theoretical Studies in the Social Organization of the Prison* (New York: Social Science Research Council, 1960), pp. 6–8.

92. James A. Inciardi, *Careers in Crime* (Chicago: Rand McNally, 1975), p. 70.

93. Sykes, *Society of Captives*, pp. 81–83.

94. John Irwin and Donald R. Cressey, "Thieves, Convicts, and the Inmate Culture," *Social Problems* 10 (Fall 1962): 143.

95. Richard A. Cloward, "Social Control in the Prison," in *Theoretical Studies in the Social Organization of the Prison* (New York: Social Science Research Council, 1960), pp. 35–48.

96. Esther Heffernan, *Making It in Prison: The Square, the Cool and the Life* (New York: Wiley, 1972).

97. For descriptive material on women's prisons, see Kathryn W. Burkhart, *Women in Prison* (New York: Doubleday, 1973).

98. See Susan K. Datesman and Frank R. Scarpitti, eds. *Women, Crime, and Justice* (New York: Oxford University Press, 1980).

99. Edwin Powers and Helen Witmer, *An Experiment in the Prevention of Delinquency* (New York: Columbia University Press, 1951).

100. See, for example, Walter C. Bailey, "Correctional Outcome: An Evaluation of 100 Reports," *Journal of Criminal Law, Criminology, and Police Science* 57 (June 1966): 153–160; Roger Hood, "Research on the Effectiveness of Punishments and Treatments," in European Committee on Crime Problems, *Collected Studies in Criminological Research* (Strasbourg: Council of Europe, 1967).

101. Douglas Lipton, Robert Martinson, and Judith Wilks, *The Effectiveness of Correctional Treatment: A Survey of Treatment Evaluation Studies* (New York: Praeger, 1975).

102. Robert Martinson, "What Works?—Questions and Answers About Prison Reform," *The Public Interest* 35 (Spring 1974): 22–54.

103. Bailey, "Correctional Outcome."

104. Hood, "Research on the Effectiveness of Punishments and Treatments."

105. James Robison, "The Irrelevance of Correctional Programs," *Crime and Delinquency* 17 (January 1971): 67–80.

106. James Q. Wilson, " 'What Works?' Revisited: New Findings on Criminal Rehabilitation," *The Public Interest* 61 (Fall 1980): 3–17.

107. See, for example, Carl B. Klockars, "The True Limits of the Effectiveness of Correctional Treatment," *The Prison Journal* 55 (Spring–Summer 1975): 53–64; Ted Palmer, "Martinson Revisited," *Journal of Research in Crime Delinquency* 12 (July 1975): 133–152.

108. Cited by Reid, *Crime and Criminology*, p. 558.

109. See, for example, James A. Inciardi, "The Evaluation of Addiction Treatment," *The Addiction Therapist* 1 (Autumn 1975): 1–5.

16

Prison Conditions and Inmate Rights

A convicted felon . . . has, as a consequence of his crime, not only forfeited his liberty, but all of his personal rights except those which the law in its humanity accords to him. He is for the time being the slave of the State.
— RUFFIN V. COMMONWEALTH, 1871

There is no iron curtain drawn between the Constitution and the prisons in this country.
— WOLFF V. MCDONNELL, 1974

The Constitution does not mandate comfortable prisons.
— RHODES V. CHAPMAN, 1981

Prisoners are not stripped of their constitutional rights, including the right to due process, when the prison gate slams shut behind them.
— UNITED STATES EX REL. GEREAU V. HENDERSON, 1976

If you're not safe in prison from armed robbery, where are you safe?
—SUPERINTENDENT BARRY AHRINGER OF FLORIDA'S POMPANO BEACH COMMUNITY CORRECTIONAL FACILITY, 1984, AFTER A GUNMAN ROBBED TWO CONVICTS IN THEIR CELL

A jailhouse lawyer in a prison library

Until only recently, the opinion expressed in *Ruffin* v. *Commonwealth*,[1] which maintained that prisoners have no legal rights, accurately reflected the judicial attitude toward correctional affairs. The conditions of incarceration and every aspect of institutional life were left to the unregulated discretion of the prison administration. Since prisoners were "slaves" of the state, privileges were matters of custodial benevolence, which wardens and turnkeys could "giveth or taketh away" at any time and without explanation. The courts, furthermore, maintained a steadfast hands-off position regarding correctional matters. They unequivocally refused to consider inmate complaints regarding the fitness of prison environments, the abuse of administrative authority, the constitutional deprivations of penitentiary life, and the general conditions of incarceration.

Not until the 1960s did the ideology expressed in *United States* ex rel. *Gereau* v. *Henderson* begin to take noticeable form.[2] The **"hands-off" doctrine** began to lose its vitality, and during that decade and the years that followed, prisoners were given the right to be heard in court regarding such matters as the widespread violence that threatened their lives and security, the problems of overcrowding, the nature of disciplinary proceedings, the conditions affecting health and safety, the regulations governing visitation and correspondence, and the limitations on religious observance, education, work, and recreation.

When the prisoners' rights movement began just over two decades ago, the higher courts across America became the instruments of change in correctional policy. But only a few years after the movement had begun in earnest, there was a major event and human tragedy that served to dramatize the problems with prisons and the character of inmate life. That event was the inmate uprising at New York's *Attica* Correctional Facility on September 9, 1971. And although the riot at Attica occurred some two decades ago, it continues to be a case study of the typical conditions and situations that tend to bring about most prison unrest — even now as American corrections moves through the 1990s.

"Hands-off" doctrine: The refusal of the courts to hear inmate complaints about the conditions of incarceration and the constitutional deprivations of penitentiary life.

ATTICA, 1971

Condemned by the Wickersham Commission for its maintenance of Auburn and Clinton prisons, New York State will have an answer to charges of inhuman penal conditions when the new Wyoming State Prison opens at Attica within the next few months with its full quota of 2,000 convicts. Said to be the last word in modern prison construction, the new unit in the State's penal system will do away with such traditions as convict bunks, mess hall lockstep, bull pens, and even locks and keys.

In their places will be beds with springs and mattresses, a cafeteria with food under glass, recreation rooms and an automatic signal system by which convicts will notify guards of their presence in their cells. Doors will be operated by compressed air, sunlight will stream into cells and every prisoner will have an individual radio.

—NEW YORK TIMES, AUGUST 2, 1931

Perhaps because of the depression economy, or perhaps for other reasons, when Attica Prison opened during the latter part of 1931 it was hardly the convict's paradise alluded to by the *New York Times*. None of the facilities mentioned in the *Times* article were present. In fact, the style of imprisonment at Attica was no different from that found at Auburn and Sing Sing prisons a hundred years before. Men were locked in their cells, harshly disciplined under a system of rigid rules and regulations; the food was poor and medical services were lacking; and programs for inmate diversion and rehabilitation were almost nonexistent. Forty years after its opening, however, the *Times* would be given a second opportunity to write about Attica Prison.

Conditions at Attica

For prisoners at Attica in late 1971, "correction" meant little more than daily degradation and humiliation. They were locked in cells for fourteen to sixteen hours each day; they worked for wages that averaged thirty cents a day at jobs with little or no vocational value; and they had to abide by hundreds of petty rules for which they could see no justification. In addition, their mail was read, their radio programs were screened in advance, their reading material was restricted, their movements outside their cells were tightly regulated, they were told when to turn lights out and when to wake up, their toilet needs had to be taken care of in the full view of patrolling officers, and their visits from family and friends took place through a mesh screen and were preceded and followed by strip searches probing every opening of their bodies.

In prison, inmates found deprivations worse than they had encountered on the street: meals were unappetizing and not up to nutritional standards. Clothing was old, ill-fitting, and inadequate. Most inmates could take showers only once a week. State-issued clothing, toilet articles, and other personal items had to be supplemented by purchases at a commissary where prices did not reflect the meager wages inmates were given to spend. To get along in the prison's economy, inmates resorted to "hustling."

The sources of inmate frustration and discontent did not end there. Medical care, while adequate to meet acute health needs, was dispensed in a callous, indifferent manner by doctors who feared and despised most of the convicts they treated; inmates were not protected from unwelcome homosexual advances; even the ticket to freedom for most inmates — parole — was burdened with inequities or at least the appearance of inequity.

For officers, "correction" meant a steady but monotonous forty-hour-a-week job, with a pension after twenty-five years' service. It meant maintaining custody and control over an inmate population that had increasing numbers of young blacks and Puerto Ricans from the urban ghettos who were unwilling to conform to the restrictions of prison life and ready to provoke confrontation — men whom the officers could not understand and were not trained to deal with. It meant keeping the

The increase in criminality has produced an alarming overpopulation in penitentiaries. The consequence is that no country has been spared in the last few years from prison uprising from the often intolerable conditions.

—FRENCH SOCIAL CRITIC, BERTRAND LE GENDRE, 1987

inmates in line, seeing that everything ran smoothly, and enforcing the rules. It did not mean, for most officers, helping inmates to solve their problems or to become citizens capable of returning to society. For the correction officers, who were always outnumbered by inmates, there was a legitimate concern about security; but that concern was not served by policies that created frustration and tension far more dangerous than the security risks they were intended to avert.

For both inmates and officers at Attica, "correction" meant an atmosphere charged with racism.

Above all, for both inmates and officers, "correction" meant an atmosphere charged with racism. Racism was manifested in job assignments, discipline, self-segregation in the inmate mess halls, and in the daily interactions of inmate and officer and inmate and inmate. There was no escape within the walls from the growing mistrust between white middle America and the residents of urban ghettos. Indeed, at Attica racial polarity and mistrust were magnified by the constant reminder that the keepers were white and the kept were largely black or spanish-speaking. The young black inmate tended to see the white officer as a symbol of a racist, oppressive system that put him behind bars. The officer, his perspective shaped by his experience on the job, knew blacks only as belligerent unrepentant criminals. The result was a mutual lack of respect that made communication all but impossible.[3]

The Dewer Incident

The majority of Attica's inmates were housed in four main cell blocks: A, B, C, and D Blocks. Each block had three tiers of cells, and each group of about forty cells was referred to as a "company."

The uprising against the conditions in Attica was not the result of a planned revolt inspired by a core of inmate revolutionaries. Rather, it was the product of building dissatisfactions and frustrations and was sparked by two related incidents.

Tensions had been growing between inmates and correction officers amidst a setting of rising expectations of improved conditions. But the anticipated changes in the prison environment seemed to be slow in coming. During the summer of 1971 there had been a number of organized protest efforts, but these accomplished no more than the disciplining of the organizers.

On September 8, an incident occurred that provoked the particular resentment and anger of inmates in two companies of Block A. An exercise-yard misunderstanding led to an unusually intense confrontation between officers and inmates, during which a lieutenant was struck by inmate Leroy Dewer. The officers were forced to back down. That evening, however, Dewer and another inmate were removed from their cells and placed in solitary confinement. It was widely believed that the two were subsequently beaten by several of the guards.

The Revolt

On the following morning, September 9, officers found the men of five-company, to which one of the inmates involved in the Dewer incident belonged, to be especially belligerent and troublesome. Thus, they decided to return the members of five-company to their cells immediately after breakfast without allowing them their usual time in the exercise yard. This decision came at a point when the inmates were lined up in one of the prison's many "tunnels."

Attica's four cell blocks form a square enclosing a large open area. Narrow corridors ["tunnels"] running from the middle of one block to

During riots at Attica Prison, prisoners raise their hands in clenched fists as a show of unity.

the block opposite divide the central area into four exercise yards. The "tunnels" intersect at a junction that is called "Times Square," inside of which is a locking device that controls access to all of the cell blocks.

The "tunnels" to "Times Square"

As the inmates of five-company were being escorted through the "tunnels" back to their cells, several attacked the officer on duty. Others joined in, and after an initial outburst of violence, the A Block inmates regrouped and set upon the locked gate at Times Square. A defective weld, unknown to officers and inmates alike, broke and the gate gave way. This gave the prisoners access to Times Square and the keys that unlocked the gates to all other directions. From Times Square the inmates spread throughout the prison, attacking officers, taking hostages, and destroying property.

By afternoon, the New York state police had regained control of part of the prison, but most of the inmates assembled in one of the exercise yards along with their thirty-nine hostages, whom the rioters threatened to kill if their demands were not met.

The Negotiations

Initially, the rebellious inmates released a series of five demands, including complete amnesty and safe transportation to a "nonimperialistic" country. These, however, were quickly rejected and more serious negotiations began. New York's Commissioner of Corrections Russell Oswald ultimately came up with a twenty-eight-point proposal that represented major advances in penal reform. It included a general liberalization of prison life, combined with provisions for more adequate food, political and religious freedom, realistic rehabilitation programs, reductions in cell time, removal of most communications censorship, recruitment of black and Hispanic correction officers, better education and drug treatment programs, and more adequate legal assistance services. In addition, Oswald agreed to recommend the application of the New York state minimum wage law standards to all work done by inmates.

But for four days the negotiations dragged on because of one major stumbling block: *amnesty*. During the initial revolt, one of the correction officers, William Quinn, sustained serious skull injuries at the hands of the inmates. Two days later he died. Without total amnesty, the inmates realized there would be murder charges—which would subject any prisoner already serving a life sentence to a possible death sentence.

The Assault

Governor Nelson Rockefeller was asked to make a personal appearance at Attica to help with the negotiations and prevent a bloodbath, but he refused. Instead, he authorized Commissioner Oswald to end the rebellion by force if necessary.

On the morning of September 13, 1971, a local state police troop commander planned and led an assault to retake Attica Prison. Within fifteen minutes, the Attica uprising was over. However, the armed state troopers had killed twenty-nine inmates and ten of the officer hostages, wounding hundreds more. Ironically, it was the bloodiest one-day encounter between Americans since the Civil War.[4]

IN PURSUIT OF PRISONERS' RIGHTS

The Attica revolt was a dramatic symbol of the enduring struggle that had been developing for almost a decade. Prior to the 1960s, it was a matter of law that offenders were deemed to have forfeited virtually all rights and to have retained only those expressly granted by statute or correctional authority. Thus, inhuman conditions and practices were permitted to develop and continue in many correctional systems, despite the Eighth Amendment's ban on cruel and unusual punishment. The courts, furthermore, generally refused to intervene in correctional matters. Their justifications were twofold:

> Judges felt that correctional administration was a technical matter to be left to experts rather than to courts, which were deemed ill-equipped to make appropriate evaluations. And, to the extent that courts believed the offenders' complaints involved privileges rather than rights, there was no special necessity to confront correctional practices, even when they infringed on basic notions of human rights and dignity protected for other groups by constitutional doctrine.[5]

The Writ of *Habeas Corpus*

Whenever an individual is being confined in an institution under state or federal authority, he or she is entitled to seek *habeas corpus* relief. This is guaranteed by Article I, Section 9 of the United States Constitution,

Inmate no. 3409, buried in a small cemetery on the grounds of New York's Greenhaven Prison in 1962, remains but a number in death as in life. His name was John Baldwin.

which states: "The privilege of the Writ of *Habeas Corpus* shall not be suspended." *Habeas corpus* relief also has statutory bases, in the Federal Habeas Corpus Act as well as in state *habeas corpus* laws.

By applying for a writ of **habeas corpus,** the person seeking relief is challenging the lawfulness of his confinement. *Habeas corpus* is a Latin term that means "you should have the body." In practice, *habeas corpus* relief involves a writ issued by a court commanding the person who holds another in captivity to produce the prisoner in court so that the legality of the prisoner's confinement can be adjudicated.[6]

Traditionally, the writ was limited to contesting the legality of confinement itself. However, in *Coffin* v. *Reichard,*[7] decided in 1944, the Sixth Circuit U.S. Court of Appeals held that, in the Sixth Circuit, suits challenging the *conditions* of confinement could be brought under the Federal *habeas corpus* statute. The court reasoned that:

> A prisoner is entitled to the writ of *habeas corpus* when, though lawfully in custody, he is deprived of some right to which he is lawfully entitled even in his confinement, the deprivation of which serves to make his imprisonment more burdensome than the law allows or curtails his liberty to a greater extent than the law permits.

Although the United States Supreme Court has never fully resolved the question of whether the writ of *habeas corpus* is available to seek relief from allegedly unconstitutional conditions of confinement, most federal courts have elected to follow the logic of *Coffin* v. *Reichard.*[8] Nevertheless, from the prisoner's perspective, the process of bringing a habeas petition to a federal court is unwieldy and time consuming. This is because existing law required (and continues to require) that the inmates of state institutions exhaust all state judicial and administrative remedies before they apply for the federal writ of *habeas corpus.* Thus, most prisoners remained (and continue to remain) effectively barred from the most direct mechanism for challenging the conditions of their confinement.

Habeas corpus: A writ that directs the person holding a prisoner to bring him or her before a judicial officer to determine the lawfulness of imprisonment.

The privilege of the Writ of Habeas Corpus shall not be suspended, unless when in Cases of Rebellion or Invasion the public safety may require it.

—Article I, Section 9, Constitution of the United States

Civil Rights and Prisoners' Rights

The civil rights movement of the late 1950s and early 1960s created a climate more conducive to a serious reexamination of the legal rights of prisoners. The specific vehicle that opened the federal courts to inmates confined in state institutions was **Section 1983** of the Civil Rights Act of 1871, which provides:

> Every person who, under color of any statute, ordinance, regulation, custom, or usage of any State or Territory subjects, or causes to be subjected, any citizen of the United States or other person within the jurisdiction thereof to the deprivation of any rights, privileges, or immunities secured by the Constitution and laws shall be liable to the party injured in an action at law, suit in equity or other proper proceeding for redress.

Section 1983: The section of the Civil Rights Act of 1871 that state prisoners use as a vehicle for access to the federal courts to litigate inmate rights.

The long-dormant Section 1983 was resurrected in *Monroe* v *Pape,*[9] decided by the Supreme Court in 1961 and holding that citizens could bring Section 1983 suits against state officials to the federal courts without first exhausting state judicial remedies.

Monroe v. *Pape:* The Supreme Court ruling that citizens can bring Section 1983 suits against state officials in federal courts without first exhausting state judicial remedies.

Three years later, in *Cooper* v. *Pate,*[10] the High Court made it clear that the *Pape* holding applied to state prisoners who could articulate cognizable constitutional claims against state prison officials or employees. However, in *Preiser* v. *Rodriguez,*[11] the Court held that although a Section 1983 is a proper remedy to make a constitutional challenge to the *conditions* of prison life, it could not be used to challenge the *fact* and *length* of custody.

The major advantages of a Section 1983 suit, as opposed to a *habeas corpus* petition, are that a Section 1983 suit does not require that available state remedies be exhausted before the federal district courts will have jurisdiction, and that an award of money damages is possible. However, the remedy of release from imprisonment is not available under a Section 1983 suit. As the High Court stated in *Preiser* v. *Rodriguez,* only the writ of *habeas corpus* could secure such release.

LEGAL SERVICES IN PRISON

The state and its officers may not abridge or impair petitioner's right to apply to a federal court for a writ of habeas corpus.
— Ex parte Hull, 1941

In *ex parte Hull,*[12] a state prison regulation required that all legal documents in an inmate's court proceedings must be submitted to an institutional official for examination and censorship before they are filed with the court. The Supreme Court found this and similar prison regulations invalid, holding that whether a petition is properly drawn and what allegations it must contain were issues for the court, not the prison authorities, to decide.

Johnson v. Avery

In spite of the rule established by *Hull,* an inmate's right of access to the courts proved to be more theoretical than actual. In many prison systems, disciplinary actions for inmates pursuing legal remedies or wholesale confiscation of a prisoner's legal documents were quite common. Furthermore, court access was either curtailed or totally inhibited because most prison officials withheld from inmates any services related to their legal needs. In most instances, inmates seeking remedies were provided with no more than a few outdated law books and occasionally the services of a notary public. Since most prisoners were indigent and lacked the funds to secure the help of an attorney, the courts were essentially closed to them. Many correctional institutions had "jailhouse lawyers"—inmates who claimed legal expertise and who provided advice and counsel to their fellow prisoners, with or without compensation. Yet even this aid was severely restricted by prison officials, thus further denying inmates their basic constitutional right of access.

Johnson v. *Avery* in 1969 acknowledged and resolved a number of these problems.[13] The case involved the constitutionality of a Tennessee prison regulation which provided that

> no inmate will advise, assist or otherwise contract to aid another, either with or without a fee, to prepare writs or other legal matters. . . . Inmates are forbidden to set themselves up as practitioners for the purpose of promoting a business of writing writs.[14]

The petitioner in *Johnson* was a jailhouse lawyer serving a life sentence who had spent almost a year in solitary confinement for repeatedly violating the rule against writ writing.

In its analysis of the Tennessee rule, the Supreme Court addressed the fact that many prisoners are illiterate and are frequently unable to find legal help from sources beyond the prison walls. Thus, the justices held that unless the state could provide some reasonable alternative type of legal assistance to inmates seeking postconviction relief, a jailhouse lawyer must be permitted to aid inmates in filing *habeas corpus* petitions.

Although the decision in *Johnson* was a significant one, it failed to delineate many of the specifics of inmates' mechanisms for legal access. In the years that followed, the courts began to address this vagueness:

Younger v. *Gilmore*,[15] 1971   The state must maintain an adequate number of law books in prison libraries and other legal materials sufficient enough to inform prisoners of what is legally relevant.

Johnson v. *Avery:* The Supreme Court ruling that unless a state provides some reasonable legal assistance to inmates seeking postconviction relief, a jailhouse lawyer must be permitted to aid inmates in filing *habeas corpus* petitions.

Darrell Adams, a Texas prisoner in protective custody. After joining the "Texas Mafia," a powerful prison gang, Adams informed on a fellow gang member. The only way to protect him from reprisals was to move him to an institution in another jurisdiction.

Wolff v. *McDonnell,*[16] 1974   Inmates have a right to the legal assistance of a jailhouse lawyer not only for seeking *habeas corpus* relief, but also for filing civil rights actions against prison officials.

Procunier v. *Martinez,*[17] 1974   Regulations that prohibit law students and legal paraprofessionals from entering prisons to assist attorneys in case investigations do not satisfy the requirements of *Johnson* v. *Avery.*

Bounds v. *Smith,*[18] 1977   Even when prison policy permits mutual legal assistance among inmates, officials are nevertheless obligated to establish either a legal services program or a law library that will meet the needs of the inmate population.

Jailhouse Lawyers

The prison regulations that forbade inmates from assisting or receiving counsel from fellow inmates in the preparation of legal documents was an outgrowth of several factors. Initially, the rule was a reflection of the general custodial attitude toward prison inmates. That is, the convict was a ward of the state who possessed no civil rights, and the privilege of obtaining legal help from other convicts was simply unthinkable. In addition, there were a number of security issues involved. "Writ-writers," as they were often called, were seen as potential troublemakers. Officials often felt that the jailhouse lawyer, in advising inmates of their legal rights, might create dissatisfactions within the prison population that could lead to belligerence and revolt. Furthermore, the phenomenon of inmates conferring about legal matters was interpreted by some as plotting against administrative authority. Finally, there was the fear that jailhouse lawyers would provide their clients with inferior representation and false hopes of success while they flooded the courts with spurious claims.

Most of these administrative and custodial concerns had some basis in fact, but in general, the problems that jailhouse lawyers caused in correctional institutions were more often ones of inconvenience rather than of discipline and security. Since *Johnson* v. *Avery* and numerous subsequent state and federal court decisions, the activities of jailhouse lawyers in many jurisdictions have been relatively unrestricted.

During the past few years, public and private agencies have begun to furnish grants to law schools for the development of legal aid programs for prisons and jails. But as Justice William O. Douglas pointed out in his concurring opinion in *Johnson,* such programs rest on a shifting law school population and often fail to meet the daily needs and demands of inmates. As a result, the jailhouse lawyer remains a significant figure in many American prisons. In some states, Washington and Massachusetts, for example, jailhouse lawyers are permitted — and even encouraged — to work *with* volunteer law students and paralegals, usually under the supervision of an attorney, in providing legal advice to the inmate population.[19] Moreover, the courts have continued to recognize the right established by *Johnson* v. *Avery.* In 1984, for example, a Wisconsin prisoner was charged with the unauthorized practice of law for helping two of his fellow inmates draft postconviction motions. Not only was the charge dismissed on the ground that his activity was constitutionally protected, but in a subsequent proceeding a federal jury assessed $22,000 in damages against his jailers for malicious prosecution.[20]

CONSTITUTIONAL RIGHTS AND CIVIL DISABILITIES

Historically, persons convicted of serious crimes could lose much more than their liberty or their lives. Under the early English common law an offender, in addition to his sentence, was also "attaint." Under this status, he lost all of his civil rights and forfeited his property to the Crown. Furthermore, his entire family was declared corrupt, which made them unworthy to inherit his property. The U.S. Constitution forbids bills of attainder,[21] and similar provisions against the attainder or its effects are found in the constitutions and statutes of the states. Yet in spite of these, every state has enacted civil disability laws that affect convicted offenders. Depending on the jurisdiction, civil disabilities may include losses of the rights to vote, hold public office, sit on a jury, be bonded, collect insurance or pension benefits, sue, hold or inherit property, receive worker's compensation, make a will, marry and have children, or even remain married. The most severe disability is the loss of all civil rights, or **"civil death."** Under current Idaho statutes, for example:

Bills of attainder

> 18-310. A sentence of imprisonment in a state prison for any time less than for life suspends all the civil rights of the person so sentenced, and forfeits all public offices and all private trusts, authority or power during such imprisonment.
> 18-311. A person sentenced to imprisonment in the state prison for life is thereafter deemed civilly dead.

Civil death: The loss of *all* civil rights.

Technically, a civil right is a right that belongs to a person by virtue of his or her citizenship.* Since civil rights include constitutional rights, it would seem that state statutes and provisions that place civil disabilities on convicted and imprisoned offenders would be in direct conflict with the Constitution. However, the Supreme Court has not interpreted these statutes as complete denials of prisoners' civil rights, but as restrictions and conditions of their expression. And with respect to many rights that have some direct bearing on the Constitution, the Court's position in recent years has been to remove a number of these restrictions.

Religion

The First Amendment of the Constitution provides that "Congress shall make no law respecting an establishment of religion, or prohibiting the free exercise thereof." Generally, or at least historically, freedom of religion was rarely a problem in correctional institutions. In fact, participation in religious instruction and worship services was always encouraged. Infringements on this right began only with the rise of minority religions and the demands of their members to have the same rights as those of conventional faiths.

The leading cases involving religious expression occurred with the growing influence of the Black Muslim movement within prisons during the 1960s. Issues such as the right to attend services, obtain literature, and wear religious medals were raised by the Black Muslims because, unlike Protestant or Catholic inmates, the Black Muslims had been

---

* Other than the right to vote and freedom from being subject to deportation, civil rights also apply, generally, to noncitizen residents of the United States.

Fulwood v. *Clemmer*

denied the right to engage in such practices. The threshold question was the recognition of the Muslim faith as a religion. This was quickly answered by a federal court in 1962 with its decision in *Fulwood* v. *Clemmer,*[22] and in subsequent cases,[23] with the assertion that Black Muslims retain the same constitutional protection offered to members of other recognized religions. However, although these cases established the Black Muslims' right to hold religious services, the courts have refused to extend that right in specific circumstances. In some institutions and at certain times, for instance, assemblages of Black Muslims were considered by custodial authorities to be revolutionary in character and to represent "clear and present dangers" to security. In several decisions, the courts ruled that although Black Muslims had the right to worship, their right to hold religious services could be withheld if they represented potential breaches of security.[24]

Importantly in this respect, for example, in *O'Lone* v. *Estate of Shabazz,*[25] decided by the Supreme Court in 1987, it was ruled that prison policies which had the effect of depriving Muslim inmates of the opportunity to attend *Jumu'ah*—a weekly congregational service—did *not* violate the free exercise clause of the First Amendment, because: (1) the policies were reasonably related to legitimate penological interests, and (2) there were other reasonable alternative methods for accommodating the Muslims' religious rights.

Cruz v. *Beto*

Other cases involving religious freedom in prisons dealt with inmate access to clergy, special diets, and the right to wear religious medals. A case to reach the U.S. Supreme Court in this regard was *Cruz* v. *Beto* in 1972.[26] Cruz, a Buddhist, had been barred from using the chapel in a Texas prison and was placed in solitary confinement for sharing his religious material with other inmates. The Court ruled that the Texas action was "palpable discrimination" in violation of the equal protection clause of the Fourteenth Amendment. On the other hand, the federal courts have held that placing limits on the practice of "satanism" is not a violation of prisoners' First Amendment rights.[27]

Mail and Media Interviews

Prison officials in the United States have traditionally placed certain restrictions on inmates' use of the mails. These restrictions generally include limiting the number of persons with whom inmates may correspond, opening and reading incoming and outgoing material, deleting sections from both incoming and outgoing mail, and refusing to mail for an inmate or forward to an inmate certain types of correspondence. The reasons for these restrictions follow security and budgetary requirements. Contraband must be intercepted, escape plans must be detected, and material that might incite the inmate population in some way must be excluded. Furthermore, correctional budgets do not allow for the unlimited use of the mails. Prisons have also used the goal of rehabilitation to justify certain restrictions on inmate correspondence. The courts have generally accepted these justifications for mail censorship and limitation, and in years past rarely intervened in prison mail regulations. More recently, however, a range of situations have been examined by the courts, with major rulings in *Wolff* v. *McDonnell* and *Procunier* v. *Martinez,* both decided by the Supreme Court in 1974.[28]

In *Wolff,* at issue was whether prison officials could justifiably open correspondence from an inmate's attorney. The Court ruled that officials are permitted to open a communication from an attorney to check for contraband, but (1) it must be done in the presence of the inmate and

(2) the contents must not be read. (*Wolff* is discussed in more detail later.) ***Procunier* v. *Martinez*** dealt with the broader issue of censorship of nonlegal correspondence. The Supreme Court held that prison mail censorship is constitutional only when two criteria are met: (1) the practice must further substantial government interests such as security, order, or rehabilitation; and (2) the restrictions must not be greater than necessary to satisfy the particular government interest involved.

The decision in *Martinez* also confirmed the earlier opinions of other courts with related matters. In the 1970 case of *Carothers* v. *Follette*,[29] a federal district court castigated officials at New York's Green Haven Prison for refusing to mail a letter from an inmate to his parents. The letter contained remarks critical about prison conditions. In the 1971 case of *Nolan* v. *Fitzpatrick*,[30] inmates contested the legality of a Massachusetts prison regulation that totally banned letters to the news media. Officials claimed that such communications could inflame the inmates and, hence, endanger prison security. Furthermore, they maintained that complaint letters would retard rehabilitation and create administrative problems since they would encourage media representatives to seek interviews with inmates. *Martinez* specifically invalidated prison censorship of statements that "unduly complain" or "magnify grievances"; expressions of "inflammatory political, racial, or religious, or other views"; and matter deemed "defamatory" or "otherwise inappropriate."

Importantly, ***Thornburgh* v. *Abbott*,**[31] decided by the Supreme Court in 1989, partially overruled the Court's earlier holding in *Martinez*. In *Abbott*, the mail censorship regulations of the Federal Bureau of Prisons were upheld. But what was most significant was that the High Court jettisoned the "substantial government interests" test of *Martinez* in favor of a "reasonableness" standard as the proper analysis to be applied when courts evaluate prison restrictions on *incoming* mail or publications. In *Abbott*, the *Martinez* standard was held to apply only to *outgoing* mail, which in the High Court's opinion presented a security concern of a "categorically lesser magnitude" than incoming mail. By rejecting the *Martinez* "substantial government interests" test as the foundation for reviewing incoming publications and correspondence, *Abbott* reversed much of the existing case law on prison mail censorship, since most of those cases involved inmate challenges to restrictions on incoming mail. As such, *Thornburgh* v. *Abbott* has been considered by a number of constitutional scholars as an example of the Supreme Court's retreat to a modified hands-off doctrine.

Rehabilitative Services

There is agreement among many clinicians, legislators, and members of the general public that in addition to confinement, one purpose of imprisonment is rehabilitation. Furthermore, in the constitutions and statutes of many states, the rehabilitation of prison inmates is at least implied, if not directly stated. For example, the New York state correction law indicates:

> Correctional facilities shall be used for the purpose of providing places of confinement and *programs of treatment* for persons in the custody of the department. Such use shall be suited, to the greatest extent practicable, to the objective of assisting persons to live as law abiding citizens.[32] [emphasis added]

The courts, however, while supporting the rehabilitative ideal, have not defined rehabilitative treatment as a constitutional right. In

***Procunier* v. *Martinez*:** The Supreme Court ruling that prison mail censorship is constitutional only when the practice furthers government interests in security and rehabilitation and when the restrictions are no greater than necessary to satisfy the particular government interest involved.

***Thornburgh* v. *Abbott*:** The Supreme Court ruling that federal prison regulations restricting prisoners' receipt of publications from outside prison pass First Amendment muster if they are reasonably related to legitimate penological interests.

O'Connor v. *Donaldson*[33] decided in 1975 (a case involving the rights of institutionalized mental patients), the Supreme Court refused to decide on the matter of rights to treatment. Other courts have approached the issue more directly:

- *Wilson* v. *Kelley* in 1968 stated that the duty prison officials owed to an inmate was "to exercise ordinary care for his protection and to keep him safe and free from harm." [34]
- *Padgett* v. *Stein* more specifically ruled that there is no constitutional duty imposed on a government entity to rehabilitate prisoners.[35]

While the courts may not have extended constitutional status to the right to treatment, they have taken a strong stand against several "rehabilitative" practices of questionable moral and legal status. During the early 1970s, for example, a number of behavior modification techniques were imposed on inmates, ostensibly for their therapeutic value. Several of these techniques seemed to have been taken directly from Anthony Burgess's *A Clockwork Orange,* George Orwell's *1984,* and Aldous Huxley's *Brave New World.* Especially applicable to a number of these practices was the "Clockwork Orange" theme presented by Burgess. His story is set in a near-future semitotalitarian state in which thugs roam the streets of London engaging in assorted acts of intimidation and violence. Alex, a fifteen-year-old psychopath, is caught by the police and subjected to "corrective brainwashing." He is bound to a chair and forced for weeks on end to view films of brutal violence until he himself becomes sickened by it. His destructive behavior is destroyed along with his will, and the State succeeds in transforming him into a "good," unthinking, obedient automaton. In the real-life parallel, Connecticut's

A therapist administers aversive conditioning treatment to a convicted child molester by showing photos of young girls and giving the subject unpleasant electric shocks to break up his tendency to associate children with sexual pleasure.

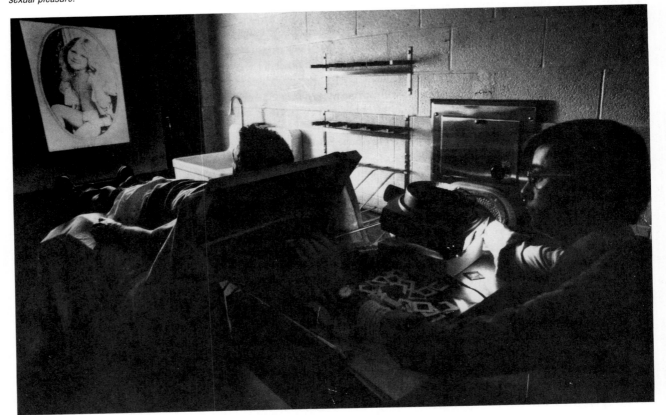

maximum-security prison at Sommers instituted an electroshock program for habitual child molesters in 1973.[36] The "patient" viewed slides of children and adults, and received an electric shock every time a picture of a naked child appeared. The rationale of the program—as with the "corrective brainwashing" in *A Clockwork Orange*—was to repress the offender's ability to think of children as sex objects. In a similar case that reached the federal courts in 1973, severely nauseating injections were used to produce an aversion to minor infractions of prison rules.[37]

A Clockwork Orange

In this case, it was ruled that the procedure was not "treatment" but "punishment"—and cruel and unusual as well, in violation of the Eighth Amendment.

However, the courts have supported some prison requirements that mandate enrollment in certain institutional programs (such as class attendance by illiterate convicts) and disciplinary measures for those who refuse to participate.[38]

Similarly, in *Washington* v. *Harper,*[39] decided by the Supreme Court in 1990, it was held that the due process clause of the Fourteenth Amendment permits a state to treat a prison inmate, who has a serious mental illness, with antipsychotic medication, against his will, if the inmate is dangerous to himself or others and the treatment is in his medical interests.

Medical Services

In principle, inmates have a right to "adequate" and "proper" medical care on several grounds. The right is protected by common law and state statutes, by the Civil Rights Act of 1964, by the due-process clause of the Fifth and Fourteenth Amendments, and by the Eighth Amendment ban against cruel and unusual punishment. Prisoners have made claims regarding the adequacy and nature of medical care received, improper and inadequate care, and the total denial of medical and health services.

In *Estelle* v. *Gamble* in 1976,[40] the U.S. Supreme Court enunciated its position on the medical rights of inmates:

> Deliberate indifference to serious medical needs of prisoners constitutes the "unnecessary and wanton infliction of pain" proscribed by the Eighth Amendment. This is true whether the indifference is manifested by prison doctors in their response to the prisoner's needs or by prison guards in intentionally denying or delaying access to medical care or intentionally interfering with the treatment once prescribed.

Estelle v. *Gamble:* The Supreme Court ruling that the deliberate indifference of prison officials or personnel to the serious medical needs of inmates constitutes cruel and unusual punishment proscribed by the Eighth Amendment.

Beyond this statement, the High Court has generally left the specifics of medical rights to the lower courts. The federal judiciary has taken the position that what amount of medical aid is "adequate" is largely dependent upon the facts of each case.[41] Thus, no uniform definition of "adequate" health care has been specified. Furthermore, in *Priest* v. *Cupp,*[42] an Oregon court made it clear that the constitutional prohibition against cruel and unusual punishment does not guarantee that an inmate will be free from or cured of all real or imagined medical problems while he or she is in custody. Thus, although prison officials cannot deny medical aid, inmates cannot expect perfect medical services.

The most recent medical issue in the prisoners' rights arena relates to AIDS. In some jurisdictions significant numbers of prison inmates are infected with HIV (human immunodeficiency virus), the virus that causes AIDS (acquired immune deficiency syndrome). Yet as noted in Chapter 15 (Exhibit 15.2), prison management policies for infected inmates vary widely. In this regard, there are two major areas of AIDS

● EXHIBIT 16.1 ●

HIV, AIDS, and Prisoners' Rights

Through the beginning of 1992, no prisoners' rights cases involving HIV and AIDS had reached the United States Supreme Court, and few had come to the attention of the federal courts in general. As the following cases indicate, the majority of decisions rendered by the courts supported correctional agency regulations, based on the belief that AIDS is a disease easily transmitted in institutional settings.

Muhammad v. *Carlson* (43 CrL 2131 [1988])

Inmate Imam 'Shahid Muhammad was transferred to the U.S. Medical Center for Federal Prisoners in Springfield, Missouri (MCFP) because he had lost coordination in his limbs. Blood tests indicated that he had developed HIV antibodies. He was classified as "Pre-ARC" (AIDS Related Complex—defined in Bureau of Prisons regulations as a confirmed positive blood test for infection with HIV plus one or more symptoms of AIDS but no conclusive damage to the body's immunological system), and was placed in the restricted AIDS unit at MCFP where he was isolated from the general inmate population. No hearing

was held in connection with Muhammad's placement. Approximately seven months later, the Bureau of Prisons changed its regulations and released Muhammad and other restricted inmates back into the general prison population of MCFP.

In his petition to the U.S. Court of Appeals, Muhammad claimed that his transfer to and seven-month confinement in the restricted AIDS unit violated his due process rights to a hearing and stigmatized him as having AIDS. The Court of Appeals ruled against Muhammad, however, holding that the transfer was not intended to punish him but to fulfill legitimate medical purposes. As such, the court stressed that the transfer raised no due process violations since the new conditions of confinement were constitutionally acceptable within the purview of Muhammad's sentence.

Roe v. *Fauver* (43 CrL 2174 [1988])

In a similar case, a New Jersey prison policy that forbids inmates diagnosed as having AIDS from being commingled with the general prison population, even when the disease is in remission, was upheld by the U.S.

District Court for the District of New Jersey. The female inmate in this case had already spent nine months in a hospital room and faced spending the rest of her prison term either there or in a special AIDS unit under construction at the prison. While she argued that her continued confinement in the hospital amounted to cruel and unusual punishment, the court agreed with prison officials that isolating her from the general population was a reasonable medical approach and was in the best interests of both the inmate and the rest of the prison population. The court noted that the fact that she was, in effect, in solitary confinement, was regrettable. It pointed out, however, as had the U.S. Court of Appeals in *Muhammad* v. *Carlson,* that prison officials' reasons for separating her from other prisoners was done on humane medical grounds.

Doe v. *Coughlin* (DCNY No. 88-CV-964 [1988])

In contrast with the decisions in *Muhammad* and *Roe, Doe* v. *Coughlin* reached an alternative conclusion. Through September 15, 1988, some twenty-one New York State inmates had been

litigation involving correctional clients—segregation and privacy rights on the one hand, and screening on the other—and several important cases have come before the courts during the past few years (see Exhibit 16.1).

Prisoner Labor Unions

Although the courts have recognized the rights of prison inmates to adequate medical care, religious expression, and access to the courts, their opinions on the issue of prisoner collective bargaining has been a

transferred to dormitory D-2 at Greene Correctional Facility. The dormitory had been set aside for inmates who tested positive for HIV antibodies, or who were diagnosed with AIDS. The transfer of these inmates had purportedly been for the purpose of improving and facilitating their medical care, not for the sake of segregating them so as to protect other inmates and prison personnel from the risk of infection.

Inmate John Doe, on behalf of himself and other New York State inmates who were infected with HIV or had AIDS, filed a class action suit against the prison system claiming that his scheduled transfer to dormitory D-2 represented a nonconsensual disclosure of his medical diagnosis. The transfer, Doe argued, would violate the United States Supreme Court's ruling a decade earlier in *Whelan* v. *Roe* (429 U.S. 589 [1977]). In the latter case, Justice John Paul Stevens had identified two interests encompassed by the right to privacy: (1) the individual interest in avoiding disclosure of personal matters, and (2) the interest in independence in making certain kinds of important decisions.

The U.S. District Court ruled in favor of John Doe, holding that he could not be involuntarily transferred to D-2, arguing that:

Those who are currently at D-2 and those who would be placed in D-2 all share a common characteristic. Each is fully aware that he is infected with a disease which at the present time has inevitably proven fatal. In the court's view there are few matters of a more personal nature, and there are few decisions over which a person could have a greater desire to exercise control, than the manner in which he reveals that diagnosis to others. An individual's decision to tell family members as well as the general community that he is suffering from an incurable disease, particularly one such as AIDS, is clearly an emotional and sensitive one fraught with serious implications for that individual. Certain family members may abandon the AIDS victim while others may be emotionally unprepared to handle such news. Within the confines of the prison the infected prisoner is likely to suffer from harrassment and psychological pressures. Beyond the prison's walls the person suffering from AIDS is often subject to discrimination.

The holding in *Doe* v. *Coughlin* has been used in subsequent decisions, but until the matter is ruled upon by the United States Supreme Court, procedures will continue to vary from one jurisdiction to the next.

Dunn v. *White* (45 CrL 2360 [1989])

On the alternative issue of mass testing of inmates for the presence of HIV antibodies, an Oklahoma case brought the matter before the U.S. Court of Appeals on August 1, 1989. In this particular case, inmate Terry Dunn claimed that prison officials had violated his Fourth Amendment rights by requiring him to submit to a blood test for HIV antibodies. Up until that point, no court in the nation had decided whether a non-consensual HIV antibody test violated a prisoner's right to be free from an unreasonable search. The court ruled in favor of the Oklahoma prison officials, holding that the prevention of the spread of HIV in prison justified the intrusion of a blood test. In evaluating the prisoner's position in the matter, the court pointed out that the Fourth Amendment permits blood to be drawn from drunken drivers, and that an inmate's privacy interest is at least as limited as that of a motorist. In either case, the court concluded that the invasion of privacy is far outweighed by the special interests of public health and safety.

different matter. In a number of institutions across the nation, inmates have sought to establish what are typically referred to as "labor unions," organized for the purposes of advocating increased pay for inmate labor, improving safety and working conditions, increasing inmate participation in handling matters affecting their welfare, ending contract labor, expressing dissatisfaction with prison programs, and gaining official recognition for inmate workers as public employees having statutory rights under state labor laws.[43] For prisoners, then, unions could operate as channels for communicating complaints that might otherwise not be brought into the open and to official notice. For prison officials, however,

Jones v. North Carolina Prisoners' Labor Union: The Supreme Court ruling that prison regulations prohibiting the organized activities of inmate labor unions are not violative of the freedom of association clause of the First Amendment.

How do you like that? The next thing you know they're going to demand the right to keep women in their cells, shoot drugs, and take weekend vacation trips to the south of France.
— AN IDAHO STATE PENITENTIARY OFFICIAL IN 1988, AFTER AN INMATE UPRISING RESULTING FROM PRISONERS' REFUSAL TO LET GUARDS CONFISCATE THEIR HOMEMADE LIQUOR

unions represent a foundation for concerted inmate actions that could represent significant threats to institutional safety and control.

Throughout the 1970s, prisoner unions attempted to organize in a number of jurisdictions. It was not until *Jones v. North Carolina Prisoners' Labor Union* in 1977,[44] however, that the U.S. Supreme Court ruled on the matter. The case began when the North Carolina Prisoners' Labor Union (PLU), whose statewide membership included some 2,000 inmates, alleged that correctional regulations were in violation of First and Fourteenth Amendment rights by denying it the opportunity to hold meetings, solicit additional members, and receive organizational materials from the outside and distribute them in-house.

The Supreme Court disagreed with the contentions of the PLU, however, holding that inmates have no constitutional right to organize a prisoners' labor union, and hence, prison regulations that prohibit the organized activities of an inmate union are not violative of the freedom of association clause of the First Amendment. The High Court went on to emphasize that prison regulations may constitutionally ban union solicitation, group meetings of members, and bulk mail privileges of the organization as long as such regulations are reasonable and rationally related to such legitimate objectives as maintenance of security, prevention of escapes, safety of inmates and prison personnel, and the rehabilitation of inmates.

Although constitutional scholars generally agree that the restrictive conditions of incarceration make the formation of inmate unions a real and distinct threat to prison security, many nevertheless feel that the High Court's decision in this case heralded the return of a "modified hands-off doctrine."

PRISON DISCIPLINE AND CONSTITUTIONAL RIGHTS

Many readers may be familiar with the story of *Papillon.* Written by French novelist Henri Charriere and produced as a motion picture in 1973 starring actors Dustin Hoffman and the late Steve McQueen, it told the story of two convicts confined to several French penal colonies and of the determination of one to escape. The colonies included several camps in French Guiana, and Devil's Island — a patch of rock less than a mile in circumference some ten miles off the Guiana coast. Most striking in *Papillon* were the severe disciplinary procedures for escape attempts and other rule violations: slow starvation; confinement for years at a time in small, dark, vermin-infested cells; or even a short interlude with what Frenchmen called "the widowmaker"—the infamous guillotine.[45]

Many may think of such practices as utterly foreign to American soil, or at least far removed in time from contemporary standards. But only a few short years ago, long after the French penal colonies were abolished during World War II, discipline at least as barbaric as the Devil's Island tradition was practiced in the very heart of America.

The Arkansas Prison Scandal

Arkansas has the best prison system in the United States.
— KNOX NELSON, ARKANSAS STATE SENATOR, FEBRUARY 8, 1967

Ninety-five percent of the complaints of convicts are lies. . . . I don't believe none of that stuff.

    — LLOYD SADLER, ARKANSAS STATE REPRESENTATIVE, JANUARY 17, 1967

The deserted end of Devil's Island where French political criminals and murderers were sent from 1852 through 1951

In 1966, Winthrop Rockefeller, grandson of industrialist and philanthropist John D. Rockefeller, was elected governor of Arkansas. As a candidate, he had pledged to eliminate corruption in state government and to hire a professional penologist to reform the state prison system. The following year, the late Thomas O. Murton, a professor of criminology from Southern Illinois University, was put in charge of the Arkansas prisons. (Murton was the real Warden Brubaker, as portrayed by actor Robert Redford in the 1980 20th Century-Fox film *Brubaker.*)

What Murton found was a prison system that had been operated on fear for over a century.[46] The traditional methods of instilling inmate compliance included beatings, needles under the fingernails, starvation, and floggings with the "hide"—a leather strap five inches wide and five feet long. At Tucker Prison Farm, as recently as 1968, there was a contraption known as the "Tucker telephone" used to punish inmates and to extract information:

> The telephone, designed by prison superintendent Jim Bruton, consisted of an electric generator taken from a crank-type telephone and wired in sequence with two dry-cell batteries. An undressed inmate was strapped to the treatment table at Tucker Hospital while electrodes were attached to his big toe and to his penis. The crank was then turned, sending an electrical charge into his body. In "long distance calls" several charges were inflicted—of a duration designed to stop just short of the inmate's fainting. Sometimes the "telephone" operator's skill was defective, and the sustained current not only caused the inmate to lose consciousness but resulted in irreparable damage to his testicles. Some men were literally driven out of their minds.[47]

For more than fifty years, many boasted that the Arkansas prison system was a symbol of efficiency, for no state appropriations were needed to support the convicts. But Murton found that this was so only because of the exploitation of inmate labor. Furthermore, the control of inmates, work assignments, promotion, food rations, bed assignments, visiting privileges, commissary privileges, laundry and clothing procedures, and the very survival of the inmate had been delegated to a select few powerful convicts who operated the prison. To make such a system operable, these "trusties" had been granted many privileges, including graft obtained from all inmate goods and services, freedom to sell liquor and narcotics, to gamble and loan money, to live in squatter shacks outside the prison and spend nights with female companions, and to profit from the illegal trafficking in prison produce. Thus, there were no traditional custodial officers. Rather, the institutions were run by a powerful structure of convict guards who used bribery and torture to maintain the status quo and to profit from the inmate slavery. In Arkansas's Cummins Prison Farm, it was alleged that inmates had been routinely murdered as punishment for disciplinary infractions and then buried in a remote cow pasture. The total number of these killings was estimated to be over 100.[48]

The barbaric conditions in the Arkansas prisons came to national attention in January 1968, as a result of Murton's discoveries and efforts at reform. However, for fear that Murton was damaging the image of Arkansas with the *Arkansas prison scandal,* on March 2, 1968, he was fired from his post and placed under house arrest. Governor Rockefeller at a press conference the following day simply explained that Murton had been a "poor prison administrator."

In the years following Murton's departure, the Arkansas prisons were in constant turmoil. On several occasions, inmates protesting prison conditions were shot at by prison officials.[49] Explanations for the continuing difficulties focused on racial conflicts and efforts at integration.

Holt v. *Sarver:* The federal court decision declaring the Arkansas prison system to be in violation of the Eighth Amendment.

When the courts finally listened to the Arkansas prisoners, the savage discipline and inhumane conditions were more fully acknowledged. A federal court decision, ***Holt* v. *Sarver*** in 1970,[50] declared the entire Arkansas prison system to be in violation of the Eighth Amendment ban against cruel and unusual punishment (see Exhibit 16.2).

Solitary Confinement

Solitary confinement has been variously referred to as "isolation" or "segregation" in "the hole" or in a "strip cell." It is the total separation of an inmate from the general prison population in a special cell of meager size and comfort, combined with the revocation of all prisoner privileges and constitutional rights, and often with a restricted diet or other physical abuse. Placement in "solitary" generally occurs for serious violations of prison regulations, such as escape attempts, forced homosexual advances, assaulting guards or other inmates, or being excessively troublesome.

The use of solitary confinement in the United States is as old as the nation's prison system, and its application is acknowledged in many state statutes. For example, Title 41 of the current *Tennessee Code* states:

> If any convict neglects or refuses to perform the labor assigned him, or wilfully injures any of the materials, implements, or tools, or engages in conversation with any other convict, or in any other manner violates any of the regulations of the penitentiary, he may be punished by solitary confinement for a period not exceeding thirty (30) days for each offense, at the discretion of the warden, or person acting in his place.[51]

● EXHIBIT 16.2 ●

Arkansas State Penitentiary

For the ordinary convict a sentence to the Arkansas Penitentiary today amounts to a banishment from civilized society to a dark and evil world completely alien to the free world, a world that is administered by criminals under unwritten rules and customs completely foreign to free world culture.

After long and careful consideration the Court has come to the conclusion that the Fourteenth Amendment prohibits confinement under the conditions that have been described and that the Arkansas penitentiary system as it exists today, particularly at Cummins, is unconstitutional.

Such confinement is inherently dangerous. A convict, however cooperative and inoffensive he may be, has no assurance whatever that he will not be killed, seriously injured, or sexually abused. Under the present system the state cannot protect him.

Apart from physical danger, confinement in the penitentiary involves living under degrading and disgusting conditions. This Court has no patience with those who still say, even when they ought to know better, that to change those conditions will convert the prison into a country club; the Court has not heard any of those people volunteer to spend a few days and nights at either [penitentiary] incognito.

The peril and degradation to which Arkansas convicts are subjected to daily are aggravated by the fact that the treatment which a convict may expect to receive depends not at all upon the gravity of his offense or the length of his term. In point of fact, a man sentenced to life imprisonment for first-degree murder and who has a long criminal record may expect to fare better than a country boy with no serious record who is sentenced to two years for stealing a pig.

It is one thing for the State to send a man to the penitentiary as a punishment for crime. It is another thing for the State to delegate the governance of him to other convicts and to do nothing meaningful for his safety, well-being, and possible rehabilitation. It is one thing for the State not to pay a convict for his labor; it is something else to subject him to a situation in which he has to sell his blood to obtain money to pay for his own safety, or for adequate food, or for access to needed medical attention.

However constitutionally tolerable the Arkansas system may have been in former years, it simply will not do today as the twentieth century goes into its eighth decade.

SOURCE: From the federal court opinion in *Holt* v. *Sarver,* 309 F. Suppl. 362 (E. D. Ark. 1970).

As with other aspects of prisoners' rights, prior to the 1960s the courts maintained their hands-off doctrine with respect to inmate complaints concerning isolated confinement. During the past two decades, however, numerous actions concerning the practice have been brought to the courts by both state and federal inmates. Some suits have argued that the very practice of solitary confinement is unconstitutional. The federal courts, however, have flatly rejected this contention. In *Sostre* v. *McGinnis,*[52] for example, circuit judge Irving R. Kaufman remarked: "For a federal court . . . to place a punishment beyond the power of the state to impose on an inmate is a drastic interference with the state's free political and administrative processes."

Despite the courts' unwillingness to ban solitary confinement on constitutional grounds, they have taken a stand on how it can be imposed and administered. Using standards established by the Supreme Court for interpreting what constitutes cruel and unusual punishment,[53] the federal courts have examined the duration of an inmate's confinement, the physical conditions of the cell, the hygienic conditions

● EXHIBIT 16.3 ●

Delaware's Infamous "Red Hannah"

The semiannual whipping and pillorying of criminals convicted at the present term of the court, of theft and other crimes, took place on Saturday. The attendance was small, probably not exceeding one hundred people, most of whom were boys. The following are the names of the "candidates," and the offenses for which they were sentenced:

Joseph Derias, colored, horse stealing, twenty lashes, one hour in the pillory.

Scott Wilson, larceny of clothing, twenty lashes.

John Carpenter, colored, four cases of larceny (ice cream freezers, carriage reins, and a cow).

He received ten lashes in each case.

John Conner, larceny of tomatoes, five lashes.

John Smith, colored, house breaking, twenty lashes.

John Brown, horse stealing, twenty lashes and one hour in the pillory.

—Delawarean, May 27, 1876

For centuries, the whipping post was a conspicuous part of Delaware's penal tradition. The first person to suffer the sanction was Robert Hutchinson, convicted of petty theft and sentenced to thirty-nine lashes on June 3, 1679. Each town and county had its own whipping post, but the one that earned a prominent place in the history of American corrections was the notorious "Red Hannah." As the Wilmington *Journal Every Evening* once described it:

In days gone by, the whipping post down in Kent County stood out brazenly in the open courtyard of the county jail not far from the old state house. It looked like an old-time octagonal pump without a handle. It had a slit near the top of it in which the equally old-time pillory boards might be inserted when needed for punitive use. There also were iron shackles for holding the prisoners while they were being whipped. That whipping post was painted red from top to bottom. Negro residents bestowed upon it the name of "Red Hannah." Of any prisoner who had been whipped at the post it was said, "He has hugged Red Hannah!"

of the inmate, the exercise allowed, the diet provided, and the nature of the infraction that resulted in punitive isolation.

The courts have been reluctant, however, to establish rigid criteria for deciding on the unconstitutionality of solitary confinement. In *Jordan* v. *Fitzharris,*[54] for example, the "strip cells" in California's Soledad Prison were deemed "cruel and unusual" due to their poor sanitary conditions. In contrast, in *Bauer* v. *Sielaff,*[55] since the inmate was not denied the minimum necessities of food, water, sleep, exercise, toilet facilities, and human contact, the Federal Court of the Eastern District of Pennsylvania held that the deprivation of a comb, pillow, toothbrush, and toothpaste for seven to ten days in a segregation cell with continuous lights, a few mice and roaches, and no reading material was not unconstitutional. Furthermore, although the stereotyped solitary confinement meal of "bread and water" has been disapproved of by the courts,[56] it has been deemed satisfactory when supplemented by a full meal every third day.[57]

Red Hannah was a survivor. Despite public and local congressional pressure to ban whipping in the state, during the second half of the twentieth century, almost 300 years after Robert Hutchinson received his thirty-nine lashes, old Red Hannah was still very much alive.

In 1963, the statutes that permitted whipping were challenged in the Delaware Supreme Court. The case was *State* v. *Cannon,* and the presiding judge held that the use of flogging to punish certain crimes did *not* violate either state or federal bans on cruel and unusual punishment. However, Red Hannah was ultimately laid to rest in 1973, when the statute authorizing the use of the lash was finally repealed by the Delaware legislature.

SOURCES: Robert G. Caldwell, *Red Hannah: Delaware's Whipping Post* (Philadelphia: University of Pennsylvania Press, 1947); *Delawarean,* May 27, 1876, p. 3; *Journal Every Evening,* August 2, 1938, p. 8; *State* v. *Cannon,* 55 Del. 587 (1963).

Old Red Hannah, Delaware's whipping post

The Lash

Whipping (or flogging) has been a common sanction in most Western cultures. In American tradition, it was used as a punishment for crimes and for preserving discipline in domestic, military, and academic environments. And curiously, although whipping has been viewed by most as uncivilized brutality, its final abolition in American penal practice has only been recent. In Delaware, for example, whipping was a constitutionally permissible punishment for specified crimes from the seventeenth through the twentieth centuries (see Exhibit 16.3). Furthermore, in many jurisdictions, flogging was a form of convict discipline.

The end of whipping as an official means of enforcing prison rules and regulations evolved from an Arkansas case, *Jackson* v. *Bishop,*[58] decided by a federal circuit court in 1968. In the Arkansas prison system, whipping was the primary disciplinary measure. Facilities for segregation and solitary confinement were limited, and inmates had few

Jackson v. *Bishop:* The federal court decision declaring that whipping was in violation of the Eighth Amendment.

privileges that could be withheld from them as punishment. Prison regulations, furthermore, allowed whipping for such infractions as homosexuality, agitation, insubordination, making or concealing weapons, participating in or inciting a riot, and refusing to work when medically able to do so. Using the criteria of "broad and idealistic concepts of dignity, civilized standards, humanity, and decency," the court declared whipping to be a violation of the Eighth Amendment ban on cruel and unusual punishment, for the following reasons:

(1) We are not convinced that any rule or regulation as to the use of the strap, however seriously or sincerely conceived and drawn, will successfully prevent abuse. . . .

(2) Rules in this area often seem to go unobserved. . . .

(3) Regulations are easily circumvented. . . .

(4) Corporal punishment is easily subject to abuse in the hands of the sadistic and the unscrupulous.

(5) Where power to punish is granted to persons in lower levels of administrative authority, there is an inherent and natural difficulty in enforcing the limitations of that power.

(6) There can be no argument that excessive whipping or an inappropriate manner of whipping or too great frequency of whipping or the use of studded or overlong straps all constitute cruel and unusual punishment. But if whipping were to be authorized, how does one, or any court, ascertain the point which would distinguish the permissible from that which is cruel and unusual?

(7) Corporal punishment generates hate toward the keepers who punish and toward the system which permits it. It is degrading to the punisher and to the punished alike. It frustrates correctional and rehabilitative goals. . . .

(8) Whipping creates other penological problems and makes adjustment to society more difficult.

(9) Public opinion is obviously adverse. Counsel concede that only two states will permit the use of the strap.

Prison Disciplinary Proceedings

Throughout the history of corrections, disciplinary actions against prison inmates have often been arbitrary administrative operations controlled solely by wardens, their deputies, or other custodial personnel. Without a formal hearing, and at the discretion of an institutional officer, inmates could be placed in solitary confinement, lose some or all of their privileges, or be deprived of "good time" credits. Even in those correctional settings where disciplinary hearing committees were convened to review serious infractions of prison regulations, decisions could be made entirely on the basis of a custodial officer's testimony. Evidence was generally not required, prisoners were rarely permitted to speak in their own behalf, and the rules of due process were typically ignored. When the prisoners' rights movement first brought these practices to the attention of the federal courts during the 1960s, the due-process clauses of the Fifth and Fourteenth Amendments were applied sparingly and only in specific circumstances. The position of the courts seemed to be that due process should prevent only "capricious" or "arbitrary" actions by prison administrators. In the 1966 case of *Landman* v. *Peyton*,[59] for example, a federal appeals judge stated:

Where the lack of effective supervisory procedures exposes men to the capricious imposition of added punishment, due process and Eighth Amendment questions inevitably arise.

During the 1970s, however, the courts began to focus on the specific procedures used in prison disciplinary proceedings, seeking to resolve the wider issue of due-process requirements. The principal case was *Wolff* v. *McDonnell,*[60] decided by the U.S. Supreme Court in 1974. The ruling in *Wolff* held the following:

1. Advance written notice of the charges against an inmate must be provided to him at least twenty-four hours prior to his appearance before the prison hearing committee.

2. There must be a written statement by the fact finders as to the evidence relied upon and the reasons for the disciplinary action.

3. The prisoner should be allowed to call witnesses and present documentary evidence in his defense providing such actions would cause no undue hazards to institutional safety or correctional goals.

4. The inmate must be permitted representation by a counsel substitute (a fellow inmate or staff member) when the prisoner is illiterate or when the complexity of the case goes beyond the capabilities of the person being charged.

5. The hearing committee must be impartial (suggesting that those involved in any of the events leading up to the hearing — such as the charging or investigating parties — may not serve as members of the committee).

In establishing these requirements, the full spectrum of due process was *not* extended. The Court made it clear that neither retained or appointed counsel, nor the right to confrontation and cross-examination, were constitutionally required. The decision stressed some additional points. First, the ruling in *Wolff* did not apply retroactively. Second, in writing the Court's opinion, Justice White emphasized that the limitations on due process imposed by the decision were "not graven in stone"; future changes in circumstances could require further "consideration and reflection" of the Court. Third, the due-process requirements set forth applied only to proceedings that could result in solitary confinement and the loss of "good time." Left unresolved, however, were the procedures to be observed if other penalties were to be imposed.

In recent years, the High Court has not gone much beyond *Wolff* in protecting inmates' rights in prison disciplinary proceedings. A case in point is *Superintendent, Massachusetts Correctional Institute at Walpole* v. *Hill,*[61] decided in 1985. As noted earlier, *Wolff* set forth certain safeguards that must be provided when a disciplinary hearing may result in the loss of good time credits, but that ruling did not require either judicial review or a specific quantum of evidence to support a disciplinary board's decision. The matter of evidence was the issue addressed in *Hill.* The Court ruled that only "some evidence" was necessary. In this case, the evidence consisted of a prison guard's report that he had heard a commotion, discovered an inmate who had apparently been assaulted, observed three other inmates, including those in this case, fleeing down an enclosed walkway, and noticed no other inmates were in the area. Justice Sandra Day O'Connor, in delivering the Court's opinion, emphasized that although the evidence presented in the disciplinary proceeding was "meager," it was nevertheless sufficient to meet due process requirements, adding:

QUESTION: Exactly how much evidence *is indeed* required by the due process clause to support a prison disciplinary hearing board's finding of guilt? Proof beyond a reasonable doubt? Clear and convincing evidence? Substantial evidence? A preponderance of evidence? **ANSWER:** In *Superintendent, Massachusetts Correctional Institute at Walpole* v. *Hill,* the Supreme Court ruled that such a decision will pass constitutional muster if there is "some evidence" to support the board's conclusions.

. . . the relevant question is whether there is *any* evidence in the record that could support the conclusion reached by the disciplinary board.

THE CONDITIONS OF INCARCERATION

As crime rates rise, state legislators react by passing stiff laws requiring longer minimum prison sentences. Result: more prisoners stay longer in prisons that are already crammed well past their planned capacity. Tensions rise as up to five inmates crowd into one-man cubicles. Gang rule prevails, as the toughest convicts abuse and torment the meek or nonviolent, and guards on undermanned correction staffs fear to intervene.
— TIME, JUNE 8, 1981

Prisons are as safe as the inmates want them to be.
— CUSTODIAL OFFICIAL, ATTICA CORRECTIONAL FACILITY, 1981

In here, not having a knife is a death sentence.
— INMATE, JACKSON PRISON, 1981

The Arkansas prison scandal in 1968 pointed to many problems within that state's correctional system. Not only was there corruption and brutality, but as the Supreme Court noted, there was also confinement under degrading and disgusting conditions. Although Arkansas during

As the rights of smokers versus non-smokers are debated and legislated in the wider community, so too are they argued in prison settings. Calls for smoke-free workplaces and other environments are an outgrowth of the growing body of evidence documenting the harmful effects of both second-hand and side-stream tobacco smoke, particularly the 1986 Report of the Surgeon General. Several prisoners' rights cases involving the lack of nonsmoking areas in correctional institutions reached the federal courts during the late 1980s and early 1990s. Significantly, in *Clemmons* v. *Bohannon* (48 CrL 1120), decided in 1990, the U.S. Court of Appeals for the Tenth Circuit ruled that prison policies that permit the double-celling of smokers with nonsmokers against their expressed will amount to deliberate indifference to the health on non-smoking inmates in violation of the Eighth Amendment and the due process clause of the Fourteenth Amendment.

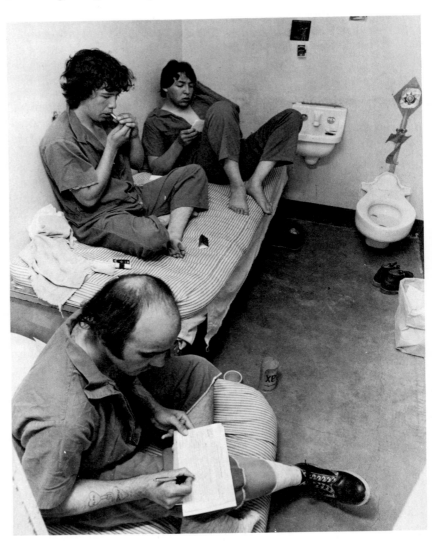

the 1960s may have been unique in its sanctioned administration by convicts under a system of unwritten rules, its general prison conditions were not an isolated phenomenon. Similar problems of overcrowding and extreme physical danger were commonplace all across the nation.

In general, the courts have held that most aspects of prison life are dictated by the needs of security and discipline, thus giving custodial authorities wide discretion in their regulation of inmate comforts. At the same time, however, the federal courts have monitored some conditions of confinement, taking the position that while offenders are sent to prison for punishment, prison should not impose extra punishments of a barbaric and uncivilized nature. For example, prison overcrowding itself has not been declared unconstitutional. Yet, as was pointed out in *Costello* v. *Wainwright* in 1975,[62] overcrowding can be a factor, when combined with other conditions, in declaring the circumstances of incarceration to be in violation of the Constitution. Thus, the federal courts have indicated that it is their duty to protect inmates from conditions of confinement that serve to add punitive measures to those already meted out by a sentencing court. The courts have also ruled, as in the 1974 case of *People* v. *Lovercamp*,[63] that the situations and circumstances some inmates face inside prison walls may serve as a defense for the crime of escape (see Exhibit 16.4).

People v. Lovercamp

The Texas Prison Suit

The people of Texas don't want prison reform.

— SENATOR CHET BROOKS, 1981

The Texas prison suit, a matter that was in the courts for more than a decade, reflects the kaleidoscope of conditions of confinement and attempts at prison reform. Just over a decade ago, the penitentiary system in the Lone Star state was the largest in the nation, with some 30,000 inmates at the close of 1980.* All nineteen Texas prisons were built as maximum-security institutions, and they were designed as such to foster rigid discipline and inhibit escape. Overcrowding was a major problem. With only 14,000 cells for its tens of thousands of inmates, the system was operating at 230 percent of capacity. That represented a doubling of the prison population since 1974. The reasons for this overcrowding were numerous. In Texas, long sentences have always been the rule. As of 1980, almost 10 percent of the inmates were serving life sentences; an additional 45 percent had terms of ten years or more. Since 1977, the Texas legislature has passed several laws ordering mandatory sentences for a variety of offenses and requiring inmates convicted of certain crimes to serve at least one-third of their terms before becoming eligible for parole. Furthermore, parole recommendations are frequently vetoed by executive authority. In 1980, for example, Texas Governor William Clements denied 2,241 of 7,886 parole recommendations, or more than 28 percent.

Overcrowding was not the only problem in the Texas prison system; there was also violence. During 1981, eleven prisoners were murdered by fellow inmates, and during one seven-day period, more than seventy inmates and guards were injured in a series of altercations.[64] Two factors contributing to this violence were understaffing and the use of prisoners

Jerry Ray Bolden is a former inmate trustie, known in Texas prisons as a "building tender" authorized to help restore order from within.

---

* By the close of 1990 Texas ranked third, with 50,042 inmates. California was the largest, with 97,309 inmates, followed by New York, with 54,895.

• EXHIBIT 16.4 •

The Defense of Necessity and the Right to Escape from Prison

Rather early in the legal history of the offense of prison escape, it became clear that all departures from lawful custody were not necessarily escapes. Two and a half centuries ago it was written that if a prison caught fire and an inmate departed to save his life, then the necessity to save his life "excuseth the felony."[a] Yet despite this pre–Revolutionary War holding, the courts traditionally have not favored the defense of necessity in escape cases. The principal justification for this hostility has been the frequently expressed fear that the availability of the defense might lead to an increase in prison escapes. This consideration has led some courts to hold that even the most intolerable of prison conditions will never justify an escape.[b] In *People* v. *Lovercamp,* however, decided by the California Court of Appeals in 1974, the conditions under which the defense of escape might be used were established.

In *Lovercamp,* two women inmates had escaped from the California Rehabilitation Center and were promptly captured in a hayfield just a few yards away. They had been in the institution just a few months and during that time they had been threatened by a group of lesbian inmates who told them that they were to perform certain lesbian acts — the exact expression was "fuck or fight." They complained to prison authorities on

several occasions but nothing was done. On the day of the escape, ten or fifteen of these lesbian inmates approached them and again offered the alternative — "fuck or fight." A fight ensued, and the two women were told that they would see the group again. Fearing for their lives, and on the basis of what occurred, the threats made, and the fact that the prison officials had not done anything for their protection, the two women felt that they had no choice but to leave the institution to save themselves.

In considering these facts, the court ruled:

We conclude that the defense of necessity to an escape charge is a viable defense. However, before *Lovercamp* becomes a household word in prison circles and we are exposed to the spectacle of hordes of prisoners leaping over the walls screaming "rape," we hasten to add that the defense of necessity to an escape charge is extremely limited in its application. . . . We hold that the proper rule is that a limited defense of necessity is available if the following conditions exist:

[1] the prisoner is faced with a specific threat of death, forcible sexual attack, or substantial bodily injury in the immediate future;

[2] there is no time for a complaint to the authorities or there exists a history of futile complaints which make any result from such complaints illusory;

[3] there is no time or opportunity to resort to the courts;

[4] there is no evidence of force or violence used towards prison personnel

or other "innocent" persons in the escape; and

[5] the prisoner immediately reports to the proper authorities when he has attained a position of safety from the immediate threat.

In subsequent cases, although the courts have agreed that the *Lovercamp* criteria are generally relevant to the defense of necessity in escape cases, they have disagreed on the role that the criteria should play. As a result, three approaches have emerged.[c] Under the most restrictive approach, the jury is not permitted to consider the evidence offered in support of the defense if any one of the *Lovercamp* criteria has not been met. The second approach, that taken by the *Lovercamp* court, requires that all five criteria be met before illegal conduct will be excused, but allows the jury, rather than the judge, to make this determination. The third approach treats the *Lovercamp* criteria only as factors to be considered by the jury in assessing the credibility of the evidence offered to establish the defense. As such, under this third approach all of the *Lovercamp* criteria need not be met.

SOURCES:
a. 1 Hale P. C. 611 (1736).
b. Comment, "From Duress to Intent: Shifting the Burden in Prison Escape Prosecutions," *University of Pennsylvania Law Review* 127 (1979), pp. 1142–1173.
c. Case Comment, "Intent, Duress, and Necessity in Escape Cases," *Georgetown Law Journal* 68 (1979), pp. 249–266.

as building tenders, turnkeys, counters, and in supervisory roles. A Texas statute specifically prohibited the use of inmates in such administrative and supervisory capacities, but it was generally ignored by institutional officials. Furthermore, and ironically, for a long time these inmate su-

pervisors *were permitted to carry weapons* — weapons that would have been denied them outside the prison walls.[65]

In June 1972, **Ruiz v. Estelle** was instituted as a class action suit in behalf of all past, present, and future Texas Department of Corrections (TDC) inmates.[66] After many years of discovery efforts, a trial finally began on October 2, 1978. At its conclusion, the court had heard 349 witnesses and had received 1,565 exhibits into evidence. The case involved issues of overcrowding, inmate security, and numerous prison services. Presiding over the case was federal judge William Wayne Justice.

In 1980, Judge Justice declared the Texas prison system to be unconstitutional. The court ordered the addition of new facilities to alleviate overcrowding; the abolition of arrangements that placed some prisoners in charge of others; the placement of any new prisons near urban areas of 200,000 population; changes in the staff-to-inmate ratio; the limiting of inmate populations; an adherence to the due process rights guaranteed by *Wolff;* and improved medical, educational, occupational, and mental health services. As Judge Justice noted in the opinion in *Ruiz* v. *Estelle:*

> It is impossible for a written opinion to convey the pernicious conditions and the pain and degradation which ordinary inmates suffer within TDC prison walls — the gruesome experiences of youthful first offenders forcibly raped; the cruel and justifiable fears of inmates, wondering when they will be called upon to defend the next violent assault; the sheer misery, the discomfort, the wholesale loss of privacy for prisoners housed with one, two, or three others in a forty-five square foot cell or suffocatingly packed together in a crowded dormitory; the physical

Ruiz v. Estelle: The federal court decision declaring the Texas prison system to be unconstitutional.

The United States Constitution must be enforced within the confines of TDC prison walls by court decree.
— JUDGE WILLIAM WAYNE JUSTICE, 1980

suffering and wretched psychological stress which must be endured by those sick or injured who cannot obtain adequate medical care; the sense of abject helplessness felt by inmates arbitrarily sent to solitary confinement or administrative segregation without proper opportunity to defend themselves or to argue their causes; the bitter frustration of inmates prevented from petitioning the courts and other governmental authorities for relief from perceived injustices.

For those who are incarcerated within the parameters of TDC, these conditions and experiences form the content and essence of daily existence.

Despite the ruling in *Ruiz,* many Texas officials maintained that their prison system was the best in the nation, and the Texas Department of Corrections sought relief in the United States court of appeals on the argument that the reforms ordered by Judge Justice were beyond the jurisdiction of his court and should not be required. In 1982, the court of appeals upheld the lower court order,[67] but the reforms were not immediately forthcoming. By 1983, conditions in the Texas system had gotten worse, and there were allegations of corruption, graft, and mismanagement. Moreover, there were serious charges of brutality by prison officials. In fact, inmate Eroy Brown was acquitted of murdering his warden after he was able to convince a jury that he was being taken to a remote corner of the prison in Huntsville to be beaten to death.[68] In 1984, there was a new prison administration imposed in Texas, and a host of new reforms were set into action. Although overcrowded conditions persisted, lower levels of prison violence were achieved.[69]

A shakedown in a Texas prison

The New Mexico Inmate Massacre

The vilest deeds, like prison weeds
Bloom well in prison air.
It is only what is good in man
That wastes and withers there.
                              —OSCAR WILDE

In 1971, the Attica riot distinguished itself as the bloodiest one-day encounter between Americans since the Civil War. On February 1, 1980, New Mexico State Penitentiary distinguished itself for having the most gruesome prison riot in U.S. history. Nearly a thousand inmates seized the institution and took fifteen guards as hostages. Prisoners threatened to kill all of the captives if state officials refused to meet their demands for improved conditions.[70]

The New Mexico institution, built in 1957 for 850 convicts, had been housing almost 1,200. A 1977 lawsuit by inmates described the prison as unsanitary and lacking medical facilities, and an investigation in 1979 found the facility to be dangerously understaffed and the guards poorly trained. When the riot broke out on February 1, only eighteen guards were on duty. Inmates looted the prison hospital for drugs and set fires that gutted all five cell blocks. They had essentially two demands: relief of overcrowded conditions and an end to harassment by guards. The prison was quickly retaken by police and the National Guard, but not before many inmates had died from drug overdoses, burns, and smoke inhalation.

The aftermath of thirty-six hours of rioting at New Mexico State Penitentiary in 1980

New Mexico's prisons are no different now than they were a decade ago. They are poorly managed, understaffed, and overcrowded with vicious inmate predators.

— A NEW MEXICO CORRECTIONS
OFFICIAL, 1988

But the New Mexico incident was not just another prison riot. It was unmatched in savagery in terms of the nature of inmate violence. Investigators found that during the riot, there had been a seven-man inmate execution squad to exact revenge on convict informers. One prisoner was beheaded; another was found with a metal rod driven through his head; several had their arms and legs cut off or their eyes gouged out; and still others were charred by blowtorches or beaten beyond recognition.[71] In all, thirty-three fellow prisoners were brutally murdered.

In the wake of the New Mexico holocaust, numerous reforms were proposed, but one commentator reflected:

> Perhaps a disaster such as this can open the windows and allow fresh thinking to enter. But many are not optimistic. Little was learned from Attica. It is hoped more may be learned from Santa Fe.[72]

Several years later, New Mexico State Penitentiary appeared to be no less a slaughterhouse. The trials of those charged with the killings inspired further bloodshed. As one prison official explained it: "Everybody is a potential witness against everybody else. No one knows who will testify against them, and that breeds tension." [73]

From Texas and New Mexico to Attica and Beyond

There are so many ways that trouble can start — violence over money, drugs, property, territorial rights, and turf, snitching and homosexuality; there's the inmate gangs, "Bloods" and "Crips," unpaid debts, protection racket scams and extortion; then there's the overcrowding, the macho guards who "get-off" by playing "tough-guy," write-ups and disciplinary hearings, the food, and on and on. Just about anything can light the fuse.

— CALIFORNIA PRISON OFFICIAL, 1991

Anytime they want you, they've got you.
— CUSTODIAL OFFICER, ATTICA CORREC-
TIONAL FACILITY, 1982

We can't do anything unless the inmates let us.
— CUSTODIAL OFFICER, ATTICA CORREC-
TIONAL FACILITY, 1985

It's all going to fall on us real soon. A real bloodbath. I think about it every day. And I have nightmares about it every night.
— CUSTODIAL OFFICER, ATTICA CORREC-
TIONAL FACILITY, 1988

When you look around, it all looks so safe and calm — TV sets in the cells, an honor block, all kinds of new rights. But you never know where you stand — not the inmates, not the officers — and that's when the trouble comes.
— CUSTODIAL OFFICER, ATTICA CORREC-
TIONAL FACILITY, 1991

Despite federal court intervention and concerted plans for change, conditions in many prisons across the nation in the 1980s remained unconstitutional and in a constant state of chaos. In the aftermath of the riot at Attica Correctional Facility in 1971, a number of reforms were proposed and implemented. But as the years passed, conditions there began to deteriorate again. By the early 1980s, Attica had become overcrowded; it had absorbed inmates from two state hospitals for the criminally insane; most of the population were violent offenders; and the number of assaults on correction officers was steadily increasing. In September 1981, just a few days before the tenth anniversary of the riot, one officer who had been on duty during the 1971 rebellion commented that tensions at Attica once again were reaching the boiling point. "We have all the ingredients for a disaster here," he remarked. Another guard said, "This place could go right now." [74] By the early 1990s, the same comments were being heard.

While Attica has not again exploded, along with other correctional institutions across the nation it was undergoing a series of what might be called "prison riots in slow-motion." In 1983, inmates at Attica took part in a general strike to protest prison conditions. At the peak of the protest, most of the institution's more than 2,100 prisoners refused to leave their cells for food, to participate in programs, or to work in the shops.[75] The following year, Attica came to the brink of explosion when a group of 182 inmates went on an eight-hour rampage in protest of the shooting of a fellow prisoner by guards.[76] Throughout the nation during the balance of the decade, protests and disturbances continued, capped by the riot at the Pennsylvania State Correctional Institution at Camp

Hill in October 1989. During the Camp Hill uprising, seventeen staff members were taken hostage, 123 employees and inmates were injured, and fifteen of the prison's thirty-one buildings were either damaged or destroyed. A subsequent investigation of the incident found overcrowding as the major cause of the riot, but indicated that poor staff training, lack of communication between top officials and institutional staff, and indecisive action on legitimate grievances were also to blame.[77]

In addition, during 1990, there were seventy prison disturbances in fifteen states and the federal system.[78] At the same time, a number of institutions were experiencing lengthy **lockdowns,** situations in which inmates were confined to their cells around the clock — denied exercise, work, recreation, and visits. Lockdown status typically results from inmate violence, and is intended to separate prisoners from one another in an effort to prevent further violence.

The reasons for the numerous riots and other disturbances were twofold. As of 1991 prisons in more than half the states had been found unfit by the federal courts. The deplorable conditions of confinement, combined with the very *fact* of confinement, produces anger, frustration, and emotions that are difficult to control. Moreover, penitentiaries are very dangerous places to live. Prisoners, many of whom have been incarcerated for violent crimes, assault and kill one another. There is sexual assault and racial unrest. The strong prey upon the weak and rivalries and jealousies are common. Seeking protection and status, many inmates join gangs. But the very presence of gangs within prison walls means additional violence, resulting from struggles over power, turf, and contraband (see Exhibit 16.5).

Finally, and for those who thought the New Mexico incident was a unique and isolated event, history repeated itself — in Montana, during

A guard tower at the federal penitentiary in Marion, Illinois. Faced with the daunting task of controlling mostly "lifer" inmates who have little incentive to obey authority, officials at this penitentiary initiated a "permanent lockdown" in the wake of widespread inmate violence in 1983. The lockdown continues today and includes nearly continuous confinement to cells, frequent body cavity searches, the use of shackles for discipline, and a ban on group activities. In Bruscino v. Carlson (43 CrL 2371 [1988]), the U.S. court of appeals called these conditions "sordid and horrible," but said that under the circumstances, they do not amount to cruel and unusual punishment in violation of the Eighth Amendment. Furthermore, the court found that "piecemeal dismantling" of the lockdown "would destroy the system's rationale and impair its efficacy."

Lockdown: A situation in which inmates are confined to their cells around the clock, denied exercise, work, recreation, and visits.

● EXHIBIT 16.5 ●

Sidelights on Criminal Matters
Inside the Walls of Folsom Prison

When you walk into Folsom Prison, your muscles begin to tense, your chest begins to tighten, and you begin to breathe hard. Inmates and guards fear each other, hate each other, plot against each other.
— A CALIFORNIA PRISON OFFICIAL, 1988

Inside the Walls of Folsom Prison, a 1951 Warner Brothers film, was the first of several media events to focus on California's monument to an age of corrections that had long since passed. Sometime later the institution became further immortalized by Johnny Cash's *Folsom Prison Blues,* played in jukeboxes in thousands of honkytonks, road houses, and saloons across America. In 1985, Folsom Prison was again in the media, but on that occasion the portrayal was neither fictional nor lyrical.

Built in 1880 and located at the base of the Sierra foothills just northeast of Sacramento, because of its antiquated conditions Folsom had been a problem since its very beginning. In the last few years, however, it has become a caricature of everything that could possibly be wrong with prison life. Originally designed for some 1,700 inmates, by the mid-1980s the population had passed the 3,000 mark. In stock-pen conditions, prisoners were living two to a

East Gate at Folsom Prison is part of the original building and is still in use today.

six-foot by eight-foot cell. Most were violent offenders; and less than half the population was working or attending classes. The result was the turning of inmates' pent-up, nothing-to-lose ferocities upon one another. The outgrowth was the formation of gangs along racial lines.

By the close of the 1980s, the situation at Folsom Prison was out of control, with no immediate solution in sight. For the

most part, the prison was being run by its three dominant gang syndicates — the Bloods, the Mexican Mafia, and the Aryan Brotherhood, all struggling for power in a situation fueled by racial animosities. What evolved was a vicious cycle of blood-feud vengeance. At one point, inmate stabbings averaged almost one a day. As one Folsom inmate put it: "They stab someone, and we get 'em back."

late September 1991.[79] In Montanta State Prison at Deer Lodge, prisoners seized control of the maximum security unit, and for much the same reasons as in the New Mexico case eleven years earlier. The targets were suspected inmate "snitches" being held in protective custody. After an assault team broke into the prison and quelled the takeover with tear gas, five inmates were found dead — three had been hanged by electrical cords from a cellblock balcony; two others had been stabbed and their heads smashed with fire extinguishers. A sixth had been left for dead, his throat cut and twenty-seven staples jammed into his skull. Not surprisingly, the riot set the rest of the nation's crowded prison systems on edge.

REFORM VERSUS LAW AND ORDER

While the 1960s ushered in the era of prisoners' rights and the 1970s witnessed agitation for prison reform, calls for "law and order" in the 1980s and early 1990s brought into focus a dilemma for American corrections that had been evolving for decades. Initially, civil libertarians had agitated for the rights of prison inmates. The federal courts responded by casting aside the "hands-off" doctrine and strengthening mechanisms for inmates in their attempts to file suits against their keepers. Prisoners were no longer the complete slaves of the state, and they slowly won significant victories with respect to legal and medical services, religious expression, access to the media, and their general treatment inside penitentiary walls. Moreover, the courts began to take a more balanced look at the conditions of incarceration. The result was that correctional systems in most jurisdictions in the United States were declared unconstitutional and ordered to reform.

At the same time, however, a slow erosion of the rights of the accused, combined with calls for strict and certain punishment of criminal offenders in the 1980s and early 1990s, led to an unprecedented escalation in the size of prison populations. The ultimate consequence was an American corrections system that, while in the throes of reform, experienced deterioration at a more rapid rate.

Added to this state of affairs were indications that there was an emergent trend aimed at limiting the rights of prisoners. In 1979 the Supreme Court handed down its ruling in *Bell* v. *Wolfish*,[80] a decision upholding the constitutionality of "double bunking," broad room search powers, frequent body cavity searches, and other restrictions imposed on federal pretrial detainees on the ground that such restrictions were rational responses to legitimate security concerns. Writing for the majority, Justice Rehnquist commented that he did not see "some sort of 'one man, one cell' principle lurking in the Due Process Clause of the Fifth Amendment." The High Court upheld the double bunking, in part, on the ground that pretrial detainees would rarely remain incarcerated for more than sixty days.

Bell v. *Wolfish*

Then there was ***Rhodes*** v. ***Chapman***,[81] decided by the Supreme Court in 1981. The suit, filed in 1975, came from Kelly Chapman, an armed robber being held at the Southern Ohio Correctional Facility in Lucasville. Chapman argued that the one-man cell he shared with another prisoner gave him only thirty-two square feet of personal living space, an area about four feet wide and eight feet long. That was less, he contended, than Ohio law required for five-week-old calves in feed lots. The district court agreed that the double-celling violated the Eighth Amendment and subsequently ordered Lucasville to reduce its inmate population. Governor James Rhodes of Ohio filed an appeal for the state, but the lower federal court's decision was affirmed by the U.S. court of appeals.

Rhodes v. *Chapman:* The Supreme Court ruling that cell overcrowding, in and of itself, is neither cruel nor unusual.

A dog in a California pound gets more running space than we do.
—CALIFORNIA INMATE, 1984

In an 8-to-1 decision, the Supreme Court reversed the lower court ruling, holding that the double-celling was *not* unconstitutional at the Ohio prison. The court was not claiming that double-celling was itself constitutional, but rather, that given the nature of other services and conditions at the institution, the cell overcrowding was neither "cruel

Hudson v. *Palmer:* The Supreme Court ruling that a prisoner has no reasonable expectation of privacy in his prison cell entitling him to Fourth Amendment protection.

"I sentence you to twenty years or until your prison becomes overcrowded, whichever comes first."

Wilson v. *Seiter:* The Supreme Court ruling that an inmate alleging that the conditions of his confinement violate the Eighth Amendment's prohibition against cruel and unusual punishment must show deliberate indifference on the part of the responsible prison officials.

The whole system is groaning and wobbling toward collapse. California is headed toward disaster in corrections.

—CALIFORNIA ATTORNEY GENERAL JOHN
VAN DE KAMP, 1987

nor unusual" nor the cause of physical or mental injury. Thus, as Justice Brennan pointed out, the Court had used the "totality of circumstances" test and found the double-celling to be constitutional. Over the past decade, *Rhodes* v. *Chapman* has resulted in a reduction—but not a drastic reduction—in the number of cases in which prisoners successfully challenged overcrowding on Eighth Amendment grounds.

In *Hudson* v. *Palmer,*[82] decided by the Supreme Court in 1984, it was made clear that prison inmates had little, if any, privacy rights. On September 16, 1981, Ted S. Hudson, an officer at the Bland Correctional Center at Bland, Virginia, along with a fellow officer, conducted a shakedown search of inmate Russel Palmer's prison locker and cell. Looking for contraband, the officers discovered a ripped pillow case in a trash can near Palmer's cell bunk. Charges were instituted against Palmer for destroying state property, and he was ordered to reimburse the state for the material destroyed.

In petitioning the U.S. district court, Palmer asserted that Hudson had intentionally destroyed letters from his wife, pictures of his children, legal papers, and other noncontraband items. He also claimed that the search of his cell and the destruction of the noncontraband items were violations of his Fourth Amendment rights. The High Court ruled that a prisoner has no reasonable expectation of privacy in his prison cell entitling him to the protection of the Fourth Amendment against unreasonable searches. The Court noted that it would be impossible to accomplish the prison objectives of preventing the introduction of weapons, drugs, and other contraband into the premises if inmates retained a right of privacy in their cells. Imprisonment, the Court emphasized, carries with it the loss of many rights as necessary to accommodate the institutional needs and objectives of prison facilities, particularly internal security and safety. Moreover, the Court held that since the state of Virginia provided an adequate postdeprivation remedy by which Palmer could bring suit for any losses he suffered from the destruction of his personal property, he was not entitled to bring a civil rights suit against Hudson in federal court.

The evisceration of the rights of prisoners continued into the 1990s. A key case in this behalf was *Wilson* v. *Seiter,*[83] decided in 1991. In *Seiter,* the Supreme Court ruled that prisoners filing lawsuits over inhumane living conditions must show not only that conditions are so deplorable as to violate the Constitution, *but also that prison officials have acted with "deliberate indifference" to basic human needs.* This standard of "deliberate indifference" previously applied only in medical care cases, as ordered by *Estelle* v. *Gamble* in 1976. The *Seiter* decision will make it considerably more difficult for prisoners to prevail in Eighth Amendment lawsuits.

It would be difficult to predict how correctional systems will fully deal with prison overcrowding and the other problematic conditions of incarceration. Some jurisdictions have instituted procedures for early parole while others have placed a portion of their excess prisoners in local jails. But these are only temporary measures. Moreover, the early paroling of convicted offenders is unpopular with the public; the placement of prison inmates in local facilities further strains the already excessive jail populations; and neither approach addresses the basic need for better institutional conditions. A number of states and the federal system have allocated funds for new prison construction. But correctional facilities are costly to build, equip, and properly staff; the prison population continues to expand; and the funding for new institutions must come from increased taxation. Yet although citizens continue to ask for more

swift and certain punishment for criminal offenders, they tend to be unwilling to bear the financial and social burden for new prison construction. As both taxpayers and the victims of crime, they feel that they would be paying twice for the misbehavior of lawbreakers. One new approach to the problem has been the **privatization of corrections** — the construction, staffing, and operation of prisons by private industry, *for profit*. Such an approach might be highly cost-effective, but there has been strong opposition to the privatization model. Opponents raise a variety of moral, legal, and ethical questions, including whether it is appropriate for the state to hand over incarceration to a profit-making organization, how liability and disciplinary issues will be handled, and whether private firms will end up lobbying for more and longer prison sentences instead of alternatives to incarceration.[84] Yet despite the debate, the private prison movement appears to be gaining ground. Privatization began in 1982 in Florida.[85] By the close of 1990, there were more than forty facilities holding some 20,000 inmates.[86]

Privatization of corrections: The construction, staffing, and operation of prisons by private industry for profit.

SUMMARY

For the better part of U.S. history, prisoners were considered "slaves" of the state. Upon conviction, defendants experienced "civil death." The conditions in prison were generally brutal, and inmates had no recourse. The Supreme Court, furthermore, maintained a "hands-off" doctrine regarding correctional matters, refusing even to consider inmates' complaints.

The prisoners' rights movement began in 1961 when the High Court ruled in *Monroe* v. *Pape* that the long-dormant Section 1983 of the Civil Rights Act of 1871 was an appropriate mechanism for challenging the constitutionality of the conditions of prison life. Through a rush of petitions to the federal courts, convicts secured favorable decisions regarding legal services, the use of jailhouse lawyers, religious expression, media and mail services, medical programs, rehabilitative services, disciplinary proceedings, and the use of solitary confinement and corporal punishment.

During this period of prisoners' rights activity, however, many institutions across the nation continued to maintain archaic conditions. In the late 1960s, the Arkansas prison scandal erupted. It was the event upon which the 1980 film *Brubaker* was based, and it demonstrated that, as stated in a federal court's opinion in *Holt* v. *Sarver,* "a sentence to the Arkansas Penitentiary today amounts to a banishment from civilized society. . . ." In 1971, news from New York's Attica prison reached the press around the world. Attica's inmates revolted because of the conditions of incarceration, and the seige to recover the prison resulted in the deaths of scores of inmates and guards. In 1980, New Mexico State Prison distinguished itself for having the most gruesome riot in U.S. history. A year later, the entire Texas prison system was declared unconstitutional. The persistent problems across the nation continue to be overcrowding, poor programs, and a general lack of inmate safety. One solution that has been offered is the somewhat controversial privatization of corrections.

KEY TERMS

civil death **(593)**
Estelle v. *Gamble* **(597)**
habeas corpus **(589)**
"hands-off" doctrine **(584)**
Holt v. *Sarver* **(602)**
Hudson v. *Palmer* **(618)**
Jones v. *North Carolina*
  Prisoners' Labor Union **(600)**

Jackson v. *Bishop* **(605)**
Johnson v. *Avery* **(591)**
lockdown **(615)**
Monroe v. *Pape* **(590)**
privatization of
  corrections **(619)**
Procunier v. *Martinez* **(595)**

Rhodes v. *Chapman* **(617)**
Ruiz v. *Estelle* **(611)**
Section 1983 **(590)**
Wolff v. *McDonnell* **(607)**
Thornburgh v. *Abbott* **(595)**
Wilson v. *Seiter* **(618)**

QUESTIONS FOR DISCUSSION

1. Why was the Supreme Court's decision in *Cruz* v. *Beto* based on Fourteenth Amendment rather than on First Amendment grounds?
2. How are inmates' rights to proper and adequate medical care protected by the Constitution?
3. By applying the criteria and reasoning of the court in *Jackson* v. *Bishop,* what other penal practices — in addition to whipping — could be considered cruel and unusual punishment? Why?

4. The decision in *Wolff* v. *McDonnell* was not retroactive to disciplinary proceedings that had failed to follow the established due-process requirements. In this case, can the loss of "good time" credits through prior unconstitutional disciplinary hearings be reconciled? If *Wolff* were retroactive, how might prison authorities deal with sanctions already imposed?
5. Do you agree with the decision in *Doe* v. *Coughlin?* Why or why not?

FOR FURTHER READING

Bowker, Lee H. *Prison Victimization.* New York: Elsevier, 1980.
Cohen, Fred. "The Law of Prisoners' Rights." *Criminal Law Review* 24 (July–August 1988): 321–349.

Martin, Steve J, and Sheldon Ekland-Olson. *Texas Prisons: The Walls Came Tumbling Down.* Austin: Texas Monthly Press, 1987.
Wicker, Tom. *A Time to Die.* New York: Ballantine, 1975.

NOTES

1. *Ruffin* v. *Commonwealth,* 62 Va. (21 Gratt.) 790, 796 (1871).
2. United States ex rel. *Gereau* v. *Henderson,* 526 F. 2d 889 (1976). For a history of the "hands-off" doctrine, see Kenneth C. Haas, "Judicial Politics and Correctional Reform: An

Analysis of the Decline of the Hands-Off Doctrine," *Detroit College of Law Review,* Winter 1977–78, pp. 795–831.
3. *Attica: The Official Report of the New York State Special Commission on Attica* (New York: Bantam, 1972), pp. 3–15.
4. See Tom Wicker, *A Time to Die* (New York: Ballantine, 1975).

5. National Advisory Commission on Criminal Justice Standards and Goals, *Corrections* (Washington, D.C.: U.S. Government Printing Office, 1973), p. 18.

6. David A. Jones, *The Law of Criminal Procedure* (Boston: Little, Brown, 1981), p. 574.

7. *Coffin* v. *Reichard,* 143 F. 2d 443 (1944).

8. See Kenneth C. Haas, "The Comparative Study of State and Federal Judicial Behavior Revisited," *Journal of Politics,* 44 (August 1982); 729–739.

9. *Monroe* v. *Pape,* 365 U.S. 167 (1961).

10. *Cooper* v. *Pate,* 378 U.S. 546 (1964).

11. *Preiser* v. *Rodriguez,* 411 U.S. 475 (1973).

12. *Ex parte Hull,* 312 U.S. 546 (1941).

13. *Johnson* v. *Avery,* 393 U.S. 483 (1969).

14. Cited by Kenneth C. Haas and Anthony Champagne, "The Impact of *Johnson* v. *Avery* on Prison Administration," *Tennessee Law Review,* 43 (Winter 1976–1977); 275.

15. *Younger* v. *Gilmore,* 404 U.S. 15 (1971).

16. *Wolff* v. *McDonnell,* 418 U.S. 539 (1974).

17. *Procunier* v. *Martinez,* 416 U.S. 396 (1974).

18. *Bounds* v. *Smith,* 430 U.S. 817 (1977).

19. Kenneth C. Haas and Geoffrey P. Alpert, "American Prisoners and the Right of Access to the Courts," in Lynne Goodstein and Doris MacKenzie (eds.), *The American Prison: Issues in Research and Policy* (New York: Plenum, 1989), pp. 68–72.

20. *National Law Journal,* December 24, 1984, p. 6

21. See Article I, Section 9.

22. *Fulwood* v. *Clemmer,* 206 F. Supp. 370 (D.C. Cir. 1962).

23. *Howard* v. *Smyth,* 365 F. 2d 28 (4th Cir. 1966); *State* v. *Cubbage,* 210 A. 2d 555 (Del. Super. Ct. 1965).

24. *Jones* v. *Willingham,* 248 F. Supp. 791 (D. Kan. 1965); *Cooke* v. *Tramburg,* 43 N.J. 514, 205 A. 2d 889 (1964).

25. *O'Lone* v. *Estate of Shabazz,* 482 U.S. 342 (1987).

26. *Cruz* v. *Beto,* 405 U.S. 319 (1972).

27. *Childs* v. *Duckworth,* CA 7, 33 CrL 2120 (1983).

28. *Wolff* v. *McDonnell,* 418 U.S. 539 (1974); *Procunier* v. *Martinez,* 416 U.S. 396 (1974).

29. *Carothers* v. *Follette,* 314 F. Supp. 1014 (S.D. N.Y. 1970).

30. *Nolan* v. *Fitzpatrick,* 451 F. 2d 545 (1st Cir. 1971).

31. *Thornburgh* v. *Abbott,* 109 S. Ct. 1874 (1989).

32. State of New York, *Correction Law,* Article 4, Section 70 (2).

33. *O'Connor* v. *Donaldson,* 422 U.S. 563 (1975).

34. *Wilson* v. *Kelley,* 294 F. Supp. 1005 (N.D. Ga. 1968).

35. *Padgett* v. *Stein,* 406 F. Supp. 287 (M.D. Pa. 1976).

36. William E. Cockerham, "Behavior Modification for Child Molesters," *Corrections* (January–February 1975); 77.

37. *Knecht* v. *Gillman,* 488 F. 2d 1136 (8th Cir. 1973).

38. *Rutherford* v. *Hutto,* 377 F. Supp. 268 (E.D. Ark. 1974); *Jackson* v. *McLemore,* 523 F. 2d 838 (8th Cir. 1975).

39. *Washington* v. *Harper,* 110 S. Ct. 1029 (1990).

40. *Estelle* v. *Gamble,* 429 U.S. 97 (1976).

41. For example, see *Gates* v. *Collier,* 390 F. Supp. 482 (N.D. Miss. 1975).

42. *Priest* v. *Cupp,* 545 P. 2d 917 (Ore. Ct. App. 1976).

43. Barbara B. Knight and Stephen T. Early, *Prisoners' Rights in America* (Chicago: Nelson-Hall, 1986), p. 113.

44. *Jones* v. *North Carolina Prisoners' Labor Union,* 433 U.S. 119 (1977).

45. For further study of Devil's Island and the other French penal colonies, see George J. Seaton, *Isle of the Damned* (New York: Farrar, 1951); Aage Krarup-Nielson, *Hell Beyond the Seas* (New York: Dutton, 1940); Mrs. Blair Niles, *Condemned to Devil's Island* (London: Jonathan Cape, 1928).

46. Tom Murton, "Too Good for Arkansas," *The Nation,* January 12, 1970, pp. 12–17.

47. Tom Murton and Joe Hyams, *Accomplices to Crime: The Arkansas Prison Scandal* (New York: Grove Press, 1969), p. 7.

48. *Newsweek,* February 12, 1968, pp. 42–43.

49. Thomas O. Murton, *The Dilemma of Prison Reform* (New York: Holt, Rinehart and Winston, 1976), pp. 35–38

50. *Holt* v. *Sarver,* 309 F. Supp. 362 (E.D. Ark. 1970).

51. *Tennessee Code,* 41–707.

52. *Sostre* v. *McGinnis,* 442 F. 2d 178 (2d Cir. 1971).

53. *Wilkerson* v. *Utah,* 99 U.S. 130 (1878); *Weems* v. *United States,* 217 U.S. 349 (1910); *Trop* v. *Dulles,* 356 U.S. 86 (1958); *Robinson* v. *California,* 370 U.S. 660 (1962).

54. *Jordan* v. *Fitzharris,* 257 F. Supp. 674 (N.D. Cal. 1966).

55. *Bauer* v. *Sielaff,* 372 F. Supp. 1104 (E.D. Pa. 1974).

56. *Landman* v. *Royster,* 333 F. Supp. 621 (E.D. Va. 1971).

57. *Novak* v. *Beto,* 453 F. 2d 661 (5th Cir. 1972).

58. *Jackson* v. *Bishop,* 404 F. 2d 571 (8th Cir. 1968).

59. *Landman* v. *Peyton,* 370 F. 2d 135 (4th Cir. 1966).

60. *Wolff* v. *McDonnell,* 418 U.S. 539 (1974).

61. *Superintendent, Massachusetts Correctional Institute at Walpole* v. *Hill,* 471 U.S. 491 (1985).

62. *Costello* v. *Wainwright,* 397 F. Supp. 20 (M.D. Fla. 1975).

63. *People* v. *Lovercamp,* 43 Cal. App. 3d 823, 118 Cal. Rptr. 110 (1974).

64. *New York Times,* December 13, 1981, p. 44.

65. Fred Cohen, "The Texas Prison Conditions Case: *Ruiz* v. *Estelle,*" *Criminal Law Bulletin* 17 (May–June 1981): 252–257.

66. *Ruiz* v. *Estelle,* 74–329 (E.D. Tex., Dec. 19, 1980).

67. *Ruiz* v. *Estelle,* F. 2d 115 (5th. Cir. 1982).

68. *New York Times,* July 8, 1984, p. E5

69. Ben M. Crouch and James W. Marquort, "Resolving the Paradox of Reform: Litigation, Prisoner Violence, and Perceptions of Risk," *Justice Quarterly,* 7 (March 1990), pp. 103–123.

70. *New York Times,* February 2, 1980, p. 1; *U.S. News & World Report,* February 18, 1980, p. 68.

71. Kinesley Hammett, *Holocaust at New Mexico State Penitentiary* (Lubbock, TX.: C. F. Boone, 1980).

72. *Time,* October 26, 1981, p. 26; Adolph Saenz, *Politics of a Prison Riot: The 1980 New Mexico Prison Riot: Its Causes and Aftermath* (Corrales, NM: Rhombus, 1986).

73. *Newsweek,* September 7, 1981, p. 11.

74. *New York Times,* September 1, 1991, p. 34.

75. *New York Times,* October 2, 1983, p. 48.

76. *New York Times,* July 22, 1984, p. 27.

77. Linda R. Acors, "Camp Hill Riots Lead to Pennsylvania DOC Overhaul," *Corrections Today,* July 1991, pp. 72–74.

78. *Corrections Compendium,* June 1991, pp. 13–14.

79. *Washington Post Weekly Edition,* October 7–13, 1991, p. 31.

80. *Bell* v. *Wolfish,* 441 U.S. 520 (1979).

81. *Rhodes* v. *Chapman,* 452 U.S. 337 (1981).

82. *Hudson* v. *Palmer,* U.S. Sup Ct (1984) 35 CrL 3230.

83. *Wilson* v. *Seiter,* 49 CrL 2264 (1991).

84. Ira P. Robbins, "Privatization of Corrections: Defining the Issues," *Judicature,* 69 (April–May 1986), pp. 325–331; United States General Accounting Office, *Private Prisons: Cost Savings and Bureau of Prison's Statutory Authority Need to be Resolved,* February 1991; Christine Bowditch and Ronald S. Everett, "Private Prisons: Problems Within the Solution," *Justice Quarterly,* 4 (September 1987), pp. 441–453.

85. *U.S. News & World Report,* July 2, 1984, p. 45.

86. Randy Welch, "Private Prisons—Profitable and Growing," *Corrections Compendium,* April 1990, pp. 1, 5–8, 16.

Probation, Parole, and Community-Based Correction

Community-based corrections is the most promising means of accomplishing the changes in offender behavior that the public expects—and now demands—of corrections.
—NATIONAL ADVISORY COMMISSION ON CRIMINAL JUSTICE STANDARDS AND GOALS, 1973

The public has assumed that the worst offenders—murderers, rapists, drug traffickers—serve substantial terms, but statistics show how easy it is for hardened criminals to get back on the streets.
—WILLIAM FRENCH SMITH, FORMER U.S. ATTORNEY GENERAL, COMMENTING IN 1984 ON THE NEED TO ABOLISH PAROLE

Why don't you just deport me?
—SIRHAN SIRHAN, PALESTINIAN ASSASSIN OF ROBERT F. KENNEDY, AFTER LOSING HIS NINTH BID FOR PAROLE, 1987

Community-based correction: Rehabilitative activities and programs within the community that have effective ties with the local government.

Situational offenders include essentially noncriminal types who feel that circumstances have forced them into illegal acts (such as an unemployed father who steals money to buy food or purchase Christmas gifts for his children).

The ostensibly self-defining principle of community-based correction rests on the fundamental dichotomy that offenders are either incarcerated or they are not. Logically, this suggests that the concept refers to all correctional strategies that take place within the community. Accordingly, there have been many types of court-determined sentences that could be viewed as community-based correction. Colonial sanctions of placement in the stocks and pillory, the ducking stool, the brank, and the wearing of the scarlet letter were certainly community-based. The same might be said of floggings in the public square and the more contemporary imposition of fines in lieu of imprisonment. But these are oversimplifications of the community-based correctional philosophy, for considerably more than the factors of sanction and location are involved. **Community-based correction** includes activities and programs within the community that have effective ties with the local environment. These activities and programs are generally of a rehabilitative rather than a punitive nature, and can include arrangements with employment, educational, social, and clinical service delivery systems. Many also involve supervision by a community or governmental agency.

Within this context, the more typical forms of community-based correctional services include pretrial diversion projects; probation and parole; work and education release activities; and furlough, restitution, and halfway house programs.

The reasons for community-based correctional strategies are numerous, encompassing a range of humanitarian, fiscal, and pragmatic motives. First, with the growth of the humanitarian movement in corrections, the notions of mercy and compassion combined with considerations of human dignity began to infiltrate sentencing practices and correctional decision making. For offenders who could not help themselves, and for others who represented diminished risks to society, it was felt that custodial coercion might be unnecessary. Second, for an untold number of lesser and situational offenders, many reformers held that the unfavorable consequences of imprisonment — the loss of liberty and self-esteem, the placement in physical jeopardy, and the fact that penitentiaries can be "schools of crime" — would impede successful rehabilitation and community reintegration. Third, from an economic point of view, it would cost far less to supervise criminals in the community than to maintain them in institutions. Furthermore, the families of those sent to prison often became financial burdens to the state. Fourth, many community-based correctional strategies were deemed to have the practical value of helping offenders to achieve positions in their neighborhoods and communities as opposed to the more negative implications of institutional banishment. Fifth, with the recent trends in prison overcrowding, reducing or altogether eliminating the offender's period of confinement has been viewed as a more pragmatic approach to the management and control of the less seriously involved criminal offenders. And sixth, since the onset of the 1960s, there seems to have developed a "last resort" philosophy in corrections which maintains that the traditional avenues of punishment and correction have not been working, and new, innovative approaches must be tested.

CRIMINAL JUSTICE DIVERSION

Criminal justice **diversion** refers to the removal of offenders from the application of the criminal law at any stage of the police and court processes.[1] It implies the formal halting or suspending of traditional criminal proceedings against persons who have violated criminal statutes, in favor of processing them through some noncriminal disposition or means. Thus, diversion occurs prior to adjudication; *it is a preadjudication disposition.*

Diversion: The removal of offenders from the application of the criminal law at any stage of the police or court processes.

The Development of Diversion

Diversion is not a new practice in the administration of justice. It has likely existed in an *informal* fashion for thousands of years, since the inception of organized law enforcement and social control. In ancient and modern societies, informal diversion has occurred in many ways: A police officer removes a public drunk from the street to a Salvation Army shelter; a prosecutor decides to *nolle pros.* a petty theft; a magistrate releases with a lecture an individual who assaulted a neighbor during the course of an argument. These are generally discretionary decisions, undertaken at random and off the record, and they tend to be personalized, standardless, and inconsistent. They are often problematic in that they may reflect individual, class, or social prejudices. Furthermore, they serve only to remove offenders from the application of criminal penalties with no attempt to provide appropriate jurisprudential alternatives.

Although these haphazard and unsystematic practices will continue, more formalized diversion activities impose social-therapeutic programs in lieu of conviction and punishment. These latter seem to have emerged within the juvenile justice system during the early part of this century. Among the first was the *Chicago Boys' Court,* founded in 1914 as an extralegal form of probation. As explained many years ago by Chicago municipal court judge Jacob Braude, the rationale of the Boys' Court was to process and treat young offenders without branding them as criminals:

The Chicago Boys' Court

> While the facility of probation is available to court, it is used at a minimum because before one can be admitted to probation he must first be found guilty. Having been found guilty, he is stamped with a criminal record and then telling him to go out and make good is more likely to be a handicap than an order.[2]

The Boys' Court system of supervision placed young defendants under the authority of one of four community agencies: the Holy Name Society, the Chicago Church Federation, the Jewish Social Service Bureau, and the Colored Big Brothers. After a time, the court requested a report of the defendant's activities and adjustment, and if they were favorable, he would be officially discharged from the court having no criminal record.

Later developments in youthful diversionary programs included New York City's Youth Counsel Bureau. This agency was established during the early 1950s for handling juveniles alleged to be delinquent or criminal but not deemed sufficiently advanced in their misbehavior to be adjudicated and committed by the courts.[3] Referrals came from police, courts, schools, and other sources. The bureau provided counseling services and discharged those whose adjustment appeared promising. In many instances, the youthful defendants not only avoided criminal convictions, but arrest records as well. Alternative programs in the developing area of juvenile diversion included the District of Columbia's Project Crossroads, aimed at unemployed and underemployed first offenders ages sixteen to twenty-five years who were charged with property offenses.[4] Upon agreement to enter the program, a youth's charge was suspended for ninety days, during which counseling, education, and employment services would be made available. At the end of the three-month period, project staff would recommend a *nolle pros.* of the charges, further treatment, or return to the court for resumption of prosecution.

Patterns of Diversion

As criminal justice diversion continued to evolve, the arguments in its favor increased. It was felt that its practice would reduce court backlog, provide early intervention before the development of full-fledged criminal careers, ensure some consistency in selective law enforcement, reduce the costs of criminal processing, and enhance an offender's chances for community reintegration. More importantly, however, it had been the conclusion of many social scientists and penal reformers that the criminal justice process, which was designed to protect society from criminals, often contributed to the very behavior it was trying to eliminate. This was typically accomplished by:

1. Forcing those convicted of criminal offenses to interact with other, perhaps more experienced criminals, thus, becoming socialized to a variety of criminal roles, learning the required skills and the criminal value system.
2. Denying convicted felons the opportunity to play legitimate roles.
3. Changing the individual's self-concept to that of a criminal. This occurs as a result of an individual being told by the courts that he or she is a criminal and being placed in an institution where inmates and guards define the individual as a criminal.[5]

Both the President's Commission on Law Enforcement and Administration of Justice in 1967 and the National Advisory Commission on Criminal Justice Standards and Goals in 1973 heavily endorsed the diversion concept, holding that it would not only offer a viable alternative to incarceration, but also minimize the potential criminal socialization and labeling of first offenders.

Primarily as a result of massive federal funding allocated by the Law Enforcement Assistance Administration for the prevention and reduction of crime, diversion programs of many types emerged and expanded throughout the nation during the 1970s. Most, however, were designed for youths, for minor crimes (such as assaults, simple thefts, and property damage resulting from neighborhood disputes), and for special offenders whose crimes were deemed to be related to problem drinking or narcotics use.

Youth Service Bureaus Specifically recommended by the President's Commission and begun in California during 1971, youth service bureaus became common by the mid-1970s. They were similar in concept to New York's original Youth Council Bureau, but many operated as adjuncts to local police departments. They offered counseling, tutoring, crisis intervention, job assistance, and guidance with school and family problems for truants, runaways, and delinquent youths.

Public Inebriate Programs   In municipalities where public intoxication has remained a criminal offense, several diversionary alternatives to prosecution have been structured for public inebriates. Some are placed in alcohol detoxification centers rather than in jails. Others are referred before trial to community service agencies for more intensive treatment and care.

Civil Commitment   Based on a medical model of rehabilitation, civil commitment programs were founded on the notion that some types of criminality resulted from symptoms of illness rather than malicious intent. Such offenders as drug users, sexual deviants, and the mentally ill could be diverted either before or after trial to a residential setting for therapeutic treatment. Community protection was promised by the removal of offenders to a rehabilitation center, while those diverted received treatment instead of criminal sanctions and stigma. Civil commitment programs were most common in California, New York, and the federal system for the treatment of narcotics users.

Citizen Dispute Settlement   Citizen dispute settlement programs were designed to deflect from the criminal justice system complaints related to family and neighborhood quarrels and evolving from petty crimes, simple assaults, property damage, threats, and bad checks. Cases are diverted to mediation by a disinterested third party at the family or neighborhood level, and identified problem areas receive help through arbitration combined with help from local community service agencies.

Treatment Alternatives to Street Crime   Treatment Alternatives to Street Crime, better known as TASC, is a program designed to serve as a liaison between the criminal justice system and community treatment programs. As a program for substance-abusing arrestees, probationers, and parolees, its more than 120 sites in twenty-five states make it the most widely supported form of court diversion in the United States (see Exhibit 17.1).

Specialized Drug Courts

In addition to TASC, there are "TASC-like" programs in numerous jurisdictions, the majority of which were established during the past half decade in conjunction with specialized drug courts. For example, New York's Drug Treatment Alternatives to Prison program, sponsored by the drug court, allows individuals arrested for nonviolent drug-related felonies to enter an eighteen- to twenty-four-month residential treatment program rather than being indicted on criminal charges.[6] In South Florida, drug courts in several counties permit those arrested for first-time cocaine possession to opt for treatment in lieu of trial.[7] Similar programs are emerging in other jurisdictions.

The Impact of Diversion

It is difficult to assess the overall value and impact of the national diversion effort. Many programs have never been evaluated, and estimations

● EXHIBIT 17.1 ●

Treatment Alternatives to Street Crime

Treatment Alternatives to Street Crime (TASC) provides an objective and effective bridge between two separate institutions: the *justice system* and the *treatment community*. The justice system's legal sanctions reflect community concerns for public safety and punishment, whereas the treatment community emphasizes therapeutic relationships as a means for changing individual behavior and reducing the personal suffering associated with substance abuse and other problems. Under TASC supervision, community-based treatment is made available to drug-dependent individuals who would otherwise burden the justice system with their persistent and associated criminality.

TASC programs were initiated in 1972 in response to recognized links between substance abuse and criminal behavior. The mission of TASC is to participate in justice system processing as early in the continuum as acceptable to participating agencies. TASC identifies, assesses, and refers appropriate drug-and/or alcohol-dependent offenders accused or convicted of nonviolent crimes to community-based substance abuse treatment as an alternative or supplement to existing justice system sanctions and procedures. TASC then monitors the drug-dependent offender's compliance with individually tailored progress expectations for abstinence, employment, and improved social and personal functioning. It then reports treatment results back to the referring justice system component. Clients who violate conditions of their justice mandate, TASC, or treatment agreement are usually sent back

to the justice system for continued processing or sanctions.

TASC combines the influence of legal sanctions for probable or proven crimes with the appeal of such innovative justice system dispositions are deferred prosecution, creative community sentencing, diversion, pretrial intervention, probation, and parole supervision to motivate treatment cooperation by the substance abuser. Through treatment referral and closely supervised community reintegration, TASC aims to permanently interrupt the vicious cycle of addiction, criminality, arrest, prosecution, conviction, incarceration, release, readdiction, criminality, and rearrest.

TASC programs not only offer renewed hope to drug- and alcohol-dependent clients by encouraging them to alter their lifestyles while remaining in their own communities, but they also provide important incentives to other justice and treatment system participants. TASC can reduce the costs and relieve many processing burdens related to substance abuse within the justice system through assistance with such duties as addiction-related medical situations, pretrial screening, and posttrial supervision.

The treatment community also benefits from TASC's legal focus, which seems to motivate and prolong client cooperation in treatment programs and ensures clear definition and observation of criteria for treatment dismissal or completion. Public safety is also increased through TASC's careful supervision of criminally involved clients during their community-based treatment.

Although there has not been a *national* evaluation of the entire TASC effort, more than forty local programs were assessed from 1972 through 1982. In general, it was found that the majority effectively linked criminal justice and treatment systems, identified previously untreated drug-involved offenders, and intervened with clients to reduce drug abuse and criminal activity. Moreover, two recent examinations—one in 1986 and another in 1988—suggest that the TASC initiative in meeting its intended operational goals.

In short, the TASC experience has been a positive one, TASC has been demonstrated to be highly productive in: 1) identifying populations of drug-involved offenders in great need of treatment; 2) assessing the nature and extent of their drug use patterns and specific treatment needs; 3) effectively referring drug-involved offenders to treatment; 4) serving as a linkage between criminal justice and treatment systems; and, 5) providing constructive client identification and monitoring services for the courts, probation, and other segments of the criminal justice system.

Perhaps most importantly, evaluation data indicate that TASC-referred clients remain longer in treatment than non-TASC clients, and as a result, have better post-treatment success.

SOURCE: James A. Inciardi and Duane C. McBride, *Treatment Alternatives to Street Crime: History, Experiences, and Issues* (Rockville, Md.: National Institute on Drug Abuse, 1991).

of their effectiveness have been based on little more than clinical intuition and hunch. Among those that have undergone rigorous assessment, the findings have ranged from promising to bleak. Furthermore, several projects became steeped in controversy, resulting in some negative commentary on the entire trend of diversion.

On the more positive side, many early programs seemed to be effecting measurable change with certain defendants. An example was the Manhattan Court Employment Project, operated by New York's Vera Institute of Justice from 1967 through 1970. Its focus was on male and female offenders charged with misdemeanors and minor felonies. Subjects were given job training and placement. Those who failed to show any progress were returned to the courts for prosecution. An evaluation in 1972 demonstrated that the recidivism rate among defendants whose charges were dropped was half that of the defendants returned for prosecution.[8] Conversely, the experience with the youth service bureaus was considerably less impressive. Although the bureaus were touted as models for diverting juveniles from the criminal justice system, a national assessment survey of the projects found that they contributed little to any community in helping solve the problem of youth crime.[9]

The concept of pretrial diversion continued through the 1980s, but with somewhat less enthusiasm. Despite the problematic character of many of the programs, a few new and innovative operations nevertheless emerged. A striking example is the Weekend Intervention Program (WIP) in Dayton, Ohio. Begun in 1978 and sponsored by the Wright State University School of Medicine, the WIP was structured in response to the growing concern over drunk drivers. First and second DWI (driving while intoxicated) offenders are given the option of conviction and sentence or a three-day program of intensive therapy and alcohol education. Persons diverted to the WIP pay a fee for the services provided, making the operation self-supporting.

In 1983 the National Highway Traffic Safety Administration supported an evaluation on WIP.[10] The research identified, from court dockets, virtually every alcohol-related vehicular conviction in a ten-county area in southwestern Ohio. These cases, almost 6,000 of them, were followed for a two-year period. The research compared the rates of repeated DWI offenses among three groups of convicted offenders—those who were sentenced to jail for two or three days, those who received suspended sentences or fines, and those who were remanded to Wright State's Weekend Intervention Program. This research found that the rate of repeated DWI offenses among first-time offenders was 7

A DWI work force cleans up litter along the highway.

percent lower for those sent to the WIP than for those receiving jail sentences or suspended sentences/fines. Moreover, among more serious drunk driving cases—those involving drivers with prior DWI conviction—the repeat offense rate for drivers sent to the WIP was 22 percent lower than the rate for drivers receiving jail or suspended sentences.

The Focused Offender Disposition Program

Given the growth of prison populations resulting from the "drug wars," interest in diversion reemerged as the nation moved into the 1990s. The apparent success of TASC programs, for example, generated new federal support for TASC as part of the White House *National Drug Control Strategy.*[11] Moreover, a variety of new and experimental activities were initiated. The *Focused Offender Disposition (FOD) Program,* for example, funded by the Bureau of Justice Assistance and implemented in Birmingham, Phoenix, and Chicago, tested new mechanisms for assigning court-referred drug offenders to community-based treatment. A feature of the FOD program was the development of the Offender Profile Index, a treatment assessment instrument which suggested the most appropriate treatment alternative for each client—either long-term residential, short-term residential, or outpatient treatment, or periodic drug testing only.[12]

PROBATION

In the month of August, 1841, I was in court one morning, when the door communicating with the lock-room was opened and an officer entered, followed by a ragged and wretched looking man, who took his seat upon the bench allotted to prisoners. I imagined from the man's appearance, that his offense was that of yielding to his appetite for intoxicating drinks, and in a few moments I found that my suspicions were correct, for the clerk read the complaint, in which the man was charged with being a common drunkard. The case was clearly made out, but before sentence had been passed, I conversed with him for a few moments, and found that he was not yet past all hope of reformation. . . . He told me that if he could be saved from the House of Correction, he never again would taste intoxicating liquors; there was such an earnestness in that tone, and a look of firm resolve, that I determined to aid him; I bailed him, by permission of the Court. He was ordered to appear for sentence in three weeks from that time. He signed the pledge and became a sober man; at the expiration of this period of probation, I accompanied him into the courtroom. . . . The Judge expressed himself much pleased with the account we gave of the man, and instead of the usual penalty—imprisonment in the House of Corrections—he fined him one cent and costs, amounting in all to $3.76, which was immediately paid. The man continued industrious and sober, and without doubt has been by this treatment, saved from a drunkard's grave.
—JOHN AUGUSTUS, 1852

John Augustus, the father of probation

This incident during the latter part of 1841 gave birth to the concept of probation in the United States. Augustus was a Boston shoemaker, and his method was to bail an offender after conviction, to provide him with friendship and support in family matters, as well as in job assistance. When the defendant was later brought to court for sentencing, Augustus would report on his progress toward reformation and request that the judge order a small fine and court costs in lieu of a jail sentence.[13] As such, *John Augustus* was the first probation officer. By 1858, he had bailed almost 2,000 defendants. His efforts led to the first probation statute, passed in Massachusetts in 1878. By 1900, four other states had enacted similar legislation, and probation became an established alternative to incarceration.

The Nature of Probation

Probation can be a rather confusing concept, for in the field of corrections the term has been used in a variety of ways. First of all, probation is a sentence. It is a sentence of conditional release to the community. More specifically, as defined by the American Bar Association, probation is a sentence not involving confinement that imposes conditions and retains authority in the sentencing court to modify the conditions of sentence or to resentence the offender if he or she violates the conditions.[14]

In addition to being a disposition, the word *probation* has also been used to refer to a status, a system, and a process.[15] As a status, probation reflects the unique character of the probationer: he or she is neither a free citizen nor a confined prisoner. As a system, probation is a component in the administration of justice, as embodied by the agency or organization that administers the probation process. As a process, probation refers to the set of functions, activities, and services that characterize the system's transactions with the courts, the offender, and the community. This process includes the preparation of reports for the courts, the supervision of probationers, and the obtaining and providing of services for them.

The Probation Philosophy

The premise behind the use of probation is that many offenders are not dangerous and represent little, if any, menace to society. It has been argued that when defendants are institutionalized, the prison community becomes their new reference point. They are forced into contact with hard-core criminals, the prison experience generates embitterment and hostility, and the "ex-con" label becomes a stigma that impedes social adjustment. Probation, on the other hand, provides a more therapeutic alternative. The term comes from the Latin *probare,* meaning to test or prove, and the probationer is given the opportunity to demonstrate that if given a second chance, more socially acceptable behavior patterns will result.

The probation philosophy also includes elements of community protection and offender rehabilitation. Probationers are supervised by agents of the court or probation agency. These are trained personnel with dual roles. They are present to ensure that the conditions of probation are fulfilled and to provide counseling and assistance in community reintegration. Furthermore, as with all types of community-based correction, it is generally agreed that the rehabilitation of offenders is more realistically possible in the natural environment of the free community than behind prison walls.

While these are the ideal philosophical underpinnings of probation, several more pragmatic issues have also entered into its use as an alternative to imprisonment. First, and as noted in the previous chapter, correctional institutions throughout the nation have become painfully overcrowded. With the almost prohibitive costs of new prison construction,

Probation: A sentence not involving confinement that imposes conditions and retains authority in the sentencing court to modify the conditions of sentence or to resentence the offender if he or she violates the conditions.

The term probation comes from the Latin *probare,* meaning to test or prove, and the probationer is given the opportunity to demonstrate that if given a second chance, more socially acceptable behavior patterns will result.

probation is seen by many as a more economically viable correctional alternative. Second, and also as a matter of simple economics, the probation process is considerably cheaper than the prison process. The cost of maintaining an inmate in prison has been estimated to average some $25,000 per year.[16] Probation costs approximate one-tenth of that amount. Third, within some sectors of the criminal justice community, imprisonment is being viewed more and more as cruel and unusual punishment. Prisons are dangerous places to live. Inmates are physically, sexually, and emotionally victimized on a regular basis. Probation, within this context, is considered to be the more humane avenue of correctional intervention.

Suspended Sentences and Conditional Release

There are a variety of terms that tend to be used interchangeably with probation, but which represent things that are quite different. The best known of these is the **suspended sentence,** a disposition that in and of itself implies supervision of the offender with a set of specified criteria and goals. The suspended sentence is a quasi-freedom that can be revoked at the pleasure of the court. Suspended sentences, furthermore, are of two types: *suspension of imposition* of sentence and *suspension of execution* of sentence. In the case of suspension of imposition, there may be verdict or plea, but no sentence is pronounced. Although uncommon, the presiding magistrate releases the defendant on the general condition that he or she stay out of trouble and make restitution for the crime. With the suspension of execution, the sentence is prescribed but is postponed or not carried out. In a number of jurisdictions, a sentence can be suspended, and this suspension is followed by an order for probation.

Alternatively, the New York Penal Law, in addition to probation, provides for sentences of *conditional discharge* and *unconditional discharge.* The sentence of conditional discharge is similar to a suspended sentence:

> The court may impose a sentence of conditional discharge for an offense if the court, having regard to the nature and circumstances of the offense and to the history, character, and condition of the defendant, is of the opinion that neither the public interest nor the interests of justice would be served by a sentence of imprisonment and that probation supervision is not appropriate.[17]

Under the New York law, the period of conditional discharge is one year for a misdemeanor and three years for a felony, and the conditions generally involve making restitution or reparation for losses suffered by the victim. The sentence of unconditional discharge goes one step further, and the defendant is released without imprisonment, fine, probation, or any conditions whatsoever. Such a sentence is used when it is the opinion of the court that no proper purpose is served by the imposition of any conditions. For all purposes, such a discharge is a final judgment of conviction.[18]

The Presentence or Probation Investigation

Probation in the United States is administered by hundreds of independent government agencies, each jurisdiction operating under different laws and many with widely varying philosophies. In some jurisdictions,

Suspended sentence: A court disposition of a convicted person, pronouncing a penalty of a fine or commitment to confinement, but unconditionally discharging the defendant or holding execution of the penalty in abeyance upon good behavior.

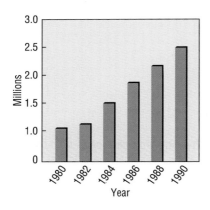

Probationers in the U.S., 1981–1990
SOURCE: Bureau of Justice Statistics

such as Hawaii, a single state authority provides services for all probationers. In other jurisdictions, probation descends from county or municipal authority, functioning under state laws, and guidelines, but is
administered by the lower courts. In some areas, such as South Carolina,
probation and parole are combined into a single state unit. In the federal
system, probation is administered as an arm of the federal district courts.

The presentence investigation is one of the basic services provided by
the probation agency, and, as noted in Chapter 13, such reports are
generally mandatory if probation appears to be a possible sentence. In
their examination of the backgrounds and characteristics of defendants,
these reports can vary widely in depth, content, and usefulness. In some
regional offices in South Carolina, for example, selected presentence
investigation reports are less than a single page in length, and contain
only the basic facts of the defendant's criminal history and current offense, followed by a brief statement of the offender's prognosis and the
probation agent's recommendation for sentencing. In contrast, some
presentence investigations conducted in Kings County (Brooklyn), New
York, have exceeded thirty single-spaced legal-sized pages, and recount
numerous aspects of the defendant's life including whether he or she was
the product of a normal birth delivery. The norm, however, is somewhere between these two extremes, and includes the characteristics of the
offender, the circumstances of his offense, an evaluative summary, and a
recommendation. (See Exhibit 17.2.)

Studies have demonstrated that in most sentences involving probation, there is a high correlation between the presentence or probation
officer's recommendation and the judge's sentencing decision.[19] This
should not suggest, however, that judicial decision making is dictated by
the content of a presentence report recommendation, or that judges and
presentence investigators interpret defendants' life histories and background characteristics in remarkably the same way. Rather, there are a
number of more logical factors at work. First, since probation is one of
the most common sentences, the simple laws of chance are operative.
Second, most criminal convictions occur as the result of guilty pleas. The
details of the plea negotiation and the prosecutor's sentencing recommendation are generally known to the presentence investigator, and
these typically influence his or her recommendation. Third, presentence
or probation officers tend to be aware of the sentencing recommendations that will be acceptable to specific judges for given kinds of cases,
and they often take the path of least resistance.[20]

The U.S. Supreme Court has upheld the validity of the presentence
investigation as meeting the due-process requirements of the Constitution. In **Williams** v. **New York**,[21] decided in 1949, the Court held that,
at sentencing, a convicted defendant does not have a Sixth Amendment
right to cross-examine persons who have supplied information to a court
(in a presentence report) regarding sentencing. However, the Supreme
Court has provided defendants with some safeguards in this matter. In
the 1977 case of *Gardner* v. *Florida*,[22] for example, the Court ruled that a
defendant is denied due process when a sentence is based, even in part,
on confidential information contained in a presentence report that the
defendant is not given the opportunity to deny or explain. Although
both *Williams* and *Gardner* involved examinations of the nature of the
presentence report in the context of capital cases, subsequent decisions
in state courts of appeals served to apply the Court's rulings to noncapital cases as well.

Presentence investigation is an investigation undertaken by a probation
agency or other designated authority at
the request of a court into the past behavior, family circumstances, and personality of a person who has been convicted of a crime, in order to assist the
court in determining the most appropriate sentence.

Williams v. *New York:* The Supreme
Court ruling that at sentencing, the
defendant does not have a Sixth
Amendment right to cross-examine
persons who have supplied information to a court (in a presentence
report) regarding sentencing.

● EXHIBIT 17.2 ●

A Presentence Report

United States District Court Central District of New York

Name: John Jones
Address:
　1234 Astoria Blvd.
　New York City
Legal Residence: Same
Age: 33
Date of Birth: 2-8-40
　New York City
Sex: Male
Race: Caucasian
Citizenship: U.S. (birth)
Education: 10th grade
Marital Status: Married

Dependents: Three (wife and two children)
Soc. Sec. No.: 112-03-9559
FBI No.: 256 1126
Date: January 4, 1974
Docket No.: 74–103
Offense: Theft of mail by Postal Employee (18 U.S.C. Sec. 1709) 2 cts.
Penalty: Ct. 2–5 years and/or $2,000 fine
Plea: Guilty on 12-16-73 to Ct. 2 Ct.1 pending
Verdict:

Custody: Released on own recognizance. No time in custody
Asst. U.S. Attorney: Samuel Hayman
Defense Counsel: Thomas Lincoln, Federal Public Defender
Drug/Alcohol Involvement: Attributes offense to need for drinking money
Detainers or Charges Pending: None
Codefendants (Disposition): None

Disposition:

Date:

Sentencing Judge:

Offense: **Official Version.** Official sources revealed that during the course of routine observations on December 4, 1973, within the Postal Office Center, Long Island, New York, postal inspectors observed the defendant paying particular attention to various packages. Since the defendant was seen to mishandle and tamper with several parcels, test parcels were prepared for his handling on December 5, 1973. The defendant was observed to mishandle one of the test parcels by tossing it to one side into a canvas tub. He then placed his jacket into the tub and leaned over the tub for a period of time. At this time the defendant left the area and went to the men's room. While he was gone the inspectors examined the mail tub and found that the test parcel had been rifled and that the contents, a watch, was missing. The defendant returned to his work area and picked up his jacket. He then left the building. The defendant was stopped by the inspectors across the street from the post office. He was questioned about his activities and on his person he had the wristwatch from the test parcel. He was taken to the postal inspector's office, where he admitted the offense.

Defendant's Version of Offense. The defendant admits that he rifled the package in question and took the watch. He states that he intended to sell the watch at a later date. He admits that he has been drinking too much lately and needed extra cash for "drinking money." He exhibits remorse and is concerned about the possibility of incarceration and the effect that it would have on his family.

Prior Record			
DATE	OFFENSE	PLACE	DISPOSITION
5-7-66 (age 26)	Possession of policy slips	Manhattan CR. CT. N.Y., N.Y.	$25.00 Fine 7-11-66
3-21-72 (age 32)	Intoxication	Manhattan CR. CT. N.Y., N.Y.	4-17-72 Nolle

Personal History. The defendant was born in New York City on February 8, 1940, the oldest of three children. He attended the public school, completed the 10th grade, and left school to go to work. He was rated as an average student and was active in sports, especially basketball and baseball.

The defendant's father, John, died of a heart attack in 1968, at the age of fifty-three years. He had an elementary school education and worked as a construction laborer most of his life.

The defendant's mother, Mary Smith Jones, is fifty-five years of age and is employed as a seamstress. She had an elementary school education and married defendant's father when she was twenty years of age. Three sons were issue of the marriage. She presently resides in New York City, and is in good health.

Defendant's brother, Paul, age thirty-two years, completed 2½ years of high school. He is employed as a bus driver and resides with his wife and two children in New York City.

Defendant's brother, Lawrence, age thirty years, completed three semesters of college. He is employed as a New York City firefighter. He resides with his wife and one child in Dutch Point, Long Island.

The defendant after leaving high school worked as a delivery boy for a retail supermarket chain then served two years in the U.S. Army as an infantryman (ASN 123 456 78). He received an honorable discharge and attained the rank of corporal serving from 2-10-58 to 2-1-60. After service he held a number of jobs of the laboring type.

The defendant was employed as a truck driver for the City of New York when he married Ann Sweeny on 6-15-63. Two children were issue of this marriage, John, age eight, and Mary, age six. The family has resided at the same address (which is a four-room apartment) since their marriage.

The defendant has been in good health all of his life but he admits he has been drinking to excess the past eighteen months, which has resulted in some domestic strife. The wife stated that she loved her husband and will stand by him. She is amenable to a referral for family counseling.

Defendant has worked for the Postal Service since 12-1-65 and resigned on 12-5-73 as a result of the present arrest. His work ratings by his supervisors were always "excellent."

Evaluative Summary. The defendant is a thirty-three-year-old male who entered a plea of guilty to mail theft. While an employee of the U.S. Postal Service he rifled and stole a watch from a test package. He admitted that he planned on selling the watch to finance his drinking, which has become a problem, resulting in domestic strife.

Defendant is a married man with two children with no prior serious record. He completed ten years of school, had an honorable military record, and has a good work history. He expresses remorse for his present offense and is concerned over the loss of his job and the shame to his family.

Recommendation. It is respectfully recommended that the defendant be admitted to probation. If placed on probation the defendant expresses willingness to seek counseling for his domestic problems. He will require increased motivation if there is to be a significant change in his drinking pattern.

Respectfully submitted,

Donald M. Fredericks
U.S. Probation Officer

SOURCE: Administrative Offices of the U.S. Courts, Division of Probation, "The Selective Presentence Investigation Report," *Federal Probation* 38 (December 1974): 53–54.

Conditions of Probation

Most states have statutory restrictions on the granting of probation. In some jurisdictions, defendants convicted of such crimes as murder, kidnapping, and rape are ineligible for probation, as are second and third felony offenders. Others tend to be less specific, but structure their penal codes in such a manner as to preclude a sentence of probation for most serious offenders. In Alabama, for example, persons convicted of crimes that typically call for sentences of death or imprisonment for ten years or more are ineligible for probation.[23] In North Carolina, "a person who has been convicted of any noncapital criminal offense not punishable by a minimum term of life imprisonment may be placed on probation. . . ."[24]

Thus, in most jurisdictions, probation is a statutory alternative to imprisonment for most felony convictions. Judges differ, however, in their approaches to granting it. As noted earlier, both plea bargaining and factors contained in the presentence report enter into the decision. In addition, there are such elements as the prosecutor's recommendation, anticipated community reaction, political considerations, court backlog, the availability of space in the prison system, and the judge's own feelings toward the particular offense or the offender. A Delaware judge commented, for example:

> Although the statutes permit it, I find sentences of imprisonment for convictions of marijuana possession to be unreasonable. . . . However, in *my* court, any person found guilty of a felony offense involving the exploitation of a child, sexually or otherwise, will receive the maximum term of imprisonment that the law allows.[25]

Upon the granting of probation and as part of their probation agreement, defendants are required to abide by a variety of regulations and conditions. These conditions are fairly standard from state to state. In New York, for example, which is typical of most jurisdictions, the conditions exhort the probationer to live a law-abiding and productive life, to work, to support his or her dependents, to maintain contact with the supervising probation officer, and to remain within the jurisdiction of the court (see Exhibit 17.3).

Special conditions of probation may also be imposed, by either the sentencing judge or the supervising probation agency. Many of these have been challenged by probationers as "improper," but most have been upheld by state apellate courts. Recent court decisions have affirmed the correctness of such special requirements as undergoing treatment for drug abuse,[26] abstaining from the use of alcohol,[27] serving a short jail sentence prior to release on probation with no credit for prior confinement,[28] refraining from operating a motor vehicle during the period of probation,[29] submitting to a search by the supervising probation officer,[30] and payment of restitution.[31] Some special conditions have been very specific yet at the same time trivial, but these too have been affirmed by the courts. In a 1980 New York case, for example, the court found proper a condition of probation that required a person convicted of embezzling from the bank account of a cemetery association to mow the lawn in the local cemetery during the grass-cutting season.[32]

Since the beginning of the 1980s, a new condition of probation has become common. In more than half the states, probation clients are being assessed a fee for services. Supervision services typically range from

---

● EXHIBIT 17.3 ●

Conditions of Probation

1. Conditions relating to conduct and rehabilitation

(a) Avoid injurious or vicious habits:

(b) Refrain from frequenting unlawful or disreputable places or consorting with disreputable persons;

(c) Work faithfully at a suitable employment or faithfully pursue a course of study or of vocational training that will equip him for suitable employment;

(d) Undergo available medical or psychiatric treatment and remain in a specified institution, when required for that purpose;

(e) Support his dependents and meet other family responsibilities;

(f) Make restitution of the fruits of his offense or make reparation, in an amount he can afford to pay, for the loss or damage caused thereby. When restitution or reparation is a condition of the sentence, the court shall fix the amount thereof and the manner of performance;

(g) Post a bond or other security for the performance of any or all conditions imposed;

(h) Satisfy any other conditions reasonably related to his rehabilitation.

2. Conditions relating to supervision

(a) Report to a probation officer as directed by the court or the probation officer and permit the probation officer to visit him at his place of abode or elsewhere;

(b) Remain within the jurisdiction of the court unless granted permission to leave by the court or the probation officer; and

(c) Answer all reasonable inquiries by the probation officer and promptly notify the probation officer of any change in address or employment.

SOURCE: State of New York, *Penal Law*, 65.10.

$10 to $30 per month, with presentence investigation costs running $100 to $300.[33] Although there are waivers for the indigent, nonpayment must be sanctioned by the court or probation agency. In Dade County, Florida, for example, all probation orders specifically state, as a condition of probation:

> You will make payments of thirty ($30.00) dollars per month, as instructed by your probation supervisor, to the state of Florida, pursuant to Ch. 945.30 Florida Statutes to cover part of the cost of your supervision, while on probation, unless such payments are waived according to the law.

Generally, conditions of probation are considered constitutional and proper unless they bear no reasonable relationship to the crime committed or the defendant's probationary status. Thus placement in a drug treatment program becomes an appropriate condition of probation only when the defendant's offense is considered to be a consequence of a drug-abuse problem. Conversely, abstinence from alcohol would be an improper condition for probationers who never had problems with

In *Griffin* v. *Wisonsin,* the Supreme Court upheld warrantless searches of probationers' homes by probation officers pursuant to a state statute authorizing such searches whenever a probation officer has "reasonable grounds" to believe contraband is in the home.

drinking. Furthermore, in *Griffin* v. *Wisconsin,*[34] decided in 1987, the Supreme Court ruled that state regulations permitting probation officers to conduct searches of probationers' homes, without warrants and upon "reasonable grounds" (rather than probable cause) to believe that contraband might be found, do not violate the Fourth Amendment. However, while warrantless searches of probationers, their automobiles, and premises are permissible conditions if carried out by probation officers with just cause, the courts have ruled that such searches cannot be extended to all law enforcement officers.[35]

Restitution Programs

Restitution: A condition of probation requiring offenders to compensate their victims for damages or to donate their time in service to the community.

Among the more widely endorsed conditions of probation in recent years is **restitution:** requiring offenders to compensate their victims for damages or stolen property (monetary restitution), or donate their time to community service (community service restitution).

The rationales for restitution are numerous. First, while fines imposed go directly into court or government treasuries, monetary restitution goes directly to the victims of crime, compensating them for injuries, time lost from work and other losses. Second, it forces the offender to take personal responsibility for his or her crime. Third, it has the potential for reconciling victims and offenders. Fourth, it can be incorporated into a probation program without the need for additional programs and expenditures. And fifth, it provides a vehicle for including the victim in the administration of justice.[36]

Despite these apparent virtues, restitution does have critics. It has been suggested that restitution can be a punitive sanction rather than a rehabilitative one, since it places an additional burden on offenders that they might not ordinarily have. Even more importantly, it carries the potential for nullifying any deterrent effects of punishment by allowing criminals to "write a check" and "pay a fee" for their offenses. Finally, it can be argued that restitution serves only the interests of those of reasonable financial ability, thus prohibiting such an option to the indigent. Although in many ways this latter argument is true, there are a number of alternatives that make restitution available to offenders at all levels of the socioeconomic ladder. There are, for example, community service restitution outlets through which juvenile vandals can work to repair the damage they caused, drunk drivers can work in alcohol detoxification centers, and other offenders can work in hospitals, nursing homes, or in juvenile counseling programs.[37]

Probation Services

At least in theory, probation service incorporates the casework approach. During the probationer's initial interview with his or her probation officer, an evaluation is made to determine what type of treatment supervision is most appropriate. Based on information contained in the presentence investigation and on his or her skills in counseling and problem solving, the officer plans a treatment schedule designed to allow the probationer to make a reasonable community adjustment. This diagnostic aspect of probation intake examines the probationer's peer relationships, family problems, work skills and history, educational status, and involvement with drug or alcohol abuse. During the course of the probation period, the officer works with the offender in these designated areas as required. The treatment may be limited to one-to-one counseling, or it may involve referral to community service agencies for drug abuse treatment, vocational skill enhancement, or job assistance. Some probation agencies have special supervision units with officers specifically trained in these areas. Others provide psychiatric services or structured group counseling programs. Since probationers are convicted criminal offenders and one of the officer's roles involves community protection, a second function of the intake interview is to determine what level of community supervision appears necessary. Such supervision planning can involve regular visits to the probationer's home and place of employment, and can require the client to report to the probation office on a weekly, semimonthly, or monthly basis.

Although many probation agencies do operate in the manner outlined, in practice few probationers receive such individualized treatment and supervision, for many different reasons. First, the educational backgrounds, skills, and experiences of probation officers vary widely. A number of agencies require graduate education and related experience for a career in probation work, but others have no such prerequisites. This often results in the recruitment of inexperienced college graduates, and probation becomes an entry-level position for employment in the criminal justice field. Furthermore, in some states high school graduates with no training in counseling, psychology, social work, or any other behavioral field have managed to secure work in the probation area. Second, as with all occupations and professions, many probation officers have little dedication or interest in their work. This often results in apathy toward their clients' needs and problems, an avoidance of responsibility, and the "stealing of time" during business hours. As one probation supervisor in a southern state once illustrated the point:

> Our field office in ——— County gets first honors in truancy. It's staffed by only two people—the agent and a secretary, both of whom hate themselves and their jobs. . . . The clients know not to call in or show up for a report on Wednesday afternoons. It's well known throughout the county that ——— and ——— close up the office at noon and shack up for the rest of the day.[38]

A third problem is the low level of career mobility in probation work. Combined with moderate to low salaries in many jurisdictions are limited opportunities for advancement. This results in frustration, dissatisfaction, cynicism, and high staff turnover. Additionally, there is the issue of case-load size. Work loads range from a dozen probationers per officer in a few agencies to over 300 per officer in others. The treatment and supervision aspects of probation become even further diluted by the requirements to perform presentence investigations. In consequence, treatment becomes reduced to making a telephone call every other week to determine if a job is being maintained, and supervision amounts to as little as a mail contact each month to determine if the probationers are residing where they say they are.

Some jurisdictions have met this challenge by recruiting volunteers and paraprofessionals to assist in probation offices. In Travis County, Texas, for example, volunteers assist regular probation officers to manage the many thousands of clients.[39] Volunteers include both men and women and some 25 percent are members of minority groups. Furthermore, many are law students from the University of Texas who assist in the preparation of presentence reports.

Finally, as is the case in police work, probation officers can differ dramatically in approaches to their work and attitudes toward their clients. There are probably many who can successfully mediate their dual

The working styles of probation officers

roles as clinicians and supervisors. However, there are also many "social workers" and "rule enforcers" who operate only from these diverse ends of the spectrum. In addition, there are the "legalists," who stress the upholding of law for its own sake; there are "company agents," who focus almost exclusively on their upward mobility in the probation organization; and there are the stereotyped "civil service hacks," who seem to think of little else than the number of years left until retirement and in the meantime work hard at getting the lion's share of days off, sick pay, fringe benefits, lunch hours, and coffee breaks. Each of these types can negatively affect a probationer's potential for readjustment.

As a final note here, most clinicians will agree that even the most dedicated workers, including probation officers, often limit the impact of the assistance they provide by not giving sufficient help to those who could benefit most. Throughout the human service delivery network, including offender rehabilitation agencies, the nature and extent of client types vary widely. At one end of the spectrum, perhaps 5 to 25 percent, there are those with a minimum of problems. Many are highly motivated to fulfill the terms of their probation, and no matter what support and assistance is or is not provided, their chances for success are high. At the opposite end there is another 5 to 25 percent who are so dysfunctional and committed to an antisocial lifestyle that little can change them. With or without service and treatment, most of these typically fail. Those in the middle, the remaining 50 to 90 percent, can go either way, depending on the nature and intensity of the service and supervision provided. These are the persons who could benefit most from rehabilitation programs. Yet there seems to be a tendency within the helping professions — an inclination based on humanitarian concern — to focus the majority of energy and services on those who appear to need them most. As a result, within the probation system it is the most dysfunctional clients — those who will potentially profit the least — who receive most of the treatment and supervision available. In consequence, the middle group, that large percentage whose behavior is most receptive to change, tends to be neglected.

Shock Probation

Shock probation: Allows for brief incarceration followed by suspension of sentence and probation.

In 1965, the Ohio state legislature passed the first **shock probation** law in the United States, allowing judges to incarcerate an offender for a brief part of the sentence, suspend the remainder, and place him or her on probation. Under the Ohio statute, shock probation (also known as a *mixed* or *split* sentence) is not part of the original sentence. Rather, the defendant can file a petition requesting it between thirty to sixty days after sentencing, or the judge can order it in the absence of any petition. Its "shock" effect comes from the contention that the staggering effect of exposure to prison or jail can be a significant deterrent to crime. Eligibility for shock probation procedures follows the same statutory guidelines that govern the granting of probation in general.

Sentiments regarding the suitability of shock probation as a rehabilitative tool have been mixed. On the one hand, it represents a way for the courts to do the following:

- impress offenders with the seriousness of their actions without a long prison sentence
- release offenders found by the institutions to be more amenable to community-based treatment than was realized by the courts at the time of sentence

- arrive at a just compromise between punishment and leniency in appropriate cases
- provide community-based treatment for rehabilitable offenders, while still observing their responsibilities for imposing deterrent sentences where public policy demands it[40]

In addition, since imprisonment is only short-term, it inhibits absorption of the offender into the "hard rock" inmate culture. At the same time, the fiscal costs of shock probation are significantly lower than those of a full period of incarceration.

Opponents of shock probation argue vigorously that it is counterproductive as a rehabilitative tool. First, its deterrent effect is limited or totally negated by the job loss and broken community ties that occur with incarceration, however brief. Second, the purpose of probation is to *avoid* incarceration, not supplement it. Third, even a short period of incarceration has the potential for contaminating offenders through exposure to hardened criminals and the hostilities and resentment of prison life. Fourth, it stigmatizes offenders for having been in jail or prison and may add to their confusion of status and self-concept. Fifth, and perhaps most importantly, prison and probation are at opposite ends of the punishment and rehabilitation scale; they are mutually

Shock probation gives an offender a little taste of the bars.
—AN OHIO PROSECUTOR, 1987

exclusive and therefore should not be mixed.[41] As one commentator expressed it:

> Once having determined that a person can be trusted in the community and can benefit most under community supervision, no appreciable benefits can be derived from committing [him or her] to a short period of incarceration.[42]

Although shock probation may be functional from the perspective of the criminal justice system in terms of the lower costs of probation versus imprisonment and the alleviation of prison overcrowding, there is no evidence yet that demonstrates that it reduces recidivism. Several empirical studies have examined the shock probation experience, but the findings remain inconclusive.[43]

Intensive Probation Supervision

Intensive probation supervision: A program of closer surveillance and more exhaustive services that serve to place a probationer under tighter control than he or she might experience under regular probation.

Intensive probation supervision is a program of closer surveillance and more exhaustive services that place a probationer under tighter control than he or she might experience under regular probation. Although it is not a particularly new concept, it has received considerable attention in recent years because of the dual purposes it appears to serve in these times of overcrowded penitentiaries and escalating criminal justice costs. *First,* it restrains the growth of prison populations and associated costs by controlling selected offenders in the community. *Second,* and at the same time, it satisfies at least a part of society's demand that offenders be punished for their crimes.[44]

The degrees of surveillance vary considerably from one intensive probation supervision to another. In general, *all* involve small caseloads and frequent contacts between the probationer and probation officer in the home, on the job, and at the probation office. The Georgia program is widely regarded as the most stringent, with standards including:

- five face-to-face contacts per week
- mandatory community service
- mandatory employment
- mandatory curfew
- weekly checks of local arrest records
- routine alcohol and drug testing[45]

As for the effectiveness of intensive probation supervision, the data appear to be inconclusive. An evaluation of the program in Montgomery County (Dayton), Ohio, from its inception in 1984 through the middle of 1986 generated results that were clearly mixed.[46] As indicated in Exhibit 17.4, a comparison of the performance of 163 intensive probationers with that of 130 regular probationers yields no statistically significant differences. However, one could argue that since the probationers under intensive supervision were in that program in lieu of incarceration, and hence, were at higher risk for recidivism than regular probationers, then the Montgomery County program appears to have been somewhat effective. While 66.9 percent of the regular probations were not rearrested during the follow-up period and 78.4 percent were not convicted of new crimes, the figures for the intensive probationers were 65.6 percent and 73.6 percent, respectively. In an analysis of data for eight programs in six states by the U.S. General Accounting Office, intensive probation supervision appeared to be a promising community-based correctional approach, but that further evaluation was in order.[47]

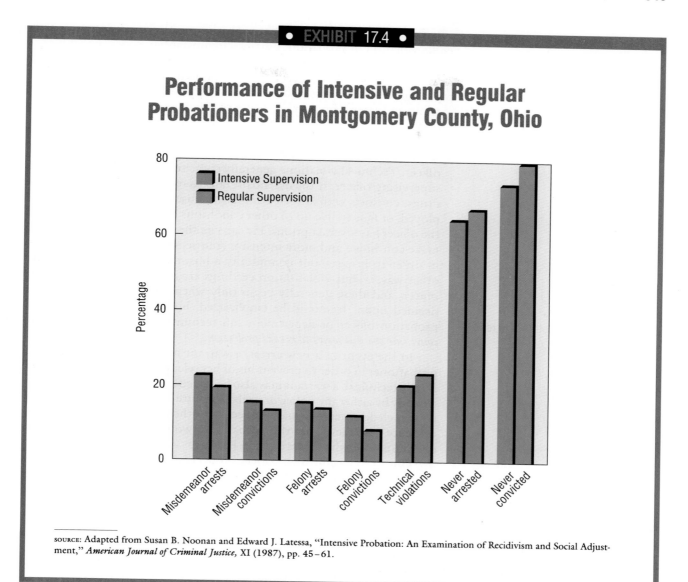

● EXHIBIT 17.4 ●

Performance of Intensive and Regular Probationers in Montgomery County, Ohio

- Intensive Supervision
- Regular Supervision

Percentage

Misdemeanor arrests / Misdemeanor convictions / Felony arrests / Felony convictions / Technical violations / Never arrested / Never convicted

SOURCE: Adapted from Susan B. Noonan and Edward J. Latessa, "Intensive Probation: An Examination of Recidivism and Social Adjustment," *American Journal of Criminal Justice,* XI (1987), pp. 45–61.

Probation Violation and Revocation

Since probation is a conditional release, it does not guarantee absolute freedom. Arrests for new crimes or technical violations of the conditions of probation can result in *revocation of probation* and the imprisonment of the offender.

Revocation of probation

As noted earlier in this chapter, the conditions of probation are established by statute and special conditions can be applied by the sentencing court. There has been little argument as to whether a new arrest constitutes a violation of probation. Furthermore, the appellate courts have given the lower courts considerable latitude in imposing conditions of probation. Thus, such technical violations as nonpayment of a fine imposed as a condition of probation, failure to pay off civil judgments for fraud although able to pay, failure to make child support payments, failure to report to one's probation officer, and driving while intoxicated, to name only a few, have been grounds for violation and revocation. *Absconding* from probation supervision, that is, failing to report and concealing oneself from the probation authorities, represents a serious violation of probation. Finally, circumstantial evidence that a probationer engaged in illegal conduct can also be grounds for revocation. In one Texas case, evidence that demonstrated that before a burglary the probationer had been in contact with those who had committed the crime and later shared in the fruits of the offense was found to justify revocation.[48]

The issue of probation violation tends to underscore the tremendous discretionary authority that is at the disposal of the probation officer. Technical violations generally come to the attention of only the supervising officer. If the defendant fails to report, reverts to the use of drugs, consorts with known criminals, refuses to remain gainfully employed, or fails to live up to other conditions of the probation contract, the officer has several options. He can cite the probationer for violation, make continued and more intensive counseling and supervision efforts in order to bring about community adjustment, or simply "look the other way." Thus violation proceedings are initiated by the probation officer, and these generally begin only when revocation is the course decided upon. It should be emphasized, however, that although the probation officer or department can recommend revocation, *only the court has the authority to revoke probation.*

In the event of a new arrest, a warrant may be lodged against the probationer in order to prevent his or her release on bail. If the violation is only technical, a warrant may also be issued and the violator taken into custody by either the police or probation authorities. Some jurisdictions issue such detainers as a matter of course; others do so only when there is evidence to believe that the probationer would abscond if left in the community pending a revocation hearing.

Once revocation is the direction decided on by the probation authorities, the offender is given notice of such, the probation officer prepares a violation report, and a formal court hearing is scheduled. Until only recently, revocation hearings reflected few procedural safeguards. In 1967, however, the U.S. Supreme Court held in ***Mempa v. Rhay*** that a probationer had a constitutional right to counsel at any revocation proceeding where the imposition of sentence had been suspended but would be enjoined following revocation.[49] In 1972, the Court ruled in ***Morrissey v. Brewer*** that when the potential for parole revocation was at issue, an informal inquiry was required to determine if there was probable cause to believe that the parolee had indeed violated the conditions of parole.[50] The Court added the mandate of a formal revocation hearing as well, within minimum due-process requirements. While *Morrissey* was a parole case, its significance for probationers came the following year with ***Gagnon v. Scarpelli.***[51] In *Gagnon*, the Court extended the holding in *Morrissey* to probationers, and also held that both probationers and parolees have a constitutionally limited right to counsel during revocation proceedings (see Exhibit 17.5).

Since *Mempa, Morrissey,* and *Gagnon,* both state and federal courts have made a number of significant decisions regarding revocation proceedings. In *United States* v. *Reed,*[52] while reversing a revocation order, a U.S. circuit court of appeals stressed the rehabilitative nature of probation and indicated that the accumulation of a few minor technical violations should not necessarily be grounds for revocation. In *United States* v. *Pattman,*[53] it was ruled that hearsay evidence that was "demonstrably reliable" need not be subject to confrontation and cross-examination in revocation proceedings. In other decisions, courts have held that revocation can be based on conduct occurring prior to the actual granting of

Only the court has the authority to revoke probation.

Mempa v. ***Rhay:*** The Supreme Court ruling that the right to counsel applies to state probation revocation hearings at which deferred sentence may be imposed.

Morrissey v. ***Brewer:*** The Supreme Court ruling that a parolee facing revocation is entitled to both a preliminary hearing to determine whether he or she actually violated parole and a final hearing to consider not only the facts in question but, if there was a violation, what to do about it.

Gagnon v. ***Scarpelli:*** The Supreme Court ruling that the holding in *Morrissey* v. *Brewer* also applies to probationers and that neither probationers nor parolees are entitled to counsel as a matter of right at revocation hearings.

probation,[54] that a probationer may not invoke the Fifth Amendment privilege against self-incrimination in revocation proceedings when asked to testify about technical violations of probation,[55] and that evidence to support a revocation of probation need not establish guilt "beyond a reasonable doubt."[56]

The Effectiveness of Probation

Probation is by far the most widely used criminal sanction. At the beginning of 1990, for example, of the more than 4.4 million persons in the American correctional population, some 62 percent were probationers. By contrast, 27 percent were in prisons and jails and only 11 percent were on parole.[57] There are many reasons for this, most of which evolve from the economic and humanitarian considerations that characterize the probation philosophy. In addition, some observers believe that probation is the most effective phase of the criminal justice process. This notion, however, can be called into serious question. The vast majority of the studies or probation effectiveness are at least two decades old. Moreover, they may not be meaningful as indicators of the success of probation.[58] Further, more recent data even contradict the findings of the earlier research.

One of the more recent studies of probation effectiveness found that most felony offenders placed on probation were still a considerable threat to the community. Commissioned by the National Institute of Justice and conducted by the Rand Corporation during the early 1980s, the study examined 1,672 felony cases from California's Los Angeles and Alameda counties. During the forty-month follow-up period of the study, 65 percent of those placed on probation were rearrested. Almost 80 percent of these, or 51 percent of the entire sample, were convicted of new crimes. Of the sample, 18 percent were reconvicted of serious violent crimes, and 34 percent were reincarcerated. Charges were filed against 53 percent of the felony probationers: 19 percent had only one charge, 12 percent had two charges, and 22 percent had three or more charges against them. As the figure in Exhibit 17.6 indicates, 51 percent of the entire study population experienced a filing for property crime, 24 percent for violent crime, and 14 percent for a drug law violation. (The percentages were based on 2,608 charges; some of the 1,672 cases had multiple charges.)[59]

The Rand Study, however, is descriptive of only one population. In 1986, researchers at Southeast Missouri State University replicated the Rand report for the state of Missouri.[60] A total of 2,083 felons from the most urban population in Missouri were tracked for the same forty-month period used by Rand, with very different results. As indicated in the following table, the rearrest rates in Missouri were considerably lower than in California. This suggests that the effectiveness of probation tends to vary from one jurisdiction to the next and that individual studies of probation effectiveness may not be representative of felony probation in general.

Outcomes	Percentage in California	Percentage in Missouri
Rearrests	65.0	22.3
Reconvictions	51.0	12.0
Major new crime	18.0	7.1

SOURCE: Johnny McGaha, Michael Fichter, and Peter Hirschburg, "Felony Probation: A Re-Examination of Public Risk," *American Journal of Criminal Justice*, XI (1987), pp. 1–9.

• EXHIBIT 17.5 •

Due Process and Revocation Hearings

Mempa v. *Rhay*, 398 U.S. 128 (1967)

On June 17, 1959, seventeen-year-old Jerry Douglas Mempa was convicted in a Spokane, Washington, court of the offense of "joyriding" (riding in a stolen automobile). His conviction was based on a guilty plea entered with the advice of his court-appointed counsel. The court suspended the imposition of his sentence, and placed him on probation for a period of two years.

Several months later, the county prosecutor moved for the revocation of Mempa's probation on the allegation that he participated in a burglary on September 15, 1959. At the revocation hearing, he was not represented by counsel, nor was he asked if he wished counsel. Mempa admitted participation in the burglary, and the sole testimony connecting him with the crime came from a probation officer. There was no cross-examination of the officer's statements. Without asking Mempa if he had anything to say or any evidence to supply, the court revoked his probation and sentenced him to ten years in the state penitentiary.

In 1965, Mempa petitioned for a writ of *habeas corpus,* claiming he had been deprived of his right to counsel at the revocation proceeding at which the sentence was imposed. The Washington Supreme Court denied his petition, however. On appeal, the United States Supreme Court ruled in Mempa's favor. In its opinion, the Court did not question the authority of the state of Washington to provide for a deferred sentencing procedure coupled with its probation provisions. However, it emphasized that the "appointment of counsel for an indigent is required at every stage of a criminal proceeding where substantial rights of a criminal accused may be affected."

Mempa v. *Rhay* resulted in a variety of judicial interpretations. The Supreme Court's holding required that counsel be provided only at those revocation proceedings involving deferred sentencing, and did not apply to cases when the probationer was sentenced at the time of trial. Many lower courts treated the decision in exactly that way. However, other courts extended *Mempa* to all revocation proceedings, with the view that any revocation hearing was a "critical stage" that required due-process protection. Furthermore, although *Mempa* applied only to probation revocation hearings, a number of courts interpreted it to apply to parole as well.

Morrissey v. *Brewer*, 408 U.S. 471 (1972)

The decision in *Morrissey* v. *Brewer* related to parole revocation, but since parole and probation revocation are similar in nature, it had potential significance for both types of proceedings.

In 1967, John Morrissey was convicted in an Iowa court of falsely drawing checks, and he was sentenced to a maximum term of seven years' imprisonment. He was released on parole the following year, but within seven months, Morrissey was cited for violation of his parole. He was arrested, and admitted to purchasing an automobile without permission, obtaining credit under an assumed name, having become involved in an automobile accident, and failing to report these and other matters to his parole officer. He maintained that he had not contacted his parole officer due to sickness.

One week later, the parole violation report was reviewed, parole was revoked, and Morrissey was returned to prison. On a *habeas corpus* petition to the U.S. district court, Morrissey claimed that he had been denied due process under the Fourteenth Amendment in that his parole had been revoked without a hearing. The district court denied his petition, the U.S. court of appeals affirmed the lower court decision, and the U.S. Supreme Court granted *certiorari.*

The Court began its opinion stating that the revocation of parole is not part of a criminal prosecution and thus the full panoply of rights due a defendant in such a proceeding does not apply. However, the Court went on to state that parole revocation involves the potential termination of an individual's liberty, and therefore, certain due-process safeguards are necessary to ensure that the finding of a parole violation is based on verified facts to support the revocation.

In establishing procedural safeguards, the Court considered parole revocation to be a two-stage process: (1) the arrest of the parolee and a preliminary hearing, and (2) the revocation hearing. In designating a preliminary hearing for all parole violators. The Court held:

Such an inquiry should be seen in the nature of a preliminary hearing to determine whether there is probable cause or reasonable grounds to believe that the arrested parolee had committed acts which would constitute a violation of parole condition.

The Court also specified that at this preliminary review, the hearing officer should be someone not involved in the case, and that the parolee should be given notice of the hearing and the opportunity to be present during the questioning of persons providing adverse information regarding the alleged violation. Subsequently, a determination should be made to decide if the parolee's continued detention is warranted.

In reference to the revocation hearing, the Court held:

The parolee must have an opportunity to be heard and to show, if he can, that he did not violate the conditions or if he did, that circumstances in mitigation suggest the violation does not warrant revocation. The revocation hearing must be tendered within a reasonable time after the parolee is taken into custody. A lapse of two months as the state suggests occurs in some cases would not appear to be unreasonable.

And in terms of due process at revocation hearings:

Our task is limited to deciding the minimum requirements of due process. They include (a) written notice of the claimed violation of parole; (b) disclosure to the parolee of evidence against him; (c) opportunity to be heard in person and to present witnesses and documentary evidence; (d) the right to confront and cross-examine adverse witnesses (unless the hearing officer specifically finds good cause for not allowing confrontation); (e) a "neutral and detached" hearing body such as a traditional parole board, members of which need not be judicial officers or lawyers; and (f) a written statement by the fact finders as to the evidence relied on and reasons for revoking parole.

However, the Court left open the question of counsel: "We do not reach or decide the question whether the parolee is entitled to the assistance of retained or appointed counsel if he is indigent."

Gagnon v. *Scarpelli,* 411 U.S. 778 (1973)

During the year following *Morrissey,* the issue of right to counsel at revocation proceedings again came before the Court.

In July 1965, Gerald Scarpelli pleaded guilty in a Wisconsin court to a charge of armed robbery. He was sentenced to a term of fifteen years of imprisonment, but the judge suspended his sentence and placed him on probation for a period of seven years. The following month, he was arrested on a burglary charge, his probation was revoked without a hearing, and he was incarcerated in the Wisconsin State Reformatory to begin serving his original fifteen-year sentence.

Some three years later, Scarpelli applied for a writ of *habeas corpus.* After the petition had been filed, but before it had been acted upon, Scarpelli was released on parole. A U.S. district court judge ruled that the petition was not moot because of Scarpelli's parole status, because the original revocation carried "collateral consequences," namely, the restraints imposed by his parole. The district court then held that the revocation of probation without a hearing and counsel was a denial of due process. The court of appeals affirmed, and the state of Wisconsin appealed to the United States Supreme Court.

In its decision, the Court made two points:

Probation revocation, like parole revocation, is not a stage of a criminal prosecution, but does result in loss of liberty. Accordingly, we hold that a probationer, like a parolee, is entitled to a preliminary hearing and a final revocation hearing in the conditions specified in *Morrissey* v. *Brewer.*

Furthermore:

Counsel should be provided in cases where, after being informed of his right to request counsel the probationer or parolee makes such a request based on a timely or colorable claim:

1. that he has not committed the alleged violation of the conditions upon which he is at liberty; or
2. that, even if the violation is a matter of public record or is uncontested, there are substantial reasons which justified or mitigated the violation and made revocation inappropriate and that the reasons are complex or otherwise difficult to develop or present.

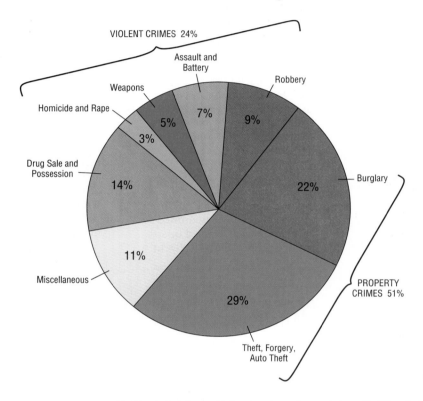

Charges Filed against Probationers: The Rand Study

NOTE: The percentages were based on a total of 2,608 criminal charges filed against the study population of 1,672 probationers.

SOURCE: Joan Petersilia, Susan Turner, James Kahan, and Joyce Peterson, *Granting Felons Probation: Public Risks and Alternatives* (Santa Monica, Calif.: Rand, 1985), p. 24.

PAROLE

I believe there are many who might be so trained as to be left on their parole during the last period of their imprisonment with safety.
— DR. SAMUEL G. HOWE, 1846

The granting of parole is an act of grace, comparable to the pardoning power that was once the prerogative of the monarchy. As such, it is infected from the outset with the arbitrariness and unpredictability that is characteristic of penal institutions and other autocracies.
— JESSICA MITFORD, 1974

Parole, from the French meaning "word of honor" and first used in 1846 by the Boston penal reformer Samuel G. Howe,[61] refers to the practice of allowing the final portion of a prison sentence to be served in the free community. Or more specifically, parole is:

> the status of being released from a penal or reformatory institution in which one has served a part of his maximum sentence, on the condition of maintaining good behavior and remaining in the custody and under the guidance of the institution or some other agency approved by the state **until a final discharge is granted.**[62]

Thus parole actually refers to two operations: (1) "parole release," the procedures used to establish the actual periods of confinement that prisoners serve, and (2) "parole supervision," the conditions and provisions that regulate parolees' postprison lives until the final discharge from their sentence.

For almost a century, parole has been an established part of American correctional theory and practice. It has had the ostensible purposes of ensuring that imprisonment is tailored to the needs of the inmate, ameliorating the harshness of long prison sentences, and hastening the offender's reintegration into the community when it appears that he or she is able to function as a law-abiding citizen. In addition, it has had the more subtle designs of alleviating the overcrowded conditions of correctional institutions, and assisting in maintaining prisons' social control through the threat of parole denial for instances of misbehavior.

The Origins of Parole

As a combination and extension of penal practices, parole has a long history. It seems to have first appeared in a most rudimentary form when the British economy declined during the latter part of the sixteenth century.[63] In its colonies, the need for cheap labor was critical. The British government began granting reprieves and stays of execution to felons physically able to work so they could be transported to the New World. The pardoned convicts became indentured servants, whose labor was sold to the highest bidder in the colonies. The newly arrived felons were required to work off their indenture, and the only other condition of their pardon was that they did not return to England.

Captain Alexander Maconochie of Norfolk Island, however, was the "father of parole" in its purest form. As noted in Chapter 14, Maconochie established a "mark system" whereby an inmate could earn early release by hard work and good behavior. Sir Walter Crofton's "Irish System" was a refinement of Maconochie's ideas, by which inmates could earn a conditional release through a "ticket-of-leave."

The concept of parole continued to evolve in the United States with the principles of *"good time" laws* and indeterminate sentencing. The notion underlying "good time" laws was modest. If, in the opinion of prison authorities, inmates maintained an institutional record of hard work and good conduct, they could be released after a shorter period than that imposed by the sentencing court. The purposes of the laws, however, were somewhat more complex. They were attempts to assist in the reformation of criminals, combined with endeavors to mitigate the severity of the penal codes; to solve the problems of prison discipline; and to get good work from inmates, thereby increasing the profits of the prison industries and contract labor.[64]

The first "good time" law was passed in New York in 1817. It provided that first-term prisoners on sentences of five years or less could reduce their sentences by one-fourth for good behavior. Although the New York statute was not immediately put into practice, shortly after

Parole: The status of being released from a penal or reformatory institution in which one has served a part of his or her maximum sentence, on the condition of maintaining good behavior and remaining in the custody and under the guidance of the institution or some other agency approved by the state until a final discharge is granted.

The purposes of parole

"Good time" laws

● EXHIBIT 17.7 ●

A Parole Agreement

STATE OF CONNECTICUT
BOARD OF PAROLE

PAROLE AGREEMENT

You have been granted a parole by the Board of Parole. It will be effective on the date indicated or as soon thereafter as your parole program is approved by the Division of Parole.

Parole gives you the opportunity to serve the remainder of your sentence outside of the institution. The Board of Parole may grant you a certificate of early discharge from your sentence at the recommendation of your parole officer after you have shown satisfactory progress while you are on parole. Until that time, or until the maximum expiration date of your sentence, you will remain in the legal custody of the Board of Parole and under the supervision of the Division of Parole of the Department of Correction.

A parole officer will be assigned to work with you and help you to adjust to life in the community. The parole officer will attempt to help you and will be available for counseling should any problems arise. You are urged to talk over any difficulties with the parole officer. The parole officer will also submit reports on your progress to the Commissioner of Correction, and, if requested, to the Board of Parole.

It is also the parole officer's duty to make sure that you abide by the conditions of parole found on the other side of this page. Those conditions have been carefully designed as guidelines for acceptable behaviour while you are on parole. If you should violate any of those conditions of parole, the officer has the authority from the Chairman of the Board of Parole and the Commissioner of Correction to return you to custody so that your parole status may be reviewed by the Board of Parole. By signing your name to the other side of this page you indicate your consent to abide by the standard and individual conditions of your parole listed there, as well as your awareness that failure to abide by those conditions will constitute a violation of parole and may result in your return to custody.

It is the hope of the Board of Parole in granting you this parole that you will accept it and its conditions as an opportunity to prove to yourself and to others that you are capable of living as a responsible, law-abiding citizen of society and of your community.

midcentury more than half the states had provisions for time off for good behavior. Then, in 1869 Michigan adopted the first indeterminate sentencing law. In 1876, as a result of the efforts of Elmira Reformatory warden Zebulon Brockway, similar legislation was passed in New York. Under its provisions, an offender could be released at such time that his behavior demonstrated that he could be returned to society. Since the offender was being released prior to the expiration of sentence, special provisions were made for community supervision, and thus parole became a reality. By the second decade of the twentieth century, most states had indeterminate sentencing laws, and the nature of parole as it is understood today had become firmly established.[65]

Parolee _____ No. _____ Release on or after _____

CONDITIONS OF PAROLE

1. Upon my release I will report to my parole officer as directed and follow the parole officer's instructions.
2. I will report to my parole officer in person and in writing whenever and wherever the parole officer directs.
3. I agree that the parole officer has the right to visit my residence or place of employment at any reasonable time.
4. I will maintain such gainful employment or other activity as approved by my parole officer.
5. I will notify my parole officer within forty-eight hours of any changes in my place of residence, in my place of employment, or of any change in my marital status.
6. I will notify my parole officer within forty-eight hours if at any time I am arrested for any offense.
7. I will not at any time have firearms, ammunition, or any other weapon in my possession or under my control.
8. I will not leave the State of Connecticut without prior permission of my parole officer.
9. I will obey all laws, and to the best of my ability fulfill all my legal obligations.
10. I will not at any time use, or have in my possession or control, any illegal drug or narcotic.
11. Your release on parole is based upon the conclusion of the Parole Panel that there is a reasonable probability that you will live and remain at liberty without violating the law and that your release is not incompatible with the welfare of society. In the event that you engage in conduct in the future which renders this conclusion no longer valid, then your parole will be revoked or modified accordingly.
12. I also agree to abide by the following INDIVIDUAL CONDITIONS:

Signed _____

Witness _____ Date _____

For the Board of Parole _____

Chairman   *Secretary*

Parole Administration

The terms *parole* and *probation* have often been mistakenly used interchangeably, but as is already apparent, there are many differences between the two. Probation involves a sentence by the court to community supervision in lieu of imprisonment; parole is a conditional release from a correction institution after a period of imprisonment has already been served. Beyond this preliminary distinction, there are numerous administrative differences. First, the authority to both grant and revoke probation falls within the realm of the lower courts. The authority to grant and revoke parole is held by an administrative board that can be (1) an

Parole versus probation

independent state agency, (2) a unit within some larger state department, or (3) the same body that regulates the state's correctional institutions. Second, the supervision of probationers can be the function of a single court, a county agency, a state department or division, or some combination thereof in any given jurisdiction. Parole supervision services, however, are under the authority of a single state agency in all instances but are not necessarily under the leadership of the parole board.

The advantages and disadvantages of the various models of parole administration have been heavily debated. As to which model is actually followed, however, is generally a matter of state politics. In recent years, as both parole and correctional agencies have become more professionalized, the trend has been to combine administration of the two.

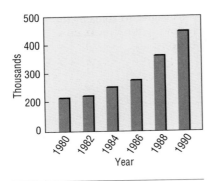

Parolees in the U.S., 1981–1990

SOURCE: Bureau of Justice Statistics

The Parole Board   The functions of parole boards are essentially fourfold: (1) to select and place prisoners on parole; (2) to provide continuing control over parolees in the community; (3) to discharge parolees from supervision when they complete their sentences; (4) to review parole violations and determine whether revocation and return to prison is appropriate. Thus the overall task of the parole board is the implementation of indeterminate sentencing.

Since parole boards make decisions on parole release and revocation, as well as create policy regarding planning and supervision services, it seems logical that the efficiency and viability of the entire parole system depends on the qualifications, skill, and experiences of the members of the board. The American Correctional Association recommended that parole board members command respect and public confidence; be appointed without reference to creed, color, or political affiliation; possess academic training that would qualify them for their professional practice; and have intimate knowledge of the common situations and problems confronting offenders.[66] To these, the National Advisory Commission on Criminal Justice Standards and Goals added:

No single professional group or discipline can be recommended as ideal for all parole board members. A variety of goals are to be served by parole board members, and a variety of skills are required. Knowledge of at least three basic fields should be represented on a parole board: the law, the behavioral sciences, and corrections. Furthermore, as a board assumes responsibility for policy articulation, monitoring and review, the tasks involved require persons who are able to use a wide range of decision-making tools, such as statistical materials, reports from professional personnel, and a variety of other technical information. In general, persons with sophisticated training and experience are required.[67]

However, surveys sponsored by the American Correctional Association and the National Council on Crime and Delinquency indicate that qualifications such as these are required by statute in only a minority of jurisdictions.[68] Independent observations have shown that in a number of states, some parole board members have had *no* exposure to the criminal justice system or offender problems prior to their appointments. This seemed to be especially the case in two selected jurisdictions where decision making was in the hands of part-time boards. Board membership included physicians, ministers, retail sales clerks, and small business operators — most of whom had an interest in correctional issues but few of whom had training or experience in law, social work, corrections, or related skills. This should not suggest, however, that all parole board members are ill-equipped for the responsibilities they share. Quite the contrary: there are many whose career experiences include law, probation, and parole, plus graduate degrees in one or more of the social or behavioral sciences.

Parole Officers

The characteristics of parole officers, or "agents" as they are referred to in some jurisdictions, vary as widely as those of board members. Some states require a graduate degree in an appropriate field; others expect only a high school diploma. Furthermore, what has already been stated regarding probation officers can be applied to parole officers, for in many ways the requirements and skills are similar. This is especially the case in such states as Delaware and South Carolina, where both probationers and parolees are supervised by the same individuals and agency.

Eligibility for Parole   There are numerous statutory restrictions on the granting of parole. As a result, inmates are not automatically paroled as a matter of right. Parole eligibility, then, refers to the earliest date that an inmate can be considered for parole. However, due to the nature of their offenses and sentences, some prisoners can never be paroled.

A key factor in the determination of parole eligibility are the statutes regarding "good time." "Good time" refers to the number of days deducted from a sentence for good behavior, meritorious service, particular kinds of work, or other considerations. Some states have a fixed formula for allocating "good time," such as two or three days for each month served. In others it is left to the discretion of the prison authorities, but cannot exceed a certain portion of the term imposed by the court. "Good time," however, is not a matter of right; it must be earned, and as noted in the discussion of prison disciplinary proceedings, it can be forfeited for poor behavior.

The Parole Hearing   Parole hearings are generally private and are attended only by the inmate, the board, a representative of the institution in which the inmate is incarcerated, and a stenographer or stenotypist to record the proceedings. The board reviews the inmate's case as well as any institutional reports that may have been submitted; questions the inmate regarding his or her adjustment, plans if released, and perhaps

Who are the Best Parole Risks?

Who, indeed, do the best on parole without repeating the crimes for which they were initially convicted? Rapists? Robbers? Prostitutes? Burglars? Check forgers? Shoplifters? Who?

Actually, it's none of the above. Quite surprisingly, the answer is murderers. There are several explanations. Many murderers tend to be first offenders who have committed crimes of passion and emotion. Another explanation is *age*: since the majority of convicted murderers serve long prison sentences, they tend to be older when released — well beyond the high-crime-risk years of adolescence and young adulthood. Finally, the so-called "felony murderers" — the killers-for-hire, robber-murderers, and serial killers — who one would expect to be repeaters never really get the chance, at least not on the street. Most of these end up on death row, or receive terms of life without parole.

the circumstances of the instant offense; and then offers the inmate an opportunity to make a statement on his or her own behalf. The inmate is then dismissed, and the board discusses the case and makes its decision.

The specific procedures used by different boards vary. In years past, one board member examined the institutional records and interviewed each inmate under consideration. He or she would then make a recommendation, and the entire board would either ratify or modify the recommendation in an executive session. Currently, several models exist. Some boards meet *en banc* for every case; others break up into groups to hold hearings in different parts of the jurisdiction. Since the mid-1970s, the U.S. Board of Parole and many of the larger states have been using hearing examiners, who make recommendations on which the board acts. Regardless of the particular procedure, parole authorities have been given wide discretion as to how hearings are actually conducted. This discretion, furthermore, has been uniformly supported by the courts. In *Menechino* v. *Oswald,*[69] decided by the U.S. court of appeals in 1970, the petitioner argued that his due-process rights had been violated by the general manner in which his parole hearing had been conducted. He claimed that the Constitution required that he be given:

Menechino v. Oswald

1. notice
2. fair hearing with right to counsel, cross-examination, and presentation of witnesses
3. specification of the reasons used by the parole board in its determination

The court, however, ruled that the due-process clause did not apply to parole hearings since inmates, who are already imprisoned, do not have "present private interests" that require protection. The following year, though, the court did hold that written reasons for the denial of parole must be given to an inmate.[70] Finally, in 1979, the U.S. Supreme Court in *Greenholtz* v. *Inmates of Nebraska Penal and Correctional Complex* affirmed previous decisions that parole hearings need not have all the elements of due process that are required at criminal trials.[71]

In *Greenholtz* v. *Inmates of Nebraska Penal and Correctional Complex*, the Supreme Court ruled that parole hearings need not have all the elements of due process that are required at criminal trials.

Parole Selection   An overview of contemporary parole practice suggest that many release decisions often reflect variable, arbitrary, and sometimes whimsical standards. A variety of legislative mandates, for example, express the vague policy that a prisoner should be paroled only when such action is not incompatible with the welfare of the community.[72] More specific criteria have included such factors as the offender's prior criminal record, his personality and physical condition, social history, employment record, intelligence, family status, institutional conduct, parole plan, prior probation or parole history, and his stated intentions for the future, among others. Yet questions exist as to how these variables should be weighted in determining if or when a prisoner should be released. Factors that are deemed significant may be emphasized although they may indeed have no significance at all.

In a number of settings the decision to release falls within a political arena. The recommendations of a sentencing judge, a prosecuting attorney, or an active press can invariably affect the paroling process when such gestures have implications for the political power base held by a member of the parole board. Moreover, in some state jurisdictions and the federal system, crime victims are permitted to testify at the release hearings of inmates convicted of victimizing them—a practice with a probable impact on parole decision making.

Selection decisions that emerge from such a nexus of policy, autocracy, and whim typically fall within the spectrum of "intuitive prognosis," "common sense," expediency, and hunch. The members of a paroling board *guess,* or give their premonitory feeling on a minimum of information submitted to them; they may observe potential candidates and make predictions based on insight, intuition, and inductive assumption; or they may examine various types of more or less scientific data to arrive at a decision. Further confounding this process is the inclination to rest decisions on a majority rule or, in some jurisdictions, on unanimous verdict.

Finally, predictions of human behavior are especially problematic when the subjects under review have already demonstrated a reduced capacity to function in a socially approved manner. Selection decisions may totally bypass *all* those considered less likely to succeed. Indeed, conservative parole boards have been known to release only those prisoners who are seen to be good risks while denying parole to the remainder.[73]

Statistical Prediction Methods

Scientific **parole prediction** emerged as an attempt to inject some degree of precision into the selection of prospective parolees. The goal was to increase the number of conditional releases to those likely to succeed, and to reduce the numbers granted to those likely to fail.

Essentially, parole prediction refers to "the estimate of probability of violation or nonviolation of parole on the basis of experience tables, developed with regard to groups of offenders possessing similar characteristics."[74] An *experience table* summarizes the postinstitutional experience of a given release group. The table classifies offenders by their admission characteristics and uses only those characteristics that are the most differentiating as to postrelease response or adjustment in an aftercare setting. The experience table is similar to an actuarial table, which calculates or estimates insurance risks, but rather than indicating mortality or morbidity rates for each type of person, it points to violation or recidivism rates.[75]

However, *parole prediction tables do not predict,* and for a variety of reasons. First, they are often heavily based on factors present in the inmate's social situation prior to arrest, and thus generally do not include postsentence variables such as institutional behavior and relationships. Second, they cannot anticipate differences in parole officers' attitudes and willingness to revoke parole. Third, they are based on data from presentence reports, a portion of which is of questionable accuracy. Fourth, the solely empirical approach of prediction methods is weakened by the absence of any theoretical basis for selecting particular variables for their predictive accuracy. In the final analysis, then, statistical prediction methods seem to generate the same level of accuracy as the success rate in parole systems not using such methods.[76]

American Law Institute Guidelines

Given the lack of specific criteria for parole decision making in many jurisdictions, combined with the weakness in the various prediction methods, the American Law Institute in its *Model Penal Code* has suggested an alternative approach. Rather than determining who should be paroled, the emphasis should be on who ought *not* to be paroled, using the following primary reasons for denial:

Parole prediction: An estimate of probability of violation or nonviolation of parole on the basis of experience tables, developed with regard to groups of offenders possessing similar characteristics.

Parole prediction tables do not predict

1. There is a substanial risk that he will not conform to the conditions of parole.
2. His release at that time would depreciate the seriousness of his crime or promote disrespect for law.
3. His release would have substantially adverse effect on institution discipline.
4. His continued correctional treatment, medical care, or vocational or other training in the institution would substantially enhance his capacity to lead a law-abiding life when released at a later date.[77]

Even this, however, has problems, since it includes no criteria for determining when the inmate denied parole should ultimately be released.

Mandatory Release One final matter here is the issue of repeated denials of parole in spite of an inmate's eligibility for conditional release. It is not uncommon, for example, for a parole board to request a recommendation from the district attorney or chief prosecutor from the county in which a defendant was convicted. Depending on the nature of the case, the prosecutor's parole recommendation can influence the board's decision. Similarly, there can be opposition to an inmate's parole by the police, the news media, the victims of the crime, and the public at large. Consider, for example, the case of Richard Speck, convicted and sentenced to a life term for the brutal murder of eight student nurses in Chicago in 1966. Given the sentiment of Illinois residents and the agitation of the victims' families, Speck's bids for parole were repeatedly denied, and he died in prison on December 5, 1991. For similar reasons, it is likely that Sirhan Sirhan (Robert F. Kennedy's assassin) and Charles Manson will never be paroled.

In less notorious cases, where inmates are serving indeterminate sentences and parole is repeatedly denied, or certain types of definite ("flat") sentences, another factor comes into play—"good time" credits. As noted earlier, **good time** refers to the number of days deducted from a sentence for good behavior, meritorious service, particular kinds of work, or other considerations. Moreover, good time falls into three categories. There is *statutory good time* that is given automatically when inmates serve their time without problems. In addition, there is *earned time* for participation in work, educational, or treatment programs. In a few jurisdictions there is *meritorious time,* earned for some exceptional act or service (such as fire fighting or other life-saving efforts).

As indicated in Exhibit 17.8, almost all jurisdictions provide for some type of good time, ranging from 4.5 days per month in the federal system to 75 days a month in Alabama.[78] Although the maximum number of good time days are fixed by statute, in some jurisdictions "earned time" credits are applied beyond this upper limit. In Florida, for example, where there is no parole and the maximum amount of good time is thirty days per month, in 1990 inmates were serving an average of less than a third of their original sentences.[79] Florida correctional officials explained in 1991 that despite the statutory limitations, most drug offenders were earning time off at a five days for every day served.[80]

The accumulation of good time days ultimately results in **mandatory release**—release as a matter of law. In New York and Missouri, inmates who are mandatory releases are subject to the same conditions as parolees and are under the supervision of a parole officer. In all other jurisdictions, however, mandatory release is *unconditional.*

Conditions of Parole

As with probationers, all individuals released on parole are released under a series of conditions, the violation of which can result in revoca-

Richard Speck, before his death in 1991, had been denied parole repeatedly. The families of his victims, eight student nurses whom he had stabbed and strangled in a Chicago townhouse in 1966, had carried on a constant battle to keep Speck from being paroled, making emotional appearances at his yearly parole hearings. In 1990, the Illinois Prisoner Review Board received more than twenty-one thousand signatures opposing Speck's parole. He died in prison from heart failure, at age forty-nine.

Good time: The number of days deducted from a sentence for good behavior, meritorious service, particular kinds of work, or other considerations.

Call it good time, gain time, earned time, statutory time, meritorious time or commutation time. Identify it as provisional credits, good conduct credits, disciplinary credits. Whatever the term, it's corrections' carrot for good behavior, and a mangement tool of long standing in the United States prisons.

—Su Park Davis, 1990

Mandatory release: A release from prison required by statute when an inmate has been confined for a time period equal to his or her full prison sentence minus statutory "good time" if any.

• EXHIBIT 17.8 •

Good Time Laws in the U.S.

More than 30 days a month
Alabama
Colorado
Illinois
Mississippi
North Carolina
Oklahoma
South Carolina
Texas

30 days a month
Arkansas
California
Florida
Indiana
Louisiana
Montana
New Mexico
Virginia
West Virginia

20 days a month
Iowa
Massachusetts
Nevada
New Jersey
Ohio

15 days a month
Arizona
Connecticut
Delaware
District of Columbia
Kentucky
Maine
Minnesota
Nebraska
Rhode Island
South Dakota
Vermont
Washington
Wyoming

Less than 15 days a month
Alaska
Federal Bureau of Prisons
Michigan (disciplinary credits)
Missouri
New Hampshire
New York
North Dakota
Oregon

No good time given
Georgia
Hawaii
Idaho
Pennsylvania
Utah
Wisconsin

Maximum amount of good time given, including both statutory (good behavior) and meritorious (earned good time). (All states' provisions translated to an approximate equivalent per month.)

States not responding to survey: Kansas, Maryland and Tennessee

SOURCE: *Corrections Compendium*, May 1990

---

tion and return to prison. These are the "dos and don'ts" of parole, and they originated under the ticket-of-leave system.

Parole conditions are fairly uniform from state to state and can be grouped into two general areas: *reform conditions,* which urge parolees toward a noncriminal way of life; and *control conditions,* which enable the parole agency to keep track of them. The most common conditions include the following:

Reform Conditions:

Comply with the laws.

Maintain employment and support dependents.

Refrain from use of drugs.

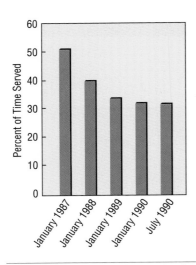

Average Percent of Sentence Served for all Florida Inmates Released

SOURCE: *CORRECTIONS COMPENDIUM*, September 1991

Control Conditions:

Report to parole officer upon release and periodically thereafter.

Cooperate with the parole officer.

Get permission (or notify) to change employment or residence.

In addition, as with probationers, there may be special conditions of parole geared to the particular treatment and control needs of a given person.

In many jurisdictions, the list of parole regulations tends to be extreme, designed to control almost every aspect of the parolee's life. Since 1970, however, a number of states, such as Alaska, Connecticut, Massachusetts, and Ohio, have abandoned a number of the restrictions, including regulations on marriage and divorce, association with undesirables, motor vehicle usage, and alcohol use. Until the late 1960s, the conditions of parole in New York included a prohibition against "having sexual relations with anyone other than your lawful spouse." This restriction allegedly crept into the New York rules as a result of the moralistic Irish Catholic influence that dominated that system during its early years. However, such a condition was considered unreasonable and unenforceable, and both parolees and parole officers alike tended to ignore it. On the other hand, some conditions have been abolished because they were violations of broad constitutional rights. In *Hyland* v. *Procunier,*[81] for example, a condition that required a parolee to secure permission before making a public speech was ruled invalid. Similarly, in *Sobell* v. *Reed,*[82] the court struck down a rule that denied a parolee the right to make an antiwar speech. In both cases, the courts held that conditions that impinged upon First Amendment rights of free speech were beyond the parole authority.

Parole Supervision and Services

Like probation officers, parole officers are responsible for supervising, aiding, and controlling the clients assigned to their case loads. As counselors, officers serve to ease parolees' reentry into society and to aide them in overcoming any obstacles to community adjustment. In addition to individual counseling, they may help in the development of employment plans and job readiness, work with families in the resolution of problems, and orchestrate referrals to community agencies for the handling of certain persistent difficulties. Some parole agencies have special units that focus on such areas as alcoholism, drug use, and unemployment, or on the more unique concerns presented in the supervision of mentally ill or retarded offenders.

Parole officers, on the other hand, also have conflicting roles. In addition to being counselors, they have the duty to police the behavior of those under their supervision. In many other states, parole officers are armed peace officers, and as such, as one officer put it:

It's a rather contradictory bag to be in. We're what you might call "gun-carrying social workers." Or better yet, how about if we refer to it as the discipline of "authoritarian casework"?[83]

Although quasi–law enforcement responsibilities are apparent in probation supervision, they are considerably more pronounced with respect to parole. Parolees tend to be more dangerous and serious offenders. Many have been incarcerated for long periods of time, with intensive exposure to prison violence and the inmate culture. Furthermore, the stigma of the ex-con label and former inmate status lessen the potential for community adjustment. All of these combine to stress the law enforcement role of the parole officer and hinder the effective pursuit of rehabilitative goals.

Parole Violation and Revocation

The violation and revocation process in parole is very similar to that described for probation. After a new arrest or serious technical violation, a warrant is issued and the parolee is taken into custody. Pursuant to the Supreme Court decision in *Morrissey* v. *Brewer,* the delinquent parolee is given a measure of due process during his or her preliminary and revocation hearings, and the parole board can make one of two decisions: "restore to supervision" or "return to prison."

Should parole be revoked, the next issue involves exactly how much time the parolee must serve in prison. This decision is made by the parole board either at the revocation hearing or during the next board meeting at the institution. A bitterly disputed matter in this regard is whether *"street time"* — the period spent under parole supervision prior to violation — should be credited against the remaining sentence. In some jurisdictions, the parole board establishes the violator's "date of delinquency" — the point at which the violation occurred. From that date on, any time served on the street is considered *"dead time."* Thus, if an inmate with a fifteen-year sentence is paroled after three years, serves two years in the community in good standing but is then declared delinquent, five years of his sentence will be considered as having been completed. The parole board may put a three-year "hold" on him, meaning that he will be eligible for parole consideration in three years. However, in other jurisdictions, the time spent on the street in good standing is not credited in this manner.

This issue has also been addressed with respect to probation violation, and in regard to both probation and parole revocation, the denial of street-time credit represents a nonjudicial increase in sentence. This argument notwithstanding, the courts have consistently upheld the right of states to deny street-time credits. They have done so on the theory that since the probationer or parolee was not physically in custody, he was not "serving a sentence."[84]

"Street time"

"Dead time"

Parole Discharge

Individuals can be discharged from parole in a number of ways. First, they can "max out." That is, they can reach their **maximum expiration date** — the date that their entire full sentence formally terminates. Second, in more than half the states and the federal system, parolees can be discharged by the parole board prior to their maximum expiration date. In this instance, however, a number of jurisdictions require that some minimum parole period must be served. In Ohio, for example, discharge can occur after one year of satisfactory supervision, and after five years in the case of a life sentence. Under New York's *executive clemency* statute, if the time remaining on the maximum sentence at the time of parole is more than five years, the board can issue a discharge after five consecutive years of satisfactory supervision. Third, discharge can occur through commutation of sentence or pardon by the governor. Pardon also represents the chief mechanism through which the civil rights lost upon conviction and imprisonment can be restored in about half the states. In the

Maximum expiration date: The date on which the full sentence ends.

Executive clemency

balance, they are automatically restored upon release from the penitentiary, discharge from parole, or at the final expiration of sentence. In Hawaii, Indiana, Massachusetts, Michigan, and New Hampshire, however, a defendant's civil rights are not lost upon conviction of a felony offense.[85]

TRENDS IN COMMUNITY-BASED CORRECTION

As of January 1991, the prison population in the United States was approaching 800,000. This represented an increase of 55 percent since 1985 and an almost 140 percent since 1980. At the beginning of the 1990s, there were more than 450,000 parolees and mandatory releasees under the supervision of parole authorities, an additional 400,000 under the supervision of various community agencies, plus over 2.5 million under court-ordered probation. Given the overcrowding in contemporary prisons and the pressures on state corrections systems to remedy the unconstitutional conditions of many of their facilities, combined with the trend toward mandatory prison sentences for violent offenders and drug traffickers, the character of inmate populations across America will likely undergo some change. More and more, prisons and penitentiaries will become places for holding the serious criminals, at least for a time, and there will be an increased use of community corrections for other types of offenders. Thus probation, court diversion, and other forms of community-based supervision and service will become even more significant in the overall correctional spectrum. The criminal justice system has long since begun its attempts to meet this challenge of community-based supervision. However, many issues and alternatives remain problematic, casting considerable doubt over the effectiveness and future use of community supervision.

Furlough and Temporary Release

Furlough: An authorized, unescorted absence from a correctional institution or a specified period of time.

As a generic concept, the **furlough** is an authorized, unescorted absence from a correctional institution for a specified period of time.[86] It is a temporary release from prison granted for the purpose of enabling inmates to reestablish community contacts and family ties on a gradual basis. It has emerged in a variety of forms, including the home furlough, work release, and educational release.

Home Furlough A home furlough is a short leave of absence from the institution, often taken on weekends, and lasting anywhere from twenty-four hours to a week. As defined in the New York State Correction Law:

> "Furlough program" means a program under which eligible inmates may be granted the privilege of leaving the premises of an institution for a period not exceeding seven days for the purpose of seeking employment, maintaining family ties, solving family problems, seeking post-release housing, attending a short-term educational or vocational training course, or for any matter necessary to the furtherance of any such purposes.[87]

The furlough serves a number of rehabilitative, humanitarian, and pragmatic purposes. It is a mechanism of release transition whereby inmates can begin the normalization of family relationships, reestablish contacts with the outside community, and prepare for eventual permanent release. In addition, prison administrators view the furlough as an avenue for better institutional management, feeling that the promise of a home visit for good behavior fosters better compliance with custodial regulations. In settings where conjugal visitation is either impractical or not permitted, the furlough also has the benefit of reducing sexual frustrations among segments of the inmate population.

Virtually unknown before the late 1960s, home furloughs have been adopted by most states as well as the federal system. Eligibility criteria vary, however, from one jurisdiction to the next. In some states, it is a matter of legislative statute and applies only to inmates who are within one year of parole eligibility or conditional release, and who have not been convicted of any escape, absconding, or violent offenses. In others, eligibility is a matter of legislative, judicial, or correctional policy, with the criteria ranging from highly specific to hopelessly vague.[88]

Work Release In many ways similar in concept and purpose to the home furlough, work release is an alternative to total incarceration whereby inmates are permitted to work for pay in the free community but must spend their nonworking hours back at the institution. Work release is not a recent correctional innovation; it was initiated under Wisconsin's Huber Law (introduced by Senator Huber for the temporary release of jailed misdemeanants) in 1913. However, the idea has been only slowly accepted, and it was not until the early 1970s that work release became a widespread correctional practice for felony offenders.[89] Eligibility criteria are similar to those adopted for home furloughs, restricting release to those nearing parole or conditional release who do not represent significant risk to the community.

In addition to the advantages of furloughs in general, work release offers the benefit of potentially reshaping an offender's self-image and

© Copyright Sidney Harris. Reproduced by permission of *Playboy Magazine.*

*"We'll continue this tomorrow. I'm on a work-release program
and I have to be back in my cell by six o'clock."*

• EXHIBIT 17.9 •

Temporary Release from Prison:
Theory and Practice
by Duane C. McBride

Temporary release from prison has a notable history in American corrections. Its justification draws upon a variety of theoretical and empirical traditions that emphasize the importance of maintaining significant, nondeviant roles outside the prison community. Participating in a temporary release program is considered to facilitate reintegration into the social and economic worlds of the general society and thereby reduce the probability of recidivism. In addition, when the release also involves *work*, the offender is afforded opportunities to make restitution, pay fines, support dependents, obtain job training and experience, and perhaps make contacts for permanent employment upon release from prison. It has also been noted that stable, meaningful employment in a *real* job, as opposed to what inmates define as the "make work" jobs in prison, may enhance inmates' feelings of self-worth and may lower the probability of both behavioral problems while in prison and recidivism upon release.

Since their inception, temporary release programs have been controversial. For those who emphasize the societal protection and the punitive purposes of offender management, temporary release programs are seen as providing significant risk to public safety by extending neither sufficient nor stringent enough deterrence. Advocates of temporary release note that most prisoners are in fact paroled or otherwise released after serving their sentences and that it is crucial in the control of an individual's future criminal behavior to encourage enconomic and social integration with the general society. Isolating individuals for long periods of time and then releasing them without viable outside contacts, they argue, does not bode well for successful community integration. From this perspective, temporary release is interpreted to be effective crime control.

Currently, all fifty states, the District of Columbia, and the federal system report at least some type of temporary release. In the majority of jurisdictions, eligible inmates must be on minimum security status, be relatively close to their parole or promoting the process of decarceration. Furthermore, releases can assume some financial responsibilities by paying their own transportation to and from the institution, contributing to their room and board, supplementing any welfare benefits that are being given to their families, and beginning payments on any court-ordered restitution. Thus work release can also serve in the interests of the taxpaying community.

However, work release has been faced with many obstacles to its effective implementation. It has been opposed on the grounds that prisoners take jobs away from law-abiding citizens; releasees have been exploited by some employers who feel that "cons" should not be paid at normal wage levels; and prison-based training has not always been usable in the modern employment market. The distance between many correctional institutions and active job centers has also restricted work release efforts. Most prisons are in isolated rural areas, and it is generally neither feasible nor cost-effective to transport inmates over long distances on a daily basis. This has been mitigated, to some extent, by the housing of inmates nightly in jails and detention centers located near their job sites. Some jurisdictions have provided for residential work release centers. These offer not only living facilities for working inmates,

mandatory release date, and have a good institutional record. The majority of states exclude sex and violent offenders. In some systems, local law enforcement must be notified, and several consider information from the community or victims.

As for the effectiveness of temporary release, surveys of state and federal programs in 1988 and 1989 by the Contact Center in Lincoln, Nebraska, indicated that criminal justice administrators considered temporary release an effective component of correctional management. Yet few evaluations have been comprehensive. Most simply report the percentage of offenders committing new crimes while on release or the recidivism rates subsequent to parole or mandatory release. Based on these criteria, federal and state reports have generally concluded that temporary release programs are effective. A few studies have noted that temporary release programs have positive impacts on inmate morale and community reintegration, as well as on prison management and overcrowding. Not surprisingly, however, the majority of these studies have been criticized for their failure to followup adequate comparison groups of inmates who were *not* placed on temporary release. As such, although temporary release does indeed serve to reduce tensions within prison walls, its effectiveness in community reintegration remains inconclusive.

SOURCES: Contact Center, *Survey: Furloughs Part I & II and Furloughs for Lifers* (Lincoln, Nebraska: Contact Center, 1988): M. Davies, "Determinant Sentencing: Reform in California and Its Impact on the Penal System," *British Journal of Criminology,* 25 (January 1985), pp 1–30; J. F. Katz and S. F. Decker, "Analysis of Work Release: The Institutionalization of Unsubstantiated Reforms," *Criminal Justice and Behavior,* 9 (June 1982), pp. 229–250; W. E. Knox and J. A. Humphrey, "Granting of Work Release," *Criminal Justice and Behavior,* 8 (March, 1981), pp. 55–77; S. Sylvester, "Crime Prevention and Criminal Justice: In Search of a Silver Bullet," *Annals of the American Academy of Political and Social Science,* 494 (November 1987), pp. 119–128; *New York Times* (National edition), October 12, 1988, p. 12; Marjorie Marlette, "Furloughs Tightened, Success Rates High," *Corrections Compendium,* Jaunary–February 1990, pp. 1, 6–8.

but counseling and supervised recreation during evening and weekend hours.

Study Release   As a natural extension of the work release principle, study release is offered to minimum security, parole-eligible inmates with the motivation for vocational or academic enrichment. Following the criteria and regulations of a state's work release project, study release provides opportunities for full-time, onsite participation in vocational school and college programs.

Experiences with Temporary Release   Temporary release programs also have their critics, and crimes committed by inmates on work release or home furlough are quickly made conspicuous. A work release center in New York City came to national attention during the mid-1970s when it was learned that almost half of its residents had either escaped or were returned to prison for disciplinary violations, and that 70 percent of the absconders were ultimately arrested for new crimes.[90] Similarly, the work release project at Chino prison in California was terminated when it was discovered that a number of the participating inmates were engaging in

armed robberies instead of going to work, and that others not actually in the program had somehow obtained weeklong passes out of prison.[91] And during 1988, there were few Americans who were unaware of the name of Willie Horton — sentenced to life without parole in Massachusetts for a homicide in 1974 only to be released on a weekend furlough during which he committed a brutal rape.[92]

In spite of such incidents of bad publicity, the concept of temporary release continues to hold promise as a form of partial incarceration, as a bridge between the prison and open society, and as another treatment mechanism in the spectrum of community-based correctional services. Perhaps many of the difficulties in existing programs might be eliminated, or at least minimized, with better screening of candidates and monitoring of releasees. However, the kind of public outrage that can be generated when even a few isolated violent crimes are comitted by persons who are supposed to be behind bars provides little support for its use as an acceptable correctional tool. This, combined with many unresolved questions as to whether temporary release actually reduces recidivism, and the political realities associated with rehabilitative risk-taking at the potential expense of public safety, suggest only a guarded prognosis for the implementation of such programs on a continuing basis (see Exhibit 17.9).

Partial incarceration, halfway houses, and prerelease centers

In contrast are the *halfway houses* and *prerelease centers* that have been developing since the 1960s. Designed for inmates who are just a few months away from their parole dates, these residential facilities in urban locations provide individual counseling, vocational guidance, and job placement. Residents are required to abide by minimum security regulations, attend counseling and therapy sessions, and actively seek employment when ready.

Whether halfway houses are effective mechanisms for community reintegration is open to question. Studies of their experience found significant levels of escape, recidivism, and returns to prison for disciplinary violations. But, since recidivism seemed to be no higher among prerelease center residents than among other newly released inmates, it was recommended that the halfway house concept be expanded.[93] There seems to be little likelihood that this will occur, however, not only because of the sensitive political nature of the concept, but also due to the opposition of many communities to "placing convicts in our backyards."

New Community-Based Alternatives

In this 1990s era of increased numbers of drug offenders, overloaded prisons, and unmanageable state budget deficits, a number of new and innovative community-based correctional alternatives have become apparent. For example:

Oklahoma's Preparole Conditional Supervision Program

- At the close of the 1980s, Oklahoma established a *Preparole Conditional Supervision Program* as a regular part of the state's correctional process.[94] The program allows prisoners to leave the penitentiary, under strict supervision, before they are eligible for regular parole. *Any inmate* who has completed 15 percent of his or her sentence and is within one year of a regularly scheduled parole eligibility date may be considered for the program. Only those on death row or serving life without parole are excluded. The vast majority of the releasees in the program have histories of substance abuse. All are required to be employed, and pay $20 per month for their supervision, plus restitution and child support where appropriate. Although the new preparole release program alleviated some of the prison crowding in Oklahoma, 26 percent of the offenders released through January 1, 1991 were considered "unsuccessful," primarily for drug use and failure to report.

- Under consideration for drug offenders in a number of jurisdictions are joint ventures between parole systems and Treatment Alternatives to Street Crime (TASC) programs. TASC, as described earlier in Exhibit 17.1, can be structured to both enhance and complement parole supervision in a number of ways.[95]

  (1) In the area of *preparole screening,* TASC assists the institutional correctional system in its role as a specialist in the identification and assessment of drug-involved offenders. Preparole screenings conducted through TASC tend to provide more comprehensive background data on drug abuse and related behaviors upon which to make informed release decisions.

  (2) In the area of *service delivery,* TASC offers advantages for both corrections and parole. TASC case managers specialize in developing and implementing aftercare plans for drug-involved offenders. In addition to drug abuse treatment, TASC provides urine monitoring, employment advocacy, client referral to other segments of the local human service delivery network, and follow up. As such, treatment and support services can be offered within a "clinical" rather than a "correctional" setting.

  (3) In the area of *clinical efficacy,* the literature suggests that TASC would represent an effective adjunct to parole. In this regard, a variety of research efforts have documented that: a) the key variable most related to successful outcome in drug treatment is *length of stay in treatment;* and, b) clients coerced into treatment tend to stay longer than those admitted voluntarily.[96] The TASC model, as a variety of coerced treatment, has been proven effective in retaining clients in treatment, in that TASC clients remain in treatment longer than noncriminal justice system referrals.[97]

  (4) In the area of *alleviating prison crowding,* TASC can assist in two ways. First, by relying on a TASC recommendation for treatment, scarce treatment slots can be allocated to those drug users most in need of, and responsive to, treatment. An accurate assessment of client need will increase the chances of success in treatment while reducing the chances of relapse and future criminal behavior, arrest, and incarceration. Second, TASC aids the parolee in successfully completing his/her term of supervision. Periodic urine tests, site visits, and case conferences tend to become a useful deterrent fostering program compliance.

- Perhaps the newest and most unique community-based correctional strategy is *Delaware's Crest Outreach Center,* the nation's first dedicated therapeutic community work release center (see Exhibit 17.10). Perhaps most interesting about Crest is that it is a state correctional facility operated totally by a university department, by university faculty and staff.

TASC and Parole

Delaware's Crest Outreach Center

● EXHIBIT 17.10 ●

Crest Outreach Center, and the Staging of Corrections-Based Therapeutic Community Treatment for Drug Offenders

Research and experience with correctional systems and populations, with corrections-based drug treatment, and with the evaluation of a whole variety of correctional programs suggest that the most appropriate strategy for effective therapeutic community (TC) intervention with inmates would involve a three-stage process. Each stage in this regimen of treatment should correspond to the inmate's changing correctional status—incarceration, work release, and parole (or whatever other form of community-based correction operates in a given jurisdiction).

A Crest resident shares a verbal "learning experience" with other residents.

The *primary stage* should consist of a prison-based therapeutic community designed to facilitate personal growth through the modification of deviant lifestyles and behavior patterns. Segregated from the rest of the penitentiary, recovery from drug abuse, and the development of pro-social values in the prison TC would involve essentially the same mechanisms seen in other therapeutic community settings.

The initial freedom after release from prison exposes many inmates to groups and behaviors that can easily lead them back to substance abuse, criminal activities, and reincarceration. Even those receiving intensive thera-

peutic community treatment while in the institution face the prospect of their recovery breaking down. Work release environments in most jurisdictions do little to stem the process of relapse. Since work release populations mirror the institutional populations from which they came, there are still the negative values of the prison culture. In addition, street drugs and street norms tend to abound. Thus, a *secondary stage* of TC treatment is warranted. This secondary

stage is a transitional TC—the therapeutic community work release center or "halfway house."

In the *tertiary stage,* clients will have completed work release and will be living in the free community under the supervision of parole or some other surveillance program. Treatment intervention in this stage should involve out-patient counseling and group therapy. Clients should be encouraged to return to the work release TC for refresher/reinforcement sessions,

Abolish Parole?

In 1938, FBI Director J. Edgar Hoover commented that the biggest job of law enforcement was the chasing down of the "canny recidivists," "mad dogs," and "predatory animals" who have been "cloaked by the mantle of parole."[98] In response to Hoover and other critics of parole, the late Edwin H. Sutherland wrote in 1947:

Although Crest is a community-based correctional facility, residents view themselves as members of a family and look to one another for help in their recovery.

to attend weekly groups, to call on their counselors on a regular basis, and to participate in monthly one-on-one and/or family sessions. They should also be required to spend one day each month at the program, and a weekend retreat every three months.

During the closing months of 1990, the Center for Drug and Alcohol Studies at the University of Delaware was awarded a five-year NIDA treatment demonstration grant to establish such a

work release therapeutic community. Known as "Crest Outreach Center," it has been designed to incorporate the three-stage treatment process just outlined. Such a staging process is possible since a prison-based therapeutic community already exists in Delaware.

The treatment regimen at Crest Outreach Center follows a five-phase model over a six-month period:

Phase One is composed of entry, assessment and evaluation, and orientation, and lasts approximately two weeks.

Phase Two emphasizes involvement in the TC community, including such activities as morning meetings, work, group therapy, one-on-one interaction, confrontation of other clients who are not motivated toward recovery, and the nurturing of the newer people in the environment. This phase lasts approximately eight weeks.

Phase Three continues the elements of Phase Two, and stresses role modeling and overseeing the working of the community on a daily basis (with the support and supervision of the clinical staff), and lasts for approximately five weeks.

Phase Four initiates preparation for gainful employment, including on mock interviews, and seminars on job seeking, making the best appearance when seeing a potential employer, developing relationships with community agencies, and looking for ways to further educational or vocational abilities. This phase lasts approximately two weeks.

Phase Five focuses on reentry, i.e., becoming gainfully employed in the outside community while continuing to live in the facility and serving as a role model for those at earlier stages of treatment. At the end of approximately seven weeks, which represents a total of twenty-six weeks at Crest Outreach Center, residents have completed their work release commitment and are free to live and work in the community as program graduates.

In all phases of treatment at Crest, urine is monitored on a regular, however unscheduled basis. Most interestingly, although *all* work releases are under the supervision and custody of Delaware Department of Correction, Crest Outreach Center is operated by University of Delaware personnel. There is no "correctional presence" at Crest.

All Crest "graduates" are urged to periodically return to the facility, to participate in the groups, the one-on-one interactions, family sessions, and retreats that represent stage three of prison-based TC treatment.

SOURCE: James A. Inciardi, Dorothy Lockwood, Steven S. Martin, and Bruce M. Wald, "Therapeutic Communities in Corrections and Work Release: Some Clinical and Policy Considerations," *National Institute on Drug Abuse Technical Review Meeting on Therapeutic Community Treatment Research,* Bethesda, Maryland, May 16–17, 1991.

The antagonism toward parole is probably greater than toward any other penal policy. This is surprising, for there is no well-known student of penology who is not wholeheartedly in favor of the principle of parole, and who does not insist that parole in practice is better than any available alternative in practice. These students insist, first, that parole should be evaluated not as an abstract principle but in comparison with the only available alternative, which is the determination in court at the time of the trial of the definite date of release, and the complete release at that time without subsequent supervision. They insist, second, that those who are released on parole serve at least as long inside prison walls for a specific type of crime as do those sentenced on definite terms, and in addition remain under supervision outside the prison for periods which generally range from one to three years, and that parole therefore is not leniency but on the contrary is more severe and is a better method of protecting society against crime than the alternative method. They insist, third, that persons released from prison on parole do not commit more crimes than persons released at the expiration of sentences without supervision, for the same offenses.[99]

Arguments about parole

Arguments about parole still persist. In 1971, for example, as a conclusion to its study of criminal justice in America, the American Friends Service Committee called for the abolition of parole.[100] The former U.S. Bureau of Prisons Director Norman Carlson, Attorney General Griffin Bell, and Senator Edward M. Kennedy have also argued for the abolition of parole.[101] The reasons of this antiparole position have generally been the same for all opponents:

1. The procedures of parole decision-making are unguided by explicit standards and by traditional elements of due process;
2. The tasks which parole is supposed to perform—the accurate prediction of the offender's likelihood of recidivism, and the monitoring of rehabilitative progress—are beyond our present capacities; and,
3. Aside from questions of effectiveness, it is unjust to base decisions about the severity of punishments on what the offender is expected to do in the future.[102]

Senator Kennedy added that sentencing disparities are compounded by parole, since it encourages some judges to impose the kind of harsh sentences that the community expects. He suggested that if flat or determinate sentencing policies were adopted, parole would not be needed:

Under this system of judicially fixed sentences, parole release would be abolished and whether or not a prisoner has been "rehabilitated" or has completed a certain prison curriculum would no longer have any bearing on his prison release date.[103]

From the perspective, too, of many inmates, parolees, civil libertarians, criminal justice reformers, and informed observers, parole is not without faults. The parolee has often been described as a "walking suspension of the Constitution,"[104] a status that seems to have evolved from the alternative theories upon which the concept of parole is based. First, there is the *grace theory,* which holds that parole is a privilege, a gift from the state and board of parole that must be returned if certain conditions are violated. Second, there is the *custody theory,* which states that parolees, although walking the streets in the free community, are legally in the custody of the parole board. As a result, they remain in a quasi-prisoner status, they are not fully at liberty, and their constitutional rights remain limited and abridged. And finally, there is the *contract theory,* which argues that since parolees are required to agree to certain terms and conditions in return for their conditional freedom, the violation of those conditions represents a "breach of contract," which can result in revocation of parole. As parole antagonist Jessica Mitford has put it, it is "a curious sort of 'contract,' in which one side has all the bargaining powers and in which the contracting parolee, if accused of breaking it, has no redress in the courts."[105]

With this context, one parolee has commented:

Stayskal/Tampa Tribune.

"I'm sentencing you to 25 years in prison with no hope of parole until after 3 p.m. tomorrow afternoon!"

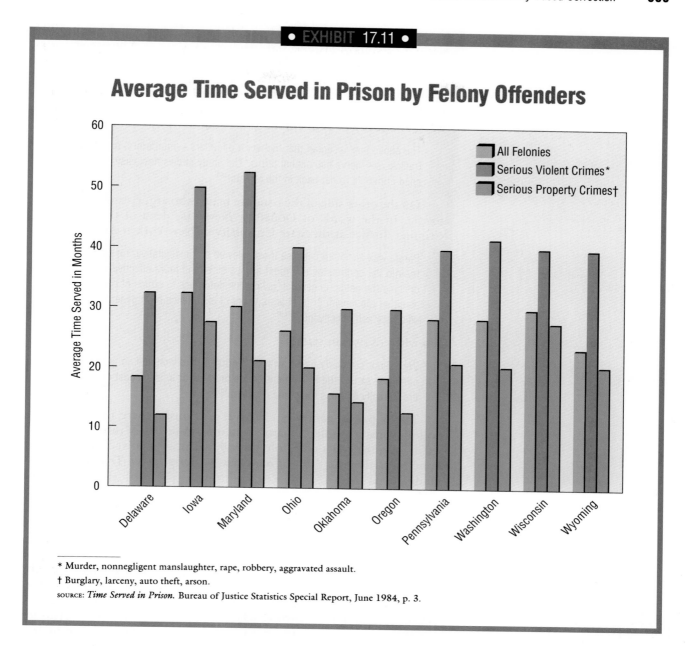

● EXHIBIT 17.11 ●

Average Time Served in Prison by Felony Offenders

Legend:
- All Felonies
- Serious Violent Crimes*
- Serious Property Crimes†

Y-axis: Average Time Served in Months (0–60)

States: Delaware, Iowa, Maryland, Ohio, Oklahoma, Oregon, Pennsylvania, Washington, Wisconsin, Wyoming

* Murder, nonnegligent manslaughter, rape, robbery, aggravated assault.

† Burglary, larceny, auto theft, arson.

SOURCE: *Time Served in Prison.* Bureau of Justice Statistics Special Report, June 1984, p. 3.

They've set up the whole system to make you fail. I guess they have a business going in this state and once they get you hooked into the system they don't want to let you go. They want you to come back. They let you out of here on a yo-yo. You're out there a little while, then they pull the string, zap, you're back. They got a good thing going here, man, can't you see it. They don't want to lose you.[106]

Similarly, another parolee has said:

If your parole officer, or the system, decides that they want you back inside, there's nothing you can do to prevent it. . . . My last time out I was doin' real good—a job, reporting, the whole thing. Then my PO gives me a toss and finds an ad for a toy gun in my pocket. With two "priors" for armed robbery I didn't stand a chance. I was gonna get it for my nephew, but to the board, as they put it, I was "about to lapse into criminal ways and company."[107]

The current system is actually a nonsystem. It defeats the reasonable expectation of the public that a realistic penalty will be imposed at the time of conviction, and that the sentence received will be the sentence served.
—SENATOR EDWARD KENNEDY, 1984

The movement to abolish parole earned renewed vigor in 1984 when the results of a twelve-state study by the Bureau of Justice Statistics documented that the average prison stay for felony offenders was three years or less — with 3.3 to 6.5 years for murderers and 2.1 to 5.3 years for rapists (see Exhibit 17.11).[108] In reaction to the study, U.S. Attorney General William French Smith called for the abolition of parole nation-wide, and further commented:

> The public has assumed that the worst offenders — murderers, rapists, drug traffickers — serve substantial terms. The study shows how easy it is for hard-ened criminals to get back in the streets.[109]

On the other side of the issue are many who argue strongly to retain parole. In the words of Donald J. Newman, dean of the College of Criminal Justice at the State University of New York at Albany:

> Parole was accepted because it was viewed as rehabilitative, for supervised reen-try into the community is almost always safer and more effective than simply opening the gates. In general, giving due deference to critics of parole who see it as either too lenient or too harsh, years of experience have generally proved its efficiency and effectiveness.[110]

Elsewhere Newman stated:

> We cannot cavalierly throw away a reform so hard won and so generally effective simply to satisfy the frustrations of the moment or to scapegoat our deeper fail-ure to really address the crime problem.[111]

But is parole generally effective? Curiously, there have been few comprehensive studies of parole outcome. A review of nineteen studies examining the effect of parole on recidivism, as reported in the highly controversial book, *The Effectiveness of Correctional Treatment,* con-cluded that

> men released on parole are likely to return to prison at a lower rate while on pa-role than men discharged from prison without parole. However, *after release from parole the rate of return to prison is similar to that of dischargees.*[112]

Beyond this rather bleak picture, there has been no recent compre-hensive research on parole effectiveness. Prior studies and other research suggest, however, that parole just may *not* be all that effective. First of all, in studies of parole outcome, how are "success" and "failure" defined? Generally, a failure is anyone who was returned to prison for parole violation, was arrested and convicted for a new offense while under parole supervision, or was an absconder at the time of the follow up. Thus recidivism subsequent to "maxing out" is generally not accounted for. Second, studies have shown that many parole violations that could conceivably result in revocation go undetected.[113] Third, and perhaps most importantly, it has been well documented that official criminal statistics are poor measures of the incidence and prevalence of offense behavior. As pointed out in Chapter 4, arrest rates reflect only a small portion of the crimes actually committed. If the sole measures of parole failure are technical violations, new arrests, and absconding, then little faith can be placed in available rates of parole success.

This argument would certainly serve in the interests of those who wish to abolish parole. Yet to abolish parole at this point would be premature. There are too many unanswered questions. For example, can parole be justified on grounds other than rehabilitation? Are *all* of pa-

role's functions without usefulness? Are there any viable alternatives to parole?

The movement toward parole abolition began during the late 1970s in Maine, and by the 1990s several other jurisdictions had either abolished parole or severely restricted its use. It is unlikely, however, that this trend will move with any due haste in the immediate future. Prisons are already overcrowded, and the inescapable fact is that parole remains one of the few economically viable alternatives to long-term imprisonment.

After serving almost seventeen years on Florida's death row, fifty-five-year-old Howard Douglas was resentenced to a life term in 1991, making him eligible for parole in 1998. In 1973, Douglas had been convicted of the first-degree murder of Jesse Atkins. Atkins' widow opposed the resentencing. "When he's released, he's going to kill me," she commented. "He promised that and I believe him."

SUMMARY

Community-based correction involves programs and activities within the community that are generally of a rehabilitative, nonpunitive nature. Such correctional approaches include criminal justice diversion, probation and conditional release, restitution programs, and furlough and temporary release.

Criminal justice diversion refers to the removal of offenders from the application of the criminal law at any stage of the police or court processes. Diversion as such began with the Chicago Boy's Court in 1914. Today its use is widespread for both juvenile and adult offenders, but its impact is difficult to assess.

The concept of probation emerged in 1841 with the work of John Augustus. Today probation is a status, a system, and a process. As an alternative to imprisonment, it is the most widely used adjudication disposition, encompassing elements of both community protection and offender rehabilitation.

Parole, common in the United States for almost a century, refers to the practice of allowing the final portion of a prison sentence to be served in the community. In contrast to probation, which involves community supervision in lieu of imprisonment, parole occurs after some part of the prison term has been completed.

Both probation and parole are subject to conditions, the violation of which may result in incarceration. The United States Supreme Court, through a series of decisions during the 1970s, has established guidelines regarding the due-process requirements at probation and parole revocation proceedings.

Other forms of community-based corrections include furlough and temporary release programs, restitution, and the use of halfway houses.

KEY TERMS

community-based
  correction (624)
diversion (625)
furlough (660)
Gagnon v. *Scarpelli* (644)
intensive probation
  supervision (642)

good time (656)
mandatory release (656)
maximum expiration date (659)
Mempa v. *Rhay* (644)
Morrissey v. *Brewer* (644)
parole (649)

parole prediction (655)
probation (631)
restitution (638)
shock probation (640)
suspended sentence (632)
Williams v. *New York* (633)

QUESTIONS FOR DISCUSSION

1. What are the differences between probation and parole in terms of organization and administration, eligibility and selection, supervision and services, and conditions and revocation?

2. In *Mempa* v. *Rhay*, why did the Court restrict its ruling on right to counsel to cases involving deferred sentencing?

3. Which would appear to be the more effective form of parole authority structure: an independent parole board or a board housed within the state correctional system? Why?

4. Should parole be abolished? Why?

FOR FURTHER READING

Erwin, Billie S., and Lawrence A. Bennett. "New Dimensions in Probation: Georgia's Experience with Intensive Probation Supervision," National Institute of Justice, *Research in Brief,* January 1987.

Hirsch, Andrew, and Kathleen J. Hanrahan. *Abolish Parole?* Washington, D.C.: U.S. Government Printing Office, 1978.

Leukefeld, Carl G., and Frank M. Tims. *Compulsory Treatment of Drug Abuse: Research and Clinical Practice.* Rockville, MD: National Institute on Drug Abuse, 1988.

Morris, Norval, and Michael Tonry. *Between Prison and Probation: Intermediate Punishments in a Rational Sentencing System.* New York: Oxford University Press, 1990.

NOTES

1. Duane C. McBride, "Criminal Justice Diversion," in *Crime and the Criminal Justice Process,* ed. James A. Inciardi and Kenneth C. Haas (Dubuque, Iowa: Kendall/Hunt, 1978), p. 246.

2. Jacob M. Braude, "Boys' Court: Individualized Justice for the Youthful Offender," *Federal Probation* 12 (June 1948): 9–14.

3. Daniel Glaser, James A. Inciardi, and Dean V. Babst, "Later Heroin Use by Marijuana-Using, Heroin-Using, and Non-Drug-Using Adolescent Offenders in New York City," *The International Journal of the Addictions* 4 (June 1969): 145–155.

4. Leon G. Leiberg, *Project Crossroads: Final Report* (Washington, D.C.: National Committee for Children and Youth, 1971).

5. McBride, "Criminal Justice Diversion," p. 250.

6. *Alcoholism and Drug Abuse Week,* May 22, 1991, pp. 2–3.

7. *Miami Herald,* July 2, 1991, p. 2B.

8. *The Manhattan Court Employment Project: Final Report* (New York: Vera Institute of Justice, 1972).

9. Arnold Schechter and Kenneth Polk, *Youth Service Bureaus, National Evaluation Program, Phase I Assessment* (Washington, D.C.: U.S. Government Printing Office, 1977).

10. National Highway Traffic Administration, *Impact of a Driver Intervention Program on DWI Recidivism and Problem Drinking* (Washington, D.C.: U.S. Department of Transportation, 1985).

11. *National Drug Control Strategy* (Washington, D.C.: The White House: 1992).

12. James A. Inciardi, "Designing Process Evaluations for TASC Programs," *Paper Presented at the TASC Executive Forum,* Key West, August 18–21, 1991; James A. Inciardi, Duane C. McBride, Richard Dembo, and Beth A. Weinman, *Drug Offender Assessment* (Washington, D.C.: Bureau of Justice Assistance, 1992).

13. See John Augustus, *A Report of the Labors of John Augustus, for the Last Ten Years, in Aid of the Unfortunate* (Boston: Wright & Hasty, 1852); reprinted as *John Augustus, First Probation Officer* (New York: National Probation Association, 1939).

14. American Bar Association Project on Standards for Criminal Justice, *Standards Relating to Probation* (New York: Institute for Judicial Administration, 1970), p. 9.

15. National Advisory Commission on Criminal Justice Standards and Goals, *Corrections* (Washington, D.C.: U.S. Government Printing Office, 1973), p. 312.

16. *DOCS Today,* August 1990, p. 5.

17. State of New York, *Penal Law,* 65.05.

18. State of New York, *Penal Law,* 65.20.

19. James A. Inciardi, "The Impact of Presentence Investigations on Subsequent Sentencing Practices," *Paper presented at the Annual Meeting of the American Sociological Association,* August 1976, New York, N.Y.

20. Robert M. Carter and Leslie T. Wilkins, "Some Factors in Sentencing Policy," *Journal of Criminal Law, Criminology, and Police Science* 58 (December 1967): 503–514.

21. *Williams v. New York,* 347 U.S. 241 (1949).

22. *Gardner v. Florida,* 430 U.S. 349 (1977).

23. *Code of Alabama,* 15–22–50.

24. *General Statutes of North Carolina,* 15A–1341 (a).

25. Personal communication, October 1979.

26. *Cox v. States,* 283 S.E. 2d 716 (Ga Ct. App. 1981).

27. *People v. Mitchell,* 178 Cal. Rptr. 188 (Cal. Ct. App., 1981).

28. *State v. Behrens,* 285 N. W. 2d 513 (Neb. Sup. Ct., 1979).

29. *State v. Wilson,* 604 P. 2d 739 (Idaho Sup., 1980).

30. *Wood v. State,* 378 So. 2d 111 (Fla. Dist. Ct. App., 1980).

31. *State v. Alexander,* 267 S. E. 2d 397 (N.C. Ct. App., 1980).

32. *People v. Sprague,* 430 N.Y.S. 2d 260 (N.Y. Sup. Ct. App. Div., 1980).

33. Denny C. Langston, "Probation and Parole: No More Free Rides," *Corrections Today,* August 1988, pp. 90–93.

34. *Griffin v. Wisconsin,* 483 U.S. 868 (1987).

35. See *Barber v. State,* 387 So. 2d 540 (Fla. Dist. Ct. App., 1980).

36. See Gilbert Geis, "Restitution by Criminal Offenders: A Summary and Overview," in *Restitution in Criminal Justice,* ed. Joe Hudson and Burt Galaway (Lexington, Mass.: Lexington, 1977), pp. 246–264.

37. Richard Lawrence, "Restitution Programs Pay Back the Victim and Society," *Corrections Today,* February 1990, pp. 96–98; Michael Courlander, "Restitution Programs: Problems and Solutions," *Corrections Today,* July 1988, pp. 165–167.

38. Personal communication, April 1977.

39. E. Kim Nelson, Howard Ohmart, and Nora Harlow, *Promising Strategies in Probation and Parole* (Washington, D.C.: U.S. Government Printing Office, 1978), pp. 16–17.

40. Paul C. Friday and David M. Petersen, "Shock of Imprisonment: Comparative Analysis of Short-term Incarceration as a Treatment Technique," *Paper presented at the InterAmerican Congress of the American Society of Criminology and the InterAmerican Association of Criminology,* Caracas, Venezuela, November 1972.

41. Friday and Petersen, "Shock of Imprisonment"; Harry E. Allen and Clifford E. Simonsen, *Corrections in America* (New York: Macmillan, 1981), p. 161; Kenyon J. Skudder, "In Opposition to Probation with a Jail Sentence," *Federal Probation* 23 (June 1959): 12–17; National Advisory Commission, *Corrections,* p. 321.

42. Eugene N. Barkin, "Sentencing the Adult Offender," *Federal Probation* 26 (June 1962): 11–16.

43. See David M. Petersen and Paul C. Friday, "Early Release from Incarceration: Race as a Factor in the Use of 'Shock Probation,'" *Journal of Criminal Law and Criminology* 66 (March 1975): 79–87; Joseph A. Waldron and Henry R. Angelino, "Shock Probation: A Natural Experiment on the Effect of a Short Period of Incarceration," *The Prison Journal* 57 (Spring–Summer 1977): 52.

44. Billie S. Erwin and Lawrence A. Bennett, "New Dimensions in Probation: Georgia's Experience with Intensive Probation Supervision," National Institute of Justice, *Research in Brief,* January 1987.

45. Ibid.

46. Susan B. Noonan and Edward J. Latessa, "Intensive Probation: An Examination of Recidivism and Social Adjustment," *American Journal of Criminal Justice,* XI (1987), pp. 45–61. See also, Frank S. Pearson, "Evaluation of New Jersey's Intensive Supervision Program," *Crime and Delinquency,* 34 (October 1988), pp. 437–448.

47. *Intermediate Sanctions: Their Impacts on Prison Crowding, Costs, and Recidivism Are Still Unclear* (Washington, D.C.: General Accounting Office, September 1990).

48. *Villarreal v. State,* 166 Tex. Cr. R. 610, 217 S. W. 2d 207 (1958).

49. *Mempa v. Rhay,* 398 U.S. 128 (1967).

50. *Morrissey v. Brewer,* 408 U.S. 471 (1972).

51. *Gagnon v. Scarpelli,* 411 U.S. 778 (1973).

52. *United States* v. *Reed*, 573 F. 2d 1020 (8th Cir., 1978).

53. *United States* v. *Pattman*, 535 F. 2d 1062 (8th Cir., 1976).

54. *United States* v. *Jurgens*, 626 F. 2d 142 (9th Cir., 1980).

55. *Watson* v. *State*, 388 So. 2d 15 (Fla. Dist. Ct. App., 1980).

56. *United States* v. *Lacey*, 661 F. 2d 1021 (5th Cir., 1981).

57. "Probation and Parole 1990," *Bureau of Justice Statistics Bulletin,* November 1991.

58. For a discussion of probation effectiveness studies, see Harry E. Allen, Chris W. Eskridge, Edward J. Latessa, and Gennaro F. Vito, *Probation and Parole in America* (New York: Free Press, 1985), pp. 256–266.

59. Joan Petersilia, Susan Turner, James Kahan, and Joyce Peterson, *Granting Felons Probation: Public Risk and Alternatives* (Santa Monica, Calif.: Rand, 1985).

60. Johnny McGaha, Michael Fichter, and Peter Hirschburg, "Felony Probation: A Re-Examination of Public Risk," *American Journal of Criminal Justice,* XI (1987), pp. 1–9.

61. G. I. Giardini, *The Parole Process* (Springfield, Ill.: Thomas, 1959), p. 9.

62. Edwin H. Sutherland, *Principles of Criminology* (Philadelphia: J. P. Lippincott, 1947), p. 534.

63. Harry Elmer Barnes, *The Story of Punishment: A Record of Man's Inhumanity to Man* (Montclair, N.J.: Patterson Smith, 1972), pp. 68–80.

64. See E. C. Wines, "Commutation Laws in the United States," *Report of the Prison Association of New York,* 1868, pp. 154–170.

65. See David Dressler, *Practice and Theory of Probation and Parole* (New York: Columbia University Press, 1969), pp. 56–76; Marjorie Bell, ed., *Parole in Principle and Practice* (New York: National Probation and Parole Association, 1957).

66. National Advisory Commission, *Corrections,* p. 399.

67. National Advisory Commission, *Corrections,* p. 399.

68. William Parker, *Parole: Origins, Development, Current Practices and Statutes* (College Park, Md.: American Correctional Association, 1975); Vincent O'Leary and Kathleen J. Hanrahan, *Parole Systems in the United States* (Hackensack, N.J.: National Council on Crime and Delinquency, 1976).

69. *Menechino* v. *Oswald*, 430 F. 2d 403 (2d Cir., 1970).

70. *Johnson, U.S. ex. rel.* v. *Chairman, New York State Board of Parole*, 363 F. Supp. 416, aff'd, 500 F. 2d 925 (2d Cir., 1971).

71. *Greenholtz* v. *Inmates of Nebraska Penal and Correctional Complex*, 422 U.S. 1 (1979).

72. See, for example, *Tennessee Code,* 40–3614.

73. James A. Inciardi and Duane C. McBride, "The Parole Prediction Myth," *International Journal of Criminology and Penology* 5 (August 1977): 235–244.

74. Peter P. Lejins, "Parole Prediction—An Introductory Statement," *Crime and Delinquency* 8 (July 1962): 209–214.

75. James A. Inciardi and Dean V. Babst, "Predicting the Postrelease Adjustment of Institutionalized Narcotic Addicts," *Bulletin on Narcotics* 23 (April–June 1971): 33–39.

76. Inciardi and McBride, "Parole Prediction Myth."

77. Don M. Gottfredson, Peter B. Hoffman, Maurice H. Sigler, and Leslie T. Wilkins, "Making Paroling Policy Explicit," *Crime and Delinquency* 21 (January 1975): 36.

78. Su Park Davis, "Good Time," *Corrections Compendium,* May 1990, pp. 1, 4–11.

79. James Austin, "The Consequences of Escalating the Use of Imprisonment," *Corrections Compendium,* September 1991, pp. 1, 4–8.

80. Personal communication, May 1991.

81. *Hyland* v. *Procunier*, 311 F. Supp. 749 (N.D. Cal., 1970).

82. *Sobell* v. *Reed*, 327 F. Supp. 1294 (S.D. N.Y., 1971).

83. Personal communication, October 1981.

84. See Richard C. Hand and Richard G. Singer, *Sentencing Computation Laws* (Washington, D.C.: American Bar Association, 1974).

85. See O'Leary and Hanrahan, *Parole Systems.*

86. E. Eugene Miller, "Furloughs as a Technique of Reintegration," in *Corrections in the Community,* ed. E. Eugene Miller and M. Robert Montilla (Reston, Va.: Reston, 1977), p. 201.

87. State of New York, *Correction Law,* 26, 851–4.

88. *Corrections Compendium,* January–February 1990, pp. 9–15.

89. Elmer H. Johnson and Kenneth E. Kotch, "Two Factors in Development of Work Release: Size and Location of Prisons," *Journal of Criminal Justice* 1 (March 1973): 44–45.

90. *New York Times,* September 2, 1975, p. 23; *New York Times,* December 27, 1977, p. 24.

91. Michael S. Serrill, "California," *Corrections* (September 1974): 39–40.

92. *Time,* November 14, 1988, p. 20.

93. Richard P. Seiter, *Halfway Houses: National Evaluation Program* (Washington, D.C.: U.S. Government Printing Office, 1977).

94. Nancy Hicks, "Preparole Release in Oklahoma," *Corrections Compendium,* August 1991, pp. 1, 5–8.

95. See James A. Inciardi and Duane C. McBride, *Treatment Alternatives to Street Crime: History, Experiences, and Issues* (Rockville, Md.: National Institute on Drug Abuse, 1991).

96. Carl G. Leukefeld and Frank M. Tims (eds.), *Compulsory Treatment of Drug Abuse: Research and Clinical Practice* (Rockville, Md.: National Institute on Drug Abuse, 1988); Robert L. Hubbard, Mary Ellen Marsden, J. Valley Rachel, Henrick J. Harwood, Elizabeth R. Cavanaugh, and Harold M. Ginzburg, *Drug Abuse Treatment: A National Study of Effectiveness* (Chapel Hill: University of North Carolina Press, 1989).

97. Robert L. Hubbard, J. Valley Rachel, S. Gail Craddock, and Elizabeth R. Cavanaugh, "Treatment Outcome Prospective Study (TOPS): Client Characteristics Before, During, and After Treatment," in Frank M. Tims and Carl G. Leukefeld (eds.), *Drug Abuse Treatment Evaluation: Strategies, Progress, and Prospects* (Rockville, Md.: National Institute on Drug Abuse, 1984), pp. 42–68.

98. J. Edgar Hoover, *Persons in Hiding* (Boston: Little, Brown, 1938), pp. 189–190.

99. Sutherland, *Principles of Criminology,* p. 551.

100. American Friends Service Committee, *Struggle for Justice: A Report on Crime and Punishment in America* (New York: Hill & Wang, 1972).

101. Bob Wilson, "Parole Release: Devil or Savior?" *Corrections Magazine* 3 (September 1977): 48.

102. Andrew von Hirsch and Kathleen J. Hanrahan, *Abolish Parole?* (Washington, D.C.: U.S. Government Printing Office, 1978), p. 1.

103. Edward M. Kennedy, "Toward a New System of Criminal Sentencing: Law with Order," *The American Criminal Law Review* 16 (Spring 1979): 361.

104. Jessica Mitford, *Kind and Unusual Punishment: The Prison Business* (New York: Vintage, 1974), p. 238.

105. Mitford, *Kind and Unusual Punishment,* p. 239.

106. Mitford, *Kind and Unusual Punishment,* p. 237.

107. Personal communication, November 1979.

108. *Time Served in Prison,* Bureau of Justice Statistics Special Report, June 1984.

109. *USA Today,* June 25, 1984, 1A.

110. Donald J. Newman, *Introduction to Criminal Justice* (Philadelphia: J. P. Lippincott, 1978), p. 358.

111. Donald J. Newman, "No, Don't Abolish Parole," *New York Times,* February 10, 1981, p. A23.

112. Douglas Lipton, Robert Martinson, and Judith Wilks, *The Effectiveness of Correctional Treatment: A Survey of Treatment Evaluation Studies* (New York: Praeger, 1975), p. 150.

113. See, for example, James A. Inciardi, "The Use of Parole Prediction with Institutionalized Narcotic Addicts," *Journal of Research in Crime and Delinquency* 8 (January 1971): 65–73.

PART

FIVE

Juvenile Justice

CHAPTER 18
The Juvenile Justice System

CHAPTER

18

The Juvenile Justice System

The selectmen of every town are required to keep a vigilant eye on the inhabitants to the end that the fathers shall teach their children knowledge of the English tongue and of the capital laws, and knowledge of the catechism, and shall instruct them in some honest lawful calling, labor, or employment. If parents do not do this, the children shall be taken away and placed with masters who will so teach and instruct them.

—THE CODE OF 1650, GENERAL COURT
OF CONNECTICUT

We drove from Second Avenue to Eleventh Avenue—most of the enemy was inside. They knew there was gonna be a retaliation, but, like idiots, some of 'em were out that night. We pulled the van up to the end of the street, got out real slow . . . then we started shooting. Everyone who was standin' in front of the house got hit. I remember there was one girl, she had on a black bomber jacket with white fur on the collar. She was the first to get hit, and I remember that fur just goin' red— bam—just like that. Looked like red flowers comin' out all over white.

—ONE OF THE "CRIPS," AS QUOTED IN
DO OR DIE BY LÉON BING, 1991

ost Americans are generally aware that juvenile offenders are handled differently by the justice system than are adults. This is apparent to almost anyone who happens to know a child who has "gotten into trouble." For the rest, there are newspaper reports, editorials, and other commentaries that decry how some young offenders, because of their tender years, literally "get away with murder," or they address the inadequate services available for troubled youths. In the main, however, few people fully understand the real and philosophical differences between juvenile and adult processing. And what appears in the media is of little help in making this differentiation. Consider, for example, some of the cases that have made national headlines in recent years:

- Kevin's mother was a drug addict, his father a drug dealer. At fourteen, Kevin got his first .38-caliber revolver. In 1991, by the time he was fifteen, Kevin was an enforcer for a Jamaican drug trafficking posse, and shot someone in the face at point blank range over a suspected theft.[1]

- In August 1991, six New York youths, ages eleven and seventeen, beat a retarded man on the head with bottles, stole his money, slit his pants with a razor, and sodomized him with a stick.[2]

- In Wisconsin during August 1985, a nine-year-old boy refused to share his bicycle with three playmates. In retaliation, the three youths — ages eleven, twelve, and fourteen — beat and stabbed the child to death. The two older youths were charged with delinquency and held in detention while the eleven-year-old was declared "in need of protection and services" and placed in a foster home.[3]

- John Cruse, a fifteen-year-old brought before the courts for homicide, was sentenced in 1982 to life imprisonment by an Alabama judge. When he entered Draper Correctional Facility, a medium-security prison for adult offenders, he became the youngest convict in Alabama's entire penitentiary population.[4]

- April Savino was fifteen years old when she became one of the nation's 1.2 million runaway and so-called throwaway children. Living among the homeless, the drugs, and the violence in the tunnels of New York City's Grand Central Terminal, life was little more than a never ending episode of despair. One summer evening in 1987, April sat down on the steps of a church a few blocks from Grand Central and put a bullet through her head.[5]

- In 1987 Chester Jackson, one of Detroit's high school heroes, got into an argument with a fourteen-year-old freshman. The youth pulled out a .357 magnum and shot Jackson to death.[6]

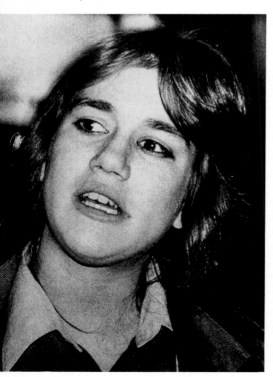

April Salvino

To these cases can be added six-year-old Nancy Jo Burch, tried in a Florida *criminal* court for having allegedly struck a schoolmate with a stick[7]; a twelve-year-old California girl, held in isolation in a juvenile detention center refusing to testify against her father;[8] the many thousands of juvenile "delinquents" found to have committed serious crimes yet immediately returned to the streets; and the almost equal number of juvenile runaways, truants, and "dependent and neglected children" who, although not having committed crimes, reside in juvenile institutions for "custody, care, and service" (see Exhibit 18.1).

On June 4, 1984, the United States Supreme Court delivered its opinion in *Schall* v. *Martin*,[9] a decision that made the activities of juvenile justice in the United States appear even more perplexing. The ruling in *Schall* upheld a New York State statute that permits the preventive detention of accused juvenile delinquents who are considered "serious risks" to the community. The decision was puzzling, not so much because it was permitting the pre-**adjudication** detention of some youths, but because it brought attention to what juvenile justice processing seemingly had wrought: *before* they are even tried, some arrested youths are sent to jail; *after* they have been adjudicated, many are released to the streets. This would suggest that in practice, the justice system wishes to prevent some youngsters from committing crimes while it goes about determining whether they already have. If it finds that they have, the system generally reverses itself and places rehabilitation above incarceration.

To understand the paradoxical character of juvenile justice processing in the United States, a number of questions must be addressed. What constitutes a juvenile? What is the jurisdiction of the juvenile justice system? Why are juveniles treated differently than adults? What is the philosophy that circumscribes juvenile justice? Why is it that some juveniles who are not necessarily "delinquent" are nevertheless dealt with by the juvenile courts? How is juvenile justice different from the rest of the criminal justice system? And since a special justice system has been designed for youths, why are many juvenile cases transferred to the adult criminal courts?

THE NATURE OF JUVENILE JUSTICE

An *adult* is a person who has reached "the age of majority"—some "magic number" (usually eighteen) which indicates that the individual is legally responsible for his or her actions and behavior. An adult has the right to vote, to marry, to hold government office, and to enter into contracts. Furthermore, if an adult should violate the criminal law or be accused of a crime, he or she is processed through a justice system that is grounded in the "due process of law" guaranteed by the Constitution of the United States.

A *juvenile* is a person who has not reached the age of majority—and therefore is deemed to have a "special status." Juveniles are held to an alternative standard of behavior than are adults. Children are required to attend school from the ages of six to sixteen; they are expected to obey their parents; they are forbidden to drink alcohol, smoke cigarettes, or drive motor vehicles; they may not marry without parental permission; they cannot enter into business or financial contracts; and they are not permitted to vote, enter the military, or run away from home. Some

Adjudication: In juvenile proceedings, the court's decision or judgment.

These young gang members elicit adult-size fears, but they are children in the juvenile justice system.

• EXHIBIT 18.1 •

Sidelights on Criminal Matters
Juveniles and Crack-Cocaine

As part of a larger study of juvenile delinquency and drug use, conducted at the close of the 1980s in Miami, Florida, 254 street youths were interviewed extensively regarding their involvement with crack. Of particular interest in the research was the relationship of the extent of the youths' crack use and their involvement in the crack business. As indicated in Table 1, all but fifty (19.7 percent) had some type of involvement in the crack business. The twenty subjects designated as having "minor" involvement sold the drug only to their friends, served as a lookout for dealers, or steered customers to one of Miami's 700 known crack houses. A "dealer" was anyone involved directly in the retail sale of crack, and a "dealer+" not only sold the drug but manufactured or smuggled it as well.

Not unexpectedly, it was found that the extent to which a youth was tied to the crack distribution network was directly related to his or her use of the drug. This is illustrated in Table 1, which lists the amount of money spent on crack by those youths (242 of them) who had used crack one or more times over the ninety-day period prior to being interviewed for the study. In spite of their intimate connections with the crack market place, those in the dealer and dealer+ groups nevertheless spent the most on the drug. By contrast, youths with only minor involvement in the crack trades spent considerably less on the drug — a median of $225 over the ninety-day period or the equivalent of less than $20 per

Addicts smoking crack-cocaine

Crack Business Involvement

Level of Involvement	Number	Percentage	Median Amount Spent on Crack for Own Use
None	50	19.7	$ 75*
Minor	20	7.9	225
Dealer	139	54.7	2000
Dealer+	45	17.7	2500
Totals	254	100.0	$1750

* The value in the "none" category was based on a sample number of thirty-eight youths who used the drug out of the total fifty.

week. Those with no crack business involvement spent even less on the drug.

As a final note, most of the money spent on crack was obtained illegally — through drug sales, prostitution, theft, robbery, or exchanging crack for stolen goods.

Adapted from: James A. Inciardi, Ruth Horowitz, and Anne E. Pottieger, *Street Kids, Street Drugs, Street Crime: An Examination of Drug Use and Serious Delinquency in Miami* (Belmont, CA: Wadsworth, 1993).

jurisdictions may place other restrictions on juveniles, such as curfews, or laws against "incorrigible" or "immoral" behavior. But like adults, children *can* be charged with violations of the criminal law. Yet because of their special status of being below the age of majority, an alternative system has evolved for dealing with juvenile lawbreakers.

The juvenile justice system in the United States was designed with the philosophy that the special status of children requires that they be protected and corrected, not necessarily punished. But as the system evolved, it failed to accord to juveniles any individual rights. For after all, in American society a juvenile is essentially in the "custody" of parents or guardians, or failing either, the state.

Beyond the philosophical orientation stemming from the special status of children, there are other differences between adult and juvenile justice systems. For adults to fall within the jurisdiction of the criminal courts, there is only one mechanism. They must be charged with some violation of the criminal law. A young person's coming to the attention of the juvenile courts, however, can occur through a variety of ways. First, and quite logically, the juvenile may be found to have violated the criminal law. Second, he or she can be charged with having committed a **status offense** — an act declared by statute to be a crime because it violates the behavior standards expected by children. Because of their status, only juveniles can be charged with the offenses of running away, truancy, or being incorrigible. Third, a child may fall within the jurisdiction of the court because of the behavior of an adult. Should a juvenile be the victim of abuse, neglect, or abandonment by a parent or guardian, the courts may intervene.

Perhaps the major difference between the adult and juvenile justice systems involves the purpose and nature of the sanctions imposed when intervention occurs. As noted in Chapter 13, there are five competing philosophies that circumscribe sentencing in the adult courts — retribution, vengeance, isolation, deterrence, and rehabilitation. By contrast, the actions taken in the juvenile courts, at least in theory, are those deemed to be "in the best interests of the child." The juvenile justice system, then, has been structured in the notion that every child is treatable, and that judicial intervention will result in positive behavioral change. One would thus assume that juvenile court sanctions are based on a rehabilitation model and do not include any other sentencing objectives.

Status offense: An act declared by statute to be a crime because it violates the standards of behavior expected of children.

You gotta be prepared — people shoot you for your coat, your rings, chains, anything.

— A 15-YEAR-OLD BALTIMORE JUNIOR HIGH SCHOOL STUDENT IN 1988, PROUDLY DISPLAYING HIS .25 CALIBER BERETTA

The Emergence of Juvenile Justice

From the early days of colonial America through the better part of the nineteenth century, juvenile offenders were handled in essentially the same way as adults. Children beyond the age of reason (about seven years old) were held to adult standards of behavior. For criminal offenses, they were subject to the same sanctions, placed in the same institutions, and hung from the same gallows.*

---

* To cite a case in point, in 1786 a twelve-year-old girl was sentenced to be hanged in New London, Connecticut, for the killing of a playmate. A local clergyman who witnessed the child's execution described her last few days of life: "About a fortnight before her execution she appeared to realize her danger, and was more concerned for herself. She continued nearly in the same state until the Monday night before her execution, when she appeared greatly affected, saying that she was distressed for her soul. She continued in tears most of Tuesday, and Wednesday, which was the day of execution. At the place of execution she said very little, appeared afraid and seemed to want somebody to help her. She then passed into that state which never ends." (From Henry Channing, *God Admonishing His People of their Duty as Parents and Masters,* a sermon preached at New London, December 20, 1786.)

● **EXHIBIT** 18.2 ●

The House of Refuge

The New York City House of Refuge, composed of a bleak set of barracks leased from the federal government, was the first house of correction for juveniles in the United States. It was dedicated on January 1, 1825, to its first nine inmates. Its founder, Reverend John Stanford, stated to his charges:

You are to look at these walls which surround the building, not so much as a prison, but as a hospitable dwelling, in which you enjoy comfort and safety from those who once led you astray. And, I may venture to say, that in all probability, this is the best home many of you ever enjoyed. You have no need for me to tell you, that the consideration of all these favors should stimulate you to submission, industry, and gratitude. You are not placed here for punishment, but to produce your moral improvement.

The first director of the House of Refuge was Joseph Curtis, an educator whose aims were to develop the individuality of his wards and to enhance their powers of self-expression.

Although progressive in philosophy, Curtis could do little to control the behavior of his wards and he quickly became a strict disciplinarian. At the table, children "must be silent, holding up a hand if they want water, a thumb for vinegar, three fingers for bread, and one finger for salt." Violation of these and the many other rules he instituted could result in corporal punishment and solitary confinement. Curtis lasted only one year, for the chief characteristic of his tenure was a high rate of escape.

Curtis was succeeded by N. C. Hart, a high school teacher who shifted the focus of the House of Refuge from education to work. The juvenile inmates labored eight hours each day at weaving, and the making of brass nails, shoes, and cane seats for chairs. Children were also sent out to labor on distant farms, or were indentured in the service of others. Records indicate that the first child to be so indentured in a foster home was thirteen-year-old Diana Williams, sent to the House of Refuge for stealing. The covenant, signed by Diana, charged that she faithfully serve her mistress and obey every lawful command:

She shall not waste her mistress's goods, nor lend unlawfully to any; she shall not commit fornication, nor contract matrimony within the said term. At cards, dice, or any other unlawful game she shall not play; not haunt alehouses, taverns, nor playhouses, but in all things behave herself as a faithful apprentice ought to.

Although the philosophy that led to the establishment of the New York City House of Refuge may have been praiseworthy at the time, in actual practice the institution was a juvenile prison. Structured to hold children securely, its interior was designed to implant the notions of order and rationality. Rooms were small and windowless and, much like jail cells, their doors were of iron-lattice slab. The treatment also paralleled that of

The House of Refuge

Reformation in the treatment of juvenile offenders began during the early decades of the nineteenth century, but it was piecemeal at best, and limited to only a few jurisdictions. Historically notable was New York City's *House of Refuge,* established in 1825 as the first systematic attempt to separate juvenile offenders from adult criminals and to provide "correction" rather than punishment (see Exhibit 18.2). Also significant in this regard was Massachusetts, which in 1847 became the first jurisdiction to establish training and industrial schools for juveniles on a statewide basis. In the courts, the separation of juveniles from adults in trial proceedings occurred in Chicago in 1861, followed by Massachusetts in the early 1870s and New York and Rhode Island in the 1890s.[10]

Parens Patriae

The early changes in the processing and treatment of juvenile offenders in Chicago and several eastern states were only the beginnings of widespread reforms yet to come. During the latter part of the nineteenth century there was an increasing awareness of explanations of criminal

a penitentiary. As children were admitted, they were given identical clothing and haircuts. "Troublemakers" were always punished. The milder sanctions included either a diet of bread and water or the depriving of meals altogether. For more serious cases there was bread and water coupled with solitary confinement, manacling with a ball and chain, or whipping with a cat-o'-nine-tails. The most troublesome offenders were typically shipped off to sea.

The House of Refuge grew rapidly, accepting not only those children who had been adjudicated for delinquent acts, but also the poor, the destitute, the orphaned, the incorrigible, and others who were simply in danger of getting into trouble. Rather than a house of "refuge," the institution had become a reformatory for delinquents and a repository for "street waifs" that New York had nowhere else to put. But to the society at large, the House of Refuge was a

model juvenile institution. A "refuge movement" began, and by the late 1840s similar facilities had been established in most eastern cities. By then, however, New York had already begun to phase out the refuge system.

In 1854, a facility large enough to hold more than a thousand juveniles was opened on Randall's Island — a small strip of land in New York's East River northeast of Manhattan. It was the new House of Refuge. Although it had retained its original name, it represented the state's first of many juvenile reformatories yet to come. In practice, youths placed in the Randall's Island facility were in prison at hard labor. In 1901, reformers exposed the Randall's Island refuge as an immense "chamber of horrors." Crusading journalists declared that beyond the waters of the East River and behind the bastions of Randall's Island lay a barbaric prison colony. An investigation was launched, but the Refuge

somehow endured, at least for a time. Finally, in 1935, the edifice on Randall's Island was closed, the inmates were moved to a new juvenile prison recently built by the New York State Department of Corrections some fifty miles north of New York City, and the House of Refuge passed into history, remaining only as a curious anecdote in the annals of juvenile justice.

SOURCES: B. K. Pierce, *A Half Century with Juvenile Delinquents: The New York House of Refuge and Its Times* (New York: Appleton, 1869); Homer Folks, *The Care of Destitute, Neglected and Delinquent Children* (New York: Macmillan, 1902); Negley K. Teeters and John Otto Reinemann, *The Challenge of Delinquency* (Englewood Cliffs, N.J.: Prentice-Hall, 1961), pp. 429–443; David J. Rothman, *The Discovery of the Asylum* (Boston: Little, Brown, 1971); Robert S. Pickett, *House of Refuge: Origins of Junvenile Reform in New York State, 1815–1857* (Syracuse: Syracuse University Press, 1969).

behavior suggesting that the roots of crime and delinquency were not necessarily to be found within individual offenders but, rather, were products of the culture and greater environment in which they lived. This new awareness, coupled with an ongoing concern for the abuse and neglect of children both in and out of institutions, led to the emergence of a new juvenile justice philosophy based on an already established concept of **parens patriae.**

Under the common law in England at the time, the Court of Chancery had the authority to intervene in property matters to protect the rights of children. This jurisdictional focus was adopted and expanded in the United States to include the handling of "dependent and neglected" children. Court intervention was justified by the theory that a child's natural protectors — the parents — were unable or unwilling to provide the appropriate care. The court took the place of the parents, and hence, *parens patriae* — the state as the parent.

Reformers merged the concept of *parens patriae* with the medical model of treatment to establish a system of juvenile justice in the United States designed to reform and rehabilitate young offenders. The under-

Parens patriae: A philosophy under which the state takes over the role of parent.

lying philosophy was that if a child "went astray," it was the *parents* who had failed. The court could take over the role of the parent, diagnose the problem, and prescribe the appropriate treatment. It did not matter what the child had done. His or her deviant behavior was merely a symptom of the problem. The court was not to blame the child or to bring a finding of guilt, but to identify and treat the underlying problem. Moreover, the youth's welfare was to be the central concern of the court. This would not only protect the future of the child, but also permit an informal court process that considered the entire history and background of the child's difficulties, without being hampered by the limitations and requirements of official criminal procedure. Thus, juvenile processing would be a civil rather than a criminal matter. Or as described by an early commentator on the new juvenile justice process:

> Since the fundamental purpose of juvenile court procedure is not to determine whether or not a child has committed a specific offense, but to discover whether he is in a condition requiring the special care of the state, it follows that the chancery or civil, rather than the criminal, procedure is best adapted to the end in view. Under the criminal procedure—with apprehension by warrant and arrest, trial on specific charges, strict application of the rules of evidence, conviction, and sentence—the punitive aspects of the process are repeatedly emphasized. The judgment must depend on the technical evidence presented, and the vital social facts of home and environmental conditions and the child's physical and mental make-up can be given, at best, limited consideration. In contrast to this complicated legal machine is the simple chancery procedure, under which the judge in an informal hearing can utilize all the information that has been obtained about the child and his family, decide whether or not the child is in a condition of delinquency or neglect, and apply the remedies best suited to the correction of the condition.[11]

The early juvenile justice reform efforts were heavily promoted by a number of penologists, philanthropists, and women's organizations—a group who have become known as the *"child savers"* (see Exhibit 18.3). The child-savers movement crystallized in the passage of the **Illinois Juvenile Court Act** in 1899, which established the first statewide juvenile court system in the United States. The Illinois statute mandated a system that was to "secure for each minor such care and guidance, preferably in his own home, as will serve the emotional, mental and physical welfare of the minor and the best interests of the child; to preserve and strengthen the minor's family ties whenever possible." Only when necessary was the court to provide "custody, care, and discipline as nearly as possible equivalent to that which should be given by his parents."[12]

Illinois Juvenile Court Act: Legislation that established the first statewide juvenile court system in the United States.

Modern Juvenile Courts

By 1945, a juvenile court system was present in every state jurisdiction in the United States. Currently, there are some 3,000 courts across the nation hearing juvenile cases. While they all reflect the same general underlying philosophy, their sophistication and procedures tend to vary. Some systems are highly organized, having extensive and well-trained support staffs and large probation and treatment components. Others are less so, relying for their services on the resources of the adult criminal courts and correctional systems. Moreover, exactly *where* juvenile cases are heard within a jurisdiction's overall court structure varies greatly. In a

Dealing cocaine on the street corner on the Lower East Side of Manhattan

Autonomous, coordinated, and designated juvenile courts

number of states, such as Utah and Wyoming, there are *autonomous juvenile courts,* in which the court is organizationally separated from all others and the judges spend all of their time on juvenile matters. More commonly, as in New York and Delaware, for example, there are *coordinated juvenile courts,* wherein the proceedings occur in the state's family or domestic relations courts. Most jurisdictions, however, have *designated juvenile courts.* In these, judges who preside over criminal and civil cases also hear juvenile cases. On the latter occasions, the judge becomes the juvenile court. In North Carolina, for example, juvenile cases are heard in the district courts by judges who volunteer to specialize in such matters. Where no judge volunteers, the chief district court judge assigns individual magistrates to serve as the juvenile court on a rotating basis.[13]

Juvenile courts, regardless of how they may be organized, have a jurisdiction defined in terms of youth's age and alleged offense. Typically, the maximum age is eighteen, although age sixteen is the upper limit in some locations. Furthermore, juvenile courts have authority over delinquency and status offenses. **Delinquency** involves criminal law violations, such as those listed in the FBI's *Uniform Crime Reports,* that would be considered crimes if committed by an adult. As such, a **delinquent** is a juvenile offender who has been adjudicated by an officer of a juvenile court. Status offenses, as noted earlier, are specific acts (truancy, running away) and general conditions (incorrigibility, uncontrollable behavior) that are unique to the status of being a juvenile. Although delinquents and status offenders compose the great majority of the juvenile justice population, there is yet a third category— dependent and neglected children, the deprived, and the abused. These juveniles are victims rather than offenders, and the court's intent is to provide assistance "in their best interests."

Delinquency: Criminal law violations that would be considered crimes if committed by an adult.

Delinquent: A juvenile offender who has been adjudicated by an officer of a juvenile court.

● EXHIBIT 18.3 ●

The "Child Savers"

The civic-minded and humanitarian citizens who became concerned about the problem of juvenile misconduct in the nineteenth century have become popularly known as the "child savers." These social reformers (some call them social "do-gooders") were instrumental in the development of the houses of refuge, the later reform schools, and ultimately, the juvenile court. Some, such as Charles Loring Brace and his Children's Aid Society, hit upon the further idea of placing vagrant and poor children with western frontier farm families. They sought to "drain the city" of its problem children and ship them westward. The pioneer spirit, fresh air and wide open spaces, and hard work were apparently considered desirable for wayward youth. . . .

The child savers advocated specialized institutions for children, as noted, but they were also advocates of stern, regimented discipline, which they considered essential to reform. It was for this reason that the institutions had to be given extensive discretionary authority over children, again in the name of *parens patriae*.

As indicated, the state reform and industrial schools for juveniles followed the houses of refuge. The first of these was opened in Massachusetts in 1847. These institutions were aimed at teaching children an honest trade and at instilling re-

spect for advancement through hard work, in addition to teaching discipline. The reform schools developed rapidly, and between 1850 and 1890 almost every state had opened one or more of them. These institutions were congregate care facilities which, in addition to institutional jobs and learning a trade, also emphasized basic education. Unfortunately, the reform schools were also characterized by racial and sexual segregation and the resulting discriminatory treatment, by harsh discipline and corporal punishment, and by poor physical care. Commitments by courts to the reform schools were indeterminate (that is, unlimited in time) until the legal age of majority, which in most states was age twenty-one.

Judge Irving R. Kaufman indicates that two principles were central to the reform school idea:

First, youths could be properly treated as criminals for offenses peculiar to their status as minors; for example, truancy, running away, incorrigibility. Second, because the mission of the reform school was a benign, rehabilitative one, the normal procedural protections of the adversary criminal trial—the rights of confronting witnesses, prior disclosure of specific charges, of counsel and of trial by jury—could be abrogated with no constitutional qualms.[a]

The child savers' response to the urbanization, industrialization, immigration, poverty, and aftermath of the Civil War, was to expand the institutional care

of children—particularly through the houses of refuge and reform schools, and to further extend the reach of *parens patriae*. Youthful offenders were incarcerated in order to incapacitate them, to keep them from committing criminal acts; they were taught the principles of Christian morality to save them from a future life of crime; and they were placed in rural foster homes away from urban poverty in order that they may benefit from the rugged, pioneer life style.

This historical period in American juvenile justice is particularly interesting and controversial. Many scholars have discussed it and written about it, especially about the role of the child savers. The motivations of the reformers in creating and expanding the juvenile justice system have been interpreted generally in one of two ways. The first and more traditional interpretation is that these reformers held a positivistic philosophy that emphasized individual values and judgments in the care of children. Individual treatment was the order of the day. The reformers believed, according to this view, that childrens' problems should be handled in the best interests of both the state and the child, so as to help the child develop into a law-abiding and productive adult.

One version of this perspective describes the evolution of juvenile justice as emanating

THE PROCESSING OF JUVENILE OFFENDERS

Each year, more than a million juveniles are arrested by the police in the United States. The offenses cover all crime categories, from the most serious violent crimes of murder, forcible rape, and robbery, to such status offenses as running away, truancy, and curfew violations. Al-

from the development of free public education in the early 1800s. . . .

A system of free public education was created in the early and mid-nineteenth century to ensure education for the lower classes. Attendance was made compulsory (with laws against truancy) in order to safeguard the child's future interests (in being an educated adult) against the immediate pressures of his or her parents (to have the child work instead) and against any shortsighted tendency of the child to remain idle. . . . The reformers succeeded in persuading counties and states to create specialized institutions, whose staff members would be trained to respond to the special problems of juveniles, and whose goal would be rehabilitation, not punishment.[b]

At least some of those who adopt this first perspective or interpretation have been referred to as "march of progress" theorists.[c] [Alexander W.] Pisciotta says the march of progress theorists "believe that the purpose of the juvenile justice system has been to provide delinquent and dependent children with humane care while protecting society from more youthful offenders. . . . Reformers and administrators have been portrayed as humanitarians who alleviated the plight of unfortunate children."[d]

A second, what can be termed critical and revisionist interpretation, is much less glowing in recounting the motives of the child savers. According to this view, the reform movement expressed the vested interests of a particular group, namely the middle and upper classes. The concept of *parens patriae* was exploited in order to continue middle- and upper-class values, to control relevant political systems such as education, and to further the child labor system. The emphasis was on controlling and perhaps resocializing young miscreants. Five motives have been attributed to the child savers in accordance with this perspective:

1. An interest (on the part of police and other community officials) in removing idle youths from the street, where they might cause trouble or commit crimes.
2. A desire (especially among upper-class leaders) for ways to remove the child from the home (particularly immigrant homes), in order to educate and socialize the young to accept "American" values.
3. A demand (by businessmen) that young people be taught the discipline and minimal skills necessary to permit the expanding factory system to absorb them and operate efficiently.
4. A need (on the part of some women in the "child-saving" movement) to find acceptable social and professional roles in an industrializing, urbanizing society.
5. Perhaps least important, a concern that young people be given the tools and education needed to earn a living within the existing economic and social structure. . . .[e]

The reality seems to lie somewhere between these two perspectives, as misguided and as ambivalent as that reality might be. Undoubtedly there were reformers guided only by benevolent and humanitarian concerns for helping the young. But there were also those who sought to control, to repress, and only maybe resocialize children who were viewed by them as being dangerously deviant. This curious blend resulted in a juvenile justice and corrections system which can best be described as ambivalent or even schizophrenic. . . .

---

[a] Irving R. Kaufman, "Juvenile Justice: A Plea for Reform," in *Criminal Justice 80/81: Annual Editions* (Guilford, Ct.: Dushkin), p. 162.

[b] Jameson W. Doig, "For the Salvation of Children: The Search for Juvenile Justice in the United States," in *Crime and Criminal Justice,* ed. John A. Gardiner and Michael A. Mulkey (Lexington, Mass.: Heath, 1975), p. 140.

[c] Alexander W. Pisciotta, "Theoretical Perspectives for Historical Analyses: A Selective Review of the Juvenile Justice Literature," *Criminology* 19, no. 1 (May 1981).

[d] Pisciotta, "Theoretical Perspectives," p. 122.

[e] Doig, "For the Salvation of Children," pp. 141–142.

SOURCE: From *Juvenile Delinquency and Corrections* by James O. Finckenauer, copyright © 1984 by Harcourt Brace Jovanovich, Inc. Reprinted by permission of the publisher.

though perhaps a third of these offenses result in release with no more than a warning, the majority are referred to the courts for official processing. However, given the less formal nature of juvenile justice combined with the dynamics of police discretion, it was once estimated that for each arrest of a juvenile there occurs some 500 "probable cause" arrest situations.[14]

Juvenile Arrests, 1990

Total	1,471,431
Murder and nonnegligent manslaughter	2,192
Forcible rape	3,563
Robbery	30,204
Aggravated assault	42,240
Burglary	85,010
Larceny-theft	324,533
Motor vehicle theft	60,092
Arson	5,150
Violent crime	78,199
Property crime	474,785
Crime Index total	552,984
Other assaults	101,108
Forgery and counterfeiting	5,576
Fraud	8,135
Embezzlement	681
Stolen property	29,107
Vandalism	84,630
Weapons; carrying, possessing, etc.	28,056
Prostitution and commercialized vice	1,157
Sex offenses	10,140
Drug abuse violations	55,398
Gambling	731
Offenses against family and children	2,198
Driving under the influence	10,756
Liquor laws	95,123
Drunkenness	16,587
Disorderly conduct	86,754
Vagrancy	2,173
All other offenses (except traffic)	205,946
Suspicion	2,732
Curfew and loitering law violations	61,506
Runaways	109,953

SOURCE: *Uniform Crime Reports*—1990.

Youths and the Police

Police officers who encounter status offenders or juveniles involved in delinquent activities have several alternatives at their disposal. First, the officer may simply release the youth with a reprimand. Second, the officer may take the youth to the police station, where a "juvenile card" is prepared that briefly describes the incident. The parents may then be called in for a discussion, after which the youth is released. A typical "adjustment" of this type was recently described by a Maryland sheriff's deputy after a homeowner complained that "a group of tough-looking kids" was "drinking, taking drugs, swearing, and raising hell" behind his garage:

> When I got there it wasn't really all that bad. There were these three kids, two boys and a girl, all about thirteen years old, passing around a "joint" and a pint of wine. A little loud, maybe, but none of them were drunk or stoned and they didn't seem to be making any kind of trouble. I made them grind out their joint and pour out the rest of the wine and told them to sit in the patrol car. The complainant said he would be satisfied if the kids promised not to return, so I drove them around for fifteen minutes lecturing them on the virtues of neighborliness, good deeds, and wholesome all-American conduct. They said they'd behave themselves, so I let them go with just a warning.[15]

This discretionary power of the police is generally unreviewed. The style of the officer, the circumstances of the incident, and the policies of the department typically play a role in the decision to release or to detain juveniles. Studies have demonstrated, however, that numerous other factors can come into play: the attitude of the victim; the juvenile's prior record; the seriousness of the offense; the age, sex, race, and demeanor of the offender; the likelihood of adequate parental handling of the matter;

It is the police officer's decision to detain or to release a juvenile.

the time and location of the incident; the availability of a service agency for referral; and the officer's perception of how the case will be handled by the court.[16] Consideration of these factors by a police officer, consciously or otherwise, is more likely to result in an "on the street disposition" or no action at all. Beyond these, there is the third option — taking the juvenile into custody.* Yet even in this event, the police still have alternatives. Some law enforcement agencies in large urban areas have their own diversion and delinquency prevention programs to which they may send a juvenile, while status offenders may be brought to social service agencies for counseling and treatment. With felony offenses, and particularly those involving violence, there is the fourth police option — referral to the juvenile court.

Petition and Intake

The mechanism for bringing juveniles to the attention of the courts is through a **petition,** as opposed to an arrest warrant. This can be filed by the police, a victim, parents, school officials, or a social worker. Like an arrest warrant, the petition specifies the alleged offense or delinquency, the name and address of the child, the names and residences of his or her parents, and a description of the circumstances of the offense. This petition initiates the formal judicial processing of a juvenile (see Exhibit 18.4).

After the petition is filed an **intake hearing** is held, conducted by the court as a preliminary examination into the facts of the case. However, it is not presided over by a judge nor does it occur in open court. Rather, the hearing officer is usually a referee with a background in social work or one of the behavioral sciences, an attorney, a probation officer, or someone else assigned by the juvenile court. The purpose of this hearing is to protect the interests of the child and to quickly dispose of cases that do not require the time and expense of formal court processing.

In effect, the intake officer makes a legal judgment of the probable cause of the petition, and this may be the only time that the sufficiency of the evidence is evaluated. The officer may also conduct a brief investigation into the background of the juvenile, have an informal hearing with the child and parents, or discuss the case with the police and attorneys. Depending on the hearing officer's judgment of the sufficiency of the evidence, the seriousness of the offense, and the need for court intervention, there are three alternatives:

1. The hearing officer can dismiss the case, in which instance the matter is over — no further court processing is required and the child can go home.
2. The officer can make an informal judgment, such as arbitration, restitution, or referral to some social agency.
3. The officer can authorize an inquiry before the juvenile court judge.

Although the intake process represents an excellent mechanism for screening juvenile cases, it is not without its problems and shortcomings. First, the "social service" worker in charge of the hearing is making

Petition: In juvenile proceedings, a document alleging that a youth is a delinquent, a status offender, or a dependent child and asking that the court assume jurisdiction over the juvenile.

Intake hearing: An early stage in juvenile court proceedings in which a court officer makes a legal judgment of the probable cause of the petition.

* It should be noted here that there are twenty-nine jurisdictions in the United States that avoid the term *arrest* with respect to juveniles, preferring the expression *taking into custody.* Moreover, in the juvenile codes of ten of these jurisdictions, it is expressly stated that *taking into custody* is *not* arrest. Although for all practical purposes being taken into custody is the same as being arrested, the latter term is avoided to protect youths from a criminal record.

● EXHIBIT 18.4 ●

The Juvenile Justice System

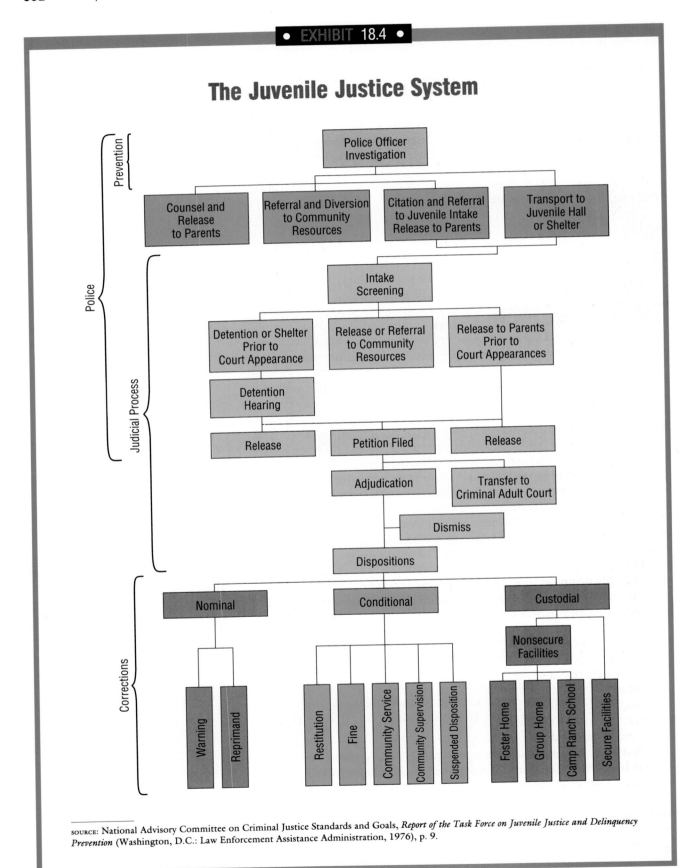

SOURCE: National Advisory Committee on Criminal Justice Standards and Goals, *Report of the Task Force on Juvenile Justice and Delinquency Prevention* (Washington, D.C.: Law Enforcement Assistance Administration, 1976), p. 9.

A Polaroid photo found by police in a gang member's house during a raid. The young men are proudly showing their guns. This photo was used in court as evidence.

legal judgments about probable cause. The hearing decision, in large measure, determines the immediate future of the child. Yet most hearing officers have no formal legal training and may be ill-prepared to deal with the complexities of law. In some jurisdictions, such as California, there has been an increasing trend to involve prosecutors in screening hearings.[17] Although this addresses the issue of legal judgments, it can also change the focus and effect of juvenile court intake procedures.

Second, as is the case with plea negotiation in the adult criminal courts, the intake hearing places pressures on the juvenile and his or her parents to proceed in a particular way. Statutes in most jurisdictions hold that if a child maintains his or her innocence or the parents so demand it, the case must be sent before a judge. However, the child's liability in the matter might not be disputed in an effort to avoid formal court inquiry.

Third, there are the issues of reliability and objectivity of case file data. The file begins at intake and the hearing officer gathers facts about the case and the juvenile. Quite often, none of these are verified. The file may contain opinions of the intake officer, the police, and the victim that cannot be effectively challenged. Yet this file information is generally accepted by the court as accurate. It is permanently entered and used as "fact" throughout the remainder of the process.

Fourth, there is the matter of discretion. Hearing officers, like police and judges, can exercise a considerable degree of discretion as to how a case ought to be handled. Decisions are often based on opinions as well as the factors used in deciding to take the juvenile into custody—both of which may be tainted by bias, resulting in the potential for arbitrary and discriminatory judgments.[18]

Such difficulties as these, however significant, do not warrant the elimination of the juvenile intake process. Rather, they suggest areas of needed improvement. In the final analysis, intake continues to serve the dual purposes of protecting the juvenile from exposure to the formal adjudication process and to preserve court resources for more serious cases. The intake procedures in the juvenile court thus fulfill much the same role as does plea negotiation in the adult court.

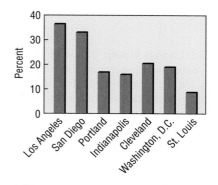

Drug Use Among Juvenile Arrestees Percentages based on positive urinalysis for cocaine, opiates, PCP, marijuana, or amphetamines.

SOURCE: National Institute of Justice, April 1991

Detention hearing: The stage in juvenile court proceedings in which it is determined whether a child is to be released to a parent or guardian or retained in custody.

Detention and Bail

Subsequent to the intake decision that recommends a hearing before the juvenile court judge, most state statutes require a **detention hearing** to determine whether the child should be released to a parent or guardian, or retained in custody. The issues addressed include: (1) whether there is a need to protect the child; (2) whether the child presents a serious threat to the community; and (3) the likelihood that the child will return to court for adjudication.

In theory, the temporary detention of juveniles should meet three basic objectives:

1. secure custody with good physical care that will offset the damaging effects of confinement
2. a constructive and satisfying program of activities to provide the juvenile with a chance to identify socially acceptable ways of gaining satisfaction
3. observation and study to provide screening for undetected mental or emotional illnesses as well as diagnoses upon which to develop appropriate treatment plans[19]

During every 100 hours on our streets we lose more youths than were killed in 100 hours of ground war in the Persian Gulf.
—Louis Sullivan, Secretary, Dept. of Health and Human Services, 1991

The gun is your best friend.
— fifteen-year-old South Central Los Angeles gang member, 1991

Should these goals be met, the detention experience might actually aid both the child and the court. In practice, however, most children in detention are housed in facilities that provide little more than security. Many are held in police lock-ups or local jails; even now in the 1990s, for some tens of thousands of juveniles annually, temporary detention occurs in secure state correctional facilities and local jails for adults.[20]

Should the detention hearing decision be to release the juvenile, the question of bail arises. Although there is a trend in some states to establish bail procedures in the juvenile courts, the federal courts have deemed it unnecessary to rule on the matter. On the one hand, there are liberal statutory alternatives for juveniles, including release on recognizance or release to parents. On the other, there is considerable opposition to the use of bail bonds and other financial conditions of release.[21] A bail agreement is a contract that is not binding on a minor. Moreover, children are unlikely to have the independent financial means to make bail, thus making it necessary for them to rely on others for the needed funds or collateral. This would provide the juvenile with little personal motivation to appear in court as required. And finally, as is the case with adult defendants, bail tends to discriminate against the poor.

Adjudication inquiry: The stage in juvenile court proceedings in which a judge determines whether the facts of the case warrant a formal hearing by the court.

Adjudication and Disposition

At the **adjudication inquiry,** which is generally closed to the public and the media, the judge determines whether the facts of the case and the child's behavior warrant a formal hearing by the court.* This inquiry is similar in purpose to the intake hearing, but now it is a magistrate who rules on the need for further processing. The magistrate can dismiss the case, order a formal adjudication hearing, or refer the juvenile elsewhere.

In recent years, the juvenile justice system in the United States has sought out any number of alternatives for avoiding the official adjudica-

---

* Many jurisdictions have "masters" or "commissioners" who have been given the authority to hear cases on behalf of judges. Intake workers may refer the more routine cases to these quasi-judicial officers, a process established for the sake of relieving judges of the burden of the less serious matters. However, in the event that the juvenile is dissatisfied with the master's decision, the case is subject to review before a juvenile court judge.

tion of youths. The major mechanism is diversion out of the court system into community agencies for counseling and treatment. However, a youth may refuse diversion and request a formal adjudication hearing.

The **adjudication hearing** is not a trial. Given the chancery court and *parens patriae* roots of juvenile justice processing, the adjudication hearing is legally classified as a civil rather than a criminal proceeding. The judge presides *on behalf of* the child to determine if he or she actually committed the alleged offense, and, if so, to use the misconduct described to determine if the youth's parents are providing adequate care, supervision, and discipline. The judge relies on any clinical, social, or diagnostic reports that may have been prepared. Should the judge determine that no misconduct occurred, the case is dismissed. If youthful misconduct *is* apparent, a disposition hearing is scheduled.

At **disposition hearings,** juvenile court judges have extremely broad discretion. They have the authority to dismiss a case, give the juvenile a warning, impose a fine, order the payment of restitution, require the performance of community service, refer the offender to a community agency or treatment facility, place the child on probation under the supervision of a court officer, place the child on some *informal* probationary status, put the child in a foster home, enter an order against the parents for the protection of the child, or mandate commitment into a juvenile institution. In practice, the most common dispositions are probation, court-sponsored restitution programs, and institutional commitment.

Adjudication hearing: The stage in juvenile court proceedings in which a judge presides on behalf of the child to determine if he or she actually committed the alleged offense

Disposition hearing: The stage in juvenile court proceedings in which the judge exercises his or her discretionary authority to choose among a variety of alternatives for resolving a case.

JUVENILES AND THE CONSTITUTION

The juvenile court process, as noted earlier, is not a criminal proceeding. It is not a matter of "*State* v. *Child*": there is no prosecutor who acts in behalf of the state to prove the guilt of the youth, and there is no jury. Rather, it is a civil process designed, at least in theory, to aid and protect the child. But is the youthful defendant in the juvenile court protected by the Bill of Rights? Does the juvenile have the same constitutional rights enjoyed by adult defendants in criminal trials? For the most part, the answers are *no,* and until the Supreme Court's decision in *Kent* vs. *United States* in 1966,[22] juvenile courts seemed to accord few, if any, rights at all. In *Kent,* for the first time in its long history the High Court evaluated juvenile court proceedings and the constitutionally guaranteed rights of children. The Court noted that youths involved in juvenile proceedings were deprived of constitutional rights and denied the rehabilitation promised under juvenile court philosophy. (The details in *Kent* are discussed later in this chapter.)

Due Process and Juvenile Proceedings

The issue in *Kent* did not give the Court the opportunity to render a decision on the content of juvenile delinquency proceedings. The next year, however, the Court did not have the occasion to do so. The case was *In re Gault,*[23] an appeal involving the detention of a fifteen-year-old in a state industrial school for allegedly having made an obscene telephone call (see Exhibit 18.5). The *Gault* decision extended to juvenile court proceedings the requirement of notice of charges, the right to counsel, the right to confrontation and cross-examination of witnesses, the privi-

In re Gault: The Supreme Court ruling that extended some—but not all—due process privileges to juvenile court proceedings.

● EXHIBIT 18.5 ●

In re Gault

On June 8, 1964, fifteen-year-old Gerald Francis Gault and a friend, Ronald Lewis, were taken into custody by the sheriff of Gila County, Arizona. Gerald was then still subject to a six-month probation order as a result of having been in the company of another boy who had stolen a wallet from a woman's purse. Gerald and Lewis's trip to the police station on that day in June was the result of a verbal complaint by Mrs. Cook, a neighbor of the two boys, about a telephone call made to her in which lewd and indecent remarks allegedly had been made.

At the time Gerald was picked up, both his mother and father were at work. No notice that he was being taken into custody was left at the home, and no other steps were taken to advise the Gaults that their son had, in effect, been arrested. Gerald was taken to a children's

detention home. When his mother returned home that evening she learned from the Lewis family that Gerald was in custody. Mrs. Gault went to the detention home and was informed by deputy probation officer Flagg that her son was indeed there and that a hearing would take place at the juvenile court the following day.

Officer Flagg filed a petition with the court on the hearing day, but a copy was not served on Gerald's parents. The petition was formal, but very brief. It made no reference to any factual basis for the court action, but merely recited that "said minor is under the age of eighteen years, and is in need of protection of this Honorable Court"; and that "said minor is a delinquent minor."

On June 9, Gerald, his mother, his older brother, and probation officers Flagg and

Henderson appeared before the juvenile court judge. Mrs. Cook, the complainant, was not there. No one was sworn at the hearing, no transcript or recording of the proceedings was made, and no record of the substance of the proceedings was maintained. From later testimony it appeared that presiding Judge McGhee had questioned Gerald about the phone call, but there were differences of opinion as to how he answered. Judge McGhee and Officer Flagg stated that Gerald had admitted making one of the obscene statements. Mrs. Gault recalled that her son said he only dialed Mrs. Cook's number and handed the telephone to his friend Ronald. At the conclusion of the hearing the judge said he would "think about it." Gerald was not sent home, but returned to the detention center. Several days later, however, he was driven home

---

In re Winship: The Supreme Court ruling that required proof "beyond a reasonable doubt" for an adjudication of delinquency.

Breed v. Jones: The Supreme Court ruling that extended the Fifth Amendment protection against double jeopardy to juveniles.

McKeiver v. Pennsylvania: The Supreme Court ruling that due process does not require a jury in juvenile court hearings.

lege against self-incrimination, and the rights to a transcript of proceedings and appellate review.

Prior to *Gault* the juvenile courts had almost unchecked power, and most constitutional rights were totally denied. Or as Supreme Court Justice Abe Fortas put it: "Under our Constitution, the condition of being a boy does not justify a kangaroo court."

Subsequent to *Gault,* additional rights were applied to juvenile proceedings. In the case of **In re Winship,**[24] addressed by the Supreme Court in 1970, it was held that proof "beyond a reasonable doubt" was required for an adjudication of delinquency. Prior to that, in juvenile matters guilt needed to be established only by the lower "preponderance of evidence" standard. In **Breed v. Jones,**[25] decided in 1975, the Fifth Amendment protection against double jeopardy was extended to juveniles. **McKeiver v. Pennsylvania,**[26] on the other hand, held that due process of law does not require a jury in juvenile court hearings. However, the Supreme Court was careful to note in *McKeiver* that there "is nothing to prevent a juvenile court judge in a particular case where he feels the need is demonstrated from using an advisory jury."

Although *Gault* changed the juvenile court into a *court of law* with needed due-process safeguards, there have been numerous transitional

with no explanation as to why he had been held in custody for almost a week. Then, at 5 P.M. on the day of Gerald's release, Mrs. Gault received the following note, on a plain piece of paper, signed by Officer Flagg:

Judge McGhee has set Monday, June 15, 1964 at 11 A.M. as the date and time for further hearings on Gerald's delinquency.

s/Flagg

Present at the June 15 meeting were Gerald and his parents, Ronald Lewis and his father, Officers Henderson and Flagg, and Judge McGhee. Again there was conflict about what Gerald actually admitted to, and again Mrs. Cook was not there. In fact, the judge denied Mrs. Gault's request that her son's accuser be present. The only contact the court ever had with Mrs. Cook was a telephone call from Mrs. Flagg on June 9.

At the June 15 hearing a "referral report" was filed with the court, yet its contents were not disclosed to the Gaults. This report charged Gerald with "lewd phone calls." At the conclusion of the hearing, the judge committed Gerald Francis Gault as a juvenile delinquent to the State Industrial School until age twenty-one. Since Gerald was only fifteen years old, that meant a term of incarceration of almost six years for a crime which, if committed by an adult, would have resulted in a fine of $50 or less. Furthermore, no appeal was permitted by Arizona law in juvenile cases.

Under a writ of *habeas corpus,* the Gaults managed to initiate the appeals process, but both the local superior court and the Arizona Supreme Court dismissed the writ. Meanwhile, Gerald Gault remained in detention at the State Industrial School.

In 1967 three years after Gault's arrest, the United States Supreme Court reviewed the case. The Supreme Court ruled against the Arizona courts, holding that Gerald Gault had been denied the following basic rights:

1. notice of charges
2. right to counsel
3. right to confrontation and cross-examination of witnesses
4. privilege against self-incrimination
5. right to a transcript of the proceedings
6. right to appellate review

The result of the Supreme Court's decision was to extend these constitutional guarantees to every case in every juvenile court in the United States.

SOURCE: *In re Gault,* 38 U.S. 1 (1967).

problems. During the pre-*Gault* era, there was no need for prosecutors, since the sufficiency of the evidence was not in dispute — only the needs of the child. There was no need for defense attorneys, since due-process requirements were not at issue. Probation or hearing officers simply prepared the cases and presented them to the court. The adjudication hearing was an informal one where the evidence was not usually questioned. And typically, there was pressure on juveniles to admit their guilt so as to initiate the rehabilitation process.

Gault introduced defense attorneys to the adjudication hearing, and prosecutors for the sake of balance. Hearings became more formal and greater attention was paid to legal sufficiency. Although this initiated more focused attention on the issue of "justice," particular in those courtrooms and cases where it was needed, in many juvenile courts it also brought about conflict — conflict that was not necessarily in the best interest of the juvenile. Many defense attorneys who attempted to turn adjudication hearings into adversarial proceedings found themselves confronted with magistrates who fully adhered to the *parens patriae* philosophy. Through both subtle and obvious methods, they influenced attorneys to cooperate with the court and to repress their adversarial roles. As one Delaware defense attorney explained the situation in 1985:

Percent of U.S. High School Students Who Report Carrying Weapons to School, 1990

RACE/ ETHNICITY	MALES	FEMALES	TOTAL
White	28.6%	5.3%	16.8%
Black	39.4%	16.7%	27.2%
Hispanic	41.1%	12.2%	25.8%
Total	31.5%	8.1%	19.6%

SOURCE: Youth Risk Behavior Surveillance System, 1991

I'm representing this 15-year-old who was brought to the court for burglary. The evidence against him is a shaky eyewitness who says he saw the kid running from the scene. There's also this statement from the defendant that was made under questionable circumstances. The probation officer is recommending an adjudication of delinquency for a misdemeanor trespass so the kid can go on probation with counseling. You see, he's got some severe adjustment problems over his parents' divorce and his mother's remarriage. The court usually follows the probation officer's recommendation.

The judge, who has frequently expressed his opinion on how difficult it has become to deal with wayward children since the *Gault* ruling, opens the hearing by saying, "Well, this looks like a straight-forward case, unless someone wants to get tough on technicalities. And I can get just as tough and technical as the next guy."

My client had a prior arrest for burglary. The new juvenile code provides for a six-month sentence for a second offense. So there I was. I figured I might be able to get the confession thrown out or at least impeach the credibility of the witness, but what a risk. So what do you do?[27]

Faced with similar problems, many defense attorneys simply act in the spirit of accommodation and serve as little more than observers in what become "traditional" adjudicatory proceedings.

Recent research has uncovered an additional curiosity associated with the post-*Gault* era. Based on data collected by the National Juvenile Court Data Archive, University of Minnesota law professor Barry C. Feld examined the availability of counsel and its effects on delinquency and status offense dispositions in six states — California, Minnesota, Nebraska, New York, North Dakota, and Pennsylvania.[28] He found that in three of the states, nearly half or more of the juvenile offenders did not have lawyers, including many youths who received secure confinement dispositions. In all of the jurisdictions, such legal variables as seriousness of the offense and prior juvenile court record was associated with more severe dispositions. But so too was legal representation. That is, all things being equal, the presence of an attorney appeared to exert an additional, independent effect on the severity of dispositions.

Police Encounters and Juvenile Rights

Juveniles and Miranda

While *Gault* addressed the rights required at the adjudication stage of the juvenile justice process, the High Court left other due-process issues to the state and lower federal courts. For the most part, many of these issues have remained unsettled, particularly with regard to juvenile rights and police encounters. The Court has not ruled specifically, for example, on the applicability of the *Miranda* safeguards to the juvenile process.[29] Although *Gault* held the privilege against self-incrimination applicable to juveniles in the same way it is applicable to adults, elsewhere in its opinion the Court qualified the scope of its ruling in general:

We do not in this opinion consider the impact of these constitutional provisions upon the totality of the relationship of the juvenile and the state. We do not even consider the entire process relating to juvenile "delinquents." For example, we are not here concerned with the procedures or constitutional rights applicable to the pre-judicial stages of the juvenile process.

The Uniform Juvenile Court Act

In 1968, the National Conference of Commissioners on Uniform State Laws drafted the *Uniform Juvenile Court Act* and recommended its enactment in all states.[30] The purpose of the act was to encourage uniformity of purpose, scope, and procedures in the juvenile justice system.

One of its provisions dealt with the issue of self-incrimination. Jurisdictions that adopted the Uniform Juvenile Court Act, in whole or in part, have similar provisions. Moreover, following *Gault* other jurisdictions enacted statutes designed to implement the *Miranda* safeguards during the investigatory stage of juvenile proceedings.

Thus, it would appear that in most jurisdictions, juveniles have the protections accorded by *Miranda*. The more perplexing issue, however, focuses on a juvenile's *waiver* of his or her *Miranda* rights. Does a minor — without the guidance of a parent, attorney, or other friendly adult — have the competence to make an intelligent, voluntary waiver of these rights? In *Fare* v. *Michael C.,*[31] the Supreme Court said yes given the "totality of circumstances." Moreover, in *West* v. *United States,*[32] the U.S. court of appeals set forth the circumstances to be considered in determining the validity of a minor's waiver of *Miranda* rights:

1. the age of the accused
2. the education of the accused
3. the knowledge of the accused as to both the substance of the charges and the nature of his or her rights to consult with a parent or attorney and remain silent
4. whether the juvenile was held incommunicado or was allowed to consult with relatives
5. whether the interrogation was held before or after the filing of the formal charges
6. the methods of interrogation
7. the length of the interrogation
8. whether the juvenile refused voluntarily to give statements on prior occasions
9. whether the accused had repudiated an extralegal statement given at a later date

A juvenile is legally capable of waiving his or her rights under the Fourth, Fifth, and Sixth Amendments depending on these conditions and whether the juvenile is able to comprehend the meaning and possible effect of any statements given to the police.

In light of Supreme Court action in 1985, juveniles' rights under the Fourth Amendment protection against illegal search and seizure are less clear. Almost two decades earlier, when the opinion in *Gault* emphasized that it was concerned with due-process requirements at the adjudicatory stage of juvenile proceedings, and *not* to those at the pre-judicial stages, it also reiterated a point made in *Kent* — that the purpose was not to extend to the juvenile process all of the rights required in adult criminal proceedings. Nevertheless, the state courts interpreted *Gault* to require the application of the Fourth Amendment and the exclusionary rule to juvenile cases, and no court has held the rule to be inapplicable. On the other hand, there is the principle of ***in loco parentis*** — literally, "in the place of the parent." The principle emerges with reference to searches of students and their lockers by school officials.

The Supreme Court has long since held that the Fourth Amendment does not protect individuals from searches conducted by private persons acting in behalf of the government. When searches of students occur, four questions emerge:

1. Is the school official acting as a private individual or as a government agent?
2. Is the official authorized to conduct a search on the basis of his or her *in loco parentis* relationship to the student?

There was nothing to do.
— Fifteen-year-old Terrance Wade in 1991, on why he and a companion allegedly raped, stabbed, and murdered a Boston woman on Halloween night

Is this going to take long? I've got someplace to go tonight.
— An eight-year-old Chicago boy being questioned by detectives in 1992, after he shot a classmate in the spine with a semi-automatic handgun

In loco parentis: A position in reference to a child of that of lawful guardian or parent.

Juveniles and the Fourth Amendment

• EXHIBIT 18.6 •

New Jersey v. T.L.O.

A teacher at a New Jersey high school discovered Ms. T.L.O., a fourteen-year-old freshman, and her companion smoking cigarettes in a school lavatory in violation of a school rule. The two girls were taken to an office, where they were questioned by a vice principal. When T.L.O. denied smoking and claimed that she was not a smoker, the vice principal demanded to see her purse. Upon opening it, he observed cigarettes and the rolling papers typically associated with marijuana use. He then searched the purse thoroughly and found marijuana, a pipe, plastic bags, a substantial amount of money, an index card listing students who owed T.L.O. money, and two letters that implicated T.L.O. in marijuana dealing. The police were called, and delinquency charges were brought against Ms. T.L.O. in juvenile court. The court denied T.L.O.'s motion to suppress the evidence found in her purse on Fourth Amendment grounds, declared the search to be a reasonable one, and adjudicated T.L.O. to be delinquent. T.L.O. appealed the decision. Eventually the New Jersey Supreme Court reversed the decision in T.L.O.'s favor

and ordered that the evidence be suppressed, holding that the search of the purse was unreasonable. On appeal to the U.S. Supreme Court, entered by the Reagan Administration in behalf of the state of New Jersey, the High Court ruled in favor of New Jersey, and stated:

1. The Fourth Amendment's prohibition on unreasonable searches and seizures applies to searches conducted by public school officials and is not limited to searches carried out by law enforcement officers. Nor are school officials exempt from the Amendment's dictates by virtue of the special nature of their authority over schoolchildren. In carrying out searches and other functions pursuant to disciplinary policies mandated by state statutes, school officials act as representatives of the State, not merely as surrogates for the parents of students, and they cannot claim the parent's immunity from the Fourth Amendment strictures.

2. Schoolchildren have legitimate expectations of privacy. They may find it necessary to carry with them a variety of legitimate, noncontraband items, and there is no reason to conclude that they have necessarily waived all rights to privacy in such items by bringing them onto school grounds. But striking the balance between schoolchildren's legitimate expecta-

---

New Jersey v. *T.L.O.:* The Supreme Court ruling that school officials, with reasonable grounds to believe that the law or school rules are being violated, may conduct reasonable searches if needed to maintain safety, order, and discipline in a school.

3. Does the *in loco parentis* relationship give to a school official a parent's immunity from the Fourth Amendment?
4. Is the search reasonable?

These questions were addressed by the Supreme Court in *New Jersey* v. *T.L.O.*,[33] decided on January 15, 1985 (see Exhibit 18.6). The Court held that in spite of the *in loco parentis* relationship, schoolchildren have legitimate expectations of privacy and public school officials are not exempt from the Fourth Amendment ban. Nevertheless, the Court added, school officials, with reasonable grounds to believe that the law

tions of privacy and the school's equally legitimate need to maintain an environment in which learning can take place requires some easing of the restrictions to which searches by public authorities are ordinarily subject. Thus, *school officials need not obtain a warrant before searching a student who is under their authority. Moreover, school officials need not be held subject to the requirement that searches be based on probable cause to believe that the subject of the search has violated or is violating the law* [italics added]. Rather, the legality of the search should depend simply on reasonableness, under all the circumstances of the search. Determining the reasonableness of any search involves a determination of whether the search was justified at its inception and whether, as conducted, it was reasonably related in scope to the circumstances that justified the interference in the first place. . . . Such a search will be permissible in its scope when the measures adopted are reasonably related to the objectives of the search and not excessively intrusive in light of the student's age and sex and the nature of the infraction.

The Court's ruling in *T.L.O.* left a number of questions unanswered. There were no views expressed on whether evidence obtained by school authorities through an *illegal* search could be used in court; whether the standard announced also applied to searches of desks and lockers; what standard would apply to searches undertaken at the request of police; and whether authorities require "individualized suspicion" before searching a particular student.

As for fourteen-year-old T.L.O. — as she was designated in court records — when the High Court delivered its opinion in early 1985 she was eighteen years old. When the incident originally took place, in 1980 at New Jersey's Piscataway High School, T.L.O. was ordered expelled. That action was postponed, however, given the litigation. Moreover, as the case moved up the judicial ladder, a New Jersey trial court affirmed the juvenile court's original finding that there had been no Fourth Amendment violation. At the same time, however, the trial court also vacated T.L.O.'s adjudication of delinquency. In June, 1984, Ms. T.L.O. graduated from Piscataway High School.

SOURCE: *New Jersey* v. *T.L.O.,* 105 S.Ct. 733 (1985).

or school rules are being violated, may conduct reasonable searches if needed to maintain safety, order, and discipline in the school.

One could interpret the decision in *T.L.O.* as the signal of a retreat from the trend to give juveniles full procedural due-process rights. Whatever the trend, state and federal court decisions since the mid-1960s have opened the juvenile courts to defense lawyers and prosecutors, and have instilled greater regard for the rights of juvenile defendants. It would appear that the days of the closed, protected, benevolent, and sometimes unfair system based on the philosophy of *parens patriae* are now little more than history.

CRITICAL ISSUES IN JUVENILE JUSTICE

Much like criminal justice, juvenile justice in America has often been described as a *system*. There are similar diagrams and flow charts that depict juvenile justice as a system — how the various agencies and components fit together as each case is being processed and what decisions are possible at each stage. In many ways, at least on the surface, juvenile justice seems indeed to function as a system. Juveniles violate laws; police take juveniles into custody; detention facilities admit juveniles; juveniles and their parents or guardians appear at hearings in court; attorneys are present in behalf of juveniles and the state; judges enter rulings; and adjudicated youths are placed on probation, assigned to group homes, or committed to institutions.[34] Yet also like criminal justice, there is considerable tension and dissonance within the juvenile justice system. As former juvenile court judge H. Ted Rubin once described it:

> Below the surface, police get tired and angry when they arrest the same youth time and again, detention centers admit youngsters who don't require being locked up and experience the release of other youngsters who will shortly be reapprehended by the police, youngsters dislike the way someone in the system handled them, parents feel they are on trial when they accompany their youngsters to court, lawyers may fulfill only a limited advocacy role, the judge is unsure whether he made the right dispositional choice, the probation officers and group home and institutional staffs meet their new client and tell him they will help him as much as he will let them.[35]

Juvenile justice is an imperfect system, suffering from the same lack of unity of purpose and organized interrelationships that are apparent within the adult system. Yet beyond this, juvenile justice also has a number of unique problems — problems that raise some serious questions about the efficacy and fairness of a process that is structured to handle children "in their best interests."

Status Offenders: PINS, MINS, CHINS, CINS, JINS, and YINS

In New York they are "persons in need of supervision" (PINS); in Illinois they are "minors otherwise in need of supervision" (MINS); in Colorado they are "children in need of supervision" (CHINS); in Florida they are also "children in need of supervision," but by a different acronym (CINS); in New Jersey they are "juveniles in need of supervision" (JINS); in Montana they are "youths in need of supervision" (YINS); and elsewhere they are known, however informally, as "ungovernable" or "unruly" or "wayward." Whatever the name or acronym, these are the **status offenders** — the runaways, truants, and other "incorrigibles" who, because of their special status as children, can be brought to the attention of the juvenile courts for certain kinds of noncriminal behavior.*

The creation of the PINS, CHINS, and other designations was an outgrowth of a movement during the 1960s and 1970s to decriminalize status offense behavior. Prior to that time, such acts fell under statutory definitions of "delinquency." [36] Under the South Dakota Juvenile Court Act, for example, which endured for half a century (it was finally repealed in 1968), the range of behaviors defined as delinquent was so inclusive that it likely applied to the majority of American youth (see Exhibit 18.7). The need for decriminalizing status offenses was obvious. Children who were runaways, curfew violators, truant, or otherwise "incorrigible" were handled in the same manner as juvenile law violators, given the same delinquent status, and housed in the same reform and industrial schools. A case in point involved New York's Girls' Term Court. Under the state's Wayward Minor Act of 1923, the juvenile courts had jurisdiction over youths ages sixteen to twenty-one who had been arrested on criminal charges or who were "developing habits and associations that may lead to crime." This latter category was for status offenders, and the Girls' Term Court handled the females as wayward minors. [37] The court procedures followed the *parens patriae* concept of informal hearings and individualized planning, but many of the Girls' Term "respondents," as they were called, were status offenders who were mixed with hard-core delinquent offenders in state correctional institutions. Moreover, "respondents" who earned early release from these institutions were supervised in the community by the New York State Division of Parole — the adult parole authority — by the same parole

Status offenders: Youths who, because of their special status as children, can be brought to the attention of the juvenile courts for certain kinds of noncriminal behavior.

The movement to decriminalize status offenses

---

* Statutory definitions of status offenders are actually more inclusive. In California, for example, a status offender is defined as follows: "Any person under the age of eighteen years who persistently or habitually refuses to obey the reasonable and proper orders or directions of his parents, guardian, custodian or school authorities, or who is beyond the control of such person, or any person who is a habitual truant from school within the meaning of any law of this state, or who from any cause is in danger of leading an idle, dissolute, lewd, or immoral life, is within the jurisdiction of the juvenile court which may adjudge such person to be a ward of the court." In 1971, the phrase "or who from any cause is in danger of leading an idle, dissolute, lewd, or immoral life" was found to be unconstitutionally vague, causing the California legislature to redraft its status offender definition. (See *Gonzalez* v. *Mailliard*, No. 50424 N.D. Calif. 1971.)

• EXHIBIT 18.7 •

What Constitutes a Juvenile Delinquent?
From the South Dakota Revised Code

Any child who, under the age of eighteen years, violates any law of this state or any ordinance of any city or town of this state; who is considered incorrigible, or intractable by parents, guardian, or custodian; who knowingly associates with thieves, vicious, or immoral persons; who, without cause and without the consent of its parents, guardian, or custodian, absents itself from its home or place of abode; who is growing up in idleness or crime; who fails to attend school regularly without proper reason therefor, if of compulsory school age; who repeatedly plays truant from school; who does not regularly attend school and is not otherwise engaged in any regular occupation or employment but loiters and idles away its time; who knowingly frequents or visits a house of ill repute; who knowingly frequents or visits any policy shop or place where any gaming device is operated; who patronizes, visits, or frequents any saloon or dram shop where intoxicating liquors are sold; who patronizes or visits any public poolroom where the game of billiards or pool is being carried on for pay or hire; who frequents or patronizes any wine-room or dance hall run in connection with or adjacent to any house of ill-fame or saloon; who visits, frequents, or patronizes, with one of the opposite sex, any restaurant or other place where liquors may be purchased after the hours of nine o'clock; who is found alone with one of the opposite sex in a private apartment or room of any restaurant, lodging house, hotel, or other place at nighttime or who goes to any secluded place or is found alone in such place, with one of the opposite sex, at night-time with the evident purpose of concealing their acts; who wanders about the streets in the nighttime without being on any lawful business or lawful occupation, or habitually wanders about any railroad yards or tracks, or jumps or attempts to jump onto any moving train, or enters any car or engine without lawful authority; who writes or uses vile, obscene, vulgar, profane, or indecent language, or smokes cigarettes or uses tobacco in any form; who drinks intoxicating liquors on any street, in any public place, or about any school house, or at any place other than its own home; or who is guilty of indecent, immoral, or lascivious conduct.

SOURCE: *South Dakota Revised Code,* Section 43.0301 (repealed 1968).

These street youths may well satisfy at least some of the "requirements" of delinquency listed in the repealed section of the South Dakota Revised Code *—yet in one way or another, so could most other young people in the United States. Decriminalization attempts to eliminate lumping status offenders—runaways, curfew violators, truants, and the like—with hard-core juvenile offenders.*

officers, under the same conditions, and reporting to the same offices that were used for convicted felons. The results were sometimes disastrous. As one New York parole officer recalled a 1967 case:

> I'll never forget Rebecca. The Girls' Term system really worked against her. She was a bright and beautiful child, and a woman by the time she was sixteen. She did well in school, but her parents—wealthy New York socialites—just couldn't deal with the way Rebecca slept around, particularly with *older* men. . . . When she contracted VD from one of her sleeping partners, Mr. & Mrs. B. really flipped. In the hope of scaring Rebecca into straightening out, they hauled her off to Girls' Term Court. But the judge sent her to Westfield State Farm for "correction." There she was brutally raped and sodomized on more than one occasion. She also made some new friends there—heroin addicts, hookers, and some pretty vicious people. *I know,* I was supervising *all* of them. . . . To make a long story short, Rebecca ended up as a heroin addict, a junky prostitute, and on her twenty-first birthday we found her dead of a drug overdose in a sleazy Times Square hotel.[38]

While the decriminalization of status offenses in most states was a positive step, what seems warranted is the total repeal of status offender jurisdiction and shifting the care and management from the juvenile courts to the social service delivery network. In many jurisdictions, status offenders continue to be detained or incarcerated with hard-core offenders—sometimes including detention in adult jails and state correctional facilities.

Perhaps the most significant problem faced by the juvenile courts in dealing with status offenders is their sheer number. Some 40 percent of juvenile court dispositions involve status offenders, and the time, attention, and resources spent on these youths significantly reduce the ability of the courts to effectively deal with youths who are serious criminal offenders. Perhaps this accounts for the apparently misplaced priorities in some juvenile sentences. Nationally, in fact, some status offenders are more likely to be incarcerated than are juvenile burglars.[39]

A move towards the repeal of the current process was the passage in 1974 of the *Juvenile Justice and Juvenile Delinquency Prevention Act.*[40] This federal legislation specified that states' receipt of federal funds for delinquency programs was dependent on their reform of status offender management. It required by 1985 the deinstitutionalization of status offenders, their removal from the justice system, and the detaining and incarceration of delinquents in separate facilities from adults. Currently, while a few jurisdictions have complied with the mandates of the Juvenile Justice and Juvenile Delinquency Prevention Act and most have separated status offenses from the former delinquency classifications, tens of thousands of status offenders continue to be incarcerated each year in the most unfavorable of conditions.

The Juvenile Justice and Juvenile Delinquency Prevention Act

Juveniles in the Adult Courts

Although federal and state laws have specified the ages at which the criminal courts gain jurisdiction over young offenders (see Exhibit 18.8), for as long as there have been juvenile court systems in the United States there have also been statutory exceptions. As indicated in a 1919 publication of the U.S. Department of Labor, for example:

> In the District of Columbia, Georgia, Iowa, Louisiana, Massachusetts, New Jersey, New York, Utah, and Vermont, the law specifically excludes the juvenile court

---

● EXHIBIT 18.8 ●

Ages at which Criminal Courts Assume Jurisdiction over Young Offenders

Age 16	Age 17	Age 18		
Connecticut	Georgia	Alabama	Kansas	Oklahoma
New York	Illinois	Alaska	Kentucky	Oregon
North Carolina	Louisiana	Arizona	Maine	Pennsylvania
Vermont	Massachusetts	Arkansas	Maryland	Rhode Island
	Michigan	California	Minnesota	South Dakota
	Missouri	Colorado	Mississippi	Tennessee
	South Carolina	Delaware	Montana	Utah
	Texas	District of Columbia	Nebraska	Virginia
		Florida	Nevada	Washington
		Hawaii	New Hampshire	West Virginia
		Idaho	New Jersey	Wisconsin
		Indiana	New Mexico	Wyoming
		Iowa	North Dakota	Federal districts
			Ohio	

They call me C.K. That mean "Crip Killer." I kill Crips.
—A member of the Bloods, 1990

from jurisdiction in such cases [of felonies or crimes punishable by death or life sentence]. In the great majority of states in which the juvenile court may have jurisdiction, the judge may in his discretion dismiss the case and allow the child to be tried in the regular criminal courts or under ordinary procedure.[41]

Not altogether inconsistent with the *parens patriae* philosophy upon which the juvenile court system was founded, such statutes were grounded in the notion that certain young offenders—specifically, those accused of serious felonies—were simply not amenable to the guardianship and special form of treatment found in the juvenile courts. That is, such youths were deemed unwilling to follow the advice of the juvenile court and be submissive to its authority. By the late 1940s, however, many states had changed their statutes in favor of young offenders, granting to the juvenile courts exclusive jurisdiction over youths regardless of the offenses involved.[42]

In recent decades, there has been a reversal in this trend. With the *Gault* decision in 1967 combined with increased rates of juvenile crime in the 1960s and 1970s, many state jurisdictions lowered the age at which youths could be tried as adults. Although such changes had the coincidental effect of extending the full complement of the rights of the accused to some juveniles, the actual purpose of the new statutes was to subject youths found guilty of serious offenses to the same sentences and punishments that would befall adults convicted of the same crimes.

The process of transferring a case from the juvenile to the adult criminal court has become known as **waiver of jurisdiction.** The effect of such a transfer is to deny a youth the protection and ameliorative treatment afforded by the juvenile process. Most state statutes provide the waivers of jurisdiction, but the provisions of these statutes vary widely. In California and Oregon, for example, waivers can be applied to all juveniles ages sixteen and over, regardless of the offense involved. By contrast, in the states of Alabama, Colorado, and Pennsylvania, waivers can occur for juveniles as young as fourteen years, but only in the case of felony offenses. In Florida, where the waiver age is fourteen, juveniles or their parents can demand waivers. It is for this reason that six-year-old Nancy Jo Burch, mentioned in the opening paragraphs of this chapter, was tried in a Florida criminal court for striking a schoolmate. Her parents had demanded a jury trial.

The waiver statutes in a number of other jurisdictions permit extremely young children to be tried in the adult courts. In Mississippi and Illinois the age is thirteen. In Indiana, ten-year-olds charged with murder can be transferred to the criminal courts. In New Hampshire and Wyoming, waivers are permitted but no age is indicated in their statutes, which theoretically means that seven- or eight-year-olds can face official criminal proceedings. Ironically, depending on the jurisdiction children may commit crimes so serious that they do not understand their gravity, but they come before the courts as adults. Yet if they steal candy and comic books from the local convenience store, they are still "youths" in the eyes of the law and their understanding of the nature of their crimes are not at issue.

Although the decision to waive jurisdiction is critical in its effect on a juvenile offender's subsequent treatment, for a long time youths had no protection against procedural arbitrariness in the waiver process. Change finally occurred in 1966 with ***Kent* v. *United States,*** the first Supreme Court evaluation of the constitutionality of juvenile court proceedings (see Exhibit 18.9). The ruling in *Kent* held that there must be waiver hearings, and although such hearings need not conform to all

Waiver of jurisdiction: The process by which the juvenile court relinquishes its jurisdiction over a child and transfers the case to a court of criminal jurisdiction for prosecution as an adult.

Kent.* v. *United States: The Supreme Court ruling that the waiver of jurisdiction is a critically important stage in juvenile proceedings and must be attended by minimum requirements of due process and fair treatment.

James Terry Roach was sentenced to death for a multiple rape/murder committed when he was a juvenile. He was executed in South Carolina's electric chair on January 10, 1986. Since the Furman *decision in 1976, only three others have been executed for crimes committed as juveniles: Charles Rumbaugh in Texas (1985), Jay Pinkerton in Texas (1986), and Dalton Prejean in Louisiana (1990).*

● EXHIBIT 18.9 ●

Kent v. United States

Morris A. Kent, Jr., had first come under the authority of the District of Columbia juvenile court in 1959. He was age fourteen at the time and had been apprehended as a result of several housebreakings and an attempted purse snatching. He was placed on probation, in the custody of his mother, and from time to time he was contacted by the juvenile court officials.

Two years later, on September 2, 1961, an intruder broke into the home of a District of Columbia woman, took her wallet, and raped her. Fingerprints found in the apartment matched those of Kent, having been taken during his juvenile court contact in 1959. At this point sixteen years of age and still on juvenile probation, Morris Kent was taken into custody by the police. After almost two days of interrogation, he admitted his involvement in these and several other housebreakings, robberies, and rapes.

Following Kent's apprehension, his mother obtained an attorney, who promptly conferred with the social service director of the juvenile court. In a brief meeting, they discussed the possibility that the court might waive its jurisdiction and transfer the case to the district court for trial — a waiver that the attorney indicated he would oppose. Meanwhile, Kent was being held in detention, during which time there was neither an arraignment nor a hearing by a judicial officer to determine probable cause for arrest. Kent's attorney, however, arranged for psychiatric examinations of his client, after which he filed two motions with the juvenile court. The first was for a hearing on the question of the waiver of juvenile court jurisdiction; accom-

panying it was a psychiatrist's affidavit certifying that Kent "is a victim of severe psychopathology" and recommending hospitalization for psychiatric evaluation. The second motion, in behalf of effective assistance of counsel, was for access to the social service file that had been compiled by the staff of the juvenile court during Kent's probation period.

The juvenile court judge did not rule on these motions; he held no hearing; and he did not confer with Kent, his mother, or his attorney. Rather, the judge entered an order stating that after "full investigation, I do hereby waive" jurisdiction of Kent and directing that he be "held for trial for [the alleged] offenses under the regular procedure of the U.S. District Court for the District of Columbia." The judge made no findings; he did not recite any reason for the waiver; and he made no reference to the motions filed by Kent's attorney.

After the juvenile court waived its jurisdiction, Kent was indicted by the grand jury and received a jury trial in the criminal court. On the rape, he was found not guilty by reason of insanity. Yet he was found guilty on six counts of housebreaking and robbery, for which he was sentenced to a term of thirty to ninety years. On appeal to the U.S. court of appeals, Kent's attorney argued that the detention, interrogation, and fingerprinting were unlawful. As to the proceedings by which the juvenile court waived its jurisdiction, he attacked them on statutory and constitutional grounds: " . . . no hearing occurred, no findings were made, no reasons were stated before the waiver, and counsel was denied access to

the social service file." The court of appeals affirmed the lower court decision, and the United States Supreme Court granted *certiorari.*

By a 5-to-4 majority, the High Court nullified the juvenile court's waiver of jurisdiction, holding that such a waiver is a "critically important" stage in the juvenile process and must be attended by minimum requirements of due process and fair treatment as required by the Fourteenth Amendment. Specifically, the Court set forth four basic safeguards required by due process during waiver proceedings:

1. If the juvenile court is considering waiving jurisdiction, the juvenile is entitled to a hearing on the waiver.
2. The juvenile is entitled to representation by counsel at such hearing.
3. The juvenile's attorney must be given access to the juvenile's social records on request.
4. If jurisdiction is waived, the juvenile is entitled to a statement of reasons in support of the waiver order.

The ruling in *Kent* was initially limited in scope, since it was seemingly based on an interpretation of the waiver requirements under District of Columbia statutes rather than on constitutional principles. However, following the many references to *Kent* in *In re Gault* and subsequent cases, the requirements stated in *Kent* have taken on constitutional dimension and are applicable to *all* juvenile court waiver decisions.

source: *Kent* v. *United States,* 383 U.S. 541 (1966).

the requirements of a criminal trial, they must measure up to the essentials of due process and fair treatment.

Although *Kent* accorded a measure of constitutional safeguards to waiver proceedings, the question remains as to whether *any* juvenile should be dealt with in the adult criminal courts. On the one hand, there is the pragmatic issue of community protection and the state's right to wage war against its enemies. On the other, there is the more abstract and philosophical consideration of confinement in a penitentiary as an appropriate treatment for what is defined under state statutes as delinquent behavior. Of even greater significance is the matter of juveniles and capital punishment. Thirty states currently permit the execution of criminals regardless of their age. Although the majority of nations around the world have set eighteen as the minimum age for capital punishment, 288 juveniles have been executed in the United States under laws that permit some young offenders to be tried as adults.[43] The last such execution was in 1964, when the state of Texas electrocuted James Andrew Echols, convicted of a rape—a crime that is no longer punishable by death as the result of *Coker* v. *Georgia*[44]—committed at age seventeen. The youngest person to be executed during the current century was a thirteen-year-old, electrocuted in Florida in 1927.[45]

As of 1992, there were thirty-six residents of death row in America who were juveniles at the time of their capital offense.[46] Opponents of the death penalty argue that the execution of any juvenile is "cruel and unusual punishment" in violation of the Eighth Amendment. Moreover, they hold, a child's behavior is different from that of an adult. On the other hand, supporters of the death penalty insist that youthful offenders should not be permitted to wrap themselves in the shield of age in order to escape responsibility for their crimes. Interestingly, the U.S. Supreme Court remained silent on the matter of juveniles and the death penalty until only recently. In *Thompson* v. *Oklahoma*,[47] decided in 1988, the Court put forth the somewhat narrow ruling that a state may not execute a person who was less than age sixteen at the time of the offense, *unless* the state legislature had spoken clearly on the matter by setting a minimum age for the death penalty. In *Stanford* v. *Kentucky*,[48] however, decided in 1989, the Court made the more specific ruling that the imposition of the death penalty for a crime committed at sixteen or seventeen years of age does not constitute a violation of the Eighth Amendment ban against cruel and unusual punishment (see Exhibit 18.10).

Interestingly, one of the few recent empirical studies of the juvenile death penalty found that in general, the public is unwilling to sentence juveniles to death—even when it feels that the circumstances warrant it. More specifically, the data suggest that juvenile murder cases resulting in a death sentence tend to involve more heinous crimes than those of the adults receiving the same sentence.[49]

Children on death row

Thompson v. *Oklahoma*

Stanford v. *Kentucky:* The Supreme Court ruling that the imposition of the death penalty for a crime committed at age sixteen or seventeen does not constitute cruel and unusual punishment merely because of the accused's age.

Juvenile Detention

The temporary detention of youths pending juvenile court action presents significant problems for both juvenile justice officials and those youths held in custody. As noted in the first section of this chapter, the Supreme Court's ruling in *Schall* v. *Martin* sanctioned the practice of preventive detention for certain juvenile arrestees. In that case, on December 13, 1977, fourteen-year-old Gregory Martin, along with two other youths, had been arrested on charges of robbery, assault, and weapons violations. For fifteen days Martin had been held in detention, after which he was adjudicated a juvenile delinquent and placed on

Schall v. *Martin:* The Supreme Court ruling that preventive detention is permissible for accused juvenile delinquents when there is evidence that the youth presents a serious risk of committing a crime before adjudication of the case.

• EXHIBIT 18.10 •

Stanford v. Kentucky

Kevin N. Stanford's crime was described as particularly "grisly and inhuman," as well as "exceedingly violent." On January 7, 1981, during a gas station robbery in Jefferson County, Kentucky, Stanford repeatedly raped and sodomized twenty-year-old Baerbel Poore, who happened to be his next-door neighbor. Stanford then drove her to a secluded area, shot her point-blank in the face, and then again in the back of her head. The proceeds from the robbery were roughly 300 cartons of cigarettes, two gallons of fuel, and a small amount of cash. Stanford was seventeen years and four months of age at the time of the robbery–rape–murder, and he was tried as an adult. He was ultimately convicted of murder, first-degree sodomy, first-degree robbery, and receiving stolen property, and was sentenced to death and forty-five years in prison. The Kentucky Supreme Court affirmed Stanford's death sentence, and the United States Supreme Court granted *certiorari.*

In tandem with *Stanford,* the High Court also considered *Wilkins* v. *Missouri. Wilkins* involved the stabbing death of twenty-six-year-old Nancy Allen, who was working behind the sales counter of a convenience store in Avondale, Missouri. Heath Wilkins committed the murder on July 27, 1985, when he was approximately sixteen years and six months of age. When Wilkins first stabbed Allen, she fell to the floor. He then stabbed her three more times in her chest. Two of these wounds penetrated her heart.

When she began to beg for her life, Wilkins stabbed her four more times in the neck, opening her carotid artery. The robbery netted liquor, cigarettes, and $450 in cash and checks. Wilkins was eventually arrested, tried as an adult, convicted of murder that was considered by the trial court as "wantonly vile and inhuman," and sentenced to death. The Supreme Court of Missouri affirmed, and the United States Supreme Court granted *certiorari,* to decide in both cases whether the Eighth Amendment precludes the death penalty for individuals who commit crimes at sixteen or seventeen years of age.

On June 26, 1989, in a 5-to-4 majority, the High Court ruled that as far as the Eighth Amendment's prohibition of cruel and unusual punishment is concerned, a person who commits capital murder at sixteen years of age is old enough to be subjected to the death penalty. Writing for the majority, Justice Antonin Scalia announced that since there can be no claim that the imposition of the death penalty in *Stanford* and *Wilkins* would have been considered cruel and unusual at the time that the Bill of Rights was adopted, the appropriate focus is whether it would be contrary to the "evolving standards of decency that mark the process of a maturing society." The most relevant indications of society's attitude in this behalf, Scalia noted, are the statutes passed by its elected representatives. Of the thirty-seven states that have a death penalty statute, the Court reasoned, fifteen decline to im-

pose it on sixteen-year-olds and twelve on seventeen-year-olds. Those numbers are not sufficient to "establish a national consensus this Court has previously thought sufficient to label a particular punishment as cruel and unusual."

In portions of the opinion, joined by Chief Justice Rehnquist and Justices White and Kennedy, Scalia discounted the relevance of state laws that draw lines at age eighteen or above for such activities as driving, drinking, and voting. Justice O'Connor cast the crucial fifth vote in a concurring opinion, agreeing that the Eighth Amendment does not forbid the imposition of the death penalty on sixteen- and seventeen-year-old defendants. Justices Brennan, Marshall, Blackmun, and Stevens dissented, arguing that imposing the death penalty on an offender aged sixteen or seventeen at the time of the offense does indeed violate standards of decency.

As for the public's overall reaction to the decision in *Stanford,* a poll conducted for *Time* and *CNN* just two days after the High Court released its opinion found that only 17 percent of adults opposed the death penalty in general, and only 35 percent opposed its imposition on sixteen- and seventeen-year-olds.

SOURCES: *Stanford* v. *Kentucky,* 45 CrL 3203 (1989); *Time,* July 10, 1989, p. 48; *New York Times,* June 27, 1989, pp. A1, A18; Ron Rosenbaum, "Too Young To Die," *New York Times Magazine,* March 12, 1989, pp. 33–35, 58–61.

probation. While still in detention, however, Martin instituted a *habeas corpus* class-action suit on behalf of *all* youths being held in preventive detention pursuant to New York's Family Court Act. When the case reached the U.S. Supreme Court, it was held that preventive detention was permissible with respect to an accused juvenile delinquent when there was evidence that he or she presented a "serious risk" of committing a crime before adjudication of the case. The New York procedure was upheld because it served the legitimate purpose of community protection and because there were numerous procedural safeguards in the New York Juvenile Court Act intended to safeguard against erroneous deprivations of liberty.

Schall v. *Martin* is the most significant to the issue of juvenile detention, not just because it validated the constitutionality of New York's statute, but because of the perspective on juvenile justice reflected in the High Court's opinion:

> Juveniles, unlike adults, are always in some form of custody. Children, by definition, are not assumed to have the capacity to take care of themselves. They are assumed to be subject to the control of their parents, and if parental control

falters, the State must play its part as *parens patriae.* In this respect, the juvenile's liberty interest may, in appropriate circumstance, be subordinated to the State's *parens patriae* interest in preserving and promoting the welfare of the child.[50]

In addition to its contention that preventive detention acts in behalf of the welfare of a child, the Court also noted that such detention is for a limited period of time, as most youths are released after only a few days. And therein lies the dilemma for both youths "in trouble" and the juvenile justice system as a whole. Jails and detention centers, particularly those that mix juveniles with adults, can be depressing and exceedingly dangerous places. For example:

The victimization of juveniles by adults during detainment

- In California, a fifteen-year-old girl arrested for assaulting a police officer hanged herself after four days of isolation in a local jail.
- In Illinois, a seventeen-year-old boy was taken into custody and detained for owing $73 in unpaid traffic tickets, only to be tortured and beaten to death by his cellmates.
- In a West Virginia jail a truant was murdered by an adult inmate; in an Ohio jail a teenage girl was raped by a guard.
- In Kentucky, fifteen-year-old Robbie Horn hanged himself in a local jail where he had been held for only thirty minutes. His offense: arguing with his mother.[51]

Although one might argue that these are just isolated cases, in fact no one really knows the full extent of the problem. As is the case with crime victims in the general population, victimizations within jails are reported only infrequently. What *is* known, however, is the relative extent to which youths find themselves in contact with jail populations — both juvenile and adult. At the close of the 1980s, for example, well over 600,000 youths were being placed in juvenile detention and correctional facilities annually, with an average commitment period of 109 days.[52] Moreover, a fourth of these were non-adjudicated youths, and literally tens of thousands were status offenders and dependent, neglected, and abused children. And finally, these figures do not include the many thousands more being held in *adult* facilities.

Juvenile Corrections

Although data periodically emerge as to the number of juveniles held in jails and correctional institutions, relatively little is known about the extent of juvenile delinquency and youth crime, the number of status offenders and the nature of their "misbehavior," the size and character of the juvenile justice population as a whole, the dispositions that result from both informal and formal juvenile hearings, and the recidivism rates of adjudicated youths. The reason is that in many jurisdictions juvenile laws require that records of youthful offenders be sealed or destroyed to protect minors from being labeled as criminals. In fact, findings from a U.S. Bureau of Justice Statistics survey indicated that twenty-six states do not retain police and court records pertaining to juveniles.[53] As a result, any conclusions as to the nature and effectiveness of juvenile corrections are at best tentative.

Diversion   The juvenile due-process requirements derived from *Kent, Gault,* and *Winship,* combined with rising costs of operating correctional institutions, have resulted in the wider use of community-based

treatment for adjudicated juveniles. A recent trend has been the greater use of diversion programs, with many young offenders being placed in remedial education and drug abuse treatment programs, foster homes, and counseling facilities. The effectiveness of these programs has not been demonstrated. However, a recent examination of studies of juvenile diversion initiatives concluded:

> One common component to all rationales for diversion seem to be that *less* intervention is better than *more* intervention. Thus, whatever else it involves, diversion necessarily implies an attempt to make the form of social control more limited in scope. Studies of diversion programs indicate that instead of limiting the scope of the system, diversion programs often broaden it. They do this by either intensifying services or by taking in more cases. The latter is referred to as a "widening of the net" effect.[54]

Probation   Probation is by far the primary form of community treatment in the juvenile justice system, and the probation process for youths is essentially the same as that for adults. At any given time as many as 500,000 youths are on probation in the United States. The tendency toward such widespread use of juvenile probation evolved from the same rationales as diversion, combined with the findings of studies conducted decades ago that found that most juvenile probationers had been discharged from supervision under favorable circumstances.[55] In other words, most had finished their probation time with no new arrests or technical violations or at least none severe enough to warrant revocation of probation. However, "discharge under favorable circumstances" is hardly what one could call a forceful measure of probation effectiveness. As noted in the examination of self-reported criminal behavior in Chapter 4, relatively few criminal and delinquent acts ultimately result in arrest. Moreover, for most juveniles on probation, supervision is generally minimal. Therefore, violations of the conditions of probation rarely come to the attention of court officials.

Correctional Institutions   Finally, there are the juvenile correctional institutions, which are generally of two types. There are the *cottage systems* similar to many of the nation's facilities for women offenders. They are typically structured as campuslike environments with dormitory rooms rather than cells. For serious juvenile offenders there are secure *training* and *industrial schools,* which generally resemble medium-security penitentiaries for adults.

Nearly all juvenile correctional facilities have a variety of treatment programs — counseling on an individual or group basis, vocational and educational training, recreational and religious programs, and medical and dental facilities. A number of these institutions also provide legal services for juveniles, and a few have substance abuse treatment programs.

Regardless of the settings and available services, juvenile facilities are still places of confinement that militate against rehabilitation in the same ways as adult penitentiaries do. They have been described as "crime schools" offering only an "illusion of treatment" under conditions that represent "legalized child abuse." [56]

As to the effectiveness of juvenile corrections, and the juvenile justice process as a whole, the lack of comprehensive evaluative data leads only to speculation. However, data from the largest follow-up study of juveniles ever conducted provide at least a few insights. In 1985, researchers at the University of Pennsylvania's Center for Studies of Criminology and Criminal Law released a preliminary report on a study of 13,160 Philadelphia male youths born in 1958.[57] Data were gathered from schools, the police, and the juvenile court on each youth, and the findings, however tentative, were nevertheless significant because they were based on a generalizable urban population.

Of the 13,160 juveniles in the 1958 birth cohort, 4,315 — or some 33 percent — had at least one police contact prior to reaching age eighteen. Of these, 42 percent were one-time offenders, 35 percent were

Gang members discussing a recent drive-by shooting

nonchronic recidivists, and the remaining 23 percent were chronic recidivists. The 4,315 offenders had committed a total of 15,248 delinquent acts and, significantly, the chronic recidivists were responsible for almost two-thirds of all the delinquencies. In other words, most of the offenses had been committed by the 992 chronic delinquents. An analysis of the juvenile court dispositions of all of the delinquent youths and their subsequent recidivism suggested that lenient treatment for serious crimes early on in delinquent careers tended only to exacerbate subsequent lawbreaking behavior. Based on these and other data, the researchers concluded:

> Juvenile courts should consider close probation supervision for perhaps first- and certainly second-time violent Index offenders [those committing FBI Index crimes]. When these offenses occur early in the life of delinquents (as they do for chronic offenders) there is a temptation to be lenient and give the delinquent the opportunity for self-induced change. Yet we know that the chronic offender is detached from the schools and other community-based socialization and control agents. Failure to impose sanctions, failure to impose necessary controls early can encourage further delinquency.

The study suggested that the majority of delinquents were one- or two-time offenders, that most of the serious delinquencies were perpetrated by a small group of hard-core offenders, and that the juvenile justice system in the United States might have had a greater effect on reducing subsequent delinquent behavior if it took somewhat stronger measures with young offenders when they *first* came to its attention.

SUMMARY

The juvenile justice system in the United States was designed with the philosophy that, as minors, young offenders have a "special status" which requires that they be protected and corrected, and not necessarily punished. Given this special status, juveniles can come to the attention of the courts as delinquents, for having violated the criminal law; as status offenders, for having departed from the behavior expected of youths; and as dependent or neglected children, for having been the victims of abuse, neglect, or abandonment.

Juvenile justice processing is grounded in the notion of *parens patriae,* a position which holds that a child's natural protectors have been either unwilling or unable to provide the appropriate care. Thus, the state must take over the role of parent. As an outgrowth of *parens patriae,* juvenile offenders were rarely treated with the "due process of law" accorded to adults by the Bill of Rights.

Much of juvenile justice processing is informal, with a wide degree of discretion permitted at every stage. Police who take juveniles into custody have the options of releasing youths with a reprimand, referring them to police-based diversion programs, or detaining them for court processing. Similar discretionary alternatives are apparent in the juvenile courts. The actual court process is considered a civil matter. Moreover, it is not a trial, there is no jury, and the judge presides *in behalf of* the child.

It was not until 1966 that the United States Supreme Court first evaluated juvenile court proceedings and the constitutional rights of children. During that year, *Kent* v. *United States* brought the juvenile justice system within the framework of the Constitution and the Bill of

Rights. Subsequently, *In re Gault* in 1967, *In re Winship* in 1970, and *Breed* v. *Jones* in 1975 extended basic due-process rights to juvenile court proceedings.

Although juvenile justice philosophy and procedure have attempted to provide fair and beneficial treatment for children, the system as a whole suffers from a number of serious difficulties. First, the persistence of status offender laws in many jurisdictions places nondelinquent youths in contact with criminals and reduces the ability of the juvenile courts to more effectively deal with youths involved in serious criminal conduct. Second, there are many questions as to the wisdom of transferring delinquents to the adult courts for formal criminal processing. Third, the widespread practice of confining juveniles in detention facilities has placed the health and welfare of many youths at high risk. Fourth, regardless of the disposition of juvenile delinquents and status offenders, little is known as to the effectiveness of juvenile correctional approaches.

KEY TERMS

adjudication **(681)**
adjudication hearing **(695)**
adjudication inquiry **(694)**
Breed v. *Jones* **(696)**
delinquency **(687)**
delinquent **(687)**
detention hearing **(694)**
disposition hearing **(695)**

Illinois Juvenile Court Act **(686)**
in loco parentis **(699)**
In re Gault **(695)**
In re Winship **(696)**
intake hearing **(691)**
Kent. v. *United States* **(707)**
McKeiver v. *Pennsylvania* **(696)**

New Jersey v. *T.L.O.* **(700)**
parens patriae **(685)**
petition **(691)**
Schall v. *Martin* **(709)**
Stanford v. *Kentucky* **(709)**
status offenders **(703)**
status offense **(683)**
waiver of jurisdiction **(707)**

QUESTIONS FOR DISCUSSION

1. Given the *parens patriae* philosophy of the juvenile justice system in the United States, would delinquent youths be better off in the adult criminal courts with its strict guarantees of due process of law?

2. Do status offender laws serve any real purpose for today's youth? Should such laws be fully abolished? Why?

3. Should individuals who committed murders as youths be given capital sentences, placed on death row, and executed?

4. How might contemporary juvenile correctional programs and procedures be best upgraded or reformed? What ought to be done with juvenile offenders?

FOR FURTHER READING

Bing, Léon. *Do or Die,* New York: Harper Collins, 1991.

Feld, Barry C. "*In re Gault* Revisited: A Cross-State Comparison of the Right to Counsel in Juvenile Court." *Crime and Delinquency* 34 (October 1988): 393–424.

Chesney-Lind, Meda. "Girls in Jail." *Crime and Delinquency* 34 (April 1988): 150–168.

Kramer, Rita. *At a Tender Age: Violent Youth and Juvenile Justice.* New York: Henry Holt, 1988.

Streib, Victor L. "Imposing the Death Penalty on Children" in Kenneth C. Haas and James A. Inciardi [eds.] *Challenging Capital Punishment: Legal and Social Science Approaches.* Newbury Park, CA: Sage, 1988, pp. 245–267.

NOTES

1. *U.S. News & World Report,* April 8, 1991, p. 26.
2. *New York Times,* August 4, 1991, p. 39.
3. Wilmington (Delaware) *News-Journal,* August 7, 1985, p. A3.
4. *New York Times,* February 14, 1982, p. 39; *New York Times,* October 10, 1982, p. 24.
5. For the full story of April Savino, see Dennis Hevese, "Running Away," *New York Times Magazine,* October 2, 1988, pp. 30–31, 42, 59–64.
6. *Newsweek,* May 11, 1987, p. 74.
7. *Miami Herald,* March 27, 1982, p. 2.
8. *New York Times,* January 8, 1984, p. 19.
9. *Schall* v. *Martin,* 35 CrL 3103 (1984).
10. President's Commission on Law Enforcement and Administration of Justice, *Task Force Report: Juvenile Delinquency and Youth Crime* (Washington, D.C.: U.S. Government Printing Office, 1967), pp. 2–3.
11. Evelina, Beldon, "Courts in the United States Hearing Children's Cases," *Children's Bureau Publication* 65 (Washington, D.C.: U.S. Department of Labor, 1918), p. 8.
12. Illinois Juvenile Court Act, *Illinois Statutes,* 1899, Section 131.
13. U.S. Department of Justice, *A Comparative Analysis of Juvenile Codes* (Washington, D.C.: U.S. Government Printing Office, 1980), p. 7.
14. Norval Morris and Gordon Hawkins, *The Honest Politician's Guide to Crime Control* (Chicago: University of Chicago Press, 1969), p. 91.
15. Personal communication, October 15, 1982.
16. Irving Piliavin and Scott Briar, "Police Encounters with Juveniles," *American Journal of Sociology* 70 (September 1964), pp. 206–214.
17. H. Ted Rubin, "The Emerging Prosecutor Dominance of the Juvenile Court Intake Process," *Crime and Delinquency* 26 (July 1980), pp. 299–318.
18. See Charles E. Silberman, *Criminal Violence, Criminal Justice* (New York: Random House, 1978), pp. 309–370.
19. H. Ted Rubin, *Juvenile Justice: Policy, Practice, and Law* (Santa Monica, Ca.: Goodyear, 1979), pp. 86–108.
20. *Jail Inmates, 1990,* Bureau of Justice Statistics, June 1991.
21. H. Ted Rubin, *Juvenile Justice,* 86–108.
22. *Kent* v. *United States,* 383 U.S. 541 (1966).
23. *In re Gault,* 38 U.S. 1 (1967).
24. *In re Winship,* 397 U.S. 358 (1970).
25. *Breed* v. *Jones,* 421 U.S. 519 (1975).
26. *McKeiver* v. *Pennsylvania,* 403 U.S. 548 (1971).
27. Personal communication, December 2, 1985.
28. Barry C. Field, "*In re Gault* Revisited: A Cross-State Comparison of the Right to Counsel in Juvenile Court," *Crime and Delinquency,* 34 (October 1988), pp. 393–424.
29. *Miranda* v. *Arizona,* 384 U.S. 436 (1966).
30. The Uniform Juvenile Court Act has been reprinted in its entirety in Sanuel M. Davis, *Rights of Juveniles: The Juvenile Justice System* (New York: Clark Boardman, 1983), pp. A1–A53.
31. *Fare* v. *Michael C.,* 442 U.S. 707 (1979).
32. *West* v. *U.S.,* 399 F.2d 467 (5th Cir. 1968).
33. *New Jersey* v. *T.L.O.,* 105 S.Ct. 733 (1985).
34. H. Ted Rubin, *Juvenile Justice,* p. 269.
35. H. Ted Rubin, *Juvenile Justice,* p. 270.
36. Herbert A. Bloch and Frank T. Flynn, *Delinquency: The Juvenile Offender in America Today* (New York: Random House, 1956) p. 471.
37. Bloch and Flynn, *Delinquency,* p. 471.
38. Personal communication, September 17, 1985.
39. Charles E. Silberman, *Criminal Violence, Criminal Justice,* pp. 309–370.
40. *Juvenile Justice and Delinquency Prevention Act of 1974* (P.L. 93–415).
41. Sophonisba P. Breckinridge and Helen R. Jeter, "Juvenile Court Legislation in the United States," *Children's Bureau Publication* 70 (Washington, D.C.: U.S. Department of Labor, 1919), p. 19.
42. Negley K. Teeters and John Otto Reinemann, *The Challenge of Delinquency* (Englewood Cliffs, N.J.: Prentice-Hall, 1950), pp. 290–313.
43. *National Law Journal,* August 8, 1983, p. 4.
44. *Coker* v. *Georgia,* 433 U.S. 583 (1977); *Echols* v. *State,* 370 S.W. 2d 892 (1963).
45. *National Law Journal,* August 8, 1983, p. 4.
46. *Death Row, U.S.A.,* NAACP Legal Defense and Education Fund, August 2, 3, 1991.
47. *Thompson* v. *Oklahoma,* 43 CrL 4084 (1988).
48. *Stanford* v. *Kentucky,* 45 CrL 3203 (1989).
49. Gennaro Vito and Thomas J. Keil, "Selecting Juveniles for Death: The Kentucky Experience, 1976-1986," *Journal of Contemporary Criminal Justice,* 5 (1989) 181–198.
50. *Schall* v. *Martin,* 35 CrL 3103 (1984).
51. *Newsweek,* May 27, 1985, pp. 87–89.
52. *Sourcebook for Criminal Justice Statistics — 1990,* (Washington, DC: U.S. Department of Justice, 1991), pp. 570–572.
53. *New York Times,* October 21, 1985, p. A17.
54. Sharla Rausch and Charles Logan, "Diversion from Juvenile Court: Panacea or Pandora's Box?" *Paper presented at the thirty-third Annual Meeting of the American Society of Criminology,* Toronto, November 6, 1982.
55. For example, see Frank Scarpitti and Richard Stephenson, "A Study of Probation Effectiveness," *Journal of Criminal Law, Criminology, and Police Science* 59 (1968), p. 361.
56. Kenneth Wooden, *Weeping in the Playtime of Others: America's Incarcerated Children* (New York: McGraw-Hill, 1976).
57. Paul E. Tracy, Marvin E. Wolfgang, and Robert M. Figlio, *Delinquency in Two Birth Cohorts: Executive Summary* (Philadelphia, Pa.: Center for Studies in Criminology and Criminal Law, The Wharton School, University of Pennsylvania, 1985). This effort was a replication of the original *Delinquency in a Birth Cohort* study which followed up more than 10,000 Philadelphia youths born in 1945. See Marvin E. Wolfgang, Robert M. Figlio, and Thorsten Sellin, *Delinquency in a Birth Cohort* (Chicago: University of Chicago Press, 1972).

EPILOGUE

The Changing Face of Criminal Justice in America

> The Supreme Court is an institution far more dominated by centrifugal forces, pushing toward individuality and independence, than it is by centripetal forces pulling for hierarchical ordering and institutional unity.
>
> —WILLIAM H. REHNQUIST, ASSOCIATE JUSTICE, U.S. SUPREME COURT, OCTOBER 20, 1984

> Having been appointed by a Republican president and being accused now of being a flaming liberal on the court, the Republicans think I'm a traitor, I guess, and the Democrats don't trust me. And so I twist in the wind, I hope, beholden to no one, and that's exactly where I want to be.
>
> —SUPREME COURT JUSTICE HARRY BLACKMUN, 1991

Many decades ago, a prominent American statesman described the administration of criminal justice in the United States as "a disgrace to our civilization." [1] He had little use for the privilege against self-incrimination and he would give police a freer hand to interrogate suspects. He referred to the protection against unreasonable search and seizure as "another constitutional restriction which has been used to save men from conviction." The rule that a defendant must be confronted by the witnesses who testify against him he considered to be "undue tenderness toward the defendant." In addition, criminal procedure had become "a mere game in which the defendant's counsel play with loaded dice"; the jury had become a "box of nondescripts of no character"; and the trial by jury had come to be regarded as a fetish to such an extent that "the verdict becomes rather the vote of the town meeting than the sharp, clear decision of the tribunal of justice." And finally, he lamented, if the guilty ever did manage to get convicted, the punishment was likely to be far too mild.

These observations on the nature of American constitutional-criminal procedure were not offhandedly disregarded as the impromptu remarks of a frustrated political conservative. Many found them to be both challenging and foreboding, for they had come from the only person in American history to occupy the two most exalted offices the nation had to offer. The remarks had been made by William Howard Taft, president of the United States from 1909 to 1913, and chief justice of the United States Supreme Court from 1921 to 1930.

Taft's harsh words had not been made without basis. They came at a time when the nation seemed to be overrun by a growing legion of criminals against which the courts appeared to be powerless. "Mafia" and "Black Hand" extortion threats were stealing front-page headlines, as syndicated writers warned of Italian conspiracies to export secret criminal societies across the ocean to America. Muckraking journalists spoke of the many "crooks," "vile sluts," and "shameless politicians" who had become millionaires while honest citizens faced rising prices and scarce jobs. In the East and Midwest, organized crime syndicates were becoming visible, prostitution and police corruption were widespread and working hand in hand, racketeering had become a scare word attached to labor organizations, and such names as Johnny Torrio and Al Capone were beginning to receive national recognition. And too, there was the Black Sox scandal of 1919, when gambler Arnold Rothstein fixed the World Series by bribing eight star players of the Chicago White Sox to suddenly "lose their talent." The police and courts were accomplishing so little against the march of crime that one *Washington Post* writer commented: "There is no time to waste on hairsplitting over the infringement of liberty." [2]

In reflecting on Taft's opinions, it is curious how history seems so often to repeat itself, and how approaches to the problem of crime in America have cyclical paths. In this regard, this epilogue examines how sentiments about crime and justice have changed over time, with a shift toward the Taft philosophy during the closing decades of the twentieth century.

THE UNITED STATES VERSUS CRIME IN THE STREETS: TWO MODELS OF CRIMINAL JUSTICE

In retrospect, it would appear that the procedures for crime control, the processing of criminal defendants, and the sentencing, punishment, and management of convicted offenders are unshakably tied to the guarantees and prohibitions found in the Bill of Rights and their interpretations by the Supreme Court. Interestingly, however, an overview of the major criminology and criminal justice textbooks used during the first half of this century finds no mention of either the Bill of Rights or the United States Supreme Court.[3] Not until the 1960 publication of the notable text *Crime, Justice, and Correction* by lawyer-sociologist Paul W. Tappan did High Court decisions begin to creep into discussions of criminal justice processing.[4] But actually, this should *not* be particularly surprising. As is apparent throughout this text, concerted Supreme Court activity in matters of criminal justice did not begin until the early 1960s. In the years hence, the High Court has been extremely active within two alternative models.

The Due-Process Model

In the 1960s, the **Warren Court** — the Supreme Court under the leadership of Chief Justice Earl Warren — announced a large number of decisions that were in accord with what the late Herbert Packer called the **due-process model** of the criminal justice system.[5] This model stresses the possibility of error in the stages leading to trial and thus emphasizes the need for protecting procedural rights even if the implementation of these rights prevents the legal system from operating with maximum efficiency. Although no model can possibly describe reality in a completely satisfactory manner, the Warren Court's decisions in the area of criminal law extended a relatively strict version of the due-process model to cover the arrest-through-trial stages of the criminal process. This was accomplished as the Court incorporated one provision after another of the Bill of Rights into the due-process clause of the Fourteenth Amendment, thereby obligating the states to guarantee criminal defendants many of the constitutional safeguards that were already routinely accorded those accused of federal crimes. By 1969, nearly all of the Bill of Rights's provisions relating to criminal violations were binding upon the states as elements of Fourteenth Amendment due process. Among these were the Fifth Amendment right to be free from compulsory self-incrimination[6]; the Sixth Amendment rights to counsel,[7] speedy trial,[8] confrontation of hostile witnesses,[9] and compulsory processes for obtaining witnesses;[10] and the Eighth Amendment prohibition of cruel and unusual punishments.[11] The process of *nationalizing the Bill of Rights* reached its climax in two decisions announced shortly before the end of the Warren Court era. In 1968, the Court held that the Sixth Amend-

Chief Justice Earl Warren

Warren Court: The Supreme Court under the leadership of Chief Justice Earl Warren.

Due-process model: The model of the criminal justice system that stresses the possibility of error in the stages leading to trial and emphasizes the protection of procedural rights over system efficiency.

The nationalization of the Bill of Rights

ment's guarantee of trial by jury applies to state criminal trials involving serious or nonpetty offenses.[12] One year later, the Court finally ruled that the Fourteenth Amendment makes the Fifth Amendment's proscription of double jeopardy binding upon the states,[13] thus overruling the famous 1937 *Palko* decision, which had upheld the validity of a Connecticut statute permitting the state to bring criminal defendants to trial twice for the same offense upon a showing of legal error prejudicial to the state's case in the original trial.[14]

Of all of the Warren Court decisions forcing the states to institute procedural changes in their criminal justice processes, none was more controversial than *Mapp* v. *Ohio*,[15] which established the basic parameters of illegal search and seizure in state cases. Decided in 1961, *Mapp* is generally credited with being the "opening gun" of the *constitutional criminal law revolution*.

The constitutional law revolution of the 1960s

If *Mapp* can be termed the opening gun, then *Miranda* v. *Arizona* can be said to have constituted the most damaging direct hit — at least as far as law enforcement authorities and states' rights theorists of interposition were concerned.[16] *Miranda* was actually the Warren Court's attempt to clarify its earlier holding in *Escobedo* v. *Illinois*,[17] that when a police inquiry into an unsolved crime shifts from the investigative to the accusatory stage, the police must warn the suspect of his right to remain silent and honor his request to consult with his attorney. Many state and lower federal court judges who disapproved of the thrust and spirit of *Escobedo* had interpreted the majority opinion as applying only in cases where the accused had requested counsel, thus rendering the decision inapplicable to the vast majority of confession cases. Consequently, the High Court expanded the doctrine further in the 1966 *Miranda* case. By a five-to-four majority, the Court established a series of procedural prerequisites that had to be met before a suspect could be subjected to a process of custodial interrogation.

Despite the claims of dismayed and disappointed law enforcement officials that *Miranda* was unwise and would unduly hamper legitimate police and prosecutorial practices, the Court displayed little hesitancy in applying the *Miranda* guidelines to the line-up stage of the criminal justice process. In 1967, another five-man majority, in *United States* v. *Wade*,[18] concluded that the Sixth and Fourteenth Amendments entitle suspects required to appear in a police line-up to have an attorney present to observe the fairness of the proceedings. Accordingly, Justice Brennan's majority opinion held that any in-court identification of a defendant by a prosecution witness would be inadmissible if it had been "tainted" by either a line-up conducted in the absence of counsel or by a line-up that the defendant's attorney had shown to be unfair. Once again, the Court provoked the anger of police officials and prosecutors, who complained that they were being forced to fight criminals while "handcuffed" and "with three strikes against them."[19]

The Crime Control Model

Crime control model: The model of the criminal justice system that views the repression of criminal conduct as its most important function.

What occurred during much of the 1970s and 1980s undoubtedly brought great pleasure to those who were critical of the Court's prior judicial activism on behalf of defendants' rights. Whereas the Warren Court clearly was attuned to Herbert Packer's due-process model of criminal justice, the Court, under the tutelage of Chief Justice Burger, could best be described as predisposed to support Packer's alternative model of the legal process — the **crime control model,** which emphasizes the virtues of managerial efficiency and is based upon the proposition that the repression of criminal conduct is the most important function of the criminal process, not the promulgation of procedural rules that may occasionally prevent the prosecution of an innocent man, but more frequently result in the release of the factually guilty. Proponents of this model, according to Professor Packer, put a premium on the values of speed and finality, prefer that truly guilty suspects be convinced of the rationality of entering a guilty plea, and cannot understand why obviously guilty defendants should go free simply because of errors on the part of police or court personnel.

The **Burger Court's** greater sensitivity to the crime control model and the new majority's inclination to seriously limit the Warren Court's criminal procedure work first became clearly evident in the 1971 case of *Harris* v. *New York*.[20] At his trial for two counts of selling heroin, Harris, the petitioner, had taken the witness stand in his own defense to categorically deny the first alleged sale and to claim that the second sale actually involved only a small quantity of baking soda. In an effort to impeach the credibility of Harris's testimony, the prosecutor read a statement in which Harris had admitted both sales in response to police interrogation immediately after his arrest. However, no *Miranda* warnings had been given to Harris prior to his questioning by police. Thus, the question for the High Court to resolve was whether a statement obtained in violation of *Miranda* standards could be introduced into evidence for the limited purpose of cross-examining the defendant and discrediting his testimony. In a strongly worded opinion, Chief Justice Burger, speaking for the majority, argued that *Miranda* applies only to the prosecutor's presentation of the state's case; if the defendant voluntarily takes the witness stand, the prosecutor must be permitted to introduce statements ordinarily barred by *Miranda* because of the necessity of preventing perjury. Accordingly, Harris's conviction was affirmed, and the process of weakening or qualifying *Miranda* had begun.

Three years later, in *Michigan* v. *Tucker*,[21] the High Court further blunted *Miranda's* applicability in cases involving evidence obtained as the result of an improper interrogation. While undergoing interrogation concerning a rape case, Tucker was advised of all of his rights except the right to have a court-appointed attorney if he were unable to afford counsel. In response to questions about his activities on the night of the crime, Tucker told the police of a friend who could corroborate his alibi. Unfortunately for Tucker, his "friend" offered testimony that was highly damaging to the defense's case and that was a major factor in Tucker's subsequent conviction. Thus the Court had to decide whether evidence that had been obtained as a result of an interrogation in which the defendant had not received the full *Miranda* warning nevertheless should be admissible in the courtroom. Speaking for the majority in a somewhat ambiguous opinion, Justice Rehnquist answered this question in a positive manner, a result that continued the trend toward the erosion of *Miranda*.

Paralleling the Burger Court's movement away from *Miranda* has been its undercutting of the *Wade* guarantee of an attorney's presence whenever a suspect is asked to participate in a police line-up. In *Kirby* v. *Illinois*,[22] a five-man majority held that the *Wade* ruling entitles only defendants who have been indicted or otherwise formally charged with a serious crime to have an attorney present to observe the line-up procedure. The majority relied upon the argument that the Sixth Amendment right to counsel does not become a constitutional necessity until the

Burger Court: The Supreme Court under the leadership of Chief Justice Warren Burger.

Chief Justice Warren Burger

A far greater factor is the deterrent effect of swift and certain consequences; swift arrest, prompt trial, certain penalty and — at some point — finality of judgment
— CHIEF JUSTICE WARREN BURGER, 1982

"critical stage" of the criminal justice process, which is marked by the onset of formal prosecutorial proceedings. Since the large majority of line-ups take place well before the accused is indicted, *Kirby* clearly constitutes an evisceration of the principles underlying the *Wade* decision. Indeed, one wonders why the majority did not simply overrule *Wade* rather than attempt to justify the highly debatable proposition that the dangers of unfairness and mistaken identity against which *Wade* had been directed were somehow more likely to be present after the indictment than in the time period immediately after arrest.

Due Process versus Crime Control

In retrospect, the 1960s and 1970s reflect a scenario of contradiction for criminal justice in America. With the advantage of hindsight, it is highly ironic that while the tumultuous and crime-ridden sixties provoked a call for "law and order" resulting in a "war on crime," the United States Supreme Court, much to the dismay of numerous observers, particularly law enforcement officials, announced a series of decisions that were regarded as anything but sympathetic to the mounting war on crime. Through *Mapp, Miranda, Wade,* and other opinions, the Warren Court affirmed and gave tangible substance to the due-process model of criminal justice. The legal rights of the accused were strengthened and constitutional guarantees were more fully solidified. Furthermore, the number of executions in America dramatically declined during the 1960s, in part because of widespread anticipation that, if given the opportunity, the Supreme Court would be inclined to declare the death penalty to be violative of the cruel and unusual punishment clause of the Eighth Amendment. The activities of the High Court had offered credibility to a concept of "justice" in America; but in so doing, the court drew considerable criticism for "handcuffing" the police and prosecutors at a time when "crime in the streets" was perceived to be at epidermic levels.

Conversely, while crime and violence were less visible during the 1970s, Supreme Court decision making began to erode the foundation of criminal due process. Although the impact of the war on crime was seemingly apparent in the decreased visibility of street violence and a deceleration in the rates of many serious crimes, many of the High Court's key decisions diverted from a due-process model to crime control model. In the *Harris, Tucker,* and *Kirby* decisions, for example, defendants' rights were narrowed considerably.

THE SUPREME COURT IN THE REAGAN–BUSH ERA

Our legal system has failed in the protection of the innocent and the punishment of the guilty. The rights of victims must come before the rights of the accused.
— PRESIDENT RONALD REAGAN, 1981

As the United States moved into the 1980s, the rights of the accused achieved few gains. Moreover, limitations were placed on the police use of deadly force. More noticeable, however, was the fact that the crime control model of criminal justice was further strengthened by a broad-based assault on the exclusionary rule. Perhaps the most significant issue to face the Court in this behalf was the "good faith" exception. At its center was the argument that evidence obtained illegally by the police should be admissible in court if it had been gathered in a "good faith" effort to respect civil liberties. The Supreme Court's long-standing exclusionary rule barring tainted evidence was assailed on the ground that it helped criminals escape prosecution while failing to deter police misconduct. Civil libertarians maintained that the rule placed important limits on searches, thereby preserving the full integrity of the Fourth Amendment.

In 1981, a bill was sponsored by South Carolina Senator Strom Thurmond to eliminate the exclusionary rule entirely, replacing it with a civil remedy for defendants whose rights were violated. A second bill, introduced by Arizona Senator Dennis DeConcini, was designed to modify the rule, permitting judges wide discretion in deciding when to admit illegally seized evidence. Moreover, bills were introduced in several states to create the "good faith" exception.[23] But debate on these bills was postponed in anticipation of the High Court's ruling in several cases that were working their way up the judicial ladder.

The 1982–1983 Supreme Court term began with the expectation that the justices would resolve the controversy over the "good faith" exception. Pending in this behalf was *Illinois* v. *Gates,*[24] a case in which the "probable cause" for the issuance of a search warrant was called into question. There was the feeling, too, that the long-awaited exception would be established with *Gates,* for it appeared that even the High Court looked upon the exclusionary rule with some disfavor. As Chief Justice Burger had commented in an earlier case:

> I see no insurmountable obstacle to the elimination of the Suppression Doctrine if Congress would provide some meaningful and effective remedy against unlawful conduct by government officials.[25]

In *Gates,* however, the Court avoided the "good faith" issue, as a majority of the justices determined that it would be inappropriate to consider a matter which had not been addressed as the case had been moving through the state courts. The *Gates* decision was significant nevertheless, for it removed one of the cornerstones of the Fourth Amendment's suppression doctrine by overruling the *Aquilar–Spinelli* standards for testing the reliability and credibility of informants' information about suspects' criminal activities.[26] During the following term, however, in the companion cases of *U.S.* v. *Leon* and *Massachusetts* v. *Sheppard,*[27] a limited "good faith" exception was adopted. The High Court ruled that the Fourth Amendment rule should *not* be applied so as to bar the use of evidence obtained by officers acting in reasonable reliance on a search warrant issued by a detached and neutral magistrate but ultimately found to be invalid.

Beyond *Gates, Leon,* and *Sheppard,* the Supreme Court established further modifications of the exclusionary rule, particularly during its 1983–1984 term. In *Oliver* v. *U.S.* and *Maine* v. *Thornton,*[28] the Court reaffirmed the "open fields" exception to the Fourth Amendment's warrant requirement that it had recognized sixty years earlier.[29] The Court's explanation in these cases was that landowners had "no reasonable expectation of privacy" because "open fields do not provide the setting for those intimate activities that the amendment is intended to shelter from Government interference or surveillance."

Nix v. *Williams, New York* v. *Quarles,* and *Berkemer* v. *McCarty,*[30] all decided in 1984, represented further erosions of the holding set forth almost two decades earlier in *Miranda* v. *Arizona.*[31] *Nix* v. *Williams* established the "inevitable discovery" exception to the exclusionary rule. It was a follow-up to the case in which the "Christian burial speech" of an Iowa law enforcement agent had led to Robert Williams's confession of where he had hidden the body of ten-year-old Pamela Powers, whom he

Republicans have the same mindless passion for throwing money at defense and crime that Democrats have over welfare, education, and poverty — with the same results.

—FORMER MINNEAPOLIS POLICE CHIEF
ANTHONY V. BOUZA, 1990

had raped and murdered on Christmas Eve in 1968. The finding of the body had led to Williams's conviction, but this was overturned by the High Court in *Brewer* v. *Williams*[32] in 1977. The reason the Court indicated was that the accused's attorney had not been present when the location of the body was pointed out. At Williams's second trial, evidence about the body was admitted, but not the accused's involvement in its discovery. The High Court held in its 1984 ruling that Pamela's body was admissible since under the circumstances of the search, it would have been "inevitably discovered" by lawful means.

In *Quarles,* the Court put forth a narrow "public safety" exception to *Miranda,* holding that police officers may "ask questions reasonably prompted by concern for the public safety." And finally, it was declared in *Berkemer* v. *McCarty* that although anyone in police custody and accused of a crime — no matter how minor the offense — must be formally advised of the right against self-incrimination prior to questioning, an ordinary traffic stop does not constitute custody. The police may question motorists without first warning them against self-incrimination.

The fact that a number of the High Court's decisions in the early 1980s served to modify both *Miranda* and the exclusionary rule has led some observers to label the Burger Court as conservative. Moreover, they predicted a trend aimed at unraveling the rights accorded to suspects during the era of the Warren Court. Without question, the Court under Chief Justice Burger broke less ground in the area of civil liberties than it did under the fifteen-year tutelage of Chief Justice Earl Warren. At the same time, the Burger Court restricted some Warren Court decisions that afforded broad protections to the accused in criminal proceedings. But to label the Burger Court as conservative would be an overstatement. On more than one occasion, "conservative" justices Rehnquist, Powell, and O'Connor came down hard in favor of civil liberties claims. Moreover, "liberal" justices Marshall and Brennan occasionally supported tighter constraints on the rights of the accused. If anything, the U.S. Supreme Court during the first half of the 1980s was a divided court, composed primarily of strong individualists who did not necessarily follow the lead of Chief Justice Burger.

The Rehnquist Court

When Warren Burger retired as Chief Justice of the U.S. Supreme Court in 1986 and was replaced by Associate Justice William H. Rehnquist, there was considerable speculation as to how much more conservative the Court would become in the years to come. Rehnquist, appointed to the High Court during the Nixon administration, had clearly established himself during the ensuing fifteen years as the Court's most consistent conservative. Then, when the associate justice seat he vacated to become Chief Justice was filled by U.S. Court of Appeals Judge Antonin Scalia, court watchers were convinced that the Bench had taken two giant steps to the conservative right. As such, it was anticipated that the new court would serve to implement President Reagan's crime control agenda.

During the Court's first term (1986–87), the **Rehnquist Court** appeared to continue the Burger Court's counterrevolution in criminal procedure, escalating both the pace and the intensity of the conservative trend.[33] The Court's adherence to a crime control philosophy was evident in *U.S.* v. *Salerno,*[34] decided by a six-to-three majority, in which the pretrial detention provision of the Bail Reform Act of 1984 was upheld.

The Burger Court is not as conservative as some liberals feared, and not as conservative as some conservatives hoped.

— ARTHUR J. GOLDBERG, FORMER
SUPREME COURT JUSTICE, 1985

Rehnquist Court: The Supreme Court under the leadership of Chief Justice William Rehnquist.

A continuation of the philosophy was demonstrated in *McCleskey* v. *Kemp*,[35] in which the Court rejected a claim that the Georgia death penalty system was unconstitutional because black defendants who kill white victims statistically are more likely to receive the death sentence.

The first term of the Rehnquist Court also reflected some hostility toward the judicially created exclusionary rule. In *New York* v. *Burger*,[36] for example, the Court upheld a warrantless search of an automobile junkyard, conducted pursuant to a New York statute authorizing such a search. Similarly, in *Griffin* v. *Wisconsin*,[37] the Court rejected a Fourth Amendment challenge to a Wisconsin statute that permits probation officers to conduct warrantless searches of a probationer's home when there are reasonable grounds to believe that contraband is present. And perhaps the greatest threat to Fourth Amendment interests during the 1986–87 term was the Court's decision in *Illinois* v. *Krull*.[38] *Krull* involved evidence seized during a warrantless search of an auto wrecking yard, conducted pursuant to an Illinois statute that authorized such, but was later declared unconstitutional.

Fifth Amendment claims fared equally poorly in the first year of the Rehnquist Court. Most significant in this behalf was *Colorado* v. *Connelly*,[39] in which the Court held that a confession is not inadmissible as involuntary simply because it is prompted by mental illness. The Justices reasoned that there must be some official compulsion or coercion present for a confession to be deemed involuntary under the Fifth Amendment.

When Justice Lewis F. Powell retired from the Supreme Court at the close of the 1986–87 term, speculation began once again as to the nature of the Court's future direction. Powell had been a centrist, often casting the decisive votes in five-to-four decisions on major issues, and both liberal and conservatives began to wonder how President Reagan would fill the vacancy. His first nominee, Judge Robert H. Bork, quickly became surrounded with controversy. Bork's writings and published opinions clearly indicated that he was a trenchant critic of dozens of Supreme Court decisions that had expanded civil rights and liberties.

Prominant during Bork's fiery confirmation hearings was the debate over "judicial activism" versus "judicial restraint." **Judicial activism** refers to the High Court's use of its power to accomplish social goals that elude — or are opposed by — legislatures. By contrast, **judicial restraint** refers to the idea that the Justices should defer to legislative and executive decisions unless a clear constitutional right has been violated. Bork, along with many conservatives across the nation, had special scorn for the High Court's expansion of the rights of the accused during the Warren Court years. Yet what appeared to be Bork's narrow reading of the Constitution drew considerable opposition, resulting in his rejection in the Senate by a vote of fifty-eight-to-forty-two.

The Powell seat was ultimately filled by U.S. Circuit Judge Anthony M. Kennedy. Supporters of the Reagan agenda rejoiced at his confirmation, for they saw him as conservative enough to cement a solid majority on the Bench to roll back years of liberal decisions and give the President a legacy on social issues that would last well into the twenty-first century.

George Bush and the Conservative Shift

The conservative majority that had been emerging in slow-motion during the Reagan years had fully solidified by the close of 1991. When George Bush took office in 1989, the High Court's relatively liberal

Chief Justice William Rehnquist

Liberal, moderate, conservative shouldn't apply to judging. The correct philosophy is to judge according to the intent of the legislature or the intent of the constitution's framers.

— Robert H. Bork

Judicial activism: The High Court's use of its power to accomplish social goals.

Judicial restraint: The High Court's deference to legislative and executive decisions unless a clear constitutional right has been violated.

Would you like to remind me, too?
— Supreme Court Justice Sandra Day O'Connor in 1991, after attorney Harry McCall commented in court that "I would like to remind you gentlemen" of a legal point.

Just "Justices" would be fine.
— Supreme Court Justice Byron White, after McCall later referred to the court as "Justice O'Connor and gentlemen"

justices included three of its oldest members — William J. Brennan, Thurgood Marshall, and John Paul Stevens. All were in their early eighties at the time, and it was assumed that they would retire soon.

In 1990, Justice Brennan retired and was replaced by Bush-nominee fifty-one-year-old David Souter. By the close of the 1990–1991 term, Souter's conservative influence was clear. Rulings in which he declared decisive votes included:

- *Riverside County, Calif.* v. *McLaughlin,*[40] holding that persons may be jailed for as long as forty-eight hours before a judge determines the validity of their arrests;

- *Barnes* v. *Glen Theater,*[41] holding that state public decency laws may prevent women from shedding their last bits of clothing while performing erotic dances at bars and nightclubs;

- *Wilson* v. *Seiter,*[42] holding that substandard, even inhumane, conditions at prisons are not unconstitutional unless there is proof of "deliberate indifference" on the part of public officials;

- *Harmelin* v. *Michigan,*[43] holding that severe mandatory penalties do not necessarily violate the Eighth Amendment ban against cruel and unusual punishment; and,

- *Arizona* v. *Fulminante,*[44] holding that criminal convictions may stand despite the use of certain coerced confessions (see Exhibit E.1).

Justice Thurgood Marshall announced his retirement in 1991, and President Bush's nomination of Clarence Thomas was steeped in controversy from the very beginning. A black, conservative federal judge,

● EXHIBIT E.1 ●

Arizona v. Fulminante
Coerced Confessions and the
Harmless Error Doctrine
by Kenneth C. Haas

If any one case symbolized the U.S. Supreme Court's increasingly conservative criminal-law jurisprudence during the 1990–91 term, it was *Arizona* v. *Fulminante*,[a] decided March 26, 1991. Since *Malinski* v. *New York* in 1945,[b] cases involving a coerced or involuntary confession have been governed by the so-called "rule of automatic reversal."[c] Under this rule, the use of a coerced confession in a criminal trial could never be considered a "harmless error"; an appellate court was duty bound to overturn a criminal conviction resting in whole or in part on a coerced confession, regardless of how much evidence of guilt existed, apart from the confession, to support the conviction. In past decades, the Court had repeatedly stressed that coerced confessions were not only untrustworthy, but that their use in a criminal trial would undermine the integrity of the entire judicial process and offend the principle that ours is an accusatorial and not an inquisitorial system of criminal justice.[d] In a significant 1967 case, *Chapman* v. *California*,[e] the Court reaffirmed that the use of a coerced confession, whether true or false, constituted a denial of the defendant's right to due process of law under the Fourteenth Amendment. The *Chapman* Court specifically identified three kinds of constitutional errors that were so serious that they could never be categorized

as harmless error: depriving a criminal defendant of counsel, trying a defendant before a biased judge, and introducing a coerced confession during a criminal trial.

The Court's decision in *Arizona* v. *Fulminante* clearly overruled *Chapman* with respect to the question of whether the introduction of a coerced confession during a criminal trial can ever be regarded as harmless error. But the *Fulminante* ruling was an unusually convoluted one, marked by shifting coalitions on three different questions answered by the Court.

Oreste Fulminante's erroneously admitted confession, around which the case revolved, was obtained in a federal prison by a fellow inmate, one Anthony Sarivola, who was working as a paid informant for the FBI in an investigation of the murder of Fulminante's eleven-year-old stepdaughter in Arizona. Sarivola told Fulminante that he knew Fulminante was starting to get some "tough treatment and whatnot" from other inmates because he was rumored to be a child murderer. He then offered to protect Fulminante from his fellow prisoners, but only if Fulminante told him the truth. Fulminante promptly told Sarivola that he had killed his stepdaughter, a confession the state introduced at Fulminante's trial. Fulminante was convicted of the murder and sentenced to death, but the Arizona Supreme Court

ultimately ruled that the confession had been coerced and reversed the conviction, pointing out that *Chapman* v. *California* forbade the use of harmless-error analysis in the case of a coerced confession.

In the first of its three *Fulminante* rulings, the U.S. Supreme Court affirmed the Arizona high court's finding that Fulminante's confession to Sarivola was indeed a "coerced confession." Writing for a five-justice majority that also included Justices Marshall, Blackmun, Stevens, and Scalia, Justice Byron White reasoned that Sarivola had conveyed "a credible threat of physical violence" to Fulminante and that it was the fear of physical violence, absent protection from Sarivola, that had motivated Fulminante to confess. Although the jailhouse use of undercover police officers or inmates acting as police informants to elicit incriminating statements from criminal suspects is not in and of itself unconstitutional,[f] the problem in this case, as the majority saw it, was that Fulminante's confession was obtained as a direct result of his belief that his life would be in jeopardy if he did not confess.

The second—and most important—issue decided in the *Fulminante* case was whether to overrule *Chapman* and the many other past precedents that had required the automatic reversal of any conviction obtained with

continued on pg. 730

continued from pg. 729

the aid of a coerced confession. On this question, Chief Justice Rehnquist commanded a five-justice majority that included Justices O'Connor, Kennedy, Scalia, and Souter. The Chief Justice's majority opinion took the position that a harmless-error approach to the use of a coerced confession was preferable to the automatic reversal rule because the introduction of a coerced confession was simply a "trial error" that can be "quantitatively assessed in the context of other evidence presented." This kind of error, according to the Chief Justice, is fundamentally different from the other two errors identified by the *Chapman* Court. The total deprivation of the right to counsel and the presence of a judge who is not impartial, he reasoned, are "structural defects" in a trial that are far more serious than the admission of an involuntary confession. These kinds of "structural defects" and others, such as the deprivation of the right to a public trial or the unlawful exclusion of members of the defendant's race from a grand jury, taint "[t]he entire conduct of the trial from beginning to end" and thus can never be considered harmless.

The erroneous admission of a coerced confession, the Chief Justice contended, is different—a mere "trial error," "similar in both degree and kind to the erroneous admission of other types of evidence." The eviden-

tiary impact of a coerced confession is indistinguishable "from that of a confession obtained in violation of the Sixth Amendment—of evidence seized in violation of the Fourth Amendment—or of a prosecutor's improper comment on a defendant's silence at trial in violation of the Fifth Amendment." These kinds of errors are quite properly subjected to harmless-error analysis by appellate courts because of the importance of preserving the truth-seeking function of trials and the need to promote public respect for the criminal justice process "by focusing on the underlying fairness of the trial rather than on the virtually inevitable presence of immaterial error." Chief Justice Rehnquist concluded by issuing succinct instructions for the nation's appellate judiciary:

When reviewing the erroneous admission of an involuntary confession, the appellate court . . . simply reviews the remainder of the evidence against the defendant to determine whether the admission of the confession was harmless beyond a reasonable doubt.

In a bitter dissenting opinion, Justice White, joined by Justices Marshall, Blackmun, and Stevens, accused the majority of overruling a "vast body of precedent" and of dislodging "one of the fundamental tenets of our criminal justice system." The majority's holding, he charged, was based on "a meaningless di-

chotomy between 'trial errors' and 'structural defects' in the trial process." He asserted that coerced confessions are different in kind from other types of errors that can be subjected to harmless-error analysis. The ban on coerced confessions was intended not only to protect the accused from a conviction based on a false confession but to reinforce the all-important principle "that in the end life and liberty can be as much endangered from illegal methods used to convict those thought to be criminals as from the actual criminals themselves." The right of a defendant not to have his or her coerced confession used against him, Justice White concluded, should be viewed as one of those fundamental rights that "are not, and should not be, subject to harmless-error analysis because those rights protect important values that are unrelated to the truth-seeking function of the trial."

Although he was on the losing side on the major constitutional question presented by the *Fulminante* case, Justice White, ironically, wrote the majority opinion for still another lineup of justices on the third question—the one that determined the ultimate disposition of Oreste Fulminante's case. Writing for a five-to-three majority (Justice Souter, without explanation, did not participate in this portion of the decision) that included Justices Marshall, Blackmun, Stevens, and Kennedy, Justice White reviewed the evidence presented at trial and reached the conclusion that the trial judge's erroneous decision to permit the prosecutor to use the coerced confession"was not harmless beyond a reasonable doubt." Without the confession, said Justice White, "it is unlikely that Fulminante would have been prosecuted at all." Consequently, Oreste Fulminante was entitled to a new trial at which his confession to Anthony Sarivola could not be introduced. Interestingly, after reviewing the same trial record, Chief Justice Rehnquist, joined by Justices O'Connor and Scalia, dissented, calling the use of Fulminante's confession "a classic case of harmless error."

The decision in *Fulminante* provides a good barometer of the Court's criminal-law jurisprudence of the 1990s. It is important to note that the fifth vote to permit harmless-error review in coerced-confession cases was tendered by Justice David Souter, President Bush's first Supreme Court appointee. Based upon his voting behavior during the 1990–91 term, it appears that Justice Souter can be counted on as a fairly reliable vote in favor of the state and against criminal defendants—in stark contrast to Justice William Brennan, the justice he replaced. The *Fulminante* holding also portends the Rehnquist Court's willingness—indeed, eagerness

—to jettison well-established past precedents that afford criminal defendants constitutional protections. The manner in which the Court dismantled *Chapman* probably is typical of how the conservative majority will deal with other past precedents it doesn't like—by replacing clear, ironclad rules of criminal procedure such as the automatic-reversal rule with various "balancing" or "reasonableness" analyses that will often permit the affirmance of criminal convictions despite the presence of errors by police, prosecutors, or judges. The *Fulminante* ruling, for example, arguably sends a signal to the nation's appellate courts that the harmless-error doctrine is now available to them whenever they are determined to uphold the tainted conviction of a defendant who appears to be "truly guilty."

It is still too early to predict the impact of *Fulminante* on the criminal justice process. There may be relatively little effect in terms of reversal-of-conviction rates. A coerced confession will still have to be shown "harmless beyond a reasonable doubt," and confessions—usually the most damaging of all evidence admitted against a criminal defendant—are rarely harmless beyond a reasonable doubt. Courts are still required to reverse convictions based mainly on coerced confessions, just as the Supreme Court ultimately did in *Fulminante*. On the other

hand, the demise of the automatic reversal rule may encourage a growing number of police officers to coerce confessions, especially if they believe that they are likely to obtain other evidence of guilt not directly traceable to the confession. Similarly, a prosecutor, armed with a coerced confession, may decide to gamble by seeking to introduce the confession in the hope that the trial judge will admit it and an appellate court will view it as harmless error. By giving appellate courts a tool for affirming otherwise invalid confessions, the *Fulminante* decision arguably gives police and prosecutors subtle encouragement to break the rules.

---

a. *Arizona* v. *Fulminante,* 111 S. Ct. 1246 (1991).

b. *Malinski* v. *New York,* 324 U.S. 401 (1945).

c. The Supreme Court has long used the terms "coerced confession" and "involuntary confession" interchangeably. Such a confession should not be confused with a *Miranda* violation, which "does not mean that the statements received have actually been coerced, but only that the courts will presume the privilege against compulsory self-incrimination has not been intelligently exercised" (*Oregon* v. *Elstad,* 470 U.S. 298, 310 [1985]).

d. See especially *Payne* v. *Arkansas,* 356 U.S. 560 (1958); *Rogers* v. *Richmond,* 365 U.S. 534 (1961); and *Jackson* v. *Denno,* 378 U.S. 368 (1964).

e. *Chapman* v. *California,* 386 U.S. 18 (1967).

f. *Illinois* v. *Perkins,* 110 S. Ct. 2394 (1990).

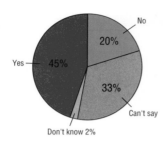

Should Thomas Be Confirmed?

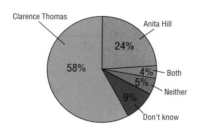

Whom Do You Believe More?   Based on telephone interviews of 501 adults conducted Oct. 13.

SOURCE: *New York Times* poll of October 13, 1991

I felt that I had to tell the truth.
— ANITA HILL, OCTOBER 10, 1991

This is a high-tech lynching for uppity blacks.
— CLARENCE THOMAS, OCTOBER 11, 1991

Thomas was immediately opposed by a number of civil rights groups because of his disagreement with affirmative action policies. Numerous liberal senators and "pro-choice" groups also opposed him because he refused to discuss his views on abortion and *Roe* v. *Wade.* Others felt that he was unqualified on the basis of his legal experience and scholarship. In fact, Judge Thomas was the first of the last twenty-two High Court nominees who failed to receive a unanimous "qualified" rating from the American Bar Association.[45]

But the most heated controversy came when law professor Anita Hill accused Judge Thomas of having sexually harassed her when the two had worked together a decade earlier. What followed was a public circus with real victims and no nets. For days, tens of millions of Americans watched the "he said–she said" charges and counter charges.[46] Senate Judiciary Committee Chairman Senator Joseph R. Biden had opened the inquiry into harassment allegations with the comment: "This is not a trial. This is not a courtroom." [47] But it was indeed a trial—for Judge Thomas, whose Supreme Court nomination hung in the balance; for Professor Hill, whose credibility was at stake; for the Senate, which had been accused of insensitivity and mismanagement of the case; and for American politics, which seemed to have become driven by viperous personal attacks and exhaustive examinations of character.

In the end, although Clarence Thomas was ultimately confirmed as the 106th Justice of the United States Supreme Court, political observers felt that there were no real winners—not even Thomas. His fifty-two-to-forty-eight confirmation vote represented the closest winning margin in more than a century. About the only things that supporters and opponents of Thomas agreed on was that the American system of selecting Supreme Court justices had gone awry, and that the process was in need of overhaul.

SUMMARY

Over the last three decades, noticeable changes occurred in the directions of Supreme Court decision making. During the 1960s, the Warren Court stressed a model that looked to the need for protecting the procedural rights of the accused. In contrast, the Burger Court of the 1970s established the position that the repression of criminal conduct was the most important function in the administration of justice. This crime control model was further strengthened in the 1980s through a broad-based assault on the exclusionary rule. Also during the 1980s, the country seemed to shift to the more conservative right, which suggests a continued trend toward strict punishment for criminal offenders and an erosion of the rights of the accused. In the 1990s, as the result of President Bush's appointments to the High Court, the conservative shift became solidified.

KEY TERMS

Burger Court (723)
crime control model (722)
due-process model (721)

judicial activism (727)
judicial restraint (727)

Rehnquist Court (726)
Warren Court (721)

QUESTIONS FOR DISCUSSION

1. How will the conservative trend affect future prospects for punishment and correction? Will the conservative trend indeed continue?

2. Where do you stand on the High Court's rulings in *Arizona* v. *Fulminante*?

FOR FURTHER READING

Cronin, Thomas E., Tania Z. Cronin, and Michael E. Milakovich. *U.S.* v. *Crime in the Streets.* Bloomington: Indiana University Press, 1981.

Gordon, Diana R. *The Justice Juggernaut: Fighting Street Crime, Controlling Citizens.* New Brunswick, NJ: Rutgers University Press, 1990.

NOTES

1. See Yale Kamisar, "A Man of Strong Words," *National Law Journal,* October 26, 1981, p. 15.

2. See Frank Browning and John Gerassi, *The American Way of Crime* (New York: G. P. Putnam's, 1980), pp. 299–360; Craig Thompson and Allen Raymond, *Gang Rule in New York* (New York: Dial, 1940); The Vice Commission of Chicago, *The Social Evil in Chicago* (Chicago: Gunthorp-Warren, 1911); John Kobler, *Capone* (New York: G. P. Putnam's, 1971); Herbert Asbury, *The Gangs of New York* (Garden City, N.Y.: Garden City, 1928); Herbert Asbury, *Gem of the Prairie* (New York: Knopf, 1940).

3. See, for example, Philip Parsons, *Crime and the Criminal: An Introduction to Criminology* (New York: Alfred A. Knopf, 1926); Harry Elmer Barnes, *The Repression of Crime* (New York: George H. Doran, 1926); Marcus Kavanagh, *The Criminal and His Allies* (Indianapolis: Bobbs-Merrill, 1928); Fred E. Haynes, *Criminology* (New York: McGraw-Hill, 1930); Harry Best, *Crime and the Criminal Law in the United States* (New York: Macmillan, 1930); Nathaniel F. Cantor, *Crime, Criminals, and Criminal Justice* (New York: Henry Holt, 1932); Edwin H. Sutherland, *Principles of Criminology* (Philadelphia: J. B. Lippincott, 1924, 1939, 1947); Harry Elmer Barnes and Negley K. Tetters, *New Horizons in Criminology* (Englewood Cliffs, NJ: Prentice-Hall, 1959).

4. Paul W. Tappan, *Crime, Justice, and Correction* (New York: McGraw-Hill, 1960).

5. Herbert Packer, *The Limits of the Criminal Sanction* (Stanford, Calif.: Stanford University Press, 1968), pp. 154–173.

6. *Malloy* v. *Hogan,* 378 U.S. 1 (1964).

7. *Gideon* v. *Wainwright,* 372 U.S. 335 (1963).

8. *Klopfer* v. *North Carolina,* 386 U.S. 213 (1967).

9. *Pointer* v. *Texas,* 380 U.S. 400 (1965).

10. *Washington* v. *Texas,* 388 U.S. 14 (1967).

11. *Robinson* v. *California,* 370 U.S. 660 (1972).

12. *Duncan* v. *Louisiana,* 391 U.S. 145 (1968).

13. *Benton* v. *Maryland,* 395 U.S. 784 (1969).

14. See *Palko* v. *Connecticut,* 302 U.S. 319 (1937).

15. *Mapp* v. *Ohio,* 367 U.S. 643 (1961).

16. *Miranda* v. *Arizona,* 383 U.S. 436 (1966).

17. *Escobedo* v. *Illinois,* 378 U.S. 478 (1964).

18. *United States* v. *Wade,* 388 U.S. 218 (1967).

19. For a more scholarly and restrained analysis of the Warren Court's codification of the constitutional rights of the criminally accused, see Fred P. Graham, *The Due Process Revolution: The Warren Court's Impact on Criminal Law* (New York: Hayden, 1970); Philip B. Kurland, *Politics, the Constitution, and the Warren Court* (Chicago: University of Chicago Press, 1969); and Archibald Cox, *The Warren Court: Constitutional Decision as an Instrument of Reform* (Cambridge, Mass.: Harvard University Press, 1968).

20. *Harris* v. *New York,* 401 U.S. 22 (1971).

21. *Michigan* v. *Tucker,* 417 U.S. 433 (1974).

22. *Kirby* v. *Illinois,* 406 U.S. 682 (1972).

23. *National Law Journal,* August 8, 1981, pp. 1, 32.

24. *Illinois* v. *Gates,* 103 S. Ct. 2317 (1983).

25. *Bivins* v. *Six Unknown Federal Narcotics Agents,* 403 U.S. 388 (1971).

26. *Spinelli* v. *U.S.,* 393 U.S. 410 (1969); *Aguilar* v. *Texas,* 378 U.S. 108 (1964).

27. *U.S.* v. *Leon,* U.S. SupCt (1984) 35 CrL 3273; *Massachusetts* v. *Sheppard,* U.S. SupCt (1984) 35 CrL 3296.

28. *Oliver* v. *U.S.,* U.S. SupCt (1984) 35 CrL 3011; *Maine* v. *Thornton,* U.S. SupCt (1984) 35 CrL 3011.

29. *Hester* v. *U.S.,* 265 U.S. 57 (1924).

30. *Nix* v. *Williams,* U.S. SupCt (1984); *New York* v. *Quarles,* U.S. SupCt (1984) 35 CrL 3135; *Berkemer* v. *McCarty,* U.S. SupCt (1984) 35 CrL 3192.

31. *Miranda* v. *Arizona,* 384 U.S. 436 (1966).

32. *Brewer* v. *Williams,* 430 U.S. 387(1977).

33. Charles H. Whitebread and John Heilman, "The Counterrevolution in Criminal Procedure," *National Law Journal,* August 17, 1987, pp. S6–S7.

34. *U.S.* v. *Salerno,* 107 S. Ct. 2095 (1987).

35. *McCleskey* v. *Kemp,* 107 S. Ct. 1756 (1987).

36. *New York* v. *Burger,* 55 U.S.L.W. 4890 (June 19, 1987).

37. *Griffin* v. *Wisconsin,* 55 U.S.L.W. 5156 (June 26, 1987).

38. *Illinois* v. *Krull,* 197 S. Ct. 1160 (1987).

39. *Colorado* v. *Connelly,* 197 S. Ct. 851 (1987).

40. *Riverside County, Calif.* v. *McLaughlin,* 49 CrL 2103 (1991).

41. *Barnes* v. *Glen Theater,* 49 CrL 2289 (1991).

42. *Wilson* v. *Seiter,* 49 CrL 2264 (1991).

43. *Harmelin* v. *Michigan,* 49 CrL 2350 (1991).

44. *Arizona* v. *Fulminante,* 111 S. Ct. 1246 (1991).

45. *National Law Journal,* September 16, 1991, p. 5.

46. See *Newsweek,* October 21, 1991, pp. 24–32; *Time,* October 21, 1991, pp. 34–51.

47. *New York Times,* October 12, 1991, pp. 1, 8.

GLOSSARY

accessory In criminal law, any person not present at the commission of a crime who commands, advises, instigates, or conceals the offense.

acquittal The judgment of the court, based on the verdict of a jury or a judicial officer, that the defendant is not guilty of the offense(s) for which he or she has been tried.

adjudication The process by which a court arrives at a decision regarding a case. In juvenile proceedings, the court's decision or judgment.

adjudication hearing The stage in juvenile court proceedings in which a judge presides on behalf of the child to determine if he or she actually committed the alleged offense.

adjudication inquiry The stage in juvenile court proceedings in which a judge determines whether the facts of the case warrant a formal hearing by the court.

administrative law A branch of public law that deals with the powers and duties of government agencies.

adultery Sexual intercourse between a man and woman, at least one of whom is married to someone else.

adversary system of justice A system in which the innocence of the accused is presumed and the burden of proof is placed on the court.

affirm The decision of an appellate court to let stand the conviction obtained (and/or the sentence imposed) in a trial court.

aggravating circumstances Circumstances relating to the commission of a crime that cause its gravity to be greater than that of the average instance of the given type of offense.

alias Any name used for an official purpose that is different from a person's legal name.

allocution The right of a convicted offender to address the court personally prior to the imposition of sentence.

anomie A condition within a society or group in which there exists a weakened respect or lack of adherence to some or most of the norms.

appeal A complaint to a superior court of an injustice done or an error committed by a lower court, whose judgment or decision the higher tribunal is called upon to correct or reverse.

appeal case A case filed in a court having incidental or gerneral appellate jurisdiction, to initiate review of a judgment or decision of a trial court, an administrative agency, or an intermediate appellate court.

appeal proceedings The set of orderly steps by which a court considers the issues and makes a determination in a case before it on appeal.

appellant The person who contests the correctness of a court order, judgment, or other decision and who seeks review and relief in a court having appellate jurisdiction, or the person in whose behalf this is done.

appellate jurisdiction Jurisdiction restricted to matters of appeal and review.

Argersinger v. _Hamlin_ The Supreme Court ruling that a defendant has the right to counsel at trial whenever he or she may be imprisoned for any offense, even for one day, whether it is classified as a felony or as a misdemeanor.

arraignment Strictly, the hearing before a court having jurisdiction in a criminal case, in which the identity of the defendant is established, the defendant is informed of the charge(s) and of his or her rights, and the defendant is required to enter a plea.

arrest The action of taking a person into custody for the purpose of charging with a crime.

arrest report The document prepared by the arresting officer describing an arrested person and the events and circumstances leading to the arrest.

arrest warrant A document issued by a judicial officer that directs a law enforcement officer to arrest an identified person who has been accused of a specific offense.

arson The willful or malicious burning or attempt to burn, with or without intent to defraud, any dwelling, other building, vehicle, or personal property.

assault An intentional attempt or threat to physically injure another.

assault and battery An assault carried into effect by doing some violence to the victim.

asset forfeiture The governmental seizure of personal assets obtained or used for a criminal enterprise.

autrefois acquit A plea of "formerly acquitted" in not guilty proceedings on double jeopardy grounds.

autrefois convict A plea of "formerly convicted" in not guilty proceedings on double jeopardy grounds.

auxiliary police Trained and uniformed (but unarmed) volunteer civilians who work with local police.

bail Security posted guarantee that a defendant in a criminal proceeding will appear and be present in court as required.

bailiff A court officer whose duties are to announce the arrival and departure of the judge and to maintain order in the courtroom.

Barron v. Baltimore The Supreme Court ruling that the Bill of Rights was added to the Constitution to protect citizens only against the action of the federal, not the state or local, government.

Batson v. Kentucky The Supreme Court's ruling that a prosecutor's use of peremptory challenges to exclude from a jury members of the defendant's race solely on racial grounds violates the equal protection rights of the defendant.

battery The nonlethal culmination of an assault.

Beccaria, Cesare The founder of the classical school of criminal law and criminology.

bench trial A trial in which the judge, rather than a jury, determines innocence or guilt.

bench warrant A document issued by a court directing that a law enforcement officer arrest and bring the person named therein before the court (usually) one who has failed to obey a court order or a notice to appear.

Benton v. Maryland The Supreme Court ruling that overruled *Palko* and extended the double jeopardy protection to state actions.

Betts v. Brady The Supreme Court ruling that the Fourteenth Amendment's due process clause does not require states to supply defense counsel to defendants too poor to employ their own attorney.

bifurcated trial In criminal proceedings, a special two-part trial proceeding in which the issue of guilt is tried in the first step and, if a conviction results, the appropriate sentence or applicable sentencing statute is determined in the second step.

bigamy The act of marrying while a former marriage is still legally in force.

bill of particulars A written statement that specifies additional facts about a charge.

Bill of Rights The first ten amendments to the Constitution of the United States, which restrict government actions.

bind over Based on the decision by a court of limited jurisdiction, to require that a person charged with a felony appear for trial on that charge in a court of general jurisdiction, as the result of a finding of probable cause at a preliminary hearing held in the limited jurisdiction court.

blackmail The taking of money or property through threats of accusation or exposure.

booking The police administrative procedures for officially recording an arrest.

Bow Street Runners Henry Fielding's unofficial band of constables who were paid as thief-takers.

Brady v. United States The Supreme Court ruling that upheld the use of plea negotiation.

breach of the peace The breaking of the public peace by any riotous, forcible, or unlawful proceeding.

breaking and entering The forcible entry into a building or structure, with the intent to commit a crime therein.

Breed v. Jones The Supreme Court ruling that extended the Fifth Amendment protection against double jeopardy to juveniles.

Brewer v. Williams The Supreme Court ruling that the use of subterfuge or trickery to elicit incriminating information from a suspect constitutes "custodial interrogation" and is bound by the holding in *Miranda*.

brief A document prepared by counsel to serve as the basis for an argument in court, setting out the facts of and the legal arguments in support of the case.

Buck v. Bell The Supreme Court ruling that Virginia did not violate the Fourteenth Amendment's due process guarantee when it sterilized, without her consent, a mentally defective mother.

Burger Court The Supreme Court under the leadership of Chief Justice Warren Burger.

burglary *See* breaking and entering.

capacity In criminal usage, the legal ability of a person to commit a criminal act; the mental and physical ability to act with purpose and to be aware of the certain, probable results of one's conduct.

capias A bench warrant.

capital offense 1. A criminal offense punishable by death. 2. In some penal codes, an offense that may be punishable by death or by imprisonment for life.

carnal knowledge The act of having sexual bodily connecton. Under many statutes, there is carnal knowledge if there is the slightest penetration of the sexual organ of the female by the sexual organ of the male; it is not necessary that the vaginal canal be entered. Sexual contact without any penetration is generally referred to as carnal abuse.

Carrier's Case A person in possession of another's packaged goods, who opens the package and misappropriates its contents, is guilty of larceny.

Carroll Doctrine The ruling, from the Supreme Court's decision in *Carroll* v. *United States*, that warrantless searches of vehicles were permissible where reasonable suspicion of illegal actions existed.

case law Law that results from court interpretations of statutory law or from court decisions where rules have not been fully codified or have been found to be vague or in error.

case load 1. In corrections, the total number of clients registered with a correctional agency or agent on a given date or during a specified time period, often divided into active supervisory cases and inactive cases, thus distinguishing between clients with whom contact is regular, and those with whom it is not. 2. In the courts, the number of cases requiring judicial action at a certain time, or the number of cases acted upon in a given court during a given time period.

certiorari, writ of A writ issued by the Supreme Court ordering some lower court to "forward up the record" of a case it has tried so the High Court can review it.

challenge for cause A challenge to

remove a potential juror on the basis of a sound legal reason to do so.

change of venue The movement of a case from the jurisdiction of one court to that of another which has the same subject matter jurisdictional authority but is in a different geographic location.

charging document A formal written accusation submitted to a court, alleging that a specified person(s) has committed a specific offense(s).

charging the jury An order by the judge directing the jurors to retire to the jury room, consider the facts of the case and the evidence and testimony presented, and from their deliberations return a just verdict.

child molesting The handling, fondling, or other contacts of a sexual nature with a child.

Chimel v. California The Supreme Court ruling that a search incident to a lawful arrest in a home must be limited to the area into which an arrestee might reach in order to grab a weapon or other evidentiary items.

civil commitment A nonpenal commitment to a treatment facility resulting from findings made during criminal proceedings, either before or after a judgment.

civil death The loss of *all* civil rights.

civil law The body of principles that determines private rights and liabilities.

civilian review boards Citizen-controlled boards empowered to review and handle complaints against police officers.

classical school of criminal law and criminology A body of ideals from Enlightenment philosophers and reformers for transforming criminal law and procedure.

classification The process through which the educational, vocational, treatment, and custodial needs of an offender are determined.

clearance rate The proportion of crimes that result in arrest.

Coker v. Georgia The Supreme Court ruling that the sentence of death for the crime of rape is an excessive and disproportionate penalty forbidden by the Eighth Amendment.

commitment The action of a judicial officer ordering that a person subject to judicial proceedings be placed in a particular kind of confinement or residential facility, for a specified reason authorized by law; also, the result of the action, the admission to the facility.

common law Customs, traditions, judicial decisions, and other materials that guide courts in decision making, but that have not been enacted by the legislatures into statutes or embodied in the U.S. Constitution.

community-based correction Rehabilitative activities and programs within the community that have effective ties with the local government.

commutation The reduction of a sentence to a less severe one.

complaint Any accusation that a person(s) has committed an offense(s), received by or originating from a law enforcement or prosecutorial agency, or received by a court.

conditional release The release by executive decision from a federal or state correctional facility of a prisoner who has not served his or her full sentence and whose freedom is contingent upon obeying specified rules of behavior.

confidence games The obtaining of money or property by means of deception through the confidence a victim places in the offender.

conjugal visitation The practice of permitting inmate and spouse to spend time together in private quarters on prison grounds, during which time they may engage in sexual relations.

consent of the victim Any voluntary yielding of the will of the victim, accompanied by his or her deliberation, agreeing to the act of the offending party.

conspiracy Concert in criminal purpose.

constitutional law The legal rules and principles that define the nature and limits of governmental power, and the duties and rights of individuals in relation to the state.

contempt of court Intentional obstruction of a court in the administration of justice, or an act calculated to lessen its authority or dignity, or failure to obey its lawful orders.

contract system A form of prison industry in which the labor of inmates was leased to an outside contractor, who furnished the machinery and raw materials and supervised the work.

conviction The judgment of a court, based on the verdict of a jury or judicial officer, or on the guilty or *nolo contendere* plea of the defendant, that the defendant is guilty of the offense(s) with which he or she has been charged.

Coolidge v. New Hampshire The Supreme Court ruling that a police search based on a warrant by a magistrate who is not "neutral and detached" is invalid; the arrest of a suspect inside his house does not justify the search of his automobile parked in his driveway.

corporal punishment Punishment applied to the body such as whipping or branding.

corrections A generic term that includes all government agencies, facilities, programs, procedures, personnel, and techniques concerned with the intake, custody, confinement, supervision, or treatment, or presentencing or predisposition investigation of alleged or adjudicated offenders.

counterculture Associated with the "hippies" of the 1960s, it was a complex of ideas and behavior patterns that ran counter to those of traditional society.

counterfeiting The making of imitation money and obligations of the government or a corporate body.

court An agency or unit of the judicial branch of government, authorized or established by statute or constitution, and consisting of one or more judicial officers, which has the authority to decide upon cases, controversies in law, and disputed matters of fact brought before it.

court calendar The court schedule; the list of events comprising the daily or weekly work of a court, including the assignment of the time and place for each hearing or other item of business, or the list of matters that will be taken up in a given court term.

court clerk An elected or appointed court officer responsible for maintaining the written records of the court and for supervising or performing the clerical tasks necessary for conducting judicial business; also, any employee of a court whose principal duties are to assist the court clerk.

court reporter A person present during judicial proceedings who records all testimony and other oral statements made during the proceedings.

courts of general jurisdiction Courts authorized to try *all* criminal and civil cases.

courts of limited jurisdiction The entry point for judicial processing, with jurisdiction limited to full processing of *all* minor offenses and pretrial processing of felony cases.

courts of record Courts in which a full transcript of the proceedings is made for all cases.

crime An intentional act or omission in violation of criminal law, committed without defense or justification, and sanctioned by the state as a felony or misdemeanor.

crime clock A display used by the FBI in its *Uniform Crime Reports* to illustrate the annual ratio of crime to fixed time intervals.

crime control model The model of the criminal justice system that views the repression of criminal conduct as its most important function.

Crime Index The sum of Part I offenses reported in a given place for a given period of time.

crime rate The number of Part I offenses that occur in a given area per 100,000 inhabitants living in that area.

criminal bankruptcy The fraudulent declaration of excessive indebtedness or insolvency in an effort to avoid partial or full payment of one's debts.

criminal justice The structure, functions, and decision processes of those agencies that deal with the management of crime: the police, the courts, and corrections.

criminal justice process The agencies and procedures set up to manage both crime and the persons accused of violating the criminal law.

criminal law The branch of jurisprudence that deals with offenses committed against the safety and order of the state.

criminal nuisance Any conduct that is unreasonable and endangers the health and safety of others.

criminal proceedings The regular and orderly steps, as directed or authorized by statute, of a court of law, taken to determine whether a person accused of a crime is guilty or not guilty.

criminal trespass Crimes that are generally misdemeanors or violations, and are differentiated from burglary when breaking with criminal intent is absent or when the trespass involves property that has been fenced in a manner designed to exclude intruders.

critical stage Any decision or processing point made by criminal justice agencies or personnel that is so important that the U.S. Supreme Court has attached to it specific due-process rights.

culpability Blameworthiness; responsibility in some sense for an event or situation deserving of moral blame.

curtilage The yard or other ground inside a fence.

custody Legal or physical control of a person or thing; legal, supervisory, or physical responsibility for a person or thing.

de facto In fact, in reality.

defendant A person formally accused of an offense(s) by the filing in court of a charging document.

defense Any number of causes and rights of action that serve to mitigate or excuse an individual's guilt in a criminal offense.

definite sentence A sentence of incarceration having a fixed period of time with no reduction by parole.

Delaware* v. *Prouse The Supreme Court ruling that police may not randomly stop motorists, without any probable cause to suspect crime or illegal activity, to check their driver's license and auto registration.

deliberation The full and conscious knowledge of the purpose to kill.

delinquency Criminal law violations that would be considered crimes if committed by an adult.

delinquent A juvenile offender who has been adjudicated by an officer of a juvenile court.

desecration The defacing, damaging, or mistreatment of a public structure, monument, or place of worship or burial.

detainee Usually, a person held in local, very short-term confinement while awaiting consideration for pretrial release or first appearance for arraignment.

detention The legally authorized confinement of a person subject to criminal or juvenile court proceedings, until the point of commitment to a correctional facility or until release.

detention hearing The stage in juvenile court proceedings in which it is determined whether a child is to be released to a parent or guardian or retained in custody.

determinate sentence A sentence of incarceration for a fixed period of time.

deterrence A sentencing philosophy seeking to prevent criminal acts by making an example of persons convicted of crimes.

deviance Conduct which the people of a group consider so dangerous, embarrassing, or irritating that they bring special sanctions to bear against the persons who exhibit it.

directed verdict A judge's order to a jury to acquit the accused.

discretion The authority to choose between alternative actions.

dismissal The decision by a court to terminate adjudication of all outstanding charges in a criminal case, or all outstanding charges against a given defendant in a criminal case, thus terminating court action in the case and permanently or provisionally terminating court jurisdiction over the defendant in relation to those charges.

disorderly conduct Any act that tends to disturb the public peace, scandalize the community, or shock the public sense of morality.

disposition hearing The stage in juvenile court proceedings in which the judge exercises his or her discretionary authority to choose among a variety of alternatives for resolving a case.

disturbing the peace Any interruption of the peace, quiet, and good order of a neighborhood or community.

diversion The removal of offenders from the application of the criminal law at any stage of the police or court processes.

double jeopardy The Fifth Amendment protects an accused from both multiple prosecutions for the same offense and multiple punishments for the same crime.

Downum* v. *United States The Supreme Court ruling that double jeopardy begins at the point where the second trial jury is sworn in.

driving while intoxicated (DWI) *or* driving under the influence (DUI) The operation of a motor vehicle while under the influence of alcohol or narcotics.

Drug Use Forecasting (DUF) A Dept. of Justice program which compiles data on drug use by arrestees in selected cities.

drunkenness The condition of being under the influence of alcohol to the extent that it renders one helpless.

dual court system Courts at the state and federal levels.

due-process model The model of the criminal justice system that stresses the possibility of error in the stages leading to trial and emphasizes the protection of procedural rights over system efficiency.

due process of law A concept that asserts fundamental principles of justice and implies the administration of laws which do not violate the sacredness of private rights.

Duncan* v. *Louisiana The Supreme Court's ruling that the Fourteenth Amendment's guarantee of due process requires states to provide trial by jury to persons accused of serious crimes.

duress and consent Any unlawful constraints exercised upon an individual forcing him or her to do some act that would not have been done otherwise.

Durham Rule An accused is not criminally responsible if he or she suffers from a diseased or defective mental condition at the time the unlawful act is committed.

embezzlement The fraudulent appropriation or conversion of money or property by an employee, trustee, or other agent to whom the possession of such money or property was entrusted.

en banc "In bank," or on the bench; the court with all its qualified judges presiding in a case.

entrapment The inducement of an individual to commit a crime not contemplated by him or her.

Escobedo* v. *Illinois The Supreme Court ruling that when the process shifts from the investigatory to the accusatory and its purpose is to elicit a confession, the accused may be permitted to consult with an attorney.

Estelle* v. *Gamble The Supreme Court ruling that the deliberate indifference of prison officials or personnel to the serious medical needs of inmates constitutes cruel and unusual punishment proscribed by the Eighth Amendment.

evidence Any species of proof, through the medium of witnesses, records, documents, concrete objects, and circumstances.

evidence in chief The first or direct examination of a witness.

ex post facto After the fact.

exclusionary rule The constitutional guarantee that prohibits, in court, the use of illegally obtained evidence.

excusable homicide Deaths from accidents or misfortunes that may occur during some lawful act.

extradition The surrender by one state to another of an individual accused or convicted of an offense in the second state.

Federal Bureau of Investigation The chief investigative body of the Justice Department, with jurisdiction extending to all federal crimes that are not the specific responsibility of some other federal enforcement agency.

felony A crime punishable by death or by imprisonment in a state or federal penitentiary.

felony-murder doctrine If a death occurs during the commission of a felony, the person committing the primary offense can also be charged with murder in the first degree.

Fielding, Henry The eighteenth-century British novelist and magistrate who laid the foundation for the first modern police force.

fine The penalty imposed upon a convicted person by a court, requiring that he or she pay a specified sum of money to the court.

Florida* v. *Bostick The Supreme Court ruling that police officers' conduct in boarding stopped passenger buses and approaching seated passengers to ask them questions and to request consent to search their luggage does not constitute a Fourth Amendment "seizure" in every instance, but must be evaluated in each case.

forcible rape Having sexual intercourse with a female against her will and through the use of threat of force or fear.

forgery The making or altering of any document or instrument with the intent to defraud.

fornication Sexual intercourse between unmarried persons.

fraud Theft by false pretenses; the appropriation of money or propery by trick or misrepresentation, or by creating or reinforcing a false impression as to some present or past fact that would adversely affect the victim's judgment of a transaction.

frisk A pat-down search of a suspect's outer clothing.

fruit of the poisonous tree The doctrine that evidence seized illegally is considered "tainted" and cannot be used against a suspect.

full enforcement The tenacious enforcement of every statute in the criminal codes.

furlough An authorized, unescorted absence from a correctional institution for a specified period of time.

Furman v. Georgia The Supreme Court ruling that statutes which leave arbitrary and discriminatory discretion to juries in imposing death sentences are in violation of the Eighth Amendment.

Gagnon v. Scarpelli The Supreme Court ruling that the holding in *Morrissey* v. *Brewer* also applies to probationers and that neither probationers nor parolees are entitled to counsel as a matter of right at revocation hearings.

gambling The playing or operation of any game of chance that involves money or property of any value that is prohibited by the criminal code.

Gideon v. Wainwright The Supreme Court ruling that an indigent defendant charged in a state court with any noncapital felony has the right to counsel under the due process clause of the Fourteenth Amendment.

Gitlow v. New York The Supreme Court ruling that the First Amendment prohibition against governments abridgement of the freedom of speech applies to state and local governments as well as to the federal government.

good time The number of days deducted from a sentence for good behavior, meritorious service, particular kinds of work, or other considerations.

grand jury A body of persons who have been selected according to law and sworn to hear the evidence against accused persons and determine whether there is sufficient evidence to bring those persons to trial, to investigate criminal activity generally, and to investigate the conduct of public agencies and officials.

Gregg v. Georgia The Supreme Court ruling that (1) the death penalty is not, in itself, cruel and unusual punishment; and (2) a two-part proceeding—one for the determination of innocence or guilt and the other for determining the sentence—is constitutional and meets the objections noted in *Furman* v. *Georgia*.

Griswold v. Connecticut The Supreme Court ruling that a right of personal privacy is implicit in the Constitution.

habeas corpus A writ that directs the person holding a prisoner to bring him or her before a judicial officer to determine the lawfulness of the imprisonment.

habitual offender A person sentenced under the provisions of a statute declaring that persons convicted of a given offense, and shown to have previously been convicted of another specified offense(s), shall receive a more severe penalty than that for the current offense alone.

hands-off doctrine The refusal of the courts to hear inmate complaints about the conditions of incarceration and the constitutional deprivations of penitentiary life.

harassment Any act that annoys or alarms another person.

hearing A proceeding in which arguments, witnesses, or evidence are heard by a judicial officer or *administrative* body.

Holt v. Sarver The federal court decision declaring the Arkansas prison system to be in violation of the Eighth Amendment.

homicide The killing of one human being by another.

Hudson v. Palmer The Supreme Court ruling that a prisoner has no reasonable expectation of privacy in his prison cell entitling him to Fourth Amendment protection.

hung jury A jury that after long deliberation is so irreconcilably divided in opinion that it is unable to reach any verdict.

Hurtado v. California The Supreme Court ruling that the due process clause of the Fourteenth Amendment does not require states to use grand jury indictments or presentments in capital cases.

Illinois Juvenile Court Act Legislation that established the first statewide juvenile court system in the United States.

Illinois v. Gates The Supreme Court ruling that in establishing probable cause for the issuance of a search warrant, magistrates may make a commonsense decision, given all the circumstances set forth in the affidavit, whether there is a fair probability that contraband can be found in a particular place.

In forma pauperis The characterization of an appeal by a poor person.

in loco parentis A position in reference to a child of that of lawful parent or guardian.

in re In the affair of; concerning.

In re Gault The Supreme Court ruling that extended some—but not all—due process privileges to juvenile court proceedings.

In re Winship The Supreme Court ruling that required proof "beyond a resonable doubt" for an adjudication of delinquency.

incest Sexual intercourse between parent and child, any sibling pair, or between close blood relatives.

indecent exposure (exhibitionism) Exposure of the sexual organs in a public place.

indeterminate sentence A sentence of incarceration having a fixed minimum and a fixed maximum term of confinement.

indictment A formal charging document returned by a grand jury based on evidence presented to it by the prosecutor.

inferior courts The lower courts, or courts of limited jurisdiction.

information A formal charging document drafted by a prosecutor and tested before a magistrate.

initial appearance The first court processing stage after arrest, in which the accused is taken before a magistrate, given formal notice of the charge, and notified of his or her legal rights.

inmate code The unwritten rules of the prison subculture, which, if violated, can result in sanctions ranging from ostracism to death.

inquiry system of justice A system in which all participants in a proceeding are obliged to cooperate with the court in its inquiry into the crime.

inquisitorial system of justice A system in which the accused was considered guilty until he could prove himself innocent.

insanity Any unsoundness of mind, madness, mental alienation, or want of reason, memory, and intelligence that prevents an individual from comprehending the nature and consequences of his or her acts or from distinguishing between right and wrong conduct.

inside cells Cells constructed back to back, with corridors running along the outside shell of the cell house.

intake hearing An early stage in juvenile court proceedings in which a court officer makes a legal judgment of the probable cause of the petition.

intensive probation supervision A program of closer surveillance and more exhaustive services that serve to place a probationer under tighter control than he or she might experience under regular probation.

intent The state of mind or attitude with which an act is carried out; the design, resolve, or determination with which a person acts to achieve a certain result.

intermittent sentence A sentence to confinement interrupted by periods of freedom.

Interpol An international police organization of 120 member countries that serves as a depository of intelligence information on wanted criminals.

isolation A sentencing philosophy seeking to remove the offender from society.

Jackson v. Bishop The federal court decision declaring that whipping

was in violation of the Eighth Amendment.

jails Local facilities for temporary detention.

Jim Crow laws A number of ordinances that were passed in southern states and municipalities in the 1880s legalizing segregation of blacks and whites.

Johnson v. Avery The Supreme Court ruling that unless a state provides some reasonable legal assistance to inmates seeking post-conviction relief, a jailhouse lawyer must be permitted to aid inmates on filing *habeas corpus* petitions.

Johnson v. Zerbst The Supreme Court ruling that the Sixth Amendment right to counsel applies to all defendants in federal prosecutions.

Jones v. North Carolina Prisoners' Labor Union The Supreme Court ruling that prison regulations prohibiting the organized activities of inmate labor unions are not violative of the freedom of association clause of the First Amendment.

judicial activism The High Court's use of its power to accomplish social goals.

judicial circuit A specific jurisdiction served by a judge or court, as defined by given geographical boundaries.

judicial restraint The High Court's deference to legislative and executive decisions unless a clear constitutional right has been violated.

judges Public officers who preside over courts of law.

judgment Any decision or determination of a court.

jurisdiction The territory, subject matter, or persons over which lawful authority may be exercised by a court or other justice agency, as determined by statute or constitution.

jury nullification The refusal or marked reluctance on the part of a jury to convict, because of the severe nature of the sentence involved.

jury panel The group of persons summoned to appear in court as potential jurors for a particular trial, or the persons selected from the group of potential jurors to sit

in the jury box, from which second group those acceptable to the prosecution and the defense are finally chosen as the jury.

jury poll A poll conducted by a judicial officer or by the clerk of the court after a jury has stated its verdict but before that verdict has been entered into the record of the court, asking each juror individually whether the stated verdict is his or her own verdict.

"just deserts" The philosophy that the punishment should fit the crime; that punishment should be the prime consideration in sentencing.

justices of the peace The judges in many lower courts in rural areas, who are typically not lawyers and are locally elected.

justifiable homicide Those instances of death that result from legal demands.

justification Any just cause or excuse for the commission of an act that would otherwise be a crime.

Kefauver Committee A special Senate committee targeting organized crime in the United States. With exciting drama of the courtroom variety, its disclosures demonstrated the extent to which racketeers had established themselves in American society.

Kent v. United States The Supreme Court ruling that the waiver of jurisdiction is a critically important stage in juvenile proceedings and must be attended by minimum requirements of due process and fair treatment.

Klopfer v. North Carolina The Supreme Court ruling that the Sixth Amendment right to a speedy trial applies in state as well as federal proceedings.

Lambert v. California The Supreme Court held that due process requires that ignorance of a duty must be allowed as a defense when circumstances that inform a person as to the required duty are completely lacking.

larceny The taking and carrying away of the personal propery of another, with the intent to deprive permanently.

law and order A political ideology and slogan that sought a return to the morality and values of earlier times and rejected the growing permissiveness in government and social affairs.

Law Enforcement Assistance Administration (LEAA) A federal bureaucracy created to involve the national government in local crime control by supplying funds to the states for training and upgrading criminal justice agencies.

lease system A form of prison industry under which contractors assumed complete control over prisoners.

lewdness Degenerate conduct in sexual behavior that is so well known that it may result in the corruption of public decency.

lockdown A situation in which inmates are confined to their cells around the clock, and denied exercise, work, recreation, and visits.

Lockhart v. McCree The Supreme Court ruling that a prosecutor's removal for cause, at the start of the guilt phase of a capital trial, of prospective jurors so opposed to the death penalty as to be unable to perform their duties at sentencing, is not a violation of the Fifth Amendment.

loitering Idling or lounging upon a street or other public way in a manner that serves to interfere with or annoy passersby.

mala in se crimes Criminal acts, such as murder and rape, that are considered to be in and of themselves, or inherently and essentially, evil.

mala prohibita crimes Criminal acts that are not necessarily evil in and of themselves, but that are wrong because they have been prohibited by the state.

malice aforethought The intent to cause death or serious harm, or to commit any felony whatsoever.

mandamus, writ of A command issued by a court to perform a certain duty.

mandatory release A release from prison required by statute when an inmate has been confined for a time period equal to his or her full sentence minus statutory "good time," if any.

mandatory sentence A statutory requirement that a certain penalty shall be set and carried out in all cases upon conviction for a specified offense or series of offenses.

manslaughter The unlawful killing of another, without malice.

Mapp v. Ohio The Supreme Court ruling that evidence obtained in violation of the Fourth Amendment must be excluded from use in state as well as federal trials.

Marbury v. Madison The Supreme Court decision that established the High Court's power to review acts of Congress and declare invalid those it found in conflict with the Constitution.

"mark system" Started by Alexander Maconochie at Norfolk Island, a system by which inmates could earn early release by hard work and good behavior.

maximum expiration date The date on which the full sentence ends.

maximum-security prisons Correctional institutions designed to hold the most aggressive and incorrigible offenders.

McKeiver v. Pennsylvania The Supreme Court ruling that due process does not require a jury in juvenile court hearings.

Meachum v. Fano The Supreme Court ruling that the unfettered discretion of prison officials to transfer inmates extends to disciplinary and punitive transfer as well as administrative transfers.

Mempa v. Rhay The Supreme Court ruling that the right to counsel applies to state probation revocation hearings at which deferred sentence may be imposed.

Mens rea (criminal intent) A person's awareness of what is right and wrong under the law with an intention to violate the law.

Miranda v. Arizona The Supreme Court ruling that the guarantee of due process requires that suspects in police custody be informed that they have the right to remain silent, that anything they say may be used against them, and that thay have the right to counsel—before any questioning can permissibly take place.

misdemeanor A crime punishable by no more than a $1,000 fine and/or one year of imprisonment, typically in a local institution.

misprision of felony The concealment of a felony committed by another.

Missouri Plan A method of selecting judges in which the governor, the bar association, and the voters all participate in the process.

mistake of law Any want of knowledge or acquaintance with the laws of the land insofar as they apply to the act, relation, duty, or matter under consideration.

mistrial A trial that has been terminated without a verdict and declared invalid by the court because of some circumstance that creates a substantial and uncorrectable prejudice to the conduct of a fair trial.

M'Naghten Rule The "right-or-wrong" test of criminal responsibility.

Monroe v. Pape The Supreme Court ruling that citizens can bring Section 1983 suits against state officials in federal courts without first exhausting state judicial remedies.

moral turpitude Depravity or baseness of conduct.

Morrissey v. Brewer The Supreme Court ruling that a parolee facing revocation is entitled to both a preliminary hearing to determine whether he or she actually violated parole and a final hearing to consider not only the facts in question but, if there was a violation, what to do about it.

motion A formal application or request to the court for some action.

murder The felonious killing of another human being with malice aforethought.

mutual agreement program A program providing for a form of contract between a prisoner and state prison and parole officials wherein the prisoner undertakes to complete specified self-improvement programs in order to receive a definite parole date, and the agency promises to provide the necessary educational and social services.

mutual pledge Alfred the Great's system of internal policing that organized the people into tithings, hundreds, and shires.

nationalization of the Bill of Rights The extension of the constitutional protections guaranteed by the Bill of Rights to defendants in state criminal trials.

natural law A body of principles and rules, imposed upon individuals by some power higher than man-made law, that are considered to be uniquely fitting for and binding on any community of rational beings.

negligence In legal usage, generally, a state of mind accompanying a person's conduct such that he or she is not aware, though a reasonable person should be aware, that there is a risk that the conduct might cause a particular harmful result.

New Jersey v. *T.L.O.* The Supreme Court ruling that school officials, with reasonable grounds to believe that the law or school rules are being violated, may conduct reasonable searches if needed to maintain safety, order, and discipline in a school.

no bill A grand jury's refusal to indict an accused.

nolle prosequi A formal entry in the record by which the prosecutor declares that he or she "will no further prosecute" the case.

nolo contendere A plea of "no contest" or "I do not wish to contest," with the same implication as a guilty plea.

obscenity That which is offensive to morality or chastity and is calculated to corrupt the mind and morals of those exposed to it.

occasional property crime Burglary, forgery, larceny, and other thefts undertaken infrequently or irregularly, and often quite crudely.

official criminal statistics The enumerations of crimes that come to the attention of law enforcement agencies; arrest compilations; and characteristics of offenders and crimes based on arrest, judicial, and prison records.

Omnibus Crime Control and Safe Streets Act A piece of federal "law and order" legislation that was viewed by many as a political maneuver aimed at allaying fears of crime rather than bringing about criminal justice reform.

open institutions "Prisons without walls," such as correctional camps, farms, and ranches.

opinion The official announcement of a decision of a court together with the reasons for that decision.

Organized Crime Drug Enforcement Task Force Program A joint federal, state, and local law enforcement initiative against high-level drug trafficking organizations.

organized crime Business activities directed toward economic gain through unlawful means.

organized robbery and gang theft Highly skilled criminal activities using or threatening to use force, violence, coercion, and property damage, and accompanied by planning, surprise, and speed to diminish the risks of apprehension.

Palko v. *Connecticut* The Supreme Court ruling that the due process clause of the Fourteenth Amendment does not require the states to observe the double jeopardy guarantee of the Fifth Amendment.

pardon A "forgiveness" for the crime committed that bars any further criminal justice processing.

parens patriae A philosophy under which the state takes over the role of parent.

parole The status of being released from a penal or reformatory institution in which one has served a part of his or her maximum sentence, on the condition of maintaining good behavior and remaining in the custody and under the guidance of the institution or some other agency approved by the state until a final discharge is granted.

parole prediction An estimate of probability of violation or nonviolation of parole on the bases of experience tables, developed with regard to groups of offenders possessing similar characteristics.

parole revocation The administrative action of a paroling authority removing a person from parole status in response to a violation of lawfully required conditions of parole including the prohibition against commission of a new offense, and usually resulting in a return to prison.

parole supervision Guidance, treatment or regulation of the behavior of a convicted adult who is obliged to fulfill conditions of parole or other conditional release, authorized and required by statute, performed by a parole agency, and occurring after a period of prison confinement.

parole violation An act or a failure to act by a parolee that does not conform to the conditions of parole.

parolee A person who has been conditionally released by a paroling authority from a prison prior to the expiration of his or her sentence, and placed under the supervision of a parole agency, and who is required to observe conditions of parole.

Part I offenses Crimes designated by the FBI as the *most serious* and compiled in terms of the number of reports made to law enforcement agencies and the number of arrests made.

Part II offenses Crimes designated by the FBI as *less serious* than the Part I offenses and compiled in terms of the number of arrests made.

parties to offenses All persons culpably concerned in the commission of a crime, whether they directly commit the act constituting the offense, or facilitate, solicit, encourage, aid or attempt to aid, or abet its commission; also, in some penal codes, persons who assist one who has committed a crime to avoid arrest, trial, conviction, or punishment.

patrol A means of deploying police officers that gives them responsibility for policing activity in a defined area and that usually requires them to make regular circuits of that area.

peacekeeping role The legitimate right of police to use force in situations in which urgency requires it.

Pear's Case A person who has legal control of another's property, and converts that property so as to deprive the owner of his possessory rights, is guilty of larceny.

per curium An unsigned opinion of the court.

per se By itself; alone.

peremptory challenge A challenge to remove a potential juror on the basis of any reason or no reason at all.

perjury The intentional making of a false statement as part of testimony by a sworn witness in a judicial proceeding on a matter material to the inquiry.

perpetrator The chief actor in the commission of a crime, that is, the person who directly commits the criminal act.

petit jury A trial jury (as opposed to a grand jury).

petition 1. A written request made to a court asking for the exercise of its judicial powers, or asking for permission to perform some act where the authorization of a court is required. 2. In juvenile proceedings, a document alleging that a youth is a delinquent, a status offender, or a dependent child and asking that the court assume jurisdiction over the juvenile.

pickpocketing The theft of money or articles directly from the garments of the victim.

piece-price system A variation of the contract system of prison industry in which the contractor supplied the raw material and received the finished product, paying the prison a specified amount for each unit produced.

plagiarism The copying or adopting of the literary, musical, or artistic work of another and publishing or producing it as one's own original work.

"plain view" doctrine The rule, from the Supreme Court decision in *Harris* v. *United States*, that any-

thing police officers see in plain view when they have a right to be where they are, is not the product of a search and is therefore admissible as evidence.

plaintiff The customary name for the person who initiates a civil action. In some states the prosecution in a criminal case (that is, "the people," as represented by government) is called the "plaintiff." "Complaint," "complaining party," and "complaining witness" are also used to mean the plaintiff.

plea A defendant's formal answer in court to the charge contained in a complaint, information, or indictment, that he or she is guilty or not guilty of the offense charged, or does not contest the charge.

plea negotiation The negotiation of an agreement among the prosecutor, the judge, and the accused's attorney as to the charge(s) and sentence imposed if the accused pleads guilty.

police brutality The unlawful use of physical force by officers in the performance of their duties.

police corruption Misconduct by police officers in the forms of illegal activities for economic gain and accepting gratuities, favors, or payment for services that police are sworn to carry out as part of their peacekeeping role.

police cynicism The notion that all people are motivated by evil and selfishness.

police discretion The freedom to choose among a variety of alternatives in conducting police operations.

"police presence" The almost continuous presence of police officers in a place of business for the crime deterrent effects it affords.

police professionalism The notion that brutality and corruption are incompetent policing.

police subculture The values and behavior patterns characteristic of experienced police officers.

political crime Illegal activity considered by offenders to be essential and appropriate in achieving necessary changes in society, including treason, sedition, espionage, sabo-

tage, war collaboration, and radicalism and protest.

polygamy The practice of having several spouses.

pornography Literature, art, film, pictures, or other articles of a sexual nature that are considered obscene by a community's moral standards.

Posse comitatus The able-bodied men of a county who were at the disposal of a sheriff when called for service.

postconviction remedy The procedure or set of procedures by which a person who has been convicted of a crime can challenge in court the lawfulness of a judgment of conviction or penalty or of a correctional agency action, and thus obtain relief in situations where this cannot be done by a direct appeal.

Powell* v. *Alabama The Supreme Court ruling that an indigent charged in a state court with a capital offense has the right to the assistance of counsel at trial under the due process clause of the Fourteenth Amendment.

prejudicial error In criminal proceedings, an error of such substance that it serves to compromise the rights of the accused.

preliminary hearing A hearing before the court designed to protect defendants from unwarranted prosecutions.

premeditation A design or conscious decision to do something before it is actually done.

presentence investigation An investigation into the background and character of a defendant that assists the court in determining the most appropriate sentence.

presentment A written notice of accusation issued by a grand jury, based on its own knowledge and observation.

President's Commission on Law Enforcement and Administration of Justice A series of task forces appointed by President Johnson to study crime and justice in the United States and to make recommendations for change.

presiding judge The title of the judicial officer formally designated for some period as the chief judicial officer of a court.

presumptive fixed sentence A fixed determinate sentence within a limited range established by statute.

pretrial conference A meeting of the opposing parties in a case with the judicial officer prior to trial, for the purposes of stipulating those things that are agreed upon and thus narrowing the trial to the things that are in dispute, disclosing the required information about witnesses and evidence, making motions, and generally organizing the presentation of motions, witnesses, and evidence.

pretrial detention Any period of confinement occurring between arrest or other holding to answer a charge, and the conclusion of prosecution.

pretrial discovery Disclosure by the prosecution or the defense prior to trial of evidence or other information that is intended to to be used in the trial.

pretrial release The release of an accused person from custody, for all or part of the time before or during prosecution, upon his or her promise to appear in court when required.

prima facie case Meaning "at first sight," it refers to a fact or other evidence presumably sufficient to establish a defense or a claim unless otherwise contradicted.

prisons Correctional institutions maintained by federal and state governments for the confinement of convicted felons.

prisonization The socializing process by which the inmate learns the rules and regulations of the institution and the informal rules, values, customs, and general culture of the penitentiary.

privatization of corrections The construction, staffing, and operation of prisons by private industry for profit.

proactive patrol A police patrol model characterized by active search for criminal activity or suspicious behavior.

probable cause Facts or apparent facts that are reliable and generate a reasonable belief that a crime has been committed.

probation A sentence not involving confinement that imposes conditions and retains authority in the sentencing court to modify the conditions of sentence or to resentence the offender if he or she violates the conditions.

probation revocation A court order in response to a violation of conditions of probation, taking away a person's probationary status, and usually withdrawing the conditional freedom associated with the status.

probation termination The ending of the probation status of a given person by routine expiration of probationary period, by special early termination by court, or by revocation of probation.

probation violation An act or failure to act by a probationer that does not conform to the conditions of his or her probation.

probationer A person who is placed on probation status and required by a court or probation agency to meet certain conditions of behavior, who may or may not be placed under the supervision of a probation agency.

procedural due process The procedures that are required before the life, liberty, or property of a person may be taken by the government.

Procunier v. _Martinez_ The Supreme Court ruling that prison mail censorship is constitutional only when the practice furthers government interests in security and rehabilitation and when the restrictions are no greater than necessary to satisfy the particular government interest involved.

professional theft Nonviolent forms of criminal occupation pursued with a high degree of skill to maximize financial gain and minimize the risks of apprehension.

prosecutor A government attorney who instigates the prosecution of an accused and represents the state at trial.

prostitution The offering of sexual relations for monetary or other gain.

Protective sweep doctrine The rule that when police officers execute an arrest on or outside private premises, they may conduct a warrantless examination of the entire premises for other persons whose presence would pose a threat, either to their safety or to evidence capable of being removed or destroyed.

public intoxication The condition of being severely under the influence of alcohol or drugs in a public place to the degree that one may endanger persons or property.

public order crime Crimes against public order and safety, mostly misdemeanors, that account for a considerable portion of criminal justice activity.

ransom The demanding of money for the redemption of captured persons or property.

rape The unlawful carnal knowledge of a female without her consent and against her will.

reactive patrol A police patrol model whereby the police respond only when there is a call for assistance.

reception center A central receiving institution where all felony offenders sentenced to a term of imprisonment are committed for orientation and classification.

recidivism The repetition of criminal behavior.

recidivist A person who has been convicted of one or more crimes, and who is alleged or found to have subsequently committed another crime or series of crimes.

reformatory A prison model generally for youthful or young adult offenders.

rehabilitation A sentencing philosophy seeking to reintegrate the offender into society.

Rehnquist Court The Supreme Court under the leadership of Chief Justice William Rehnquist.

release on recognizance (ROR) The release of an accused from jail in his or her own obligation rather than on a monetary bond.

removal of landmarks The relocation of monuments or other markings that designate property lines or boundaries for the purpose of fraudulently reducing the owner's interest or holdings in lands and estates.

reparole A release to parole occurring after a return to prison from an earlier release to parole, on the same sentence to confinement.

reprieve The postponement of the execution of a sentence for a definite period of time.

respondeat superior The doctrine under which liability is imposed upon an employer for the acts of his employees that are committed in the course and scope of their employment.

respondent The person who formally answers the allegations stated in a petition that has been filed in a court; in criminal proceedings, the one who contends against an appeal.

restitution A condition of probation requiring offenders to compensate their victims for damages or to donate their time in service to the community.

retribution A sentencing philosophy seeking to create an equal or proportionate relationship between the offense and the punishment.

Rhodes v. Chapman The Supreme Court ruling that cell overcrowding, in and of itself, is neither cruel nor unusual.

robbery The felonious taking of the money or goods of another, from his person or in his presence and against his will, through the use or threat of force and violence.

Robinson v. California The Supreme Court ruling in 1962 that sickness may not be made a crime, nor may sick people be punished for being sick. The Court viewed narcotic addiction to be a "sickness" and held that a state cannot make it a punishable offense.

Rochin v. California The Supreme Court ruling that evidence acquired in a manner that "shocks the conscience" is in violation of the Fourth Amendment.

Ruiz v. Estelle The federal court decision declaring the Texas prison system to be unconstitutional.

Rule of Four The decision of at least four Supreme Court justices that a case merits consideration by the full Court.

Schall v. Martin The Supreme Court ruling that preventive detention is permissible for accused juvenile delinquents when there is evidence that the youth presents a serious risk of committing a crime before adjudication of the case.

search and seizure The search for and taking of persons and property as evidence of crime.

search warrant A written order, issued by a magistrate and directed to a law enforcement officer, commanding a search of a specified premises.

Section 1983 The section of the Civil Rights Act of 1871 that state prisoners use as a vehicle for access to the federal courts to litigate inmate rights.

seduction The act of enticing or luring a woman of chaste character to engage in sexual intercourse by fraudulently promising to marry her or by some other false promise.

self-reported crime Crime statistics compiled on the basis of self-reports by offenders.

sentence review The reconsideration of a sentence imposed on a person convicted of a crime, either by the same court that imposed the sentence or by a higher court.

separate system Solitary confinement in an isolated cell for the purpose of eliminating evil association in congregate quarters.

separation-of-powers doctrine The principle that power is distributed among three branches of government—the legislative, the executive, and the judicial—for the purpose of ensuring that no one person or group will make the law, interpret the law, and apply the law.

sequestration The removal of the jurors (and alternates, if any) from all possible outside influences.

severance In criminal proceedings the separation, for purposes of pleading and/or trial, of multiple defendants named in a single charging document, or of multiple charges against a particular defendant listed in a single charging document.

sexual assault Any sexual contact with another person (other than a spouse) that occurs without the consent of the victim or is offensive to the victim.

sheriff The elected chief officer of a county law enforcement agency, usually responsible for law enforcement in unincorporated areas and for the operation of the county jail.

shock incarceration A three- to six-month regimen of military drill, drug treatment, physical exercise, hard labor, and academic work in return for having several years removed from an inmate's sentence.

shock probation A program of brief incarceration followed by suspension of sentence and probation.

shoplifting The theft of goods, wares, or merchandise from a store or shop.

silent system Confinement under a rigid rule of absolute silence at all times.

Sixth Amendment The right to a speedy and public trial, by an impartial jury, in the district where the offense was committed; notice of charges; confrontation with witnesses; compulsory process for obtaining witnesses; and assistance of counsel.

sodomy Certain acts of sexual relationship including fellatio (oral intercourse with the male sex organ), cunnilingus (oral intercourse with the female sex organ), buggery (penetration of the anus), homosexuality (sexual relations between members of the same sex), bestiality (sexual intercourse with an animal), pederasty (unnatural intercourse between a man and a boy), and necrophilia (sexual intercourse with a corpse).

sovereign immunity The principle that the state cannot be sued in its own courts or in any other court without its consent and permission.

speedy trial The Sixth Amendment guarantee that protects an accused from indefinite incarceration prior to coming to trial.

Speedy Trial Act A Congressional measure that established a 100-day deadline between arrest and trial in federal cases.

split sentence A sentence explicitly requiring the convicted person to serve a period of confinement in a local, state, or federal facility followed by a period of probation.

Stack* v. *Boyle The Supreme Court ruling that bail set at a figure higher than an amount reasonably calculated to assure the presence of the accused at trial and at the time of final submission to sentence is "excessive" under the Eighth Amendment.

state account system A form of prison industry in which inmate production was directed by prison officials, goods were sold on the open market, and inmates received a share of the profits.

state use system A form of prison industry in which inmate-produced goods were used in state institutions and bureaus.

status offenders Youths who, because of their special status as children, can be brought to the attention of the juvenile courts for certain kinds of noncriminal behavior.

status offense An act declared by statute to be a crime because it violates the standards of behavior expected of children.

statute A written law enacted by legislation.

statutory law Law created by statute, handed down by legislatures.

statutory rape Having sexual intercourse with a female under a stated age (usually sixteen or eighteen, but sometimes fourteen), with or without her consent.

stay of execution The stopping by a court of the carrying out or implementation of a judgment, that is, of a court order previously issued.

stop and frisk The detaining of a person by a law enforcement officer for the purpose of investigation, accompanied by a superficial examination by the officer of the person's body surface or clothing to discover weapons, contraband, or other objects relating to criminal activity.

street crime A class of offenses, sometimes defined with some degree of formality as those that occur in public locations, that are visible and assaultive, and that thus constitute a group of crimes which are a special risk to the public and a special target of law enforcement preventive efforts and prosecutorial attention.

subpoena A written order issued by a judicial officer, prosecutor, defense attorney, or grand jury, requiring a specified person to appear in a designated court at a specified time in order to testify in a case under the jurisdiction of that court, or to bring material to be used as evidence to that court.

substantive due process Due process protection against unreasonable, arbitrary, or capricious laws or acts.

superior courts The courts of record or trial courts.

suppression hearing A hearing to determine whether or not the court will prohibit specified statements, documents, or objects from being introduced into evidence in a trial.

surety A third party who posts a bond for an accused.

suspect A person considered by a criminal justice agency to be one who may have committed a specific criminal offense, but who has not been arrested or charged.

suspended sentence A court disposition of a convicted person, pronouncing a penalty of a fine or commitment to confinement, but unconditionally discharging the defendant or holding execution of the penalty in abeyance upon good behavior.

Tennessee* v. *Garner Deadly force against a fleeing felon is proper only when it is necessary to prevent the escape *and* when there is probable cause to believe that the suspect poses a significant threat to the officers or others.

Terry* v. *Ohio The Supreme Court ruling that when a police officer observes unusual conduct and suspects a crime is about to be committed, he may "frisk" a suspect's outer clothing for dangerous weapons.

Texas Rangers Founded by Stephen Austin in 1823, the first territorial police agency in the United States.

theft The unlawful taking, possession, or use of another's property, without the use of threat of force, and with the intent to deprive permanently.

thief-takers Citizens who receive a reward for the apprehension of a criminal.

Thornburgh* v. *Abbott The Supreme Court ruling that federal prison regulations restricting prisoners' receipt of publications from outside the prison pass First Amendment muster if they are reasonably related to legitimate penological interests.

ticket of leave Started by Sir Walter Crofton of Ireland, a system of conditional release from prison that represented an early form of parole.

Tison* v. *Arizona The Supreme Court ruling that a "nontriggerman" who does not intend to commit murder may be executed when he or she participates in a felony that leads to murder and is found to have exhibited "reckless indifference" for human life.

tort A civil wrong for which the law gives redress.

total institutions Places that furnish barriers to social interchange with the world at large.

transactional immunity Immunity against prosecution given to a grand jury witness in return for testifying.

trial The examination in a court of the issues of fact and law in a case, for the purpose of reaching a judgment.

trial *de novo* A new trial, on appeal from a lower court to a court of general jurisdiction.

true bill A grand jury's endorsement of the charge or charges specified in the prosecutor's bill.

Uniform Crime Reports The annual publication of the FBI presenting official statistics on the rates and trends in crime in the United States.

United States* v. *Calandra The Supreme Court ruling that refused to extend the exclusionary rule to grand jury questions based on illegally seized evidence.

United States **v.** *Leon* The Supreme Court ruling that the Fourth Amendment exclusionary rule does not bar the use of evidence obtained by police officers acting in objectively reasonable reliance on a search warrant issued by a magistrate but ultimately found to be unsupported by probable cause.

United States **v.** *Wade* The Supreme Court ruling that a police line-up identification of a suspect, made without the suspect's attorney present, is inadmissible as evidence at trial.

U.S. Courts of Appeals The federal courts of appellate jurisdiction.

U.S. district courts The trial courts of the federal judiciary.

U.S. Magistrates Federal lower court officials whose powers are limited to trying lesser misdemeanors, setting bail, and assisting district courts in various legal matters.

U.S. Supreme Court The highest court in the nation and the court of last resort.

use immunity A limited immunity that prohibits the government only from using a grand jury witness's compelled testimony in a subsequent criminal proceeding.

usury The taking of or contracting to take interest on a loan at a rate that exceeds the level established by law.

vacated sentence A sentence that has been declared nullified by action of a court.

vagrancy The condition of being idle and having no visible means of support.

vengeance A sentencing philosophy seeking satisfaction from knowing or seeing that offenders are punished.

venire A writ that summons jurors.

verdict The decision of the jury in a jury trial or of a judicial officer in a nonjury trial, that the defendant is guilty or not guilty of the offense for which he or she has been tried.

vicarious liability The doctrine under which liability is imposed upon an employer for the acts of employees that are committed in the course and scope of their employment.

victimization surveys Surveys of the victims of crime based on interviews with representative samples of the household population.

vigilante justice Extralegal criminal justice activities by individuals or groups who take the law into their own hands for the sake of establishing "law and order."

violation Offense defined in criminal codes to be less serious than a misdemeanor (also called "infraction" in some jurisdictions).

violation of privacy Any unlawful trespass, interception, observation, eavesdropping, or other surveillance that serves to infringe on the private rights of another.

violent personal crime Criminal acts resulting from conflicts in personal relations in which death or physical injury is inflicted.

void-for-vagueness doctrine The rule that criminal laws which are unclear or uncertain as to *what* or *to whom* they apply violate due process.

voir dire An oath sworn by a juror regarding his or her qualifications.

voyeurism (peeping) The surreptitious observance of an exposed body or sexual act.

waiver of jurisdiction The process by which the juvenile court relinquishes its jurisdiction over a child and transfers the case to a court of criminal jurisdiction for prosecution as an adult.

Walnut Street Jail The first American penitentiary.

warrant Any of a number of writs issued by a judicial officer that direct a law enforcement officer to perform a specified act and afford him protection from damage if he performs it.

Warren Court The Supreme Court under the leadership of Chief Justice Earl Warren.

Weeks **v.** *United States* The Supreme Court ruling that a person whose Fourth Amendment rights of security against unreasonable search and seizure are violated by federal agents has the right to require that evidence obtained in the search be excluded from use against him or her in federal courts.

Weems **v.** *United States* The Supreme Court ruling that a sentence disproportionate to the offense is in violation of the Eighth Amendment ban against cruel and unusual punishment.

white-collar crime Offenses committed by persons acting in their legitimate occupational roles.

The Wickersham Commission A federal inquiry into crime and the organization of justice in the United States.

Williams **v.** *New York* The Supreme Court ruling that at sentencing, the defendant does not have a Sixth Amendment right to cross-examine persons who have supplied information to a court (in a presentence report) regarding sentencing.

Wilson **v.** *Seiter* The Supreme Court ruling that an inmate alleging that the conditions of his confinement violate the Eighth Amendment's prohibition against cruel and unusual punishment must show deliberate indifference on the part of the responsible prison officials.

Witherspoon **v.** *Illinois* The Supreme Court ruling that states cannot exclude from juries in capital cases *all* persons opposed to the death penalty.

Wolff **v.** *McDonnell* The Supreme Court ruling that the due process clause of the Fourteenth Amendment protects, in part, state prisoners facing loss of good-time credit or punitive confinement.

working personality A personality characterized by authoritarianism, cynicism, and suspicion developed in response to danger and the obligation to exercise authority.

writ A formal written order issued by a court commanding specified individuals to do (or abstain from doing) some specified act.

zero tolerance A federal anti-drug measure that permits the confiscation of planes, vessels, or vehicles found to be carrying a controlled substance.

ACKNOWLEDGMENTS

TEXT AND TABLES

Page 3 From *The Gangs of New York* by Herbert Asbury. Copyright © 1928 by Alfred A. Knopf, Inc. and renewed 1956 by Herbert Asbury. Reprinted by permission of the publisher.

Page 54 Material from the "Public Opinion Quarterly," 47, 1983 p. 206. Article entitled, "John Hinkley Jr. and the insanity defense: The Public Verdict," by Valerie P. Hans and Dan Slater. Reprinted by permission of The University of Chicago. Copyright © 1983 by The Trustees of Columbia University.

Pages 57, 229, 720, and 725 Excerpts from *The Police Mystique: An Insider's Look at Cops, Crime and the Criminal* by Anthony V. Bouza. Reprinted by permission of the author and Plenum Publishing Company. Copyright © 1990.

Page 75 Article entitled "Robbery by Reptile" from the *Time* Magazine issue date, August 11, 1980. Copyright © 1980 Time Warner Inc. Reprinted by permission.

Page 83 Results of *Time/CNN* poll on rape entitled, "Attitudes about Rape in the U.S." Copyright © 1991 by the *Time* Inc. Magazine Company. Reprinted by permission.

Page 216 Article entitled, "Stolen Late-Model Auto — Officer Inside" by Robert McFadden appeared in The New York Times, March 30, 1991 edition. Copyright © 1991 by The New York Times Company. Reprinted by permission.

Page 225 Results of Newsweek/Gallup poll entitled, "Up with the Cops." Newsweek issue date May 29, 1989. Copyright © 1989 from Newsweek Inc. All rights reserved. Reprinted by permission.

Page 275 Excerpt from, "Clubs, Clubbers and the Clubbed" in *The Autobiography of Lincoln Steffens* by Lincoln Steffens, copyright © 1931 by Harcourt Brace Jovanovich, Inc. and renewed 1959 by Peter Steffens, reprinted by permission of the publisher.

Page 281 Excerpt from *Boss: Richard J. Daley of Chicago* by Mike Royko. Copyright © 1971 by Mike Royko. Used by permission of the publisher, Dutton, an imprint of New American Library, a division of Penguin Books USA Inc.

Page 291 Excerpt from "Writing on the Wall," from *Time* Magazine issue date April 1, 1991. Copyright © 1991 The *Time* Inc. Magazine Company. Reprinted by permission.

Page 295 Poll entitled, "Nationwide, how much police brutality do you think exists against minorities?" Conducted March 14–15, 1991. From *Newsweek*, March 15, 1991. Copyright © 1991 Newsweek, Inc. All rights reserved. Reprinted by permission.

Page 296 Results of New York Times/CBS News poll entitled, "The Public Views the Police," conducted April 1–3, 1991. Copyright © 1991 by "The New York Times" Company. Reprinted by permission.

Page 297 Poll entitled, "How much police violence is used against citizens in your community?" Poll conducted by *Time/CNN*. Copyright © 1991 The Time Inc. Magazine Company.

Page 344 Excerpt from "South Florida" Magazine, by Lona O'Connor. Copyright © "South Florida Magazine." Reprinted with permission from "South Florida Magazine."

Page 360 Material from "Sentences for Drug Felonies." Copyright © 1990, The Los Angeles Times. Charts reprinted by permission. All rights reserved.

Page 382 "Sanctions Imposed on Lawyers by State Courts 1981–1989," copyright © 1989. Reprinted by permission of the American Bar Association.

Page 383 Article entitled, "Bare Justice" appeared August 19, 1991. Reprinted with permission from *Insight* Magazine. Copyright © 1991 *Insight* Magazine. All rights reserved.

Page 540 "Assaults on Prison Staff by Inmates, 1984–1990" reprinted by permission of Corrections Compendium, published CEGA Services, Inc. Copyright © 1990.

Page 550–551 Article by James Inciardi entitled, "AIDS and the IV Drug User in the Criminal Justice System." Reprinted with permission. Copyright © *Journal of Drug Issues* 20(2), 1990.

Pages 566 and 567 Excerpt from, "Michigan Program Makes Children's Visits Meaningful," by Christina Jose-Kampfner, August 1991 *Corrections Today,* Vol. 53, No. 5. Reprinted with permission of the American Correctional Association.

Page 568 "Prison Violence in the United States, 1984–1990," reprinted by permission of Corrections Compendium, published by CEGA Services, Inc. Copyright © 1990.

Page 569 Excerpt from *The Prison Community,* copyright 1958 by Donald Clemmer and renewed 1986 by Rose Emelin Clemmer, reprinted by permission of Holt, Rinehart and Winston.

Page 571 "Security Levels of New Prison Beds." Reprinted by permission of Corrections Compendium, published by CEGA Services, Inc. Copyright © 1991.

Page 575 "Inmate Suicides, 1984–1990." Reprinted by permission of Corrections Compendium, published by CEGA Services, Inc. Copyright © 1990.

Page 657 "Good Time Laws in the United States." Reprinted by permission of Corrections Compendium, published by CEGA Services, Inc.

Page 658 "Average percent of sentence served for all Florida inmates released." Reprinted by permission of Corrections Compendium, published by CEGA Services, Inc.

Page 689 Excerpt from "The Child Seekers" from *Juvenile Delinquency and Corrections* by James O. Finckenauer, copyright © 1984 by Harcourt Brace Jovanovich, Inc., reprinted by permission of the publisher.

Pages 729, 730, and 731 "Arizona v. Fulminante—Coerced Confessions and the Harmless Error Doctrine," by Kenneth C. Haas. Reprinted with permission of Dr. Kenneth C. Haas/University of Delaware. All rights reserved.

Page 732 Charts from The New York Times, "Should Thomas Be Confirmed?" and "Whom do you Believe More?" from the October 13, 1991 edition. Copyright © 1991 by The New York Times Company. Reprinted by permission.

PHOTOS

Chapter 1 Wide World Photos, **xviii**; The Bettmann Archive, **3**; Culver Pictures, **4**; UPI/Bettman, **5**; 1986 The James Dean Foundation under License Authorized by Curtis Licensing Corp, **9**; UPI/Bettman, **10**; Wide World Photos, **10**; Doug Menuez/Reportage, **11**; Photo Trends, **12**; Frankie Frost, **14**; AP/Wide World Photos, **15**; AP/Wide World Photos, **15**; AP/Wide World Photos, **15**; AP/Wide World Photos, **15**; Chicago Tribune, 1985, **15**; Tony Schwartz, **16**; UPI/Bettmann, **21**; Wide World Photos, **23**; White House Photo, **26**; Bill Gentile/SIPA Press, **32**

Chapter 2 Bruce Davidson/Magnum Photos, **36–37**; Tony O'Brien/JB Pictures, **38**; 1989 The Detroit News, **41**; Gerald Davis/Contact Press, **42**; Frank Cotham/National Law Journal, **46**; John Barr/Gamma Liaison, **49**; Courtesy of American Professional Captains Association, **58**; Declan Haun, **60**

Chapter 3 S. Feld/H. Armstrong Roberts, **66**; Wide World Photos, **69**; Reuters/Bettmann, **71**; Abbas/Magnum, **73**; Sidney Harris, **75**; Frank Cotham/Penthouse, **77**; G. Marche/FPG, **79**; Manny Crisostomo, **85**; Dan Miller/Woodfin Camp, **87**; Miller's Crossing 1990 Twentieth Century Fox Film Corp All Rights Reserved, **94**; Sidney Harris/Playboy, **97**; UPI/Bettmann, **100**; Reuters/Bettmann, **102**; AP/Wide World Photos, **103**

Chapter 4 Fusco/Magnum, **106**; Richard Hutchings/Photo Researchers, **110**; UPI/Bettmann, **112**; Jeff Lowenthal/Woodfin Camp, **115**; 1988 Mathew Neal McVay/Stock Boston, **116**; Kenneth Siegel, **120**; UPI/Bettmann, **121**; Alon Reininger, Contact/Camp, **122**

Chapter 5 Stuart Nichol/Katz/Woodfin Camp, **132**; Culver Pictures, **136**; Wide World Photos, **141**; Brown Brothers, **142**; UPI/Bettmann, **143**; UPI/Bettmann, **145**; Laima Druskis/Photo Researchers, **146**; P. Steiner 1982 The New Yorker Magazine, **147**; Patrice Chauvel/Sygma, **151**; Sidney Harris, **152**; U.S. Government Printing Office, **157**

Chapter 6 Lynne Sladky/AP Wide World Photos, **160–161**; Jose Azel 1989/Contact Press, **162**; Culver Pictures, **167**; Library of Congress, **172**; Western History Collections, University of Oklahoma Library, **169**; U.S. Coast Guard, **171**; Library of Congress, **172**; Wide World Photos, **176**; Okamoto/Rapho/Photo Researchers, **177**; Larry Mulvehill/Photo Researchers, **181**; Pinkerton's Inc., **184**; Pinkerton's Inc., **185**; Pinkerton's Inc., **185**; Pinkerton's Inc., **185**; Library of Congress, **186**; Greg Rummell, **187**; Movie Still Archives, **188**; Movie Still Archives, **189**; Michelle v. Agins/NYT Pictures, **191**

Chapter 7 Van Bucher/Photo Researchers, **194**; Sebastian Papenberg/Photo Edit, **197**; UPI/Bettmann, **198**; Jose Azel 1984 Contact/Woodfin Camp, **201**; Jill Freedman, **206**; Cynthia Johnson/Time Magazine, **210**; Marty Katz, **213**; Eli Reed/Magnum, **220**; Jim Anderson/Stock Boston, **221**; Jose Azel/Contact/Woodfin Camp, **224**; UPI/Bettmann, **225**

Chapter 8 1986 J. B. Diederich/Contact Press, **228**; Eugene Richards/Magnum, **234**; Uniphoto Picture Agency, **235**; Lester Sloan 1987/Woodfin Camp, **237**; Wide World Photos, **242**; Chon Day/Penthouse, **247**; 1986 J. B. Diederich/Contact Press Images, **249**; Eli Reed/Magnum Photos, **253**; Reprinted by Permission of UFS Inc., **257**; Wide World Photos, **261**; Wide World Photos, **266**

Chapter 9 H. Armstrong Roberts, **272**; Eli Reed/Magnum Photos, **276**; UPI/Bettmann, **283**; Ricard Ferro/NYT Pictures, **284**; Reuters/Bettmann, **288**; Jose Azel 1989, Contact Press, **290**; UPI/Bettmann, **292**; Steve Benson/Reprinted with permission of Tribune Media Services, **293**; Alex Webb/Magnum Photos, **293**; AP/Wide World Photos, **297**; James Inciardi, **302**

Chapter 10 Steve Chenn/H. Armstrong Roberts, **306–307**; Bill Ross/H. Armstrong Roberts, **308**; Missouri Historical Society, **311**; Allen Hess/Library of Congress, **312**; Arnie Levin, National Law Journal, **316**; Western History Collections/University of Oklahoma Library, **319**; James Inciardi, **331 Left**; HBJ Collection, **331 Right**; Library of Congress, **333 Top Left**; Wide World Photos, **333 Top Right**; Supreme Court Historical Society, **333 Bottom Left**; Supreme Court Historical Society, **333 Bottom Middle**; Wide World Photos, **333 Bottom Right**; Erich Salomon/Magnum, **334**; D. Fradon, 1967 The New Yorker Magazine, **336**; Wally McNamee 1991/Woodfin Camp, **338**

Chapter 11 Ron Slenzak/H. Armstrong Roberts, **342**; Stacy Pick/Stock Boston, **345**; John Baynham/Tremmel T-Shirt Co., **355**; Frank Capri/SAGA, **359**; Western History Collections/University of Oklahoma Library, **361**; Bettmann, **368**; Flip Schulke/Life Magazine, **373**;

Daniel S. Brody/Stock Boston, **375**; Sidney Harris, **380**; Reprinted Courtesy Penthouse Magazine 1986, **381**

Chapter 12 S. Meiselas/Magnum Columbie, **386**; James Inciardi, **393**; James Inciardi, **394**; Michael O'Brien/Archive, **395**; Lester Sloan/H. Armstrong Roberts, **396**; 1983, Jaydie Putterman, **399**; Joseph Farris/National Law Journal, **407**; Eli Reed/Magnum Photos, **408**; 1990 Sidney Harris, **411**; Robert Mills/Library of Congress, **412**; Michael Grecco, **421**; Lorenz, 1977, The New Yorker Magazine, **422**; J. Twohy, National Law Journal, 1987, **427**

Chapter 13 Glen Stubbel/The Washington Times, **436**; Culver Pictures, **439**; Keystone-Mast Collections, California Museum of Photography, University of California, Riverside, **443**; David Burnett/Woodfin Camp, **446**; USA Today, **448**; Wide World Photos, **458**; Bettmann Archive, **462**; Wide World Photos, **463**; Granger Collection, **464**; Wide World Photos, **467**; Wide World Photos, **469**; Eddie Adams/Time Magazine, **470**; Owen Franken/Stock Boston, **471**; Chris Troyanna/Huntsville Item, **475**; Yvonne Hemsey/Gamma Liaison, **477**; Mark Richards, **478**; Wide World Photos, **479 Top**; Gamma-Liaison/Dennis Hamilton, **479 Bottom**; Phoenix Newspapers Inc., **482**; Wide World Photos, **484**

Chapter 14 Larry Downing/Woodfin Camp, **492**; Insight Magazine/Richard Kozak, **494**; Culver Pictures, **496**; Culver Pictures, **497 Top**; Culver Pictures, **497 Bottom**; Culver Pictures, **498**; Courtesy Sarasota County, Florida, **499**; Robert McElroy/Woodfin Camp, **504**; Norinne Betjemann, **505 Top**; H. Armstrong Roberts, **505 Bottom**; U.S. Bureau of Prisons, **506 Left**; Courtesy of American Correctional Association, **506 Right**; Courtesy of the American Correctional Association, **508**; Library of Congress, **509**; Bettmann Archive, **512**; Robert McElroy/Woodfin Camp, **513**; Courtesy of the New York Department of Correctional Services, **514**; Bettmann Archive, **518 Top**; Frank Micelotta/Time Magazine, **518 Bottom**; Courtesy of the American Correctional Association, **521**; James Inciardi, **522**; Brooklyn Historical Society, **525**; Michael Soluri, **526**; H. Armstrong Roberts, **527**

Chapter 15 Newsweek/Robert McElroy, **532**; H. Armstrong Roberts, **535**; Lester Sloan 1990/Woodfin Camp, **538**; Michael Soluri, **541**; Gern Ludwig 1989/Woodfin Camp, **542**; Steve Hanson/Stock Boston,

544; Courtesy of the American Correctional Association, **547**; Robert Mass/Photo Reporters, **550**; Michael Douglas/Image Works, **553**; Peter Cross/Miami Herald, **557**; Michael Soluri, **558**; Robert McElroy/Woodfin Camp, **560**; Pamela Price/The Picture Cube, **565**; Woodfin Camp, **570**; Seth Resnick 1989/Stock Boston, **576**

Chapter 16 Insight Magazine/Richard Kozak, **582**; Wide World Photos, **587**; James Inciardi, **589**; Robert McElroy/Woodfin Camp, **591**; Ernie Hearion/NYT Pictures, **596**; Wide World Photos, **601**; Delaware State Archives, **605**; Michael L. Abramson/Woodfin Camp, **608**; Robert McElroy/Woodfin Camp, **609**; Jack Deland/Library of Congress, **611**; Danny Lyon/Magnum Photos, **612**; UPI/Bettmann, **613**; Larry Downing/Woodfin Camp, **615**; Courtesy California Department of Corrections, **616**; Bob Englehart, Hartford Courant, **618**; Larry Downing/Woodfin Camp, **619**

Chapter 17 Billy E. Barnes/Stock Boston, **622**; Tom Lankes/Texastock, **629**; MacDonald Photographers/The Picture Cube, **641**; James L. Shaffer/Photo Edit, **652**; Lloyd Degrane, **656**; Sidney Harris/Playboy, **661**; MacDonald Photographers/Unicorn Stock Photos, **663**; Jack Buxbaum, **666**; Jack Buxbaum, **667**; Stayskal, Tampa Tribune, **668**; Wide World Photos, **671**; Douglas R. Burrows, **676–677**; Michael Newman/Photoedit, **678**; Black Star/NYT Pictures, **680**; J. P. Laffont/Sygma, **681**; Eugene Richards/Magnum Photos, **682**; Marty Katz, **683**; Ira Berger, **687**; Patricia Hollander Cross/Stock Boston, **690**; Ken Geiger/Texastock, **691**; Mark Richards/Picture Group, **693**; McCarten/Photo Edit, **702**; J. P. Laffont/Sygma, **704**; Roberts/Amberg/The State Newspaper, **707**; Carlos Guarita/Reflex/Picture Group, **711**; McCarten/Photo Edit, **713**; Vicki Silbert/Photo Edit, **714**

Epilogue Ed Kashi, **718**; Wide World Photos, **721**; Wide World Photos, **723**; Wide World Photos, **727**; Wide World Photos, **728**

Endpapers Mark Peterson/JB Pictures (*front*); Norinne Betjemann (*rear*)

Foldout (*from left to right*) UPI/Bettman; Durand/SIPA Press; E. Roth/Picture Cube; John Running/Stock Boston; Lester Sloan/Woodfin Camp; Comstock; Mitch Kezar/Black Star

CASE INDEX

NAME INDEX

SUBJECT INDEX